Fiscal Administration

John L. Mikesell is Chancellor's Professor of Public and Environmental Affairs Emeritus at Indiana University. His work in government finance, budgeting, and taxation has appeared in such journals as *National Tax Journal, Southern Economic Journal, Public Finance Review, Public Budgeting & Finance, Public Finance and Management, State Tax Notes, Public Choice, International Journal of Public Administration, Tax Notes,* and *Public Administration Review* and he is internationally regarded as an expert in general sales taxation. He is coauthor with John F. Due of *Sales Taxation: State and Local Structures and Administration*, a standard guide for policy discussions about that tax. He was editor-in-chief of *Public Budgeting & Finance*, the journal of the American Association for Budget and Program Analysis and the Association for Budgeting and Financial Management for fifteen years. He has served on the Revenue Forecast Technical Committee of the Indiana State Budget Agency for over thirty years, has been a David Lincoln Fellow in Land Value Taxation with the Lincoln Institute for Land Policy, has been Senior Research Fellow, Peking University–Lincoln Institute Center for Urban Development and Land Policy, Beijing, People's Republic of China, and has been visiting scholar at the Congressional Budget Office. He has served as chief fiscal economist and chief of party with the USAID Barents Group/KPMG Peat Marwick fiscal reform project with the Government of Ukraine, as Moscow-based director for assistance in intergovernmental fiscal relations with the USAID Georgia State University Consortium Russian fiscal reform project, and has worked as consultant on World Bank missions to the Kyrgyz Republic, Kazakhstan, Azerbaijan, Tajikistan, and Turkmenistan, He has been the sales tax expert on tax reform research and discussions in Indiana, Hawaii, Nebraska, Minnesota, and New York. He holds a BA from Wabash College and MA and PhD in economics from the University of Illinois and is a member of Phi Beta Kappa. He received the 2002 Wildavsky Award for Lifetime Scholarly Achievement from the Association for Budgeting and Financial Management and the 2015 Steven D. Gold Award for Outstanding Contributions to State and Local Fiscal Policy from the National Tax Association.

To Karen, Elizabeth, Thomas, and Daniel

Preface

This book seeks to provide a perspective on how and why fiscal systems have developed, to build a basis for understanding the principles and structural dynamics that promise to shape the future of fiscal systems, and to develop a foundation of techniques necessary to become a practitioner of fiscal administration. It is not a training manual, but it does provide the foundation for becoming a functional practitioner and does develop the skills appropriate for a midlevel public manager. The skills in budgeting and finance it develops are equally applicable to governments, nonprofit organizations, and private entities because, in many respects, budgeting is budgeting and finance is finance and it doesn't matter what the context is. Because of the nature of the topic, the text uses elements from economics, political science, law, accounting, business management, and bits of other stuff as it goes along, but it is not a text for any of these disciplines. It is directly aimed at those studying public administration, public affairs, and public policy, all areas that require an understanding of applied public budgeting and finance.

This edition sticks with two distinguishing features. First, a public affairs student and practitioner of public finance needs to understand from where the money comes and to where it goes—not just in general, but quite specifically—and that the ultimate focus should be on service results. Quoting an earlier edition: "If armies move on their stomachs, then governments certainly crawl on their purses." Public administrators who do not understand revenue systems, options, and policies, who do not understand the basic concepts of borrowing and debt management, who do not understand that they are spending other people's money, and who do not track the use of that money to the delivery of appropriate services become the sinister "public bureaucrats" that conservative commentators revile: "spend, spend, spend is all they know." To be a useful contributor to the public, the graduate of a public affairs program needs familiarity with the practice of all components of public finance.

Second, a public affairs student hasn't learned enough if he or she hasn't crunched some numbers (probably a lot of numbers) during a public budgeting and finance class. Most chapters in this text are followed by questions and exercises that require some calculations to come up with an answer. That is how you learn what is going on and that is how you become useful to a prospective employer. You will discover that many exercises are much easier with a spreadsheet program, and if you don't know how to use these, this would be an outstanding time to learn. But learning how to plug numbers into a spreadsheet template provided you will not do; you need to know why you are doing what you are doing and what it means. The preparation of spreadsheets is something you can learn on your own, outside of class, so this textbook concentrates on developing the "what and why" behind the problems and asking the questions that can be answered with that logic. If you understand the principles involved, plugging the numbers into your own spreadsheet will be easy. The ideas always precede the numbers. If you start by plugging numbers into a spreadsheet template prepared by someone else, you will not be able to do independent analysis. Of course, every exercise can be done with paper and pencil. It just takes longer.

This edition updates all statistics of government finance reported in the text and in the tables to the most recent year available. It includes fiscal actions through the official end date of the Great Recession and beyond, and it includes new legal actions that form government fiscal processes. It includes the Budget Control Act of 2011, the act that established new spending constraints and debt ceiling for the federal government and that Congress quickly worked to violate; the continued inability of the federal government to meet its fiscal deadlines or to put finances on a long-term path of sustainability; the state and local government struggles to close fiscal gaps even as they rush to reduce the productivity of their tax systems; the municipal defaults, bankruptcy filings, and state receiverships that have characterized recent years even though they continue to be rare; the financial problems with state and local government pension programs and our social insurance systems; the arguments about the tax that should be paid by the top 1 percent of earners (the people who are not the 99 percent); and the possibly hopeless struggle to repair the federal income tax. There are new and revised cases, sidebars, and exercises. All text materials have been updated where needed to reflect new literature, new laws, and new data.

Instructor's Manual/Test Bank

The Instructor's Manual/Test Bank is available online at the password-protected Instructor's Companion Site (via cengage.com). It provides answers to many review exercises or study questions mentioned in the text, as well a detailed bank of exam questions for each chapter. Interested instructors can find it by looking up this edition of the book on Cengage.com.

Acknowledgments

I want to thank my colleagues at Indiana University and friends at other institutions for their comments and suggestions of ways in which the text could be improved. Many generations of students also have been generous with their thoughts about the text, serving as the best force for quality control that I know. I am particularly grateful to my former students who have gone on to great careers with governments, financial institutions, and research organizations around the world and have given comments from their experience that helped to improve each edition of this text. I would like to thank the reviewers, who made comments and suggestions to help the revision of this book: Dr. Nancy S. Lind, Illinois State University; Dr. Natalia Ermasova, Governors State University; and Dr. Rosa Leung, California State University, Dominguez Hills. Diana Worman provided outstanding secretarial assistance when I couldn't figure out how to make tables, graphs, or figures that were clear and presentable. Finally, I thank my wife Karen for complaining only moderately about the time that I was devoting to this revision.

John L. Mikesell
Indiana University

Contents

CHAPTER 1

Fundamental Principles of Public Finance

Chapter Contents

Before the following chapters help you with the skills necessary to become a productive participant in the work of government finance, it is important for you to understand why a functioning public sector is critical for a comfortable, civilized existence. Despite the centuries of human, economic, and social success accommodated by government operations, loud voices declare the importance of markets and free enterprise and declaim a desire for governments to shrink away. In the face of such noise, it is important for anyone contemplating work in the public sector to understand the unique and critical role that this sector must play in even the most vibrant of market economies. Both markets and governments must succeed if people are to be comfortable. Therefore, this first chapter delves into the vital role that government must play and explains why mindless downsizing of government would be a horrible idea. Sound public finances are a prerequisite for making government function.

Why Public Finance and Budgeting?

Why do public managers, whether they work for the government or for a not-for-profit organization, need to study public budgeting and finance? Here is your top ten list:

1. They must make choices about how resources are utilized, and working through the finances gives a good start in organizing the options.
2. They operate in the public trust and need to be able to control the use of public resources—they are using *other people's money*, and those people get mad when the money disappears.
3. They need to make sure they don't run out of money before they run out of need for the service being provided with the money.
4. They need to make a case for the resources appropriate to provide services to their constituents and clients to legislative and executive bodies.
5. They need to understand the case being made by other managers.
6. They don't want to go to jail for misuse of resources that belong to the public or to their organization.
7. The people in any organization who actually understand what the organization is doing are the people who understand the finances of the organization.
8. Not-for-profit organizations frequently have abysmal financial management practices in place.
9. Government crises, regardless of whether the government is national, state, or local, often have financial underpinnings that could have been avoided with better budget systems and mechanisms for finance.
10. It is simply fun to understand what is going on in public organizations, and understanding finance is the most important single step in gaining that understanding.

Unless you have no interest in providing services to people through the public sector, at least one item on this list of reasons will resonate with you. If none does, then you probably need to reconsider your professional goals and objectives. When you have worked through the chapters, cases, and exercises that follow, you will have at least a start at dealing with everything in that list, and you will have made a substantial start to becoming more useful to whoever your employer is.

Public Finance versus Business Finance

Public finance is not the same as business finance, although the two are related and use many of the same tools. One difference is in ultimate objectives. Financial management in business seeks to increase the value of the firm to its owners by judicious allocation and control of its resources.[1] Public financial management uses similar analytic, technical, and managerial tools to allocate and control finances, but governments differ from private businesses in terms of resource constraints, ownership, and objectives. Four important differences exist: governments may tax to enlarge their resources; "ownership" of the government is not clear because many stakeholders—including at least taxpayers, those benefiting from particular government services, and those providing government services—share a legitimate interest in government decisions; the value of government services is neither easy to quantify nor reflected in a single measure (like the sales or profits of a business enterprise); and governments are dealing with the public trust and reputations of all the citizenry. Default on obligations and financial bankruptcy may be seen as interesting and possibly useful financial tools for a private business and stair steps to eventual private wealth, but they are indelible stains on governments and their citizens because they represent violations of contracts with employees, suppliers, lenders, or those receiving services—and breaking contractual promises is not acceptable behavior.

Businesses operate by generating an income stream from the sale of goods and services on the market. Production requires inputs that must be paid for from that income stream; efficient producers can end up with money left over (profit) after the inputs have been paid for, and that is mostly what interests business owners. Business executives may point with pride to the number of people they employ, but if the business isn't profitable, those people are gone. Governments similarly provide goods and services that are valued by the community, but the nature of these goods and services is such that the government cannot capture that value in a voluntary sales transaction. The value of the government service is collective, for the community as a whole, as opposed to the individual value received by purchasers of business services. The fundamental idea that the provider of a valued product can capture a portion of that value—a link between creating value and receiving revenue from that value—is broken for government operations. Government finance, for this reason, is fundamentally different from business finance.

The absence of that link does not mean that governments are financially powerless because governments have the unique power to tax, prohibit, and punish, which makes all the difference when the government is providing a service whose benefits are collective. These coercive powers make governments different from proprietary businesses and voluntary organizations (in this respect, not-for-profits

---

[1]The collapse of financial institutions in 2008 and 2009, such as Merrill Lynch, Northern Trust, and AIG, exposed several instances in which managers and officers of these institutions enriched themselves while the value of the businesses to the stockholders was declining dramatically toward bankruptcy or government takeover. This divergence of interest between owners (the shareholders) and managers (executive officers) has plagued American capitalism since the emergence of the modern corporation in the early twentieth century. Nevertheless, business finance presumes maximization of corporate value, not plunder by high executives, as the objective. That is a simpler objective than the maximization of the interests of those governed because not everyone has the same interests. For example, I like soccer (what the world calls football) and you like American football, but the public park has room for only one size playing field and set of goals. Whose "best interests" will win? Business managers do not face such balancing dilemmas. They just go for profit.

are more like proprietary businesses than like government); the reflection of those differences makes public financial administration distinct from business finance. Those powers are not, however, without limit, and those limits may be political (the people may get fed up and throw the public officials out, both figuratively and literally) and economic (the economy and the population cannot support a limitless draw to support government operations). Both private and public entities are interested in *fiscal sustainability*: that is, the ability to operate over the long term without reducing the standards of life below those currently enjoyed and even to improve that standard. If fiscal actions now reduce the capacity of future generations to live at least as well as we do now, then those actions violate the standard of sustainability. Much more about violations of fiscal sustainability appears in later sections because American lawmakers seem to have an ingrained desire to violate those standards.

Many different organizations—private businesses, nonprofit organizations, and government agencies—provide the goods and services that we use every day, including both those necessary for life itself and those that make life more enjoyable. Private businesses sell us food and clothing, cars and television sets, and so on: a vast range of commodities that we purchase for survival and enjoyment. The same applies to services: we go to movies run by private companies, travel across the country on privately operated airlines, and hire the neighbor to feed our cats when we go on vacation. All these and many more goods and services are provided under market principles of voluntary exchange: privately owned businesses provide those services to us in exchange for the payment we make to them. No payment, no service. Markets do a pretty good job of getting those goods and services to people willing and able to pay for them, and there isn't much reason for governments to get involved when markets are working. Much the same applies for many nonprofit organizations, such as hospitals and social service organizations, that operate on the basis of charges and government contracts. Other services come from voluntary associations or clubs: the services of the county historical museum, the local neighborhood association, or a local youth soccer organization. Their operations are financed by a variety of contributions and fees. Although voluntary organizations may not require payment before service is rendered, they still need to be paid by someone, voluntarily, in order to survive. After all, those who provide the resources that are used in providing services (utilities, rents, supplies, etc.) need to be paid for those resources.

Finally, we receive the services of police departments, school systems, the judicial and regulatory systems, the social safety net, and so on from governments. But these services are financed differently. Rather than operating from finance by voluntary exchange (market sales) or by voluntary contribution, governments provide goods and services paid for by taxes or other revenues raised by law. This revenue comes not from voluntary purchase or contribution, but, even in a democracy, from the operation of a revenue system based on the legal requirement for payment—ultimately backed by threat of force. Why have a public sector? The reason is not that government services are uniquely essential to life: most countries leave the provision of life's necessities—food, clothing, and usually shelter—to the private sector. But when government fails, the private sector cannot function, and citizens are "bereft of even the most basic conditions of a stable existence: law and security, trust in contracts, and a sound medium of exchange."[2] In short, the public sector exists to provide valued services when the market fails to provide them appropriately, including services needed for proper functioning of markets. Public budgeting and finance sees to the operations of the public sector.

Functions of Government: Market Failures

Why can't private businesses selling their products in free markets be relied upon to provide all goods and services that ought to be available? The argument for the efficiency of markets is powerful. The President's Council of Economic Advisers explains:

> If markets are competitive and function smoothly, they will lead to prices at which the amount sellers want to supply equals the amount buyers demand. Moreover, the price in any market will simultaneously equal the benefit that buyers get from the last unit consumed (the marginal benefit) and the cost of producing the last unit supplied (the marginal cost). These two conditions ensure efficiency: when they hold in all markets, the Nation's labor and other resources are allocated to producing a particular good or service if and only if consumers would not be willing to pay more to have those resources employed elsewhere.[3]

Markets cause the productive capacity of the economy to be used to produce what people want most and cause the least possible amount of resources to be used in that production. In a world of limited resources, it is a valuable result. Markets make people better off and economize on the use of scarce resources.

But there remains an important role for government, even if private markets can deliver most goods and services reliably and at low cost. Indeed, there is an important cooperative relationship between healthy government and healthy markets. Markets need government to function efficiently: "Deals must be enforced and fraud discouraged. Without a government legal system to guarantee property rights and enforce contracts, corporate organizations and market exchange would be virtually impossible. Anarchy and the free market are not synonymous."[4] Markets are useful for government. Governments can obtain important information from market data, use markets as efficient mechanisms for implementing public policy, and acquire goods and services in market transactions to provide government services.

---

[2]International Bank for Reconstruction and Development/World Bank, *World Development Report 1997* (New York: Oxford University Press, 1997): 19.
[3]*Economic Report of the President Transmitted to the Congress February 1997* (Washington, D.C.: U.S. Government Printing Office, 1997): 191.
[4]Ibid., 192.

The market economy needs government to function properly, and governments need the market economy if they are to serve the public interest.[5]

The role of government, however, extends beyond simply allowing markets to operate because a system of markets is not always able "to sustain 'desirable' activities or to stop 'undesirable' activities."[6] What makes some services a government responsibility? Why can't private action be relied upon to provide public safety, primary education, environmental protection, public health, national defense, and so on? Individuals demand these services, and we expect businesses to respond to customer demand in their quest for profit. Why do markets fail, and thereby create an economic need for government? The role for government begins with what are called "public goods."

Public Goods[7]

Some goods will not be supplied in the market or, if supplied, will be supplied in insufficient amounts because of their very nature. The problem comes from two properties: (1) *nonexhaustion,* or nonrivalry, occurs when benefits of the service can only be shared, meaning that a given quantity of the service can be enjoyed by additional people with no reduction in benefit to the existing population; and (2) *inability to exclude nonpayers* occurs when benefits cannot be easily limited to those who have paid for the services. The properties reflected in Figure 1–1 distinguish private goods, public goods, and two intermediate kinds of goods—toll goods and common-pool goods.

What do these public-good properties mean? When services are nonrival, use of the service by one person does not preclude concurrent full use by others at no additional cost of providing that service. To give an extreme example, should some extraordinarily rich individual decide to build a bridge across the Mississippi River for his personal use and because he thought it would look pretty, the extra cost of allowing someone else to use the bridge is nothing. Once the service has been provided for one, the cost of providing the service to additional users equals zero (its marginal cost is zero, in microeconomic terms). Economic efficiency requires that the price paid by the buyer (the value of resources given up by the buyer to make the

---

[5]Some doubt that governments do anything useful. For instance, they point to high crime rates in areas with heavy police presence: why aren't the cops doing their job? But maybe the police are there because of the crime and maybe the crime rate would be even higher if the police weren't there. No sense sending lots of police where there isn't much crime. In terms of gauging impact, there sometimes are natural experiments. After the 9/11 attacks, there was much increased policing in the District of Columbia for reasons unrelated to amounts of criminal activity there. Did crime levels go down when alert levels (and intense policing) were high? Yes, evidence indicates that a 50 percent increase in police presence led to a decrease in crime of around 15 percent, a pretty good return from policing (Jonathan Klick and Alexander Tabarrok, "Using Terror Alert Levels to Estimate the Effect of Police on Crime," *Journal of Law and Economics* 48 (April 2005): 266–79.

[6]Francis M. Bator, "The Anatomy of Market Failure," *Quarterly Journal of Economics* 72 (August 1958): 351.

[7]Some argue that individuals make "wrong" decisions. The idea is that the market underprovides museums, ballets, and symphonies because people do not understand their true value and government needs to step in to support such "merit goods." On the other hand, junk food and reality television starring yokels could be viewed as "merit bads." The line between good and bad is not scientific and ends up in special-interest political battles. My idea of what things are "good," in all likelihood, would not match your idea and that is why the "merit good" idea ends up being somewhat squishy as a standard for determining what governments should pay for.

Figure 1–1
The Elements of Nonappropriability

	Rival	Nonrival
Excludable	Pure private goods Examples: food, clothing, television sets	Toll goods Examples: satellite broadcasts, toll bridges, turnpikes, concerts
Nonexcludable	Common property resources Examples: fisheries, aquifers, petroleum reserves	Pure public goods Examples: national defense, system of laws, vector control

purchase) not exceed the additional cost of producing the purchased good or service. A private business will charge a price higher than zero, the efficient price, because it cannot afford to do otherwise. Therefore, too little of the good or service will be purchased and consumed, and its price will be too high, compared with quantities and prices in a fully functioning market.

Now suppose a private business has no way of excluding people who have not paid from using the service. That's a big problem: if the business can't keep nonpayers away, it will be hard to get anyone to pay (only the suckers), and the business will have no incentive for providing the service. It has little chance of covering its costs, let alone make a profit. Again, this is a market failure because the seller can't successfully charge a price, and without being able to charge a price, the service won't be available. Within the range of exclusion failure, if someone provides the service, all receive that service. When one structure in an urban area receives fire protection, given the propensity of fires to spread, nearby structures receive protection as well. (The public good is fire protection, not firefighting; when the equipment is putting out the fire at Smith's house, it is not available to put out the fire anywhere else. Extinguishing Smith's fire, however, provides fire protection equally to many neighbors.) Obviously, there are geographic limits to that range of impact: fire protection provided in Bloomington, Indiana, will not extend to the people in Jackson, Mississippi. Sidebar 1–1 provides further discussion about the provision of fire protection. Within a specific geographical area, however, all receive the service regardless of payment, whether they want it or not. Such is the special monopoly position of governments: not only are alternative providers unavailable, but also residents do not have the option of not paying for the service because public revenue systems operate independently from service delivery. A governor of Kentucky recognized the difference between operating the state and operating his successful business: "Hell, governing Kentucky is easier than running Kentucky Fried Chicken. There's no competition."[8] Payment regardless of preference or consumption is, of course, a unique feature of government provision.

---

[8]The Honorable John Y. Brown Jr., quoted in *Newsweek* (March 30, 1981). Mr. Brown qualified to be governor by once heading Kentucky Fried Chicken, so he had some evidence behind his claim. However, he did not face a legislature with dramatically different policy philosophies than his. Perhaps President Obama might find heading Kentucky Fried Chicken to be a relief after being president of the United States.

Sidebar 1–1
Fire Protection as a Private Good

Households expect fire protection as a part of civilized life, an expectation that includes extinguishing any fires on the household's property and preventing any fire from spreading from the neighbor's property. Although property owners may install sprinkler systems for protection, there remains a presumption that some firefighting service will be available to combat any fire that erupts. There are alternative ways in which this service could be provided, sometimes by governmental entities, sometimes by volunteer community groups, and sometimes by private firms.

In colonial America, it was common for fire insurance companies to provide fire protection and firefighting services. Property owners paid a fee in advance, and an insurance mark was placed on the property. Fire companies would fight fires only in buildings for which that payment had been made. The companies fought the fire to reduce the loss that the insurance company would need to pay for the loss experienced by insured clients. That gave the fire insurance company a considerable incentive to extinguish the blaze as expeditiously as possible. Property owners had an incentive to pay for the insurance mark because otherwise the fire company would not extinguish the fire. But in built-up areas, fire companies ultimately had to extinguish all fires, even those on uninsured properties, because of the danger that the fire would spread to adjacent insured parcels. It was advantageous to be a free rider, certain in the knowledge that the company would fight the fire, even if the fee hadn't been paid, and private provision fell apart. Municipal fire companies supported by tax revenue became the rule throughout the world.

Insurance companies still are involved in firefighting in the western United States, however. American International Group (the AIG involved in the financial collapse of 2008) and some other insurers of high value properties operate fire protection operations for their private clients in California, Colorado, and Idaho. For example, in the Castle Rock, Idaho, wildfires of 2007, AIG sent in its own fire truck with retardant chemicals to protect seven extremely expensive properties that it covered (the homes were valued at around $35 million, so the insurance company had a lot at risk, and this was not an exercise in charity).[1] The public-good problem is that fires tend to spread, and if your neighbor does not have fire protection, the fire on his property will threaten your property. That protection of property owned by others is the public-good feature. You can be reasonably certain that AIG wasn't there fighting the fire because of these public benefits.

In a number of other parts of the country, fire protection companies are privately run and privately financed by fire protection fees paid by property owners. These are true fees for services and not disguised taxes, such as the Fire Prevention Fee collected in California. For that fee, there is a collection process associated with nonpayment, not withholding of service and paying the fee is not optional. Governments usually impose such fees because some legal or political constraints make it difficult to finance the service through straightforward taxes. Truly privatized provision is financed by voluntary payments, and failure to pay means service will not be rendered. Consequences can be tough, as the following example illustrates.

[1]William Yardley, "The Wealthy Get an Extra Shield for Wildfires," *New York Times,* August 28, 2007.

Residents of Obion County, Tennessee, have the option of paying a $75 fee for fire protection from the city of South Fulton. In October 2010, the house of a family that had chosen not to pay caught fire, the firefighters did not respond, and the house burned down. They did respond when the neighbor's field caught fire and endangered his house—the neighbor had paid the fee. Amazingly enough, the same thing happened in December 2011. Another house whose owner had not paid caught fire, and the South Fulton firefighters watched as it burned to the ground. Apparently, there are slow learners in the county.[2] The South Fulton mayor notes that the costs of the fire department have to be covered, and if the department responded to nonpayers, there would be no reason for anyone to pay. People in the city, of course, get the service automatically because it is financed by city taxes.

Other private firefighting companies have somewhat different operating procedures when confronted with a fire in a parcel that has not paid the fee. The Rural Metro Fire Department in the Maricopa County, Arizona, area battles the fire and then bills the property owner for the cost of the service. One couple in Surprise, Arizona, were surprised to receive a bill for $19,825 with charges of $1,500 per fire truck and $150 per hour for firefighters for their mobile home fire.[3] A similar approach is used by the Southside Fire Department in Georgia.

The ability to handle firefighting through private provision depends on the operating environment. When properties are densely situated, fires are likely to spread from one property to another, which makes it generally infeasible to ignore a fire on a nonpaying parcel because of the likelihood that it will spread to adjacent properties. In that environment, fire protection has public-good characteristics, and providing service through the market is of doubtful feasibility (but a private company might be contracted to produce the service that is being provided by the government). In less dense areas, fire protection is less definitely a public good and alternate approaches may be feasible. But if private financing is the choice, then the system will work only if there is a clear policy about what will happen if the property of a nonpayer catches fire.

[2]Jason Higgs, "Home Burns While Firefighters Watch." http://www.wpsdlocal6.com/news/local/Home-burns-while-firefighters-watch-again-135069773.html
[3]David Lohr, "Arizona Firefighters Charge Family Nearly $20,000 After Home Burns Down," *Huffington Post*, November 8, 2013.

Public goods include national defense, mosquito abatement, pollution control, and disease control, for example. The common characteristics of these services are the previously described nonexclusion and nonexhaustion or nonrivalry. Consider mosquito abatement. When a given level of control is provided, all people in the area receive the same service. Other people could enter the control district and simultaneously receive that same service without any additional abatement cost (marginal cost equals zero). Furthermore, there is no way to deny service to those not paying for it. Individuals in the service area may value the abatement service differently (reaction to mosquito bites varies among individuals; some people swell up in alarming fashion, and others don't—and the consequences of some mosquito-borne diseases, like Zika, are considerably more devastating to some people), but all receive the same service in terms of mosquito reduction. Public goods are the domain of public provision and public finance.

Toll goods and common-pool goods have one public-good characteristic, but not both (as shown in Figure 1–1). Toll goods are nonrival: one person can consume the service to its fullest while not reducing the amount of service someone else may consume. For these goods, however, exclusion is feasible; boundaries can separate payers and nonpayers. Examples include wifi at Starbucks, drive-in movies, and toll roads: up to a congestion point, a larger number of people can consume these services without exhausting the service concurrently available to others. All are, however, subject to exclusion: those not paying for the service may be kept from receiving the service through passwords, walls, and toll booths.

Common-pool goods are goods or services for which exclusion is not feasible but for which there are competing and exhaustive uses. Examples include aquifers, oil and gas deposits, and fisheries. There are no normal means of exercising exclusive property rights on the resource, but when used, the resource becomes unavailable for others. Left to private processes, the resource may be rapidly exhausted because it is valuable and is not, in its natural state, subject to normal ownership controls. (First-come-first-served is a normal allocation principle, so getting those resources out of the ground as quickly as possible is advantageous to any private user and is the reason governments frequently intervene in markets for natural resources. That is another element of market failure.) However, Eleanor Ostrom, Nobel Prize winner in economics, observes that self-organized local systems can successfully manage many common-pool resources without either well-defined property rights or government intervention, so analysis of the problem requires considerable attention to the institutional circumstances. Sidebar 1–2 describes one common-pool resource problem and how government action sought to remedy it.

Externalities

Government also may have a role when market transactions between buyer and seller affect third parties. The consequences may be negative (as with the exhaust fumes from automobiles) or positive (as with the protection provided pregnant women when a boy receives a rubella vaccination), but either way that value is unlikely to be fully recognized in the market transaction. For these goods and services, the private return from their consumption is substantial, so the market will not fail to provide. It will not, however, provide at a socially reasonable level.

A positive externality causes the good in question to be underproduced. In the case of the rubella vaccination, those people who are vaccinated receive the benefit of reduced probability that they will contract the disease, a direct benefit to them for which they could be expected to pay. But they also provide protection against the disease to others in that they will not infect others if they themselves do not have the disease. That is a third-party, or external, effect of the vaccination. It is unlikely that everyone considering the vaccination will take full account of these benefits when weighing the advantages of vaccination against the disadvantages (minimal discomfort and some small risk of adverse reaction, time spent and inconvenience in receiving the injection, and the out-of-pocket price of the service), and some will decide not to be vaccinated. Fewer people would be vaccinated than would be in the

Sidebar 1–2
Government Creates a Market for Fishing Rights

Market failure does not always require direct government provision of a service as a remedy. Sometimes, the government may intervene in ways that create a market where none could exist before. The Council of Economic Advisers provided one example in the *Economic Report of the President* for 1993:

> There is no practical way to establish ownership rights of ocean fish stocks. Traditionally, fish have been free for the taking—a common pool resource. Theory teaches that such underpricing leads to overconsumption. In the halibut fisheries off Alaska, fishing fleets caught so many halibut that the survival of the stock was threatened. No single fishing boat had an incentive to harvest fewer fish since the impact on its own future catch would be minimal and others would only increase their take. This is an example of what is known as "the tragedy of the commons."

> Officials tried limiting the length of the fishing season. But this effort only encouraged new capital investment such as larger and faster boats with more effective (and expensive) fishing equipment. In order to control the number of fish caught, the season was shortened in some areas from 4 months to 2 days by the early 1990s. Most of the halibut caught had to be frozen rather than marketed fresh, and halibut caught out of season had to be discarded.

> In late 1992, the federal government proposed a new approach: assigning each fisherman a permit to catch a certain number of fish. The total number of fish for which permits are issued will reflect scientific estimates of the number of fish that can be caught without endangering the survival of the species. Also, the permits will be transferable—they can be bought and sold. By making the permits transferable, the system in effect creates a market where one did not exist previously. The proposed system will encourage the most profitable and efficient boats to operate at full capacity by buying permits from less successful boats, ensuring a fishing fleet that uses labor and equipment efficiently. Moreover, the transferable permits system establishes a market price for the opportunity to fish—a price that better reflects the true social cost of using this common resource.

The cap-and-trade system for dealing with environmental protection applies a similar approach. Sources of emissions (like sulfur dioxide) are allocated an initial emissions limitation. The entity is permitted to meet the limit by whatever means it chooses (conservation, revised production technology, end-of-pipe controls, etc.), so each will select whatever method is least expensive. But the entity can exceed its limit by purchasing limit caps from other entities—those who have excess cap because of particularly efficient methods for limiting their emissions. By this means, the intended overall emission reduction is achieved at minimal cost to the economy. The market price for emission limits emerges, exactly in the same way as the price for the opportunity to fish was established.

Both are clever ways to employ market-based approaches to deal with problems of initial market failure and achieve an efficient, effective, and low-cost solution.

The permit system provided a control on overfishing for Alaska halibut and has also been applied in New Zealand with considerable success. By 2007, it was being considered for codfish and haddock in the American northeast because of rampant overfishing in the eastern Georges Bank. Establishing a market provides a way of controlling abuses associated with management of a common-pool resource.

SOURCES: Council of Economic Advisors, *Economic Report of the President, 1993* (Washington, D.C.: U.S. Government Printing Office, 1993); and Bret Schulte, "One Fish, Two Fish, No Fish," *U.S. News & World Report,* August 27, 2007.

best interests of society because of the external benefits from the personal choice about vaccination. Governments require young boys to get rubella vaccinations not simply to protect them—rubella itself is not much worse than a common cold for most otherwise healthy people—but also because we do not want them to give the disease to a pregnant woman and cause birth defects in her child. Sidebar 1–3 examines in greater detail the external impacts of vaccination.

An undesirable (or negative) externality—think of it as a "public bad"—has the opposite effect, an overproduction of the good. Automobile operators pay the operating costs of their cars to enjoy the great personal mobility that cars provide,

---

Sidebar 1–3
Vaccine Deniers and Externalities

Public health officials refer to the concept of "herd immunity": if enough of a population is immunized against an infectious disease, even those without immunization will be protected because any invading germ will not be able to spread. There is no chain of transmission. An individual receiving a vaccination does not get the disease (the internal benefit) and does not infect anyone else with the disease (the external benefit). This external benefit is particularly important because it stops epidemics and protects individuals who are unable to have the vaccination because of age or medical conditions. The economic issue is not with direct benefit to the child (families can work that out for themselves) but with the full social costs of choosing not to get the child vaccinated. The family choice is not likely to include the external benefits from the vaccination, and, as a result, there is likely to be underprovision of vaccinations and excessively high levels of disease without government intervention.

When the "herd" is sufficiently immunized, those without immunization are able to enjoy free-rider protection. But if overall immunization levels fall below a critical threshold percentage of the population, that herd protection is gone. Hence, public health officials work to maintain immunization levels even when prevailing incidence of the disease is low because protection of that "herd immunity" protects everyone and stops epidemics before they can start. That is why states require all children to have received vaccinations for childhood diseases, particularly measles/mumps/rubella, before they can enroll in school.

Here is an illustration of the importance of the vaccination cocoon: infants under two months old are particularly vulnerable to pertussis with fatal consequences. However, infants this young cannot be vaccinated for that disease because their immune systems are not fully developed. Older children are vaccinated partly to provide protection for younger children—it's the externality that matters. So parents who do not vaccinate are being particularly selfish.

There is also a measles problem. Measles is an extremely contagious disease: prior to vaccinations, one case in a classroom and everyone in the class, all siblings of everyone in the class, and probably everyone in the entire school has the disease. (Long ago, second grade got me.) Data for early years are not good, but researchers believe that the number of cases probably approached 3.5 million per year in the United States prior to the middle of the twentieth century (in other words, the entire birth cohort, because everyone got measles), although official reports are of around 500,000 cases reported each year with around 400 deaths. Things changed: a measles vaccine was licensed in 1963, vaccination rates increased, and the number of cases began to fall. By 1990, the Centers for Disease Control reported 28,000 cases and, by 2000, when 90 percent of children had the appropriate vaccination, the number was 86. In 2012, the total was 55 cases. That is close to eliminating the disease in the population.

A problem developed: most state laws allow parents to decline required immunizations for their school-age children for philosophical or religious reasons. Unfortunately, an antivaccination movement developed a few years ago, particularly amidst some celebrities who wanted greater control over what medical treatments their children received ("My child, my choice" was the view), fueled by pseudoscientists who proclaimed the risk from vaccination. The "vaccine deniers" certainly were not concerned with the impact on others of individual vaccination choice, and their children were pretty much protected because of the vaccinations received by others. However, the vaccination rate declined, with exactly the anticipated result: there were 634 cases in 2014, as a disease that had been virtually exterminated in the United States started to return. Public health workers strive to increase the vaccination rate to reestablish herd immunity and to protect vulnerable third parties. As with other vaccines, medical conditions do prevent some people from receiving the vaccination, so the only protection they receive is through third parties.

The deniers got some well-publicized consequences: sometime in December 2014, someone with measles visited Disneyland in California (located in Orange County, not only a hotbed of the antivaccination movement, but also a destination for tourists from all over the world, including from some countries where measles continue to be widespread.) Unfortunately, that person came in contact with people who had not had the measles vaccination, and the disease spread from there. By the time the outbreak was finally over, 147 people from 17 states in the United States and 159 people in Canada got the disease, and one person died (the first measles fatality in the United States since 2003), an outbreak that would never have happened if children had had their proper vaccinations. People can get away with having their children forgo vaccination as long as there is a high level of herd immunity; they can ride on the coattails of positive externality from those who have had vaccinations. When that protection is gone, cases and their consequences will rise.

In the 2015 state legislative session, California eliminated the personal and religious belief exceptions to the childhood vaccination requirement, joining Mississippi and West Virginia with such a strict requirement. Only children with serious health issues that made vaccinations dangerous to them would be allowed to opt out of the requirement. Unvaccinated children would need to be homeschooled because they would not be permitted in any public or private school in the state. It seems to be a bad idea to mess with the Magic Kingdom in California.

Just so you know that vaccine deniers are loonies without borders, a six-year-old boy in Spain died from diphtheria in July 2015, the first case in the country in twenty-eight years, because his parents accepted the idea of antivaccine activists. The disease still exists in Russia, India, and Africa, and antitoxin was flown in from Russia, but its use was not successful. Eight other children tested positive for the bacteria that carries the disease, but all had received the vaccination and none developed the disease. Spain had wiped out the disease about twenty years ago with vaccination rates of 95 percent or so—until the dawn of the deniers.

without full attention to the undesirable health and aesthetic effects of the exhaust fumes produced by their vehicles or of the congestion delays caused by having many vehicles competing for highway space. Again, this leads to a misallocation of resources: more car miles traveled than would be the case if their operators based their choices on the full social cost (internal plus external) of using the car. Here is another example of negative externality: in 2014, residents of Toledo, Ohio were warned not to drink city water because of contamination from toxic algae blooms in Lake Erie, the city's water source, caused by phosphorus run-off from farms. Excessive phosphorus fertilizer use had a negative externality not accounted for by the farmers applying it.

Governments regularly subsidize or tax to try to correct these market failures caused by externalities.[9] For instance, governments may pay producers or consumers of goods with positive externalities to encourage more consumption of the good in recognition of benefits to third parties. They may also levy corrective taxes to make purchasers and sellers respond to the external damage done by other products. The idea is to make buyers and sellers respond to the external effects of the product, to bring the third-party effect into their decision making in an economically tangible way.

Incomplete Markets and Imperfect Information[10]

Governments often intervene in markets when customers have incomplete information about products. Governments test (or supervise the testing of) new drugs, guard against the sale of hazardous products, establish certain financial disclosure standards, and so forth. The market may ultimately provide information—but not until after much grief and suffering by the unwary. Problems in the past few years with the safety of peanut butter, spinach, and dog food; the collapse of financial instrument values; and the like remind us of what happens when the regulation is broken. Consumers do not have the information on their own to protect themselves against dangers in the global economy, and if the government inspection and assurance system fails, the consequences are considerable.[11]

---

[9]When transaction costs are negligible, bargaining between users of resources can internalize external effects and cause an efficient level of output with no more government action (i.e., no taxes, no subsidies, and no prohibitions) than to establish private rights to the use of resources. (Ronald Coase, "The Problem of Social Cost," *Journal of Law and Economics* 3 (October 1960): 1–44.) Of course, that assumes neither party pulls out a gun and shoots the other, following an undesirable approach to dispute resolution.

[10]Governments also may get involved when barriers to entry (such as extreme economies of scale or trade restrictions) allow firms to exercise monopoly power to charge prices higher than justified by market conditions. These government actions normally involve regulation of various types, not fiscal mechanisms. Because big money is involved, regulated firms may capture control over the regulator and use that regulation to keep potential competitors out of the business.

[11]The classic argument for market failure in the medical care market driven by uncertainty, moral hazard, and other imperfections appears in Kenneth J. Arrow, "Uncertainty and the Welfare Economics of Medical Care," *American Economic Review,* 53 (December 1963): 941–73. Medical care markets suffer from a double market failure. First, patients don't have the information necessary to evaluate medical treatments, so there is an imbalance of knowledge problem. Second, people normally purchase insurance to cover the risk of encountering hugely expensive medical treatments, and insurance companies profit not from providing efficient care but from trying to limit insurance sales to people who won't need much care, the adverse selection problem. In sum, it is unreasonable to expect good solutions coming from this market.

Several private markets, particularly those in insurance and finance, can present special problems of adverse selection and moral hazard. *Adverse selection* occurs when insurance purchasers impose higher-than-average costs on sellers (in health insurance, for instance, those more likely to purchase insurance are those more likely to need care) or when sellers exclude such potential purchasers (health insurance companies seek to exclude those more likely to require care). The ultimate adverse selection problem in health insurance is that, in a purely unregulated private insurance system, we all would lose our health insurance if we live long enough. The cost of providing modern medical care typically rises as we get older. Insurance companies would thus keep their costs down by dropping coverage of older people, the policyholders systematically having higher medical costs. Medicare, the federal insurance program for the elderly, saves Americans from this adverse selection problem. One provision of the Affordable Care Act (Obamacare) prohibits insurance companies from denying coverage on the basis of a pre-existing condition, thus saving the nonelderly population from adverse selection.

Moral hazard is a problem when those with insurance have an incentive to cause the insured event to happen or to be less than diligent in averting the insured event. In other words, people behave in a riskier fashion when someone else stands behind them to pick up the pieces if things do not turn out well. A "heads, I win; tails, you lose" gamble is going to induce you to play the game a lot and take more risks. For example, with health insurance, there is a tendency for people to seek more treatment when the third party, the insurance company, is paying for it.[12] In a case of government failure, federally subsidized flood insurance (premiums for the federal National Flood Insurance Program, established in 1968 to cover property owners in flood-prone areas that private insurers regarded as having too much risk, represent only about 38 percent of what a full premium would be) makes people more willing to build in floodplains and in coastal areas, thus increasing the loss when the inevitable flood occurs, as with Hurricane Katrina in 2005. Indeed, it has been observed that nature produces floods, but that humans create flood damage. Subsidized flood insurance enables flood damage because few people would build in areas prone to flooding (the probability of flooding is reasonably easy to predict) without insurance being sold to them at less than market rates. Residents of the rest of the country, the ones not building in flood-prone areas, pay for the dangerous behavior of others. For example, the 2005 hurricane damage required that the subsidized flood insurance program receive $20 billion in payment from taxpayers. Some properties have been rebuilt time after time in the same location after receiving flood insurance payments. Indeed, a disproportionate share of total program losses annually comes from "repetitive loss properties." That is moral hazard in action.[13]

---

[12]Another moral hazard example: safer automobiles make it possible for drivers to behave with less caution. Do you think NASCAR drivers would drive with such reckless abandon if they did not have marvelous safety equipment installed in their cars? Do you think American football players would be tempted to use their heads in tackling if they did not have protective helmets that weaponize their heads?

[13]Another moral hazard from baseball: pitchers in the American League do not bat, so they do not face direct retaliation in the batter's box and are thus more likely to throw at opposing batters than are their counterparts in the National League, who do have to bat for themselves. J. C. Bradbury and D. J. Drinen, "Crime and Punishment in Major League Baseball: The Case of the Designated Hitter and Hit Batters," *Economic Inquiry* 45 (January 2007): 131–44.

One argument made against the federal rescue ("bailout") of financial firms in 2008–2009 was that of moral hazard: the firms and their officers were being compensated for their risky behavior, which created the financial crisis, and they would get the message that, should the opportunity for taking huge risks arise again, it was a risk worth taking because the consequences of failure would be cushioned by the federal government. But others argued that the rescue was still necessary because of an externality issue: if the financial institutions were not rescued, their problems would infect other institutions, thereby endangering the entire financial system. It is rather like the problem of fighting fires caused by careless behavior (e.g., smoking in bed): bringing the fire department to put out the fire backstops poor behavior by reducing the personal consequences of a poor choice, but it does protect neighboring properties, whose owners have done nothing wrong. Letting the fire burn teaches the careless person a lesson that likely won't be forgotten (if the person survives), but it stands a good chance of harming the innocent neighbors. The idea of trying to stop the problem of financial collapse from spreading ultimately won the day in the financial rescue program.

Reasoned government intervention involves securing widespread coverage (to prevent adverse selection) and regulating markets to ensure that decision makers feel the accurate cost implications of those choices (to prevent moral hazard). Adverse selection and moral hazard keep markets from functioning properly and require government intervention to fix the problem. Social insurance systems (public pension, health and disability, unemployment, etc.) throughout the world stem from these market problems.

Functions of Government: Economic Stabilization

Governments seek to stabilize the macroeconomy, in other words, prevent high unemployment, control inflation that could erode purchasing power and distort financial markets, and improve the prospects for economic growth and higher quality of life. The private economy experiences cycles of economic activity that translate into episodes of slow improvements in standards of living (slow or no economic growth) and general price increases that erode purchasing power of incomes and assets, distort financial and other markets, and otherwise make life miserable for the citizenry. Modern democracies accept the principle that they should attempt to mitigate the depth of downturns, to prevent high rates of price increase, and to make prospects for growth better. The Great Recession (December 2007–June 2009: those are the official dates from the National Bureau of Economic Research, the group that gauges these things. If you don't agree with those dates, complain to them, not to me.) brought public and political attention to the important role that governments can play in mitigating the misery that macroeconomic decline will produce and, more important, in reversing that decline. Few responsible leaders now take the view that, because recessions will eventually end on their own, it would be best for government to do nothing. To do nothing seems to be irresponsible. When politicians crow "Jobs! Jobs! Jobs!" they are implicitly agreeing that the private market has failed and accepting the stabilization role of government. Not many will now admit to holding the view expressed by President Herbert Hoover's Secretary of Treasury in the early days of the Great Depression of the 1930s that a good, solid recession was a beneficial way of purging the rottenness from the economic system and that no government intervention would be appropriate.[14] And those that do usually enjoy considerable job security and have no expectation that the job that intervention would save would be their own.

The stabilization policy that is expected to be the first line of defense is monetary policy. In the United States, this policy is normally in the hands of the Federal Reserve System, our central bank. (Other countries have similar institutions with similar functions.) Through various mechanisms, the Federal Reserve manipulates the supply of money available to the public and the terms under which credit is provided. These manipulations influence interest rates, and, in turn, these rates influence business investment. The impact on national aggregate demand—what policy makers are trying to stimulate to boost economic performance and reduce unemployment—occurs when businesses and other borrowers increase their investment spending because of those lower rates. Monetary policy is the first line of defense in economic stabilization because it does not have to flow through the delays of the political process that other stabilization tools must surmount. So long as the Federal Reserve is independent of the national government, it can respond to economic forces rather than political advantage.[15] The problem with monetary policy in the Great Recession was that, even when the Federal Reserve got interest rates almost to zero, businesses still did not borrow and invest in productive infrastructure, and individual households did not borrow to build houses. Without that induced capital investment, monetary policy will not stimulate aggregate demand, and the economy continues to lag. That brought a need for fiscal policy.

Fiscal policy involves making changes in government spending and in tax collections to influence aggregate demand in the economy. Government purchases directly increase aggregate demand, and reducing tax collections (a tax cut) operates indirectly by leaving households and businesses more after-tax income that they are free to spend. Government, household, and business spending gives other households and businesses income that they will spend in turn, bringing income to others—and so it goes. Only spending gives the hoped-for boost to aggregate demand. And, in terms of inducing a recovery of the economy, it doesn't much matter whether the initial government spending is to buy Buicks to drive off into the Atlantic or to build wind turbines to provide electricity without using fossil fuel—spending is spending

---

[14]Andrew Mellon was Secretary of Treasury during the Harding, Coolidge, and Hoover administrations. In line with many current politicians, he never saw a tax cut that he didn't like—except when the Great Depression hit and he thought that cutting government spending and raising taxes was just the ticket for economic recovery.

[15]Federal Reserve System profits are returned to the federal government, its operations are subject to regular financial audit, and its leadership is approved by Congress. (In 2010–2011, Congress refused to approve appointment of a Nobel Prize–winning economist to the Board of Governors because some members doubted that he had strong enough credentials in economics. Really? How dumb is that? Probably not the dumbest congressional position taken in recent years, but it has to rank pretty high on the dumbness scale.) But its policies are not subject to government approvals.

and both provide income to suppliers, who will then use that income to do stimulative spending of their own. In severe recession, it is more spending (increased aggregate demand) that is needed for economic stimulation, and how that happens is of secondary concern.

The problem with fiscal policy is its slowness—it takes time to reach consensus that a problem exists, to get legislative approval for the fiscal changes needed to implement the policy, and to get the changes into the economy. Fortunately, there is a short-cut system for fiscal policy—the automatic stabilizers. These stabilizers are integral and permanent elements of the tax and transfer system that tend to mitigate fluctuations in aggregate demand without requiring any actions by lawmakers. When income declines in a recession, tax liabilities fall, giving households more disposable income, and more households become eligible for transfer programs (such as food stamps and unemployment compensation). Those programs work to stabilize consumer spending, thus constraining the potential depth of an economic downturn. They work in the opposite way when the economy is expanding so rapidly that great price increases (high inflation) are a danger.[16]

The federal government has considerably greater flexibility to work for fiscal stabilization than do the states and localities because it has better access to debt markets (increasing spending and reducing taxes will create a higher fiscal deficit that needs to be covered) and, ultimately, because it can even print money to cover the gap.[17] State and local governments, however, usually must cover all spending in a year with revenue collected in the year (in other words, they must balance their budgets), and, as economic activity declines, they have real trouble doing this. Demand for their services rises and revenue from their taxes falls in a recession. Being fiscally responsible, as they must ultimately be, too often means tax increases and expenditure reductions—exactly the wrong medicine for the ailing economy. State and local fiscal programs can significantly counterbalance federal stabilization efforts, a reason the federal government has sometimes included grants to these governments as part of its stabilization efforts.

Governments also attempt industrial policy, meaning an effort to direct economic development in particular directions through support of particular sorts of economic activity that has been politically defined to be appropriate for the future. The targeted subsidies and tax advantages (part of the fiscal structure) are designed to stimulate particular industries, in the belief that they can increase economic

---

[16]Congressional Budget Office, *The Effects of the Automatic Stabilizers on the Federal Budget as of 2013* (Washington, D.C.: Congressional Budget Office, 2013) explains the stabilizer impact and estimates their impact on strengthening economic activity in fiscal years 2009 through 2012.

[17]Printing money to cover government expenditures even makes sense in some extremely rare economic circumstances (generally, extreme underemployment of resources in the nation), but it often creates substantial and even self-perpetuating inflation. The problem goes like this. The national government prints money to cover its spending. This spending competes for economic resources along with spending by private entities (no tax has been levied to reduce their demand for those resources). Private and government competition for limited resources causes prices to rise. To cover its spending at the higher prices, the government has to print more money, which adds to demand for resources, causes prices to rise, requires more money printing, and so it goes. This was a problem in the early days of new countries emerging from the old Soviet Union, in Zimbabwe, and, more recently, in Venezuela. The problem became so bad in Venezuela that orders for new banknotes stressed the capacity of printing plants to produce them. (Kejal Vyas, "Venezuela Orders Planeloads of Bank Notes," *Wall Street Journal,* February 4, 2016.)

growth and reduce unemployment by boosting activities destined to be national or even global leaders. Politicians and bureaucrats have a remarkably bad record at identifying industries or firms whose support will be critical for the long-term success of the nation or a region. Johnson and Kwak give us an idea about why: "the openness of the American political system has always made it possible for the current business elite to use its political power to shift the economic playing field in its favor. Any growing and profitable sector can take this route, from railroads, steel, and automobiles to defense and energy. Each of these industries has used the argument that 'what's good for (fill in the blank) is good for America' in order to obtain preferential tariffs, tax breaks, or subsidies."[18] Politicians and bureaucrats are ripe targets for these arguments, even though there is abundant evidence that targeted support is a sucker bet in which a favored group cashes in without much return for the general public. The 2011 bankruptcy of Solyndra, a solar panel maker that had received more than half a billion dollars in federal loans because it was judged to be a leader in promising clean energy technology, was one recent example.[19]

There is also not much evidence to support the idea that subnational government use of targeted tax and expenditure programs can have much of an effect on overall development of a state or local economy, but that does not stop state and local politicians from trying. The *Economist* succinctly explains why industrial and economic development policy, whether national, state, or local, has such a low success rate: "Neither economists nor emperors can be relied upon to pick winners. The best bet is entrepreneurial trial and error."[20] Government money spent to assist particular industries is, sadly, often badly spent because even the well-advised government usually guesses wrong. If lawmakers really knew how to do effective development, would there be poverty anywhere?

Functions of Government: Redistribution

One of the great strengths of a free market system is that individual effort provides the mechanism for distribution of economic rewards. Successful efforts get rewarded and that encourages people to even greater effort and society benefits. No central directorate establishes who gets what based on support for that directorate or whims of those in power. Markets distribute products of the economy to those people having and using resources (talents, properties, etc.), without distinguishing whether those resources were earned by going to medical school, serving an

---

[18]Simon Johnson and James Kwak, *13 Bankers: The Wall Street Takeover and the Next Financial Meltdown* (New York: Vantage Books, 2011), 24.

[19]The federal government—representing both political parties—has a dismal record in its support of energy schemes, including such failures as the Clinch River breeder reactor, Synthetic Fuels Corporation, clean coal, and hydrogen-powered automobiles. Steven Mufson, "Before Solyndra, a Long History of Failed Government Energy Projects," *Washington Post,* November 12, 2011.

[20]"Finding Your Niche," *Economist* 21 (March 2003): 70. There are a few success stories of government support, including commercialization of penicillin (pharmaceutical companies were reluctant to undermine the market for their profitable sulfa drugs) and, possibly, development of the Internet.

apprenticeship as a plumber, spending many days in the gymnasium perfecting a jump shot, inherited from rich parents, stolen, or whatever. Those who have the most valuable resources and put them to productive use get the goods. People with few resources—property or skills—may be destined to a life of poverty. Governments may correct perceived injustices in the distribution of affluence in society. Some argue for a degree of redistribution out of a social conscience and a desire for a safety net for all humanity; others argue for a degree of redistribution out of a fear that the poor will revolt, taking property from the affluent (the less affluent have numbers on their side in any such struggle). More recently, it has been argued that high levels of inequality reduce the rate of economic growth in the economy, thus hurting the prospects for everyone.[21] The counterargument for limited redistribution is that generous support programs will blunt individual work effort and that will cause a loss for everyone. Most politicians believe that the public wants some protection for the very poor and at least some mild redistribution by the government of the result produced by pure operation of the market. The issue is more how much and how rather than whether there should be some programs.

A dilemma of recent years in the United States is that the highest-income households have done extremely well relative to the rest of the population. Figure 1–2 shows the percent of total income earned in the nation by the highest 10 percent of families. In 2012, the latest year for which data are available, this fortunate 10 percent received half of all income earned. That is roughly 15 percentage points higher than was the case in the years from the start of World War II until the early 1980s and higher than at any other time in the 1917–2012 period. Some argue that this is no major problem, but simply reflects rewards to talent, intellect, skill, and effort applied to satisfying the demands of the American public.[22] Others argue that the system is rigged and held captive by the fortunate few and that radical reactions are appropriate. And some argue that, if not managed, inequality will get worse. Thomas Piketty provides evidence that the return on capital exceeds the rate of growth in the economy, resulting in an increasing share of income going to capital (i.e., the rich) and that this promises to continue.[23] For whatever reason, income inequality has risen in recent decades, and American governments do give attention to redistribution, paying particular attention to providing a guaranteed safety net to those at the bottom of the income scale.

Governments employ a variety of approaches toward redistribution. These include tax structures that levy relatively higher tax burdens on high-affluence households than on low-affluence ones (e.g., income taxes that levy higher effective rates on high-income households), direct income payments to low-affluence families (e.g., the earned income tax credit), programs that provide assistance services for

---

[21]Organization for Economic Cooperation and Development, *In It Together: Why Less Inequality Benefits All.* Paris: OECD, 2015.

[22]There is evidence that the fortunate few aren't the same people every year and that there is a degree of mobility across the deciles. Gerald Auten and Geoffrey Gee, "Income Mobility in the United States: New Evidence from Income Tax Data," *National Tax Journal* 62 (June 2009): 301–28. However, income class mobility in the United States appears to be somewhat less than found in some European counties.

[23]Thomas Piketty, *Capital in the 21st Century.* Cambridge, Massachusetts: Belknap Press of Harvard University Press, 2014.

Figure 1–2
The Top Decile Income Share in the United States, 1917–2012

Notes: In 2012, top 10% decile includes all families with annual income above $114,000.

SOURCE: Emmanuel Saez, "Striking It Richer: The Evolution of Top Incomes in the United States" http://eml.berkeley .edu/~saez/saez-Ustopincomes-2012.pdf.

which only low-affluence families qualify (Medicaid, a medical insurance program for the poor), or programs available to all that low-income families use more heavily (unemployment benefit programs).[24] The Social Security system provides income assistance to the disabled and the elderly, although neither program is directed only to low-income families, and Medicare provides guaranteed health insurance to the elderly. Combined, these programs have quite successfully broken the near-guarantee that growing old would mean income distress and that elderly parents would have to move in with their children out of economic necessity. However, the United States makes less aggressive use of active tax and transfer programs to handle problems of poverty than do other wealthy nations, preferring programs of economic expansion that benefit everyone, trusting that economic expansion will take care of the economic bottom as it benefits the economic top. As a result, the gap between highest and lowest incomes and the level of unrelieved poverty in the United States are considerably greater than in other wealthy nations; upward income mobility from one generation to the next is similarly less here than in many countries in Europe. Evidence is clear that in the United States people born into the top of the

---

[24]Countries in Europe attempt less redistribution through the tax system and more redistribution through direct payments than is done in the United States.

income ladder and people born into the bottom of the income ladder are likely to remain in those positions throughout their lives.[25] Given that reality, many believe that government needs to ensure that the fortunate provide some assistance for the less fortunate.

Another distribution dilemma emerges because there are considerable geographic differences in affluence within the United States. In 2014, per capita income in Connecticut was 82 percent higher than in Mississippi, a huge disparity that certainly translates into more and better options for those living in Connecticut and raises the potential for economic transfers. However, around those averages, there is the fact that there are poor people living in Connecticut and wealthy people living in Mississippi. Which is a better option: a federal redistribution approach that provides assistance to poor places or that provides assistance to poor people? The most prominent program with a location-based focus is the urban enterprise zone, a program for significant tax incentives to businesses locating in poor areas and federal grants for training, investment, and business assistance to those areas. Evidence of zone effectiveness is mixed, but it does not support the conclusion that the effort increases employment in the area. Place-based programs providing infrastructure and education have better results.[26] But it remains unclear whether direct assistance to poor people would provide better results.

Privatization

Modern societies argue about the size of government, that is, the line between government provision and market provision of goods and services. Many governments have downsized the public sector to achieve efficiency in the belief that market provision may offer more service options to the public, more flexibility in service response, and lower operating costs. Other governments have sold government assets or functions to get immediate cash. And others have maintained responsibility for provision of the service, but have arranged for its production by private firms ("outsourced").[27] After considering the appropriate functions of government, as we did in the previous section, it is also reasonable to explore the range for which various forms of privatization may be reasonable and to sort out the various meanings of privatization.

---

[25] Pablo Mitnik and David B. Grusky, *Economic Mobility in the United States*, Pew Charitable Trusts and Russell Sage Foundation, July 2015.

[26] David Neumark and Helen Simpson, "Do Place-Based Policies Matter?" *FRBSF Economic Letter*, 2015–07, March 2, 2015.

[27] An excellent analysis of the economics of privatization is John Vickers and George Yarrow, "Economic Perspectives on Privatization," *Journal of Economic Perspectives* 5 (Spring 1991): 111–32.

Why Privatize?

Several arguments have been offered to support privatization.[28] Here are three of the most frequently used:

1. **Smaller government.** Some argue for a smaller government and fewer public employees largely as a matter of philosophy, a blind faith in the badness of government. Because governments may spend without producing services (e.g., the check writing of the American Social Security system) and may be deeply involved in the private economy without even spending (e.g., the safety regulations applied to private industry or tax credits to support certain activities), privatization may reduce government production without reducing at all the size of government or state involvement in the economy. This therefore provides a weak basis for privatization. Whatever size of government provides best, not big or small out of a philosophical stand, would seem to be a more appropriate guide for public policy.

2. **Operating efficiency and response to clients.** Governments often consider privatization of public service production as a means for lower-cost or higher-quality services to the public. Governments produce under the political-bureaucratic system of central command and control, often driven from a desire to employ people with minimal attention to the need to cover costs of operation. State enterprises frequently lack a hard budget constraint and receive a government subsidy to cover any losses. This situation blunts the incentive for efficient operations and for responsiveness to clients. To survive, private businesses must respond to direct customer demand and must constrain prices out of concern for competition from other businesses. That environment drives private business toward operating efficiency (lower production cost) and improved responsiveness to customers, but only if the new private businesses face a competitive business environment. There is no reason to believe that a private monopolist city water company would be more efficient and responsive than a government monopolist city water company serving the same territory under the same regulatory conditions.

   The cost reduction associated with improved operating efficiency is a frequent objective of government privatizations in the United States. However, it is not always the case that a private system will outperform

---

[28]A desire to stem corruption was a major influence in nineteenth-century decisions for local government ownership and management of gas, electric, and water utilities and public transport enterprises. Reformers believed that managers of public organizations would have weaker incentives to capture profits for the enterprise from corrupt activities if profits were not received personally. The study also suggests that public ownership is likely to create inefficient operation and excessively high government payrolls. Edward L. Glaeser, "Public Ownership in the American City," *National Bureau of Economic Research Working Paper 8613,* December 2001. The anticorruption argument may have continued applicability in privatization discussions in the developing and transition environment, but it is not a clear call.

a government one.[29] Here are a couple of examples. The Internal Revenue Service found that it could do a better job of collecting revenue from difficult taxpayers than could private contractors forced on it by a Congress determined to prove the private sector is always more efficient. Also, the Transportation Security Administration, the agency that frustrates all air travelers, found that private air passenger screeners cost around 3 percent more than did federal screeners, although there are problems in making the comparisons.[30] For best results for the citizenry, it is best to take an agnostic attitude when considering private-public supply. Contracting does not assure cost savings, better quality, or better response. Private sector efficiencies are most likely when the task to be performed is well-defined, easily measured, and subject to competition. Otherwise, all bets are off.

3. **Cash.** Sale of government-operated enterprises may bring government revenue. Operating profits (or losses) in the future would disappear, although the enterprise would then be subject to the tax system (unless the buyer arranged a tax preference as part of the deal). If the asset was producing revenue, a toll bridge, for instance, then its sale is logically equivalent to borrowing the amount of the sale and using toll proceeds to pay off that debt. In terms of fiscal sustainability, it is exactly the same as borrowing and the sale brings no new revenue to the government. Unfortunately, many assets that governments would like to sell produce no revenue or produce revenue that is less than operating cost. That makes their market value extremely low. This is a problem that countries of the former Soviet Union had to face as they tried to move into a market economy. Many state enterprises had high production costs, and, even with private ownership, the product would not sell on national or international markets at a price sufficient to cover those costs. Although the old central plans invested heavily in these plants, their privatized value proved to be low—except in natural resource sectors (oil, gas, etc.). In other environments, the revenues have proved substantial. In some parts of the world, notably Russia, some de-privatizations have occurred, at least in part for political reasons and not because of the economic fundamentals. And a number of localities around the United States have reacquired water supply systems in recent years, often in reaction to higher water rates imposed to finance system upgrades.[31] States and localities have also sold assets (office buildings, parking lots, etc.) that they have

---

[29] Kirkpatrick, Parker, and Zhang find no evidence of better performance by private water utilities than by state-owned utilities in Africa, a continent with many nations suffering great loss from an absence of safe and affordable water services. Colin Kirkpatrick, David Parker, and Yin-Fang Zhang, "An Empirical Analysis of State and Private-Sector Provision of Water Services in Africa," *World Bank Economic Review* 20, no. 1 (2006): 143–63.

[30] Government Accountability Office, "Aviation Security: TSA's Revised Cost Comparison Provides a More Reasonable Basis for Comparing the Costs of Private-Sector and TSA Screeners," March 4, 2011. Many air travelers would gratefully face three percent higher cost of air travel if passenger screening could be made less irritating and less likely to cause flights to be missed.

[31] Jim Carlton, "Calls Rise for Public Control of Water Supply," *Wall Street Journal,* July 17, 2008, A-6. In some instances, the utility had been sold to a private firm in an effort to raise revenue for the municipality.

then leased back, the asset sale having given them quick cash to close budget gaps. These are effectively pawn shop loans, often undertaken because the government faces strict controls on its regular borrowing, and they violate fiscal sustainability principles because the government uses borrowed funds to support current operations, thus kicking the cost of government to the future. It is just disguised borrowing. If the assets have no public use, then selling them makes perfect sense—except the asset often is so specialized for government use that it has little alternative value.[32] A surplus military tank would be extremely interesting to have, but its impracticality dramatically limits prospective purchasers.

Other motives behind privatization include to provide more appropriate personnel or expertise to perform the service, to permit greater operating flexibility and reduced personnel cost (particularly fringe benefits), to quicken implementation of new programs, to increase the pace of innovation, and to improve quality of service.[33] And one suspects that sometimes the privatization was partially driven by an effort to escape unionized public provision for nonunionized private operators. Owners of privatized operations also can become important campaign contributors to those officials who have transferred public operations to them, something not possible if the operations stayed in government hands. However, all government services are not equally susceptible to outsourcing and not all motives will be satisfied in any particular privatization program. And not all motives are clearly in the public interest.

The largest transactions involve formerly nationalized industries under old concepts of the economic role of government or of the need to keep "socially or economically significant" industries under state control: telecommunications, petroleum and petrochemicals, gas distribution, automobile manufacturing, electricity generation and distribution, airlines, steel making, and so on.[34] Government operation of these industries has been notoriously bad because of political influences on service decisions (e.g., a city gets served by the national airline because an important politician lives there) and on operations (e.g., the industry is seen as employer of last resort and the resulting bloated payrolls prevent it from ever producing its

---

[32]One fiscal myth is that the federal deficit could be substantially reduced if the federal government were to sell its excess property. Although getting properties in better use is a good idea, the revenue potential is modest (a lot of what the federal government owns isn't worth much in alternative use), establishing a disposal process would be complex, and it would have only a single-shot impact. Theresa Gullo, Testimony: Selling Federal Property before the Committee on Oversight and Government Reform, U.S. House of Representatives, July 27, 2011.

[33]All of these motives, along with a need for cash, were drivers behind the privatization requirements placed on the Greek government in 2015 as one of the conditions for fiscal rescue. Among the state properties targeted for privatization: the Athens airport, Hellenic Petroleum, the state electric utility, offshore gas and oil parcels, partial ownership of commercial banks, and parcels of land and buildings.

[34]The largest of all was the sale of Nippon Telegraph and Telephone by the government of Japan. Share offerings in 1987 and 1988 raised almost $80 billion; the $40 billion offering in November 1987 is the largest security offering in history. William L. Megginson, *The Financial Economics of Privatization* (New York: Oxford University Press, 2005), 27–28.

product at a competitive cost).[35] These inefficient operations require subsidization from somewhere and, as former UK Prime Minister Margaret Thatcher observed, "They always run out of other people's money." Without other people's money, such operations will collapse.

Governments in the United States have historically been less active in privatization in the sense of sale of government assets than those in Western Europe, Latin America, Asia, Japan, New Zealand, and Australia.[36] On a global basis, Western Europe has been preeminent in privatization, largely because countries there had many state-owned enterprises and, accordingly, had lots of property with potential for privatization. Many of the big international privatizations, however, have been in industries never publicly owned in the United States. Privatization of roads, airports, the postal system, schools, and the like raise much more interesting social, political, and economic issues than the state sale of telephone or petrochemical companies, which have produced the largest privatization revenue globally.[37] The services of roads, airports, schools, and so on are different because their services have a degree of publicness and external impact that other publicly owned capital assets may lack. But some providers of apparently public goods have been sold: the United Kingdom sold 70 percent of Royal Mail for 1.98 billion pounds in 2013 and has plans now to sell the rest, and Austria, Germany, Belgium, and the Netherlands privatized their postal services sometime earlier.

In recent years, there have been a number of large public asset sales or extraordinarily long-term leases in the United States.[38] These include the 99-year lease of the Chicago Skyway for $1.8 billion, the 75-year lease of the Indiana Toll Road for $3.8 billion, the 99-year lease of Chicago's Midway Airport for $2.5 billion (a deal that seems to have collapsed when the lessors were unable to obtain sufficient financing), the 50-year lease of parking facilities by Ohio State University for $483 million, the 99-year lease of the Pocahontas Parkway in Virginia for $548 million (plus some additional highway construction), and the 75-year lease of parking meter revenue in Chicago for $1.16 billion. The City of Cleveland in 2011 leased Seneca Golf Course for 99 years to Cleveland Metroparks, a special-purpose local government encompassing Cuyahoga County and part of Medina County, primarily to get rid

---

[35] National airlines can face difficult political barriers to efficient operations. Keith Johnson and Luca Di Leo, "Alitalia Can't Stanch Red Ink," *Wall Street Journal,* April 21, 2004, A-16. Staff reductions then being proposed would have brought Alitalia down to about 1,100 passengers per employee, compared with about 9,000 passengers per employee for the competing discount carrier Ryanair.

[36] In the 1977–2000 peak period for privatizations internationally, privatization revenues in Japan and the United Kingdom greatly exceeded those of any other developed country. Bernardo Bortolotti and Domenico Siniscalco, *The Challenges of Privatization, An International Analysis* (Oxford, England: Oxford University Press, 2004), 43.

[37] The pioneer of privatization in the last decades of the twentieth century, Britain, has been unable to fully privatize its coal industry, so apparently technically simple decisions do get muddled by politics and other factors.

[38] Federal tax law regards lease of an asset for a period longer than its useful life to be a sale. Following that reasonable logic, these long-term leases can reasonably be discussed as sales regardless of the packaging of the deal. Edward D. Kleinbard, Testimony at a Hearing of the Subcommittee on Energy, Natural Resources, and Infrastructure of the Committee on Taxation on Tax and Financing Aspects of Highway Public-Private Partnerships, July 24, 2008. http://finance.senate.gov/hearings/testimony/2008test/072408ektest.pdf.

of a loss-making enterprise. In the typical asset sale, the government is trading the future user charge revenue from the asset for the payment of immediate revenue, a mechanism for "securitizing" (borrowing) that revenue flow. Because each of these assets is unique, it is extremely difficult to determine whether the sale price was too high or too low. In all the sales cited above, there are at least some who claim that the payment received was far below the market value of the asset, a claim that is impossible to either confirm or refute with certainty, although we do know that the entity that purchased the Indiana Toll Road went bankrupt. And because all these sales are relatively recent, it is impossible to know whether the public will feel it is getting good-quality service for the prices being charged by the private operators. The transactions involve changing the timing of revenue rather than the creation of a new revenue source. The public body is collecting the revenue when the lease is made at the sacrifice of the revenue that it would have collected from the public asset in future years.

Great care must be used in the selection of government assets for sale and in the use of the proceeds of those sales. Here is the most important point to be made about the sale of public assets: using proceeds from the sale of government assets as revenue to cover operating costs and thinking you have made the public better off is about the same as burning pieces of your house for heat and thinking that you are better off because you haven't had to buy firewood. That is a long-term losing strategy that will make future generations less able to enjoy the standard of life enjoyed now. It uses resources bought by previous generations to subsidize current consumption and leaves a lowered resource endowment for the future. That violates fiscal sustainability—although it is always popular with current politicians because it allows them to kick the problem ahead to another set of politicians. Whether sale of public assets for cash will also lead to improved performance for the public is an open question and should be a point for analysis rather than an operating assumption.

Versions of Privatization: Production/Provision

The American privatization issue frequently concerns the provision–production dichotomy.[39] Goods and services provided by a government because of market failure need not be produced by that government. Provision means government intervention to ensure and control availability or, generally, to finance the service; it does not require production by the government. The production choice should be made according to which entity—a government department, a private entity (profit or nonprofit), or another government—would supply the desired quantity and quality of service at least cost to the citizenry.

---

[39]It also encompasses application of user-pay concepts, including sale of service and tax payments based on the benefits received from particular government services. These mechanisms bring some market like principles but do not alter public provision and thus are discussed in the revenue section of this book.

The distinction between government and private production and provision can be clarified by examples:

1. *Government provision/government production.* The city street department plows the streets after a heavy snowfall. The job uses department managers, department employees, department equipment, and department supplies.

2. *Government provision/private production.* The county hires a private appraisal firm to estimate values of real estate in the county for use in computing property tax bills. The firm does the work with its managers, employers, equipment, and supplies. Or a library board contracts with Library Systems and Services International for operation of its library branches. At the federal level, the U.S. Department of Defense hires private firms to provide food and other support services to military units in the field. The military has almost always relied on private suppliers for equipment and material rather than trying to produce those resources itself. Outsourcing/contracting out is almost certainly the most common privatization practiced in the United States.[40] Some local governments (e.g., Weston, Florida) rely on contract suppliers for all the services they provide.[41] Such "outsourcing" works best when the contract pays for a concrete and observable outcome, prevents operations that deliver only in the easy areas ("cream-skimming"), and ensures that the measured outcome cannot be gamed. The contractor will concentrate on providing the measure for which it is being paid.[42]

3. *Private provision/government production.* A racetrack pays a city for extraordinary traffic control services on race days.

4. *Private provision/private production.* A private manufacturer patrols its factory site with its own security employees.[43] Neighboring properties may receive some protection spillover from this security activity.

Even parts of the judicial system may be privately produced: California permits litigants to hire private jurists when court congestion or special expertise makes such a procedure attractive to both parties, and private firms have undertaken contractual

---

[40]U.S. General Accounting Office, *Privatization: Lessons Learned by State and Local Governments,* GAO/GGD-97–48 (Washington, D.C.: U.S. Government Printing Office, 1997).

[41]Jonas Prager, "Contract City Redux: Weston, Florida, as the Ultimate New Public Management Model City," *Public Administration Review* 68 (January/February 2008): 155–66. An earlier version of this is the California Lakewood Plan. Robert Bish, *The Public Economy of Metropolitan Areas* (Chicago: Markham, 1971), 85.

[42]Some governments use "public-private-partnerships" or P3s to build and operate highways, prisons, water facilities, and so on. The idea is that the private firm covers the up-front costs and then operates and collects revenue from tolls or other revenue produced by the facility. Any project that has substantial capital cost that the government would have trouble financing (for instance, because of debt restrictions) but has potential for yielding revenue as it goes into operation is a P3 candidate.

[43]Businesses and individuals in the United States spend over twice as much for private security as governments spend on providing public safety. "Welcome to the New World of Private Security," *Economist* (April 19, 1997): 21.

operation of corrections facilities.[44] School systems have similarly chosen private production through vouchers or charter schools.[45] In these systems, the school district provides financing, but the educational service is produced by another entity.

If government seeks to provide services of desired quantity and quality at the least cost to the public, privatized production should always be kept as an open option. When might contracting not be an efficient option? One study suggests that in-house production may be warranted when "(1) there are very few potential suppliers, (2) costs of switching from one producer to another are high, (3) information about the production process and supplier performance is expensive to obtain, and (4) the good or service being provided cannot be clearly defined."[46] In other words, the option would be difficult if contracts would be especially difficult to write and the public would end up being confronted with a monopoly supplier. Otherwise, out-of-government production can be an efficient option. A study of the use of private contractors to support military operations in Iraq also noted that security contracts would not need to be renewed if needs declined, whereas military units doing the work would need to remain in the force structure even with the declining need.[47]

The federal government has defined the boundaries for its privatization by contract actions:

> An inherently governmental activity is an activity that is so intimately related to the public interest as to mandate performance by government personnel. These activities require the exercise of substantial discretion in applying government authority and/or in making decisions for the government. Inherently governmental activities normally fall into two categories: the exercise of sovereign government authority or the establishment of procedures and processes related to the oversight of monetary transactions or entitlements.[48]

---

[44]"California Is Allowing Its Wealthy Litigants to Hire Private Jurists," *Wall Street Journal*, August 6, 1980; and U.S. General Accounting Office, *Private and Public Prisons: Studies Comparing Operational Costs and/or Quality of Service*, GAO/GGD-96–158 (Washington, D.C.: U.S. Government Printing Office, 1996). Corrections Corp. of America, the largest private prison operator in the United States, operates sixty-four facilities spread across around twenty states and the District of Columbia. Correction facilities face an interesting incentive problem: it is against their economic interests to rehabilitate criminals in their care because successful rehabilitation reduces demand for their incarceration services, so it is quite important to make sure that their performance contract provides the appropriate incentives and performance metrics. Stephanie Chen, "Growing Inmate Population Is Boon to Private Prisons," *Wall Street Journal*, November 19, 2008, A4.

[45]Gary Putka, "Baltimore Test of Privatization Gets a Bad Start," *Wall Street Journal*, September 23, 1992. Voucher systems provide families an education grant—a subsidy for the purchase of education—that may be spent on services from a variety of producers. Charter schools allow private entities to create schools outside the public system, with financing from public funds. Families pick among schools.

[46]John C. Hilke, *Competition in Government-Financed Services* (New York: Quorum Books, 1992), 8. Why does the federal government run its own printing house, the Government Printing Office? To learn more about mixed motives, see Graeme Browning, "Stop the Presses?" *National Journal* 25 (October 16, 1993): 2483–85.

[47]Congressional Budget Office, *Contractors' Support of U.S. Operations in Iraq* (Washington, D.C.: Congressional Budget Office, 2008).

[48]Executive Office of the President, Office of Management and Budget, Circular No. A-76 (Revised), Subject: Performance of Commercial Activities, May 29, 2003, A–2.

If an activity is "inherently governmental," it should not be carried out by a contractor, but should be undertaken by government employees. Of course, the boundaries of this standard are subject to considerable debate, even though the concept is clear.

Privatization of provision is a more difficult problem. For public goods, the market will not function because the private supplier will not charge an efficient price for the service because of nonrivalry and inability to exclude. Business firms provide goods and services because they intend to make money, not for the sheer enjoyment of providing the goods or services. If it is not possible to charge people for the good or service, a business firm will seldom provide it. Furthermore, the price will exceed the cost of providing service to an additional consumer (recall that the additional cost is zero).

The expectation of government provision of public goods is strong, but occasionally governments will provide private goods as well and often do a very bad job of it. Organizational problems, particularly lack of appropriate production incentives, cause high costs, undesirable production strategies, and a bland product designed by an uneasy consensus. Governments provide toll goods (highways, bridges, etc.), and sometimes they do about as well as the private producer would do. But even some toll goods are provided by private businesses. For instance, in France eight public-private joint ventures and one private company operate the toll highway/tunnel system, the most extensive auto toll system in Europe. Private toll roads have a long history in the United States, starting with the Philadelphia Lancaster Turnpike in 1792. Recent enterprises are the Dulles Greenway in Virginia, dating from the 1990s, along with the privatized Chicago Skyway and Indiana Toll Road, as mentioned earlier. In addition, there are over 2,000 privately owned toll bridges in the United States.

Some observers of public fiscal problems have suggested that private provision would relieve pressures on government finances. That is a realistic response if the service being privatized in fact lacks substantial public-good features; one wonders why, in such a case, the government got involved in its provision. On the other hand, to expect private firms to provide public goods at desirable levels is folly. At best, the private firm may be contracted to produce the public good provided (paid for) by the government.

Building Public Choices from Individual Preferences

Public choices in a democracy do not come from a czar, but rather through some variety of voting, either directly or indirectly. To understand how results emerge through votes, it is helpful to consider how individual choices are translated into public decisions. The logic of moving from individual choice to choices made by society is built on three fairly simple tenets. First, individuals are the best judges of their own well-being and generally act to improve that well-being as they see it. There is no scientific principle that leads us to reject or accept the judgments made by individuals about their own lives. Second, the welfare of the community depends on the welfare of the individuals in that community. In other words, communities are made up of people, and community welfare increases only if the welfare of those in the community is improved. From that comes the third tenet, judging the impact of a social action on the welfare of the community. The Pareto criterion, named after a nineteenth-century economist, holds that if at least one person is better off from a policy action and no person is worse off, then the community as a whole is unambiguously better off for the policy.[49] Does a social action harming anyone, despite improving the condition of many individuals, improve the welfare of society as a whole? It cannot be indisputably argued that such an action improves the well-being of society, regardless of the numbers made better off, because the relative worth of those harmed cannot scientifically be compared with that of those helped. Such a proposed policy would fail the Pareto criterion for judging social action.[50]

With those standards, we can analyze the implications of nonappropriability for public provision. Suppose that only five people would be influenced by construction of a levee to protect a small area from periodic flooding. The cost of that levee is $20,000. Each individual in this community knows the maximum sacrifice that he or she would be willing to make to have that levee as compared to having no levee at all. Presumably, it would not be larger than the individual damage avoided by having levee protection. The property owners have a pretty good idea of what they would lose in a flood that the levee could protect against. These are the individual benefit numbers in Table 1–1. The levee would be a public good because each individual could use it without diminishing its availability to anyone else in the community (stopping the flooding for one person wouldn't alter the amount of flood averting available to others behind the levee), and exclusion of nonpayers is not feasible (if your property is behind the levee, it will be protected even if you didn't pay the levee charge).

First, would the levee be built without public action, that is, by individual action only? The cost of the levee is $20,000; the most that any single individual (individual D) will pay to get the levee built is $9,000. Thus, the levee would not be produced by

Table 1–1
Individual Benefits from the Project: Example 1

Individual	Individual Benefit	
A	$8,000	
B	$7,000	
C	$6,000	*Total cost* $20,000
D	$9,000	
E	$6,000	
Total benefit	$36,000	

---

[49] Vilfredo Pareto, *Manuel d'Economie Politique,* 2d ed. (Paris: M. Giard, 1927), 617–18.
[50] Benefit-cost analysis, an analytic technique discussed in a later chapter, employs a less restricting and somewhat less appealing rule than the Pareto criterion. This is the Kaldor criterion, which holds that a social action improves community welfare if those benefiting from a social action could hypothetically compensate the losers in full and still have gain left over. Because no compensation need actually occur, losers can remain, and the Pareto criterion would not be met.

any single individual. If the levee only cost $8,500 to construct, however, we suspect individual D would build the levee for his or her benefit, and four other people in the community would receive benefits from the levee without payment. (The four would be *free riders,* but D would still be better off for having built the levee.) Once the levee is there, it serves all because of its public-good features.[51] The initially presumed construction cost, however, is such that the maximum individual benefit is less than the cost of the project, so the levee will not be built by private action.

Is the levee a good economic choice for the community; that is, do total benefits exceed total construction and operating cost? The social cost, the value of the resources being used in the construction of the levee, equals $20,000. The social benefit of the levee, the sum of the improved welfare of the individuals with the levee, equals $36,000. Because social benefits are greater than social costs, it is a desirable project.[52] A responsive government would act to provide the levee and would raise sufficient funds through the revenue structure to finance the project. If the government levied an equal per capita tax—a payment based on the coercive power of government rather than the voluntary payment of market exchange—on the community to finance the levee ($4,000 each), all individuals would still be better off with the levee and the tax than without the combination.[53] Government can thus provide a desired service that public-good features prevent private action from providing.

A second example yields additional insights. Assume that the community receives benefits from a project as shown in Table 1–2. The project, a levee in another location, is a public good. The cost of the project is $20,000. Because the sum of individual benefits ($19,000) is less than the cost of the project, the project resources would be worth more in uses other than a levee. Suppose, however, that the project decision will be made at a referendum among the people in the community, with a

Table 1–2
Individual Benefits from the Project: Example 2

Individual	Individual Benefit	Cost Share	Individual Gain
A	$5,000	$4,000	$1,000
B	$5,000	$4,000	$1,000
C	$2,000	$4,000	–$2,000
D	$1,000	$4,000	–$3,000
E	$6,000	$4,000	$2,000
Total	$19,000	$20,000	

---

[51] Voluntary associations (clubs) represent an intermediate option between a government with sovereign powers and individual action. Neighborhood associations offer an example popular in some regions.
[52] A small number of people may construct the levee without the full coercion of government. For instance, individuals A, B, and D could form a small property-owners association; the sum of benefits to those three exceeds the cost. These people might privately agree to build the levee for their protection—and benefits would spill over to C and E.
[53] This tax "system" is selected for convenience alone. It is not a "model" or an "ideal" in any sense.

simple majority required for passage. The referendum also includes the method to be used to finance the project: an equal per capita tax (project cost divided by number of people in the community, or $4,000 per person). If the people in the community vote according to their individual net gain or loss from the project (as computed in Table 1–2), it will be approved (three for, two against). Does voter approval make the project desirable for the community? Not at all because the project misallocates resources: its cost is greater than the amount of benefits that it yields. The majority vote may misallocate resources.

A third example further illustrates the problems of public decision making. Table 1–3 presents individual benefits from a project with a total cost of $12,500 and an equal per capita tax method of distributing project costs. Total benefits do exceed total cost, so the project apparently represents an appropriate way to use scarce resources, and the project would be approved by majority vote if the people voted according to their individual gains or losses. The project, however, does leave one individual worse off. Is the loss to E less important to the community than the gains of A, B, C, and D? That answer requires a value judgment about the worth of the individuals to society, a judgment with which science and Pareto cannot help. One option would be to distribute costs in exactly the same proportion as individual benefits. That is the approach shown in the last column of Table 1–3. Any project for which total benefits exceed total cost has possible cost distributions from which all will be made better off. There is no redistribution of individual cost from which all will be made better off for projects like that demonstrated in Table 1–2, but choices about situations like that shown in Table 1–3 are difficult. Politicians make such decisions regularly, but not with scientific justification.

One voting rule would ensure that only projects that pass the Pareto criterion could be approved. That rule is unanimity, if we assume that people will not vote for policies contrary to their own best interest. This rule is seldom used because reaching decisions often requires substantial costs. Certain decisions are more dangerous to minorities (the losers in decisions) than others, and those decisions may require unanimity. For instance, many juries must reach a unanimous verdict because of the very high external costs that juries can place on people. For similar reasons, constitutional revision has high-percentage vote requirements.

Table 1–3
Individual Benefits from the Project: Example 3

Individual	Individual Benefit	Cost Share	Individual Gain	Individual Share of Total Benefits	Benefit-Based Cost Share
A	$3,000	$2,500	$500	15%	$1,875
B	$5,000	$2,500	$2,500	25%	$3,125
C	$8,000	$2,500	$5,500	40%	$5,000
D	$3,000	$2,500	$500	15%	$1,875
E	$1,000	$2,500	–$1,500	5%	$625
Total	$20,000	$12,500		100%	$12,500

Politics, Representation, and Government Finance

Decisions about public spending, revenue raising, borrowing, and so on are intensely political and involve personal interests, interest groups, political parties, and the process of representation. Therefore, irrational choices will be made, resources will be misallocated, and scams will be implemented. Sound governance processes and institutions can improve the odds of reasonable choices, but that's all. Even the clearest preferences of any particular individual are usually filtered through representation, and that one preference becomes part of a vote that may or may not be in the majority whose choice prevails. The many elements that produce a fiscal choice are diverse, but a framework devised by Anthony Downs for exploring the process of representation can help with an understanding of what influences these decisions.[54] He hypothesizes that political parties in a democracy operate to obtain votes to retain the income, power, and prestige that come with being in office. Parties are not units of principle or of ideals, but are primarily seekers of votes. A lack of perfect knowledge, however, permeates the system: parties do not always know what citizens want; citizens do not always know what the government in power or its opposition has done, is doing, or should be doing to try to serve citizen interests. Information that would reduce this ignorance is expensive to acquire. The scarcity of knowledge obscures the path that would lead from citizen preferences to their votes. Neither political parties nor elected representatives know exactly what the voters want, and the voters do not know exactly what the government is up to.

Several consequences for the representative process result. First, some people are politically more important than others because they can influence government action. One person, one vote is the ideal slogan, but it doesn't represent political influence particularly well. Having lots of money to contribute to campaigns helps. Second, specialists in influencing people will appear, and some will emerge as representatives of the people. These individuals will try to convince the government that the policies they support, and that directly benefit them, are good for and desired by the electorate. Information provided by these individuals will be filtered to provide only data consistent with the supported cause. A rational government will discount these claims, but it cannot ignore them. Third, imperfect information makes a government party susceptible to bribery simply because the party in power needs resources to persuade voters to keep it in power. Parties out of power are susceptible as well, but they have less to sell. It is no accident that corruption scandals involve more Republicans when the Republicans are in power and more Democrats when the Democrats are in power. Political influence is a necessary result of imperfect information combined with the unequal distribution of income and wealth in society. Parties have to use economic resources to provide and obtain information.

Lobbying is a rational response to the lack of information, but an important imbalance of interests influences the lobbying process. Suppose a direct subsidy to industry is being considered. This subsidy is of great total value to that industry. The total subsidy paid by taxpayers, of course, exactly equals the subsidy received by the

---

[54]Anthony Downs, *An Economic Theory of Democracy* (New York: Harper & Row, 1956).

industry. However, each taxpayer bears only a small individual share of that total subsidy. Who will undertake the expense of lobbying on the measure? The industry will, not the taxpayer, because the net benefit of lobbying is positive for the industry (comparing the substantial cost of lobbying with the substantial direct benefit to the industry) and negative for any taxpayer (because the substantial lobbying cost overwhelms the small individual share of the subsidy that could be saved).

These efforts to influence fiscal decisions take two general forms. Traditional lobbying is personal: "Affable men in suits would hang around swarming, sweaty legislative chambers, buttonholing lawmakers as they swaggered through lustrous bronzed doors, whispering in ears, slapping backs, winking knowingly."[55] The lobbyists know the elected representatives and have access to them, know the unelected administrators carrying out public policies, and use these contacts to deliver the message of their clients on issues. Many former legislators and agency administrators—federal and state—develop lucrative careers as lobbyists, using contacts and friendships to help deliver the message of the interests they represent; their value is in their access to the people who remain in government. In one recent example, the member of Congress primarily responsible for the Medicare Prescription Drug Improvement and Modernization Act of 2003 (P.L.108173), an act that provided significant new revenue for the pharmaceutical industry and avoided price constraints on prescription medicines, left Congress for a position as chief lobbyist for brand-name drug companies.[56] Many call this easy mobility between legislative or executive positions and interested private entities "a revolving door," and few believe it to be contributory to the public interest. But it is part of the way in which public policies get adopted today.

Grassroots lobbying is the mobilization of constituent action, reflected in letters, phone calls, emails, faxes, and other direct contacts to the elected representative. Mass campaigns had great successes in getting civil rights legislation and in shaping other policies, but communications and information technologies make it much easier to generate what appears to be a groundswell of interest and masses of constituent communications on public policy questions, including those of government expenditure and taxation. Such manufactured communications are called "Astroturf lobbying" because they are only an artificial reflection of public concerns, not the true grassroots. And social media experts are valuable for mobilizing supporters and directing views to lawmakers.

A final important point in the process of representation deals with the intensity of preference. In ordinary voting, intensity of preference is not registered. Each vote has equal weight. In a legislative body, however, the flow of many issues allows

---

[55] Ron Faucheux, "The Grassroots Explosion," *Campaigns and Elections* (December 1994–January 1995). Lobbying state legislators can be crass: "It's one of the accepted rules in the unwritten guide to being a lobbyist. The way to get a lawmaker's ear is to get him a drink first." Christi Parsons and Rick Pearson, "Springfield Has a Gift for Grab," *Chicago Tribune,* July 6, 1997.
[56] As Robert L. Livingston, former head of the House Appropriations Committee who became president of a lobbying firm, said about lobbying: "There's an unlimited business out there for us." Jeffrey H. Birnbaum, "The Road to Riches Is Called K Street," *Washington Post,* June 22, 2005, A1. K Street in Washington is where the offices of the major lobbyists are located.

legislators to trade a vote on a minor issue (according to that person's preferences) for a vote on a more important one. Trading votes allows adjustments according to intensity of preference. For example, a member of Congress may be interested in getting a bridge built in her district, another may want a levee in his district, and a third may want work done on a military base in his district. They don't care one way or another about the other projects—the cost of any one isn't big enough to have a discernible impact on tax rates, so they see no obvious impact. In this circumstance, the members of Congress may trade their votes—I'll support your project if you support mine—to get a project approved. This process, called *logrolling,* can produce wasteful spending (an irrigation project yielding benefit to a small area at great national cost, for instance).

How does vote trading create wasteful spending? Refer to the example in Table 1–4 for those three projects previously noted. The table indicates the net benefit or cost to voters in five legislative districts of each of the three projects. Suppose that the members of Congress vote according to what benefits the people in their districts and that the projects are considered separately (no logrolling here). In this case, four out of five will vote against each project, and the projects, each with benefits less than project cost, all get defeated. Now suppose that the three members of Congress with project proposals get together and create a bundled proposal with all three projects and an agreement to trade votes. On a bundled basis, district A benefits in total (plus 12 from the bridge, minus 4 from the levee, and minus 4 from the military base), district B benefits in total (minus 8 from the bridge, plus 12 from the levee, and minus 2 from the military base), and district C benefits in total (minus 2 from the bridge, minus 4 from the levee, and plus 12 from the military base). Districts D and E do not gain from the bundled/logrolled package of projects, but their negative votes don't matter because the three members of Congress have a majority in favor of the bundle. Of course, legislative bodies, like Congress, have lots more members, but everybody has pet projects, and by combining the projects and logrolling, lots of money gets wasted. It's as simple as that.[57]

Table 1–4
Logrolling, Project Bundling, and Government Waste
(Net Benefits [+] or Net Costs [–] to Voters in District)

District	Bridge in A	Levee in B	Military Base in C	Bundled Net
A	12	–4	–4	4
B	–8	12	–2	2
C	–2	–4	12	6
D	–2	–4	–6	–12
E	–4	–4	–2	–10
Net for Project	–4	–4	–2	–10

---

[57] Example based on James Gwartney and Richard L. Stroup, *Microeconomics: Private and Public Choice,* 8th ed. (Chicago: Dryden Press, 1997), 503.

The majority in a referendum can inflict severe cost on the rest of society with dramatic consequences for the social fabric. The major disadvantage of the referendum process must emerge from the absence of minority power in the direct legislation system. An initiated referendum has no provision for executive veto, creation of political stalemates in the legislative process, or changed negotiating positions in committees, all vital positions of lawmaking that can serve to protect minorities.[58]

The Layers of Government

In the United States, three layers of government with sovereignty of their own (not a single government) provide public services, levy taxes, and borrow money. Indeed, Americans must really love governments because we have so many of them: at last count, we had 90,107 of them—1 federal government, 50 state governments, and 38,910 local governments (of these, 3,031 were counties, 19,519 were municipalities, and 16,360 were townships, all general purpose governments) and 51,146 were special-purpose units, including school districts.[59] Or maybe we don't trust governments at all, so we want to keep them small and weak. Whatever the reason, the United States certainly sets the standard for numbers of independent governments.[60]

Not all nations are governed in this fashion. Some governments are unitary, meaning that a single national government has legislative authority over the entire country. There may be local councils with certain powers, but they function only on the approval of the national government. In many unitary states, local revenue and expenditure programs must be approved by the national government, and a single consolidated financial program (or budget) exists for the entire country. Unitary states include Belgium, France, the Netherlands, Norway, Poland, and many countries of the former Soviet Union (but not Russia). The United Kingdom, historically unitary, is devolving some powers to regional parliaments in Scotland and Wales.

Other nations are federal. In the United States, states exist as an independent layer of government with full powers (including independent financial authority) and all residual powers.[61] Other important federal states include Argentina, Australia, Austria, Brazil, Canada, Germany, India, Mexico, and the Russian Federation (although recent changes there to reduce sovereign powers of regional and local governments and move them to the national government have moved the nation closer to being a unitary state—the national administration frets about the "power vertical" from national to subnational governments, a clear indication of less than robust

---

[58]John L. Mikesell, "The Season of the Tax Revolt," in *Fiscal Retrenchment and Urban Policy,* ed. John P. Blair and David Nachimaias (Newbury Park, Calif.: Sage, 1979), 128.

[59]U. S. Bureau of Census, Governments Division, *2012 Census of Governments.*

[60]China has far more local entities, but these units do not have the degree of sovereignty necessary to count them as governments.

[61]The national government under the Articles of Confederation, precursor to the Constitution, lacked the power to tax. Payments from the states proved inadequate, so it is no wonder that it resorted to finance by printing money, which proved to be disastrously inflationary.

commitment to the federalism concept). In each instance, to understand government finances—spending, taxing, and borrowing—one must understand the intergovernmental structure in the country. In no way are the subnational governments in these federal countries dependent departments of the central government, as they would be in a unitary state.

In the U.S. federal system, constitutional terms define the elemental financial powers and limits under which the levels function. First, there are powers and limits to national (federal) authority: Article I, section 8, lists fiscally significant powers. These include the powers

> To lay and collect taxes, duties, imposts and excises, to pay the debts and provide for the common defense and general welfare of the United States; but all duties, imposts and excises shall be uniform throughout the United States.

> To borrow money on the credit of the United States.

> To regulate commerce with foreign nations, and among the several States, and with the Indian tribes.

> To coin money, regulate the value thereof, and of foreign coin, and fix the standard of weights and measures.

> To establish post-offices and post-roads.

> To raise and support armies, but no appropriation of money to that use shall be for a longer term than two years.

> To provide and maintain a navy.

Article I, section 9, establishes some fiscal constraints on the federal government:

> No capitation, or other direct, tax shall be laid, unless in proportion to the census of enumeration herein before directed to be taken.

> No tax or duty shall be laid on articles exported from any State.

> No money shall be drawn from the Treasury, but in consequence of appropriations made by law; and a regular statement and account of the receipts and expenditures of all public money shall be published from time to time.

Of course, legislation and court decisions have, over the years, specifically defined what these powers and constraints mean in practice.

The major constitutional provision for states appears in the Tenth Amendment of the Constitution: "The powers not delegated to the United States by the Constitution, nor prohibited by it to the States, are reserved to the States respectively, or to the people." The states thus have *residual powers*. The Constitution does not need to provide specific authority for a state government to have a particular power: constitutional silence implies that the state can act in the area in question, thus establishing states as the sovereign "middle layer" in the federal system. Much of what states do in regard to their finances falls within these residual powers.

The Constitution similarly identifies, in Article I, section 10, what states cannot do. Of fiscal significance is the prohibition against coining money. Therefore, states cannot bail themselves out of a sticky fiscal problem by printing currency to cover the gap. The Commerce Clause (Article I, section 8, paragraph 3, listed above) prevents state interference with international commerce and commerce among the states, a particularly significant limit on taxing power and regulatory authority in a global economy. A later amendment (Article XIV, section 1) requires states to follow due process in their actions and to afford equal protection of the law to all within their jurisdictions.[62] The federal equal-protection clause often has been copied in state constitutions. The dramatic change in school finance in California generated by the court case *Serrano v. Priest (Cal. 3d 584 P. 2d 1241, 97 Cal. Rptr. 601 (1971))* resulted from state constitutional provisions copied after those in the federal Constitution.

Local governments in the United States typically appear as captive creatures of their states unless state action has specifically altered that relationship. This principle was defined by Judge J. F. Dillon of Iowa:

> It is a general and undisputed proposition of law that a municipal corporation possesses and can exercise the following powers and no others: First, those granted in express words; second, those necessarily or fairly implied in or incident to the powers expressly granted; third, those essential to the declared objects and purposes of the corporation— not simply convenient, but indispensable. Any fair, reasonable, substantive doubt concerning the existence of power is resolved by the courts against the corporation, and the power denied.[63]

Dillon's rule holds that if state law is silent about a particular local power, the presumption is that the local level lacks power. In state-local relationships, state government holds all powers. That is a critical limitation on local government fiscal activity.

Several states have altered Dillon's rule by granting home-rule charter powers to particular local governments. Such powers are particularly prevalent in states containing a small group of large metropolitan areas with conditions substantially different from the environment in other areas of the state. The special conditions of such large cities can be handled by providing them with home-rule charter power to govern their own affairs. When charter powers have been provided, local governments can act in all areas unless state law specifically prohibits those actions. Many times, however, fiscal activities are included in the range of areas that are prohibited under charter powers. Thus, it is better to presume limits than to presume local freedom to choose in fiscal affairs. That presumption is accurate if Dillon's rule applies or if charter powers have been constrained in fiscal activities.

---

[62] Two examples: public schools, as examined in Rosemary O'Leary and Charles R. Wise, "Public Managers, Judges, and Legislators: Redefining the 'New Partnership,'" *Public Administration Review* 51 (July/August 1991): 316–27; and jails, as examined in Jeffrey D. Straussman and Kurt Thurmaier, "Budgeting Rights: The Case of Jail Litigation," *Public Budgeting & Finance* 9 (Summer 1989): 30–42.

[63] John F. Dillon, *Commentaries on the Law of Municipal Corporations*, 5th ed. (Boston: Little, Brown, 1911), vol. 1, sec. 237. See *City of Clinton v. Cedar Rapids and Missouri Railroad Company*, 24 Iowa 455 (1868).

Conclusion

An overview of the basis for government action certainly indicates that government choices made in budgeting and raising revenue will not be simple. Government will be unable to sell its services because these services are nonappropriable (neither excludable nor exhaustible). That means that government will not have market tests available to help it with choices and sales revenue will not finance operations.

Governments surely do not want to waste resources—after all, resources are scarce, and most things used by government do have alternative uses—so the benefits to society from government action ought to exceed the cost to society from that action. Determining whether actions really improve the conditions of the community gets complicated, however, when there is no basis for comparing the worth of individuals. The Pareto criterion for the welfare of a community does not require interpersonal judgments, but it leaves many choices open to political decision. Despite sophistication and rigor, science and analysis will not provide definitive answers to many government choices. Votes, either on issues or for representatives, will settle many decisions. Direct votes, however, will guarantee neither no wasteful public decisions nor choices that satisfy the Pareto criterion for improving society. They may well impose substantial costs on minorities. Some problems of direct choice are reduced when representatives make decisions, but there will remain imbalances of influence and posturing to continue in office rather than following clearly defined principles. Lobbying—direct or grassroots—is one way in which some interests obtain extra influence.

Finance in a representative democracy is not simple. Governments should be judged on their responsiveness to public preferences and on their refusal to ignore minority positions. Not all governments can meet those simple standards, and not all budget systems used in the United States do much to contribute to those objectives. The U.S. structure delivers and finances services using three tiers of government: federal, state, and local. Although independent in some respects, there are important mutual constraints. The federal level has powers delimited in the Constitution; the states have residual powers. Local governments—under Dillon's rule—have only powers expressly granted by their states. Some states grant local home rule, giving localities all powers save those expressly prohibited. Few home-rule authorizations are complete, however. Thus, budget and finance functions vary widely across the country.

QUESTIONS AND EXERCISES

1. A business improvement district is considering the installation of a new lighting system for the district. If the lighting system is installed, all the businesses in the area will benefit, and there will be no way in which a business that does

not pay for a share of the system can be denied full benefits from the system. The system will cost $4,000 and will benefit the five members of the district as follows:

	Individual Benefit (in $)	Cost Share (in $)
A	1,500	800
B	1,500	800
C	700	800
D	600	800
E	600	800

   a. Is the project economically feasible?

   b. Would any individual business be willing to install the lighting system (and pay for it) by itself?

   c. Would the project be approved by a majority of the businesses at a referendum?

   d. Does the project as currently structured meet the Pareto criterion?

   e. If possible, revise the cost shares to allow the project to meet the Pareto criterion and to pass a referendum.

2. Determine for your state the budget and finance constraints that the state places on local government. Does Dillon's rule apply? Do some units have home-rule powers? What is the extent of any such powers?

3. Private businesses have a great interest in quality primary and secondary education because today's students are tomorrow's employees. However, private businesses make limited financial contributions to this sector of education (excluding the taxes they pay to public school systems), even to market-oriented programs like vouchers and charter schools. What do you suppose explains this low contribution level? (*Hint:* Consider what sort of good primary and secondary education might be.)

4. The City of Dobra Kleb has decided to provide all citizens with a loaf of wholesome, nutritious bread every day to improve public health. The bread is to be distributed free of charge at city distribution centers located conveniently around the city. Does this program make bread a public good? Explain why or why not.

5. Many local governments in the United States operate public libraries that provide books, reference materials, Internet access, public meeting space, genealogical assistance, and other information/education services at no charge. Are the services of these local libraries pure public goods? What government functions are they seeking to serve? What privatization options might be possible? What services should be free and what could be subject to a charge? What would be the concerns raised if many services were made available only on a charge basis? Would your reaction be different if charging for services were the only alternative that allowed the library to remain open?

CASE FOR DISCUSSION

CASE 1–1

Market Interplay, Municipal Utilities, and a Common-Pool Resource

Governments often are surprised by private responses to what appear to be relatively straightforward and sensible public decisions. It should be no surprise that businesses respond to higher prices for their purchases by trying to economize on their use of those more expensive resources. What may be surprising is how these reactions themselves create even more complex problems for the government. In the case described here, the normal business response is particularly interesting because it crosses between the operation of a municipal utility and the exploitation of a common-pool resource. Here is a case from the *Wall Street Journal*.

Consider These Questions

1. Identify the various types of goods (private, public, and in between) involved in this case. Explain how each involves feasibility of exclusion and rivalry in use. What was the primary objective of the government program, and how was it being financed? Explain the unintended consequences of the financing approach. Is that financing approach appropriate for the type of good involved?

2. What options might governments in the Boston area have for financing of their objective?

City Dwellers Drill for Precious Fluid

As water rates go up, some Bostonians are going down—about 900 feet to find water. Average water and sewer bills in Boston have more than tripled since 1985 to cover costs of cleaning up Boston harbor. To cut their bills, several Boston businesses have recently drilled their own wells.

"It's a very alarming trend," says Jonathan Kaledin, executive director of the National Water Education Council, a Boston-based group that tracks water project funding issues. As customers "leave the system," those who remain must shoulder higher funding burdens.

If such drilling becomes a trend, it could undermine funding in a number of cities for projects to comply with clean-water laws. New York City water projects, for example, are expected to cost more than $10 billion during the 1990s, according to a recent report by Mr. Kaledin's group. Boston officials also worry that buildings in the city's Back Bay area, a fill-in swamp, may sink if wells lower the water table. Structures there rest on immersed wooden pilings that "will rot in two or three years" if exposed to air as the water level drops, warns Boston City Councilman David Scondras. City officials, citing over 400 known hazardous-spill sites in Boston, also fret that wells may tap into polluted water.

But the economic arguments for drilling are overwhelming, says Roger Berkowitz, co-owner of Legal Sea Foods, a Boston restaurant chain that recently drilled a well. Its 15,000 gallon-a-day gusher saves the company $2,500 a month by providing water for laundry and other uses. Though it isn't used for drinking, Mr. Berkowitz says, tests show water from the chain's well surpasses Boston's municipal water in purity.

CHAPTER 2

The Logic of the Budget Process

Chapter Contents

The budget process provides the medium for determining what government services will be provided and how they will be financed. Depending on how controlling the lawmakers want to be, it may also establish how the services will be provided. The basic budgeting problem, simply stated, is the following: "On what basis shall it be decided to allocate X dollars to activity A instead of activity B?"[1]

---

[1] V. O. Key Jr., "The Lack of a Budgetary Theory," *American Political Science Review* 34 (December 1940): 1137. As it turns out, the title of the article is wrong now (and arguably was wrong when the article was written) because there has been no absence of a budget theory for many years. Indeed, there is a cornucopia of theories both of how governments ought to behave (prescriptive) and of how governments actually behave (descriptive). This point is discussed in greater detail in John L. Mikesell and Daniel Mullins, "Innovations in Budgeting and Financial Management," in R. Durant, ed., *The Oxford Handbook of American Bureaucracy* (New York: Oxford University Press, 2010). Budget practitioners have not been befuddled by the alleged absence of theory and have gone about their business completely unfazed.

That is a pretty simple-sounding question, but, like many things in life, the problems lurk in its application. How many dollars should be moved from private businesses and individuals to government, and, once moved to government, how much should go to each government activity? Indeed, the logical answer is remarkably clear: move money from private to public use and among alternative public uses until it is not possible to move one dollar from one use to another without losing for the public as much value from where you took it as you gain in value from where you put it. It's not a big deal conceptually. There is no lack of theoretical guidance as to how things should work. Markets for private goods do the allocation invisibly, as prices and profits provide the resource allocation signals and private businesses and individuals take it from there. But, as discussed in Chapter 1, markets don't work for public goods, the home turf of governments, so here come the lawmakers to do the allocation job that markets can't. They may bungle the job (in a democracy, we elected them, so it is our collective fault), but the budget process is where those choices get made for government operations, not so quietly and we hope not so invisibly, but definitely politically. When governments tax and spend, making decisions within the framework of the budget process, they are doing for the public sector what the private market does for the provision of private goods and services. They are deciding how big government will be relative to the private sector and, within government, the relative sizes of the various programs and agencies that the government provides. They even make decisions about how programs and agencies will operate. Each government has some method for making these fiscal choices, although the degree of formality varies widely. But we do know what the budget process ought to be doing—moving resources to the best advantage of the population. Nevertheless, one should never underestimate the capacity of politicians to do exactly the wrong thing—either by making a poor decision or by making no decision at all.

Except for the limited number of town meeting processes, referendum decisions, and participatory budget processes, elected representatives make the primary spending and financing decisions. However, in budget preparation and in the delivery of services supported by the budget, nonelected public employees make many crucial decisions. Although these employees enjoy at least some measure of job security and may be less responsive to voters than elected officials, the logic of representative government presumes that such bureaucrats, and certainly the elected executives and legislators who guide their work, will be responsive to the citizenry.[2] And if they aren't, those elected officials deserve to be voted out of office.

Public organizations can operate with a haphazard budget process. Many local governments manage with casual or ad hoc processes, and most nonprofit

---

[2] This is an example of the "principal/agent problem": bureaucrats and elected officials (the agents) are inclined to pursue their own self-interests, which may well differ from the interests of the citizenry (the principals). "Participatory budgeting," discussed in Chapter 6, provides an alternate and direct channel for getting citizen priorities into the deliberations on a portion of a budget.

organizations are informal and unstructured with budget documents of limited utility. Of course, having a well-organized and well-designed budget process is no guarantee that the organization will actually use the process. A number of observers note that the federal government recently has barely been following its own rather rigidly laid-out processes, as is discussed in Chapter 4.[3] However, a system designed with incentives to induce officials to respond to public demands is more likely to produce decisions in the public interest, and thereby provide citizens with the quality and quantity of desired public services at the desired times and locations and at the least cost to society. At a minimum, the process must recognize competing claims on resources and should focus directly on alternatives and options. A major portion of the process involves presentation of accurate and relevant information to individuals making budget decisions on behalf of the citizenry. At its best, the budget process articulates the choices of the citizenry for government services (and how those services will be paid for) and manages efficient delivery and finance of those services. Before considering the logic of the budget, however, it is good to understand some basic facts about government expenditure.

Size and Growth of Government Expenditure[4]

Government spending can be divided into two primary categories: purchases and transfers. Both purchases and transfers need to be financed (as must interest payments on outstanding government debt, another spending category), and both entail a government payment, but their impacts on the economy differ, so the categories are differentiated in the national economic accounts. Furthermore, transfers and purchases are commonly treated differently by government budget processes, which is discussed in considerable detail in later chapters.[5]

---

[3]Irene Rubin, "The Great Unraveling: Federal Budgeting, 1998–2006," *Public Administration Review* 67 (July/August 2007): 608–17. Congressional leaders in 2015–2016 have argued for a return to "regular order" in their budget processes. This simply means that all the steps in the budget process are followed in their established order, that deadlines for action be met, and that all pieces of the process established in law and regulation be followed. As of the middle of 2016 (for the 2017 federal budget), regular order has not been followed.

[4]One might also measure the size of government by the public sector share of total employment in the nation. According to recent International Labor Organization data, this is around 16.2 percent in the United States (14.5 percent in Germany). However, the governments in the United States (and other nations) do lots of purchasing without hiring government workers. For example, when the Department of Defense purchases a new aircraft, it buys from a private company, and the aircraft is built by employees of that private firm. Looking up government employment data will not give much information about the size of government.

[5]Two easily available explanations of economic statistics as they relate to analysis of government finances are Congressional Budget Office, *The Treatment of Federal Receipts and Expenditures in the National Income and Product Accounts* (Washington, D.C.: Congressional Budget Office, 2007); and Enrico Giovannini, *Understanding Economic Statistics: An OECD Perspective* (Paris: Organization for Economic Cooperation and Development, 2008).

1. **Government purchases** divert productive resources (land, labor, capital, natural resources) from private use by businesses and individuals to government use in the provision of education, national defense, public safety, parks, and all the other services that governments provide. Some of this spending pays wages and benefits to government employees, some pays suppliers of items or services used by these employees in the production of government services, and some pays private entities who have agreed to produce government services under contract. Most of this spending is for the provision of current services, but part of this spending is government investment—the purchase of long-life capital assets such as roads, buildings, and durable equipment.[6] In the national income accounting system, the system that is used to keep track of national economic activity, this direct provision represents the government contribution to gross domestic product (GDP). In other words, when a city outfits its fire department to provide services during the year, pays its firefighters, or purchases a new fire truck, it will be purchasing from *private* suppliers. (In contrast with a socialist system, productive resources in the United States are mostly privately owned.) Some purchases will provide services within the year of purchase (consumption), and others will yield services over the longer useful life of the asset purchased (gross investment). These purchases represent direct acquisition of resources by the government, and these resources will provide services to the public as they are used by the government. They represent the direct contribution of government to aggregate demand in the national economy.

2. **Transfer payments** constitute the other major element of government spending. These payments provide income to recipients without service being required from the recipient. Such direct payment transfers to individuals include Social Security benefits, unemployment insurance payments, and cash payments by governments to low-income individuals. These payments amount to almost 40 percent of all current government expenditure in the United States, so they represent an important contributor to the financing requirements of government and an important concern for government operations. Although the government is not directly spending the money, it will need to find the money to pay for the transfers, using the revenue resources available to it (taxes most of the time). In contrast to government purchases, the direct impact on GDP is through spending by the transfer recipients, not through spending by the government. The transfers certainly will make things better for the individual who receives them, but they do not involve direct purchases of anything by the government, nor do they represent direct provision of services by the government.

---

[6]This gross investment—meaning spending to purchase new assets without taking account of the depreciation (wearing out) of the existing capital stock—amounts to a bit more than 10 percent of total U.S. investment.

Table 2–1 shows the path of federal, state, and local government spending in the United States from 1960 to 2013. These data focus on the movement of resources between private and public sectors, that is, the way in which sectors of the economy claim production of the economy. They do not exactly coincide with the fiscal year, cash-outlay data that later chapters use, but they do make important points needed for understanding U.S. government finances.[7] (The fiscal year is the financial year used for maintenance of financial records.)

Total spending by all government in the United States—federal, state, and local combined—was 37.5 percent of total economic activity (measured by GDP) in 2013. That is considerably higher than the 26.2 percent fifty years earlier, and even higher than the 30.4 percent in 2000. State and local government spending as a share of the economy increased from 9.6 percent in 1960 to 14.6 percent in 2013, and federal spending increased from 17.8 percent to 22.9 percent. The federal increase was primarily driven by the cost of wars in Iraq and Afghanistan and economic stimulation efforts to combat the Great Recession, whereas the state and local increase was driven heavily by expanded health care spending.

Data in the table also highlight two other significant patterns in government expenditure: the importance of transfer payments (spending without making purchases) and of payments to government employees. These transfer payments are payments made to people without a current work requirement made of them. At the federal level, these are predominantly Social Security payments to the elderly, people with disabilities, and the surviving dependents of covered individuals and Medicare payments for health care to the elderly; at the state and local levels, the payments are predominantly retirement benefits for former employees, Medicaid for the poor, and unemployment compensation. These payments have increased substantially as a share of total spending. At the federal level, the increase has been from 21.2 percent of the total in 1960 to 47.1 percent of the total in 2013 and, at the state and local levels, from 9.1 percent to 23.1 percent over the same years. This expansion of share raises considerable concern for fiscal sustainability and is a topic discussed at length in later chapters.

Compensation of current employees, as the table shows, represents an important component of the cost of government services—many government services are labor intensive. The share of total spending for state and local governments was 49.3 percent in 2013, about half the total, but not quite as high as in some earlier years. This high share reflects the importance of teachers, firefighters, and police officers

---

[7]The 1995 revision of the national income and product accounts brought significant change in how the accounts treat government expenditure, especially for capital asset purchases. The components in the new structure include the following: gross government investment includes total government expenditures for fixed assets; "government consumption expenditures" replaces "government purchases" and includes the estimated value of the services of general government fixed assets, as measured by consumption of fixed capital (as well as the purchases for use in the year); and government consumption and investment expenditures show the total current-year government contribution to GDP. See Robert P. Parker and Jack E. Triplett, "Preview of the Comprehensive Revision of the National Income and Product Accounts: Recognition of Government Investment and Incorporation of a New Methodology for Calculation Depreciation," *Survey of Current Business* 75 (September 1995): 33–41.

Table 2–1
United States Government Spending in Relation to Gross Domestic Product (GDP), 1960–2013

	1960	% Total	1970	% Total	1980	% Total	1990	% Total	2000	% Total	2010	% Total	2013	% Total
Federal Government														
Employee Compensation ($B)	22.6	24.1%	48.3	23.5%	102.5	16.8%	193.9	14.8%	233.0	12.3%	466.3	11.9%	402.8	10.5%
Current Transfer Payments to Persons ($B)	19.9	21.2%	55.6	27.1%	219.6	36.1%	445.1	34.0%	769.1	40.5%	1708.3	43.7%	1806.8	47.1%
Total Expenditures ($B)	93.7	100.0%	205.3	100.0%	608.4	100.0%	1307.4	100.0%	1900.6	100.0%	3906.9	100.0%	3839.4	100.0%
Total Expenditures as % GDP	17.80%		19.80%		21.8%		22.5%		19.1%		26.9%		22.9%	
State and Local Government														
Employee Compensation ($B)	25.5	50.5%	71.1	53.7%	193.0	53.1%	415.9	51.9%	679.0	48.3%	1064.2	47.6%	1206.4	49.3%
Social Benefit Payments to Persons ($B)	4.6	9.1%	16.1	12.2%	51.2	14.1%	127.7	15.9%	271.4	19.3%	534.6	23.9%	565.4	23.1%
Total Expenditures ($B)	50.5	100.0%	132.3	100.0%	363.3	100.0%	801.7	100.0%	1404.5	100.0%	2237.0	100.0%	2449.2	100.0%
Total Expenditures as % GDP	9.60%		12.70%		13.0%		13.8%		14.1%		15.4%		14.6%	
All Governments														
Employee Compensation ($B)	48.1	34.9%	119.4	38.1%	295.5	33.5%	609.7	30.8%	912.0	30.2%	1530.5	27.6%	1609.2	25.6%
Current Transfer Payments to Persons ($B)	24.4	17.7%	71.7	22.9%	270.8	30.7%	572.7	29.0%	1040.6	34.4%	2242.9	40.5%	2372.2	37.7%
Total Expenditures ($B)	137.7	100.0%	313.2	100.0%	883.1	100.0%	1976.9	100.0%	3021.5	100.0%	5538.8	100.0%	6288.6	100.0%
Total Expenditures as % GDP	26.20%		30.20%		31.7%		34.1%		30.4%		38.1%		37.5%	

SOURCE: U.S. Department of Commerce, National Income and Product Accounts.

Note: No adjustment has been made for intergovernmental transfers.

in the service delivery of these governments. Employee compensation is a much smaller component of federal spending—10.5 percent in 2013, down from 24.1 percent in 1960. The federal government more heavily contracts out work to private firms and also spends more on materials made by private firms (such as military equipment and supplies).

Special attention should be given to the difference between price and physical effects on purchases. Government spending increased from $137.7 billion in 1960 to $6,288.6 billion in 2013. That increase resulted from two forces: (1) purchases of more "stuff" (trucks, computers, workers' time, etc.) and (2) payment of higher prices for the items purchased. The total increase encompasses both change in prices and change in physical (real) purchases. Because only the latter represents greater capacity to deliver service, it is important to divide the components of change. Sidebar 2–1 describes the basic mechanics of making price adjustments. The division of total spending into the portion that represents paying higher prices and the portion that represents purchasing more resources is one of the most basic tools of fiscal analysis

---

Sidebar 2–1
Deflating: Dividing between Real Change and Price Change

The amount of money spent depends on how many items are purchased and what the price of each item is: 400 gallons of motor fuel at $2.10 per gallon means $840 spent on fuel. More money spent in 2016 than in 2015 does not mean that more things have been purchased if the prices of those things have changed between the two years. It is useful to know whether higher spending is the product of higher prices or more things purchased: more spending because prices are higher gives no reason to believe that more government services are being provided. So how can analysts compare real purchasing power of money spent across periods when prices are different? The answer lies in the use of price indexes.

Suppose a set of purchases (commodities and services) cost $100 at 2016 prices, but only $75 at 2009 prices. That means that between 2009 and 2016, prices have risen on average by 33 percent ([100 − 75]/75, converted to percentage form), or the ratio of 2016 prices to 2009 prices is 1.33, (i.e., 100/75). This ratio of the value of a group of commodities and services in current dollars (or "then-year" dollars) to the value of that same group in base-year dollars (or constant dollars) is a price index. If 2009 is the base year, its index would be 100 and the index for 2016 would be 133 (or 33 percent higher than the base year). The index could also be stated in ratio form. In this case, 2009 would be 1.00 and 2016 would be 1.33. A price index provides a method for identifying to what extent higher expenditure reflects real change (more items purchased) and price changes (higher prices); the index shows how prices, on average, differ from those in a base year.

Here is an example from the budget of the U.S. government. Federal spending for health research and training increased from $28,828 million in 2006 to $30,911 million in 2015. The deflator for nondefense spending, using 2009 as the base year, went from 0.9408 in 2006 to 1.0893 in 2014. That implies a 15.8 percent increase in prices between the years [(1.0893 − 0.9408)/0.9408]. Total spending for natural resources and the environment increased by 7.22 percent, but how much was due to more "stuff" to be used to provide services? In other words, how much of the increase was real? In constant (base-year 2009) dollars, health research and training spending in 2006 was $30,642 million [28,828 / 0.9408], and in 2014, it equaled $28,377 million [30,911 / 1.0893]. That means that the real change was negative—a decline of 7.4 percent. Agencies performing services in that area had fewer resources to work with in 2014 than they had in 2006.

Analysts use many different price indexes, depending on the expenditure category being analyzed; the Bureau of Economic Analysis of the U.S. Department of Commerce reports price indexes appropriate to many activities on its website (www.bea.gov). The data used here came from the federal budget. Prices of all items do not change by the same amount. Some go up a lot, some go up a little, some don't change, and some even decrease. All those changes are captured in a single index by computing a weighted average in which the price change for big purchase items counts for more than the price change for small purchase items. Traditional indexes have used fixed weight measures: the base-year spending patterns establish fixed weight values for computing the averages. This practice creates a problem when there is considerable difference in the amount of price change among items: purchasers substitute those items whose price has risen less for those items whose price has risen more. The fixed weights become wrong. Analysts now remedy the problem by using a rolling average, or chain weights, instead of fixed base-year weights. The system sets the weights by taking the average growth of the current year and the preceding year. Price weights are thus constantly updated for changes in relative prices.

Spending calibrated in prices from one year can be easily converted into prices for another. Suppose the price indices for 1990 is 0.6958 and for 2010, 1.1256 in some reference year. If you were to change to 1990 as the reference year, then the price index for 1990 is 100.0 [= (0.6958/0.6958) × 100], and the price index for 2010 is 161.8 [= (1.1256/0.6958) × 100]. The absolute level of the index and the absolute difference between years in the index differ according to the base year used, but the percentage change remains the same across base years. Price indexes and deflated (constant or real) values have meaning only in a relative sense.

Whenever an analyst is examining spending data over a time span of several years, it is important to make adjustments for changes in prices. In most eras, annual rates of price change in the United States have been relatively modest, but even a small annual rate maintained for a decade will make for a large difference between beginning and end. And price changes in some other countries have been much more dramatic than in the United States. When data from different years are being compared, it is always a good practice to make adjustment for changes in prices. It is never completely wrong to do so, and it can sometimes be catastrophic to fail to do so.

because purchasing more resources creates the possibility of providing more services, whereas paying higher prices creates no such expectation.[8] When adjusted to reflect constant prices (2009 = 100.), the increase was from $1,145.7 billion to $5,789.6 billion, a big increase, but certainly less than the current dollar comparison would have suggested.

How does the size of the American public sector compare with that of other countries? Table 2–2 reports data for several countries of the Organization for Economic Cooperation and Development (sort of a club for industrialized, market-oriented democracies). Although the conventions used in these measures do not exactly match those of the national income and product accounts just discussed, the basic logic is comparable and can be interpreted in the same way. Measured by final consumption expenditure, the countries ranged from 20.3 percent of GDP in Denmark to 6.1 percent in the United States; the mean is 12.3 percent. As noted previously, purchases do not measure the full extent of public sector involvement in the economy. Total general government expenditure percentages range from 32.3 percent of GDP in Korea to 57.7 percent in Denmark. The United States percentage, 41.9 percent, is below the mean of 45.9 percent.[9]

The nature of these government expenditures—in other words, the kinds of services governments provide—are examined in Chapters 4 and 5 But it is now important to learn the general elements of the budget process and the language that applies in fiscal systems.

---

[8]The real and price changes do not add to the total change, but they are mathematically related. If X_{10} = total expenditure in 2010, X_{80} = total expenditure in 1980, and t = the percentage increase in total expenditure between the years; if D_{10}, D_{80}, and g are the similar variables for deflated (real or constant dollar) expenditure; and if F_{10}, F_{80}, and p are similar variables for price levels, then

$$X_{10} = X_{80} + (X_{80} \times t) = X_{80}(1 + t)$$
$$D_{10} = D_{80} + (D_{80} \times g) = D_{80}(1 + g) \ and$$
$$P_{10} = P_{80} + (P_{80} \times p) = D_{80}(1 + p)$$

In other words, start with the value in 1980 and add to it the increase to 2010 and you will have the value for 2010.

Thus, total expenditure in 2010 equals real expenditure in 2010 times the 2010 price level:

$$X_{10} = D_{10} \times P_{10}$$

Substituting into this equation yields the following:

$$X_{80} (1 + t) = D_{80} (1 + g) \times P_{80}(1 + p)$$

Rearranging terms, we obtain:

$$X_{80} (1 + t) = D_{80} \times P_{80} (1 + g)(1 + p)$$

Because $X_{80} = D_{80} \times P_{80}$, then $(1 + t) = (1 + g)(1 + p)$. In other words, one plus the rate of price increase times one plus the rate of increase of deflated expenditure equals one plus the rate of total expenditure increase.

[9]Governments also interact with the private sector through regulations, legal requirements, and mandates. These effects are difficult to measure, but many would place the United States considerably higher in the league table than its ranking according to government spending share.

Table 2–2
Government Expenditures in Selected Industrialized Countries, 2011

	Total General Government Expenditure (% GDP)	General Government Consumption Expenditure (% GDP) Final
Australia	35.2	11.0
Austria	50.7	11.2
Belgium	53.6	15.6
Canada	41.9	
Czech Republic	43.2	10.8
Denmark	57.7	20.3
Estonia	37.6	10.7
Finland	55.2	16.4
France	55.9	16.0
Germany	45.2	12.2
Greece	51.9	7.1
Hungary	49.9	10.8
Iceland	47.4	16.7
Ireland	47.1	12.9
Israel	41.9	12.7
Italy	49.7	11.9
Japan	41.9	11.9
Korea	32.3	6.8
Luxembourg	42.6	10.3
Netherlands	49.8	17.1
New Zealand	45.1	11.7
Norway	43.9	14.1
Poland	43.4	10.4
Portugal	49.3	10.8
Slovak Republic	38.9	8.7
Slovenia	49.9	12.4
Spain	45.7	12.3
Sweden	51.5	19.1
Switzerland	33.7	6.2
United Kingdom	48.2	13.8
United States	41.6	6.1
Mean	45.9	12.3

SOURCE: Organization for Economic Cooperation and Development (OECD).

What Is a Budget?

A budget is a critical document in the operation of any modern public organization; this includes both governmental and non-profit organizations. It has an explicit meaning, and it has several expected components. In simplest terms, a budget is a financial plan that carries forward the financial implications of carrying out a particular planned response to the anticipated operating conditions in a future period, normally a year. It has been prepared to fit expenditure programs within the constraint of revenues available in that future period. Fitting programs into available resources is the heart of budgeting; everything else is subservient to that effort.

The budget takes a policy plan for provision of physical services and translates it into the cost of providing that plan. It is not a forecast of future spending by the organization, but it represents the intended response of that organization to the conditions that the organization expects to face in the future. It isn't a projection of government spending and revenue collections, and it isn't a target. It isn't a wish list of what the organization would like to do if it had no limits on its resources. And it isn't a shopping list of the things that the organization intends to purchase in a future year. A good budget says, in essence, these are what we believe are likely to be the operating conditions in the budget period (sorts of problems that will emerge, level of prices that the organization will have to pay for what it purchases, resources that we expect to have available within the period, etc.), and here is what we intend to do about the problems and opportunities. The expected operating conditions may not materialize as we have expected, but if they do, here is our operating response. If they don't, we will make adjustments on the fly. The first rule of budgeting is simple: the ideas (policy) always precede the numbers. If you don't have the ideas, the numbers are just fluff.

Here are the blunt facts: If a program manager knows what she is doing and intends to do, she will be able to produce a budget. If she doesn't and is just filling a chair, she won't be able to do it. If she believes that producing a budget is keeping her away from the important tasks of running the operation, she should be relieved of duties before she creates any more damage. If she works with budget numbers without first devising her operating plan for the budget year, she doesn't know what she is doing. And she ought to be happy about doing the plan because that offers her a way of communicating her good ideas for service to the public. If you know what you are doing, you can do a budget and can and should use it as an important tool for management, evaluation, and communication.

The complete budget will include at least three distinct segments: a financial plan that reflects expenditures intended to carry out the planned response to the operating conditions expected in the budget year, a revenue forecast that reflects how much revenue the government expects to collect in the budget year based on the anticipated state of the economy and the revenue structure that the government intends to have in place, and a plan for managing any difference (surplus or deficit) between the expenditure plan and the revenue forecast. The budget begins with a narrative discussion of what the government expects and how it plans to deal with those expectations; it then moves to a financial section that provides budget numbers. Later chapters of this text will go into considerable detail about the meaning of the sections of the budget, the methods used to prepare each section, and the tools used to analyze the sections. Later chapters will also discuss the revenue side of the budget process, including the development of revenue policies and revenue forecasts.

Federal, state, and larger local governments divide responsibility for pieces of the full budget. For instance, state budget managers seldom are directly involved in the revenue forecast, but they will be operating within revenue constraints developed by others. However, managers in smaller local governments and nonprofit organizations will need to be intimately involved in all parts of the budget. Our first emphasis is on the expenditure portion of the budget, but keep in mind that this is only one element of the full public budgeting and finance process.

Budget Process and Logic

The market allocates private resources without a need for outside intervention; price movements serve as a signaling device for resource flows. In the public sector, decisions about resource use cannot be made automatically from price and profit signals because of four special features of government decisions, as discussed in Chapter 1. First, public goods, the primary service focus of governments, are difficult, if not impossible, to sell, and, even where sales may be feasible, nonrevenue concerns may be as important as the cash collected. For instance, national parks may serve a conservation purpose in addition to being a recreation facility. In that case, money collected from recreation charges would not be a complete guide to decisions about those facilities. Profit can neither measure success, nor guide resource allocations, nor serve as an incentive to efficient operations. When markets have failed, it is a mistake to try to use simple market information as a first guide for decisions. Second, public and private resource constraints differ dramatically. Whereas earnings and earnings potential constrain spending of private entities, governments are limited only by the total resources of the society.[10] Resources are privately owned, but governments have the power to tax. There are obvious political limits to tax extractions, but those limits differ dramatically from resource limits on a family or a private firm. Third, governments characteristically operate as perfect monopolies. Consumers of government services cannot purchase from an alternate supplier, and, more important, the consumer must pay whether the good provided is used or not. Again, this makes market-proxy data based on traditional government operations suspect as a guide for resource allocation. Finally,

---

[10]Few have dared suggest natural limits to the ability of governments to extract resources from society since Colin Clark's proposition many years ago: "25 percent of the national income is about the limit for taxation in any nontotalitarian community in times of peace" ("Public Finance and Changes in the Value of Money," *Economic Journal* 55 [December 1945]: 380). That limit was based on zero inflation—so it may not have been truly tested. However, most successful modern democracies exceed that level with minimal general price increases (recall the OECD data in Table 2–2).

governments operate with mixed motives. They are trying to achieve more goals than the single objective of maximizing value of the firm that characterizes private business decisions. In many instances, not only the service provided but also the recipients of the service (redistribution) or the mere fact of provision (stabilization) is important. For example, the federal Supplemental Nutrition Assistance Program (SNAP, formerly the food stamp program) seeks to make healthy food available to low-income families by supplementing the money these families have to buy food. But the program is administered by the U.S. Department of Agriculture. In other words, it seeks to help low-income families, but it also aims to increase the income of American food producers (farmers), even though there may be more economical means of achieving either of these objectives by itself. Accordingly, more may hinge on the provision of a public service than simply the direct return from the service compared with its cost. Because these multiple and mixed objectives cannot be weighed scientifically and because achievement of objectives cannot be easily measured across programs, the budget process is political, involving both pure bargaining or political strategies and scientific analysis.

The Parts of the Public Expenditure/ Public Revenue Process

Government spending must be financed: receiving the benefits of a good or service is linked in the private sector to paying for it (you have to buy it before you can use it), whereas in the public sector what the government provides does not determine how its operations will be financed. When a business makes shirts, it knows exactly from whom the financing will be received: the people to whom it sells those shirts. If people don't buy the shirts, the business is in trouble. But when the federal government decides to increase its provision of national defense, it must make another decision: Who will pay? It isn't going to sell the service; there is no link between who receives the service and how it will be financed. That means that there will be two separate planning processes: public expenditure and public revenue. Payment for a government service is not a precondition for benefiting from that service; if the mosquito abatement district has seen to its job, both those who pay taxes to the district and those who don't will be free of mosquito bites.

There are two distinct components of public finance. The *expenditure* side of budgeting should set the size of the public sector, establishing what is provided, how it is provided, and who gets it. The *revenue planning* side, on the other hand, determines whose real income will be reduced to finance the provision of the budgeted services. Although the total resources used must equal the total resources raised (including current revenues, borrowing, and, for national governments, the creation of new money to spend), the profile of government expenditure does not ordinarily indicate how the cost of government should be distributed. In some instances—for example, the Holland Tunnel that connects New York and New Jersey under the Hudson River—it is feasible to identify the direct beneficiaries of the public service and to charge them to finance the tunnel, thus causing the operators of the facility to be more like a private business than a government, but the range of public services for which such financing would be practical is limited. (Charge financing is discussed in Chapter 12.) More often than not, government services are more like mosquito abatement than the Holland Tunnel, and revenue planning will be distinct from decisions about spending.

Figure 2–1 shows how dollars, resources, and public services logically flow from the revenue system to the procurement process to service delivery. The public procurement process involves exchange transactions (purchase on the open market) and, with few exceptions (eminent domain purchase of property and military draft being two), is economically (but possibly not politically) comparable to procurement by private firms. That is, it matters in the political process what firm the government does business with, not just the quality and cost of the product being sold, sometimes for apparently benign reasons (a requirement that all firms selling resources to the government must be American) and sometimes for less honorable and usually illegal reasons (a requirement that all firms must donate to the right political campaign). And legislators at all levels of government seek to bring government business to their own constituencies, often with minimal regard to whether that is the most efficient way of delivering services to the public as a whole. The unique public sector features of the flow involve revenue-generation and service-delivery decisions, the concerns of the following chapters. Governments devote much of their attention to the part of the budget process that deals with expenditure and service-delivery processes; the next several chapters examine this part of the budget. Revenue planning is examined in later chapters.

The basic communication device of the process is the budget, a government's plan for operation translated into its financial implications. Governments prepare budgets as a means for (1) elaborating and communicating executive branch intentions, (2) providing legislative branch review and approval of those plans, (3) providing a control-and-review structure for implementation of approved plans, and

Figure 2–1
Service-Delivery and Revenue Systems as Separate Planning Processes

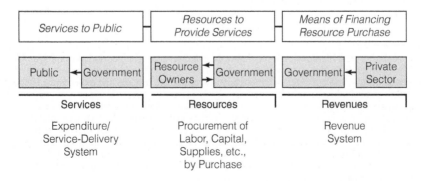

(4) providing a template for external review of the legality of what the government has done with funds entrusted to it.[11] Nonprofit organizations prepare budgets for all those reasons, and they also need the budget to show prospective and actual funders how their money is being used. Budgets are forward-looking and action-oriented. Although they ideally will also contain some historical information to provide a foundation for the budget proposals, their real focus is on the future for the government or other organization. The budget—by explicitly spelling out provisions for spending and identifying responsibility for all money to be spent—provides the first and most critical defense against public corruption. Governments can use the budget to communicate their program intentions for the future to the public, although not enough governments think of the budget in such terms and the public is not accustomed to looking at budgets at all.[12] The media can serve as a useful device for that communication, but budgets have insufficient glitz to capture the attention of many traditional outlets, despite the significance of government program intentions for the public.

Budget Classification, Structure, and Presentation Years

The expenditure side of government budgets deals with plans for spending to deliver services to the public. Logically, the agency develops plans to provide services and estimates the cost of purchasing the resources necessary to execute those plans. In that respect, government operations are similar to those of private business: resources are acquired and used to deliver a valued output. The public agency's budget is its business plan for the next year, subject to the approval of certain representatives of the people.

The information in that plan can be organized in various ways to facilitate policy formulation, resource allocation, fiscal discipline, and compliance with the law. Three fundamental categorizations are:

1. **Administrative.** An identification of the entity that is responsible for management of the public funds and for provision of public services with those funds. In other words, the budget would be classified according to funds to the police department, the fire department, and so on in the city government. This classification is critical for identification of responsibility and for ongoing execution of the budget.

---

[11]Only appropriation and historical reports of spending and revenue are mentioned in the U.S. Constitution, Article I, section 9[7]: "No money shall be drawn from the Treasury, but in consequence of appropriations made by law; and a regular statement and account of the receipts and expenditures of all public money shall be published from time to time."

[12]Some governments make considerable effort to have their budget serve as a communication device, with colors, pictures, and charts that try to show what has been accomplished already and what intends to be accomplished with the programs in the budget proposal. It is not clear that the public has paid much attention, however, and not many budget analysts are particularly impressed. Perhaps governments should embed YouTube videos in their presentations to draw more attention. Because budgets of many governments are now posted on websites, such videos would be entirely possible. Mayors could introduce their budgets with a nice song-and-dance routine.

2. **Economic.** An identification of the type of expenditure: compensation of employees, utilities to be purchased, supplies, and so on. This classification is also called line item (the items in a purchase list) or object of expenditure. This represents something like a shopping list for the government and may be built with varying levels of detail (i.e., it may list "utilities," or it may have separate lines for each utility: "electricity," "water," "gas," etc.).

3. **Functional.** An identification of spending according to the intended purposes and objectives of the government. This classification organizes government operations into their broad purposes (such as education or national defense) without regard for the entity responsible for the resources. It is a classification particularly suitable for fundamental resource allocation choices.

The three classifications are independent of each other, and many governments present all three in their budget document in an effort to provide for full transparency of finances.

The Budget of a City Police Department: Organization, Items, and Years

The most basic (and most traditional) classification is economic or line item, with its focus on inputs to the flow of service provision, that is, on the resources (line items or inputs)—labor, equipment, supplies, and the like—purchased by the government in the course of responding to the demand for service. Each administrative unit prepares its own budget to provide control and responsibility. The budget for the police department of the city of Kirkland, Washington, for 2015–2016 illustrates that classification (Figure 2–2) and provides an excellent starting point for understanding budget presentation.[13] Kirkland uses a biennial budget system, so it does its budgeting in two year rather than one year blocks. The 2011–2012 column reports the most recent budget execution, the 2013–2014 budget columns represents the expected amounts that will be spent during the current biennium (when the 2015–2016 budget is being adopted) and the amounts budgeted for that period, and the proposed budget for the 2015–2016 biennium.

The 2013–2014 estimates column reports how budget execution is proceeding (some categories have had to be increased, either by internal transfers or by more money being approved by the legislative body), and the 2015–2106 column represents the program plan for the upcoming fiscal period. The budget items are for expenditures to be made (purchases) by the department. This format is the basic structure for budget development in that it is the template an agency would use for estimating the cost of carrying out its plan for service. The presentation gives the line items for the department as a whole and totals distributed to each of the divisions of the department.

---

[13]Kirkland provides greater detail about expenditure plans elsewhere in its budget presentation.

Figure 2–2
City of Kirkland, Washington, Budget Summary for Police Department, 2015–2016

2015–2016 Financial Overview

POLICE

Financial Summary by Object

	2011–2012 Actual	2013–2014 Estimate	2013–2014 Budget	2015–2016 Budget	Percent Change
Salaries and Wages	20,764,629	23,369,165	23,633,063	24,637,506	4.25%
Benefits	7,909,973	9,541,753	9,662,239	10,324,420	6.85%
Supplies	850,043	481,594	668,466	626,629	−6.26%
Other Services	6,658,271	7,483,663	7,766,269	8,659,761	11.50%
Government Services	5,835,034	7,232,028	6,656,196	5,462,510	−17.93%
capital Outlay	66,591	89,440	89,440	—	−100.00%
TOTAL	42,084,541	48,197,643	48,475,673	49,710,826	2.55%

Financial Summary by Division

	2011–2012 Actual	2013–2014 Estimate	2013–2014 Budget	2015–2016 Budget	Percent Change
Administration	9,622,954	10,200,158	10,309,650	12,142,519	17.78%
Police Investigation	4,033,497	4,457,234	4,402,319	4,659,666	5.85%
Patrol	18,008,864	18,986,935	19,299,788	19,786,060	2.52%
Traffic	2,136,833	2,646,327	2,608,681	2,769,141	6.15%
Police Services	7,738,690	11,281,263	11,229,140	9,732,078	−13.33%
Community Services	543,703	625,726	626,095	621,362	−0.76%
TOTAL	42,084,541	48,197,643	48,475,673	49,710,826	2.55%

Position Summary by Division

	2011–2012 Actual	Adjustments	2013–2014 Budget	Adjustments	2015–2016 Budget
Administration	11.00	0.00	11.00	−1.00	10.00
Police Investigation	11.00	0.00	11.00	0.00	11.00
Patrol	75.00	−4.00	71.00	1.00	72.00
Traffic	6.00	0.00	6.00	0.00	6.00
Police Services	32.50	2.00	34.50	0.50	35.00
Community Services	2.00	0.00	2.00	0.00	2.00
TOTAL	137.50	−2.00	135.50	0.50	136.00

The budget in Figure 2–2 demonstrates some important features. First, this display is for the police department. There will be a similar budget component for each administrative agency of the city. Budgets to agencies provide a mechanism for control and responsibility in the process. Administrators of the police department are responsible for this appropriated money. Second, the budget display includes information for the upcoming budget period (the plan). But it also includes comparable information for the current year—in this instance, both the initially budgeted amounts and the amounts revised to reflect likely actual execution—and for the most recently completed period. This presentation of these years provides a basis for the analyst (or for an inquisitive member of the general public) to get an idea of what changes might be in store for the city in the next year.[14] Multiyear presentations are standard for government budgets. Unfortunately, nonprofit organizations frequently submit only single-year budgets to their boards to get approval of plans. It is not clear what these boards are supposed to do with only a single year. Possibly check the math? Third, the budget provides details on the amount spent by each of the divisions of the police department. That gives information about the resources being devoted to the several different services provided by the department. Fourth, this budget provides a distribution of staffing in the department, a useful presentation in light of the high share of total spending devoted to salaries and wages. Not all budgets provide this detail, but it does contribute to better understanding the operations of the department. The full budget document (not reproduced here, but available at the city website [http://www.kirklandwa.gov]) also provides a statement of the mission of the department, a description of the functions of each division of the department, and a short identification of what program changes (plans) are reflected in the budget request.

The years appearing in a budget logically are these:

1. **The budget year.** The document focuses on the budget year (or years if the process is biennial), 2015–2016 in this example. These numbers reflect what the agency plans for operations, what it has requested for approval by various stages of review, and what resources will be required for the execution of these plans. These columns are the action items for consideration and legislative approval and, once enacted into law, become the template against which the agency will be held responsible. Some executive budgets will report what the agency requested initially, along with the amount recommended by the executive; this one does not. The Kirkland budget also presents the percentage change for the budget period in comparison with the prior period budget.
2. **The progress-report year.** The budget for 2015–2016 will have been considered during the 2013–2014 budget period. The 2013–2014 columns in this budget report what was budgeted for that biennium and what the actual result is likely to be. (Frequently, only the likely result for the current year is reported; the figures initially adopted are not reported.)

---

[14]Remember that expenditure changes may need to be adjusted for price changes to understand what any change in resources available to the department might be.

3. **The final-report year.** This column reports the fiscal figures for the most recently completed fiscal year, 2011–2012 in this illustration. These figures provide a standard for comparison.
4. **Out-years.** Some budgets (but not the one in Figure 2–2) also carry figures for out-years, or years beyond the budget year in the request cycle. Some governments prepare a multiyear financial framework with budget estimates for from three to five years into the future so that a longer perspective on finances is possible. However, these out-years are not part of the basic budget appropriations, and the extent to which they make much difference in the decision process varies widely across organizations. In many instances, those forecasts aim to produce warning signs that induce actions which are intended to actually make the forecast wrong. For example, a forecast of expanding deficits in the out-years may induce current actions to reduce programs that would be contributing to those deficits, thus making the forecasts wrong. Out-year numbers are almost always wrong as indicators of eventual outcomes.

The federal government has recently used a budget year plus four years in executive budget summary presentations.[15] However, the Obama administration's first budget framework, *A New Era of Responsibility, Renewing America's Promise,* returned to a ten-year horizon in its budget summaries, a horizon that was used in presidential budgets from 1997 through 2002. The longer horizon reflects a concern with future implications of fiscal decisions, even though specific actions on those future figures seldom will be taken in that particular cycle. Nor should those fiscal choices be locked in early; priorities, needs, and fiscal circumstances may well change. The earliest multiyear presidential budget presentations date from the Reagan administration. Skeptics suggest that these were developed so that control over the federal deficit could be shown eventually, although the deficit reductions were only in years at considerable distance from anything actually proposed in the budget. Later Obama budgets provide a five-year horizon in most presentations. Both Congress and the administration do work with a ten-year horizon even if most attention is given the current budget year.

Administrative and Functional Classification

Budget classification in functional form provides the same budget proposal as an administrative presentation, but it organizes the information to highlight resource allocation choices as opposed to highlighting the entities that are to be responsible for the funds. Table 2–3 illustrates the point with information from the federal budget.

---

[15]In the middle of 1996, the Congressional Budget Office started doing ten-year budget estimates. Nobody but politicians and the media took these seriously, particularly the more distant years of the estimating horizon. It is hard enough to get reasonable estimates for the five years required in laws establishing budget procedures. Rudolph G. Penner, "Dealing with Uncertain Budget Forecasts," *Public Budgeting & Finance* 22 (Spring 2002): 1–18.

Table 2–3
Federal Outlays by Function and by Administrative Organization, Fiscal 2013

Superfunction and Function	$ Million	Department or Other Unit	$ Million
National Defense	**633,385**	Legislative Branch	4,334
Human resources	**2,417,949**	Judicial Branch	7,063
Education, Training, Employment, and Social Services	72,808	Department of Agriculture	155,872
Health	358,315	Department of Commerce	9,140
Medicare	497,826	Department of Defense—Military Programs	607,800
Income Security	536,511	Department of Education	40,910
Social Security	813,551	Department of Energy	24,670
(On-budget)	56,009	Department of Health and Human Services	886,291
(Off-budget)	757,542	Department of Homeland Security	57,217
Veterans Benefits and Services	138,938	Department of Housing and Urban Development	56,577
Physical resources	**89,997**	Department of the Interior	9,607
Energy	11,042	Department of Justice	29,745
Natural Resources and Environment	38,145	Department of Labor	80,307
Commerce and Housing Credit	0	Department of State	25,928
(On-budget)	−81,286	Department of Transportation	76,322
(Off-budget)	−1,913	Department of the Treasury	399,068
Transportation	91,673	Department of Veterans Affairs	138,464
Community and Regional Development	32,336	Corps of Engineers—Civil Works	6,299
Net interest	**220,885**	Other Defense Civil Programs	56,811
(On-budget)	326,535	Environmental Protection Agency	9,484
(Off-budget)	−105,650	Executive Office of the President	380
Other functions	**185,174**	General Services Administration	−368
International Affairs	46,418	International Assistance Programs	19,740
General Science, Space, and Technology	28,908	National Aeronautics and Space Administration	16,975
Agriculture	29,492	National Science Foundation	7,417
Administration of Justice	52,601	Office of Personnel Management	83,867
General Government	27,755	Small Business Administration	477
Allowances	....	Social Security Administration (On-Budget)	109,849

(continues)

**Table 2–3
(continued)**

Superfunction and Function	$ Million	Department or Other Unit	$ Million
Undistributed offsetting receipts	**−92,785**	Social Security Administration (Off-Budget)	757,542
(On-budget)	−76,617	Other Independent Agencies (On-Budget)	28,180
(Off-budget)	−16,168	Other Independent Agencies (Off-Budget)	−1,913
Total, Federal outlays	**3,454,605**	Allowances	....
		Undistributed Offsetting Receipts	−249,450
		(On-budget)	−127,632
		(Off-budget)	−121,818
		Total outlays	3,454,605

SOURCE: Office of Management and Budget, *Budget of the Government of the United States, Fiscal Year 2015, Historical Tables*. (Washington, D.C.: U.S. Government Printing Office, 2014.)

Federal outlays are organized according to function in the left side of the table and according to administrative department in the right. Total spending for both sides of the table is the same, just categorized differently. The functional classification identifies spending for provision of a particular service or purpose category, without regard for the responsible entity. So spending to provide service for support of natural resources and the environment is considerably different from spending by the Environmental Protection Agency because a number of agencies are involved in supporting services for natural resources and the environment. And so it is with each function and for most agencies—several agencies contribute to the functions and single agencies are contributing toward multiple functions. The functional classification gives a view of fundamental resource allocations to deal with the array of public problems.[16]

Alternative classifications of budgets, including the strengths and weaknesses of each classification, are discussed in greater detail in later chapters. However, behind any budget classification lurks some "grocery list" of inputs that will be needed for the service plan regardless of the vision or strategy for providing services that has produced that plan. Just as a cook has to decide whether to bake cherry pies or angel food cakes before preparing a grocery list (the inputs), a government executive needs to have a service plan before creating the list of inputs to be purchased. And both the cook and the government executive will eventually need a grocery list to carry out the plan. Hence, the input classification is the most basic and durable format of all. In many small governments and nonprofit organizations, it is the only classification structure for the budget. However, this grocery list should not be the focus of budgetary analysis. The focus should be on what the agency does with the resources it has purchased.

---

[16]The federal budget provides the standard multiple years for both administrative and functional classifications. They are not included in the table because of space limitations.

What the Budget Process Should Contribute

Governments exist to provide services. The budget process provides a time for decisions about the services desired by the public and the options available to the government for providing these services. A traditional expectation is that properly working budget processes act to constrain government and to prevent public officials from stealing. Indeed, public budgeting in the United States developed first at the municipal level to prevent thievery, pure and simple. Budgets should do that, but they should also do more, particularly with regard to seeing that governments fulfill their appropriate role in delivering the services demanded of them by businesses and individuals through choices made in the democratic process and that resources available to government are reasonably used. The process allocates resources among government activities and between government and private use.

The great struggle in the budget process is between "needs" and "availability." On one hand, the resources available to the government are limited by economic conditions and the extent to which the government is willing to apply its fiscal authority to draw revenue from the private economy. On the other hand, agencies and departments of government have commitments and opportunities to deliver services to the citizenry. Long-term fiscal sustainability—the ability of the government to maintain its operations on behalf of the public without deterioration of services or dramatic increases in taxation—requires that actual spending be within resource availability. That means continuing tension because opportunities for service always exceed resource availability. The budget process has to work that out as part of the agenda for sustainability.[17] Budget presentations that extend several years into the future, well beyond the term of current budget proposals, are primarily documents for fiscal sustainability.

Public financial managers expect budget procedures to (1) provide a framework for fiscal discipline and control, (2) facilitate allocation of government resources toward uses of highest strategic priority, and (3) encourage efficient and effective use of resources by public agencies as they implement public programs.[18] They also expect budget procedures to be the primary mechanisms for creating transparency in the fiscal operations of the government, an objective made much easier by the ability to post significant documents on a government website for anyone to see. The procedures work through budget planning and development, budget deliberations, budget execution, and audit. The processes of analysis and management apply equally to government and nonprofit organizations, although they are usually more highly developed and more routine in governments.

---

[17]Many nations have instituted what are called *medium term expenditure frameworks (MTEFs)* in an effort to provide this balancing of needs and availability over a three- to five-year horizon. The MTEF involves development of a top-down (from the central budget office or Ministry of Finance) resource constraint from a macroeconomic model, a bottom-up (from the agencies) estimation of the medium-term cost of delivering services according to current policies, and a reconciliation against government priorities. The framework feeds into the annual budget process to give better responsiveness to national priorities and some greater predictability of funding to agencies.

[18]*Public Expenditure Management Handbook* (Washington, D.C.: The World Bank, 1998), 17.

1. **Fiscal discipline and control.** The expenditure-control function in budgeting restrains expenditures to the limits of available finance, ensures that enacted budgets are executed and that financial reports are accurate, and preserves the legality of agency expenditures. The control function—making sure that expenditures agree with the legal intent of the legislature—helps develop information for cost estimates used in preparation of future budgets and preserves audit trails after budget years are over.[19] Much of the control comes from within the spending unit, to ensure that funds are being spent within legal intentions because it is better to prevent misuse than to try to punish it after it has occurred. Sending public officials to jail may provide some satisfaction, but it won't bring the stolen resources back. It is better to have a framework in place to prevent theft than to concentrate on punishing violators after it has happened. Budgeting and appropriating given dollar amounts to purchase given quantities of goods or services simplifies the fundamental external audit questions: Do financial statements of the agency tell the truth, is the agency sufficiently protective of public resources, and did the agency use the resources provided it in the intended way? If the appropriation was for the purchase of 10 tons of gravel, was that gravel actually purchased and delivered in a responsible manner, was the gravel adequately protected while it was in the agency's hands, and do the agency's financial reports accurately reflect the gravel transaction?

   Restructuring the notion of control away from inputs purchased toward services provided presents a great challenge for government responsiveness. Unfortunately, the definition of accountability in government has remained relatively constant over the past fifty years: "limit bureaucratic discretion through compliance with tightly drawn rules and regulations."[20] If government is to be flexible, responsive, and innovative, narrow control and accountability to the legislature and within the operating agencies almost certainly must change from internal operations to external results.

2. **Response to strategic priorities.** The budget process should work to deliver financing to the programs that are of greatest current importance to the citizenry. Governments face many fruitful opportunities for providing useful services. Their resources are limited, so they must choose among useful options, recognizing that their choices both influence and must be influenced by community, state, and national environments. They should not have to work around legal or administrative constraints that protect certain activities without regard for their relative importance. All

---

[19]An audit trail is a sequence of documents—invoices, receipts, canceled checks, and so forth—that allows an outside observer to trace transactions involving appropriated money: when the money was spent and who received it, when purchases were delivered and what price was paid, and how the purchases were cared for and used.

[20]Paul C. Light, *Monitoring Government: Inspectors General and the Search for Accountability* (Washington, D.C.: Brookings Institution, 1993), 12.

resources controlled by the government should be available to respond to the legitimate demands of the country; the competition for those scarce resources ought to be balanced among the alternatives, with the final decision about how the funds are used driven by the return from the competing uses, not barriers that hinder allocation of those funds. This is difficult for politicians and interest groups because both have an innate tendency to want to tie the hands of future generations with what they believe to be timelessly good ideas. Making sure that fire department horses had access to hay and water was critical in the nineteenth century; it isn't an issue today. Permanent dedication of certain taxes to provision of particular services, called tax earmarking, is popular with lawmakers but ties the hands of future governments, thus inhibiting response to strategic priorities.

3. **Efficient implementation of the budget.** Budgets serve as a tool to increase managerial control of operating units and to improve efficiency in agency operations. The important concern is the relationship between the resources used and the public services performed by the unit. The public budget—as in a private business plan—serves as the control device and identifies operational efficiency. For this purpose, the agency must consider what measurable activities it performs, an often difficult, but seldom impossible, task. The process should induce agencies to economize in their operations, identify the services of greatest importance to the populations they serve, choose best available technologies and strategies for delivering those services, and respond quickly when service demands or operating conditions change. Not spending funds appropriated to the agency is not praiseworthy if the agency has also failed to provide desired public services. And it certainly is not praiseworthy if other agencies have pressing service demands that budget limitations have prevented them from meeting.

Delivering Those Budget Process Functions

The budget process should enforce aggregate fiscal discipline, facilitate allocation of government resources to areas of greatest current public priority, and encourage efficient agency operations. Some process features that help to realize those promises are (1) realistic forecasts of receipts and other data useful for development of budgets; (2) comprehensive and complete application of the budget system to all parts of the government; (3) transparency and accountability as the budget is developed, approved, and executed; (4) hard and enforced constraints on total resources provided to agencies, but with considerable flexibility in how agencies may use these resources in service delivery; (5) use of objective performance criteria for agency and government accountability; (6) reconciliation between planned and executed budgets; and (7) capable and fairly compensated government officials to prevent susceptibility to corruption.[21] The budget should be authoritative, in the sense that spending will occur only according to the budget law, and that records will be accurate in recording actual transactions and flows.

The budget should also be forward looking, in the sense that, while being prepared and adopted for the short fiscal period of only a single year or two, it sets the stage for years in the future. Therefore, the public is best served if the budget is formulated within a medium-term economic framework of four or five years (or the ten years in federal budgeting), so that the chances of fiscal sustainability will be improved. That doesn't mean that the budget should be adopted for four or five years at a time.[22] Indeed, the expectations of the budget process are better served if the budget is adopted on an annual basis for better fiscal discipline and responsiveness to changed conditions. It does mean that an effort should be made to track the implications of fiscal decisions made in the current budget process into the medium term as a way to provide better guidance for decisions being made now.[23]

Overarching all the budget process, all budget procedures, and all budget documents is a concern with *fiscal transparency*. This interest is inherent in democratic governance: If the public cannot see what the government has done, is doing, and intends to do, how can it give its informed consent to that government? Fiscal transparency requires that the general public, analysts, and the media have easy access to information about service delivery, financing arrangements, debt management, and the other elements that explain what is going on. Transparency does not mean pictures and pie charts in the budget document, but it does mean provision of accessible information about operations, achievements, and intentions. And it does not mean a data storm of discrete operating details, provided en masse in an arcane data format when inquiries are made by analysts, researchers, or the media. Sidebar 2–2 provides some guidance about what contributes to fiscal transparency, as well as what does not. Closing the information door, responding to legitimate information requests in an unhelpful way, dumping a pile of uncategorized transaction records, and presenting heroic pictures rather than operational information are inconsistent with public transparency and with democratic governance. It is, indeed, appropriate for government officials to believe that someone is watching them closely. After all, it isn't their money that they are spending, and they aren't operating programs according to their own tastes and preferences. It is the public's business, not theirs.

---

[21]Ed Campos and Sanjay Pradhan, *The Impact of Budgetary Institutions on Expenditure Outcomes: Binding Governments to Fiscal Performance,* Working Papers Series (Washington, D.C.: The World Bank, Policy Research Department, 1996).

[22]In 2008, the Duma of the Russian Federation passed an actual three-year budget covering 2009–2011, an exception to the multiyear budgets that offer only an advisory framework. Apparently, the budget had to be abandoned in 2009 because of political and economic developments. They continued to adopt three-year budgets. However, the 2016 budget that was part of the 2015–2017 package was replaced with a single year budget in fall 2015 when economic prospects soured. That is the problem with multiyear budgets: actual events interfere with the forecasts envisioned for the budget period. Russia returned to a three-year budget for 2017 and later, at least until the next economic difficulty develops.

[23]The approach to development of a medium term expenditure framework (MTEF) is explained in World Bank, *Public Expenditure Management Handbook* (Washington, D.C.: World Bank, 1998) 31–58. Anyone interested in economic development activity should become familiar with the MTEF procedures because development assistance agencies expect recipient governments to have them in place.

Sidebar 2–2
Fiscal Transparency for Modern Democracies

Fiscal transparency means openness and accountability in fiscal operations whereby budget processes from development through implementation and audit are subject to public scrutiny. It includes full disclosure of activities in the fiscal sphere, whether involving spending, collecting revenue, or borrowing. Complete and reliable disclosure helps participants in financial markets have confidence in government claims, provides an understanding of budgeting options and decisions for the citizens, and allows the public to participate in fiscal decisions on an informed basis. Transparency is a foundation for fiscal accountability and should be embraced by budget processes in a democracy. It is said that fresh air has great cleansing properties.

The International Monetary Fund Code of Good Practices on Fiscal Transparency provides a good template with its four general principles:

1. Clarity of roles and responsibilities. Government and commercial activities should be clearly distinguished, and there should be clear legal and institutional frameworks for governing fiscal relations with the private sector. Fiscal documents should include the full picture of receipts and expenditures, and there should be no pockets of semigovernmental operations excluded from public view.
2. Open budget processes. Budgets should be prepared, presented, and discussed to facilitate analysis of policies and assist accountability.
3. Public availability of information. The public should have easy access to past, current, and expected fiscal activity, and that access should be timely. Online availability is an appropriate approach, although libraries and government offices should also make documents available.
4. Assurances of integrity. Fiscal data should meet accepted quality standards and should be subject to independent audit. Reports should be reliable—actual receipts and expenditures should be reasonably correlated to the adopted budget.

The code was developed primarily for national government finances (and particularly with regard to extraction of natural resources, an area in which history shows large sums of public revenues disappearing into private hands), but it makes sense as a guide for all governments.

What fiscal information should be easily, promptly, and freely available to media, interest groups, and the general public? Given that providing online availability is rather inexpensive (preparing the materials for posting will cost more), lots of information should be provided, and it should be provided in a format that permits easy access, searching, and analysis. Types of information that could reasonably be provided include:

1. All budget documents, including historical tables in downloadable spreadsheet or database formats. Governments should also provide a "budget in brief" document that summarizes revenues, expenditures, and debt included in the budget.[1] Documents should include the executive budget proposal, the enacted budget (appropriations), midyear execution reports, and end-of-year reports.

---

[1]Organization for Economic Cooperation and Development, *OECD Best Practices for Budget Transparency* (Paris: OECD, 2002) provides greater detail on the specific budget documents that should be available.

(continues)

Sidebar 2–2
(continued)

2. Economic forecasts upon which revenue forecasts and expenditure plans were based.
3. External audit reports. The reports should cover both financial status and compliance with laws.
4. Contracts entered into by the government. Data could include the name of the contractor, the type of activity being performed, and the financial details of the contract.
5. Economic development incentives and grants provided by the government. Data could include the recipient, the type of subsidy, amounts provided, promised developmental impact, and any clawback provisions for return of funds if development promises are not kept.
6. Tax expenditure report. Data could include the amounts of revenue lost by subsidy provisions embedded in the tax code.
7. Tax abatements. Governmental Accounting Standards Board Standard 77 requires governments to disclose information about their tax-abating agreements: the purpose of the abatement program, the tax being abated, the dollar amount of taxes abated, provisions for recapture if the recipient fails to carry out promised activities, types of commitments made by abatement recipients, and other commitments made by the government in the agreement, such as construction of infrastructure.
8. Comprehensive annual financial report.
9. Data from the government's checkbook. Data on all payments made by the government, including to whom the payment was made, the amount of payment, and the agency receiving the contracted service.

Transparency postings matter for citizens who want to understand and to participate knowledgeably in the political process. For this interest, it is important that fiscal data be organized in a usable fashion: for what is the government spending the money (what services, not what purchases), from where is the government getting its money (what taxes and charges are being collected), and what is the government doing about its debt? Ease of access, useful categorization of gross fiscal data, and timeliness are what matters here. A useful and meaningful categorization matters if citizens are to be able to participate in policy discussions.

It is often argued that transparency requires that deliberations about revenue and expenditure programs need to be public sessions to prevent deals that are contrary to the public interest. However, it is just as likely that open sessions will create public posturing and an atmosphere in which absolutely nothing gets accomplished except through deals made outside of the formal process. Compromise is critical in the U.S. system of political checks and balances, and barriers to compromise offer an open invitation to policy gridlock.

Another sort of transparency posting matters for those who perpetually smell a rat and believe that having all the data will show the problems. If the external observer doubts the controls of the fiscal system and is focused on finding funny business, then the data that matters are information on checkbook transactions, contract awards, and development incentives. For most analysis, these raw data won't answer interesting questions; it will be no surprise that the state police make a lot of payments to purchase gasoline, for instance. To know that a city has purchased quite a lot of asphalt to pave its streets doesn't indicate whether the price it paid per ton was high or low, whether the purchase went through the accepted appropriation and contracting procedures, and whether the asphalt was used well. The checkbook information can provide useful information for competitors interested in bidding for city work. Trying to reconstruct the policy choices that led to the spending is tedious, and not many ordinary citizens or members of the media have the capacity to make sense of raw data. Systems controls and contracting regulations, backed up by external audit, should handle protection of public resources. If those structural procedures are inadequate, then the remedy would be improved systems and structures, not self-appointed watchdogs replicating work that should have been done by internal controls and external audit. The objective of transparency is to increase public understanding, not to catch the crooks.

As a practical matter, the transparency objective should be timely, clear and relevant, complete, accurate, and meaningful provision of fiscal data provided in an accessible fashion. That means reliance on systems for basic protection of fiscal resources. Total data dumps such as the checkbook can be provided, but that would not provide effective fiscal control and would be no substitute for proper systems. Former Texas Deputy State Comptroller Billy Hamilton has a useful insight in his definition of transparency: "Burying the truth under piles of otherwise useless data."[2]

[2]Billy Hamilton, "The Devil's Dictionary of Tax Politics and Legislative Phraseology," *State Tax Notes*, December 9, 2013, 619.

The Budget Cycle

Recurring (and overlapping) events in the budgeting and spending process constitute the "regular order" of the budget cycle. Although specific activities differ among governments, any government that separates powers between the executive and legislative branches shows many of the elements outlined here.[24] The four major stages of the cycle—executive preparation, legislative consideration, execution, and audit and evaluation—are considered in turn. The cycles are linked across the years because the audit and evaluation findings provide important data for preparation of future budgets. The four phases recur, so at any time an operating agency is in different executive and legislative roles. But the budget still must be prepared and adopted in phases of different budget years. Suppose an agency is on an October 1 to September 30 fiscal year and it is December 2017. That agency would be in the execution phase of fiscal year 2018 (fiscal years are normally named after their end year). It would likely be in the legislative consideration phase of fiscal year 2019, just at the beginning of the executive preparation phase of fiscal year 2020, and in the audit and evaluation phase of fiscal 2016 and prior years. Thus, the budget cycle is both continuous and overlapping, as Figure 2–3 illustrates.

---

[24]A parliamentary government would not neatly fit this cycle because there is no separation between executive and legislative branches. The city manager approach to local government does not easily fit the separation either.

Figure 2–3
Phases of a Budget Cycle

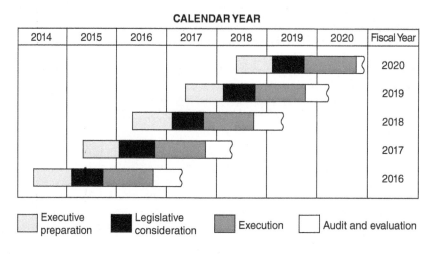

The federal fiscal year begins in October; many local governments have fiscal years beginning in January; all state governments except Alabama, Michigan, New York, and Texas start fiscal years in July. The fiscal year in Alabama and Michigan starts in October, New York has an April start, and Texas's is in September. Nonprofit organizations typically use either a January or July start, although they may select any start that is most convenient for their flow of operations. Governments relying heavily on transfers from a higher government often start their fiscal years some months after that of the higher government so that they will be more likely to know the amount of transfers they will receive before they enact their budgets.

Executive Preparation

The executive budget is a message of policy; the financial numbers on spending, revenues, and deficits or surpluses are driven by those policies. Dall Forsythe, who once served as New York State budget director, emphasizes the point for governors (and all chief executives): "If you cannot use the budget to state your goals and move state government in the direction you advocate, you are not likely to make much progress towards those goals."[25] For the budget process to meet its expectations, the executive presentation for legislative deliberation should (1) be comprehensive (i.e., cover all government revenues and expenditures), (2) be transparent (i.e., present a clear trail from details to aggregate summaries of revenue and expenditure so that the implications of policy proposals and operating assumptions are clear), (3) establish accountability (i.e., clarify who will be responsible for funds, in what amount, and

---

[25]Dall W. Forsythe, *Memos to the Governor, An Introduction to State Budgeting* (Washington, D.C.: Georgetown University Press, 1997), 84–85.

for what purpose), (4) avoid revenue dedications (earmarks) or other long-term commitments that could hinder response to new priorities or problems, and (5) establish as clearly as possible for what public purpose (i.e., desired result, not administrative input) the funds will be spent. The executive will set the tone for preparation with a statement of his or her priorities (e.g., improving the business climate, protecting the most vulnerable groups in the population, improving inter-city transportation networks, upgrading early childhood education, etc.), and agencies are expected to devise program plans that honor those priorities.

Beyond priorities, preparation requires standard technical instructions. These instructions (sometimes labeled the "call for estimates") include (1) a timetable for budget submissions, (2) instructions for developing requests, (3) indication of what funds are likely to be available (either in the form of an agency ceiling or in terms of a percentage increase), and (4) overall priority directions from the executive. The federal instructions, Circular A-11 revised annually, appear on the Office of Management and Budget website (www.whitehouse.gov/omb) for all to see. Many states also place their instructions on their budget agency's website. The instructions may also, but not necessarily, provide forecasts of certain operating conditions for the fiscal year, including things like input price increases, service population trends, and so on, with an eye toward making sure that all agencies work with the same basic data. An important element in developing the instructions is a forecast of the economic climate and what it means in terms of revenue and expenditure claims on the government. A forecast of difficult economic conditions and limited revenue growth usually means instructions with limited prospects for the expansion of existing programs or the development of new programs, and possibly instructions to reduce spending.

The agency request builds on an agency plan for service in an upcoming year (the agency response to public demands for service) and an agency forecast of conditions in the upcoming year (the group of conditions influencing the agency, but not subject to agency control). These forecasts ought to be best estimates of conditions in the future. They are not necessarily projections, or simple extensions, of current conditions into the future because the agency may believe that those conditions will change. And the request is definitely not a forecast or projection of agency spending. For example, a state highway department request for snow-removal funds would involve a forecast of the number of snowy days and a planned response for handling that snow. For any snow forecast, the agency budget request will vary depending on how promptly the agency responds to snowfall (after trace snowfall, after 1 inch, after 3 inches, etc.), which roadways will be cleared (arterial, secondary, residential, etc.), and so on. Each planned response will result in a different budget request. The forecast does not dictate the request.

Unfortunately, some agencies build their plans on inputs (the highway department bought 120 tons of road salt last year, so it will request about that amount for the budget year); this approach makes changes in service-delivery methods and practices difficult and is a pretty good indicator that the agency isn't doing the taxpayers any favors. In sum, the public service demands and operating conditions will be forecasts, but the amount requested by the agency will reflect its planned response to those forecast conditions. Different response plans will mean different budget requests.

An agency develops not only a cost estimate for providing the services it plans to deliver, but also a narrative justification for the requests. The estimate and its justification reflect the large number of program decisions the agency has made. The chief executive's budget office gathers the requests made by many operating agencies and consolidates these requests. The budget office reviews budget requests for consistency with the policies of the chief executive, for reasonable cost and logical content, and for total consistency with spending directions. Often there are administrative hearings for reconciliation of an agency request and budget office adjustments. Finally, the executive budget document is transmitted to the legislature for its consideration. Law usually establishes the date of transmission to the legislature.

The budget document, or executive budget, incorporates all agency requests into a government-wide request or plan. The requests by the agencies have been accumulated and aggregated according to the policy plan of the chief executive. Some legislative bodies, including the U.S. Congress, propose their own alternative budgets. Agency requests will almost always be reduced by the chief executive to produce an overall executive plan. And, of course, the expectation is that the vision or priorities of the chief executive will dominate the direction of the final plan. As is discussed later, the substantial changes made in agency requests before proposals are seen by the legislature reflect differences in attitudes and service clienteles of the agencies and the chief executive.

Legislative Consideration

In a government with distinct legislative and executive branches, the budget document is transmitted to the legislature for debate and consideration. The legislature typically splits that budget into as many parts as appropriation bills will ultimately be passed and submits those parts to legislative subcommittees. This consideration usually begins with the lower house of a bicameral legislature. In subcommittee hearings, agencies defend their budget requests, often calling attention to differences between their initial request and what appears in the executive budget. After the lower house has approved the appropriation, the upper house goes through a similar hearing process. When both houses have approved appropriations, a conference committee from the two houses prepares unified appropriation bills for final passage by both houses. Appropriation acts are the outcome of the legislative process. These laws provide funds for operating agencies to spend in a specified fashion in the budget year. The initial requests by the agency reflect the plans of that agency; appropriation converts these plans (or portions of them) into law.

The chief executive normally must sign the appropriation bill before it becomes law, and thus gives operating agencies financial resources to provide services, but not all executives have the same options. Some executives may sign parts of the bill, while rejecting others (called *item-veto power*); others must approve it all or reject it all, thus returning the bill to the legislature. Most state governors have item-veto power, but the president does not. Some observers feel the item veto provides a useful screening of projects that political clout, rather than merit, has inserted in the appropriation bill. Others are skeptical about such power because of its use for executive vendettas against selected groups, legislators, or agencies.[26]

In a non-profit organization, it is normal for the executive director to prepare a budget for entity operations in the upcoming year, using the same logic as previously outlined for governments. In its preparation, the director will ideally discuss problems and opportunities with organization stakeholders, and then will present the budget to the organization's executive board for approval. Of course, the approved budget does not constitute an adopted law, but it does provide a guidance for operations of the agency.

Execution

During execution, agencies carry out their approved budgets. Appropriations are spent, and services are delivered. The approved budget becomes an important device to monitor spending and service delivery. Although there are other important managerial concerns during execution, spending must proceed in a manner consistent with appropriation laws. Law typically forbids (often with criminal sanctions) agencies from spending more money than has been appropriated. The Anti-Deficiency Act of 1906 is the governing federal law; similar laws apply at state and local levels and in other countries with well-developed fiscal systems. Spending less than the appropriation, although a possible sign of efficient operation, may well mean that anticipated services have not been delivered or that agency budget requests were needlessly high. Thus, finance officers must constantly monitor the relationship between actual expenditures and planned/approved expenditures (the appropriation) during the fiscal year. Failure to spend the full appropriation is not necessarily a good achievement. A standard tool used to analyze the quality of budget processes is to compare the amounts approved for government services with the amounts actually spent on delivery of those services. The question is: was the adopted budget actually executed?

Central budget offices (the Office of Management and Budget for the federal government) normally handle the monitoring and release of funds during execution of the budget. Most governments have some pre-expenditure audit system to determine the validity of expenditures within the appropriation and some controls to keep expenditures within actual resources available. It is normal that funds will be maintained in a single treasury account rather than being distributed among separate agency bank accounts. That means that an agency pays for its purchases by ordering

---

[26]Strangely enough, former Governor Rick Perry of Texas was indicted for abuse of power when he used his item-veto power on an appropriation to the Travis County Public Integrity Unit following the drunken-driving arrest and guilty plea of the person in charge of the unit. That unit is responsible for corruption investigations of state government, and its head was of a different political party from the governor. (Nathan Koppel, "Texas Gov. Perry Indicted After Veto of Funding," *Wall Street Journal*, August 15, 2014.) Governors have freely exercised item-veto powers, so the indictment puzzled public finance experts. It was dismissed completely in 2016.

the central treasury to issue the payment, rather than having the agency itself make payment. The single treasury account provides better protection of public funds and reduces the need for carrying high cash balances to meet the flow of payments.

Spending is the direct result of appropriations made to carry out the service envisioned in the agency's initial budget plan.[27] However, because expenditures can involve the purchase of resources for use both in the present and in the future, it would generally be incorrect to expect the expenditure to equal the current cost of providing government services. Some of the current expenditure will provide services in later periods. (In simplest terms, part of the road salt purchased this year may be used next year, but much of the difference between expenditure and service cost will be caused by purchase of capital assets, such as buildings, trucks, computers, etc.) The cost of government would equal the amount of resources used, or consumed, during the current period—some resources coming from expenditure in that period and some from previous expenditures. Focus on expenditure thus renders an inaccurate view of the cost of government. Figure 2–4 outlines the flow of transactions and accompanying management information requirements between budget authority and service cost: (1) *budget authority* provides funding (the appropriation law approves agency Z's plan to publish an information bulletin), (2) *obligation* occurs when an order is placed (agency Z orders paper from business A), (3) *inventory* is recorded when material is delivered (business A delivers the paper to agency Z), (4) *outlay* occurs when the bill is paid (agency Z pays for the paper), and (5) *cost* occurs when the materials are used (agency Z prints an information bulletin on the paper).

Some reference to the federal structure may help clarify. Budget authority—provided through appropriation, borrowing authority, or contract authority—allows agencies to enter into commitments that will result in immediate or future spending.[28] Budget authority defines the upper limit for agency spending without obtaining

Figure 2–4
Financial Information for Management

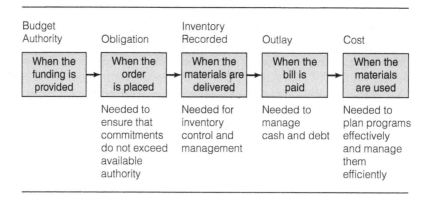

Budget Authority	Obligation	Inventory Recorded	Outlay	Cost
When the funding is provided	When the order is placed	When the materials are delivered	When the bill is paid	When the materials are used
	Needed to ensure that commitments do not exceed available authority	Needed for inventory control and management	Needed to manage cash and debt	Needed to plan programs effectively and manage them efficiently

---

[27]Not all expenditure, however, results from appropriation. This complication is explained later.
[28]Borrowing authority permits an agency to borrow funds and to spend the proceeds for qualified purposes. Contract authority allows an agency to make obligations before appropriations have been passed.

Figure 2–5
Relationship of Budget Authority to Outlays, 2017

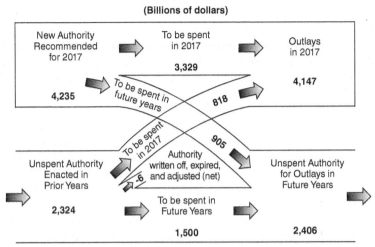

SOURCE: Executive Office of the President, Office of Management and Budget, *Budget of the United States Government, Fiscal Year 2017: Analytical Perspectives. Budget Process* (Washington, D.C.: OMB, 2016): 110.

additional authority. Figure 2–5 illustrates the relationship between budget authority and outlays envisioned in the 2017 federal budget. The budget plans outlays of $4,147 billion. Most of the outlays are based on proposals in this budget ($3,329 billion), but $818 billion (19.7 percent of the total) is based on unspent authority enacted in prior years. Therefore, budget authority in a particular year differs from outlays for the year; outlays may result from either present or previous budget authority.

Operating agencies should have managerial flexibility in the use of funds, allowing them to change the particular mix of inputs they purchase, so long as they can provide the level of service to the public that was envisioned in the adopted budget. Agencies almost certainly know more about new technologies, changes in prices of inputs that could allow cost savings, and emerging problems than does the legislature or the budget agency. Hence, locking agencies to the line-item details of the proposed and adopted budget usually inhibits efficiency and innovation. Ideally, the operating agency should be responsible for budget totals and agency results, not the details of exactly how money was spent (within laws of theft and corruption).

Audit and Evaluation

An audit is an "examination of records, facilities, systems, and other evidence to discover or verify desired information."[29] The audit seeks to discover deviations from accepted standards and instances of illegality, inefficiency, irregularity, and

---

[29]Peter F. Rousmaniere, *Local Government Auditing—A Manual for Public Officials* (New York: Council on Municipal Performance, 1980), 83.

ineffectiveness early enough to take corrective action, to hold violators accountable, and to take steps to prevent further losses. The audit may be internal (in other words, the auditors are subordinate to the heads of the departments being audited) or external (the auditors are outside the structure being audited and, for governments, are ultimately responsible to the citizenry). In general, the auditors verify the assertions made by the audited entity. Information is documented on the basis of a sample of transactions and other activities of the entity—a judgment about purchasing practices, for instance, is made from a review of a sample of transactions, not from an examination of all invoices.

Post-expenditure audits determine compliance with appropriations and report findings to the legislature (or to a judicial body if laws have been violated).[30] At the federal level, the Government Accountability Office (GAO), an agency of Congress, supervises audits of agencies, although the actual auditing is typically done by agency personnel.[31] States frequently have elected auditors or independent agencies that audit state agencies and local governments. Local governments sometimes have audits done by independent accounting firms as well as by government bodies, although some such governments have not frequently had independent audits.[32]

Government audits may be classified according to their objectives into two types: financial and performance. Financial audits include financial statement audits, which "determine (1) whether the financial statements of an audited entity present fairly the financial position, results of operations, and cash flows or changes in financial position in accordance with generally accepted accounting principles, and (2) whether the entity has complied with laws and regulations for those transactions and events that may have a material effect on the financial statements,"[33] and financial-related audits, which "include determining (1) whether financial reports and related items, such as elements, accounts, or funds are fairly presented, (2) whether financial information is presented in accordance with established or stated criteria, and (3) whether the entity has adhered to specific financial compliance requirements."[34] These audits test financial records to determine whether the funds were spent legally, receipts were properly recorded and controlled, and financial records and statements are complete and reliable. They concentrate on establishing compliance with appropriation law and on determining whether financial reports prepared by the operating agency are accurate and reliable. The financial audit still must determine, however, whether there has been theft by government employees or their confederates, although this part of the task should be minor because of

---

[30]A pre-expenditure audit ascertains the legality or appropriateness of making payment. Such an analysis often occurs, for instance, prior to the delivery of payroll checks.

[31]The international group of audit bodies is the International Organization of Supreme Audit Institutions (INTOSAI). This group establishes international principles of organization and operation for these supreme audit institutions. The GAO is the U.S. member.

[32]Federal general revenue sharing required an audit at least once in three years for general-purpose governments receiving such money. The aid program is long gone, but the tradition of regular audits fortunately continues.

[33]U.S. General Accounting Office, *Government Auditing Standards,* 1998 rev. (Washington, D.C.: GPO, 1998), 2–1.

[34]Ibid., 2–2.

protections created by controls within the agency (internal controls). But if nothing else has provided the protection, it is expected that the financial audit will protect public resources and see that thieves get dealt with appropriately by the judicial system.

Performance audits similarly encompass two classes of audits: economy and efficiency audits, which seek to determine "(1) whether the entity is acquiring, protecting, and using its resources (such as personnel, property, and space) economically and efficiently, (2) the causes of inefficiencies or uneconomical practices, and (3) whether the entity has complied with laws and regulations concerning matters of economy and efficiency,"[35] and program audits, which examine "(1) the extent to which the desired results or benefits established by the legislature or other authorizing body are being achieved, (2) the effectiveness of organizations, programs, activities, or functions, and (3) whether the entity has complied with laws and regulations applicable to the program."[36] Economy and efficiency audits might consider questions of procurement, safeguarding of resources, duplication of effort, use of staff, efficiency of operating procedures, management to minimize cost of delivering appropriate quantity and quality of service, compliance with laws governing use of resources, and systems for measuring and reporting performance. Program audits emphasize the extent to which desired results are being achieved, what factors might inhibit satisfactory performance, whether there might be lower-cost alternatives for obtaining the desired results, and whether there may be conflict or overlap with other programs. Some states link performance audits with sunset reviews: "a set schedule for legislative review of programs and agencies and an automatic termination of those programs and agencies unless affirmative legislative action is taken to reauthorize them. Thus, the 'sun sets' on agencies and programs."[37] States with such legislation typically include a performance audit as part of the preparation for action on agencies or programs eligible for termination.

A simple example may illustrate the focus of each audit. Consider a state highway department appropriation to purchase road salt for snow and ice removal. A *financial audit* would consider whether the agency had an appropriation for salt purchased, whether salt purchased was actually delivered, whether approved practices were followed in selecting a supplier, and whether agency reports showed the correct expenditure on salt. An *efficiency and economy audit* would consider whether the salt inventory is adequately protected from the environment, whether the inventory is adequate or excessive, and whether other methods of selecting a supplier would lower the cost. A *program audit* would consider whether the prevailing level of winter highway clearing is an appropriate use of community resources and whether approaches other than spreading salt would be less costly to the community.

---

[35]Ibid., 2–3.
[36]Ibid.
[37]Advisory Commission on Intergovernmental Relations, "Sunset Legislation and Zero-Based Budgeting," *Information Bulletin,* no. 76–5 (December 1976): 1.

Government Accounting and Financial Reporting

Proper accounting and reporting makes government finances more transparent to constituencies, including public officials, the public, and the investment community. They should improve accountability to the public, including allowing the public to see whether current revenues are sufficient to cover current expenditures; they should make it possible to evaluate the operating results of the government for the year, including determining how financial resources are obtained and how they are spent; and they should help with assessment of the level of services that the government can afford to provide, including supplying information about the financial condition of the government.

Standards

Independent authorities or boards establish the standards (or rules) for accounting and financial reporting; in the United States, the Financial Accounting Standards Board (FASB) sets the standards for the private sector, the Federal Accounting Standards Advisory Board (FASAB) issues standards and guidance for federal accounting, and the Governmental Accounting Standards Board (GASB) sets them for the state and local governments. Similar bodies do the work in other countries. These standards establish the practices that the accounting system will implement and allow any interested party to understand the finances of the government and to make certain comparisons of finances across governments. However, the accounts, even when prepared according to recognized or "generally accepted" standards, are not statements of scientific validity, as anyone even slightly familiar with the Enron experience of rigged accounts that showed profitability as the company went bankrupt in 2001 will understand. At best, they seek fair representation, not unassailable truth or scientific validity.

The accounting system allows the manager to assemble, analyze, and report data for the essential work expected of the budget process. The data must be complete, accurate, timely, and understandable for all public constituencies. The focus of the system is on revenues and expenditures, on financial balances, and on financial obligations of the government. The financial reporting system is expected to provide understandability (reports should be sensible to the general public as well as to experts), reliability (reports should be comprehensive, verifiable, and without bias), relevance (information provided should meet the needs of users), timeliness (reports should be issued shortly after the close of the fiscal year), consistency (the basis should be the same for all transactions and across fiscal years), and comparability (it should be possible to compare reports across governments). The accounting system is expected to provide the framework for financial control, but it is also expected to be a ripe source of information for government decision makers and the public.

The full accounting system combines several elements:

1. **Source documents:** These are the receipts, invoices, and other original details of transactions.
2. **Journals:** These are chronological summary lists of all transactions.

3. **Ledgers:** These are reports at varying levels of detail that present the balance in any revenue, expenditure, or other account.
4. **Procedures and controls:** These are the forms and instructions for classifying, recording, and reporting financial transactions in the source documents, journals, and ledgers.

Government accounting focuses on cash flows and improved transparency, control, and accountability to constituencies rather than the profit-and-loss emphasis of private sector accounting. This difference brings several normal practices in government accounting:

1. Governments use fund accounting to permit compliance with legal restrictions on the use of revenue and to facilitate strong financial administration of multiple government operations.
2. Debt is segregated. Bonds to be repaid from general financial resources of the government are reported as obligations of the entire government; bonds to be repaid from specific funds (bonds issued to build a parking garage being repaid through parking garage revenue, for instance) are reported as such.
3. The budget of a government is at the heart of its system of "checks and balances." Demonstrating compliance with the adopted budget is a critical part of the accounting and reporting process. In the private sector, budgets are more on the order of an initial flexible plan, not an adopted appropriation law. Nonprofit organization budgets are somewhere in between.

Governments have historically made little attempt to account for fixed assets in their financial records. They built an infrastructure for the operations of general government, but did not account for its condition in their financial records. That meant that any balance sheet of the government's assets did not accurately portray the true financial situation of the government. It did not reflect depreciation and deferred maintenance of these critical assets. Accordingly, financial reports could portray a misleading sense of the condition of the government: failure to maintain infrastructure eventually adds to the costs of operation, can lead to more borrowing than would be otherwise necessary, can cause previous capital investment to be wasted if not adequately protected, can cause economic development in the community to be impeded because of low-quality government services, and misleads about the total cost of providing services. A GASB standard (GASB 34) now requires larger governments to account for these infrastructure costs in their accounts, and the standard will eventually extend to all governments.[38] The change is driven by the effort to ensure that governments provide information about the full cost of

---

[38]A symposium in *Public Budgeting & Finance* analyzes several major implications of the new reporting model produced by Statement 34: Robert S. Kravchuk and William R. Voorhees, "The New Governmental Financial Reporting Model under GASB Statement No. 34: An Emphasis on Accountability"; Terry K. Patton and David R. Bean, "The Why and How of the New Capital Asset Reporting Requirement"; Earl R. Wilson and Susan C. Kattelus, "The Implications of GASB's New Reporting Model for Municipal Bond Analysts and Managers"; John H. Engstrom and Donald E. Tidrick, "Audit Issues Related to GASB Statement No. 34"; and James L. Chan, "The Implications of GASB Statement No. 34 for Public Budgeting," *Public Budgeting & Finance* 21 (Fall 2001).

providing government services, something that the omission of a reflection of cost from the existing infrastructure has prevented in the past. How critical this omission might be is open to dispute: there is little reason to know the "going concern" value of a government because nobody is going to buy or sell it. The value of most physical assets owned by governments is particularly speculative because they are so specialized for governmental service that they lack a meaningful market value, and nobody should make much of those values in considering annual reports.

Funds

In private sector accounting, a single set of accounts reports all material transactions and details of financial condition. Government accounting, however, segregates funds or accounts because there are legal restrictions on the use of government revenues and on the purposes of government expenditure. Mixing money prevents a clear demonstration of compliance with restrictions. Therefore, distinct funds ("cookie jar accounts") provide the necessary controls. They have much in common with the "envelope system" presented by personal finance guru Dave Ramsey as a tool for managing household finances.

Governments prepare financial reports in a number of separate funds or accounting entities that are expected to be self-balancing (equal credits and debits across accounts). Generally accepted accounting principles (GAAP) define funds to be interrelated accounts that record assets (revenues) and liabilities (expenditures/obligations) related to a specific purpose. Municipal accounting divides funds into three basic types: governmental funds, proprietary funds, and fiduciary funds, each with subcategories.

1. Governmental Funds
   a. General fund: general revenues to the government, including taxes, fines, licenses, and fees. Most taxes and expenditures are in this fund. There is only one general fund.
   b. Special revenue funds: account for operations of government that are supported by dedicated revenue sources—dedicated taxes, fees, or intergovernmental assistance. Transportation trust funds are one example.
   c. Debt service funds: account for payment of interest and repayment of principal due on long-term debt.
   d. Capital projects funds: include resources used for construction and acquisition of capital facilities or major capital equipment purchases. The fund is dissolved when the project is completed.
   e. Permanent funds: account for resources held in trust, where earnings, but not principal, may be used for public purposes.
2. Proprietary Funds
   a. Enterprise fund: includes the financial records of self-supporting operations, like water or sewer utilities. Accounts for business-type activities of the entity, which are operated for the general benefit of the public, but are expected to support themselves from their own revenue.
   b. Internal service fund: includes the financing of goods or services provided by one agency or department to other agencies or departments of the

government on a cost-reimbursement basis, like the operations of a motor vehicle maintenance department.

3. Fiduciary Funds: account for assets held by a government as a trustee for others. Fiduciary funds include (1) pension funds that are used to pay public employees' retirement benefits and (2) trust funds that are used to pay for management of resources. Their use is usually tightly controlled.

In a mature fiscal system, an independent auditor prepares an evaluation of government financial operations at the end of the fiscal year. If the auditor renders a so-called clean opinion, then the way that the government prepared its financial report is considered to have been fair and accurate. Among other things, the auditor's report requires that the agency's statements be prepared according to GAAP. Clean budget processes also bring all government operations together, regardless of the fund structure, in order to preserve the comprehensiveness of public financial decisions.

Accounting Basis: Cash or Accrual

The accounting basis—the method of matching revenues and expenditures over time—may be cash (revenue posted when cash is received, expenditure posted when cash payment is completed), full accrual (revenue posted when earned, expenses posted when good or service is used), or modified accrual (revenues posted in period in which they are measurable and available, expenditure posted when liability is incurred). The traditional standard, cash accounting, records money inflows when received and spending when money is disbursed, generally following the flows of the government checkbook. Those flows can substantially lag changes in the true condition of the government, and capital assets (buildings, highways, etc.) require a cash payment when they are acquired, but no purchase payments over their many years of useful life. GAAP requires a modified accrual basis for governmental accounting, in which inflows are called revenues, not the receipts of cash accounting, and outflows are called expenditures, rather than the disbursements of cash accounting. The revenue measure requires an estimate of taxes owed, but not yet paid; the expenditure measure requires inclusion of purchases for which payment has not yet been made. Expenditure is recorded when liability is recognized, generally meaning when the good or service is delivered to the purchaser and normally well before any check is written to pay for the purchase. GAAP also requires that individual government operations expected to be self-supporting use full accrual accounting, the method of the private sector. In full accrual, outflows, called expenses, are recorded in the period in which benefit is received from the resource.[39]

---

[39]Accrual accounting applies in the preparation of financial reports. Accrual concepts can also be applied in the budget process. Accrual budgeting is used in some countries, including Australia, New Zealand, the Netherlands, Switzerland, and the United Kingdom, and partly used in many more. M. Peter van der Hoek, "From Cash to Accrual Budgeting and Accounting in the Public Sector: The Dutch Experience," *Public Budgeting & Finance* 24 (Spring 2005): 32–45; and Jon R. Blondal, "Issues in Accrual Budgeting," *OECD Journal on Budgeting* 4, no. 1 (2004): 103–19.

The accrual basis provides more information for decision makers and for managers, particularly in regard to the distribution of cost over time, and is not susceptible to end-of-year cash manipulations. It has the capacity to place costs properly in the relevant period. Only a handful of national governments around the world prepare financial statements on an accrual basis, although that is the evolving pattern for American state and local governments, and even fewer provide for depreciation of their capital assets in their accounts.[40] The federal government does prepare the *Annual Financial Report of the United States Government* and that is done on an accrual basis, but it is not clear that the report matters much to either the public or government decision makers. The cash basis controls flows of cash and does not distribute cost accurately to periods, but it is less complex than the accrual system and is less subject to fundamental manipulation for impact on financial statements. As *The Economist* summarizes, cash "is far harder to disguise or invent."[41] Either system can be functional, depending on the needs of the entity.[42]

Comprehensive Annual Financial Report (CAFR) and Monitoring Financial Performance

The public, government officials, those lending money to governments, and others doing business with government all want to understand the financial well-being of the government. Will it be able to sustain its operations, to provide services, and to pay its bills in the future? Future obligations will include service on outstanding debt (interest and repayment of amounts borrowed), pension and other benefits promised workers when they retire, costs associated with infrastructure for provision of public services, and so on; it is important that these financial requirements do not take up so much of revenue available in the future that provision of services to that population is endangered. A single year snapshot of finances—the flow of expenditures and revenues within the year—cannot provide the whole story. Also, neither perform out-year analysis in a medium-term financial forecast. Although there is no single indicator that can answer those questions of fiscal health and sustainability definitely, some elements of the government's current financial condition do offer some guidance. However, the annual report tells where the government has been

---

[40]Because many capital assets owned by government have little value in anything but governmental use, except as scrap, the value of capital assets in government balance sheets is dodgy, and there is little likelihood that anyone would want to buy them. That means the value number is entirely arbitrary and hypothetical and not subject to any accuracy test. This is not a big deal because people are concerned with the services that they receive from the government and what they have to pay for those services and are little concerned with the overall value of the government. Nobody specifically owns the government and nobody is going to buy the government.

[41]"Badly in Need of Repair," *The Economist* 362 (May 4, 2002): 67.

[42]A number of countries that moved to accrual accounting have recently become concerned by some lack of transparency thus created, and others have delayed a move for similar reasons. Andy Wynne, "Accrual Accounting for the Public Sector—A Fad That Has Had Its Day?" *International Journal on Governmental Financial Management* 8 (2008): 117–32. What makes sense for private businesses may not be transferrable to governments.

recently; that is what accountants do well. It does not tell where the government is likely to be headed in the medium or long term.

The CAFR is a general-purpose report prepared annually according to the standards promulgated by the GASB to meet the information needs of public officials, citizens, auditors, bond rating agencies, and investors. It is expected to be a publicly available document that encompasses all funds and accounts controlled by the government entity. The CAFR should provide a comprehensive, reliable, and internally consistent source of information about the finances and structure of the government, with financial data presented according to generally accepted accounting principles, so that an external observer can understand the situation of that government without having to do additional research on definitions or context. It is comprehensive in depth and breadth, reported in sufficient detail to provide full disclosure. States and many larger cities, counties, school districts, and special districts post their CAFRs on their websites, and you can easily trace the sections noted below in that document. The report includes three sections:

1. An introductory section that seeks to explain the structure of the government, the nature and scope of its activities, and the specific details of its legal environment.

2. A financial section that provides a comprehensive overview of the government's operations and includes an independent auditor's report on the finances. The section will provide a balance sheet for the end of the period and statements of revenues, expenditures, and changes in fund balances over the period. The balance sheet will provide the value of assets owned by the government (the value of cash, equipment, buildings, etc.) and of liabilities (the value of its obligations to be paid). It pays attention to liabilities that lurk in the future, such as benefits eventually to be paid to pensioners. The difference in these values equals net assets, which measures the government's financial position at a point in time. Just as the revenues and expenditures making for the budget position of deficit or surplus are based on some critical assumptions about conditions in the upcoming budget year, portions of both assets and liabilities are based on assumptions about future conditions. But the balance sheet takes a longer view. Some assets can be converted to cash to pay bills quickly (they are liquid) and others cannot.[43]

3. A statistical section that provides details on government operations and its major financial trends. The section will provide details on the tax base (particularly property tax for local governments), the condition of the ambient economy, outstanding debt, and often information about government operations.

---

[43]One important rule for anyone trying to compare CAFRs across entities: read the footnotes. Not all lines in the CAFR have exactly the same computation from one report to another, and to understand their meaning, the footnotes must be read. Beware of values of real assets owned by the entity: lots of property owned by a government has limited alternative uses and, in actual market terms, limited value, although quite critical for operation of the government. Similarly, some liabilities—such as the obligations to pay pensions and other post-employment benefits to workers—are estimated as well, and alternative assumptions will yield differing liability estimates. The balance sheet value is more hypothetical than might be expected by the casual observer.

This report gives a complete overview of finances, prepared according to GAAP, and is critically interesting to those involved in public capital markets. In other words, people who might be loaning money to the government really want to know what the financial condition of the government is, and the CAFR gives them the basic information they want to find out. The budget reflects the plans of the government and recent history of fiscal operations, whereas the CAFR gives a picture of government finances at a point in time past and considers some estimated future obligations that may not be reflected in the government's budget. Anyone using a CAFR has to read the footnotes because governments have options with regard to how they treat some transactions, and it is not possible to understand the full financial situation without knowing exactly what options have been taken.

There have been efforts to use balance sheet and related data about state and local governments to provide fiscal condition indexes that give a concise overall assessment of the condition of that government, both at present and as it promises in the future. If it were possible to capture the salient elements into a simple index, that would be useful for formation of government policy, for citizen assessment of the quality of government operations, and for those who might be inclined to loan money to that government, among other uses. However, there is no single indicator, and analysts employ different data elements in producing their condition indicators. Table 2–4 provides one set of factors recently used in evaluating the fiscal conditions

Table 2–4
Financial Condition Analysis: Measures for Estimating Four Types of Solvency

Cash Solvency Ability to pay bills on time, tests liquidity and effectiveness of cash management system.

Measured by	Cash Ratio: (cash + cash equivalents + investments) / current liabilities
	Quick Ratio: (cash + cash equivalents + investments + receivables) / current liabilities
	Current Ratio: current assets / current liabilities

Budget Solvency Ability to meet current year spending obligations without deficit

Measured by	Operating Ratio: total revenue / total expenses
	Surplus (Deficit) per capita: change in net assets / population

Long-Run Solvency Ability of the government to pay all its costs, including those that may occur into the future

Measured by	Net asset ratio: restricted and unrestricted net assets / total assets
	Long-term liability ratio: long-term (noncurrent) liabilities / total assets
	Long-term liability per capita: long-term (noncurrent) liabilities / population

Service Level Solvency Ability to provide and pay for level and quality of services required to meet community's general health and welfare needs

Measured by	Tax per capita: total taxes / population
	Revenue per capita: total revenues / population
	Expenses per capita: total expenses / population

Note: Data for ratios would be taken from annual financial reports of each entity.

Source: Xiaohu Wang, Lynda Dennis, and Yuan Sen (Jeff) Tu, "Measuring Financial Condition: A Study of U.S. States," *Public Budgeting and Finance,* 27 (Summer 2007): 1–21.

of the fifty states, but there are other approaches in use.[44] Indeed, the Canadian province of Nova Scotia prepares a Fiscal Condition Index for each of municipalities so that municipal councils and the public can have a better idea of financial operations and challenges.[45] The dimensions of that index include revenue, budget, and debt and capital. Although the indicators are thorough, the province warns: "The FCI is not a substitute for a comprehensive examination of a municipality's financial performance."[46] Looking backward is not necessarily a good way to see where one is headed in the future.

Budgets and Political Strategies

Most of this text aims to provide technical skills required for work in and around public finance and budgeting. Much of it strives to organize the best evidence to help guide decisions toward the best interests of the community. However, spending and taxing decisions emerge from an intensely political process. They do not spin out of an analytic "black box" programmed by purveyors of information technology and program analysis. Presidents, governors, mayors, and other public executives cannot ignore political forces when they develop their fiscal proposals, and legislators certainly do not ignore these forces as they pass budget laws.[47] Understanding the budget process is vital for shaping public policy, and so is the analysis necessary to innovate and implement programs most likely to be in the public interest. But budget proposals do need to be delivered and defended in a political environment: truth and beauty alone will not save the day. There will be negotiations, and some participants in the process will be less than straightforward in their participation. (Yes, they might lie.) Hence, an understanding of some strategic behavior is important for practitioners of the budget process.

---

[44]For another similar approach: Judith A. Kamnikar, Edward G. Kamnikar, and Keren H. Deal, "Assessing a State's Financial Condition," *Journal of Government Financial Management* (Fall 206): 30–36.

[45]http://novascotia.ca/dma/finance/indicator/fci.asp.

[46]In a recent study, Benjamin Y. Clark, using data from Ohio cities, questions whether a financial condition index is capable of providing a meaningful assessment of city fiscal condition. ("Evaluating the Validity and Reliability of the Financial Condition Index for Local Government," *Public Budgeting & Finance,* 35 (Summer 2015): 66–88.) Public finance professionals working for a government have a pretty good idea of the fiscal condition of that government and have little need for an index to tell them how things are going. The indexes are mostly for the use of those outside that particular government.

[47]Natural disasters are about as nonpolitical as can be—hurricanes and tornados, for example, are indifferent to the political affiliation of their victims. However, research shows that rates of disaster declarations are higher in states of greater electoral importance, the rate of disaster declaration is higher in election years than in nonelection years, and states with congressional representation on the committees with oversight over the Federal Emergency Management Agency receive larger relief payments than states lacking that voice. Even with natural disasters, spending is driven by politics. Molly D. Castelazo and Thomas A. Garrett, "In the Rubble of Disaster, Politicians Find Economic Incentives," *The Regional Economist* (July 2003): 10–11. This article summarizes several studies of disaster declarations and payments.

The Incrementalist Insight

The incrementalist concept holds that budgeting is mainly a process of political strategy. It downplays the service-delivery attitude of models from public finance economics and the attempts at rationality from policy analysis. As outlined by Aaron Wildavsky and Naomi Caiden,

> The largest determining factor of this year's budget is last year's. Most of each budget is the product of previous decisions. The budget may be conceived of as an iceberg; by far the largest part lies below the surface, outside the control of anyone. Many items are standard, simply reenacted each year unless there is a special reason to challenge them. Long-range commitments have been made, and this year's share is scooped out of the total and included as part of the annual budget. . . . At any one time, after past commitments are paid for, a rather small percentage—seldom larger than 30 percent, often smaller than 5—is within the realm of anybody's (including congressional and Budget Bureau) discretion as a practical matter.
>
> The beginning of wisdom about an agency budget is that it is almost never actively reviewed as a whole every year, in the sense of reconsidering the value of all existing programs as compared to all possible alternatives. Instead, it is based on last year's budget with special attention to a narrow range of increases or decreases, i.e., changes in service response plans. General agreement on past budgetary decisions combined with years of accumulated experience and specialization allow those who make the budget to be concerned with relatively small increments to an existing base. Their attention is focused on a small number of items over which the budgetary battle is fought. Political reality, budget officials say, restricts attention to items they can do something about—a few new programs and possible cuts in old ones.[48]

Incremental budgeting is handy for lazy government, lazy administrators, and lazy lawmakers. Each agency receives roughly the same amount as it did the year before with only marginal changes. The temptation to behave incrementally is huge. Leaving the base largely alone minimizes conflict, and nobody has to make difficult choices. Resources do not get moved to deal with problems or opportunities that have developed. Absence of substantial change requires less admission of past errors and gives the impression of prudence. It preserves flexibility for the future. Administrators are comfortable but the citizenry has every reason to believe that it has been short-changed as the important choices do not get made.

Dramatic changes in federal expenditure programs, beginning with the end of the Cold War, the Republican Contract with America in the mid-1990s, the beginning of wars in Iraq and Afghanistan, the Katrina hurricane disaster, the Great Recession of 2007–2009; dramatic changes in leadership of some state governments; and other political and economic changes in the recent past have raised some questions about whether government budget processes are as simple as Wildavsky and Caiden claim. Recent research by Anderson and Harbridge questions the basic argument of incrementalism: "This year's spending may very well be a function of last year's

---

[48]Aaron Wildavsky and Naomi Caiden, *The New Politics of the Budgetary Process,* 3rd ed. (New York: Longman, 1997), 45.

spending, but [our] analysis shows that the changes are surprisingly large ... [There] is little stability in year-to-year budgeting, especially at the subaccount and appropriations bill levels."[49] More than half of budgetary changes are more than 10 percent, and more than one-fifth are greater than 50 percent. There have been dramatic fiscal changes within extremely short time periods.

The fact remains that some policies—and resulting expenditure and revenue implications—do remain in place over the years; that most spending agencies at all levels of government do begin their new budget development by considering their approved budgets and the changes that should be made to them to adjust to new operating conditions; that the facilities of the agency are established in certain locations and are not going to be moved quickly; that budget comparisons in central budget offices, in legislative committees, and in the media are made between the proposed and prior-year budgets; and that the *most rational* place to get insights about the near future is from the immediate past. Information from looking at incremental change—positive or negative, big or little—ought not to be ignored simply because there have been major shifts in the direction of government spending, especially federal. Looking at change is a tool, not a religion, after all. Indeed, some states and many local governments build budgets from percentage increments to the historical budget base (the prior-year budget) in accord with some notion of fair shares to each agency—the ultimate in operational laziness. In many administrative systems, the base is assumed when the next budget cycle begins.[50] Of course, some local governments are so poorly staffed that they really don't know how to do anything better than build the budget by making additions to the existing line items. They really have no capacity to plan a response to anticipated conditions, and adding some percent to recent spending is all they are up to.

Roles, Visions, and Incentives

Service-delivery choices in the budget process involve several roles, each with different approaches and biases. Participants in the budget process recognize and expect those approaches and are aware of the errors, incentives, and organizational blind spots inherent in each. The major attitude orientations are those of operating agencies, the office of the chief executive, and the legislature. All participants in the budget process seek to provide service to the public (except for the lazy, time-servers noted in the previous section). Each, however, works from different perspectives, resulting in different incentives and different practical definitions of that objective. A full understanding of the budget process obviously requires recognition of those roles.

---

[49]Sarah Anderson and Laurel Harbridge, "Incrementalism in Appropriations: Small Aggregation, Big Changes," *Public Administration Review* (May/June 2010), 471.

[50]What is certainly incremental is tax law. For most major taxes, a tax code is adopted, and it remains in effect until explicitly changed or repealed. Tax changes are made by amending the existing code rather than by adopting a whole new tax. That is completely incremental.

1. **Operating agencies.** Operating agencies (e.g., the Fish and Wildlife Service, the Department of Parks and Recreation, or Immigration and Customs Enforcement) spend money for the delivery of government services. These agencies focus on the clientele they serve. The agency will not be concerned with services provided by other agencies or be interested in relative priorities among other agency services. The agency probably is not much concerned with comparisons of service cost with service value. The agency recognizes the value of services it provides to its clients and ordinarily tries to increase those services regardless of overall budget conditions of the government. There will be a virtually limitless expanse of service opportunities, many of which go unfunded simply because other uses of public resources are of higher priority to those making fiscal choices. Agencies, however, seldom recognize those competing uses and often complain about their own lack of resources. Large agencies have both operating people who have little direct contact with the budget and budget people who have little direct contact with service delivery. Both groups, however, can be expected to have essentially the same point of view and clientele orientation.

   Operating agencies usually have identifiable proponents in the legislature—particular people who support the agency in hearings and in committee deliberations—but it is seldom appropriate for the agency to make direct proactive contact with those people to go around budget decisions made by the chief executive. In most situations, the operating agency is not responsible for raising the revenue that it spends for delivery of services and accordingly can be excused for regarding those resources as free. Service to clientele is the principal focus.

2. **Chief executive.** The office of the chief executive, whether that of president, governor, mayor, or whatever, has budget specialists acting on its behalf. The offices have different names (federal: Office of Management and Budget; state: state budget agencies; etc.), but their function and role are the same regardless of name. Analysts in that agency conform to the chief executive's priorities, not their own. The analysts pare down requests from operating agencies until total spending is within available revenue. Reductions are typical for items (1) not adequately justified, (2) not closely related to achieving the agency's objective, and (3) inconsistent with the chief executive's priorities. Whereas agencies have a clientele orientation, the chief executive (selected by the entire population) must balance the interests of the total population. Thus, priorities for an individual agency should not be expected to coincide with those of the chief executive because specific client-group priorities seldom match those of the general public. The interests of Corn Belt farmers, for instance, are not the same as those of the general population. And the chief executive is going to be responsible for raising revenue, so she is going to be doing some balancing that simply is not part of the operating agency viewpoint.

3. **Legislature.** The priorities of elected representatives can be expected to follow interests of their constituents. Representatives are concerned with

programs and projects serving the people who elect them. Representatives focus on a specific subset of the population, as is the case for operating agencies. Representatives, however, are oriented to a region rather than a specific client group. A legislator with a particular constituent interest can be particularly helpful when he or she is the chair of an important committee in the legislature.

Forsythe offers another guide for chief executives in understanding the budgetary vision of legislators: "assume that legislators will apply a simple calculus in reviewing your budget proposals: they will want to take credit for spending increases and tax cuts, and they will want to avoid blame for budget cuts and tax increases."[51] The rule may not work all the time in every legislature—sometimes legislators take an ideological stand that all government is bad and happily cut spending—but otherwise it is a reasonable beginning assumption. It is particularly difficult to find legislators in favor of tax increases, especially of broad-based taxes that are not entwined in a complex package. Fiscal responsibility in practice seldom resonates with the general public.

Strategies

Budget proposals must be championed within operating agencies to be included in the agency request, within the administration for inclusion in the executive budget, and within the legislature to receive appropriation. A number of strategies, defined by Wildavsky and Caiden as "links between intentions and perceptions of budget officials and the political system that both imposes restraints and creates opportunities for them,"[52] are regularly used in these processes at every level of government and, indeed, in many different countries. They may also be considered devices for marketing and communicating the agency position.

Two ubiquitous strategies are always in use for the support of budget proposals. The first is cultivation of an active *clientele* for help in dealing with both the legislature and the chief executive. The clientele may be those directly served (as with farmers in a particular program provided by the Department of Agriculture) or those selling services to the particular agency (such as highway contractors doing business with a state department of highways). The best idea is to get the client groups to fight for the agency without having the agency instigate the action when the chief executive proposes the reduction; such instigation would look like insubordination, and the agency might ultimately suffer for it. Agencies unable to develop and mobilize such clientele find defending budget proposals difficult. The media can also deliver the support indirectly, but only with some preparations; agencies normally

---

[51]Forsythe, *Memos,* 48.
[52]Wildavsky and Caiden, *New Politics,* 57.

get coverage because they have bungled something.[53] A strategy can help: "Try to stay in the news with interesting stories that do not put the agency in a bad light and that help you maintain good relations with reporters. Then, when you come close to budget time, you can give them press stories that show how well the agency has done with limited resources, and how well its pilot programs are working. Unstated is the premise that with a little more money you could do wonderful things and that if you are cut the public will lose valuable services."[54] The National Aeronautics and Space Administration (NASA) is a master at using the media to deliver its story through the budget process and serves as a model for any agency interested in learning how the strategy is played. It even has its own cable television channel, a delivery system that bypasses the media. With the exception of some reporters for the national papers of record—*New York Times, Washington Post,* and *Wall Street Journal,* in particular—journalists are mostly uninformed about government finances and are susceptible to manipulation by interest groups and agencies. Websites, including those offering blogs, are often more specialized, and their writers may have great expertise, but they often have considerable political bias and are subject to no editorial supervision, so they can be both valuable and dangerous.

A second ubiquitous strategy that an agency may use is developing *confidence* in the agency among legislators and other government officials. To avoid being surprised in legislative hearings or by requests for information, agency administrators must show results in the reports they make and must tailor their message's complexity to their audience. All budget materials must clearly describe programs and intentions. Strategically, budget presenters develop a small group of "talking points" that concisely portray their program. If results are not directly available, agencies may report internal process activities, such as files managed or surveys taken. Confidence is critical because, in the budget process, many elements of program defense must derive from the judgments of the administrators, not hard evidence. If confidence has been developed, those judgments will be trusted; if not, those judgments will be suspect.

Contingent strategies depend on whether the discussion concerns (1) a reduction in agency programs below the present level of expenditures (the budget base), (2) an increase in the scope of agency programs, or (3) an expansion of agency programs to

---

[53]If a member of the media is itself involved as the agency, it becomes more interesting for mobilizing clientele. For example, in developing the fiscal 2006 appropriation bill for health, education, and labor programs, the House subcommittee proposed a reduction of about one-quarter of the funds for the Corporation for Public Broadcasting and an end to all funding within two years. Public radio and television stations mobilized their listeners to contact their congressional representatives in a blitz of announcements throughout the nation. The full House voted by a wide margin to restore the funds even as other attractive programs in that bill—such as community health care for the uninsured, literacy training for prisoners, maternity group-home funding, and so on—were being eliminated. The fifty-seven programs being terminated did not have the capacity to mobilize clientele as public broadcasting did regardless of their probable value to society. Shailagh Murray and Paul Farhi, "House Vote Spares Public Broadcasting Funds," *Washington Post,* June 24, 2005, A6. A similar saga occurred in 2011 (Elizabeth Jensen, "Public Broadcasting Faces New Threat in Federal Budget," *New York Times,* February 27, 2011), and listeners were mobilized yet again.

[54]Irene S. Rubin, "Strategies for the New Budgeting," in *Handbook of Public Administration,* 2nd ed., ed. James Perry (San Francisco: Jossey Bass, 1996), 286.

new areas. Some strategies seem strange or even preposterous; they are used, however, and should be recognized because the budget choices involved are vital parts of government action.[55] It cannot be emphasized enough, however, that strategy and clever rhetoric alone are not sufficient; they do not matter at all if the basics of the budget—its logic, justifications, mathematics, and internal consistency—are faulty.

Several strategies are applied as a program administrator responds to proposals for *reduction in base* (if a program may be terminated or reduced from its existing level of operation). These include the following:

a. **Propose a study.** Agency administrators argue that rash actions (such as cutting their programs) should not be taken until all consequences have been completely considered. A study would delay action, possibly long enough for those proposing cuts to lose interest and certainly long enough for the program administrator to develop support for the program.

b. **Cut the popular programs.** The administrator responds by proposing to cut or eliminate programs with strong public support. By proposing that the school band or athletic programs be eliminated, for instance, the administrator hopes to mobilize sufficient outcry to ensure no budget cuts.

c. **Dire consequences.** The administrator outlines the tragic events—shattered lives of those served, supplier businesses closed, and so on—that would accompany the reductions. For instance, a zoo in Boston threatened to euthanize its animals if it didn't get more state funding.[56]

d. **All or nothing.** Any reduction would make the program impossible, so it might as well be eliminated.

e. **You pick.** The administrator requests that those proposing the cut should identify the targets, thereby clearly tracking the political blame for the cut and hopefully scaring away the reduction.

f. **We are the experts.** The agency argues that it has expertise that the budget cutter lacks. The reduction is shortsighted, based on ignorance, and thus should not occur.

g. **The Washington Monument.** A time-honored strategy of program administrators is to respond with a dramatic gesture. In other words, the federal National Park Service says that it will close the Washington Monument, a popular tourist attraction, if the relevant appropriation bill is not passed by Congress (as it did for two days every week in 1969 to deal with a budget battle), or the local police department proclaims that it will no longer respond to vehicle break-ins because its fuel budget is being exhausted. Another example: when a 2015 request for additional subsidy from participating local governments by the Washington Metropolitan Area Transit Authority was denied, the Authority responded by a threat to cut all bus service to all

---

[55]Important sources on strategy are Aaron Wildavsky, *The Politics of the Budgetary Process*, 4th ed. (Boston: Little Brown, 1984), chap. 3; Robert N. Anthony and David W. Young, *Management Control in Nonprofit Organizations*, 4th ed. (Homewood, Ill.: Irwin, 1988), 459–536; and Jerry McCaffery, *Budgetmaster* (privately printed).

[56]"Zoo May Close, Euthanize Animals," WCVB Boston, July 11, 2009. http://www.thebostonchannel. com/r/20021259/detail.html.

Washington area airports, one of the most heavily used and most popular services it provides.[57]

h. **Spread the bucks.** If the suppliers to a program can be distributed across enough legislative districts, the representatives of those districts can become valuable guardians of the program, should any executive attempt to reduce or eliminate the program. The most striking example of an application of this strategy is the defense of the V-22 Osprey, a tiltrotor aircraft capable of vertical takeoff and landing, as well as short takeoff and landing. The aircraft struggled with difficult development, an embarrassing tendency to crash, failure to meet performance specifications, cost overruns, and a lurking suspicion that it added no actual capability that the Defense Department wanted very much. Defense secretaries tried to kill the program—but it lived on. The prime contractor for the project had made sure that subcontractors for the program were salted around key congressional districts so that people in legislative power would be trusted to make sure that the next piece of acquisition cost would be included in the adopted appropriation.

Other strategies apply when the agency seeks to *augment operations* of its existing program:

a. **Round up.** Rounding program estimates—workload, prices, costs, and the like—upward to the next highest hundred, thousand, or million creates substantial slack when consistently done.

b. **"If it don't run, chrome it."** The budget presentation sparkles with data, charts, graphs, glittering PowerPoint, and other state-of-the-art management trappings. The presentation may not relate directly to the decision at hand, and the data may not be particularly accurate, but the quality of the show aims to overpower weak substance.

c. **Sprinkling.** Budget items are slightly increased, either in hard-to-detect general categories or across the board, after the basic request has been prepared. The layer of excess is spread so thinly that it cannot be clearly identified as padding.

d. **Numbers game.** Agency administrators may discuss physical units—for example, facilities operated, grants initiated, or acres maintained—rather than the funds requested and spent to divert attention from substantially increased spending for each unit.

e. **Workload and backlog.** Administrators often base their request on greater client demands or a backlog of unfilled requests. The argument is reasonable if the workload measure is germane to the agency's function, if the agency is doing something that needs to be done, and if the backlogs are not caused by poor management of existing resources.

---

[57] This strategy appears not to be just American. Mikhail Piotrovsky, the director general of the Hermitage Museum in St. Petersburg, Russia, announced that security police would stop guarding the art treasures of the museum as of November 1, 2015, because of layoffs in the Russian Ministry of the Interior (*Tass*, August 18, 2015).

f. **The accounting trap.** Either side in the budget process may argue that a proposed expenditure must be made (or is forbidden) because the accounting system controls such transactions. However, accounting systems exist to help management implement policy and to provide information for policy decisions. Policy choices should not be made difficult by the accounting system.

g. **Play the inevitable.** Constrain proposed spending in a line in the budget that is so critical that it will be augmented if money runs out during the year, while increasing spending elsewhere. For example, a police department may not increase its request for motor fuel, a major purchase category in most police budgets, even as prices are expected to increase, because it knows that the legislative body will come up with the needed money later in the year if money for fuel runs low. The department can use the slack created by not requesting an increase for motor fuel to expand other parts of the budget.

h. **Hire a consultant.** Some departments try to build a case for increased budgets by enlisting the support of an expert review of the operations of the department. For example, in 2015, the Boston Public Library hired a consultant to review management of its world-class art collection to give them a frank assessment of what needed to be done. The expert found benign neglect, along with a considerable need for increased resources.[58] What a surprise! Outside experts who specialize in the programs being examined can reliably be expected to conclude a need for more money in their frank assessments.

Proposals for a new program entail special challenges because the new program lacks any inertia from prior budget cycles. Some budget processes even place new programs in a separate decision structure that considers new programs only after available revenues have covered all requests from existing activities. Other processes cause trouble for proposed programs simply because clients and constituents who could provide political support have not yet developed. Some strategies are characteristic of the *new proposal*:

a. **Old stuff.** Administrators may disguise new programs as simple extensions or growth of existing operations. When the new operation has developed directors, clients, and political allies, it can be spun off into an independent life, having been nurtured through early development by existing agency operations.

b. **Foot-in-the-door financing.** A project starts with a small amount of funding, possibly under the guise of a pilot or demonstration program or as a feasibility study. Modest amounts build each year until the program is almost operational and has developed a constituency. By the time full costs are identified, it may be more economical to spend more money to finish the task rather than irretrievably abandoning the costs sunk into the project. Here is a classic example: In 1991, the Royal Thai Air Force purchased a squadron

---

[58]Meghan E. Irons, "More Resources Needed for Boston Library, Report Says," *Boston Globe*, June 24, 2015.

of F-16 fighters. The military lacked sufficient money to make the purchase, so the planes were purchased without engines. Delivery was scheduled for 1995, which left plenty of time to gather the extra funds. But a new Thai government took office in 1992. Although it wanted to exert control over military spending, its options were to approve more money for the engines or to pay for nonflying (probably undeliverable) airplanes. Rather than getting no return from the $560 million spent on airplanes, training, and a new radar system, the purchase was approved—even though the new government sought to constrain military spending and to devote its scarce resources to domestic use.[59]

c. **It pays for itself.** Supporters of new programs sometimes argue that the program will produce more revenue than it will cost. Examples include arguments made by law enforcement agencies concerning collections of fines and, with growing frequency, by economic development departments concerning induced tax collections from economic activity lured by the project.

d. **Spend to save.** Expenditure on the proposal would cause cost reduction somewhere else in the government. The net budget impact would be nil, or even positive, if spending $1 in agency A would allow spending to be reduced by $1 or more either in that agency or somewhere else in government.

e. **Crisis.** The proposal may be linked to a catastrophe or overwhelming problem—Zika, economic underdevelopment, homelessness, homeland security, and so on—even though the link may be tenuous. But an agency must use caution because skeptics will question why it did not deal with the problem before it reached crisis proportions. A substrategy that might merit a category of its own is "Tie it to Terror." For many years (at least since 1966), the National Park Service has sought an underground visitors center at the Washington Monument. When the proposal emerged again in 2003, its name had changed from "Washington Monument Visitors Center Plan" to "Washington Monument Permanent Security Improvements." One critic observes: "As soon as you say that it's for security, any project—however questionable—is able to move forward because everyone is afraid that one of these great monuments might be destroyed on their watches. But in reality, [the underground proposal] has nothing to do with security."[60] At least so far, it hasn't gotten the visitors center, and the link between the center and security still is being used as justification.

f. **Mislabeling.** The actual nature of a program may be hidden by mixing it with another, more politically attractive program. Examples abound: military installations may have blast-suppression areas that look strangely like golf courses; university dormitories or office buildings may have roofs that have seats convenient for viewing events on the football field; the rigid upper-surface covers for the new sewers may support vehicular traffic. These strategies, however, require an essentially supportive environment; all

---

[59]Cynthia Owens, "And Now They'll Sneak in Orders for Aviation Fuel and Parachutes," *Wall Street Journal,* January 28, 1993, C-1.

[60]Monte Reel, "Washington Monument Dispute Resurfaces," *Washington Post,* August 4, 2003, A01.

key participants in the budget process must be in agreement on the proposal because budget people remember and make allowances in later years. It is a bad idea to try to trick a budget analyst.

g. **What they did makes us do it.** An action taken by another entity may place demands on the agency beyond what could be accommodated by normal management of existing programs. If school libraries were to be closed and teachers continued to assign reference work, local public libraries might argue for new programs to accommodate student requests for assistance. Harsh federal sentencing guidelines for certain classes of drug offenses means that new federal prisons must be built.

h. **Mandates.** Some external entity (a court, a federal agency, the state, etc.) may legally require an agency action that would entail greater expenditure. Rather than rearranging operations to accommodate the new requirement, an agency may use the mandate as an argument for additional funds. The agency may in fact have requested that the external entity issue the mandate as a budget strategy. The approach can be compelling, but analysts need to determine the grounds for and authority of the mandate and the extent to which revised operations can accommodate the mandate before simply accepting the argument for an increased budget. The approach also has applications for base expansion and, if the time frame is sufficient, for defense against cuts.

i. **Matching the competition.** Agencies often compare their programs with those operated by others and use the comparison as a basis for adding new programs. (Seldom does the comparison lead to a proposal that some programs be eliminated because similar agencies do not have them.) The argument is also used to expand existing programs.

j. **It's so small.** Program proponents may argue that a request is not large enough to require full review, that its trivial budgetary consequences do not make the review a reasonable use of time. Those who understand foot-in-the-door financing are naturally wary of such arguments and generally respond that smallness makes activities natural candidates for absorption by the agency without extra funds. Everett Dirksen, a senator from Illinois of many years ago, holds everlasting fame for saying: "A million here, a million there, pretty soon you're talking about real money." Of course, inflation has changed the idea to billions, not millions—and it starts with small stuff.

k. **It's the local economy.** Public projects are often supported on the basis that they will bring local economic development and prosperity. For instance, the development of a local arts program may be supported because of the incomes it will generate and the business activity that spending from those incomes will create. But this impact is not the result of the arts program. It is the result of spending. Building a new city dump would have the same outcome in terms of incomes and business activity. Legitimate arguments for an arts program need to hinge on the services of the arts program, not impacts that are generic to any spending (particularly spending financed by those from outside the locality).

Conclusion

The budget process is where choices about the allocation of public resources get made. The flow of budget decisions from plan to expenditure is accomplished in a four-phase cycle involving executive preparation, legislative consideration, execution, and audit. Although budgets are constructed and approved in a political environment, it is not clear that appropriations are the simple product of adding a small increment to the prior-year appropriation. There is at least some room for attempts at rational choice in budget structures. Later chapters will prepare you to do the tasks required in the budget process and to understand how the process is carried out in practice.

QUESTIONS AND EXERCISES

1. The relative size of government has been a continuing public policy concern. Size and growth questions have been important at the state and local levels, as demonstrated by several state referenda to limit federal, state, or local expenditures. Some evidence for those discussions can be drawn from data on trends of spending activity, using information from the Department of Commerce's National Income and Product Accounts and the Census Bureau's Government and the Bureau of Economic Analysis website (www.bea.gov). From those sources, prepare answers to these questions about the size of government in the United States.

    a. Has the public sector grown relative to the private sector? How does the size of the federal government compare with that of state and local governments? (A benchmark for comparison is the percentage of GDP or personal income accounted for by the appropriate sector.)

    b. Which sectors have grown fastest? Compare growth of the public sector in your state with that of its neighbors and of the nation. Why might a comparison based on expenditure growth differ from one based on employment?

    c. Calculate national defense spending as a percentage of total federal government outlays and as a percentage of GDP. Can you identify the impact of the end of the Cold War and the beginning of the wars in Afghanistan and Iraq on these data?

    d. Which functions account for the greatest share of federal, state, and local government expenditures? Does the pattern differ much among states?

    e. What is the relative significance of local government expenditure compared to state government expenditure in your state? (Make the comparison first counting state aid to local government as state expenditure. Then omit that portion from state expenditure.) How does your state compare with its neighbors and the nation?

The following data are from a recent federal budget:

2. **Federal government discretionary outlays ($ billions)**

	2000	2014
Defense outlays	294,363	603,457
Nondefense outlays	1,494,587	2,902,632
Composite outlay deflators (2009 = 1.00)		
Defense	0.7235	1.0510
Nondefense	0.8134	1.0893

a. Compute the percentage change for federal defense and nondefense outlays in current-year dollars from 2000 to 2014. Divide that change into its real and price components.
b. For nondefense outlays, convert the deflator base to 2000 = 1.0000, and recalculate the absolute change in these real dollars and compare that with the absolute change with 2009 = 1.000. Why might budget strategists try to use one or the other of these two numbers to argue for more or less spending? Is either of the two base years more correct? Explain. Compute and compare the real percentage increases using the two different base years.

3. Identify the strategy represented in each of the following arguments taken from budget discussions:

a. A bill to increase the number of women eligible for Medicaid-funded prenatal assistance in this state would not only save lives, but also cut state costs for care of low-birth-weight babies and children with disabilities. Studies have shown that every dollar spent on prenatal care reduces long-term health-care expenditures by $3.38.
b. The change in the Board of Health sanitation position from full-time to part-time will demolish the inspection program. Rather than accepting the weakened program, we would prefer that the program be terminated.
c. Faculty salaries at Enormous State University rank seventeenth among eighteen universities with which it competes. Substantial improvements in pay must come in this budget year if major defections are to be prevented.
d. In March, the second of two school-funding referenda failed (by a 2–1 margin) in the Riverside-Brookfield (Illinois) School District. The school board responded by proposing the elimination of the girls' badminton, swimming, and cross-country teams; the boys' soccer, tennis, and wrestling teams; seven additional coaching programs; the cheerleading program; and the Pup-ettes (a pompom squad). A phase-out of the German language program at the school had been started before the failure of the referendum.
e. The Unipacker II will return its full purchase cost in lower labor and maintenance expense within two years of initial operation.
f. An editorial in the *Philadelphia Inquirer* (September 24, 2008) argues for a regional sales tax to support funding for the arts on these grounds: "Making

sure attractions thrive is about more than satisfying the need for creative outlet. It's about dollars and good economic sense: The groups surveyed for the
study provide 19,000 jobs, generate $657 million in yearly revenue, and raise
$526 million in contributions."

g. The AIDS education program I have proposed for the biennial budget carries
a price tag of only $200,000. This cost represents an absolutely trivial percent-
age of the $10 billion the state spends each year and will have no impact on
the state fiscal crisis. Furthermore, the medical expense to the state associated
with even one AIDS case is more than $100,000, so it is the most misguided,
mean-spirited, and shortsighted of economies to deny this proposal.

h. The governor proposes major reductions (80 percent of the $321 million per
year program) in state general assistance, a program that provides medical
coverage at about $120 per month to its 131,000 recipients (adults with no
children or other dependents). This reduction may cost more than the amount
it saves if only a fraction of the recipients end up in mental institutions or
shelters. For example, keeping one-tenth of the current recipients in the state
psychiatric hospital for ninety days would cost more than $200 million, and
keeping one-tenth of the recipients in a shelter for ninety days would cost
$22 million. The reduction is clearly a false economy.

i. In response to budget reductions driven by a declining tax base, the Detroit
school system announced that parents would have to purchase toilet paper
for the public schools for the upcoming school year.

j. An internal memo leaked to the media said that cuts to the National Weather
Service budget in FY 2005 would have a critical impact on its life-saving
mission. For instance, "warning lead times will shorten and tornado detec-
tion rates will decrease (as will most other NWS performance standards)
leading to the troubling and tragic conclusion that there will be unwarranted loss of life." Its operating budget for FY 2005 had been reduced by
2 percent.

k. Former President George W. Bush left his request for funding to support the
wars in Iraq and Afghanistan out of his budget submission for the total government and then submitted a separate request a few months later.

l. In response to a countywide instruction to constrain spending, the Fairfax
County, Virginia, fire department announced that it would eliminate "First
Team," a program of support to family members of injured firefighters, for an
annual saving of $6,000.

m. The police department of the City of Palm Bay, Florida, announced that, in
response to a reduced budget and higher fuel costs, it would discontinue
responses to burglaries in which the home or car owner had failed to lock his
home or car.

n. In response to a state fiscal crisis, the director of the Michigan Department of
Human Services proposed cutting money for food banks and homeless shelters and for burials for the dead.

o. Economist and former Secretary of Treasury Larry Summers argues in the
Washington Post (October 13, 2015): "if we were able to raise the gas tax by

40 cents and repair our highways and roads, we would create no new net burden on consumers: the benefit in reduced vehicle operating costs would at the very least offset their higher gas bills. In fact, since our cost estimate is conservative, the net effect on consumers would most likely be positive."

If confronted by such arguments and strategies, what questions would you raise?

4. Go to the website of a city or county of your choosing and look for documents relating to that unit's budget and finances. Look for the following:

   a. Find the chief executive's budget message. What is the tone of that message? What are the major priorities?
   b. Find the budget timetable and budget instructions if they are available on the website.
   c. Does the government use an annual or biennial budget process?
   d. Locate the budget presentation, including any agency narrative and the budget data. Does the budget give you an understanding of the mission of each agency and what new proposals might be causing changes in the budget proposal? Look for budget year, progress year, and report year. Are any out-years provided? Does the budget give other information (e.g., agency request versus council recommendation)? Does the presentation for each agency explain what the agency does, does it provide an organization chart for the agency, and does it explain what its primary objectives for the budget year are? What is the distribution of revenue by source and of expenditure by agency and function?
   e. Pick one agency. What is the first question you would ask the administrator of that agency about the budget proposal?

5. Find the comprehensive annual financial report of a state or local government of your choosing at that entity's website. Identify the sections of the report and examine the data provided in each. How might the data you locate there be helpful to the decisions made by a government executive?

6. Compute a financial condition index for two states or cities of your choosing. Use the index structure provided in this chapter as your starting point, but make revisions as you feel necessary. Using the entity's CAFR and other sources you might find useful, compute the index for the most recent year and for a year five years ago so that you will have a time comparison. On the basis of the indices of the two entities, what conclusions would you have about their relative financial condition? Does their financial position seem to be improving or worsening?

7. Determine whether the outlays of your favorite department of the federal government have been increasing, decreasing, or staying the same over the past twenty years. Check the percentage increase in terms of current dollars, constant dollars, and share of total federal outlays.

   Based on your analysis of the budget proposal, what does the most recent presidential budget submission have in mind for the operations of that department in the next five years?

You will find all the data you need to answer these questions in the current federal budget's historical tables. Check at the website of the Office of Management and Budget for the relevant tables.

8. In a period in which motor fuel prices have been increasing at an annual rate of 30 percent, the chief of police submits a budget request to the city council that shows no increase in the budget line for purchases of gasoline, a budget category that constitutes around 15 percent of the department total and is second only to costs associated with personnel in the department budget. Other city departments have increased their fuel budget requests by at least 20 percent and some by even more because, along with higher motor fuel prices, the city has been experiencing considerable population growth. The chief says that the department can hold the line on fuel costs because of smarter management of patrol resources. Should the chief be applauded for his efficient management, or is he using a cynical budget strategy?

9. The data that follow report the damage caused by named hurricanes that caused damages of $500 million or more (nominal or current dollars) in the mainland United States. What is the ranking of the hurricanes in terms of real dollars? (You can find various deflators (the implicit gross domestic product deflator would be one option) at the Bureau of Economic Analysis website (www.bea.gov).) Does that ranking differ from the ranking according to nominal damages? What do deflated values tell you that the nominal values do not? Hurricane categories gauge the intensity of the storm, with 5 being the highest. Do storms of the same category produce roughly the same damage?

Hurricane	Year	Category	Nominal Damages ($ Millions)	Hurricane	Year	Category	Nominal Damages ($ Millions)
Allison	1989	0	500	Elena	1985	3	1,250
Alberto	1994	0	500	Betsy	1965	3	1,421
Frances	1998	0	500	Camille	1969	5	1,421
Ernesto	2006	0	500	Juan	1985	1	1,500
Erin	1998	2	700	Bob	1991	2	1,500
Bonnie	1998	2	720	Alicia	1983	3	2,000
Diane	1955	1	832	Allison	2001	0	5,000
Agnes	1972	1	2,100	Jeanne	2004	3	6,900
Dennis	2005	3	2,230	Hugo	1989	4	7,000
Frederic	1979	3	2,300	Frances	2004	2	8,900
Opal	1995	3	3,000	Rita	2005	3	11,300
Fran	1996	3	3,200	Charley	2004	4	15,000
Isabel	2003	2	3,370	Ivan	2004	4	15,000
Floyd	1999	2	4,500	Wilma	2005	3	20,600
Lili	2002	1	860	Andrews	1992	5	26,500
Gloria	1985	3	900	Katrina	2005	3	81,000
Georges	1998	2	1,155				

CASE FOR DISCUSSION

CASE 2–1

Politics and Budget Strategies in Building the Tenn-Tom Waterway

Consider These Questions

1. What budget strategies do the supporters of the project appear to have employed? Could they have been as effective if the waterway were financed by the states of Mississippi and Alabama instead of being federally financed?

2. Explain how this project might have been part of a logrolling or vote-trading strategy. This project was done in an era in which laws that provided financing (appropriation bills) were adopted without any ceilings or controls. In the 1990s, the system was briefly changed to put rigid ceilings on how much money Congress would allow itself to spend in any single year. How would those controls have changed the ability to logroll projects?

3. Explain how the political power structure built into the legislative process contributed to the success of the project.

4. Would you judge the Tenn-Tom to have been a good use of public funds? Explain your position, whatever it may be. Would your assessment differ, depending on whether you live in the Mississippi-Alabama region through which the waterway flows or in some other part of the country?

Geography

The Mississippi River provides a natural waterway—with significant help from locks and other government assistance along the way—through the central United States to the Gulf of Mexico at New Orleans. But for 200 years, some have dreamed of a cutoff farther east—a waterway linking the Tennessee River and the Tombigbee River to the Gulf at Mobile, Alabama, a shortcut to the sea for industrial cities of the North and a remedy for chronic unemployment in the areas through which the waterway would pass. In the French colonial era, the leaders of Mobile proposed a canal and towpath link to the Tennessee, but the King of France thought it extravagant. In the 1870s, the idea surfaced again as a way to allow the year-round shipping on the Tombigbee that sandbars prevented during low-water season. The full waterway would provide a shorter route for cargoes passing through the Ohio River system from the direction of Louisville, Cincinnati, Pittsburgh, and beyond. The trip would be shorter, the nation's economy would be stimulated, and thousands of new jobs would be created. The system is shown in the accompanying figure.

Case 2–1
Map Showing the Tenn-Tom Waterway

SOURCE: S. Chang and P. R. Forbus, "Tenn-Tom Versus the Mississippi River," Transportation Journal 25 (Summer 1986). Copyright © Tennessee-Tombigbee Waterway Development Authority. Reprinted with permission.

Congress

The U.S. Congress authorized the project in 1946, but construction of the 234-mile waterway did not begin until 1972.[61] It opened for business in 1985, stretching from the Tennessee River immediately above the Yellow Creek port in northern Tishomingo County to the Demopolis lock connecting to the Tombigbee River, which empties into the Gulf at Mobile, Alabama. For any cargo heading to the Gulf of Mexico from the east, the system of ten locks, dams, and ten manmade lakes in the states of Alabama and Mississippi reduced the trip by 235 miles. The project—five times longer than the Panama Canal—was the largest civil works project ever undertaken by the U.S. Army Corps of Engineers, the primary public works agency of the federal government.

The Tenn-Tom Waterway had strong supporters in the U.S. Congress. It was the grand plan of powerful southern politicians who steered the public works project

---

[61]In the federal budget process, public infrastructure spending must first be authorized (or approved as a part of government policy) and then appropriated (or provided funds, usually in one-year blocks to the agency responsible for the project). Many more projects get authorized than end up being constructed.

through Congress in the 1970s and 1980s. While the project was under consideration and construction, the chairman of the House Appropriations Committee, the committee that must approve all federal appropriations, was Jamie Whitten of Mississippi, the member of Congress representing the part of northeastern Mississippi through which the waterway would flow. Chairman Whitten said, "Everything is in someone's district. I've got the position in Congress I most want. It doesn't mean you can run [the Appropriations Committee]. It just means you've got the first say."[62] And the chair of the House Appropriations Subcommittee on Energy and Water, the subcommittee through which all waterway development projects must go, was Tom Bevill of Alabama. But even these friends didn't provide complete political insulation. In 1981, when Congress threatened to stop funding, floodlights were installed on the waterway so that digging could continue through the night, getting the project so close to completion that its supporters could argue that to stop the canal would be a horrible waste of public funds.

The Numbers

U.S. Army Corps of Engineers estimates in the late 1970s showed a cost-benefit ratio of 1.2 to 1, meaning that each dollar spent on the project would generate $1.20 in benefits, based on a construction cost of $1.6 billion and $250 million that would be necessary for maintenance during the fifty-year useful life of the waterway. For these estimates, the Corps followed the requirements of the Water Resources Development Act of 1974 and used a discount rate of 3.25 percent, the rate for federal borrowing. A rate estimated for tax funds would have been around 6.625 percent, and the cost-benefit ratio would then have fallen to 0.64 to 1. Construction cost of the waterway finally amounted to $1.992 billion, compared with the initial appropriation estimate of $323 million (and only $117 million when the project was authorized). Its maintenance cost is now around $22 million per year.

Operations

Doubts expressed during development of the waterway about the generosity of other parts of the analysis have proven accurate. The U.S. Army Corps of Engineers estimated that the waterway would move 27.3 million tons of cargo in its first year of operation, eventually expanding to 40 million tons. However, actual traffic has proven to be much less. In 1993, 7.6 million tons of cargo were shipped; in 1988, when a drought made transport on the Mississippi difficult, 10 million tons were shipped. In general, shippers preferred the free-flowing Mississippi to the west, and there have been few new industrial plants springing up along the waterway. The major products shipped on the waterway have been wood products (especially wood chips) and logs (about half the traffic), followed by coal. None of these are high-value, time-sensitive products for which speedier transit is critical. Indeed, transit via the Tenn-Tom appears to be more expensive than using the Mississippi because of the many locks and narrow path of the waterway.[63]

---

[62]David Rogers, "Rivaling Cleopatra, A Pork-Barrel King Sails the Tenn-Tom," *Wall Street Journal,* May 31, 1985, 1.

[63]S. Chang and P. R. Forbus, "Tenn-Tom versus the Mississippi River," *Transportation Journal* 25 (Summer 1986): 47–54.

CHAPTER 3

Budget Methods and Practices

Chapter Contents

Many tasks in the budget cycle can be learned only by dealing nose-to-nose against and elbow-to-elbow with other participants. However, understanding some methods and perspectives before that first crunch is important. This chapter introduces some methods and activities in each phase of the budget cycle. In particular, it deals with (1) preparation of agency budget requests, (2) review of agency requests, (3) construction of the final executive budget, (4) management of budget execution, and (5) audit.

The first weapon in the arsenal of those responsible for the preparation and analysis of budgets is the calculation of annual growth rates. They are useful for the development of budget proposals, the analysis of what has been proposed, and the examination of what actual spending has occurred. This is a basic tool for fiscal analysis and for development of budget cost estimates.

Growth Rates and Simple Forecasts

The first principle about budgets is that the narrative comes before the numbers. That is, the description of what the budget proposes should be done before budget numbers are developed. Because many public finance novices are apprehensive about preparing the budget estimate (the numbers), this section will violate that first principle—it will discuss some numbers first. Just don't develop your budgets in this order.

Budgets are prepared for future years, and that means that somebody is going to have to be forecasting what the future will bring in terms of the operating conditions for government. The forecast is not of spending for those future years, but rather of the conditions in which the government providing services will operate in the future. What will the demands for government services be in the budget year? What will prices for the things that governments need to buy to produce those services be in the budget year? What technologies will be available for use of those resources in providing services? What revenue will the government collect in the budget year? One of the most fundamental tasks that those who prepare and analyze budgets have is that of preparing forecasts. In much of this work, the methods used in actual practice are relatively simple. Simplicity in these forecasts is appropriate because seldom will there be time, resources, or data to do much else. In addition, simplicity is a virtue for process transparency. Fortunately, the accuracy of simple techniques can be quite good.

Annual growth rates can be extremely useful in analyzing budgets and fiscal results, as well as in providing a useful grounding for the forecasts upon which budgets are prepared. Here is an example of their applicability and the technique.

At what annual rate has the population—those expecting to receive government services—grown over the years? Suppose the state population increased from 1.8 million in 1990 to 6.7 million in 2015. The compound rate of growth is computed according to the formula

$$R = (Y/X)^{(1/N)} - 1$$

where

R = the growth rate,

Y = the end value,

X = the beginning value, and

N = the number of periods of growth.

In this case, the population growth rate would equal the following:

$$R = (6.7/1.8)^{(1/25)} - 1 = 0.054 \text{ or } 5.4\%$$

That isn't as imposing as it looks, so long as you have an inexpensive calculator in your pocket or an Excel (or other) spreadsheet program on your computer. Using a spreadsheet, think of the calculation like this:

$$R = [(6.7/1.8) \wedge (1/25)] - 1 = 5.4\%$$

For calculator users, look for the y^x key to do the work.

The calculation done here says that, on average, over that twenty-five year period, each year has a population that is 5.4% higher than the year before. That will be the basis for forecasting the population for years beyond 2015. If you have insights that allow you to use a forecast that you believe to be more accurate, then use that forecast. But you always have some historical growth rate to fall back on.

Annual growth rates are useful for comparing changes in data series when the numbers of years of observation are different and, as a result, comparing overall percentage changes won't help. For instance, suppose you have population levels for 1985 and for 2005 and total income levels for 1983 and 2007. Has income increased more or less rapidly than population? You can't tell by comparing percentage change between beginning and ending years because they are different for the two sets of data and because the data cover different spans of time. But you can compare annual growth rates, calculated as above, to learn which was growing faster, and that is useful for analysis.

So why not just calculate the total percentage change over several years and divide by the number of years? Mostly because it will give you the wrong answer. Back to the original data: that calculation would look like this:

Wrong $R = [(6.7 - 1.8)/1.8]/25 = 0.109$ or 10.9%

To see whether this is the right answer, start with 1.8 and increase it by 10.9 percent, then increase that result by 10.9 percent, then increase that by 10.9 percent, and so on until you have gone out twenty-five years. If 10.9 percent is the right annual growth rate, you should have reached 6.7. But running the numbers shows a result of 23.9. So that calculation does, indeed, produce the Wrong R! Remember, that calculation approach is wrong, not even approximately right. Do not do it!

What happens if you use the right growth rate—the one calculated to be 5.4 percent? Go through the same process of starting with 1.8 and increase it by 5.4 percent for twenty-five years. You get 6.7, which is what you would expect from doing it right.

It is useful to know the annual growth rate for analysis, but you can also use that growth rate to do a simple and easy forecast. In other words, you are assuming that growth into the future will be roughly the same as has been experienced in the recent past. That might not be right, but it is likely to be the best you can do, and most of the time such a forecast will produce a usable result. Suppose you wanted to forecast the number of clients your agency would need to serve in the next year. The amount is probably more than in recent years, but how many more? Assuming growth comparable to the recent past is at least a good first approximation. You might want to revise a little from your personal knowledge about what is going on, but you might not want to change at all. Suppose your agency served 14,450 clients in 2008 and 17,680 in 2015. You don't have complete data for 2016 because the year is not completed, and you need a forecast for preparation of the 2017 budget. Compute the growth rate between 2008 and 2015:

$R = (17{,}680/14{,}450)^{(1/7)} - 1 = 0.029$ or 2.9%

And use that rate to forecast 2017 client workload:

Clients in 2016 $= 17{,}680 \times 1.029 = 18{,}193$

Clients in 2017 $= 18{,}193 \times 1.029 = 18{,}721$

You could get to the forecast number without the two calculations by using this simple equation:

$C = A (1 + R)^N$ or $C = A (1 + R)$ ^ N on your calculator or computer spreadsheet.

where

C = the future value you want to forecast,

A = the base year from which your growth forecast will be made,

R = the growth rate used for the forecast, and

N = the number of periods between the base year and the future year.

In our case, $C = 17{,}680 \times (1.029)^2 = 18{,}721$.

That's your forecast and it is pretty simple. But, as it turns out, this sort of forecast is used very often in the construction of annual budgets for forecasting elements of the operating environment in which services are to be provided, likely workloads, the prices that might be paid by the agency for the things that it purchases, and so on. Figure out how to calculate annual growth rates and how to use them for simple forecasts. You will do these calculations all the time when you are preparing budgets. You will also discover that such growth rates, not some complex forecasting model, are regularly used in the preparation of long-term fiscal scenarios. The ability to create credible forecasts for periods many years in the future is extremely limited, so complexity provides minimal improvement over the simple growth rates. You will learn more complex forecasting methods in a later chapter about revenue forecasting, but you will use simple forecasts like these most often when you are developing and analyzing the expenditure sections of an annual budget. Just don't use growth rates to create your expenditure requests directly (i.e., "spending has grown at a rate of 3 percent over the past five years, so I will just add 3 percent to spending this year to get the spending request"). That means that you haven't a clue about developing an action plan for your agency, but are simply willing to go with the flow and aren't doing your job. Forecast the operating conditions; then develop your spending proposal around your planned response to those conditions.[1] This approach puts you in command of building your planned response, rather than projecting on the basis of a history that mixes changes in plan and changes in operating conditions in some

---

[1]Many economic and fiscal variables are subject to regular variation across the months of the year, influenced by the calendar (holidays), weather, and other regular patterns. For instance, construction work in the northern United States tends to decline in winter months, and retail sales throughout the country tend to rise before Christmas, both regardless of the underlying economic strength. Therefore, economic variables for quarters or months are often reported on the basis of their implied annual levels. In other words, recognizing patterns of economic activity through the year, personal income for the fourth quarter would be reported at what personal income would be for the year if income were to be generated through the full year at the rate experienced for the fourth quarter. The logic is this: if the historical pattern is for 30 percent of annual personal income to be earned in the fourth quarter and if unadjusted personal income reported in the fourth quarter was $ 3,500,000, then the annual rate, based on the fourth quarter, would be $11,666,667 (calculated as 3,500,000 divided by 0.30). That is the nature of quarterly data normally presented in the Bureau of Economic Analysis reports, for example. The data aren't quarterly totals but are annual rates based on activity in the quarter.

unknown mix. The budget should reflect your plan for action, i.e., your response to what you believe to be the opportunities for service (sometimes referred to as problems) that will emerge in the upcoming year.

Preparation of Agency Budget Requests

Operating agencies work from the budget instruction transmitted by the central budget office to develop their operating plans for the year and the budget requests that will accommodate those plans. Ideally, the instructions provide (1) the chief executive's main goals for the people, (2) forecasts of critical operating conditions for the budget year (inflation, service populations, etc.), (3) a format for the budget proposal (usually including prescribed forms that tell you what expenditure categories to use in your request), (4) a time schedule to be followed in developing the budget, and (5) some indication of the amount of money that the agency ought to build its budget around (either a ceiling control total or an estimated maximum increase from prior years).

How do the chief executive and central budget office know whether the instructions to agencies should emphasize extreme fiscal constraint, allow modest expansion of existing programs, or permit consideration of sound new programs? Many governments prepare, as a starting point, a preliminary *baseline forecast* of the surplus or deficit. The baseline provides the projected budget conditions if policies embedded in existing law are maintained.[2] In this analysis, the budget office forecasts revenue for the budget year and compares that forecast with the cost of continuing existing programs at their current level of operations under the conditions expected for the next year (prices, workloads, etc.). In many instances, the simple projection approaches presented earlier in this chapter are used, although sometimes more complex forecasting models may be applied. The gap, either positive or negative, between revenue and expenditure under current law gives a first guidance for the budget instruction: Will agencies be allowed to propose new programs? Will they work under hiring freezes? Will they be constrained in their capacity to request new equipment or to make capital outlays? What sort of ceilings will they face in making their requests? How the chief executive feels about deficits and surpluses and whether that executive is willing to propose revenue increases (tax or charge increases) also shape the instruction.

A good place for the agency administrator to start her budget development, along with making sure she understands what the chief executive wants, is to reflect on where the agency's operations have been in the recent past and to consider where

---

[2]Establishing exactly what the baseline should entail is not without controversy. See Timothy J. Muris, "The Uses and Abuses of Budget Baselines," in *The Budget Puzzle: Understanding Federal Spending,* ed. John F. Cogan, Timothy J. Muris, and Allen Schick (Stanford, Calif.: Stanford University Press, 1994): 41–78. The argument concerns what exactly current policy should mean.

she would like the agency to head in the near future—three to five years, with more attention to the near years than to the distant years. This reflection provides, along with the instruction, the basis for creating the service policy that will shape her budget proposal. After she gets into the numbers, it will be too late to do much policy reflection and revision, so she should start by thinking.

Within that instruction and service intention, the agency develops the three important pieces of its budget proposal: (1) a *narrative,* which describes the agency (mostly the same from year to year), indicates its managerial objectives for the budget year and beyond (probably changing from year to year), and is keyed to the agency mission statement; (2) *detail schedules,* which translate the managerial objectives into requests for new agency appropriations; and (3) *cumulative schedules,* which aggregate the new initiatives into existing activities to form the complete request. The presentation also probably includes *workload, productivity,* and *performance measures* for the agency. The workload identifies measurable activities of the agency with historical trends and projections for the future. Productivity relates these workload measures to numbers of personnel, and performance measures identify quantity and quality of service delivered to the public, sometimes including the results of citizen satisfaction surveys (Chapter 6 discusses the use of performance indicators in the budget in some detail).

The most important lesson for the neophyte to learn about budget preparation, and possibly the most surprising, is that narrative dominates the numbers. The request narrative must describe and justify the plan; the numbers follow from that. Budgeting is logic, planning, justification, and politics, not mathematics or accounting. The narrative, detail schedules, and cumulative schedules are all critical because they provide governments with the "how much" and "what it does" information needed for successful public decisions. The whole process begins with the agency's explanation of what it intends for the budget year. The narrative explains the policy response that the agency has decided to make in response to the operating conditions it believes it will face in the budget year. The basic rule: "The words come before the numbers." When the words (the narrative) are clearly provided, the numbers easily fall out. An agency administrator who builds his or her budget request by projection of historical patterns of expenditure categories is not serving the public well and really does not understand the job. That sort of budget is easy to produce, but does not serve the public interest.

Agency budget documents are likely to include details not just on how money has been and is intended to be spent, but also on agency performance and accomplishments. It is a reasonable expectation that an agency be able to explain what it has done with the money—besides spend it!—and to explain what the public can expect to receive from the planned operations of the agency in the upcoming budget year. This performance information and these plans may be embedded as an important element of the budget narrative, but, increasingly, the budget proposal has a distinct and identifiable section that deals with performance. Central administrations, legislatures, and the citizenry all seek performance information as they consider budget requests and operating plans of public agencies.

Budget Justification

Program status reports, requests for supplemental funding, supporting explanations for increased staff, budget increases, and so on require justification for any planned agency action. Well-developed justifications are the key to successful agency budget requests.[3] The standard rules of English prose apply, but there are also several general and specific guidelines for effective budget justifications.

1. The justification must avoid jargon and uncommon and unexplained abbreviations because its audience includes individuals less familiar with the details of the proposed activity than the operating agency's personnel. Neither budget-agency examiners nor legislators are likely to approve poorly described projects. Never create your own acronyms. The justification should follow the basic standards of expository writing: short sentences, short words, active voice, no footnotes, and no unnecessary words.[4]

2. The justifications must be factual, provide documented sources, and go through ordinary review and revision to produce a polished presentation. Some of the justification may be technical; however, the technical parts cannot overwhelm the rest or be left unexplained. The justification has to focus on the small number of points that the reader should pay attention to and remember.

3. The justification structure must address the current situation, additional needs, and expected results from honoring the request. One section of the justification should describe the current program in terms of measurable workloads, staffing, funding, or productivity trends. It should briefly and specifically inform the budget examiner of existing conditions, without extraneous detail that might misdirect the examiner's attention. Another section of the justification should describe the additional needs. It must specifically identify additional funds, personnel, and materials needed for the budget activity at issue. The reason for the need must be explicitly developed. The examiner must not have to guess what and why.

4. The request must indicate what beneficial results will come from granting the request. It must make clear that something important will be made better if the requested activity is carried out and that the agency has the capacity to carry it out.

A good simple guidance about the request narrative is that it be clear, concise, and compelling. Be direct without jargon and omit the math and footnotes, make the points succinctly, and push your idea as hard as possible. The reviewer is looking at many budget requests and a bloated narrative will not help.

The details of what belongs in the justification are ordinarily covered in the instructions. Hence comes the basic rule for doing budget justifications: *read the*

---

[3] They are also critical for grant proposal writing for public and nonprofit organizations.
[4] Be a Hemingway, not a Faulkner. Check with an English-major friend if you don't understand.

instructions and follow them. If the instructions leave you with any uncertainty about what the justification should include, you won't go wrong by explaining (1) what resources the agency wants for the budget year, (2) what it intends to do with those resources, and (3) what good will result from that intention.

Common reasons for requesting funds include the following:

1. **Higher (or lower) prices.** Prices of supplies and services needed to maintain agency operations at their existing level may be increasing (or decreasing). For instance, the local electric utility may have received approval for a rate increase during the next year. That could elicit a request for a budget increase to accommodate the increased cost of the service.

2. **Increased demand for service (workload).** The clientele served by the agency may increase. To maintain service levels, the agency's budget may need to increase. An agency providing education to children of the homeless, for instance, could argue for a larger budget if the population of such children is expected to increase.

3. **Methods improvement.** Administrative changes or innovations can alter the budgets of agencies. An operating unit can become more productive and generate fewer errors if it has more space, if it has more modern equipment, or if it has better information technology. That would require a budget request. Methods improvement can also allow savings, in which case the budget change would be negative. Some improvements may have been mandated or required by the courts, the legislature, or a higher level of government.

4. **Full financing.** Agencies frequently start new operations at some point other than the start of a fiscal year. Initial appropriations for new operations are thus partial; to cover full operations would require larger appropriations, a change that needs to be described in the agency request.

5. **New services.** New services, enlarged services, improved services, or services to an expanded clientele should be identified and justified. Because new services would not have been previously considered in legislative deliberations, they do require separation in the budget. New services are likely to be closely linked to initiatives in the basic narrative. As with method improvements, some new services may have been mandated.

There may be other categories of justification that would be applied to allow agencies to identify the underlying case for their request. For instance, some federal agencies recognize a judicial restraining order as a separate category. Those noted here, however, are among the most common.

The narrative should describe expected results from the proposal and try to convince the budget office and the legislature of the need for the proposed activity. The narrative should describe the consequences if the requested resources are or are not provided. Because the reviewer will want to know whether partial funding will help, whether critical program objectives will be endangered without funding, whether workload can be backlogged to get around the problem, and what the implications of the request will be for future requests, answers to those questions should be available and defensible. The justification should make a solid case for a realistic increase.

Table 3–1
Checklist for Budget Justification

Completeness	Are the major elements (objective of program, magnitude of need, benefits, or results) covered?
Explicitness	Are program benefits and related funding increases clearly stated?
Consistency	Are the statements or data appearing in several places the same or easily reconcilable?
Balance	Are the most important programs and issues given the most prominence? Do the programs' objectives adequately support the budget level requested?
Quantitative data	Are quantitative data used appropriately and effectively?
Organization	Is the material well organized to bring out only the significant matters? Are appropriate headings or titles used? Is introductory or summary material used appropriately?
Relevance	Is the material in the justification relevant to the proposal?
Purpose	Does the justification explain why the program is necessary to achieve a desirable purpose?
Directions	Does the justification follow the guidelines presented in the budget instructions?

SOURCE: U.S. Office of Personnel Management, *Budget Presentation and Justification* (Washington, D.C.: Office of Personnel Management, 1982) with additions.

There is no reason to spread a justification thin to defend a large increase when a solid case for a smaller increase is possible.[5] Table 3–1 presents a brief checklist for elements to include in a sound justification.

An agency should never assume that its request for additional resources, no matter how reasonable it may appear to agency staff, will automatically bring more funds. When an agency does not receive its full budget request, the agency cannot complain that it has not been "fully funded." Its legislative masters, the representatives of the citizenry, have not agreed to the plan proposed by the agency, but it has fully funded the plan that it has accepted. The agency is expected to execute the plan that has been accepted and approved.

An important thing to keep in mind is that policy drives budgets. The budget needs to reflect policy decisions, and when policies change, budgets will need to change as well. For instance, when states and the federal government began adopting "get-tough-on-crime" programs and an expanded battle against illegal drugs that brought greater incarceration rates, prison costs increased dramatically. And as states became concerned about the great increase in the prison share of state budgets, a number of states began work on revamping state criminal codes to reduce prison terms.[6] The debate continues at the federal level.

---

[5] There is some debate about whether it is better to over-promise, but under-deliver or to under-promise, but over-deliver in budget requests and agency operations. That will be something for you to decide when you are on the job.

[6] Neil King, "The Right Way? As Prisons Squeeze Budgets, GOP Rethinks Crime Focus," *Wall Street Journal*, June 21, 2013, A1.

Elements of Cost Estimation

Estimates of what the cost would be of fulfilling the agency service plan for the budget year may be developed and organized through one or more of the following classification structures. First, the cost may be grouped by the *organization* (branch, section, division, etc.) incurring the cost. The estimates originate in the offices where the costs occur. The costs thus follow the organizational chart. For example, if a city has six organizational units (police, fire, parks, public works, streets, and mayor and council), a cost estimate would be prepared for each unit. The estimates would entail each unit's planned responses to forecast operating conditions. Some plans and forecasts would ideally be common; that is, everybody has integrated into their plans the closing of a military establishment on the edge of town. But some plans would almost exclusively affect one department; for example, the street resurfacing program matters for the streets budget, but not for the others. Second, costs may be grouped by *task, purpose, function,* or *program cost center* or by program outcome group. For instance, program cost centers for a police department might include central administration, the jail, criminal investigations, crime prevention, traffic, training, communication, and records. Each represents an identifiable task for which operating plans and budget cost can be identified. Alternatively, cost may be divided by outcome program: transportation, public safety, environmental protection, and so on. Sometimes, the organizational breakdown coincides with these task or program breakdowns, but often organizational costs are attributable to several different tasks or programs. Third, the costs may be broken down by *object* (or economic) class, that is, by the nature of goods and services to be purchased (personnel, utilities, motor fuel, etc.). This amounts to the agency's planned shopping list. Agencies organize their cost estimates according to the uniform object classification required and provided by the budget office of that particular government.

The beginning of any budget cost estimation, regardless of eventual focus on department, task cost center, or program outcome, is the object class. This is the basis for estimating resource requirements regardless of how costs will eventually be organized. Ideally, the agency would determine what it intends to do, determine what resources it needs to do it, estimate the price of those resources, and multiply the price by the number of input units to get a cost total. In routine budget preparation, some of the estimates for smaller input categories are based on what the agency has experienced in the recent past ("last year plus 5 percent," for instance, implicitly says we aren't changing our operating plan and costs of inputs associated with that plan haven't changed very much). Such an incremental estimation for significant budget categories is not appropriate or acceptable—it does not distinguish the reason for the change. Is it because service demand is higher, because prices of inputs have changed, because policy for responding to public service demands has changed, because of some combination of reasons, or because of something else? The public and the legislative body need to know the reason, as must the program administrator. Budget costs occur as agencies acquire resources (personnel, materials, and facilities) to provide public services. Somewhat different estimating techniques apply to each class, with a particular distinction between personnel and non-personnel costs. The agency is always working toward estimating the cost of carrying out the plan described in the narrative.

Personnel Costs: Paying the Staff

Agencies need workers if they are to produce government services or, even if production is contracted out to private firms, to monitor this production by others. Indeed, payments to employees—wages and salaries plus other agreed benefits (pensions, insurance, etc.)—usually represent the largest single component in government agency budget requests and a major element in the total cost of government. For instance, compensation of employees amounts to more than 70 percent of state and local government consumption expenditures, with some agencies even much more labor intensive. A considerable portion of the total cost of modern government is determined by compensation paid to employees, even though the wage-and-salary component of spending has declined through the years as governments provide more services by contract with private firms and by transfer payments and as they substitute technology for personnel to improve service quality and constrain cost.

Wages and Salaries

The task is to estimate personnel cost for a budget request: to determine the kind and amount of personnel services needed (established by the agency's planned response to forecast operating conditions)—the time to be spent by employees at work—and then apply prevailing wage and salary rates to compute the total cost. In other words, total personnel cost equals the number of workers in each pay category multiplied by the payment per worker in that category. A standard procedure uses personnel data on individuals in each pay category, adjusted for anticipated movements to the next pay step in the budget year. Thus, if there are fifty people in the Tax Auditor I category with five years' experience this year, there will likely be fifty people in the Tax Auditor I category with six years' experience next year, assuming the tax department plans about the same operating pace as in the prior year. The budget estimate for them would be 50 times the annual pay of a Tax Auditor I with six years' experience. Governments normally maintain a position management system that charts authorized positions by pay class, which positions are filled and which are vacant, and the pay rate in each class. The system both provides a control over employment and its costs and offers an excellent tool for cost estimation.

The request for payment of staff must be supplemented by lapses that reduce total cost: turnover (retirements, quits, and terminations) with replacement at lower pay grades or nonreplacement, delays in filling vacant positions, and so on. Such lapses may be estimated from experience with the agency workforce. Requests for new personnel ordinarily are based on greater expected workload, on a desire to improve the quality of service, or on new programs. At least at the agency request level, staffing decisions have moved away from regarding government as the employer of last resort, where those unable to find jobs elsewhere can turn, and toward staffing to ensure the agency delivers planned services and achieves its objectives.

But how much should each employee be paid? This question is critical for sound government finances and for the delicate political balance between, on one hand, the interests of public employees and the groups that represent them and, on the other, the concerns of taxpayers/service recipients who both receive what governments provide and pay the bill for that provision. A reasonable objective in determining pay rates for government finances might be to ensure delivery of government services at least cost to the taxpayer. If employees are overpaid, the taxpayer pays too much for services provided; if employees are underpaid, the taxpayer receives subsidization at the expense of those employees. In practice, pay rates may come (1) from law or tradition, as with the salaries of elected officials; (2) from pay rates established in a civil service classification structure that attempts wage comparability across position factors; or (3) from collective-bargaining agreements.[7] Most governments establish some salaries in each of these ways. For example, a city could well have the salaries of the mayor and the members of the council established by state statute, the wages and salaries in most city department employees established in a personnel classification system, and the wages of police officers, firefighters, and sanitation workers established in a collective-bargaining agreement.[8]

NON-WAGE-AND-SALARY PERSONNEL COSTS

The total cost of workers includes both direct compensation (wages and salaries) and fringe benefits associated with employment, including the cost of post-employment benefits promised the employees. At least some fringe-benefit payments are included in object classes separate from wage-and-salary payments, but they must be considered when estimating total compensation and when developing budget estimates. These payments may include payments into public employee pension systems, health and life insurance premiums, clothing or uniform allowances, employer Social Security or other payroll tax payments, and so on. Most such benefits are computed by applying formulas, which are established by law, labor contract, or (less frequently now) prevailing practices. Cost is normally driven either by the number of employees (hospital insurance premiums, for example) or by the amount paid to employees (e.g., payments into a public employee pension fund based on a certain percentage of wages). Calculation is thus relatively straightforward (although the formulas can sometimes be quite complicated). Some costs associated with employing workers may be in budgetary accounts other than those of the agency in which the person works. For example, the government may put employee benefits (pensions, vacation pay, etc.) in the budget of a Department of Personnel. That complicates the work of analysts who are trying to discern how much a government is spending to provide a particular service—looking at the spending in the police department will not provide the whole answer if some police officer benefits are being covered in the personnel department budget.

---

[7]See Charles A. Pounian and Jeffrey J. Fuller, "Compensating Public Employees," in *Handbook of Public Administration,* 2nd ed., ed. James Perry (San Francisco: Jossey-Bass, 1996), for more discussion of pay systems.

[8]There are perpetual battles over whether public employees are over-paid or under-paid relative to their private sector equivalents; that argument is not going to be opened here. A problem in assessing the evidence is that too often the person doing the analysis knows what he or she wants to prove before starting the research and that spoils the reliability of the finding. But surely there are differences according to skill levels and specializations, how employment stability is accounted for, the way in which various fringe benefits are included, the extent to which locational distinctions or hostile environments are considered, and so on. Suffice it to say that, if an agency is having difficulty hiring qualified staff for certain positions or losing good staff to private employers, then compensation is probably less than the market requires.

Non-Personnel Costs

Other object costs may be more difficult to estimate than personnel costs.[9] Non-personnel costs are often computed using estimating ratios, as adjusted by recent experience. Much information for the request can be located in prior-year budget materials. Five estimation techniques are frequently used in these computations:

1. **Volume × unit price.** This method is attractive when an identifiable quantity and a single average price are applicable to a relatively high-ticket object class. Candidates for this approach include requests for items such as automobiles or personal computers. These items represent fairly homogeneous categories that can constitute a large share of cost in an object class. If the police department plans to purchase ten new vehicles, each of which would likely cost $35,000, the estimated cost of the plan is $350,000.

2. **Workload × average unit cost.** This approach uses recent cost experience with adjustments for changed plans, inflation, or productivity changes. For instance, food expenses for a training class could be estimated by such a method (300 trainee days at $20 per trainee day, for a request of $6,000).

3. **Workforce ratios.** Some categories of cost, particularly small categories of miscellaneous costs, can be estimated by relating them to the workforce. For example, office supply expenses for a revenue department district office could be related to the size of the staff stationed there. A proposal to hire new police officers may bring with it the need to purchase new police vehicles. (Similar estimates can be made by linking the expense category to the clientele being served by the local office.)

4. **Ratios to another object.** When there is some relationship between certain categories and other resources used in the production process, that expense group can be estimated by use of ratios to the non-personnel object class. As an example, a parts inventory for motor vehicles can be linked to the number of vehicles in the motor fleet. Purchase of ten new police vehicles would require some additional costs for operation and repair.[10]

5. **Adjustment to prior-year cost.** Small, heterogeneous cost categories can be estimated by adjusting prior-year lump sums, using whatever adjustment percentage seems right. This method may be necessary when other means are not feasible or economical, but it lacks the attempted precision of other techniques and should not be used for any substantial cost category.

---

[9]See Susan A. MacManus, "Designing and Managing the Procurement Process," in *Handbook of Public Administration,* 2nd ed., ed. James Perry (San Francisco: Jossey-Bass, 1996), for an excellent analysis of the procurement of goods and services.

[10]Sometimes things do not work out well. For instance, a federal judge ordered LaPorte County, Indiana, to remedy chronic jail overcrowding, and the county spent $23 million on a jail renovation and expansion, completed in 2004. Unfortunately, the county did not have enough money to hire additional jailers, so a new wing with space for 200 inmates had to remain empty. Too bad the judge did not order jailers to accompany the jail space.

No formula or ratio can be automatically applied without hazard. Cost ratios and other relationships may change if operating methods are altered, prices of inputs change, or production technologies change. All of these change in a dynamic economy, often with great impact on operating cost. Sidebar 3–1 describes break-even analysis, an estimating device often used by managers in public, private, and nonprofit agencies as they develop fiscal plans.

Screening for Errors

Budget estimates must be carefully prepared because the quality of the presentation shapes the impressions that budget analysts (and others) develop about agencies. Analysts are less likely to trust judgments of budget officers who prepare sloppy budget requests. Several simple errors are particularly frequent, although they should never occur. The budget should not be transmitted outside the agency until

---

Sidebar 3–1
Break-Even Analysis

Break-even analysis is a helpful tool for certain managerial problems, including budget estimation, subsidy determination, scaling, and the like. Agencies that have sales revenue can make more frequent direct use of the technique, but most managers will find some applications. The technique plots cost against revenues as the quantity of service (output) provided varies.

That comparison allows the manager to identify the service level at which service revenue equals service cost (the break-even point) and the required subsidy or contribution (profit) at other operation levels. With the costing model developed here, a budget administrator can easily see how changing demand for a service (or workloads) will influence the agency's spending pace, and that can be useful in both developing a budget request and monitoring spending within budget execution.

The logic of the method is illustrated with this example. Suppose the Smithville Solid-Waste Management Authority has a trash collection fee of $2 per 40-gallon container; that means its revenue in a particular time period will equal the number of containers of trash collected multiplied by $2. Algebraically,

$$TR = P \times Q$$

where TR equals the total revenue, P equals the price per unit, and Q equals the number of units or service level. Thus,

$$TR = 2Q$$

(continues)

**Sidebar 3–1
(continued)**

The Authority faces two types of cost, some that are fixed (they do not change with the quantity of service provided, at least within normal service ranges) and some that are variable (the cost increases with the level of service). Authority estimates show the following costs:

Fixed (Annual)	
Administration (staff, utilities, etc.)	$35,000
Equipment lease	85,000
Total	$120,000
Variable (per container)	
Landfill tipping charge	$1.00
Equipment operation on collection routes (fuel, maintenance, etc.)	0.15
Collection crew payment	0.25
Total	$1.40

An algebraic statement of total cost would be

$$TC = FC + (VC \times Q)$$

where TC equals the total cost, FC equals the fixed cost, and VC equals the unit variable cost. Thus,

$$TC = 120,000 + 1.40Q$$

The Authority can now estimate the level of collections at which the operation will break even and, probably more important, the necessary subsidy at actual levels of operation. The break-even service level is the one at which TR equals TC:

$$2Q = 120,000 + 1.40Q$$

$$0.60Q = 120,000$$

$$Q = 200,000$$

The break-even Q is 200,000; collection levels above that will provide a surplus (or contribution) for use elsewhere, and collection levels below that will require a contribution from elsewhere (maybe a tax) to cover the cost. By substituting the manager's best guess for actual service level into the equation, the actual contribution or subsidy requirement may be estimated. The analysis can also help the manager identify the relative impact of controlling fixed or variable costs in reducing the overall subsidy requirements.

Managers need to recognize the limitations of the analysis, even as they use it. Costs may be difficult to estimate and may not be easily divided into fixed and variable categories. There may also be cost discontinuities. In other words, certain costs may be fixed up to some production level, but need to increase to support further service production. Service levels almost certainly vary with the price charged, especially with larger price changes. The assumption of linearity can only be seen as a working approximation. The technique, however, remains one of great applicability. Managers often develop break-even charts to visualize the costs and revenues of their operations as level of operations changes. The charts plot total cost and total revenue against service (or output) levels, as shown here.

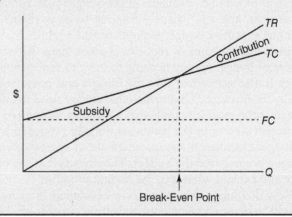

a check has been made for the following errors because these errors will be the first things that the central budget examiner will look for:

1. **Instructions not followed.** Budgets may not coincide with current budget instructions, budget guidelines, and forms. A budget may be developed using the prior-year budget as a guide, but the submission itself must coincide with current regulations. Failure to follow instructions produces needless embarrassment and may put the request at extra risk.

2. **Missing documentation.** Budget submissions may lack required supplemental documents, or the documentation may not be properly identified. Budget examiners are not inclined to give the benefit of the doubt to budgets with missing materials.

3. **Internal inconsistency.** Cost estimate detail columns may not add to totals carried forward in the presentation. One must continuously cross-check to preserve the internal consistency of the budget request.

4. **Math.** The math may not be right. Failure to check all calculations can lead not just to professional embarrassment, but also to rejected budget requests and to terminated employment. Even spreadsheet calculations need to be verified to ensure that formulas do what is expected and that the formulas are right. The computer does exactly what it is told to do, even when you tell it to do the wrong thing.

It is not a sign of weakness to have a colleague review your request before you move it up the administrative channels.

Review of Budgets

Agency requests are reviewed by a central budget office before proposals are included in the executive budget (and by legislative committees after inclusion in the proposal). The central budget office is working under a total resource constraint—revenue forecast to be available in the budget year, funds to be borrowed during the budget year, and any balances forecast to be available from prior years—and the sum of all executive budget requests must be within that constraint. In almost every circumstance, the sum of requests is more than the money available to spend, so the central budget agency is going to have to reduce some requests. But the budget agency is also concerned that the budget and operating plan finally approved can actually be executed. That means that it may need to add omitted items from some requests if the examiner finds that a program supported by the chief executive cannot be executed with the resources initially proposed by the agency. Furthermore, the budget examiner is less informed about agency operations than are those in the agency who prepared the budget. That means that the budget must clearly communicate and explain what is in the budget proposal.

How do budget examiners review budgets? In many respects, the budget examiner will "reverse engineer" the budget proposal to get behind the gross numbers to see what is driving them, to see what policies are being implemented, to see what environmental forecasts are involved, and to see what the internal logic of the proposal actually is. The examiner will have the budget narrative as a road map, but will deconstruct the numbers to make sure that she understands how the service delivery plan works and how that matches the narrative. The examiner will be less knowledgeable about details of the program under review than those who run the program, but will not be uninformed and powerless to review.

Agency budget requests will often be analyzed twice within the executive branch. First, an analyst within an agency is looking to bring forward a request that best reflects the program of that agency and stands the best chance of ultimately being approved and executed. The objective is to produce the best case for the agency's proposals against those from other agencies. Second, an analyst within a central budget office is reviewing a request to ensure that it best reflects the program interests of the chief executive and, if approved, can be executed as intended. Both examiners ultimately have the interests of the public as their objective, but their particular twists on the analysis will be slightly different, as you can appreciate.

Reviewing a Budget Request

A budget reviewer will go through several steps in the analysis of a department or division budget. The materials used in the review will include (1) the budget instruction under which the budget proposal has been prepared (chief executive priorities, ceilings, standard price increases for categories such as motor fuel that are purchased by many departments, etc.), (2) the narrative for that agency, (3) the budget request numbers for that agency, (4) prior-year budgets and appropriations to that agency, and (5) a report of execution of that budget for the current year (budgets are always being reviewed in the midst of budget execution, and those reports give useful information about the budget proposal because the execution gives the freshest fiscal information about the agency—a first review step is to determine whether the current pace of spending will use up the appropriation and whether what is found is consistent with the budget request).[11] With those information sources, the analyst considers these questions:

1. **Policy.** The reviewer must consider what the policy rationale is for the agency's proposal. Among the questions to be considered are these: Is the problem real? Is the problem something that this government should be doing something about? Is the strategy that the agency is proposing likely to be successful? Will the program make any difference? What is the chief executive's view on the policy under consideration? Does the narrative reflect the chief executive's expressed priorities? If not, it is unlikely that the chief executive will want the budget transmitted for legislative approval to be heavy on that sort of proposal. The analyst would normally check with the agency to see whether or not it might want to try again, no matter what the submission timetable was.

2. **Arithmetic.** The math gets checked again. The reviewer must verify the arithmetic used to produce program requests. Errors and overambitious rounding seem to increase requests more often than they reduce them.

3. **Linkages.** Reviewers should check linkages between justifications and dollar requests. Is there reason to believe that the request will have the expected result, or will things stay about the same regardless of the money requested? Requests in the latter category are good candidates for elimination. Does the budget narrative get reflected in the budget request? Suppose the police department narrative emphasizes a new program that moves the police out of cars and onto bicycles as a program of heavier engagement in the community and of environmental sensitivity. If that is there, the analyst would look for bicycles in the budget and maybe for less motor fuel. The words need to be reflected in the numbers because the words establish the intended policy response to the expected service environment.

4. **Agency competence.** Does the budget request suggest that the agency understands what is going on? If the request appears to have been prepared by an extrapolation or projection of expenditure categories in prior years, then the agency administrator is either lazy or inept or has no understanding of the

---

[11]In other words, if the budget request is being analyzed with three months left in the fiscal year, divide actual spending by the agency to date by 9 and multiply by 12 to see whether the resulting number is considerably above or below the appropriation. If it is considerably below, is the budget request for the next year reduced, and, if not, why not? At least ask questions about the request on the basis of the comparison.

process of providing the assigned service. This person is officially a wiener, and it is the job of the budget examiner to roast him or her. Projections of prior growth do not make a legitimate budget request—no policy, no expectations about operating conditions, no idea how the agency fits together.

5. **Spending drivers.** Figure out what drives the budget and make sure that relationships are reasonable. For instance, many city police department budgets are driven by cops and cars—those two inputs, and inputs closely associated with them (e.g., motor fuel and fringe benefits), create much of the budget and changes from one year to the next. The budget analyst needs to ensure that changes in these critical inputs are consistent with the narrative and that internal relationships between these inputs are reasonable. For instance, is the police budget request being manipulated by a change in the established replacement cycle for police cars? If so, is this a reasonable and conscious policy, or is it simply an attempt to kick the problem down to later years? Agencies will differ in terms of what the drive inputs are—a city water utility is likely to have different critical inputs than the city police department, and the U.S. Department of Defense will be completely different. Part of the reverse engineering that the budget examiner does will involve identifying the major spending drivers.

6. **Omissions.** The reviewer must seek omissions from the budget requests. Some years ago a major university constructed a large center for performing and creative arts, but neglected to request money to cover electricity and other utilities needed for its operation. That created significant budget problems during the first year because major reductions had to be imposed on other university activities (but not football) to cover that utility bill. The reviewer should also consider whether the agency is planning to mix capital funds with operating funds.

7. **Ratios, shares, execution, and trends.** The reviewer must use all resources available for analysis, particularly the prior-year budget and actual expenditure, the current-year budget and reported expenditure to date, and the proposed budget. A comparison of these documents can be made without undue trouble, especially as the analyst has been keeping track of the agency throughout the operating year. The analyst should establish the cause of any deviations from trends apparent in those comparisons. The analyst often computes ratios and shares of cost elements over time and across agencies to identify variances and to raise questions for the agency (Sidebar 3–2 discusses ratios and shares in greater detail). Ratios, shares, and trends seldom answer questions by themselves, but they frequently do open up topics for further inquiry. Compare the budget request with the requests and appropriations for previous years and, crucially, with the execution report for the current year. Are there significant changes in trends and relationships between inputs and programs, and are any changes explained in the narrative? Are changes based on different service policies or on changing prices for inputs? Are certain input categories likely to be underspent or overspent this year, based on the execution reports, and is there a reasonable adjustment in the budget request?

Sidebar 3–2
Ratios and Shares

Management guru Peter F. Drucker writes, "A database, no matter how copious, is not information. It is information ore. For raw material to become information, it must be organized for a task, directed toward specific performance, applied to a decision. Raw material cannot do that itself."[1]

Budget documents provide a rich lode of data about agencies, but those data are raw. Budget analysts regularly calculate ratios and shares from that data to convert them into information that might help make a decision. For example, it may be interesting to know that East Liverpool spends $400,000 on police salaries, but real insight requires the number to be related to something, often through a ratio or a share. What ratio or share might help, given the considerable array of possible computations that could be made? Ratios matter for forming decisions. For instance, one alligator in the swimming pool in ten years means extra care when the dog goes outside; one alligator per week means moving back to New Jersey.

Here are some fundamental data questions:

1. What period-to-period increase or decrease appears in the categories being examined? What reasons induce the changes, and are they likely to continue in the future?
2. What are the growth rates of elements in the budget totals? Which categories are driving the overall growth, what appears to be causing those patterns, and what are the prospects for the future?
3. To what should the data be compared? You have a number. Against what other value does it need to be compared to give information? What goes in the denominator of the ratio helps make sense of the data. An irrelevant comparison number leads to misguided decisions.
4. How large is the element under consideration, relative to the entity under consideration? Is it big, considering the economy, population, geography, or whatever else may be important?

Ratios and shares do not, by themselves, answer analytic questions, but they can highlight avenues for further inquiry. The analyst spends much time computing them and deducing what additional questions need to be asked. Much of the effort involves comparisons of ratios across units and across time. There will be no "right" value for a particular ratio. Rather, the ratios provide clues that may open avenues of understanding for the analyst and decision-makers.

[1] Peter F. Drucker, "Be Data Literate—Know What to Know," *Wall Street Journal*, December 1, 1992, A-16.

8. **Choices within limits.** The reviewer must understand that resources are finite and choices must be made among worthwhile programs. Government programs to improve adult literacy and to reduce fatalities at rural intersections both yield a return that is important for society. But if government resource constraints prevent both programs from being included in the executive budget at the full amount requested by the operating agencies

proposing them, a choice has to be made between the two—and there is no common denominator (a social value "converter" between more literate adults and fewer deaths in the country) between the two programs. The choice will be fuzzy, imprecise, and somewhat discomforting. But it is a choice (one of many) that has to be made. Also, if the request involves moving some activities to outside contractors or moving some previously contracted activities back into the agency, the reviewer needs to question the reason and the justification to see whether performance improvement or cost reduction has been sufficiently demonstrated (movements in and out are costly, so they should not be done on whim).

9. **Performance.** The reviewer considers the performance documentation provided by the agency, the extent to which the measures provided are consistent with the mission and goals of the agency, the extent to which accomplishment is appropriate to the budgetary resources available to the agency, and how the performance plan relates to the budget request of the agency. It is important to consider the extent to which measures are germane to the mission of the agency and extend beyond just measuring things that are easily measured. Poor performance may, if the work of the agency is sufficiently important to the citizenry, provide a reason for increasing the budget of the agency rather than for cutting its budget. It is expected that there will be a link between achievement of the performance measures and the implementation of the budget.

The reviewer is examining the budget request as representative of the chief executive and of the taxpaying/service-receiving public. The objective is not to irritate the person who prepared the request, although that may happen along the way, but to make sure that planned services get provided as effectively, efficiently, and economically as possible.

The Budget Presentation

Although the budget has been presented in written form, agency administrators usually will need to make a formal, oral presentation of the budget to a budget policy committee, a legislative group, or others. There are varying degrees of formality to the presentation and of tension associated with the event. In many instances, the ⟨...⟩ to which the budget is being presented, although well-meaning and serious,

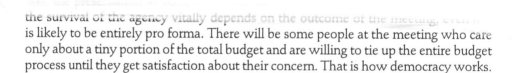

the survival of the agency vitally depends on the outcome of the meeting, even if is likely to be entirely pro forma. There will be some people at the meeting who care only about a tiny portion of the total budget and are willing to tie up the entire budget process until they get satisfaction about their concern. That is how democracy works.

The presentation should provide an overview of what the budget is about and, in particular, how each segment contributes to the fundamental objectives of the organization. It should direct special attention to the larger elements of the budget, even though nonexperts will feel more comfortable discussing smaller items. The administrator's objective in the presentation is to bring the committee into support of the agency budget, and that includes support for the large elements, even though their understanding may be somewhat imperfect. In many respects, the administrator seeks to teach the committee about the agency, its reason for existence, the things it intends to achieve, and how the budget works to reach those objectives.

Some administrators take a hide-and-seek approach with their budget presentations. In other words, there are problem areas in the budget request, but the review committee will have to find them on their own if they can. An alternate approach is entirely opposite. The administrator directs the attention of the committee to the problem areas and then takes the offensive in terms of building the agency view (or spin) on the topic. In this approach, the agency position sets the standard, establishes the environment, and draws the boundaries for the committee discussion. Many administrators are more comfortable with this approach and find it to be extremely useful. It also has the advantage of better following the governance principle of transparency than does the hide-and-seek approach.

Budget committee processes are ultimately uncontrollable by the agency administrator making the budget presentation, and a committee member can raise an entirely unpredictable question of fact, one that even the best administrator would not be able to answer without doing considerable background research. In this eventuality, the administrator has a choice: (1) admit that he or she does not know the answer, but will provide the answer soon after doing some checking, or (2) give a ballpark answer from out of thin air with great confidence and great precision, knowing full well that nobody will be able to verify whether the answer is right or not and that the answer has no real bearing on the operations of the agency. Both approaches are regularly used, but the former is much to be preferred for the sake of good governance. When that approach is taken, the follow-through must be quick and complete.

The Executive Budget: The Plan and the Balancing

The executive budget document delivers the financial plan for the government, provides a clear statement of the policy vision that shaped that plan, tells the legislature and the public what enactment of the plan would bring, and provides an archive of information about the government and its agencies. It also includes information about the operating performance of the government and about the performance plan that is inherent in the financial support that is requested. In all these areas, the message needs to be communicated clearly, but concisely; many participants in the process immediately conclude malicious intent for everything

and the public.

Many governments post their budget, in detail ranging from summary to complete, on the government's website for easy access by all. Some governments also post the budget requests transmitted by the agencies to the central budget office.

The budget, like that delivered to Congress by the president or presented by other executives to their legislative bodies, typically contains four basic elements:

1. **The budget message** is an introduction, from the chief executive, that highlights the major conditions surrounding the budget's preparation (economic conditions, perceived social problems, service priorities, etc.) and the primary changes proposed in the budget. The message sets the tone for the budget ("hard times," "new beginnings and new challenges," "change," "emerging from severe fiscal crisis," "new hope," "new era of responsibility," etc.); in simple budgets, this may be the only narrative in the entire document.[12] The message is where the executive (president, governor, mayor, etc.) makes a statement about which goals matter to him or her and what initiatives are planned.

2. **Several summary schedules,** the type and number of which vary by budget, gather the major aggregates planned in the full document. These schedules include both revenue and expenditure categories, each organized by classification schemes seen as important by the government (revenue by source, expenditure by object class, expenditure by organizational unit, expenditure by function, etc.). Schedules ordinarily include the budget-year amounts and comparable figures for the current and most recently completed years.

3. **Detail schedules,** the heart of the budget, explain why the administrative departments seek the money they hope to spend. Estimates may also be presented for several out-years to provide information about long-term trends and impacts on budgets of decisions now and of external developments (e.g., economic or demographic change). The details are presented in at least one and usually more of the following organizational structures: by administrative unit (the department, division, etc., responsible for spending and delivering services), by program or function (the type of service delivered), or by object of expenditure (the input classes to be purchased). Most governments also include a performance plan and report for each agency. These schedules state the actual results in terms of measured indexes for the closed fiscal year and planned accomplishments for the budget year.

4. **Supplemental data** also may be included in the budget document, depending on the information requirements placed on the executive by the legislative body and on the special problems or opportunities encountered by the subject government. Most budgets, including the federal budget, include supplemental tables and displays that are useful and interesting, but have no direct bearing on the key tasks of the budget. Other examples of displays

---

[12]For more about the strategy of that message, see Henry W. Maier, *Challenge to the Cities: An Approach to a Theory of Urban Leadership* (New York: Random House, 1966). Maier was the longtime mayor of Milwaukee.

that governments use include detailed historical tables on tax rates, analysis of grant revenue, debt schedules, and special detail on pension and other trust funds.

Building the executive budget from the agency plans requires a serious struggle to get program plans to fit within resources available to the government. Using executive priorities as a guide, the central budget office crafts the budget on behalf of the chief executive by cutting some plans, scaling back other plans, stretching out the pace of programs, and even proposing revenue options to enhance available resources. Controls on filling vacant positions, cuts in supply and equipment purchase proposals, and reduction of inflation adjustments are reasonably uncomplicated mechanisms for dealing with minor imbalances; such adjustments, along with the savings resulting from normal review of agency proposals within the template offered by the chief executive's vision for the future, provide orderly accommodations to resources that "meat-ax" approaches (such as reducing all proposals by a flat percentage, denying all plans for new services, or cutting any proposed increases that exceed a prescribed rate) do not afford. The responsible budget office makes a spending program proposal that can be executed within the funds that the government has for the year. This is the place where the avalanche of good to the public gets adjusted to fit within the resources available to the that year, where fiscal sustainability ultimately gets enforced (or not

Making Budget Reductions for Fiscal Sustainability

When the crunch hits and service programs have to be reduced for the government as a whole, there is no easy approach. It is assumed that the poorly justified and unjustifiable programs have been purged from the proposal and that options for increasing revenues have been rejected—and that the jurisdiction has rejected the policy of deliberately not paying its bills or of delaying their payment into future budget years. So how does a budget executive proceed with making the reductions among good public programs? There is no standard "best practice" for this task. Here are some approaches that administrators have regularly used to make the reductions:

1. **Make across-the-board reductions.** If proposed spending exceeds anticipated revenue by 5 percent, then reduce all budget proposals by that flat amount. It punts the hard choices to the program administrators who then have to decide how to manage the reduction. But at least the program administrators make the detailed adjustments; because they understand program operations better than the central administration, the odds of preserving the most significant elements of programs are improved. It is certainly a better approach than alternatives like the next one.

2. **Make centrally determined reductions in certain expense categories.** In this alternative, the central executive directs what changes will

3 percent, contracted services by no more than 5 percent, and so on, until a given expense saving is produced. Or save personnel and operating costs by reducing hours in which service units are open, reduce frequency with which certain services (e.g., trash collection or mosquito spraying) are provided, increase the number of students in each classroom, and so on. The problem is that opportunities for economization are not the same in all departments and the administrator of the program is far more likely to know what those alternatives are than is the central executive. The cutback program needs to utilize the knowledge and skills of program administrators to the greatest degree possible, and these category constraints stand in the way of that.

3. **Postpone all new programs.** This approach protects existing programs and those who benefit from them. As a result, it can help politically because the new programs have not developed a constituency yet. It may not be a good result for the public, however, because some of the new programs may be far more valuable than the existing ones.

4. **Stop or slow capital spending.** The purchase of new capital infrastructure usually involves large-ticket items. One such delay can have a far greater fiscal impact in the year than lots of decisions about operating expense categories. Some capital equipment, such as police cars or computers, may be on a standard replacement cycle, and money can be saved by stretching out that cycle (so that cars are kept four years rather than three). But that piece of new capital equipment may provide lots of service for the public and may reduce the cost of operating old equipment. Therefore, the cost saving may come at considerable expense to the public. Deferred maintenance is also a regular strategy, at least until the bridges start collapsing.

5. **Fire people, furlough people, leave vacant positions vacant, pay people less, cut benefits.** Government programs tend to be labor intensive, so a considerable share of total spending for operations each year is for personnel. If the administrator looks for cuts in places where there is money, the personnel line item will pop up. This is a tough choice politically. It also is tough for efficiency: losing people hurts the productivity of those remaining, requires readjustment in how services are delivered, and creates gaps that will be hard to fill when government operations expand in the future. In addition, some governments operate under terms of union contracts, and this can significantly complicate the process. Some governments have reduced spending by contracting out provision of certain services to a surrounding or overlapping government, as when Pontiac, Michigan, disbanded its police department in 2010, replacing the service with a contract with the Oakland County sheriff's department.[13] Cost may be reduced—and probably also the level of service.

6. **Draw down supply inventories.** Service production requires some inventories of materials and supplies (fuel, road salt, paper and forms, etc.). Agency

---

[13]Mike Martindale, "Pontiac Disbanding Police Department," *Detroit News,* October 13, 2010.

operations over time will have developed a particular supply system that automatically orders more when the inventory falls below a set level. Moving that level lower will reduce the ordering pace and the amount spent in a particular year. Similarly, agencies may stretch out the replacement cycle for some operating equipment, for instance, delaying the cycle for replacement of police vehicles for a year. Operating and maintenance costs will increase, but probably by less than postponed vehicle cost.

7. **Suck it up and make the hard choice.** Somebody got elected to make the tough choices on behalf of the people. That person or group of people has to decide what services are most important to the public as a whole and what services are less important and, on that basis, make the appropriate shifts in resources. Cut where the return to the public is less and protect where the return is greatest. That's what executives are supposed to do. You wanted the job, so do it. The choices can't be contracted out.[14] Once the choices about what services are most important and what services can be reduced have been made, it is reasonable to leave the detailed management choices to the program administrators. Within their range of competence (fire protection, parks and recreation, etc.), they know more about operations than do the central executives and are better positioned to deal with the spending reductions.

8. **More revenue.** A final budget balancing approach is to behave more like a private business. When demand for product increases or when costs of operation increase, a business increases its prices. In a similar vein, governments should consider revenue increases to deal with their budget imbalances. In other words, they should consider increasing their tax and user charge rates. This alternative will usually be politically difficult, but quite possibly more consistent with the public interest than taking the expenditure reducing (and service cutting) actions previously noted.

Managing Budget Execution

The appropriations approved by the legislature, not the budget proposed by the executive, determine the amount of funds available for delivery of services during the budget year. This approved budget becomes the standard against which actual operations are controlled, and thus the critical managerial tool in execution, both guiding agency operations and ensuring that spending does not exceed appropriations. Appropriation is the tool that legislatures use to keep check on the actions of the executive. The approved budget establishes the control standard; other elements

---

[14] In a classic dereliction of responsibility, Alexandria, Virginia, city officials hired a professional ethicist to guide their budget priorities in 2008. What did those people think their job was when they assumed their positions? Only to make choices when the choices meant more for everybody? Michael Laris, "A

of the execution process measure actual performance against that standard and implement control systems to correct the variance.[15] In practice, systems institute several budget controls:

1. **Preventive controls** are established to block actions that would violate standards. To prevent such violations, some governments establish extraordinary procedures for reviewing planned purchases with price tags that exceed a set limit; the limits tend to be lower when funds are tight. Even more governments apply special pre-audits to establish the appropriateness of payment before checks are written, often requiring approval by multiple independent authorities before spending occurs. (Some of these approvals may represent needless red tape.)

2. **Feed-forward controls** perform diagnostic or therapeutic actions in the spending process. Variance reports may automatically place stop orders on certain accounts when differences between actual expenditures and budgeted expenditures exceed certain levels.

3. **Feedback controls** start corrections into the budget cycle for the future. The comparison between budgeted expenditures and actual expenditures within the fiscal year is important information for those preparing, reviewing, and directing budgets for the next year.

Ordinarily, budgets are approved for an entire fiscal year, but execution of the budget occurs on a day-to-day, week-to-week basis. How can the annual budget establish a control standard for this execution? Well-functioning fiscal systems divide the total budget appropriation to operating units for the year into quarterly (or monthly) allotments by agreement with the central budget office. Suppose the Department of Streets and Storm Sewers has an appropriation of $4 million for the fiscal year from January 1 to December 31 and relatively constant expenditure rates are anticipated during the year. An allotment plan adopted by the department and the city budget office could then be as follows:

	Allotment to Quarter	Cumulative Allotments
January 1	$1,000,000	$1,000,000
April 1	1,000,000	2,000,000
July 1	1,000,000	3,000,000
October 1	1,000,000	4,000,000
Total	4,000,000	4,000,000

---

[15]In developing and transition countries, problems have arisen with "arrears," or payment obligations that the government has been unable to discharge in an acceptable time period. That stresses the economy as workers, pensioners, and suppliers who have not been paid cannot, in turn, pay their bills, and the people they owe cannot pay their bills, and so on. The problem may emerge from unrealistic budgets built on unrealistic revenue forecasts, inadequate monitoring of budget execution, or poor controls on budget administrators. The remedy, along with correcting the problems previously mentioned, is a system of commitment controls that requires clearance from a treasury or similar central entity before an operating agency can order goods or services to assure that funds/appropriations are available for paying the resulting obligation. An accurate revenue forecast should prevent the arrears problem from developing.

A comparison of actual expenditure at each quarter's end with the allotment provides an early warning for controlling department activity and preventing over-spending or unnecessary underprovision of service. If reports of spending plus com-mitments to spend (encumbrances) through the end of June exceed $2 million, the pace of operations would need to be reduced to keep within appropriations. The comparison between expenditure plan and spending activity must include both pay-ments made and contractual commitments made that will involve payment later. These latter totals have different titles in different fiscal systems (encumbrances and obligations are two), but, regardless of title, they reduce the available spending authority and must be included in the comparison against the plan. Although the accounting system (correctly) would not regard the money as having been spent, the manager must recognize that the budget resource is gone as soon as the com-mitment occurs.

Service delivery, and hence spending profiles, for many agencies is not spread equally throughout the year. A typical outdoor swimming pool in the northern United States will be in service during the summer months only, so its operating expenditures concentrate in these months; equal quarterly allotments would not be useful for control and management. Activities that produce uneven expenditure flows during the year (seasonal needs, major capital equipment acquisitions, open-ing or closing new facilities, etc.) require uneven allotments. The allotment schedule must be consistent with both the approved budget and the activity-flow expecta-tions if it is to be useful for control and management.

Comparisons of the allotments and expenditures to date (variances) can suggest (1) areas in which expenditure may have to be curtailed, (2) areas in which surpluses may be available for use against deficits in other areas, (3) patterns that may be helpful in the preparation of future budgets, and (4) the possible need to request a supplemental appropriation (funds beyond those initially appropriated for the fiscal year). Some faster-than-allotment spending may simply be accelerated acquisition (e.g., transfer between quarters to take advantage of low prices not anticipated when the budget was prepared). Other spending may imply spending above the approved appropriation. These latter overruns require spending-unit action to control the flow, generally according to budget office direction. Both agencies and finance officers can thus maintain better control of budget execution with these periodic allotment-to-expenditure comparisons. Although the objective of execution is delivery of services to the public, funds must not be spent in a fashion contrary to the appropriation.

Some government units find that there is no special seasonal pattern to their major expenditure categories. Those units may use simple budget-status reports, which compare the percentage of total budget used (spent and obligated) at a par-ticular date with the percentage of the fiscal year expired. If the percentage of budget used exceeds the percentage of year expired, a problem may exist in that portion of the agency operations. Such a budget-status (or budget-variance) report for a trans-portation authority appears in Figure 3–1. This report is for the midpoint in the fiscal year and works to focus attention on spending categories in which the rate of spend-ing appears to vary from the full plan. Note that there are dangers in being lulled into inattention by percentages: a small percentage variance in a large budget line can be

Figure 3–1
A Budget-Variance Report: Capital Metropolitan Transportation Authority (Austin, Texas)

Capital Metropolitan Transportation Authority
Statement of Revenues, Expenses, and Changes in Net Position for Q2FY 2015

		FY 2015 Year-to-Date			YTD (Actuals)
	YTD Budget Q2 FY2015	YTD Actual Q2 FY2015	YTD Variance Fav/(Unfav)	YTD Var % Fav/(Unfav)	YTD % of Total
Operating Revenues:					
Passenger Fares	$ 7,704,278	$ 7,909,674	$ 205,396	2.7%	8.0%
Third Party Fares	2,685,760	2,918,205	232,445	8.7%	2.9%
Freight Rail Revenue	2,402,519	2,514,857	112,338	4.7%	2.5%
Other Revenue	1,176,098	1,155,785	(20,313)	-1.7%	1.2%
Total Operating Revenue:	**13,968,655**	**14,498,521**	**529,866**	**3.8%**	**14.6%**
Operating Expenses:					
Salaries & Benefits	17,106,542	16,625,720	480,822	2.8%	16.7%
Professional Services	13,008,342	9,676,026	3,332,316	25.6%	9.7%
Materials and Supplies	2,058,060	806,300	1,251,760	60.8%	0.8%
Fuel & Fluids	10,055,977	7,489,736	2,566,241	25.5%	7.5%
Utilities	1,280,226	1,116,412	163,814	12.8%	1.1%
Insurance	1,682,558	1,757,714	(75,156)	-4.5%	1.8%
Taxes	528,270	513,518	14,752	2.8%	0.5%
Purchased Transportation	59,348,283	60,258,593	(910,310)	-1.5%	60.7%
Other Expenses	3,927,045	274,856	3,652,189	93.0%	0.3%
Interest Expense	300,546	301,248	(702)	-0.2%	0.3%
Lease/Rental	846,396	463,770	382,626	45.2%	0.5%
Total Operating Expenses	**110,142,245**	**99,283,893**	**10,858,352**	**9.9%**	**100.0%**
Operating Income/(Loss)	**(96,173,590)**	**(84,785,372)**	**(10,328,486)**	**10.7%**	**-85.4%**
Non-Operating Revenue/(Expenses):					
Sales Tax	97,996,882	101,711,444	3,714,562	3.8%	102.4%
Investment Income	44,215	75,562	31,347	70.9%	0.1%
Operating Grant Revenue	10,142,758	10,412,763	270,005	2.7%	10.5%
Capital Grant Revenue	1,191,809	1,805,499	613,690	51.5%	1.8%
Total Non-Operating Revenue/(Expenses)	**109,375,664**	**114,005,268**	**4,629,604**	**4.2%**	**114.8%**
Change in net position available for financing and capital activities	**$ 13,202,074**	**$ 29,219,896**	**$ 16,017,822**	**121.3%**	**29.4%**

caused by price surprises, demands for service, supply problems, or alternative uses of resources in providing the service. There should not be a variance because the agency changed its basic service provision plan, however. The figure is for an agency that sells its services, so its variance report includes revenues as well as spending. A governmental department would not be expected to have that component because revenue collection is done by a department specializing in that work.

Governments establish special rules within which their agencies may move funds around in response to conditions not foreseen when appropriations were made. At the federal level, *reprogramming* is the use of funds within an appropriation account for purposes other than those contemplated at the time of appropriation. Consultation between the agency and the appropriate substantive and appropriation committees of Congress usually precedes the action, which may involve formal notification and an opportunity for disapproval by the committees. *Transfers* move all or part of budget authority in an account to another account or subdivision of an account (e.g., moving funds from Operation and Maintenance to Personnel). Such changes require statutory authority, although some agencies have transfer authority within an established percentage or absolute limits.[16] State and local governments have similar, although often less formal, procedures. Often states establish interim committees to provide needed flexibility during periods of legislative recess, a vital adjustment feature where the legislature meets only periodically. Executives of nonprofit organizations would usually have considerable flexibility, although major shifts might require discussion with a board of directors.

Internal Controls

Program managers are obviously concerned with delivery of services according to plan. Financial managers are simultaneously concerned with maintaining internal control, defined as the methods and procedures within the agency established to safeguard assets, check the accuracy and reliability of financial and other data, promote operational efficiency, and encourage adherence to the prescribed policies and procedures of the agency.[17] Internal controls represent the first line of defense against fraud and corruption.

Some basic steps in establishing internal control include the following:[18]

1. **Provide qualified personnel, rotate duties, and enforce annual leaves/ vacations.** This policy ensures capable handling of tasks and ensures that irregularities can be found when new staff take over tasks on rotation or on temporary assignment. Every person involved in financial operations

---

[16] General Accounting Office, *Budget Reprogramming, Department of Defense Process for Reprogramming Funds,* GAO/NSIAD-86-164BR (Washington, D.C.: General Accounting Office, July 1986).

[17] Paul E. Heeschen and Lawrence B. Sawyer, *Internal Auditors Handbook* (Altamonte Springs, Fla.: Institute of Internal Auditors, 1984), 36.

[18] The federal standards for internal controls appear in OMB Circular A-123, available on the OMB website. Internal control checklists are easily available from many organizations.

should be required to take a vacation of one week each year so that another employee will be in a position to see fraudulent activities. Personnel who are required to work beyond the limits of their capabilities are dangerous because they hold employment more tenuously and are thus more susceptible to requests for inappropriate actions.

2. **Segregate responsibility.** Dividing related duties and operating responsibilities among two or more qualified people reduces the chance of error or fraud by providing checks and balances on work performed. The bank statement must be sent to and reviewed by a person who does not have check signing authority. If the entity issues credit cards, statements must be reviewed by a person other than the ones using the cards and credit cards outstanding have to be closely controlled.

3. **Separate operations and accounting.** Divide the responsibilities for operational transactions (purchasing, receiving, collecting, etc.) from maintenance of accounting records to reduce chances for error or theft. Maintain a separate reconciliation of transaction records.

4. **Assign responsibility.** This ensures that tasks are performed and that the appropriate party in questioned transactions can be identified.

5. **Maintain controlled proofs and security.** Maintain segregated bank accounts and closely control cash and negotiable documents. Issue sequentially numbered receipts for collections, and avoid cash payments as much as is feasible. Make orders only from numbered and controlled standard purchase orders. Make payments only according to standard separate authorizations, and require bonding for any employees with access to significant amounts of organization funds. Require dual signatures on checks so that no single person in the organization can write a check. Regularly review and test internal control systems. Mark invoices as "paid" as soon as payment is made.

6. **Record transactions and safeguard assets.** Promptly record and accurately classify events and transactions. Limit access to source records and government assets to authorized individuals. Immediate deposit of receipts with "for deposit only" endorsement, daily list of all deposits, separation of responsibility between person who has custody of deposits and person who records them.

These steps can help implement the internal control standards of the International Organization of Supreme Audit Institutions, of which the Government Accountability Office is a part: documentation, prompt and proper recording of transactions and events, authorization and execution of transactions and events, separation of duties, supervision, and access to and accountability for resources and records.[19] These control devices can reduce the chances of theft, error, and fraud. Although they offer no protection against poor public choices, they can help ensure

---

[19] Internal Control Standards Committee, International Organization of Supreme Audit Institutions, *Guidelines for Internal Control Standards* (June 1992), 9.

that choices get executed as they have been made, for better or worse. So many instances of theft from government could have easily been prevented with the most rudimentary system of internal controls.

An Intra-Year Cash Budget

A cash budget is a detailed translation of the enacted budget into revenue and expenditure flows through the operating year. It yields a forecast of disbursements, receipts, cash balances, and needs for financing over the budget period, taken at regular points throughout the year. It is based on likely (or known and controllable) patterns.

1. The pay cycle for employees is known, as are the wage-and-salary commitments in the enacted budget. From that information, the payment amounts can be forecast throughout the year—employees will be paid agreed amounts on certain days of the month throughout the year.
2. The pattern of payments to suppliers (contractors, utilities, etc.) is established, along with the budgeted amounts of those payments.
3. Large payments—payments of principal and interest of debt or purchases of large equipment—are in the adopted budget and are known in advance. Purchases of some large-ticket items may even be controlled within the budget year, so that payment is made shortly after large revenue inflows, not shortly before, to ensure that sufficient cash is on hand without any need for short-term borrowing.
4. Tax and charge revenues are usually driven by regular seasonal patterns. Collections are high in some months and low in others because of the fluctuations of economic activity within the year (high season and low season for some industries, due dates for quarterly payments, etc.). For instance, analysis of data from several recent years might show that sales tax payments received in January are typically 8.5 percent of the annual total. With these patterns known, the revenue forecast for the budget year can easily be translated into its likely monthly flow. Multiply the total sales tax forecast for the entire year by 8.5 percent to get the expected collections in January and so on through the rest of the months.

The cash budget is helpful to execution of the annual budget because it shows when the government might not have sufficient funds to cover the bills coming due at particular points during the year. That warns when the government might need to arrange a very short-term loan from local banks to tide it over the cash shortage and may allow the government to adjust some flows in or out to avoid the need for such a loan. That would save the interest that otherwise would need to be paid on the loan. Preparing such an estimated cash budget is a helpful practice for government fiscal officers. Furthermore, careful estimation of the payment outflows can be helpful in establishing allotment patterns for dividing the annual appropriation for

Audit and Evaluation

When the budget year is over, several questions should be asked. One basic question is whether the budget was executed as it was passed. The adopted budget should reflect priorities for government expenditures and the intentions for funding that spending. If the budget was responsibly developed and became, by legislative action, the legal fiscal plan, then it should be executed intact, subject to emergency changes beyond accommodation within the enacted budget.

A first key check is to establish that the executed budget and the adopted budget do coincide. Did spending occur according to plan or did it have to be reduced because of revenue shortfalls? Do the plans reflected in the budget match actual expenditure patterns at the close of the year? If they do not, have appropriate procedures been followed during execution to make the changes? In other words, the budget law must be followed if the budget process is to be meaningful in terms of legally adopted plans to be executed. This highlights the need to make sure that, during execution of the budget, expenditures get accounted for properly. For instance, an agency likely has more than one budget account to administer—for example, an account for central office administration and another one for field delivery of services. As the agency works through the year, it will spend from both accounts. It is important that, when payments get made, the accounting system takes payment from the proper account—the telephone bills for the field get paid from the field account and not the central account, for instance. A correct accounting is necessary to keep operations in line with the adopted plan reflected in the budget, prevents illegal movement of funds from one account to another, and provides a sound information base for development of future budgets.

Other questions are asked through the external audit process. Many audits are conducted using a prescribed checklist of steps to establish uniformity in how several different auditors perform a class of audits. Much of the audit focuses on controls built into the systems of the agency. If the internal control/internal audit system operates satisfactorily, the external audit agency need not be concerned with tracing the body of individual transactions because the system produces substantial compliance. The audit does, however, test that system. Accounting controls prevent fraud and waste, ensure the accuracy of operations, ensure compliance with applicable laws, and promote adherence to stated policies (including legislation). The audit determines whether those control systems work. In their audit, examiners look for errors and abuses such as those listed in Table 3–2. Much of the audit employs statistical sampling to permit probabilistic inferences about the extent of error in the total record population. There is seldom reason to scrutinize all records.

What Audits Need to Prevent: Some Methods of Stealing from Government

Stealing from government is normally rare in the twenty-first century. A robust budget process, including strong internal controls, clear appropriations and fiscal

Table 3–2
Some Errors, Abuses, and Manipulations Sought by Auditors

- Year-end accounting manipulations that push revenues and expenditures from one year to the next to increase or decrease totals in the year
- Unrecorded liabilities: commitments to vendors that are suppressed by withholding written agreements and purchase orders from the paperwork system
- Overforecasting of revenues to keep tax rates down or spending up
- Failure to reserve adequately for nonpayment of taxes
- Miscalculation of utility, hospital, and other service bills
- Unauthorized transfer of funds between appropriation accounts
- Recording of grant receipts in the wrong funds
- Use of a commingled cash account to disguise use of restricted funds for unauthorized purposes
- Failure to observe legal requirements for review and approval of budgets
- Failure to compile and submit financial reports to state and federal agencies punctually
- Improper computation of state aid claims

SOURCE: Peter F. Rousmaniere, *Local Government Auditing—A Manual For Public Officials* (New York: Council on Municipal Performance, 1980), 10 with revisions.

responsibilities, and capable external audit, usually keeps theft in check. (Waste is another matter.) Nevertheless, thefts from government do still happen and receive extensive publicity when they are discovered, and they do make headlines when they occur. It is worthwhile to review some of the methods that have historically been used to steal from government.

GHOSTING

Theft through phantom resources—receiving payment for resources not actually delivered—can take several forms. One method, the ghost employee, involves placing on an agency payroll an individual who does not work for that agency. The person receives pay, but provides no service. A second method is payment for supplies or services that are not delivered. Invoices sent by the firm show delivery, but the agency never receives the supplies or services. A third method is double payment for supplies or services. The services are performed once, but invoices show delivery of two shipments. Each method causes the government to pay for resources not delivered, and each artificially increases the cost of public service.

BID RIGGING

The procurement fix involves rigging bids on supply contracts. Suppose a section of highway is to be repaved. Potential suppliers would establish beforehand the bid winner and the winning price; other firms would submit noncompetitive bids. Firms would cooperate in the collusion because their turn to win would come on another project. The collusion increases the profits of the firms and increases the cost of government. Government employees may or may not profit from the procurement fix, depending on the arrangements of the scheme.

HONEST GRAFT

"Honest" graft uses advance information or information known only to a small number of government officials to produce private profit for the individual employee. The reminiscences of George Washington Plunkitt, Tammany Hall leader of early twentieth-century New York City, describe the process:

> There's an honest graft, and I'm an example of how it works. I might sum up the whole thing by sayin': I seen my opportunities and I took' em.
>
> Just let me explain by example. My party's in power in the city, and it's goin' to undertake a lot of public improvements. Well I'm tipped off, say, that they're going to lay out a new park at a certain place.
>
> I see my opportunity and I take it. I go to that place and I buy up all the land I can in the neighborhood. Then the board of this or that makes its plan public, and there is a rush to get my land, which nobody cared particular for before.
>
> Ain't it perfectly honest to charge a good price and make a profit on my investment and foresight?[20]

That profit measures the extent to which the honest grafter, through use of inside information, steals from the public by forcing excess payments for a resource. Honest graft may similarly involve acquisition or establishment of companies to do business with a government. Bid specifications may be written so that a company would be the only one qualified. Requirements for the commodity or service would be artificially increased for the enrichment of the government employee.

DIVERSION[21]

Public assets or the service of employees may be stolen for private use. Office supplies, equipment, gasoline, and so on are as usable for private purposes as for government activities. Public employees may be diverted to private uses, including construction or maintenance projects on property owned by government officials. Employees are sometimes used as workers in political campaigns while on government time—a special illegal advantage of incumbency. These activities involve straightforward stealing because individuals use assets owned by the government without payment. But there are other approaches: poor controls over the use of government credit cards can provide modern thieves a highly effective tool for diverting public assets far beyond the dreams of corrupt public employees of earlier years. Too many government credit cards floating in a local government represent an improvised explosive device waiting to be detonated in the local Wal-Mart, at least in figurative terms.

---

[20] William L. Riordon, *Plunkitt of Tammany Hall* (New York: E. P. Dutton, 1963), 3.
[21] For good illustrations of how diversion and shoddy material approaches to corruption work, watch *Catch 22,* a 1970 movie based on Joseph Heller's novel of the same name and pay particular attention to the work of First Lieutenant Milo Minderbinder.

SHODDY MATERIAL

Because low-quality supplies and materials can generally be delivered at lower cost than can higher-quality supplies and materials, government contract specifications require delivery of quality material. A contractor who provides lower-than-specified quality (shoddy material) can thus profit at public expense. The Chicago experience goes back to 1869 when city officials painted City Hall, but used cheap whitewash and pocketed the amount that would have been spent on more costly paint.[22]

KICKBACKS

Public officials who have power to select who receives contracts to do business with governments, what banks receive public deposits, and who works for government agencies may profit by arranging for artificially high contract awards or artificial wage payments with a portion of that payment kicked back to the government official. The favored individual or firm receives higher than the appropriate price for the contracted service and thus is able to profit even after making the payment to the contracting agent. Also, legislators have opportunities to shape appropriation bills to include the goods or services sold by a particular vendor. Sometimes, the payment goes to the public official or a relative, or the business purchases something from the official or the legislator at an inflated and highly profitable price. Sometimes, the payment is in the form of giving a job to a relative of the official or the legislator. Sometimes, the payment assists the finances of the election campaign of that official or of that official's political party; in the language of the politics of the 2000s, the former is "hard money" and the latter is "soft money." Unfortunately, kickbacks and special deals seem to have become an important influence in American politics and policymaking.[23]

Corrupt businesses in less developed countries and countries in transition to market economies use political power to steal in slightly different ways from those found in developed democracies. Johnson and Kwak summarize some standard approaches: "An emerging market oligarchy uses its political power and connections to make money through such means as buying national assets at below-market prices, getting cheap loans from state-controlled banks, or selling products to the government at inflated prices."[24] Transparency, regularized fiscal processes, and internal controls normally prevent such easy pickings in other nations, although they do remain a problem in subnational governments of the United States where unskilled government officials and inadequate systems make public resources ripe for picking.

---

[22] "Corruption in Illinois: Where's Mine?" *The Economist*, June 6, 2015, 24.

[23] At one time, it was an accepted practice for firms interested in doing financial work for local governments to make significant financial contributions to local politicians before they were to be even eligible to bid for the work, a practice called "pay to play." Those requirements are now banned almost universally.

[24] Simon Johnson and James Kwak, *13 Bankers* (New York: Vantage Books, 2011), 133. Such purchases of government-owned assets, particularly involving natural resources, when the socialist economy was privatized was a source of the vast wealth of many of the "oligarchs" who are so important in the Rus-

The twenty-first century provides interesting new twists for corrupt behavior. For example, the finance director of the Los Angeles Memorial Coliseum put the purchase of new sound equipment for the government-owned facility on his personal credit card, earning a fabulous number of reward points.[25] Not only did the action violate procurement policy that forbade use of personal cards for major acquisitions, but also it raised questions about conflict of interest in choices made by the director, evaded financial controls for the jurisdiction, and probably caused the warranty on the equipment to be voided. Major purchases are done by purchase orders and checks, not credit card, because such payments are more readily controlled against unauthorized use of public funds.

Conclusion

Budget skills combine techniques that can be taught with a cunning that comes only with experience. The start for all budgets must be a sound understanding of what the agency request intends to accomplish. Without that foundation, no amount of tricks can help much. As in many government operations, the great problem is information—those who have that information and are able to communicate it have greater-than-average success. Beyond that, there are few general truths.

QUESTIONS AND EXERCISES

1. The data in the following table present revenues and expenditures by categorized type for the School of Public Affairs at Enormous State University. As with most elite programs at state universities, the school has accepted missions of teaching, research, and service to the university, state, and nation. The data include budgeted and actual data for three years and the proposed budget for fiscal 2014–2015. Your task as a budget analyst is to learn as much as possible about the operations of the school and its plans for the budget year just from these data. In particular, you should look for trends, changes in shares and ratios, and the categories that are particularly important in driving the finances of the school. A few notes about the reported data: First, the state appropriates money to the university and then the central administration distributes that money to the various operations on campus. That is the source of the state appropriation number—it has been assigned to the school, so this number for 2014–2015 is an actual. All others are part of the request. Second, the central administration charges the school for the services that it provides (central library, computer networks, etc.). This charge is the assessment number in the table. It is based on

[25] Paul Pringle and Rong-Gong Lin II, "Coliseum Finance Director Earned Visa Points on Stadium Upgrade," *Los Angeles Times*, December 10, 2011. http://articles.latimes.com/2011/dec/10/local/la-me-coliseum-20111211

	FY 2011–2012		FY 2012–2013		FY 2013–2014		FY 2014–2015
	Budget	Actual	Budget	Actual	Budget	Estimated	Budget
Student Fees	14,691,883	14,617,508	14,852,883	15,505,988	16,290,202	14,648,218	17,356,000
State Appropriation	5,391,233	5,391,233	5,155,353	5,155,353	5,100,703	5,100,703	5,150,000
Indirect Cost Income	850,000	1,048,415	900,000	943,279	900,000	1,256,485	900,000
Other Revenue	130,622	136,561	97,750	111,031	104,450	121,263	120,000
(Assessments)	(7,297,873)	(7,079,459)	(7,497,632)	(7,356,908)	(8,072,512)	(8,249,461)	(8,100,000)
TOTAL REVENUE	13,765,865	14,114,258	13,508,354	14,358,743	14,322,843	12,877,208	15,426,000
UG Financial Aid	28,000	22,500	28,000	29,075	32,000	27,000	36,000
Grade Financial Aid	1,184,510	1,181,212	1,100,510	1,147,754	1,200,442	1,358,033	1,400,000
Total Financial Aid	1,212,510	1,203,712	1,128,510	1,176,829	1,232,442	1,385,033	1,436,000
Compensation	11,616,746	11,202,082	11,674,484	10,979,134	11,563,133	11,253,420	1,204,1159
General Expenses	974,359	732,636	937,150	801,710	949,267	886,242	950,125
Travel	286,400	232,158	254,700	193,637	265,250	231,331	265,755
Capital Outlay	11,667	0	0	0	0	14,231	0
Transfers for Indirect Cost	286,848	412,080	326,304	1,164,942	439,491	688,102	458,650
Total Expenditures	14,388,530	13,782,668	14,321,148	14,316,252	14,449,583	14,458,359	15,151,689

school operations during the year, so it is an estimate and counts as a negative component in school revenue. Your answer to this exercise should include both your conclusions from your analysis and a list of questions that your analysis has led you to have for the person who prepared the 2014–2015 budget. Suppose the central administration has asked for each school to reduce its spending by 5 percent. Where would you suggest that the school turn to make that reduction?

2. The Department of Revenue wants to add more people to the unit that attempts to collect unpaid taxes through telephone contact. What questions would you, as a budget analyst, have after you receive the following request justification memorandum?

   Date: June 19, 2017

   Subject Collection Telephone Pursuit

   Currently, nineteen employees work on telephone pursuits on a full-time basis. Each employee can make an average of twenty-five to forty phone calls per day. The amount collected by the nineteen employees for the past year is $17,858,623. If we could add an automated phone system and increase our staff by ten full-time employees, we could double the number of phone calls made and increase our collections by 59 percent, or $8,900,000.

3. This table shows the staffing and pay rates of the Marshall City Fire Department:

Employee Grade	Number in Grade	Salary (in $)
Chief	1	$125,000
Shift commander	3	$90,000
Firefighter 1	12	$49,000
Firefighter 2	26	$35,000
Clerical (part-time)	3	$15,000

   The city is part of the federal Social Security system. The city and the employee each pay Social Security payroll taxes of 6.2 percent of all salary paid up to $118,500 per employee to finance federal retirement and disability insurance and 1.45 percent of all salary paid to finance Medicare. The city pays a portion of the cost of health insurance for each full-time employee, an amount equal to $180 per month. Employees are part of a pension system financed by a city payment of 20 percent of the employee's salary and an employee payment of 5 percent of the employee's salary. Full-time employees receive an allowance for uniforms of $750 per year.

   Estimate the city's full cost of fire department labor during the fiscal year, assuming no change in staffing. Separate that cost into salary and fringe-benefit components.

4. Write budget requests and justifications for each of the following program conditions. Start your request by categorizing each request as (1) new service, (2) other continuing, (3) workload change, (4) change in service level, (5) price change, (6) full financing, or (7) methods improvement. The program conditions are as follows:

a. The agency sends about 275,000 pieces of mail each year. The postal rate has increased by 2 cents per ounce.
b. The division travel appropriation has been $15,000 per year short of actual expenditure for the last three years, after internal transfers of funds.
c. Fifteen account examiners process 115,000 assistance files per year. Client growth estimates indicate that, in the next budget biennium, files will increase to 125,000 in the first year and 130,000 in the second year. (Account examiners' salaries are $3,775 per month plus fringe benefits of 25 percent.)
d. The city council appropriated $18,000 for a program to track down those not paying traffic fines. The program began in the second quarter of the fiscal year and has produced fine revenue far greater than its cost. The legal affairs division wants to continue the program throughout the entire new fiscal year.
e. The division wants to replace the computer workstations for five administrative assistants. Each workstation includes a personal computer, laser printer, and standard office workstation software.

5. The local water utility has maintained records over several years of its monthly purchases of raw water from the state water authority. The monthly averages are shown in the following table.

   Assume that the city pays a flat rate per thousand gallons of water purchased and that the fiscal year begins on July 1. Payment is made in the month after use. Prepare quarterly allotments for $8 million appropriated for water purchase.

Gallons (000s)		Gallons (000s)	
January	35,000	July	125,000
February	35,000	August	125,000
March	50,000	September	90,000
April	65,000	October	60,000
May	68,000	November	50,000
June	100,000	December	40,000

6. A progress report for the division of tourism promotion prepared for transactions through March 31 of the fiscal year, which runs from July 1 to June 30, shows that the travel account, with a total appropriation of $9,000, has expenditures to that date of $2,500 and encumbrances of $3,500. Because of an important trade fair in May, the allotment distribution for the division had 40 percent of the division budget planned for expenditure in the last quarter of the fiscal year. What is the status of the division's travel account? What managerial actions are appropriate?

7. Analyze this budget justification:

   Workload Change—Biennial Cost: $84,300

   Because of the recognition of new social procedures, our psychometricians are now able to obtain valid test results and scores, enabling our valuators to make sociological recommendations that are realistic and not stereotyped views of battering. Our evaluation professionals, plus specialty counselors with spe-

strides in bringing together battered spouses throughout the state. To achieve maximum effectiveness, an additional four counselor teams to be strategically located are essential. This success factor that we have experienced has also brought about an increase in the referral of abused children, which will also require additional case service funds.

a. List the questions you would raise about the justification if you were a budget analyst.
b. Rewrite the justification according to your understanding of what the request intends.

8. A 9-1-1 emergency telephone line provides a single telephone number to be called when help is needed. An operator receives the call and directs police and/or fire-fighter assistance as needed. The address of the call is displayed on a computer screen, along with other information appropriate to guiding a response. Calls are also recorded, providing full information about the nature of the conversation. In a major metropolitan county, the cost is around $3.6 million per year, after an installation cost of $4.5 million. The system would be financed by a tax of 1.5 percent of the monthly line charge paid to the local telephone company.

Prepare a narrative justification for initiation of such a system.

9. The Public Budgeting and Finance Association is planning its annual conference. The conference hotel has quoted the following prices for services:

Thursday afternoon	Conference facilities rental: $425
	Coffee-break service: $10 per person
	Audiovisual equipment rental: $55
	Evening reception: $25 per person
Friday	Conference facilities rental: $750
	Coffee-break service, morning and afternoon: $15 per person
	Continental breakfast: $15 per person
	Luncheon: $20 per person
	Audiovisual equipment rental: $150
Saturday morning	Conference facilities rental: $375
	Continental breakfast: $15 per person
	Coffee-break service: $10 per person
	Audiovisual rental: $75

Program materials and marketing would cost about $550. The association charged $130 for each participant last year and would like to use the same price this year.

a. Prepare a break-even chart for the conference and determine the break-even attendance level.
b. Suppose the association wanted to encourage student participation by charging a rate that would cover only the costs directly caused by their attendance. What price would you charge?
c. Prepare a budget for the event if you expect 110 people to attend.

10. Suppose you work for the city budget office. The chief budget officer for the city reports to the staff that revenues are 7.3 percent below the forecast level of $6.8 million for the first five months of the budget year. She asks for ideas on what, if anything, should be done to deal with the problem. The city is legally forbidden to borrow to cover operating deficits.

11. The manager of a municipal ice rink is concerned that the flow of patrons will not be sufficient to maintain the long-standing policy of keeping the rink on a self-supporting basis. Revenues come mainly from the hourly rental of ice time (the city has set that at $2.50 per hour per person) and skate rental ($1.50 per pair). The average ice time per patron over the last three years has been about 1.5 hours. Approximately half the patrons rent skates. Salaries, scheduled maintenance, and other overhead expenditures amount to $94,500 per year; these costs do not vary with the number of patrons. Costs that vary with the number of patrons (direct maintenance and supplies) are estimated to be $1.80 per patron hour. The number of patrons has been averaging 85,000 per year for the last three years. Is the manager right to be concerned?

12. When state finances get tough, many governors have special impoundment authority available to them. Indiana's governor is one of those. A section of the budget law states that the state may "withhold allotments of any or all appropriations . . . if it is considered necessary to do so in order to prevent a deficit financial situation." In the middle of fiscal year 2009, the Indiana governor informed the public radio station that is associated with Indiana University that it would not receive its fourth-quarter allotment. The payment was not delayed; it was gone forever. This took away revenue upon which the station had built its budget. That revenue distribution was the following: support from Indiana University, 36 percent; individual gifts, 22 percent; corporate underwriting, 17 percent; miscellaneous, 12 percent; federal support, 10 percent; and state support, 3 percent. The station reports that it has frozen hiring, cut down on travel, and postponed equipment purchases to deal with the unexpected shortfall. It also initiated a number of announcements over the air, outside of its regular fundraising events, in which it asked current donors to increase their donations and for new donors to step up. What is your assessment of this situation? What is your view of this power to suspend appropriations?

13. Federal outlays for air transportation increased from $16,743 million in 2004 to $20,923 million in 2014. The deflator for nondefense federal expenditures increased from 0.8838 in 2004 (2009 = 1.000) to 1.0893 in 2014. Answer these questions:

    a. What is the real rate of change in spending for air transportation over this period?
    b. Suppose the rate of change of prices continued through 2017 at the same rate as from 2004 to 2014. What outlay level in 2017 would provide the same real level as in 2014?

14. Governments and nonprofit organizations need systems for providing fiscal discipline and control, for directing resources to uses with the highest priority of the

not all such organizations have developed these budget and finance systems to the same degree, and those with systems do not have them structured in the same way. Select a local government or nonprofit organization in your area and analyze the budget and finance processes that it employs. This entity may be a local government (city, county, township, school district, solid-waste district, library district, etc.) or a nonprofit organization located in this area. The entity should be chosen because you are interested in the service it provides and because the entity will cooperate with your review and assessment.

a. Investigate the budget, revenue, and financial management processes and practices of that entity. The topics that should be investigated include, but are not limited to, the following: (i) *budget process*—how the budget is developed, what the cycle is, how decisions are made in developing the budget, what the review procedure is, who adopts the budget, how the process was established, what the style/nomenclature of the budget is, whether processes are transparent, whether there is a separate capital budget and budget process, whether there are extrabudgetary funds or earmarked revenues, whether appropriate internal controls are in place, what the external audit arrangement is, and so on; and (ii) *budget analysis*—explore expenditure patterns and trends to the extent possible, analyze inputs and performance results, and examine the extent to which the entity operates with fiscal discipline and control.

b. On the basis of your investigation, what do you conclude about the fiscal situation, processes, and procedures of the entity? Be specific. Link your conclusions to the information developed in your analysis. Outline and defend your proposals for reform or restructuring of the entity you have examined.

For the entity you select, you will need to talk with the administrators responsible for the entity's finances; to analyze budget preparation materials, budgets, and annual financial reports; and to examine laws or other documents establishing and governing the entity's framework. You may locate other source materials on some entities (debt rating reports, newspaper stories, etc.).

15. The Midwest Reptile Society, a nonprofit organization housed at the University of Illinois, sends a newsletter to its members three times per year. The objective of the newsletter is to provide information on the care and feeding of reptiles, to communicate information about reptile seminars and workshops, and to facilitate reptile exchange among society members. Provision of this information to the membership is a primary goal of the society. The newsletter is not particularly time sensitive (reptiles are slow moving), and society members tend to be well educated and have higher-than-average family incomes. There is no expense for preparation of the substance of the newsletter because all materials are submitted by society members in electronic form, ready to put into the newsletter, and the university donates the technological equipment appropriate for preparation of the newsletter. Physically, the newsletter has four printed pages on a single, folded sheet of paper. The newsletter is mailed at the standard first class rate.

The society executive director is preparing her budget for the year, and the newsletter is an important service to the membership. However, newsletter costs are constraining the ability of the society to provide other important member benefits. Here are some data she has available:

	2012	2013	2014	2015 est.
Society Members, Average for Year (#)	5,570	5,800	5,550	5,700
Postage Expense ($)	6,786	7,139	7,400	7,540
Printing Expense ($)	13,050	14,160	14,280	15,660

The director expects that the postage rate will increase by 2 cents per newsletter in May 2016; it increased from 46 to 48 cents in May 2014. Prepare the newsletter budget for 2016 under at least two different plans for providing this service to the membership. Explain and justify your budget, along with providing the dollar request.

16. The state budget director has asked you to create a medical care cost inflation index to use in evaluating certain items in the state budget. You are to use 2013 as the base year (2013 = 100.0) for your index. If costs have risen at an average annual rate of 4.35 percent in recent years and the budget director believes that this rate will continue, what is the value of your index in 2018?

17. Many city governments post their full budgets on a public website. Go to one of these websites, pick a department of that city government (e.g., police, fire, parks and recreation) and analyze the budget of that department. Questions that you should explore include the following:

    a. What inputs to the production process are the primary drivers of the budget? In other words, what expenditure categories are most important in the total spending by the department?
    b. Compare the planned expenditure for the budget year with the actual expenditures in prior years. Where are there significant changes? Is there a narrative that accompanies the budget that could help explain the differences?

18. Absurdistan must develop a medium-term budget condition baseline to qualify for credits from the International Monetary Fund. In the current year (2017), it expects revenues of A$135,000 million, discretionary spending of A$98,000, and formula assistance spending for the dependent population of A$50,000. In the medium term, the government expects revenue to grow at the same rate as gross domestic product, discretionary spending to grow at the same rate as inflation, and formula assistance to increase with population and inflation (in other words, for real per-capita formula assistance to remain the same as in 2017). Gross domestic product increased from A$180,000 to A$270,000 from 2010 to 2016, population increased from 35,780,000 to 68,550,000 over the period from 2000 to 2010, and the GDP deflator rose from 98 to 107 from 2010 to 2016. Calculate the following for the period 2018 through 2022: revenue baseline, dis-

CASES FOR DISCUSSION

CASE 3–1

Green Felt-Tip Pens, a Tape Recorder, and Embezzlement: Where Did the Budget Process Fail?

The New Hope/Solebury School District serves students in part of Bucks County, Pennsylvania. The county, just north of Philadelphia, has been a peaceful refuge since its colonial beginnings as a stopover on the road between New York and Philadelphia. But modern telemarketing reaches even the quietest parts of the county and can expose even the most straightforward budget-execution tasks to million-dollar fraud.

Consider These Questions

1. What standards of internal control were violated here?

2. How would you revise financial practices in the District to prevent similar fraud in the future?

3. Compare the roles of internal control and post-audit in the war against waste, fraud, and abuse.

The scam involved the business manager of the District, Kathryn Hock, and American Corporate Supplies, an office supplies distributor operated as a telemarketer by Marc and Teresa Suckman. The district serves about 825 students, with an annual budget of $6.6 million. Hock, business manager since 1978, had worked her way up from school secretary. Some school board members had questioned her ability to deal with more sophisticated accounting systems and methods and had expressed doubt about her qualifications. She had managed to keep her job, although uneasily.

American Corporate Supplies, located in California, made phone calls to prospective purchasers (public, private, nonprofit—it mattered not) around the country, offering products at discount. Often the discounts were from artificially inflated prices. Their business was to induce customers to purchase felt-tip pens from them; the scam was that the pens often had not been ordered at all or, if ordered, were never delivered. Their business was good: along with the school district, victims included an Idaho priest ($66,000), a St. Louis businessman ($40,000), and a Pennsylvania man ($155,000). But the $2 million from the school district apparently was their best.

Hock received a long-distance call from American Corporate Supplies in 1983, offering green felt-tipped pens. Because district teachers had requested the color, she placed an order. The shipment arrived as promised, and she paid the bill.

Through the year, the business manager made more pen orders. Eventually, her contact, William Chester of American Corporate (possibly Suckman), informed her that her good-customer status entitled her to receive a pocket tape recorder, a gift that she accepted. That put Hock in jeopardy, although she did not realize it.

After a few weeks, Chester called in regard to filling her back order. There actually was none, but he convinced her that such an order did exist and that she had a legal obligation to complete the order. Mr. Chester then proceeded to call one or two times each month to obtain a new order from her.

By April 1984, the district definitely needed no more markers. They had arrived in regular batches, and there was room for little else in the storage closet. Hock tried to stop the flow, but Chester told her that the district had an outstanding balance of $3,547.14 and that she should send a check to close the account. The claim was excessive, Hock objected, but Chester threatened to tell the school board about the gift she had accepted for placing the orders. That would cause her to be fired, so she settled the account and stopped the orders.

Or so she thought. A month later Chester called again, this time with an outstanding balance of $4,229.53. She again objected, but Chester threatened to inform both the school board and the police about the unauthorized payment for goods not received. The stakes for her were higher.

Hock felt in even greater jeopardy and, because of this vulnerability, was going to be called on to provide even greater sums of money. *U.S. News & World Report* describes her response:

> Hock knew then she was in deep water. "I was panic-stricken," she says. "I had never come up against anything like this and didn't know how to handle it." She paid that bill, and then another the following month, and dozens more, sometimes three in a month. "Each time he said it would be the final order, but it never was," she says. When the amounts Chester demanded escalated as high as $30,000, she started breaking up the payments with several different checks so they would be easier to hide in the books. She had authority to sign checks and stamp them with the signatures of two board officials. When the canceled checks came back from the bank, she would white out American Corporate Supplies and type in the name of the local fuel oil company and other regular suppliers, inflating their costs. Then she would alter the computerized accounts accordingly.

This process continued until 1988, when the accumulated overspending had grown so large that Hock could no longer conceal it. She quit in June, just as the district superintendent who had supported her against the skeptical board retired. The new superintendent and business manager soon found discrepancies and performed a special audit. The FBI and the U.S. Attorney received the results, and Hock confessed.

In July 1989, Hock pled guilty to embezzling $2,043,903 from the district; evidence indicated that she kept none of the money, but sent it all to Suckman. She was sentenced to sixteen months in prison and ordered to pay back the money she had stolen. She cooperated in further investigations to help find the Suckmans. The district had to borrow $1 million to replace the missing funds.

In April 1990, a federal grand jury indicted the Suckmans on thirty-eight counts of transporting stolen securities obtained by fraud, twenty counts of engaging in monetary transactions in criminally derived property, and single counts of conspiracy to commit interstate transportation of stolen money and securities. Marc Suckman was also indicted on three counts of blackmail. The Suckmans were arrested in Costa Rica and transported to Philadelphia for trial. They pled guilty shortly before jury selection; Marc Suckman faced up to six years in prison and Teresa Suckman up to four years and three months. They agreed to help in further investigations of telemarketing scams. U.S. District Court Judge James McGirr Kelly ordered restitution (the Suckmans claimed all proceeds had been "dissipated" by high living) and forbade them from working in telemarketing again.

SOURCES: References used for this case include Thomas Moore, "A New Scam: Tele-blackmail," *U. S. News & World Report* 108 (June 11, 1990): 51; "An Alert Reader Lends a Hand to the FBI," *U. S. News & World Report* 108 (June 25, 1990): 8; and Joseph A. Slobodzian, "Telemarketer Sentenced in New Hope Scam," *Philadelphia Inquirer*, January 31, 1991, B-1.

CASE 3–2

Another Way to Lose Money on Horses

Small towns are vulnerable to considerable financial crime. The citizenry tends to be trusting, and government operations are frequently informal and in the hands of people who, although entirely well-meaning, lack the education appropriate for public financial management. Because they know no better, their systems lack some of the important controls appropriate to safeguard public funds or to guide public decisions. This case shows how those vulnerabilities can be exploited in a trusting environment.

Consider These Questions

1. What violations of internal controls are present?

2. What questions should have been asked but were not?

3. How would you outline an alternative scenario in which the crimes would not have occurred?

Dixon, Illinois, is the hometown of Ronald Reagan. Its population in 2010 was 17,733 and in 2009, the Illinois legislature named it "The Catfish Capital of Illinois" (it hosts an annual catfish tournament on the Rock River). It has an annual budget of between $6 and $8 million. And its city treasurer, Rita Crundwell, embezzled $53 million from the town over two decades, according to federal prosecutors, the biggest municipal embezzlement in U.S. history.

Ms. Crundwell started with the city in 1970 while she was still in high school and decided to stick with the city rather than attend college. She moved into the finance function, and in 1983 she became treasurer and comptroller, a position she retained for roughly thirty years. Toward the end of her tenure, she was earning a salary of $80,000. She was widely regarded as a nice person, generous to others, and a credit to the community. One city official told the city council in 2011: "Rita Crundwell is a big asset to the city. She looks after every tax dollar as if it were her own." How true the last part of the remark was. And, while she worked for the city, she built a remarkable quarter horse breeding operation, RC Quarter Horses LLC, with a large ranch in Dixon, expensive horse trailers and motor homes for travel to competitions, and 400 horses, including 52 world champions recognized by the American Quarter Horse Association. Along with the horse farm, she had several residences and expensive personal vehicles. The spending was not consistent with the salary, but Dixon residents presumed there must be outside investors.

The money actually came from the city. She started the scheme in December 1990 when she opened a secret bank account for the City of Dixon at First Bank South (eventually becoming part of Fifth Third Bank). The city was the primary account holder, and "RSCDA c/o Rita Crundwell" was the second account holder. She was signatory on the account, which was called the Reserve Sewer Capital Development Account–Reserve Fund (RSCDA), and she was the only person who knew about the account. She took care to gather all statements on the account when they arrived in the mail. Obviously the account was not authorized by the city council and the city had no professional manager.

In the next year she started the embezzlement. She transferred funds from the city's Money Market account to its Capital Development Fund account, then wrote checks on the council-authorized Capital Development Fund payable to "Treasurer" (that's her), which she deposited in the RSCDA. She created fictitious invoices from the state of Illinois to justify the payments. (Although Dixon procedures required a purchase requisition and approval from an appropriate employee to support an invoice, none of the invoices had the requisition.) The U.S. Attorney's Office gave the following illustrative transactions: "on September 8, 2009, Crundwell wrote checks for $150,000 and $200,000 drawn on two of the city's multiple bank accounts. She deposited both checks into Dixon's Capital Development Fund account and, later the same day, wrote a check for $350,000 payable to "Treasurer" and deposited that check into her secret RSCDA account. Crundwell created a fictitious invoice to support the payment of $350,000 to the state of Illinois that falsely indicated the payment was for a sewer project in Dixon that the state completed. Later on September 8, 2009, Crundwell wrote a check drawn on the RSCDA account for $225,000, which she deposited into her personal RC Quarter Horses account."

Ms. Crundwell was the person who received, signed, and deposited all checks. She balanced checkbooks, made deposits, and received all financial statements that came to the city mailbox. She started out by stealing $181,000 in 1991 and kept at it until 2009. She got $5.8 million in 2008 and $5.6 million in 2009, her two best years. When city officials would mention that city finances were a little tight, Ms. Crundwell would blame it on slow payments by the state of Illinois. Nobody questioned that response.

City finances were audited regularly, in some years by auditors from a major CPA firm and sometimes by small practitioner firms. The city received an unqualified audit opinion with each audit—no questions of internal control, fair presentation of financial condition, no material noncompliance.

How did she get caught? Ms. Crundwell went on an extended vacation. A city clerk opened the mail in her absence, discovered the RSCDA account, and told the mayor. The mayor called the FBI. Eventually, Ms. Crundwell was sentenced to nineteen years and seven months in prison, and her assets were sold to recover some of the lost money. At last report, Ms. Crundwell was suing to recover some of the trophies her horses had won, but the feds were resisting. They may have a trophy room of their own to display them.

SOURCES: Bryan Smith, "Rita Crundwell and the Dixon Embezzlement," *Chicago Magazine*, December 2012; and U. S. Attorney's Office, Northern District of Illinois, "Former Dixon Controller Rita Crundwell Pleads Guilty to Federal Fraud

CHAPTER 4

Federal Budget Structures and Institutions

Chapter Contents

Federal Spending

The Fiscal Control Record

Legal Framework for Federal Budgeting

Phases in the Federal Budget Cycle
 Executive Preparation and Submission Phase
 Legislative Review and Appropriation Phase

Execution/Service Delivery
Audit

Sorts of Budget Authority

Mandatory and Discretionary Spending

Federal/Trust, On-Budget/Off-Budget

Conclusion

Budgets perform the same functions for choice making, management, and control for governments, businesses, and nonprofit organizations. The particular institutions and structures that an entity uses, however, are subject to much individuality, sometimes because of real differences in the mission, size, opportunities, and so on of the entity, but sometimes only because of institutional history ("That's just the way we do it here because that's the way we always have."). In addition, federal institutions and practices change as administrations change—if a new president or congressional leadership wants things done differently, this process changes. The federal process is described as "regular order" and, as you will discover later in this chapter, Congress and the President have recently had extreme difficulty in maintaining regular order. Details may change, but the intentions and expectations of the process will remain. In this chapter, we examine what sort of services the federal government provides with its expenditures and how federal budget structures and institutions operate to plan, execute, and control the spending that provides those services. Most of this chapter focuses on budget processes aimed at establishing fiscal discipline, the first role noted earlier for budgeting. In other words, it seems like a pretty good idea to budget to spend for services provided in the year only as much money as you are collecting during the year. There may be some exceptions involving major crises (big wars, big collapses of the national economy) or extraordinary purchases of long-life assets, but otherwise not much good can be said for overspending current revenue.

As you will learn, the federal government struggles with maintaining discipline and doesn't do a very good job of it.

As earlier described, a budget is a financial plan, either explicitly or implicitly. A government budget, however, reflects choices well beyond those of finance. A congressional agency report makes the point: "Not only is the budget a financial accounting of the receipts and expenditures of the federal government; it also sets forth a plan for allocating resources—between the public and private sectors and within the public sector—to meet national objectives."[1] Even in a market economy, the budget represents the basic national economic plan—the chosen mix of public and private sector uses of national resources. It doesn't have sectoral production quotas across industries or assignment of resources to industries that characterized the old and ineffective structure of socialist economic systems, but it does represent a plan, first, for dividing resources between the public and private sectors and, second, for allocating resources across the public operations.

The executive plan for federal operations is the president's budget, which is delivered early in the calendar year for the fiscal year starting on October 1. The legislative plan for federal operations is the congressional budget resolution delivered a bit later in the calendar year. However, neither of these budgets actually provides resources for delivery of services. That happens only after Congress has passed legislation providing authority to spend and the president has signed it into law, and that action will be much later.

Federal Spending

The first task is to understand what services federal government expenditure provides. Some summarize the federal government by describing it as a heavily indebted, heavily armed insurance company. Here is why: from 2015 outlay data, the federal government spends 16 percent of its total outlays on national defense (plus more for homeland security and even more on benefits paid to military veterans), about one-quarter of its total outlays on Social Security, about one-quarter percent of its total outlays on Medicare plus Medicaid, 4 percent on military veterans' benefits, 14 percent on income security (federal retirement programs, unemployment compensation, etc.), and 6 percent on interest (a significant portion paid on debt accumulated to support defense spending).[2] That doesn't leave much else. Social Security, Medicare, Medicaid, and net interest are spent according to an automatic formula spending process that is outside the annual budget process. That makes control and discipline over federal spending even more of a challenge.

---

[1] Congressional Budget Office, *An Analysis of the Administration's Health Proposal* (Washington, D.C.: U.S. Government Printing Office, 1994), 41.
[2] Where does that put the federal government on the moral scoreboard? Quoting Martin Luther King Jr.: "A nation that continues year after year to spend more money on military defense than on programs of social uplift is approaching spiritual death." (Martin Luther King Jr. "Beyond Vietnam: A Time to Break Silence," "Meeting of Clergy and Laity Concerned at Riverside Church in New York City," April 4, 1967.)

Table 4–1 provides expenditure data for selected years from 1960 through 2015 for the major federal functions. Two-thirds of outlays are for human resources, including income maintenance, health, support for the elderly and people with disabilities, and education and training. The largest block in the category, almost one-quarter of all outlays, is for Social Security (the income support program for the elderly, for surviving spouses and children, and for persons with disabilities). Medicare, the health program for the elderly, constitutes another 15 percent of total spending; and Medicaid, a health program for low-income people, constitutes another 8 percent. Other significant insurance-like expenditures are for veterans and federal employee benefits. Much of this human resource expenditure occurs through legal formulas that determine who is eligible and to how much those eligible are entitled. Most elements in this spending category have grown at rates significantly greater than the growth rate for total outlays since 1970, and most are expected (or feared) to continue this rapid growth in the future. The share for interest payments would be higher except for extremely low interest rates at which the federal debt can be financed.

National defense was once the predominant interest of the federal government. This is not to say that defense is no longer a significant interest: it remains the largest nonhuman resource program of the federal government by a considerable margin. However, 1961 was the last year in which defense amounted to half or more of federal outlays; it had been over 70 percent for 1942 through 1946, with a maximum of 89.5 percent in 1945, no surprise in light of the expense (and importance) of fighting World War II. The secular decline in the defense share of federal outlays was interrupted for 1981 through 1987. Many believe that this increase, by forcing a reaction from the Soviet Union that its inefficient socialist economy could not support, caused the collapse of the Soviet Union and an end to the Cold War. That defense buildup essentially won a war without firing a shot, undoubtedly the best way to fight a war, and a record not repeated in the twenty-first century. There was also an increase in the first decade of the twenty-first century, created by the cost of the wars in Iraq and Afghanistan and political pressures.[3] Unfortunately, quite a few shots were fired in these adventures, not quite as good a record as with getting an end to the Soviet Union. This increased share remains far below its level of the 1960s and 1970s and, with luck, will not approach those levels again. Indeed, the share isn't even up to its level in 1990, let alone the huge share during the WWII years. The lower spending share is more an indicator that we are safer than we were when

---

[3]The costs of the Department of Homeland Security are not included as part of national defense in the federal budget. In the spending categorizations in the budget, its spending is categorized as part of transportation, disaster relief and insurance, and law enforcement functions, not national defense. In light of the fact that the department's own strategic plan states that "the Department was created to secure our country against those who seek to disrupt the American way of life," this may seem a little strange. And, of course, benefit payments to veterans appear as a separate subfunction, not in the national defense function, even though they are clearly deferred costs of provision of national security. Hence, true total spending for national defense is even greater than the numbers reported in Table 4–1. In the functional classification of federal expenditure, Function 050 National Defense does not include military assistance to allies, the Transportation Security Administration, or Veterans Benefits and Services.

Table 4–1
Federal Outlays by Function, 1960–2015 ($ Millions)

	1960	% Total	1970	% Total	1980	% Total	1990	% Total	2000	% Total	2010	% Total	2015	% Total
National Defense	48,130	52%	81,692	42%	1,33,995	23%	2,99,321	24%	2,94,363	16%	6,93,485	20%	5,89,564	16%
Human resources	26,184	28%	75,349	39%	3,13,374	53%	6,19,297	49%	11,15,517	62%	23,86,633	69%	27,06,820	73%
Education, Training, Employment, and Social Services	968	1%	8,634	4%	31,843	5%	37,171	3%	53,764	3%	1,28,598	4%	1,22,061	3%
Health	795	1%	5,907	3%	23,169	4%	57,699	5%	1,54,504	9%	3,69,068	11%	4,82,223	13%
Medicaid	....		2,727	1%	13,957	2%	41,103	3%	1,17,921	7%	2,72,771	8%	3,01,472	8%
Medicare	....		6,213	3%	32,090	5%	98,102	8%	1,97,113	11%	4,51,636	13%	5,46,202	15%
Income Security	7,378	8%	15,655	8%	86,557	15%	1,48,668	12%	2,53,724	14%	6,22,210	18%	5,08,843	14%
Social Security	11,602	13%	30,270	15%	1,18,547	20%	2,48,623	20%	4,09,423	23%	7,06,737	20%	8,87,753	24%
Veterans Benefits and Services	5,441	6%	8,669	4%	21,169	4%	29,034	2%	46,989	3%	1,08,384	3%	1,59,738	4%
Physical resources	7,991	9%	15,574	8%	65,985	11%	1,26,011	10%	84,925	5%	88,835	3%	1,15,170	3%
Energy	464	1%	997	1%	10,156	2%	3,341	0%	-761	0%	11,618	0%	6,838	0%
Natural Resources and Environment	1,559	2%	3,065	2%	13,858	2%	17,055	1%	25,003	1%	43,667	1%	36,034	1%
Commerce and Housing Credit	1,618	2%	2,112	1%	9,390	2%	67,599	5%	3,207	0%	-82,316	-2%	-37,905	-1%
Transportation	4,126	4%	7,008	4%	21,329	4%	29,485	2%	46,853	3%	91,972	3%	89,533	2%
Community and Regional Development	224	0%	2,392	1%	11,252	2%	8,531	1%	10,623	1%	23,894	1%	20,670	1%
Net interest	6,947	8%	14,380	7%	52,533	9%	1,84,347	15%	2,22,949	12%	1,96,194	6%	2,23,181	6%
Other functions	7,760	8%	17,286	9%	44,996	8%	60,634	5%	1,13,777	6%	1,74,048	5%	1,69,360	5%
International Affairs	2,988	3%	4,330	2%	12,714	2%	13,758	1%	17,213	1%	45,195	1%	48,576	1%
General Science, Space, and Technology	599	1%	4,511	2%	5,831	1%	14,426	1%	18,594	1%	30,100	1%	29,412	1%
Agriculture	2,623	3%	5,166	3%	8,774	1%	11,804	1%	36,458	2%	21,356	1%	18,500	1%
Administration of Justice	366	0%	959	0%	4,702	1%	10,185	1%	28,499	2%	54,383	2%	51,903	1%
General Government	1,184	1%	2,320	1%	12,975	2%	10,460	1%	13,013	1%	23,014	1%	20,969	1%
Undistributed offsetting receipts	-4,820	-5%	-8,632	-4%	-19,942	-3%	-36,615	-3%	-42,581	-2%	-82,116	-2%	-1,15,803	-3%
Total, Federal Outlays	92,191	100%	1,95,649	100%	5,90,941	100%	12,52,993	100%	17,88,950	100%	34,57,079	100%	36,88,292	100%

SOURCE: Office of Management and Budget, *Budget of the Government of the United States, Fiscal Year 2017, Historical Tables* (Washington, DC: U.S. Government Printing Office, 2016).

shares were much higher than a suggestion that we might be dangerously unsafe from inattention to defense. The real question is how much is enough, and there is no definitive answer to that. However, any efforts to constrain federal spending do have to include defense spending in the discussion, because there isn't much left outside of the insurance-type spending of the federal government.

Other functional outlays are much smaller parts of the federal total. The federal government devotes a surprisingly small portion of its total outlays to provision of nondefense programs: transportation, education, energy, environmental protection, law enforcement, parks, and so forth. Outlays for physical resources, including infrastructure or the federal capital stock, are modest in share. The shares were much higher in the 1990s and earlier. Many believe increased public infrastructure investment is critical for improved standards of living, indeed for maintaining the health and safety of the public, but the outlay patterns show physical resource growth to be slow. Spending on other functions is both relatively small and slow growing; the rates of increase often have not kept pace with the combined effects of population increase and inflation. Many critics of federal spending point to "foreign aid" as a category to cut or eliminate to constrain the growth of spending and the deficit, but that spending amounts to less than 1 percent of the total and completely eliminating that spending would have minimal impact on federal operations.

Changing directions is not impossible, but, as the incrementalists remind us, it may be difficult to accomplish. The great counterexample of how spending directions can dramatically change, however, is national defense through the past forty years. Spending shares can change substantially when operating conditions change, no matter what the incremental inertia is. Indeed, we started to reallocate resources away from national defense, enjoying victory in the Cold War, even before the collapse of the Soviet Union at the end of 1991, and spending quickly ratcheted up after the attacks of September 11, 2001. In no way are spending shares replicated year after year, without regard to what might be happening in the external environment.

The Fiscal Control Record

The first expectation of a budget process is that it will be a tool for fiscal discipline. The experience over the past century does not speak well for the ability of the federal government to maintain a balance between available revenues and expenditures. Figure 4–1, using data from historical tables provided in the *Budget of the United States Government* and *Historical Statistics of the United States,* shows that most years since 1900 are in deficit, meaning that expenditure exceeded revenues, and that the deficit has been a significant share of total outlays in a number of years. The share numbers in the figure indicate the portion of total outlay in that year that had to be financed by borrowing, as opposed to being paid for with revenue raised that year. In other words, it indicates the extent to which the cost of federal government services in that year has been punted on to the future.[4]

Figure 4–1
Deficit/Surplus as Percentage of Federal Outlays, 1901–2015

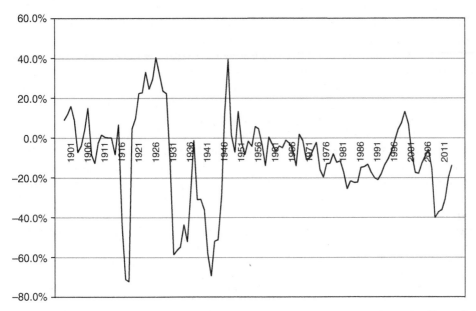

SOURCE: Office of Management and Budget, Budget of the United States Government, Fiscal Year 2017, Historical Tables (Washington, D.C.: U.S. Government Printing Office, 2016).

The deficits never threatened the capacity of the government to finance them in the modern era, in other words, the credit of the federal government has remained good, but periodically they have been large enough to make the trend seem aimed toward an unpleasant conclusion. Bond drives were regularly used during World War II to encourage private purchases of debt for patriotic reasons, but in other recent times special efforts to sell the bonds have not been needed to support the deficit.[5] The credit of the federal government is strong, the federal government currently faces extremely low interest rates when it borrows, and its debt is denominated in United States dollars so that, in a pinch, the government could print new

---

[4]The surplus/deficit concept employed here is called the current fiscal balance, representing the difference between current revenue (CR) and current expenditure (CE) or (CR − CE). It measures the draw on capital markets needed to finance the operations of government. Another deficit concept used in some analysis is the primary fiscal balance or primary deficit. This measure excludes net interest payments (NI) from spending and equals [CR − (CE − NI)]. It gauges the extent to which the government is capable of paying for the services it provides, excluding the impact of fiscal choices from the past. For fiscal 2014, the current surplus/deficit was −$484,602 million (2.81 percent of GDP) and the primary surplus/deficit was −$255,634 million (1.48 percent of GDP). The difference in the measures can be much greater than seen in the United States and in some other countries.

[5]Data aggregated for 1789 to 1849 show a 6.4 percent surplus, and data aggregated from 1850 to 1900 show a 6.4 percent deficit. Individual year data are not easily available.

money to pay its debts if the revenue system were to collapse.[6] Chronic absence of fiscal balance, in both good and bad economic times, is irritating, but not worth going into crisis mode, and it may not even be violating the fiscal sustainability standard. If the imbalance is going to the purchase of long-life infrastructure assets (highways, bridges, airports, etc.), then future generations will be paying for the assets whose services they are receiving when they deal with the debt. And scrimping on maintenance spending to keep a balanced budget is no bargain for future generations. But the American problem is that the imbalances, even when the economy is expanding, are consistently supporting current services, not building up productive infrastructure, and that does violate sustainability.

You can see that deficits get big during big wars (World Wars I and II) and big economic downturns (the Great Depression and the Great Recession). Then there is that long period from 1970 through the mid-1990s—the longest peacetime economic expansion in American history—where there is mostly no good reason for the deficits. English economist John Maynard Keynes wrote: "The boom, not the slump, is the right time for austerity at the Treasury,"[7] but the federal government didn't get the message. As you can see, recently around 40 percent of total spending was financed by borrowing, and that is not a pattern that should be continued. The present budget structures developed through the years largely to provide a process for controlling the deficit—and Figure 4–1 may have spoiled the story by showing that the structures haven't exactly done their job of maintaining fiscal discipline particularly well.

Expenditure decisions are made through a political process that is governed by a set of laws designed to provide open deliberations about options, attempt to direct resources to the areas of greatest need, ensure accountability and prevent corruption, and provide a mechanism for fiscal control. The politicians who pass those controlling laws frequently ignore or bypass those laws or change them when they become inconvenient. Because they intend that fiscal constraint apply to other members of Congress and not to programs that interest their own constituency, actual restraint remains a difficult challenge. This problem is made clear by Robert Gates, Secretary of Defense in the George W. Bush and Obama administrations: "I was constantly amazed and infuriated at the hypocrisy of those who most stridently attacked the Defense Department for being inefficient and wasteful, but would fight tooth and nail to prevent any reduction in defense activities in their home state or district no matter how inefficient or wasteful."[8] Every program has its constituency, either because of services rendered or inputs purchased, and it didn't get into federal spending by accident, and those who got it in are interested in keeping it in, regardless of deficit impact.

That brings forth a lesson: unless there is operational political will to maintain fiscal discipline, budget control laws and procedures stacked ten feet high are not going to produce results consistent with fiscal sustainability because members of Congress can figure out gimmicks to evade any control system. It is far easier to pass

---

[6]In other words, the United States is not like Greece, a highly-indebted nation whose debt is denominated in Euros, a currency its national government does not control.

[7]John Maynard Keynes, *Collected Writings of John Maynard Keynes*, vol. 21 (London: Palgrave Macmillan, 1937/1983), 390.

[8]Robert M. Gates, *Duty: Memoir of a Secretary at War* (New York: Alfred A. Knopf, 2014), 580.

legislation to control the deficit than it is to pass legislation that actually controls or reduces the deficit. The choices are hard, and lawmakers shy away from making them when they might entail reducing expenditure or raising revenue—and some combination of those actions are the only options for closing a budget deficit.

Legal Framework for Federal Budgeting[9]

The federal budget process—its practices, timing, and institutions—is the product of both law and tradition aimed at solving perceived problems with how the fiscal control structure was performing. More often than not, the problem was that of controlling the deficit (Figure 4–1), meaning that spending was more, sometimes considerably more, than revenue being taken in, and it was believed that elimination of the deficit—or at least controlling it—was important for the economic prosperity of the country. Several laws establish the structure for federal fiscal control.

United States Constitution Fundamental federal law—the United States Constitution—grants the "power of the purse" to Congress, but provides only limited instruction about the fiscal process: "No Money shall be drawn from the Treasury, but in Consequence of Appropriations made by Law; and a regular Statement and Account of the Receipts and Expenditures of all public Money shall be published from time to time" (Article 1, section 9).[10] Thus, Congress must make appropriations before money is spent, and there must be periodic financial reports. That's it: no budget requirements and not even a regular reporting schedule. Until the late 1800s, agencies submitted their requests as needed directly to Congress without involving the president and, obviously, with no central executive coordination. In the last part of the nineteenth century and the early years of the twentieth century, agencies were prohibited from making direct request to Congress, and all individual department and agency requests were gathered in an uncoordinated "Book of Estimates" for congressional review. The process concentrated on appropriating, the operation mentioned in the Constitution. Financing of World War I brought large deficits and a concern about establishing a real budgetary process because nobody in the process was paying much attention to the totals, just focusing on the individual appropriation laws.

---

[9]Office of Management and Budget, *Budget System and Concepts, Fiscal Year* (Washington, D.C.: U.S. Government Printing Office)—a document revised each year—explains the system, process, legal requirements, and concepts used to formulate the president's budget each year. It is available through the Office of Management and Budget website (http://www.whitehouse.gov/omb/). For absolutely everything about the appropriation system and the laws that govern it, the source is Government Accountability Office, *Principles of Appropriations Law,* a three-volume monster referred to as the "Red Book," that is provided on the GAO website (www.gao.gov).

[10]It may be argued that the requirement for a "regular Statement and Account of the Receipts and Expenditures" was not fulfilled until the Chief Financial Officers Act of 1990 (PL 101-576) created the capacity and requirement for annual accrual-based financial statements for funds and accounts and for their annual audit, with audits done either by inspector generals or by public accounting firms hired by the inspector generals. The GAO audits the Internal Revenue Service, the Bureau of Public Debt, the Federal Deposit Insurance Corporation, and the consolidated financial statements of the U.S.

One controlling effort then was enactment of debt ceilings (the level of debt equals the accumulation of all deficits since the start of the federal government less any surpluses). The first federal debt ceilings were established in the World War I era as Congress became concerned about the great sums of money spent for the war and the resulting borrowing to support the spending. Debt ceilings were a substitute for budget system control and were applied not to the authorization for expenditure (the appropriation) but rather on the payment to the supplier. If the Treasury lacked the money to make the payment out of prior receipts, it could not borrow to make up the difference. When the budget system came into being, the statutory debt ceilings continued as well, even though the reason for their existence had ended.[11]

The laws outlined in the following paragraphs created the budgetary structure in place today, the first coming shortly after WWI.[12] In general, each new law does not replace the structure from the existing law but adds some new wrinkles to the old. Table 4–2 summarizes the laws creating the budget structure for fiscal control and discipline.

Budget and Accounting Act of 1921 (67th Congress, 1st session, chap. 18, 47 Stat. 20) The 1921 Act initiated the *presidential budget process* and created the institutions needed for its implementation. Important elements of that law include:

a. The Act required a presidential budget message to Congress at the beginning of its legislative session. It would be a consolidated plan for federal operations and individual agencies would no longer transmit requests directly to Congress.

---

[11]A complete review of the debt limits appears in D. Andrew Austin, *The Debt Limit: History and Recent Increase*, CRS Report for Congress, Order Code RL 31967 (Washington, D.C.: Congressional Research Service, 2008). For decades, the federal government has operated with statutory limits on the amount of debt that could be outstanding, thereby constraining the capacity to run a deficit (i.e., add to the debt) when the ceiling is reached. These laws have historically had little effect because debt limits have been regularly increased. Spending had already been approved in the appropriation bill, and obligations had been made, so the only thing remaining was to have the funds necessary to cover the purchases already made. If necessary, the cash could easily be raised by new borrowing—so long as the ceiling would permit. None doubted the capacity of the federal government to meet its debt obligations, and none doubted the ability of the federal government to borrow. However, in the summer of 2011, a group of members of the House of Representatives chose to delay allowing an increase in the statutory debt ceiling that would permit the federal government to make payments for purchases already made. Although the ceiling increase finally was approved, it was not before there was significant concern about the willingness of the federal government to meet its financial obligations and not before federal debt had lost its previous gilt-edge status with some investors. The House of Representatives managed to score an "own-goal" in a game with no opposition!

[12]A more complete listing would include the following: (1) the Federal Credit Reform Act of 1990 (part of the Budget Enforcement Act of 1990), which requires budgetary treatment of direct loans and loan guarantees, not on a purely cash basis, but on estimated present values (see Chapter 7 for an explanation of present values) of the long-term cost of the loans or guarantees to the government; (2) the *Report of the President's Commission on Budget Concepts* (Washington, D.C.: U.S. Government Printing Office, 1967), which, although it has no legal status, remains the only authoritative statement on federal budget accounting; (3) the Chief Financial Officers Act of 1990, which required audited financial statements and increased powers of financial management authorities; and (4) the Government Performance and Results Act of 1993, which required agencies to develop strategic plans, measure performance, and integrate budgeting with performance improvement programs. The rules and procedures for budget execution appear in the Anti-deficiency Act (codified in Chapters 13 and 15 of Title 31, United States Code). Procedures for submission of the president's budget and information to be contained in it are in Chapter 11, Title 31, United States Code.

Table 4–2

Highlights of Major Acts Establishing the Federal Budget Process

---

Budget and Accounting Act of 1921 (67th Congress, 1st session, chap. 18, 47 Stat. 20)

- Established fiscal year from July 1 to June 30
- Supplemental appropriation
- Bureau of Budget (now Office of Management and Budget [OMB])
- General Accounting Office (now Government Accountability Office [GAO])
- Required president's budget message (first day of session)
- No direct agency submission of appropriation requests

Congressional Budget and Impoundment Control Act of 1974 (Public Law 93–344)

- Established fiscal year from October 1 to September 30
- Established Congressional Budget Office (CBO)
- Established House and Senate Budget Committees
- Required Current Services Budget presentation by president (what budget levels would be in the future if no policy changes occur)
- Required congressional budget resolutions (first and second)
- Established functional classification in president's budget
- Required tax expenditure analysis
- Established rescission/deferral instead of impoundment

Balanced Budget and Emergency Deficit Control Act of 1985 (Public Law 99–177, revised in 1987)

- Established deficit targets
- Formula sequestration to enforce targets
- Required earlier presidential budget message (first Monday after January 3)
- No second congressional budget resolution

Budget Enforcement Act of 1990 (Title XIII, Public Law 101–508)

- Established mandatory and discretionary spending categories
- Pay-as-you-go (PAYGO) requirement for mandatory spending categories and revenue provisions
- Established discretionary spending controls
- Required presidential adjustment of ceilings for sequester
- Supplemental appropriations included in outlay controls, except for wars and dire emergencies

---

Statutory Pay-As-You-Go Act of 2010 (Public Law 111–139)

- New legislation changing taxes, fees, or mandatory expenditures, taken together in a year, must not increase projected deficit
- Enforced by sequestration against a select group of mandatory programs (most Medicare payments, farm price supports, vocational rehabilitation state grants, mineral leasing payments to states, social services block grants), but not Social Security, most unemployment benefits, veterans' benefits, debt interest, federal retirement, and low-income entitlements
- OMB calculates whether there is a violation at the end of the congressional session, and the president issues any required sequestration order (none required yet)

(continues)

Table 4–2 (continued)

Budget Control Act of 2011 (Public Law 112–25)

- Create discretionary spending caps through 2021
- Require congressional vote on balanced budget amendment to Constitution
- Create Congressional Joint Committee on Deficit Reduction to propose at least $1.5 trillion in cumulative budget savings over ten years (*Note:* Joint Committee did not meet deadline to report program)
- Upon failure of Joint Committee, sequestration program for fiscal 2013 through 2021 to cut $1.5 trillion over ten years, cuts divided equally between defense and nondefense spending (exempt Social Security and low-income programs)
- Increase statutory debt ceiling in three tranches

---

    b. The Act created a Bureau of the Budget (initially in the Department of Treasury, but moved to the Executive Office of the President in 1939 and converted to the Office of Management and Budget, or OMB, in 1970) to assist the president in preparing that budget. The president appoints its director. Its staff, including both political and professional appointees, is expected to carry out the policies of the president.[13] The OMB consolidates agency requests for appropriations within the guidelines provided by the president. After appropriation, the OMB meters the flow of spending to ensure that agencies do not spend more than their appropriation.[14]

    c. The Act created for Congress and the American people the General Accounting Office (now the Government Accountability Office, or GAO) to ensure that agencies were operating as intended by Congress. The GAO holds accountable the operations of federal departments and agencies and is the primary "watchdog" agency. As the external (i.e., outside the operating agency) audit agent for the federal government, it supervises the accounting done by the executive agencies, but much of its work emphasizes investigations to improve the effectiveness of government. Much audit detail, in fact, is done by the audit staff of the executive agencies themselves, subject to GAO agreement. The head of the GAO, the comptroller general, is appointed by the president with the consent of the Senate for a single fifteen-year term; the comptroller general is almost unremovable within term.[15] The current emphasis of the GAO's work

---

[13]Other countries have central budget agencies as well. John Wanna, Lotte Jensen, and Jouke de Vries, eds., *Controlling Public expenditure: The Changing roles of Central Budget Agencies—Better Guardians?* (Northampton, Mass.: Edward Elgar, 2003), provide a cross-national comparative overview of these agencies, including the OMB.

[14]Complete studies of the agency appear in Percival Flack Brundage, *The Bureau of the Budget* (New York: Praeger, 1970); and Larry Berman, *The Office of Management and Budget and the Presidency, 1921–1979* (Princeton, N.J.: Princeton University Press, 1979). Brundage was budget director for President Eisenhower.

[15]Two major studies provide a detailed view of the GAO. In *The GAO: The Quest for Accountability in American Government* (Boulder, Colo.: Westview Press, 1979), Frederick Mosher traces the development of the GAO to the end of the 1970s; and Erasmus H. Kolman, ed., *Cases in Accountability: The Work of the GAO* (Boulder, Colo.: Westview Press, 1979), collects several cases that illustrate the kinds of audits or evaluations done by the GAO.

is the evaluation of government programs, sometimes at the request of a single member of Congress, sometimes at the request of a congressional committee.

d. The Act established a fiscal year that ran from July 1 to June 30 and provided a process for supplemental appropriations in unexpected instances in which agencies were in danger of exhausting their appropriations before the fiscal year was over.

The fiscal 1923 budget was the first budget submitted under this system.

Congressional Budget and Impoundment Control Act of 1974 (Public Law 93–344) The 1921 Act got the nation through the extremes of the Roaring 1920s, the Great Depression, and World War II. In the early 1970s, confidence in government began to erode with the Vietnam War, the Watergate break-ins, and the conflict between Congress and President Nixon. The president had assured the nation that he was "not a crook," but many in Congress did not believe him. Many members of Congress believed that the OMB was not trustworthy, that the deficit was out of control, that Congress needed to develop its own budget plan, that the president was selectively using his impoundment power (all presidents had had the authority to exercise fiscal management by not spending all money that had been appropriated) to punish his enemies, that the budget did not include all data necessary for responsible deliberations, and that Congress needed more time between when the president submitted his budget and the start of the fiscal year. The 1974 Act, signed into law by President Nixon only three weeks before his resignation, provided greater congressional budgetary authority, power, and responsibility. Provisions of the Act include the following:

a. The Act established a congressional budget process and Budget Committees in both houses of Congress to deal with the federal budget as a whole.
b. It created the Congressional Budget Office (CBO) to provide Congress generally and the congressional Budget Committees specifically with expertise similar to that of the OMB. The CBO provided a permanent, nonpartisan professional staff to supply Congress with three basic services: help in developing a plan for the budget (macroeconomic forecasts, baseline budget projections, deficit-reduction options, analysis of the president's budget), help in staying within its budget (cost estimates for bills, scorekeeping or maintaining frequent tabulations of bills that affect the budget, sequestration reports), and help in considering issues of budget and economic policy.[16]
c. It required that Congress pass a budget resolution, the product of the House and Senate Budget Committees, in April to establish revenue, expenditure, and deficit controls for the budget year and another budget resolution in August to modify those controls (the second resolution was eliminated in 1985). The Act changed the start of the fiscal year to October 1 to ensure that the appropriation laws were approved before the fiscal year began.

---

[16]Philip G. Joyce, *The Congressional Budget Office: Honest Numbers, Power, and Policymaking* (Washington, D.C.: Georgetown University Press, 2010). Because the CBO has maintained its reputation as both extremely qualified and aggressively nonpartisan, its forecasts and recordkeeping are the gold standard in

d. The Act required the president to submit a Current Services Budget that indicated what budget levels would be if no policy changes were made in the future.

e. The Act required a functional classification in the budget, in addition to the traditional administrative organization classification, and a tax expenditure analysis, a statement of the fiscal cost of tax preferences. (Tax expenditures are discussed in a later chapter.)

f. The Act eliminated presidential impoundment power, substituting a process whereby the president could defer or rescind appropriated spending, but only with congressional approval. More will be said about this in a later section.

The Congressional Budget and Impoundment Control Act of 1974 was thought to induce greater fiscal responsibility because Congress was required to approve a deficit or surplus appropriate to the existing macroeconomic circumstances and to adopt revenue and appropriation laws within that standard. No longer would spending increases and tax reductions be free additions; now they would have to be balanced within the ceilings of the resolution. Shortly after the law was passed, deficits increased (see Figure 4–1). Some suggest that this shows the conceptual inability of Congress to budget and practice fiscal constraint and that budgeting should be exclusively a presidential responsibility. The nonpartisan neutrality that makes the Congressional Budget Office a beacon of trustworthy fiscal data, estimates, and reports cannot convert politically driven lawmakers into responsible budget makers. But maybe deficits at the wrong time and for the wrong reason would be even worse without the CBO. The Act continues to be in effect.

Balanced Budget and Emergency Deficit Control Act of 1985 or the Gramm-Rudman-Hollings Act (Public Law 99–177, revised in 1987) Although the 1974 Act made significant procedural improvements to the fiscal system, it did not repair the tendency for substantial federal deficits. In contrast to the first two Acts, which sought fiscal discipline by changing procedures, the 1985 Act took a direct approach. It established firm and declining deficit targets for upcoming fiscal years (leading to balance in 1993) and established an automatic sequestration (cutting of appropriations) formula if the targets were violated. The amount of the violation would be established, initially by the GAO and later by the OMB because of a constitutional issue, and the amount of sequestration necessary to get to the target would be divided equally between military and domestic spending (exempting Social Security, Medicare, debt interest, and some antipoverty programs from the calculation and the cuts). The targets were mandatory, and, if violation was forecast at the start of a fiscal year and legislative changes did not correct the violation, a sequestration process reduced spending by formula to restore the target deficit.[17]

---

[17]Violations were based on expenditure and revenue forecasts. Had the process remained in place longer, it is entirely possible that sequestrations would have been easily avoided by fudging the forecasts.

Cuts were to be made by the percentage needed to get the deficit back to the legal target, without regard to priorities.[18] Gramm-Rudman-Hollings was, because of its mindless reductions, intended to be so politically distasteful that Congress would exert extreme caution to prevent a sequester. Instead, Congress chose to kill the process. Three years were sequester-eligible: 1986 (carried out), 1988 (rescinded), and 1990 (replaced by the Budget Enforcement Act of 1990). The 1985 Act became a dead letter, although the sequestration concept emerged in later deficit-controls. The Act applied to fiscal years from 1986 through 1990.

Budget Enforcement Act of 1990 (Title XIII, Public Law 101–508) The 1990 Act (BEA90), renewed twice and finally expiring in 2002, created an effective deficit-control structure by focusing on direct control over spending and taxing directly, rather than on estimated deficits. Several elements of the Act continue to shape budgetary discussions, even though the Act no longer controls in full.

a. BEA90 created two federal spending categories: mandatory and discretionary. Discretionary spending goes through the congressional appropriation process, and mandatory spending occurs automatically, by legislated formula. Roughly speaking, discretionary spending supports operations of federal agencies (defense is the biggest category) and mandatory spending supports programs such as Social Security, Medicare, and interest on the national debt.[19]

b. Mandatory spending and revenue provisions are subject to a pay-as-you-go (PAYGO) requirement. A provision to make a mandatory spending formula more lucrative (e.g., to extend the weeks of eligibility for unemployment compensation from thirty-nine to fifty-two) would have to be accompanied by a provision to cover its cost. Revenue lost with tax reductions would similarly need to be recovered. Changes are thus required to be deficit-neutral.[20] PAYGO meant that revenue reductions or entitlement enhancements had to be internally financed by accompanying revenue increases or entitlement reductions.

c. Discretionary spending was subject to rigid annual outlay caps for several years into the future (and caps were extended each time the Act was renewed). Sequesters would apply if any violation occurred.

d. Supplemental appropriations were included in the outlay controls. The only exception was in the case of war or a "dire emergency." Only in such cases, outlays could be added without violating the spending caps.

---

[18]The 1985 version scheduled balance in 1991, but that date was stretched in the 1987 version. The initial act assigned the enforcement of sequestration orders to the comptroller general. In *Bowsher, Comptroller General of the United States v. Mike Synar, Member of Congress,* 478 U.S. 714 (1986), the Supreme Court held that this assignment of powers by Congress to the comptroller general violated the constitutional command that Congress play no direct role in the execution of laws. The 1987 act remedied the problem by assigning the task to the OMB, an executive agency.

[19]Other countries make similar distinctions. For instance, Canada divides spending into "voted appropriations" and "statutory expenditures" in its budget process.

[20]The process of estimating the revenue impact of a tax change or the spending impact of a mandatory program formula change is called "scoring." There has been a continuing dispute about whether this scoring should include the impact of changes in the macroeconomy resulting from those statutory changes. This argument about "dynamic scoring" is examined in a later chapter.

Some observers, reacting to the many adjustments and diffusion of responsibility, labeled BEA90 as a start toward "no fault budgeting,"[21] but outlay ceilings constrained appropriations until 1998. After that budget year, annual adjustments to original statutory caps allowed considerable expansion of outlays. The Omnibus Budget Reconciliation Act of 1993 (P.L. 103–66) extended new ceilings through fiscal 1998, and the Balanced Budget Act of 1997 (P.L. 105–33, the 1997 budget reconciliation) continued ceilings through fiscal year 2002.[22] The discretionary caps and the PAYGO mechanism expired in September 2002. After its expiration, federal deficits did increase dramatically. Other portions of the Act continue to apply and much discussion continues to involve the mandatory and discretionary categories of spending first established in the Act.

Statutory Pay-As-You-Go Act of 2010 (Public Law 111–139) The deficits after 2002 eventually brought legislation to partially restore controls of the past. The 2010 Act establishes a control provision that legislation changing taxes, fees, or mandatory spending, taken together in a year, cannot increase the projected deficit. Any legislation that reduces revenue must be offset by cuts to mandatory programs or by other revenue increases, and any legislation that increases mandatory expenditure must be accompanied by revenue increases or cuts in other mandatory spending. The system requires the OMB to determine whether there has been a violation at the end of the congressional session (it works with both five- and ten-year budget windows for its estimates) and, if there has been, the president issues the required sequestration. (No such sequestrations under this law have been required so far.) Sequestration applies to certain mandatory programs (most Medicare payments, farm price supports, vocational rehabilitation state grants, etc.) but not to Social Security, most unemployment benefits, veterans' benefits, debt interest, federal retirement, and low-income entitlements. The Act applies to all laws enacted after February 12, 2010.

Budget Control Act of 2011 (Public Law 112–25) The 2011 Act emerged from arguments about increasing the statutory federal debt ceiling in the summer of 2011. The Act established firm discretionary spending caps through fiscal 2021 (accomplished by amending the 1985 Act to reinstate spending limits on discretionary budget authority for 2012 through 2021), required Congress to vote on a balanced budget amendment to the Constitution (done, but it did not pass), and created a Congressional Joint Committee on Deficit Reduction to propose at least $1.5 trillion in cumulative budget deficit savings over a ten-year period (the committee did not meet the deadline for making the proposal, so it expired). The spending caps do remain in place, so the top line for the budget process has been established for some years to come. The caps are enforced by OMB-initiated across-the-board sequestrations with cuts divided equally between national defense and all other budget functions. Nondefense cuts would come from both discretionary and some

---

[21]Richard Doyle and Jerry McCaffery, "The Budget Enforcement Act of 1990: The Path to No Fault Budgeting," *Public Budgeting & Finance* 11 (Spring 1991): 25–40.
[22]PAYGO would continue, but without any enforcement mechanism. Other legislation provided caps on highway and mass transit outlays (through 2003) and on conservation outlays (through 2006).

mandatory programs. However, the caps can be overridden by congressional vote, just as sequesters and caps have been in the past. The Act applies to fiscal years from 2012 through 2021. No sequestrations have been applied through fiscal 2015.[23] The caps created a problem for fiscal 2016. The resulting Bipartisan Budget Act of 2015 increased discretionary spending caps for both security and nonsecurity spending for fiscal 2016 and fiscal 2017 with some alleged offsets from revenue and mandatory spending to prevent a deficit impact; another part of that act extended the public debt limit through March 15, 2017.[24]

Three gimmicks used to get around the control of the caps are worth noting. The first is the Overseas Contingency Operations Fund (or war spending), a sort of slush fund to deal with unexpected war-fighting needs.[25] The fund is outside the spending caps (and its level tends to be larger than requested by the Department of Defense), so Congress sticks various defense items into the fund as an escape technique. That permits defense spending to exceed the cap while maintaining the façade of sticking to the cap.[26] The second is cost timing. The controls work with a ten-year budget window in regard to control of deficits. Thus, legislation is structured to put spending for long-term programs into years just beyond the tenth year or to accelerate tax payments just inside the tenth year to avoid the constraint. One approach proposed in 2015 was a gimmick called "pension smoothing," a program that would have employers reduce employee pension contributions initially (thus reducing operating costs and increasing taxable profits to boost tax collections now) but increase pension contributions later (thus increasing operating costs, reducing taxable profits, and reducing tax collections) beyond the budget window. And third are the offsets that are used to keep expenditure increases within the control caps. For instance, to manage increased spending for highways, the Senate in 2015 used such added revenue as from indexation of customs fees for inflation, using private debt collectors to collect overdue taxes, sell oil from the Strategic Petroleum Reserve, revoke or deny passports for those with seriously delinquent taxes, and so on. Are any of these revenues anything more than phantoms? Who knows and

---

[23]Office of Management and Budget, *OMB Final Sequestration Report to the President and Congress for Fiscal Year 2015* (January 20, 2015).

[24]Because deficits have continued, the level of federal debt has continued to increase. That means there may be yet another debt ceiling crisis awaiting in 2017. Rather than eliminate the ceiling or eliminate the deficits, the root causes of the problem, some members of Congress have apparently been working on legislation that would prioritize what bills would be paid and what bills would not in case of a Treasury cash crisis. Such prioritization of who to stiff was an important issue (the "arrears" problem) in the era of major financial mismanagement in the countries of the former Soviet Union in the early years of their independence, but should never be an issue in a modern democracy.

[25]The Forest Service is less devious. Its funding has been constrained by the caps as severe wildfires have plagued the western United States in recent years. That has meant that other Forest Service programs have been substantially constrained as the firefighting share of service spending has increased from 16 percent in 1995 to roughly 50 percent now. (U.S. Department of Agriculture, "The Rising Cost of Wildfire Operations: Effects on the Forest Service's Non-Fire Work," August 4, 2015). Its solution: passage of the Wildfire Disaster Funding Act that would provide fire suppression funds outside the sequestration cap limits. That approach would ease the situation of any federal agency.

[26]An "unfunded priorities list," an inventory of items the Defense Department would like to buy if it got a few extra billion dollars, is actually maintained, so Congress knows where to go for purchases outside

who cares?[27] It lets the Senate do what it wants to do, which is to accommodate more highway spending. The actual amounts are beside the point, because the objective is to develop a reason for more highway spending.

Because the caps are themselves gimmicks that interfere with congressional intentions, it is no surprise that Congress responds to them with evading gimmicks. Control gimmicks are no substitute for political will. To the American politician, appearing to reduce the federal deficit is far more important than taking the necessary actions to actually reduce that deficit.

Phases in the Federal Budget Cycle[28]

The federal budget cycle involves operations by both the executive and the legislative branches of government. Spending cannot occur without the approval of both branches, and the budget cycle involves movement of work between the branches of government. Figure 4–2 provides a diagram of the process to help with the discussion that follows.[29]

Executive Preparation and Submission Phase

The executive preparation and submission phase begins about eighteen months before the start of the fiscal year.[30] The president establishes general budget and fiscal policy guidelines, and the OMB works with federal agencies to translate them into agency programs and budget requests.[31] Table 4–3 shows the key budget cycle events, as outlined in Circular A-11, the primary budget instruction from the OMB. The requests are compared with the presidential program objectives, expenditure ceilings set by the president, Department of Treasury revenue forecasts (from the

---

[27]The offset from sale of oil from the Strategic Petroleum Reserve was based on a price of oil of $84–$89 per barrel when the spending bill was introduced. Before the appropriation bill passed, the price of oil was below $45 per barrel, so there was no way that the sale revenue would actually offset the spending. But nobody cared. The bill also used a transfer of capital from the Federal Reserve system as part of the offset. That is bizarre because the Federal Reserve already transfers its revenue less its operating cost to the U.S. Treasury every month or so. That means that this offset—allegedly new revenue to prevent the extra spending from adding to the deficit—is actually money that the Treasury already receives. It isn't an actual offset, it is double-counting! Again, nobody cared because Congress was interested in spending, not in constraining the deficit.

[28]More detail on the process appears in U.S. Government Accountability Office, "Appendix 1, Overview of the Development and Execution of the Federal Budget," *A Glossary of Terms Used in the Federal Budget Process*, GAO-05-734SP, September 2005.

[29]I am indebted to my colleague Denvil Duncan for providing this diagram.

[30]The federal fiscal year begins on October 1. That has not always been the case. The first federal fiscal year began on January 1, 1789. Congress changed the start to July 1 in 1842 and to October 1 for 1977 and onwards.

[31]The Department of Defense is so large a part of federal government finances that the OMB directly works with the department as its budget is prepared, so OMB is involved even before the budget is transmitted for OMB review. That is not the case with other government operations.

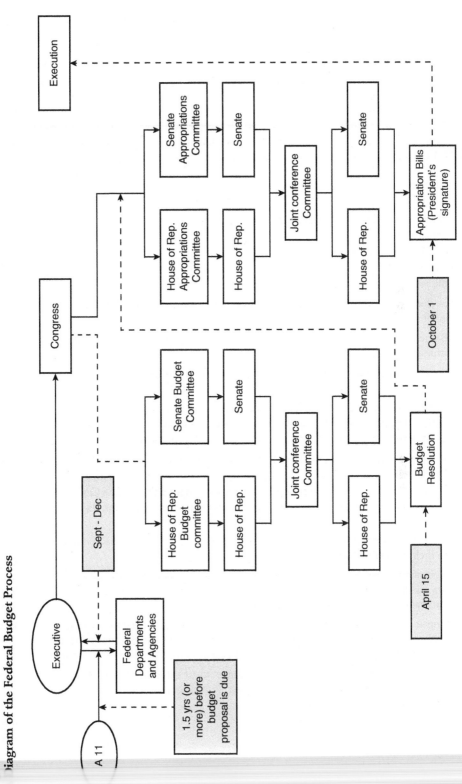

Table 4–3
Events in the Federal Budget Cycle

Major Steps in the Formulation Phase

What Happens?	When?
OMB issues spring planning guidance to Executive Branch agencies for the upcoming budget. The OMB Director issues a letter to the head of each agency providing policy guidance for the agency's budget request. Absent more specific guidance, the outyear estimates included in the previous budget serve as a starting point for the next budget. This begins the process of formulating the budget the President will submit the following February.	Spring
OMB and the Executive Branch agencies discuss budget issues and options. OMB works with the agencies to: • Identify major issues for the upcoming budget; • Develop and analyze options for the upcoming fall review; and • Plan for the analysis of issues that will need decisions in the future.	Spring and Summer
OMB issues Circular No. A-11 to all Federal agencies. This Circular provides detailed instructions for submitting budget data and materials.	July
Executive Branch agencies (except those not subject to Executive Branch review) make budget submissions. See section 25.	September*
Fiscal year begins. The just completed budget cycle focused on this fiscal year. It was the "budget year" in that cycle and is the "current year" in this cycle.	October 1
OMB conducts its fall review. OMB staff analyzes agency budget proposals in light of Presidential priorities, program performance, and budget constraints. They raise issues and present options to the Director and other OMB policy officials for their decisions.	October–November
OMB opens the MAX A-11 Data Entry (MAX) application for all agencies to submit their prior year budget data.	November
OMB briefs the President and senior advisors on proposed budget policies. The OMB Director recommends a complete set of budget proposals to the President after OMB has reviewed all agency requests and considered overall budget policies.	Late November
Passback. OMB usually informs all Executive Branch agencies at the same time about the decisions on their budget requests.	Late November
All agencies, including Legislative and Judicial Branch agencies, enter all MAX budget schedule data and text materials. This process continues until OMB must "lock" agencies out of the database in order to meet the printing deadline.	Late November to early January*
Executive Branch agencies may appeal to OMB and the President. An agency head may ask OMB to reverse or modify certain decisions. In most cases, OMB and the agency head resolve such issues and, if not, work together to present them to the President for a decision.	December*
Agencies prepare and OMB reviews congressional budget justification materials. Agencies prepare the budget justification materials they need to explain their budget requests to the responsible congressional subcommittees.	January
President transmits the budget to the Congress.	First Monday in February

*OMB provides specific deadlines for this activity.

(continues)

Table 4–3 (continued)

Major Steps in the Congressional Phase	
What Happens?	When?
Congressional Budget Office (CBO) reports to Budget Committees on the economic and budget outlook.	January
CBO reestimates the President's Budget based on their economic and technical assumptions.	February
Other committees submit "views and estimates" to House and Senate Budget Committees. Committees indicate their preferences regarding budgetary matters for which they are responsible.	Within 6 weeks of budget transmittal
The Congress completes action on the concurrent resolution on the budget. The Congress commits itself to broad spending and revenue levels by passing a budget resolution.	April 15
The Congress needs to complete action on appropriations bills for the upcoming fiscal year or provides a "continuing resolution" (a stop-gap appropriation law).	September 30

Major Steps in the Execution Phase	
What Happens?	When?
Fiscal year begins.	October 1
OMB apportions funds made available in the annual appropriations process and other available funds. Agencies submit apportionment requests to OMB for each budget account by *August 21* or within *10 calendar days* after the approval of the appropriation, whichever is later. OMB approves or modifies the apportionment specifying the amount of funds agencies may use by time period, program, project, or activity.	September 10 (or within 30 days after approval of a spending bill)
Agencies incur obligations and make outlays to carry out the funded programs, projects, and activities. Agencies hire people, enter into contracts, and enter into grant agreements, etc., in order to carry out their programs, projects, and activities.	Throughout the fiscal year
Agencies record obligations and outlays pursuant to administrative control of funds procedures (see Appendix H), report to Treasury (see the Treasury Fiscal Requirements Manual and section 130), and prepare financial statements.	
Fiscal year ends.	September 30
Expired phase (no-year funds do not have an expired phase). Agencies disburse against obligated balances and adjust obligated balances to reflect actual obligations during the period of availability. Agencies continue to record obligations and outlays pursuant to administrative control of funds procedures, report to Treasury, and prepare financial statements.	Until September 30, fifth year after funds expire.

SOURCE: Executive Office of the President, Office of Management and Budget, Preparation, Submission, and Execution of the Budget, Circular No. A-11 (Washington, D.C.: Office of Management and Budget, 2016).

Office of Tax Analysis), and economic forecasts from the Council of Economic Advisers and the Federal Reserve System.[32] The economic estimates—inflation rate, interest rates, level of unemployment, growth rate of GDP, and so on—are especially important because many budget totals are sensitive to the state of the economy. For example, Congress passes laws that provide for spending that depends on the number of unemployed workers who qualify for assistance, and several programs (most notably Social Security) index spending to inflation. Furthermore, federal revenues are particularly sensitive to economic activity, and, given the considerable amount of federal debt outstanding, total outlays change significantly depending on the rate of interest the federal government must pay. As a result, the economic forecast can substantially affect the budget's spending and revenue plans.

The *budget baseline*—a forecast of the receipts, outlays, and deficits that current law would produce—provides a warning of future problems, gives a starting point for formulating the current budget, and offers a "policy-neutral" benchmark against which the president's (and other) budget proposals can be compared[33] without complication from the ways the economy can alter those numbers. Indeed, when Congress discusses budget cuts for out-years, it almost always is considering cuts against some increasing future budget baseline (an extension of present spending under certain projection assumptions, and differing assumptions can create different baselines), not a reduction in comparison with present actual spending levels. What is called a "cut" often involves no reduction in spending from the prior year.[34]

The long-term budget baseline is constructed on the basis of current law, and that means that it should not be taken as a prediction of what longer-term budget outcomes are actually going to be because laws may change. In its 2001 long-term budget outlook, the nonpartisan and highly respected CBO produced an outlook that found that budget surpluses then being run and projected for the next few years would allow the redemption of all federal debt by the end of the 2002–2011 period.[35] Of course, the CBO was working within the tax and expenditure framework then in place, the projected surpluses quickly became huge actual deficits, and the elimination of the federal debt never became a problem. Indeed, it probably is the case that

---

[32]The Council of Economic Advisers, another part of the Executive Office of the President, advises on macroeconomic conditions and overall fiscal policy and on microeconomic issues. *The Economic Report of the President,* which the council prepares, is an important source document for information and policy discussion. The Federal Reserve System is the American central bank.

[33]The Current Services Budget, one part of the Analytical Perspectives volume of the president's budget, provides a baseline. In general, receipts and mandatory spending (spending that occurs according to a formula, not annual appropriation) are estimated according to current law; funding that must be approved each year is estimated by adjusting the most recently approved appropriation for inflation. The CBO also prepares a budget baseline for its analysis; the CBO baselines have been more widely used in recent years. Nobody knows exactly what the baseline should be. For an excellent discussion of the problem of defining a baseline, see Timothy J. Muris, "The Uses and Misuses of Budget Baselines," in John F. Cogan, Timothy J. Muris, and Allen Schick, *The Budget Puzzle: Understanding Federal Spending* (Stanford, Calif.: Stanford University Press, 1994), 41–78.

[34]And the cuts can be imaginative. In cuts announced in spring 2011, the Census Bureau got credit for a budget cut of $6 billion, an impressive reduction until you realize that it is simply the result of not doing the decennial 2010 census in 2011.

[35]Congressional Budget Office, *The Budget and Economic Outlook: Fiscal Years 2002–2011* (Washington, D.C.: CBO, 2001).

those projected surpluses provided some political support for the new expenditure programs and tax reduction that caused the surpluses never to be realized.

From discussions between agencies and the OMB during budget preparation, agencies submit requests in the fall for OMB review.[36] Most issues are resolved between the OMB and the agency, but some require a final policy decision by the president. Transmission of the final document—the president's budget message—occurs no later than the first Monday in February (exceptions happen in the transition from one presidential administration to the next because there is too little time between when the president takes office and the February date). This document presents the president's program plans, with requests for funds to carry out those plans, for the upcoming fiscal year. That means for the fiscal year beginning on October 1, 2017 (the 2018 fiscal year), the message would be delivered in early February 2017.[37] The final budget is both printed and posted on the OMB website for public disclosure.[38] (Before electronic dissemination, budget release day brought an army of staffers and lots of interns to the Government Printing Office to pick up paper copies of the budget documents, each set about a foot high, to take back to offices throughout the country. The Internet has destroyed that high drama.) The president's budget has no legal impact, but it provides the basis for congressional deliberations about providing budget authority, the result of appropriation legislation. The president's budget is sometimes claimed to be "dead on arrival" with no chance of passage, a view expressed by Bruce Bartlett, an advisor in Reagan and George H. W. Bush administrations: "The president's budget has been 'dead on arrival' for years, and the White House now treats it more as a chore to be done and gotten out of the way than the showcase of its legislative program."[39] In fact, the budget is never completely dead for the process, just as no budget is enacted exactly as presented.[40]

Many months separate the budget message from the end of its fiscal year. Not only can there be economic, international, and social surprises to upset plans, but also Congress may not agree with the presidential agenda. Nevertheless, differences between presidential plans and actual spending have been surprisingly small in relative terms. Total budget outlays seldom differ from the initial executive proposal

---

[36]Budgets for the legislative and judicial branches are included in the executive budget without change from their initial transmission.

[37]Unless the transmission date changes—the 1921 Act specified the first day of each regular session; the Budget and Account Procedures Act of 1950 changed the date to within the first fifteen days of the session; Gramm-Rudman-Hollings specified the first Monday after January 3; and BEA90 established the current date. Congress and the president have also changed the date by mutual consent. The Obama administration has characteristically been late in presenting its budget: 64 days late for 2014 and 28 days late in 2015, a very long delay for years in which there has been no change in presidential administrations. Since BEA90, outgoing presidents have had the option of leaving the last budget to their successor, and both Bushes and Clinton took that option. Thus, budgets in those transition years have been abnormally late.

[38]http://www.whitehouse.gov/omb/budget.

[39]Bruce Bartlett, "Where to Find Nuggets of Data in the Budget," *New York Times*, March 18, 2014.

[40]In spring 2016, Congress demonstrated how dead it regarded President Obama's budget for 2017 by failing to schedule a presentation of that budget by the head of OMB. That set a new record for ignoring the executive budget. Nevertheless, it is likely that much spending in that budget will, in fact, turn out to be appropriated when the process is finally over.

by more than 2 percent (although that is still a lot of money). This suggests the key role of the executive in aggregate expenditure control. If the president is not willing to make the difficult choices necessary for fiscal discipline, it is extremely unlikely that Congress will take on the task. There are, of course, much greater differences in individual programs than appear in these aggregates.

Legislative Review and Appropriation Phase[41]

The legislative review and appropriation phase of the federal cycle includes several committee pathways and many political quirks. The budget structure laws establish the budgeting framework, but the fiscal committees of Congress structure the appropriation laws. Appropriation laws are important because, for general operations of government, agencies are unable to spend (and operate) if they lack an appropriation that provides obligation authority for the fiscal year. Expenditure and tax laws must be passed by both the Senate and the House of Representatives, but the work to create those laws is done in committees of Congress and, indeed, often in subcommittees of those committees.

Federal fiscal decisions must follow four fiscal committee paths through the houses of Congress, each path with different responsibilities, focuses, and interests.[42]

Authorizing Committees In the spending process, the authorization committees set policies and create programs for agencies to carry out but do not provide funds for programs. Committees with legislative jurisdiction over subject matter (e.g., agriculture) consider (1) enabling, or organic, legislation that creates agencies, establishes programs, or prescribes a function; and (2) appropriation authorization legislation that authorizes appropriation of funds to implement the organic legislation. The latter may be part of the organic legislation, or it may be separate. There is no general requirement that specific authorization precede appropriation committee work, but operating rules make this the expected sequence. Some programs require annual authorization; others have authorizations for a set number of years or for an indefinite period. Authorizations usually establish funding ceilings for particular programs, but they provide no money for programs. Many authorized programs never receive any appropriation.[43]

---

[41]A detailed description of the appropriation process is presented in Jessica Tollestrup, "The Congressional Appropriation Process: An Introduction," Congressional Research Service 7-5700 (November 14, 2014). The previously-referenced "GAO Red Book" provides even more details.

[42]Another significant fiscal committee is the Joint Committee on Taxation, a nonpartisan committee with representation from both House and Senate. Although the committee does not produce legislation, it does assist the tax-writing committees in development and analysis of legislation and prepares revenue estimates of all tax legislation considered by Congress, along with other tasks. It operates with a strong professional staff for assistance of all members of Congress on tax legislation.

[43]Authorization acts also carry legislation that has little to do with the basic purpose of the programs being authorized. For instance, the defense authorization act being considered in late 2014 included provisions to create six national parks, expand nine other parks, and establish a bipartisan commission on building a national women's history museum. It's a good place to insert legislation because the defense authorization bill is almost certain to pass. (Ed O'Keefe, "Nonmilitary Provisions Snag Defense Bill," *Washington Post*, December 4, 2014.)

Appropriations Committees The appropriations committees, working through their subcommittees, develop the appropriation bills that provide funds for federal agency operations. Appropriation subcommittee and authorization committee jurisdictions do not match up: the agencies falling under the jurisdiction of a particular authorizing committee may have appropriations in several different appropriation subcommittees. Table 4–4 lists the twelve appropriation subcommittees for the House and for the Senate in 2014, each with its own appropriation law to write. Congress can juggle its committees as it wishes. For instance, when the Department of Homeland Security was created in 2003, subcommittee jurisdictions were shifted to create a homeland security subcommittee within a total of thirteen subcommittees. The number was later reduced to twelve. Appropriations can be made in a single, consolidated appropriation act or through a number of separate appropriation acts. However, the last regular (in other words, fully intentional) consolidated appropriation was the General Appropriation Act of 1951 (P.L. 81–759). More recently, Congress has lumped several individual appropriation bills into a consolidated appropriation because it was unable to reach resolution on the individual bills and it had to act because agencies were running out of money as the new fiscal year began. For example, the Consolidated Appropriations Act of 2012 (P.L. 112–74) passed in December 2011, several weeks after the fiscal year had started. It lumped appropriations for much of the federal government together, not because of any decision that this was the right way to do it, but because of an inability to act on a timely basis on the individual bills. During legislative consideration, the president's view on proposed budgetary legislation is communicated, through the OMB, in Statements of Administration Policy (SAPs).

Table 4–4
Senate and House of Representatives Appropriation Subcommittees, 2014

Agriculture, Rural Development Food and Drug Administration, and Related Agencies
Commerce, Justice, Science, and Related Agencies
Defense
Energy and Water Devleopment
Financial Services and General Government
Homeland Security
Interior, Environment, and Related Agencies
Labor, Health and Human Services, Education, and Related Agencies
Legislative Branch
Military Construction, Veterans Affairs, and Related Agencies
State, Foreign Operations, and Related Programs
Transportation, Housing and Urban Development, and Related Agencies

SOURCES: "United States Senate Committee on Appropriations." http://appropriations.senate.gov; "United States

Financing Committees The financing committees are Senate Finance and House Ways and Means. These committees have jurisdiction over federal tax and revenue measures, an obviously critical part of government finance, but they also have jurisdiction over spending through the Social Security system, the Medicare and Medicaid structures, unemployment compensation, and payment of debt interest, a span that includes more than half of all federal expenditure. Hence, these committees are extremely important for the finances of the federal government. More about their spending functions is discussed in a later section on entitlements. This spending does not go through the annual appropriation process (the mandatory category from BEA 1990).

Budget Committees The budget committees, one for each house of Congress, were created by the 1974 Act. Their primary role in the process is the development of the Budget Resolution—the Congressional Budget that establishes the ceilings and floors for spending and revenue intended to guide the work of all the other fiscal committees. The Budget Committee works with "views and estimates" of spending and revenue transmitted to it from congressional committees, along with CBO input, in preparing the resolution. The resolution establishes what are called 302(d) allocations that set the amount of money to be spent by the appropriation committees; the appropriation committees then divide the allocation among the twelve subcommittees that produce the appropriation bills. The budget committees do not, however, provide actual spending authority through their action. The budget resolution must include at least five fiscal years: the budget year plus four subsequent out-years. The resulting Budget Resolution is approved by both houses of Congress but is not signed by the president.

Legislating: Budget Creation in Congress The budget committees develop the congressional budget (the budget resolution). Before the 1974 Act, Congress considered the federal budget only as the several appropriations bills; Congress did not consider the budget as a whole. The budget was fragmented into general administrative department "chunks," and each chunk was considered by a separate appropriations subcommittee. This microlevel budget analysis permitted scrutiny of individual department requests, but it did not permit the overall comparison of revenue, expenditures, and the accompanying surplus or deficit. More important, this practice did not permit consideration of government-wide priorities—transportation versus defense, national parks versus urban housing, and so on—that effective budget choices require, and there was nothing in the system that balanced the funds added to one department against the need to finance that increase through either more revenue or less spending somewhere else. Appropriation committees scrutinized appropriations within their individual bill, and Congress appropriated to the appropriation bills, and that was that.

    The revised process, used initially for the 1977 budget, produced an additional flow through Congress: the appropriations committees work as before, but separate budget committees, with staff assistance from the CBO, draft a budget resolution that encompasses budget levels for five years.[44] The resolution presents recommended aggregates for new budget authority, budget outlays, direct loan obligations,

---

[44]That's the budget year and four out-years. Appropriations continue to be predominantly for only the single budget year. Other parts of the process use a ten year horizon.

primary loan guarantee commitments, revenues, surplus or deficit, and public debt and recommends aggregate revenue change. New budget authority, budget outlays, direct loan obligations, and primary loan guarantees are also divided among twenty functions of government (the major national priorities served by the federal government, such as national defense, transportation, agriculture, and administration of justice). The explanatory statement with the resolution allocates budget authority and outlays in functional categories to committees with jurisdiction over programs in the function. The appropriations committees must allocate budget authority and outlays among their subcommittees. Allocations to each House and Senate committee are called 302(a) allocations; their allocations to the twelve subcommittees are called 302(b) allocations. This budget resolution is macro level; it does not work directly from the detailed agency requests, and it does not provide funds for any agency to spend, although the budget committees (and their staff) are well versed in what agencies have in mind and they do receive budget recommendations from each standing committee of Congress as they develop the resolution.

The concurrent budget resolution is approved by both houses of Congress in the spring, before the appropriation consideration begins in earnest.[45] The budget resolution does not go to the president for approval, it is not a law, and it provides no funds for any agency. The deadline for its passage is frequently missed, and Congress has approved no budget resolution in some recent years. The resolution was always passed in the years from 1976 through 1998, but the record has been more spotty in recent years. From 1999, a resolution passed in nine years and was not passed in nine years. Although the resolution passed for fiscal 2016, none passed from 2011 through 2015. The 2017 Resolution was not passed on time and might not pass at all. (In fairness, it should be noted that some argue that the 2011 Budget Control Act, with its required ceilings, might have superseded part of the need for the budget resolution.) The congressional budget provides a template against which the microbudget actions of appropriations committees can be judged for control and constraint. The timetable that Table 4–3 showed for the congressional budget and appropriation process would have Congress complete all appropriations actions before the start of the fiscal year (it usually doesn't).

There is a final element to the congressional budget process: reconciliation. The 1974 Act created reconciliation as a mechanism for getting the year's tax and expenditure policies to coincide with the targets in the congressional budget. It has come to be viewed as the most powerful congressional tool for deficit reduction: rather than minor, one-year adjustments to targets, it now entails five-year instructions to committees for tax or fee increases and for spending cuts. The amounts involved can be large.[46] The reconciliation bill can be powerful, if Congress chooses

---

[45]The formal Clinton fiscal 1994 budget was the first since the 1974 Act received by Congress after it had passed the budget resolution. President Obama presented a budget outline in late February, followed by passage of a congressional budget resolution, followed by a traditional presidential budget. Appropriation subcommittees normally start hearings before the resolution.

[46]The reconciliation in 1981 was the medium for implementing President Reagan's economic reconstruction for fiscal 1982 (the 1982 executive budget had originated with President Carter, so this was the best place for President Reagan to revise those plans). The 1993 reconciliation was similarly the medium used by President Clinton.

to use its full clout, because (1) the bill gives binding instructions for changes in taxes and spending by formula or for reductions in spending to all committees except for appropriations committees, which are subject to other ceilings; (2) the bill cannot be filibustered, so it requires only a simple majority to be approved in the face of considerable objection (when majority parties in the Senate lack sixty votes, they like the reconciliation process as a legislative approach); (3) amendments must be germane, and committees cannot add extraneous provisions (both are subject to a sixty-vote test in the Senate); and (4) a committee that fails to meet its reconciliation target is subject to a motion to return its report to committee and return with a proposal that meets the target.[47]

The congressional budget process permits Congress to develop its own spending priorities, particularly with the assistance of the CBO, and to consider the appropriate macroeconomic impact for its fiscal actions. Without the congressional budget, the system would have the president being responsible for budget aggregates and overall policy plans and Congress responding to adjust those priorities by moving funds in the appropriation process. The congressional budget process adds a congressional view on priorities and responsibility for aggregates.[48]

Legislating: Structuring Appropriations Appropriations normally provide funds through distinct appropriation acts (see Sidebar 4–1), which emerge through the individual appropriations committees. These subcommittees work with pieces of the president's executive budget that reflect the requests from agencies within their jurisdiction. In this stage of legislative deliberation, elements of agency operation are examined, and agencies make the case for their fiscal plans. Committee staff and committee members develop considerable expertise in the subjects of their jurisdiction and watch programs very carefully. However, their focus is exclusively on the operations in their jurisdiction, not on other segments of the federal government, and many members become champions for the programs they are reviewing. They are not inclined to work toward budgetary balance by cutting programs in their bill so that more can be spent in some other bill.

The appropriation bills are traditionally expected to originate in the House. Each bill is approved by the appropriation subcommittee, then by the full appropriations committee, and then by the House before starting a similar flow through the Senate. In recent years, however, Senate appropriation subcommittees have often started hearings before House action is complete. Both House and Senate must approve the bill before it can be transmitted to the president for signature into law.

---

[47]A complete discussion of the reconciliation process appears in Robert Keith and Bill Heniff Jr., *The Budget Reconciliation Process: House and Senate Procedures,* CRS Report for Congress, Order Code RL33030 (Washington, D.C.: Congressional Research Service, August 10, 2005).

[48]Not everyone considers this an improvement. Louis Fisher writes, "By looking to Congress for comprehensive action, the unity and leadership that must come from the President have been unwittingly weakened. Creation of multiple budgets opened the door to escapism, confusion, and a loss of political accountability." "Federal Budget Doldrums: The Vacuum of Presidential Leadership," *Public Administration Review* 50 (November/December 1990): 699.

Sidebar 4–1
The First General Appropriation Act

Here is the first general appropriation act passed by Congress (1789):

> Be it enacted by the Senate and House of Representatives of the United States of America in Congress assembled. That there be appropriated for the service of the present year, to be paid out of the monies which arise, either from the requisitions heretofore made upon the several states, or from the duties on impost and tonnage, the following sums, viz. A sum not exceeding two hundred and sixteen thousand dollars for defraying the expenses of the civil list, under the late and present government; a sum not exceeding one hundred and thirty-seven thousand dollars for defraying the expenses of the department of war; a sum not exceeding one hundred and ninety thousand dollars for discharging the warrants issued by the late board of treasury, and remaining unsatisfied; and a sum not exceeding ninety-six thousand dollars for paying the pensions to invalids. [1 stat. 95]

That is a total of $639,000: $216,000 for civil or administrative governments, $137,000 for defense, $190,000 to retire short-term debt issued by the prior government, and $96,000 for pensions to the disabled.

Compare this act with any of the recent appropriation acts for a contrast in complexity, length, and money. For instance, the fiscal 2010 appropriation for the Department of Homeland Security alone was for over $42,800,000,000, and the act making the appropriation was forty-nine pages long.

Congress usually passes appropriations in lump sums to accounts that group related activities together, such as "Construction, General."[49] The appropriations are not organized according to line-items. Agencies may move spending around within the lump sum account, but they normally may not move funds from one account to another without congressional approval.[50] As the U.S. Supreme Court held, "the very point of a lump sum appropriation is to give an agency the capacity to adapt to changing circumstances" (*Lincoln v. Virgil,* 508 U.S. 182 (1993)). The appropriation committees are not supposed to get into policy, just financing. However, the

---

[49]Operating agencies are not permitted to move money from one account to another without congressional permission. In 2012, the National Weather Service moved funds from various long-term capital projects to pay employees without asking permission. The NWS believed the account for pay was under-funded and the capital project account was overfunded. Of course, that is a call to be made by Congress, not the agency. The actions did not cause spending that was above appropriation, but it violated the appropriation account structure, and it appeared that the NWS has been making unapproved reprogramming for some time. After the problem was discovered, it for a time appeared that the NWS would have to furlough 5,000 employees in the summer because of a lack of funds. Finally, Congress acted to make a reallocation to preserve the agency. The NWS's director abruptly retired and other staff were replaced. Lisa Rein, "Congress to Allow National Weather Service to Reconfigure Budget," *Washington Post,* June 20, 2012. The appropriation accounts are serious business.

[50]For instance, in summer 2015, the Veterans Administration faced a huge shortfall in its health-care operations and wanted to move money to that account from an account created to support medical care outside the VA system. It could not do this without approval from Congress even though both accounts

appropriation act may designate some funds for particular purposes or particular locations. The provisions may be in committee reports and explanatory statements rather than in the law itself. Agencies generally regard these notes as binding because they do not want to jeopardize their relationship with Congress in future budget cycles. The designation may also be in the appropriation bill itself. Here is an example. In the Omnibus Appropriation Act, 2009, the Army Corps of Engineers received an appropriation for construction of $2,141,677,000. The Act also included the following statement shortly after the appropriated amount: *"Provided further,* That the Chief of Engineers is directed to use $8,000,000 of the funds appropriated herein for planning, engineering, design or construction of the Grundy, Buchanan County, and Dickenson County, Virginia, elements of the Levisa and Tug Forks of the Big Sandy River and Upper Cumberland River Project." Purists might object that such matters are those of policy or substance, thus belonging in the authorization and not in a law providing financing. Purists seldom serve on appropriation committees.

Appropriation bills are supposed to deal with financing and not with policy. However, questions of substance can impede the smooth passage of legislation, sometimes involving topics not directly linked to the substance of the appropriation. For instance, the deliberations on the fiscal 2016 appropriation for Interior-Environment were halted because of an amendment concerning the Confederate flag that had been added to the spending legislation. That's not a financing question, but proponents of particular ideas use any means at their disposal, regardless of procedural standards, to further their cause.

Members of Congress historically coveted membership on the appropriations committee because programs and projects of special constituent interest may be developed, expanded, and protected there. The assignment isn't as attractive as it once was, given the concern about federal deficit control, but it still helps to be among the group that is making the control selections. All members are elected from geographically specific electoral bases, and their constituencies can benefit from location-specific projects—pork-barrel spending or "ZIP code designated expenditure"—that have dubious return to the nation but bring federal money into the home economy.[51] (Of course, programs that do have national importance have to be situated somewhere, and directing those to the home jurisdiction can be

---

[51]The effectiveness of Robert Byrd as chair of the Senate Appropriations Committee for his home state of West Virginia was legendary, but there are many other successful practitioners as well. For entertaining, but troubling examples, see Brian Kelly, *Adventures in Porkland: How Washington Wastes Your Money and Why They Won't Stop* (New York: Villard, 1992). A more scholarly study of appropriations legislation is Richard Munson, *The Cardinals of Capitol Hill* (New York: Grove Press, 1993). Cardinals are the chairs of the appropriation subcommittees. Ronald Utt notes that the pork projects often do not fit the priorities of the recipient locales. Ronald D. Utt, "How Congressional Earmarks and Pork-Barrel Spending Undermine State and Local Decision-Making," *The Heritage Foundation Backgrounder,* no. 1266, April 2, 1999. More on how it works: Representative John Murtha chaired the House Defense Appropriations Subcommittee and made sure that multiple millions of defense and other federal spending got directed to the Johnstown, Pennsylvania, airport (named after him). The airport has modest activity—two commuter round-trips to Washington per day now—and much of the military equipment there is disused. Mr. Murtha argued that upgrades to the airport were important so that it could serve as a backup to Pittsburgh in a crisis. Critics argue that the spending was pure pork, driven solely by the congressman's control over defense appropriations. Carol D. Leonnig, "Murtha Airport Got Military Upgrades," *Washington Post,* April 30, 2009. Mr. Murtha died in 2010.

helped by membership on the appropriations committee as well.) Although pork-barrel spending often includes highway projects (the Transportation Equity Act for the 21st Century, H.R. 2400, included 1,850 location-designated projects alone—but that was an authorization bill, so the projects may not have been carried out), university institutes and research programs, airports, government office buildings, and the like, no appropriation bill is immune.[52]

What makes a particular project "pork" as opposed to being a program that simply happens to be physically in a particular location? Using standards akin to Supreme Court Justice Potter Stewart's statement about pornography ("I know it when I see it," *Jacobellis v. Ohio,* 378 U.S. 184 [1964]), the media can easily identify wasteful government spending, but more careful discussion attempts to hone the concept more precisely. Counting up pork is a slippery task because what an external observer sees as wasteful spending will usually be seen as highly productive by those benefiting from it.

Some common features of identified pork include the following: the project is created as an earmark (a location-specific line item) in the appropriation bill; the project emerges from a member of Congress rather than from the administrative agency review process; and the project is added to the appropriation bill after the regular hearings and deliberations that produced the bill and without any discussions about the particular project.[53] Thwarting such items seems a way to constrain wasteful spending and to constrain the deficit, although some believe that a bit of pork is useful as a means of lubricating the legislative process. They argue that without the pork deals would be harder to consummate and Congress would do even less than it does already. However, congressional earmarks were one critical element in the lobbyist influence scandals of 2005–2006 that sent people to jail.[54]

The Office of Management and Budget, in the later years of the George W. Bush administration, tracked the amount of earmarks in the appropriation bills, defining earmarks as "funds provided by the Congress for projects, programs, or grants where

---

[52]A defense illustration: the Army maintains that it has a sufficient number of the 70-ton Abrams tank at $7.5 million each. Congress keeps putting more money in the budget to purchase the tanks. The nation's only tank plant is in Lima, Ohio, and the purchases are heavily supported by the senators and members of Congress from the state. It also helps that the manufacturer of the tanks (General Dynamics) has developed a supply chain of more than 560 subcontractors located throughout the country to help continue tank production as an employment program. (Richard Lardner, "Army Says No to More Tanks, but Congress Insists," *Military Times,* Aril 28, 2013.) And this goes on at a time when the Defense Department operates under a spending ceiling that limits its capacity to develop systems that it believes it actually needs.

[53]For a thorough examination of the earmarking process as it worked for transportation projects, see Gian-Claudia Sciara, "Peering Inside the Pork Barrel: A Study of Congressional Earmarking in Transportation," *Public Works Management Policy* 17 (3: 2012): 217–37.

[54]Pork is in the eyes of the beholder. Governor Jindal of Louisiana denounced wasteful spending on volcano monitoring in his response to President Obama's message to Congress on the large fiscal stimulus bill of 2009. That got a quick eruption from both senators from Alaska, Republican and Democrat, who pointed out the significance of that work for protection of life, limb, and property in areas with volcanos—like Alaska. Shortly after Jindal's speech, Mount Redoubt in Alaska erupted, but damage was not as severe as it could have been because the volcano monitors worked to provide some advance warning. George Bryson, "Alaskans Fume over Jindal Volcano-Monitoring Remark," *Anchorage Daily News,* February 25, 2009.

the purported congressional direction (whether in statutory text, report language, or other communication) circumvents otherwise applicable merit-based or competitive allocation processes, or specifies the location or recipient, or otherwise curtails the ability of the executive branch to manage its statutory and constitutional responsibilities pertaining to the funds allocation process."[55] OMB counted as earmarks (1) add-ons: when the appropriation was more than requested by the administration and had restrictions on how the additional money was to be spent (particularly involving locations); (2) carve-outs: restriction on how some portion of the appropriation was to be used; and (3) provisions that are so restrictive that only one recipient can qualify for funding. Over the years of tracking, the amounts earmarked did decline, from around $18.9 billion in 2005 to around $11 billion in 2010, possibly the result of improved transparency provided by these tallies. The largest number of earmarks and the largest dollar amount always appeared in defense appropriations. One suspects that defending the nation from foreign threats was not what was at the top of the agenda in how that money was spent. However, it should be kept in mind that total earmarks in each year amounted to only a small share of total discretionary spending, never more than 2 percent in any year. Earmarks just do not make much contribution to the overall fiscal position of the U.S. government. Indeed, a number of observers suggest that earmarks do not increase spending but simply direct where money will be spent.[56] If not for the earmarks, the money would still have been spent, just for something else or at some other location.

It is easy and appropriate to be enraged about earmarks and pork—efficient and effective provision of government services is not served by such interventions into a system that should make decisions based on carefully balancing the returns from various alternatives to spending public money. But there is no simple solution when choices, by their nature, must be political.[57] Rules approved by the Senate and House in early 2011 ban earmarking for the 112th Congress and the ban continues. Members of Congress use less transparent mechanisms, including convincing federal agencies to roll what would have previously been a congressional earmark into the agency budget request. In fact, members of Congress have a pretty good idea into what congressional district money will flow if particular agency operations are funded, even without formal earmarking. In addition, members of Congress have

---

[55]Office of Management and Budget, "Guidance to Agencies on Definition of Earmarks." http://earmarks.omb.gov/earmarks-public/earmarks_definition.html.

[56]Savage correctly points out that there are significant administrative costs associated with handling the earmarks, over and above the funds directly involved in the earmark. James D. Savage, "The Administrative Costs of Congressional Earmarking: The Case of the Office of Naval Research," *Public Administration Review* 69 (May/June 2009): 448–57.

[57]For many years, the sponsors of earmarks have been anonymous—the member of Congress who inserted an earmark was not identified. In recent years, an OMB database tracks each earmark, identifying the member of Congress who inserted it and what geographic area it would benefit. The idea probably was to shame the transgressors of public efficiency. It didn't work. Members of Congress could now definitively claim credit for bringing back the bucks to their district. In matter of fact, the public likes earmarks when they bring money back home. It is money going elsewhere that the public resents.

developed what is called a "soft earmark." This approach involves insertion into legislation along the lines of the committee "endorses" a particular program or "urges" or "recommends" agency finance for the program. That doesn't have the force of a full earmark and it hides both the supporter of the effort and how much money is involved, but agencies still get the word about congressional expectations.[58] Overall, banning earmarks provides little impact on federal spending and presents only a modest impediment to spending to benefit congressional constituencies.[59] Given that earmarks and pork-barrel projects have been the deal-making mechanism in Congress, maybe the result should be applauded.

Final Presidential Approval After Congress passes an appropriation bill, it must be signed by the president before it becomes law. The president can veto the bill or sign the bill in its entirety. For almost a century and a half, every president has sought the line-item veto, the power to strike individual parts of spending and taxing bills, while signing the remaining sections into law. The Line-Item Veto Act (P.L. 104–130, April 9, 1996) revised the Congressional Budget and Impoundment Control Act by granting the president additional power to shape federal finances. For calendar years 1997 through 2004, the president was given the power to cancel (1) any dollar amount of discretionary spending authority, (2) any item of new direct spending (roughly, new entitlements), or (3) any limited tax benefit (defined to be a revenue-losing provision with 100 or fewer beneficiaries; the Joint Committee on Taxation was to establish the list of eligible provisions and append the list to the bill sent to the president) within five days of signing into law the act containing the item. The president could cancel whole individual amounts in the appropriation acts or in the reports accompanying the acts, but could not reduce the amounts. The cancellation required that the president determine that the action would (1) reduce the federal budget deficit (and special controls ensured that this would occur), (2) not impair any essential government function, and (3) not harm the national interest. Congress had the ability to override the cancellation within a thirty-day review period.[60] In fiscal 1998 appropriation bills, which were the first approved under the item-veto cloud, President Clinton vetoed 77 items, accounting for about 0.10 percent of discretionary budget authority proposed in those bills. Of these, 87 percent were taken from defense and military construction bills, and Congress overrode the

---

[58]Ron Nixon, "Pork Barrel, by a Softer Name, Remains Hidden in the Budget," *New York Times*, April 7, 2008.

[59]Members of Congress now use "phone-marking" or direct contact with the executive branch to lobby for projects in their districts. They also use specific language in authorization bills to direct purchases to one particular product. For instance, a member of Congress sought to include language in the 2015 National Defense Authorization Act on purchase of "lightweight carbon fiber composite ladders" ($1,900 each) made by a firm in his district. Not officially a banned earmark, but with the same impact. (Christian Davenport, "The Earmark End-around? Pork-barrel is Out, Reviews of Military Ladder Options Are In," *Washington Post*, May 12, 2015).

[60]The first use of the line-item veto: three provisions in the 1997 reconciliation laws. See Jackie Calmes and Greg Hitt, "Clinton Uses Line-Item Veto for First Time," *Wall Street Journal*, August 12, 1997, Z-3. This was a surprise for Congress. The Republican majority had passed the veto law to strengthen the hand of the Republican president it expected to be elected in 1996. But Bill Clinton was reelected.

veto of the latter. This was the last use of this power because in *William J. Clinton, President of the United States v. City of New York*, 524 U.S. 417 (1998), the U.S. Supreme Court ruled that the line-item veto authority departed from the "finely wrought" constitutional procedure for enactment of law. If the president is to have line-item veto power, the Constitution must be amended; the power cannot be provided by simple legislation.

Not all agree that such power would improve government finances or even have much impact. The power can provide the president with a tool to prevent pork-barrel and other wasteful spending, but it also gives the president a valuable weapon to punish recalcitrant members of Congress—those who have managed to get on a presidential "enemies list"—by making sure that programs they support receive meager funding. And it cuts the president in on the deal making that builds appropriations and other pieces of legislation: the president can assure a representative's vote on a program by promising not to veto a project dear to the member of Congress. Indeed, the president may be wary of vetoing any pet projects of members of Congress with leadership roles, the people whose support is needed for presidential programs, while other members are not thus protected. Overall, the tool would shift the balance of power toward the president. Many are willing to accept these potential problems for the sake of greater fiscal responsibility and because the president's national constituency might make him less controlled by narrow interests than members of Congress. Others regard it as an inappropriate change in the balance of powers between the legislative and executive branches and believe that it carries the potential for great political evil. For now, only congressional action can rescind an appropriation or tax benefit that the president wishes out of a law.

Execution/Service Delivery

The end dates of the fiscal year set the bounds for the execution phase, the third stage of the process. In this period, appropriated monies are spent and public services are delivered. Fiscal control is critical in budget execution, and budget accounts are used to control funds provided through the appropriations. These appropriation accounts are the mechanism Congress employs to control how government services are provided. Appendix 4–1 explains and illustrates the linkage between appropriations (the legal articulation of the financial plan that is the budget) and these budget accounts. The fact that money is appropriated for a purpose, however, does not automatically and immediately lead to public expenditure or even to agencies having money to obligate/spend. To prevent agencies from exhausting funds before the end of the fiscal year and to use expenditure timing for macroeconomic purposes, the OMB divides total agency obligation authority into sums for distribution over the year (apportionments), and agencies obligate those portions as the year progresses.

Historically, appropriations were regarded as the maximum authority available to spend. The president could spend up to the appropriated amount, but not more.

Presidents, starting with John Adams, regularly impounded budget authority, acting on their own, to control spending during budget execution. It was regarded as a reasonable device for constraining the pace of spending and for efficient operations. Although it might irritate members of Congress whose pet projects got caught in the trap, the amounts were modest, and the process was accepted as part of executive financial management. However, President Nixon took the impoundment authority to new heights in the early 1970s, both in size (around 12 percent of appropriations) and targets (members of Congress who were deemed enemies of the president had projects in which they were interested hit by the impoundment axe).[61] Congress responded with provisions in the Congressional Budget and Impoundment Control Act. After the 1974 Act, impoundments became subject to congressional review and were divided into two categories: rescissions of budget authority, or permanent cancellation, and deferrals, or temporary withdrawal, of budget authority in the fiscal year. Rescissions proposed by the president must be approved by Congress within forty-five days of the proposal. (Congress may also initiate rescissions.) If not approved within the deadline, the funds must be released for expenditure. Deferrals require a message to Congress reporting the action; the deferral may not involve a change in policy but may be justified by a need to provide for contingencies or to achieve savings from changed requirements or operating efficiency. The deferral cannot extend beyond the fiscal year.[62] "Programmatic" delays—when "operational factors unavoidably impede the obligation of budget authority, notwithstanding the agency's reasonable and good faith efforts to implement the program"[63]—do not need to be reported.

Table 4–5 traces the historical record of rescissions since their beginnings. That record clearly shows a number of things. First, compared to total government spending, rescissions—both proposed and enacted—have been modest. Second, rescissions coming from Congress have been larger than those coming from the president. And, third, the success rate of presidential rescission proposals has not been high. President Clinton had the best luck with over 50 percent of the dollar value of his proposals enacted. President Ford fared the worst, with only 16 percent of his proposals enacted. Presidents George W. Bush and Barack Obama did not make any proposals. About one-third of all presidential rescissions have been enacted, both in numbers and in volume. Congress has been more aggressive in rescissions than have the presidents. In contrast to most chief executives, the president does have clearly constrained powers of control in budget execution.

---

[61]The events that caused the change are chronicled in Louis Fisher, *Presidential Spending Power* (Princeton, N.J.: Princeton University Press, 1975), especially chapters 7 and 8.

[62]Congress may enact legislation disapproving a deferral. Under the initial act, either house could prevent the deferral by passing an impoundment resolution. This was ruled to be an unconstitutional legislative veto in *City of New Haven v. United States*, 809 F.2d 900 (D.C. Cir. 1987), and was replaced with the current system.

[63]Office of the General Counsel, General Accounting Office, *Principles of Federal Appropriations Law* (Washington, D.C.: U.S. Government Printing Office, 2004), 21. This is the principal reference on federal budget authority and appropriations for the federal government.

Table 4-5
Summary of Proposed and Enacted Recissions and Total Outlays, Fiscal Years 1974–2011

Fiscal Year	Recissions Proposed by President Number	(Millions $)	Proposals Accepted by Congress Number	(Millions $)	Recissions Initiated by Congress Number	(Millions $)	Total Enacted	Total Rescinded (Millions $)	Total On-Budget Outlays (Millions $)	President Proposing Rescissions
2011	0	$0.00	0	$0.00	157	$20,980.10	157	$20,980.10	$2,901,531.00	B. Obama
2010	0	$0.00	0	$0.00	132	$10,917.06	132	$10,917.06	$3,000,661.00	B. Obama
2009	0	$0.00	0	$0.00	92	$12,716.57	92	$12,716.57	$2,507,793.00	G.W. Bush/B. Obama
2008	0	$0.00	0	$0.00	126	$12,201.18	126	$12,201.18	$2,275,049.00	G.W. Bush
2007	0	$0.00	0	$0.00	56	$8,035.71	56	$8,035.71	$2,232,981.00	G.W. Bush
2006	0	$0.00	0	$0.00	89	$33,361.18	89	$33,361.18	$2,069,746.00	G.W. Bush
2005	0	$0.00	0	$0.00	76	$6,351.13	76	$6,351.13	$1,913,330.00	G.W. Bush
2004	0	$0.00	0	$0.00	49	$10,515.46	49	$10,515.46	$1,796,890.00	G.W. Bush
2003	0	$0.00	0	$0.00	47	$3,123.44	47	$3,123.44	$1,655,232.00	G.W. Bush
2002	0	$0.00	0	$0.00	76	$4,621.09	76	$4,621.09	$1,516,008.00	G.W. Bush
2001	0	$0.00	0	$0.00	67	$5,148.14	67	$5,148.14	$1,458,185.00	G.W. Bush
2000	3	$128.00	0	$0.00	61	$3,757.77	61	$3,757.77	$1,381,064.00	W. Clinton/G.W. Bush
1999	3	$35.04	2	$16.80	105	$5,081.43	107	$5,098.23	$1,335,854.00	W. Clinton
1998	25	$25.26	21	$17.28	43	$4,180.81	64	$4,198.09	$1,290,490.00	W. Clinton
1997	10	$407.11	6	$285.11	96	$7,381.25	102	$7,666.36	$1,259,580.00	W. Clinton
1996	24	$1,425.90	8	$963.40	104	$4,974.85	112	$5,938.25	$1,227,078.00	W. Clinton
1995	29	$1,199.82	25	$845.39	248	$18,868.38	273	$19,713.77	$1,182,380.00	W. Clinton
1994	65	$3,172.18	45	$1,293.48	81	$2,374.42	126	$3,667.89	$1,142,799.00	W. Clinton
1993	7	$356.00	4	$206.25	74	$2,205.34	78	$2,411.59	$1,129,191.00	W. Clinton
1992	128	$7,879.47	26	$2,067.55	131	$22,526.95	157	$24,594.50	$1,082,539.00	W. Clinton
1991	30	$4,859.25	8	$286.42	26	$1,420.47	34	$1,706.89	$1,027,928.00	G.H.W. Bush/W. Clinton
1990	11	$554.26	0	$0.00	71	$2,304.99	71	$2,304.97	$932,832.00	G.H.W. Bush
1989	6	$143.10	1	$2.05	11	$325.91	12	$327.97	$860,012.00	G.H.W. Bush
1988	0	$0.00	0	$0.00	61	$3,888.66	61	$3,888.66	$809,243.00	G.H.W. Bush
1987	73	$5,835.80	2	$36.00	52	$12,359.39	54	$12,395.39	$806,842.00	R. Reagan/G.H.W. Bush
1986	83	$10,126.90	4	$143.21	7	$5,409.41	11	$5,552.62	$769,396.00	R. Reagan
1985	245	$1,856.09	98	$173.70	12	$5,458.62	110	$5,632.32	$685,632.00	R. Reagan
1984	9	$636.40	3	$55.38	7	$2,188.69	10	$2,244.06	$660,934.00	R. Reagan
1983	21	$1,569.00	0	$0.00	11	$310.61	11	$310.61	$594,892.00	R. Reagan
1982	32	$7,907.40	5	$4,365.49	5	$48.43	10	$4,413.92	$542,956.00	R. Reagan
1981	133	$15,361.90	101	$10,880.94	43	$3,736.49	144	$14,617.43	$477,044.00	R. Reagan
1980	59	$1,618.10	34	$777.70	33	$3,238.21	67	$4,015.90	$404,941.00	J. Carter/R. Reagan
1979	11	$908.70	9	$723.61	1	$47.50	10	$771.11	$369,585.00	J. Carter
1978	12	$1,290.10	5	$518.66	4	$67.16	9	$585.82	$328,675.00	J. Carter
1977	20	$1,926.93	9	$813.69	3	$172.72	12	$986.41	$77,281.00	J. Carter
1976	50	$3,582.00	7	$148.33	0		7	$148.33	$301,098.00	G. Ford/J. Carter
1975	87	$2,722.00	38	$386.30	1	$5.00	39	$391.30	$270,780.00	G. Ford
1974	2	$495.64	0	$0.00	3	$1,400.41	3	$1,400.41		G. Ford

SOURCE: Government Accountability Office, *Updated Recission Statistics, Fiscal Years 1974–2011*, B-322906 (July 19, 2012).

Audit

The audit phase of the federal cycle, supervised by the GAO, formally begins at the end of the fiscal year. Some audit functions, however, do begin during the fiscal year as agencies work to prevent illegal and irregular transactions by various approval stages. In an important sense, the audit phase ensures that everything else in the budget process matters: unless the decisions made elsewhere in the process are carried through, the process is irrelevant. The audit phase determines whether those directions were followed. The GAO reports to the House and Senate Committees on Government Operations, and those reports are accessible at the GAO website.[64]

Sorts of Budget Authority

Budget authority gives agencies the ability to enter into obligations that will eventually result in outlays (from the Treasury) of federal funds. Agencies receive this authority rather than actual funds to spend. The authority may be one-year, multiyear, or no-year authority; the law providing the authority will define how long the agency will have the authority before it expires. The action may be permanent and amounts may be indefinite. Several types of authorities to make commitments (obligations) result in government outlays (or expenditures). Important types include the following:

1. **Appropriations authority**, the most common authority, permits "federal agencies to incur obligations and to make payments from Treasury for specified purposes."[65]
2. **Contract authority** provides authority for agencies to enter into binding contracts before the agency has an appropriation to make payments under the contract or in amounts greater than existing appropriations.[66] Eventually, an appropriation must cover the contracts, and, because the contracts legally commit the U.S. government, Congress would have little choice but to provide the appropriation. At one time, contract authority provided a device for "backdoor spending," a way that substantive committees could force the more conservative appropriations committees to accept more aggressive government programs. Now new contract authority can be provided only to the extent appropriations are also provided for that fiscal year.
3. **Borrowing authority** appearing in either a substantive law or an appropriation act allows an agency to incur and liquidate obligations from borrowed funds. That authority may involve some combination of borrowing

---

[64]http://www.gao.gov.
[65]Accounting and Financial Management Division, Government Accountability Office, *A Glossary of Terms Used in the Federal Budget Process.* http://www.gao.gov/new.items/d057345p.pdf.
[66]Most federal highway programs operate with contract authority. U.S. Department of Transportation, Federal Highway Administration, *Financing Federal-Aid Highways,* Publication No. FHWA-PL-92-016 (May 1992), explains this system.

from the Treasury, borrowing directly from the public (selling agency debt securities), or borrowing from the Federal Financing Bank (selling agency securities to it). Again, this authority now is limited to amounts provided in appropriation acts.

4. **Loan and loan-guarantee authority** consists of statutory authorizations for the government's pledge to pay all or part of principal and interest to a lender if the borrower defaults; no obligation occurs until the contingency (default) occurs. Such commitments, after the Federal Credit Reform Act of 1990, now require specified treatment in appropriation acts of estimated long-term costs (defaults, delinquencies, etc.).

5. **Entitlement authority provides authority** "to make payments (including grants and loans) for which budget authority is not provided in advance by appropriation acts to any person or government if, under the provisions of the law containing such authority, the U.S. government is obligated to make the payments to persons or governments who meet the requirements established by the law."[67] Entitlements provide payments according to formula: Social Security, Medicare, Medicaid, and veterans' benefits (pensions and education) are some important examples. Farm price supports fall in this category as well; they were replaced by a firm appropriation for a time. Entitlement spending results not directly from the appropriation process, but through the extent to which beneficiaries qualify under the formulas erected in substantive law. Entitlements now fall within the scope of the reconciliation process. As noted earlier, much growth in federal spending comes from entitlements. A later section examines the nature of entitlements and "mandatory" expenditure in greater detail.

Regular appropriation is now the checkpoint for most important sources of budget authority, entitlements being the major exception. And controlling the granting of budget authority is the way in which Congress and the president could control the growth of government spending, should they be so inclined. There are three types of appropriation measures: regular appropriation bills, continuing resolutions, and supplemental appropriation bills. Regular appropriations come in several durations (periods of legal availability) with different rules attached to each. The traditional appropriation is *annual* (one-year) authority, which provides funds for obligation during a specific fiscal year.[68] Such appropriations usually finance the routine activities of federal agencies; unless specified otherwise, appropriations are annual and may not be carried beyond the current fiscal year for obligation later (funds expire). There is evidence of an agency spending surge at the end of the fiscal year to make certain no funds remain unspent (possible evidence that their budget requests are excessive), that such spending is more wasteful than other spending during the year,

---

[67]GAO, *Glossary.*

[68]Congress may appropriate for less than a full fiscal year. A fiscal 1980 appropriation to the Community Services Administration for emergency energy-assistance grants specified that awards could not be made after June 30, 1980. Congress wanted to help with heating, not air conditioning (P.L. 96–126), but there was a severe heat wave, and Congress extended the program to include fans; the appropriation was extended to the full fiscal year (P.L. 96–321).

and that allowing rollover into later years would reduce the waste.[69] *No-year* appropriations provide funds for obligations with no restrictions placed on year of use. Most construction funds, some funds for research, and many trust fund appropriations have been handled in this fashion. *Multiple-year* appropriations provide funds for a particular activity for several years. General revenue sharing, a program of federal assistance to state and local governments of the late 1970s and early 1980s, was funded on that basis to provide greater predictability for the recipients. *Advance* appropriations provide agencies with funds for future fiscal years. This structure is seldom used, although it can facilitate agency planning and has been strongly urged for use in defense-system procurement. *Permanent* appropriations provide funds for specified purposes without requiring repeated action by Congress. To add greater certainty to public capital markets, interest on the federal debt is handled with such appropriations. All but annual appropriations reduce the ability of the legislative and executive branches to realign fiscal policy when economic or social conditions change, even though they increase agency ability to develop long-range plans. The trade between control and planning is not an easy one, but responsibility and accountability probably weigh the balance toward annual appropriation, especially in regard to the difficulty of forecasting operating environments many months in advance.

Budget authority not obligated within the time period for which it was appropriated expires. Congress may act to extend the availability of funds, either before or after their scheduled expiration, through reappropriation. The federal budget structure counts these funds as new budget authority for the fiscal year of reappropriation.

Two other methods of providing agency funds, in addition to these normal appropriations, should be mentioned. First, a *continuing resolution* allows agencies to function when a new fiscal year begins before agency appropriation laws have been approved for the year. The resolution—an agreement between both legislative houses—authorizes the agency to continue operations.[70] The resolution level may be the same as the prior year, may entail certain increases, or may encompass the appropriation bill as it has emerged from one house of Congress; the resolution may be for part of the fiscal year or for the entire year. Without some action, however, the agency without appropriations could not spend and would not be able to provide services.

How often are continuing resolutions necessary? In the fiscal years from 1948 through 2016, all appropriation acts were signed into law by the first day of the new fiscal year only in 1989, 1995, and 1997—and it was done for 1997 only by rolling six appropriation bills (defense; commerce, justice, state, and the judiciary; foreign operations; interior; labor, health and human services, and education; and treasury)

---

[69]Jeffrey B. Liebman and Neale Mahoney, "Do Expiring Budgets Lead to Wasteful Year-End Spending? Evidence from Federal Procurement," National Bureau of Economic Research Working Paper 19481 (September 2013). Before the change in fiscal year start, this was called the "spring spending spree." Somehow the "fall spending spree" doesn't have the same panache.

[70]A good guide to the construction of and experience with continuing resolutions is Thad Juszczak, "Living with Continuing Resolutions," *The Public Manager* 40 (Fall 2011): 40–44.

into an omnibus appropriation bill approved on September 30, 1996, just in the nick of time.[71] The timetable for nicely defined appropriations in place with the new fiscal year is not always met, and continuing resolutions are so regular that they might as well be considered normal.

Sometimes an impasse between Congress and the president prevents the continuing resolution from being passed in time, and there is an appropriation gap. This has occurred in fiscal years 1977, 1978, 1979, 1980, 1982, 1983, 1984, 1985, 1987, 1988, 1991, 1996, and 2014.[72] When there is an absence of obligation authority, agencies must shut down, excluding those associated with protection of human life and property. Parks, museums, and monuments get closed, operations get delayed, passports and visas don't get issued, inspections don't get performed, and so on.[73]

Continuing resolutions have many trappings of appropriations, but their continued use raises three special issues. First, the continuing resolution in theory would have few, if any, new programs. A steady pattern of such funding could hinder an agency's program development and response to changing service conditions. And, in similar fashion, programs that are scheduled to be terminated, even when there is agreement between the president and Congress on the termination, continue in operation. Second, the omnibus continuing resolution may partly impede the president's veto power. A veto of an omnibus package could harm the flow of services throughout the government, a consequence the president ordinarily would want to avoid, even though there may be some included appropriation bills that might individually be vetoed. Third, the omnibus package may tempt members of Congress to add special favors for their constituencies, causing an inordinate number of pet projects to be included, well above the number of those in a smaller appropriation bill, where they are more easily open to scrutiny and rejection. The continuing resolution deserves an uneasy life. Many countries have systems of automatic continuing resolutions to ensure that government does not close. Similar programs have been proposed for the federal government, but as yet there has been no agreement on what formula to use.[74]

---

[71]The ideal is for twelve separate appropriation bills to be passed before the start of the fiscal year. However, many of the individual bills may be combined into a single "omnibus" appropriation bill, passed either just before the start of the new year or sometime thereafter. When only a few are included in a single bill, that has been termed a "minibus" appropriation bill. Neither approach would be seen as part of "regular order" in federal finance.

[72]Kevin Kosar, *Shutdown of the Federal Government: Causes, Effects, and Process,* CRS Report for Congress, Order Code 98-844 GOV (Washington, D.C.: Congressional Research Service, September 20, 2004) and updates from news media.

[73]The effect from failing to increase the federal debt limit is different. If the federal government hits its debt limit, it loses its ability to borrow to obtain cash to finance its obligations, and it has to borrow because current receipts now cover only 40 percent of outlays. Agencies can continue to spend if they have budget authority (from appropriation or continuing resolution), but the bills for that spending cannot be paid when they come due. Thus, fiddling with the debt limit gives the worst of all worlds: no control over federal spending and the federal government becomes a deadbeat.

[74]There is a special provision for national defense. The Food and Forage Act (41 U.S.C. § 11), a law passed during the Civil War, allows a Department of Defense contracting office to incur obligations in excess of appropriation to obtain food, fuel, forage, and related items necessary to meet current year needs. In more recent times, it was used during Vietnam, during the first Gulf War, and in 2001 (after September 11). Failure to appropriate won't stop (or cripple) a war.

A second special form of providing funds is the *supplemental appropriation,* an appropriation of funds to be spent during the current fiscal year. (Requests and appropriations are normally for future budget years.) The supplemental appropriation may be part of a presidential budget submission, or it may be separate. Typical reasons include the need to (1) cover the cost of programs newly enacted by the legislature, (2) provide for higher-than-anticipated prices or workloads, or (3) cope with surprise developments. The request is for appropriation in addition to funds previously approved by the legislature. Forecasts of operating environments are seldom perfect, so most budget seasons include some supplementals. One exceptional example: the terrorist attacks of September 11, 2001, induced an emergency supplemental appropriation for $40 billion—for funds to be spent as required in any fiscal year, pretty much money to be spent anytime, anywhere, for anything. Other examples include supplementals to help deal with the Northridge (Los Angeles) earthquake in 1994, flooding in the Dakotas in 1998, military operations in the 1990s and later, and fiscal 2011 funding for disaster relief for Hurricane Irene. Emergency circumstances produce supplementals outside the normal cycle. The most famous (or infamous) recent supplemental appropriation is the American Recovery and Reinvestment Act of 2009 (P.L. 111–5), more popularly called the "fiscal stimulus bill," that was signed into law on February 17, 2009, shortly before enactment of the omnibus appropriation for 2009 and just as Congress would ordinarily have been starting work on the president's budget proposals for fiscal 2010. Some members of Congress were likely confused by the flurry of appropriation acts coming through at the same time. Certainly, the media and the public were.

The Bush administration chose to finance the wars in Iraq and Afghanistan almost entirely through supplemental appropriations, leaving these costs out of its regular budget message and adding them through the year. This practice is contrary to accepted budget practice because it hinders the capacity to maintain fiscal discipline and to direct limited resources to areas of greatest national priority. It is as if fighting these wars is an afterthought in finance that must automatically be added to the deficit. It is a good way to cripple the national economy. The Obama administration added them into the regular budget.

Supplementals that must pass become a great vehicle for special earmarks: the 2005 military supplement had provisions involving oil drilling, the National Park Service, a new baseball stadium in Washington, tsunami relief, aid for Palestinians, and emergency watershed protection in Utah attached to it. A supplemental titled "Kosovo and Other National Security Matters" included funds for a Coast Guard Great Lakes icebreaker. Of course, supplementals are sometimes necessary because someone made a major mistake. For example, the Department of Veterans Affairs needed a supplemental appropriation for fiscal 2005 to cover health services for veterans because it based its budget request on demand in fiscal 2002, before the invasion of Iraq and the resulting significant surge in demand for medical treatment for returning service personnel, even though the request was prepared after the war had started.[75] The supplemental for Superstorm Sandy included appropriations

---

[75]Thomas B. Edsall, "VA Faces $2.6 Billion Shortfall in Medical Care," *Washington Post,* June 29, 2005, A19.

for Alaskan fisheries, new cars and equipment for the Departments of Justice and Homeland Security, roof repair for the Smithsonian Institution, and money for the Kennedy Space Center and the National Park Service.[76] Nevertheless, net supplemental appropriations constitute a relatively modest share of total outlays in most years. They averaged 3.2 percent of outlays in fiscal years from 1962 through 2014 and 2.7 percent from fiscal 2000 through 2014. There were no supplementals at all in fiscal 2011 and 2012.[77]

Mandatory and Discretionary Spending

The Budget Enforcement Act of 1990 established the useful categorization of federal spending into mandatory and discretionary classes. Discretionary spending is spending that flows through the annual appropriation process—the process through which the discussion of the phases has taken you—and shows up in one of the twelve appropriation laws (or in a continuing resolution). It is the spending for agency operations involving both defense and nondefense (domestic) services. Mandatory spending includes outlays that are made according to definitions of eligibility and benefit or payment formulas rather than directly through the appropriation process. Table 4–6 divides the major types of mandatory federal spending into the programs that are *means-tested* (i.e., payments are determined by the economic status of the recipient) and those that are *non-means-tested* (transfers are made without regard to economic status, but on the basis of other characteristics of the recipient).[78] Social Security, Medicare, and Medicaid constitute the largest components of mandatory spending. Sidebar 4–2 provides more insight into the financing of Social Security and Medicare. You can see that non-means tested programs are, in total, much larger than are the means tested ones.

Congress and the president still control mandatory spending, but they exercise control by establishing the definitions and rules, not through annual appropriation acts; when those conditions have been met, however, the government has a legal obligation to pay funds to the eligible person, corporation, or other entity. The government cannot plead lack of funds or more important uses for its funds.[79] Congress and the president cannot increase or decrease the outlays for a given year without

---

[76]"Pork for Christmas," *Wall Street Journal*, December 21, 2012.

[77]Supplementals had increased substantially over the fiscal 1997 through fiscal 2006 period, roughly a fivefold increase over the previous ten-year period. (Government Accountability Office, *Supplemental Appropriations, Opportunities Exist to Increase Transparency and Provide Additional Controls*, GAO-08-314 [Washington, D.C.: Government Accountability Office, January 2008], 3.)

[78]Means-testing looks like a sensible approach to making sure that assistance goes to those people who need it most, thus providing a way for fiscal responsibility while helping the less fortunate. But it is also argued that means-testing damages incentive for work effort. The return that a household receives from successful work effort gets reduced by loss of mean-tested assistance. The net result could be to discourage that effort, and nothing good can be said about such an incentive.

[79]However, Social Security spending is limited to the amount of money in its trust fund. If that money should be completely exhausted, payments going out would be limited to payments coming in—a total return to a pay-as-you-go system and a violation of the entitlement concept.

Table 4–6
Mandatory and Discretionary Federal Spending, 1975–2013 (In Billions $)

	1975	1980	1985	1990	1995	2000	2005	2010	2013
Important Means-Tested Programs									
Student Loans	0.1	1.4	3.5	4.4	4.4	1.0	15.0	8.9	n.a.
Medicaid	6.8	14.0	22.7	41.1	89.1	117.0	182.0	273.0	265.4
Food Stamps	4.6	9.1	12.5	15.9	25.6	18.0	33.0	70.0	84.1
Child Nutrition	1.5	3.4	3.7	5.0	7.5	9.0	13.0	17.0	n.a.
Earned Income Tax Credit	—	1.3	1.1	4.4	15.2	26.1	34.6	54.7	57.5
Supplementary Security Income	4.3	5.7	8.7	11.5	23.6	29.5	35.3	43.9	50.2
Family Support	5.1	7.3	9.2	12.2	18.1	21.0	24.0	28.0	24.7
State Childrens Health Insurance	—	—	—	—	—	2.0	5.0	8.0	9.5
Veterans Pensions	2.7	3.6	3.8	3.6	3.0	3.0	*	*	80.0
Important Non-Means-Tested Programs									
Medicare	14.1	34.0	69.7	107.0	177.1	216.0	335.1	520.5	585.2
Social Security	63.6	117.1	186.4	246.5	333.3	406.0	519.0	701.0	807.8
Federal Civilian, Military, Veterans and Other	18.3	32.1	45.2	59.9	75.2	88.0	148.0	197.0	241.0
Unemployment Compensation	12.8	16.9	15.8	17.1	21.3	21.0	32.0	159.0	67.3
Deposit Insurance	0.5	(0.4)	(2.2)	57.9	(17.9)	(3.1)	(1.0)	(32.0)	4.3
Farm Price and Income Supports	0.6	2.8	17.7	6.5	5.8	30.0	19.0	n.a.	23.8
Social Services	2.9	3.7	3.5	5.1	5.5	4.0	*	n.a.	n.a.
Veterans Benefits	10.2	11.0	12.9	13.4	18.3	24.0	*	*	*
General Revenue Sharing	6.1	68.0	4.6	—	—	n.a.	—	—	—
Flood Insurance	n.a	n.a.	n.a.	n.a.	n.a.	n.a.	1.0	1.3	n.a.
Universal Service Fund	—	—	—	—	—	n.a.	6.0	8.9	9.2
Offsetting Reciepts	(18.3)	(29.2)	(47.1)	(58.7)	(79.7)	(78.6)	(126.0)	(184.0)	(106.8)
Total Mandatory and Related Programs	151.1	262.0	40.1	568.1	738.8	951.2	1,320.0	1,912.9	2,032.0
Net Interest	23.2	52.5	129.5	184.3	232.1	222.9	184.0	196.2	220.9
Total Discretionary	15.0	276.3	415.8	500.6	544.9	614.8	968.0	1,347.2	1,202.2
Total Outlays	332.3	590.9	946.6	1,253.2	1,515.8	1,789.1	2,472.0	3,457.1	3,455.0

n.a., data not available.
*Included with federal civilian, military, veterans, and other retirement and disability.

SOURCES: Congressional Budget Office, *Budget and Economic Outlook* (Washington, D.C.: CBO, various years) and Office of Management and Budget, *Budget of the United States Government, Fiscal Year 2015, Historical Tables* (Washington, D.C.: US GPO, 2014).

Sidebar 4–2
The Biggest Entitlements: Social Security and Medicare

The two largest federal entitlement programs—61.9 percent of mandatory spending in fiscal year 2015—are Social Security and Medicare, both social insurance programs primarily for the elderly. (Medicaid, the health program for low-income people that is a shared state-federal program, amounts to another 15.2 percent of mandatory spending and is the third largest entitlement, but it is financed through general revenue and is not subject to the same financing issues as Social Security and Medicare.)

Social Security—more formally the Old-Age, Survivors, and Disability Insurance (OASDI) Program—provides benefits to retired and disabled workers, their dependents, and survivors that replace income lost to a family by retirement, death, or disability of a worker. It originated with the Social Security Act of 1935, although its coverage and role, as well as many structural features, have changed over the years.

Medicare is a national health insurance program for the aged and certain disabled people. Part A Medicare covers inpatient hospital services, posthospital skilled nursing facility care, home health services, and hospice care and is available automatically to almost everyone older than age 65. Part B Medicare covers physicians' services, laboratory services, durable medical equipment, outpatient hospital services, and other medical services; payment is generally limited to 80 percent of an approved Medicare fee schedule after the patient has met an annual $100 deductible amount, and the insurance is provided only to those individuals who purchase it. Part C or Medicare Advantage is a Medicare-approved private insurance health plan for those enrolled in Part A and B. Part D Medicare provides prescription drug coverage through premiums paid to private insurers and general fund subsidies.

Social Security and Part A Medicare are financed by payroll taxes paid by workers covered by their programs (roughly 96 percent of the paid workforce) and their employers and by a tax on the net annual earnings of the self-employed. Part B Medicare is financed by premiums paid by people in the program and by general federal revenues. Any fund balances are invested in U.S. Treasury securities to earn interest. Benefits are paid as entitlements; the benefit formulas are determined by Congress. The funds do not go through the annual appropriation process.

Social Security and Medicare are reasonable candidates for "self-financing" (or "actuarial funding") schemes associated with social insurance trust funds because of their focus on the elderly. And we also know that conditions of moral hazard and adverse selection make private medical insurance for the elderly expensive at best and unavailable at worst. With a social insurance system, people must pay into the social insurance fund during their work life and qualify for guaranteed benefits from the fund during that work experience. The idea is that, on retirement, sufficient funds will have accumulated—payments in, plus interest earned on balances held—to support pension payments and health insurance coverage for the population cohort. The life cycle of the fund is one of accumulation during work years and disbursement during retirement; the fund will be "fully funded" or "actuarially sound" when the system accumulations are sufficient to cover benefits estimated to be owed to system beneficiaries.

Unfortunately, the American social insurance system for too long operated on a pure "pay-as-you-go" system of finance, wherein people qualified for benefits during their work life, but insufficient money was accumulated to support those benefits on retirement. The scheme worked because it was possible to use revenues collected from the current workforce to support benefits paid to current retirees. But demographic forces create a problem: there were about five workers for each Social Security recipient in 1960, but there are expected to be only about two workers per recipient by 2030—the immediate transfer from worker to recipient cannot be supported anymore. With that demographic distribution, the money accumulated in the Social Security trust funds rapidly disappears. Payments into the system and interest earned on the accumulation are insufficient to finance the system as people live longer, as "baby-boomers" retire, and as labor force growth slows—all demographic forces now in place. On top of that is the rapid escalation of health-care costs. That hits all sectors of the health system—private insurance, Medicare, and Medicaid. The social insurance trust funds, both Social Security and Medicare, have been in surplus for a number of years and have provided a partial cushion against the deficits of the general fund, but the cruel truth is that those surpluses are too small to cover the benefits being earned by workers.

The economic numbers for both programs are chilling. Social Security expenditures have exceeded payments into the fund since 2010, the first year in which that had happened since 1983, roughly the time at which the system was converted from a pay-as-you-go to an actuarial funding logic. A deal at the time of the conversion in the mid-1980s made some adjustments to the formula for taxes in and benefits out, and the adjustments were estimated to handle the Social Security funding problem for about twenty-five years. It was assumed that, before that period had expired, statesman-like lawmakers would come back for a permanent fix to the system. They were right about the fix lasting about twenty-five years; they were wrong about the statesman-like lawmakers.

The trust funds accumulate and invest balances. Surpluses in the Social Security and Medicare trust funds (and other federal trust funds that have accumulations) are invested in federal fund debt, in the same way that private endowment and pension funds invest their annual surpluses in various interest-bearing assets. Because of the desire that these trust fund assets be entirely secure, federal debt is the only asset the trust funds have been permitted to purchase, thus providing some financing of the federal funds deficit; indeed, the Social Security Trust Fund is the largest single holder of United States government debt. (The stock market declines of the recession that began in late 2007 likely have dampened any efforts for more aggressive investment strategies for some years.) However, just as is the case with private investment funds, the debt is owned by the social insurance and other trust fund programs. The problem with the Social Security and Medicare accumulations is that they are not large enough to support the future outflows of benefits without eventual subsidization from other budgetary resources. The Social Security and Medicare (off-budget) surpluses give little reason for satisfaction: the accumulated surpluses are intended to finance benefits for the current workforce when those people retire, and actuarial forecasts show that these accumulations will run out. In other words, the Social Security and Medicare surpluses are too small to cover the benefit obligations that are being accrued by the current workforces.

Fund assets are U.S. government bonds (physical bonds kept in a safe in the Bureau of Public Debt in Parkersburg, West Virginia), so the federal government will have to raise taxes, borrow more (from some lender other than the Social Security system), or cut federal fund spending to repay the debt being liquidated by the Social Security system. If the federal government

(continues)

Sidebar 4–2
(continued)

---

is unable to repay the debt owned by the Social Security system as it comes due, then the financial problems of the Social Security system will be only one of the fiscal disasters that the country will face.

The trustees of the Social Security system now estimate that Social Security trust funds will be exhausted in 2034. Thereafter, the fund would be supported only by annual payments into the fund, and that would require an immediate reduction of around 20 percent of benefits across the board and the cut would increase over time. When the fund is exhausted, the system essentially reverts to the old pay-as-you-go structure in which payments by current employees immediately are paid out as benefits to current retirees.

The trustees find an even worse profile for the portion of Medicare financed through its trust fund. The trust fund will be exhausted in 2030. From that point, either Medicare benefits will need to be dramatically reduced or revenues into the system will need to be significantly increased, either by dedicated Medicare taxes or by transfers from the regular federal revenue system. Medicare costs are estimated to have been reduced and life of the trust fund extended because of provisions in the Patient Protection and Affordable Care Act of 2010 (i.e., Obamacare), but by far less than what is necessary to make the program sustainable.

As with other elements of government finance, the general options are clear: (1) increase current revenues into the system, (2) constrain benefits paid from the system, or (3) increase returns earned while balances are in the system by expanding the investment options available to fund administrators. The rules of the funds provide that, should the fund not have enough money to cover benefits in a year, the benefits will be reduced to no more than the money available—the entitlement promise goes away. Of course, making both programs for the elderly a private responsibility is another option, but returning society to pre-1930 conditions, with individuals being solely responsible for their own old age—an environment in which growing old typically meant being forced to move in with family or to the county poorhouse—is not an attractive prospect for most Americans and is not consistent with expectations for a modern, industrialized democracy. What is clear is that neither the Social Security nor the Medicare problem will go away by itself and, while the options for action are clear, the courage of lawmakers to pursue the options is microscopic.

SOURCE: Social Security and Medicare Board of Trustees, *Status of the Social Security and Medicare Programs: A Survey of the 2014 Annual Reports* (Washington D.C.: Social Security Administration, 2014); Office of Management and Budget. *A New Era of Responsibility, Renewing America's Promise* (Washington, D.C.: Office of Management and Budget, 2009); and Congressional Budget Office, *Social Security: A Primer* (Washington, D.C.: Congressional Budget Office, 2001).

---

changing the law that created the eligibility and the payment rules; these rules coming from authorization legislation, not appropriation actions, determine outlay. Because the spending is outside the annual appropriation process, it frequently is called uncontrollable spending; the annual appropriation checkpoint is gone. And those expenditures have taken larger shares of all federal outlays. Mandatory spending also

Figure 4–3
Discretionary Federal Outlays as % Total Outlays, Fiscal 1962–2014

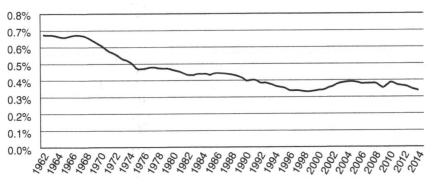

SOURCE: Office of Management and Budget, Budget of the United States Government, Fiscal Year 2016, Historical Tables (Washington, D.C.: U.S. Government Printing Office, 2017).

includes offsetting receipts—certain fees and charges that are regarded as negative budget authority and outlay. These receipts are collected from other government accounts or from the public in business transactions (like rents and royalties from oil and gas drilling leases on the Outer Continental Shelf or fees to the Citizenship and Immigration Service) and operations financed by such receipts are largely outside of congressional control. Payment of interest on the federal debt, although not strictly considered a mandatory category, is also outside the annual appropriation process.[80]

Mandatory spending and discretionary spending have taken dramatically different paths over recent decades. Figure 4–3 shows the trend for discretionary spending. Discretionary spending has fallen from almost 70 percent of total outlays in 1962 to under 35 percent in 2014. The annual growth rate over this long period for mandatory spending (8.7 percent) is much greater than that for total discretionary spending (5.4 percent), and that compounds to a considerable difference in shares over time. The recent bumps upward for discretionary spending are largely caused by defense spending (wars are expensive), although nondefense discretionary spending did increase in the early years of the century.

Two social insurance programs—Social Security and Medicare—are major components of mandatory spending. Social Security, the largest single element of mandatory spending, has been around 20 percent of total outlays since the mid-1970s and now is close to one-quarter of outlays (in earlier years, it seldom exceeded 15 percent).[81] The aging of the U.S. population guarantees the growth of this outlay.

---

[80]Salaries of members of Congress and the president are also deemed mandatory, although they are not entitlements. Some entitlements, such as Medicaid and some veterans' programs, are funded through annual appropriations; these are called appropriated entitlements, but are driven by benefit and eligibility criteria.

[81]The best single source on entitlement spending is "The Green Book": Committee on Ways and Means, U.S. House of Representatives, *Background Material and Data on Programs within the Jurisdiction of the Committee on Ways and Means* (Washington: U.S. Government Printing Office). The book is published periodically and includes major entitlements not strictly in Ways and Means jurisdiction.

Congress could reduce spending growth by changing the law and increasing retirement age, lowering benefit levels for more affluent retirees, and so on, but without such changes, the spending is predestined. The second largest category is Medicare, the federal health-care program for the elderly, a demographic group that would be unable to purchase private health insurance at reasonable rates because of the adverse selection problem. (Remember that private medical insurance companies make their money by selling insurance to people who don't get sick—a group that generally does not include the elderly.) Spending there has gone from 3.2 percent of outlays in 1970 to 15 percent in 2015, a large increase caused by higher prices for medical care in general, but also by enhancements in program coverage and increases in the number of old people.

Neither of these programs is means-tested. That is, all those who meet eligibility standards receive assistance according to a payment formula, regardless of their general affluence; changes in either are closely watched by recipient groups. Any changes would be in the domain of the Finance/Ways and Means Committees, not the annual appropriation process. Both are financed through a trust fund arrangement, by which dedicated taxes on payroll, plus interest income received from investment of trust fund balances, are expected to support benefits paid out. More about financing these two large entitlements—and their dismal financial condition—is discussed later. Other, larger non-means-tested entitlement programs are federal civilian and military retirement programs and unemployment compensation. The long national economic expansion kept unemployment compensation spending low during the 1990s. The Great Recession (December 2007–June 2009) brought increases.[82]

A second, but smaller, block of mandatory spending is means-tested; only those with limited affluence qualify to receive benefits from the program. Medicaid, a program providing medical assistance for low-income people, people with disabilities, members of families with eligible dependent children, certain other pregnant women and children, and elderly people needing nursing home care, is the largest such program, amounting to 8 percent of federal outlays in 2015, and outlays have grown rapidly.[83] The two federal medical care entitlement programs—Medicare and Medicaid—combined amount to 23 percent of federal outlays, causing many to observe that the key to controlling the federal budget ultimately lies in the ability to constrain the cost of medical care. Other important means-tested programs include (1) Supplemental Nutrition Assistance Program (SNAP, formerly Food Stamps), a program designed to allow low-income households to buy a nutritionally adequate

---

[82]Mandatory programs like those for unemployment insurance and income security are a significant component of the "automatic stabilizers" that provide a countercyclical fiscal stimulus when the economy falls toward recession, boosting the economy without requiring any legislative action. (Mindy R. Levit, D. Andrew Austin, and Jeffrey M. Stupak, "Mandatory Spending Since 1962," Congressional Research Service Report 7-5700, March 18, 2015.)

[83]Medicaid is jointly financed by the federal and state governments. The programs are funded by each of the states within guidelines established by federal legislation. While the poor without Medicaid coverage have access to emergency rooms, charity care, and free clinics, Medicaid program participants have higher health-care utilization, lower out-of-pocket medical care expenses and lower debt, and better physical and mental health. Amy Finkelstein et al., "The Oregon Health Care Experiment: Evidence from the First Year," National Bureau of Economic Research Working Paper 17190, Cambridge, Mass., July 2011.

low-cost diet;[84] (2) the Earned Income Tax Credit, an income subsidy program for families to encourage work; (3) the Supplemental Security Income program, a cash assistance program for very low-income persons who are elderly, are blind, or have other disabilities; and (4) Temporary Assistance for Needy Families, the former Aid to Families with Dependent Children, which provides family support through federal block appropriations to states rather than on an individual entitlement basis. Such means-tested spending constitutes "safety net spending." The data in Table 4–6 show that, although spending on most means-tested programs has grown more rapidly than has spending on non-means-tested programs, the non-means-tested programs are much larger and create a greater challenge for the budget. In gross budget-control terms, the major financial concern is with the latter programs, especially Medicare and Social Security, the programs for the elderly.

Are Congress and the president powerless to alter the path of mandatory spending? Of course not. They may lack the political will (what a surprise!), but they do not lack the political power. Options include (1) capping entitlements (essentially limiting the total amount that can be spent in a program each year, generally causing them to be annual appropriations), (2) making entitlement provisions less generous or at least constraining movements to make them more generous, and (3) making more entitlements means-tested (ensuring that only those classified as needy according to a broader measure of affluence receive benefits). And, for the trust-fund entitlements, another prospect is for increasing revenues into the trust funds by either increasing the taxes dedicated for their support or increasing the income from investment of balances in the funds. The point is that mandatory spending and its impact on the federal deficit can be controlled.[85] History shows, however, that Congress and the president have not been very good at doing the job, particularly when the entitlements being considered are Social Security, Medicare, or Medicaid.

Discretionary spending represents the rest of federal spending, the spending that flows through the annual appropriation process and the appropriation bills. Appropriation acts provide funding (the budget authority discussed earlier), and that funding will be used to make financial commitments or obligations. Outlays (spending) occur when the obligations get paid. This spending is for federal programs and the federal bureaucracy. Operations of agencies—the Department of Defense, the Fish and Wildlife Service, the Internal Revenue Service, and so on—fall in the discretionary category. Being "discretionary" does not mean that the spending is unimportant or that the nation could easily go without the program. It means that the spending goes through the traditional appropriation process and is not automatic.

---

[84]SNAP also is a powerful force for reducing poverty, particularly childhood poverty, in addition to improving nutrition. Laura Tiehen, Dean Jolliffe, and Craig Gundersen, "Alleviating Poverty in the United States: The Critical Role of SNAP Benefits," Economic Research Report No. 132, U.S. Department of Agriculture Economic Research Service, Washington, D.C., April 2012.

[85]Conversion of the Social Security system into a personal retirement savings program is hardly a solution to underprovision for retirement. The federal government currently offers more than a dozen tax-advantaged retirement savings programs, and creating another is not going to do much to provide more retirement security. Diverting some payments into the system to individual accounts serves to reduce the pool available to pay current benefits, thus accelerating the point at which that pool will be insufficient to meet promised payments.

The continuing question for Congress and the president is how much should be appropriated. Sidebar 4–3 provides some thoughts about the question of how much defense spending (the biggest single chunk of discretionary spending) might be considered to be adequate. This matters if one is concerned with the growth in federal government spending (and, by implication, in constraining the deficit): federal spending is driven by defense and social insurance spending, so meaningful control must focus on those areas.

Sidebar 4–3
How Much Is Enough?: Relative to What?

Policy discussions, budget presentations, and performance investigations are laden with numbers. Indeed, numbers are the mechanism for making a case for a particular decision, and when properly presented, they can be the means for closing off deliberations. The numbers show the facts, and the facts cannot be disputed. Case closed.

Not really. It isn't quite that simple. Numbers can be deployed badly, sometimes unintentionally, but often with a willful intent to deceive. As discussed in an earlier chapter, a big part of the problem lies in the importance of making sure the presentation provides some way of judging the magnitude of the numbers. Often, the question is "relative to what?" or "how big is big?" For instance, in fall 2014 Governor Cuomo of New York pointed with pride to the fact that the unemployment rate in the state had fallen to 6.2 percent, the lowest rate since the early days of the Great Recession in 2008. Evidence of a pretty good accomplishment for the state. But he didn't point out that the national unemployment rate was 5.9 percent and that, too, was the lowest rate since 2008. So, when put into the proper comparison terms, the New York accomplishment wasn't such a big deal: unemployment falling with the national patterns but still higher unemployment than in the nation as a whole.

The comparison has to be proper, however, if it is to provide meaningful insights for decisions. It matters particularly for national security discussions in the United States, the single largest service provided by the federal government. The national defense establishment expresses great concern that outlays for national security are planned to average 3 percent of gross domestic product in the 2015 through 2020 fiscal years, falling to only 2.7 percent in 2019 and 2020. That level is below the 3.9 percent average for the 2001 to 2014 period (roughly the era of the war on terror), and much below the 4.6 percent average over the longer 1970 to 2014 period, and way below the 7.1 percent average during the Cold War (1947 to the demise of the Soviet Union in 1991). The defense defenders point to these ratios as sure evidence that the defense budget is slated to fall into what surely must be the danger zone.

But is that the appropriate standard for comparison? The share of gross domestic product might give an indication of what the economy could afford (for instance, NATO expects its member countries to spend at least 2 percent of their gross domestic product on defense, a level actually met by only the United States, the United Kingdom, Greece, and Estonia in 2013), but it does not give a clear indication of relative strength of the national military. The United States economy is big, and that 3 or 4 percent of gross domestic product spent on national security translates into a large amount of money. If amounts spent translate into quantity and quality of security, then the country would probably be pretty secure. The fact that, for instance, Saudi Arabia spends 10 percent of its gross domestic product on defense would not be a major issue because U.S. gross domestic product is roughly 15 times that of Saudi Arabia—our 3 percent purchases a lot more defense stuff than does their 10 percent. In addition, Saudi Arabia is almost certainly an ally and not an international foe. The gross domestic product share does not provide the appropriate relative comparison.

A more meaningful comparison would likely be a comparison of total amounts spent, under the assumption that the more money spent, the higher the quantity and quality of defense being purchased. One might protest, arguing that in the American case, a portion of the money is spent to support local economies by producing weapons and other supplies, not because the military wants them but because the local member of Congress wants to support local employment, and that doesn't translate into increased security. However, this probably goes on in other countries as well, so that is not likely a big comparison problem. So how does the United States spending compare with that of other nations? Data for 2014 indicate that the United States spends more than the next seven countries do combined, and five of the next seven (Saudi Arabia, France, United Kingdom, India, and Germany) seem to be allies rather than enemies.[1] As someone once quipped, "Money isn't everything, but it sure has a big lead on whatever is in second place." The United States certainly seems to have a big lead in terms of money spent, even if we might not be devoting as big a chunk of the total economy to defense as we once did.

Is the United States planning to spend too much or too little on national security? That has to be thrashed out between people who know about military operations and national security. But it is clear that understanding the issues requires making some comparisons, and not all comparisons have the same information content. The amount of spending relative to gross domestic product doesn't provide much useful information about how much is enough.

---

[1]Stockholm International Peace Research Institute, *SIRPI Military Expenditure Database*, April 2015. Data are for 2014.

Federal/Trust, On-Budget/Off-Budget

Another group of federal spending distinctions needs to be noted. Federal spending is divided into spending from federal funds, spending from trust funds, spending that is on-budget, and spending that is off-budget. The budget documents also include reports for a number of government-sponsored enterprises whose finances are not included in the budget totals. The distinctions are primarily technical, often created for political reasons alone, and they do not help make the process more transparent. Indeed, it is a challenge to identify any real use that they serve except to make sensible policies a bit more difficult. Table 4–7 shows how the several distinctions create different patterns of surplus or deficit for the unified operations of the federal government.

Table 4–7

Surplus or Deficit (−): Total, Type of Fund, Off-Budget and Total as % GDP, 1940–2015 ($ millions)

Fiscal Year	Total	Federal Fund	Trust Fund	Off−Budget	Total, % GDP
1940	−2,920	−4,045	1,125	564	−3.0
1941	−4,941	−6,360	1,419	653	−4.3
1942	−20,503	−22,496	1,992	830	−13.9
1943	−54,554	−57,648	3,094	1,041	−29.6
1944	−47,557	−51,818	4,261	1,178	−22.2
1945	−47,553	−52,972	5,419	1,167	−21.0
1946	−15,936	−19,847	3,910	1,028	−7.0
1947	4,018	577	3,441	1,157	1.7
1948	11,796	8,834	2,962	1,248	4.5
1949	580	−1,838	2,417	1,263	0.2
1950	−3,119	−3,055	−65	1,583	−1.1
1951	6,102	2,451	3,651	1,843	1.9
1952	−1,519	−5,005	3,486	1,864	−0.4
1953	−6,493	−9,921	3,427	1,766	−1.7
1954	−1,154	−3,151	1,997	1,677	−0.3
1955	−2,993	−4,173	1,180	1,098	−0.7
1956	3,947	1,313	2,634	1,452	0.9
1957	3,412	1,657	1,755	773	0.7
1958	−2,769	−3,017	248	546	−0.6
1959	−12,849	−11,271	−1,578	−700	−2.5
1960	301	791	−490	−209	0.1
1961	−3,335	−4,193	858	431	−0.6
1962	−7,146	−6,847	−299	−1,265	−1.2
1963	−4,756	−6,630	1,874	−789	−0.8
1964	−5,915	−8,588	2,673	632	−0.9
1965	−1,411	−3,910	2,499	194	−0.2
1966	−3,698	−5,165	1,467	−630	−0.5
1967	−8,643	−15,709	7,066	3,978	−1.0
1968	−25,161	−28,373	3,212	2,581	−2.8
1969	3,242	−4,871	8,112	3,749	0.3
1970	−2,842	−13,168	10,326	5,852	−0.3
1971	−23,033	−29,896	6,863	3,019	−2.1
1972	−23,373	−29,296	5,924	2,695	−1.9
1973	−14,908	−25,683	10,774	338	−1.1
1974	−6,135	−20,144	14,009	1,063	−0.4
1975	−53,242	−60,664	7,422	906	−3.3
1976	−73,732	−76,138	2,405	−4,306	−4.1
1977	−53,659	−63,155	9,495	−3,726 ·	−2.6
1978	−59,185	−71,876	12,691	−3,770	−2.6
1979	−40,726	−59,061	18,335	−1,093	−1.6
1980	−73,830	−82,632	8,802	−689	−2.6
1981	−78,968	−85,791	6,823	−5,109	−2.5
1982	−127,977	−134,221	6,244	−7,384	−3.9
1983	−207,802	−230,874	23,072	−110	−5.9
1984	−185,367	−218,272	32,905	−98	−4.7

(continues)

Table 4–7 (continued)

Fiscal Year	Total	Federal Fund	Trust Fund	Off–Budget	Total, % GDP
1985	−212,308	−266,457	54,149	9,222	−5.0
1986	−221,227	−283,120	61,893	16,688	−4.9
1987	−149,730	−222,348	72,618	18,627	−3.1
1988	−155,178	−252,902	97,724	37,087	−3.0
1989	−152,639	−276,122	123,483	52,754	−2.7
1990	−221,036	−341,181	120,145	56,590	−3.7
1991	−269,238	−380,971	111,733	52,198	−4.4
1992	−290,321	−386,338	96,018	50,087	−4.5
1993	−255,051	−355,436	100,385	45,347	−3.8
1994	−203,186	−298,508	95,322	55,654	−2.8
1995	−163,952	−263,211	99,259	62,415	−2.2
1996	−107,431	−222,052	114,621	66,588	−1.3
1997	−21,884	−147,826	125,942	81,364	−0.3
1998	69,270	−91,927	161,197	99,195	0.8
1999	125,610	−87,120	212,730	123,690	1.3
2000	236,241	1,629	234,612	149,819	2.3
2001	128,236	−100,513	228,749	160,681	1.2
2002	−157,758	−360,156	202,398	159,659	−1.5
2003	−377,585	−555,977	178,392	160,833	−3.3
2004	−412,727	−605,365	192,638	155,234	−3.4
2005	−318,346	−555,093	236,747	175,265	−2.5
2006	−248,181	−537,271	289,090	186,313	−1.8
2007	−160,701	−409,395	248,694	181,452	−1.1
2008	−458,553	−724,621	266,068	183,295	−3.1
2009	−1,412,688	−1,539,978	127,290	136,993	−9.8
2010	−1,294,373	−1,417,705	123,332	77,005	−8.7
2011	−1,299,593	−1,396,740	97,147	67,182	−8.5
2012	−1,086,963	−1,176,827	89,864	61,913	−6.8
2013	−679,544	−765,931	86,387	39,463	−4.1
2014	−484,627	613,175	128,548	29,512	−2.8
2015	−438,406	−549,975	111,569	27,295	−2.5

The distinctions discussed here should not confuse the fact that the federal government uses a *unified budget*, meaning that trust funds and federal funds are in the same overall budget, as are on-budget and off-budget operations, and that the budget does not distinguish between budgets for operating expenditures and budgets for capital infrastructure. (The latter distinction might even make for better and more transparent public policy, but of course it is not used.)[86]

---

[86]General Accounting Office, *Report to the Chairman, Committee on Government Operations, House of Representatives: Trust Funds and Their Relationship to the Federal Budget,* GAO/AFMD-88-55 (Washington, D.C.: General Accounting Office, September 1988); and Office of Management and Budget, *Budget of the United States Government, Fiscal Year 2016, Historical Tables* (Washington, D.C.: U.S. Government Printing Office, 2015).

Federal Funds Federal funds amounted to 72.5 percent of federal total gross outlays in fiscal 2015. In terminology, these funds are designated general, special, intragovernmental revolving or management, and public enterprise revolving funds. *General fund* accounts are financed by undesignated receipts and provided for use by regular appropriation. *Public enterprise revolving funds* receive revenues generated by business-type operations with the public, such as Postal Service operations, and are available without appropriation for those operations. Of course, the operations are controlled by Congress, so they aren't really like private businesses. *Special fund* receipts are designated for specific uses, deposited into separate accounts, and available for use under statutorily prescribed conditions (the Nuclear Waste Fund receives fees from civilian nuclear power operators; funds can be used only for disposal of high-level nuclear waste). *Intragovernmental revolving funds* collect receipts from government agencies selling services to other government agencies. All federal funds are on-budget, as described later.

Trust Funds Trust funds totaled 45.3 percent of federal total gross outlays in fiscal 2015. These are budget accounts that receive specially designated (or earmarked) receipts and have been designated by law as trust funds. Some of the largest federal trust funds, in terms of receipts, are the Federal Old-Age and Survivors Insurance Trust Fund, the Federal Hospital Insurance Trust Fund, the Civil Service Retirement and Disability Fund, the Military Retirement Fund, the Federal Supplementary Medical Insurance Trust Fund, the Unemployment Trust Fund, the Federal Disability Trust Fund, the Highway Trust Fund, the Airport and Airway Trust Fund, the Foreign Military Sales Trust Fund, and the Railroad Social Security Equivalent Benefit Account. Most lack the fiduciary relationship present in the normal meaning of trust funds: beneficiaries do not own the funds, and Congress may unilaterally alter tax rates, benefit levels, or other features of the program. Furthermore, for most of the trust funds, expenditures go through the congressional appropriation process. The shares of the federal fund and trust fund categories do not add up to 100 percent because of interfund transfers. The trust fund total is typically in surplus (every full fiscal year since 1960). But that does not mean that each trust fund is in surplus or that it has sufficient funds to meet the service responsibilities it is expected to cover. In particular, the Highway Trust Fund, intended to provide support for state and local highway and transit operation and maintenance programs of national interest, suffers chronic financial difficulty because of increased costs of such programs coupled with congressional unwillingness to increase the taxes (on motor fuel and other motor vehicle related items) intended to support the fund. The fund was created to provide orderly support for such programs, but it now may erect a barrier to appropriation to support an important national need.

On-Budget and Off-Budget The Federal Old-Age and Survivors Insurance Trust Fund and the Federal Disability Trust Fund are legally off-budget. All other trust funds and all federal funds are on-budget (79.9 percent of federal gross outlays in fiscal 2015 were on-budget). Both on- and off-budget operations are in the federal budget statements. There is currently no particular significance to the distinction. The off-budget concept was created in the early 1980s because social insurance funds were in deficit, and by removing them from the calculation, what became the on-budget deficit was lower. The distinction was a scam to provide what appeared to be a lower budget deficit then by directing attention to the on-budget operations. However, reform of social security finances in the mid-1980s caused the system to be in surplus, and the off-budget portion of the budget is now typically in surplus—but a surplus not large enough to accommodate the future spending demands placed on the system.

Government-Sponsored Enterprises The budget document includes detailed self-reports of financial operations and conditions of several government-sponsored enterprises (GSEs), although these enterprises are neither on-budget nor off-budget, strictly speaking. These enterprises were initiated by the federal government, but are classified as private: the Student Loan Marketing Association, the College Construction Loan Insurance Association, the Federal National Mortgage Association (Fannie Mae), the Banks for Cooperatives and Federal Farm Credit Bank, the Federal Agricultural Mortgage Corporation, the Federal Home Loan Mortgage Association (Freddie Mac), the Federal Savings and Loan Insurance Corporation, and the Resolution Funding Corporation. The GSEs are intended to be independent of the federal government, to provide federal support, and not to be subject to any actual federal guarantees. Although the legal documents produced by Fannie Mae and Freddie Mac stated that their securities did not have a guarantee by the federal government, the private investors assumed that this was just window dressing and invested in them at low rates because of that implicit backing. It turns out that the private investors guessed right, because the U.S. Treasury bailed both institutions out in 2008 when they suffered the effects of the recession and collapse of the housing market.

The budget document also reports the administrative budget of the Board of Governors of the Federal Reserve System (the Fed), the independent central bank of the United States. The Fed is neither on-budget nor off-budget, and the system is not a government-sponsored enterprise. However, the federal Treasury does receive profits earned by the Fed, and the Fed is subject to regular financial audit with results provided to Congress and the public. In 2015, that amounted to $96.5 billion, mostly representing interest earned on the Fed's portfolio of Treasury securities and mortgage-backed securities it had purchased to reduce interest rates in order to stimulate economic activity. Before the Great Recession, Fed contributions to the Treasury were much lower (averaging $23 billion per year in the five prior years) because the Fed portfolio was much smaller. When the Fed eventually tightens monetary policy by selling securities, that portfolio will again diminish in size.

Conclusion

The federal government prescribes a precise budget cycle with clearly defined boundaries between the executive and legislative branches and clearly defined dates for steps in the cycle to follow. But the process is in disarray. Administrations have submitted budgets that intentionally omit major expenditures that are transmitted later in supplemental requests. Executive budgets are not transmitted on schedule. Congress regularly fails to pass its own budget (the budget resolution). Fiscal years begin without appropriations in place, and, in some fiscal years, no appropriations are actually made. Two programs that contribute a major share of mandatory expenditure are in severe fiscal distress. The congressional budget process functions with no meaningful controls, the appropriation process faces an unclear future, and prospects are for significant deficits throughout the planning horizon. Federal finances are in deficit in both economic expansion and economic recession. The process pays little attention to fiscal and economic effects of choices made now on the future sustainability of the U.S. economy. It is not the picture of a government on a sustainable path.

The response has been to create more process, controls, and constraints. But the congressional establishment is full of bright and clever people and so is the Executive Office of the President. Absent a real will to operate within fiscal constraints, controls will be thwarted. A major reconsideration of what the federal government intends is important, and it must include policy choices as well as following the prescribed process.

Former U.S. Treasury official Eugene Steuerle points out that federal lawmakers have little fiscal freedom now because a vast share of tax revenue has already been committed to Social Security, Medicare, and other entitlements plus interest on the national debt before they even consider any programs for infrastructure, education, disaster relief, or the like.[87] The problem is worse because tax increases are anathema to many lawmakers. Revenue from a growing economy has already been committed to cover the cost of permanent programs put in place by legislatures of long ago. Present lawmakers are constrained by choices made by Congresses of long ago, and the extent of constraint will only get worse. Refusal to reform entitlement programs and to consider increasing revenue flows is a formula for colossal violation of fiscal sustainability standards.

QUESTIONS AND EXERCISES

1. Using the *Historical Tables* available at the budget tab of the website of the U.S. Office of Management and Budget, prepare an analysis of the trends in the following data: total federal outlays, total defense spending, and total mandatory spending. Do the analysis in both current and constant dollars. Provide your interpretation of what forces are driving the patterns that you observe.

2. Use the following federal agencies for this exercise: Fish and Wildlife Service, Forest Service, Bureau of Land Management, Bureau of Reclamation, National Oceanic and Atmospheric Administration, U.S. Geological Survey, Army Corps of Engineers, Environmental Protection Agency, and U.S. Coast Guard. You will be able to locate the answers in the *Budget of the United States Government,*

---

[87]Eugene Steuerle, *Dead Men Ruling*. New York: The Century Foundation Press, 2014.

available through the OMB website, and through the various appropriation acts passed by Congress.

a. Determine where each agency lies in the administrative structure of the federal government. Is it in an executive department, or is it an independent agency?
b. Determine which of the appropriation subcommittees has jurisdiction over each agency's budget request (i.e., what appropriation bill contains the agency's financing).
c. Determine where each agency's operations fall in the functional classification of the budget.
d. Pick one agency and, for a recent budget year, determine (1) the budget authority and outlays proposed for the agency and (2) the actual outlays and budget authority for the agency in that year.

3. Identify the congressional committees to which the member of Congress representing your district has been assigned. If the member is on the appropriations committee, identify the subcommittee as well. Try to determine why those committees are interesting to him or her. Thinking about economic interests and major employers in the district is a good start. (Your member of Congress almost certainly has a website that lists his or her committee and subcommittee assignments. Check that first.) Another basic source is Congress's own website (http:// thomas.loc.gov). It lists all committees and the membership of each. ("Thomas" is for Thomas Jefferson, the spirit behind the Library of Congress.)

4. Pick a federal agency of your choice. Find that agency's appropriation for a recent fiscal year. That may be located in an annual appropriation act or in a consolidated appropriation bill that lumps a number of normal appropriation acts together. Are there provisions of a somewhat substantive nature that are included in the appropriation act?

5. The U.S. Treasury statement for August 2015 reports the following:

Receipts

Individual Income Tax	$103B
Social Security & Other Payroll Taxes	83B
Corporate Income Tax	2B
Other Taxes, etc.	23B

Outlays by Function

Defense	$ 40B
Social Security	75B
Medicare	24B
Interest on Debt	25B
Other	111B

Calculate (i) the total surplus (or deficit) and (ii) the primary surplus (or deficit). What is the logical reason for distinguishing between the two measures?

APPENDIX 4–1

Appropriations, Departments, Agencies, and Budget Accounts

Congress appropriates funds for the operation of the federal government. These funds go through the appropriation acts, to departments, and then to agencies within those departments. The funds are controlled within accounts within agencies. Departments do not, no matter how they might wish it to be true, receive funds that they might spend as they see fit. Instead, Congress maintains a reasonably close control over those funds.

The system of control operates through a system of budget accounts. These budget accounts also serve as the basis that program administrators use to build their budget requests that eventually become part of the president's budget request (and, they hope, come back as congressional appropriations). OMB Circular A-11 describes the accounts as follows: "A budget account generally covers an organized set of activities, programs, or services directed toward a common purpose or goal. Budget accounts are the basic building blocks of the President's Budget.... In addition, budget accounts are the basis for congressional action on the budget."[88] The budget accounts receive a defined funding amount available for a prescribed time period to be used by a specific organization in the agency to support the cost of similar programs or activities.

The following example shows how the budget account system functions.[89] Table 4A–1 show the numbers of accounts in the several departments in the U.S. government.

The number of accounts varies widely among departments, and there is no relationship between the amount of money being spent by the department and the number of budget accounts. For instance, spending levels by Interior and State are roughly comparable, but Interior has eighty-one budget accounts, whereas State has only thirty-four. How many budget accounts a department has is determined by how Congress chooses to appropriate the funds. Adding accounts provides Congress with an additional degree of control over the money it provides a department.

The next step in understanding the process involves looking within a department at its bureaus or main organization units. Table 4A–2 shows the budget accounts within the bureaus of the Department of Interior.

As with the budget accounts within departments, these accounts within bureaus are determined by Congress. More accounts within a bureau usually mean more congressional desire to control, and, again, there is little relationship between amounts to be spent and number of accounts. The funds provided each are part of the congressional appropriation.

---

[88]Office of Management and Budget, Circular A-11, Section 71-1.

[89]The accounts described here are from the perspective of the OMB and are from a high-level view. Agencies themselves use an even more detailed account framework in budget execution and reporting to Treasury. Each separate account in the Treasury database has additional codes to identify the fiscal year of the appropriation and whether funding is single-year, multiyear, or indefinite. Treasury, in cooperation with the OMB, establishes and maintains the official set of accounts in its FAST book (http://www.fms.treas.gov/fastbook/index.html). All of these are crosswalked to an OMB account.

Table 4A-1
Budget Accounts and Spending by Department, Fiscal Year 2006

Agency Code	Department	Number of Accounts	Spending ($ Billions)
005	Agriculture	103	102.0
006	Commerce	33	6.6
007	Defense	111	538.8
018	Education	27	90.4
019	Energy	35	25.0
009	Health and Human Services	43	908.9
024	Homeland Security	64	33.1
025	Housing and Urban Development	44	49.4
010	Interior	81	16.4
011	Justice	40	23.1
012	Labor	26	52.1
024	State	34	13.8
021	Transportation	61	65.1
015	Treasury	43	472.7
029	Veterans Affairs	21	74.3

SOURCE: Arthur W. Stigile, Chief, Budget Concepts Branch, Budget Review, U.S. Office of Management and Budget. Reprinted by permission.

Table 4A-2
Bureau Accounts and Spending by Bureau, Department of Interior, Fiscal Year 2006

Bureau Code	Bureau	Accounts	Spending ($ Millions)
04	Bureau of Land Management	11	2,883
06	Minerals Management Service	7	2,585
08	Office of Surface Mining Reclamation and Enforcement	2	351
10	Bureau of Reclamation	10	1,105
11	Central Utah Project	2	34
12	United States Geological Survey	2	972
18	United States Fish and Wildlife Services	16	2,072
24	National Park Service	9	2,593
76	Bureau of Indian Affairs	7	2,397
84	Departmental Management	3	372
85	Insular Affairs	3	424
86	Office of the Solicitor	1	55
88	Office of the Inspector General	1	39
90	Office of the Special Trustee for American Indians	5	464
91	Natural Resources Damage Assessment and Restoration	1	37
92	National Indian Gaming Commission	1	12
	Department Total	81	16,395

SOURCE: Arthur W. Stigile, Chief, Budget Concepts Branch, Budget Review, U.S. Office of Management and Budget. Reprinted by permission.

Table 4A–3
Spending by Budget Account for the National Park Service, Fiscal Year 2006

Account ID	Account Title	Spending ($ Millions)
010-24-1036	Operation of the National Park System	1,719
010-24-1039	Construction and Major Maintenance	335
010-24-1042	National Recreation and Preservation	54
010-24-1049	United States Park Police	80
010-24-5035	Land Acquisition and State Assistance	47
010-24-5140	Historic Preservation Fund	72
010-24-9924	Other Permanent Appropriations	100
010-24-9928	Recreation Fee Permanent Appropriations	166
010-24-9972	Miscellaneous Trust Funds	20
	National Park Service—Total	2,593

SOURCE: Arthur W. Stigile, Chief, Budget Concepts Branch, Budget Review, U.S. Office of Management and Budget. Reprinted by permission.

Financing within the bureaus is based on the funds within the budget accounts. Table 4A–3 provides the details of the budget accounts in the National Park Service. Its authorizing legislation defines the mission of the Park Service to be to "preserve unimpaired the natural and cultural resources and values of the national park system for the enjoyment, education, and inspiration of this and future generations." Its park system includes 388 units covering 88 million acres in forty-nine states, the District of Columbia, American Samoa, Guam, Puerto Rico, the Northern Mariana Islands, and the Virgin Islands.[90] It provides these services through the funds provided by these budget accounts.

The account structure is determined by Congress and defines the activities of the National Park Service that it intends to support. This is the level at which Congress does its budget analysis and makes its appropriations. It is also the level at which the National Park Service prepares its budget proposals for inclusion in the president's budget. It should be noted that one large account is for operation of the national park system. This account gives the Park Service the flexibility to devote its attention to whatever park in that system needs greatest attention, whether that be the result of visitors or repairs after a natural disaster. The accounts do not go down to the level of individual parks. The budget account structure is particularly important for administrators because it is forbidden to move funds from one budgetary account to another, even within a single bureau, without congressional approval. Therefore, the budget accounts are a critical control device for Congress—the broader the account, the greater the flexibility that the organizational unit has in responding to what it sees as the important public demands that it faces.

The last important step to help develop an understanding of how the appropriation and budget account system operates is to look at the text of an appropriation act. An example, the Environment and Related Agencies Appropriations Act of 2006 (P.L. 109–54), is presented in Figure 4A–1.

---

[90]"National Park Service Budget Highlights, Fiscal Year 2006" [http://www.doi.gov/budget/2006/06Hilites/BH71.pdf].

Within the Act, notice these elements:

1. The act identifies the funding as going to the Department of Interior and for the 2006 fiscal year and then for the operation of the National Park Service. It also is worth noting that the Act was passed before the beginning of the fiscal year, something of a rarity in this era. Other accounts for the National Park Service are funded in later provisions of the Act.
2. The Act describes the purposes for which the funds may be used and the total amount of money being appropriated.
3. The Act indicates how some portions of the total appropriation are to be used. A purist would object that this is mixing policy with funding and would properly belong in authorization rather than appropriation, but these provisions are a normal element of the modern appropriation process.
4. The Act explicitly limits the extent to which funds in this budget account may be used for the United States Park Police. Recall from Table 4A–3 that there is a separate budget account (010-24-1049) for them, which will be provided for later in the Act.

In summary, the budget account structure provides the framework for preparation of agency budget requests, the basis for congressional review of those requests and for congressional appropriation of funds to agencies, the basis for agency provision of services to the public, and, ultimately, the basis for an external audit of agency spending. It represents the basis for congressional oversight and control over agency operations.

Figure 4A–1
2006 Appropriation Act Language for National Park Service

Making appropriations for the Department of Interior, Environment, and Related Agencies
   For the fiscal year ending September 30, 2006, and for other purposes.

NATIONAL PARK SERVICE
OPERATION OF THE NATIONAL PARK SERVICE

For expenses necessary for the management, operation, and maintenance of areas and facilities administered by the National Park Service (including special road maintenance service to trucking permittees on a reimbursable basis), and for the general administration of the National Park Service, $1,744,074,000.

Of which $9,892,000 is for planning and interagency coordination in support of Everglades restoration and shall remain available until expended.

Of which $97,600,000, to remain available until September 30, 2007, is for maintenance, repair or rehabilitation projects for constructed assets, operation of the National Park Service automated facility management software system, and comprehensive facility condition assessments;

And of which $2,000,000 is for the Youth Conservation Corps for high priority projects.

Provided, that the only funds in this account which may be made available to support United States Park Police are those funds approved for emergency law and order incidents pursuant to established National Park Service procedures, those funds needed to maintain and repair United States Park Police administrative facilities, and those funds necessary to reimburse the United States Park Police account for the unbudgeted overtime and travel costs associated with special events for an amount not to exceed $10,000 per event subject to the review and concurrence of the Washington headquarters office.

SOURCE: Department of the Interior, Environment, and Related Agencies Appropriations Act, 2006, (P.L. 109–54), August 2, 2005.

CHAPTER 5

State and Local Budgets

Chapter Contents

Budgeting by subnational governments—states and localities in the United States—is different from budgeting at the national level. For one thing, subnational governments operate in open economies, meaning that economic activity and populations served can easily move across jurisdictional boundaries. In other words, moving a family or a business from Des Moines to Urbana is much easier than moving from Mexico to the United States. People living on the outskirts of a city can enjoy many public services provided by that city government without paying for them, and people can move from one locality to another in a metropolitan area, picking among the mix of local services and means of providing them, without having to change jobs.[1] The prospect of telecommuting makes worker flexibility even greater. Efforts by the city to stimulate its local economy will immediately spill over to other areas. Jurisdictions are watching what their neighbors are doing in terms of taxing and provision of services in an effort to gain economic advantage for their populations and to encourage businesses to relocate. And many tax bases are easily mobile: for instance, residents of a city can respond to a sharply increased city sales tax rate by shopping in the suburbs. Easy border crossing makes the service delivery and financing different for subnational governments.

---

[1] In many respects, the several localities operating in a metropolitan area operate like firms competing in a marketplace. See Charles Tiebout, "A Pure Theory of Local Public Expenditures," *Journal of Political Economy* 64 (1956): 416–24. Their competition for residents and economic activity leads to efficient provision of government services, much in the way that competition between firms leads to efficient allocation of resources in private markets.

Another fundamental difference between national and subnational governments is that subnational governments lack one powerful fallback tool. The national government, when pushed to it, can create spending power out of thin air: it can print money (actually, it can create bank accounts for itself to use). That is something not available to states and localities, and it can be a powerful cushion for support of deficit finance. Of course, it is a power that cannot be heavily employed even by national governments because of concern about rampant inflation, but it is a power that has its uses, and only the central government has it. Governments able to practice independent monetary policy (i.e., have control of their own national currency) do have a big advantage in dealing with economic problems—and that is definitely relevant to countries trapped in the Euro-zone whose economic situation could be improved by a currency devaluation (for instance, Greece and Finland in 2015).

Finally, subnational governments operate in a different legal environment than do national governments. National governments frequently limit the fiscal powers of the lower tiers, for instance, in terms of what taxes subnational governments might adopt, what services they are to provide, and what fiscal constraints they must operate under. However, that is not the case in the United States. Subject to a few constitutional fundamentals (due process, equal protection under the law, etc.), state governments in the United States have great freedom in regard to the revenue devices they use, the government services they provide, and how they operate. There are few national standards that must be followed, and, where there are such provisions, they are frequently attached to federal assistance programs that the states may choose not to participate in. In contrast to most of the world, American states are close to being fiscal free agents with lots of discretion in their operations. However, state governments often establish their own fundamental and constitutional limits to their fiscal operations, for instance, with regard to how much debt they can have outstanding, the revenue sources they can draw upon, permitted growth in state spending, and so on. And local governments usually must operate under the narrow confines permitted them by their state, including sometimes a requirement that a state agency review and approve the local budget before it can be adopted. Furthermore, a number of states have provisions under which the state may take over the operations of a local government that is in extreme financial difficulty and, as will be discussed later, a number of states allow their localities to declare bankruptcy for protection from their creditors.[2] Of course, there are 50 states and more than 90,000 local governments within them, so there is great variety among budget

---

[2]Several states have provisions that allow the state government to take over the finances of local governments that experience extreme fiscal problems. For instance, in early 2011, New York State took over the finances of Nassau County, and a state-installed manager took over operations of Benton Harbor, Michigan. Michigan has taken over finances of more than a dozen localities since a program was established in 1990. The takeover of Detroit finances ultimately led to a formal bankruptcy filing, and Wayne County entered financial emergency status in 2015. Atlantic City ceded fiscal management to the state of New Jersey in 2010. Various cities in Pennsylvania have fallen into a state recovery program in past years. The federal government would not take over finances of a state (or a locality) in the American system: under the U.S. Constitution, states have residual powers, and localities are created by the states and not by the federal government. State takeovers are discussed in greater detail in Chapter 15.

processes. The best this chapter can do is to give some idea of the general nature of state budget structures and processes. The details must remain for individual state research.[3]

State and Local Spending and Services Delivered

Table 5–1 reports expenditures by state and local governments in the United States. Both levels devote most of their attention to services closely related to the general public—education, public safety, welfare, sanitation and health, and so on—not the more global reach of international affairs and disputes that is the province of the national government.[4] Those are the larger spending categories seen in the table. But before commenting on the spending patterns, a couple of reporting conventions need to be noted. States transfer considerable sums to their local governments; this table tallies such spending at the recipient level only (which makes the expenditures "direct"). The table also follows the convention of separating general expenditure from expenditures of government-operated utilities, liquor stores, and insurance trust systems (unemployment compensation, public employee retirement, etc.). Surpluses from the utilities and liquor stores may ultimately support general government operations (or their losses may have to be subsidized); insurance trust operations, especially unemployment compensation, have little direct link to general finances, although general finances of the government do have to maintain employee retirement programs and may need to make up fund shortfalls.[5] Problems associated with state and local government retirement programs—and those problems are substantial—are discussed later in this chapter.

Local government expenditure is dominated by elementary and secondary education, amounting to 39.3 percent of total spending. Much of this spending is by independent school districts, local governments with a single purpose. However, a number of large cities (e.g., New York and Chicago) operate their schools as a department of city government. A considerable portion of school spending is financed by state aid, even though the local unit administers the program. Often the aid comes with requirements about how the money will be spent, usually to the irritation of local authorities who are convinced that they know local needs better than do those

---

[3]The National Association of State Budget Officers (NASBO) and the National Conference of State Legislatures (NCSL) are excellent sources for individual state details and comparisons of how state budget processes operate.

[4]And if those identified public services aren't enough to convince you of the importance of state and local government to providing a civilized and comfortable society, how about the fact that these governments are responsible for running the elections used for selection of officials for all levels of government, including federal? A mishandled election in an individual state can cause national (and international) confusion and repercussions, such as Florida in 2000.

[5]Surpluses in these trust funds, if invested in government debt, normally are invested in federal rather than state-local debt. Hence, merging them with general state-local operations as is done at the federal level would not be appropriate.

Table 5–1
State and Local Expenditures, 2012 ($ in thousands)

Description	State and Local	% Direct General Expenditure	State	% Direct General Expenditure	Local	% Direct General Expenditure
Direct expenditure	$3,147,545,020		$1,500,100,718		$1,647,444,302	
Direct general expenditure, total	2,587,317,474	100.0%	1,167,333,919	100.0%	1,419,983,555	100.0%
Direct general expenditure, capital outlay	285,133,018	11.0%	114,955,101	9.8%	170,177,917	12.0%
Education	869,195,706	33.6%	271,117,301	23.2%	598,078,405	42.1%
Higher education	259,735,781	10.0%	220,266,001	18.9%	39,469,780	2.8%
Elementary and secondary	565,403,215	21.9%	6,794,590	0.6%	558,608,625	39.3%
Other education	44,056,710	1.7%	44,056,710	3.8%	0	0.0%
Libraries	11,446,701	0.4%	419,770	0.0%	11,026,931	0.8%
Public Welfare	485,588,136	18.8%	433,312,083	37.1%	52,276,053	3.7%
Hospitals	155,755,495	6.0%	65,514,468	5.6%	90,241,027	6.4%
Health	84,397,654	3.3%	42,005,549	3.6%	42,392,105	3.0%
Employment Security Administration	5,116,142	0.2%	5,065,317	0.4%	50,825	0.0%
Veteran's Services	838,031	0.0%	838,031	0.1%	0	0.0%
Highways	158,562,139	6.1%	97,508,989	8.4%	61,053,150	4.3%
Air Transportation	21,533,229	0.8%	1,891,646	0.2%	19,641,583	1.4%
Parking Facilities	1,896,808	0.1%	10,262	0.0%	1,886,546	0.1%
Water Transportation	5,300,028	0.2%	1,578,515	0.1%	3,721,513	0.3%
Police Protection	96,972,215	3.7%	12,848,203	1.1%	84,124,012	5.9%
Fire Protection	42,404,755	1.6%	0	0.0%	42,404,755	3.0%
Corrections	72,576,605	2.8%	46,020,671	3.9%	26,555,934	1.9%
Protective Inspection	13,578,032	0.5%	8,849,279	0.8%	4,728,753	0.3%
Natural Resources	29,008,682	1.1%	18,856,123	1.6%	10,152,559	0.7%
Parks and Recreation	37,404,429	1.4%	4,631,908	0.4%	32,772,521	2.3%
Housing and Community Development	53,141,353	2.1%	10,080,093	0.9%	43,061,260	3.0%
Sewerage	51,711,843	2.0%	772,754	0.1%	50,939,089	3.6%
Solid Waste Management	24,247,114	0.9%	2,451,082	0.2%	21,796,032	1.5%
Financial Administration	38,984,349	1.5%	21,819,452	1.9%	17,164,897	1.2%
Judicial and Legal	43,157,218	1.7%	21,148,068	1.8%	22,009,150	1.5%
General Public Buildings	14,033,783	0.5%	3,617,445	0.3%	10,416,338	0.7%
Other	27,756,896	1.1%	4,424,863	0.4%	23,332,033	1.6%
Interest on General Debt	109,117,652	4.2%	47,342,438	4.1%	61,775,214	4.4%
Miscellaneous Commercial Activities	5,056,048	0.2%	2,543,161	0.2%	2,512,887	0.2%
Other and Unallocable	207,020,633	5.0%	42,666,448	3.7%	85,869,983	6.0%
Utility expenditures	128,536,431		23,796,134		183,224,499	
Water Supply	61,239,779		420,194		60,819,585	
Electric Power	76,470,245		10,391,513		66,078,732	
Gas Supply	7,041,003		10,670		7,030,333	
Transit	62,269,606		12,973,757		49,295,849	
Liquor store expenditures	6,696,872		5,607,711		1,089,161	
Insurance trust expenditures, total	346,510,041		303,362,954		43,147,087	
Unemployment compensation expenditure	95,553,860		95,317,830		236,030	
Employee retirement expenditure	233,227,038		190,315,981		42,911,057	
Workers' compensation benefit payments	10,923,109		10,923,109		0	
Other insurance trust benefit payments	6,806,034		6,806,034		0	

SOURCE: U.S. Bureau of Census, Governments Division, Annual Survey of State and Local Government Finances. www.census.gov.

people in the state capital. No other category amounts to as much as 10 percent of the total, but welfare (3.7 percent), hospitals (6.4 percent), and police protection (5.9 percent) are the largest remaining categories. Categories that have grown rapidly in recent years include corrections, health, air transportation, solid-waste management, and interest payments.

The largest single category of state government spending is public welfare programs (37.1 percent). The 1996 changes in the federal welfare program—converting Aid to Families with Dependent Children (a federal entitlement paid to individuals) to Temporary Assistance for Needy Families (a grant program with conditions that assign responsibility to state governments)—place even greater responsibility on states and provide them with a great incentive to administer carefully and move people off assistance rolls. Medicaid, the federal-state health-care program for the poor that states operate according to federal guidelines with both federal and state funding, is a major component of this category and a major factor in its expansion. Of the other functions, only higher education (18.9 percent) amounts to as much as 10 percent of the total. Larger shares go to highways (8.4 percent), hospitals (5.6 percent), corrections (3.9 percent), and health (3.6 percent). Although there are major interstate differences, particular problems for state finances emerge from corrections—an area in which both growth of inmate populations and judicial requirements for humane treatment of inmates have increased spending—and from health, especially Medicaid. Greater expenditure by Medicaid is one expected impact of the Affordable Care Act, and many observers see rapid growth in Medicaid cost as a huge challenge to finances of state government, a cost expansion that threatens to swamp the other important public services states are expected to provide. And there is considerable variation across states. For instance, eleven states—Michigan, Oregon, Arizona, Vermont, Colorado, Pennsylvania, New Hampshire, Delaware, Rhode Island, Massachusetts, and Connecticut—spend more on corrections than on higher education, sometimes by a wide margin.[6]

The data in the table are for the nation as a whole, and there are variations from one state to another. States and localities make their own decisions and are not guided by any national standards. Jurisdictions differ dramatically in how they allocate their fiscal resources. The patterns shown here provide a first guess of how any jurisdiction is allocating its budget, but only by looking at the specific government's finances can you be certain how it is spending its money. In making comparisons across states and localities, it is particularly important to consider operating environments. For example, two school districts—one serving an affluent, educated, homogeneous suburb and another serving a low-income, poorly educated, distinctly heterogeneous inner city—are likely to have to spend radically different amounts to provide the same level of learning because of the operating conditions, not because one is more efficient than the other.

---

[6]National Association of State Budget Officers, State Expenditure Report: Examining Fiscal 2012–2014 State Spending (Washington, D.C.: NASBO, 2014).

Fiscal Control and Conditions

Individual state and local governments characteristically do not run large surpluses or deficits. This results from some combination of legal constraints, tradition, concern about access to capital markets, and worries about being unable to service accumulated debts (these governments lack the power to print money, after all, either through the printing presses or through loans from the national central bank).[7] That does not mean that every state and local government spends no more than it takes in every year or that all state and local governments in total will run a surplus. However, a continuing concern for all government finances is the extent to which fiscal discipline is maintained. We have seen that, for the federal government, the answer is not very well, with deficits experienced on an apparently perpetual basis. It is appropriate to consider the same question for states and localities. Of course, the answer differs across the governmental entities, with some showing an excellent record of discipline and others with great problems. A few cities and other local governments have gone bankrupt in the past few years (municipal bankruptcy is discussed later), so things have not gone well for all subnational governments in the United States. But what does the overall situation look like for these governments in totality?

Figure 5–1 presents a measure of aggregate government fiscal condition called "net saving," measured by the totaled difference between current receipts and current expenditures of each state and local government, using data from the national income and product accounts reported by the U.S. Department of Commerce Bureau of Economic Analysis from 1960 through 2013. Net saving is divided by total current expenditure to allow an assessment of relative fiscal condition over the long period of time from 1960 through 2013. The data show that, for most of the early years of that period, local governments overall showed net savings. Recessions (like those in 1973, 1980–81, 1991, 2001, and 2007–2009) dramatically reduce net saving, and recent recoveries have not restored pre-recession saving rates. The measure fell into negative territory in the Great Recession and it remains there in recent years. These deficits are, however, considerably smaller relative to expenditure than seen for the federal government. State government finances show fewer periods of net saving than do local government finances. Indeed, since the late 1980s, all years have shown negative savings, and the negative savings rate increased dramatically in both the 2001 and 2009 recessions. The 2009 level is a record for the half-century. State net savings have, however, increased somewhat since the end of the Great Recession when compared to the experience of local governments, and state savings increased substantially after the 2001 recession. As will be discussed later, state governments rely on revenue sources that are much more sensitive to the state of

---

[7]It may also reflect the limited effectiveness of state and local expansionary fiscal policy. Any stimulus from a tax reduction or an expenditure increase would quickly leak outside the political (and electoral) boundaries of the government. The beneficiaries of the new deficit would be outside the local citizenry.

Figure 5–1
State and Local Net Saving as % Total Expenditure, 1960–2013

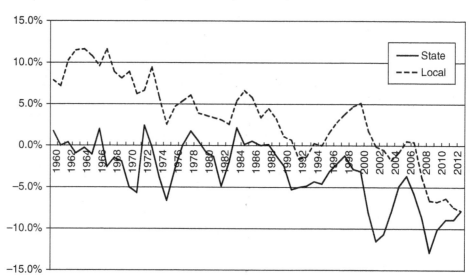

the national economy (income and retail sales taxes) than do local governments (real property taxes), and that has had an important impact on the relative fiscal experience of state versus local governments. In general, there has been a secular decline in net savings ratios for both states and localities over the half century examined here, and a continuation of that trend does not give a happy result.[8] But some states and localities have behaved differently from the results shown in the national aggregates.

That overall fiscal control record does not look good. However, the extent to which spending is not covered by current revenues is far smaller for both states and localities than was seen for the federal government, net saving being an approximation of a cumulative surplus measure, and local governments do regularly show net savings. It is generally the case that, within state and local governments, there is a fervent understanding that continuing deficits are not sustainable and that there is an expectation that finances will be roughly in balance over time. That is a difficult target for subnational governments to achieve in a climate of higher expectations for education, health, highways, public safety, environmental protection, and other state-local services; restrained interest in providing financing from the federal government; and resistance against increasing state and local taxes. More important for fiscal sustainability is the fact that for both states and localities gross government investment in each year exceeds the amount of negative net savings. Although deficit operations are moving costs to the future, this suggests that government operations are also purchasing capital stock available in the future. That does not imply a

---

[8]The GAO is upset: U.S. Government Accountability Office, *State and Local Governments' Fiscal Outlook, 2014 Update,* GAO-15-224SP (December 2014).

net loss for the future in current state and local government operations. In contrast, the federal deficit in each year far exceeds the amount of federal investment expenditure, so there is no fiscal sustainability advantage there.

State and Local Budget Processes

The federal government uses a closely defined (but frequently shifting) budget process with narrowly drawn deadlines (that are often missed), regulations (that are ignored), roles, and authority that specify the flow of resources from the germination of an idea for service through the audit of outcomes. Virtually all states and larger localities use the familiar four-phase budget cycle. However, it should be no surprise, in light of the great diversity of state and local governments, that there is no one process that all such entities use.[9] Therefore, the process must be learned within the context of the government at hand. The way it works in Wichita may not apply in Altoona, and both governments may have budget processes that function perfectly well where they are applied—or they may not work so well. Hence, the discussion about the state and local government budget process can only be general in nature. Justice Louis Brandeis observed in *New State Ice Co.* v. *Liebman,* 285 U.S. 262 (1932) that "it is one of the happy incidents of the federal system that a single courageous State may, if its citizens choose, serve as a laboratory; and try novel social and economic experiments without risk to the rest of the country." And so it is with the budget process. (Appendix 5–1 at the end of this chapter describes the budget process in Texas as an example of one system.[10]) Because so many federal lawmakers started their political careers in state or local government and are familiar with fiscal processes used there, it is no surprise that ideas for restructuring the federal budget process have their genesis at the state or local level even though the operating environment at the federal level is considerably different from that found at the subnational level.

State and local budget processes and staffing may be comparable to that of the federal government, except in scope, but many, especially local processes, are remarkably informal, in part because nobody in the process has any training in government finance and budgeting. Indeed, there may be no executive budget for the locality. Agency heads may submit their requests directly to a legislative body (e.g., a city or county council) without any executive directive for developing those requests. Those local requests, especially for small governments, may be transmitted according to no regular schedule, but simply as agencies run out of funds or

---

[9]Some sense of the range is shown in Edward J. Clynch and Thomas P. Lauth, eds., *Governors, Legislatures, and Budgets: Diversity across the American States* (New York: Greenwood Press, 1991). National Association of State Budget Officers, *Budget Processes in the States* (Washington, D.C.: NASBO, 2015), provides the most complete overview of the structure of each state's budget processes.

[10]The websites of most states and some localities provide descriptions of the jurisdiction's budget process, sometimes also including the most recent set of budget preparation instructions distributed by the chief executive.

encounter new program options, rather like the federal government did before the 1921 Act.

States are more formal and more controlling in their processes: "the days of agencies having the freedom to request budgets in whatever amounts they see fit are gone, and in their stead are various control mechanisms or types of ceilings that must be observed when requesting funds."[11] That guidance may involve (1) formal rankings of executive priorities; (2) instructions in regard to allowed program improvements, maintenance of current services, or continuance of only minimum services; or (3) specific dollar-level ceilings within which to prepare proposals. State budgets are frequently driven by a baseline (or current services) revenue forecast that gives budget participants a hard budget constraint under which the spending totals must fall if operations are to be sustainable in the long term, and either the state budget office or a state legislative services agency may have prepared a current services baseline for analyzing expenditure proposals. Although the state budget office may be housed in various places (e.g., in the governor's office, in a freestanding executive agency, or in a larger department of administration or finance), it provides supervision of the entire process, review of proposals as they are assembled into the budget, and control of the execution of the adopted budget. And there may be a nonpartisan legislative fiscal office to provide many of the services provided by the CBO at the federal level (many of these offices actually predate the CBO).

Among localities, however, a wider range of practices exists, with and without much budget guidance and control. Some of the more glaring problems emerge in budget preparation and legislative consideration. First, many localities continue *Christmas list budgeting,* in which department heads prepare requests without any executive guidance about budget targets or conditions. This practice leads to unrealistic requests that are usually cut without much attention given to programs and priorities or that flow unchanged to the legislature. The proposals from the various departments may be at odds with each other and may have been created without any particular policy guidance. Telling an agency head to prepare a budget request according to what the agency needs, without any guidance about fiscal constraint, is not likely to lead to a carefully managed proposal. Second, some state and local operating agencies may have elected heads (e.g., a county sheriff); these officials may not feel bound by such directions constraining their proposals. The elected sheriff believes that he or she has just as much standing from the people as an elected mayor or county executive, so how can the sheriff budget be subject to review by another executive? Third, agency requests may not have been reviewed by an executive budget office, often because there is no such staff or because the staff is small and untrained. Therefore, the requests may arrive for legislative review in inconsistent format, following no particular standards in preparation, with no unifying plan for service delivery, and without screening for technical or presentation errors, internal inconsistency, or even math mistakes. In essence, the budget message has been prepared with a stapler only, not according to an analytic

---

[11]Robert D. Lee, "The Use of Executive Guidance in State Budget Preparation," *Public Budgeting & Finance* 12 (Fall 1992): 29–30.

template or generally consistent executive vision. Such a system (or nonsystem) swamps the legislative body with details. Members of the legislative body must verify arithmetic and often fall into deliberations about each proposed purchase (or line item). Rather than considering policy questions, they plunge into the intimate cost estimates of the particular requests and usually exhaust their deliberative time and energy before they reach higher-order questions of program, performance, efficiency, or missions. Seldom do members of the legislature have any skill in budget analysis, so poor reviews are no surprise. Finally, any executive guidance may focus entirely on the things that the government purchases and not on what services the government provides. A local county government may instruct departments to build their budget request by giving everyone a 4 percent raise and holding all other spending categories constant. That is not a particularly useful way to make sure that the public gets good government services for the money they are paying. But those sorts of inefficiencies and ineffectiveness are the result of having limited capacity for budgeting and finance in local government. They are good shortcuts but not good governance.

Many state and local governments also differ from the federal government in the audit phase of the budget cycle. Although most of these governments have a public agency serving as external auditor, much in the way that the Government Accountability Office (GAO) serves Congress, a number have privatized the function by allowing audits to be done under contract with qualified private accounting firms. So long as audit procedures, audit standards, and audit questions are prescribed and audit firms are qualified for technical competence before they may bid, there is no particular reason states need to establish their own version of GAO for financial and compliance audits.[12] In a number of states, a non-partisan legislative agency performs performance audits separately from the financial audits. In contrast to the recommended model, some states place the audit agency in the executive branch; some states have both executive and legislative audit units.

Executive-Legislative Powers and Functions[13]

The federal budget process has, over the years, created an uneasy and shifting balance of fiscal power between the executive and legislative branches of government. The balance that has emerged there does not immediately transfer to state and local governments.

---

[12]There is some concern that a private audit firm may be less willing to produce negative audit reports out of fear that the contracting government will replace it with a more flexible competitor.

[13]Most states and many large cities post a description of their budget process on their websites. (Processes for Minnesota and St. Louis are particularly accessible.) In addition, local processes frequently involve some supervision, review, or even approval by state agencies to assure that the budget does not violate state controls. Recall from Chapter 1 that localities are legally creatures of their states, so this involvement is not surprising. When local governments have gotten into great financial difficulty, it is not unusual for states to take over their operations, installing managers with the capacity to override local decisions, replace local officials, and the like.

First, not all state and local governments have an executive budget in the normal sense, although a budget proposal is prepared everywhere. Some states have budgets prepared by the legislature, and others have budgets prepared by the governor and the legislature in a joint budget committee. These joint budgets are difficult to categorize without understanding the details of each state; in some instances, they may be truly joint, built by a consensus between the governor and the legislature, but in others, the committees may be arranged in such a way that the governor has sufficient votes to guarantee that the budget is an executive budget regardless of its official title. Some local governments, including cities, counties, and school districts, have budgets prepared by professional managers working at the direction of a legislative body, much in the manner of a budget prepared by the executive director of a nonprofit organization. In these governments, there is considerable blurring of the preparation and legislative consideration phases of the budget cycle. Indeed, a council-manager system has, for purposes of the budget, more similarity to parliamentary structure (i.e., a governmental structure with no clear distinction between the legislative and executive branches of government) than to the system of separation of powers between the legislative and executive branches that characterizes our federal and state governments. In many cities, it is common for the council and the mayor to meet before budget deliberations to discuss priorities for the next year and sometimes to work together in creating the final budget document. This can be an important contributor to getting a consensus when the budget is presented, but what results could hardly be seen as an executive budget.

Second, state and local government executives often possess extraordinary fiscal powers in regard to expenditure during the fiscal year. Many states do not have year-round legislatures; the body meets in the early months of the calendar year, passes the state appropriations (and other laws), and adjourns for the year. More important, states and localities have limited capacity to deal with budget deficits (i.e., ability to borrow) that might emerge during budget execution because of unexpected economic or other problems. To deal with interim surprises, the governor may have broad impoundment powers—the ability to postpone or cancel expenditures in approved appropriations. The governor may also be able to spend for certain emergencies without appropriation, although almost always with agreement of some interim legislative committee.[14] These accommodations give governors considerable ability to manage finances during budget execution. They do not face a rescission process like the one that the president must deal with. They can simply adjust the approved budget to match fiscal resources.[15] Most state and local governments have allotment processes to control spending through the budget year, with

---

[14]The executive may also have substantial contingency funds provided for various emergencies or surprises.

[15]The authority of the mayor to make unilateral budget adjustments was an issue of serious contention in San Diego in 2007. The city switched from a city manager system, in which the mayor was primarily the chair of the city legislative body, to a system in which the mayor was chief executive in 2006. The mayor made budget adjustments, and the council objected on the ground that such changes required their approval. The city has experienced great financial problems in the past half-decade for reasons that may or may not be related to the change in systems.

funds parceled out quarterly or, when times are tight, monthly. Unfortunately, some governments have sought to recapture balances not obligated in that control period, thereby eliminating any incentive for agencies to economize—spend the money quickly before the governor takes it away.

Third, state and local governments differ in the accommodating mechanisms that provide funds for operations when the legislative and executive branches cannot agree and fiscal years end without new appropriations in place.[16] Some operate with near-automatic continuing resolutions, whereas others provide governors with considerable discretion or rely on passage of short-term appropriation bills to cover the gaps. Illinois appeared to be able to pay certain state workers (but not all) even in the absence of a passed appropriation law for fiscal 2016 (based on court rulings), but it could not pay out winnings on the state lottery, make scholarship awards at state universities, or distribute funds to nonprofit social service agencies.[17] Other states have no stop-gap option clearly available and are required to shut down if the budget has not been passed by the start of the new fiscal year (usually with some provision to preserve "essential" services, as somehow determined). Parks and museums are often closed during the impasse. Contract providers (both private firms and nonprofit organizations) do not get paid, and local governments do not receive expected transfer payments. Minnesota state government shut down for about two weeks in 2011 because of a legislative impasse between the governor and the legislature, causing agency and facility shutdowns and work stoppage by state contractors. (A shorter shutdown occurred there in 2005.) California regularly has experienced the sort of budget impasse one would expect in a comic republic, in large part because state budgets there required a two-thirds majority for passage, a unique feature among the states, and a requirement that was reduced to a simple majority in 2011. In the previous system, a small minority of disgruntled legislators could prevent adoption of the budget, even as the fiscal year was ending and authority for state spending was expiring. As a result, the state regularly experienced fiscal crises in which it could not pay its bills—rather bizarre for a state whose economy, if it were a nation, would be in the top ten in the world.[18] Sidebar 5–1 discusses the unique approach the state employed to deal with the impasse in 2009. Pennsylvania went many months without appropriations passed for the 2016 fiscal year: the state Senate borrowed money from a commercial bank to pay salaries and benefits to senators and staff, and the House opened a bank line of

---

[16]Some agencies that operate largely on the basis of user charge revenue may not be affected at all because they do not rely on appropriated funds.

[17]Kim Geiger, "Downstate Judge Rules State Workers Should Be Paid in Full," *Chicago Tribune*, July 9, 2015. An earlier ruling had allowed payment only at the federal minimum wage level. Apparently a state constitutional requirement that only the governor and legislature could decide how money would be spent did not apply. In February 2016, the governor of Illinois submitted his 2017 state budget, even though the budget for fiscal 2016 (which started in July 2015) still had not been passed and state agencies continued to stumble around without clear financing. The state went more than eleven months with appropriations being passed.

[18]California hopes to accelerate the process through a state constitutional amendment that prevents legislators from getting paid if the budget is not approved on time—and prevents them from ever getting back pay for the delayed period when the budget is passed.

Sidebar 5–1
Scrip and Irregular Finance

Scrip is a form of currency issued by an irregular entity—that is, not the entity in charge of issuing official legal tender for the country (the nation's central bank or treasury)—as a means of accommodating some irregular problems. This irregular currency lacks the full status of legal tender, meaning that its acceptance for all private and public obligations is not assured, but it will be accepted in some instances by some entities. In many respects, scrip amounts to a loan, usually non–interest bearing and usually not voluntary, to the issuer of the scrip by the entity receiving the scrip (someone who is owed money by the issuer). In a normal transaction, the issuer would pay its bills with a regular payment in the national currency, and that currency can then be used by the recipient in any transaction within the nation. In a scrip transaction, the issuer pays with scrip, and the recipient can use that scrip anywhere it is accepted. However, the number of places accepting scrip will be limited, and its acceptance is not assured. The use of scrip is not a feature of acceptable government finance and, unlike the national currency, scrip is not legal tender in all economic transactions.

How has scrip been used in irregular government finance? One example was the state of California in 2009. The legislature and the governor could not agree on a budget that was within revenues available to the state (the recession had hit state revenues very hard), and the fiscal year started in July without appropriation laws having been passed to cover state spending. Legislative power of the purse means that payment cannot be made unless a law has authorized that payment, and the legislature had not passed the law. That meant that the state could not pay its suppliers or its employees or issue tax refunds in the normal way—it was not authorized by state law to make those payments. The state couldn't simply shut down, but there was no mechanism available to accommodate short-term spending gaps. Some governments pass short-term, stopgap appropriations to accommodate operations until the appropriation laws for the full year are passed, and some governments have automatic continuation of prior-year appropriations to tide the systems over, but California did neither. The state could have done the former, but the governor refused the option because he wanted some policy changes along with a budget deal and believed a short-term deal would reduce his leverage for getting those changes.

California law permitted a different response. The state issued "individual registered warrants," essentially IOUs, to those receiving tax refunds and to its suppliers. It could not issue them to its employees because federal law prohibits such payment to workers. These warrants amounted to forced loans to the state, made somewhat more palatable by the state promise to pay 3.75 percent annual interest on the warrants. (The warrants were issued in July and repayment was promised for October.) The warrants looked much like a bank check, except they stated "This REGISTERED WARRANT will be honored on or after 10/02/2009 . . ." rather than directing payment to the order of the recipient. Some of those who received the warrants found the interest promise to be attractive and held onto them as a short-term investment, but lots of other recipients needed cash to pay their bills. In the beginning, local banks accepted the scrip in exchange for cash and accumulated the IOUs to receive the promised interest. And the state of California accepted the scrip as payment for any tax owed the state, making it immediately useful without any need to exchange it for cash for many businesses and individuals.

So long as the scrip could be used as cash or could easily be exchanged for cash, the system could function (anything will work as money, so long as everyone accepts it as such). But banks did not have an unlimited appetite for this state debt, and after about two months, they stopped making the exchange. And that made it unattractive for suppliers to continue doing business with the state. Fortunately, the legislature resolved its impasse at about the same time, possibly because the creditors were becoming restless, and finally the appropriations were passed. The state issued more than 194,000 registered warrants with a face value of $1.03 billion during the crisis; total state expenditure during fiscal 2010 was over $257 billion.

credit with several banks for the same purpose; without approved appropriations, the lawmakers were reluctant to obtain money for payroll from the state Treasury. Because Pennsylvania school districts are dependent on state transfer payments for their operations, they had to borrow large sums to operate while the state lawmakers fumbled.

States with part-time legislatures often require that special legislative sessions be called when the constitutionally designated regular session ends without a new set of appropriations in place. (Local governments are more likely to have year-round legislative meetings, so the process may become continuous and without year-end crises.) The specific accommodation depends on the institutions and laws of the particular state. When state legislatures are close to the time that their session must end and are also close to passing a state budget, it is not uncommon for them to agree to stop the hands of the official clock to keep the legislative day from ending until the job is done. (Too bad Cinderella did not have this option—the fairy tale might have had its happy ending without forcing the prince to bear the cost of travel around the countryside looking for her.)

Finally, most governors have long-established line-item veto power.[19] Indeed, only five—the governors of Indiana, Maine, Nevada, New Hampshire, and Rhode Island—may veto only an entire appropriations bill, giving them the same all-or-nothing authority as the president of the United States. If the state has a single appropriation bill that covers all government operations, the governor is in the difficult situation of having to put all government services in jeopardy because one or two parts of the bill are objectionable. Of those governors with line-item veto power, forty may delete funding for a particular line item, and thirty-two may even veto funding for an entire program or agency. Eleven may reduce an appropriation line without full veto. Although specifics of these line-item vetoes vary, all allow the governor to alter the bill approved by the legislature and sign

---

[19]Louis Fisher, "Line Item Veto Act of 1996: Heads Up from the States," *Public Budgeting & Finance* 17 (Summer 1997): 3–17, reviews state experiences with the line-item veto, including legislative strategies for avoiding the executive control that it might bring.

the remainder into law, with the legislature having the power to override that partial veto.[20] These, along with impoundment authority previously mentioned, are powers presidents can only dream about having. But free use of the item-veto power may not have great fiscal impact. For instance, Governor Paul LePage of Maine used his item-veto power to reject sixty-four items totaling $6.7 million from the 2016 budget passed by the legislature. It was significant news because no Maine governor had used the power before, and supporters of programs losing budget authority certainly felt it. However, the total approved budget for the biennium was $6.7 billion, meaning that the vetoed parts amounted to only 0.9 percent of total proposed spending, not enough to have much impact on overall state finances.[21]

Budget Features

State and local government budgets show great basic variety. First, budgets may be annual or biennial (Table 5–2 gives a recent tally). At one time, state legislatures usually met only every other year. That meant making appropriations for two years in one legislative session. Even as legislative sessions became more frequent, several states continued the biennial budgets. These annual sessions became distinguished as the budget session and the policy session (or, in less-dignified terminology, the correction session). States have generally moved toward annual sessions and toward single-year budgets; local governments have no biennial tradition, probably because they tend to meet throughout each year. In cities, administrators commonly rebudget and adjust the approved appropriations in midyear.[22] Some local governments are in rebudgeting-and-appropriating mode almost all the time, at every meeting of the council or governing board, even though a budget has been passed before the start of the fiscal year. Because of the difficulty of foreseeing what problems may face the state beyond a single fiscal year, states are inclined to regard the single-year budget as best suited to responding to public problems and to maintaining fiscal discipline.[23]

---

[20]The Wisconsin governor has the most sweeping line-item veto powers, including the ability to strike words and numbers without much limit, even to the extent of reversing the meaning of the bill (try striking the "not" from "thou shalt not commit adultery" to see what the power could do). Until recently, the governor could veto letters in words, thus permitting a game of legislative anagrams. Governor Tommy Thompson had 457 vetoes in the single 1991–1993 biennial budget bill. Dennis Farney, "When Wisconsin Governor Wields Partial Veto, the Legislature Might as Well Go Play Scrabble," *Wall Street Journal,* July 1, 1993, A-16.

[21]Douglas Rooks, "Governor Line-Item Vetoes Biennial Budget Bill," *State Tax Notes,* June 22, 2015, 900.

[22]John P. Forrester and Daniel R. Mullins, "Rebudgeting: The Serial Nature of Public Budgeting Processes," *Public Administration Review* 52 (September/October 1992): 467–73.

[23]Converting the federal government to a biennial budget is a perennial reform idea brought forth by members of Congress who have state government experience. Only if the president and Congress absolutely foreswear any reopening of the budget in off years, an almost impossible temptation, would there be any time saved, and there would be guaranteed inability to respond quickly to new issues. General Accounting Office, Biennial Budgeting: Three States' Experiences, GAO-01-132 (Washington, D.C.: General Accounting Office, October 2000).

Table 5–2
State Budget Cycles

Annual Budget (30 states)	Biennial Budget (20 states)
Alabama	Arkansas
	Connecticut
Alaska	Hawaii
Arizona	Indiana
	Kentucky
California	Maine
Colorado	Minnesota
Delaware	Montana
Florida	Nebraska
Georgia	Nevada
Idaho	New Hampshire
Illinois	North Carolina
Iowa	North Dakota
Kansas	Ohio
Louisiana	Oregon
Maryland	Texas
Massachusetts	Virginia
Michigan	Washington
Mississippi	Wisconsin
Missouri	Wyoming
New Jersey	
New Mexico	
New York	
Oklahoma	
Pennsylvania	
Rhode Island	
South Carolina	
South Dakota	
Tennessee	
Utah	
Vermont	
West Virginia	

SOURCE: National Association of State Budget Officers, *Budget Processes in the States*. Washington, D.C.: NASBO, 2015.
NOTES:
AZ: largest agencies on annual by statute, others are annual by recent practice
CT: revisions made to second year, creating *de facto* annual
HA: biennial in law, annual in practice
MN: regular supplemental budget for second year
NB: regular supplemental budget for second year
NC: regular adjustment process for second year
ND: enacts consolidated two-year budget, not two years at one time
OH: governor presents mid-biennium budget review bill
VA: regular consideration of budget amendments
WA: regular adjustment process
WV: regular adjustment process

Second, state and local governments may have a single appropriation law covering all expenditures, or they may have many appropriation laws. In other words, the legislature may pass a complete budget in a sense not traditionally practiced by Congress, or there may really be no budget as ordinarily considered. The range is vast—about one-third of the states typically pass a single appropriation bill, but, at the other extreme, Arkansas passes around 500 appropriation bills. When there is a single appropriation bill, however, line-item veto power is probably more important for the executive. With a large number of appropriation bills, it is difficult to have any sort of unified plan for services being delivered by the state.

Third, in contrast to the unified federal budget, many state and local governments use a dual budget system in which recurring operating expenses are controlled in one budget and acquisition of capital infrastructure is managed in a separate capital budget. Capital budgeting is discussed in Chapter 7. For now, suffice it to say that regularization of infrastructure purchases can be particularly important in maintaining fiscal stability in smaller budget processes. But some governments go beyond dual budgets. Cities are likely to establish appropriation ordinances for each fund that the government has established, with something like a separate budget process for each fund. And, violating the budgetary principle of comprehensiveness, many of these governments do not move monies between funds, despite the appropriateness of directing public resources to the highest priority and greatest public need. (Capital and operating budgets are reasonably kept separate, however.)

Fourth, state and local governments historically have passed firm appropriations. They have not passed formula legislation (entitlements), which allow spending to occur at whatever level results from qualifying activities during the year. An exception is the Medicaid program, the federal-state program for providing medical care for certain low-income families. State assistance to local schools, a program for aiding primary and secondary education, distributes aid according to formula, but state funds ordinarily enter the distribution by appropriation, not by entitlement, and the formula may well be underfunded in a particular year. Some states also employ formulas for distribution of funds to institutions of higher education, with funds distributed according to various indicators of institutional operations and performance, and for distribution of funds to localities for maintenance of streets and roads.[24] States also do not separate authorizing and appropriating in their legislative processes.

Fifth, state and local governments have historically been unable to accommodate deficits with the easy access to borrowing that the federal government enjoys. Furthermore, the vast majority faces statutory or constitutional restrictions against deficit operations. This has induced many to develop rainy-day or budget stabilization funds to stabilize their finances in an economic downturn, when revenues are likely to decline. All states except Colorado, Illinois, and Montana plus the District of Columbia now operate some sort of rainy-day/reserve/budget stabilization

---

[24]Formulas based on more than enrollment numbers create considerable tension among institutions with differing educational objectives. (Eric Kelderman, "Iowa Budget Proposal May Spark 'Family Feud' Among Universities," *Chronicle of Higher Education*, June 2, 2014.)

fund.[25] Table 5–3 provides the names of these savings funds across the states and indicates what sort of target or cap they operated under. It is apparent that there is a wide range in the amounts that are intended to be accumulated in the funds, meaning that some states have greater capacity to weather a fiscal shock than others. Some funds are financed by whatever the surplus happens to be, with funds accumulating until the amount in the fund reaches a target or cap. Others require that a particular percentage of general fund appropriations or revenue be dedicated to the fund, again until a target amount is reached. Arizona, Indiana, and Michigan determine required payment into the fund according to growth in state personal income. Along with providing a degree of stability in finances, properly designed budget stabilization funds—by reducing perceived default risk on state debt—can reduce the borrowing cost of state debt.[26] There is evidence that such state funds played a significant role in propping up state spending in the recession that began in 2001, although there remained some significant budget shortfalls in the first years of the twenty-first century.[27] The funds certainly provided a cushion for some states in the Great Recession, but no states had enough money in their funds to insulate them from that fiscal shock. Lawmakers forget how severe the problems are in a recession as the years pass by after the recession and become reluctant to let the fund continue to accumulate. Indeed, the fiscal challenge of the Great Recession stretched the imagination of everyone. The funds just don't get big enough to cover the problems of a severe recession. Local governments are less likely than states to have such stabilization funds, although some do. They tend to rely on real property taxes for revenue, and this source is less sensitive to changes in ambient economic activity than are the income and sales taxes upon which states rely. Local government revenues tend to be much more stable than those of either state or federal governments. However, localities that rely heavily on local sales taxes do face considerable revenue instability.[28]

---

[25]"Why States Save: Using Evidence to Inform How Large Rainy Day Funds Should Grow," A report from the Pew Charitable Trusts, December 2015. Similar budget stabilization funds, although aimed at stabilization over the long term rather than in a business cycle, have been established in a number of resource-rich countries, such as Kazakhstan, Kuwait, Russia, Norway, and Kiribati, to ease the transition when the resource has been depleted.

[26]There is evidence that the rainy-day funds are something of an illusion. One study indicates that rainy-day funds simply substitute for general fund savings that would have occurred without the rainy-day funds. The evidence is that every dollar deposited into a rainy-day fund increases total savings (rainy-day plus general fund balance) by between $0.44 and $0.49. Gary A. Wagner, "Are State Budget Stabilization Funds Only the Illusion of Savings? Evidence from Stationary Panel Data," *Quarterly Review of Economics and Finance,* 43 (Summer 2003): 213–18. Other studies argue that regular rainy-day funds driven by stringent rules can allow states to overwhelm political resistance to building up reserve funds and make a contribution to accommodating revenue swings. James Douglas and Ronald Keith Gaddis, "State Rainy Day Funds and Fiscal Crises: Rainy Day Funds and the 1990–1991 Recession Revisited," *Public Budgeting & Finance* 22 (Spring 202): 19–30.

[27]Elaine Maag and David F. Merriman, "Understanding States' Fiscal Health during and after the 2001 Recession," *State Tax Notes,* August 6, 2007, 359–77.

[28]Members of Congress periodically call for the federal government to establish a federal rainy-day fund, following in the successful footsteps of state governments. Possibly a useful idea, but it would first require the federal government to get into surplus. Otherwise, the federal government would effectively be establishing the rainy-day fund with borrowed funds. That being the case, it might as well wait until the rainy day to do the borrowing and avoid the interest cost between the establishment of the fund and the date of its use.

Table 5–3
State Rainy-Day Fund Balance Caps Targets

State	Fund Name	Cap or Target
Alabama	General Fund Rainy Day Account	10% of previous year's General Fund appropriations minus prior years' rainy-day account withdrawals that have not been repaid
Alaska	Constitutional Budget Reserve Fund and Statutory Budget Reserve Fund	No caps
Arizona*	Budget Stabilization Fund	7% of current fiscal year's General Fund revenue
Arkansas	Rainy Day Fund	$125 million
California	Special Fund for Economic Uncertainties	No cap or target
Colorado	No fund	–
Connecticut	Budget Reserve Fund	15% of current fiscal year's General Fund Appropriation
Delaware	Budget Reserve Account	5% of current fiscal year's estimated General Fund revenue
Florida	Budget Stabilization Fund	10% of prior fiscal year's General Fund revenue
Georgia	Revenue Shortfall Fund	15% of prior fiscal year's net revenue
Hawaii	Emergency and Budget Reserve Fund	10% of prior fiscal year's General Fund revenue
Idaho	Budget Stabilization Fund	10% of prior fiscal year's General Fund revenue
Illinois	No fund	–
Indiana*	Countercyclical Revenue and Economic Stabilization Fund	7% of current fiscal year's General Fund revenue
Iowa	Economic Emergency Fund	2.5% of current fiscal year's estimated General Fund revenue
Kansas	No fund	–
Kentucky	Budget Reserve Trust Fund Account	5% of current fiscal year's General Fund revenue
Louisiana	Budget Stabilization Fund	4% of prior fiscal year's total state revenue
Maine	Budget Stabilization Fund	18% of prior fiscal year's General Fund revenue
Maryland	Revenue Stabilization Account	7.5% of current fiscal year's estimated General Fund revenue
Massachusetts	Commonwealth Stabilization Fund	15% of prior fiscal year's budgeted revenue
Michigan*	Countercyclical Budget and Economic Stabilization Fund	10% of prior fiscal year's combined School Aid Fund and General Fund–General Purpose revenue
Minnesota	Budget Reserve Account	$810,992,000
Mississippi	Working Cash-Stabilization Reserve Account	7.5% of current fiscal year's General Fund appropriations
Missouri	Budget Reserve Fund	10% of current fiscal year's net general revenue
Montana	No fund	–
Nebraska	Cash Reserve Fund	No cap or target
Nevada	Account to Stabilize Operation of State Government	20% of current fiscal year's General Fund appropriations

*Required payment into fund determined by growth in state personal income.

SOURCE: "Why States Save: Using Evidence to Inform How Large Rainy Day Funds Should Grow." A report from the Pew Charitable Trusts, December 2015.

Table 5–3
(Continued)

State	Fund Name	Cap or Target
New Hampshire	Revenue Stabilization Reserve Account	10% of prior fiscal year's General Fund revenue
New Jersey	Surplus Revenue Fund	5% of current fiscal year's estimated General Fund and Property Tax Relief Fund revenue
New Mexico	General Fund Operating Reserve and General Fund Tax Stabilization Reserve	8% of prior fiscal year's aggregate recurring General Fund appropriations and 6% of the prior fiscal year's aggregate recurring General Fund appropriations
New York	Tax Stabilization Reserve Fund and Rainy Day Reserve Fund	2% of current fiscal year's General Fund expenditures and 5% of next fiscal year's projected General Fund expenditures
North Carolina	Savings Reserve Account	8% of the prior fiscal year's General Fund operating budget
North Dakota	Budget Stabilization Fund	9.5% of current fiscal biennium's General Fund appropriations
Ohio	Budget Stabilization Fund	8.5% of prior fiscal year's General Fund revenue
Oklahoma	Constitutional Reserve Fund	15% of prior fiscal year's certified General Revenue
Oregon	Rainy Day Fund	7.5% of prior fiscal biennium's General Fund revenue
Pennsylvania	Budget Stabilization Reserve Fund	6% of current fiscal year's General Fund revenue
Rhode Island	Budget Reserve and Cash Stabilization Account	5% of current fiscal year's estimated state general revenue
South Carolina	General Reserve Fund and Capital Reserve Fund	5% of prior fiscal year's General Fund revenue and 2% of prior fiscal year's General Fund revenue
South Dakota	Budget Reserve Fund	10% of prior fiscal year's General Fund appropriations
Tennessee	Reserve for Revenue Fluctuations	8% of current fiscal year's estimated sales tax revenue for the General Fund and Education Trust Fund
Texas	Economic Stabilization Fund	10% of prior fiscal biennium's general revenue
Utah	Budget Reserve Account	9% of current fiscal year's General Fund appropriations
Vermont	General Fund Budget Stabilization Reserve and Rainy Day Reserve	5% of prior fiscal year's General Fund appropriations and 5% of prior fiscal year's General Fund appropriations
Virginia	Revenue Stabilization Fund	15% of prior three fiscal year's average annual income and retail sales tax revenue
Washington	Budget Stabilization Fund	10% of current fiscal year's estimated general state revenue
West Virginia	Revenue Shortfall Reserve Fund	13% of prior fiscal year's State Fund-General Revenue Appropriation
Wisconsin	Budget Stabilization Fund	5% of current fiscal year's estimated General Fund expenditures
Wyoming	Legislative Stabilization Reserve Account	No cap

Sixth, because local governments are closest to the people of any tier of government, they are most able to get ordinary citizen input into the fiscal choice processes. It is quite common for cities to integrate citizen hearings and citizen comments into both executive preparation and legislative consideration phases of the budget process. (A later chapter discusses participatory budgeting, a formalized system for introducing this input into the process for portions of the budget. But citizens participate in local budget processes without that system.) This is input from ordinary citizens, not the lobbyist representation of interest groups that is common in the federal process. Such broad opportunity to include individual concerns in budget deliberations would not be feasible at state or federal levels. Even without formal integration of citizens into the process, citizen input is easier at the local level—the general public runs into their city council members, mayors, and the like on a regular basis at school events, the grocery, the hardware store, and so on, and they feel free to let their elected representatives know how they feel about public policy. Of course, in parts of New England, the fiscal business of small local governments gets transacted in town hall meetings in which everybody gets their say and their opportunity to vote on what the government will do. Such a system of direct citizen input can work with such governments, although transaction costs would become an issue if the system were to be tried for a larger city or state.

Seventh, state and local budgets and appropriations frequently include details about what the money is to be spent for; that is, the details of the grocery list of supplies (the line items) that the agency will be expected to purchase. This is in marked contrast to the budget account appropriations that characterize the control structures of the federal government. Such object-level appropriations hamper the flexibility of response by these agencies and represent a throwback to the narrow control orientation that was a driving force for the earliest public budgets.

Eighth, state and local governments often earmark or dedicate portions of some broad revenue sources, such as personal income or general sales taxes, to particular uses. For example, a state may earmark a percentage of the state sales tax to primary and secondary education. That would mean that proceeds from that portion of the tax would be tracked to that purpose regardless of any other needs the state might have. Around ten states earmark more than one-third of their tax collections to some purpose or another, thereby reducing the ability of the fiscal system to respond to changing public priorities. The average for states is around 20 percent; it is probably somewhat higher for general-purpose local governments. Although there is some possible logic to directing tax and charge revenue directly associated with a public function to that function, in the way that motor-fuel tax collections are frequently dedicated to operation and maintenance of highways, there is no economic sense to locking in general revenue to a specific use; that is a choice that priority balancing in the budget process should make. Not only does it hinder the capacity to respond, but it also adds an extra degree of complexity to the fiscal system. Furthermore, revenue is fungible (or easily mixed) in a general-purpose government, allowing easy substitution between uses. In short, earmarking may not have the impact that its supporters expect. In an analysis of state earmarking programs for highways, education, and non-school local government assistance, Dye and McGuire discovered either nonchange in spending for these programs, or increases less than the amount of revenue set aside for the earmarked program. Much of the earmarked revenue replaced money that would have been spent on the supported function anyway.[29] In other words, the earmarking just clogs up the budget process with no discernable impact on spending allocations.

Ninth, states and localities differ considerably in the extent to which they devise long-term fiscal frameworks to identify issues that may be developing in the future. Among the states that develop and publish such detailed analyses are California, New York, Washington, Massachusetts, Michigan, and Oklahoma.[30] Some others provide estimates in lesser detail, but less than half the states provide expenditure estimates. The idea of such frameworks is to identify potential imbalances that may be emerging as a result of demographic change, economic transformations, inflation, and other factors so that lawmakers have sufficient time to make adjustments to reduce the negative impact of the dynamic changes. Illustrations of these long-term frameworks can be found on state websites. The Governmental Accounting Standards Board is working to require longer-term financial condition reporting on financial statements to support decisions that increase fiscal sustainability.

Finally, state and local governments show considerable difference with regard to transparency in the presentation of their budgets and finances. State budget agencies typically post the budget proposed by the governor on a state website, but the presentation is often considerably less accessible than is that of the federal government. Seldom are substantial historical data provided for analysis of patterns and trends, and presentation formats do not allow easy transmission into analytic software. States do regularly post their comprehensive annual financial reports on state websites, although the posting often occurs a half-year or more after the end of the fiscal year. Most of the reports are lengthy and technical, not intended as communication to the typical citizen. As with any financial report, a careful review of footnotes is necessary to understand exactly how reports are to be interpreted. Local government budgets range widely in their accessibility and in both internal and external utility. Some provide a clear expression and communication of fiscal intentions of the government and some provide virtually uninterpretable accounting spreadsheets of questionable provenance. The latter mean little for those operating within the government and even less for the general public. There is similar variety in regard to both preparation and presentation of comprehensive annual reports, ranging from units preparing no such report, to those preparing a report so late as to have little meaning, to those using the report as a tool for communication and analysis. It should be no surprise that transparency of fiscal intentions and results has great variation.

---

[29]Richard Dye and Therese McGuire, "The Effect of Earmarked Revenues on the Level and Composition of Expenditures," *Public Finance Quarterly* 20 (October 1992): 543–556.
[30]Elizabeth C. McNichol, Vincent Palacios, and Nicholas Johnson, *Budgeting for the Future: Fiscal Planning Tools Can Show the Way*, Center for Budget and Policy Priorities, February 2014.

Legal Constraints

It is extraordinarily rare for a state to operate without legal limitations—statutory, constitutional, or both—on its capacity to spend or tax, and states quite regularly place additional limits on the fiscal operations of their local governments. The limits are placed on the state by itself, not by the federal government. Both limits, taxing and spending, may constrain the size of government and change the manner of finance (strong local limits may, for instance, induce a larger state contribution to joint responsibilities). Some fiscal decisions, like increasing a tax or borrowing to build a new school, may be made only after referendum approval, and that vote may require a supermajority. Many state and local governments operate under limitations, or caps, on spending (or revenues to be collected) in the fiscal year; the limit may be linked to personal income, population growth, or inflation. For instance, overall appropriations are limited to the state personal-income growth rate in Oregon, North Carolina limits appropriations to 7 percent of the state's personal income, and appropriation growth is limited to the combined growth of population and inflation in Alaska.[31] Sometimes the state may be required to refund excess revenues to taxpayers (Colorado, Florida, Indiana, Louisiana, Massachusetts, Michigan, and Missouri), and sometimes appropriations may be limited to anticipated revenues (for instance, Mississippi limits appropriations to 98 percent of projected revenue).[32] Limits, caps, referenda requirements, and supermajorities are common features of state and local fiscal processes; they are not characteristic of the federal government.

State and local governments usually have balanced budget requirements, a fact often noted when comparisons are made between them and the federal government. Indeed, Indiana and Vermont are the only two state governments that do not face a balanced budget requirement. That requirement, however, has various meanings across the states, including (1) the governor's proposed budget must be balanced when presented, (2) the enacted budget must be balanced, and (3) the budget must be balanced when the year is over. Some states may, within the requirement, carry a deficit into the next year, making the standard much easier to achieve. In addition, the language of the requirements can be interesting. For instance, the Massachusetts constitutional requirement for balance reads as follows: "The governor shall submit a budget which shall contain a statement of all proposed expenditures of the commonwealth for the fiscal year, including those already authorized by law, and of all taxes, revenues, loans, and other means by which expenditures shall be defrayed" (Massachusetts Constitution, Article LXIII, paragraph 2). By that standard, federal budgets have always been balanced because deficits have been successfully covered by loans! Although requirements usually extend well beyond the state or local general fund to include trust funds, special funds, and funds set up to operate federal programs, they typically do not include capital budgets set up to fund capital

---

[31]National Association of State Budget Officers, *Budget Processes in the States, Spring 2015* (Washington, D.C.: NASBO, 2015), Table 11.
[32]Mandy Rafool, "State Tax and Expenditure Limits," *The Fiscal Letter* 18, no. 5 (1996): 4–7; Philip G. Joyce and Daniel R. Mullins, "The Changing Fiscal Structure of the State and Local Public Sector: The Impact of Tax and Expenditure Limitations," *Public Administration Review* 51 (May–June 1991): 240–53.

improvements (highways, buildings, etc.) and financed by bonded indebtedness (borrowing). One study of state balanced budget provisions observes that "it is the tradition of balancing budgets, the mindset this tradition creates, and the importance placed on balanced budgets that result in states complying with their requirements."[33] The same probably applies for local governments. As discussed later in the chapter, states and localities have developed a fabulous arsenal of gimmicks for escaping the balance requirement, meaning that the balance mindset is more significant than the requirement in the pursuit of fiscal sustainability.[34]

Both state and local governments must remain concerned about access to capital markets; profligate behavior will eventually restrict their ability to borrow, and they lack the ultimate backstop of finance by money creation that the federal government has. These requirements by themselves are not sufficient to ensure the long-term fiscal health of state or local governments because, if there is political will, there will always be a way to get around the limits.[35] It is that will, not the legal limits, that provides the constraint—absent a will, there will always be a gimmick that can be found to get around the limit.

State and local governments also typically face limits on their capacity to issue debt, either to finance capital construction (building highways, schools, prisons, etc.) or to cover operating deficits. These limits may involve a requirement that the voters specifically approve the borrowing or dollar limits on debt that can be outstanding, either in absolute terms or in some relationship to the tax base (e.g., constrained to 5 percent of a county's total property tax base). As is described in Chapter 15 on public debt, governments have devised many legal mechanisms to surmount these legal obstacles without much difficulty.

Budget Balance Tricks

States and localities often face a legal requirement for a balanced budget, and many find it inconvenient to actually balance the budget or may want to reduce the apparent level of the deficit.[36] As a result, governments have developed a number of devices to "cook" budget numbers; many are widely and regularly used to avoid the difficult tasks of actual deficit reduction (increasing revenue or reducing expenditure). None

---

[33]National Association of State Budget Offices, "State Balanced Budget Requirements: Provisions and Practice," *State Tax Notes* 3 (July 27, 1992): 117.

[34]Remember that budgets are plans and forecasts, not an accounting of actual finances. Thus, calls for preparation of budgets on an accrual rather than a cash basis will not close the door on fiscal tricks.

[35]By implication, those who believe that a balanced budget amendment to the U.S. Constitution is the solution to the federal deficit problem do not understand the lessons of state experience. The limits are easily circumvented unless there is political will to maintain balance. Political will trumps legal barriers (plus the barriers themselves aren't very rigid). Rule of thumb: if a government's finance officers cannot find a way around whatever balance requirement the lawmakers have erected, they are not very good.

[36]Richard Briffault, *Balancing Acts, The Reality behind State Balanced Budget Requirements* (New York: Twentieth Century Fund, 1996), explains that state balanced budget requirements are not nearly so binding as a casual observer might assume. An operating budget would include the expenditures to be made for services delivered within the year; the resources purchased from the operating budget would largely be used within that year.

of these approaches represents sound financial management. Even if the budget is balanced in terms of producing sufficient revenue to cover expenditures, the manner in which it is balanced may violate the fiscal sustainability standard.

1. **Rosy scenarios.** Any budget must be constructed with revenue forecasts for the upcoming fiscal year. Phantom budget balances, therefore, can be developed by using artificially high forecasts for that year. Such forecasts can be produced by assuming unrealistically high economic activity (income and sales taxes are sensitive to the level of economic activity),[37] by positing impossibly diligent administration of the tax, or by presuming that the link between revenue collections and economic activity has improved. Local property taxes ordinarily could not be overestimated because rates are set on the basis of assessed value on a prior valuation date (more about this in a later chapter). The estimated revenue can be manipulated, however, by assuming unrealistically low delinquency (or noncollection) levels: if 90 percent of the levy has historically been collected, a budget boost is possible by assuming 95 percent collection. During its fiscal troubles of the late 1970s, New York City apparently got such boosts toward balancing the budget by presuming 100 percent collection, a completely unrealistic basis for budgeting. In 2010, California eliminated $1.4 billion of its proposed budget deficit by deciding to use a more optimistic revenue forecast.[38] That is much easier than figuring out how to reduce spending or increase revenue to close the gap. Similar effects may result from overly optimistic assumptions about intergovernmental assistance from either federal or state sources or about the possibility that some other government or a private organization will assume responsibility for a service previously provided through this budget. New York State has, for a few years, included around $150 million in revenue from collection of cigarette taxes on Indian reservations in its budget— in spite of doubts that such taxes can be enforced—but they do help with the budget gap. Estimates of revenue from newly adopted taxes or other revenue sources are always a bit chancy; there is no history upon which an estimate can be based. Thus, state administrations have helped their deficits with robust estimates of extra revenue coming from such sources as contracting out the lottery operation, allowing online gaming, auctioning off facilities, and so on. Rosy scenarios also can reduce planned expenditures: a healthy (forecasted) economy reduces social program needs and entitlement flows, and artificially low inflation will constrain spending in many areas. Chapter 13 explains the best methods for forecasting revenues, but using these approaches will not insulate a government from forecast manipulation.

---

[37]In a review of revenue forecasting evidence, John L. Mikesell and Justin Ross, "State Revenue Forecasts and Political Acceptance: The Value of Consensus Forecasting in the Budget Process," *Public Administration Review* 74 (March/April 2014): 188–202 find no evidence that revenue forecasts are systematically too high or too low across all state governments. That is not to say that manipulations of the forecast for budget advantage do not occur in some entities in some budget cycles.

[38]Vauhini Vara, "California Budget Plan Draws Skepticism," *Wall Street Journal*, October 3, 2010.

2. **One-shots.** An unrepeatable revenue boost can be produced by the sale of property or other assets held by the government, a "one-shot." As long as that revenue is not viewed as a long-term boost to the fiscal base and the asset is truly no longer needed for government service, the sale may be perfectly reasonable. But this is not always the case. Arizona sold its state capitol complex in 2009 for money to close a hole in the state budget, but, of course, immediately leased back the facilities so it could conduct state business—closing the deficit in one year but increasing spending in later years. The "green sale-leaseback" is a recent reincarnation. Providence, Rhode Island transferred three city buildings, including City Hall, to the city's Public Building Authority. The building authority borrowed $35 million, using the buildings as collateral. The city will lease the buildings back for fifteen years and those rental payments will cover debt payments. Of the bond issue, about $5 million will go for building energy-efficiency upgrades and $30 million will cover the city's budget deficit.[39] These are all, of course, simply borrowing in a disguised format, not actions to support fiscal sustainability. Other examples include privatization proceeds, the more profitable of which may bring in substantial revenue in the sale year but mean the loss of profit flows in later years.[40] An eastern state took the one-shot to its ridiculous extreme. A state hospital was declared surplus, was appraised at a handsome value, and was advertised for sale, and the anticipated revenue from that sale was included in the state revenue estimate. It helped balance a tight budget. But the facility did not sell, so the anticipated sales revenue was included as part of revenue expected for the next budget year! As long as the property remained for sale, the state felt justified in including appraised proceeds as anticipated revenue. In the budget process for 2016, the Pennsylvania legislature got its deficit down to an acceptable level by including revenue from privatizing the state wine and liquor store system even though it had not yet passed legislation to do the privatization and even though the governor vetoed the proposal after the legislature had passed the law.[41] The sales have not taken place as planned in the budget presentation; whether gimmick or plan is for others to decide. Sale of an asset reduces the financial resources of the government by an amount equivalent to the amount of the sale and should not be treated the same as sustainable operating revenue (like taxes or charges).[42]

---

[39]Michael Corkery, "Cities Deep in Red Turn to Green Deals," *Wall Street Journal,* September 9, 2011, C1.
[40]Privatization is best defended to improve operating efficiency and delivery of service, not as a one-shot revenue enhancer.
[41]Federal budgets are not immune from such manipulations. Recent presidential budgets have included revenue from the sale of AMTRAK, oil leases in the Arctic National Wildlife Refuge, the Naval Petroleum Reserves, the telecommunications spectrum, and so on. Portions of the spectrum have, in fact, been auctioned—but not as soon as the revenue started appearing in budgets. In budget scorekeeping, revenue from asset sales do not count against deficit targets.
[42]International standards hold that sales of government-owned assets should be treated as means of financing the deficit, not revenue, because they are asset conversions only, not continuing sources of revenue. For instance, this is the required treatment for privatization receipts from sales of state-owned properties in countries of the former Soviet Union.

As noted in Chapter 1, in recent years a number of states and localities have sold various infrastructure assets—bridges, highways, and the like—for a quick jolt of revenue, sometimes wisely used and sometimes not. Such proceeds are capital revenue, not current revenue, inasmuch as they are not repeatable. They do not reduce the cost of government, do not improve the revenue prospects of the government, and do not repair a fundamental fiscal gap. Another favorite one-shot during the Great Recession was the state tax amnesty, programs whereby tax cheats would be forgiven consequences of their cheating (penalties and interest) if they would pay previously evaded taxes in a brief amnesty period—a quick revenue boost, no matter the questions about rewarding dishonest taxpayers and potentially losing future revenue from the demonstrated success of cheating.

3. **Interbudget manipulation.** State and local governments often have capital budgets in addition to and separate from operating budgets. Capital budgets finance purchases of assets with long, useful lives (as discussed in Chapter 7) and often have no requirement for balance because such long-life assets may logically be financed on a pay-as-you-use basis through the issuance of debt. Some governments have shifted activities that would ordinarily be included in the operating budget to the capital budget to produce the desired balance in the operating budget. For instance, in its fiscal 1992 budget, New York City included an $80 million bond issue to finance the four-year job of painting 872 city bridges "Yankee Blue," clearly a basic and continuing maintenance expenditure, but not included in the operating budget.[43] The shift can destroy the logic of the capital budget and, more important, can endanger the capability to finance the government's capital infrastructure.

4. **Bubbles and timing.** Deficits may be managed by accelerated collection of revenue to create a cash "bubble" in the year of acceleration.[44] The advantage accrues only in the acceleration year without influencing the fundamental revenue base. The bubble can be duplicated in forthcoming fiscal years only by further accelerating collections, an unlikely possibility. Here is how acceleration can work: Suppose a state requires that vendor collections of sales-and-use taxes in one month (say, May 2017) be paid to the state by the end of the next month (June 2017). The payment from the vendor then will be received by the state early in the next month (July 2017). If the state changes the due date from the end of the month to the 20th, however, the checks will almost certainly be received by the state in that month, that is, in late June rather than early July. But for a July 1 fiscal-year state, June is in the 2017 fiscal year, and July is in the 2018 fiscal year; fiscal 2017 thus receives thirteen months of sales-and-use tax collections. Because a similar schedule applies for 2018 and beyond, each year continues to receive twelve months of collections. (Acceleration gets more complicated when payments are electronic

---

[43]John J. Doran, "New York City Comptroller Kills Bonding Plans for Bridge Painting; Cites Mistakes of 1970s," *Bond Buyer,* July 16, 1991, 2.
[44]In New York State, these accelerations are called "spin-ups."

rather than by checks in the mail, but it still can be done. Most of the accelerations were done in the era of mailing checks.) Only a return to a slower schedule would leave a fiscal year a month short of revenue. States started the speed-up approach in the 1970s and extended it with early payment and prepayment requirements in later years. Well over half of the states require either early payment of collections within the month (e.g., partial payment of May collections in May) or prepayment of estimated collections with reconciliation against actual collections later (estimated May collections paid in May with adjustment against actual collections later) for some major taxes remitted by businesses. Virginia is a recent participant: in fiscal 2010, retailers with annual sales of at least $1 million were required to make advance payment of sales tax owed, bringing thirteen months of tax revenue into that fiscal year. These manipulations are politically less difficult than raising statutory tax rates and can provide added revenue for a problem.[45]

The balance problem also may be concealed by manipulating the timing of expenditure.[46] One approach loads the cost of multiyear programs in later fiscal years rather than in a sequence consistent with normal project-development flow. The low current budget-year request may help achieve balance in that year; the result, however, may well be greater problems in achieving balance in future budget years. A somewhat different method of expenditure manipulation, particularly within a fiscal year, delays payment for purchases made toward the end of a fiscal year until the next fiscal year (and the next year's appropriations).[47] The technique artificially reduces the operating deficit in the first year and amounts to short-term borrowing from suppliers across the two fiscal years. In general, the technique kicks the deficit down the road and reduces funds available for the next year. Unless the imbalance is corrected, similar problems will result in following years, and the operating deficit carryover will expand with time.[48] In another example

---

[45]Similar shifts may substitute for ordinary borrowing. For instance, the city of Philadelphia used a property tax provision: businesses willing to pay estimated 1978 taxes along with their 1977 taxes were given a special discount on their 1978 tax bill. See "Early Taxpayers Can Get a Break in Philadelphia," *Louisville Courier-Journal,* April 3, 1977. This shift, however, does reduce aggregate collections, whereas acceleration does not.

[46]For example, in 1980 the city of Chicago, to avoid bank loans in a cash crisis, delayed payments to vendors who regularly did business with the city. The problem emerged because property tax bills were not mailed as scheduled because of a judicial challenge of a homestead exemption program. The city had short-term borrowing authority, but feared it was insufficient to cover the shortage. "City May Delay Payment to Suppliers," *Chicago Tribune,* August 19, 1980. Because the taxes were actually levied, there was no borrowing across fiscal years in this instance; the strategy was simply one of cash-flow management.

[47]A federal example: the federal government temporarily stopped payments to Medicare providers for the last six business days of fiscal 2006—moving the spending from one fiscal year to the next.

[48]In 1992, New York City required 2,104 police recruits to begin training at 11:59 p.m. on June 30, the last minute of the fiscal year. These orders met a state requirement for starting the new class in the 1991–1992 fiscal year, but deferred required city pension contributions for them ($20 million) until the 1993–1994 fiscal year. Kevin Sack, "Fiscal Footwork Is Fancy in Plan for Police Recruits," *New York Times,* June 30, 1992, B-3.

of expenditure timing, in 2013, New Jersey sent out property rebate checks in August, instead of May, so that $400 million would show up in spending for the next fiscal year.[49]

The federal system creates a somewhat different version of the timing game. Budget presentations work with an out-year window of five or ten years. To conceal the long-term impact of fiscal policies being proposed, legislation may be proposed that has its largest impact on the deficit just outside the budget window. That can involve when provisions expire, when tax rates change, or when other changes will have a significant impact on the deficit. If the change were within the presentation window, the impact would stir controversy. By being just beyond, it can slide through with a minimum of attention.

5. **Ducking the decision.** A balanced executive budget may omit some activities that political pressures would prevent the legislature from excluding. The executive may thus claim a balanced budget (or a smaller deficit), even though the hard choices have not been made; appropriations actually made will likely produce a deficit, or proposals will be radically realigned before appropriation. An illustration: Texas requires that its Legislative Budget Board (LBB), the body responsible for preparing the budget document for appropriations, submit a balanced budget. In the fall of 1984, after substantial work had been done on the document for presentation to the 1985 session, the state comptroller substantially reduced the official estimate of oil and natural gas tax revenue (a major source of Texas state revenue). The revision occurred just before the LBB reviewed higher education requests, the last item on its schedule. Rather than altering recommendations for all state agencies, the LBB opted to balance the budget entirely through reductions in higher education and recommended a 26 percent appropriation decrease. Possibly the LBB intended to stimulate efficiency in higher education, but it is more likely that it was practicing phantom balance. In any case, the legislature made substantial readjustments; virtually all reductions were restored, and some institutions received increases.[50]

An artificially balanced budget may even be passed, with the legislature relying on supplemental appropriation in the next year to provide required funds. Such proceedings may go largely unnoticed by the media and the citizenry because emphasis traditionally focuses on the budget presentation and consideration, not on what actually happens during the budget year. In a similar fashion, the imbalance may be handled by shifting expenditures normally planned for the early part of the coming budget year into a supplemental request for the current budget year. Unfunded public employee pension

---

[49]Kate Zernike, "Christie Embraces Budget Strategies He Scorned as a Candidate," *New York Times*, October 29, 2013.
[50]Lawrence Biemiller, "How the University of Texas, Flexing Its Political Muscle, Foiled Budget Cutters," *Chronicle of Higher Education* 30 (June 19, 1985): 12–15.

promises are probably the largest American example in gross dollar terms of ducking the decision.

6. **Playing the intergovernmental system.** States regularly manage their budget problems by transferring the problems to their local governments. First, states can assign local governments responsibility for services that have previously been state-financed. For instance, highway maintenance is usually a shared state-local responsibility, with certain roads being state and others local. By moving more of the statewide network to the local system, the state can reduce its expenditure requirement. Second, states can reduce the amount of aid they provide local governments. For example, state aid to school districts represents a considerable share of total state spending (the national average is around 15 percent of state spending). By reducing the amount distributed to schools, the state can reduce its budget problem. Cutting aid to local governments, actually presented as loans to the state, was one approach that the state of California used in its budget-balancing fiasco in the summer of 2009. During the Great Recession, states responding with reduced assistance to cities or other local governments included Ohio, Nebraska, New York, and Michigan, among others.[51] Third, states can delay appropriated aid payments to local governments, moving expenditure from one state fiscal year to another. When the dates of local fiscal years do not match those of the state year, the change may not even alter the total funds to the localities in their fiscal year, just the timing within their year. Suppose the state is on a July 1 fiscal year and its school districts are on January 1 fiscal year, a common situation in the United States. The state owes school districts twelve monthly aid payments during a year. Suppose that the June payment is made in July rather than June. This saves the state one payment during the first fiscal year, although it still pays the school districts the same amount through their calendar fiscal year. But all these strategies do have considerable potential for moving state fiscal problems to their localities. Indeed, states sometimes simply skip a payment to local governments, kicking the problem down to them.

7. **Magic asterisk.** The "magic asterisk" is a federal creation, although it is regularly employed in state budget documents. David Stockman, President Reagan's first director of the Office of Management and Budget, coined the phrase to mean budget savings to be identified later, or "whatever it took to get a balanced budget . . . after we totaled up all the individual budget cuts we'd actually approved."[52] Because so much media and public attention focuses on proposed deficits, the fact that the budget provides no clear funding plan gets overlooked. Many times the asterisk will be linked to "administrative savings," which no one has the foggiest idea about how to achieve. The same kind of unspecified savings appears in many gubernatorial

---

[51]Michael Cooper, "States Pass Budget Pain to Cities," *New York Times*, March 23, 2011.
[52]David A. Stockman, *The Triumph of Politics* (New York: Harper & Row, 1986), 124.

budgets, especially during the first year of office when there is little time between election and budget presentation. The new governor may have almost no idea about how to get some outcome promised in the campaign, but the public still remembers the promise. A magic asterisk permits the desired bottom line and gives the administration some time to figure out how to do it.

8. **Punt the pension.** Most public employee pension funds are established in such a way that payments are made by the government employer into the fund during the working life of an employee cohort with the expectation that the total of these payments plus interest earned over the years will cover the pensions paid to the cohort. It was common during the last few decades for state and local governments to close their deficits by failing to make the pension payment or by making an inadequate payment. The employees weren't concerned because they were entitled to their pensions, regardless of the balance in the government pension fund; and the citizenry wasn't concerned because nonpayment into the fund meant that taxes could be a bit lower. So failure to contribute became a common approach to balancing a budget. The practice violated fiscal sustainability standards because it kicked a current cost into the future, but it balanced the budget.[53]

9. **Securitization.** "Securitized" revenue brings a large revenue boost in a single fiscal year. One of the most popular securitization targets has been revenue paid from the tobacco Master Settlement Agreement between five large tobacco companies and forty-six states concerning illegal marketing, promotion, and advertising of cigarettes. Under the agreement, the states are paid tobacco revenue into the future, and several states have securitized the revenue, essentially borrowed on the basis of that revenue flow, to obtain revenue in a particular year. States have used this revenue to close a budget gap in the year, but at the sacrifice of revenue that would have come in future years—thus mortgaging the future for the present.

If you have been paying attention, you should realize that balanced budgets and balanced budget requirements are largely a myth. If there is no political will to maintain fiscal sustainability, legal requirements will be no barrier.[54]

---

[53]In only one example, New Jersey passed a law in 2011 that restructured its public employee pension program and included a promise that the state would pay into the program enough to cover required future benefit payments (governors in the past had regularly short-changed or totally ignored required payments into the fund). The state made the required payments for two years, but cut them back in 2014 and 2015 because Governor Christie said he could not balance the state budget otherwise. His plan was to skip payment entirely for 2016. (Kate Zernike, "New Jersey's Top Court Rules Christie Can Skip Pension Payments," *New York Times*, June 9, 2015.) And the New Jersey court decided that the governor had the legal right to skip the pension payment to prevent a current budget crisis. So much for fiscal sustainability.

[54]One good review of state balanced-budget requirements and how they are avoided is Institute for Truth in Accounting, "The Truth about Balanced Budgets: A Fifty State Study," February 2009. http://www.truthinaccounting.org/news/listing_article.asp?section=451&section2=451&CatID=3&ArticleSource=572.

The Elephant in the Room: State and Local Pensions and Other Post-Employment Benefits[55]

A normal element of the traditional employment relationship in the United States is the promise of a pension upon retirement that will be provided through the employer. That is true for both public and private employers.[56] The financing of these pensions (and other post-employment benefits) has become a significant issue for state and local governments. When a government has to compensate both current employees and past employees at the same time, the total cost can become unmanageable. That is the problem that many state and local governments now face. They made promises of post-employment benefits (pensions, health insurance, etc.) as a part of employee compensation, but they did not make financial allowances for these promises while the employees were delivering services to the government. The financial crunch hits when the government faces the cost of paying both current and past employees out of current revenue. Various benefits may be involved, but the area of greatest recent concern has involved pensions. These pension programs may be state employee pension systems, state-operated local pension systems, or pension systems operated by individual local governments.

The programs may be for all employees of the particular government, but there are frequently different systems for public school teachers, for police officers, and for firefighters. They all face similar concerns.

To understand the problem requires an understanding of the distinction between two different sorts of pension arrangements. One style of pension is a *defined contribution* pension.[57] In this system, the employer is obligated to make a regular payment into a pension account for the individual employee during the work-life of the employee. Payment amounts are usually driven by the salary of the employee; that is, the payments equal some defined percentage of the employee's salary. The employee may also be required to make a payment. The combined total in the employee's account is then invested on behalf of the individual employee with the idea that the payments into the fund plus the return earned on the fund will ultimately provide the pension for the employee. The amount that has accumulated

---

[55]This section focuses primarily on pension issues. However, there are other post-employment benefits. The most critical other benefit involves promises of health insurance for the retiree. Because many public employees, particularly police and firefighters, have arranged full retirement well before the age at which Americans qualify for Medicare, the promise is an expensive one. Unfortunately, not many local governments have made allowance for these costs during the working life of employees—one study suggests that they are only 6 percent funded, a status even worse than pension funding—so the costs must be covered on a pay-as-you-go basis, an expensive proposition that violates fiscal sustainability standards.

[56]Although much of the language is the same, these pensions are different from Social Security. The pensions are part of the employer–employee compensation relationship, whereas Social Security is part of the government–beneficiary social insurance relationship. Employees of ten states (Alaska, California, Illinois, Louisiana, Maine, Massachusetts, Nevada, Ohio, and Texas), as well as local governments in many other states, are not part of the Social Security system, neither paying taxes in nor receiving benefits out from that employment.

[57]These programs are similar to private-sector 401(k) pension plans.

in the fund for that particular employee will determine what pension payment the retiree will receive. The retiree is not guaranteed a particular pension level, but the employee is promised that a set amount will regularly be put into the retirement account. Thus, the contribution is defined, and what it ultimately accumulates to— total payments plus returns from their investment—will define the pension amount. Defined contribution plans, by their nature, require that the government bear the cost of future retirement benefits at the time the employee earns those benefits.

The other style of pension is a *defined benefit* pension. In this system, the level of benefit upon retirement is determined according to a formula driven by such factors as the number of years the retiree worked for the employer, the final salary earned by the employee, cost of living adjustments, the age of the employee upon retirement, and possibly other factors. The employer maintains a fund that is intended to cover benefit payments, but there are no individual employee accounts. Employees may be required to contribute payments into the fund with each paycheck, but the employer is obligated for the defined benefit payments and not for particular payments into the fund. It is expected that, in total, those payments plus fund earnings will be sufficient to cover the promised benefits when employees retire. If the fund does not have sufficient resources to meet the contracted payments, then the employer is expected to come up with the payment from other resources. Payments are guaranteed by state statute, constitution, or contract law. The vast majority of public employee pension programs historically have been defined benefit programs.[58]

Many state and local governments have operated defined benefit pension programs without making proper current allowance for future benefit promises, which has created a fiscal dilemma. The problem is that government administrations, when facing difficult fiscal choices, have given their employees improved pension benefits (earlier full retirement, higher benefits, lower individual contributions into the system, more generous calculation of salaries upon which pension payments are based, or some combination of all) rather than giving them higher wages and salaries. The wages and salaries would come from current resources, whereas the pensions will need to be paid at some point in the future—and the total spending in the years in which pensions were earned could be reduced if the government failed to make the required contribution. It was a sort of deal between governments (mayors, governors, legislators, administrators) and employee groups (unions): the government offered an attractive benefit package to the employees, financed in a politically attractive but fiscally unsustainable way, and the employee groups, seeing a fine deal presented, took the offers. Taxpayers also were in on the scam: they got artificially reduced taxes and maybe the burden could be kicked down the road many years into the future. Of course, a responsible government would accumulate funds to meet those future payments as the pension promise is earned. The problem is that it can be convenient to delay those payments (the payment is called the Actuarially Determined Employer Contribution) in difficult fiscal times (or even in good

[58]Exceptions to the rule that government employees are in defined benefit programs: faculty at many state universities are in the TIAA/CREF defined contribution program and federal employees in the Federal Employee Retirement System Thrift Savings Plan. In 1996, Michigan established a defined contribution plan for all new employees. In 1991, West Virginia school employees were put in such a plan.

times) on the assumption that later administrations will make up for the missed contributions. Except each administration does the same thing, kicking the date of fiscal reckoning further into the future. When employees do retire, the jurisdiction faces a fiscal squeeze because prior administrations have not been making the required contribution and the required pension payment may become an unsustainable share of the total budget. That is when the reckoning from a failure to make regular and sufficient annual payments into the pension fund actually hits.

Employee groups are not particularly inclined to protest these failures by the government to put aside enough to meet future promises because the pension promise is the future benefits and it is the problem for the government to find the money to do it. The employees are not directly affected by the failure to make the necessary payments; the impact is on the taxpayers and citizenry in the future. If accumulations are insufficient to meet the promised pensions, the government will need to significantly reduce current services or dramatically increase revenues to meet the pension promises that have been made to employees of the past. The politics are that it is better to boot the cost of government to the future than it is to pay the costs now because, by the time those deferred costs actually come due, those administrators and lawmakers who have deferred the costs will have moved on to other things and it won't be their problem.

That is not the end to the dilemma. The defined benefit pension requires the accumulation of a pension fund from which promised pensions will be paid. There are two particular problems with these funds. First, there are questions about how much money needs to be accumulated in these funds to make them actuarially sound. That amount depends on how long payments will be made into the fund, what the benefits paid out will be, how long retirees will be drawing benefits, and, crucially, what rate of return will be earned on the money in the fund. The higher the rate of return that will be earned on the money in the fund, the less the employer will need to place into the fund. A set of benefit obligations in the future can be supported with a lower fund accumulation the higher the rate of return is, and any gap between money that needs to be in the fund and actual funds accumulated (the unfunded liability) will be lower when the rate is higher. The low interest rates of the Great Recession and its aftermath have brought more financing troubles for the pension funds because the earning power of money in the fund is reduced. Of course, nobody knows what that actual future rate of return will be, so the fund liability will be based on an estimated rate.[59] In recent years, there has been a heated debate about what rate should be used. It has been common practice (approved by the Government Accounting Standards Board) to use a rate of 8 percent for these

---

[59]Some governments have been guilty of absolutely horrible fund management. For instance, Detroit and some other cities were in the practice of issuing "bonus checks" to retirees whenever the pension fund rate of return exceeded the target rate used to determine necessary government payments into the system. In 2014, Philadelphia paid a bonus to its retirees of $62.4 million because the five-year average return for the fund exceeded the rate used to calculate required fund balances, even though its pensions were only 47 percent funded. They paid $7.7 million in bonuses in 2015 for the same reason, even though the fund lost $218 million in value during the year. Good heavens! Did they levy a "return clawback" whenever actual returns fell below the target? No wonder many city pension funds are in trouble and that Detroit had to receive bankruptcy protection.

investments, but critics have pointed out that this is higher than the returns that have been recently earned (a fair market approach to estimating the required payments). In 2012, the Government Accounting Standards Board revised its rules for pension accounting and reporting of financial condition in annual financial reports. Pension systems that are adequately funded may use their historical average returns in estimating liability (according to the National Association of State Retirement Administrators, the average return assumption was 7.68 percent in 2015). Systems lacking adequate funding must use a return equal to the yield on a tax-exempt 20-year AA-or-higher rated municipal bond, a much lower rate. When lower rates are used, the unfunded liability of state and local pension funds becomes shockingly large.[60] The gap is large enough to raise questions about the financial viability of some governments, and unfunded pension liabilities has been an important issue in recent local government bankruptcy filings, although the new gap is only from reporting rules and not from any change in the condition of the funds. With the few exceptions of cities entering into bankruptcy proceedings, pensions continue to be paid as scheduled. Fortunately, the unfunded liability does not come due immediately, but the governments do need to reform their programs and initiate efforts to build their pension fund balances.

Second, even though state and local pension funds fall far below levels necessary for actuarial soundness, they still amount to a large pool of money. That makes the funds attractive to those with interests possibly contrary to maintaining the security of pension promises. Investment advisors and other participants in the financial services industry seek business from the funds for the commissions that can result, and because of the considerable sums of money involved, shadowy financial arrangements involving bribes, campaign contributions, hiring of relatives, and so on may emerge. Even without corrupt practices, the management fees paid pension investment advisors are often substantial, far exceeding the amount of increased return to the fund that their recommendations will bring. Business may not be directed in a way that best serves the public interest. In similar fashion, the pension funds may be seen as a pot of money to be used to stimulate the local economy (providing low-cost financing for economic development, using local investment advisors rather than national professionals, etc.), practices that are contrary to the best interests of the funds. Even inadequate fund balances create the temptation for misuse, a temptation that is particularly great when benefit payments are a number of years in the future and the beneficiaries are not directly depending on amounts in the fund. It will be the taxpayers in those future years who will face the implications of misuse now, so they are not paying much attention.

In 2014, public pension funds had $3.78 trillion of assets invested. Almost 60 percent of payments to beneficiaries came from investment income.[61] Although

---

[60]Novy-Marx and Rauh are particularly critical of the return assumption and, when using what they believe to be a more realistic rate, find unfunded liabilities on the order of 24 percent higher than gross domestic product. Robert Novy-Marx and Joshua D. Rauh, "The Liabilities and Risks of State Sponsored Pension Plans," *Journal of Economic Perspectives* 23 (Fall 2009): 191–210.

[61]National Association of State Retirement Administrators, NASR Issue Brief: Public Pension Plan Investment Return Assumptions, May 2015.

Sidebar 5–2
Pension Obligation Bonds (POBs): The Costless Approach to Public Pension Funding?

When public employee pension fund balances are insufficient to cover the actuarial estimate of future benefit payments, fund managers have difficult options for improving the financial condition of the funds to make them fiscally sustainable. They can increase the contributions into the pension funds to cover the promises that have been made to the current cohort of employees and to cover the promises made in the past that were not paid for when the benefits were being accrued. They can negotiate with pension beneficiaries, current and future, to reduce the value of benefits that will be paid in the future or, in some recent instances, get those benefit reductions imposed through a bankruptcy court decision. Or the fund managers can work to improve the return earned on money while it accumulates in the pension fund by investing in more risky investment media, taking a greater chance that balances will be lost when the investment does not do well. None of these alternatives is politically easy, and all impose extra costs on either taxpayers or on public employees. Nobody will accept the cost cheerfully. It is not surprising that lawmakers are reluctant to make those difficult choices.

Because of political costs associated with dealing with underfunded pensions in a straightforward way, lawmakers in some jurisdictions have taken a different approach. They have, in essence, become semi-amateur investment bankers. Here is how the scheme, first implemented by the City of Oakland, California, in 1985, works. The POB is a classic arbitrage instrument: take advantage of different prices in different markets to profit on that difference, in this case by borrowing at one rate of interest to invest for a higher rate of return. The difference between the rate paid and the rate earned represents profit from the transaction. Easy and involving no sacrifice by either taxpayers or pension recipients: the pension fund liability was made transparent (it was the amount being borrowed by the fund, so the fund liability was made obvious to everyone), and the profit from the arbitrage was going to reduce the unfunded liability. The POBs do not change the total indebtedness of the fund, but simply changes its nature, converting a somewhat flexible commitment to pensioners into a firm commitment to lenders.

When the POBs started, making a profit on the operation was pretty easy: state and local governments were able to borrow at an artificially low rate of interest because the interest they paid was excluded from the federal income tax and their bonds made a marvelous tax shelter for those subject to high federal tax rates (more about that in a later chapter) and the return they could earn came from much higher yielding taxable investments, but the state and local governments were not subject to the federal income tax. Thus, the state and local government pension funds were almost certain to profit from the POBs: borrow tax-free and invest taxable (but owe no tax on the profitable difference). Even fund managers not capable enough to manage pension funds on a sound basis were pretty certain to come out ahead on these investments. It was almost a classic no-brainer, and these were just the people qualified to take advantage of the opportunity. Congress, however, was not amused because the POB scheme involving sale of tax-free bonds cost the federal treasury tax revenue: the Tax Reform Act of 1986 did away with the tax exemption for the POBs.

However, the POB did not disappear because the lure of repairing the underfunded public pensions without appearing to burden either taxpayers or pension beneficiaries, and even of

(continues)

**Sidebar 5–2
(Continued)**

allowing the government to skip a required annual payment, was too great. In the 1990s, the stock market was booming. Pension funds, traditionally investors in fixed income securities (e.g., bonds), had started moving toward heavier investment in the stock market and returns seemed good. Some pension funds, particularly those in California and Illinois and particularly those with fiscal stress, started issuing taxable bonds and investing the proceeds in these apparently attractive markets. The spread between the interest paid on the taxable pension fund bonds and the return from the assets in which the funds were invested boosted the return that the pension fund earned. The strategy, essentially a gamble on the spread between rates for borrowing and investing, promised to increase the return earned on pension assets overall, reducing the unfunded balance and reducing the potential pressure on taxpayers or retirees. However, for the strategy to work, the timing and selection of investments has to be correct because, as everyone relearned in the Great Recession, market prices can fall. Get the market timing wrong and the finances of the issuing entities will be in even greater trouble than before. Entities that got the timing right made money, and those that didn't lost money. Pension funds that were in strong financial condition were less likely to use POBs. What is clear is that the POB will make money for investment advisors and the financial intermediaries charged with selling these new bond issues.

But changes in government accounting rules add a new wrinkle. The POBs are particularly attractive because of an accounting trick. Covering the unfunded liability by issuing a POB does not alter the total indebtedness of the pension fund, but the borrowed funds cut the measured unfunded liability—the fund has the proceeds of the debt issue available to cover its ultimate liabilities. That means, according to Governmental Accounting Standards Board rules, that the fund may estimate that future liability using the historical average rate earned on its invested funds rather than the much lower tax exempt municipal bond rate. Using that higher estimated return rate makes the liability gap less and makes the balance sheet more attractive. Borrowing to cover the unfunded pension liability makes the unfunded pension liability less, even though the practical amount of indebtedness changes only in form and not in total. So much for thinking that balance sheets and accounting reports represent the scientific truth. Under these circumstances, the attractiveness of POBs is clear, even with the risk associated with a changed investment strategy.

the Great Recession had a substantial impact on the value of assets invested in stocks, values are recovering. A 2012 GAO report concluded that the funds have sufficient assets to cover all benefits for a decade or more, even as the funds are making changes to improve long-term sustainability.[62] State and local governments are paying more attention to the finances of their pension funds and to the need to maintain required payments into the funds. Governments still use shortchanging the required pension contribution to deal with fiscal problems, but at least there

---

[62]Government Accountability Office, *State and Local Government Pension Plans: Economic Downturn Spurs Efforts to Address Costs and Sustainability,* GAO-12-322 (Washington, D.C.: Government Accountability Office, March 2012).

is more likely to be public outcry about this violation of fiscal sustainability than historically was the case.

Some jurisdictions are working to negotiate benefit levels downward (lower benefits have been a remedy argued in local bankruptcies, a court-protected unilateral change in contract provisions for current and retired workers), and some are increasing payments into their funds, including getting increased employee contributions. Some have explored converting their pension programs to defined contribution systems, a switch that is expensive because the jurisdiction has to continue payments to their traditional program beneficiaries at the same time as it makes contributions under the new program.[63] Sidebar 5–2 discusses another approach to covering the funding gap, the pension obligation bond, an approach that makes the long-term obligation explicit, provides funds to invest, and opens the door to an interesting balance sheet trick.

Although pension contributions are typically a relatively small part of the total operating budget—roughly 3.8 percent in 2010, but promising to grow significantly if funding levels do not increase[64]—state and local governments have become more concerned about appropriate management of their cost and more focused on the impact of making promises that require significant future financial obligations. The best way to avoid pension fund sustainability problems is simply to pay the appropriate required pension contribution each year and not dodge the payment when the budget is tight.

Conclusion

State and local governments provide services close to property and persons: education, public safety, public welfare, highways, and so on. Each state establishes its own budgeting system and procedures and makes service choices largely according to the preferences of its citizens, without standards or requirements from the federal level. Local governments largely work within systems and expectations established by their state. States put more constraints and limits on their spending than the federal government puts on its spending.

One considerable budgetary challenge for states and localities is the absence of a long-term perspective on fiscal decision making. Few of these entities prepare meaningful fiscal assessments beyond the budget year. Even those with biennial budget cycles do little real examination of future challenges, but rather proceed with passage of two similar budgets in a single legislative session. Some, but far from all, present a couple of out-years in their budget presentations, and even fewer develop

---

[63]Defined contribution programs do, however, deal directly with the early retirement issue. Employees will have funds accumulated in their personal retirement accounts, and it is financially immaterial to the employer when the employee retires.

[64]A. Munnell, J. Aubry, and L. Quinby, "The Impact of Public Pensions on State and Local Budgets," State and Local Issue Brief, Center for Retirement Research, Boston College, October 2010.

a medium- or long-term fiscal framework going five or more years into the future to identify the prospects of lurking financial issues.[65] And these governments are inclined to make decisions that boot costs to the future, particularly in regard to the cost of post-employment retirement benefits.

Many of these subnational governments face balanced budget requirements, either constitutional or statutory, with varying requirements to make spending stay within currently available revenue resources. In spite of that, these governments regularly run deficits in their finances through a variety of avoidance mechanisms. Just as with federal government finances, if there is a will to run a deficit, the deficit will be run because sometimes—particularly in recession—the impact of running a deficit is less catastrophic for the long term than taking the actions necessary to prevent the deficit. Controls, constraints, and gimmicks cannot substitute for the will of lawmakers. It is will that can protect fiscal sustainability, not requirements. Net savings by both states and localities has been decreasing and has become regularly negative over the years, stark evidence of overall deficits from these governments. As the years pass following the end of the recession, continued negative net savings do suggest a need for some corrections in state and local finances.

QUESTIONS AND EXERCISES

1. Look at the budget preparation instructions issued by a state budget agency on the state's website. What is the timetable for submission, what is the basic format for preparation of the submission, and are certain displays explicitly required? Do the instructions give suggestions about important areas that the governor wants to emphasize or indications about limits to increases in funding?

2. Identify these key elements of your state budget process:

   a. Does your state have an annual or a biennial budget? Does it appear to have a separate budget for acquisition of capital assets (buildings, roads, bridges, etc.)?
   b. What units direct the preparation of the executive budget? (Not all states have an executive budget.)
   c. How many appropriation bills are usually passed?
   d. How much object-of-expenditure detail appears in these bills?
   e. What item-veto power, if any, does the governor have? Can the governor change the amounts in appropriation bills or is the veto limited to total amounts?
   f. Is the budget process described on a state website? Does the website have the budget instruction issued to state agencies?

---

[65]When longer-term fiscal framework budget numbers are provided, one never knows how serious the thought was that went into them. Because no legislative action is associated with the future years, they may be simple projections of the recent past and provide little to no useful information for the decision process. Requiring additional years in the process does not guarantee anything particularly useful.

    g. Is the state budget easily accessible on the state website?

    h. Does the website provide information on the agency requests, in addition to the executive proposal and adopted appropriations?
The National Association of State Budget Officers provides much of this information in its publication *Budget Processes in the States,* which may be accessed at its website [http://www.nasbo.org].

3. Go to the website of a city or county of your choosing and look for documents relating to that unit's budget and finances. Look for the following:

    a. Find the chief executive's budget message. What is the tone of that message? What are the major priorities?

    b. Find the budget timetable and budget instructions if they are available on the website.

    c. Locate the budget presentation, including any agency narrative and the budget data. Look for budget year, progress year, and report year. Are any out-years provided? Does the budget give other information (e.g., agency request versus council recommendation)? Does the presentation for each agency explain what the agency does, does it provide an organization chart for the agency, and does it explain what its primary objectives for the budget year are? What is the distribution of revenue by source and of expenditure by agency and function?

    d. Does the budget give you enough information to allow you to understand what the tasks of the agencies are?

    e. What is your overall evaluation of the budget presentation? Does it meet your transparency standard? What information did you not find that you would have found useful?

APPENDIX 5–1

An Illustrative State Budget Process: Texas[66]

State and local governments apply the standard four-phase budget cycle involving the executive and legislative branches of government, but there are many individual characteristics in each application. The differences reflect the particular characteristics of government in the various entities and the differing attitudes of the citizenry regarding the appropriate powers of the executive and legislative branches of government. The state of Texas offers an interesting illustration because there are a number of features that operate somewhat differently from those seen in the federal process.

The general flow of the preparation and legislative consideration/adoption phases of the biennial Texas budget cycle is shown in Figure 5A–1. (Execution and audit are not shown in the figure; those phases are generally comparable to

---

[66]Based on House Research Organization, *Writing the State Budget,* State Finance Report No. 79-1 (Austin, Tex.: Texas House of Representatives, February 4, 2005); and Senate Research Center, *Budget 101: A Guide to the Budget Process in Texas* (Austin, Tex.: Texas Senate, 2005).

Figure 5A–1
Texas Biennial Budget Cycle

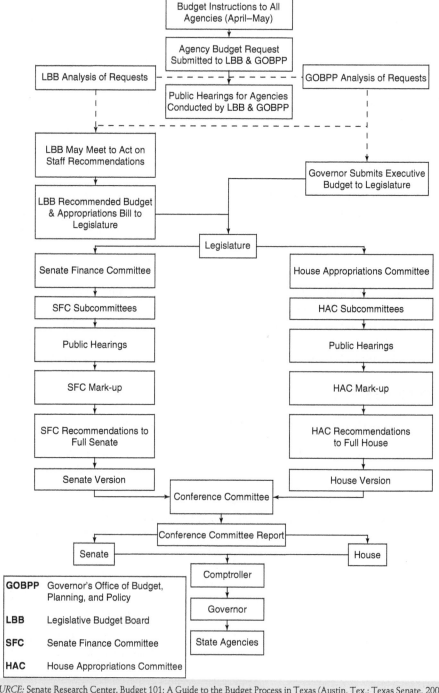

SOURCE: Senate Research Center, Budget 101: A Guide to the Budget Process in Texas (Austin, Tex.: Texas Senate, 2005).

the federal scheme.) In general, agencies prepare appropriation requests in one year, the legislature passes a General Appropriations Act in the next, and the budget is executed over the next two years. And, of course, the cycle continues and overlaps. Notable differences from the federal system are seen in terms of legislative power, item-veto, role of a second elective executive agent (the comptroller), a single appropriations bill, and constitutional restraints.

Budget Preparation

The process begins with cooperation between the governor and the Legislative Budget Board (LBB), an entity not seen in the federal system. The LBB consists of the lieutenant governor; the speaker of the House; the chairs of the Senate Committee on Finance, Senate Committee on State Affairs, House Committee on Ways and Means, and House Committee on Appropriations; two members of the Senate appointed by the lieutenant governor; and two members of the House appointed by the speaker. The LBB has a permanent staff and is responsible for adopting a spending limit; preparing the general appropriations bill (the budget); preparing agency performance reports; guiding, reviewing, and finalizing agency strategic plans; identifying the probable cost of proposed legislation (these are called fiscal notes); and managing transfers among purposes within agencies or among agencies. The LBB provides staff support for the appropriation process during the legislative session: tracking committee decisions, answering committee member inquiries, performing analyses, and providing testimony.

The executive branch is involved through the Governor's Office of Budget, Planning, and Policy (GOBPP; reflecting the governor's policies) and, of course, the agencies that develop their requests for funds according to instructions issued to them. The governor and the LBB develop goals for each state agency to use in developing strategic plans and develop the instructions (Legislative Appropriation Request or LAR instructions) the agencies must use in preparing their appropriation requests. The LARs are submitted to the governor, and hearings are held on those requests in conjunction with the LBB. The governor submits a budget within the first six days of the legislative session and delivers a general appropriations bill within thirty days after the start of the session. The governor's budget is often seen as the statement of policy, and the LBB bill is used as the appropriations bill.

The budget is biennial, and both legislative and executive branches are involved in preparation of the budget and the strategies upon which it is based.

Legislative Consideration and Adoption

The legislature receives the budget and general appropriations bill. It also receives from the comptroller of public accounts (comptroller), an elected state official, a *Biennial Revenue Estimate* of funds expected to be received during the budget period. This is important because the Texas Constitution prohibits the legislature from appropriating an amount greater than estimated revenue collections.

The two houses of the legislature take turns acting as the originating chamber for the general appropriations bill and chairing the conference committee that works out differences between the bills ultimately passed by each house.

The House bill goes through the House Appropriations Committee; the Senate bill goes through the Senate Finance Committee. The general appropriations bill has the following articles: general government, health and human services, education, judiciary, public safety and criminal justice, natural resources, business and economic development, regulatory, general provisions, legislature, savings clause, and emergency clause.

After approval of the appropriations bill, the comptroller must certify that the state will have sufficient revenue to cover the money approved. In case of an "emergency and imperative public necessity" (Article 3, section 49a of the state's constitution), appropriations may exceed revenue on approval of four-fifths of the membership of each house. Normally, the comptroller can certify; appropriations bills are not passed if they violate the revenue provision. If the comptroller does not certify the bill, it returns to the house of origin.

The governor has the power to veto specific items in the appropriations bill. Some agencies have received "lump sum" appropriations, in which case the governor can only veto the entire agency appropriation, not individual components of the agency's appropriation.

Supplemental appropriations are possible when agencies are in danger of running out of funds before the end of a budget period. The legislature may also reduce appropriations during the budget period.

The growth of spending is constitutionally forbidden (Article 8, section 22) to exceed the LBB's official estimate of growth of the state economy. However, spending from dedicated tax revenue is outside the limit. The state constitution also prohibits deficit spending (Article 3, section 49a) and requires that any unanticipated deficit at the end of a biennium be eliminated in the subsequent budget.

Execution

Execution is by state agencies within the biennium that begins on September 1 of odd-numbered years, subject to monitoring by the LBB and the State Auditor's Office (SAO). The SAO operates under the direction of the Legislative Audit Committee, which consists of the lieutenant governor, the speaker of the House, the chairs of the Senate Finance Committee and the House Appropriations and Ways and Means Committees, and a member of the Senate appointed by the lieutenant governor. The LBB is heavily concerned with agency performance objectives.

The governor and the LBB have joint authority to transfer funds within or between agencies.

Audit

The SAO, a legislative agency, is the external auditor of state agencies. It conducts financial, compliance, and performance audits of agencies and reports its findings to the legislature.

CHAPTER 6

Budget System Reforms: Trying to Make Better Choices

Chapter Contents

The budget process discussion in previous chapters has focused primarily on fiscal discipline and control, important concerns if government operations are to be fiscally sustainable. Making sure that government resources are not stolen and that governments do not spend more money than they have are important roles for the budget process, but we ought to expect more than that from government. Surely we can consider how government spending and the resulting services provided might be useful, not just how spending can be controlled. We now move to considering how the budget process can serve in facilitating choices among government programs and in inducing efficient use of resources within programs, the other two roles expected from a budget process.

Governments may provide many different valuable services, but they cannot do everything. At some point, they have to make choices among good ideas, not just sort out the bad ideas (although killing off bad ideas is a good start). To make those choices, government decision makers need good financial information and effective systems to help assist those choices. This chapter and Chapter 7 deal with structures and processes that can inform those choices, sometimes through entire systems for budget development and sometimes through smaller changes in what sort of information is provided and how it is organized.

Budget processes can help governments allocate public resources, control agency operations, manage service delivery, and communicate intentions and accomplishments to the public. Budgets can be clear statements of plans, priorities, performance, and costs, as well as the basic template for administrative control. Unfortunately, prevailing practices often impede the full use of budgeting for planning and analysis to guide public choices. Too often our systems and decision processes cause budget participants to bounce between Oscar Wilde's cynics and sentimentalists, as defined in the exchange between Cecil Graham and Lord Darlington in *Lady Windermere's Fan*:

Cecil Graham: What is a cynic?

Lord Darlington: A man who knows the price of everything and the value of nothing.

Cecil Graham: And a sentimentalist, my dear Darlington, is a man who sees an absurd value in everything, and doesn't know the market price of any single thing.[1]

The fiscal process must avoid the seductions of both cynic and sentimentalist to understand that reasonable choice entails both value and what must be paid, and although good ideas are limitless, to recognize that resources to finance those good ideas are not. Choices cannot be made solely on either cost or solely on value but should be made on the basis of comparing cost and value.

The budget process isn't helped by the fact that it often does not even give information on what the cost of a program is, let alone provide a usable assessment of what the value is. Knowing neither the value of a service nor its cost of provision leaves the decision maker rather uncertain about making a decision. However, some budget structure reforms, as we shall see, at least help with providing a better idea of actual costs of services and of better organizing choices.

The basic concern of a budget process is to create an executable annual budget using economic (line-item) classification, with effective controls on budget execution, reliable financial reporting, and control over payments from a treasury. The first concern is spending control, not resource allocation. In the United States, this emphasis was critical because public budgeting processes emerged in the first decades of the twentieth century when theft of public resources was rampant, especially at the municipal level, and budget procedures sought to put a stop to this. Hence, early budgets focused on control of resources (or inputs) and little else. Modern governments have moved beyond that stage, but too much of budgeting retains that old preoccupation (although these first principles remain relevant because of their absence in developing and transition countries around the world).[2]

Governments provide valued services, so budget processes must serve as more than devices for restraining thieves, for stopping spending, and for limiting the extent to which political hacks provide employment for inept friends and relatives. Narrow controls designed almost exclusively to provide fiscal constraint thwart innovation,

---

[1]Oscar Wilde, *Lady Windermere's Fan* (London: Methuen, 1908), 134.
[2]It should be noted that public corruption survives even today and appears to influence how governments spend public money in U.S. states: John L. Mikesell and Cheol Liu, "The Impact of Public Officials' Corruption on the Size and Allocation of State Spending," *Public Administration Review* 74 (May/June 2014): 346–58.

constrain capacity to respond to citizen clients, and increase the unit cost of services. Decision makers must control waste and make allocation choices among the government services desired by the public; budget structures need to facilitate this work, not just tie the hands of managers.

Logically, budget allocation is simple: allocate funds among government programs until an additional dollar moved to any program yields an additional return to society equal to the return lost from the program from which that dollar was taken.[3] That is the public sector equivalent of the familiar resource allocation rule for profitability in business operations. But the private decision maker maximizes a clear and measurable objective—profit—and measuring profitable return from several lines of operation is feasible because the standard is clearly calibrated, uniform, and measured with a common denominator (profit). Public sector operations usually (1) have multiple objectives (e.g., subsidized school lunches both feed children and support the income of farmers), (2) have conflicting objectives (e.g., the reservoir needs to be nearly empty to provide flood control and to be nearly full to allow water skiing), and (3) have no standard measure or common yardstick to compare the return from various programs (e.g., the gains from cleaner rivers are not measured in the same units as are reduced traffic fatalities). Furthermore, the beneficiaries of the various programs often are not the same people, so choices among programs cause there to be distributional winners and losers, in violation of the Pareto criterion. In addition, taxpayers paying for the programs may well not be the people benefiting from the public services being provided, complicating the decision process even more, as does the fact that program beneficiaries are not evenly distributed among the electoral districts of the lawmakers deciding what programs will receive appropriations. Hence, the simple public program allocation rule, so easy to define, may only be a glimmer in the foggy politics of budget decisions. Lawmakers working in the public interest face tough choices, well beyond the complexities a business executive will confront.

The budget process is where choices are made among program alternatives. It will be far from perfect, but some budget classifications and structures may make the allocation choices more likely to improve conditions of society, and some processes do a better job of opening decisions to the public view than do others. Certainly more transparency and more open government will not hurt the democratic process. Thinking about format is important because, as Fenno says, "the form of the budget determines what the conversation will be about."[4] A line-item format invites discussion about what the government is purchasing, whereas a format organized to

---

[3]This rule also applies for a perfectly altruistic nonprofit organization. However, most nonprofit organizations are narrow interest groups, aiming to protect the environment, to ease the plight of the homeless, to care for the indigent sick, and so on. Hence, the budgetary allocation rule for a nonprofit organization is more related to that of a private, proprietary business than to that of a general-purpose government—allocations among its operations should work toward the particular purpose of the organization, just as the business aims for the highest profit, not the multiple competing objectives of society that governments have to balance. Otherwise, all tools of public budgeting—budget development, review, adoption, execution, audit, and so on—apply to these entities just as they apply to governments.

[4]Richard F. Fenno, "The Impact of PPBS on the Congressional Appropriation Process," in *Information Support, Program Budgeting, and the Congress,* ed. Richard L. Charhand, Kenneth Janda, and Michael Hugo (New York: Spartan, 1968), 183.

highlight services provided will invite discussions about services. It would be good if the conversation focused on decisions to improve the public interest rather than choices designed primarily to line the pockets of major campaign contributors.

Considering the Flow of Provision of Government Services: The Logic of the Service System and Budget Classifications

Government agencies may be thought of as operating entities that buy resources, use those resources in the performance of certain tasks, and, as a result of performing those tasks, achieve certain results that are valued by society. Total government expenditure equals the sum paid by agencies for purchases of inputs; for contractual services to be delivered by others; for transfer payments made to individuals, businesses, or other governments; for interest paid on debt outstanding; for post-employment benefits paid to retirees; and so on, but budget classification schemes may organize and control that spending in a variety of ways. Figure 6–1 provides a simple outline of service provision. The following explains the terms in that outline:

1. **Inputs.** Inputs are the resources an agency purchases to use in its service-delivery operations. A city's street department buys resources (asphalt,

Figure 6–1
The Flow of Public Service Provision

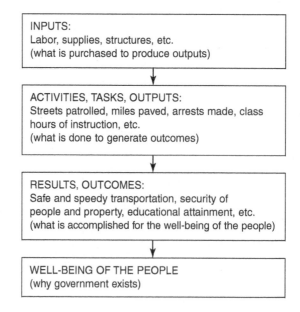

crushed stone, fuel to operate its equipment, the services of its employees, etc.). The funds in the budget are not inputs; the funds are what the agency uses to purchase the inputs. The inputs are the items on the shopping list of the government (i.e., the line items).

2. **Outputs.** Outputs are direct products or services produced by the agency. With the resources it has purchased, the department undertakes certain tasks or activities (fills potholes, resurfaces roadways, teaches students, audits taxpayers, rescues stray animals, etc.). However, these are the steps taken toward the end objective, not the end itself. Outputs are important for measuring internal operations of the agency (i.e., for telling us what the agency is doing), but they do not indicate the extent to which the agency's purpose is being achieved. For example, if dangerous childhood diseases could be prevented without giving children vaccinations, the world could be a better place: we want an absence of sick children, not lots of children vaccinated.

3. **Results or Outcomes.** Because of the activities undertaken, desirable outcomes result (e.g., people and property can move through the city more quickly and safely, with less damage done to vehicles, or fewer children suffer from whooping cough, measles, etc.). The measured result or outcome indicates progress by the agency toward achievement of its purposes of improving the economic or social condition of the citizenry. The measures can reflect successful events, occurrences, or conditions and may also indicate the quality of the service being rendered. Citizen satisfaction surveys may play a role in the measurement of outcome performance, particularly with regard to service quality, and they may be the basis for evaluating public goods that cannot be sold and are equally available to all.[5] The practice of budgeting regularly confuses outputs and outcomes. Here is a guideline for determining whether a particular measure is outcome or output: we would be happy to reduce an output if doing so would not reduce the outcome; we are not happy about reducing the outcome.

4. **Consequences for Society (Well-Being).** The outcome improves the standard of life for the public. This is why the agency exists—to improve life for the citizenry. Something about why the agency matters to the standard of living should appear in the agency's mission statement, and that should be helpful in specifying the results produced by the agency and the outputs that help in accomplishing those results.[6]

---

[5]Uwe Deichmann and Somik V. Lall, "Are You Satisfied? Citizen Feedback and Delivery of Urban Services," World Bank Policy Research Working Paper 3070 (Washington, D.C., June 2003), reviews the return from citizen feedback surveys.

[6]Sometimes events will permit evidence of impacts. For instance, a mass layoff of Oregon State Police in 2003 (a 35 percent reduction in highway troopers) dramatically reduced traffic citations. As a natural experiment, DeAngelo and Hansen were able to combine these data with other sources to estimate that a highway fatality can be prevented with $309,000 of state police expenditures. (Gregory DeAngelo and Benjamin Hansen, "Life and Death in the Fast Lane: Police Enforcement and Traffic Fatalities," *American Economic Journal: Economic Policy* 6 (No. 2, 2014): 231–57).

The budget may include performance measures to assist in reporting accomplishments and intentions. As discussed later in this chapter, those measures may be either outputs, outcomes, or some combination of the two.

Budget classifications follow the flow of public service provision previously outlined. Classifications found in public budgets include the following:

1. **Line item or object of expenditure.** This is the grocery list classification discussed in Chapter 2. The focus is on what the government buys, either directly from its suppliers or indirectly through transfer, subsidy, and loan programs. The input format is basic and traditional and has been around as long as governments have been constructing budgets. It is the building block for budget cost estimates and provides the focus for the control structures of government operation. The spending on inputs is categorized according to the administrative unit (the department or agency) responsible for use and control over the items that are purchased. This classification is critical for assigning organizational *responsibility* for delivery of services and *accountability* for public resources.

2. **Activities or tasks (outputs).** This format classifies according to the intermediate product, the activities the government engages in, or the tasks it performs. The classification emphasizes measurable tasks: lane miles paved, pupil class hours taught, prisoners incarcerated, arrests made, tons of solid waste managed, number of border inspections, and so on.

3. **Function, purpose, or program.** This format classifies expenditure according to broad public purpose. The orientation is toward the final customer, the people served by the government. Classification focuses on the reasons that the government exists: for example, protecting people and property or maintaining a healthy citizenry.[7]

Budgets for governments and public organizations mix these classifications in several ways as they attempt to provide information useful for planning the utilization of resources, for devising efficient operations of agencies, and for controlling use of resources. Most actual budgets now are hybrids, but Table 6–1 provides information on some fundamental features of traditional budgets, traditional performance budgets, program budgets, and new performance budgets. The elements in the table will become clearer in the discussion that follows.

Budget presentations increasingly provide performance measures for each agency, and increasingly these measures attempt to gauge outcomes or results of agency operations, not just the activities that the agency is engaged in. Simply

---

[7]Budget systems do not use a consistent language in distinguishing between concepts of performance (activity or task) and program (function or purpose). In some budgets, "program" means a service area (such as street maintenance), for which a cost center is established; in other budgets, "program" means an outcome group (such as safe and speedy transport of people and property), which can be balanced against other purposes of government. In the discussion here, "what governments do" means task, activity, direct output, or intermediate product, and "why governments exist" means achievement, consumer output, final product, or outcome. "Program" refers to the latter. The distinction is particularly important in examination of municipal budget processes. The two uses of "program" might be considered "service area programs" and "outcome programs."

Table 6–1
Features of Alternative Budget Formats

Format	Characteristics	Primary Organization Feature	Budgetary Focus
Traditional	Economic or object of expenditure classification to administrative units	Inputs purchased	Fiscal responsibility and control
Traditional Performance	Spending by unit of workload	Tasks/activities/ outputs	Managerial control and technical efficiency
Program or Functional	Spending according to common public goals or purposes	Outcomes, final products, results	Resource allocation
New Performance or Results-Oriented	Performance measures by administrative unit	Outcomes (outputs)	Resource allocation

spending appropriations without stealing too much is no longer an acceptable indicator of accomplishment. Agencies are expected to provide services for the common good and are held accountable for serving the public.

Budget classifications focus on different stages of the expenditure-delivery system, from resources purchased (*line item*) through activities performed (*traditional performance*) to services delivered (*program*). Line-item and performance systems maintain traditional departmental structures in the organization of expenditure plans; program budgets classify government outputs (or services provided) without regard for the administrative unit charged with service provision. All seek to improve the job done by the government and to keep government operations consistent with the wishes of the citizenry, but their fundamental concerns differ. Line-item budgets have as their foremost concern expenditure control and accountability. Performance budgets seek to improve internal management and cost of services provided. Program budgets emphasize arranging details in a manner to improve decision capacity for rational choice. (See the budget illustration in Chapter 2 for a reminder of how the line-item format looks.)

This chapter examines several alternative budget formats and budget systems, including traditional budgets, traditional performance budgets, program budgets, zero-based budgets, new performance budgets, and participatory budget systems. It also examines the idea of evidence-based budget decision making, a concept with growing popularity. Each effort has reform of particular parts of the public-expenditure/ service-delivery process as its primary focus, and each has weaknesses in application. A review of each provides good insights into the practice of government finance in many different environments. But the place to start is with the most frequently utilized structure, the budget organized by administrative departments and purchases intended to be made by those departments.

Traditional Budgets: A Flawed Tool for Decision Making (but Pretty Good for Control and Accountability)

Traditional budgets, line-item purchases organized by administrative department, devote a lot of energy to figuring out what to buy and not enough energy on what results to achieve. Traditional budget procedures embody several impediments to efficient and effective public management and planning. These include (1) the administrative department basis for budget requests and appropriation; (2) the short-period concept for costs in budget considerations; (3) the focus on agency inputs rather than services provided, outputs, or outcomes; and (4) weak tools for comparing program costs with the value of the program. Budget details often take on such bulk that they intimidate inexperienced users and discourage those with limited time from extracting the budget's policy plans. Unfortunately, legislators—the people who are supposed to review and approve the plans inherent in the budget document—may be just as inexperienced and short of time as the general public. Traditional budgets do not present information in a way that is well organized for making decisions.

ADMINISTRATIVE DEPARTMENT BASIS

Traditional budget processes are driven by cost estimates but may not provide cost information in a way that is helpful to program decisions. Budgets are proposed and appropriations are made on an administrative department basis, not on the basis of what departments intend to achieve.

Such categorizations blur the allocation process and impede consideration of alternatives, the essence of resource allocation. Categories of administration—departments of defense, transportation, or justice at the federal level; departments of public works, economic development, public safety, or social services at the state-local levels—are too broad for judgments about the appropriate amounts of resources to be allocated to each. Some activities of a particular department may be of extreme importance for social goals, whereas others could be of considerably lower consequence and less significant than activities proposed by other departments. But the traditional budget approach tends to focus on departments, treating all work within them as being of equal contribution to public well-being. An important consequence of traditional budgets is that *where you are establishes what you get*. Departments and even agencies within them include activity conglomerations; some of those activities are related more to the work of other agencies than to that of the rest of their own agency. The Army Corps of Engineers' work in U.S. rivers and the services of security officers in city park departments offer two examples of work not matching larger titles or primary operations of the larger department. Budgets and appropriations that go through organizational charts complicate identification of the cost of achieving a particular objective because most agencies have multiple outputs. Edmond Weiss notes the "fallacy of appellation . . . the rhetorical act of obscuring the distinction between the name of a budget category and the actual phenomenon generally associated with that name."[8] In short, intelligent resource allocation decisions are unlikely to emerge from budget considerations based on administrative departments. Activities rise and fall, based on their departmental location, not always because of what the activity does. For instance, military bands are in the Department of Defense budget and, as defense spending moves, so does support for the bands—significantly increasing during the Reagan administration military buildup and diminishing in the more recent era of outlay caps and concern with defense sequestration. No success or failure or change of mission had anything to do with the budgetary changes.[9]

Administrative Conventions

Budgets and appropriations to administrative units can conceal the full cost of delivery of government services. For example, cities frequently have departments of public works that are responsible for maintenance of all infrastructure and even for some new construction and departments of human resources that provide employee fringe benefits (pensions, vacation pay, etc.) for all employees of the government through its budget. That makes management of related activities easier and allows for specialization in performing and supervising tasks, but it doesn't help with fiscal decision making. In this circumstance, identifying the amount the city spends for provision of a city service—such as parks and recreation or police protection—would require analysis of the operations of the primary department, but also analysis of some spending of these other departments that have no immediately visible link to that agency's role. This violates the transparency standard for government operations and lessens the utility of the budget document in making public choices.

Single-Year Basis

Traditional budgets are developed and considered on a single-year basis without developing cost profiles over time. If they do extend to the out-years (the years beyond the budget year), the numbers are frequently simple extrapolations of recent expenditures rather than reflecting careful thought about future policy intentions. Appropriation decisions usually cover a single year of agency operation[10]—an appropriate period for fiscal control—even though many activities proposed by an agency have significant future cost implications. The single-year cost may be little more

---

[8]Edmond H. Weiss, "The Fallacy of Appellation in Government Budgeting," *Public Administration Review* 34 (July/August 1974): 377.
[9]Richard L. Hudson, "Spending for B1s and MXs Is Rising, So the Tubas Got an Increase, Too," *Wall Street Journal*, 1981; and Carol Ann Alaimo, "Facing Cuts, Military Bands Face Budget Blues," *Army Times*, August 24, 2011. The Department of Defense spent over $400 million on its 130 military bands in 2015, even as defense advocates complained about inadequate resources to protect the nation.
[10]Some governments have biennial budgets, but these are essentially single-year budgets times two. Only by accident will the complete cost of a project be captured in a biennial budget.

than a program down payment with many installments ahead. Reasonable decision making requires that the total cost of a project be examined, not just the single-year cost. Because full project cost data are seldom a part of the annual budget process, budget choices must be made without appropriate information.

The federal budget process now produces the budget year plus nine out-years (four out-years in many displays). Few appropriation decisions are locked in choices for full program life, so the impact on decision processes is not clear, but those numbers can give an early warning of unsustainable fiscal conditions for the future. (The detailed department-by-department presentations from which the appropriation committees work include only the single budget year.) The out-years can contain much mischief when governments try to prove their fiscal conservatism by showing how they will control deficits—in the future. Nevertheless, good-faith attempts to identify future (out-year) cost implications of current choices are necessary for reasonable budgetary deliberations.[11]

Input Orientation

Reasoned choice requires a comparison among alternative methods of reaching a desired objective. The input orientation of traditional line-item budgets blocks operational vision and traps agencies into conventional operations.[12] Agencies traditionally build budgets from existing input combinations. The agencies lock themselves into "normal" operating techniques and overlook alternative methods, and legislatures appropriate into definite line items. Public agencies and legislatures focus on what they buy (inputs) to the near exclusion of what they provide (services or outputs): a budget presentation of line items invites attention to purchases. Ordinary reviews emphasize changes in the objects of expenditure—that is, the personnel to be hired (or fired) and their pay grades, changes in the pay of current staff, and the supplies and equipment to be purchased. An input orientation produces the following logic: If the price of gasoline increases by 25 percent, agency operation requires a 25 percent increase in the appropriation for those purchases. Otherwise, the agency must cut back its services.

This logic implies that the objective of the agency is the purchase of given amounts of specific inputs. A budget process should induce consideration of alternative production strategies to economize on the use of resources that have become more expensive; are there ways of accomplishing the agency mission that do not use as much gasoline? Seldom is there but a single way to provide a service, and budget processes need to consider alternatives, especially when the price of some inputs has increased dramatically. A simple analog to traditional budgeting would be a baker who purchases flour, milk, and sugar without considering either the number of cakes, cookies, breads, and so on to be sold or alternative recipes for their production. That would be a silly way to run a business, and it is a silly way to run a government. How is it possible to make reasonable choices between programs that offer different services to the population

---

[11]A medium-term fiscal framework is an expected feature of good fiscal governance in international assistance programs.
[12]David Osborne, "Escaping from the Line-Item Trap," *Governing* 5 (September 1992): 69.

when the budget presentations focus on what the government agencies will be buying? It isn't a responsible way to make decisions across government agencies, and it isn't a responsible way for agencies to make decisions about their internal operations. Unfortunately, that is the emphasis of traditional budget classification systems, and change from that emphasis has been agonizingly slow.

These physical input requirements are selected before any cost estimation and without reference either to alternative production methods or to the programs sacrificed if a particular choice is made.[13] Indeed, some governments treat final appropriations to input class so rigidly that agencies, faced with a burdensome series of approvals should they adjust to changed operating conditions during the budget year, choose to do nothing. The language of the appropriation law defends them against the need to respond to the legitimate service demands of the public.[14]

The Question of Value

The toughest, but most fundamental problem of all is that public decisions must weigh the cost of public programs against their worth to society. The line-item costs in traditional budgets are financial, out-of-pocket costs. They exclude social costs not directly paid; they reflect financial transactions, not the value of opportunities not chosen; and they do not distinguish between sunk and incremental costs of actions. Thus, the cost data presented may not be quite right for making decisions. Yet budget costs are often all decision makers consider. The needed comparison between cost and program value, vital to intelligent resource allocation, is not a regular component of budget processes because the value of programs delivered is seldom reported or formally considered. For public goods, value is just plain hard to measure. Without such regular comparison, poor public decisions are likely, and they certainly are not going to be driven by precise value information. Public decisions based only on program cost—because costs are either remarkably high or affordably low—will not consistently lead to a wise use of scarce resources; neither will consideration based solely on project worth to the exclusion of cost. A society with scarcity must require consideration of worth against cost, if only in the sense of considering how society would be poorer in the absence of the service. Regardless of whether worth is easily measurable, no choices are possible solely on a cost basis, and decisions should not focus on the inputs being purchased.

---

[13]William Niskanen, Gordon Tullock, and others point out that agency administrators have individual incentives to spend as much as possible (conduct any project at the highest feasible cost). See Gordon Tullock, *The Politics of Bureaucracy* (Washington, D.C.: Public Affairs Press, 1965); and William A. Niskanen Jr., *Bureaucracy and Representative Government* (Chicago: Aldine, 1971). Whether the budget-maximizing bureaucrat is an accurate reflection of reality has been empirically argued many times over the years. One recent answer ("no") appears in Julie Dolan, "The Budget-Minimizing Bureaucrat? Empirical Evidence from the Senior Executive Service," *Public Administration Review* 62 (January/February 2002): 42–50.

[14]In the old Soviet Union, budgets were constructed on the basis of national "norms": the planners would decide where a facility (factory, school, hospital, etc.) would be located, and the norms would dictate what resources (staff, supplies, etc.) would be dedicated to that facility. Those resource requirements defined the budget. The system didn't pay attention to citizen demand for services (who cares what the people want, after all?), differences in prices of resources, new technological options, and so on. Unfortunately, traditional budget construction contains too much of this "norm" logic.

Traditional Performance Budgets

One of the oldest budget reform inclinations is to put agency performance information together with agency spending. The principal idea behind performance budgets, both the traditional format discussed here and a newer format discussed later in the chapter, is that putting performance information alongside budget numbers will improve public decisions and will keep agencies focused on productive use of funds. Traditional performance budgets emphasize agency activity performance objectives and accomplishments, not the purchase of resources. The traditional performance budget presents the cost of performing measurable accomplishment units during the budget year, so the budget process has the dual role of providing funds and establishing performance objectives.

The idea of performance budgets is not new. Performance budgeting dates to the mid-1910s in New York City, and offspring of that attempt survive in present-day state and local governments.[15] The primary impact of performance budgeting on the service-delivery process, however, dates from the first Hoover Commission (Commission on Organization of the Executive Branch of the Government) report of 1949.[16]

The performance budget concept entails certain shifts in thinking from that of the traditional line-item budget.

1. Budget information should be organized in terms of activities (repairing roads, planting trees, treating patients, teaching students, making arrests, etc.) rather than in terms of individual line-item spending only.
2. Activities should be measured, costs should be identified for these activities, and efficiency in performance (unit costing) should be evaluated.
3. Performance should be monitored by comparing actual cost and accomplishment against the planned levels.
4. Although the performance measures would ordinarily not be "end products" of government, the activities ideally should be associated with these beneficial results or outcomes. In modern terminology, these performance measures are on the order of "means to an end" rather than being the end themselves.

The performance classification promises better services at lower cost from more accountable officials; improved legislative review as attention and debate shift away from issues of personnel, salaries, supplier contracts, and the like toward activity issues more related to how resources are used; and decentralized decision making, allowing top management to concentrate its attention on policy matters. Classification of requests follows the activities of the agency, not the inputs it purchases. Performance budgets link costs with activities. This linkage permits unit-cost comparisons across agencies and over time within agencies to emphasize improvements in operating efficiency.

---

[15]General Accounting Office, *Performance Budgeting: State Experiences and Implications for the Federal Government,* GAO/AFMD-93-41 (Washington, D.C.: General Accounting Office, 1993), surveys these experiences.

[16]Commission on Organization of the Executive Branch of the Government, *Budgeting and Accounting* (Washington, D.C.: U.S. Government Printing Office, 1949).

Figure 6–2 further illustrates the performance classification. It includes performance budget material for snow removal from the 1981-1982 Salt Lake City budget, a historical document noted for its faithfulness to the performance concept. Note the following elements:

1. **The demand section** defines the expected operating environment for the budget year, with prior- and current-year levels for comparison.
2. **The workload section** establishes how the operating unit intends to respond to expected demand by allocation of staff time.
3. **The productivity section** presents the cost per activity unit that emerges from the budgeted costs. This is the special identifying feature of full performance budgets. Most budget documents will not, for instance, allow easy identification of either historical or proposed costs of dealing with snow removal after a snowstorm; the performance classification does because it links costs to measured units of activities. Even budgets with cost centers identified within departments will not provide answers to those sorts of questions.
4. **The effectiveness section** shows the unit's performance against criteria that indicate whether the unit is accomplishing its intended objectives. This is important because one avenue to lower cost is lower quality of service— one pickle slice fewer per hamburger will reduce the cost of producing hamburgers by millions of dollars in a national restaurant chain, and the same goes for government services.

The performance structure has some special implications. First, the budget should become a powerful tool for management responsibility and accountability. In that structure, budgeting must be a central management responsibility because activity levels and their costs are specifically presented in a document that guides agency operation. Operating supervisors can no longer permit separate budget personnel to prepare budget requests (it is bad practice to do this, in any case, of course) because they become detailed operating plans for the budget year.[17] Many agency managers do not like the performance budgeting concept because it exposes the agency's operating details (demand estimates, workload trend, etc.) to outsiders— such as taxpayers and legislators. Second, legislatures must change their review and appropriations procedures from traditional line-item reviews to agency activity reviews. The legislature may feel uncomfortable considering something other than objects of expenditures, particularly where there is no apparent linkage to revenue and budget balancing and when the activities may be difficult to measure or relate to what the citizenry really wants. Third, a performance budget can make a management-by-objectives program easier to operate. The objectives would be the performance measures (activities) appearing in the budget. Performance and budget attainment can thus be monitored throughout the fiscal year.

The performance budget hinges on the quality of its performance measures and a legislative-executive consensus that those measures are the proper ones for agency attention. Some performance measures may be misleading or irrelevant, despite the

---

[17]Traditional budgets are operating plans as well, except they do not contain identifiable operating objectives. That addition provides the new constraint on the agency.

Figure 6–2
The Salt Lake City Performance Budget

Program: Snow Removal   Department: Public Works
Program Description: To remove snow and ice from city streets for safe travel during inclement weather conditions.

| | Program Operating Expense | | | |
Resource Requirements	1979-1980 Actual	1980-1981 Budget	1980-1981 Estimated	1981-1982 Recommended
Personnel/personal services	19.5/$279,318	16.9/$325,358	11.25/$190,618	4.7/$111,975
Operating and maintenance supplies	39,081	48,300	29,763	47,720
Charges and services	61,774	193,169	111,864	199,379
Capital outlay	0	17,596	12,570	0
Work order credits	(212)	0	0	0
Total	$379,961	$584,423	$344,815	$359,074
Program Resources				
General fund	$379,961	$584,423	$344,815	$359,074
Total	$379,961	$584,423	$344,815	$359,074

Program Budget Highlights
The 1980-1981 budget indicators had an overallocation of man hours in the snow and ice program which has been rectified by midyear adjustments and is now correctly reflected in the 1980-1982 request. During 1980-1981, a study was conducted analyzing the past five winters. It was obvious as a result of this study that our projections for the 1980–1981 budget year were unrealistic, so we reassigned employees' time to other programs causing other program expenditure levels and personnel allocations to rise.

Performance Objectives
1. To review "scale" of snow fighter program.
2. To develop an expanded U.D.O.T. and S.L.C. responsibilities exchange where practical.
3. To evaluate an "exceptional storm" emergency backup system.

Performance Review	1979-1980 Actual	1980-1981 Budget	1980-1981 Estimated	1981-1982 Recommended
Demand				
1. Lane miles of priority snow routes	400	400	460	460
2. Inches of snowfall	63	68	45	68
3. Storms requiring crew mobilization	15	19	16	19
4. Storms requiring salt only	7	10	10	10
5. Storms requiring snow plowing	8	9	6	9
Workload				
1. Man hours salting streets	n.a.*	12,640	1,000	2,060
2. Man hours plowing streets	n.a.	18,960	1,400	3,090
3. Tons of salt applied	7,410	8,000	4,900	8,000

(continues)

**Figure 6–2
(continued)**

Performance Review	1979-1980 Actual	1980-1981 Budget	1980-1981 Estimated	1981-1982 Recommended
Productivity				
1. Cost/priority lane mile	962	1,418	874	765
2. Average cost/storm	25,663	29,864	25,138	18,513
Effectiveness				
1. Vehicle accidents in which snow and ice are a contributing factor	253	250	135	250
2. Complaints received	49	50	35	50

*n.a. = Not available.

fact that they can be measured and reported. Audit quality, for instance, may be more important than simply the number of audits conducted. The number of audits could well be the performance measure however, simply because it is more easily quantified. If the Department of Parks and Recreation is going to be responsible for maintaining flower beds, then it will need to define a standard flower bed to calculate unit costs. Furthermore, the performance budget does not ask whether the performance being measured is the service the public actually wants. Of course, there is no necessary consideration of alternate ways to do a particular task. The drive to lower a government's unit cost of performance should induce development of improved methods, not sacrifice the unit's quality—but the technique is not geared to handle that problem.

The performance budget structure does not question whether objectives are appropriate or a service is worth its cost of production. They only consider whether the activity is being done at low cost. And that brings up the Achilles heel of performance budgets: they are extremely expensive to develop. Unless the government really will use them as an integral part of public management and decision making, they are not likely to be a worthy use of government resources. Because of these limitations, such budgets have been extremely rare.

Program Budgets

The program budget format organizes proposed expenditure according to output/outcome or contribution to public objectives.[18] Program budgets focus on the critical question for public choices: what are agencies doing that is valued by the public? They don't focus on what governments buy or the tasks that agencies perform. They get

---

[18]These programs are linked to fundamental missions. In recent years, some jurisdictions have started to identify service areas (such as street cleaning) of government agencies as programs. That obviously creates some confusion in discussion of budget structures.

to the heart of the matter: what of value are you doing? Programs are constructed on the basis of their contributions to those objectives without regard to administrative organizations responsible for delivery of the particular service. In essence, the program format requires the government—and agencies in the government—to identify what products or services it provides and then to organize its budget requests and budget execution along those product or service lines. The format redirects focus from the expenditure objects or economic classifications (the things that the government purchases) or from those doing the spending (the administrative departments) to the subjects of that expenditure (the services to society that the government provides), and it breaks down the administrative boundaries between government agencies. A complete program budget combines services that contribute to a similar objective so that competition for funds occurs among real alternatives, contrary to the style of an ordinary budget, in which agencies or departments compete for funds, as do service units within agencies or departments. In a program budget, similar service options compete with each other, not with dissimilar programs housed in an administrative agency, and budget decision makers can see proposed spending organized according to services to be provided, in addition to what agencies might be doing the spending.[19]

Program budgeting defines the goals of the government and classifies organizational expenditure contributing to achievement of each goal. To focus competition for resources on objectives and alternative programs for achieving objectives, items are grouped by end product. The program structure identifies agency products; it does not focus on the inputs used by the agency or on the agencies. Table 6–2 illustrates the program budget classifications used by the Commonwealth of Pennsylvania. The format classifies by service provided to the public rather than by individual department (several services would in fact be provided by more than one department), input purchased, or department activity. The structure seeks a final product orientation. For example, you will see that several agencies are providing services in the Protection of Persons and Property program. To look at only one of these—the State Police, for instance—would provide a misleading view of the significance of the program in the budget. The Direction and Supportive Services classification is normal in program budgets; those functions provide inputs unallocable to the provision of the other services. The Pennsylvania display shows that many agencies contribute to several programs and that most programs include operations of more than one agency (Transportation is the exception in the Pennsylvania structure).

Program budgeting requires careful definition of programs, an exercise in taxonomy that is the essence of such budgets. The logical criteria for program design provided by Arthur Smithies are generally helpful:

1. **Facilitate comparisons.** Design programs so they "permit comparison of alternative methods of pursuing an imperfectly defined policy objective."[20]

[19]Conversion from line item to program budget formats is not solely an American experiment: for instance, see John M. Kim, ed., *From Line-item to Program Budgeting, Global Lessons and the Korean Case.* Seoul: Korea Institute of Public Finance and World Bank, 2007. The concept is applicable to operations of any government.

[20]Arthur Smithies, "Conceptual Framework for the Program Budget," in *Program Budgeting,* 2nd ed., ed. David Novick (New York: Holt, Rinehart & Winston, 1969), 42.

Table 6–2

Program Budget Structure Illustration: Commonwealth of Pennsylvania, 2013-2014 to 2019-2020

Direction and Supportive Services. The goal of this commonwealth program is to provide an efficient and effective administrative support system through which the goals and directives of commonwealth programs can be attained. This commonwealth program supports the administration's goals to streamline state government and achieve efficiencies. (2.7 percent of actual expenditures, 2013-2014)

Agencies include the Governor's Office, Executive Offices, Lieutenant Governor, Auditor General, Treasury, Civil Service Commission, departments of General Services and Revenue, Ethics Commission, Health Care Cost Containment Council, eHealth Partnership Authority, the State Employees' Retirement System, Government Support Agencies, and the Legislature.

Protection of Persons and Property. The goal of this commonwealth program is to provide an environment and a social system in which the lives and property of individuals and organizations are protected from natural and man-made disasters and from illegal and unfair actions. This commonwealth program supports the administration's goal to protect the public health and safety of Pennsylvania's citizens. The program addresses consumer and environmental protection, certain regulatory activities, the criminal justice system, and mitigation of effects of disasters. (13.3 percent of actual expenditures, 2013-2014)

Agencies include State Police, Department of Banking and Securities, Attorney General, Department of Corrections, Public Utility Commission, Liquor Control Board, Pennsylvania Emergency Management Agency, Board of Probation and Parole, the Judiciary, Milk Marketing Board, Department of State, and Insurance Department. Some activities of Executive Offices, Department of Environmental Protection, Agriculture, Labor and Industry, Military and Veterans Affairs, and Transportation.

Education. The goal of this commonwealth program is to provide a system of learning experiences and opportunities that will permit each individual to achieve his or her full potential intellectual development through high-quality basic education and special education programs and through high-quality career and technical education and higher education. This commonwealth program supports the administration's goals to support an agenda for excellence, a world-class education that enables all Pennsylvania children to achieve their full potential and to expand educational opportunities and alternative pathways to teaching and leadership. (21.9 percent of actual expenditures, 2013-2014)

Agencies include Department of Education, Department of Human Services, Department of Revenue, Department of Labor and Industry, Higher Education Assistance Agency, and Tax Equalization Board.

Health and Human Services. The goals of this commonwealth program are to ensure access to quality medical care for all citizens, support people seeking self-sufficiency, provide military readiness and assistance to veterans and maximize opportunities for individuals and families to participate in society. The program addresses the following substantive areas: research; prevention and treatment of physical, mental health, and intellectual disabilities; maternal and child health care; financial assistance for older Pennsylvanians, medically needy individuals and families in transition; and other programs to address the various issues individuals encounter in a complex society. (47.0 percent of actual expenditures, 2013-2014)

Agencies include Departments of Aging, Health, Human Services, and Drug and Alcohol Programs. Contributions from Departments of Agriculture, Labor and Industry, Military and Veterans Affairs, and Revenue.

Economic Development. The goal of this commonwealth program is to invest public resources to create jobs for Pennsylvanians. To do so, this program offers a variety of grants, loans, and loan guarantees designed to stimulate economic investment, growth, and expand employment. This commonwealth program supports the administration's goal to create and maintain a business climate in which good, family-sustaining jobs can grow and communities can prosper. (3.2 percent of actual expenditures, 2013-2014)

(continues)

Table 6–2 (continued)
Program Budget Structure Illustration: Commonwealth of Pennsylvania, 2013-2014 to 2019-2020

Agencies include Department of Community and Economic Development, Pennsylvania Economic Development Financing Authority, and the Infrastructure Investment Authority (PENNVEST). Contributions from Executive Offices, Auditor General, Housing Finance Agency, and Departments of Education, Labor and Industry, and Revenue.

Transportation. The goal of this commonwealth program is to provide a system for the fast, convenient, efficient, and safe movement of individuals and goods within the commonwealth that is interfaced with a national and international system of transportation. The commonwealth program supports the administration's goal to create and maintain a business climate in which good, family-sustaining jobs can grow and communities can prosper. (9.2 percent of actual expenditures, 2013-2014)

Agency is Department of Transportation.

Recreation and Cultural Enrichment. The goal of this commonwealth program is to improve the quality of life in Pennsylvania's urban, suburban, and rural communities. This program focuses resources on our recreational and cultural amenities ensuring that Pennsylvanians can fully enjoy the natural beauty of the commonwealth. The program also ensures that residents and visitors can explore the diversity of cultural traditions, the creativity of our artistic community and the bountiful history of our state and its prominence in forming the heritage of our nation. (0.9 percent of actual expenditure, 2013-2014)

Agencies include the Department of Conservation and Natural Resources. Contributions from Department of Education, State Library, Historical and Museum Commission, Fish and Boat Commission, Game Commission, and Council on the Arts.

Debt Service. The goal of this commonwealth program is to provide sufficient financial resources necessary to meet the timely payment of commonwealth debt obligations. (1.8 percent of actual expenditures, 2013-2014)

Agency is Treasury Department.

SOURCE: Derived from Office of the Governor, Commonwealth of Pennsylvania, *2015-2016 Pennsylvania Executive Budget.* Harrisburgh, Penn.: Office of Governor, 2015.

If there are competing ways of reducing some social problem, make certain they end up in the same program.

2. **Include complementary resources.** Programs must include complementary components that cannot function separately. Thus, health programs require physicians, nurses, physical facilities, and the like in appropriate proportions, and those elements must all be in the program. And all costs associated with acquisition of the resource must be included, even if some costs (such as fringe benefits) are acquired in another department (e.g., a human resources department). In addition, public infrastructure used to provide a service requires upkeep and maintenance, and those costs should be associated with the program.

3. **Recognize the unallocable.** When one part of a government serves several other parts of that government, separate supporting service programs may be needed. Thus, centralized electronic data processing, personnel administration, and so forth may permit operating economies that would not be possible

if each agency handled them separately. These activities can be handled as programs, even though their outputs are not government objectives (e.g., the Direction and Supportive Services program in Pennsylvania). It isn't reasonable to try to allocate the time of the mayor or governor to the specific programs. In addition, eliminating a particular program element to which part of the mayor's office has been allocated is not going to cause a change in the mayor's office cost, so any such allocated costs are not relevant to the program decision. Joint costs are just that, joint, and trying to divide them up is folly, as well as adding no useful information to the decision-making process.

4. **Multiple structures.** Governments may need overlapping program structures to achieve their objectives. Many revenue departments, for instance, have structures arranged both functionally and geographically. That approach appears when both national and regional (or statewide) objectives are important. Unless the government chooses to reorganize along pure program lines, appropriations will be made to agencies and departments in order to maintain fiscal control, so there will be an organization chart financial structure on top of the program budget.

5. **Recognize long-term activities.** Some activities involving research, development, or long-term investment may be considered separate subprograms because of the long time span over which the expenditures take effect. Uncertainties preclude reasonably reliable estimates of resource requirements beyond short portions of their lives.

It can be assumed that all government activities seek to improve the general welfare. The goal of program budgeting is to identify the components of that broad objective so that choices can be made among those components and among alternative approaches to achievement of that objective. Devising a program budget requires a reclassification of expenditures from their organization across the traditional agencies. Each such effort brings its special challenges, but Sidebar 6–1 provides some basic steps involved in that conversion.

Program construction is the identifying feature, but program budgets often include other elements. First, budget time horizons expand beyond an annual appropriation to the program's lifetime. Although appropriation remains annual, decision makers are presented with the total program cost, not simply a single-year down payment. Second, steps in preparation induce agencies to consider alternate operating methods and to propose only those that require the least cost to achieve the desired results. Because agency administrators traditionally have incentives toward larger budgets for prestige or advancement, such steps are difficult to enforce. Third, program budgets often include some cost-benefit analysis of the resource use of proposed programs (a technique discussed in Chapter 7). Programming combines costs for achieving particular objectives, so an important piece of the data needed for cost-benefit analysis is provided.

All these elements appeared in the federal planning-programming-budgeting system (PPBS) experiment, applied initially to the Department of Defense in 1961, expanded to other federal agencies in 1965, and officially terminated in 1971. The Department of Defense continues with a formal system renamed in 2003 the

Sidebar 6–1
Administrative Budget to Program Budget

For resource allocation choices, lawmakers and the public need to know the amount of public resources being devoted to provision of different services to the citizenry. That means the full amount being spent for provision of public safety, transportation, recreation, and so forth is important to know, and looking at appropriations to administrative departments (a listing of amounts being spent to purchase inputs) will not always provide that information because agencies often have mixed missions and not all similar sorts of services are the responsibility of the same agency. Restructuring budget data into programs promises greater transparency and a classification of great use to lawmakers.

The budget organization specifics vary across jurisdictions so there cannot be a general template for converting administrative to program formats. It requires some digging into operations of agencies and thought about what services are being provided. However, there are some standard steps in making the transformation:

1. Determine what each part of operating agencies does. The name of the agency often does not capture its actual range of operations. Some may be more closely related to what other administrative agencies are doing than to other parts of the host agency. For instance, the U.S. Forest Service mission is to "sustain the health, diversity, and productivity of the Nation's forests and grasslands to meet the needs of present and future generations," and it proclaims itself to be the largest natural resource research organization in the world. However, almost half of its budget is devoted to fighting wildfires to protect people and property, a public safety activity.
2. Move similar services into the same program. For instance, services involving protection of people and property, a public safety program, may be in fire, police, and emergency services departments. They would be organized together in a program budget.
3. Move all costs associated with purchase of service inputs together. For instance, some governments organize their administrative budgets so that fringe benefits provided all employees appear in a human resources department. The program classification requires that these costs be in the same program as the wage or salary paid the employee: the cost of pension obligations provided as part of compensation to firefighters must be in the same program as wages paid to the firefighters. Similar transitions may be necessary if a single public works department does work on infrastructure throughout the government.
4. Put services that might be considered to be competitive ways of dealing with public desires together. If adult literacy improvement efforts are being provided by the school system, by the public library, and by a social services department, they should be included in the same program in the budget, even though their providers differ and their target clients might be somewhat different.
5. Leave general administration in a separate program category that covers all costs of overall supervision and legislation. It may seem tempting to allocate compensation of the chief executive (mayor, county executive, etc.) among the various governmental programs, reasoning that the executive spends time dealing with administration of their operations. This exercise is not worthwhile because payment to the executive is not driven by work of any particular agency but is more appropriately regarded as a fixed cost to the government enterprise.

**Sidebar 6–1
(continued)**

The program budget seeks to identify costs directly associated with providing the service, in other words, on the costs that would go away if the program were to be terminated. It is not useful to attach a share of overall administration to programs because those costs would not be avoided if the program were to end.

The budget will be divided into programs intended to provide services to the citizenry (such as public safety), and these programs will then ordinarily be categorized into subprograms with more specific purposes (such as police protection and fire protection). And the subprograms will likely be divided into subprograms as well such as police patrol and investigations. Program costs will be identified down to the sub-subprogram level, using the same standards as apply to identifying costs to the programs. The budget is divided into these programs as opposed to being divided along the administrative structure.

Planning Programming Budgeting and Execution System (PPBES).[21] The system provides a link between the missions or programs of the Department of Defense and the departments within Defense (Army, Navy, Air Force, etc.) charged with delivery of those missions and, through the secretary of defense, provides an important element in the principle of civilian control of the military force.

The logical steps of the PPBES system—extending beyond organizing the budget in program format—are these:

1. **Planning.** Define, identify, and examine alternative strategies for dealing with the environment of the future. In defense terms, the planning involves analysis of trends, adversary capability, threats, strategies, technologies, and long-term implications of current choices. The process determines service requirements. The plans are long-term and multiyear.

2. **Programming.** Balance resources among the various program options. The programming process considers alternatives for meeting the previously established service requirements. It will derive what are believed to be the best programs for meeting those requirements.

3. **Budgeting.** Formulate, justify, execute, and control the budget that embodies those selected programs. The programs previously established are rolled into a budget request for approval by department leadership, the president, and Congress. Resources will be controlled according to the relevant appropriation law.

---

[21]An excellent description and analysis of the budget and other financial management systems in the Department of Defense, including PPBES, is L. R. Jones and Jerry L. McCaffery, *Budgeting, Financial Management, and Acquisition Reform in the U.S. Department of Defense* (Charlotte, N.C.: Information Age Publishing, 2008).

Elements of the old PPBS system remain in budget frameworks of many federal agencies. In addition, the PPBES process has recently been expanding, as it has now been adopted by the National Oceanic and Atmospheric Administration (NOAA), the Department of Homeland Security, the Library of Congress, and the National Aeronautics and Space Administration (NASA). It continues in various versions among several states and localities.[22] The advantages: it provides a long-term connection to objectives and strategic plans, it ends a process in which budgets were constructed on an annual increment basis, and it focuses on distributing available resources reasonably among competing programs in the agency. Its process is ideal when the department has separate units that are performing similar or interrelated tasks. It does move fundamental decision making higher in the department.[23]

The functional classification required by the 1974 Congressional Budget and Impoundment Control Act provides something along the lines of a program format for federal expenditures that appears alongside the traditional administrative classification in the congressional budget resolution and in the president's budget. The functions frequently include more than a single department (the national defense function, for instance, encompasses activities of the Defense and Energy Departments), and departments may have activities in more than a single function. Appendix 6–1 presents the United Nations classification of functions of government (COFOG), a functional classification that applies to services provided by all levels of government. This classification, because of its breadth, provides a good thinking template for any government—national, regional, or local—that is developing a functional classification for its operations, and it serves as the basic template for making comparisons of government operations across countries.

As is characteristic of program budgets, the federal functional classification cuts across agencies so that decision makers may think about use of public resources to the advantage of the citizenry without regard for organizational boundaries. Figure 6–3 shows the extent to which functions are distributed to agencies and the extent to which agencies support multiple functions in the U.S. government. A Government Accountability Office (GAO) report describes the situation for fiscal 2003:

> Sometimes there is a "match" between a function and a department—for example, the Department of Transportation is associated almost exclusively with the Transportation function (400) and over 80 percent of spending within the Transportation function (400) is by the Department of Transportation. Sometimes, however, there is an imbalance between the importance of an agency in a mission area and the importance of the mission area within the department. For example, while almost all obligations in the Agriculture function (350) are by USDA [U.S. Department of Agriculture], that function

---

[22]See Allen Schick, *Budget Innovation in the States* (Washington, D.C.: Brookings Institution, 1971), for a review of state use of program and performance structures. About thirty-five states have implemented modified PPBS at one time or another.

[23]West and colleagues identify complaints and resistance in the recent introduction of PPBES to NOAA. William F. West, Eric Lindquist, and Katrina N. Mosher-Howe, "NOAA's Resurrection of Program Budgeting: Déjà vu All over Again?" *Public Administration Review* 69 (May/June 2009): 435–47. Agencies never like change in how they do things. People cherish the power that comes from understanding a process, and changing any process erodes that power.

Figure 6–3
Federal Spending by Agency and Function: Multiple Agencies for Functions and Multiple Functions for Agencies

Budget Function	National Defense (050)	International Affairs (150)	General Science, Space, and Technology (250)	Energy (270)	Natural Resources and Environment (300)	Agriculture (350)	Commerce and Housing Credit (370)	Transportation (400)	Community and Regional Development (450)	Education, Training, Employment, and Social Services (500)	Health (550)	Medicare (570)	Income Security (600)	Social Security (650)	Veterans Benefits and Services (700)	Administration of Justice (750)	General Government (800)	Net Interest (900)	Number of functions charged by agency
Executive Branch																			
Department of Agriculture		●		●	●	●	●		●		●		●				●		9
Department of Commerce					●		●		●								●		4
Department of Defense	●	●			●						●		●		●		●		7
Department of Education										●			●						2
Department of Energy	●		●	●													●		4
Department of Health and Human Services										●	●	●	●				●		5
Department of Homeland Security	●				●			●	●		●		●			●	●		8
Department of Housing and Urban Development							●		●				●			●			4
Department of Justice	●	●														●			3
Department of Labor	●									●	●		●		●	●			6
Department of State		●			●						●								3
Department of Transportation	●							●											2
Department of Veterans Affairs															●				1
Department of the Interior					●			●	●	●							●		5
Department of the Treasury		●			●		●		●	●	●		●			●	●	●	10
Environmental Protection Agency					●														1
Executive Office of the President		●					●										●		3
General Services Administration							●										●		2
Independent Agencies	●	●		●	●	●	●	●	●	●	●		●		●	●	●		14
National Aeronautics and Space Administration			●					●		●									3
National Science Foundation	●		●																2
Nuclear Regulatory Commission				●															1
Office of Personnel Management											●		●				●		3
Postal Service							●												1
Small Business Administration							●		●										2
Social Security Administration													●	●	●				3
Number of Executive Agencies Charging this Function	8	7	3	4	9	2	9	5	8	7	9	1	11	1	5	6	12	1	
Judicial Branch													●			●			2
Legislative Branch		●					●			●		●	●			●	●		7
Number of Agencies Charging this Function		1					1			1		1	2			2	1		
All	8	8	3	4	9	2	10	5	8	8	9	2	13	1	5	8	13	1	

SOURCE: Government Accountability Office, Federal Budget: Agency Obligations by Budget Function and Object Classification for Fiscal Year 2003, GAO-04-834 (Washington, D.C.: Government Accountability Office, 2004).

represents only about 41 percent of the spending by the department. Over 40 percent of USDA's obligations are for the Income Security function (600).[24]

---

[24]Government Accountability Office, *Federal Budget: Agency Obligations by Budget Function and Object Classification for Fiscal Year 2003,* GAO-04-834 (Washington, D.C.: Government Accountability Office, 2004). The numbers in parentheses refer to function numbers in the classification system.

One classification focuses on resource allocation choices for the federal government; the other focuses on establishing responsibility and accountability. Barring a reorganization to make functions (or programs) and agencies match, a crosswalk between functions and agencies is critical for getting all that is expected from the budget process. Without an easy, quick, and understandable crosswalk, the function or program format yields numbers that are not usable by budget decision makers, and choices continue to be made in the familiar setting of the traditional budget. That problem contributed heavily to the demise of the earlier federal PPBS. Linked computer spreadsheet and database programs make translation between classifications—from function or program to administrative agency accounts, for instance—almost instantly possible. That was not the case in the 1960s when the Johnson administration tried it.

Three operational problems with program budgets require special attention. First, many public services contribute to more than one public objective, and the best programmatic classification for them is not always apparent. Whatever choice is made will emphasize one set of policy choices at the expense of another. For example, federal expenditures on military academies might be attributed to higher education or to national security. The placement of that expenditure establishes which analysis it faces, so placement must depend on the most important current issues raised by the expenditure. Any long-maintained program structure produces the bureaucratic blindness associated with continued examination of the same issues from the same approach. Furthermore, difficult interrelationships among public programs remain. Thus, highway transportation activities may influence urban redevelopment or complicate environmental protection. These interrelationships can baffle any budget navigator.

Second, cost estimates for programs may be less meaningful for public decisions than imagined. There is no scientifically defensible method to allocate substantial joint agency costs or administrative overhead costs. Because most agencies work with several programs, many resources used by an agency are shared and are not attributable to a single program. Furthermore, public decisions require concern for social implications—not simply money out of pocket—but program budgets still focus on agency cost alone. Thus, the program cost data are unlikely to be directly usable for decision making.

Third, programs cannot entirely replace departments to deliver all expectations from the budget process because responsibility and accountability for performance and for funds must be assigned to an organizational unit. Programs cannot be accountable; departments (and the people in them) can be. Hence, fiscal discipline, in the final analysis, requires a budget and appropriation structure beyond that provided by a program format.

Finally, program budgets may have little impact on appropriations. Legislatures, lobbyists, and government departments have experience with the traditional budget format. Participants know where their allies are located, and the location is in a department. All are familiar with that construction and have developed general guidelines for its analysis. New presentations require new guidelines and extra effort by all. Unless the major participants in the budget process want the improved presentation, it will be ignored in favor of the format to which they are accustomed.

But, ultimately, that may not matter.[25] The program budget and a process like PPBES are initially for development of an executive budget. As a tool for developing that budget, the executive branch can find it extremely useful in developing its policy responses, in choosing among options, and in creating its proposal to the legislative branch. Therefore, even if the legislature insists on looking at the traditional budget, what is in that traditional budget will have been created according to the PPBES principles.

If the executive believes the format to be useful for making fiscal choices and a crosswalk can be created at little cost, there is no reason not to use the system. As with all higher-order budget processes (in other words, those that try to go beyond line items and organization charts), there are costs associated with program budgets, so they should be created only if they are going to be used. As we know, the current federal budget comfortably crosswalks from agency appropriations and functional categories without problems, surely creating more transparency, if nothing else.

An Illustration of an Expenditure in Alternative Classifications

The budget system reforms discussed so far involve recategorization of spending to provide information in alternative formats. How this would affect information is demonstrated in Figure 6–4. How might the salary of a teacher employed in a state correctional facility appear in traditional, performance, and program budget formats? With a traditional budget, that salary would appear as a part of the personnel (wage-and-salary) line of the state Department of Corrections budget. It would thus compete for funds, in the first instance, within that department. Money received could well depend on how the governor and legislature viewed the overall prison system. More money appropriated to the corrections system could end up being directed to the educational systems in the institutions.

If that budget was classified according to performance, that expenditure would appear as part of the cost of achieving a target number of departmental instruction hours. Again, competition for resources would be with other activities of that department. It would be distinguished, however, from activities not related to instruction. There would be a distinction between money for the education program and money devoted to stronger security and detention apparatus.

A program structure might classify that expenditure as a part of a human development program, separating the expenditure from its link to incarceration and causing it to be considered with training and education activities. It would be considered with primary and secondary education, job training, and other education activities, and not with money associated with improving and maintaining public safety.

---

[25] And confusing the lobbyists, even for a legislative session or two, might be a good thing. Never fear, they will figure things out soon enough.

Figure 6–4
Salary Classification in Traditional, Performance, and Program Budgets

Morris Hall is employed by the Green Valley Correctional Facility as a teacher in the basic literacy program. His salary is $25,000 per year. Where would Mr. Hall's salary appear in different budget classifications? Follow the asterisk (*).

Traditional Departmental	Performance	Program
Department of Corrections	Department of Corrections	Human Resource Development
Green Valley Correctional Facility	Activity: Adult literacy	Service: Adult literacy
Personnel	Personnel*	Local
Director	Supplies	State facilities*
Clerical	Cost per student	Service: Vocational education
Guards	instructional hour	
Instructors*	Activity: Incarceration	Protection of Persons and Property
Supplies and equipment		
Contractual services	Department of Highways	Provision of Safe and Speedy Transportation
Jackson State Correctional Facility		
Department of Highways		
Department of Education		

The salary expenditure is the same dollar amount, but the different budget classifications require different treatment to accommodate different budget purposes. The budget classification undoubtedly would influence the questions asked about the expenditure and, possibly, the size of its appropriation. In creating a budget classification system other than one following the traditional administrative unit system, it will be necessary to reclassify funds away from their accounting location to provide information groups more appropriate for the public decisions being made. The funds need to be associated with an administrative unit for fiscal control and responsibility, but other classifications will be more useful for other budgetary purposes.

The Zero-Based Budget System

Systems called zero-based budgeting (ZBB) come in several different varieties. What all have in common is an effort to prevent pure incremental budgeting, in which the budget from the prior year is taken as the starting point with a presumption that the new budget will be some upward adjustment to the old budget. The ZBB implication is that the budget would be developed without reference to the previous year's budget, that there are no foundation presumptions about what will be in the new budget, and, very definitely, that there is no assumption that agencies are assured of an appropriation at least as great as their current level. Everything starts with a clean slate, and all options for service and how the services are to be delivered are on an even competitive basis.

It is fundamentally preposterous to believe that the new budget will actually start from scratch, as if decisions about budgets in prior years had not been made and everything is new. Any government starts the year with lots of carryovers—for instance, a city has four fire stations, three city parks, a police station in a particular location, probably a collective-bargaining agreement with city employees that sets compensation rates and possibly staffing levels, and a history of decisions that previous administrations and city councils have reached over the years about city policies, responsibilities, and limits. The budget is going to be built from those foundations because many choices are not going to change (indeed, they may be legally binding), and, even with any instruction to ignore the recent past, capable administrators are going to pay attention to the information from that experience in building service programs, policies, and budget requests.

But zero-based thinking is a good approach. What one hopes is that the agency administrators will build their budget proposals with an open mind with regard to serving the public and with regard to ways in which services might be provided, that the budget gets built from a plan for providing outcomes, and that *nobody*—not agencies, budget agencies, lawmakers, or the public—can accurately assume that current levels of funding are guaranteed, that increments only go up, and that adding 2 percent or so to last year's budget lines is how to create a budget. That is a far more effective approach than to make the unrealistic claim that budgets are being prepared entirely from scratch every year.[26] And it does mean that the budget will be built with a thought toward service delivery plans, not as a series of adjustments to expenditure levels in the prior year.

When Jimmy Carter became president in 1976, he instituted a zero-based budgeting system for the federal government, one based on what he had used as governor of Georgia some years earlier. Similar systems have been applied periodically by state and local governments, most using procedures and terminologies like those in this federal system.[27] His idea was to implement a rational program to reallocate

[26]The House Appropriations Committee instructed that the appropriation proposal for the legislative branch for fiscal 2013 be constructed on a zero base. "The Committee believes that there are considerable opportunities to realize meaningful savings by carefully reviewing each agency's budget requirements from a zero base, rather than by reviewing only incremental changes to the base. Such a review would not only assist the Committee in its appropriating and oversight responsibilities, but would also require agencies to systematically examine all of their budgetary requirements as they relate to the individual mission. Therefore, the Committee directs each and every agency of the Legislative Branch to develop and present their budget requirements from a zero base. The individual reviews should examine and justify each and every program, project, and activity (PPA) as if the PPA were nonexistent." Committee Reports, 112th Congress, House Report 112–148, Legislative Branch Appropriations Bill, 2012. A recent legislative proposal would extend a ZBB concept to all federal operations: the Zero-based Budgeting Ensures Responsible Oversight (ZERO) Act of 2013 (H.R.239, 113th Congress) would require the president to submit a budget for each agency that would describe the activities of the agency; identify the legal basis for each agency activity; propose three funding levels for each activity (two below current funding levels), summarize priorities accomplished by each level, and identify increments of value from each higher funding level; and provide for each activity one or more measures of cost efficiency and effectiveness. It has not progressed legislatively.

[27]A National Conference of State Legislatures report tallies seventeen states as recent users of some form of ZBB plus more legislatures actively considering bills to require its use. It also notes an Illinois Legislative Research Unit study that finds no evidence of actual ZBB in most of the states reporting its use. (Ronald Snell, *NCSL Fiscal Brief: Zero-Base Budgets in the States*, January 2012.)

public resources to areas of greatest public need and to break the limitations ingrained in an incrementalist budgetary system (recall the incrementalist insight discussed in Chapter 2). In theory, the zero-based budget (ZBB) annually would require each agency to defend its entire budget.[28] Deliberations in both executive preparation and legislative approval would be about the full budget, not just the proposed increase, and the assumed incremental lock on fiscal decision making would be broken. The system would make government more flexible, eliminate low-return programs, allocate resources to the highest-return programs, improve government effectiveness by forcing programs to be justified in their entirety every year, and simplify reallocations of government spending in response to changed program demands—all good objectives. Choices about programs and funding would be made based on a system of internal rankings of those options, and the whole budget would be put together on that totally rational basis.

ZBB systems in implementation had individual peculiarities, but many included the elements diagrammed in Figure 6–5.[29] In the first stage, unit managers prepare *decision packages,* which are alternatives for performing a particular function with differing amounts of money. Each package includes funding levels and increments, a description of the activity, and a statement of the activity's impact on major objectives of the agency (Note: performance measures again required in the system). The decision package also describes the implications of not providing funds for the package.[30]

Unit managers submit their ranked decision packages to agency heads. Agency heads consolidate the packages received from the several unit managers, rank the packages, and transmit the packages forward in the government hierarchy. The packages flow through successive consolidations and rankings to the department level. The final consolidation and ranking produces the budget request transmitted to the central budget office for eventual inclusion in the president's budget.[31] As many packages as can be afforded within available revenue will be in the budget, all priority-ranked.

The process has several potential strengths. It will produce much operating data—workloads, performance indicators, and so on—for use in management and should induce consideration of alternative delivery approaches. Furthermore, it will require formal consideration of priorities throughout the organization, something not done when the process takes previous operations as given in budget preparation. Budget construction builds from the bottom of the organization, where the best

---

[28]The federal PPBS process just discussed was intended to start budget development from a zero base as well. The development of President Carter's ZBB system is described in Lawrence A. Gordon and Donna H. Heivilin, "Zero-Base Budgeting in the Federal Government: An Historical Perspective," *GAO Review,* 13(Fall 1978): 57–64.

[29]Executive Office of the President, Office of Management and Budget, "Zero Base Budgeting" (Bulletin No. 79–9), April 19, 1977, provides a full description of the federal version of ZBB.

[30]The ZBB system in Georgia and at the federal level didn't start with zero; agencies were to start with 80 percent of the previous year's appropriation. But 80 percent-based budgeting doesn't sound so impressive. Robert N. Anthony, "Zero-Base Budgeting Is a Fraud," *Wall Street Journal,* April 27, 1977.

[31]President Carter claimed that, as governor of Georgia, he did the final ranking of the thousands of decision packages flowing up through the state government. Had he done so, he would have had time for little else during the year.

Figure 6–5
Decision Package Flow in the Federal ZBB System, Late 1970s

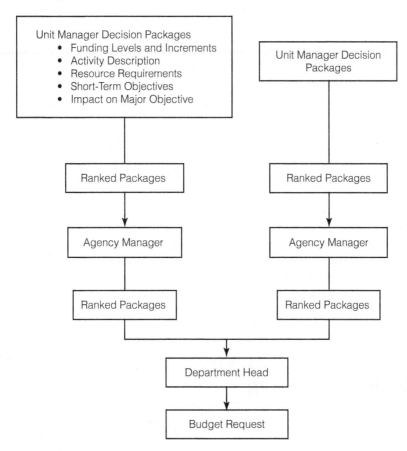

operating information resides, not from the top down, as is characteristic of most budget processes. Finally, ZBB requires considerable thought about the objectives of the agency.

There are problems. First, package development generates package options that have absolutely no chance of serious consideration. Some programs cannot realistically be considered candidates for zeroing out, some packages will never be seriously considered for funding, and some production alternatives will not be meaningful contenders. Many capable administrators, recognizing all that, will not take ZBB seriously. Second, performance information may not be germane to agency operations. Measures may be accurate, but not meaningful—and they may not be accurately reported. Third, many spending activities will not be amenable to zero-based treatment. Several such categories include mandates at the state and local levels, activities controlled by earmarks, contractual payments (debt service and pensions), and, especially, formula entitlements. These constitute a considerable share of many budgets. Finally, the rankings from those in the program delivery flow may not reflect the rankings of society. One suspects that administrators will have protection of their programs shaping their rankings. It is not unreasonable to expect people to rank their programs high and to rank those of others low—and that inclination may be inconsistent with best fiscal choices for the public. The idea that federal programs could be objectively ranked from highest to lowest priority misses the basic fact that most programs cannot be evaluated on numerical terms and, even where programs can produce numbers, the numbers are not comparable from one program to another. The numbers from veterans' benefits are not the same as numbers from farm price supports.

Most observers doubt that federal ZBB had much impact on federal spending. The Reagan administration terminated it as soon as it took office. Allen Schick says that zero-based budgeting "changed the terminology of budgeting, but little more."[32] Zero-based budgeting probably directs too much attention to the routine of the budget process and away from the tough questions of that process—the questions of program objectives and social values. Some pieces continue in federal, state, and local budget systems, including elements of target-based budgeting processes in which budget units develop alternative budget proposals based on different levels of potential funding.[33] Proposals for new implementations are a perennial reform because starting everything from zero and having total flexibility in resource allocation seems like such a good idea.[34]

Results-Based, Outcome-Driven, New Performance Budgeting

There has been a continuing fascination with the potential for improving government operations if only agency performance could be formally integrated into the budget cycle and that fascination has brought outcome-oriented, results-oriented, or new performance budgeting. As David Osborne and Ted Gaebler write, "Cynicism about government runs deep within the American soul."[35] Nothing will dislodge this cynicism. American popular discussions refer to the public as "taxpayers," not "service recipients," focusing on how much government costs and not on the services government provides, so the traditional input focus may be no surprise. However, giving a clearer view of what the results or outcomes of government expenditures are and providing some assurance that government agencies are focused on performance

---

[32]Allen Schick, "The Road from ZBB," *Public Administration Review* 38 (March/April 1978): 178.

[33]Robert K. Goertz, "Target-Based Budgeting and Adaptations to Fiscal Uncertainty," *Public Productivity and Management Review* 16 (Summer 1993): 425–29.

[34]Shayne C. Kavanagh, *Zero-Base Budgeting, Modern Experiences and Current Perspectives*. Chicago: Government Finance Officers Association, 2011.

[35]David Osborne and Ted Gaebler, *Reinventing Government, How the Entrepreneurial Spirit Is Transforming the Public Sector* (Reading, Mass.: Addison-Wesley, 1992), xv.

accountability may assuage some skeptics and might improve the extent to which the public trusts the government. At least that is a hope.

There is nothing wrong about expecting a decent return from money spent. It should be no surprise that there is a demand for performance reports and performance targets for the budget year—and that this information would logically be attached to the policy proposals for spending public money. As the only high-stakes annual (or biennial in some jurisdictions) event that considers all operations of a government, the budget process is the ideal place to consider government performance, and being able to link performance to decisions about spending should make it even better. A budget that looks for results and reallocation based on that evidence is certainly more reasonable than one that has as its primary focus money being spent and inputs being purchased.[36]

A discussion of new performance budgeting is complicated by the fact that there "never has been an agreed-on definition of performance budgeting."[37] The systems proposed and implemented have varied features, they operate at different points in the fiscal structure, and their intentions are not always the same. Some seek efficiency, some seek to cut the size of government, some seek to make the case for expanded government, some seek improved transparency and information flow, and some want to stop the crooks. Some (mostly those individuals naïve to operations and purposes of government) even have aspired to creation of a formula that, having plugged performance measures in for all parts of government, will spit the appropriate budget amounts out, bypassing the realities that legislatures might have different ideas about performance (citizens have different preferences in regard to public services provided) and that there is no common denominator for measurement of performance accomplishment. Joyce helpfully suggests that, in describing budgeting practices, it is better to talk about "performance-informed budgeting" because that terminology better captures the political reality and accepts the idea of performance data as an input to budgeting, not the ultimate allocator of resources.[38] It is difficult to generalize, but the basic elements of new performance budgeting include (i) budgets with information about objectives and results (key *outcome* indicators, not just outputs) and (ii) a budget process that integrates this information into budget preparation and execution by agencies and into appropriation decisions by legislatures, including presentation of performance measures (achieved and intended)

---

[36]But an agency performance focus will not provide a tool for everything expected of a budget process. From Estonian evidence from 2008 to 2010, Raudla and Savi cast doubt on the use of performance measures for fiscal discipline when cutbacks are required, indeed with evidence of less use of such measures in crisis than in normal times. (Ringa Raudla and Riin Savi, "The Use of Performance Information in Cutback Budgeting," *Public Money & Management* 35, no. 6 (2015): 409–16.)

[37]William C. Rivenbark, "Defining Performance Budgeting for Local Government," *Popular Government* 69 (Winter 2004): 2. A good summation of the ideal of performance budgeting is Marc Robinson and Duncan Last, *A Basic Model of Performance-Based Budgeting* (Washington, D.C.: International Monetary Fund, 2009). Because of this imprecision about the meaning of performance budgeting, this section mingles various strands from practices with labels involving outcome-based budgeting, performance-based budgeting, results-oriented budgeting, etc. They have common intentions, even with some variation of emphasis, and the systems in place are almost always some jumble of various budget system ideas.

[38]Philip G. Joyce, "The Obama Administration and PBB: Building on the Legacy of Federal Performance-Informed Budgeting," *Public Administration Review* (May/June 2011): 356–67.

directly in budget documents.[39] A GAO report induced by the OMB Circular A-11 for budget formulation with instruction to develop performance-based budgets in some agencies identified four themes for results-oriented budget practices in federal agencies: (i) performance will inform budget formulation and implementation; (ii) agencies will produce reliable estimates of costs and resources; (iii) agencies can relate performance, budgeting, spending, and workforce information; and (iv) agencies will continuously seek improvement.[40] New performance budgeting aspires to make outcome measures integral to the budget cycle and, ideally, to link funding to measured agency results. These elements may help improve allocation of fiscal resources among alternatives and may encourage agencies to spend more efficiently and effectively.[41]

The idea of such outcome-driven budgeting is that the societal goal, the outcome or result that agencies provide, is what matters for government performance, not the output or activity of the agency or what it purchases. That is the same logic that drove program budgeting, but this new approach does not cross agency lines to put operations with similar societal objectives together. This focus on results is comparable to that of the private sector—auto companies manufacture cars to make a profit (the outcome), not to buy materials (the focal point for traditional government budgets) or even to build cars (the activity or output). Although governments won't be expected to yield profits, they can be expected to produce beneficial results for society. The outcome orientation flips the input control focus of traditional budgets on its head. That identifying results may be difficult, time consuming, sometimes bordering on the impossible, and even embarrassing for administrators, does not mean that the inquiry is inappropriate.

A quick perusal of budgets presented on government websites will show that, one way or another, performance measurement has gotten tied into many budget presentations and deliberations. Traditional performance budgets tended to link costs to the outputs or activities of government agencies and to calculate unit costs of these activities, whereas the new performance budgets are more likely to simply present performance results and targets associated with departmental operations. They do not attempt unit costing.

The ideal results-oriented performance budget would have sparse details on what the agency would purchase—the line items would not be controlled in plan or execution—because control should be on what services the agency would provide. Agencies might have some focus on operational outputs or tasks (e.g., caseloads or miles of highway patrolled), but that would be for internal management, not for indicating agency performance success. By focusing on results, governments could become more responsive to the interests of the citizenry; by allowing greater flexibility, governments could become more entrepreneurial and efficient in service delivery.

---

[39]Performance measurement reports not integrated into the budget process are not performance budgets.
[40]U.S. General Accounting Office, *Results-Oriented Budget Practices in Federal Agencies,* GAO-01-1084SP, August 2001.
[41]The effort to link performance is not limited to the United States. Organization for Economic Cooperation and Development, *Performance Budgeting in OECD Countries* (Paris: OECD, 2007).

New performance budgeting integrates information on government outcome performance into the budget process and involves these principles:

1. **Objectives/strategic plan.** The agency should state what it is trying to accomplish that matters for the citizenry. The agency normally develops a strategic plan (Sidebar 6–2, an outline of the Government Performance and Results Act of 1993 [GPRA], shows the requirements for federal agency strategic plans), but it must also consider why it exists in the first place (its mission). Annual performance plans and annual budgets are to be linked to the strategic plan, but the thinking about mission (and its justification) comes first.[42] The strategic plan should show how the agency intends to achieve results.

2. **Performance measures.** From that strategic plan must be developed measures that will gauge progress toward meeting objectives. Performance measurement should provide the connection between the strategic plan and the results. In contrast with traditional budget processes that focus on inputs (the resources purchased by the agency) or direct outputs (the agency's activities or tasks), the performance budget measures outcomes (the results or the extent to which agency activities have their intended effect). Table 6–3 illustrates the activity (direct output) to outcome shift for several basic government functions.

Some performance measures can be observed from existing social, economic, demographic, or health status data, but some may require new tests or surveys to gauge performance. The focus is intended to be on performance outcomes—not the number of passengers (silver-haired grandfathers, infants, and all) subjected to search by the Transportation Security Administration, but whether flying is safer from terrorist threats. If you can't contract out with real terrorists to test the performance, the success at finding weapons brought in by testers from the Department of Homeland Security inspector general's office would be a good proxy, and recent tests gave the TSA a 95 percent *failure* rate at finding weapons.[43] That's not excellent performance, and you will not be surprised to learn that such a measure does not appear in the Department of Homeland Security's annual performance report, a document that is full of activity (not outcome) measures.[44] An important bureaucratic principle: if you can't identify an outcome, or if the outcome is not good, provide an activity (or output) measure and hope no one notices.

There are six critical principles in selecting outcome performance measures:

a. *External focus.* The measure should relate to the client or customer, not to internal procedures of the agency.

---

[42]The National Aeronautics and Space Administration states that the goal of the Space Science Program is to "chart the evolution of the universe from origin to destiny." Performance measures would likely not be easy to spin from this goal. They might need assistance from Neil DeGrasse Tyson to get it straightened out and understandable.

[43]Ashley Halsey III, "Why the TSA catches your water bottle, but guns and bombs get through," *Washington Post*, June 3, 2015.

[44]Each department's annual performance report accompanies its budget justification to Congress, but it is not formally integrated with the budget.

Sidebar 6–2
Federal Performance Measurement and the Budget Process

The federal government does have systems for performance measurement with a linkage to the budget process, although the measures do not appear in the formal budget document. The Government Performance and Results Act of 1993, Public Law 103-62 (GPRA), requires all agencies to submit to OMB an annual performance report for each program in the agency's budget.[1] The report should be consistent with the agency's strategic plan and have these features: the establishment of goals to define performance to be achieved by each program activity; goal statements that are objective, quantifiable, and measureable; performance indicators to measure relevant outputs, outcomes, or service levels; and a description of operational processes and resources required to meet the performance goals. The GPRA report provides a descriptive program evaluation of outcomes and implementation and assesses them against goals. The program outcomes may or may not be the direct result of program efforts.

GPRA has three important elements that seek to reduce inefficiency and ineffectiveness in government programs by directing attention to agency performance and results:

A. Multiyear (three- to five-year) strategic plans that identify the fundamental mission of the agency, the general goals that will be used to accomplish the mission, and resource requirements consistent with the mission. Strategic plans are to be updated at least every three years. The Act provides for the following required parts of the strategic plan:

(1) a comprehensive mission statement covering the major functions and operations of the agency;
(2) general goals and objectives, including outcome-related goals and objectives, for the major functions and operations of the agency;
(3) a description of how the goals and objectives are to be achieved, including a description of the operational processes, skills and technology, and the human, capital, information, and other resources required to meet those goals and objectives;
(4) a description of how the performance goals included in the plan required by section 1115(a) of title 31 shall be related to the general goals and objectives in the strategic plan;
(5) an identification of those key factors external to the agency and beyond its control that could significantly affect the achievement of the general goals and objectives; and
(6) a description of the program evaluations used in establishing or revising general goals and objectives, with a schedule for future program evaluations. (5 U.S.C. § 306)

B. Annual performance plans that drive day-to-day operations. The plans include objective, quantitative, and measurable performance goals: measurable indicators to determine whether programs are meeting goals: and a summary of funding and staffing resources being used to achieve the goals. The plans are expected to link to the strategic plan.

C. Annual performance reports to be made six months after the end of the fiscal year to relevant committees and subcommittees for evaluating the agency record. The report is based on achievement of planned measurable performance indicators.

The intent was that these performance activities would link into a performance budget process and that federal appropriations would be made on a more rational basis. As a federal law, GPRA has had considerably greater staying power than budget systems established by presidents for development of their executive budgets. However, the president is free to develop the executive budget without paying any attention to GPRA.

**Sidebar 6–2
(continued)**

GPRA's main legacy is a greatly increased supply of agency performance data. GPRA performance reports are posted on department websites for easy accessibility. Along with plans for each program, they provide a number of performance measures reports for the prior year and targets for the future year that are sometimes outcome in logic but often are output measures.

[1]GPRA was revised by the Government Performance and Results Act (GPRA) Modernization Act of 2010 (GPRAMA, Public Law No. 111-352). In general, it established new performance routines to try to encourage greater performance measure use by federal managers. Moynihan and Kroll find evidence that GPRAMA did get managers more interested in using performance measures, but Congress continues to show little interest. (Donald P. Moynihan and Alexander Kroll, "Performance Management Routines That Work? An Early Assessment of the GPRA Modernization Act," *Public Administration Review*, DOI: 10.1111/puar.12434) A GAO report, however, found a decrease in agency use of performance measures over the 2007 to 2013 period. (U.S. Government Accountability Office, "Managing for Results: Agencies' Trends in the Use of Performance Information to Make Decisions," GAO-14-747 (September 2014))

   b. *Truly measurable.* It should be possible to gauge success or failure and whether performance is improving, deteriorating, or staying the same.

   c. *Outcome based.* It should measure service delivery to the citizenry rather than impact within the entity.

   d. *Significant.* The measure should encompass the essence of the agency's mission. More of what is measured must clearly be good for society.

   e. *Manageable.* The number of measures should be no greater than necessary to cover the scope of agency operations. There should be no danger of user overload.

   f. *Verified.* Measures should be independently verifiable if not produced by a third party.

Getting the measures right is extremely important for the functioning of a results-driven budget system, as Campbell's Law makes clear: "The more any quantitative social indicator is used for social decision-making, the more subject it will be to corruption and the more apt it will be to distort and corrupt the social processes it is intended to monitor."[45] Choosing the wrong measures is worse than having no measures at all, and choosing measured targets that are easy to achieve does little to further agency efficiency.

3. Flexible execution. Agencies should not be constrained by control of how resources get used during budget execution. Accountability should focus on outcomes, not expenditures. Agencies might also be allowed to retain at least some portion of unexpended funds for use in upcoming fiscal years, rather

---

[45]Donald T. Campbell, "Assessing the Impact of Planned Social Change," in *Social Research and Public Policies,* ed. G. M. Lyons (Hanover, N.H.: The Public Affairs Center, Dartmouth College, 1976), 54.

Table 6–3
Outputs (Activities or Tasks) versus Outcomes (Results)

One of the most difficult tasks in measuring government performance is that of identifying what performance to measure. The concept of inputs is easy to understand, and their measurement does not differ much from one program or department to another. Inputs are the resources, such as labor, building materials, utilities, and so on, that go into the production of government services. They are measured the same whether they are purchases by the fire department or by the department of environmental protection. There are more problems with regard to outputs and outcomes.

Outputs are the tasks that agencies perform as they go about their business. They are not ends in themselves, but are intermediate measures leading toward achieving the objectives of the organization. Indicators of output focus on the amount of measured work accomplished or on the quality of the processes used to accomplish that work. It is expected that the outputs are working toward the agency's intended purpose.

Outcomes are the final desirable results that the agency hopes to accomplish. They are results that directly contribute to the objectives of the agency and represent measures of the agency's reason for existence.

The following material gives some examples of outputs and outcomes (or results) for a number of government functions.

Fire Department

Outputs: inspections performed, fire calls answered, arson investigations performed, hours of educational programs offered, property value protected in service area

Outcomes: ISO fire insurance rating, dollars of fire loss (negative), number of fire-related injuries and fatalities (negative), number of traffic accidents during fire runs, number of reported and unreported fires

Police Department

Outputs: hours on patrol, responses to calls for assistance, crimes investigated by category, number of arrests, police officer presentations to school children

Outcomes: deaths, injuries, and property losses from crime in service area, crime clearance rate, citizen complaints about officer abuse

Elementary and Secondary Education

Outputs: instructional days, students promoted or graduated

Outcomes: test score results, parent/student satisfaction ratings, percent of graduates employed

Public Health

Outputs: number of persons served, number of vaccinations given, number of restaurant inspections, training program days

Outcomes: mortality rates, morbidity rates, cases of infectious diseases by category

Table 6–3
(continued)

Public Welfare

Outputs: number of clients, number of clients by type of assistance category

Outcomes: former clients leaving the welfare system

Solid-Waste Management

Outputs: waste collected and processed, residences served, miles of road cleaned

Outcomes: proportion of streets rated as clean, incidence of vector-borne disease, citizen satisfaction ratings, achievement of environmental standard

Tax Department

Outputs: returns processed, processing time, delinquency rates

Outcomes: overall compliance rate, taxpayer complaint rates, measured uniformity of treatment of taxpayers

Environmental Protection and Management

Outputs: permits granted, inspections performed

Outcomes: percent of state residents living where air quality meets state or federal standard, percent of groundwater that meets drinking water standard, release and generation of solid waste as percent of base-line year

Juvenile Justice

Outputs: number of children in the system, worker caseload

Outcomes: juvenile justice recidivism rate, juvenile justice system clients leaving system for school or employment

Employment Training Program

Outputs: number of trainees in class, number of hours taught

Outcomes: number of placements in improved employment

---

than following the traditional practice of having unspent funds returned to the general treasury, so that agencies would not face the "use it or lose it" choice.[46]

4. **Reporting.** At the end of the year, agency reports should include service outcomes with their financial reports and in budget presentations. Audit and evaluation emphasize outcomes and de-emphasize details of how money was spent. Performance measures for individual agencies appear in the

---

[46]A strong internal control structure is necessary if agencies are to have greater flexibility regarding their finances. A strong control structure frees auditors to focus on performance rather than financial issues.

budget documents of well over half the states and many cities, although the extent to which responsibility and control focus on these measures, as opposed to the input categories, is generally limited.[47]

Performance, Outcome-Budgeting Experience

The outcome-based budget (as the city describes it) prepared by the City of Baltimore, Maryland, provides an excellent model of the format. In the budget, the mayor's office identifies six outcomes: better schools, safer streets, stronger neighborhoods, a growing economy, innovative government, and a cleaner and healthier city (one might call these programs). Specific operations of government are linked to these outcomes/programs, and service areas are responsible for achieving performance results that contribute to the objectives. Figure 6–6 shows how performance measures are integrated into the budget presentation for the animal services operations of the city Department of Health.

The budget clearly describes the service being provided, it summarizes funds for the service for the budget year and two earlier years, and provides performance measures—distinguishing between output, effectiveness, and outcome indexes—for the years. (The budget gives a detailed breakdown of the expenditures and of personnel devoted to the service in a section not reproduced here.) The budget presentation supports focuses on results and how they contribute to the city outcome areas. The outcome measure here—the percent of animals adopted, transferred to rescue organizations, or returned to owners—is designed to capture a clearly desirable result. Note that the raw number of adoptions, transfers, and returns would have been inappropriate: if the number of animals entering the shelter declines because there are fewer unwanted pets (a desirable result), then raw adoption numbers would decline, suggesting that the shelter performance was deteriorating, almost certainly not the case. The percentage conversion provides a supportable outcome indicator.

Performance, results-oriented budgeting has been introduced by national governments, including that of the United States, and many states and localities.[48] The most extensive application of these concepts onto U.S. federal budgeting was the Program Assessment Rating Tool (PART) system used in the administration of

---

[47]Melkers and Willoughby find that all but three states require strategic planning regarding agency mission, goals, and objectives and a process that requires measurable data on program outcomes. See "The State of the States: Performance-Based Budgeting Requirements in 47 out of 50," *Public Administration Review* 58 (January/February 1998): 66–79.

[48]The considerable scope of international experience is reviewed and analyzed in Aidan Rose, "Results-Oriented Budget Practices in OECD Countries," Working Paper 209, Overseas Development Institute, London, February 2003; Pedro Ariziti et al., *Results, Performance Budgeting and Trust in Government* (Washington, D.C.: World Bank, 2010); and Marc Robinson and Jim Bumby, "Does Performance Budgeting Work? An Analytical Review of the Empirical Literature," IMF Working Paper WP/05/210 (November 2005). For experience in a less-developed country, see Anand P. Gupta, "Evaluation of Governance: A Study of the Government of India's Outcome Budgeting," *Journal of Development Effectiveness* 2, no. 5 (2010): 566–73. It is usually more difficult to implement than it looks.

Figure 6–6.

Performance Measures an Integral Part of City of Baltimore Budget: Animal Services in Department of Health, Fiscal 2016

Service 716: Animal Services

Priority Outcome: Safer Streets　　　　　　　　　　　　　　**Agency: Health**

Service Description: This service protects residents from zoonotic diseases and animal attacks, and protects the animal population from neglect, abuse, and cruel treatment. This service also includes the Baltimore Animal Rescue and Care Shelter, which provides housing and care for shelter animals, lost and found, pet licenses, adoptions, volunteer, foster, rescue, and low~cost vaccination and microchip clinics.

Fiscal 2014 Actual

Fund	Dollars	Positions
General	$3,017,034	20
TOTAL	$3,017,034	20

Fiscal 2015 Budget

Dollars	Positions
$3,136,122	20
$3,136,122	20

Fiscal 2016 Recommended

Dollars	Positions
$3,164,962	20
$3,164,962	20

PERFORMANCE MEASURES

Type	Measure	FY12 Actual	FY13 Actual	FY14 Target	FY14 Actual	FY15 Target	FY16 Target
Output	# of animals entering shelter	12,648	12,649	*13,000*	10,844	*13,000*	*12,000*
Effectiveness	% of top 5 priority service requests closed on time	93%	91.4%	*95%*	86%	*95%*	*95%*
Outcome	% of animal abuse cases forwarded to the State Attorney's Office for prosecution resulting in convictions	38%	73%	*100%*	87%	*100%*	*90%*
Outcome	% of animals adopted, transferred to rescue organization, or returned to owners	60%	64%	*65%*	77%	*65%*	*80%*
311 receives 65 animal control calls every day; top service requests concern endangered animals, animal attacks, aggressive animals, and animals trapped in vacant buildings.							

President George W. Bush; this system is discussed in some detail in Appendix 6–2. Because the system was administrative only, it was in place only for that administration. Several other efforts to require considerable performance measurement by federal agencies have been made, although none have been directly integrated into the budget process. For example, the Chief Financial Officers Act of 1990 requires financial officers of federal agencies to develop and report systematic measures of performance for their agencies, and, even stronger, the Government Performance and Results Act (GRPA; P.L. 103–62) directs agencies to develop strategic plans, to measure their performance, and, at least tentatively, to work toward performance budgets.[49] GPRA documents presented to Congress, easily accessible on the Internet, give excellent illustrations of materials developed for outcome performance measurement (and output measures substituting for outcomes). Sidebar 6–2

---

[49]General Accounting Office, *Performance Budgeting, Past Initiatives Offer Insights for GPRA Implementation,* GAO/AIMD-97-46 (Washington, D.C.: General Accounting Office, 1997).

explains more of the GPRA activities. However, GPRA information, even though it is often impressive, is not presented with or integrated into the president's budget submission, and Congress has not made much use of those GPRA data in considering appropriations. At the state and local levels, the Government Accounting Standard Board (GASB) seeks to have annual financial statements include a *service efforts and accomplishments* (SEA) report. And most states and many localities do claim that they use performance measures, either as performance measure reports or directly in the budget process, as part of their budget development, review, and execution.[50] A perusal of budget presentations on the web will show the extent to which measures are integrated into the process and the extent to which they reflect outcomes.

Some Challenges for New Performance Budgeting

Moving the budgetary focus away from an input orientation seems to be getting it right for making public decisions. Nevertheless, there are some crucial concerns in this transition:

1. **The usefulness of agreement on what is to be accomplished.** The agency mission statement is the starting place for measures for the performance budget. Managers have to respond to elected executives, legislative bodies, and the general public. Programs often have multiple and conflicting objectives and disagreements about the relative importance of the objectives. Without strong consensus about agency objectives, establishing performance measurement and budget systems based on those measures will be difficult. Furthermore, there has to be agreement on the need to spend the money necessary to measure performance.[51]

2. **Performance budgets do not cross agencies.** Outcome measures give minimal help with comparisons among agencies, in other words, in answering the traditional budget allocation question: "How much to agency A, and how much to agency B?" There is no standard performance yardstick that applies across all agencies, the causal link between agency effort and performance outcome differs dramatically among agencies, and the ease of measuring outcomes varies widely among agencies. The results orientation

---

[50]A National Association of State Budget Officers report provides a good overview of state experiences with bringing performance data into budgeting: National Association of State Budget Officers, *Investing in Results, Using Performance Data to Inform State Budgeting*. Washington, D.C.: NASBO, 2014.

[51]Focused measures can be a problem. Under GPRA, the Internal Revenue Service defined the objective of at least 90 percent of total taxes owed being collected (up from around 82 percent). Congress started getting complaints about aggressive enforcement and complaints showed up in the media. The IRS switched to a "balanced measures" objective involving customer satisfaction, employee satisfaction, and quality work product, making it hard to tell that this was a tax collection agency. So much for the value of precision in defining missions, goals, and performance, at least for tax collectors. (Brian Friel, "IRS Learns Results Act Lesson," *GovExec.com Daily Briefing,* September 16, 1998. http://www.gov-exec.com/dailyfed/0998/091698b1.htm.)

can guide within each department, but government budgets have to allocate between departments, not just within. Suppose, for instance, that the Department of Homeland Security did not meet its targets, and the National Endowment for the Arts (NEA) did. Would Congress move funds between agencies on that basis? Or would it be reasonable to continue to pay attention to basic national priorities, which likely still rank homeland security above the programs of the NEA? Should funds for homeland security decrease, or should they increase, based on the missed performance target?

3. **Responsibility without control.** Agencies find results-oriented goals to be difficult to accept because they correctly understand that many measured performance outcomes may be outside their control. They do not want to be held responsible for objectives that they can only influence. They prefer to focus on activities or outputs because these can be controlled. For example, diligent effort by a local job-development agency can control the number of trainees run through its seminars, but many environmental conditions—especially overall economic conditions—determine how many of those graduates end up in lasting employment from any annual crop of graduates. Great effort by local schools may produce dismal educational results if parents and the community do not cooperate in the learning process. Agencies are reluctant to be responsible for objectives that they cannot fully control.

4. **Trust and no micromanagement.** New performance budgeting requires a different relationship between operating agencies and legislatures. If the agency is to be flexible in its service delivery and to be responsible for results instead of inputs, then the legislature must leave it alone. But legislatures do intervene. For example, Congress should not dictate national security provision inputs to the Defense Department, but it does with regard to what weapons systems (the A-10 Warthog being one example) should be retired and which military bases are redundant to national security needs. Some financial controls need to be relaxed, and agencies need the flexibility to reallocate funds. It is sometimes suggested that, because elected officials find micromanagement hard to resist, they ought not to be provided with line-item expenditure information at all.

5. **Refocused audit.** Audit can no longer focus on financial detail. Agencies would still be responsible for appropriations, but the detailed use of those appropriations, within the laws of financial propriety, would no longer be an oversight concern. Attention would be directed to performance measurement, achievement of outcome expectations, and audit of the performance measurement and reporting process, not to the expenditure details.

6. **Information overload.** When performance measurement becomes an element in the budget process, large quantities of information will be produced. More measures will get introduced, and measurement will become more important in making decisions. Everyone wants his or her own favorite included when measures start to matter. Experience in the states shows that decision makers become overloaded with the details and find it difficult to locate what would be useful to them. This potential overload means that it is

critical to have a distillation process to provide the most important elements for the decision makers and limit the measures that are reported to a manageable and useful number. One or two good measures are far more useful than a long list of ones that are not so good.[52]

7. **Complicated outcome measurement.** Outcome measurement is not easy for all government agencies, and many units eventually resort to output, not outcome, indicators. Frequently, client satisfaction surveys are part of the measurement process to gauge the quality of service provided.[53] An outcome orientation generally increases the administrative expense because some outcome measures are unlikely to emerge from the normal flow of agency operations, thus requiring agencies to undertake the dreaded task of gathering more data rather than fulfilling their mission. And there are questions of interpretation. For instance, if tax auditors find few mistakes, should that be taken as evidence of poor performance by the tax auditors, poor selection of returns for audit, or evidence of success in the tax authority's efforts to induce taxpayers to pay voluntarily without being audited? Are low arrest rates evidence of little crime or poor police work? A related concern is that performance approaches will discriminate against agencies with less-easily measurable outcomes; it is conceptually easier to measure the reduction in travel time associated with a transportation project than it is to quantify the enjoyment associated with a subsidized art show.

8. **Agencies cheat and manipulate.** Perhaps the most basic concern is with honest measurement. There is a principle in economics called Goodhart's Law, popularized to say: "When a measure becomes a target, it is no longer a good measure." Before there is anything riding on a particular measure, it can provide a good idea of how things are going. When stakes increase, people start manipulating operations to improve performance as measured, which may or may not have much to do with actual improved performance. For example, in 2004, the State Council of the Chinese government set a target of fewer traffic deaths for provincial authorities and informed officials that promotion required improved performance. Recorded deaths fell by about 50 percent by 2012: officials worked to keep traffic victims alive for eight days because they counted as traffic deaths only if the death was within seven days of the accident.[54] At worst, agencies may fudge the measures. For example, high-stakes testing in Atlanta public schools with budgets and teacher pay riding on the results appears to have caused rampant cheating, and some follow-up analysis suggests that the problem is national

---

[52]Performance measures reports typically provide a long laundry list of indicators, far more than should appear in a performance budget.

[53]Some governments, both in the United States and internationally, conduct citizen "report card" surveys of satisfaction with particular public services. Along with being an element in performance budget processes, they also contribute to campaigns for more open governance, accountability, and control of corruption. The International City/County Management Association conducts "citizen surveys" on contract for local jurisdictions to assist with such evaluation measurement.

[54]Eduardo Porter, "Grading Teachers by the Test," *New York Times*, March 24, 2015.

in scope.[55] Unaudited, self-reported information is the worst option of all for high-stakes performance measurement. Trust but verify is the standard—but it does require the verify part.

The new results-oriented budget focus has brought revisions in how all levels of government develop and present their budgets; vastly greater attention to measurement, testing, and citizen satisfaction surveys; and, most important, greater focus on outcomes or results. As with any other system for budgeting, a performance budgeting system may not remain in place for the long term as elections bring in administrations with different ideas about how to operate the expenditure process.

Seldom do systems do either as much as their advocates claim or as little as their opponents argue. Whether much will change in terms of real government performance and allocation of budget resources remains an open question. As Hilton and Joyce observe, "the development of better performance and cost information can itself spur greater attention to performance, even in places where an input focus has been ascendant. Transparency concerning the relationship between funding and results can shine a light on practices that result in failing to allocate resources toward desired societal ends."[56] If nothing else, the performance budget structures can make government operations more transparent.

Even the best performance outcome measures require political judgments for resource allocation. Outcomes are not the same for all agencies, so moving resources from Agency X to Agency Y will mean less of the outcome provided by X and more of the outcome provided by Y. But the outcomes come in different measures and likely benefit different components of the population. Does the resource shift make the public as a whole better off?[57] That is a call to be made by the political process, not a choice that can be scientifically dictated.

A next-wave effort at getting better results is evidence-based budgeting. As Sidebar 6–3 describes, it does not erect a budget system but does direct a revised thought process for budget development. The last budget of the Obama administration made a great effort to embody this process in preparation of agency budget requests.

---

[55]Heather Vogell, "Investigation into APS Cheating Finds Unethical Behavior across Every Level," *Atlanta Journal Constitution,* July 6, 2011; and Heather Vogell, John Perry, Alan Judd, and M. B. Pell, "Cheating Our Children: Suspicious Test Scores across the Nation," *Atlanta Journal Constitution,* March 25, 2012.

[56]Rita M. Hilton and Philip G. Joyce, "Performance Information and Budgeting in Historical and Comparative Perspective," in *Handbook of Public Administration,* ed. B. Guy Peters and Jon Pierre (London: Sage Publications, 2003), 411. So does it work? For an international assessment, see Marc Robinson and Jim Brumby, "Does Performance Budgeting Work? An Analytical Review of the Empirical Literature," International Monetary Fund Working Paper WP/05/210, Washington, D.C., 2005. In sum, mixed results at best.

[57]The Oakland Athletics pioneered the use of player performance statistics to identify the attributes that most contributed to winning baseball games. But this approach, called "moneyball," doesn't immediately translate into improving government performance. No single measure of overall value can gauge how well a city is doing because cities provide a bunch of services. It would be no comfort to a person whose house has just burned down because of slow fire department response to learn that the city's performance number has increased because of excellent library service. Governments should use germane performance data, ideally outcome data, to guide operations and choices, but trying to capture it all in a single number—like baseball wins—represents a misunderstanding of the multiservice, multiclientele nature of democratic government. (Apparently Boston thought it was possible: Peter Schworm, "Boston Eyes Single Number to Grade City Hall," *Boston Globe,* October 8, 2015).

Sidebar 6–3
Evidence-Based Budgeting

Evidence-based budgeting, at its essence, tries to implement the principle: "Don't do stupid stuff." It does not create a new budget system, but it does seek to employ analysis of program expenditures, outputs, and outcomes to identify returns on money spent, mostly with respect to social service programs. It seeks to use rigorous evaluation methods, including information from randomized experiments with proper controls (RCTs or randomized controlled trials), to provide evidence of program effectiveness and to use that evidence to make sure programs accomplish what they intend. It doesn't look simply for improvements in performance measures but, by use of randomized controls, considers whether the program was the *cause* of any performance improvement. How can one oppose using actual evidence in making government decisions? Indeed, one might wonder why agencies and administrations haven't been using evidence in making their decisions all along and, if they weren't, what were they using? Peter Orszag and John Bridgeland, fiscal officials in the Obama and George W. Bush administrations, say decision makers sure haven't been working with the program data:

> Evidence of success is barely considered when legislation is proposed and discussed in committee and on the floor of Congress. There is no systematic way in which members of Congress or other key decision makers are informed about that evidence or lack thereof. They instead tend to rely on ad hoc assessments provided by lobbyists and interest groups. And once legislation is passed and a program is up and running, there is no mechanism for automatically tracking its effectiveness, beyond counting the number of people served by a program, no matter the impact it has on their lives.[1]

That's not particularly encouraging, although probably not surprising.

The Office of Management and Budget directed federal agencies to prepare their requests for fiscal year 2014 using an "evidence-based" structure and that has continued through preparation of the 2017 budget. The idea was to require more attention to program evaluation in budget development. An OMB memorandum instructed that submissions should "include a separate section on agencies' most innovative uses of evidence and evaluation."[2] By evidence, the memo meant that agencies should employ program performance evaluations, rigorously conducted, as part of their budget development process.

The directive invited agencies to develop new program evaluations that capitalized on administrative data or new technologies, expanded evaluation efforts in existing programs, and provided systematic measurement of costs and cost per unit of outcome. The OMB sought to encourage agencies to use evidence to compare the cost-effectiveness of how they spent their money, including both funding across and within agencies. Agencies were expected to employ such performance evidence in their grant programs of all types. Examples include Departments of Justice and Labor programs that provide payments only after successes have been shown ("Pay for Success"). Evidence was expected to be the basis for enforcement of criminal, environment, and workplace safety laws, with agency allocation and reallocation of resources based on what program evidence shows. Finally, agencies were expected to improve their capacity to conduct evaluation research. Agencies are motherlodes of operating data down to the level of the individual program beneficiary, agencies can design program operations to create control and treatment groups, and evidence-based budgeting principles

**Sidebar 6–3
(continued)**

expect agencies to mine data from operations to identify what the impact of their programs actually is.

This instruction brings new emphasis, but the effort to bring program effectiveness evidence into budget development (and, with luck, budget adoption) is more a continuation of prior intentions than an entirely new idea. What may be notable in the instruction is that it encourages agencies to devote resources to evaluation (developing evidence) even as the agencies face diminished total funds. That direction of scarce resources may not be popular with agencies, given their normal interest in delivery of services to clientele, and using constrained budgets for evaluation must mean some sacrifice of service capacity. What is somewhat new is the intent to link funding to tiered evidence: projects receiving the most support are to be those with strongest evidence of effectiveness, and the least funded are to be approaches with high potential but without clear evidence.

The effort continues the path of budget reform and restructuring: a focus on outcomes, attention to performance, willingness to reallocate budgetary resources, and attention to effective allocation of scarce resources. The continuing problem is that the evidence about programs is fundamentally internal. That is, the effectiveness of a program is directed toward the achievement of its outcomes; for example, the program does or does not reduce infant mortality, and it does or does not achieve a reduction that is or is not better than an alternative way of reducing infant mortality. This information is critical with regard to establishing which programs might well be worth terminating or expanding with regard to approaches to reducing infant mortality. However, the information doesn't help cut across programs with different objectives—say, infant mortality versus adult literacy. There is no common measure; the valuable outcomes come in different measures, and the outcomes accrue to different people in society. Even with excellent outcome information—that such and such program effectively achieves these desirable outcomes—the best that the evidence can do is to inform the lawmakers.

State governments have also developed programs to integrate evidence from evaluations into their budget processes. The programs seek to reduce spending on programs that have not delivered expected results, to expand spending on successful programs, and to improve program accountability for outcomes. A recent report identifies state laws in roughly a dozen states that are designed to implement evidence-based budget choices: laws requiring agencies to categorize their programs according to evidence of effectiveness, providing grants and other funds to promote implementation of evidence-based programs in agencies, restricting funding for programs shown to be ineffective, requiring that agencies implement only programs that demonstrate at least a minimum standard of effectiveness, and providing funds to evidence-based programs.[3] There is insufficient evidence to allow any judgment as to the impact of these laws on state budget processes and outcomes.

One hopes that operating agencies and chief executives will employ evidence in crafting budgets, and one hopes that legislatures will employ evidence in making appropriations, but the evidence itself will not make the determination. Hard political choices, not collection of useful information, continue to be the heart of budgeting. Evidence can give ammunition to the

---

**Sidebar 6–3
(continued)**

---

political process, even though it will not drive choices by itself. We know more about doing solid program evaluation than we know about how to get that evaluation evidence into budget decisions.

[1]John Bridgeland and Peter Orszag, "Can Government Play Moneyball?" *The Atlantic*, July/August 2013.

[2]"Use of Evidence and Evaluation in the 2014 Budget," Memorandum to the Heads of Executive Departments and Agencies, M-12-14, May 18, 2012.

[3]"Legislating Evidence-Based Policymaking," Issue Brief from Pew–MacArthur Results First Initiative, Pew Charitable Trusts /MacArthur Foundation, March 2015. The state of Washington is regarded as a leader in these efforts.

Participatory Budgeting

Local, and sometimes state, budget processes include an opportunity for ordinary citizens to speak their mind about proposed expenditures before the legislative body votes to approve the budget. However, by the time of those budget hearings, virtually all fiscal decisions will have been made, so it amounts to telling the public what the decisions have been and giving them an opportunity to object. It leaves minimal opportunity for meaningful citizen input, and citizens certainly are not directly involved in making decisions. Choices are made by public administrators and by elected representatives, but *direct* citizen impact on those choices will necessarily be only at the margins. With the state of communication technology, it should be possible to get the interests of the population more directly into the decision process.[58] However, the systems of participatory budgeting go beyond citizen hearings, access to budget documents on websites, or televising budget deliberations. They attempt to alter the fabric of the budget process to integrate citizen input more fundamentally throughout the budget cycle, not just at the end of the legislative consideration phase. It doesn't attach some new openness on the traditional systems.

The process typically intends to direct more resources to lower-affluence parts of the jurisdiction and mostly involves decisions on infrastructure investment. In addition, the process is expected to increase the democratic legitimacy of budgetary actions taken because citizens play an increased direct role in identifying, discussing, and prioritizing spending projects.

The participatory budget process intends that many different stakeholders debate, prioritize, and monitor choices made about public expenditure so that ultimate choices are more transparently made, so that the process is more inclusive, and so that the results are more equitable. The system is characterized by direct citizen involvement in the development of the budget, direct citizen involvement in the monitoring of budget execution, and formal engagement of civil society organizations in the budget process.

---

[58]New England town hall meetings, in which all the citizenry gather to make fiscal decisions, might be seen as the ideal for public participation. However, the cost of assembly and the cost of reaching decisions make that model impractical and inefficient for larger governments.

It seeks to connect citizens to their governments and give a better sense of ownership and trust of public decisions. Citizens and their government, in a process of prioritization and joint decision, together establish the final allocation of public expenditures. The stakeholders are broadly determined to include the general public, poor and vulnerable groups including women, private businesses, organized citizen groups, representative bodies, and, in developing and transition countries, donor groups. The process seeks a wide spectrum of views. The executive still presents the budget proposal to a legislative body, and the legislative body still makes the final choice about putting the budget into law, but the public participates quite formally in the process. It seeks transparency, responsiveness, and broad representation in the budget process.

The participatory influence can be integrated into three stages of the budget process:

1. **Budget preparation.** Citizens participate in budget allocation according to priorities they have identified in meetings and workshops. Meetings will include neighborhood assemblies, "thematic" (program-type) meetings across the jurisdiction, and delegates meeting for jurisdiction-wide coordination. Expenditure and service monitoring information flow into the preparation.
2. **Expenditure monitoring.** Citizens track whether spending is consistent with allocations made in the adopted budget and track the flow of funds to agencies responsible for the delivery of public services.
3. **Service delivery.** Citizens monitor the quality and quantity of government services relative to the expenditures made for the services.

The main features of the process are the following:

1. Clearly defined regional boundaries within the territory of the government practicing participatory budgeting. In one of the most famous applications, the town of Porto Alegre, Brazil (population 1.4 million), is divided into sixteen regions for citizen meetings. These geographical structures are crucial for decision making and service monitoring.
2. Open meetings to discuss thematic issues (Porto Alegre has five areas: transportation; education, leisure, and culture; health and social welfare; economic development and taxation; and city organization and urban development), to decide strategic priorities, to develop action plans, and to monitor current results. Meetings occur both within the regions and according to the thematic issue areas. Priorities from these meetings complement the representative democratic structures. Tens of thousands of people are reported to participate in the Porto Alegre process, vastly more people than ever are directly involved in any local budget process in the United States (or most other places). Participants in these meetings receive information directly from operating departments and transmit their views directly to the agencies as budgets get developed. Budget discussions are going on long before any formal budget hearings would be.
3. An annual cycle of participation, planning, and meeting to regularly involve the citizenry.
4. A budget decision process that brings the priorities in the regions directly into the development and approval of the budget. The Porto Alegre process is particularly focused on the public works section of the budget (or the investment budget).

It is expected that the process will lead to more responsive and effective government, more equitable distribution of government services, greater consensus among the citizenry regarding government programs, stronger nongovernmental organizations, and improved support for government reforms and restructuring. It is particularly aimed at providing a voice for the traditionally underrepresented sections of the population, particularly those of lower affluence, and at controlling government corruption through openness and monitoring. It is a tool for good governance and effective decentralization of government. However, even in the Porto Alegre case, noted as a considerable success, only about 1.5 percent of the population regularly participates in the process. In Paris, 40,000 people voted either online or at one of 200 locations around the city, a lot of people but only around 1.8 percent of the population. Does a system in which this modest number of self-selected participants make fiscal decisions represent an improvement over a system in which freely and openly elected representatives make those decisions? Is it likely to get responsible fiscal decisions in a process that establishes spending programs without an equivalent discussion about how the programs will be paid for?

Countries in which some localities practice participatory budgeting include Albania, Brazil, Bolivia, the Czech Republic, Canada, France, Ireland, India, Uganda, the United Kingdom, Portugal, Romania, and South Africa.[59] Some U.S. cities have brought direct citizen participation into parts of budget development and allocation. New York City provides one example. During the development of its 2013 budget, discretionary capital budget funds were set aside in some council districts for citizen allocation. Budget delegates selected in district assemblies prepared budget proposals for those funds, and district residents voted to select the specific proposals to include in the budget. A similar council district allocation process has been employed in parts of Chicago, Boston, and St. Louis. In these applications, the funds have been from allocations assigned to council members for discretionary use in their districts, so getting greater direct citizen involvement both is feasible and likely represents improved allocation in the public interest. In Cambridge, Massachusetts, the city set aside $600,000 of the 2017 capital budget for participatory budgeting (its total governmental expenditures exceed $620 million, so this represents a modest portion of city spending). Its solicitation brought 540 ideas to be whittled down to twenty-four options by a city committee. A city referendum would select the winning projects. In the prior year cycle, six projects were selected: 100 new trees and tree wells, 20 laptops for the Community Learning Center, bilingual books for children learning English, a public toilet in Central Square, 8 bike repair stations, and free wifi in six outdoor locations.

These experiences are not for developing and adopting a full city budget.[60] They do get the public more directly involved in public spending (one wonders

---

[59]Case studies of participatory budgeting experiences from around the world are discussed in Anwar Shah, ed., *Participatory Budgeting* (Washington, D.C.: World Bank, 2007). World Bank documents provide the best available descriptions of the participatory budget process, its implementation, and its practice.

[60]For more information about the application and outcomes of participatory budgeting, see Aimee L. Franklin and Carol Ebdon, "Are We All Touching the Same Camel? Exploring a Model of Participatory Budgeting," *American Review of Public Administration* 35 (June 2005): 168–85; and Yves Cabannes, "Participatory Budgeting: A Significant Contribution to Participatory Democracy," *Environment and Urbanization* 16 (April 2004): 27–46. Porto Alegre uses the participatory process for up to 20 percent of its budget. The share for most entities is considerably lower. For instance, in Paris, the share was 5 percent of its investment (infrastructure) budget only.

if the budget delegates would be as enthusiastic about the spending if they were also being required to raise the money to finance the spending) than do traditional systems and make portions of the system more transparent than does posting city budget documents on a website.[61] To be explicit, the New York City and Chicago experiments involve citizen decisions about dividing the budgetary spoils distributed to local council districts, something like deciding the distribution of a political kickback in the fiscal process. Citizen decisions about this part of the budget are likely better than having distributions to political cronies. These programs should not be confused with the full integration of public participation into the city budget process through greater openness of fiscal information and general opportunities for public input to the fiscal program. They should not be regarded as a substitute for better openness in general.

Conclusion

Budget reforms try to get the best possible return to society from public spending. None provides the complete solution to the budget problem; it is wrong to expect any system to provide judgments that must be made by people. These systems, however, try to organize information so that decision makers can make choices in a reasonable and flexible fashion. People will continue to make budget decisions, and that is appropriate; the useful organization of information and the erection of reasonable organizational incentives are the roles of budget systems.[62] Each of the structures described here can represent significant improvements over the traditional, line-item, administrative-unit structure if executive, bureaucratic, and legislative branches choose to use them. In addition, there is no magic bullet that will replace budget judgment and budget politics with science. Furthermore, government officials are not likely to find for agency evaluation a public sector equivalent to the easily definable, measurable, and widely accepted indicators of performance that private sector profitability comparisons afford. What budget classification reform can do is provide performance data

---

[61]Another approach to bringing service choice down to the community level is the business improvement district, a nonprofit organization of entities in an area that have privately organized to finance the provision of extra services to the area (policing, sanitation, beautification, etc.) without calling on existing local governments. The district members decide on what services are to be provided and how their cost will be divided among district members. They are spending their own money, not revenues raised by a larger government, as it the case in the participatory budget model.

[62]Embedded in most efforts to reclassify and reform government budgeting is the assumption that there is a clear understanding of the link between government spending and results or outcomes. This confidence is misplaced if it is cast too broadly. In the government service area subjected to the greatest amount and intensity of study, primary and secondary education, Eric Hanushek's extensive and intensive review of 147 separately published studies leads him to the conclusion that "there is a consistency to the results: there appears to be no strong or systematic relationship between school expenditures and student performance. This is the case when expenditures are decomposed into underlying determinants and when expenditures are considered in the aggregate." Eric A. Hanushek, "The Economics of Schooling: Production and Efficiency in Public Schools," *Journal of Economic Literature* 24 (September 1986): 1162.

and other information when political decisions are made and provide information that might contribute to discussions more likely to lead to better results for the general public. Any system that moves attention toward outcomes and toward achievement of those outcomes has a better chance of working in the public interest than do traditional systems that direct attention toward what governments purchase. Furthermore, as systems fancies come and go officially, nothing every completely leaves and each reformed system leaves some elements even after it has been replaced.

QUESTIONS AND EXERCISES

1. Refer to question 1 from Chapter 3. What alternate budget classification systems are possible for the School of Public Affairs at Enormous State University? Identify (a) the measurable performance activities, programs, and outcomes for which the school might be responsible, (b) the budget classifications you would prescribe for each, and (c) the problems you would encounter in assigning spending to the categories.

2. The new mayor of a Midwestern city has developed a list of administration goals and objectives for the city: (a) establish effective government by incorporating improved information systems and management practices; (b) improve intergovernmental cooperation for more cost-effective service delivery; (c) build public support for administration priorities through two-way communication; (d) make timely investments in roads, utilities, sewers, parks, and alternative transportation systems to encourage responsible growth and sustain a healthy economy; (e) maintain and improve the city as a place where people can live and work without fear; (f) protect the community's natural assets and enhance environmental quality; (g) work to improve the economic health of the city in an equitable manner for all citizens; (h) support and facilitate access to basic social services for all citizens; (i) establish a customer-driven city workplace; and (j) maintain and improve park services and facilities. Use this statement to structure both a program budget format and a new performance budget format for the city. For the latter, identify measurable performance indicators.

3. The U.S. Coast Guard has five central missions: search and rescue, preservation of national marine resources, enforcement of federal laws at sea, ship safety in U.S. waters, and national defense. The first of these is recognized as its main job, but dealing with pollution and preserving marine resources takes the largest share of its budget.

   An article in *The Economist*, commenting on a 1999 budget request presentation by Admiral Robert Kramek (the request was for $2.77 billion), proclaimed:

   > He dwelt on something rare in the armed services: results. In the past four years, he proudly informed the legislators, the Coast Guard has saved 20,000 lives and $9.3 billion in property, seized 370,000 pounds of illicit drugs, interdicted (or assisted) 75,000 foreigners trying to enter America, reported 64,000 cases of marine pollution

and checked 59,000 fishing boats for possible catch violations. "We're a model of better government at least cost," said the Admiral. ("The Coast Guard: Keeping All Channels Open," *The Economist* 12 [September 1998]: 28–29.)

Discuss and answer the following questions:

a. Did Admiral Kramek provide outcomes as envisioned by mission- or results-oriented performance budgeting? Explain your answer.

b. From what you understand to be the Coast Guard mission, what sort of performance measures would you propose for use by the agency?

c. How could we test whether Admiral Kramek is right when he asserts that the Coast Guard is delivering "better government at least cost"?

d. What budgetary strategy is the admiral using, and what questions would you prepare for Admiral Kramek if you were on the staff of the appropriation subcommittee considering his request?

4. Select a government agency or a nonprofit organization. From documents available to you (budgets, financial reports, mission statements, legislation, media reporting, etc.) and your general knowledge about that entity, do the following: (a) identify the inputs used by the entity (personnel, contractual services, etc.), (b) identify the activities or outputs produced by the entity, and (c) identify the measurable performance outcomes of that entity. What new data systems (testing, sampling, surveying, etc.) might be necessary to produce the outcome measures? What environmental influences outside the easy control of the entity are important in shaping those measured outcomes? What budget classification system or systems does the entity currently use in its budget processes?

5. The local historical society museum is hoping to receive a municipal operating subsidy to help it with its finances and keep from having to increase its modest admission charge. However, your municipality expects each budget entity to include outcome-oriented performance measures with every budget request. What measures would you propose for the museum, using the standards previously identified in this chapter? You should consider the purpose of the museum, the outputs or activities conducted by the museum, and the measurable outcomes that would result from successful museum operations.

6. Monroe County is putting a needle exchange program in place to stop the spread of HIV and hepatitis C. How would you devise a system for developing evidence of the effectiveness of this program?

APPENDIX 6–1

United Nations Classification of Functions of Government

The United Nations classification of functions of government (COFOG) divides the major service commitments accepted by governments as follows:[63]

---

[63]United Nations, http://unstats.un.org/unsd/cr/registry/regcst.asp?Cl=4&Lg=1.

- General Public Service (legislative, executive, fiscal management, public debt service, etc.)
- Defense
- Public Order and Safety (police services, fire protection, courts, prisons)
- Economic Affairs (general economic, commercial, and labor affairs; agriculture, forestry, fishing, and hunting; fuel and energy; mining, manufacturing, and construction; transport; communications)
- Environmental Protection (waste management, waste water management, pollution abatement, protection of biodiversity and landscape)
- Housing and Community Amenities (housing development, community development, water supply, street lighting)
- Health (medical products, appliances, and equipment; outpatient services; hospital services; public health)
- Recreation, Culture, and Religion
- Education
- Social Protection (sickness and disability, old age, survivors, family and children, unemployment, housing)

Data in these programs or functional categories provide a good basis for making international comparisons and a good start for developing the framework for a program budget.

APPENDIX 6–2

The Program Assessment Rating Tool (PART) Performance Budgeting Experience

The administration of President George W. Bush employed the Program Assessment Rating Tool (PART) to develop its budgets from fiscal 2003 through fiscal 2009 in possibly the most comprehensive and ambitious program for integrating measured performance into the budget process. The first federal budget developed using PART explained that the process "asks not merely 'How much?'; it endeavors to explain 'How well?'"[64] The system sought to link requested resources to strategic and programmatic outcomes, to shift focus from expense items to resource allocation based on program goals and measured results, to identify full costs of program activities to link them to goals, and, overall, to move beyond inputs and outputs to outcomes.

The PART process systematically applied questions about each program of the federal government (there were scores for more than 1,000 programs; OMB worked with agencies to define and categorize them throughout the federal establishment) that focused on four general sections: (1) whether the program had a clear purpose and was well designed to meet its objectives; (2) whether

---

[64]Office of Management and Budget, *Budget of the United States Government, Fiscal 2003* (Washington, D.C.: U.S. Government Printing Office, 2002), 5.

the program had a strategic plan with valid annual and long-term goals; (3) rating the management of the program, including its financial oversight and program improvement efforts; and (4) the results that the program could report with accuracy and consistency. Scores for each section were weighted in the final evaluation: program purpose and design, 20 percent; strategic planning, 10 percent; program management, 20 percent; and results/accountability, 50 percent. This system focused on summary performance measures, not the direct measures discussed previously (e.g., percent of days with clean air), although the focus was on evaluated performance.

Figure 6A–1 illustrates the PART system with the Cultural Resource Stewardship program of the National Park Service of the Department of Interior. This program seeks to protect and preserve historic structures, archaeological sites, museum objects, and other cultural resources in the national parks. The figure identifies the performance measures for the program (the presentation identifies them according to whether they are outcomes, outputs, or efficiency improvements); the full display provides the questions and answers to the PART questions for the program.[65] Scores became one factor in developing the president's budget proposal.

The process was internal to the executive branch, although its results were transparent to all. And the years in which the PART process was in place did show an improvement in program performance, at least as measured by that process. From 2002 through 2007, the percent of programs found to be effective or moderately effective increased from 30 percent to 49 percent. Whether these ratings improvements were the product of improved performance, gamesmanship on the part of program administrators, the work of consulting firms hired to boost the scores, or grade inflation is beyond the scope of the present discussion. However, it is clear that program administrators paid close attention to the PART results process because the percent of programs not demonstrating results declined from 50 percent to 19 percent.[66]

What about its impact on the fiscal system, in other words, on presidential budgets and on Congress and appropriations? Congress did not use PART in its appropriation decisions, and PART was not well integrated with GPRA strategic planning and reporting.[67] A later GAO report found that the review process got agencies to increase their evaluation capacity to meet the needs of their programs, but not necessarily evaluation for broader objectives, and that a requirement for frequent evaluation may create superficial reviews of minimal use that overwhelm agency evaluation capacity.[68] From outside of government, a study

---

[65]PART scores were once posted on an Office of Management and Budget website, along with funding levels for each program, in the interest of transparency, but the end to PART has brought an end to this easy access.

[66]Office of Management and Budget, *Budget of the United States Government, Fiscal Year 2009, Analytical Perspectives* (Washington, D.C.: U.S. Government Printing Office, 2008).

[67]Government Accountability Office, *Performance Budgeting: Observations on the Use of OMB's Program Assessment Rating Tool for Fiscal Year 2004 Budget,* GAO-04-174 (Washington, D.C.: Government Accountability Office, 2004).

[68]Government Accountability Office, *Program Evaluation: OMB's PART Reviews Increased Agencies' Attention to Evidence of Program Results,* GAO-06-67 (Washington, D.C.: Government Accountability Office, 2005).

Figure 6A–1

Program Performance Measures in the PART Process: Cultural Resources Stewardship Program of National Park Service, 2008 Report

Type of Measure	Measure
Outcome	Percent of historic and prehistoric structures in good condition
Outcome	Percent of preservation and protection standards met at park museum facilities
Outcome	Percent of recorded archeological sites in good condition
Outcome	Percent of cultural landscapes in good condition
Output	Percent of historic and prehistoric structures that have complete and accurate inventory information
Output	Percent of museum objects cataloged and submitted to the National Catalog
Efficiency	Average cost to catalog a museum object
Outcome	Condition of all NPS historic buildings as measured by a Facility Condition Index.

SOURCE: Office of Management and Budget, Detailed Information in the National Park Service—Cultural Resource Stewardship Assessment. http://georgewbush-whitehouse.archives.gov/omb/expectmore/detail/10002356.2004.html

by Gilmour and Lewis of the fiscal 2004 budget found a modest connection between performance as measured by PART scores and OMB budget decisions, and the limited influence that appeared was on programs traditionally linked to Democrats. Merit seemed to matter only with regard to programs traditionally supported by the other party.[69] But the impact on federal appropriations is certainly unclear.

As with budget processes instituted by the executive branch, PART was abandoned when President Obama took office. The new administration brought no new comprehensive system like PART, PPBS, or ZBB but stressed identification of programs with inadequate performance, relying more on input from agencies for selection, thus replacing the heavily "top down" approach of PART.

---

[69]John B. Gilmour and David E. Lewis, "Does Performance Budgeting Work? An Examination of the Office of Management and Budget's PART Scores," *Public Administration Review* 66 (September/October 2006): 742–51.

CHAPTER 7

Capital Budgeting, Time Value of Money, and Cost-Benefit Analysis: Process, Structure, and Basic Tools

Chapter Contents

Why Have a Separate Capital Budget Process?

A Process for Managing Capital Expenditure
Planning
Budgeting
Implementation/Execution
Audit

Problems in Capital Budgeting

Accounting for Time: Discounting and Compounding
Compounding
Discounting
The Annuity Formula—A Special Case

Organizing Information for Choices: Cost-Benefit Analysis
Elements in Cost-Benefit Analysis
Some Special Problems of Cost-Benefit Analysis

Conclusion

Capital expenditures purchase physical assets that are expected to provide services for several years; the outlay will yield benefits in the future without having to repeat the purchase.[1] Capital spending also includes capital improvements or rehabilitation of physical assets that extends or enhances the useful life of these assets (as distinct from the operating expenditures for repair or maintenance expenditures, which assure functionality during the expected life of the asset).

Public capital assets, also called infrastructure, become inputs into production of both private and public goods and services. The Congressional Budget

---

[1]Not everything with enduring impact is a capital expenditure. The work of teachers also lasts for many years. But compensation for teachers does not belong in the capital investment category because, if you want the services of the teacher next year, you are going to have to pay again. Teacher pay is a recurring expenditure. Public buildings are not so demanding—pay to build them once and they continue delivering services for many years without paying again. The buildings will require maintenance, but this is a recurring operating cost, not a capital expenditure.

Office (CBO) writes, "The production and distribution of private economic output depends on public transportation and environmental facilities including highways, mass transit, railways, airports and airways, water resources, and water supply and wastewater treatment plants."[2] All these fit directly into production processes yielding *private* goods and services. Roads, sewers, and transportation systems have become part of the competition between states and localities for new industrial and commercial development, so a sound system of infrastructure finance represents a crucial factor for regional economic growth. But public infrastructure also enters into production processes that deliver *public* services: elementary and secondary school buildings, park and recreation areas, state hospitals, administrative complexes, jails and police facilities, fire stations, the defense establishment, and so on, and these are critical for society as well. Therefore, the public capital stock matters for the production of both private and public goods and services. Infrastructure failure can be catastrophic, as when the Mississippi River bridge in Minneapolis–St. Paul collapsed in 2007 or when the levees broke in New Orleans in 2005. But the costs of deficient or deteriorated public infrastructure are great even without catastrophe, as with traffic delays and extra fuel use when slowed by congestion or by potholes on highways, delays and crowding on elderly public transit systems, time spent waiting to take off from congested airports, loss of drinking water through leaking pipes, pollution with poorly treated sewage, and so on. Public capital stock acquired through the capital budgeting process is an important contributor to the quality of life enjoyed by the public.[3] In the United States, spending for public infrastructure—roads, bridges, school buildings, water supply, airports, and the like—is primarily a state and local government responsibility: in 2014, 93.9 percent of gross government investment in structures was by states and localities.[4] Over half of federal investment is for national defense assets, and much of that is for equipment and intellectual property products. Slightly over 60 percent of state capital expenditure is for transportation.

Capital expenditures can be combined with operating expenditures in a unified budget and budget process, or the government may employ a dual budget process with one budget for operating expenditures and a second one for capital expenditures. Regardless of approach, capital spending is different from spending for current operations. Three obvious differences are (1) that capital asset decisions can have future impact and thus merit extraordinary care (long life), (2) that capital assets usually have high price tags and their purchase may destabilize the finances of a

---

[2]Congressional Budget Office, *How Federal Spending for Infrastructure and Other Public Investments Affects the Economy* (Washington, D.C.: Congressional Budget Office, July 1991), x.

[3]Human capital and research and development spending also contribute to long-term economic growth, so this attribute is not unique to capital spending. See General Accounting Office, *Choosing Public Investments,* GAO/AIMD-93-25 (Washington, D.C.: General Accounting Office, July 1993). But teachers and researchers expect to be paid year after year, as noted previously, so spending to pay them is considerably different from spending to build a bridge.

[4]Bureau of Economic Analysis, *National Income and Product Accounts of the United States.* http://www.bea .gov. The state and local share of all government investments, including equipment and software with structures, is lower, only 55.7 percent of the total, primarily because of federal national defense purchases.

government (high price), and (3) that capital asset purchases tend to occur at irregular intervals and may need special attention in regard to scheduling (nonrecurring). Therefore, capital spending, whether done through a separate process or not, merits special attention.

Why Have a Separate Capital Budget Process?

A budget process helps decision makers select between individual programs for funding while keeping expenditures within a total resource constraint. Identifying capital projects for special attention, possibly even creating a separate budget for them, complicates an already complex process. For special treatment of capital acquisition to be defensible, it must make a substantial contribution to improved fiscal choice.

These are the arguments for a separate capital budget. First, separate consideration can improve both the efficiency and the equity of providing and financing nonrecurrent projects with long-term service flows. These projects serve the citizenry, for good or bad, for many years beyond the year of purchase. Considering them in a process that might allow financing by borrowing, not the annual balance expected of current operating expenditures, provides important opportunities to improve equity between generations and among local citizenry pools. In other words, the spending program in a capital budget can be covered either by revenue raised currently (current taxes, charges, grants, etc.; a pay-as-you-go system) or by borrowing on the promise to repay from future revenues (a pay-as-you-use system). Incurring debt for such projects is consistent with the "golden rule" of government finance and fiscal sustainability because the borrowing is to cover the acquisition of long-life capital assets. Future generations face the debt, but they also have the infrastructure financed by that debt and they will pay for the infrastructure as they use it. The spending in the capital budget must be covered (the money is raised from current revenue or debt sources), but the budget need not necessarily be balanced (total expenditure equals current revenue). The general standard is that operating budgets typically must be balanced; capital budgets, financed. The inequity of the pay-as-you-go approach is apparent: If a local government project with a thirty-year service life is constructed and paid for this year, no construction cost will be incurred during the remaining life of the project. Anyone entering the area tax-paying pool after the construction year (by moving into the area or by growing up) may receive project service without appropriate contribution. This inequity does not occur if the project is equitably paid for over its useful life.

The use of capital budgets can improve decision efficiency. In a combined budget, big-ticket investment looks expensive relative to consumption (operating expenditures), even though the true cost of that investment (its depreciation or its "wearing out") occurs over many years. Separate consideration can avoid that bias and improve the chances for more balanced responses to service demand.[5] High ticket prices for capital assets look less daunting if they aren't put in the same budget pot as expenditures for current services.

Second, special treatment of capital expenditure can stabilize tax rates when individual capital projects are large relative to the tax base of the host government. If a city with a tax base of $1.5 billion decided to construct a $150 million water reservoir, it would undoubtedly be dissuaded if it were required to collect sufficient revenue for construction in one year. The cost would be 10 percent of the total city tax base, hardly leaving enough tax capacity for police and fire protection, street operation, and so on. However, the reservoir may have a service life of fifty years or more. It is reasonable, then, to divide the construction cost over the service life, thus reducing the burden on the tax base each year and preventing the dramatic fluctuation in tax rates that would result from financing the project in the construction year. The case for a regular capital budget process is strong whenever projects are large enough to significantly influence tax rates. However, the entire capital budget need not be debt-financed to maintain stable tax rates; recurring capital outlays should be financed from current revenue; that is, if the government is buying police cars every year, it is logical to treat the purchase as a recurring expenditure and avoid debt finance.

Third, special reviews of capital budgeting are appropriate because capital projects are permanent—mistakes will be around for many years. Kenneth Howard describes the problem:

> If a new state office building is built today, it will stay there for a long time. Everybody may know by next year that it is in the wrong place, but not much can be done about moving it then. Perhaps it is disrupting the development of a downtown business district; perhaps it is affecting traffic flows and parking facilities in a most undesirable way; or perhaps its location makes it psychologically, if not geographically, far removed from certain segments of the population. Whatever these effects may be, they are real, and they will endure awhile. They should be anticipated to the fullest extent possible before the project is undertaken.[6]

The special reviews for capital expenditure will not prevent all mistakes, but they can reduce costly errors. Those reviews and associated planning processes can produce the orderly provision of public capital facilities to accommodate economic development. Thus, the capital budget process serves to reduce errors of both commission and omission in public infrastructure construction.

Finally, special reviews of capital expenditure provide valuable tools for managing limited fiscal resources, particularly in light of the special care required to plan

---

[5]Lennox Moak and Albert Hillhouse suggest that governments having financial trouble may find that identifiable capital projects are more easily postponable than are expenditures for operating agencies. A separate capital budget can improve the chances for preserving capital projects when the operating budget is under great pressure. See Moak and Hillhouse, *Concepts and Practices in Local Government Finance* (Chicago: Municipal Finance Officers Association, 1975), 98. Cities regularly use capital spending reductions as a means of dealing with difficult fiscal conditions. See Michael A. Pagano, "Balancing Cities' Books in 1992: An Assessment of City Fiscal Conditions," *Public Budgeting & Finance* 13 (Spring 1993): 28.

[6]S. Kenneth Howard, *Changing State Budgeting* (Lexington, Ky.: Council of State Governments, 1973), 241.

activities that necessitate long-term drains on those resources. Items in this budget tend to be "lumpy." The process provides a mechanism to smooth out peaks and valleys, regularize construction activity in an effort to avoid local bottlenecks that can delay projects and inflate their costs, avoid excessive drains on the tax base when projects must be paid for, and balance spending with the resources available within political, economic, and legal tax and debt limits.

American governments are mixed in regard to their utilization of dual budgets. The states are almost evenly divided between those legislatures receiving executive capital budget requests in a separate budget document and those receiving requests with the operating budget. There is no separate capital budget or capital budgeting process at the federal level. Capital and operating expenditures are mixed together throughout the budget process, and appropriations for big capital projects are made annually to provide Congress with greater control over spending.

The reasons supporting a separate capital budget are stronger for local and state governments than for the federal level. First, critics of a federal capital budget fear that a separate capital budget would create a bias toward deficit spending or, more accurately, add to the existing bias that is apparent in the historical record. The danger is that all items potentially definable as investment (and politicians love to refer to every dollar spent for anything as "investment") would be inserted into a debt-financed capital budget, even if the spending were recurring. It has been politically much easier for the federal government to borrow than to tax, so this extra incentive is dangerous.

Second, the federal government is so large that no single infrastructure project is likely to influence tax rates. Although a careful physical inventory and planning for estimated demand conditions are helpful, scheduling of projects to control tax rates is of little practical consequence. Large projects may, however, create "spikes" in budget authority to individual agencies—but that does not make a case for the smoothing that a capital budget process might create for the federal government as a whole.

Third, the federal government does not need the careful project planning inherent in capital budgeting to preserve its debt rating. The federal government has, after all, the ultimate power of printing money to cover deficits, and capital project financing is not a factor in the federal credit rating. Its debt rating is endangered primarily by arguments among politicians, not basic financial capacity, and not by finances directly.

Finally, skeptics say that another budget would simply provide federal bureaucrats and lawmakers with another way to conceal fiscal conditions. Adding operating capital to the existing on-budget/off-budget, federal fund/trust fund complications doesn't contribute to fiscal transparency and would likely muddle citizen understanding even more, even as it satisfies fiscal purists. Thus, the gains from capital budgeting at lower government levels, particularly local, may not be translated to a similar federal case.

Even without a distinct capital budget process, the federal budget has included outlays and budget authority for federal investment—outlays that yield long-term benefits—in a special section on federal investment expenditure for more than half a century. The coverage is included in the *Analytical Perspectives* volume of the budget.[7] Outlays are divided into (1) major public physical capital investment, (2) conduct of research and development, and (3) conduct of education and training. The information about federal investment outlays is greater than is found in quite a few state and local capital budgets, despite the absence of a federal capital budget. (Note the inclusion of both recurring and nonrecurring expenditures in the listing of investments. As observed previously, U.S. politicians like to refer to any kind of spending as an "investment in . . .")

Agency proposals for capital asset investment are expected to demonstrate a projected return on the investment that is clearly equal to or better than alternative uses of available public resources. Return may include improved mission performance in accordance with measures developed pursuant to the Government Performance and Results Act; reduced cost; increased quality, speed, or flexibility; and increased customer and employee satisfaction.[8]

The federal budget and budget process, however, remain unified, in that there is no other separation between capital and operating spending. Agencies develop operating and capital projects in the same budget cycle, Congress reviews proposals and makes appropriations without distinguishing between the two sorts of spending,[9] and there are no separate rules for the finance of capital as opposed to operating programs. Agency appropriations include budget authority for both operations and capital projects on the same basis. The budget process attempts to achieve full appropriation for long-term, large-ticket capital projects (e.g., the International Space Station) by a combination of current and advance appropriations. Up-front funding for the full cost allows Congress to control spending at the time of commitment. However, it requires agencies to bear that cost in the annual budget, even though returns will accrue over the long life of the project and the cost may absorb a considerable portion of discretionary spending.[10] Critics of the current system argue that this full cost/up-front funding discriminates against and discourages capital spending because it goes up against the small price tag of operating expenditures without distinguishing the fundamental difference in flow of returns.[11]

---

[7]Office of Management and Budget, *Budget of the United States Government, Fiscal Year 2010, Analytical Perspectives* (Washington, D.C.: U.S. Government Printing Office, 2009), 33–41. However, the investment program is not extended beyond the budget year.

[8]Office of Management and Budget, *Principles of Budgeting for Capital Asset Acquisitions,* Circular A-11, part 7 (Washington, D.C.: Office of Management and Budget, 2015).

[9]A General Accounting Office study reports that federal capital project requests provided to the appropriate House and Senate committees do not always identify the total cost of proposed projects (funding has been sought in increments, not total), have not always identified funds already spent on the project, and have often provided scant descriptions of the nature of the project. General Accounting Office, *Budget Issues: Agency Data Supporting Capital Funding Requests Could Be Improved,* GAO-01-770 (Washington, D.C.: General Accounting Office, June 2001).

[10]General Accounting Office, *Budget Issues: Budgeting for Federal Capital,* GAO/AIMD-97-5 (Washington, D.C.: General Accounting Office, November 1996), offers a good review of capital investment practices of the federal government and the problems that they create.

[11]Private capital budgeting is quite concerned with proper allowances for depreciation. This is important for defining profitability and for establishing the value of the business as a going concern. These are critical concerns for owners of the business. Owners of government—that is, us—are concerned about the services provided and the taxes we pay in their support and are not focused on either profitability or the value of the government if sold. Government depreciation charges might be useful for some internal management questions, but they are not so important for the owners.

A Process for Managing Capital Expenditure

The capital budget process, whether separate from the process for operating expenditures or part of a unified budget, seeks to constrain the financial impact of capital asset acquisition on the overall budget while delivering the infrastructure needed to satisfy the citizenry's public service demands. Formal capital budget processes operate in many different ways; using various terms, steps, and the sequencing of those steps; and function separately from the process producing the annual (operating) budget. The process outlined here is based on those from several different state and local governments. The processes are concerned with selecting capital projects from the multitude of possible alternatives, timing expenditure on the projects selected, and fitting capital projects into the overall financial program of the government. The politics of capital projects can be complicated because each project is at a known and specific location and will likely have specific impacts on the area surrounding it, some desirable (a new park) and possibly some not (a new incinerator or jail). NIMBY ("not in my back yard") is about capital projects, after all. This focuses citizen interests in ways far beyond concerns about, for instance, social programs or police protection, which have general impact.[12]

The capital budget typically becomes an element of the annual budget, either as a section of the overall budget or as a separate capital budget document.[13] The capital budget should have cost estimates (requests) for all infrastructure projects that are proposed, including both the proposed investment cost and the implications for the operating budget. The budget usually goes through the normal legislative review and enactment requirements of any expenditure program, and, once approved, spending follows the same control mechanisms as faced by any public expenditures. The future years of the capital budget may or may not be appropriated when the facility proposal is first considered, and the government may or may not honor future capital expenditure requirements as later components of the plan are proposed. Executives and their priorities change, as do legislatures. One would hope that an approved capital budget does not include facilities so repugnant as to bring their cancellation when legislatures and chief executives change, but later governments do not always feel bound by decisions made by their predecessors.

A fully developed capital budget process functions in some respects separately from the process for the annual budget, although they obviously intersect in the final stages of the cycle. The four elements in the capital budget process—planning, budgeting, implementation/execution, and audit—are specific applications of the standard budget cycle, although with some variations in the tasks undertaken in each. Table 7–1 provides a general outline of a capital budget process, one that can

---

[12]Participatory budget processes often focus exclusively on capital infrastructure because of that high citizen interest in getting the good stuff located nearby and the bad stuff located somewhere else.

[13]The federal system records the full cost of a capital asset as an obligation when resources are committed, and resulting cash expenditures are counted as outlays as payments are made. Budgetary control is on obligations. Many agencies would like to spread costs over several years, rather than facing a full up-front obligation, so they do not take such a large budget hit in the year that projects begin.

Table 7–1
Logical Flow of Capital Budget Process

Phase	Step	Result
Planning		
	Update inventory and assess asset condition	Inventory of infrastructure, analyze condition and adequacy of maintenance spending
	Identify projects	Project list with cost estimates (capital improvement plan), multiyear horizon
	Project evaluation	Detailed costing, estimation of any revenues, compare with strategic plans, cost-benefit analysis for most promising
	Project ranking	Establish ranking of projects, re-rank each year
Budgeting		
	Financing	Financing arrangements for projects to be included in the budget (borrowing, intergovernmental transfers, current revenues)
	Budget	Include expenditures in budget proposals of appropriate departments, placement in resource envelope available to government, inclusion of project operating costs in budget
Implementation/Execution		
	Procurement	Process for selection of contractors for projects
	Monitoring	Review of physical and financial progress of project, coordinate spending with revenue flow
Audit		
	External audit	Ex-post review of financial records, project completion

apply regardless of whether the government uses a unitary budget that includes both capital and operating expenditures in a single budget or whether it uses a dual budget system. The steps are those that are appropriate for implementation of a capital asset management program.

Planning

Governments need to start their infrastructure development programs with a good assessment of the existing situation. The necessary information base would include an inventory of the capital facilities owned by the government with these data for each facility: (1) its age, (2) an assessment of its condition, (3) its degree of use,

(4) its capacity, and (5) how much it would cost to replace. The amount initially paid for the facility is not of much use during the decision process. Such an inventory can help the government estimate needs for renewal, replacement, expansion, and retirement of its existing capital stock. It can also contribute information for the repair and maintenance portion of the operating budget. The level of detail for the inventory and the degree of accompanying analysis vary by the significance of the facility to the operations of the government. It is not unusual for governments to have no such inventory of what properties they own.

After the inventory, a catalog of possible infrastructure projects can be developed, along with general estimates of their cost. The government may have a capital improvement program (CIP), with a list of projects coming from government agencies and, sometimes, private organizations; each project proposal includes a justifying narrative and cost data. These project proposals may be screened by a government-wide planning department or a similar body to evaluate costs, locate interrelationships, and establish initial priorities. Some decisions can be guided by established service goals of the community. For instance, if a local government has certain fire protection standards it wants to achieve for all properties in its jurisdiction and it cannot achieve that goal because of infrastructure limitations, then this unmet standard can shape an element of the investment plan.[14]

A number of priority systems are possible. These include priorities based on (1) functional areas, such as natural resources, higher education, transportation infrastructure, or assistance for local government projects; (2) problem severity, such as the health and safety of the population, critical maintenance of facilities, facility improvements, and new construction; (3) status of support, such as the governor's priorities, agency priorities, legal or federal mandate, and passage of referenda; or (4) a formal scoring system according to ranked criteria.[15] Realistically, the priorities of the chief executive (governor or mayor) have to play an important role in making the choices, and the interests of the legislature cannot be ignored. Many states provide no clear ranking, but there does continue to be some preference for maintaining existing facilities against new construction.

Evaluating projects for the capital budget is not simple because the decisions intertwine economic, political, and social forces. An Urban Institute study identified a number of criteria that were important in evaluations done by local governments:

1. Fiscal impacts, including capital, operating, and maintenance costs; revenue effects; energy requirements; and legal liability
2. Health and safety effects on both the citizenry and government employees
3. Community economic effects on the tax base, employment, incomes of people and businesses, and neighborhoods

---

[14]A good guide for developing facilities plans is Alan Walter Steiss, *Strategic Facilities Planning, Capital Budgeting and Debt Administration* (Lanham, Md.: Lexington Books, 2005).

[15]National Association of State Budget Officers, *Capital Budgeting in the States* (Washington, D.C.: National Association of State Budget Officers, Spring 2014). The participatory budgeting process outlined in the previous chapter provides one approach to making these decisions.

4. Environmental, aesthetic, and social effects on the quality of life in the community
5. Disruptions and inconvenience created during the work on the project
6. Distributional effects across age and income groups, neighborhoods, business and individuals, people with and without automobiles, and people with and without disabilities
7. Feasibility in terms of public support, interest-group opposition, special federal or state permitting procedures, consistency with comprehensive plans, and legal questions
8. Implications of deferring the project to a later year
9. Amount of uncertainty and risk with regard to cost and other estimates, technology, and the like
10. Effects on relationships with other governments or quasi-governmental agencies that serve the area
11. Effects on the cost or impacts of other capital projects[16]

The extent to which these concerns matter differs across types of projects—a new jail raises different questions than a sewage-treatment plant, for instance. Furthermore, evaluation signals may conflict for particular projects. But these are the kinds of questions that apply when evaluating such choices. Table 7–2 identifies several standard questions that budget examiners raise. Because capital projects are place-specific, political pressures can be intense. Some projects are desirable and can become parts of pork-barrel trading and rewards; others may be unattractive and subject to considerable protest from residents of the host locality. For example, controversy surrounds proposals for both a new community college and a nuclear waste storage facility.

This screening is particularly concerned with scheduling: projects should be timed to avoid waste (the new sewers should be put in before the streets are resurfaced), predetermined program emphases should be implemented, and projects that can be postponed should be identified.[17] Part of this priority review may be linked to a community (or state) master plan—a long-term (ten- to twenty-five-year), broad-gauge estimate of community growth encompassing estimated needs for public improvements and controls on private use of property. Because long-term forecasts of social, demographic, and economic behavior are inaccurate, that plan should not be taken too seriously as a guide to actions if the government intends to base its operations on what people want as opposed to the schemes of politicians and bureaucrats.

The capital program ordinarily is developed in agencies, but with central instruction, oversight, and coordination. Governments are becoming especially concerned that CIP outcomes contribute to overall government goals. The final capital improvement program has a segment scheduled for each year of its multiyear span.

---

[16]Harry P. Hatry, "Guide to Setting Priorities for Capital Investment," *Guides to Managing Urban Capital* (Washington, D.C.: Urban Institute, 1984), 5: 716.
[17]Moak and Hillhouse, *Concepts and Practices in Local Government Finance,* 104–5.

Table 7–2
Selected Questions for a Capital Budget Request

What evidence is given of the need for the project, and what happens if the project is not funded?

What benefits are claimed for the project, and how convincing are the claims?

What plans have been developed for the project?

What happens if the project is delayed another year?

How sensitive is the justification to changed circumstances: population growth or decline, major technological change, decline or increase in service demand, change in government structure, actions of other governments or businesses, and so on?

Is the capital cost comparable with experience on similar projects here and elsewhere?

Are all costs—land acquisition, planning, insurance, and the like—included in the request?

What are the operating costs for the life of the project? Are they reasonable and affordable? Could project design changes allow savings?

Can the project more properly be financed by someone else? By a private business, by another government, or through some partnership arrangement?

Are there other options? Renovating or retrofitting existing infrastructure? Leasing?

What financing options are appropriate: current budget, general obligation bonds, revenue bonds, lease-purchase agreement?

The capital budget proposal for the year includes current-year expenditures from the capital improvement program.

An analysis of project costs and time schedules in the CIP ordinarily shows a need for reprioritization of projects. Because priorities change across the years, the plan should be revised annually to create a rolling, multiyear investment plan. (Unfortunately, some governments develop a master plan with the intention that it will be permanent for years into the future and try to stick with it, even as conditions change.) The plan should include the time schedule and estimated costs for all projects in the plan. Such a multiyear plan should help the government manage its limited financial resources, induce the government to manage toward more cost-effective approaches to infrastructure development, and assist with prudence in the financial management of infrastructure acquisition.

Budgeting

The government must keep its infrastructure development program within its financial capacity. The limit to its capacity depends on several factors, including the government's operating expenditure level, the fundamental revenue capacity of the government, any revenues produced by the infrastructure facility itself, the extent to which other governments or private entities will share the cost of the infrastructure facilities or of their operation, and, if the infrastructure is to be financed with borrowed funds, the debt options available to the government. Any impact of the facility on recurring expenditures of the government must be part of the financial analysis; facilities can either reduce or increase the operating expenditures of a government.

This part of the process coordinates a financial analysis of the government with the facility additions envisioned in the capital improvement program. This interrelationship is vital because of the long-term fiscal commitments that such facilities involve. Just as a poorly conceived physical structure can disrupt a city for many years, a poorly conceived financing approach can disrupt that city's fiscal condition. Finance officers must examine the present and anticipated revenue-and-expenditure profile to determine the financial cushion available for new projects. Particularly important are the status of existing debt issues (Will any debt issues be retired soon? Will funds be available to meet contractual debt service—principal and interest—payments? Are there needs for extra funds for early bond retirement?), estimated growth profile of the tax base, and potential for new revenue sources. This fiscal profile, year by year, may then be related to the priority list of projects, again scheduled by years. In this analysis, fiscal officers usually consider the financing alternatives available for specific projects (special assessments for sidewalks, user charges for water utilities, state or federal aid for highways, etc.), and further reports will have financing sources attached to projects. Choices also need to be made about whether to finance by borrowing (general or limited obligation bonds), by use of capital reserve funds (special funds accumulated over time for future capital spending), or from current sources (pay-as-you-go financing). Some projects may involve a public-private partnership (P3), in other words, a joint ownership and financing arrangement between a government and a private business (an approach that requires a durable revenue stream to pay for the project over its life; the private firm does not participate out of a will for the common good, but out of a desire for profit). From those considerations, the project list is revised in preparation for its insertion into the annual budget process.

The capital component for the annual budget—infrastructure investment—must be prepared to be transmitted either in a capital budget or as an element of a unified budget. Cost estimates for projects need to be prepared with greater precision than was sufficient for the capital plan, and justifications must be developed in the format prescribed for that budget cycle. The financial analysis may indicate that the full project schedule can remain intact for the year, but more often fiscal conditions require choices to fit a proposal to the scarce available resources.

The Government Finance Officers Association "best practices" guide identifies the following as being necessary elements of a capital budget:

- A definition of capital expenditures for the entity.
- Summary information of capital projects by fund and category.
- A schedule for completion of the project, including phases of the project, estimated funding requirements for future years, and planned timing for acquisition, design, and construction activities.

- Description of general scope of the project, including expected service and financial benefits to the jurisdiction.
- A description of any impact the project will have on the current or future operating budgets.
- Estimated cost of the project, based on recent and accurate sources of information.
- Identified funding sources for all aspects of the project, specifically financing any financing requirement for the upcoming fiscal year.
- Funding authority based either on total estimated project cost or estimated project cost for the upcoming fiscal year.
- Any analytical information deemed helpful for setting capital priorities, including cost-benefit comparisons and related capital projects.[18]

The projects surviving agency and executive cuts become the capital section of the annual budget. The document usually provides a distribution of projects by function and agency, shows prior and estimated future costs of the project (initial appropriations may well have been annual; each year's construction plan requires a new appropriation), and summarizes sources of financing (type of debt, aid, etc.). The capital improvement program thus feeds the capital budget proposal for the next year, subject to revisions produced by the environmental conditions and the legislative process. The projects are reviewed by the legislature and sometimes are substantially modified. When projects are approved, provision must also be made in the operating budget for operation and maintenance of the completed facility. A new civic arena will not be usable if the operating budget has no money for its interior lighting, and the new convention center will not meet its expectations if no money is available for marketing.

Total government expenditure includes both operating expenditures from the operating budget and capital purchases from the capital budget. Operating expenditures are normally financed by current revenue (taxes, grants, charges, etc., collected in the current year). If operating expenditures are financed by borrowing instead of by current revenue, the current-period expenditures must be paid in the future, along with necessary interest. Thus, that future period will bear the costs of both current and past operating expenditures; the overhang from previous years can severely restrict the capacity to provide necessary services. That is why the operating portion of the budget needs to be balanced for long-term fiscal sustainability.

In terms of the comprehensive budget, the revenue that must be generated in any budget year equals the operating budget plus a capital project component. The latter equals capital items purchased without debt plus the *debt-service* requirements (interest and repayment of principal) on borrowing for capital items purchased in prior years. Those debt costs would ideally approximate a depreciation charge for capital assets acquired in the past; serial bonds (bonds in a single project issue that are to be paid off at various dates through the life of the project) can provide a rough approximation of that cost distribution. Debt financing is discussed in detail in Chapter 15.

---

[18]Government Finance Officers Association, "GFOA Best Practice: Incorporating a Capital Project Budget in the Budget Process," approved by GFOA Executive Board, January 2007.

Implementation/Execution

The third step in the capital budget process is execution of projects for which funds have been appropriated. Special attention must be given to (1) the rules (bidding, procurement, etc.) under which contracts can be issued; (2) controls to keep project work on schedule, so that facilities will be completed as planned; and (3) monitoring to keep project cost within budget. A full capital asset management program also requires a scheme for financing routine maintenance and upgrading of capital assets (not as politically attractive as building new facilities) and a system for keeping a current inventory of capital assets, thus feeding back into the beginning of the process.

Audit

External audit for capital projects typically follows the same cycle and procedures as does external audit for the rest of the budget. It can become more critical with capital spending because of the sums of money involved and the accompanying attractiveness of cheating for personal advantage.

Problems in Capital Budgeting

As is always the case with mechanisms to help make public decisions, there are problems in applying capital budgeting. First, the capital improvement/capital budget process assumes a continuous cycle of reappraisal and revaluation of project proposals. The cycle is necessary because the world changes, causing substantial changes in the value of public projects. For instance, decisions between mass transit and highways may differ, depending on whether the price of motor fuel is expected to be $3 per gallon or $6 per gallon. Unfortunately, many processes assume established priorities to be unchangeable, even in the face of different project costs and different project demands. As Howard points out, "Too often cost fluctuations do not generate a reassessment of priority rankings; original rankings are retained despite the fluctuations."[19] In a related manner, the time a project has spent in the priority queue sometimes establishes its priority rank; all old project proposals have higher rankings than any new ones. That approach makes no sense because time alone does not improve the viability of a marginal project. Indeed, items entering the priority queue some years before may, by the time they reach the top of the list, have outlived their usefulness or may have been superseded by adjustments made by people and markets. The project may have gone unfunded for many years because sensible people in the administration understood that the project would be a bad use of money. The passage of time has not made it any better.

---

[19]Howard, *Changing State Budgeting,* 256.

Second, availability of funds can alter decisions. The appropriate approach in establishing final priorities should involve a general comparison of the cost of the project with the project's return to the community—the money's source doesn't matter in this comparison. Some projects can get favored treatment, however, because earmarked funds are available (a special tax creates a fund pool that can be spent only on one class of project), because they produce revenue that can be pledged to repayment of revenue bonds without identifiable tax burden or the need to satisfy restrictions placed on general debt, because federal or state assistance is available for particular projects, or because a private partner is contributing something to the project. If somebody else (a donor or a different level of government) is paying for a large share of the cost of the project, that cannot be ignored when making project choices. The project becomes cheaper and should be evaluated on its discounted cost.

Third, capital budgeting can unduly and uneconomically favor the use of debt finance. Borrowing to purchase capital assets may not always be desirable. For instance, items that are purchased regularly and in considerable numbers—vehicles used by a larger city government, for instance, or buses for a large school district—may be more economically purchased on a regular-flow basis, even though the purchase of individual vehicles would appear to be a good candidate for debt finance.

Finally, there is a standard problem in all public decisions: establishing priorities. How do items get into the capital budget? Cost-benefit analysis, examined in a later section, provides some assistance, but as with operating programs, there are no unambiguous answers. Projects that the elected chief executive is interested in always have a good shot at being included.

Accounting for Time: Discounting and Compounding

The principles of discounting and compounding are the building blocks of most financial analysis. Not only are they used in capital budgeting but also, as is seen in later sections, they are critical for cost-benefit analysis, debt administration, fund investment, and tax policy. An understanding of the time-value concept is essential to becoming fully functional in government finance. Its application is vital in infrastructure finance. The costs and benefits of most public projects, particularly those long-life, high-price capital infrastructure projects, seldom occur in any single year. More often than not, an initial capital expenditure is made at the beginning—for instance, when a fire station is constructed—and both operating cost and program returns accrue over a long project life. In that event, special attention must be given to the timing of the flows, recognizing that a return available only at some point in the future has less value than an equal return available now.

The approach for comparing such impacts on personal, business, and public finance is discounting, a process of converting a stream of returns or costs incurred at different points in time to a single present value. The present value accounts for both the absolute size and the timing of impacts of a proposed action. It applies the concept of *time value of money*.

Why is a payment of $100 received one year from now not equivalent to $100 received now? If inflation's erosion of purchasing power and the uncertainty of the future seem to make the answer obvious, assume that the $100 is certain to be received and has been adjusted for price-level changes: the reason for discounting is related neither to inflation nor to uncertainty. The reason is simply that the $100 available now can yield a flow of valuable services (or interest) throughout the year. Or, even more to the point, the private market tells us that people must be compensated if they sacrifice current use of resources for future use. At the end of the year, the holder could have $100 plus the flow received from use of the $100 during the year. Therefore, $100 now has greater value than does $100 received at the end of the year. As the date of receipt is more distant, the present value of a given dollar amount is lower: the flow of services between now and then would be greater.

Compounding

Although the principle of time value applies to any resource or service, the mechanics are most often done using market-exchange equivalents (dollar values) of those returns, and the analysis uses investment for interest as the earned service flow. Thus, $X available now (the principal) becomes $X plus $X times the rate of interest (the principal plus interest earned on that principal) at the end of one year. Suppose the appropriate rate of interest is 5 percent; if $1,000 is invested today, it will accumulate to $1,050 by the end of the year. In other words,

$1,050 = $1,000 + ($1,000 × 0.05)

or

Amount at end of year = Original principal + Interest earned

Algebraically, if r = the rate of interest, PV = the present amount, and FV_1 = the amount at the end of a year, then

$$FV_1 = PV + PV \times r \quad \text{or} \quad FV_1 = PV(1+r)$$

that is, FV_1 equals the original principal (PV) plus accumulated interest ($PV \times r$).

Many policy and management questions involve multiple-year decisions in which the returns are permitted to compound over several years. In other words, the principal plus accumulated interest is reinvested and allowed to accumulate. An example is calculation of the amount to which $1,000 would have accumulated at the end of five years with 5 percent annual interest. Figure 7–1 shows annual account balances. There is an easier way, however, to compute compound interest. Using the symbols previously introduced for values now and values at the end of a year, the calculations look like this:

At the end of the first year:

$$FV_1 = PV(1+0.05) = PV(1.05)$$

Figure 7–1
Compounding

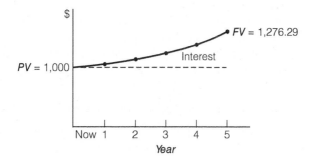

Initial Deposit, $1,000	Interest Earned (interest rate × previous balance)	Account Balance
End of year:		
1	$50.00	$1,050.00
2	52.50	1,102.50
3	55.13	1,157.63
4	57.88	1,215.51
5	60.78	1,276.29

At the end of the second year, the account balance would increase from interest earned:

$$FV_2 = FV_1(1.05) = PV(1.05)(1.05) = PV(1.05)^2$$

The same increase from interest earned occurs at the end of the third year:

$$FV_3 = FV_2(1.05) = PV(1.05)(1.05)(1.05) = PV(1.05)^3$$

For the fourth year,

$$FV_4 = FV_3(1.05) = PV(1.05)(1.05)(1.05)(1.05) = PV(1.05)^4$$

And so on. The same process applies regardless of the number of years. By now you should get the message: in general, if PV = the present amount, r = the appropriate interest rate, n = the number of periods of compounding, and FV_n = the account balance at the end of the periods, then

$$FV_n = PV(1+r)^n$$

From the previous example,

$$FV_5 = PV(1.05)^5 = \$1,000(1.05)^5 = \$1,276.28$$

With each passing year, the annual increase in value gets higher. That is because the interest compounds, which means that interest is earned on interest received in prior years. Private financial advisors talk about the "magic of compounding" and earn their living by encouraging people to invest and leave their money invested to get that magic. It isn't magic, but it does work—and not just in terms of the financial advisors getting their fee.

Financial contracts often provide for compounding more frequently than once a year. The compounding formula can easily be adjusted to allow for semiannual, quarterly, or any other regular frequency-of-interest payment. For example, suppose interest is paid twice a year. With an annual rate of 5 percent, that system would roughly mean 2.5 percent interest is paid for the first half of the year and 2.5 percent is paid for the second half of the year. Thus, principal plus interest amounts at the end of the half-years would be:

$$FV_1 = PV(1 + (0.05/2)) \qquad \text{(balance at end of one half year)}$$
$$FV_2 = PV(1 + (0.05/2))^2 \qquad \text{(balance at end of two half years)}$$
$$FV_3 = PV(1 + (0.05/2))^3 \qquad \text{(balance at end of three half years)}$$

and so on. Thus, at the end of n years,

$$FV_n = PV(1 + (0.05/2))^n$$

In general, if interest is added x times per year and other definitions are as before,

$$FV_n = PV(1 + (r/x))^n$$

More frequent compounding means the future value will be higher.

Discounting

Discounting adjusts sums to be received in the future to their present-value equivalent, the amount that will accumulate to that future sum if invested at prevailing interest rates. It amounts to going in the other direction from compounding. Recall that FV_1, the accumulated balance at the end of one year, equals $PV(1 + r)$, the balance at the start of the year multiplied by 1 plus the rate of interest. That formula can be algebraically rearranged to become

$$PV = FV_n/(1 + r)$$

This means that amount PV invested at interest rate r will grow to FV_1 by the end of the year. Suppose $1,000 will be received at the end of one year ($FV = 1,000$). If the interest rate that could be earned is 5 percent, what sum today (PV) would accumulate to $1,000 by the end of the year? Calculate the amount by use of the present-value formula:

$$PV = \$1,000/(1+0.05) = \$952.38$$

That means that $952.38 now, plus 5 percent interest earned in one year ($952.38 $\times$ 0.05 = 47.62$) equals $1,000: the present-value equivalent of $1,000 received at the end of one year when the available prevailing interest rate is 5 percent is $952.38. That prevailing rate is called the discount rate.

What happens if the return is received more than one year into the future? The same logic of adjusting for interest that could have been earned still applies, but the computations look messier because the interest earned would compound. In other words, interest earned during the first year would earn interest in the second year, and so on through the years. The general formula for compounding, $FV_n = PV(1 + r)^n$, can be rearranged in the same way that the single-year compounding formula was rearranged to produce the general present-value formula:

$$PV = FV_n / (1+r)^n$$

where

PV = the present-value equivalent,
FV_n = a value received in the future,
$\quad r$ = the discount rate, and
$\quad n$ = the number of years into the future that the sum is received.

For example, $800 received ten years in the future, assuming a 10 percent discount rate, would have a present value of $800/(1 + 0.10)^{10}$, or $308.43.

Projects yielding dramatically different returns over time can and must be compared using this technique. Suppose an agency has two projects under consideration. Each costs $1,900 (all occurring at the present), but the profile of returns from the projects differs substantially across the five years of the project:

Received at End of Year	Project A	Project B
1	1,000	480
2	300	480
3	1,000	480
4	0	480
5	0	480

Neither project lasts beyond the fifth year. Which project yields greater net benefits? Recognize that simple addition of returns—$2,300 for project A and $2,400 for project B—is wrong because the timing of those returns is not the same.

An accurate comparison requires that both streams be converted to their present-value equivalents. Suppose that prevailing interest rate conditions indicate that resources should earn a 10 percent return. Ten percent is then a reasonable discount rate to use, with the following results:

Received at End of Year	Discount Factor	Project A Return ($)	Discounted ($)	Project B Return ($)	Discounted ($)
1	$1/(1.1) = 0.909$	1,000	909	480	436
2	$1/(1.1)^2 = 0.826$	300	248	480	396
3	$1/(1.1)^3 = 0.751$	1,000	751	480	360
4	$1/(1.1)^4 = 0.683$	0	0	480	328
5	$1/(1.1)^5 = 0.621$	0	0	480	298
Total			1,908		1,818

Under those conditions, the present value of project A is $1,908 and that of project B is $1,818. Of the two projects, only A has a value exceeding its cost.

What would happen if 3 percent were the appropriate discount rate? As the following table shows, the present value of both would be above the cost of the projects.

Received at End of Year	Discount Factor	Project A Return ($)	Discounted ($)	Project B Return ($)	Discounted ($)
1	$1/(1.03) = 0.971$	1,000	971	480	466
2	$1/(1.03)^2 = 0.943$	300	283	480	453
3	$1/(1.03)^3 = 0.915$	1,000	915	480	439
4	$1/(1.03)^4 = 0.888$	0	0	480	426
5	$1/(1.03)^5 = 0.863$	0	0	480	414
Total			2,169		2,198

In fact, project B now has a present value greater than that of project A because returns in the future make greater contributions to present value when the discount rate is lower. Choice of the appropriate discount rate clearly matters for public decisions—an artificially high or low rate can lead to wasteful choices.

Analysts sometimes compare alternatives by determining what discount rate would cause the present value of projects under consideration to be equal. Thus, the present value of projects A and B would be the same at a rate around 4 percent. If the rate is above that level, A is better; if below, B is better. The discount rate that would equate the two streams is called the *internal rate of return*.

The Annuity Formula—A Special Case

In some situations, the income stream to be discounted may be constant for several years. For instance, a new maintenance garage might reduce costs by $20,000 per year for twenty-five years, and that cost savings is to be compared with the construction cost of the garage. The flow in each year could be discounted back to the present as discussed previously; a quicker approach entails use of an annuity formula to compute the present value of the income stream in a single computation. This formula does the same discounting, but it has been mathematically simplified. The present value of the annuity flow equals:

$$PV = C \times [(1 - (1/(1 + r)^n))/r]$$

Where PV = present value of annuity flow, C = amount of periodic payment, r = discount rate per period, and n = number of periodic payments.

All rules about more frequent compounding (quarterly, semiannually, monthly) apply in this formula as well. In the example here, the present value of those maintenance garage cost savings if r = 5 percent would equal

$$PV = 20,000 \times [(1 - (1/(1.05)^{25}))/.05] = \$281,880$$

This formula is used later in bond pricing (Chapter 15) and in converting a capital cost into an annualized cost equivalent.

Organizing Information for Choices: Cost-Benefit Analysis[20]

Because society cannot afford to waste its scarce resources, judging whether a particular program is worth its cost is a constant problem in public program choice. Cost-benefit analysis provides a way of organizing information about a program under consideration so that priorities may be reasonably established.[21] A private firm considers a major project (say, the purchase of a new delivery truck to replace an older, smaller one) and compares the anticipated increase in revenue from the new truck with the anticipated increase in costs. There is no sense using resources badly, whether the use is by a private firm or by a government.

Cost-benefit analysis is the government analog to that process of private capital budgeting. Governments can use the tool for assistance in making decisions as diverse as purchasing information technology systems, modernizing vehicle fleets, developing water-resource projects, developing communicable disease control programs, and building new highways and bridges. It has also been used to evaluate numerous

---

[20]Anyone intending to apply cost-benefit analysis should read Scott Farrow, "How (Not) to Lie with Benefit–Cost Analysis," *The Economist's Voice* 10 (2013): 45–50, for a statement of several best practices for use of the technique in informing policy choices.

[21]One source for more complete coverage of cost-benefit analysis is Edward M. Gramlich, *Benefit-Cost Analysis of Government Programs,* 2nd ed. (Englewood Cliffs, N.J.: Prentice Hall, 1990).

government regulations.[22] For capital budget purposes, however, cost-benefit analysis is similar to private decision-making processes: the analysis estimates whether the gain to society (benefit) from the project is greater than the social sacrifice (cost) required to produce the project. If so, the project is worthwhile; if not, the project is not worthwhile. Worthwhile projects improve economic conditions in that worthwhile projects direct resources where their use provides a greater return than would alternative uses.

Skeptics point out that what characterizes the public decision process is political bargaining, not an exercise in rational consideration by nonpolitical administrators.[23] So what service can cost-benefit analysis provide? First, the analysis augments the political influence of underrepresented potential beneficiaries and identifies the position of cost bearers. A display of costs and benefits makes it more difficult for the unrepresented to be ignored in political bargaining. In some instances, it can be a valuable weapon (for either side) in the "it pays for itself" budget strategy. Second, economic efficiency—the guiding force of cost-benefit analysis—is but one of several public goals. For example, a bus route may go a particular route to provide a low-income community access to some employment hub with an income redistribution objective that overwhelms the fact that the direct transportation benefits are less than the cost of providing the service. Even though a decision may not be based primarily on benefit-cost grounds, the potential gain sacrificed in the selection of a particular public policy is important information. Third, cost-benefit analysis forces public decision making to focus on the value of competing alternatives. Valuation and the accompanying process of competing priorities are the keys to sound decision making, so cost-benefit analysis directs attention to vital questions. Cost-benefit analysis may contribute by helping to keep governments from wasting resources. If so, it would have made a noble contribution.

The cost-benefit logic is not limited to complex projects; it can be particularly useful in more narrow public management decisions about alternative methods of accomplishing a particular task. Among the applications are repair-replace and lease-purchase decisions, fuel conversion, modernization choices, and data processing equipment acquisitions. In these decisions, the objective is simply to perform a task at least cost, often when one option involves a capital expenditure and others do not.

Elements in Cost-Benefit Analysis

Five steps make up formal cost-benefit analysis: (1) categorizing project objectives, (2) estimating the project's impact on objectives, (3) estimating project costs, (4) discounting cost and benefit flows at an appropriate discount rate, and (5) summarizing

---

[22]"Best practices" for preparing economic analyses of regulatory actions are presented in Executive Office of the President, Office of Management and Budget, *Economic Analysis of Federal Regulations under Executive Order 12866* (Washington, D.C.: Office of Management and Budget, 1996).

[23]Federal water resource projects have one of the longest histories of cost-benefit applications. Even here, Eric Schenker and Michael Bunamo indicate that these projects are strongly influenced by purely political factors when examined across regions in the United States. See "A Study of the Corps of Engineers' Regional Pattern of Investments," *Southern Economic Journal* 39 (April 1973): 548–58.

findings in a fashion suitable for decision making.[24] The content of the analysis varies according to the project considered; the following discussion focuses on common elements and their application in selected situations.

PROJECT OBJECTIVES

The project analysis should identify the project's benefits. What desirable results will happen because of the project?[25] The relationship between the project and the objective must be traceable to establish a sound foundation for the analysis. The following are some examples: a rapid transit system could increase travel speed (saving time for travelers), reduce accident costs, and reduce private-vehicle operation costs; a water project might reduce flood damage, provide water for residential and other use, and improve effluent dilution for water-quality management; a new fire station might reduce operating costs of an older facility and reduce prospective fire loss in a service area; and a word processing system might reduce labor costs, material costs, and filing expenses. The analysis must focus on the factors that are different in the options under consideration.

This simple example illustrates some elements of the necessary incremental logic. Suppose a town is contemplating a newspaper-recycling project; its garbage truck will be fitted with a rack to collect bundles of newspapers along the collection route. Cost and revenue estimates prepared by the town clerk appear in the following list:

	Annual Cost
Labor (one extra worker to gather and process papers)	$14,000
Purchase and installation of rack (one-year useful life)	400
Apportioned share of truck operation and maintenance	1,500
Apportioned share of Public Works Department administrative expense	2,000
Total	$17,900

	Annual Revenue
980 tons of paper at $15 per ton	$14,700
Annual Loss (or Required Subsidy)	($3,200)

---

[24]The Office of Management and Budget provides in Circular A-94 an instruction guide to preparing cost-benefit analyses for the federal government: Executive Office of the President, Office of Management and Budget, Circular A-94 Revised (Transmittal Memo No. 64), October 29, 1992.

[25]This is benefit-cost analysis, not economic impact analysis, so spending effects are not included in the analysis. People employed in the project are a cost, not a benefit, and expenditures net out. A new football stadium might result in increased spending at local bars and restaurants, a positive impact for those firms, but that spending comes from the pockets of their patrons and that is a negative for them. For the economy as a whole and for benefit-cost analysis, the impacts cancel out.

Although the estimates are consistent with accounting principles, the conflict is with the incremental principle: only costs or revenue that change with a decision should be considered in making the decision. In the preceding example, there is nothing logically wrong with estimates of revenue, labor cost, or rack cost: none of those would exist without the recycling, so they are incremental to the decision. There are problems, however, with the administrative, operational, and maintenance cost figures: will any of these costs be different because of the recycling program? If not (which is probably the case), they should be excluded in making the decision. When the adjustment to incremental reasoning is made, the program actually will subsidize the general government ($300 incremental revenue over incremental cost) rather than requiring subsidization. In addition, there may be further gains if costs of the traditional waste-management operation are reduced because newspapers are no longer in the stream going to the landfill.

BENEFIT ESTIMATION AND VALUATION

A Senate guide to water-project evaluation defines benefits as "increase or gains, net of associated or induced costs, in the value of goods and services which result from conditions with the project, as compared with conditions without the project."[26] The same logic applies to any project. The analyst must estimate for the life of the project both physical changes from the project and the value of these changes. No single method applies for all projects: specific techniques used to estimate benefits of a personnel-training project would not be the same as those used in water projects. Regardless of the project, however, the decision must be made from estimates, not facts. Facts in economic or social relationships can be only historical. Present decisions cannot change what has already happened, and what will happen can only be estimated. The analysis must proceed with best estimates; it cannot be paralyzed by lack of complete information because complete information is available only when it is too late to decide.

An initial step estimates the physical size of the project's expected change. Sometimes a controlled experiment on a sample can estimate probable effects before resources are committed to the entire program. For instance, the state of Virginia estimated the likely benefits of reflectorized motor vehicle plates by comparing accident frequency among a random sample of cars equipped with these plates with frequency in the remainder of the population.[27] The controlled experiment results could be used to estimate accident reduction from reflectorized plates for the entire state.

Controlled experiments (the randomized controlled trials associated with the evidence based budgeting discussed in Chapter 6), however, are seldom possible. More often, models developed from the social, physical, or engineering sciences are

---

[26]U.S. Senate, *Politics, Standards and Procedures in the Formulation, Evaluation and Review of Plans for Use in Development of Water and Related Land Resources,* 87th Cong., 2nd sess., S. Doc. No. 87-97 (May 1962).

[27]Charles B. Stoke, *Reflectorized License Plates: Do They Reduce Nighttime Rear-End Collision?* (Charlottesville: Virginia Highway Research Council, 1974). Drivers were not told and could not control the type of plates they received. The plates did not make a difference in the incidence of such collisions.

used to estimate that change. For water-resource projects, hydrological models can yield estimates of the influence of reservoirs, canals, and channelization on water flows and levels. From that information, the effects on navigation, probability of flooding, water supply, and so on can be derived. Gravity models from economic analysis and marketing can indicate likely drawing power of various public facilities. Trip-generation models can suggest traffic flows from transportation facility changes. Any model allows the analyst to apply evidence from other environments to predict the results of projects under consideration so that these changes can be valued: analytical models are the key to linking government inputs to government outputs. Harold Hovey describes the importance of models:

> To analyze any program . . . requires a model, which describes the relationship between what we put into the activity (inputs) and what we expect to get out of it (outputs). Good models explain what exact relationships are, not just that a relationship exists. . . . To require that the model be made explicit is one of the greatest potential contributions of systematic analysis to government. An explicit model can be studied, criticized, evaluated, and improved. Too often, decisions are made without explicit models. The result can never be better than if the model is explicit, it can frequently be worse.[28]

When the project's impact has been estimated, the worth of its benefits must then be gauged. Such valuation permits comparison of project cost to project returns and helps establish whether the undertaking increases the net well-being of the region. Money values are used, not to glorify money, but to provide a common yardstick to compare how individuals value the project with how they value the resources used by that project. For example, 1 million tons of concrete applied to highway construction may prolong by one year the useful life of 5,000 automobiles; resources of one type are used to save resources of another type. Will the community be better off with that use of its scarce resources? A direct comparison is impossible because units being measured (cars and concrete) are not the same. Our only meaningful alternative is to estimate the relative value individuals place on cars and concrete: how much general purchasing power are individuals willing to give up to acquire each? Those purchasing-power units provide the measuring standard.

The particular valuation approach depends on the project, but the task is always easiest when values can be connected to a private market, that is, when the public good being considered is an intermediate good (a good that becomes an input into the production of a private good). For instance, river-navigation projects may reduce shipper costs: the estimated difference between costs of river shipment and costs of the cheapest available alternative can indicate the value of an increased volume of shipping. (Recall the Tenn-Tom Waterway case several chapters ago.) The value of employment-training projects can best be estimated from differences in anticipated pre- and post-project incomes of trainees. Many capital expenditure

[28]Harold A. Hovey, *The Planning-Programming-Budgeting Approach to Government Decision-Making* (New York: Praeger, 1968), 23.

items purchased by governments may reduce operating costs, in which case those savings are the primary benefit from the project.[29]

For some projects, however, outputs are not linked to private goods or services: the output is desired for its own sake (relaxation in a city park), not because it contributes to another production process. In other words, these outputs are final products as opposed to the intermediate products that contribute to the production of a private good.[30] When the government product or service is a final product or when prices of marketed commodities change as a result of the project, a different approach is used. That approach is the estimation of *consumers' surplus*—the difference between the maximum price consumers would willingly pay for given amounts of a commodity and the price that the market demands for the commodity (which would be zero for public services provided at no direct charge). The underlying logic of consumer surplus is relatively simple, although its application is anything but simple: points along an individual's demand curve for a product or service represent the value the person places on particular amounts of the product in question. The individual would voluntarily pay a price up to the level on the demand curve rather than not have the product. He or she would not pay more, so the price on the curve represents the individual's valuation of the product.

Figure 7–2 represents an individual's demand for visits to a park; for ten visits to the park, the maximum that individual would pay is $5. If the price charged is above $5, the individual would visit fewer times (if at all); if the price is below $5, the individual receives a consumer surplus—the consumer receives the service at less

Figure 7–2
Individual Demand for a Park

[29]The public value of a National Football League (NFL) franchise has been estimated by real property rents in NFL cities compared to cities without a franchise. Gerald Carlino and N. Edward Coulson, "Compensating Differentials and Social Benefits of the NFL," *Journal of Urban Economics* 56 (June 2004): 25–50. A cost-benefit analysis of government subsidies to NFL franchises (mostly stadium subsidies) working from this benefit calculation suggests that they may be a good investment for cities.
[30]Richard A. Musgrave, "Cost-Benefit Analysis and the Theory of Public Finance," *Journal of Economic Literature* 7 (September 1969): 797–806.

than the price he or she would have willingly paid. Consumer surplus then equals the difference between the maximum price the individual would have paid and the price he or she actually pays multiplied by the number of units purchased. If the price were zero (the park has no admission charge), the total consumer surplus here would be

$$(\$10 \times 5) + (\$5 \times 5) + (\$2 \times 5) + (\$1 \times 5) = \$90$$

That is the entire area under the demand curve for the service and estimates the value of the service to this consumer.

Public services are seldom sold, so how is it possible to consider quantities demanded as a function of price? The demand curves are constructed by recognizing that implicit prices must be paid to use even free services. Individuals must bear the cost of getting from where they live to the free facility; this cost is the implicit price. User pattern analysis allows estimation of a demand curve. Use (quantity demanded) usually is greater by those who are closest to the facility (travel cost, or implicit price, is lower), following the configuration of a conventional demand curve.[31] Estimating consumer surplus is not without problems, but it provides a reasonable technique for that class of public services. Contingent valuation, as described in Sidebar 7–1, provides another approach to estimating the demand for a pure public good.[32]

ESTIMATING PROJECT COSTS[33]

A project's resource cost estimate includes construction cost and operating cost for the life of the project. Obviously, the preparation of these estimates requires the close cooperation of engineers and accountants skilled in costing, particularly if heavy public-work facilities are involved. The analyst must recognize, however, that the important cost for society is the opportunity cost of the resources used in the project: "By the opportunity cost of a decision is meant the sacrifice of alternatives required by that decision. . . . [O]pportunity costs require the measurement of sacrifices. If a decision involves no sacrifices, it is cost free."[34] The cost that matters

---

[31]An often-cited example of estimating a demand curve from travel costs is Frank Lupi et al., "The Michigan Recreational Angling Demand Model," Agricultural Economics Staff Paper 97-58, Department of Agricultural Economics, Michigan State University, January 1998, which estimates the demand for recreational fishing in the state.

[32]Jobs from the project are not a benefit. Unless there is high unemployment, the jobs with the project are moving labor from what it has been doing to work on the project and there is no net benefit at all. The cost of hiring the labor is a project cost, not a benefit.

[33]A close relative of cost-benefit analysis is cost-effectiveness analysis. This technique compares the relative costs of achieving a given objective, but does not attempt to estimate benefits of reaching that objective. For instance, a cost-effectiveness analysis of stopping aircraft hijacking found that the cost of saving one life by putting federal air marshals on aircraft would be $180 million per life saved, whereas the cost per life saved of hardening cockpit doors would be $800,000 per life saved. (M. G. Stewart and J. Mueller, "Assessing the Risks, Costs and Benefits of United States Aviation Security Measures," Center for Infrastructure Performance and Reliability, University of Newcastle (Australia) Research Report No. 267.04.08, 2008.) Hardening cockpit doors makes much more sense than putting marshals on planes. Analysts believe the TSA employs around 3,400 air marshals. Can we apply the "stop doing stupid stuff" rule here?

[34]William Warren Haynes, *Managerial Economics* (Plano, Tex.: Business Publications, 1969), 32.

Sidebar 7–1
Measuring the Value of Nonmarket Goods

The nonappropriability feature of a public good prevents direct measurement of the market value of that good. Market value emerges from the independent decisions of buyers and sellers in exchange transactions. Nonappropriability means that sellers cannot charge an appropriate price to cover the cost of resources needed for service provisions and that buyers will not pay a price sufficient to reflect the full social value of the service. Where transactions do occur, they cannot be expected to reflect the social value of the service.

So is there a way in which market-type valuation information can be obtained for a pure public good? The Council of Economic Advisers in its 1993 *Economic Report of the President* describes one approach that has been used:

> Since a public good is not traded on a competitive market, the market cannot assign it a price based on its value. Measuring the benefits public goods provide is problematic. One method is to infer the value of public goods from actual markets or observable economic behavior. For example, to estimate the value people put on scenic beauty, economists may measure the effect of scenic beauty on actual real estate prices. The value that people put on a park may be reflected in the amount of time and money that they spend to visit and use it.

> The contingent-valuation method (CVM) uses public opinion surveys. A polltaker asks people to estimate the amount they would be willing to pay to maintain or create a certain public good or the amount they would require to compensate for its loss. Advocates of the CVM argue that it can generate reliable estimates of value in cases where it is impossible to make inferences from actual markets or behavior, and in principle, it takes into account the fact that some people value a good more highly than others do.

> However, the CVM also has generated considerable criticism. For example, those surveyed do not actually have to pay the amount they report, a factor that can lead to overstatements. Responses are sensitive to the way questions are posed. (In one case, the estimated value of protection from oil spills changed by a factor of 300 when polltakers asked additional questions before eliciting this value.) CVM results can be inconsistent. (For example, one CVM study showed that people were willing to pay more money to clean up small oil spills than to clean up both small and large spills.) In many cases, CVM results cannot be verified except by another CVM study.

> These problems are exacerbated when the CVM is used to estimate the value of goods that are abstract, symbolic, or difficult to comprehend. One study showed that if the CVM were used to estimate the value of saving whooping cranes from extinction, resulting estimates might be as high as $37 billion per year (more than the Federal Government spends each year on education and Head Start programs). Finally, even if all the problems of the CVM could be resolved, care must be taken to ensure that it is not used to analyze policy in a one-sided way. For example, a proposed program to protect whooping cranes might put people out of work. The $37 billion figure could be cited by those who claim that the benefits of the program exceed its costs. But opponents of that view could undertake a CVM study of their own asking people how much they would be willing to pay to protect these jobs.

A valuation by CVM will not be perfect, but it certainly is preferable to ignoring these nonmarket impacts—which generally amounts to assuming that they have no value.

SOURCE: Executive Office of the President, Council of Economic Advisers, *Economic Report of the President Transmitted to the Congress January 1993* (Washington, D.C.: U.S. Government Printing Office, 1993), 209.

for decisions is the value of paths not taken. That complication can produce three types of cost estimate adjustments based initially on resource purchase prices. First, ordinary project cost estimates include only private or internal costs. Many public projects, however, can create undesirable effects on others, or negative externalities. Examples include the damage done to surrounding properties by pollutants produced by a municipal incinerator and the traffic delays created when streets are blocked by construction of a government office building. These are costs inflicted on parties outside the market transaction, but the costs are just as real to society as wages or payment for construction materials. These adjustments are made using the same indirect methods applied in benefit estimation—these impacts are, logically, negative social benefits.

Second, adjustments are appropriate if the project uses completely unemployed resources or resources for which there is no alternative use. If such is the case, there is nothing sacrificed in consuming those resources in the project being considered. Thus, the actual social opportunity cost of the resource to the project is zero, not the financial cost involved in paying the resource's owner. For that reason, it may be sensible to undertake programs in areas with massive unemployment when that program ordinarily would not be economically justifiable: putting the idle resources to work adds a desired product without economic loss.

Third, many public projects use property already owned by the government. Property acquisition brings no out-of-pocket cost; when sites for a new highway, incinerator, and so forth are being compared, the site using public property has the lowest financial cost. The real social cost of that site for the proposed project is the site's value in its existing (or other possible) use. What does the community lose if the site is selected for the new use? There is no justification for valuing already owned properties at zero. Furthermore, the amount paid for the resource (its historical cost) may not be a usable guide. For example, if a municipality invests $1.5 million in a new incinerator plant that will not burn the refuse mix generated by the city, the value of the plant clearly is less than $1.5 million and, unless there is some salvage value for the facility, approximates zero.

Decisions have to be based on alternatives sacrificed and opportunities forgone. Amounts paid in the past (historical costs) have no necessary bearing on cost in present decisions. Alternative uses establish the cost that matters for current choices.

SELECTING A DISCOUNT RATE

Public projects usually create a flow of costs and returns that spans several years. Therefore, both streams must be converted to present value. However, no single discount rate is immediately obvious as the appropriate rate for analysis.[35] Market imperfections and differences in risk cause a broad spectrum of interest rates in the economy. Two important alternatives for discounting are the cost of borrowed

---

[35]The Federal Reserve discount rate is the interest rate at which the Federal Reserve will make loans to banks that are members of the Federal Reserve System. Although this rate is published as the discount rate, it is not appropriate for discounting or compounding in financial management.

funds to the government (the interest rate the government must pay) and the opportunity cost of displaced private activity (the return that private resources could earn). There are conditions under which either may be appropriate.

The cost of borrowed money provides the closest analog to private project analysis—it is an interest rate that presumably must be paid by a borrower. Because most public programs are ultimately financed by tax revenues, use of the rate at which a government can borrow would not necessarily direct resources to their best-yield uses. Absence of default risk on (federal) government debt makes that rate abnormally low. Allocation using that rate would pull resources away from higher-yielding private activities to prospectively lower-yielding public use. Sidebar 7–2

Sidebar 7–2
What Discount Rate to Use?

The big three of federal government finance—Office of Management and Budget (OMB), Government Accountability Office (GAO), and CBO—all do discounting in consideration of capital expenditure programs, lease-purchase decisions, regulatory reviews, valuation of assets for sale, and so on. But the discount rates they use are not the same. Here is a quick summary of their rates.

OMB establishes the discount policy for almost all executive agencies in its Circular No. A-94. The current base case analysis prescribes a real discount rate of 7 percent, a rate to approximate the marginal pretax rate of return on average private sector investment in recent years. There are exceptions to that base policy. Water-project analysis uses a rate based on the average yield during the previous fiscal year on interest-bearing marketable securities of the United States, which have terms of fifteen years or longer to maturity. Cost-effectiveness analysis with constant-dollar costs should use the real Treasury borrowing rate on marketable securities of comparable maturity to the period of analysis. In addition, lease-purchase analysis of nominal lease payments should use the nominal Treasury borrowing rate on marketable securities of comparable maturity to the period of analysis. Internal federal investments that either increase federal revenue or decrease federal cost should generally use the comparable maturity Treasury rate.

The GAO uses a discount rate based on the average nominal yield of marketable Treasury debt with maturity between one year and the life of the project, with benefits and costs in nominal terms. The same rate applies for all evaluation uses; the GAO endorses sensitivity analysis.

The CBO uses the real yield of Treasury debt and estimates that rate to be 2 percent with a sensitivity analysis of 2 percentage points to test variability. Asset valuation uses comparable private sector interest rates.

SOURCES: Randolph M. Lyon, "Federal Discount Rate Policy, the Shadow Price of Capital, and Challenges for Reform," *Journal of Environmental Economics and Management* 18 (March 1990), Part 2; and Office of Management and Budget, Circular A-94 Revised (Transmittal Memo No. 64), October 29, 1992.

describes the different philosophies and rules in the federal government.[36] For state and local governments, the borrowing rate could be particularly misleading because the exclusion of interest on most state and local debt from federal income tax allows these governments to borrow at well below the market rate.[37]

Public authorities that generate revenue from sales of products or services might use that rate because it estimates the market attitude toward the prospects of the enterprise. Even here, however, the interest excluded from income taxes complicates the analysis.

The return that could have been achieved in displaced private spending is generally more appropriate for the logic of cost-benefit analysis (an analysis aimed at discovering actions that increase the welfare of the community). It is a rate the analyst must estimate; there is no defined interest rate. William Baumol lucidly expresses the essential argument:

> If the resources in question produce a rate of return in the private sector which society evaluates at r percent, then the resources should be transferred to the public project if that project yields a return greater than r percent. They should be left in private hands if their potential earnings in the proposed government investment are less than r percent.[38]

The problem is to estimate what the rate of return would have been on these displaced resources because that is the opportunity cost a public project must exceed if it is not to misallocate community resources. In general, this rate can be estimated according to the formula

$$r_p = k_1 r_1 + k_2 r_2 + \ldots + k_n r_n$$

where

r_p = rate of return on displaced resources (the project discount rate),

k = fraction of project cost extracted from a particular sector (usually the percentage of total taxes collected from it),

r = return on investment in a particular sector, and

n = the number of private sectors with displaced resources.

---

[36] OMB Circular A-4 (September 17, 2003), guidance for doing benefit-cost analysis for proposed regulations, suggests analysis using real discount rates of 3 and 7 percent. Because analysis of regulations involves measurement of difficult-to-value benefits and costs, this circular can be a helpful guide.

[37] An individual in the 35 percent federal tax bracket would receive the same after-tax rate of return on a taxed corporate bond yielding 15 percent as on an untaxed municipal bond yielding 9.75 percent, calculated by subtracting the tax that would be owed on that 15 percent rate to get the net after-tax rate, that is, $(15 - (.35 \times 15)) = 9.75$.

[38] William J. Baumol, "On the Discount Rate for Public Projects," in *Public Expenditures and Policy Analysis*, ed. Robert H. Haveman and Julius Margolis (Chicago: Markham, 1970), 274.

This weighted average provides a workable estimate of the private opportunity cost of the displaced resources, and the resulting discount rate is applied to the estimated benefit and cost flows.[39]

DECISION CRITERIA

The final stage in project analysis applies a decision criterion to the discounted cost and return flows to summarize the economic case for the project. The summarization can either identify whether a project is economically justifiable or establish rankings among projects to be fitted into a limited budget. Two criteria often used are the benefit-cost ratio (BCR; the present value of benefits divided by the present value of costs) and the net present value (NPV; the present value of benefits less the present value of costs). If B = project benefit, C = project cost, r = the appropriate discount rate, t = the year in the life of the project, and T = the life of the project, then

$$NPV = \sum_{t=1}^{T} \frac{(B_t - C_t)}{(1+r)^t}$$

and

$$BCR = \left. \sum_{t=1}^{T} \frac{B_t}{(1+r)^t} \middle/ \Sigma_{t=1}^{T} \frac{C_t}{(1+r)_t} \right.$$

The test of economic efficiency requires an NPV greater than 0 or a BCR greater than 1. If the test is met, resource use for the project will increase economic well-being because alternative use of those resources would produce a lower return for the community. Application of these criteria ignores politics, desires for wealth redistribution, regional problems, and other important concerns, but both NPV and BCR capture the economics of the project. Sidebar 7–3 illustrates how capital projects can be evaluated with the cost-benefit analysis tool.

Two additional measures should be mentioned briefly. These are the payback period and the internal rate of return. The payback-period method divides the estimated net annual flow of project returns into the capital cost of the project to obtain the number of years it would take to fully recover (pay back) the capital cost. Thus, if $2,000 is the net annual return from a project with a capital cost of $8,000, the payback period is four years. The shorter the period, the more attractive the project. This measure is defective in that it ignores both the time profile of returns (proceeds

---

[39]When the time span for the consequences is very long—hundreds of years, as would be the case for certain environmental policies—it is extremely difficult to identify an appropriate discount rate. The long-term ramifications may be huge, but they disappear at any normal discount rate. Some options are proposed in Paul R. Portney and John P. Weyant, eds., *Discounting and Intergenerational Equity* (Washington, D.C.: Resources for the Future, 1999).

Sidebar 7–3
An Application of Net Present Value to Evaluate a Capital Project

A major university hosted a nationally televised football game toward the end of its unsuccessful season, and the field was in such poor condition that alumni from around the country called to complain about the poor image it gave their alma mater. The university must replace the field in any case. It has two alternatives: a conventional sod field or a synthetic turf called Astro Play. The Astro Play would cost $446,000 to install, requires no annual maintenance, and can be used for eleven seasons. The sod field would cost $110,000 to replace, will last three seasons, and requires an annual maintenance cost of $20,000 in each nonreplacement year. Suppose that 5 percent is a reasonable discount rate. What is the NPV of installing the Astro Play?

The NPV of installing Astro Play is computed by comparing the NPVs of the costs for the two field options over the eleven-year period. The NPV of the cost of the sod field would equal the benefit from installing the synthetic surface because it is these costs that would be avoided with the Astro Play. The cost of Astro Play simply equals its installation cost because there are no other costs through its useful life.

The flow of costs from the alternatives, the appropriate discount factor [$(1.05)^n$ where $n =$ years since initial installation], and the discounted costs of the alternative are as follows:

	Cost of Sod Field ($)	Discount Factor	Present Value of Sod Field Cost ($)
Beginning	110,000	1.000	110,000.00
End of Year 1	20,000	1.050	19,047.62
Year 2	20,000	1.103	18,132.37
Year 3	110,000	1.158	94,991.36
Year 4	20,000	1.216	16,447.37
Year 5	20,000	1.276	15,673.98
Year 6	110,000	1.340	82,089.55
Year 7	20,000	1.407	14,214.64
Year 8	20,000	1.477	13,540.96
Year 9	110,000	1.551	70,921.99
Year 10	20,000	1.629	12,277.47
Year 11	20,000	1.710	11,695.91
Total			479,033.22

The NPV of installing Astro Play equals the difference between discounted benefits and discounted costs. Discounted benefits equal $479,033.22; discounted costs equal $446,000. The NPV equals $33,033.22 and the benefit-cost ratio equals 1.07. The internal rate of return (IRR) may also be calculated: the first term in the stream of benefits would equal negative 336,000 (the extra initial cost from choosing Astro Play), and the remaining stream would be the benefits from choosing Astro Play (the costs from grass that are saved). The IRR equals 6.788 percent.

The football team may still lose, but the cost-benefit analysis indicates that it should be playing on the synthetic turf to save the university some money. If nothing else, it will look good while losing!

Table 7–3
Payback Analysis

| Project | Capital Cost ($) | Annual Net Benefits (End of Year) | | | Payback Period |
		Year 1 ($)	Year 2 ($)	Year 3 ($)	
A	10,000	10,000	0	0	1 year
B	10,000	9,000	1,100	0	1+ years
C	10,000	3,000	4,000	7,000	3+ years

available only late in project life are valued as if equal to earlier returns) and proceeds received after the payback point. For example, consider the projects in Table 7–3. By payback-period reasoning, the project ranking (best to worst) would be A, B, C. If a discount rate of 10 percent were appropriate, the NPV of $A = 2,909$, of $B = 909$, and of $C = 1,292$. Crude payback periods are simply not generally reliable as a project guide.[40]

The internal-rate-of-return method seeks the interest rate that would equate the present value of benefits with the present value of costs. That return is compared with the discount rate: the project passes the economic efficiency test if its rate of return is higher than the discount rate. Computation of an internal rate of return may be illustrated using the data for project C in Table 7–3. The internal rate of return (r) is the rate that causes the stream of net benefits in the future to exactly equal the present capital cost:

$$10,000 = (3,000/(1+r)) + (4,000/(1+r)^2) + (7,000/(1+r)^4)$$

r may be computed only by successively trying values of r until the value for the right side equals that for the left side. The computations are relatively simple in this instance (the solution is $r = 16.23$ percent), but iterations involving flows over many years are tedious. Fortunately, computers can be programmed to do the work, and internal-rate-of-return calculations are standard features of spreadsheet programs and many electronic calculators.[41]

However, the present-value methods are "simpler, safer, easier, and more direct."[42] They can be adapted to use multiple discount rates during investment life, they avoid the problem of multiple internal rates of return that can emerge in computing internal rates, and they do not require additional tests to determine the

---

[40]However, a recent study of Canadian municipalities found a distinct preference for the payback approach in doing capital budgets, in spite of its clear deficiencies. Yee-Ching Lillian Chang, "Use of Capital Budgeting Techniques and an Analytic Approach to Capital Investment Decisions in Canadian Municipal Governments," *Public Budgeting & Finance* 24 (Summer 2004): 40–58.

[41]In an Excel spreadsheet, the internal rate of return may be calculated using the following: @irr (values, guess), where "values" is the range of cells containing the flow for which you want to calculate the internal rate of return (the first value is going to be negative) and "guess" is your guess about what the internal rate of return is. Usually, you don't need to insert a guess because the spreadsheet will use 10 percent and that will work.

[42]Harold Bierman, Jr, and Seymour Smidt, *The Capital Budgeting Decision* (New York: Macmillan, 1975), 57.

Table 7–4
Projects with Ranking Criteria Conflict

Project	Cost ($)	Benefit ($)	NPV ($)	BCR
A	150	200	50	1.33
B	500	600	100	1.20

validity of a computed rate of return. Project analysis may require not just an evaluation of the economics of a number of projects, but also selection of particular projects from several alternatives. Two ranking indexes are available: the benefit-cost ratio and net present value.[43] Project rankings are often the same with either criterion, but sometimes—especially when project sizes are substantially different—the ranks are different. Which ranking should apply: that produced by NPVs or by the BCR?

Table 7–4 presents the discounted cost and benefit data for two capital projects. If $500 is to be budgeted, should project A or project B be undertaken? Project B has the higher NPV, whereas project A has the higher BCR. Each criterion supposes particular facts about the projects. Ranking by BCR assumes that either project can be increased in any proportion without changing the return relationships. In the present comparison, ranking by BCR presumes that project A can be expanded to $3\frac{1}{3}$ times its present size at the same benefit rate ($667), yielding a NPV of $167. That expansion must be technically and economically possible if ratios are to guide the decision. Ranking by NPV presumes that the alternative investment streams are the size indicated, without the possibility of changing project size at the same BCR.

In many situations, of course, neither presumption is met entirely. When such is the case, the decision must rely on a comparison of present value of benefits from the use of available funds in feasible combinations of all project sizes. If the analysis attempts to determine economically feasible projects, not allocation within a fixed budget, either method will be satisfactory: if NPV is positive, the BCR will be greater than 1. Conflict emerges only with rankings. In public project analysis, the difficult questions involve estimating benefits, costs, and discount rates; conflict between criteria seldom is the concern. More often than not, knowing how a project stands according to either criterion is enough because the choice is whether or not to proceed with a project, not how to rank a group of projects.

Some Special Problems of Cost-Benefit Analysis

MULTIPLE OBJECTIVES

Cost-benefit analysis provides information about the economic impact of projects. Overall economic impacts, however, may not be the sole or even the most important objective of some programs, particularly those concerned with redistributing

---

[43]The ratio of excess benefit to cost (benefit minus cost, divided by cost) provides no additional information because project ranks are the same as with the BCR: $B/C = [(B - C)/C] + 1$.

income. If redistribution is important, benefits received by some groups in society will be more important than benefits received by others. Market values do not measure this objective, so benefit values would need explicit adjustment to encompass redistribution concerns.

Normal cost-benefit analysis accepts all portions of the economy as equal; who gains and who loses does not matter. It accepts the hypothetical compensation criterion of theoretical welfare economics: a public decision will be regarded as sound if those gaining from a public action receive sufficient benefits to compensate any losses, with some surplus gain remaining.[44] The principle ignores distribution of gains and losses across society and can be defended by these arguments: (1) changes affecting income distributions can be viewed as negligible;[45] (2) public investment is neither a proper nor an effective tool for redistribution, and other fiscal policies can easily correct for any investment-related maldistribution; and (3) many projects over time will have benefits randomly distributed, causing the overall effect to average out at no redistributional change. On these grounds, distribution effects can be ignored with some theoretical justification. The view has been growing, however, that such treatment assumes way too much and that some groups in society seem always to be the loser in public choices.

Two general techniques have emerged to deal with this distributional concern. Some analysts have allowed for distribution effects by weighting benefits according to a measure of the societal importance of the recipient. Benefits received by meritorious groups (those society wants to help) count more than benefits received by others. Selection of weights is obviously a problem. Burton Weisbrod has applied weights derived from past public project decisions that have not followed strict cost-benefit rankings.[46] This approach does not, however, attack the problem of how the distribution should be changed, but rather weighs analysis in the historical pattern. Besides, this pattern may simply reflect the clout of congressional delegations, not the relative importance of certain groups in society. John Krutilla and Otto Eckstein approach the problem by using marginal rates of federal taxation as weights, assuming that these rates roughly measure the importance of redistribution to society.[47] The technique does focus directly on the income distribution, but it, too, has political pressure problems. Furthermore, it ignores the difference between statutory rates (those quoted in the tax law) and effective rates (those applicable after loopholes). And whenever the tax structure changes, the evaluation of all projects would need to be revised. That does not seem reasonable. Other approaches would apply specific weights specified by the analyst. All bend the general rule that the analyst is to be an impartial observer in the analytic process. Decision makers may not recognize (or accept) the value system assumed by the analyst.

---

[44]J. G. Head, "The Welfare Foundations of Public Finance Theory," *Rivista di Diritto Finanziaro e Scienza-Della Finanze* 24 (September 1965): 379–428. The recipients of "hypothetical" compensation would much prefer actual compensation.

[45]Otto Eckstein, *Water Resource Development* (Cambridge, Mass.: Harvard University Press, 1958), 36–37.

[46]Burton A. Weisbrod, "Income Redistribution Effects and Benefit-Cost Analysis," in *Problems in Public Expenditure Analysis*, ed. Samuel B. Chase (Washington, D.C.: Brookings Institution, 1968), 177–222.

[47]John V. Krutilla and Otto Eckstein, *Multiple-Purpose River Development* (Baltimore: Johns Hopkins University Press, 1958).

An alternative, the display technique, supplements general cost and benefit totals with a tabulation of how costs and benefits are divided among the population.[48] Many distributions, such as income, age, race, sex, and geographic area, could be important. By providing such a display, the analyst need not weight the social importance of groups. Decision makers could supply their own weights to each recipient group as desired. The number and type of displays provided would not likely be the same for all projects. If the analyst's goal is to provide information for decision makers and consumers and not to yield conclusive, social-maximizing decisions, such displays seem a prerequisite.

VALUING PROJECTS THAT SAVE LIVES

A sticky problem occurs when public projects seek to reduce the loss of human life, as with transportation safety, cancer research, nutrition education, or fire protection. Life or death can rest on government allocation of resources to particular projects. Those decisions are distasteful, but they have been and will continue to be made. The real question is whether decision makers know what they are assuming about that value. Any decisions that deny resources to activities that have a lifesaving element have implicitly placed a value on life. They imply that the value is less than the cost of the rejected activity. Is that implicit value—referred to as the "value of a statistical life" in the analysis—reasonable?[49] It isn't valuing any particular person, but it is asking the question, "What does individual behavior observed in market transactions tell us about how much we are willing to pay to reduce the loss of somebody's life?" The VSL gives an estimate of how much the public is willing to spend to reduce a risk sufficiently to save one life. If government decisions are already acting on such values implicitly as they pick among programs, why shouldn't the values be provided transparently? That's what reporting agency VSLs does.

A number of methods—none flawless, but some with stronger logical foundation than others—have been proposed to value lifesaving. Historically, the first was average life insurance face-value outstanding, under the logic that this was a value on loss of life that individuals placed on themselves. It is an observable measure, and it emerges from individual market choices. The obvious problems are that individuals buy life insurance for varied motives, including some that have nothing to do with death potential (e.g., forcing themselves to save), and that individual holdings vary substantially by family characteristics. These influences render insurance values generally inappropriate as a value of life saved.

A second technique, the human capital or earnings-loss method, views the human as a machine. Thus, the value of a life saved is estimated at the present value of lifetime earnings less subsistence cost through the work career of the individual.

---

[48]Roland McKean, *Efficiency in Government through Systems Analysis* (New York: Wiley, 1958), 131–33, 208, 242.
[49]Some discussions use "value of mortality risk" instead of "value of a statistical life." It's a matter of terminology alone. The U.S. Department of Transportation must deal with two sticky valuation problems in most of its work: the value of saving a life and the value of saving time in travel. Its updated thinking on these valuations appears at its website: "Economic Values Used in Analysis." https://www.transportation .gov/regulations/economic-values-used-in-analysis.

This computation equals, it is alleged, the contribution of the individual to the economy—the lost earnings potential of the victim—and is the value of a life saved. There are questions both about what earning pattern to use and whether that narrow production view truly gauges the social worth of an individual. This approach is now seldom used.[50] Most people would be willing to pay more than their lost earnings to avoid their own death or injury—so governments using such measures probably spend less on life- and injury-saving programs than their public would prefer.

The third technique, willingness to pay, assesses what people would pay for reduced risk to life and then uses that estimate to calculate the value of a whole statistical life. A number of occupations (e.g., logging, offshore drilling) have greater death risks than other occupations requiring similar skills. The wage premiums necessary to recruit workers to high-risk occupations provide an estimate of the value of life in the labor market. Thus, lifesaving values emerge directly from the choices made by individuals. It works like this. Suppose there are two jobs, one a teacher and the other a logger. The logger faces a greater added chance of being killed on the job in any week—a risk higher by 1 in 100,000. Because of the higher risk, loggers have to be paid a bit more—assume market evidence shows that the amount needs to be $50 per week more than teachers. If 100,000 made that choice, each seeing the extra risk as being acceptable when pay is $50 higher, then collectively loggers are willing to pay no more than $5 million (100,000 × $50) to avoid one expected fatality (100,000 × 1/100,000). There are some logical questions about this method—for one, the values may be artificially low because those jobs apparently appeal to individuals whose attitudes toward risk are different from those of others (they may actually enjoy extreme danger) and possibly to those who haven't thought things through very well—but it apparently gives the soundest estimates generally available.[51]

Government decisions do generate implicit values for lifesaving every time one project alternative is accepted and another is rejected.[52] That valuation cannot be avoided. However, being explicit about the numbers can stir up controversy; for instance, there was a firestorm in the media when it was revealed that the Environmental Protection Agency was using a "value of a statistical life" of $6.9 million in 2008, compared to $7.8 million five years earlier. And agencies do not all use the same value: recently the Environmental Protection Agency increased its estimate to $9.1 million, the Food and Drug Administration was using $7.9 million, and the Department of Transportation was using $6 million.[53] Regulatory agencies

---

[50]A close variant is reportedly used in military pilot safety decisions; the value used is the cost of training a replacement. Safety-feature costs are balanced against that value estimate. Should this make military aviators a little nervous? Also, the judicial system uses this approach in wrongful death cases: one element in the awards to families is the estimated net discounted lifetime earnings of the victim.

[51]A pioneering work is W. K. Viscusi, "Wealth Effects and Earnings Premiums for Job Hazards," *Review of Economics and Statistics* 60 (August 1978): 408–16. Estimates also can be developed from contingent valuation surveys asking people what they would be willing to pay for reduced risk of death of injury.

[52]Some government decisions also involve saving human lives in the future. Should there be a discount rate for human life? One study suggests that Maryland households consider six lives saved twenty-five years in the future of equal value to one life saved today (this is about a 7.5 percent discount rate). See Maureen L. Cropper and Paul R. Fortney, "Discounting Human Lives," *Resources* (Summer 1992): 1–4.

[53]Binyamin Applebaum, "As U.S. Agencies Put More Value on a Life, Businesses Fret," *February 16, 2011.*

use widely different values in deciding whether the costs imposed on industry by their rules are merited by the benefits from lives saved from the requirements. For instance, the Mine Safety and Health Administration uses a VSL of $9.1 million for regulations reducing miner exposure to respirable coal mine dust, and the Food and Drug Administration uses a VSL of $3.5 million for regulations restricting sales of cigarettes to children.[54] Morally right or wrong? That's a matter beyond the competence of public budgeting, but it does reflect how people are willing to pay for small risk reductions in their individual behaviors. Shouldn't individual choices guide public choices in a democracy? Cost-benefit analysis must ensure that these valuations are conscious and consistent. We can hope for little else. But choices cannot avoid the implicit decisions made as some options are selected and some are rejected, so being explicit is at least appropriate for the objective of public transparency.

Conclusion

Public capital infrastructure contributes to both private and public production. Crumbling roads and bridges, inadequate sewers and outmoded sewage-treatment plants, antiquated schools and public buildings, levees that leak or are too low, low-capacity airports, and so on can have considerable national impact; therefore, governments need to attend to the public capital stock and the capital investment that renews and expands that stock. Leaving future generations with depleted capital assets is just as significant a violation of sustainability as leaving them with a huge debt burden from accumulated operating deficits. Capital budgets, providing a separate review for capital as opposed to current expenditures, establish a process for making choices about the development or replacement of long-life assets such as those just noted. Special concern is warranted because capital investment choices now can influence the quality of life for many years into the future.

Most capital projects involve payments now, when infrastructure is constructed, with a flow of services coming in the future, through the long, useful life of the project. Discounting provides a mechanism for converting these future impacts into their present equivalents. In general, discounting provides a means of converting flows occurring at different times into a standard equivalent and is an important cornerstone of analysis of debt and investments.

Many public projects, including those involving capital investment, involve the use of one sort of resource (concrete to build a highway) to obtain a different return (a saving of travel time with the new highway). Cost-benefit analysis provides a technique for organizing information for the evaluation of public programs when the resources used in the program are dissimilar from the return received from the program. The analysis uses microeconomic market evaluations of the worth of resources and program results.

---

[54]Jo Craven McGinty, "Why the Government Puts a Dollar Value on Life," *Wall Street Journal*, March 25, 2016.

QUESTIONS AND EXERCISES

1. My son informed me that a comic book I purchased for 10 cents in 1948 is worth $125 today. What has been the average annual compound rate of return on that valuable asset? (See Chapter 2.)

2. Dr. Rubin has $10,000 to invest for three years. Two banks offer a 2 percent interest rate, but bank A compounds quarterly and bank B compounds semiannually. To what value would his money grow in each of the two banks?

3. A time-sharing condominium firm offers prizes to people who visit its project and listen to a marketing presentation. One prize is a $1,000 savings account. Unfortunately, the account would not be available for forty-five years and requires that the winner pay an initial service fee of $55. If one put $55 in an investment account, what annual compound rate of return would cause that sum to reach $1,000 in forty-five years?

4. The Penn Central Railroad has not paid local taxes since 1969, under federal bankruptcy court protection. Some years later the court required Penn Central to offer municipalities a choice of two payment options to clear this liability. (Penn Central had been absorbed by Conrail, so there were no future tax liabilities involved.) The choices were (a) immediate payment of 44 percent of the total liability or (b) immediate payment of 20 percent of the liability, 10 percent paid at the end of each of the next three years, and 50 percent paid at the end of ten years. Which alternative would you recommend to a municipality and why?

5. Two public infrastructure projects have the economic profiles that follow:

	Option A			Option B		
Year	Capital Cost ($)	Operating and Maintenance Cost ($)	Benefits ($)	Capital Cost ($)	Operating and Maintenance Cost ($)	Benefits ($)
1	2,000,000	0	0	2,500,000	0	0
2	1,000,000	10,000	0	500,000	50,000	750,000
3	500,000	70,000	120,000		100,000	750,000
4		90,000	600,000		100,000	750,000
5		90,000	800,000		100,000	750,000
6		90,000	800,000		100,000	750,000
7		90,000	800,000		100,000	750,000
8		90,000	800,000		100,000	750,000
9		100,000	800,000		100,000	750,000
10		100,000	500,000		100,000	300,000

Use these data to compute for each (a) the NPV at discount rates of 10 and 5 percent, (b) the BCR at the same rates, and (c) the internal rate of return for each. Describe the facts about the projects that would dictate which criterion is appropriate, and indicate which project is preferable under each circumstance.

6. The narrow gravel road to Jehnzen Lake is open only for the summer months. At present, the county spends $750 per mile each year to prepare the road for summer traffic and another $150 per mile for maintenance during the period in which it is open. A "permanent" road could be constructed at a cost of $10,000 per mile; the county would have to spend $800 per mile for maintenance (patching, etc.) only every five years through the thirty-year life of the road. Prospects for the area suggest that the road would have to be relocated at the end of that period. If 5 percent is a reasonable discount rate, which option is less costly? What discount rate would cause the two alternatives to have the same cost in present value terms?

7. What problems involving cost-benefit analysis appear in the following statements?
   a. A public power project uses a discount rate of 8.5 percent, the after-tax rate of return for electric utilities in the area.
   b. Evaluation of a new municipal fire station uses a discount rate equal to the rate at which the city can borrow long-term funds.
   c. Evaluation of a new four-lane highway to replace an older two-lane highway shows saved travel time for truckers and for private vehicles, the value of increased gasoline sales, and increased profits of trucking firms.
   d. A cost-benefit analysis of removal of architectural barriers for people with disabilities from commercial buildings produced the following benefit estimate for a 202,000-square-foot shopping center: economic benefit during fifty-year useful life of center (1975–2024) = $4,537,700, the cumulative gross revenues from leasable area. (This increase in gross revenue per year attributable to new accessibility to people with disabilities is calculated by multiplying gross revenues per year by the ratio of persons with disabilities to nondisabled people in the area. The estimate is based on gross revenue per leasable area experienced nationally in 1969, brought forward to 1975 by the rate of consumer price index increase, and extended through the fifty-year life of the building according to the compounded rate of growth in sales revenue experienced by community shopping centers, 1966–1969. A 7 percent discount rate is employed.)
   e. A benefit-cost study done by the state Department of Environmental Management of an offshore wind power project calculates initial project cost at $811 million, but reduces that estimate by 15 percent to allow for the impact of government incentives expected to be adopted before the project actually starts construction.
   f. Some studies of the Keystone Pipeline include the 5,000 to 6,000 construction jobs as a benefit of the project.

8. Highway departments and airports need some substance that will melt ice from roads and runways so that traffic may continue to flow safely when winter storms hit. Here are some options that are available:

   Road salt costs about $30 per ton, and it works fast. More than 10 million tons are spread each year in the United States. It is corrosive to concrete, asphalt, and metal, thus eating roads, bridges, and car bodies. It contaminates drinking water and kills trees and plants. Studies suggest that this damage costs from $600 to $1,000 per ton of salt to correct.

Calcium magnesium acetate, a commercial deicer, is made from limestone and vinegar. It costs about $650 per ton and takes about 15 minutes longer than salt to melt large ice patches. It usually lasts somewhat longer. Scientists think it may actually do some good for soil and plant life, and it is not corrosive.

Contrast financial cost and social cost involved with using these products. Which cost should be used for government decision making? Why?

9. Expansion of London's Heathrow Airport, historically the busiest airport in Europe and behind only Atlanta's Hartsfield Jackson and Beijing's Capitol International airport in passengers served, could require the demolition of the twelfth-century Norman Church of St. Michael's in the village of Stewkley, and doing a benefit-cost analysis of that option requires an estimation of the cost involved with that demolition. The original cost of building the church might have been around 100 British pounds. If property values increased at an annual rate of 5 percent over the 900 years since its construction, its value, to be lost with the construction, would be 1,175,896,676,622,870,000,000 British pounds, and certainly no airport expansion is going to have benefits bigger than that. What do you think about this approach to valuation of a property? What other options might be available?[55]

CASE FOR DISCUSSION

CASE 7–1

Some Rough Cost-Benefit Numbers for a "Bridge to Nowhere"

A widely publicized federal earmark in the 2006 transportation appropriation bill was $223 million for a bridge intended to provide access to Ketchikan, Alaska's airport on lightly populated Gravina Island. The project had the misfortune to become labeled the "Bridge to Nowhere" when the earmark came to light in the 2008 presidential campaign. It is possible to do some rough cost-benefit analysis on the project.

Gravina Island has a population of around fifty, so most of the bridge traffic would likely be those using the airport. The island was not inaccessible without the bridge. A ferry serves the island, with ferries leaving every half hour. The primary impact from the bridge would be to reduce travel time on the trips. It has been estimated that the drive to the airport from Ketchikan would take thirteen minutes, compared to twenty-seven minutes by ferry. Therefore, the time saving is around fifteen minutes per passenger. Ketchikan is a port for cruise ships, which dock on the mainland, so some of the bridge traffic would be ship passengers either joining or leaving the cruise ships. Airline enplanements/deplanements (total passengers

---

[55]Based on "Fight over an Old Church Raises a Tough Question," *Wall Street Journal,* December 9, 1971.

coming and going through the airport) are on the order of 400,000, so that traffic would create 800,000 crossings of the bridge. But let's be generous and round up to 1,000,000 crossings, each saving around one-quarter hour by taking the bridge.

How much is the time saving worth? Let's assume that each visitor earns $125,000 in income per year. If the visitor works fifty weeks per year and forty hours per week, then the work year is 2,000 work hours. Some visitors are children and some are retired—and the earning level assumed here is much higher than the national average—but let's not worry about that. Work it out with different estimates on your own, if you wish. With these numbers, the value of work time equals $62.50 per hour. But this is leisure time for most of the traffic, not work time, so let's adjust the value downward by 50 percent (probably an underadjustment) to get an estimate of the value of leisure time: $31.25. Each passenger saves fifteen minutes with the bridge (compared with travel by ferry), so the saving per passenger equals $7.81. Multiply that by 1 million passengers to get $7,810,000.

We will assume that the bridge will last forever and will have no maintenance cost and that 3 percent is a reasonable discount rate (that's lower than the OMB rate of 7 percent, but probably higher than current market interest rates). Divide $7,810,000 by 0.03 (because benefits are perpetual—the value is lower if we use a finite life for the bridge) to get the present value of the services from the bridge of $260.4 million, a large number and, as it turns out, larger than the amount of the appropriation. (If you are uncomfortable with perpetual life, use 100 years and the annuity formula to get a present value of services: $(7.81/0.03)[1 - (1/1.03)^{100}] = \$246.8$ million.)

But that is not the end of the story. To make the bridge functional, the state of Alaska has to spend $165 million in addition to the federal government's $233 million. Summing up, the present value of the benefits of the bridge is at most $260.4 million, but its total cost is $398 million.

Consider These Questions

1. Would you consider the bridge to be a worthwhile use of federal resources?

2. Why might the state of Alaska be interested in getting the bridge built, even though the total cost of the bridge exceeds the present value of the benefits from the bridge? From the standpoint of Alaska, what are the relevant costs and benefits?

3. How do the benefit-cost analysis results change if the discount rate is 7 percent? What about 2 percent?

4. The analysis is made with several assumptions about use of the bridge, value of traveler time, and number of visitors. How would the analysis change with alternate assumptions that you believe to be potentially reasonable? Do your changes make the bridge more or less attractive as a public investment?

CHAPTER 8

Taxation: Criteria for Evaluating Revenue Options

Chapter Contents

Discussion about taxation is a sensitive and difficult one because nobody enjoys paying taxes and no politician enjoys levying them. It has been a difficult topic even from the earliest days of the United States. James Madison made that point in 1782, in the exciting early days of the nation: "We have shed our blood in the glorious cause in which we are engaged; we are ready to shed the last drop in its defense. Nothing is above our courage, except only (with shame I speak it) the courage to tax ourselves."[1] If we lack the courage to tax ourselves, financing government services will be a continuous challenge because governments collect most of their revenue by exercising their sovereign power to collect coercive payments—taxes—rather than by selling products or services, and reliance on free-will offerings is awfully risky. Everyone would prefer that taxes be paid by someone else, and that doesn't leave many options for making everyone happy.

These coerced payments differ from prices in that they purchase no specific good or service. Furthermore, businesses and individuals would rather not pay taxes because, by and large, the amount of government services anyone receives is independent of the tax that person or business pays. Paying tax does serve to keep the taxpayer out of trouble with the tax collectors, but, with few exceptions, if the

---

[1] William T. Hutchinson and William M. E. Rachal, eds., *The Papers of James Madison* (Chicago: University of Chicago Press, 1965), 4: 330.

neighbors pay enough to finance a government service, then what the individual pays (or doesn't pay) has no impact on the level of service that person will receive. The taxpayer doesn't get more by paying more or less by paying less. Neither are these payments voluntary contributions offered through some sense of civic duty. They are amounts established in a political process that erects a structure of laws—tax statutes and administrative regulations—to determine how the collective cost of government services will be distributed among parts of the market economy. Some services can, indeed, be sold, and it makes sense to finance them from sales revenue because that relieves those not using the service from having to pay for them and preserves the tax system for support of services that cannot be financed by sales revenue. A later chapter discusses the conditions under which user charge systems are feasible and reasonable. However, governments exist, in large measure, to provide services when the private market has failed or may be expected to fail to provide those services in sufficient quantity or quality, if at all. Attempts to sell public goods would be ineffective, so taxes are the answer.

The disconnection between tax paid and service received creates a tension for the tax administrator and, ultimately, for the public agencies that must live within the revenue raised by the tax system. In a market economy, businesses and individuals are used to the principle of exchange that says, crudely, "You get what you pay for." But that principle does not apply in the tax system financing public services. The tax is the law and the tax collectors enforce the "application of the rules of collection to a tax base"[2] (the rule of law), not the collection of prices charged for services rendered.

The tax may be structured to have quasi-market effects—particularly with regard to distributing the cost to those using a service most heavily and to inducing those consuming or producing a product that inflicts uncompensated costs on others to recognize those impacts in their decisions—but the tax remains an involuntary payment to support collective provision of certain goods and services, not a price for services rendered. Nevertheless, the power to finance by coercion reflects a faith in government that allows government to step in when markets fail, and that power is central to government operations. Once-notorious bank robber Willie "The Actor" Sutton allegedly said, "I rob banks because that's where the money is." The following chapters emphasize taxes because, for most general purpose governments in the developed world, that's where the money is.

One important point about tax policy should be emphasized before embarking on consideration of standards and, in later chapters, on specific revenue alternatives. This is that tax policy involves two basic, but distinct questions. The first is that of the appropriate *level* of taxation. How high should taxes be? The answer to this question comes from the expenditure side of the budget process. If the system is to be fiscally sustainable, whatever the outcome of the spending side turns out to be defines the amount that the revenue process must generate. The appropriate level of taxation is not directly a tax issue; it is established by those spending choices. What

---

[2]John L. Mikesell, "Administration and the Public Revenue System: A View of Tax Administration," *Public Administration Review* 34 (1974): 651.

the budget result is establishes the appropriate tax level—if taxes collected do not cover the expenditures made, there is a sustainability issue; if taxes collected consistently exceed the amount of expenditures made (there are persistent large budget surpluses), taxpayers are being overcharged for government services. Cutting taxes without first cutting expenditures is irresponsible governance.

The second question is one of tax structure because the necessary level of taxation can be generated via many different combinations of taxes designed in many alternate ways. Although the revenue capacities of the various taxes are finite, the size of the revenue task does not define how the revenue is to be raised. A proper design of the structure is important, as Henry George effectively described more than a century ago: "The mode of taxation is, in fact, quite as important as the amount. As a small burden badly placed may distress a horse that could carry with ease a much larger one properly adjusted, so a people may be impoverished and their power of producing wealth destroyed by taxation, which, if levied in any other way, could be borne with ease."[3] Even if you are not familiar with horses under stress, you can understand the idea. Care in structuring the tax is as important as the amount of tax itself.

Taxation in the United States: A Brief Overview of the Systems

Governments in the United States collect most of their own-source general revenue from taxes on income, purchases or sales, or property ownership or transfer, as Table 8–1 shows.[4] For all governments, 55.4 percent of general revenue came from taxes, or 70 percent of own-source revenue. Revenue from user charges and from miscellaneous sources (these include lotteries, interest on invested funds, royalties, profits earned by the Federal Reserve System, etc.) play a relatively small role in financing general government. Intergovernmental revenue (transfers from other governments) make a substantial contribution to general revenue. Special revenue, shown at the bottom of the table, includes the substantial collections from the payroll tax that funds the federal insurance trust system. This federal payroll tax for Social Security and Medicare is the

---

[3]Henry George, *Progress and Poverty* (1879), Book VIII, Chap. 3. Online edition: http://www.econlib.org/library/YPDBooks/George/grgPP.html.

[4]Own-source general revenue excludes (1) revenue from intergovernmental aid and (2) revenue from liquor stores, utility operations, or insurance programs (e.g., Social Security or unemployment compensation). The first exclusion takes out revenue that has been transferred from other governments and, hence, does not come from the government's own revenue system; the second excludes revenue from special operations of the government. These distinctions do not reflect laws that restrict certain revenues for certain uses (earmarking). For instance, most states earmark motor fuel tax revenue for highway use. The division used here and in census data considers that revenue to be general and not in the special category.

Table 8–1
Government Revenue by Source and Level of Government, Fiscal 2012 ($ Thousands)

	All Governments	Federal	State	Local	All: Share of Total	Federal: Share of Total	State: Share of Total	Local: Share of Total
Revenue	6,431,977,516	2,909,757,000	1,907,026,846	1,615,193,670				
General revenue	5,151,151,222	2,064,443,000	1,630,034,675	1,456,673,547	109.4%	100.0%	100.0%	100.0%
Intergovernmental revenue	1,073,164,472		533,657,604	539,506,868	22.8%	0.0%	32.7%	37.0%
From Federal	584,499,378		514,139,109	70,360,269	12.4%	0.0%	31.5%	4.8%
From State	469,146,599		0	469,146,599	10.0%	0.0%	0.0%	32.2%
From Local	19,518,495		19,518,495	0	0.4%	0.0%	1.2%	0.0%
General revenue from own sources	4,077,986,750	2,064,443,000	1,096,377,071	917,166,679	86.6%	100.0%	67.3%	63.0%
Taxes	2,855,683,804	1,467,529,000	799,350,417	588,804,387	60.6%	71.1%	49.0%	40.4%
Property	446,099,195	-	13,110,672	432,988,523	9.5%	0.0%	0.8%	29.7%
General sales	314,795,888	-	245,445,704	69,350,184	6.7%	0.0%	15.1%	4.8%
Selective sales	240,712,547	79,061,000	133,098,458	28,553,089	5.1%	3.8%	8.2%	2.0%
Motor fuel	41,447,220		40,139,259	1,307,961	0.9%	0.0%	2.5%	0.1%
Alcoholic beverage	6,492,927		5,963,492	529,435	0.1%	0.0%	0.4%	0.0%
Tobacco products	17,605,937		17,189,314	416,623	0.4%	0.0%	1.1%	0.0%
Individual income	1,439,540,718	1,132,206,000	280,693,192	26,641,526	30.6%	54.8%	17.2%	1.8%
Corporate income	291,319,858	242,289,000	41,821,318	7,209,540	6.2%	11.7%	2.6%	0.5%
Motor vehicle license	24,384,657	-	22,631,173	1,753,484	0.5%	0.0%	1.4%	0.1%
Customs duties and fees	30,307,000	30,307,000			0.6%	1.5%	0.0%	0.0%
Estate and gift taxes	18,472,843	13,973,000	4,499,843		0.4%	0.7%	0.3%	0.0%
Current charges	916,680,254	489,900,000	174,260,371	252,519,883	19.5%	23.7%	10.7%	17.3%
Higher Education	99,163,546		89,227,546	9,936,000	2.1%	0.0%	5.5%	0.7%
Hospitals	123,503,909		49,790,723	73,713,186	2.6%	0.0%	3.1%	5.1%
Highways	13,285,943		7,321,828	5,964,115	0.3%	0.0%	0.4%	0.4%
Sewerage	47,275,757		625,464	46,650,293	1.0%	0.0%	0.0%	3.2%
Postal Service	65,400,000	65,400,000			0.0%	3.2%	0.0%	0.0%
Medicare premiums	64,700,000	64,700,000			0.0%	3.1%	0.0%	0.0%
Miscellaneous general revenue	305,622,692	107,014,000	122,766,283	75,842,409	6.5%	5.2%	7.5%	5.2%
Special Revenue								
Utility revenue	151,735,218	-	13,626,445	138,108,773				
Liquor store revenue	8,339,781	-	7,114,248	1,225,533				
Insurance trust revenue (1)	1,120,751,295	845,314,000	256,251,478	19,185,817				

SOURCES: U.S. Bureau of Census, Governments Division and Office of Management and Budget, *Budget of the Government of the United States, Fiscal Year 2014, Analytical Perspectives.*
Federal user charges include offsetting receipts and offsetting collections.

second largest revenue producer among all sources at all levels; only revenue from the federal individual income tax is greater. But this payroll tax revenue is not directly available for general government and is not included in the tax contribution to general revenue.

The table reflects a distinct separation of revenue sources by level of government, although there are no national laws in the United States that assign particular taxes to particular levels of government, in contrast to the practice in many nations. The federal revenue system is not diversified among tax bases. The federal government relies predominantly on income taxes, individual and corporate, for revenue—54.8 percent of total general revenue from the individual income tax and 11.7 percent from the corporate income tax—and raises about as much from these two taxes as state and local governments raise from all taxes combined. The federal individual income tax is, by a good margin, the most productive of all the taxes; indeed, it produces more money than any tax levied by any other government in the world. Federal dominance in income taxation is even greater because the payroll tax for Social Security (almost all of the insurance trust revenue to the federal government reported in Table 8–1) amounts to a second federal income tax for individuals receiving only wage and salary income and for the self-employed. Indeed, for lower-income households, payments for this payroll tax far exceed the amounts paid in federal individual income tax.

The federal government levies no general sales tax, a rarity among economically developed countries. There is no fundamental "catch" or legal barrier that prevents the federal government from levying such a tax, but taxes on retail sales are a major source for state and local governments. This heavy reliance by states and localities has created political resistance each time the federal government has considered invading that territory, as it did periodically throughout the twentieth century. The federal government does, however, collect sales taxes on selected commodities, such as motor fuels and alcoholic beverages, and on certain imported products (customs duties). The amounts collected from these taxes pale in comparison to those from the federal income taxes—just 3.8 percent of federal general revenue. Virtually all other nations levy a general sales tax, called a value-added tax, and rely rather heavily on its revenue.

The federal government collects no property tax. The U.S. Constitution makes the adoption of a federal property tax politically difficult because it requires apportionment of any direct tax (like the property tax): "No capitation, or other direct, Tax shall be laid unless in Proportion to the Census or Enumeration herein before directed to be taken" (Article I, sec. 9[4]). This provision means that states with one-twentieth of the national population would have to pay one-twentieth of any direct tax. To produce that apportionment, a federal property tax would require high tax rates in poor states and low rates in wealthy states. Any state-by-state difference in federal tax rates would be politically impractical, and to have rates inversely related to state wealth would add an extra degree of difficulty, as the writers of the Constitution surely knew. In his economic analysis of the Constitution, Charles Beard sums up: "Direct taxes may be laid, but resort to this form of taxation is rendered practically impossible, save on extraordinary occasions, by the provision that they must be apportioned according to population—so that numbers cannot transfer the burden to accumulated wealth."[5] The framers of the Constitution, no matter what their many liberal virtues, were generally rich men who appeared not to want to have national taxes placed on their wealth by the masses.

A reasonable question at this point is, What are direct and indirect taxes? Richard Musgrave suggests the possibilities:

> Some have suggested that (1) indirect taxes are taxes which are shifted [i.e., the real burden is borne by someone other than the one paying the tax to the government], and others that (2) they are taxes which are meant to be shifted. Still others hold that (3) they are taxes which are assessed on objects [or privileges] rather than on individuals and therefore not adaptable to the individual's special position and his taxable capacity; or finally (4) that they are simply taxes which are not on income. While (3) is probably the most useful criterion, this is not the place to resolve this terminological matter. It is evident, however, that under most criteria, the classification of certain taxes is far from clear-cut.[6]

Fortunately, the difference has little economic importance, although it can complicate the legal constraints surrounding the tax. For instance, in addition to the constitutional provision previously noted, some states specify certain rate structures or collection processes that differ according to whether the tax is direct or indirect—so there must be determinations about the particular tax in question. If Professor Musgrave is not up to resolving the issue, then there is not likely to be a generally accepted resolution to the question. Indeed, governments who have to enforce the distinction do not all agree.[7] The lack of a definition periodically provides a good income for tax lawyers attacking some tax provision or another according to whether the particular tax in question qualifies as direct or indirect.

In comparison with the federal government, the revenue systems of state and local governments are broadly diversified, as demonstrated in the view of state and local revenue collections in Table 8–1.[8] The three levels of government combined, although forming tax policies independently, manage a tax system split among income, property, and sales taxes. Table 8–2 presents further information on these structures by indicating the number of states that use the major tax bases and contain localities using these bases. State governments apply income taxes (41 states levy broad individual income taxes; 44 states tax corporate income), but their aggregate collections do not approach federal government collections. Many states, however, do receive more revenue from income taxes than from any other source. State income taxes often mirror federal taxes. In fact, state tax returns often copy information directly from the federal return in computing state liability, and state tax authorities rely heavily on the efforts of the federal government in enforcing their income taxes. A number of cities levy local income taxes, but in many cases, the taxes are limited to coverage of employee payroll, not taxes on income for all sources. About 3,500 local governments levy local income taxes, but only 900 of these are outside Pennsylvania. Taxes on individual

[5]Charles A. Beard, *An Economic Interpretation of the Constitution of the United States* (New York: Macmillan, 1935), 215. As will be noted later, the federal government levied property taxes for short periods in the distant past. The taxes were apportioned.
[6]Richard A. Musgrave, *Fiscal Systems* (New Haven, Conn.: Yale University Press, 1960), 173.
[7]As discussed in a later chapter, the U.S. Supreme Court has changed its mind about whether the individual income tax was direct or indirect. The categorization was rendered irrelevant when the federal Constitution was amended to explicitly permit the tax without apportionment.
[8]Intergovernmental revenue (grants and contracts) is netted out across governments in Table 8–1. Therefore, there are no net grants for all government: one grants, one receives, and net is zero for government as a whole.

Table 8–2
Major Tax Sources for States and Localities, July 2012

Tax	States Using the Tax	States with Localities Using the Tax
General Property	Thirty-five states plus D.C. Exceptions: Colorado, Connecticut, Delaware, Hawaii, Idaho, Iowa, New York, North Carolina, Ohio, Oklahoma, South Dakota, Tennessee, Texas, Utah, and West Virginia.	All fifty states.
General Sales	Forty-five states plus D.C. Exceptions: Alaska, Delaware, Montana, New Hampshire, and Oregon. Many Alaskan municipalities and boroughs levy general sales taxes.	Thirty-six states.
Individual Income	Forty-one states plus D.C. Exceptions: Alaska, Florida, Nevada, New Hampshire, South Dakota, Tennessee, Texas, Washington, and Wyoming. New Hampshire and Tennessee levy taxes on dividend and interest income.	Fifteen states.
Corporate Income	Forty-four states plus D.C. Exceptions: Nevada, Ohio, South Dakota, Texas, Washington, and Wyoming. (Nevada levies a commerce tax, Washington levies a business and occupation tax, Texas levies a gross margins tax, and Ohio levies a commercial activity tax. All are taxes on gross, not net income, and share attributes of general sales taxes.)	Four states.
Motor Fuel	All states plus D.C.	Thirteen states.
Cigarettes	All states plus D.C.	Ten states.
Alcohol Beverages	All states plus D.C.	Eighteen states.

SOURCE: Federation of Tax Administrators; U.S. Bureau of Census, Governments Division; and CCCH Internet Tax Research Network.

income currently are the largest single source of state revenue, with the retail sales tax close behind.[9] All states receive revenue from sales or gross receipts taxes (general or selective), and only five (Alaska, Delaware, Montana, New Hampshire, and Oregon) do not use a general sales tax. Around 6,400 local governments across the thirty-eight states permitting the tax levy general sales taxes as well, making them second only to property as a local tax source. Although the sales tax shows no sign

---

[9]In recent years, the individual income tax and the general sales tax have traded off as the largest single source of state tax revenue. From 1947 to 1997, the general sales tax was the largest source, but was replaced by the individual income tax from 1998 to 2002. It returned to its position as largest producer in 2003 and 2004. Sales tax revenue held up somewhat better than did revenue from the individual income tax during the Great Recession, but the income tax held on to the position of largest-yielding state tax.

of eclipsing the property tax in overall local importance, in some large cities it is the major tax revenue producer. Contrary to the local income tax, which is frequently administered locally, local sales taxes are almost always administered by the state government in conjunction ("piggybacked") with the state tax. The U.S. Constitution prohibits states and their subdivisions from levying customs duties, which are taxes levied on imported goods.

The property tax remains the major own-source revenue producer for local government. Despite continued popular attacks on the tax, it remains the predominant local tax, possibly because it is the only major tax generally within the means of independent local administration and capable of fine statutory-rate differences between geographically small jurisdictions. A number of state governments levy their own general property tax, but its significance in state finances is modest, although it was the dominant state source before the Depression of the 1930s.

How does the tax structure in the United States stack up against that in other industrialized countries? Some comparisons are possible from the data in Table 8–3. Among the countries in the Organization for Economic Cooperation and Development (OECD), the U.S. tax burden as a percentage of gross domestic product (GDP) is toward the bottom—24.4 percent here against an OECD average of 33.7 percent.[10] Looking at shares of that total by tax source, the United States makes heavier use of taxes on personal income (37.7 percent of the total for the United States compared with a 24.5 percent OECD average); heavier use of the "other" tax category, mostly property taxes as it turns out (11.9 percent compared with a 8.0 percent OECD average); slightly higher use of taxes on corporate income (10.2 percent compared with a 8.5 percent OECD average); and much lighter use of goods-and-service or sales taxes (17.9 percent compared with a 32.8 percent OECD average). Our Social Security contributions are somewhat below the average (22.3 percent against 26.2 percent).

This point bears repeating. Among the industrialized nations of the world, the United States is a low-tax country and, as we know from our earlier discussions of deficits at federal, state, and local government levels, a country that does not levy taxes high enough to cover the cost of government services being provided. That low-tax standing does not mean that certain economic activities or individuals are not disadvantaged by provisions of the U.S. tax systems. There are all manner of disincentives and perversities in U.S. tax structures, which are discussed in later chapters, but the U.S. tax burden is, on average, low in relation to that of generally comparable countries.[11] We are, however, considerably above the average for use of the rather visible individual income tax, a fact that may contribute to the widespread complaints of high U.S. taxes. Or maybe Americans just like to complain.

---

[10]These data include operation of national social insurance systems and aggregate all levels of government.
[11]Compared with the industrialized nations, developing countries tend to have lower tax burdens, greater reliance on consumption as opposed to income taxes, and greater reliance on corporate as opposed to personal income taxes. Developing countries have trouble administering any taxes they do manage to adopt. Vito Tanzi and Howell H. Zee, "Tax Policy for Emerging Markets: Developing Countries," International Monetary Fund Working Paper WP/00/35, Washington, D.C., 2000.

Table 8–3

Tax Revenue as Percentage of Gross Domestic Product (GDP) and as Percentage from Major Taxes, 2012 (Counties of Organization for Economic Cooperation and Development)

Country	Total Tax Revenue as % of GDP	Personal Income as % of Total Taxation	Corporate Income as % of Total Taxation	Social Security Payroll as % of Total Taxation	Goods and Services as % of Total Taxation	Other as % of Total Taxation
Australia	27.3	39.2	18.9	0.0	28.1	13.8
Austria	41.7	22.9	5.3	34.1	27.6	10.1
Belgium	44.0	27.8	6.8	32.1	24.9	8.4
Canada	30.7	36.6	9.5	15.5	24.5	13.9
Czech Republic	33.8	10.6	9.9	43.6	33.9	2.0
Denmark	47.2	50.7	6.3	1.9	31.4	9.7
Estonia	32.1	16.4	4.5	35.3	42.2	1.6
Finland	42.8	29.3	4.9	29.6	33.1	3.1
France	44.0	18.0	5.6	37.4	24.5	14.5
Germany	36.5	25.6	4.8	38.3	28.4	2.9
Greece	33.7	20.6	3.3	32.0	37.8	6.3
Hungary	38.5	13.8	3.4	32.8	43.7	6.3
Iceland	35.3	37.4	5.4	10.4	35.1	11.7
Ireland	27.3	33.2	8.4	15.3	34.9	8.2
Israel	29.6	18.4	8.9	17.1	39.2	16.4
Italy	42.7	27.2	6.5	30.3	25.5	10.5
Japan	29.5	18.6	12.5	41.6	18.0	9.3
Korea	24.8	15.0	14.9	24.7	31.2	14.2
Luxembourg	38.5	21.9	13.4	29.3	28.1	7.3
Netherlands	36.3	20.2	5.1	41.2	29.3	4.2
New Zealand	33.0	37.7	14.1	0.0	38.3	9.9
Norway	42.3	23.4	24.8	22.6	26.3	2.9
Poland	32.1	14.1	6.6	37.8	36.2	5.3
Portugal	31.2	18.5	8.7	28.3	39.7	4.8
Slovak Republic	28.1	9.2	8.4	43.9	35.4	3.1
Slovenia	36.5	15.5	3.4	40.8	37.9	2.4
Spain	32.1	22.6	6.4	35.8	26.6	8.6
Sweden	42.3	28.2	6.1	23.6	29.1	13.0
Switzerland	26.9	31.7	10.5	24.9	22.9	10.0
Turkey	27.6	14.4	7.4	27.2	45.0	6.0
United Kingdom	33.0	27.5	8.1	19.1	32.9	12.4
United States	24.4	37.7	10.2	22.3	17.9	11.9
OECD—Average	33.7	24.5	8.5	26.2	32.8	8.0

SOURCE: Organization for Economic Cooperation and Development, *OECD Tax Statistics.* Paris: OECD, 2013.

Standards for Tax Policy

Jean-Baptiste Colbert, finance minister in Louis XIV's court before the French Revolution, is alleged to have summed up the task of financing government: "The art of taxation consists in so plucking the goose as to obtain the largest amount of feathers with the least possible amount of hissing."[12] Taxation based on power alone is an excellent device for inflicting costs on minorities and those with limited political clout, but power so used is inconsistent with leadership and is likely to produce policies that trade long-range damage for quick political gain.

Most people prefer taxes to be paid by someone else because an individual's payment of a tax ordinarily has no influence on whether a public service is available. Former Senator Russell Long (D-LA) elucidated a major principle of tax politics some years ago: "Don't tax you, don't tax me, tax that fellow behind the tree."[13]

That principle, combined with a public that is not familiar with tax structure and tax effects, renders pure public opinion a hazardous standard for revenue choice. Indeed, robbing Peter to pay Paul is an almost certain way to get Paul's vote, a principle that U.S. politicians understand only too well. But attention to opinion may guide approaches through which otherwise desirable changes may be implemented and may identify desirable changes that must await a beneficial political climate.

Economists George Break and Joseph Pechman describe the fundamental principle behind the evaluation of tax policy: "The primary goal of taxation is to transfer control of resources from one group in the society to another and to do so in ways that do not jeopardize, and may even facilitate, the attainment of other economic goals."[14] Those transfers include (1) shifts of purchasing power among groups in the private sector and (2) shifts of control over purchasing power from the private sector to the public sector. A tax intends to move resources away from private use and will by itself harm the private sector; tax policy seeks to achieve that shift with the least possible economic or social harm. Without this concern for minimizing harm, any revenue would be about as good as any other, and tax policy would not be a significant element in public decisions. In other words, tax policy is about damage control. To summarize, *we want a tax system that behaves like a pickpocket and not like a mugger*: the government wants the money to finance services, but doesn't want the taxpayers to lie bleeding on the sidewalk.

When public goods are financed, the tax must not be voluntary. Otherwise, rational actions of nonpayers—who could fully enjoy the service provided without financial payment—would keep the system from producing expected revenue. A tax may be distinguished from other ways of raising revenue by its *compulsory* nature.

---

[12]Mencken H.L., ed., *A New Dictionary of Quotations on Historical Principles from Ancient and Modern Sources* (New York: Knopf, 1942), 1178.

[13]Thomas J. Reese, "The Thoughts of Chairman Long, Part I: The Politics of Taxation," *Tax Notes 6* (February 27, 1978): 199.

[14]George F. Break and Joseph A. Pechman, *Federal Tax Reform, The Impossible Dream?* (Washington, D.C.: Brookings Institution, 1975), 4. The dream is just as impossible now as it was when Break and Pechman wrote the book.

If one possesses the tax base, one pays the tax regardless of whether one uses the services provided by the taxing unit. That's enforcing the rule of law. Their involuntary nature distinguishes taxes from the user charges—recreation admissions, tolls, college tuition, fees for postal service, and so on—that many governments collect. The tax is neither a price for service received nor a voluntary contribution. Furthermore, governments do not rely on "fair share" contributions because fairness is susceptible to widely different individual definitions, particularly what one's own fair share would be.

Criteria for judging taxes and tax systems have been proposed by many observers, but there has been a substantial conformity among those standards. The grandfather of evaluation standards appears in *The Wealth of Nations* (1776), as Adam Smith proposes four classic maxims that should guide taxation in a market-based economy:

I. The subjects of every state ought to contribute towards the support of the government, as nearly as possible, in proportion to their respective abilities; that is, in proportion to the revenue which they respectively enjoy under the protection of the state.

II. The tax which each individual is bound to pay ought to be certain and not arbitrary. The time of payment, the manner of payment, the quantity to be paid, ought all to be clear and plain to the contributor, and to every other person.

III. Every tax ought to be levied at the time or in the manner in which it is most likely to be convenient for the contributor to pay it.

IV. Every tax ought to be so contrived as both to take out and to keep out of the pockets of the people as little as possible, over and above what it brings into the public treasury of the state.[15]

Although the language of those standards has changed over the years and emphasis has shifted with the development of a more complex economy, modern reform still concerns essentially the same issues. Whether the deliberations involve the 1986 federal tax reform in the Reagan administration, the 1993 Clinton economic plan, design of a tax system for a newly independent nation, the Bush 2001 tax reductions, the 2005 Bush tax reform panel,[16] the proposals brought forth by candidates for president, or a state tax reform study (of which there is an almost limitless list, often labeled "Blue Ribbon" and usually producing no changes), attention will be directed to some translation of the basic criteria: equity, economic efficiency effects,

---

[15] Adam Smith, *An Inquiry into the Nature and Cause of the Wealth of Nations,* Modern Library ed. (New York: Random House, 1937), 777–79.

[16] The most recent general federal tax review, the President's Advisory Panel on Federal Tax Reform, was charged with transmitting to the secretary of the treasury revenue-neutral reform options that would "(a) simplify Federal tax laws to reduce the costs and administrative burdens of compliance with such laws; (b) share the burdens and benefits of the Federal tax structure in an appropriately progressive manner while recognizing the importance of homeownership and charity in American society; and (c) promote long-run economic growth and job creation, and better encourage work effort, saving, and investment, so as to strengthen the competitiveness of the United States in the global marketplace." Executive Order 13369, President's Advisory Panel on Federal Tax Reform, January 7, 2005. Of course, nothing came of the ideas generated.

and collection cost/simplicity (cost to government and impact on taxpayer), plus revenue consequences. Recent proposals for tax restructuring have brought renewed concern for transparency, the modern translation of the need for taxes to be certain and not arbitrary, with clear political responsibility when they are levied and enough visibility to ensure that the public does not think that government services are free. Even though transparency is a new concern from the good governance movement, in terms of taxation, it dates back to 1776 Scotland.

Adequacy of Revenue Production

Taxes serve to generate revenue necessary for the provision of government services. Other uses of the revenue system—to direct or encourage certain sorts of economic activity, for instance—are immediately suspect. Hence, the first questions to be answered in an analysis of a tax or system of taxes are in regard to yield. The adequacy question is simple: does the tax system raise sufficient revenue so that spending on services for the current generation will not place an undue burden on future generations? That is the crucial test for fiscal sustainability because if the system does not raise enough revenue, then future generations will be required to take care of the costs of the past as well as taking care of their own costs. That will negatively affect their standard of living, a sustainability violation. If you will recall the discussion about deficits of federal, state, and local governments, you will be able to form your own informed opinion about the current adequacy of these tax systems in the United States. Here is a hint: they aren't doing the job. Attention needs to be focused on tax policies and tax options—and tax levels—to get back on the sustainability track. And if lawmakers and the public aren't interested in increasing taxes, then cutbacks of services being provided are in order.

What about adequacy analysis for a particular tax rather than for a tax system? A tax levied for revenue is worthwhile only if it can generate meaningful revenue at socially acceptable rates.[17] A few taxes may be levied for reasons other than revenue—punitively high rates to stop an undesirable activity or taxes applied simply to keep track of a particular activity—but revenue is the prime objective of most taxes, and nothing good comes from needlessly high tax rates.

How much revenue will a tax yield, and how does yield change when a government changes the effective rate applied to a particular tax base? Tax yield (R), or total collections, equals the tax rate (t) times the tax base (B): if the effective resident income tax rate is 1 percent and resident income equals $200 million, then tax yield equals $2.0 million. That is the simple accounting relationship for tax revenue. If the tax rate is quadrupled, to 4 percent, the yield quadruples as well, to $8.0 million. The tax revenue equation, $R = t \times B$, is graphed in Figure 8–1 as the straight line from the origin (no revenue is produced when the tax rate is zero). There is a linear relationship between the effective tax rate and the yield from the base. Tax-rate

---

[17]Recall that Adam Smith did not include revenue production among his maxims.

Figure 8–1
Relationship between Tax Rate and Tax Revenue: The Rate-Revenue Curve

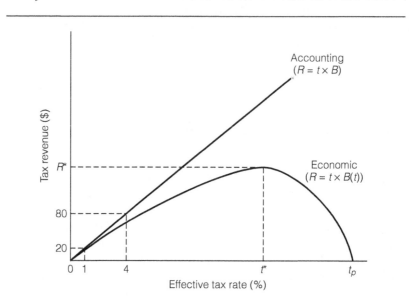

changes produce additional revenue in proportion to the rate change. For example, a 10 percent increase in rate would yield a 10 percent increase in revenue, and so on.

This accounting relationship, to avoid subtlety and any confusion, is wrong. It ignores the economic response by individuals and businesses that now face a different tax rate, and that response will cause the tax base to differ from what it was at the old rate. In other words, the tax base itself is determined in part by the effective tax rate levied against it: if the resident income tax rate increases to 4 percent, resident income will no longer be $200 million. As Robert Inman explains, "the increase in the tax on residents' income might well cause residents to work less as their incomes are taxed or even cause wealthier families to leave the taxing jurisdiction."[18] Similar economic responses apply for other taxes as well. Furthermore, higher rates provide greater return from various "fiddles" to illegally remove operations from the tax system (i.e., higher rates make cheating more attractive). Therefore, the economic relationship between effective rate and revenue yield is not linear, but is one in which the tax rate itself is one of the determinants of the tax base. In Figure 8–1, the economic response to the higher tax rate causes actual yield to be less than shown from the linear relationship. The economic relationship considers first the negative rate-to-base effect (the base as a function of rate or $B(t)$) of a rate increase

---

[18]Robert P. Inman, "Can Philadelphia Escape Its Fiscal Crisis with Another Tax Increase?" *Federal Reserve Bank of Philadelphia Business Review* (September/October 1992): 7.

Sidebar 8–1
The Workings of the Rate-Revenue Curve: Accounting versus Economics

The difference between the accounting relationship and the economic relationship in the tax rate/tax revenue relationship can be simply illustrated with an example. On June 1, 2005, Kentucky increased its cigarette tax rate from $0.03 per pack to $0.30 per pack. That is an increase of 900 percent.

Monthly sales went from around 161 million packs at the old rate to around 145 million packs, a decrease in the tax base of around 10 percent. Although other factors may be involved, it is almost certain that one extremely important factor in the sales decline in cigarette sales is the higher tax that is embedded in the price that cigarette purchasers pay. In other words, the size of the tax base is a function of the cigarette tax rate.

What is the impact on cigarette tax revenue? Revenue equals base times rate, so before the tax increase, monthly revenue would have been around $4.83 million ($0.03 × 161 million); and after the tax increase, monthly revenue would have been around $43.5 million ($0.30 × 145 million)—an increase of 800.6 percent.

The percentage increase in tax collections is considerably less than the percentage increase in the tax rate (800 percent against 900 percent) because the rate increase caused the tax base to be smaller. The base is sensitive to the tax rate, so the accounting relationship does not hold in this case. It may serve as a workable approximation when the tax rate change is small—but not here and maybe not even then. Also, although the rate increase does cause the base to be smaller, notice that it is not the case here that the base reduction causes actual collections to decline. The higher tax rate brings higher tax collections.

So where did the sales go? Some possibilities include sales lost across the Ohio River to Indiana (as well as to other nearby states) as Kentucky retailers lost some of the price advantage they had previously enjoyed, sales lost to Native American smoke shops making sales via the Internet without applying tax, and sales lost because people cut back on smoking or quit entirely.

and then estimates yield by multiplying this adjusted base by the rate ($t \times B(t)$). That causes the economic relationship to differ from the accounting relationship and in Figure 8–1.[19] Sidebar 8–1 illustrates the workings of the rate-revenue relationship in practice.

Figure 8–1 portrays a maximum yield (R^*). This peak measures the maximum economic yield from that tax base. The peak is neither the optimal nor the ideal, nor is it a target for that tax. It is simply the highest feasible amount that can be generated from the particular tax base, and there is no reason to believe that this would be

---

[19]One analysis of rate-revenue curves for each tax in a state is Michael L. Walden, "Dynamic Revenue Curves for North Carolina Taxes," *Public Budgeting & Finance* 23 (Winter 2003): 49–64. None of the state taxes had rates that pushed the state beyond the revenue peak.

or should be the objective of any government. Further tax-rate increases from t^* will cause declining yield as the revenue loss from the tax-induced decline in the base overwhelms the additional yield from the higher rate. Carrying the analysis further, there would be a rate so high (t_p) that the taxed activity would cease.[20] The profile of this rate-revenue curve would depend on how responsive the particular tax base is to the effective tax rate. At lower rates and for small relative changes, change impacts may well approximate the accounting relationship. But the economic relationship cannot be ignored for larger changes, and especially when the tax is being applied to a geographically small region or when avoidance is easy (e.g., close to borders).

Several efforts have been made to estimate what this economic relationship actually looks like for various taxes, and tax policy has sometimes been made on the basis of assertions about its configuration. President Reagan's 1981 tax reductions were based in part on the view, argued most effectively by Arthur Laffer (after whom the rate-revenue curve has popularly been named), that federal personal income tax rates were above t^* and, hence, the rate reduction would help close the budget deficit by increasing tax revenue. Laffer was by no means the first to note the possibility. John Maynard Keynes wrote in 1933: "Nor should the argument seem strange that taxation may be so high as to defeat its object, and that, given sufficient time to gather the fruits, a reduction of taxation will run a better chance, than an increase, of balancing the budget."[21] Careful analysis has shown yields to have been reduced by the Reagan reductions, however.[22] Tests for local taxes usually show actual rates to be below t^*, but not always.[23] Figuring out what might be t^* for the federal individual income tax is not a simple task, given data problems, shifting tax structure, and the like. However, some who have done an exhaustive review suggest that evidence indicates a peak at a top rate of 60 percent or higher, considerably higher than the U.S. levies now.[24] Jurisdictions that have built tax restructuring on the presumption

---

[20]It would disappear as far as the tax collectors are concerned. There may be activity in the underground economy—just as prohibition did not eliminate the production and consumption of alcohol beverages in the United States.

[21]"The Means to Prosperity," reprinted in *Essays in Persuasion: The Collected Works of John Maynard Keynes* (London: Macmillan, St. Martin's Press, 1972), 9: 338. President Reagan would doubtless have been heartbroken to have the relationship be called the Keynes Curve.

[22]Donald Fullerton, "On the Possibility of an Inverse Relationship between Tax Rates and Government Revenue," *Journal of Public Economics* 19 (October 1982): 3–22. Influences of changing the top marginal rate—the tax highest-income people pay on additional income—on revenue are far less clear. See Robert J. Barro, "Higher Taxes, Lower Revenues," *Wall Street Journal,* July 9, 1993, A–10.

[23]Studies revealing an actual rate to be below t^* include the following: for city property taxes, Helen Ladd and Katharine Bradbury, "City Taxes and Property Tax Bases," *National Tax Journal* 41 (December 1988): 503–23; for local sales tax, John L. Mikesell and C. Kurt Zorn, "Impact of the Sales Tax Rate on Its Base: Evidence from a Small Town," *Public Finance Quarterly* 14 (July 1986): 329–38; for Long Island school districts, Robert Inman, "Micro-fiscal Planning in the Regional Economy: A General Equilibrium Approach," *Journal of Public Economics* 7 (April 1977): 237–60; and for state sales taxes, Gerald E. Auten and Edward H. Robb, "A General Model for State Tax Revenue Analysis," *National Tax Journal* 29 (December 1976): 422–35. The rate was shown to be above t^* in the following: for New York City business taxes, Ronald Grieson, William Hamovitch, Albert Levenson, and Richard Morgenstern, "The Effect of Business Taxation on the Location of Industry," *Journal of Urban Economics* 4 (April 1977): 170–85; and for Philadelphia city taxes, Inman, "Micro-fiscal Planning."

[24]Emmanuel Saez, Joel Slemrod, and Seth Giertz, "The Elasticity of Taxable Income with Respect to Marginal Tax Rates," *Journal of Economic Literature* 50 (2012): 3–50.

that reduced legal rates would cause a tax base response sufficiently large to replace collections lost from the lower rate have virtually always found the presumption to be wrong.

Yield can be a difficult practical problem—before reaching the limits of economic capacity—when state restrictions limit local fiscal autonomy. For instance, a state may establish a special district to provide services financed only from a single excise tax base or may impose restrictive property-tax-rate ceilings on local governments. These limits can create considerable revenue adequacy problems. In most instances, political constraints to use of tax bases bind well before the maximum economic capacity of the tax.[25]

Another capacity problem is that of fiscal disparity or horizontal fiscal imbalance. Not all regions of a nation or localities within a region have equal tax-base endowments. For instance, some regions contain important commercial centers or valuable natural resources, whereas other regions have no significant revenue base. To the extent that these regions must finance government services from their own revenue sources, the areas with lower fiscal resources are at considerable disadvantage. For instance, Beverly Hills and Temple City are both cities in Los Angeles County, California, and both have populations of around 35,000. However, the 2013 taxable sales tax base is $62,172 per capita in Beverly Hills (shopping as a fiscal resource!), but only $3,574 per capita in Temple City.[26] That gives residents of Beverly Hills fiscal opportunities considerably different from those of residents of Temple City. Such disparity shows up across most tax bases, both state and local, because affluence and economic activity are not equally distributed geographically and those differences are reflected in tax structures. Sometimes the disparity emerges because high affluence households live in the area, but sometimes the disparity emerges because certain economic activities are located in the area. For example, a jurisdiction with substantial heavy manufacturing activity is likely to be rich in property tax base—not many affluent households live in the area because manufacturing tends not to be an attractive neighbor—and the "auto mall" can be a rich source of sales tax revenue for any local government hosting one.[27] Thus, different tax bases will often have different disparity patterns. This disparity question is examined in greater depth in a later chapter that discusses intergovernmental horizontal fiscal balance.

Adequacy also includes a dynamic dimension: is revenue stable in the short run, and does it grow in the long run? Efforts to manage the national economy have not eliminated economic fluctuations, as the Great Recession from December 2007 to June 2009 clearly demonstrated, and states and localities experience their

---

[25]There is no reason for any government to identify and use its maximum revenue capacity. That would mean the government seeks to maximize its budget, and that would almost never be in the public interest. Yet another reminder: t^* represents the maximum yield, not the optimum yield.

[26]Data from statistical reports of the California State Board of Equalization, 2012-2013 and U.S. Bureau of Census estimates.

[27]Apparently the auto mall is a California invention designed to capture local sales tax revenue and allow a very low property tax, much to the advantage of entities located in the jurisdiction. Of course, that requires that the local sales tax be collected by the location of the dealership rather than by the home address of the purchaser.

own fluctuations that may not be closely correlated to the national pattern. Government functions continue during depressed economic activity and may even grow because of social and economic tensions. A revenue source with good cyclical adequacy remains reasonably stable during periods of declining economic activity. Such stability is vital for state and local governments because they lack the borrowing flexibility and money-creating powers that can accommodate federal deficits. Any rainy-day funds that they may have accumulated are finite and probably too small to provide a complete cushion for the revenue shock. (State and local lawmakers have a tendency to underestimate the fiscal effect of a recession.) Having these governments respond to the shock can be a substantial problem in light of the significance of services provided by these governments to the workings of the nation (education, public safety, the electoral system, social services, etc.).

Subnational governments can avoid some of the problems by avoiding taxes with greatest cyclical sensitivity. In general, taxes on corporate profits are particularly unstable because of the volatility of that base. Property taxes have considerable stability, except for delinquency problems during deep depressions (including localized economic collapse). Although property tax revenues fell slightly in the period after the Great Recession, they continued to be more stable than sales and income taxes. Revenue stability, however, is a problem for government when the economy is growing (and the overall U.S. economy grows more often than it declines, although some regions of the economy are in near-permanent decline). Demand for many government services increases more rapidly than the increase in economic activity. The demand pattern can be examined using the income elasticity of service expenditure, an estimate of the percentage increase in expenditure that will result from each 1 percent increase in income. Those services for which expenditure increases more rapidly than does income have an income elasticity greater than 1, meaning that an increase in income of 1 percent generates an increase in government spending greater than 1 percent. Governments lacking revenue sources with similar growth characteristics face the prospect of increased debt, increased tax rates (or new taxes), or unmet demand for government services. Each of these options is unpleasant, so there is a general preference for responsive taxes, taxes whose revenue increases more rapidly than does income (the revenue elasticity or the elasticity of the tax base with respect to income exceeds 1). Table 8–4 reports income elasticities by individual tax bases as found in several recent tax studies.[28] Because the exact structure of each tax differs to some degree from government to government and these differences influence performance of the tax, the table provides elasticity ranges as well as the median.

Overall, the individual income tax shows greatest responsiveness (caused by both a structure that increases the tax rate as an individual's income is higher and sensitivity of the base to changes in economic activity), whereas motor-fuel and tobacco

---

[28]These *elasticities* are typically computed from a time-series regression of the form $\ln B = a + b \ln Y$, where B is the tax base analyzed, Y is the measure of economic activity, and b is the income elasticity of the tax. Other influences on the base—for instance, statutory-tax-rate changes—may also be included as independent variables. Sometimes analysis is done of *tax buoyancy*. This analysis considers tax yield (base times tax rate) rather than just the tax base.

Table 8–4

Compilation of Selected Long-Term Tax-Base Elasticities as Found in Various Tax Studies

	Low	High	Median
Personal income tax (41 states)	0.809	3.983	1.604
Retail sales tax (44 states)	0.339	1.365	0.781
Corporate income tax (9 studies)	0.72	1.44	1.1
General property tax (12 studies)	0.34	1.41	0.87
Motor-fuels tax (50 states)	1.091	0.478	0.739
Tobacco tax (8 studies)	0.00	0.54	0.26

SOURCE: D. Bruce, W. F. Fox, and M. H. Tuttle, "Tax Base Elasticities: A Multi-State Analysis of Long-Run and Short-Run Dynamics," *Southern Economics Journal* 73 (2006): 315–11; Advisory Commission on Intergovernmental Relations, *Significant Features of Fiscal Federalism, 1976–1977,* vol. 2, *Revenue and Debt* (Washington, D.C.: Advisory Commission on Intergovernmental Relations, 1977); and J. H. Bowman and J. L. Mikesell, "Recent Changes in State Gasoline Taxation: An Analysis of Structure and Rates," *National Tax Journal* 36 (June 1983): 163–82.

taxes—generally applied on a specific (volume or unit) basis rather than on a value (volume times price) basis—have the least responsiveness. The general sales tax is in an intermediate position. The property tax elasticity estimates are probably artificially high because some studies did not separate the revenue effects of increased property tax rates, so the elasticity result is not purely the outcome of automatic base growth.[29] Because responsive taxes may not be stable, the appropriate choice for adequacy over time depends on whether an environment of economic growth or economic decline is most likely and whether the government has access to debt markets and the ability to raise rates during periods of economic decline. Given that the U.S. economy has historically been in expansion more frequently than it has been in decline and that it is a pretty decent bet to continue that pattern, building a revenue structure primarily to be resilient in recession is probably poor public policy.

So what does income elasticity mean for a state government? Suppose that private economic activity is increasing at a rate of 10 percent annually. If that state has a personal income tax with typical base elasticity (from Table 8–4), personal income tax revenue would generally be increasing at a rate of 16.04 percent annually without any increase in tax rates. If the state happened to rely upon a general property tax, revenue from that tax would generally be increasing at a rate of 8.7 percent annually. This difference in elasticity can significantly influence the fiscal performance of the government. High elasticities can insulate the government in a growing area from having to increase tax rates; low elasticities can bring perpetual fiscal crises.

---

[29]A study that extracts both rate changes and general reassessments of property found a property-tax-base elasticity of 0.27 in one state (Indiana). This measurement is more comparable to those reported for sales and income tax bases because it extracts all statutory and administrative sources of base change. See John L. Mikesell, "Property Tax Assessment Practice and Income Elasticities," *Public Finance Quarterly* 6 (January 1978): 61.

Equity: Horizontal and Vertical

How should the revenue burden be distributed? Nobody is going to proclaim that it should be raised unfairly, not politicians, members of the news media, preachers, or even windbags on talk radio. Everybody wants fair and equitable taxes, but what does that really mean? This section will not attempt to answer the fundamental moral question of what *fair* means, but it will outline the concepts that tax analysts use to provide information for those who do make that judgment.

There are two general equity standards: (1) according to taxpayers' benefits from or usage of the public service (*benefits received*) and (2) according to taxpayers' capabilities to bear the burden (*ability to pay*). The approach chosen must finally be partly philosophic and partly pragmatic.

The logic of the benefits-received approach is an appealing complement to the exchange economy for private goods.[30] In this quasi-market arrangement, individuals would pay for a public service if and only if they benefit from the public service, and those who receive more benefits would pay more than those who benefit less. When governments sell services—that is, apply user charges (or public prices)—then only those who benefit must pay, assuming that the service has no considerable external benefit. (More is said about this in a later chapter.) Tax structures can be benefit-based as well if there is some tax that will cause tax payments to align closely with benefits received from a government service, even if direct charges are not collected from users of that service. One example might be a motor-fuel tax financing highways: the more a person uses highways, the more motor fuel used, and the more motor-fuel tax is paid on the fuel purchases, so those with heaviest use of the facility make the greatest payment. If the individual benefits, he or she pays a tax (or charge) consistent with that benefit; if not, he or she does not pay. There are neither the wasteful oversupply of public services that can result when a service's price is artificially low nor the equally wasteful underprovision when prices are too high. A taxpayer receiving 1 percent of the benefits of a public service pays 1 percent of the cost of providing that service; there is no cross-subsidization among taxpayers. The user pays for the service; the nonuser does not bear the burden.

Not only will fiscal cross-subsidization from nonusers to users be prevented, but also revenue production may help guide the allocation of government resources, and the benefit basis may override anti-tax sentiment among the citizenry. People may accept a tax on hunting ammunition, for instance, if proceeds are used for wildlife habitat development. Unfortunately, before tax revenue flow can tell us about the demand for a service, there must be close complementarity between the tax base and the government activity, a situation not often occurring.[31] The link between

---

[30]How might benefits be measured? The logically correct measure would be the value of the service to the individual. Failing that, less-satisfactory measures include the cost of rendering the service to the beneficiary, the insurance value of the property protected, or, according to Adam Smith's criteria, the amount of income earned by the individual (which sounds awfully much like an ability to pay standard).

[31]Earmarking a portion of a general tax—dedicating a particular share of the state sales tax for support of public education, for instance—provides no evidence of preferences for that service, so the practice cannot be justified on the basis of improving information for public decisions.

motor-fuel taxes and use of roads previously noted is a good example of such complementarity. In these instances, the tax becomes a proxy for a price paid for consumption of the government service.[32]

Problems prevent wholesale application of a benefits-received approach. For one thing, pure public goods, by their very nature, provide no divisible exchange in the public-good transaction. Any "purchaser" will buy benefits for others. Furthermore, modern governments typically try to redistribute—providing services directly aimed at transferring affluence from one group to another. In this circumstance, the benefits-received approach fails: the objective of the action is subsidization, not exchange. When circumstances of measurement and redistribution do not prohibit it, however, the benefits-received approach has strong logical support. Protection of low-affluence households is a frequent excuse for rejecting user charge finance, even though the greatest beneficiaries from general finance are actually higher-affluence households.

The benefits-received philosophy implies that for every particular mix of government services provided, there is a different appropriate distribution of the cost of government. The tax structure would identify who benefits and then tax those beneficiaries accordingly. A different mix of services implies that different people should pay. On the other hand, the ability-to-pay approach eschews the market-exchange philosophy and argues that, regardless of services being provided, those most capable of bearing the cost of government should bear the greatest amount of that cost.

The logic of the ability-to-pay principle is that appropriability (particularly its absence) makes public services and private goods fundamentally different, and only the latter are susceptible to market approaches to payment for services. The decision to provide public services can be considered separately from the choice of financial burden distribution, so the distribution may be set according to concepts of fairness or equity. Unfortunately, scientific tools do not establish what distribution is fair, and your opinion (and that is all that it is) probably differs from mine. If individual satisfaction levels could be measured and compared, tax systems might be designed to yield revenues for public use at the least loss of satisfaction to society. There remains no calibration method, so a scientific distribution of financial burden seems beyond reach. Distribution is a matter of political opinion and political power, within ethical limits that may or may not shape the political process, not a matter of establishing what is scientifically correct.

Application of the ability-to-pay approach has two decision elements: selecting an ability-to-pay measure and choosing the way tax payments should vary with that measure. The appropriateness of alternative ability measures varies with the level

---

[32]This system of highway finance is nearing collapse. Hybrid, all-electric, and some alternative-fuel vehicles break the link between motor-fuel purchase and highway use, thereby rendering the fuel taxes unable to finance highways as before. Fortunately, technology now permits direct highway charges, and states will need to make the switch soon. The state of Oregon is already experimenting with vehicle miles traveled charge systems. Billy Hamilton, "Oregon Test-Drives Replacement for the Gas Tax," *State Tax Notes,* 65 (July 16, 2012): 209–14. If insurance companies can figure out how to charge premiums on the basis of driving behavior, certainly governments should be able to employ that technology for charging for highway usage. Some people express privacy concerns, but how can information about personal behavior in the hands of insurance companies be of smaller concern that information in the hands of a government agency?

of economic development. In an agrarian society—for instance, eighteenth-century America—an effective measure of ability to pay might be property ownership, particularly of land, buildings, carriages, and cattle. Modern economic organizations and systems—the corporate form of business enterprise, the development of complex debt forms, and the importance of intangible values in total wealth—make gross values of property an unreliable measure of ability to pay. Therefore, most public discussion about ability to pay concentrates on current income as the appropriate measure. A more comprehensive measure would encompass net wealth as well because both income and wealth figure into an individual's real affluence. Others argue, as we shall see in a later chapter, that consumption by households is a superior index to income because household consumption measures exactly what the household itself believes that it can afford to buy. Exactly which index should gauge ability to pay is not a settled issue despite the tendency toward annual income in most popular discussions (and toward household consumption among many tax policy experts).

The second choice—after household ability has been measured—is the appropriate distribution of the tax burden across households. This is a social policy question (with some economic aspects), and it has both horizontal and vertical elements.

Horizontal equity—what might also be called "equal justice" or "equal protection"—considers equal treatment of taxpayers who have equal capability to pay taxes. If two taxpayers are equivalent, but one taxpayer pays significantly more tax, the tax structure lacks horizontal equity. Such a condition may emerge when taxes vary by individual taste and preference, as when taxes are levied on commodities that are used by a narrow segment of the population or when some sectors of the economy have extra access to schemes that can reduce their tax liability.[33] It may also occur when tax administration is haphazard or capricious or when the administrative task at hand is particularly challenging. For instance, property tax valuation practices may cause houses of apparently similar market value to bear considerably different tax burdens. And it may occur because the tax system taxes different sorts of income at different tax rates, for example, applying a higher tax rate to income from wages and salaries than is applied to income from capital investment.

An obvious problem here is defining equivalent taxing units: The behavior that creates the observed horizontal equity—for example, the family's taste for taxed luxury items—may itself be regarded as evidence of elevated taxpaying capability.[34] In sum, the concept of horizontal equity may have problems in application, but the principle is clear. Equal treatment, after all, is a principle implicit in the equal-protection requirements of the U.S. Constitution. In a property tax case, the U.S. Supreme Court explained that "the constitutional requirement is the seasonable attainment of a rough equity in tax treatment of similarly situated property

---

[33]For example, the federal Tax Reform Act of 1986 sought to improve horizontal equity by reducing the availability of tax shelters to the daring, slick, or cagey investor.

[34]In the world of tax politics, the idea of luxurious consumption may get mangled by political expediency. For instance, the 2016 Philadelphia soda tax, a tax of 1.5 cents per ounce on sodas, diet sodas, flavored waters, energy drinks, sports drinks, and any beverage that is not at least 50 percent milk, fruit, or vegetables (except beverages where consumers add the sweetener, like coffee), embodies the strange idea that such consumption means that the purchaser has extraordinary capacity to bear the cost of government, over and above capacity tapped by the income or general consumption tax.

owners,"[35] and that is exactly horizontal equity. The logic extends to other taxes as well. For instance, why should two households with equal income pay significantly different income taxes simply because of differences in the way that income was earned? But, as you will discover in a later chapter, they likely do.

Vertical equity concerns the proper relationship between the relative tax burdens paid by individuals with different capabilities to pay taxes. The comparison is among unequals, and the question is: by how much should tax payments differ? No scientific guides indicate what the proper differentiation might be, but most would argue that those with more capacity should pay more tax. This simple observation, however, provides minimal guidance for tax policy. And no major tax in use today does not systematically require larger payments from those with greater economic affluence. What needs to be determined further is whether the tax structure should be proportional, progressive, or regressive; that is, by how much should the tax differ across households of different measured ability?

Table 8–5 illustrates the distributions from three hypothetical tax systems, assuming a simple community with only two taxpayers, one of high income and

Table 8–5
Regressivity, Proportionality, and Progressivity in Tax Systems

Regressive System ($10,000 Total Tax)

Taxpayer Income ($)	Share of Pre-tax Income (%)	Tax Paid ($)	Effective Tax Rate (%)	Share of Post-tax Income (%)
20,000	20	3,000	15	18.9
80,000	80	7,000	8.75	81.1
100,000	100	10,000		100.0

Proportional System ($10,000 Total Tax)

Taxpayer Income ($)	Share of Pre-tax Income (%)	Tax Paid ($)	Effective Tax Rate (%)	Share of Post-tax Income (%)
20,000	20	2,000	10	20
80,000	80	8,000	10	80
100,000	100	10,000		100.0

Progressive System ($10,000 Total Tax)

Taxpayer Income ($)	Share of Pre-tax Income (%)	Tax Paid ($)	Effective Tax Rate (%)	Share of Post-tax Income (%)
20,000	20	1,200	6	20.9
80,000	80	8,800	11	79.1
100,000	100	10,000		100.0

---

[35]*Allegheny Pittsburgh Coal Company v. County Commission of Webster County, West Virginia,* 488 U.S. 336 (1989).

the other of low income. Each system distributes a tax burden of $10,000 between the taxpayers. The vertical equity concept gauges the relationship between income and effective rates (tax paid divided by the relevant affluence measurement; the examples here use current income). A tax structure is *regressive* if effective rates are lower in high-ability groups than in low (effective rates fall as ability rises), *progressive* if effective rates are higher in high-ability groups than in low (effective rates rise as ability rises), and *proportional* if effective rates are the same in all groups (effective rates remain constant as ability rises). Effective-rate behavior distinguishes whether the high-income taxpayer is paying relatively more, relatively less, or the same in relation to income as is the low-income taxpayer. That determines the extent to which the tax structure redistributes affluence in the society.

Notice in the table that the proportional structure leaves the shares of post-tax income exactly as the shares were before tax, the regressive structure improves the share of the high-income taxpayer, and the progressive structure improves the share of the low-income taxpayer. These patterns of redistribution reflected in the effective-rate patterns are the essence of vertical equity. What society wants the tax system to do in regard to redistribution establishes whether public policy should seek progressive, proportional, or regressive tax structures, and that is an ethical judgment.

At one time, public finance scholars sought scientific support for the redistribution caused by progressive rate structures through reference to diminishing marginal utility of income: those with more affluence gain less satisfaction from income (increments to affluence) than do those with less affluence. Thus, total utility loss to society to obtain a given amount of revenue would be minimized by applying higher tax rates to those with greater affluence. The diminishing-marginal-utility-of-income argument has not been provable and may be wrong, so progression remains unscientific.[36] There continues, however, a general feeling that tax systems should not place greater relative burden on the less affluent (although, as you will discover in later chapters, several of our important taxes do exactly that).

Table 8–5 also illustrates measurements that do not always indicate whether a structure is progressive or regressive. For instance, a comparison of total tax paid by high- and low-income groups does not produce meaningful information about vertical equity. For each structure here, the high-income taxpayer pays more tax, even with the regressive tax. Therefore, simply comparing total taxes paid by income groups does not distinguish the regressivity/progressivity/proportionality of the tax structure. Neither does a comparison of the proportion of total taxes paid by an income group with that group's proportion of total population. In the example, the highest-income taxpayer represents half of community population, and the regressive tax structure causes that taxpayer to pay 70 percent of community taxes, so that comparison is not useful. If the tax base per taxpaying unit is unequal among income groups (as it certainly must be), proportional, regressive, and progressive taxes all cause high-income groups to pay a disproportionately high share of taxes

---

[36]See Walter J. Blum and Harry Kalven Jr., *The Uneasy Case for Progressive Taxation* (Chicago: University of Chicago Press, 1953).

and low-income groups to pay a low share relative to share of the population. Thus, effective-rate comparisons are the only reliable guide to vertical equity of a structure.

Equity analysis requires an understanding of what entity actually bears the burden of each tax. The work is complicated because the entity legally required to pay any tax may be able to shift some or all of the real burden elsewhere. In the language of tax analysis, the *impact* or statutory incidence may not coincide with the *economic incidence* of the tax because *shifting* has occurred. We can reliably assume that businesses and households will respond to a tax obligation by trying to figure out some way to leave themselves as well-off as possible after dealing with the tax, dumping the burden on someone else if at all feasible.

The incidence question most often involves taxes with impact on businesses, like taxes on corporate net income, business property, or employee payroll. As illustrated in Figure 8–2, a business may respond in three ways to a tax:

1. **Forward shifting.** The business increases its prices to reflect the tax.
2. **Backward shifting.** The business reduces the price it pays to owners of the resources it purchases, including the wages paid workers, prices paid suppliers of raw materials, and so on.
3. **Absorption.** The business may return a lower profit to its owners.

What actually occurs depends on the form of the tax—that is, whether the tax is levied on net profits, sales, or property—and on the market conditions the firm faces, but it can be expected to respond in whatever fashion leaves its owners with

Figure 8–2
Tax Impact, Shifting, and Incidence

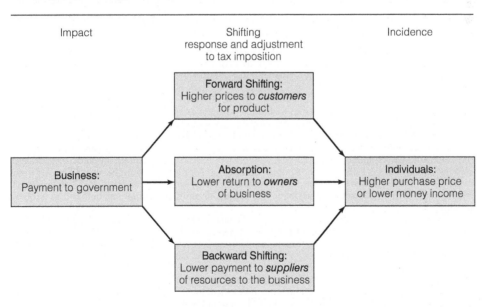

the greatest profit after tax.[37] The business will not automatically react by increasing prices because buyers will respond to the higher prices by purchasing less, and the profit lost from those sales may be greater than the tax recovered from the price increase. No matter how the business responds, however, the business tax reduces the real income of individuals by causing customers to pay higher prices, by causing workers or other resource owners to receive lower income for what they sell to the firm, or by leaving owners of the firm with lower profits. For example, the payroll tax to finance Social Security has two shares, one paid by the employer and one paid by the employee. Most analysts argue that both components reduce the real income of the employee: the payroll tax paid by the employer represents wages, salaries, and fringe benefits that would have been paid to the employee in the absence of the tax. The employer knows about the payroll tax and adjusts wages downward to cover that tax. Hence, the real burden, or incidence, of this share, along with the employee share, is on the employee. Or another example: The landlord pays property tax on his or her rental units. However, over time, the landlord may adjust the rents upward to accommodate that property tax. If so, the incidence of the tax rests on the renter.

Two important principles about tax incidence are often lost in political discussions. First, laws may define tax impacts (who makes payment to the government), but market forces determine incidence (whose real income gets reduced because of the tax); *to legislate incidence is about as effective as legislating against snowfall.* Second, all taxes are ultimately borne by individuals. Businesses serve as conduits of burdens to people, as buyers, as sellers, or as owners. The shifting process is not easy to sort out, but its determination is necessary to identify the vertical equity of a tax.[38]

To illustrate the application of vertical equity analysis, Table 8–6 displays Congressional Budget Office estimates of effective tax rates for federal taxes across families, arrayed by income-group quintiles, to permit some comparability across time in selected years from 1980 to 2013.[39] The table is calculated to include all taxes levied by the federal government; more individual attention will be given them in later chapters. The distribution in Table 8–6 makes these incidence assumptions: (1) families who pay the tax bear the burden of the individual income tax (no shifting); (2) the social insurance tax burden is allocated to employee compensation (employer share

---

[37]The responses are carefully analyzed in Richard A. Musgrave, *The Theory of Public Finance* (New York: McGraw-Hill, 1959), chap. 13; and in Joseph E. Stiglitz, *Economics of the Public Sector,* 3rd ed. (New York: W. W. Norton, 2000), chaps. 18, 23, and 27. Another good source: Executive Office of the President, Council of Economic Advisers, *Economic Report of the President Transmitted to the Congress February 2004* (Washington, D.C.: U.S. Government Printing Office, 2004), chap. 4. An excellent practical guide to shifting of state businesses taxes is Robert Cline, Andrew Phillips, Joo Mi Kim, and Tom Neubig, "The Economic Incidence of Additional State Business Taxes," *State Tax Notes,* January 11, 2010, 105–18. Any respectable report of tax burdens across households will explain its shifting assumptions before it presents its findings.

[38]If businesses serve as conduits of tax burden to individuals, why not forget about taxing businesses and concentrate only on taxing individuals directly? Is it just because of political dynamics? For a good discussion of the logic, see Thomas F. Pogue, "Principles of Business Taxation. How and Why Should Businesses Be Taxed?" in *Handbook on Taxation,* ed. W. Bartley Hildreth and James A. Richardson (New York: Marcel Dekker, 1999), 191–203.

[39]The distributions are according to "before tax income," a measure that includes wages, income from an individually owned business, retirement income, investment income, plus the value of transfer payments received (SNAP, Social Security, Medicare, Medicaid, unemployment compensation, etc.).

Table 8-6
Federal Tax Distributions and Effective Tax Rates by Income Quintiles for All Families, 1980–2013

Quintile	1980 Income Share	1980 Tax Share	1980 Effective Tax Rate	1985 Income Share	1985 Tax Share	1985 Effective Tax Rate	1990 Income Share	1990 Tax Share	1990 Effective Tax Rate	1995 Income Share	1995 Tax Share	1995 Effective Tax Rate	2000 Income Share	2000 Tax Share	2000 Effective Tax Rate	2009 Income Share	2009 Tax Share	2009 Effective Tax Rate	2013 Income Share	2013 Tax Share	2013 Effective Tax Rate
Lowest	5.7	2	7.7	4.8	2.3	9.8	4.6	1.9	8.9	4.6	1.3	6.3	4	1.1	6.4	5.1	0.8	1	5.1	0.8	3.3
Second	11	7	14.1	10.1	7.2	14.8	10	6.8	14.6	9.7	5.8	13.4	8.6	4.8	13	9.8	4.4	6.8	9.3	3.9	8.4
Third	15.7	13.3	18.7	15.2	13.2	18.1	15.1	12.6	17.9	14.9	11.4	17.3	13.5	9.8	16.6	14.7	9.2	11.1	13.9	8.9	12.8
Fourth	22.1	21.3	21.5	21.9	21.3	20.4	21.6	20.7	20.6	21.3	19.3	20.5	19.6	17.5	20.5	21.1	16.5	15.1	20.2	17.1	17
Highest	45.8	56.3	27.3	48.6	55.8	24	49.5	57.9	25.1	50.2	61.9	27.8	54.8	66.6	28	50.8	68.9	23.2	52.6	69	26.3
Top 1%	9.1	14.2	34.6	11.5	14.8	27	12.1	16.2	28.8	12.5	20.1	36.1	17.8	25.5	33	13.4	22.3	28.9	15	25.4	34

SOURCE: *Congressional Budget Office, The Distribution of Household Income and Federal Taxes, 2013* (Washington, D.C.: CB), 2016.

shifted backward to employees, no shifting of employee share); (3) excise taxes are paid by individual consumers in higher prices (forward shifting); and (4) corporate income tax is paid by families (one-quarter shifted back to workers in proportion to labor income, three-quarters shifted to owners of capital in proportion to income from interest, dividends, rents, and adjusted capital gains).[40] Notice that the impact or statutory incidence of these taxes does not always fall on the individuals who bear the final burden or incidence. For instance, product producers usually are responsible for paying the federal excise taxes, but the incidence analysis assumes that the taxes are shifted forward to purchasers in higher product prices.[41]

The distribution is progressive through the years, with rate differences between the highest quintile and the lowest somewhat greater in 2013 than in 1980. The effective rate paid by the highest-income earners is lower in 2013 than it was in 1980, but the decline is greater for the lowest quintile. The table also shows the share of pre-tax income received and the share of federal tax borne in each quintile; as is characteristic of a progressive distribution, the share of tax is greater than the share of pre-tax income for higher-income groups and the reverse for lower-income groups.[42] These are, of course, average rates for the quintiles, and around that average are considerable differences from family to family. For instance, the highest 1 percent of income earning families face a much higher effective rate than do families with lower income, but some of that fortunate few do manage to pay much less, even with that higher average. If these differences within income groups are large enough, they indicate horizontal inequity.

Analysts occasionally estimate the relative share of taxes paid by businesses and individuals, especially at the state and local levels of government. Easily identified business taxes usually include taxes on business property, corporate net income taxes, business gross receipt taxes, corporate franchise taxes, miscellaneous business and occupation taxes, licenses, severance taxes, document and stock transfer taxes, and the like. Taxes on individuals include property taxes on residences and household personal property, individual income taxes, retail sales taxes, and selective excise taxes. Special classification problems arise with taxes on agricultural property (What portion of a farmer's property tax bill is individual, and what portion is business?), unincorporated business income (the business is taxed through the individual income

---

[40]Yes, one-quarter of the corporate income tax is believed to be shifted backward to workers.

[41]Individual income tax burdens may not always end up on the individual. Here is a hypothetical illustration: the state of Florida levies no individual income tax, while the state of Ohio levies a state income tax, as do many of its localities. When LeBron James was negotiating his move back to the Cleveland Cavaliers from the Miami Heat, do you suppose that extra income tax burden entered the salary negotiations? One expects that his Cavaliers salary might have been boosted a bit to allow partial relief from the extra tax burden, shifting the burden from Mr. James to the Cavaliers, thus increasing their operating costs (and then possibly to their fans). Everyone in Ohio was probably thrilled with the outcome.

[42]Because individuals face different economic conditions and make different economic choices over their lifetimes, they are not always taxed in the same way and by the same taxes. Some economists have tried to estimate the lifetime incidence profile of a tax system and its elements, moving away from the traditional annual focus. See, for example, Don Fullerton and Diane Lim Rogers, *Who Bears the Lifetime Tax Burden?* (Washington, D.C.: Brookings Institution, 1993). A study that looks at burden over a longer time horizon appears in Congressional Budget Office, *Effective Tax Rates: Comparing Annual and Multiyear Measures* (Washington, D.C.: Congressional Budget Office, 2005).

tax system), and sales tax paid on business purchases. Those complexities are usually resolved by allocations based on a sample of taxpayers (or by making a guess).

Of course, the burden of taxes levied on businesses ultimately falls on individuals, even if the tax is collected initially from business. Those engaged in transactions with the business as its customers, suppliers, employees, or owners bear the tax. So why tax the business separately from taxing those people directly? Much of the answer is pure politics—lawmakers prefer the fiction that by taxing businesses they are sparing individuals the burden of paying for government services. But there are a couple of reasons that have some logical support. First, there is an economic reason: the business tax may charge the business for costs it generates, but otherwise would not take account of when deciding what, where, and how to produce. In other words, a carefully designed business tax may make the business recognize the cost of otherwise unpriced inputs used in production. The most important costs involved are the cost of services provided by government to the business (public safety, civil court system, and so on) and the cost of environmental damage caused by production of goods and services (air, water, and soil pollution). The business tax can provide signals about resource use to the operators of the business, thus improve the utilization of resources in the economy. Second, it may be more effective and less costly to use the business as a conduit of burden to individuals than to collect directly from the individuals. For example, collection of a retail sales tax indirectly through vendors who add the tax to the price of goods that they sell is much more efficient than trying to collect a comparable tax from individual purchasers after the sale has been made.[43] As far as the owners of a business are concerned, probably more important than the share of taxes paid by business is the amount of those taxes that cannot be readily shifted to suppliers or to customers—the taxes that, under existing market conditions, reduce the return received by owners of the business.

State and local governments are interested in relative business-individual shares, however, for reasons other than equitable burden distribution (or the politically important fact that tax paid by business has a more hidden burden on individuals—politicians are less fervent believers in transparency than are fiscal analysts). In many instances, the individuals ultimately bearing the burden of business taxes, either as owners or as customers of the business, live out of state.[44] A higher business share thus means that a greater amount of state and local government costs is exported to nonresidents. That exporting is politically attractive. Although those businesses do receive services provided by the host community, the appropriate amount of payment is always subject to dispute between businesses and the government. Furthermore, states must take care that out-of-state businesses are not treated more harshly than are domestic businesses, at least not blatantly so, because differential treatment would violate the Commerce Clause of the U.S. Constitution.[45]

---

[43]For a good discussion of the idea of business taxation, see Pogue, "Principles of Business Taxation," 191–203.
[44]Note that certain individual taxes may be substantially exported in special circumstances: for example, residential property taxes in second-home communities and lodging taxes in tourist areas.
[45]"The Congress shall have Power . . . to regulate Commerce with foreign nations and among the several States and with the Indian Tribes" (Article I, sec. 8[3]). Differential treatment by a state involves a power reserved to Congress.

The capability to use taxes with the initial impact on business to export the cost of government to nonresidents, however, does have an important limitation. Taxes may adversely affect the competitive position of business in the state (or at least state lawmakers fear that they might). If tax structures designed to export cost to nonresidents place local business at competitive disadvantage relative to out-of-state competitors, the state economy may suffer. Therefore, tax-share manipulation must be tempered with evaluation of the overall tax level in the competitive states (all of a very low total tax burden would have less influence on competitive position than would a moderate share of a very high total tax burden), but the concern with competitive balance does influence the quest for cost exporting. Thus, states frequently trade the desire to export government cost for a competitive balance for local firms.

Economic Effects

Taxes change the way people and businesses behave, often with considerable economic consequence. It is important to design taxes and their administration so that they are not needlessly harmful to the economy. There is a difference of opinion as to whether taxes can be expected to do more than simply produce revenue and cause as little economic harm as possible. Some argue that a tax should be neutral in its effect: market systems can be trusted to function well without intervention, so the most one should expect from a tax is that it disturbs the marketplace as little as possible. The federal Tax Reform Act of 1986, for instance, sought to establish a "level playing field" for types of economic endeavors. In other words, the tax should ordinarily be neutral. Others argue that a tax should have favorable economic effects: the outcome from market operations can be improved by using tax incentives to alter private behavior in some desired fashion. That means that the tax structure should be used to try to improve on the results from the market.[46] Preferences—credits, exemptions, preferential rates, and the like—are designed to bend market results in ways that certain lawmakers prefer. Rather than using the market to achieve particular purposes, they are actually working to subvert market signals, and are more consistent with state planning than the free market. Many people trust market results far more than they trust what a bunch of politicians, even the well-meaning ones who have not been heavily influenced by campaign contributors and lobbyists, would produce.[47]

Regardless of one's view about the appropriateness (or even the possibility) of trying to improve on the results from the market with tax distortions created by politicians, it is clear that taxes do influence economic behavior and that influences differ among taxes. Taxes can have important effects on economic activity, and tax incentives—good and bad—are part of tax policy discussions. Whenever a tax

---

[46]How tax structure may induce (or discourage) development in poor countries is exhaustively reviewed in the excellent survey by Robin Burgess and Nicholas Stern, "Taxation and Development," *Journal of Economic Literature* 31 (June 1993): 762–830.

[47]What we do know is that there are considerable differences both within states and across states in tax costs faced by type of business activity (retail, research and development, corporate headquarters, capital-intensive manufacturer, etc.), as estimated in *Location Matters: The State Tax Costs of Doing Business* Washington, D.C.: Tax Foundation, 2015. Some of the differences are probably intention, but many are unintended consequences of the tax structure. They violate the "level playing field" standard for resource allocation.

produces a difference in the return that can be gained between two or more competing economic activities, individuals and businesses can be expected to respond toward the alternative leaving a greater after-tax return. Individuals and businesses change their behavior in response to a tax, but the reaction depends on how the tax is structured, not just its absolute level. Furthermore, the response can come in anticipation of a change in the tax, the response may differ according to whether the tax is believed to be permanent or temporary, and the response increases as individuals and businesses have more time to adjustment to the tax.

Here are a number of different choices that a tax wedge—the difference between before- and after-tax prices, payments, or rates of return—can create, along with some examples of the effect:

1. **Work versus leisure.** High taxes on extra income earned may induce workers to choose more leisure time instead of working more hours. Working overtime is less attractive if governments tax away a very high percentage of income earned from that overtime, for instance. Suppose that, of each $100 of overtime pay that a worker earned, the government taxed away $80. Do you suppose workers would choose to work as much overtime as they would if the tax amount were only $15?

2. **Business operations.** Firms should not be induced to organize business practices—production techniques, type of business organization, distribution or marketing system, and so forth—on the basis of tax provisions. Thus, a state property tax on business inventory held on a particular date can induce firms to ship inventory out of state on that date for return later. Suppose that Indiana levies a tax of 10 percent of the value of automobiles on the showroom floor on March 1 and that the tax does not apply to automobiles owned by private owners. Do you suppose that auto dealers would have special sales events to reduce their inventory just before the tax day?[48] Taxes can even lead to the creation of new businesses. The high cigarette tax in New York City, combining to $5.85 per pack, has led to the establishment of "roll your own" cigarette shops. The shop sells loose tobacco and cigarette papers and provides machines for customers to use in producing their own cigarettes. The much lower tax on loose tobacco makes the price for these cigarettes much less than that for the regular cigarettes.[49]

---

[48]Historically, newspapers have been published in broadsheet rather than tabloid format because in 1712 Britain introduced a stamp tax on newspapers per sheet of newsprint. Papers responded by increasing the size of their pages to reduce the amount of tax that they would owe. Bigger sheets, fewer pages, lower tax. The traditional size spread globally, and only recently have newspapers started reducing the size of the sheets.

[49]Sam Roberts, "Low-Tax Cigarettes, Made in Store, Draw City Lawsuit," *New York Times*, November 21, 2011. Having pre-rolled cigarettes at these stores is, however, strictly forbidden: New York Department of Taxation and Finance, "Tax Department Raids Twelve Capital District/Hudson Valley Businesses for Possessing Untaxed Cigarettes for Sale," press release, April 25, 2013. A big difference in the federal tax on pipe tobacco (low rate), roll-your-own tobacco (high rate), big cigars (low rate) and small cigars (high rate) has also created massive shifts in purchases of the competing products. [David Gootnick, "Tobacco Taxes: Disparities in Rates for Similar Smoking Products Continue to Drive Market Shifts to Lower-Taxed Options," U.S. Government Accountability Office, Testimony before the Committee on Finance, U.S. Senate, July 29, 2014 (GAO-14-811T)].

3. **Shopping, purchases, and business location.** High tax rates on goods—cigarettes, liquor, or all retail sales, for instance—in some states induce their residents to make purchases from nearby states with lower taxes and lower prices. These and other taxes may change where entrepreneurs set up their businesses. Do you suppose that Boston residents, facing a sales tax rate of 6.25 percent, might take the short drive to New Hampshire, where there is no general sales tax, to purchase some appliances, tires, and other high-ticket items? In addition, a tax can make things disappear: In 2002, Ireland passed a tax of one-quarter of a euro on plastic bags. If you are in Ireland today, don't even dream of getting your groceries in a plastic bag when you check out because they won't even be available.[50] Washington, D.C. and some other U.S. cities have similar taxes.

4. **Personal management.** Because travel expense to professional conventions can be subtracted from income subject to the federal individual income tax, such conventions may be held in resort locations. Those attending can thus combine vacation and business, while reducing their tax obligation. Also, tax provisions can influence how people prefer to be paid. If, for instance, payments received as fringe benefits are not taxed as income, then employees will prefer more of their compensation in that form rather than in taxable wages and salaries. Suppose your employer can purchase health insurance for you, paying $6,000 per year for that insurance, compensation that is not taxed, or your employer can pay you an extra $6,000 per year, fully taxable, and then you have to purchase your own health insurance. Which option would you prefer? A tax can also change how people live. For example, King William III of England imposed in 1696 a dwelling tax determined by the number of windows in the house, providing an easily observable indicator of the value of the property (the number of windows could be counted from outside by assessors called "window peepers," and more windows meant that the house was more valuable). The tax was high, people responded by blocking up windows, and dwellings become darker and poorly ventilated.[51]

5. **Productive investment and financial portfolios.** Investment may be expected to be influenced by the after-tax rate of return and by tax-induced rate-of-return differentials between sorts of enterprise. Furthermore, high-income entities may direct investable funds to municipal bonds yielding tax-free interest rather than to other productive investment, the return on which would be taxed. Capital is usually more mobile than is labor, and

---

[50]Speaking of Ireland, at the same time that Bono, the Irish rock star and supporter of international good deeds, was pushing the Irish government to contribute more aid to Africa in 2006, he was moving U2's music publishing operation to Amsterdam to dramatically reduce their tax obligations, mostly at the expense of revenue to the government of Ireland. Timothy Noah, "Bono, Tax Avoider," *Slate,* October 31, 2006 [http://www.slate.com/id/2152580/]. Too bad he wasn't willing to pitch in to pay for the good deeds being done by the Irish government.

[51]Wallace E. Oates and Robert M. Schwab. 2015. "The Window Tax: A Case Study in Excess Burden." *Journal of Economic Perspectives* 29 (1): 163–80.

differences in rates of return can elicit considerable shift in capital investment very quickly.[52]

6. **Savings.** Taxes can distort the decision to save by making consumption postponed to the future (savings) more expensive than equivalent consumption in the present. The influence can be on personal decisions to save and on business decisions to retain or distribute earnings to business owners.

Case 8–1 shows how taxes influence a number of basic life decisions. Overall, taxes should not discourage private employment or economic activity more than the minimum needed to extract resources for government operation. Undesirable distortions should be minimized because they cause a waste of productive resources, lower rates of economic growth, and lower national living standards.

Sidebar 8–2 explains excess burden, a measure used in the analysis of distortion. This example provides a worst-case scenario because the tax yields no revenue (from Fred) but does create an economic burden (the value lost from the distorted consumer choice). The efficiency objective in tax policy seeks to yield necessary revenue (the tax burden), while keeping economic distortion (the excess burden) as low as possible. Although the illustration is of consumer choice, there is a similar concern with minimizing producer distortions. In general, excess burden can be reduced by (1) keeping tax rates low (a good reason to have broad tax bases); (2) avoiding different tax rates on similar products, similar uses for competing productive resources, or similar ways of earning an income; and (3) avoiding taxes in markets where buyers or sellers react substantially to changes in price.

These changes in taxpayer behavior represent tax avoidance. Another tax-induced economic behavior is tax evasion. Both represent efforts to reduce the amount of tax paid, but they are not the same. The difference between the two is clear in logic, but it can be complicated in actual practice.

Tax avoidance includes efforts by the taxpayer to reduce the amount of taxes that he or she owes by means that are legal. These practices include such activities as investing in debt that pays interest that is not subject to federal income tax, putting money in an Individual Retirement Account, taking advantage of tax credits for purchasing energy-saving windows for one's home, taking a deduction for contributions made to an eligible charitable organization, and so on. These actions (distortions of taxpayer behavior) reduce the taxpayer's tax liability within the intent of the tax law.

---

[52]People do move in response to tax rates, even though the response is small. When New Jersey implemented a millionaire's tax—an income tax rate increase of 2.9 percentage points on its highest-income earners—migration was minimal, mostly among those living on investment income, people working entirely in-state, and retirees. The tax produced revenue, reduced income inequality, and produced no discernible net tax flight by high earners. Cristobal Young and Charles Varner, "Millionaire Migration and State Taxation of Top Incomes: Evidence from a Natural Experiment," *National Tax Journal* 64 (June 2011): 255–84. However, an analysis of the behavior of European football superstars finds a considerable impact of differences in national income tax rates on player movement. Henrik Kleven, Camille Landais, and Emmanuel Saez, "Taxation and International Migration of Superstars: Evidence from the European Football Market," National Bureau of Economic Research Working Paper 1645, Cambridge, Mass., 2010. These are people who earn very high incomes, are young, have short careers, and have little connection to any particular location.

Sidebar 8–2
The Excess Burden of a Tax: Measuring the Value of Economic Distortion

Economists identify two components of the total burden of a tax. These are the *tax burden*, the payment made by the taxpayer to the government, and the *excess burden* (also called the deadweight loss or welfare cost), a measure of the economic distortion caused by the tax. The excess burden is the loss created by changes in producer and consumer decisions that the tax produces. In general, economists expect that free choice by producers and consumers will direct resources to those activities yielding the best return for society and that consumers will use their purchasing power to acquire those goods giving them the greatest satisfaction. Imposing the tax yields revenue to the government—the tax burden—but it also normally causes a reduction in the amount of the subject of the tax (a commodity or an input) sold. That reduction in units sold brings the deadweight loss: those now-unsold units were bringing satisfaction to the purchaser above the price the purchaser was paying and a return to the seller above the price the seller was receiving (otherwise, neither buyer nor seller would have made the exchange). This market loss is above the tax paid to the government. Indeed, we don't worry much about the tax burden—if the government is budgeting wisely, the use of the resources by the government will yield a return above that which could have been earned in the private market.

The idea of excess burden can be illustrated in a simple example. Suppose Fred ordinarily buys three compact discs (CDs) per month at a price of $15 each (spending a total of $45 per month)—he is a traditionalist and still buys CDs. The government now imposes a new CD tax that adds $3 to the price of each disc. Fred concludes that $18 per disc is simply too much to pay and no longer buys CDs. The government collects no tax revenue from Fred (his tax burden is zero), and he now has $45 per month available to spend on other things.

Does Fred bear any burden from the tax? He certainly does, under the assumption that he was making well-informed, free choices before the imposition of the tax. The tax has caused him to move from his preferred use of that $45 to the purchase of something else, a less desirable (to Fred) option. We know it is less desirable to him because he rejected it before, choosing to buy the CDs instead. Fred loses the satisfaction from the CDs and switches to a less preferred use of his money. This loss is called the excess burden by tax analysts.

That governments should avoid excess burden in structuring their tax systems is an application of the general principle that government should avoid doing things that are economically stupid. If the private market is managing its basic role of allocating resources, then the tax system should leave it alone as much as possible.

Tax evasion, on the other hand, involves actions by the taxpayer to reduce taxes by illegal means. Evasion includes failing to report income received from work done (payment for installing the water heater at a neighbor's house), overstating the amount of deductible expenditures (claiming a larger charitable deduction than was actually made), misusing a sales tax exemption (buying a television for home use without paying sales tax by claiming it was for resale), and so on.

There are different views about strategizing to reduce what would otherwise be one's tax liability. However, the U.S. Supreme Court is on the side of the tax minimizers. It has ruled the following:

> The legal right of a taxpayer to decrease the amount of what otherwise would be his [or her] taxes, or altogether avoid them, by means which the law permits, cannot be doubted.[53]

In other words, the money paid to tax lawyers, accountants, and other advisors to help minimize tax liability through legal means is entirely acceptable. Just don't move toward tax evasion—the courts do not approve of that. Concealing income is almost always seen as tax evasion; different interpretations about preferences are treated less severely.

Not all countries are as accepting of tax avoidance as is the United States. For instance, some of the Russian oligarchs being pursued for tax that led to seizure of their businesses in recent years appear to have been guilty mostly of taking advantage of provisions in the tax law as it existed at the time of their actions to reduce their liabilities. They are being treated as felonious tax evaders, if not enemies of the state, rather than as businesspeople who sought to reduce their liabilities by what they believed to be means that were legal at the time. Such violators in the United States would receive a bill for tax plus interest and maybe a penalty, not a ticket to a prison cell. If the actions were legal at the time they were taken, they wouldn't even have tax to pay.[54]

Collectability

In general, taxes and tax provisions should be designed to keep total tax collection cost as low as possible within the constraint of satisfactory equity and economic impact. Unfortunately, there are frequently trade-offs. For instance, taxes on payrolls represent the income tax format with least collection cost: collection is made by employers (there are far fewer of them to keep track of than there are employees, and the tax return from one employer will cover many employees), the problem of checking on interest and dividend income is avoided, and special questions about rents and capital gains do not arise. Unfortunately, those with interest, dividend, rental, and capital gain income tend to be more affluent than those receiving only payroll income. Thus, the tax that is simple to administer has equity problems. Narrow-based taxes, particularly selective excises, often simply cannot be collected at low cost and are poor choices for the revenue system.[55] The resources used in their collection can be more profitably used in administration of other taxes.

---

[53]*Gregory v. Helvering,* 293 U.S. 465 (1935).

[54]The failure to collect all tax owed (the tax gap from tax evasion) is a concern for all tax administrations. The nature of the problem will be discussed separately for each of the major taxes.

[55]Some excise taxes compensate for social costs associated with use of particular products or services. For example, the federal tax on ozone-depleting chemicals was imposed not for revenue purposes but rather to cause producers and consumers to recognize the dramatic external cost of use of the chemicals and thus to reduce their use in the economy.

Efficient collection "avoids complex provisions and regulations; multiple filing and reporting requirements; and numerous deductions, exclusions, and exemptions. The more complicated the tax system, the greater the costs of taxpayer compliance. A less-complicated system of taxation enables understanding of the law and enhances public confidence in the system. From the government's perspective, complexity increases the costs of administration, and frequent changes to tax laws prohibit effective fiscal planning."[56] Complexity is usually the product of well-intentioned efforts to correct some perceived inequity in the tax system or to improve some element of how the system affects economic incentives. Nina Olson, the United States Taxpayer Advocate, nails the explanation: "Tax complexity doesn't occur just because of big money special interests. It occurs because of the tax provisions that benefit each one of us. We are the special interests."[57]

The complications allow lawmakers to use the tax system for reasons other than raising revenue. There is, indeed, a demand for complexity, and with that complexity come increased costs of compliance and of administration. The quest for tax simplicity is an excellent applause line in political speeches, but members of the public rather like tax complications that reduce their own tax bills. Simplification—and the end to preferences that it would normally entail—should be applicable to somebody else; everyone wants to keep his or her own tax-saving complexities. In short, the enemy to tax simplification is us.

Naturally, politicians go along with the preference game. Milton Friedman explained: "From the citizen's point of view, the function of tax legislation is to decide who shall pay how much to finance government spending. But from Congress's point of view, tax legislation has an additional and very important function: It is a way to raise campaign funds."[58] In exchange for preferences, lobbyists are quite eager to make contributions to election committees.[59] Therefore, improving collectability in the real world of tax restructuring requires a delicate balancing of tax policy and practical tax politics. The options can be easily summarized: fair or simple, take your pick. And you have the political dynamic working against you.[60]

A complication in examining collectability arises because not all tax collection systems use the same division of responsibilities between taxpayers and the tax administrators in producing revenue. "Taxpayer-passive" systems require tax collectors to do most of the work (and bear most of the cost) of raising revenue.

---

[56]David Brunori, "Principles of Tax Policy and Targeted Incentives," *State and Local Government Review* 29 (Winter 1997): 53.
[57]Nina Olson quoted in *State Tax Notes* 79 (February 1, 2016): 375.
[58]Milton Friedman, "Tax Reform Lets Politicians Look for New Donors," *Wall Street Journal,* July 7, 1986.
[59]One study found that lobbying for a particular tax preference brought participating companies a return of 22,000 percent on their investment. Dan Eggen, "Investments Can Yield More on K Street, Study Indicates," *Washington Post,* April 12, 2009, A8. No wonder firms try to influence tax legislation.
[60]One metric of tax simplification over the past twenty-five years is provided by the value of H&R Block stock, the largest tax preparation firm in the United States. The value of its stock has increased 8.4 times, compared with 5.9 times for the S&P 500 stock index, from 1990 to 2015. The tax preparation business seems to be doing pretty well, some evidence that people are not becoming less intimidated by the requirements for doing their own tax returns. True tax simplification would not be good for their business.

For instance, real property taxes typically require little from the property holder, as government agencies perform all the tax record keeping and calculations. The total cost of tax collection with this system is almost exclusively what the government spends in administering the law. There isn't much compliance cost imposed on the taxpayer, and taxpayers don't see the complexity. Even though the property tax has many complications, taxpayers don't complain about the complexity—it isn't complicated for them. They complain about almost everything else about the property tax, just not its complexity.

"Taxpayer-active" systems privatize much of the collection effort, that is, impose most of the collection responsibility on the private taxpayer: for instance, the U.S. income tax requires the individual taxpayer to "supply all relevant information, compute the tax base, calculate the tax, and pay the tax, or some installment of it, when he files his return,"[61] while the tax collector distributes forms, verifies taxpayer reports, and manages revenue flows. The tax administrators aim to induce voluntary taxpayer compliance rather than to collect the tax directly with this sort of administrative system. When the system functions properly, most revenue comes without direct administrative action, and the bulk of collection cost is the expenses of taxpayer compliance, not government administrative cost. Less than 2 percent of total revenue collected by the Internal Revenue Service (IRS) comes from enforcement actions; the rest comes from voluntary compliance. However, this is not a free-will offering from the taxpayer. The exact motives behind why taxpayers actually do comply are not fully understood, but it is likely that many comply not because they believe they are buying government services but because they do not want a visit from the tax collector: paying their taxes is a way of keeping this unwelcome visitor away. This system involves modest administrative cost and substantial compliance cost.

Neither collection system is always best, and most taxes could be administered with different mixes of taxpayer and tax collector responsibilities.[62] The approach selected for a particular tax should reflect prevailing economic conditions, compliance environments, and technologies to best meet the tax policy criteria described previously.[63] For example, not all individual income taxes place as

---

[61]Carl S. Shoup, *Public Finance* (Chicago: Aldine, 1969), 430.

[62]And there are choices as to where compliance responsibility is assigned. For instance, an individual income tax collected via withholding by employers for wage and salary income provides an alternative to having employees remit all tax owed at the end of the year. There are also important options for operation of consumption taxes. For instance, there has been a tendency for states to move the point of collection of motor-fuel taxes from the retail gas station to the distributor or prime supplier. That reduces the number of payers involved in the process, increases the extent to which the tax is passed through to the final purchaser, and reduces the amount of tax owed but not collected by the state. (Wojciech Kopczuk *et al.*, "Do the Laws of Tax Incidence Hold? Point of Collection and the Pass-Through of State Diesel Taxes," National Bureau of Economic Research Working Paper 19410, September 2013) How a tax is administered influences administrative cost, effects of imposing the tax, and extent to which the tax is fully collected. Administration systems matter.

[63]Technology to integrate sources of information and reduce the compliance work required from taxpayers can significantly reduce compliance cost, sometimes without even altering the structure of the tax. Joseph Bankman, "Using Technology to Simplify Individual Tax Filing," *National Tax Journal* 61 (December 2008): 773–89.

much responsibility on the taxpayer as does the U.S. system. In various degrees, income tax agencies in many countries have used information on taxpayer filing status, number of children, and income received (employer wage payments, payments from financial institutions, and tax withheld/remitted by those making payments) to allow computation of a "pre-filled return" system. Those receiving only that employer-reported compensation and interest or dividends need do no tax computations. Countries with such systems for at least some households include Chile, Denmark, Finland, Malta, New Zealand, Norway, Sweden, Singapore, South Africa, Spain, Turkey, Australia, Estonia, France, Hong Kong, Iceland, Italy, Lithuania, and Portugal, so such systems are not a theoretical dream.[64] For a few years, the California Ready Return system provided certain taxpayers (those receiving only wage income who would file a simple return) with the option of filing the completed return that had been prepared by the state Franchise Tax Board on the basis of information provided it by the taxpayer's employer or of doing their own return. That system completely removed the compliance problem for these individuals. The biggest practical (i.e., nonpolitical) barrier in the United States would be reporting of income payments so slowly as to prevent calculation by the IRS on a timely basis (plus a likely popular suspicion that the IRS was going to pull a fast one and require overpayment). Going the other direction, some people argue that a self-assessment system for real property would do no worse than the current taxpayer-passive system.[65]

Because of the difference between taxpayer-active and taxpayer-passive systems, a fair comparison of collectability across taxes must focus on total collection costs, including both the cost incurred by the government in administering the tax and the cost incurred by taxpayers and their agents in complying with the tax's legal requirements (excluding tax actually paid). Although a tax agency may reduce its budget problems by shifting greater collection cost to individuals (as with requiring individuals to pick up return forms from revenue agency offices instead of mailing them to everyone on the tax roll), there is no reason to believe that such practices reduce collection cost. In fact, loss of specialization and economies of scale may actually cause total collection cost to increase. The decision focus is properly on collection cost, the combination of administrative and compliance activities.

---

[64]Great Britain did use a pre-calculated system, but now uses a system of self-assessment, a switch referred to as "privatization." General Accounting Office, *Internal Revenue Service: Opportunities to Reduce Taxpayer Burden through Return Free Filing,* GAO/GGD-92-88BR (Washington, D.C.: General Accounting Office, 1992).

[65]Some taxes are collected in advance: cigarette manufacturers purchase tax stamps from states and affix the stamps to packs of cigarettes intended for sale in the particular state. The state gets its money early, and enforcement is easy—just look for the appropriate stamp. In Belgium, residents pay administrative fees—for a passport or for a change of address—using fiscal stamps that they must purchase from post offices. They buy the stamps at the post office and use them at the administrative office, and the administrative office turns them in to the national government to get the cash. Napoleon created the system a couple of centuries ago because he didn't trust the locals to handle money. John Miller, "As Gregor Samsa Awoke to Less Red Tape . . . ," *The Wall Street Journal Europe,* May 17, 2004, A3.

Combined costs are particularly critical when comparing real property taxes and the major non-property taxes. The non-property taxes are largely taxpayer-administered. For these taxes, the individual or firm maintains records of potential taxable transactions, tabulates the tax base, computes appropriate liability, and makes payments at appropriate times. Government agencies concentrate on partial coverage audits, not direct agency collection, to ensure substantial compliance with the law. The taxpayer bears the bulk of total collection cost. Administration aimed at inducing voluntary compliance would have low administrative cost and higher compliance cost.

The real property tax, on the other hand, ordinarily does not depend on voluntary compliance. A government agent maintains parcel records, values these property parcels for tax distribution, computes the liability for each parcel, and distributes tax bills to parcel owners; the taxpayer is passive. Moreover, when overlapping units of government (city, county, special districts, school district, etc.) levy property taxes, the taxpayer typically receives a single bill for all property taxes. This reduces compliance cost even further. Unless the taxpayer appeals an assessment, payment is the only taxpayer activity and the only collection cost is from administration. Thus, comparing the cost of administering a real property tax with the cost of administering a non-property tax is not appropriate.

Table 8–7 presents administrative cost data for a selection of taxes levied by a variety of governments. Because most revenue agencies administer more than one tax and in fact undertake some nonrevenue functions, the joint cost-allocation problem makes completely accurate cost estimates impossible. The data here must thus be viewed as simply estimates prepared through reasonably consistent allocation schemes. None of these taxpayer-active broad-based taxes shows administration costs much above 1 percent of revenue produced, and many show costs substantially lower than that. In comparison, the cost of administering a high-quality property tax system has been estimated at around 1.5 percent of collections, substantially more than the cost estimates presented for other broad-based taxes.[66]

For the major non-property taxes, most revenue comes from taxpayer actions alone (voluntary compliance); relatively little of the total comes from enforcement, audit, or related revenue-department actions. For example, 2 percent of total Michigan collections, 4.5 percent of California sales and use-tax collections, 5 percent of total Arizona revenues, and 1.69 percent of IRS collections come from direct enforcement actions, including audits, penalties and interest, and delinquency collection.[67] Taxpayers—not government agencies—bear the bulk of the total collection costs (record keeping, return preparation, accounting and legal fees, etc.).

---

[66]Ronald B. Welch, "Characteristics and Feasibility of High Quality Assessment Administration," in *Property Tax Reform,* ed. International Association of Assessing Officers (Chicago: International Association of Assessing Officers, 1973), 50. There are no general-accepted estimates of what a quality real property tax costs to administer now, with the benefit of modern information technology, but the cost is certainly lower than was experienced forty years ago.

[67]These data come from the same sources as the data in Table 8–7.

Table 8–7
Administrative-Cost Estimates for Major Taxes

	Administrative Costs as a Percentage of Revenue
Income Tax	
Colorado (individual and corporate)	0.33
Michigan (individual)	0.64
U.K. individual income, capital gains, and national insurance tax	1.5
U.K. corporate income tax	0.52
General Sale and Use Tax	
California	1.23
Colorado sales	0.22
Colorado use	0.12
Idaho	0.8
Mississippi	1
North Carolina	0.68
North Dakota	0.5
South Dakota	0.41
Washington	0.7
Other Taxes	
Federal luxury excises	0.3
Twelve OECD value-added taxes	0.32–1.09
GAO estimates for 5% broad U.S. value-added tax	1.2–1.8
Taxes administered by IRS	0.53
Arizona taxes	0.61
California alcoholic beverage	0.59
California cigarette tax	3.21
California motor vehicle fuel tax	0.78
Colorado alcoholic beverage	5.27
Colorado cigarette and tobacco	0.1
Colorado gaming tax	5.88
Colorado mileage and fuels	1.44
Colorado death and gift	2.51
Idaho taxes	0.84
U.K. major excises	0.25
U.K. value-added tax	0.60

SOURCES: Colorado Department of Revenue, *Annual Report, 2007* (Denver: Department of Revenue, 2008); Idaho State Tax Commission, *Annual Report, 2007* (Boise: State Tax Commission, 2008); Internal Revenue Service, *Data Book 2011* (Washington, D.C.: Internal Revenue Service, 2012); Sijbren Cnossen, "Administrative and Compliance Costs of the VAT: A Review of the Evidence," *Tax Notes International* 8 (June 20, 1994); Michigan State Treasurer, *Annual Report, 1977–78* (Lansing: State Treasurer, 1980); John F. Due and John L. Mikesell, Sales Taxation (Washington, D.C.: Urban Institute, 1994); General Accounting Office, *Value Added Tax: Costs Vary with Complexity and Number of Businesses,* GAO-GGD-93-78 (Washington, D.C.: General Accounting Office, 1993); Cedric Sanford, Michael Godwin, and Peter J. W. Hardwick, *Administrative and Compliance Costs of Taxation* (Bath, England: Fiscal Publications, 1989); Arizona Department of Revenue, *2004 Annual Report* (Phoenix: Department of Revenue, 2005); California State Board of Equalization, *Annual Report, 2010* (Sacramento: State Board of Equalization, 2011).

Those compliance costs vary substantially among taxpayers, and estimates are hazardous. However, for most taxes, compliance cost is several times as large as administrative cost. For instance, Joel Slemrod and Nikki Sorum have estimated that the compliance cost of federal and state income taxes is between 5 and 7 percent of total tax revenue, many times the cost of administering the taxes.[68]

Transparency

The revenue system in a market democracy should be transparent in its adoption, in its administration, in its compliance requirements, and in the amounts that must be paid because democracy requires that the people know who is responsible for public actions, including what goes on with the taxes they must pay. Transparency, shining daylight on operations of the tax system, is critical for good governance in a democracy. As Lawrence Zelenak observes, "Taxation without comprehension is as inimical to democracy as taxation without representation."[69] However, politicians are not so keen on transparency. They do not like to admit that taxes are being levied at all, that people bear the burden of taxes, that taxes might need to be increased to keep up with demand for government services, that they may have inserted provisions in the tax law to benefit particular industries, or even that taxes might be necessary to finance the government services that people want. A hidden tax is the ideal tax for many U.S. politicians, and maybe for the American public so they can continue with the delusion that government services are free. But that opacity isn't a way to make democracy function for everyone.

Tax transparency has several aspects:

1. **Adoption.** Tax laws should be adopted in an open legislative process. The electorate needs to know the origin of tax proposals—who is introducing the legislation and who is voting for it—and their implication for the distribution of the cost of government. There should be a clear and accessible hearing process for receiving public input on legislative proposals. Unfortunately, just as appropriation earmarks slip into spending bills, the same technique gets used by lawmakers to insert tax provisions into tax bills. A corollary to adoption transparency is that, in order to maintain the security of contracts, tax laws should not be changed retroactively, in the sense of changing the tax treatment of transactions that already have occurred.[70]

---

[68]Joel Slemrod and Nikki Sorum, "The Compliance Cost of the U.S. Individual Income Tax System," *National Tax Journal* 39 (December 1984): 461. An extensive catalog of compliance-cost estimates appears in Francois Vaillancourt, "The Compliance Cost of Taxes on Businesses and Individuals: A Review of the Evidence," *Public Finance/Finances Publiques* 42, no. 3 (1987): 395–430.

[69]Lawrence A. Zelenak, "When We Loved Form 1040," *New York Times*, March 31, 2013.

[70]One exception on retroactivity is that when a bill is in preparation, it may establish a particular date upon which the law will be effective for certain transactions, even though the law has not yet passed on that date. That helps reduce the delay of transactions based on a desire to get more favorable treatment (or the acceleration to avoid harsher treatment) from the changed law.

2. **Administration.** Tax payments should be based on objective and explicit criteria that should be apparent to all and should appear to be reasonable to all. Taxpayers should have easy access to tax procedures and those who administer them. The tax should not be subject to negotiation on a taxpayer-by-taxpayer basis, and payments should be based on an impersonal and uniform application of the tax law, not the judgments—particularly negotiable judgments—made by a tax bureaucrat. Regulations should be developed in a predictable process, should be reasonably derived from the tax statutes, should operate without special treatment for particular taxpayers, and should be understandable, at least in broad terms, to all taxpayers.[71] Taxpayers must also know the process for appeal and what standards may be used to appeal their tax obligation, must be confident that the appeal will be judged fairly, and must be certain that the authorities will not seek revenge on anyone filing an appeal.

3. **Compliance requirements.** Tax calculation should not be a mystery. Each taxpayer should understand how the tax he or she is paying is determined, how changes by the taxpayer would change the tax, and what filing responsibilities are. Everyone should be given full information about all rules and regulations governing economic transactions so all potential competitors can base their decisions on an accurate assessment of potential costs, returns, and market opportunities.

4. **Amount of tax burden.** Each taxpayer should know how much tax he or she is paying (hidden taxes are not likely to allow sound choices to be made about the scope of government) and should know to what government the payment is being made. If taxpayers do not see the tax and believe that the tax is being paid by somebody else, they may believe that the government service has no cost, which is unlikely to produce good fiscal choices. A combined tax bill for several governments (for instance, a property tax bill with a payment that will be divided among a city, a county, and an independent school district) is convenient for collections, but not so good for ensuring that each government's tax actions are clearly understood by taxpayers. However, gauging this standard is not always easy: Is a general sales tax (either a retail sales tax or a value-added tax) with a requirement that customers receive receipts separately stating the tax paid and the tax rate on each transaction more transparent than an individual income tax collected through periodic withholding by the employer with a summary filing at the end of the year? The payments and tax rate are obvious through the year for the former, but the taxpayer has almost no idea of what his or her total payment to the government is, whereas with the latter, the taxpayer may have no running idea, but knows precisely the tax paid at the end of

---

[71]The normal practice is for tax statutes to define the general principles that define the tax. Tax administrators will then prepare the regulations and instructions that put the principles into practice. If taxpayers believe that the regulations do not accurately reflect the intentions of the statute, the court system makes the final determination.

the year. The electorate needs to know the cost of government—but which cost is more relevant? What we do know is that making taxpayers believe that taxes paid by businesses somehow involve no tax payment by individuals is fiscally dishonest.

A tax structure that is not transparent, at least in its broad outlines, is likely to be seen as unknown and probably unfair, can hide significant inequities in the treatment of taxpayers in its confused application, is subject to "rigging" to the advantage of those people in power, and opens the tax authority to the presumption—often accurate—that bribes might be taken and deals may be struck.

Some argue that tax structures can create "fiscal illusions" that conceal from the public the actual budgetary cost of government, allowing politicians to behave irresponsibly and probably causing government expenditure to be higher than a fully informed citizenry would prefer. Evidence of this influence, if any, is far from clear—partly because it is difficult to define what a completely transparent tax structure is and then to calibrate how actual systems differ from that ideal and partly because it is difficult to specify how nontransparency might alter fiscal behavior. However, it is difficult to see how tax structures that make it difficult for the public to understand taxes and to identify the cost of public programs can possibly contribute to the objectives of an open, democratic government.

State and Local Taxes and Economic Development

State and local governments are keenly interested in the impact that their taxes might have on economic development, and particularly on jobs.[72] They are cautious about raising rates, they compare their taxes with those of their neighbors, and they make tax concessions to bring businesses into their markets. Competition for industry among the states, within states, and now with the rest of the world is fierce and can serve as a powerful force for keeping these governments efficient and responsive to the service demands of their citizenry. State and local governments really want to manipulate their fiscal systems to influence business location, employment, and physical investment; market-oriented politicians seem perfectly

---

[72]National politicians do like to try to use tax policy to stimulate economic growth: Joint Committee on Taxation, *Economic Growth and Tax Policy*, (JCX-47-15), February 20, 2015. Tax analysts are suspicious of any efforts to use tax systems for anything other than producing revenue, believing that efforts to distort markets will come to no good in the long haul, probably because they trust the wisdom of free markets over that of politicians. Systems do cause differences in treatment of some activities (e.g., differences in marginal tax rates faced by certain activities), and those differences are likely to distort growth patterns across industries. However, when overall growth rates are measured from peak to peak of the national business cycle, tax cuts show no impact on those growth rates, not even the famous Reagan tax cuts of the early 1980s. An exhaustive review by the Congressional Research Service finds minimal impact of tax rates on long-run economic growth. (Jane G. Gravelle and Donald J. Marples, "Tax Rates and Economic Growth," Congressional Research Service 7-5700, January 2, 2014).

willing to manipulate market forces, thus violating the market process, if it might mean more for their electorates.[73]

But do taxes really have much impact on growth and development? Nontax influences on business profitability (access to markets, availability of usable business sites, levels of production cost, availability of a good-quality workforce and other resources, access to natural resources, etc.) vary so much between prospective locations that they could swamp the effect of taxes. And workers like amenities, some that can be provided by state or local governments and some that come with nature, and those amenities can help businesses obtain that quality workforce. If taxes are so low that these government services cannot be provided at a satisfactory level, growth prospects will be harmed. The question of what governments can do that has an impact has been argued for decades, and it is far from settled now. The evidence does seem to indicate the following with regard to the influence of the general tax climate.[74]

First, tax levels may have a small effect on interregional location of economic activity. For any particular state, the extent to which its overall tax level differs from the level of states with which it competes matters to a degree, but almost certainly less than publicized. In addition, specific tax provisions can make certain lines of business unattractive in a state or locality. The effect of total tax burden on total economic activity is certainly smaller than the impact of particular tax provisions on particular industries. For example, if a state includes the value of business inventory in its property tax base, that state is not going to be particularly attractive for a retailer's distribution and order fulfillment centers.

Second, taxes have a much larger effect on economic outcomes within a region. In other words, the effect of tax differences on location choice between Louisville and Cincinnati is much greater than between Louisville and Phoenix. Within a region, tax differences are likely to be determining because many other factors— climate, access to resources and markets, and so on—are generally the same. Even within a region, the impact is not likely to be great, although certain activities may be badly affected by particular treatment by the state or local tax structure and find

---

[73]In *Cuno v. Daimler Chrysler*, 386 F.3d 738 (6th Cir. 2004), the U.S. Court of Appeals for the Sixth Circuit ruled that Ohio's corporate investment tax credit for new manufacturing equipment and machinery (in this case, provided for a Jeep assembly plant in Toledo, Ohio) violated the Commerce Clause of the U.S. Constitution because state taxpayers who invested in Ohio received the credit, but state taxpayers who invested outside Ohio did not. That would hinder free trade between states. That is exactly what the state intended, of course—to bias the decision of the corporation toward expansion in Ohio. Although praised by some as the first step in stopping inefficient tax bidding among the states that distorts the operations of the free market, the U.S. Supreme Court reversed the decision on appeal, ruling that the taxpayers lacked standing to challenge the credits because they could not demonstrate injury from them [547 U.S. 332 (2006)].

[74]A review of recent evidence appears in Robert Tannenwald, "Do Taxes Matter? The Latest from the Tax Policy Center and CBPP," *State Tax Notes*, July 22, 2015. In particular, evidence gives little support to the idea that reducing state individual income taxes will produce state economic growth. One good and extremely influential analysis across state and local tax systems is the *State Business Tax Climate Index* prepared annually by the Tax Foundation, a nonpartisan research organization. It also is a good source of information about the details of state tax structures.

shifting location to be attractive. Secondary impacts of such relocation are likely to be small: the employees of the firm may be living and shopping in jurisdictions other than that of the activity, and other input suppliers are likely to be located elsewhere as well.

The tax influence is only part of the story of government influence on economic development. Taxing governments use the proceeds to finance public services, with some working to enhance the attractiveness of the jurisdiction to business enterprise. Education, highways and transportation, and public safety services seem to be important, but the evidence is substantially less clear than for tax influences.[75] In doing any evaluation of incentive impact, it is difficult (and necessary) to parse out what would have happened without the incentive, because it is always to a business's advantage to claim the importance of the incentive—that's a good way to get even more.

State and local governments also use various special provisions or narrow tax incentives—targeted abatements that forgive property taxes on new industrial development for specified periods, enterprise zones in which state or local taxes do not apply, deductions or credits for making certain types of capital investment or for hiring certain categories of employees, and so on—that provide exceptional treatment within a general tax to a limited number of taxpayers as an inducement for development. State lawmakers are particularly fond of giving targeted preferences. For instance, a number of states offer special tax preferences to companies making movies in the state. When a movie is made in the state, lawmakers can point with pride to it, suggesting that, without their heroic giveaway of tax dollars, the scenes occurring among the oil rigs might have been made somewhere else— without regard to the fact that the script called for the specific oil rigs of that state and that the preference given the movie company cost state revenue that would need to be made up by taxes levied on other entities within the state if state services aren't to be reduced just a bit. It should be apparent to everyone that a movie involving alpine skiing is not going to be shot in Indiana, regardless of incentives the state might offer. Because of the preferences are specific, they are more attractive to politicians than general improvements to the tax climate that might actually improve the economy. They can point with pride to the specific project accepting the incentive (and, if it is a film credit, maybe get to hang out with the stars), and that just doesn't happen with the gains from making the overall fiscal system more attractive in general for economic growth and development.

What does considerable resort to tax preferences for economic development tell us about a tax system? When the business climate of a state becomes so problematic that tax laws need to be forgiven routinely to attract business, the practice may be a symptom of problems with the tax system itself and a signal that systematic tax reform might be a more useful approach. In effect, tax reform treats existing and new firms equally, and responsible reform also systematically accounts for any tax revenue lost due to reform. Sound tax and fiscal policy probably obviates many of

---

[75]Ronald C. Fisher, "The Effects of State and Local Public Services on Economic Development," *New England Economic Review* (Federal Reserve Bank of Boston) (March/April 1997): 53–66.

the tax perks that businesses seek.[76] Tax analysts are in general agreement that the best tax policy for economic development is a sensible-base broadly defined, low-tax-rate strategy that makes business tax climates more attractive to all firms and less discriminatory among types of business activities. That approach is supported by the fact that many executives of firms that have received economic development tax credits do not know that they have received a tax incentive: Jolley, Lancaster, and Gao find that only 30 percent of executives of firms receiving a North Carolina tax credit were aware that they had the credit.[77] That makes it difficult to argue that incentives are critical for motivating economic development.

Getting elected officials to follow a policy of designing a tax structure that is economically attractive to all, as opposed to being laden with special exceptions to entice some particular footloose business or to relieve taxes paid by a particular industry, is a difficult task, however. The problem is that the geeky guy tinkering in his mother's garage is about as likely to come up with what truly transforms the economic prospects of a region as are the bureaucrat-approved scientists working at firms designated by the state as engines of economic growth. That geek could have gotten going even faster if he hadn't been burdened by paying his share of the taxes forgiven from those footloose firms. Attempts at "good discrimination" in taxation have an excellent chance of being as harmful as unintended ordinary discrimination.[78]

Taxes and Externalities

An important exception to the neutrality standard for tax efficiency occurs when private actions create important negative external effects—that is, when production or consumption by one person or firm causes adverse real consequences for some other person or firm. Market forces induce producers and consumers to react to prices that they pay, and they can be expected to economize on the use of goods and services that must be paid for. The impacts on others, the externalities, are outside the market, so producers and consumers watch out for these external interests only out of the goodness of their hearts—a motive less compelling or reliable than pressures on the pocketbook.

---

[76]Michael Wasylenko, "Taxation and Economic Development: The State of the Economic Literature," *New England Economic Review* (Federal Reserve Bank of Boston) (March/April 1997): 49.

[77]G. Jason Jolley, Mandee Foushee Lancaster, and Jiang Gao, "Tax Incentives and Business Climate: Executive Perceptions from Incented and Nonincented Firms," *Economic Development Quarterly*, 29 (2, 2015): 180–86.

[78]And sometimes truly strange: the state of Iowa provided over $19 million in tax incentives to Kum & Go, a convenience store chain, for moving its headquarters from West Des Moines to downtown Des Moines, roughly ten miles and all within Iowa. Not to bring a company in from Illinois or Texas, but to shift a company ten miles in state! (David Brunori, "Let's Get High for the Children," *State Tax Notes*, September 14, 2015).

Governments may respond to this problem in many different ways, including but not limited to regulations, subsidies, tradable pollution rights, or taxes.[79] Taxes applied under this argument do not seek neutrality in the ordinary sense of staying clear of pure market outcomes; rather, they intend to change private actions so that external effects directly enter the decision calculus. The market is then allowed to respond to consumer demand and to obtain production at least cost, but with both buyer and seller economically aware of (not just morally sensing) the external effects of their actions. Indeed, the tax makes the cost internal (i.e., the external effects get included in the price) to the decisions of both buyers and sellers. These taxes designed to have environmentally friendly effects are sometimes called green taxes. Two types of tax instruments can be applied:

1. *Emission taxes.* These instruments, often called Pigovian taxes after a British economist who proposed them long ago,[80] apply a tax per unit of measured pollution output. They require direct measurement if they are to have their desired incentive effect and ordinarily apply to only one emission type at a time. They apply at the last link in the production-distribution chain to those emitting the substance into the environment. Unlike charges, these taxes bring no expectation that the payer receives anything in return, except that he or she is not treated as a lawbreaker.

2. *Indirect taxes on goods or services.* These taxes apply to goods or services, the production or consumption of which causes environmental or other external damage.[81] Taxes on the use of carbon fuels or ozone-depleting chemicals, for example, discourage processes using them and encourage the quest for alternatives. They do not directly tax the discharge with undesirable external effect, but they seek to discourage the discharge indirectly.

Some countries levy what are called "green taxes," and high motor-fuel taxes are one such device. The United States does not levy a high motor-fuel tax (we levy one of the lowest in the developed world), but it could be sensible as a mechanism to make motorists face the full external impact of their fuel purchases. The higher tax would serve partly as an environmental measure designed to discourage emissions of the greenhouse gases associated with internal combustion engines, partly as a measure to reduce highway congestion caused by heavy use of private automobiles, and partly as a measure to reduce use of a product that helps keep the country involved in Middle Eastern politics. But the United States, in addition to failing to use the tax as a Pigouvian tool, adds to the problem by earmarking much of motor-fuel tax revenue for highway maintenance and operation, thus encouraging even further use of motor vehicles.

Governments also identify particular products or services that seem undesirable and use taxes to discourage their production or consumption. Examples include

---

[79]For greater detail, see J. B. Opschoor and H. B. Vos, *Economic Instruments for Environmental Protection* (Paris: Organization for Economic Cooperation and Development, 1989).

[80]A. C. Pigou, *The Economics of Welfare* (London: Macmillan, 1920).

[81]An excellent analysis of environmental taxation, particularly fuel taxes, is Dirk Heine, John Norregaard, and Ian W. H. Parry, "Environmental Tax Reform: Principles from Theory and Practice to Date," IMF Working Paper, WP12/180 (July 2012).

a Canadian federal tax on automobile air conditioners (an extra inducement to convince automobile purchasers to skip an accessory that reduces fuel economy) and the U.S. gas-guzzler tax (a tax applied to vehicles that do not meet prescribed fuel-economy ratings). Some other examples of green taxes include higher taxes on leaded than on unleaded motor fuel in a number of countries, taxes on batteries in Sweden, a Belgian tax on disposable razors, taxes on plastic bags in Ireland and other jurisdictions, and taxes on emissions of carbon dioxide in Denmark, Finland, the Netherlands, Norway, and Sweden.[82] The taxes intend to distort ordinary market choices by making polluters face the true (internal plus external) costs of their actions.

Conclusion

The number of handles available to governments seems almost without end. In general, the many possible handles eventually translate into taxes on incomes, taxes on wealth, and taxes on purchase or sales. Taxes require an involuntary payment; they are not collected for services received on a normal exchange basis. Because of separation of service receipt and payment, it is possible to evaluate taxes on the basis of planning criteria. Those criteria are equity (vertical and horizontal), adequacy, collectability, transparency, and economic effects. Design of tax programs for consistency with these criteria involves three steps. First, identify a tax base that is consistent with the logic of either the ability-to-pay or the benefits-received principle for dividing the cost of government. Second, structure the tax so that it is as broad as possible, including as few preferences and exceptions as possible. Third, levy the lowest possible tax rate to the base. That design will produce a broad-base, low-rate tax system that yields revenue with the least possible collateral damage, the fundamental objective of tax policy.

QUESTIONS AND EXERCISES

1. Patterns and structure of revenue for state and local government are important policy concerns because they establish who will pay for public services. Revenue revision can begin only with a clear understanding of where revenue policy leaves the state and its localities now and what available options have not been selected. Furthermore, it is useful to understand what conditions are like in surrounding areas. Evidence for such discussions can be drawn from sources such as the Department of Commerce's Survey of Current Business (monthly);

---

[82]"Taxes for a Cleaner Planet," *The Economist* (June 28, 1997): 84.

the Bureau of Economic Analysis; the Census Bureau's Census of Governments (quinquennially), Governmental Finances (annually), and State Tax Collections (annually); and state tax handbooks published annually by Research Institute of America (RIA) and Commerce Clearing House (CCH). You can find valuable data at the Bureau of Economic Analysis (www.bea.gov) and Bureau of Census (www.census.gov) websites. From those and similar sources, prepare answers to these questions about the revenue system in your state:

a. How does the burden of state, local, and state-local taxation in your state compare with that of the nation and region? (Comparisons are often made as percentages of state personal income and per capita income. What is the logical difference between the two measures?) State and local tax collections for each state are available at the website of the U.S. Bureau of Census (www. census.gov); look under the section labeled "Public Sector." How does the local share of state and local taxes compare?

b. Prepare an estimate of the relationship between business and individual tax shares for your state. How do you decide what is a business tax and what is an individual tax?

c. How rapidly have state and local taxes grown in your state during the past five years? Is that faster or slower than growth in state personal income and the rate of inflation? Have there been tax increases (decreases) affecting that growth?

d. What are the major revenue sources used by governments in your state? How does relative use of those sources compare with the nation and the region? Does your state have any major taxes not common to other states (severance, business and occupation, local income, etc.)? Are some typical taxes not used?

2. The Congressional Budget Office reports that the highest 1 percent of income-earning households paid 38.7 percent of total federal individual income tax collected in calendar year 2009. What does this information indicate about progressivity or regressivity of the federal income tax? Explain.

3. Not-for-profit organizations lack the authority to levy taxes for support of their programs and must finance their operations from a variety of revenue streams. Some are commercial and operate largely from the sale of goods or services (including revenue from service contracts with governments), others are charitable and operate with various sorts of donated support, and others combine revenue from a variety of sources. Select a not-for-profit organization in your area and analyze its revenue resources. The entity should be chosen because you are interested in the service provided by that entity and because the entity will cooperate with your review and assessment.

a. Analyze the revenues received by the entity (taxes, charges, donations, etc.— provide disaggregated data), examine trends and shifts, determine whether sources are sensitive to general economic conditions, explore limits and controls that the entity may face, and review the processes by which revenue decisions are made. You should pay particular attention to the division of revenues from use of endowment, charges for services, and annual donations. To what extent does the entity employ the principle that those using services must pay (an analog to the benefits-received principle in taxation)? In light of the purpose of the entity, to what extent is payment for service appropriate?

b. Examine how the entity manages fund development, that is, money raising. Is it self-administered, or does another entity administer the system, possibly by contract? Are protective controls properly in place? What are the costs associated with this activity?

c. On the basis of your investigation, what do you conclude about revenues available to the entity? Do you have recommendations for reform and restructuring? Be specific. Link your conclusions to the information developed in your analysis.

CASE FOR DISCUSSION

CASE 8–1

Birth, Marriage, Death, and Taxes

Scarlett O'Hara, in *Gone with the Wind,* laid it out for us: "Death, taxes and childbirth! There's never any convenient time for any of them."[83] But timing matters in all things, and it turns out that those events, plus marriage, are related. That's what the empirical evidence shows.

Consider These Questions

1. Do these impacts create social or economic losses for the country?

2. How might these influences conflict with the normal criteria for good tax policy?

3. How could revisions of tax structure reduce these influences on birth, marriage, and death?

A core economic principle is that incentives influence human behavior, and our tax system creates many incentives, some purposeful and some accidental. The incentive results when a change of behavior produces a reduction of tax liability that exceeds any cost associated with that change. (In other words, we expect behavior to change because of gain, not simply because of spiteful behavior against the tax.) We are not surprised to find that tax structures influence where and how people shop, how households and businesses invest, the way businesses structure their operations and organizational framework, and so on.

But what about impacts beyond the scope of economics and finance? Economists believe that incentives shape all behavior, so it is not surprising that they have sought and found a tax influence on some basics of humanity—namely, timing of birth, marriage, and death. Before the noneconomists explode in outrage, please

---

[83]Margaret Mitchell, *Gone with the Wind* (New York: Macmillan, 1936), vol. 2, pt. 4, chap. 38.

understand that the tax impact applies to the propensity for behavior or on its timing; it isn't the only thing that matters for the events themselves. The general principle is that wherever there are tax consequences from an action, it is reasonable to anticipate a response to the incentives provided.

The tax impact on births is a product of "all or nothing" provisions in the U.S. Tax Code: if a child is part of a family for one minute of the year, full tax advantages are provided for the year, and these advantages are lost for the old year if the child is born one minute into the next year. There are three tax advantages to families with children: the child tax credit (provided from 1998, the credit directly reduces tax liability for each child in the family), an earned income tax credit (a cash subsidy for working families) that is more generous to families with two or more children, and the personal exemption that reduces the base upon which tax is levied for each member of the family. Whether a child is born in late December or early January can have a significant consequence for total family tax liability over the two years.

Evidence does indicate a tax-influenced pattern of births. In four of the seven years from 1997 through 2003, the day with more births than any other has fallen between Christmas and New Year's. (The other three were in September, the month of most frequent birth for decades and decades, presumably the result of people spending more time inside the house during the cold and dreary days of winter.)[84] Economists Chaudra and Dickert-Conlin, using a sample of children from the National Longitudinal Study of Youth, found that the probability of birth in the last week of December rather than the first week of January is positively correlated with tax benefits from earlier birth (families with more to gain are more likely to have earlier births). They estimate that a higher tax benefit of $500 raises the probability of birth in the last week of December by 26.9 percent.[85] The technologies of caesarian birth and induced labor do seem to be used for tax advantage.

The tax impact on numbers of children also works in reverse because the IRS, something like a modern day Pied Piper of Hamelin, apparently made children disappear. In 1986, the IRS started to require that people include the Social Security number of anyone claimed as dependent on their federal individual income tax return. Tax returns for 1987 showed 5 million fewer children than had been claimed in 1986, appearing to make the IRS one of the greatest mass murderers in world history. Families who had neglected to get Social Security numbers for their children quickly repaired that omission, and 2 million children returned to the returns in the next year, but the rest were gone forever.[86]

Marriage patterns also appear to be influenced by tax incentives. Although recent years have reduced the likelihood that a married couple would pay higher tax than a similarly situated unmarried couple, for many years the impact could be significant. Sjoquist and Walker found from Census data a significant negative impact on marriages in the early 1990s: fewer couples marry in the last two months of the

---

[84]David Leonhardt, "To-Do List: Wrap Gifts, Have Baby," *New York Times,* December 20, 2006.

[85]Stacy Dickert-Conlin and Amitabh Chandra, "Taxes and the Timing of Births," *Journal of Political Economy* 107 (1999): 161–77.

[86]Ariel Rubinstein, "Freak-Freakonomics," *The Economist's Voice* 3 (December 2006): 1–6.

year relative to marriages in the early months of the year.[87] Alm and Whittington, using data from the Panel Study of Income Dynamics, found a significant impact on marriage probabilities from the last quarter of one year to the first quarter of the next.[88] Interestingly enough, although the incentive ought to work in the opposite direction as well, no impact on divorce rates has been discovered. Maybe noneconomic factors matter more for ending a marriage than for starting one. Or maybe the judicial processes necessary for divorce are more difficult to time.

The impact of deaths may appear when estate tax rates change. Kopczuk and Slemrod examine the timing of deaths around the time of changes in the U.S. estate tax system—increases or decreases—when living a little longer or dying a little sooner would significantly change tax liability. Their analysis of the timing of deaths involving taxable estates around thirteen major tax changes from 1917 to 1984 shows a clear impact. In particular, for deaths within two weeks of an estate tax change, $10,000 of tax saving (adjusted to 2000 price levels) increase the probability of dying in the lower tax period by 1.6 percent.[89] And the influence is not limited to the United States. Gans and Leigh analyzed the effect when Australia abolished its estate tax on July 1, 1979. In this case, they found that one-half of those estates that ordinarily would have been taxed in the last week of the tax managed to avoid it.[90] Further, they estimated that one in twenty likely deaths in the last week of June was delayed by enough time to escape the tax. Whether these timing changes involve choices about pulling the plug on granny's respirator, some fudging of death date reporting, or some combination of the two is unknown.

---

[87]David Sjoquist and Mary Beth Walker, "The Marriage Tax and the Rate and Timing of Marriage," *National Tax Journal* 48 (1995): 547–58.
[88]James Alm and Leslie Whittington, "Does the Income Tax Affect Marital Decisions?" *National Tax Journal* 48 (1995): 565–72.
[89]Wojciech Kopczuk and Joel Slemrod, "Dying to Save Taxes: Evidence from Estate Tax Returns on the Death Elasticity," *Review of Economics and Statistics* 85 (May 2003): 256–65.
[90]Joshua Gans and Andrew Leigh, "Toying with Death and Taxes: Some Lessons from Down Under," *Economists' Voice* 3 (June 2006): 1–3.

CHAPTER 9

Major Tax Structures: Income Taxes

Chapter Contents

In this chapter and the following two chapters, we examine the general nature of the three predominant tax bases: income, consumption, and property. Taxes on income and consumption typically apply to current transaction values; property taxes apply to the value of holdings (a stock value), not transactions (a flow value). In many respects, that difference makes property taxes more difficult to administer, although growth of the underground economy—economic activity "off the books," or outside traditional accounting records—has complicated operation of the other two taxes in recent years. It is useful to start with taxes on income. Americans apparently prefer this tax base to other options; we rely considerably more on income taxes than do other developed democracies.

This chapter outlines the structure and terminology of income taxation and provides some comparisons of types of income taxes. It examines performance of the income base and several issues that elements of income taxes raise. Some reform alternatives are discussed. However, it does not delve deeply into the darkest arts of income tax return preparation. One chapter provides far too little space for that topic given the complexities of U.S. income taxes today. This fact alone should raise questions in your mind about whether or not our income taxes, as presently structured, are entirely consistent with the transparency standard discussed in the previous chapter.

There is one important point to emphasize at the outset. All taxes labeled *income* do not operate in the same fashion, and statements about the yield response, collectability, equity, or economic effects of a particular tax must carefully define what the structure of the tax being examined actually is. (Indeed, an analyst must go behind the label to understand the structure of any tax as a first step in examination of the likely performance of that tax.)

Our investigation has to start with a consideration of how to define income, which is the starting point of the tax. Income might roughly be defined as the money or other gain received over a period of time by an individual, corporation, or other entity for labor or services rendered or from property, natural resources, investments, operations, and so on. (A formal definition is discussed later in the chapter.) But governments differ in what particular receipts are selected for taxation, how those receipts are manipulated to become the tax base, and what structure of rates applies to that base (changes to one or more those three basic elements constitutes every income tax reform program). Because of those tax policy options, general statements about burden distribution can be hazardous. For example, the federal individual income tax has a generally progressive burden distribution because statutory rates increase as income is higher and because the tax applies to a broad measure of income that includes some kinds of income that are particularly significant for affluent households; many local income taxes have a generally proportional or slightly regressive burden pattern because they often levy flat rates on a base limited to wages and salaries and do not tax types of income that are particularly important to the more affluent. Not all income taxes have progressive burden distributions; it depends on the structure of the particular tax, and manipulations in structure and rates can make any income tax more or less progressive.

Governments tax the income of individuals and corporations.[1] Unincorporated business (partnership, proprietorship) income is ordinarily taxed through the individual income tax, although some countries apply an enterprise or business income tax to income from both incorporated and unincorporated businesses. Wage and salary income (payrolls) and income of the self-employed are taxed both by the regular individual income tax and by separate taxes to finance the social insurance system (Social Security, unemployment compensation, etc.). Individual income tax yield is much greater than that of corporate income taxes, so greater attention is focused

---

[1]A corporation is an entity created by a government (state or federal) and empowered with legal rights, privileges, and liabilities of an individual, separate and distinct from those held by the individuals who own the entity. Think of the corporation as a *legal person*. Owners have liability limited to their investment in the corporation. A growing number of states now allow limited-liability companies, a business form taxed like a partnership (business income is fully distributed to the owners for taxation and is not taxed separately at the business level) and easier to establish than a corporation, but with the liability limits of a corporation. And Subchapter S corporations, a type of smaller corporate entity, are taxed like partnerships as well.

on the former. Many of the structural elements of individual taxation apply to the corporate form as well; many other corporate tax questions are too arcane for coverage here. One important issue to which there may be no answer is considered: How should corporate income taxes be related to the income tax of individual corporate stockholders? Do corporations have tax-bearing ability that is separate from that of the owners of the corporation?

Some Background

Before the Civil War, the federal government relied on excises (sales taxes on tobacco products, distilled spirits, refined sugar, carriages, etc.) and tariffs on imported goods to finance its limited activities. War, however, was too expensive to finance with that revenue alone. The northern states enacted an income tax in 1861 (3 percent on all incomes of more than $800 per year) to help finance their war expenditure, but the law was so unclearly structured that it was not put into effect. A second income tax passed in 1862 and was enforced. This tax applied an initial rate of 3 percent and a top rate of 5 percent on incomes of more than $10,000. It expired in 1872, having raised about $376 million (about 20 percent of internal revenues produced during the period).[2] Abraham Lincoln, address the "White House," shows up on the tax list as paying $1,296 on an income of $25,000 for 1864. We know about his tax situation because tax returns were public in that era, and that publicity was the primary device for ensuring that people actually paid the tax they owed. (Shame probably would not work as a substitute for Internal Revenue Service enforcement now.)

There remained an important legal question. As Chapter 8 noted, the U.S. Constitution requires federal direct taxes to be apportioned among the states, but it was not clear whether an individual income tax was legally direct or indirect.[3] If the tax were direct, it would have to be divided among the states according to population, and each state's share then raised from its population according to income. A state with lower per capita income would have to apply higher income tax rates than would a state with higher per capita income. However, the Civil War tax had the same rates for all states, and in *Springer v. United States* (102 U.S. 586 [1880]), the U.S. Supreme Court held that the income tax was, for purposes of the Constitution, indirect and hence valid. By the time of the ruling, the tax was no longer in force, so the ruling had minimal immediate importance.

In 1894, the federal government again enacted an individual income tax, this time in a package with reduced tariffs. The low-rate tax (2 percent of income above

[2]Harold M. Groves, *Financing Government* (New York: Holt, 1939), 153–55.
[3]Corporate income taxes were never regarded as direct taxes on individuals and thus were never subject to apportionment. The federal corporate tax began some years before the federal individual income tax that is in place now.

$4,000) affected only a small portion of the population, but it was challenged on constitutional grounds. This time the U.S. Supreme Court, in *Pollock v. Farmer's Loan and Trust* (157 U.S. 429 [1895] and 158 U.S. 601 [1895]), ruled that the income tax was direct and hence subject to apportionment. The tax as levied was unconstitutional and could not be collected. The decision left the federal government with no broad-based revenue source to finance the increased international role the nation was taking in the early part of the twentieth century.[4]

To levy an individual income tax with the same rates throughout the country would require a constitutional amendment. Can you imagine Americans amending the Constitution to explicitly permit an individual income tax now? How did it happen back in the early part of the twentieth century? In 1909, President William Howard Taft agreed to accept an "excise" on corporate net income (which did not require an amendment to enact because the tax was viewed as indirect) if Congress would propose an amendment for a national individual income tax. (A tax business/tax individuals deal!) Both the amendment and the excise quickly passed. Getting approval of the necessary number of states for the amendment to be approved took longer, but when Wyoming became the thirty-sixth state to ratify the Sixteenth Amendment (1913), the revenue problem was resolved: "The Congress shall have power to lay and collect taxes on incomes, from whatever source derived, without apportionment among the several States, and without regard to any census or enumeration." That provided the financial base for defense and, eventually, an expanded federal role in domestic affairs.[5] The 1913 income tax applied a normal rate of 1 percent on incomes in excess of $3,000 ($4,000 for married persons) with a top surtax rate of 6 percent (a combined rate of 7 percent) on incomes above $500,000. Only about 1 percent of the population had income sufficient to be liable for the tax.[6] There were 357,598 returns filed (so few that the Bureau of Internal Revenue audited them all), with an average tax of $78.

Only with the advent of the Second World War did the tax become a tax paid by most of the citizenry as the level of income at which the tax started to apply fell to levels earned by ordinary households.[7] In 1939, 7.6 million returns were filed to yield $1,028.8 million in that fiscal year; by 1945, the number of returns had increased to

---

[4]How desperate was the federal government for revenue at the turn of the twentieth century? So desperate that it even applied a tax to chewing gum.

[5]Revenue from the individual income tax made the Eighteenth Amendment (1919) to the Constitution feasible. Before the income tax, the federal government needed the revenue from alcoholic beverage excises to finance its operations and could not have afforded prohibition of making, transporting, and selling those beverages. With the tax, prohibition was possible (although possibly unwise).

[6]Richard Good, *The Individual Income Tax,* rev. ed. (Washington, D.C.: Brookings Institution, 1976), 3. There was a problem in the initial law. It applied the tax to "lawful income." Congress soon amended the law to remove the word "lawful," thus clearing up definitional problems and opening up additional enforcement powers. It should be pointed out that gangster Al Capone was sent to prison for tax evasion, not for the murders, bootlegging, prostitution, racketeering, or other crimes he almost certainly committed. The change in the tax law undoubtedly helped stop his villainy. Never forget that it was the Bureau of Internal Revenue, not the Federal Bureau of Investigation, that finally sent him to prison.

[7]In the early days of World War II, there was serious discussion about financing the war effort with a general sales tax rather than through increased use of the individual income tax. The income tax won out, primarily because that was the preference of President Roosevelt.

49.9 million to yield $19,034.3 million.[8] Employer withholding of individual income tax from wages began in 1943, thus dramatically simplifying the collection process and facilitating application of the tax to the general population. Until 1944, collections from the corporate income tax had exceeded those from the individual income tax in all years but 1934 and 1937; from 1944 onward, individual income tax collections have always exceeded those from the corporate income tax, now by a great margin. The corporate income tax contributed about 30 percent of federal revenue in the 1950s, but the share has fallen to around 10 percent today.

The third, and newest, portion of the federal income tax structure are the payroll taxes for support of the social insurance system. These narrow-base taxes on wage and salary income and certain income from self-employment may legally be imposed on the employer, imposed on the employee, or shared between the employer and employee; most analysts suspect that the economic incidence is on the employee regardless of who is responsible for sending payment to the government. The shifting logic is simple: the employer knows that paying a certain wage to the employee will require an accompanying payroll tax payment to the government. Why wouldn't the employer take account of that payment when deciding how much to offer employees and how many employees to hire? These taxes now support the Social Security system (old age, disability, and survivors income support), Medicare (health insurance for the elderly), and unemployment compensation. The Social Security and unemployment compensation taxes began with the Social Security Act of 1935; the Medicare tax began with amendments to that act in 1965. For most lower-income (and many middle-income) individuals and families, their social insurance payroll tax liability amounts to more than the amount of individual income tax owed.

The individual and corporate income taxes and the payroll taxes on wages and salaries are the dominant government revenue source in the United States. Table 9–1 reports the pattern for all governments from 1930 to 2014. In 2014 individual income taxes yielded $1,746.8 billion, corporate income taxes yielded $476.2 billion, and receipts for the social insurance system (largely payroll taxes for Social Security, Medicare, and unemployment compensation) produced $1,164.1 billion, 67.8 percent of the $4,995.4 billion in current receipts to all governments.[9] Revenue from individual and corporate income taxes increased dramatically as a share of gross domestic product (GDP) with the need to finance World War II, but fell modestly when the war ended. The share was from 11.5 percent to 13.5 percent of GDP until 2000, when it jumped to 14.7 percent. It has now fallen to 12.8 percent, although all post-WWII shares are well above pre-WWII levels. The percentage increased a bit in the 1990s, the product of somewhat higher rates and great prosperity of high-income individuals. The corporate income tax alone fell as percent of GDP from around 6 percent in the 1950s to around 2 percent now, partly for policy reasons and partly because businesses structure their organizations to avoid subjecting themselves to the tax. When social insurance taxes are added in, the income-base

---

[8]U.S. Bureau of the Census, *Historical Statistics of the United States, Colonial Times to 1970: Part 2,* Bicentennial Ed. (Washington, D.C.: U.S. Government Printing Office, 1975), 1107, 1110.
[9]Bureau of Economic Analysis, National Income and Product Accounts. www.bea.gov

Table 9–1

Individual and Corporate Income Taxes and Social Insurance Contributions as Percentage of Total Government Receipts and Gross Domestic Product (GDP)

	1930	1935	1940	1945	1950	1955	1960	1965	1970	1975	1980	1985	1990	1995	2000	2005	2010	2013	2014
Individual and Corporate Income Taxes as % of:																			
All government current receipts	19.0%	16.2%	24.1%	57.6%	54.6%	55.6%	49.9%	47.9%	46.8%	43.9%	47.3%	41.5%	42.1%	42.4%	46.9%	43.2%	39.1%	44%	44.5%
Gross domestic product	2.1%	2.3%	3.9%	13.3%	12.3%	13.0%	12.7%	12.0%	12.9%	11.9%	13.5%	12.0%	12.4%	12.7%	14.7%	12.5%	10.7%	13%	12.8%
Income Taxes Plus Social Insurance Contributions as % of:																			
All government current receipts	20.0%	17.1%	35.5%	67.9%	62.9%	65.0%	62.1%	61.0%	63.0%	64.2%	68.2%	64.8%	66.2%	66.5%	69.5%	67.1%	64.2%	67.1%	67.8%
Gross domestic product	2.2%	2.5%	5.8%	15.7%	14.2%	15.2%	15.9%	15.3%	17.4%	17.3%	19.5%	18.7%	19.5%	19.9%	21.9%	19.5%	17.5%	19.2%	19.5%

SOURCE: Bureau of Economic Analysis, National Income and Products Accounts. www.bea.gov

share of all government revenue is more than 64 percent and 19.5 percent of GDP. This latter percentage had been generally increasing for fifty years but has fallen somewhat since 2000.

The Argument about Taxing Income

For the System of Taxing Income

Many regard an income tax as a fair and reasonable source of revenue because of the nature of the base and the method of its administration—and it certainly is productive and heavily used in the United States. Why do many believe that the income tax is a satisfactory source?[10]

EQUITY—MEASURING ABILITY

Income is an important measure of a taxpayer's capacity to bear the cost of government. Economic well-being is significantly determined by current income. An exception is the person with substantial wealth and minimal current income, so a broader measure could include current income and net wealth converted into an income equivalent, but such logic does not appear in income tax codes. Measuring the value of an individual's net wealth each year would be difficult in comparison to measuring current income for the year, so practicality helps explain why wealth does not figure into the ability calculation. Current income remains for most people most of the time a reasonable, if not perfect, indicator of relative affluence.

EQUITY—ADJUSTABILITY

The U.S. income tax, which requires annual taxpayer returns, can be made to account for individual taxpayer conditions (family size, infirmities, special economic circumstances, etc.).[11] This offers a unique advantage over taxes not based on that filing.

---

[10]For many years, the U.S. Advisory Commission on Intergovernmental Relations conducted a nationwide survey to discover what tax Americans viewed as the least fair. The federal income tax or the local property tax was always seen as the least fair. In the last poll (1994), 27 percent viewed the federal income tax as the worst, compared with 28 percent for the local property tax. As in previous surveys, respondents viewed the state income tax as the least unfair (7 percent). This is an interesting finding, given that the state income taxes are virtually all linked copies of the federal income tax, although at lower rates. U.S. Advisory Commission on Intergovernmental Relations, *Changing Public Attitudes on Governments and Taxes 1994* (Washington, D.C.: U.S. Advisory Commission on Intergovernmental Relations, 1995). The Tax Foundation has done similar surveys in recent years, and the federal income tax and the local property taxes continue their status as regarded as least fair. Scott A. Hodge and Andrew Chamberlain, "2006 Annual Survey of U.S. Attitudes on Tax and Wealth," Tax Foundation Special Report 141 (April 5, 2006).

[11]Not all national income taxes have an annual return, but rather rely on exact withholding of tax by the employer and others paying the individual. The total amount withheld by the employer and then remitted to the government is the amount owed, and that's it. That is a simple system, but it does not allow for adjustments to the taxpayer's circumstances during the year that might reduce ability to bear the cost of government.

Table 9–2
Distribution of Federal Income Tax Payments and Effective Tax Rates By Income Quintiles for All Families, 2013

| Quintile | Individual Income Tax | | Corporate Income Tax | | Social Insurance Tax | |
	Tax Share	Effective Tax Rate	Tax Share	Effective Tax Rate	Tax Share	Effective Tax Rate
Lowest	−4	−7.2	1.6	0.8	5.4	8
Second	−1.2	−1.2	2.9	0.8	9.5	7.8
Middle	3.9	2.6	5.3	0.9	15.2	8.3
Fourth	13.3	6.1	9.5	1.2	23.8	9
Highest	88	15.5	79.4	3.7	45.9	6.7
All	100	9.2	100	2.6	100	7.7
Top 1%	38.3	23.6	46.8	7.7	4.7	2.4

SOURCE: Congressional Budget Office, The Distribution of Household Income and Federal Taxes, 2013. (Washington, D.C.: CBO, 2016). https://www.cbo.gov/publication/51361

For instance, a package of cigarettes is taxed regardless of the economic status of the purchaser because it would be too costly to do a check of taxpayer circumstances with each transaction. Adjustments when a tax return is filed can allow for circumstances that restrict tax-bearing capacity and might merit adjustment of tax owed.

Table 9–2 shows the pattern of the federal taxes on income as they are distributed across quintiles of household income, taking full account of likely shifting of taxes paid by a business (i.e., corporate income and the employer share of social insurance payroll taxes) to individuals. The pattern shows considerable progressivity of individual and corporate income taxes, even through to the highest-income taxpayers—as household income is higher, the effective tax rate paid is higher as well, and the effective rate increase appears through the quintiles. The effective tax rate for the individual income tax paid by the extremely fortunate highest income earning 1 percent of the population is 23.6 percent, dramatically different from the minus 7.2 percent effective rate paid by the lowest quintile of the population.[12] The effective corporate income tax rate paid by the top 1 percent is 7.7 percent, versus 0.8 percent for the lowest quintile. The evidence is clear that these two taxes are progressive. Although some high-income households certainly exploit provisions of the tax system to dramatically reduce the tax they owe, the evidence is that on average these households face much higher tax burdens than do lower-income households.

The social insurance taxes—Social Security, Medicare, and unemployment compensation—are narrowly based on wage and salary income (payrolls), are levied at flat (or even declining statutory rates), and make no adjustment for taxpayer

---

[12]The negative effective rate reflects the impact of fully refundable credits received by these households that exceed the amount of tax they would otherwise owe. In other words, their relationship with the federal income tax is to receive payments, rather than to pay tax. The effective tax rate is negative for first and second lowest income quintiles on average. That does not mean that all households in those quintiles are net recipients, but it does reflect the overall average.

economic circumstances. They do not apply to income from capital ownership (particularly dividends, interest, and rent). The taxes supporting the social insurance system show a pattern of regressivity at high and low ends of the income distribution and some progressivity in the middle. Extremely high-income households bear an extremely low effective social insurance tax rate, in dramatic contrast to the other income taxes.

The pattern of effective tax rates translates into a heavily concentrated income tax burden. Table 9–2 shows that the highest-income earners in the nation, the top 1%, paid 38.3 percent of total individual income tax and fully 88 percent of the net income tax bill is paid by the highest income-earning 20 percent of the population, an even greater share for the individual income tax than for the corporate income tax. This reflects both the extreme concentration of income in the United States, a concentration that has increased significantly in the past few years, and the legal structure of the taxes. High-income households have done very well, both absolutely and relative to how middle- and lower-income households have done, and their high individual income tax burdens reflect that success. In any case, these share patterns indicate that the tax is moving toward its origins as a class tax, not a tax paid by the masses that it became with the shared sacrifice to fight World War II. It is definitely not the case that the top 1 percent of the population successfully avoids paying a considerable share of the cost of federal government services.

YIELD

A broad income base permits significant revenue at socially acceptable rates, and the base grows at least as rapidly as the growth in the overall economy, possibly even somewhat more rapidly, i. e., the revenue elasticity is greater than one. Governments with income taxes need not seek rate increases as often, or apply such high nominal rates, to keep up with growing public demand for services as may governments with narrower bases or bases with lower elasticity to economic growth. The base of both individual and corporate income taxes is, however, subject to considerable cyclical variation, with corporate profits particularly being sensitive to economic decline. During the Great Recession, collections from both dropped considerably, creating special difficulty for state government finances because those governments must annually balance their budgets.

BASE BREADTH

The resource distortion with the general income tax may be less than with some narrower bases, but there will be distortions from individual and corporate income taxation.[13] Many provisions do certainly influence the economic behavior of individuals in saving, investment, housing, compensation packages, organization form

---

[13]Income taxes may distort work and investment decisions made by individuals and businesses. Thus, the resources-distortion basis for general income taxation is unclear at best. Economists seek an "optimal tax," that is, one minimizing total distortions. See Joel Slemrod, "Optimal Taxation and Optimal Tax Systems," *Journal of Economic Perspectives* 4 (Winter 1990): 157–78.

of the business, and so on. It is politically popular to place extremely heavy tax burdens on the affluent, and the data just shown demonstrate that this is exactly what we do in the United States. But there are limits to this because these affluent individuals are exactly the ones most able to take evasive action that distorts the overall production in the economy. The income taxes that politicians create do not tax all types of income at the same tax rate. That ends up creating economic distortions as individuals seek to arrange their economic affairs so that their income ends up in the favored categories. Breadth of coverage reduces that distortion. To the extent that breadth permits a low rate, there are clearly efficiency and equity advantages. Distortions of economic behavior are an important element in the case for and against income taxation.

Against the System of Taxing Income

Many others argue that the income tax system has horrible flaws and that it should be fundamentally changed. Indeed, it is often argued that consumption is a far better base for distributing the cost of government than is income. What are the elements of that anti–income tax argument? Here comes the laundry list of charges against income taxation!

Transparency and Compliance

The individual income tax is so complicated that it violates the transparency standard and compliance is too expensive. Taxpayers do not understand the system, its provisions are so arcane as to be beyond the comprehension of all but very few experts, the electorate sees little association between tax paid and the work of government, and some privileged individuals use loopholes (or tax preferences) designed in the backrooms of congressional committees to avoid paying their fair share of the tax. Billions of taxpayer hours are spent on complying with the tax, but despite all the attention, only a tiny fraction fully understands how the system works, and the withholding process conceals how much individual taxpayers actually pay. In 2005, the individual income tax law contained more than a dozen distinct retirement planning schemes with a confusing array of rules and regulations, at least nine separate preference programs for encouraging education spending, an earned income tax credit (EITC) program for low-income workers so complicated that 72 percent of those claiming the credit paid a tax preparer to complete their returns, and a second tax structure (the Alternative Minimum Income Tax) that penalizes taxpayers for qualifying for certain legal tax preferences and requires them to do two separate tax calculations, only one of which will actually produce tax revenue.[14] Changes since then have not reduced the complexity.

---

[14]Testimony of Nina E. Olsen, National Taxpayer Advocate, to the President's Advisory Panel on Federal Tax Reform, March 3, 2005.

The majority of households have a paid preparer do their taxes (56 percent of returns for tax year 2012), so the citizenry really doesn't know much about what goes on in determining their liability. For more complicated returns (taxes paid through the regular 1040 return), 95.7 percent of returns were done by a preparer.[15] That is a strong indictment of the perceived complexity of the tax, and it suggests that a large share of the population has little idea what goes on in the tax structure. Their tax is whatever the tax preparer says it is. In terms of seeing the burden, regardless of whether the taxpayer does his or her own return or hires someone else to prepare it, people are more aware of their tax refund at the end of the year (the difference between what the employer has withheld during the year and actual tax liability) than how much their tax liability is. Simplification would make the tax more transparent and would reduce its collection costs. No discussion of federal income tax issues is complete without consideration of the complexity problem, even though no serious broad simplification has occurred in the past three decades, probably because it is often the complications that deliver tax preferences for certain categories of taxpayer, and few want to sacrifice their own tax advantages.

ADMINISTRATION AND COMPLIANCE

The income tax system is expensive to collect. The IRS operating budget in fiscal 2015 was $10.9 billion. It had over 81,000 employees and dealt with more than 144 million individual income tax returns and 5.8 million corporate income tax returns. A number of critics maintain that, even with this expenditure, the IRS is poorly administered, is not particularly helpful when taxpayers request assistance, and abuses its powers to inspect individual and business records. What is clear is that the IRS has suffered severe resource reductions: its 2015 budget is about 20 percent less in current dollar terms than in 2010, its total staff is 14 percent smaller, and its enforcement staff is 20 percent less. At least as many people argue that the agency is badly under-resourced as criticize its operations. State and local governments collect their income taxes independently of the federal government, although federal and state administrations do share information, and those costs add to the overall administrative expense of collecting taxes on income.

The administrative cost per dollar collected is small—currently reported as less than 50 cents per $100 collected. But this cost is only the tip of the iceberg because these taxes are collected in a taxpayer active fashion with major compliance responsibilities placed on the taxpayer. Taxpayers compliance cost is at least ten times the cost of administration.[16] The revenues of tax preparation firm H&R Block alone exceed $3 billion per year, and all that amounts to taxpayer cost of complying with the tax. Add to that the revenues of all the other tax preparers, tax accountants, and

---

[15]Data from Tax Statistics from the Statistics of Income Division of the Internal Revenue Service. www.irs.gov/taxstats

[16]Marsha Blumenthal and Joel Slemrod, "The Compliance Cost of the U.S. Individual Income Tax System: A Second Look after Tax Reform," *National Tax Journal* 45 (June 1992): 185–202.

tax lawyers, and you will understand the concept of high compliance cost. And that is only the dollar cost, with no accounting of the mental pain and suffering individuals endure as they struggle to complete their tax returns as the filing deadline approaches each year.

Of course, things aren't getting easier: U.S. lawmakers are involved, so chances of improvement are small. The IRS is required by the Paperwork Reduction Act to estimate the time required to complete each component of the tax return and report those times in its taxpayer instructions. In 1988, completion of a standard return with itemized deductions and reported interest and dividends was estimated to require 15.1 hours for a taxpayer; in 2014, the same forms were estimated to require 16 hours. At least the perpetual calls by politicians for tax simplification didn't increase complexity even more, so maybe we should be thankful. More complicated returns with more required forms add even more to the time requirement. Even the simplest return (the form 1040EZ – only one page long) is now estimated to require 5 hours to complete, and far too many people are so flummoxed by the process that even 2 percent of these, almost half a million returns, were done by a paid preparer in 2012.

ECONOMIC EFFECTS

Critics argue that the income tax has adverse effects on the long-term prosperity of the U.S. economy by discouraging saving and investment and by discouraging earning of income in general. The argument is that income taxation distorts the choices that people make between how much income they consume in a year and how much they save for future spending because the tax applies to interest earned on the savings. By capturing part of the return from "waiting" to consume in the future, the tax distorts the choice between present consumption and future consumption, with the distortion toward present consumption. Accordingly, saving (delayed consumption) is reduced. This matters for economic growth because saving ultimately provides the basis for increased capital stock, which provides a foundation for economic growth.

The distorting effect can be even worse under our multiple income tax structure because returns to investment may be taxed once under the corporate income tax and then again under the individual income tax when the shareholder receives those corporate earnings as dividends.[17] A special lower rate for dividend income reduces the discrimination somewhat, but some extra burden remains. Evidence also shows an impact on taxable income from increased marginal tax rates—in essence, higher rates discourage households from earning income. The response is rather small, but higher for higher-income households than for lower-income households.[18] And

---

[17]Businesses have responded by organizing their operations as "pass-through" entities in which business income is taxed only at the individual owner level: partnerships, limited-liability companies, subchapter S corporations, etc.

[18]Emanuel Saez, Joel Slemrod, and Seth Giertz, "The Elasticity of Taxable Income with Respect to Marginal Tax Rates: A Critical Review," *Journal of Economic Literature* 50 (2012): 3–50.

there is no evidence that increasing tax rates, even for the most affluent, would reduce revenue production at anything close to current rates.

ECONOMIC DISTORTION

Provisions in the tax structure provide varying reliefs and punishments to different sectors of the economy as lawmakers seek to overcome the signals for resource allocation coming from market transactions. Some industries, businesses, and individuals end up facing higher effective tax rates on their capital investment and on their productive labor than do others. That causes economic resources to move because of tax advantages rather than moving according to market forces that reflect consumer demand, resource prices, and production technology. This brings considerable economic loss to the nation and decay in the competitive position of U.S. businesses in the world economy. One element of the economic loss from tax distortions is the effort that taxpayers exert to convert income that would be taxed at a higher tax rate (for instance, income from wages and salaries) into income that would be taxed at a lower rate (for instance, income from gain in value of a capital asset or capital gains).

EQUITY

Many people believe that the income tax distributes the cost of government unfairly. The distribution is, overall, strongly progressive, as the earlier table demonstrated. There are objections on both sides of progressivity. A good number believe that rates should be about the same for everyone (more proportional), and many others believe that the tax should be more progressive than it is now. But very few believe that people in similar economic circumstances should pay dramatically different effective tax rates simply because of the way they arrange their economic affairs, whether from fortunate accident, clever assistance from tax advisors, or access to special tax preferences or "loopholes" not available to everyone. That appears to be a blatant violation of horizontal equity, and the cost of government avoided by some has to be borne by the rest. Provisions of the federal income tax are such that not all income is treated equally for tax purposes, that certain sorts of economic activity are given favorable tax treatment, and that there can be significant differences in effective tax rates paid by households with similar income. A concern with this horizontal inequity was an important driving force for the 1986 federal tax reform, the last major revision of the federal tax system, but inequities have slipped back into the system.

OVERUSE

The distortions and inequities of any tax become more significant as the tax is heavily used. Problems that are minor irritants when tax rates and burdens are low can become severe when the tax is high. Businesses and individuals find it worthwhile to invest more effort to avoid paying the tax by restructuring their affairs and by hiding operations that would subject them to a tax; at lower rates, such efforts are not worth the expense. Even if the income taxes were otherwise sound in design, their extremely heavy use in the U.S. revenue system could be a reason for seeking tax alternatives. Greater balance among tax sources might relieve pressure created by the dominance of the income tax, especially in the federal tax system.

Individual Income Taxation

The following sections examine the logic of the federal individual income tax and some issues in its design. Figure 9–1 provides a schematic overview of the federal structure and captures the structural heart of the federal revenue system. The figure indicates the points at which adjustments, exemptions, deductions, credits, and so on enter into the calculations that implement the structure.

Defining Income

Tax statutes in the United States do not define income; rather, they list transactions that produce income for tax purposes. Items on the list include wages, salaries, interest, rents, royalties, net income from a business, and so on. There is no general definition for use in cases of doubt. (Instructors usually receive a copy of this book at no charge: Would its value be income for them? Would it depend on whether they sell the book when the semester ends?) Tax lawyers earn healthy incomes in part through their efforts to structure transactions that give their clients more money to spend, but do not cause income as far as the tax laws are concerned.

So how would income be defined in an ideal world? Many analysts favor the Haig-Simons income definition as a standard that can be applied outside the constructions of lawmakers who use definitions to deliver tax savings to constituents. The version proposed by Henry Simons defines personal income for tax purposes as "the algebraic sum of (1) the market value of rights exercised in consumption and (2) the change in the value of the store of property rights between the beginning and the end of the period in question."[19] In other words, Haig-Simons income equals the value of consumption plus any increase in net wealth during the year. That is the maximum amount of consumption that would be possible during the year without any reduction of the household's net wealth.

This definition can yield results that differ from application of existing tax law, as three examples illustrate. Suppose Mr. Smith owns shares of a corporate stock that increase in value by $10,000 during the year, but he does not sell the stock during the year. The Haig-Simons concept views that as income: this increase in Smith's

---

[19]Henry C. Simons, *Personal Income Taxation: The Definition of Income as a Problem of Fiscal Policy* (Chicago: University of Chicago Press, 1938), 50. A similar concept appears in Robert M. Haig, "The Concept of Income—Economic and Legal Aspects," in *The Federal Income Tax,* ed. R. Haig (New York: Columbia University Press, 1921), 7.

Figure 9–1
**Elements of the Federal Individual Income Tax Structure: How the Flow
of Calculations Produces the Tax Paid**

Total Income[1]
  Minus
Adjustments
  Equals
Adjusted Gross Income
  Minus
Standard Deduction or Itemized Deduction (Taxpayer's Choice)[2]
  And
Personal Exemptions[3]
  Equals
Taxable Income
  To which apply
Rate Schedule or Tax Table
  To calculate
Tax
  Minus
Credits
  Equals
Total Tax
  Minus
Withholding, Estimated Payments, and Other Payments
Equals
Tax Refund or Tax Due[4]

---

[1]The Internal Revenue Code does not include as income some flows that would appear to be income under comprehensive definitions of household income used by tax analysts or even under definitions that would be sensible to normal people. These exclusions may not even be reported on the tax return, although some—like interest received on tax exempt municipal bonds—are reported. Some income—like capital gain from sale of an asset and stock dividends–gets reported for taxation (at lower rates) in a special stream.
[2]Higher income taxpayers may lose a portion (or all) of the deduction.
[3]Higher income taxpayers may lose a portion (or all) of the exemption.
[4]Some taxpayers will also be required to calculate their tax according to the Alternative Minimum Income Tax scheme and then to pay the higher of the Alternative or regular tax calculation.

---

net wealth (a "capital gain") adds to his total potential command over the economy's resources. The existing tax system would not tax that gain; the system taxes such gains only as they are realized—that is, when the higher-value stock is sold.[20] Second, suppose Ms. Jones lives in a home that she owns. She thus consumes the

---

[20]Not all national tax systems regard all capital gains as income, and not all U.S. policy analysts agree that the U.S. approach makes sense in terms of equity or economic efficiency. See Bruce Bartlett, "Slaying a Pair of Cap Gains Villains," *Wall Street Journal,* June 10, 1993, A-20. Current law taxes gains as realized, but at a preferential (lower) rate. Indeed, U.S. Supreme Court decisions at various times in the past, starting with *Gray v. Darlington*, 82 US 63 (1872), a challenge involving the Civil War income tax, have held that capital gains are not income at all and, therefore, cannot be taxable in an income tax. In *Merchants Loan and Trust Co. v. Smietanka*, 255 US 509 (1921), the Court finally definitively ruled that capital gains were taxable under the income tax and that only congressional action could remove the tax.

services provided by that structure. These services (implicit rent) are a part of Jones's consumption and would be part of Haig-Simons income. The current system taxes no such imputed incomes, thus providing a significant incentive for purchase of assets, such as owner-occupied houses, that produce noncash returns to the owner. Third, suppose Mr. White's great aunt gives him $50,000. That clearly increases his net wealth (or permits increased consumption), so it would be part of Haig-Simons income. Because the transaction occurred without any work by White, however, the current system does not regard that payment as income. It could be taxable under the gift tax, but White's aunt's economic circumstance, not his, would determine that tax liability. That means the tax on the gift to White (who has an annual income of $5,000) is the same as the tax on the aunt's similar gift to his brother (who has an annual income of $60,000). Same aunt, same gift, same tax—regardless of the recipient's economic status. Defining the tax at the recipient level seems to make more sense than driving it from the owner. Our estate tax system works in this same way, driven by the estate and not the inheritor.

Policy analysts, both inside and outside government, typically use broad affluence measures for distributional analysis and for thinking about how the tax base might be revised rather than the tax base defined by the law, because that law is riddled with preferences and exclusions that make it less than a usable measure for comparing fundamental affluence. Sidebar 9–1 describes the more comprehensive measures used in analysis done by the Congressional Budget Office, the Treasury Office of Tax Analysis, and the Joint Committee on Taxation to gauge the distribution of the tax burden and in considering changes in the tax structure. All are in the spirit of the Haig-Simons concept, and all escape the legislative definitions of the current tax base to one degree or another. These are the measures used in preparation of effective rate distribution tables like those presented earlier in this chapter and in Chapter 8.

Adjusted Gross Income

Adjusted gross income (AGI) is the tax law measure of aggregate tax-bearing capacity. Because the philosophy of income taxation is that the tax should apply to net income, not gross receipts, the AGI includes, along with the listed salaries, wages, rents, dividends, and interest received by an individual, returns from individual business operation after deducting that business's operating costs.[21] But there are adjustments made to total income before applying the tax structure to calculate liability. First, adjustments are made for alimony payments made (such payments contribute

---

[21] Income from businesses organized as a sole proprietorship, partnership, limited liability company, or Subchapter S corporation (small corporation) is taxed on a "pass-through" basis, meaning it is taxed through the individual income tax structure only and not at the business level. There are disputes about what are legitimate business expenses that can be subtracted. For instance, Lamar Odom, National Basketball Association player with Los Angeles, Miami, and Dallas, deducted $190,000 in NBA fines and fitness program fees as ordinary and necessary business expenses. The IRS disagreed and sent a tax bill for $87,000. Odom appealed and ultimately largely prevailed: the IRS settled for around $7,800. Legitimate business expenses depend on what sort of business you are in.

Sidebar 9–1
More Comprehensive Income Measures for Distributional Analysis

The ideal income concept has many possible operational definitions. The tax code definition of adjusted gross income (AGI) does not meet the needs of being consistent over time, as Congress redefines what the tax system will or will not cover, or of capturing the full scope of taxpayer affluence during the year. It is infected with all manner of preferences and peculiarities and will not do for analysis of tax burden distribution across families of differing affluence. The federal agencies responsible for analysis of the tax system fully recognize the need for using a more comprehensive and stable measure in their work, but they do not agree on what the appropriate measure would be. They all recognize the Haig-Simons concept and work toward a broad concept of potential consumption without reducing wealth, although to differing degrees. Here are some examples of these broad measures.

Market Income (Congressional Budget Office)

CBO distributional analysis uses market income and before-tax income (market income plus government transfers (referred to as before-tax income)).[1] Market income includes:

(i) Labor income—Cash wages and salaries, including those allocated by employees to 401(k) plans; employer-paid health insurance premiums; the employer's share of Social Security, Medicare, and federal unemployment insurance payroll taxes; and the share of corporate income taxes borne by workers. (ii) Business income—Net income from businesses and farms operated solely by their owners, partnership income, and income from S corporations. (iii) Capital gains—Profits realized from the sale of assets. Increases in the value of assets that have not been realized through sales are not included in market income. (iv) Capital income (excluding capital gains)—Taxable and tax-exempt interest, dividends paid by corporations (but not dividends from S corporations, which are considered part of business income), positive rental income, and the share of corporate income taxes borne by owners of capital. (v) Other income—Income received in retirement for past services and other sources of income.

Government transfers consist of cash payments from Social Security, unemployment insurance, Supplemental Security Income, Temporary Assistance for Needy Families (and its predecessor, Aid to Families with Dependent Children), veterans' programs, workers' compensation, and state and local government assistance programs. They also include the value of in-kind benefits, such as Supplemental Nutrition Assistance Program vouchers (formerly known as food stamps), school lunches and breakfasts, housing assistance, energy assistance, and benefits provided by Medicare, Medicaid, and the Children's Health Insurance Program. (The value of health insurance is measured on the basis of the Census Bureau's estimates of the average cost to the government of providing such insurance.)

Family Cash Income (Obama Treasury Office of Tax Analysis)

Cash income consists of wages and salaries, net income from a business or farm, taxable and tax-exempt interest, dividends, rental income, realized capital gains, cash and near-cash transfers from the government, retirement benefits, and employer-provided health insurance (and other employer benefits). Employer contributions for payroll taxes and the federal corporate income tax are added to place cash on a pre-tax basis.

(continues)

**Sidebar 9–1
(continued)**

Expanded Income (Joint Committee on Taxation)[2]

Expanded income is narrower than the CBO concept and follows the existing tax law more closely. The concept starts with AGI and then adds:

1. Tax-exempt interest
2. Workers' compensation
3. Nontaxable Social Security benefits
4. Excluded income of U.S. citizens living abroad
5. Value of Medicare benefits in excess of premiums paid
6. Minimum tax preferences
7. Employer contributions for health plans and life insurance
8. Employer share of payroll taxes

[1]Congressional Budget Office, The Distribution of Household Income and Federal Taxes, 2011, November 2014.
[2]Joint Committee on Taxation, Overview of the Definition of Income Used by the Staff of the Joint Committee on Taxation in Distributional Analysis, February 8, 2012 JCX-15-12.

---

to the recipient's well-being and are taxed as part of that person's income, not that of the one who pays). Second, certain expenses associated with job-related moves and some business expenses are subtracted. It is always difficult to distinguish between relocation associated with earning an income and relocation associated with personal preference; the logic of taxing net income suggests that the former should be subtracted (moving for employment represents a cost of earning that income) and the latter should not (that moving expense is a result of a lifestyle or consumption choice). For example, did Charlie move to Boston because of employment opportunities there or because he likes the Red Sox? There is no simple, clear, logical line, so the error is made on the side of encouraging mobility. Third, adjustments are made to encourage certain activities by individuals: the deduction of Individual Retirement Account and other personal retirement plan payments to encourage private retirement saving, the student loan interest deduction to reduce the cost of borrowing to pay for education, and deductions to reduce the cost of private provision of health insurance.[22]

Net proceeds from some transactions simply do not show up in AGI, but appear to be income by both popular and Haig-Simons concepts.[23] Among the exclusions are interest received from certain state and local government bonds, certain transfer

---

[22]Similar provisions to encourage certain activities may appear in the itemized deductions. However, only taxpayers not opting for the standard deduction receive the benefit of these deductions. The impact of providing relief as an adjustment, rather than as a deduction, is therefore much greater. For instance, changing the preference for charitable contributions from an itemized deduction to an adjustment would significantly increase the number of taxpayers able to take advantage of the preference.
[23]Some federal tax preferences were subjected to an alternative minimum tax (AMT) in the Tax Reform Act of 1979 and continued by the 1986 law, but some exclusions remain.

payments (e.g., welfare payments, most Social Security benefits, and food stamps), many fringe benefits provided by employers (particularly pension and health plans), income from savings placed in life insurance, and gifts or inheritances. The value of fringe benefits received from an employer is taxable unless the law explicitly excludes the benefit from the tax, as is the case for many important benefits (services provided at no additional cost to the employer, certain employee discounts, working condition benefits, etc.). The system does not include unrealized capital gains and excludes imputed incomes. Most federal and state-local distributional analysis uses some larger measure of ability (such as those in Sidebar 9–1) rather than simple AGI to maintain a consistent measure of economic capacity. The impact of these exclusions can be huge. For instance, the exclusion of employer-provided health insurance is currently the largest single federal health subsidy for the nonelderly. The value of these preferences are called tax expenditures. Their measurement and how they are included in budget presentations is discussed in Chapter 13.

Several exclusions seem reasonable, particularly those directed to low-income individuals: it is not sensible to assist individuals because of their poverty and then tax away part of that assistance. Some assistance categories, however, are not limited to the poor; that is, they are not need-based, and eligible recipients may have sizable income from other sources. Thus, if one desires to apply tax according to net well-being, there is a case for including retirement pay, Social Security, unemployment compensation, and similar payments not strictly conditioned on current income or wealth. Unemployment compensation is now fully taxable; other related flows may be taxable in certain circumstances.[24]

The exclusion of interest received on state and local government debt historically stems from the principle of reciprocal immunity, that the federal government cannot destroy state or local governments (and vice versa). Because "the power to tax involves the power to destroy," the federal government historically did not tax instruments of state and local government.[25] The exclusion represents an important subsidy to state and local governments because it allows these governments to borrow at interest rates below current market rates. To demonstrate the influence of this exclusion, suppose an individual pays 35 percent of any additional income as federal income tax. A tax-exempt municipal bond paying 3.7 percent yields the same after-tax income as would a taxable bond paying about 5.7 percent.[26] Thus, the state or local government borrower automatically receives an interest subsidy through the federal tax system, allowing that government to borrow at artificially low rates. These bonds have been a favorite avenue of tax avoidance for higher-income individuals, and the value of interest subsidization to state and local governments must be balanced against the damage done to tax system equity by the exclusion.

---

[24]The link between income earned by those receiving Social Security benefits and those benefits within the tax system is troublesome for incentives. Earning income can cause more of Social Security benefits to be taxable and can cause loss of benefits, leaving little, if any, net return from work.

[25]*McCulloch v. Maryland*, 17 U.S. 316 (1819), is the source of John Marshall's famous "power to tax" quote. The reciprocal immunity doctrine, however, is enunciated in *Collector v. Day*, 78 U.S. 113 (1871).

[26]The taxable bond at 5.7 percent would leave the investor 65 percent (100 percent minus 35 percent) of its yield after tax, and 5.7 percent times 65 percent equals 3.7 percent.

Any suspicion that the nondiscriminatory taxation of interest on state and local bonds might be unconstitutional was eliminated in the 1988 U.S. Supreme Court decision in *South Carolina v. Baker:* "The owners of state bonds have no constitutional entitlement not to pay taxes on income they earn from state bonds, and states have no constitutional entitlement to issue bonds paying lower interest rates than other issuers."[27] So the provision remains as a valuable federal subsidy, a subsidy especially important to state and local governments and aggressively defended by them because it is received at their own control. The Tax Reform Act of 1986 dramatically reduced the scope of such borrowing, however, as a later chapter on government debt describes.

Personal Deductions

Personal deductions adjust the measured ability to pay the tax to the circumstances of the individual taxpayer. Personal deductions may improve the tax's horizontal and vertical equity by allowing individuals with such deductions to subtract them from the AGI and hence lower their tax base. Personal deductions may also encourage taxpayers to do things they might not otherwise do because of the tax savings that may result.

There are three types of spending that the itemized personal deductions identify as reducing the taxpayer's capacity to bear the tax below that of others with similar incomes.

(i) Some expenditures are largely outside the control of the household and reduce ability to share in covering the cost of government. Currently in this category are deductions for *medical and dental expenses* above 7.5 percent of AGI, *losses from casualty or theft* above 10 percent of AGI (less $100), and *certain state and local taxes* (either state and local income or retail sales taxes paid and property taxes). In each instance, individuals—presumably through little fault of their own—must bear these special expenses that more fortunate individuals do not incur. Thus, an adjustment of measured tax-bearing capacity is permitted.[28]

(ii) Some expenditures are deductible because the federal government has decided that private spending in those areas should be encouraged by reducing the

---

[27]*South Carolina v. Baker, Treasury Secretary of the United States,* 485 U.S. 99 (1988). South Carolina sued because it objected to a Tax Equity and Fiscal Responsibility Act of 1982 provision that requires identification of owners of such bonds. Before that requirement states could issue "bearer bonds"; whoever presented the bond received the periodic payments, and no questions about ownership were asked. They were popular with tax evaders, for money laundering, and with organized crime. The Court volunteered more answers than the state and local governments would have wished.

[28]The deduction for the state and local taxes raises some questions. These taxes represent payments for government services and reflect public decisions made to receive higher levels of those services. Why should the federal government be subsidizing (and biasing) these decisions? These payments really are not uncontrollable. The casualty loss deduction raises questions about *moral hazard*. Are people a little less cautious when the federal government is implicitly picking up some of the consequences of risky behavior?

after-tax cost of those actions. Thus, *charitable contributions* are deductible. This spending is optional (not like state taxes or medical bills), but the federal government seeks to encourage contributions. *Interest paid on home mortgages* (first and second homes) is similarly deductible as an important encouragement to home ownership, a matter of considerable importance to individuals who have borrowed to purchase homes.[29] Evidence indicates that the mortgage interest deduction has induced Americans to overinvest in owner-occupied housing, has added an incentive for urban sprawl, and reduces the progressivity of the tax because higher-affluence households are more likely to pay mortgage interest than are lower-affluence households (45 percent of tax savings goes to the top 10 percent of the income distribution) and that resources could be more productively invested in other capital assets. The preference gives little benefit to low-income households, senior citizens, or anyone without a mortgage, benefiting mostly households in higher-income brackets and younger households with high mortgage debt.[30] Indeed, some argue that its main effect is to encourage high-income borrowers to take on more debt. Public opinion puts great store in home ownership, and eliminating the provision has little political traction—although the provision now extends to only two houses per taxpayer.

(iii) Some deductions are needed to maintain the principle that the tax apply to net incomes, not gross receipts. In this category are expenses associated with *moving to a new job* and *certain job-related expenses* (education expenses needed to maintain or improve skills on the present job, union dues, work uniforms, research expenses for a college professor, occupational taxes, etc.). The latter group, combined with some *miscellaneous deductions* (tax preparation fees, fees associated with earning income from investments, etc.), are deductible only to the extent they exceed 2 percent of AGI. *Gambling losses* are fully deductible, but only up to the amount of winnings.

Each policy choice in designing the tax was made because it seemed to improve the equity or efficiency of the system. Because each provides greater tax relief to high-income taxpayers (a charitable deduction of $100 has an after-tax cost of $65 to an individual in the 35 percent bracket and a cost of $85 to someone in the 15 percent bracket), there is a special incentive for such individuals to arrange their expenses to fit into these deductible categories. Thus, professional meetings are timed to double as vacations, consumer loans are converted to home equity (mortgage) loans, and so on. As a result, these provisions can reduce the overall progression of the tax system and distort economic behavior. The system works to reduce this impact by applying

---

[29]Other personal interest payments—for credit card, automobile, education, installment, and signature loans—were fully deductible before the 1986 tax act. Furthermore, the 1997 tax reconciliation act made interest paid on certain student loans again deductible (but only for individuals with incomes up to $40,000 and for couples with incomes up to $60,000). Student loan interest now is an adjustment, subtracted in calculating adjusted gross income, even for those not itemizing deductions.

[30]James Poterba and Todd Sinai, "Revenue Costs and Incentive Effects of the Mortgage Interest Deduction for Owner-Occupied Housing," *National Tax Journal* 66 (June 3, 2011): 531–64.

a phase-out of several itemized deductions—each dollar of deduction is reduced by 3 percent for taxpayers whose AGI exceeds a limit.

Not all taxpayers, however, use the itemized personal deductions. In fact, most taxpayers do not: for tax year 2013, only 31 percent of individual returns showed itemized deductions.[31] The rest of the returns took another and potentially simpler route. Since the early 1940s, an optional standard deduction has permitted individuals to subtract from their AGI base a standard deduction regardless of itemized totals. This deduction eliminates the need for keeping records of deductible expenses. The initial idea was to make the tax simpler for the many people who became taxpayers for the first time during the Second World War (and maybe to give a psychological boost to people without substantial itemized deductions). The standard deduction has gradually increased over time and is now indexed to increase with inflation; from 1987 to 2016, for instance, it increased from $2,540 to $6,300 for a single person and is now double that for joint returns.[32] Unless taxpayers have itemized deductions totaling more than that amount, they will not itemize; home-ownership with the accompanying mortgage interest payment and local property tax typically creates the threshold to make itemization pay.[33]

For some taxpayers, the optional standard deduction certainly reduces the complexity of the tax by eliminating the need to keep records of deductible payments made through the year. But many taxpayers ultimately using the standard deduction still keep those records, with the intention of deciding which filing option to take only after comparing the tax advantage of the two. When all taxpayers have a general deduction, tax rates must be higher to generate a given amount of tax revenue, diluting the relief for the deserving and the undeserving alike. However, anyone can considerably simplify their federal income tax obligations by electing the standard deduction, no matter what. Those choosing itemization are choosing tax reduction over tax simplification.

The standard deduction/itemized deduction choice is not equally distributed across income groups. As noted earlier, only 31 percent of taxpayers itemize. However, among taxpayers with adjusted gross income of more than $200,000, the itemization rate is around 95 percent. That is why some politicians have proposed limits on the use of itemized deduction by higher-income taxpayers, even though that would certainly add to the complexity of the system and to the distortions coming from the system. There are also considerable differences across states in the propensity to itemize, from only 18 percent in West Virginia to 50 percent in Maryland, the result of differing patterns of deductible state and local taxes and home mortgage interest, two major influences on whether it is to the taxpayer's

---

[31]Michael Parisi, "Individual Income Tax Returns, Preliminary Data, 2013" *Statistics of Income Bulletin,* Spring 2015. www.irs.gov/taxstats

[32]There is an additional standard deduction for taxpayers over the age of 65 and for blind taxpayers. Plus certain real estate taxes are added to the standard deduction, so that taxpayers who do not itemize will get this preference. This special preference doesn't make much sense, but it came from Congress, so we shouldn't be surprised.

[33]For tax years 2008 and 2009, even taxpayers who took the standard deduction were allowed to deduct state and local property taxes that they had paid.

advantage to itemize or to take the standard deduction.[34] And savvy tax payers (and their tax preparers) are going to compute tax according to both approaches to make sure tax is minimized, so providing the standard deduction is not generally a complexity reducer.

Personal Exemptions

The tax law allows an exemption for each person in a taxpaying unit—the taxpayer, the taxpayer's spouse, and dependents (certain members of the household who are supported by the taxpayer, usually the taxpayer's children)—plus extra exemptions if the taxpayer or spouse is blind or older than age 65. The exemption is a flat amount for each exemption claimed: $3,950 in 2014, $4,000 in 2015, and $4,050 in 2016. (The exemption changes because it is adjusted annually for inflation.) The exemption adjusts tax payment for size of the taxpaying unit, adds some progressivity to the effective rate pattern, and removes many low-income households from the tax system. The structure provides greater tax reduction for those in higher tax brackets (subtracting $4,000 from taxable income reduces tax burden by more for a taxpayer in the 35 percent bracket than it does for someone in the 15 percent bracket), so the system provides that taxpayers above a certain AGI level (it was $309,900 for a married taxpayer filing jointly in 2015) would reduce personal exemptions by 2 percent for each $2,500 or part thereof by which AGI exceeds that threshold.

Taxable Income

Taxable income equals AGI less personal deductions, either itemized or standard, and personal exemptions. It is the base to which the tax-rate structure applies. The elemental identity of taxation is that tax yield equals tax base times tax rate. Therefore, a given tax yield may be generated through many different base and rate combinations, some involving narrow-based definitions (many deductions, exclusions, and exemptions from the Haig-Simons or other general income concepts) and high rate structures and some involving broad-based definitions (few deductions, exclusions, and exemptions) and low rate structures. The perennial mantra of federal tax reform, reflected in the 1986 Tax Reform Act, but generally eroded in later legislation, has been a movement toward a broader-based lower-rate option. The idea has been supported by the beliefs that lower rates at the decision margin do less to discourage saving, investment, and work effort than do higher rates, that broader bases leave fewer protected pockets that could harbor economic activity profitable only because of tax provisions, and that broad coverage is less likely to engender horizontal inequity. Of course, lawmakers and taxpayers generally are thinking about broadening the base to eliminate tax preferences enjoyed by others and not

---

[34]Gerald Prante, "Most Americans Don't Itemize on Their Returns," *Tax Foundation Fiscal Fact No. 95* (Washington, D.C.: Tax Foundation, July 23, 2007).

by themselves or their constituents. Thus, progress in tax reform is dreadfully slow in spite of the conceptual agreement. Broadening the base has much in common with cutting government spending—it is easier to agree on the principle than it is to identify what exactly is to be done—and everyone wants to eliminate loopholes used by somebody else, not the ones that they use themselves.

Tax Rates

Federal individual income tax rates increase in steps as income increases. At each step, the rate applicable to additional income is slightly higher than the rate on lower income. Figure 9–2 presents recent tax rate schedules for single and married taxpayers; Figure 9–3 gives one portion of the tax tables that certain filers are directed to use in determining their tax liability. The tax table—which reflects the relevant rate schedules—does the calculations from the rate schedules in $50 increments of taxable income, presumably in recognition of the diminished math skills of the American public. (Higher-income taxpayers must use the rate schedules for calculation of amounts. Either their math skills are better, or they are presumed to be hiring someone with the skills necessary for the calculations.)

The rate schedule is graduated upward with marginal rates (the percentage taxed from each additional dollar of taxable income) of 10, 15, 25, 28, 33, 35, and 39.6 percent.[35] Using the 2015 rate schedule, a single individual with taxable income of $85,000 would thus have part of that income taxed at 10 percent, part at 15 percent, and part at 25 percent. Only part of her income would face the 25 percent rate, but if she earned an extra $100, only $75 would be retained after tax. This marginal rate is critical in economic choices. The average tax rate she would pay is substantially less than 25 percent because of the lower rates in earlier brackets. In a graduated rate schedule, all taxable income is taxed at the lowest rate and, depending on how much income is received, parts of the total are taxed at each increasing rate.[36]

The number of tax rates, or brackets, by itself has no impact on computational complexity of the tax. If the taxpayer uses the tax table, she or he only looks at the amount of tax owed for the relevant income range and sees no tax brackets at all. If the taxpayer must use the rate schedule, the only computation is one involving the marginal rate in which the taxpayer's income falls. In neither instance does the taxpayer have to worry about the number of stairstepped rates that are involved in computing tax owed. Reducing the number of tax rates or their degree of upward graduation, while possibly useful for reasons of economic efficiency, has no impact on simplicity for the taxpayer.

In comparison with the recent past, the rate structure consists of fewer rate brackets (there were fourteen before the 1986 tax reform) and a lower top-rate

---

[35]There have been many more brackets in the tax structure (for instance, twenty-four rates from 20 to 91 percent in 1962), and there have been many fewer (for instance, three rates from 15 to 31 percent in 1992).
[36]In the U.S. system, that isn't exactly accurate because the tax code has a recapture system to remove the impact of the lowest tax bracket for high-income taxpayers, an extra complication in the system. This is similar to the recapture scheme previously noted for the personal exemptions.

Figure 9–2
Federal Rate Schedule for 2015

Married Individuals Filing Jointly

If Taxable Income Is:	Then Tax Is:
$0 – $18,450	10% of the amount over $0
$18,450 – $74,900	$1,845 + 15% of the amount over $18,450
$74,900 – $151,200	$10,312.50 + 25% of the amount over $74,900
$151,200 – $230,450	$29,387.50 + 28% of the amount over $151,200
$230,450 – $411,500	$51,577.50 + 33% of the amount over $230,450
$411,500 – $464,850	$111,324.00 + 35% of the amount over $411,500
$464,850 or more	$129,996.50 plus 39.6% of the amount over $464,850

Single Filers

If Taxable Income Is:	Then Tax Is:
$0 – 9,225	10% of the amount over $0
$9,225 – $37,450	$922.50 + 15% of the amount over $9,225
$37,450 – $90,750	$5,156.25 + 25% of the amount over $37,450
$90,750 – $189,300	$18,481.25 + 28% of the amount over $90,750
$189,300 – $411,500	$46,075 + 33% of the amount over $189,300
$411,500 – $413,200	$119,401 + 35% of the amount over $411,500
$413,200 or more	$119,996.25 + 39.6% of the amount over $413,200

SOURCE: Internal Revenue Service, 2015 Form 1040 Instructions, Tax Tables.

bracket (the rate was 50 percent before the 1986 tax reform). Few returns characteristically have been filed by taxpayers paying any tax at the highest marginal rate (although that has changed dramatically in the last decade with the remarkable economic success of high-income taxpayers).

In the years from 1936 through 1981, the highest marginal tax rate was 70 percent or higher (90 percent or higher from 1944 through 1963). Those high rates may harm the national economy without adding much revenue. For example, a person in the 70 percent bracket, a person with considerable income, would face this sort of choice: "I can work a bit more and earn an additional $1,000, of which $700 will be paid to the federal government (and some probably will be paid for state and local income taxes as well) and $300 I can keep for myself. Or I can use that extra time to go to some baseball games or play with my dog. Or I can hire tax advisors to try to structure that additional $1,000 so I won't have to pay so much tax." Two of these alternatives do not contribute much to the national economy and only one of those two does much for individual enjoyment (assuming you like baseball and dogs), but, given the after-tax return to the individual, many people would select them. That is an important influence behind tax structuring efforts to raise necessary revenue and achieve the desired degree of progressivity without high marginal rates. In designing tax structures, it is useful to think about what tax wedge—the tax-created difference between the total paid by the buyer (or employer in labor markets) and the net received by the seller (or worker in labor markets)—has been created. A high wedge on the margin of decision causes distortions and invites strategies (legal and illegal)

Figure 9–3
A Portion of the Federal Tax Table for 2015

If line 43 (taxable income) is—		And you are—			
At least	But less than	Single	Married filing jointly	Married filing sepa-rately	Head of a house-hold
		Your tax is—			
72,000					
72,000	72,050	13,800	9,881	13,800	12,829
72,050	72,100	13,813	9,880	13,819	12,341
72,100	72,150	13,825	9,896	13,825	12,364
72,150	72,200	13,838	9,904	13,888	12,366
72,200	72,250	13,850	9,911	13,850	12,379
72,250	72,300	13,863	9,919	13,883	12,391
72,300	72,350	13,875	9,928	13,875	12,404
72,350	72,400	13,888	9,934	13,888	12,416
72,400	72,450	13,900	9,941	13,900	12,429
72,450	72,500	13,913	9,949	13,913	12,441
72,500	72,550	13,925	9,956	13,926	12,454
72,550	72,600	13,938	9,964	13,938	12,466
72,600	72,650	13,950	9,971	13,950	12,479
72,650	72,700	13,963	9,979	13,963	12,481
72,700	72,750	13,975	9,986	13,975	12,504
72,750	72,800	13,988	9,994	13,988	12,516
72,800	72,850	14,000	10,001	14,000	12,529
72,850	72,900	14,013	10,003	14,013	12,641
72,900	72,950	14,025	10,016	14,025	12,554
72,950	73,000	14,038	10,024	14,038	12,586

SOURCE: Internal Revenue Service.

to keep from paying tax. In the period in which the highest marginal rate was over 90 percent, not much tax was generated in that bracket. Those in danger of confronting such a high tax bite had enough clout with employers to figure out nontaxed ways of getting compensated.

The average rate (tax liability divided by taxable income) always lies below the marginal rate (the increase in tax liability resulting from $1 additional income) in the federal tax structure. With that structure, an individual will never have greater after-tax income by having less income. The percentage of income going to federal tax increases as income rises, but the absolute income left over will not decline.[37]

---

[37]That may not necessarily be the case when effects from government benefit programs are added in. For an illustration, see Mary Rowland, "When Working Isn't Worth It," *New York Times,* September 26, 1993, F-15.

But the tax rates confronted by most taxpayers are more than just the graduated rates shown in Figure 9–2. First, most states (and many localities) levy their own income taxes, applying supplemental rates to federal AGI or taxable income. Each adds another layer to the rate paid, although state returns are filed separately from federal returns. The combined rate cannot be found on a single rate schedule; it has to be added up, sometimes with allowances made for differences in statutory coverage between federal and state taxes. Several states do, however, have local governments that piggyback their tax on the state tax, and liability for both state and local taxes is handled in a single return.

A second complication results because not all income is taxed in the same rate structure. Some countries, including the United States, apply multiple rate schedules, in which different sorts of income—wages, interest, or earnings from a business—are taxed at different rates. The federal government taxes income from realized long-term capital gains—increase in value of a capital asset between time of acquisition and time of sale—and dividend income at preferential rates. This income is taxed at 0, 15, or 20 percent, depending on what rate the taxpayer faces for ordinary income.[38] The idea is to encourage capital investment and to prevent a double taxation of income that is saved, but the scheme creates incentive issues. There is a considerable incentive for taxpayers to attempt to convert ordinary income into flows that would be considered capital gain income—for example, when some investment managers arrange their compensation for managing client money so that it would be taxed as capital gain (at 20 percent) as opposed to being taxed as ordinary compensation (at a 39.6 percent marginal rate).[39]

Not only does the incentive distort economic resources, but also it requires extra administrative effort to police shelter schemes established to exploit the difference in rates. A difference of 20 percentage points is sufficient to bring tax advisors calling with systems to convert income flows from one class to another.

Taxing different income sources at different rates represents a clear violation of normal principles of tax policy, as it complicates, distorts, and makes the system less certain and transparent. Special treatment of long-term capital gains is supported, however, by concerns about the unfairness of taxing gains that are nominal (inflation) but not real (purchasing power), about the danger of capital being locked in to current holdings (no capital gains tax applies when heirs receive appreciated assets

---

[38]Because capital gains are taxed only when they are realized (i.e., when the asset is sold), changes in the capital gains tax rate can have a considerable impact on realization and on revenue; when the rate is known to be increasing, as with the Tax Reform Act of 1986, investors respond by realizing a lot of gains to avoid the higher rate, and capital gains revenues jump. After the higher rate is in place, capital gains realizations go back to roughly their normal level. Congressional Budget Office, "Capital Gains Taxes and Federal Revenues," Revenue and Tax Policy Brief, October 9, 2002.

[39]The controversy was over the taxation of "carried interest," the share of profits that managers of private equity funds, hedge funds, and so on received. Although the managers had no money of their own invested, they sought to have their compensation taxed as capital gains rather than ordinary income. In the 2012 presidential campaign, the fact that Mitt Romney received "carried interest" income from his prior employment at Bain Capital and, as a result, had very high income that was taxed at a very low average tax rate was a point of some contention. He was doing nothing that was either dishonest or unethical. He was following the rules of the Internal Revenue Code.

when an estate is settled),[40] and about the possible chilling effect of the tax on saving and investment.

Not all income taxes are levied with graduated rates. At the present time, six states in the U.S. levy flat-rate income taxes, and several countries, particularly some Eastern European countries, also apply such rate structures.[41] The flat-rate tax prevents some of the distortions and disincentives that upwardly graduated rates can produce. If the coverage of the tax is broad enough—in other words, if major preferences have been eliminated—the statutory rate may be low enough to reduce some tax evasion. That may happen if the tax saved at the margin from evasion is not worth the risks associated with being caught. In these flat systems, any progressivity in effective rates is produced by other structural features, particularly large exemptions, not through graduation of the legal rates. Table 9–3 demonstrates how a relatively generous exemption by itself can convert a flat statutory rate into progressive effective rates. In essence, the large exemption creates progressive *effective* rates because the exemption provides greater relief *relative to* family income to the lower-income family: $10,000 per person is a much more significant portion of total income for Family A than for Family C (or B). That translates into a much greater impact on the effective rate. This impact on vertical equity works with any rate structure; large personal exemptions make the progressivity of an upward graduated tax structure even greater.

Tax Credits

Tax credits, direct forgiveness of tax owed, are a powerful stimulus for private activities. The credit amount reduces tax liability by an amount exactly equal to the

Table 9–3
Effective Rate Impact of a Flat-Rate Income Tax (10 percent) and a Large Personal Exemption ($10,000) on Selected Families of Three Persons

Family	Before Tax Income ($)	Total Personal Exemptions ($)	Taxable Income	Tax Paid ($)	Effective Tax Rate (%)
A	40,000	30,000	10,000	1,000	2.5
B	100,000	30,000	70,000	7,000	7.0
C	500,000	30,000	470,000	47,000	9.4

---

[40]This is called "step-up in basis." For eventual capital gains tax purposes, the value of the inherited asset becomes the value at the time of inheritance, not the value at which the asset was purchased. This increase in value from purchase to inheritance therefore escapes the income tax system. Not only is this income not taxed twice when the estate tax applies, but also it wouldn't be taxed at all if not for the estate tax. "Constructive realization," meaning taxing capital gains at the death of the owner, would allow dramatic reduction of estate taxes without substantial revenue loss, while preserving a degree of equity. This was a reform adopted in Canada.

[41]The impact of Russia's implementation of a flat-rate tax, replacing a graduated-rate tax, is analyzed in Clifford G. Gaddy and William G. Gale, "Demythologizing the Russian Flat Tax," *Tax Notes International* 43 (March 14, 2005): 983–88. Some U.S. commentators have erroneously pointed to this experience as evidence that moving from graduated-rate to flat-rate structures boosts economic activity and possibly even tax revenue, but Gaddy and Gale do not find that result in their careful analysis.

credit; it does not reduce the tax base, as is the case for exemptions or deductions, so its tax-reducing impact is not filtered through the rate structure. Therefore, the tax reduction from a given credit is the same for taxpayers in all rate brackets; deductions and exemptions, on the other hand, have greater tax-reducing impact for those in higher tax brackets.[42] But because credits reduce taxes directly, they produce greater revenue loss than do equivalent deductions or exemptions, an important concern for most governments.

Credits have been used over the years to induce political contributions, installation of energy-saving mechanisms, capital investment, and home purchase, to cite some recent federal system examples. Current credits are provided for families with children, for certain college tuitions, for child- and dependent-care expenses, for the elderly and people with disabilities, and for certain adoption expenses. Furthermore, the federal system provides a credit for low-income workers (the EITC), as described in Sidebar 9–2, a credit defined as a percentage of earned income that substantially relieves taxes for the working poor. State income taxes similarly employ credits to support desirable activities, choosing the power and evenness of support from credits against the substantial revenue loss they produce. A number of states provide their own earned-income tax credit programs.

Effective Tax Rates

The statutory, or nominal, rates appearing in the rate schedule are not the effective rates. Analysis of the income tax system usually is conducted by looking at the relationship between taxes paid and AGI (the federal tax system equivalent of net household income) or one of the broader measures in the Haig-Simons tradition (recall Sidebar 9-1). This rate is the average effective rate. The statutory rates are reduced substantially by the tax provisions removing income from the base (adjustments, deductions, exemptions, and exclusions) and forgiving tax owed (credits). These elements can be regarded as the work of tax loopholes or as the work of tax policy designed to correct inequities or to encourage socially desirable behavior.

One little-observed feature of the federal income tax is the large number of tax filers who pay no federal individual income tax. Refer to Table 9–2 for the data for 2013. In that year, households in the two lowest income quintiles paid no federal individual income tax; their tax shares and effective tax rates were negative. That means that, on average, those households received money from the government rather than paying any tax; the workings of deductions, exemptions, and adjustments made their liabilities extremely low, and then the workings of fully refundable credits made their net liabilities negative. Rather than paying income tax to the federal government, the government was paying them. A thorough study of

---

[42]A number of federal credits and other tax preferences are reduced in stages as income increases; there are about twenty different phase-out ranges and calculation methods. All add complexity and uncertainty to the system, presumably in the name of targeting relief and social engineering. Most members of Congress who voted for these provisions also claim to be supporters of tax simplification.

Sidebar 9–2
The Earned Income Tax Credit

The federal earned income tax credit (EITC) provides needy families with financial assistance, while it gives a positive incentive for work among the lower-paid members of society. It aids these people without the need for a special welfare bureaucracy and appears to reach a higher percentage of those eligible than does any other income support program, possibly because it avoids any stigma associated with programs that more specifically identify the recipients. It also avoids the major work disincentives that some welfare programs have when earning additional income causes countervailing loss of welfare benefits. Quite simply, assistance is provided through the individual income tax system with fully refundable tax credits given to those who qualify. Fully refundable means that if their credit exceeds the amount of federal income tax they would owe, they receive the difference as a refund—the reason for the negative effective tax rates earlier seen in Table 9-2. Not all credits are fully refundable, so this is a distinct advantage for the EITC.

Here is how the Council of Economic Advisers described the operation of the EITC in the 1994 *Economic Report of the President:*

> The earned income tax credit is often thought of as a type of negative income tax, but in fact it is more complicated than that. The EITC has three ranges: a "credit range" in which it functions like a wage subsidy, a "plateau" in which it has no marginal effect, and a "phaseout" range in which the credit is paid back as earnings rise. . . .
>
> To illustrate, when the increases enacted in 1993 are fully effective (in 1996), the credit will work as follows for a family with two or more children. (Less generous schedules apply to one-child and childless families.) As earnings rise from zero to $8,425 (all dollar figures are in 1994 dollars), the EITC will provide a 40 percent wage subsidy, so that each $100 of additional earnings will net the family $140. The maximum credit is $3,370, which is therefore reached when earnings hit $8,425. The credit will then be constant as earnings rise from $8,425 to $11,000. Beyond $11,000, however, the family's tax credit is reduced 21 cents for each extra dollar earned. Benefits are thus exhausted when earnings reach $27,000.

The EITC provides a marginal work incentive in the credit range (unlike a negative income tax), a marginal work disincentive in the phase-out range, and neither in the plateau. However, to the extent that labor supply decisions involve whether or not to work, rather than how many hours to work, the credit provides a positive work incentive to all recipients.

In fiscal 2011, the EITC provided $55.6 billion in benefits. That compares with $71.8 billion for the Food Stamp program (now SNAP), $49.6 billion for the Supplemental Security Income program, and $21.3 billion for Temporary Assistance for Needy Families (TANF; what is thought of as America's foundation public welfare program), three of the most important income security programs functioning through the spending side of the fiscal system. More than half of EITC payments go to families below the poverty line. The program has been of particular benefit to families at the bottom of the income ladder and represents a significant component in the economic safety net, even though administered through the tax system and not through the public assistance bureaucracy.

Around half the states have their own earned income tax program, in addition to the federal program.

SOURCES: Executive Office of the President, Council of Economic Advisers, *Economic Report of the President Transmitted to the Congress February 1994* (Washington, D.C.: U.S. Government Printing Office, 1994), 51.

nonpayment showed that, in 2014, 45.4 percent of taxpaying units had zero or negative federal individual income taxes.[43] In other words, they were not taxpayers at all. Generally about half pay no tax because they fall below the income threshold after which tax applies and about half pay no tax because of special provisions in the tax code that eliminate liabilities or even result in net payments from the government. Is it really the case that almost half of all Americans have incomes that are so low that they cannot afford to contribute to the general services provided by the federal government?[44] If so, do we conclude that the federal government is just too darn big to be affordable, that the United States is simply an impoverished country, or that some Americans are getting a free ride from others? When this tally is placed against the concentration of individual income tax payments in the upper categories of the income distribution shown previously in Table 9–2 (88 percent of individual income tax collections come from the top 20 percent of taxpayers and 38.3 percent from the top 1 percent), the extent to which the revenue system depends on a small pool of taxpayers is apparent. Of course, the uppermost income recipients have done ridiculously well, and that is the primary reason for the concentration of payment—but is it good for sound democratic decision making for the payment for public services to be so concentrated and for so many to have no liability? And are voters likely to be fully responsible when they realize that extra federal spending is likely to have no tax cost for them?

Indexation

When a tax structure has upward graduated brackets, a phenomenon known as bracket creep can occur during high inflation. Suppose a family has an AGI of $28,000, pays a tax of $3,300, and is in the 15 percent marginal tax bracket. In two years, its income has increased to, say, $33,600 (a 20 percent increase), but the cost of living has increased by 20 percent as well, so its real income has not changed. The family would, however, pay tax on that higher income even though its living standard has not really changed, and that income is subject to a higher marginal bracket. Thus, it might now pay $4,300, an increase of tax liability of more than 20 percent, because of the upward rate graduation. Of course, the real value of personal exemptions and standard deductions decreases as well.

This graduation has historically helped stabilize the economy, accelerating tax collections during inflation to provide a macroeconomic brake and slowing tax collections during recession to provide a macroeconomic stimulus without legislative action. During the long economic expansion of the 1980s, governments raised

---

[43]Tax Policy Center, "Table T15-0138 Tax Units with Zero or Negative Income Tax Under Current Law, 2011-2025," Urban-Brookings Tax Policy Center Microsimulation Model (version 0515-1), October 2, 2015.

[44]It should be noted that in 2014 only 26.9 percent of tax units paid a negative sum of individual income and payroll tax for social insurance systems. So a smaller percent of the population is paying neither tax. (*Ibid.*)

substantial revenue without statutory rate increases simply by letting growth, real and inflated, carry taxpayers into higher-rate categories. Federal and state governments enjoyed growing income tax revenues without the necessity of increasing any statutory tax rates.

After the high inflation rates in the 1980s, governments moved to remedy the problem by indexing significant features of their income taxes to prevent further bracket creep. (Note the government action to deal with the problem after the worst of the problem was over.) The adjustment works by formula to annually change personal exemptions, standard deductions, and the starting points of rate brackets to allow for any inflation that has occurred since the prior year. The federal system has done indexing since 1985, and a number of states have followed suit. The idea is to prevent stealth tax increases. Some observers have suggested that, by removing some upward trend in tax revenue, indexation contributed to increased federal deficits and state fiscal stress.

Tax Computation

The nature of income taxation can best be understood by working the mechanics of the tax. Table 9–4 provides an illustration of such a manipulation. It applies the general schematic of the federal income tax to demonstrate deductions and exemptions, as well as the computation of average, marginal, and average effective tax rates. That schematic shows how each provision that shapes tax liability comes into play and how the place in the system at which a preference is installed matters for impact on liability and effective rate. Fully refundable credits have greatest impact, followed by credits, exclusions, exemptions, adjustments, and deductions.

But this computation is not quite everything for certain taxpayers. If their income is above a specified threshold, the taxpayer must calculate an alternative minimum tax (AMT) that might mean extra tax to be paid. AMT, the stealthy federal tax that all political parties and both branches of government love to hate, but can't figure out what to do about, is described in Sidebar 9–3.

This illustrated computation seems reasonably straightforward. Where is the complexity that is claimed to infest the tax system? The requirements for collecting information about deductible expenses and for making sure that all income is reported have already been noted. But that is only the tip of the iceberg. Here is a list of a few of the complicating features:

(i) The tax code has a dozen different special preferences to help with educational expenses, with terms of eligibility and benefits differing for each, and the use of one may complicate the availability of other financial assistance for college.

(ii) There are many different preferences to encourage people to save money for retirement (IRA, Roth IRA, Keogh, 401(k), etc.), each with different terms, conditions, and eligibilities.

(iii) Deductions, exemptions, and some other preferences are subject to phase-out provisions that both complicate tax calculation and alter taxpayer incentives.

Table 9–4
An Example of Income Tax Computation

Mr. and Mrs. Gross have one dependent child. Their total income is $200,000, all from wages and salaries. They also received income from municipal bonds of $7,500, but this money is excluded from the federal individual income tax. They have adjustments of $20,000 from student loan interest, educator expenses, and Individual Retirement Account contributions, so their adjusted gross income equals $180,000 ($200,000 less $20,000). They have itemized deductions of $15,000 (state income tax paid, mortgage interest paid, and charitable contributions). Because this exceeds the amount of the standard deduction for which they would qualify ($12,600), they use the itemized deduction in their filing. Each personal exemption is $4,000, for a total of $12,000. Mrs. Gross's employer has withheld $35,000 of her salary (and paid that amount to the federal government) to cover her tax liability. They file a joint return.

Computing Taxable Income:

Adjusted Gross Income: $180,000
- Less itemized deduction ($15,000)
- Less personal exemptions ($12,000)
- Taxable income = $153,000

Computing Tax Liability:

From Tax Rate Schedule for Married Filing Jointly (Figure 9–2):
- Tax liability for taxable income from $151,201 to $230,450 equals $29,387.50 + 28% of the amount over $151,200 *or* $29,387.50 + .28 ($153,000 − $151,200) = $34,424.50
- Tax owed/tax refund (withholdings less tax liability): $35,000 − $34,424.50 = $575.50 overpayment that can be refunded

Some Important Tax Indicators:

Average tax rate = tax liability/taxable income = $34,424.50/$153,000 = 22.5% Average effective tax rate = tax liability/(total income plus exclusions) = $34,424.50/($200,000 + $7,500) = 16.59%
Marginal tax rate = change in tax liability/change in taxable income = 28% (from rate schedule

---

(iv) There are complicated rules for determining what parent can claim a child as dependent that vary according to marital status and parent income.
(v) There are special rules for taxation of unearned income (mostly dividends and interest payments) received by a child to prevent parents from shifting investment income to their children to take advantage of the child's lower marginal rate (sometimes called the "Kiddy Tax").
(vi) There are complicated rules and instructions for provisions like the earned income tax credit, a program for low-income taxpayers who may have lower educational attainment.

Sidebar 9–3
The Alternative Minimum Tax

The United States has two tax systems. The regular system encompasses the standard individual and corporate income taxes, but there is a separate system, the alternative minimum tax (AMT) system, that is designed to ensure that corporations and individuals with substantial income do not fully utilize tax preferences provided in the tax law to avoid significant tax liability. The AMT system requires the taxpayer to do two distinct calculations of tax liability, one for the regular system and one for the AMT. It has been described as "the best example of pointless complexity in the tax system,"[1] a high distinction indeed.

In 1969, Secretary of Treasury Joe Barr made news when he reported that 155 individuals with incomes over $200,000 in 1967 had paid no federal income tax. Twenty of that number were millionaires. Even though none of these taxpayers had done anything illegal, none was a tax cheat, and none was doing anything other than taking advantage of tax preferences that Congress had adopted to encourage certain economic behavior or to relieve certain perceived inequities in the tax system, a furor erupted. Congress enacted the AMT to ensure that the few high-income individuals who otherwise would pay no tax would pay at least something. The first tax enacted was a minimum tax; the tax was revised in the late 1970s to the current alternative minimum tax.

The AMT process for individual taxpayers is the following.

1. The taxpayer calculates tax liability according to the regular law.
2. The taxpayer calculates AMT liability by adding back most preferences (personal deductions and exemptions) and adjustments to regular taxable income, subtracting the special AMT exemption (the exemption phases out at higher income levels), and computing AMT liability using a simple rate structure (only two rates: 26 and 28 percent).
3. The AMT equals the excess of the alternative calculation over the regular income tax.

By itself, the AMT is simpler than the regular income tax: there are fewer tax preferences to keep track of, and the rate structure has fewer brackets. The added complexity is caused because the taxpayer has to do two tax calculations: the regular income tax and the AMT. In addition, the taxpayer can't easily know ahead of time which income tax he or she will be subject to.

The AMT was intended initially to reach high-income taxpayers, but its net now catches many middle-income taxpayers. The reasons are simple: the regular income tax is generally indexed for inflation and the AMT is not, and recent tax cuts have significantly reduced the regular income tax for many taxpayers. Inflation brings higher income, and the regular income tax adjusts its provisions upward to keep tax burdens from rising simply because of inflated incomes, but the AMT thresholds remained based on price and income levels of the late 1960s until they started to be inflation adjusted in 2013. Before then, more and more people found that their income status cast them into the AMT net. These people still are not tax cheats.

What sort of tax avoidance behavior causes people to fall prey to AMT? The people most likely to have AMT liability are those paying high state and local property and income taxes, those with large families, those with high miscellaneous deductions, and those running businesses

Sidebar 9–3 (continued)

with large operating losses. It is hard to believe that these people should be hit with an extra income tax liability, but that's the way the law works. Furthermore, the number of people hit by AMT continues to grow: in 1970, the tax hit 20,000 taxpayers, but applied to almost 8 million taxpayers for tax year 2009.

So why doesn't Congress get rid of the AMT? Quite frankly, it hardly can afford to. AMT revenue in 2015 was $28 billion, and making that sum up when lawmakers are reluctant to pass any provisions that generate extra revenue would be extremely difficult. The amounts coming from the AMT will, unless changed, continue to grow over time. In addition, the AMT works to protect Congress and the president from their own fiscally unsustainable actions: when new tax reductions get passed, the AMT works to bring back some of that lost revenue as liability lost from the reduction is recaptured by the AMT.

Critics point to increased taxpayer compliance burdens, higher IRS administrative cost, redistribution of tax burdens among taxpayers, and denial to taxpayers of entirely legal tax incentives that Congress intended to provide. For a huge number of taxpayers, it requires a second calculation of tax liability with no revenue flowing to the government—the worst sort of tax program. Similar arguments apply to the corporate AMT. The biggest barrier to AMT reform: how could the lost revenue be replaced?

Some observers have suggested a way out. The AMT by itself is simpler than the individual income tax. Why not repeal the regular income tax and change the name of the AMT to the income tax? That would allow taxpayers to make fewer calculations, to keep fewer records, and to reduce their need for costly tax advisors, in exchange for somewhat higher statutory rates. In other words, if you can't slay the dragon, why not convert it into domestic livestock?

[1]Leonard E. Burman, William G. Gale, Gregory Leiserson, and Jeffrey Rohaly, "Options to Fix the AMT," Tax Policy Center, January 19, 2007, 54.

(vii) Type of income (e.g., salary and interest versus capital gain and dividend) determines what rate structure is to be used, and there are complicated boundary rules that define the income categorization.

It is no surprise that so many Americans throw up their hands at the complexity and hire someone else to fulfill the basis task of tax compliance. It is no surprise that complexity of the system is about as big a complaint as the actual amount of tax being paid. Unfortunately, efforts to simplify run up against the fact that the elements of complication are the source of tax preference—lower taxes—for some taxpayers, and those taxpayers accept the complexity in exchange for tax relief. And those preferences cause lawmakers to erect complicated controls to try to limit those receiving the preferences to only those intended to benefit from them.

The Individual Income Tax Gap

There is a federal individual income tax compliance problem. The system relies on voluntary compliance by taxpayers, and not all taxpayers pay the tax that they owe. The IRS struggles with uncollected taxes and does have considerable success, but it estimates that the overall noncompliance rate is around 17 percent. That is money owed and not collected, effectively moving the burden from nonpayers to honest taxpayers.

The IRS works to identify the sources of noncompliance to gauge its success and, more important, to identify where it should allocate its resources to do its job as well as it can. Its primary tool is called the National Research Program, a program of research audits that is designed to identify types and size of misreporting, a difficult research task given that those taxpayers who are not paying all the tax they owe are not eager to let the IRS know about it. The results of this research, a summary of which appears in Table 9–5, show how the compliance system is functioning across various types of income.

There are three major conclusions from these data. First, withholding and reporting income at the source is really effective. The unreported income gap for nonbusiness income—wages, salaries, interest, and dividends—is substantially less than for business income, even though wages and salaries alone represent over 70 percent of total income: business income is substantially overrepresented in the income reporting gap. It is easier to enforce the tax obligation against employers than against employees; there are fewer of them to deal with, and they are serving as a conduit between their employees and the government, so they are roughly disinterested third parties in the transaction. Many individuals have their tax overwithheld through the year, probably as a scheme of forced saving, so their filing with the government is a request for a refund, not a need for payment of money owed. That is a good incentive for filing.

Second, third-party reporting helps induce compliance. Financial institutions and dividend-paying corporations must report to the IRS their interest and dividend payments made to taxpayers (the 1099 reporting system), so the IRS knows that other part of nonbusiness income has been paid. Under certain circumstances, the payers can be required to also withhold tax, as well as to report payment. As a result, the payment is difficult to hide and provides real encouragement for the taxpayer to report and remit tax owed.

Finally, pure voluntary compliance doesn't work so well. When income received by a taxpayer is subject neither to withholding nor to third-party reporting, the misreporting percentage skyrockets. That is the case with all forms of business income: farm and nonfarm proprietors and owners of rental properties in particular, but also partnerships, corporations taxed like partnerships, estates, and trusts. This income is known, in the first instance, only to the taxpayer, and whether the taxpayer reports accurately is known only to the taxpayer unless the IRS checks. However, the IRS lacks the resources to do extensive checking. The National Research Program tells the IRS that this sort of income certainly deserves special scrutiny.

Table 9–5
Federal Tax Gap: Tax Year 2006

	(Money in billions $)
Estimated Total Tax Liability	$2,660
Gross Tax Gap	450
Overall Voluntary Compliance Rate	83.10%
Net Tax Gap	385
Overall Net Compliance Rate	83.5
Nonfiling Gap	
Individual Income Tax	25
Estate Tax	3
Underreporting Gap	
Individual Income Tax	235
Nonbusiness Income	68
Business Income	122
Adjustments, Deductions, Exemptions	17
Credits	28
Corporate Income Tax	
Small Corporations (assets <$10M)	19
Large Corporations	48
Employment Tax	
Self-Employment Tax	57
FICA and Unemployment Tax	15
Estate Tax	2
Underpayment Gap	
Individual Income Tax	36
Corporate Income Tax	4
Employment Tax	4
Estate Tax	2
Excise Tax	0.1

SOURCE: Internal Revenue Service, National Research Program.

Because the income taxes require taxpayers to maintain records, calculate tax owed, and file returns, the IRS must verify that taxpayers are being reasonably honest and, indeed, to make tax compliance something that people other than suckers do. Table 9–6 shows the percentage of returns that were examined (audited) by the IRS for returns filed in calendar 2014; overall, fewer than one in one hundred returns was audited. High income taxpayers are much more likely to be audited than are low income taxpayers (unless you report no income, which is suspicious). Large

Table 9-6

Examination Coverage by IRS by Type of Return, Fiscal Year 2014

	(% returns filed)
Individual Income Tax	0.86
No AGI	5.26
$1 to under $25,000	0.93
$25,000 to under $50,000	0.54
$50,000 to under $75,000	0.53
$75,000 to under $100,000	0.52
$100,000 to under $200,000	0.65
$200,000 to under $500,000	1.75
$500,000 to under $1,000,000	3.62
$1,000,000 to under $5,000,000	6.21
$5,000,000 to under $10,000,000	10.53
$10,000,000 and over	16.22
Corporate Income Tax	1.3
Small Corporations	1
Large Corporations	12.2
Huge Corporations (assets over $20 billion)	84.2
Employment Tax	0.2

SOURCE: IRS Databook.

corporations were much more likely to get a visit from the IRS, and the largest were absolutely certain to be examined. However, given the modest examination percentages, it is obviously clear that the IRS needs to allocate its examination resources cleverly if it is to adequately police the income tax system.[45] Most tax returns will be accepted as filed and that's it.

Corporate Income Taxation

The corporation net income tax applies to the net earnings of incorporated businesses, following the theory that the legal person created by incorporation creates an economic entity with tax-bearing capacity separate from the owners (shareholders)

---

[45]Enforcement revenue collected by the IRS amounted to around 2.3 percent of total collections in fiscal 2011. That small share is not surprising for a tax that relies on voluntary compliance by taxpayers to generate the revenue.

of that business.[46] The tax applies to total corporate profit as defined by the account-ing system and the tax law, including both earnings retained by the firm and those paid in dividends to the stockholder. Although the tax lacks the personal exemptions and deductions found in the individual tax, it does allow a deduction for charitable contributions (to encourage corporate generosity), a deduction for ordinary and nec-essary costs of operating the business, including recovery of capital expenditure, and a special deduction (a Section 199 deduction) to lower the effective tax rate for corporations engaged in domestic manufacturing.

Defining the base as the profit of the corporation—total revenue received less all costs of doing business—is simpler than actually measuring it for tax purposes. There are some issues involving operating costs that will be deducted: for instance, is the rental of the skybox at the NFL stadium an ordinary and necessary business expense and hence deducted from the base upon which tax rates apply (thus causing the general taxpaying public to bear part of the cost of that corporate box), or should it be considered a use of the enterprise's profits (thus causing the corporation to bear all the cost)? However, really sticky questions come from the effort to properly deal with the cost of capital assets, those big-ticket, long-life assets discussed in a previ-ous chapter, but this time being purchased by business and not government. The problem for defining profit in a particular year requires some formula for translating the purchase price of long-life capital equipment and structures, occurring in a lump in one year, into cost for the particular years of the productive life of that asset. The cost of the infrastructure is part of the cost of making the product, but how much of the large cost incurred when the infrastructure is purchased ought to be assigned to (or recovered in) any particular year?

Ideally, the depreciation schedule should provide a "deduction profile over time that mimics the profile of the asset's true economic depreciation."[47] As the asset wears out, a comparable chunk of its purchase price would be subtracted from what would otherwise be profit of the firm. Because there is no feasible way to track actual depre-ciation for every asset (and actual measurement is mostly impossible), tax systems adopt arbitrary depreciation rules that define the useful life of broad asset classes and the speed with which the purchase price of the asset can be recovered over that life.

Many recovery schemes are possible, but one common rule is *straight-line,* a method under which an equal portion of cost is recovered in each year of the asset's estimated life. Thus, if the asset life is ten years, then 10 percent of asset cost is deductible each year. Other systems allow faster recovery of cost (*accelerated*

---

[46]Business income is not the same thing as corporate income. Many businesses, including many that are highly profitable, are not legally organized as regular corporations. These other businesses, such as sole proprietorships and partnerships, pay tax through the individual income tax structure. Also, certain corporations (Subchapter S corporations), because of the manner in which they are organized, are treated by the tax system like partnerships. All these are "pass-through" entities: their income is not taxed at the business level, but is "passed through" to the owners of the business for taxation on their individual returns. As might be expected, these entities are a popular way for organizing businesses, although some lack the limited liability of the corporation. When tax rates differ according to how the business is orga-nized, it is almost certain that competitors in the same industry are going to face different tax rates, and that is both inequitable and inefficient and probably reduces the overall revenue yield to the Treasury.
[47]Dale Chua, "Depreciation Schedules," in *Tax Policy Handbook,* ed. Parthasarathi Shome (Washington, D.C.: International Monetary Fund, 1995), 136.

depreciation), that is, larger deductions in early years of life and smaller deductions in later years. Fastest of all would be to allow expensing, in which all the cost is deducted in the year of purchase. Faster depreciation is often proposed as a means for increasing capital investment and, hence, economic growth. The federal system is called MACRS, or Modified Accelerated Cost Recovery System, in which classes of assets are placed into depreciation periods for cost recovery. Whatever the system, however, the depreciation rules, along with decisions about what will be considered ordinary and necessary business expense, are critical for determining the profit to be taxed. To spur economic activity, most machinery and equipment can now be expensed (i.e., total cost deducted) at the time of purchase.

The statutory federal corporate income tax rate is 35 percent on income over $18.3 million. There are lower rates (starting at 15 percent) provided as a concession to small enterprises, and there is a "bubble rate" of 38 percent to recover the advantage of the lower bracket rates from more profitable corporations, but most taxable corporate income hits the highest rate. This rate is currently the highest statutory corporate income tax rate in the developed world—certainly not helpful for U.S. economic development—although the effective tax rate is far less, probably a little less than average for the big industrial countries because of the many deductions and credits provided to our corporations. Reducing special interest preferences, themselves certainly causing economic distortions, would allow a lower statutory tax rate without sacrifice of corporate tax revenue.

One particularly troubling result of these preferences is that some industries end up facing much higher average effective federal corporate income tax rates than do others. Although the average rate across all industries was 26 percent in 2007-2008, effective rates ranged from 14 percent for utilities and 18 percent for mining and leasing to 31 percent for construction and the wholesale and retail trade.[48] That degree of disparity in tax rates is almost certain to distort the way in which resources are allocated in the economy—too much investment in the low-rate sectors and too little investment in the high-rate sectors—with loss of economic well-being for the nation as a whole. There is no justification for such interference in the operation of market-based resource allocation.

Corporate income tax incidence is somewhat unclear: does the corporate income tax reduce the real income of the stockholders of the corporation, produce higher prices for the corporation's products, or reduce the real income of labor and other resources used by the corporation?[49] This uncertainty is troublesome because

---

[48]White House and Department of Treasury, *The President's Framework for Business Tax Reform*, A Joint Report by the White House and the Department of Treasury, February 2012.

[49]Most analysts believe the burden is distributed to capital, either generally or to the owners of the corporation, or to employees of the corporation (employees are less mobile than capital and thus are vulnerable to tax shifting). Shifting the burden through prices charged by the firm for its products is viewed as the least likely possibility. In recent years, analysts have generally concluded that a greater share of the burden has been shifted backward to employees and that has reduced the estimated progressivity of the corporate income tax because ownership of capital and of corporate stock is more concentrated with higher-income households than is labor income. (*Modeling the Distribution of Taxes on Business Income*, Prepared by the Staff of the Joint Committee on Taxation, JCX-14-13, October 16, 2013.) The March 2013 issue of the *National Tax Journal* published a forum on the incidence of the corporate income tax and, not surprisingly, the economist participants did not agree, so the burden distribution is not a decided question.

the corporate income tax is the third largest source of federal revenue (although of diminishing importance), and that revenue would be difficult to replace from other sources.[50] Problems with the corporate income tax, however, must be considered. One is the fairness of burden distribution. If corporation stockholders bear the tax, why should dividend income be taxed more heavily than other income to the individual? Wages are taxed only once; why should dividends be taxed twice? Furthermore, because not all households within a particular income category receive dividend income, the special tax on corporate income—as translated through to stockholders—obviously violates the equal-treatment-of-equals rule for appropriate tax-burden distributions. The corporate income tax, however, does fill a gap: without it, the portion of corporate income not distributed would go untaxed.[51] In addition, the corporate income tax probably increases the progressivity of the system because dividend income tends to be more concentrated in higher-income groups. At the state level, the corporate income tax allows the state to extract compensation for benefits that the state provides to corporations whose owners may be largely out of state.[52]

One other complication. Suppose you work for a nonprofit organization. This discussion about corporate income taxation would seem pretty much irrelevant. But wait. It would be unfair and inefficient for entities to have tax advantages over similar service providers simply because of the way in which the entity is organized (i.e., proprietary versus nonprofit). And nonprofit doesn't mean zero profit, it just means that any surplus from operations can't be distributed to owners of the entity but must be used for services or business growth. Therefore, we have the Unrelated Business Income Tax, or UBIT, for nonprofit organizations and that tax is discussed in Sidebar 9–4.

Dividing the Profit Base among Governments

Business operations are seldom confined to a single jurisdiction but are multistate or even multinational. Each jurisdiction hosting operations of the business may levy a tax on business income, and that can create complications and opportunities for tax planning by the business, as well as for the jurisdictions that would like to tax them.[53] Problems created by corporate inversions—for instance, when Burger King purchased Tim Horton doughnuts of Canada in 2014 and became a Canadian

---

[50]Revenue received by state governments from corporate income taxes has been in decline as a share of state taxes for many years. Part of the reason is clever corporate tax avoidance strategies, but part is state fear that having corporations pay for state services they use will cause the firms to move elsewhere.

[51]It may increase the market value of corporate stock and create capital gain income when the stock is sold.

[52]Because capital has greater interstate mobility than labor, there is a strong probability that a considerable portion of the burden of a state corporate income tax is born by workers in that state.

[53]The worry is that companies will engage in what is called Base Erosion and Profit Shifting (BEPS), moving profits around to whatever jurisdiction levies the lowest tax. Countries would like profits to be taxed in whatever country they are earned, but that is not easy to determine when parts of a company's operation are scattered all over the world.

Sidebar 9–4
Unrelated Business Income Tax

Nonprofit organizations enjoy a special relationship with the federal tax system: their income is exempt from tax. They do not pay income tax on flows that would be fully taxable if received by an entity organized otherwise. Most file an information return Form 990 with the Internal Revenue Service.

However, certain income earned by the nonprofit may be subject to the Unrelated Business Income Tax (UBIT) if that income is produced in an activity that is not related to the exempt mission of the organization. The tax, enacted in 1954, seeks to ensure that nonprofit organizations do not gain an unfair competitive advantage over proprietary firms in the same business. It is to create a "level playing field" when both proprietary and nonprofit entities happen to be in the same business. So will the Girl Scouts be subject to income tax on their cookie sales? Will the local Red Cross chapter be taxed on the proceeds of its annual book sale? Will the museum be subject to income tax on profits from sales in the museum shop? Will the nonprofit hospital be subject to income tax on profits from its operations? Will the shelter for battered women be subject to tax on its income from sales of food and lodging? As in many questions of taxation, the answer is "It depends."

As a start, the organization must meet two requirements. First is the "nondistribution" constraint that "no part of the net earnings" of the organization can benefit any private individual or shareholder. Second is the rule that the organization may not engage in prohibited lobbying and political activities. But what about income that such an organization might earn? If it is related to the mission, no problem. But what if the income is unrelated to that mission? If so, then the exemption does not apply.

Income is considered to be unrelated if these three conditions hold:

1. The activity is undertaken as a trade or business, generally meaning that the activity is carried out to produce income by sale of goods or services.
2. The activity is undertaken on a regular basis, meaning the activity is carried out with the frequency and continuity of and in a manner comparable to commercial activities by non-exempt entities. For instance, an ice cream stand operated by the Red Cross at a fall festival would be different from an ice cream shop operated by that entity in its office building.
3. The activity is not substantially related to the exempt mission of the organization, meaning the activity does not contribute significantly to accomplishing that mission. If the activity is conducted on a scale larger than reasonably appropriate to the exempt mission, it is suspect.

The fact that income generated by the commercial activity is used by the organization to support its exempt mission is not relevant.

Even if the three conditions hold, there is an exclusion if the income comes from volunteer labor or consists of dividends, interest, rents, and some capital gains.

Any taxable income would be taxed at ordinary corporate tax rates. Unrelated, profit-making activities are allowed, but if they consume too much of the nonprofit organization's attention, the tax authorities may conclude that the organization has abandoned its exempt purpose and

---

**Sidebar 9–4
(continued)**

---

revoke its exempt status. In tax year 2008, the UBIT yielded $336.6 million, with 42,066 returns filed. Individual and corporate income taxes yielded over $1.45 trillion in that year.[1]

State income tax systems typically follow the federal standards. However, there are different state systems for determining whether nonprofit organizations are exempt from retail sales or property taxes.

The IRS provides instructions and explanations in IRS Publication 598, *Tax on Unrelated Business Income of Exempt Organizations.* Reporting is on IRS Form 990-T.

[1]Jael Jackson, "Unrelated Business Income Tax Returns, 2008," *SOI Bulletin* 31 (Winter 2012): 131–55; and Office of Management and Budget, *Budget of the Government of the United States, Fiscal Year 2013, Historical Tables* (Washington, D.C.: U.S. Government Printing Office, 2012).

---

company in order to reduce its tax liability—are discussed in Sidebar 9–5. Two other problems encompass the determination of where profits are generated in a multijurisdictional business and how to deal with transactions that occur within the business. The latter concern, the transfer price problem, involves the price that a part of the business in one country charges for supplies, services, or inventory sold to a part of the business in another. An artificially high price paid for sales to the U.S. operation will cause understated U.S. profit, and, therefore, corporate profit tax paid in the United States will be artificially low. The profit will show up in the other country. Multinational firms are frequently accused of establishing internal prices in such a way that high profits appear only in countries with low corporate profit taxes. Thus, *transfer-pricing rules* (the rules establishing what internal prices are allowed) are critical in establishing corporate liability. If the transfer price is high, profit is increased for the subsidiary where the shipment originates; if the transfer price is low, profit is increased for the subsidiary where the shipment ends up. The profit all ends up with the company owning the subsidiaries, but the total profit tax—part paid to the originating country and part paid to the destination country—differs depending on what the transfer prices are. There is evidence that multinational corporations do manage to report more of their profits where corporate tax rates are lower.

Fairness of profit distribution suggests that the transfer prices should approximate the prices that would be charged in a transaction between unrelated companies, but that is not always simple to establish. An approach that is increasingly popular for multinational companies is the *advance pricing agreement,* in which the tax authority and the company agree on what pricing approach the company will employ in calculating its profits, thereby avoiding the danger that the approach will

Sidebar 9–5
Inversions

Businesses prefer paying lower taxes and will organize their operations accordingly. An inversion provides such an opportunity. In general terms, an inversion occurs when a U.S. corporation changes its legal home to a foreign country by, in essence, converting a foreign subsidiary into the parent company or by purchasing a foreign company and transferring ownership to that company. Thus, parent Corporation XYZ with headquarters in the United States owns a foreign subsidiary Corporation XYZ-A in a low-tax country. With the inversion, the subsidiary Corporation XYZ-A becomes the parent, and Corporation XYZ becomes the subsidiary. Operations of the companies do not change, plants do not move, jobs do not move, even the chief executives may stay in the United States (although board meetings will be in the new location). Indeed, Corporation XYZ-A may be little more than a mailbox in the host low-tax country, but the new U.S. subsidiary seeks to shift as much profit as possible to the new foreign parent. Changes are not physical; the only differences are in where the headquarters is legally located and in what tax the United States gets to collect.

The tax situation works like this. The United States imposes a high statutory corporate income tax rate relative to other industrialized countries, and the tax applies to profits that domestic corporations collect from their foreign subsidiaries (although the tax does not apply until those profits are paid to the U.S. parent firm).[1] That is called a "worldwide" system of taxation, and it contrasts with the "territorial" system that other industrialized countries employ. In the territorial system, only profits generated domestically are taxed. The combination of a high statutory rate and worldwide taxation means that U.S. corporations will be taxed more heavily on foreign subsidiaries than they would if they were not U.S. corporations. Because U.S. corporations are taxed on profits no matter where they are earned and are taxed at a high rate, it is no wonder that some corporations decide to become foreign corporations. U.S. tax still gets paid on profits earned in the United States, but there is no U.S. tax on profits earned elsewhere. And the corporation may also take advantage of techniques to strip the U.S. operation of profits, for instance by charging the U.S. subsidiary royalty or license fees to move profits out of the United States and to the foreign home. By moving the domicile of the company to a country with territorial taxation, the firm pays tax on earnings from each country of operations at whatever rate that country applies.

Around fifty corporations have done inversions in the last decade, contributing to the peculiar situation in which corporation profits are an increasing share of U.S. national income at the same time that corporation income taxes are a declining share of federal tax revenue.

A good source on the tax treatment of profit earned by multinational businesses: Congressional Budget Office, *Options for Taxing U.S. Multinational Corporations*, January 2013.

[1]When a U.S. corporation repatriates income from a foreign subsidiary, it must pay a tax equal to the difference between the U.S. corporate tax rate and the rate applicable in the foreign country. For 2005, the American Jobs Creation Act of 2004 created a holiday during which repatriated profits would be taxed only at a rate of 5.25 percent. As would be expected, federal corporate-profit tax collections for 2005 increased dramatically as businesses took advantage of this one-shot window. Many argue that another such holiday should be offered. More evidence that corporations use transfer pricing for tax avoidance: Eric J. Bartelsman and Roel M. W. J. Beetsma, "Why Pay More? Corporate Tax Avoidance through Transfer Pricing in OECD Countries," *Journal of Public Economics* 87 (2003): 2225–52. A higher corporate tax rate caused reported profits to flee the country, but not the corporation's operations.

be disallowed on audit and thus bring fines and other sanctions. Unfortunately, such agreements are time consuming and may make the system a bit overly individualized in its application.

A similar issue in the United States involves division of corporate profit across the states in which the firm does business. Only Nevada, Ohio, South Dakota, Texas, Washington, and Wyoming do not currently have corporate income taxes roughly patterned after the federal tax, and the state taxes do create some special tax base distribution problems. The big complication is that corporations conduct business in more than one state. What state gets to tax what profit? Some income may be clearly defined as originating from property or other assets in a single state, but much cannot be so identified. For instance, a particular corporation may have retail outlets in forty-five states, warehouses in nine states, and factories in two states. How much of that firm's profit should be taxable in any one state?

To handle the problem, each state with a corporate income tax has adopted its own income *apportionment* formula to determine how much of the total profit earned by a multistate corporation it will tax. States employ formulas that involve the share of total corporate sales in the state, the share of total corporate property in the state, and the share of total corporate payroll in the state. (Of course, the corporation must be conducting a minimum amount of business in the state to be taxable by the state; this contact is referred to as having *nexus* with the state.) The traditional approach is the three-factor formula, in which the shares are equally weighted. With this formula, if state A has 50 percent of the firm's total property value, 25 percent of the firm's total payroll, and 60 percent of the firm's total sales, that state would apply its corporate tax rate to 45 percent [(50 + 25 + 60)/3] of the firm's total profit.[54] Other states use the same three factors, but give double weighting to the sales factor, whereas yet others use only sales in the formula.[55]

States are migrating toward formulas that give greater emphasis to sales rather than to property or payroll in an effort to favor corporations with production facilities in their borders (having production facilities means property and employees, but does not bring an allocation of profit for state taxation if these factors are not in the apportionment formula). In other words, the attempt is to improve the competitive position of the state by shifting factors from those that reflect the origin of economic activity (payroll and property) to those that reflect the destination (sales). States see this change toward heavy weight on the sales share as part of their economic development effort.[56] There is no clearly correct formula for apportionment, of course, but having production facilities in a state certainly requires the state to deliver some

---

[54]This three-factor formula is frequently called the Massachusetts formula, although Massachusetts no longer uses it.

[55]The U.S. Supreme Court, in a case involving Moorman Manufacturing Company, upheld the Iowa formula that uses only sales. See "New Flexibility on Business Tax Granted State," *Wall Street Journal,* June 16, 1978. The problem was that, when states use a variety of differing apportionment formulas, an unlucky multistate business could find that it paid state corporate income tax on more than 100 percent of its total profits. And more lucky businesses could pay tax on less than 100 percent of their profits.

[56]Austan Goolsbee and Edward L. Maydew, "Coveting Thy Neighbor's Manufacturing: The Dilemma of State Income Apportionment," *Journal of Public Economics* 75 (2000): 125–43, measures the impact of the apportionment factor on manufacturing employment in a state.

services to the business. That is the logic behind having the non–sales factors in the formula. Because many states lack sufficient audit staff to verify the factors computed by all corporate filers, they must accept the calculations done by many corporations. This problem of profit apportionment makes local corporate income taxes extremely difficult in terms of compliance and enforcement.[57]

Integration of Corporate and Individual Income Taxes and Distortion Problems

The U.S. tax system taxes profit earned by the corporation and dividends received by the individual corporate stockholder. By treating corporations and their investors as separate taxable entities, the system causes an extra tax burden on distributed, as opposed to retained, profits, puts an extra burden on income from capital, and discriminates against the ordinary corporate form of business organization. This has meant a considerable secular decline in the use of the ordinary corporate form for doing business. Returns from ordinary corporations (called C corporations in the federal system) constituted 16.6 percent of all business tax returns in 1980 and fell to only 4.9 percent of the total in 2012. The number of regular corporations fell by about one-quarter over those years, and the total number of businesses increased by two and one-half times. Over that same period, the number of multiple-owner businesses that have income taxed only at the individual level, not at the business level, almost quadrupled.[58]

A major problem with this traditional treatment of corporate and individual income is its effects on savings and real investment. The taxes probably tax dividends twice and thus reduce the rate of savings, with undesirable effects on capital formation. It definitely has stimulated the creation of business forms that are something like regular corporations (particularly with regard to offering limited liability to their owners), but whose profits are taxable only to the owners and not at the business-entity level (the Subchapter S corporation and the limited liability company, for instance, are such "pass through" entities). Furthermore, the

---

[57]Businesses have another approach to minimizing state income tax. They establish a closely held company in a low-tax or no-tax jurisdiction that owns trademarks used by the business, and that company charges a royalty for the use of those trademarks. The royalty is high enough to capture most or all of the operating profits, eliminating the profit where it would be taxed and realizing it where it is barely taxed. Good deal for the business; not so good for the state. Another example: Wal-Mart stores are on property owned by a separate, but captive Wal-Mart real estate investment trust housed in a state not taxing rental income (such as Delaware). Wal-Mart pays rent on the store property, reducing its taxable profit, and the proceeds show up in Delaware and aren't taxed by any state. Jesse Drucker, "Wal-Mart Cuts Taxes by Paying Rent to Itself," *Wall Street Journal,* February 1, 2007, A-1. Other companies do the same, and states fight by claiming that these are sham transactions. A few states counteract this shifting by requiring "combined reporting," a requirement that the parent corporation and its subsidiaries be added together for tax purposes. Corporations are not fond of the requirement because it eliminates the advantage of the strategy.

[58]Internal Revenue Service, SOI Tax Stats–Business Tax Statistics. http://www.irs.gov/uac/SOI-Tax-Stats-Business-Tax-Statistics.

corporate tax certainly influences choices by corporate executives between finance by debt (interest payments to bondholders are deductible) and finance by equity (dividend payments to shareholders are not deductible).[59] Those capital formation effects add to the productivity problems of the nation, so some change might be appropriate.

Many of the undesirable economic and equity effects would be reduced if individual income and corporate income taxes were integrated either partially or completely to mitigate the extra tax the two systems place on distributed corporate profit. Complete integration would treat the corporation in the same way as partnerships. In other words, the tax would not apply to corporate income at all, but the owners of the corporation would be taxed according to their proportionate shares of dividends and retained earnings, as in this example: if Fred and Jack are partners and their business agreement is that Fred owns 30 percent of the business, then Fred would pay individual income tax on 30 percent of profits (distributed and retained), Jack would pay individual income tax on 70 percent of profits, and that would be that. Although this would be the most direct approach (and would treat the ordinary corporation in exactly the same way as other business forms are treated), it would create some sticky issues:[60]

1. The tax would apply to income not distributed. Individuals would be taxed according to income distributed as dividends plus income the corporation retains. There is some question whether this would encourage greater corporate payout of earnings and thus might lower the rate of real investment.
2. Many holders of corporate stock are tax-exempt entities (e.g., pension funds). Under this integrated structure, those entities would not pay individual income tax on their dividends and retained earnings, and there would be no collection of tax at the corporate level either. How could that revenue loss be replaced?[61]
3. Sizable amounts of U.S. stocks are held by foreign entities. How would that income be treated? What country would be entitled to tax those U.S. dividends and retained earnings? If not the United States, how would that federal revenue loss be made up?
4. Corporations do not have single classes of stock. Corporations frequently have common stock, preferred stock, and possibly other varieties of equity ownership representations. How would corporate income be divided equitably among those various classes of stock?

---

[59]Every business requires capital to operate. Capital can come from borrowing, for which interest must be paid, or from equity invested by owners in exchange for an ownership share. Interest paid on debt is tax deductible whereas money paid to equity owners is not. That distorts toward borrowing: a chunk of the interest payment will reduce tax owed by the business, thus reducing the net cost of debt relative to equity finance.

[60]R. Glenn Hubbard, "Corporate Tax Integration: A View from the Treasury Department," *Journal of Economic Perspectives* 7 (Winter 1993): 115–32.

[61]Of course, under the current system, even though they are tax exempt, they may well be bearing a portion of the corporate income tax burden passed through to them via reduced returns.

The alternate approach is partial integration. Partial integration would provide relief only on the share of corporate earnings that is distributed as dividends, either by giving some special credit to dividend recipients to account for the corporate income tax already paid on the flow or by applying the corporate income tax only to undistributed corporate profit. That relief would cut tax collections substantially, and there is the fear that it would appear to be an unwarranted tax break for business. Those two factors have kept interest in such reform low, although there is a revival in connection with the relatively slow growth rate of the U.S. economy and the slow rate of capital formation that has worked to produce that slow growth.[62]

Payroll Taxation

In addition to the broad-based individual and corporate income taxes, there are narrow taxes on payrolls or wage and salary income, levied on the employer, the employee, or both, but normally collected by the employer each pay period and remitted by the employer.[63] Payroll taxes include those levied by the federal government on employers and employees to support the Social Security system and Medicare, those levied by federal and state governments on employers to support the unemployment compensation system, and earned-income taxes levied on employee wages and salaries by some local governments.[64] Most analysts believe the real burden of these taxes, regardless of legal impact, is largely on the employee. When labor markets permit, employers simply adjust their compensation packages to account for the payroll tax for which they know they will be liable. About two-thirds of the U.S. population pay more federal payroll tax than they do federal individual income tax.

The payroll taxes have several peculiarities. First, they are narrow and exclude types of income more likely to be received by higher-income individuals, including interest, dividends, capital gains, and so on. That exclusion increases the likelihood that the tax will cause low-income people to bear higher effective tax rates than do high-income people. Moreover, people with roughly the same income would pay

---

[62]Countries of the Organization for Economic Cooperation and Development (OECD) follow several different schemes for mitigating the extra tax. Some eliminate the extra tax at the corporate level by full deduction of dividends paid at the corporate level (Greece and Norway), and some eliminate it at the individual level by giving full credit for tax paid by the corporation (Australia, Finland, Germany [partial], Italy, New Zealand). Others reduce the extra tax by lower rates on distributed profits, partial deduction of dividends paid, or partial credit for corporate tax on dividends received (Germany [partial], Iceland, Spain, Sweden, France, Ireland, United Kingdom, Austria, Denmark, Japan, Portugal). Belgium, Luxembourg, the Netherlands, Switzerland, and the United States do not provide accommodation.
[63]Payroll taxes are also common in other countries.
[64]A good overview of the social insurance taxes appears in Committee on Ways and Means, U.S. House of Representatives, *Green Book, Background Material and Data on the Programs within the Jurisdiction of the Committee on Ways and Means* (Washington, D.C.: U.S. Government Printing Office). The 2011 version is available on the Internet: http://greenbook.waysandmeans.house.gov/.

different amounts of tax according to the kinds of income. Therefore, these are both vertical and horizontal equity questions.

Second, the federal and state payroll taxes for the social insurance system have unusual statutory rate patterns. Taxability begins with the first dollar earned, and, except for the Medicare tax, the tax rate falls to zero on pay above some maximum level earned in the year. That means the marginal rate structure is graduated downward, and, for individuals above the maximum, the average rate falls as income rises. Low-income workers are hit the hardest by the taxes. For 2015, the federal tax supporting Social Security applied at a rate of 6.20 percent on the employee and 6.20 percent on the employer, but only the first $118,500 of earnings were taxed. The rate supporting Medicare is 1.45 percent on both employer and employee, and there is no limit on the base. Since 2013, there has been an additional Medicare tax of 0.9 percent applied on income (wages plus self-employed income) above $200,000 in a calendar year (for a single filer); employers withhold, but more tax may be owed. The tax borne by a person earning $10,000 would be $1,530 (15.3 percent of total pay), whereas the tax borne by a person earning $140,000 would be $19,024 ($14,694 for Social Security—12.4 percent of the maximum taxable wage base of $118,500—plus $4,060 for Medicare—the 2.9 percent rate applied to the full $140,000). The average rate on earnings is 13.5 percent for the higher-income person and 15.3 percent for the lower-income person. As earnings increase, the average rate decreases even more.[65]

The payroll tax financing the unemployment compensation system has federal and state components. The federal tax rate is 6 percent on earnings to $7,000, paid by the employer. However, if a state has an approved unemployment compensation system (and all fifty do), then up to 5.4 percent of the state rate is a full credit against the federal liability, leaving a net federal rate of 0.6 percent. States may have a taxable wage base higher than the federal limit (forty-one do). States also can levy rates on employers that differ from the 5.4 percent standard based on the unemployment experience rating of the firm: those with fewer layoffs pay lower tax than do those with more layoffs.[66] The idea is to encourage employers to stabilize their labor force while financing the unemployment compensation system.

Finally, the federal and state payroll taxes are all earmarked. That is, their revenues are dedicated to finance only particular social insurance benefits. Because these benefits tend to be more valuable to lower-income individuals, the public generally accepts the unusual features of these taxes that make their burdens regressive. Nevertheless, they do contribute to labor market incentive effects by adding to the wedge between what employers pay and what employees retain. Any surpluses in these funds are invested in U.S. government bonds, thus helping support those markets.

---

[65]For economic stimulation purposes in the Great Recession, the payroll tax rate was reduced from its normal level. The tax returned to its normal level at the end of 2012.

[66]Rates can range from zero (sixteen states) up to 10 percent (three states). Three states also tax the employee. A number of state unemployment compensation funds ran out of money during the recession that started in December 2007 and were forced to borrow from the federal government to maintain benefit payments.

Conclusion

The income tax has been the heart of the federal revenue system from the early years of the twentieth century, providing sizable revenue for global responsibilities and domestic programs. For seventy years, the individual income tax has been the dominant source, although the payroll taxes for social insurance have become almost as significant in overall finance. Corporate income taxes now play only a small role in finances. Individual income taxes also make a major contribution to the finances of state governments.

Although achieving progressivity, the income taxes do have problems of economic inefficiency, horizontal inequity, expensive collection, and failure of transparency. Effective tax rates for individual and corporate taxes are considerably less than the statutory rates because of the flurry of preferences inserted by lawmakers. Corporate and payroll taxes raise considerable revenue, but they offer difficult challenges of equity and efficiency. There are enough preferences inserted in the income tax system to raise the belief that lawmakers have lost sight of the fact that the fundamental purpose of the system is to raise money to support government operations. The taxes are overwhelmingly complex, but efforts to simplify them fail because those complexity provisions are the means for delivering tax preferences to constituents. In the aggregate, keeping your preferences while eliminating preferences enjoyed by others is mathematically doomed to failure. The strange patterns and incentives often produced by the preferences give stark evidence of the problems created by using the tax system for something other than its unique function, that of raising money for the provision of government services.

QUESTIONS AND EXERCISES

1. Identify the important elements of the income tax in your state. Does your state levy individual and corporate income taxes; do local governments levy such income taxes and, if so, are they linked to the state taxes; are the state income taxes linked to the federal income taxes; are the rates graduated; are there preferences in the state taxes that are not also in the federal taxes; and are the state taxes indexed?

2. A midwestern state aids its institutions of higher education by giving a credit against its income tax equal to 50 percent of any gift to such institutions (subject to a limit of $50 credit per person). Two residents of that state, Mr. Blue (in the 10 percent federal tax bracket) and Ms. Jones (in the 35 percent federal tax bracket), each contribute $100 to an eligible state university.

   a. How much will the state tax liabilities of each change as a result of their gifts?
   b. State income tax payments and contributions to charitable organizations (such as universities) are both currently deductible from the base used to compute

federal tax liability. How much will federal tax liability change for Mr. Blue and Ms. Jones as a result of their contributions?

c. Considering changes in both federal and state tax liabilities, what is the net after-tax cost of Mr. Blue's and Ms. Jones's gifts? (*Hint:* Subtract the changes in state and federal liabilities from $100.)

d. Suppose the state program changed from a credit to a deduction. If the state tax rate was a flat 3 percent, how much would state liability for Mr. Blue and Ms. Jones change?

e. From the previous computations, which approach (credit or deduction) do you suppose universities in the state would favor? Why?

3. Mr. Brown is in the 10 percent federal income tax bracket and wants to invest $10,000 in interest-earning assets. Mr. Black is in the 35 percent bracket and wants to invest $15,000. The current rate on a typical high-quality tax-exempt municipal bond is 3.5 percent and on a high-quality corporate bond is 4 percent. You are the financial advisor to both. Which investment would you recommend to each individual?

4. Ms. Busch has gathered these data about her finances:

Salary	140,000
Taxable interest received	2,500
Municipal bond interest received	15,000
Total itemized deductions	8,000

The personal exemption is $3,700. The standard deduction for a single filer is $5,800. Use the rate schedule in Figure 9–2 to compute the following:

a. Her tax
b. Her average effective tax rate
c. Her average tax rate
d. Her marginal tax rate
e. Her accountant discovers a previously omitted personal deduction of $800. By how much does her federal tax liability fall with that addition?
f. Amazingly enough, the accountant now discovers a $250 credit omitted from previous calculations (but after discovering the $800 in part e). By how much does her federal tax liability fall because of this credit?

5. A proposed state income tax would require individuals with incomes of $15,000 or less to pay no tax and those with incomes above $15,000 to pay a tax of 10 percent only on the part of their income that exceeds $15,000.

a. Could an individual pay an average tax rate of 7.5 percent under this system?
b. Could an individual pay an average tax rate of 10 percent under this system?
c. What average and marginal tax rates would individuals with these income levels face: $10,000, $20,000, $40,000, and $150,000?
Explain each of your answers and provide examples to justify your conclusions.

6. The Ukrainian tax system in the late 1990s had several components. The personal income tax (calculated and paid on a monthly basis) had these brackets:

Zero	if income was below one NTM
10%	for income from 1 NTM + 1 KBV to 5 NTM
20%	for income from 5 NTM + 1 KBV to 10 NTM, plus the tax on 5 NTM
30%	for income from 10 NTM + 1 KBV to 15 NTM, plus the tax on 10 NTM
40%	for income from 15 NTM + 1 KBV to 25 NTM, plus the tax on 15 NTM
50%	for income above 25 NTM, plus the tax on 25 NTM

KBV, karbovantsi; NTM, nontaxed minimum.

The NTM was 1,400,000 KBV (one U.S. dollar was worth about 180,000 Ukrainian KBV). In September 1995, the average monthly salary was 9 million KBV. Use of the NTM provides an easy way of adjusting the entire tax structure for the impact of inflation.

Employers paid payroll taxes at these rates: 37 percent to the social insurance fund, 12 percent to the Chernobyl fund, and 2 percent to the employment fund. Employees also paid 1 percent to the employment fund.

a. Create a tax rate schedule like that in Figure 9–2 for the Ukraine personal income tax.

b. Create a tax table like that in Figure 9–3 for incomes from 9,100,000 KBV to 9,100,200 KBV.

c. Analysts calculate the tax wedge—defined to be the difference between the amount that the employer must pay to hire an employee and the amount that the employee receives net of all taxes as a percentage of the employee's net—in examining the nature of tax systems. Compute the total tax wedge for a worker at the average monthly salary, at twice the average, and at five times the average.

d. Compute the average effective tax rate and the marginal tax rate for a worker at the three salary levels from part c.

e. Comment on the likely incentive effects of this tax structure.

7. The Bartonia Company manufactures grommets in Georgia and sells them directly to industrial customers in Georgia, Florida, and South Carolina. The company's profit for last year was $20,000,000. The company has its manufacturing plant and headquarters in Georgia, warehouses in South Carolina and Florida, and sales forces in each state. Here are some of its financial statistics:

	Payroll	Property	Sales
Georgia	5,000,000	35,000,000	6,000,000
South Carolina	1,000,000	5,000,000	13,000,000
Florida	500,000	400,000	1,000,000
TOTAL	6,500,000	40,400,000	20,000,000

a. Suppose each state uses a simple three-factor apportionment formula. What share of company profit would each state tax?

b. Make that same calculation, but suppose each state double-weights the sales factor.

c. Make the calculation with each using only the sales factor.

    d. Assume now that Georgia adopts the single sales factor and the other states use double-weighted sales.

    e. Assume now that South Carolina adopts the single sales factor and the other states use double-weighted sales.

    f. Explain why manufacturing firms in some states have pressed for use of the single sales factor. Why have nationwide business organizations not made this switch an issue?

8. Warren Buffett, one of the richest men in the United States and the head of Berkshire Hathaway Corporation, a profitable investment company, complained in 2007 that he was paying a smaller percentage of his income in federal taxes (17.7 percent) than was the receptionist in his office (about 30 percent). Assuming that he was not cheating on his taxes, what factors might account for this situation? Does this information by itself suggest that the federal tax system is regressive?

9. The Georgia state income tax uses adjusted gross income as reported on the federal tax return as the starting point for calculation of its tax liability. The North Carolina tax uses federal taxable income as its starting point. What are the implications of these two different starting points?

10. The Republic of Mouton Rouge individual income tax has two components. Earned income (wages, salaries, profit of unincorporated business, and rents) is taxed according to the following rates: taxable income from 0 to GM$15,000 at a rate of 5 percent; taxable income from GM$15,001 to GM$45,000 at a rate of 10 percent; taxable income from GM$45,001 to GM$100,000 at a rate of 15 percent; and taxable income above GM$100,001 at a rate of 20 percent. Taxable income for an individual taxpayer equals earned income less an exemption of GM$10,000. Unearned income (capital gains, interest, and dividends) received by an individual is taxed at a rate of 12 percent with no exemption. (Note: GM$ is the Grand Mouton dollar.)

    Ms. LeBlanc received a salary of GM$115,000 and interest of GM$2,000. Calculate the following:

    a. Total tax paid by Ms. LeBlanc.

    b. The average effective tax rate she pays.

    c. Her marginal tax rate on earned income.

CASE FOR DISCUSSION

CASE 9–1

When Marginal Tax Rates Were Really Extreme

Raintree County brought its author fame, fortune, and serious tax liability. The serious novel was 1,066 pages long and full of betrayal, sex, and deviousness and seemed to put its author, Ross Lockridge Jr, on pace to be the next great American novelist.

It was well received by reviewers and was a hit with the public. But the success of the novel brought tax consequences and other problems that sadly brought Lockridge's suicide before he fulfilled his apparent potential. The following article takes you through the tax problems that were endemic in the system of that time.

Consider These Questions

1. Use the case to explain why tax analysts worry about marginal rates, not average rates, in looking for incentive effects of taxes.

2. Explain the relevance of this case for discussions about revisions of the federal income tax system.

3. Explain how some changes in the tax system would have made Lockridge's tax problem somewhat less now than in the 1940s.

4. In your view, was Lockridge being badly treated by the income tax system? Explain your view.

Taxes in the Shade of the Raintree by J. Fred Giertz[67]

Some critics assert that the U.S. individual income tax in its current form has never been more intrusive or complex. However, an obscure circumstance that arose 60 years ago suggests otherwise.

In early 1948, Bloomington, Ind., was the focus of the literary world. The book *Sexual Behavior in the Human Male* by Indiana University Prof. Alfred Kinsey was a national sensation, rising to number one on the *New York Times* nonfiction bestseller list. During the same period, the novel *Raintree County* by Bloomington native Ross Lockridge Jr. also reached the top of the *Times* fiction list.

Today *Raintree County* is likely remembered as the flawed 1957 film starring Montgomery Clift and Elizabeth Taylor. The movie was loosely based on the Lockridge novel that tells a complex story of an Indiana native (based on a Lockridge ancestor) from mythical Raintree County (Henry County, Ind.) through flashbacks that occur on a single day on July 4, 1892. It was a serious novel that was also a popular success despite its over 1,000-page length. It has been hailed as a failed but valiant attempt at the illusive "great American novel" and is now considered an important work in environmental fiction, becoming a staple in American studies courses.

Lockridge was not the stereotypical dissolute, self-indulgent artist. He was handsome and well-liked and an accomplished scholar and athlete who was devoted to his wife and family.[68] After excelling in his junior year at the

---

[67]J. Fred Giertz is a professor of economics at the University of Illinois at Urbana-Champaign. An earlier version of this article appeared in the NTA newsletter *NTA Network,* June 2008. *Tax Notes,* August 4, 2008, with minor editorial changes. Copyright 2008 J. Fred Giertz. All rights reserved.

[68]Much of the information about Lockridge comes from the biography written by his son Larry Lockridge: *Shade of the Raintree: The Life and Death of Ross Lockridge Jr., Author of Raintree County.* New York: Viking Penguin, 1994.

Sorbonne, he graduated in 1935 with the highest average in the history of Indiana University. He eventually went on to Harvard University to study for a Ph.D. in English. As a graduate student at Harvard and a teacher at Simmons College, a woman's college in Boston, he wrote the monumental *Raintree County* while supporting his wife and four young children.

Unlike many writers, he was also well informed about business and tax matters. After years spent writing the book and enduring a painful editorial process, the book became a literary and financial success. In addition to the normal royalties from the Houghton Mifflin publishing house, the book won an MGM prize of $150,000 (with $125,000 to Lockridge and $25,000 to the publisher) for the screen rights and became a Book of the Month Club choice, generating an additional $25,000. These values can be multiplied by 10 to provide an estimate of their purchasing power in 2008 dollars.

Lockridge went from an unknown, struggling former graduate student and teacher to a rich and famous author almost overnight. By March 1948 *Raintree County* had become the number one fiction bestseller. On March 6 Lockridge completed and mailed his wife's income tax return, wrote a detailed letter to his lawyer dealing with his own tax matters, and being a true Hoosier, made plans to listen to the radio broadcast of a Bloomington High School regional basketball game.

Later that night, he was found dead in his garage from carbon monoxide poisoning—a suicide victim at age 33. It is now known that he was severely depressed and suffered from anxiety. This problem was not well diagnosed 60 years ago and even less well treated. Clearly his suicide was the result of his depression, but in the last year of his life, his distress focused on both artistic and business problems, including taxes.

In the artistic arena, Lockridge found the editing and especially the cutting of his work very painful. The demands of the MGM prize and the Book of the Month Club selection led to the need for cuts of up to 100,000 words in what he thought was the final version. As with most authors, he was also concerned about the reception of his novel, believing that his work was not being reviewed fairly by many critics.

On the business front, Lockridge became unhappy with Houghton Mifflin, where some smaller disputes and misunderstandings eventually soured the overall relationship. He operated without a literary agent, so many issues that might have been handled at arm's length became the source of personal bitterness. Within this context, taxes also played a major role.

As a person knowledgeable about business affairs, he was also familiar with taxation issues. In 1947 the U.S. income tax was highly progressive with extremely high marginal rates.[69] There were 24 brackets, with marginal rates ranging from 19 percent to 86.45 percent—the highest rate applying to taxable income over $200,000. Also, there was no income splitting available for families before 1948—one year too late for Lockridge and his wife. All taxpayers had to

---

[69]For more detail, see Joseph Pechman, *Federal Tax Policy,* Washington, D.C.: Brookings Institution, 1987.

file single returns. Moreover, there was no explicit forward or backward averaging. Income averaging made an appearance in the U.S. income tax laws from 1964 to 1986, but it did not exist in 1947.

Realizing this, Lockridge made an unusual demand when his manuscript was submitted for the MGM prize. He wanted the proceeds of the prize to be paid over several years, not in a lump sum. He believed that this condition had been accepted at the time of submission. When he won the prize, his joy was dampened when he learned that prize was to be paid in one payment in 1947. He was bitterly disappointed about this and felt betrayed by his publisher and MGM.

This was not an inconsequential concern. Arguments for income averaging are usually based on stories similar to Lockridge's situation—a period of long gestation with little or no pay followed by a large lump sum payout. Using the tax tables for 1947, $125,000 of taxable income generated a tax liability of $85,092 for an average tax rate of 68.1 percent and a marginal rate of 84.55 percent.[70] A five-year distribution of $25,000 (or five-year averaging) would have generated a total tax bill (present value considerations aside) of $48,213 with a 38.6 percent average and 56.05 percent marginal rates.

Income splitting with joint returns was introduced in 1948. If full income splitting and a five-year distribution of the $125,000 had been available, the total tax bill would have fallen to $34,343 with a 27.5 percent average and 40.85 percent marginal rate. The overall difference between the tax on the lump sum payment and a five-year distribution with income splitting amounts to $50,749, with the lump sum tax 2.5 times the amount of the smaller tax bill.

Lockridge was deeply troubled that taxes had seriously eroded a payment (well over $1 million in today's dollars) for the best work he might ever produce that could have provided long-term security for him and his family. He spent more than five years working on the book and in 1948 had nothing in the pipeline for future publication. It should be noted that he and his wife did not object to the welfare state and the resultant high levels of taxation. They were ardent supporters of Franklin Roosevelt and were even against Indiana native Wendell Willkie in the 1940 election. Lockridge was not upset with high taxes in general, but he was unhappy with their impact and perceived unfairness on people in his particular situation.

His problems illustrate the effects of high marginal rates with extreme progressivity.[71] Some of these problems were eventually dealt with explicitly through income splitting and averaging provisions in the tax law and ultimately by lowering marginal rates and reducing the number of brackets.

In addition to attempting to spread his income over a longer period, Lockridge also devised an ad hoc splitting arrangement. Lockridge paid his wife,

---

[70]These tax calculations should be viewed as illustrative in that detailed information about Lockridge's actual situation is not available. In addition to inflation, these results are also not directly comparable to rates today because of differences in the tax base and the availability of avoidance opportunities.

[71]Heavyweight boxing champion Joe Louis was another casualty of this high marginal tax rate era. Bad business advice along with disallowed charitable contributions from the donation of fight purses during World War II resulted in a crushing tax bill and interest charges that wrecked his career.

Vernice, $25,000 for her assistance in writing *Raintree County,* which transferred income from his 84.55 marginal rate to her still high 56.05 marginal rate (and a 39 percent average rate). On the day of his death, he was still concerned about how the IRS might view this payment and went to some length to justify the arrangement in a letter to his attorney. He also made deductible charitable contributions to the Indiana University Foundation for an account that would be used by his father, who was active in promoting Indiana history and culture.

No one should conclude that taxes drove Ross Lockridge, Jr. to suicide. However, tax concerns were a source of his distress that was magnified by his depression. This also shows that even with all of its defects and problems, the income tax today could be worse and actually was much worse in the past. Think about how intrusive and disruptive the income tax would be today with marginal rates reaching 50 percent at less than $200,000 in 2008 dollars and over 84 percent at $1 million with brackets not indexed for inflation and without income splitting and tax deferred saving options. We may not live in the best of all tax worlds, but we do not live in the worst either.

CHAPTER 10

Major Tax Structures: Taxes on Goods and Services

Chapter Contents

Governments in the United States collected more than $1,213.7 billion from taxes levied on goods and services in 2014.[1] Of that amount, federal excises and customs duties (taxes on imports) yielded $137.8 billion—far behind the collections from the income base (individual income, Social Security payroll, and corporate income taxes). State and local sales and excise taxes generated $1,075.9 billion, in total the most significant base for these governments. As pointed out in an earlier chapter, however, American reliance on goods and services levies (the consumption base) overall is less than that in most industrialized democracies.

Taxes on goods and services have several desirable features as a part of a revenue system. First, they can provide considerable revenue when they apply to a broad base, thus allowing diversification from other tax bases. A range of alternative tax bases can be important because heavy use of any tax is likely to bring out all of its worst efficiency, equity, and collectability problems. Most developed nations have lower

---

[1]Bureau of Economic Analysis, National Income and Product Accounts. www.bea.gov

reliance on the income base than does the United States because they levy broad-base national taxes on consumption and the U.S. does not. Second, the consumption taxes provide a means for extracting payment from individuals with high economic capacity and low current income, including those who have successfully evaded the income tax or are living off of inherited wealth. If the income tax cheat enjoys an elegant lifestyle with purchases from honest vendors, some tax is collected when purchases are made. This can be particularly important in developing countries. Third, some taxes on goods and services may function as quasi-prices to collect for social costs or to act as surrogates for charges for certain government services. Finally, some argue that consumption taxes can have important desirable production effects because they tax according to what people take from the economy (consumption), not according to what of value they add to the economy (income), and because they encourage saving.

Goods and services taxes may be general or selective, specific or ad valorem, single stage or multistage, for general or earmarked purposes, and legally applied to the buyer or the seller; all these varieties appear in the slate of goods and services taxes that governments now levy. Before considering the taxes in detail and the special issues each may involve, here is a quick summary of some structural distinctions:

1. **General or selective.** A general sales tax applies to all transactions at a level of economic activity, except for certain listed exemptions (e.g., a sales tax applied to all retail sales of tangible personal property except those of food). A selective sales tax (commonly called an excise tax) applies only to enumerated transactions (e.g., a lodging tax applied to room rentals for thirty days or less).
2. **Specific or ad valorem.** A specific tax (or unit tax) applies to the number of physical units bought or sold (e.g., a motor-fuel tax might be 50 cents per gallon of fuel). An ad valorem tax applies to the value (number of units times price per unit) of the transaction (e.g., a lodging tax of 10 percent of the hotel bill).
3. **Multistage or single stage.** A tax may apply every time a transaction occurs (multistage tax) or only at one stage in the production and distribution process (single-stage tax). The taxed stage may be at the manufacturer level, at the wholesaler or distributor level, or at the retail level. A multistage tax would apply at more than one point of exchange.[2]

---

[2]Governments have occasionally levied gross receipts (turnover) taxes that apply at a low statutory rate on all business activities, and such taxes are sometimes still proposed. These are particularly obnoxious taxes because they violate several aspects of normal tax policy. They have burden distributions roughly like those of retail sales taxes, but because of their pyramiding nature (discussed later in this chapter), they discriminate across types of businesses and place prospective burden on the least profitable ones, harm the economic competitiveness of the jurisdiction that makes the mistake of levying them, distort the nature of business transactions in the state, violate transparency by hiding and significantly understating their actual effective rate (probably explaining why lawmakers like them), and are grossly inequitable. Their "charms" are more fully explored in John L. Mikesell, "State Gross Receipts Taxes and the Fundamental Principles of Tax Policy," *State Tax Notes* 43 (March 5, 2007): 615–32; and Charles E. McLure Jr., "Why Ohio Should Not Introduce a Gross Receipts Tax—Testimony on the Proposed Commercial Activity Tax," *State Tax Notes* 36 (April 18, 2005): 213–15. Ohio ignored his wise advice and passed the tax anyway. Experience with gross receipts taxes in West Virginia and Indiana and in Western Europe demonstrates the difficulties associated with these taxes. States levying such taxes include Washington (business and occupations tax), Delaware, Nevada, Ohio, and Texas (margin tax), along with the tax financing the baseball stadium in Washington, D.C. States repealing such taxes since 2000 include Michigan, Kentucky, New Jersey, and Indiana.

4. **General fund or earmarked.** Excise taxes often are earmarked to special funds for expenditure only on specific purposes as opposed to being collected for the general purposes of government. For example, most motor-fuel tax revenue collected by U.S. states goes into special funds for highway-associated expenditure. Unfortunately, such fund earmarking creates rigidity in the budget process, and revenue flows into these funds may not reflect need for public services.[3] Only if revenue going to the fund reflects demand for the service financed by the fund does earmarking make a positive contribution. That can happen when purchase of the taxed item is complementary to use of the government service, that is, when there is a close relationship between purchase of the taxed item and consumption of the government service.

5. **Buyer or seller.** A tax on a transaction or on something transferred in the transaction may be legally on the buyer or the seller. Usually the distinction matters for legal purposes alone because whether the tax will be reflected in price or absorbed by the seller will depend on the market conditions surrounding the transfer. More often than not, our tax burden estimates will presume that the tax is reflected in prices (shifted forward), regardless of what the statutes say. However, enforcement is usually easier against sellers (there are fewer of them than there are of buyers and liability within a reporting period is likely to be larger) and sellers may be more familiar with accounting and tax questions than are buyers, so assignment of statutory responsibility may be significant for some taxes. Assignment is particularly important for sales taxation of purchases made from out-of-state vendors, as will be discussed later in the chapter.

Table 10–1 and Table 10–2 present an overview of general and selective goods and services tax collections received by federal, state, and local governments. In the tables, the selective excises are divided into four main groups: (1) sumptuary excises applied "to control the consumption of items that are considered immoral or unhealthy,"[4] (2) transport excises potentially defensible as proxy service charges for transportation facilities, (3) environmental excises levied "to improve efficiency in the use of resources"[5] by causing recognition of damage associated with the taxed product, and (4) miscellaneous excises that have been applied for reasons that include attempting to capture extraordinary taxpaying capacity (the recent federal luxury excises) and the lure of taxing the nonresident (lodging taxes). State yields, combining selective and general taxes, are more than nine times the amount of federal excises and almost 50 percent higher than local general and selective excises. Most of the excise revenue comes from the "traditional or big three" excises on tobacco products, alcoholic beverages, and fuels.

---

[3]The revenues may also simply substitute for other government resources that would have been provided even without the dedicated tax. Because revenues are fungible, it is difficult to ensure that money supports only the dedicated purpose.

[4]Sijbren Cnossen, *Excise Systems, A Global Study of the Selective Taxation of Goods and Services* (Baltimore: Johns Hopkins University Press, 1977), 8. That is according to someone's idea of what kind of consumption is immoral. Taxes on casino gambling is a new favorite in some states. Into which category do these taxes fall? Are they taxes on extraordinary capacity or on immoral behavior?

[5]Ibid., 9.

Table 10–1
Major Federal Taxes on Goods and Services, Fiscal 2012

Tax	Collections ($K)	% of Total Federal Receipts (less Social Insurance)
Transportation		
Truck, trailer, and semitrailer chassis	3,321,701	0.21%
Tires	393,890	0.02%
Aviation fuels	364,385	0.02%
Motor fuels	33,666,013	2.10%
Fuels used commercially on inland waterways	78,246	0.00%
Transportation of persons by air	8,798,294	0.55%
Use of international air travel facilities	2,869,656	0.18%
Tax on heavy vehicle use	1,008,944	0.06%
Diesel fuel use by trains	(35,771)	−0.00%
Transportation of property by air	603,139	0.04%
Passenger transportaton by water	33,577	0.00%
Environmental		
Ozone-depleting chemicals	1,070	0.00%
Gas guzzlers	61,334	0.00%
Petroleum (Oil Spill Liability Trust)*	449,179	0.03%
Sumptuary		
Alcoholic beverage	10,028,320	0.62%
Tobacco products	15,081,717	0.94%
Other		
Luxury passenger vehicles**	(5)	0.00%
Coal	570,661	0.04%
Certain childhood vaccines	313,262	0.02%
Telephone and teletype services	773,700	0.05%
Private foundation investment income	505,692	0.03%
Firearms and ammunition	762,836	0.05%
Sport fishing equipment	109,343	0.01%
Tax on policies issued by foreign insurers	489,806	0.03%
Bows, arrows, and arrow shafts	54,347	0.00%
Medical devices	1,404,275	0.09%
Tanning tax	91,655	0.01%
Health insurance plan coverage (Patient Centered Outcome Research)	115,435	0.01%
Total Excise Collections	88,042,000	5.49%
Total Customs Duties and Fees	30,307,000	1.89%
Total Excises and Customs	118,349,000	7.38%

*Tax expired January 1, 2003
**Tax expired January 1, 1995
SOURCES: Sources of Income Bulletin and Budget of the Government of the United States, Fiscal Year 2014.

Table 10–2

State and Local Taxes on Goods and Services, Fiscal Year 2013 ($K)

	State and Local Total	Share of Total Tax Revenue (%)	State Total	Share of Total Tax Revenue (%)	Local	Share of Total Tax Revenue (%)
Taxes	1,455,498,630	100.0%	847,434,611	100.0%	608,064,019	100.0%
Sales and gross receipts	496,439,247	34.1%	394,086,475	46.5%	102,352,772	16.8%
General sales	327,065,751	22.5%	254,154,294	30.0%	72,911,457	12.0%
Selective sales	169,373,496	11.6%	139,932,181	16.5%	29,441,315	4.8%
Selective Sales: Transportation						
Motor fuel	41,410,555	2.8%	40,089,067	4.7%	1,321,488	0.2%
Selectvie Sales: Sumptuary						
Alcoholic beverage	6,618,673	0.5%	6,058,633	0.7%	560,040	0.1%
Tobacco products	18,255,711	1.3%	17,858,789	2.1%	396,922	0.1%
Amusements	7,235,121	0.5%	7,235,121	0.9%		0.0%
Pari-mutuels	124,177	0.0%	124,177	0.0%		0.0%
Selective Sales: Miscellaneous						
Public utilities	28,640,895	2.0%	14,356,400	1.7%	14,284,495	2.3%
Insurance premiums	18,094,904	1.2%	18,094,904	2.1%		0.0%
Other selective sales	48,993,460	3.4%	36,115,090	4.3%	12,878,370	2.1%

SOURCE: U.S. Bureau of Census, Governments Division.

Selective excise revenues tend to grow slowly. Because many have specific (or unit) rates, their yields do not pick up the effects of increasing prices, and substantial revenue increases require higher statutory rates. When rates have not increased over time, the share of total revenue from the excise tends to decline. Governments sometimes preserve the administrative ease of specific rates (enforcement officers need only track the items, not their value) while protecting revenue amid inflation by means of automatic adjustment formulas of various types. For instance, some countries of the former Soviet Union defined excise and import duty rates in terms of the euro (the monetary unit of the European Union) rather than their local currency. That automatically protected against both inflation (there was high inflation in prices denominated in the local currency) and exchange rate deterioration. Excise revenue also can be vulnerable to tastes and preferences of the population: for instance, in the United States cigarette tax revenue has declined dramatically as fewer people smoke. That result can be counted as a success, given that an important reason for cigarette taxes has been to reduce smoking and its damaging external effects.

Almost half of state tax revenue in the United States (and an important amount of major city revenue) comes from taxes on consumption, either from general sales taxes or from selective excise taxes. General sales tax revenue is the greater of the two, producing about one-third of all state tax revenue. Mississippi and West Virginia imposed the first general sales taxes during the early 1930s when existing state revenue sources (predominantly property taxes and state motor fuel taxes) were unable to finance state spending of the period. The retail sales taxes (RSTs) got many states through the Great Depression—they could produce revenue even when the property tax failed—and the taxes quickly spread to almost half the states before World War II. Their revenue was a significant contributor to the expansion of state government services after the war. These sales taxes were the largest single source of state tax revenue from 1947 until 1998, when their yield was surpassed by that from individual income taxes. Many local governments levy general sales taxes as well, and revenue from these taxes is second only to the property tax in overall significance to local governments. In some cities, the general sales tax yields more revenue than any other tax.

Selective excises are also widespread among state and local governments, but far less productive. All states levy excises, the most common being taxes on motor fuels, tobacco products, alcoholic beverages, public utilities, and insurance premiums. Excise taxes on casino gaming, part of the amusement excise category in Census reports, are significant in a few states (more than half a billion dollars in Pennsylvania, Indiana, Illinois, Nevada, Louisiana, and New York), but their effect is minor in aggregate.[6] Many local governments levy selective excises as well, with public utility taxes being most productive.

Items or services for consumption typically pass through several stages of production, each performed by a separate economic unit, as they go from raw material to the product desired by the user. Figure 10–1 outlines that flow, from the extraction of raw materials to use by that customer. Between each stage there is an exchange transaction, a buyer and a seller, and, at each transaction, tax may apply. Some taxes are designed to apply at more than one level of the flow, as is the case with gross receipts (or turnover) taxes and value-added taxes (VATs). Other taxes apply at only one stage of the flow: manufacture, wholesale, or retail. Unless special allowances have been made in structuring the tax (as described later in the discussion about VATs), single-stage, retail-level taxes cause the least economic damage associated with the revenue they raise and give the public the clearest idea of what their actual tax burden is.

Single-stage taxes, especially retail, are preferred for three reasons. First, price increases from tax paid by the customer will likely equal the amount received

---

[6]These are revenues from casino excises (taxes on gross receipts, number of gaming devices, or admissions) and are distinct from taxes collected on profits earned by the casinos or on their property and from the profits states receive from lotteries they operate. Revenue from taxes on casino profits is not, possibly surprisingly, a sure thing because many casinos are only marginally profitable at best and several have gone bankrupt.

Figure 10–1
Tax Points in the Flow of Production and Distribution

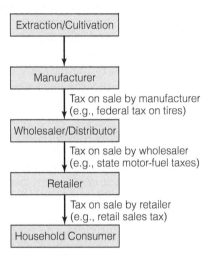

by the government, that is, there will be truth in taxation and its effect. Multistage and pre-retail taxes tend to pyramid or cascade. For example, any manufacturer-level tax paid is part of the cost seen by the wholesaler; that is, if the wholesaler buys garden tractors from a manufacturer for $1,500 plus a 10 percent excise, the wholesaler undoubtedly sees its unit cost as $1,650. When selling the tractor to a retailer, the wholesaler adds a markup percentage to that cost—say, 50 percent—for a charge of $2,475 ($1,650 plus 50 percent of the $1,650) to the retailer. The same markup process works for the retailer. When the customer finally purchases the tractor, that 10 percent excise has increased the price of the tractor by more than $150. Therefore, the price of the product increases by more than the tax that the government receives, and the effective tax rate is considerably more than the advertised 10 percent. A single-stage retail tax applied to the last transaction in the production-distribution flow would not have that impact. Second, multistage taxes strike with each market transaction (purchase and sale). Integrated firms (e.g., those that manufacture, wholesale, and retail) have fewer such transactions and, hence, lower tax embedded in product cost.[7] That would give such firms an artificial economic advantage over independent firms. Single-stage application (particularly at retail) eliminates that effect. Third, retail application causes no incentive for the production process to move to a stage of trade above the point taxed to reduce the base to which the tax applies. In general, the more of total product value produced after the tax is levied, the lower the tax. Retail application leaves no point for escape.

---

[7]Integrated firms move the product through stages of production, but these are bookkeeping transactions within the firm, not sales and purchases, so they are not taxable.

The retail application of the tax requires some greater administrative effort because there are more retailers than there are manufacturers or wholesalers and, hence, more taxpayers for tax administrators to track. Many selective excises levied by both federal and state governments—on motor fuel, tobacco products, alcoholic beverages, and so on—are collected at the manufacturer or distributor level because of those economies. These taxes are usually applied on a specific basis for ease of enforcement: the amount paid for the product at the point of taxation does not determine how much tax is owed. In other words, a tax of $1.00 per pack of cigarettes is the same amount regardless of whether it is levied on the transaction from manufacturer to distributor, on the transaction from distributor to retailer, or on the transaction from retailer to customer. That would not be the case if the tax was defined as 10 percent of the transaction price. Because the tax was applied at manufacturer or distributor level, the customer usually doesn't even know that the product was taxed.

The Equity Question

Vertical equity is a difficult policy issue for consumption. Evidence from many studies done at many different times and in many different environments shows that consumption spending is higher as a share of household income for lower-income households than it is for higher-income households. This is true for total consumption, and it is also true for most categories of expenditure. This creates an equity problem for taxes on consumption: the effective tax rate

$(t \times CE)/HI$

where t = statutory tax rate, CE = consumption expenditure, and HI = household income

is higher for low-income households than for higher-income ones because CE/HI tends to fall as household income is higher. The distribution of the tax burden is regressive. Table 10–3 shows effective rate evidence for federal excises and Table 10–4 shows the evidence for the Minnesota retail sales and excise taxes.[8] Both tables also present the effective rates for all taxes levied by the governments, totals that are dominated by individual income taxes. The federal and state excises and the state retail sales tax are all regressive, and that contrasts with the pattern for all taxes levied by the governments. This pattern is typical for virtually all excises, and it raises a difficult issue in taxation. Consumption expenditure is regarded as a reasonable base for distributing the cost of government, and consumption-based taxes are effective producers of

---

[8]The Minnesota Department of Revenue takes considerable care to detail its methodology and shifting assumptions and has been preparing incidence studies for a number of years. It provides a good model for other entities that might want to start such an analysis.

Table 10–3
Vertical Equity of Federal Excise Taxes, 2013
Effective Rates (%) by Household Income Class

	Federal Excises	All Federal Taxes
Quintile		
Lowest	1.7	3.3
Second	1.1	8.4
Third	0.9	12.8
Fourth	0.7	17
Highest	0.4	26.3
All Households	0.7	20.1
Top 1%	0.2	34

SOURCE: Congressional Budget Office, *The Distribution of Household Income and Taxes, 2013* (Washington, D.C.: CBO, 2016)

Table 10–4
Vertical Equity of Minnesota General Sales and Major Selective Excise Taxes, 2012
Effective Tax Rates Paid (%) by Income Deciles

Household Income Decile	General Sales Tax	Motor-Fuels Excise	Alcoholic Beverage Excise	Cigarette and Tobacco Excise	All Taxes
Lowest	10.2	1.39	0.16	2.52	28.35
Second	5.48	0.8	0.1	1.12	12.87
Third	4.34	0.63	0.08	0.75	11.46
Fourth	3.68	0.54	0.06	0.55	11.44
Fifth	3.17	0.46	0.05	0.41	12.3
Sixth	2.84	0.41	0.05	0.3	12.21
Seventh	2.62	0.36	0.04	0.23	12.17
Eighth	2.41	0.33	0.04	0.17	12.09
Ninth	2.13	0.28	0.03	0.12	11.79
Highest	1.4	0.12	0.02	0.03	10.51
Top 1%	0.96	0.04	0.02	0.01	9.81

SOURCE: Tax Research Division, Minnesota Department of Revenue, *2015 Minnesota Tax Incidence Study, Analysis of Minnesota's Household and Business Taxes,* March 9, 2015.

substantial revenue. However, the distribution pattern is regressive. Lawmakers must balance between the revenue productivity of such taxes and the equity issue.

These taxes also raise horizontal equity issues. Consumers have varying tastes and preferences in terms of both overall consumption and consumption of particular items. That variation in consumption patterns within household income groups creates variation in effective tax rates borne by households simply based on preferences. Therefore, on top of the vertical equity questions that consumption-based taxes raise, there are horizontal fairness problems as well. The extent to which these issues matter for policy depends on the reason for levying the tax. When revenue is the principal reason, the policy questions are greatest. However, as later sections describe, not all selective excises are levied purely for the revenue they generate (cigarette taxes are almost certainly levied to discourage smoking, for instance). For those nonrevenue excises, the equity issues are somewhat less pressing.

Selective Excise Taxation

Selective excises apply differential tax treatment to particular products or services, causing those purchasing or selling them to bear a greater tax burden than general indicators of tax-bearing capacity (income, wealth, or total consumption) would otherwise indicate. Although these excises seldom yield enough revenue to be a major factor for general government operations, their major attractiveness often lies on other grounds or with other special purposes. Indeed, their intent is often discriminatory: to try to charge people for the social cost of their actions. When that is the plan, selective excises could be judged effective, at least partly, on the basis of nonrevenue effects, not collections.[9] Selective excises, because of their relatively narrow base, require relatively high statutory rates to yield significant revenue. That high tax wedge—the difference between the price paid by the consumer (tax included) and the net price received by the seller (tax subtracted)—makes tax evasion a perennial problem as customers and vendors both seek to gain a tax-saving advantage. It gives a great temptation to begin bootlegging and smuggling when rates are high (alcoholic beverages and cigarettes in particular). That is in addition to the losses from distortions to behavior of customers and vendors in the legal market.

Governments levy, or talk about levying, narrow excises on many goods and services. Sometimes lawmakers are thinking about punishing certain purchasers or providers for what is seen as inappropriate behavior. Sometimes they need new revenue to close a budget hole but do not want the political consequences of raising a more productive, broad-based tax. Sometimes the tax is designed to approximate a charge for public services that cannot be directly priced. There is no definite way to

---

[9]The best general discussions of selective excises are Cnossen, Excise Systems (op. cit.); and Sijbren Cnossen, ed., *Theory and Practice of Excise Taxation: Smoking, Drinking, Gambling, Polluting, and Driving* (Oxford, England: Oxford University Press, 2005).

categorize these taxes. The categories used here (luxury, sumptuary, benefit-based, and regulatory/environmental) are arbitrary, and some excises could fit under more than one label.

Luxury Excises

Governments levy luxury excises on nonessential goods or services whose purchase is deemed to reflect extraordinary taxpaying ability. The definition of what, exactly, is a luxury is entirely subjective for lawmakers; luxury goods are mostly in the eye of the beholder, and one person's luxury may be seen by another as a near-necessity.[10] These excises attempt to distribute the cost of government to those best able to pay, so luxury excises may be evaluated on normal revenue policy standards. If the luxury excises raise substantial revenue, they might ease rate pressure on other taxes; seldom does that happen because the base is too small. Before most were repealed in the mid-1960s, the federal government levied excises on a surprisingly wide array of goods, including such items as photographic equipment, radios, televisions, phonographs and phonograph records, fountain and ballpoint pens, mechanical pencils, lighters, matches, playing cards, air conditioners, refrigerators, safe deposit boxes, coin-operated amusement devices, and billiard and pool tables. Recent federal luxury excises have applied to expensive aircraft, automobiles, yachts, furs, and jewelry; all but that on automobiles were repealed in 1993, and the automobile tax ended in 2003.[11] Excises continue on firearms and ammunition, sport fishing equipment, and bows and arrows.

The objections to luxury excises are several. First, such taxes distort producer and consumer choices: because the tax establishes a difference between the resource-cost ratios in production and the price ratios to which consumers respond, there is unnecessary loss of economic welfare in the economic system.[12] Purchasers and sellers change their behavior because of the tax, and that brings an economic loss to them. (Recall the discussion of excess burden in Sidebar 8–2.) The tax induces them to behave differently than they would otherwise prefer, and there is no reason to believe that the market for these products requires intervention to serve the public better. Second, and pragmatically more important, the tax distributes burdens on the basis of personal preferences for the taxed items. The tax imposes higher effective rates on people within an income class who have high taste for the taxed commodities or services. Third, there are administrative problems with these excises. Relative to the amount of revenue produced, the cost of collecting the tax is high. Because retailers would have difficulty separating the sales of the taxed luxury items from other sales and because administrators would prefer to work with the relatively few manufacturers or wholesalers compared to the numbers of retailers, these excises typically apply at the manufacturer or wholesaler

---

[10]The microeconomics definition of a luxury as being a good whose consumption increases by a percentage greater than the percentage increase in income is not relevant here, at least not to lawmakers.

[11]These taxes applied only to the amount of the transaction above a particular threshold.

[12]John A. Tatom, "The Welfare Cost of an Excise Tax," *Federal Reserve Bank of St. Louis Review* 58 (November 1976): 14–15.

level. They thus fall prey to the objections to any levy that applies earlier than retail.[13] However, another administrative problem often emerges in the definition of the taxed commodity. For example, a handful of states tax soft drinks, but what is a soft drink?[14] Are powdered drink mixes, imitation orange juice, flavored waters, bottled chocolate drink, and so forth to be taxed? Is low-alcohol beer a soft drink? How is a concentrate, sold to be mixed with water, to be equated for tax purposes with bottled drinks? In each case, a difficult administrative problem in interpreting and applying the tax may well be handled only by separate, brand-name determinations, a process that is time consuming for the tax department's rule makers. Collection costs for narrow excises usually are excessive relative to the modest revenue they produce.

Even though luxury excises can have considerable political appeal, they are not strong elements of a revenue system. Revenue growth for most luxury excises is low, largely because their specific nature does not allow capture of price effects. They do yield some revenue, although at considerable collection cost, and who but industry lobbyists (and the people who make those goods) will stand up for luxury purchases? How important is the revenue? In fiscal 1992, the last year before repeal of the federal luxury excises on boats, aircraft, jewelry, and furs, these excises produced $29 million. The federal individual income tax alone generated more than $475 billion that year.[15]

As taxes levied for revenue purposes, luxury excises do not measure up.

Sumptuary Excises

Sumptuary excises seek to discourage excess consumption of items considered unhealthy or unsafe, both for the consumer and for the public as a whole.[16] The best examples are taxes on tobacco products and alcoholic beverages: the prices paid to producers do not reflect the social cost of product use and abuse in terms of damage to health, property, and families.[17] (The taxes may also have moral overtones and are

---

[13]The recent federal luxury excises were at the retail level. They created problems because they applied only on prices above a threshold, an extra complication for compliance record keeping and enforcement.
[14]Is this an example of a luxury excise? Probably so; it doesn't make much sense as anything else and very little sense as a luxury excise either.
[15]"Selected Historical and Other Data," *Statistics of Income Bulletin* 16 (Winter 1996-1997): 167.
[16]Or unwise. The Affordable Care Act enacted a 40 percent excise tax on high-cost health coverage (often called the "Cadillac tax" for luxurious health care), applicable after December 31, 2017. The idea is that extensive health coverage, coverage lacking no deductible, no out-of-pocket for the individual, and imposing no limits (the reason the insurance premium is high-cost) leads to inefficiently large health-care costs (the moral hazard argument). The tax is intended to discourage employers from offering that high-end health-care coverage and adjust the asymmetry that now favors compensating workers in insurance rather than in cash. It is believed that extremely generous insurance plans drive up health costs and restoring the balance between insurance and cash would create more efficient use of health care. The act also imposed a tax on tanning bed use, possibly to discourage an activity associated with higher rates of skin cancer.
[17]One study estimates that a much higher excise on beer would have dramatically reduced the number of young drivers killed in automobile accidents (1,660 lives saved between 1982 and 1988). See Michael Grossman, Frank J. Chaloupka, Henry Saffer, and Adit Laixuthai, "Effects of Alcohol Price Policy on Youth," National Bureau of Economic Research Working Paper 4385, Cambridge, Mass., 1993.

sometimes labeled "sin taxes"; along with tobacco and alcoholic beverage taxes, special taxes are applied to gambling activities, and these taxes may be considered sumptuary as well.) Taxes on alcoholic beverages and tobacco products are among the oldest taxes in the United States; indeed, an early test of the new central government was the Whiskey Rebellion (1794), a violent (and unsuccessful) challenge to a federal excise put down by the military.[18] Would present-day tax protesters want to try to stand up to the 82nd Airborne? It's easier and safer to complain than to take on the troops for real nowadays, no matter the guarantees of the Second Amendment regarding firearms.

Demand for items subject to these excises is relatively insensitive to price, particularly in the short term, so consumption seldom changes much with imposition of the tax.[19] Legislatures do not propose truly prohibitive tax rates because they want tax revenue—a curious balancing between discouraging harmful activity and maintaining revenue flow from the activity. Moderate increases in sumptuary excise rates generally elicit minimal protest from consumers, although sellers complain about illegal (nontaxed) competition. Bootlegging is a continual problem because the tax rates tend to be rather high; one enforcement procedure uses stamps applied to units on which tax has been paid at the manufacturer level.[20] With stamps, the tax is collected early in the production-distribution chain (meaning fast revenue for the government), and enforcement agents need only look for the stamp to verify that tax has been paid. Sizable rate differences among states swamp control structures with evasion.[21] When the tax in a state or locality gets significantly higher than that applied in nearby jurisdictions, a resulting difference in prices charged can induce lots of cross-border shopping, and considerable revenue loss. Tax stamps are effective at making sure that vendor stock has the tax paid; they aren't effective at policing people who cross the border to get their personal supplies.[22]

---

[18]There were serious questions about the tax, among which was the fact that large producers of whiskey (a group that included President Washington) paid a considerably lower tax per gallon than did smaller producers. It also required cash payment, and cash was in short supply in the western United States at the time (which meant western Pennsylvania, the hotbed of the rebellion). Indeed, cash was so scarce on the frontier that whiskey was used for currency as well as for drinking, certainly a misallocation of resources.

[19]Cigarette tax increases do have an impact on both the number of smokers and the number of cigarettes each smokes in the long term. For instance, the Joint Committee on Taxation estimated "that the increase in the [federal] excise tax on cigarettes from $0.39 per pack to $1.00 per pack will reduce by 1.9 million the number of individuals who choose to smoke in 2017. We further estimate that those smokers will decrease their consumption of cigarettes by 4 percent." Staff of the Joint Committee on Taxation, "Modeling the Federal Revenue Effects of Proposed Changes in Cigarette Excise Taxes," JCX-101-07, Washington, D.C., October 19, 2007.

[20]NASCAR racing fans owe a great debt to liquor taxes. After Prohibition ended, governments enacted high taxes on distilled spirits, making bootlegging extremely attractive. People could imbibe lawfully and liquor upon which tax had been evaded was a good bargain. Fast cars provided an excellent delivery device because they could outrun the revenue collectors. The cars ended up on race tracks and NASCAR was born. No high liquor taxes, no NASCAR.

[21]For a review of the problem, see Advisory Commission on Intergovernmental Relations, Cigarette Tax Evasion: A Second Look, Report A-100 (Washington, D.C.: Advisory Commission on Intergovernmental Relations, 1985).

[22]Differences in federal taxation of cigarettes, roll-your-own tobacco, pipe tobacco, small cigars, and large cigars in 2009 created dramatic changes in the market for these substitutes. Government Accountability Office, Tobacco Taxes: Large Disparities in Rates for Smoking Products Trigger Significant Market Shifts to Avoid Higher Taxes, GAO-12-475 (Washington, D.C.: Government Accountability Office, April 2012).

These excises do raise some revenue with minimal public protest. The loudest complaints normally come from producers rather than consumers, and legislators are usually wary of overt support for those interests unless the producers are concentrated in the legislator's home district. The importance of producer politics is demonstrated by the fact that state cigarette taxes are lowest in the states where tobacco production is economically important (e.g., 30 cents per pack in Virginia versus a national average state rate of $1.60 per pack). Purchasers of the product are likely to bear the burden of the tax on average, but if the tax rate is lower than in other areas, it may give the producers there a competitive advantage in the market.

There are three primary objections to sumptuary excises. First, the demand for the products taxed is often highly price-inelastic, so the tax has little short-term effect on the amount of the product purchased. The tax paid by the purchaser might otherwise have been spent on desirable or beneficial activities. (The extreme example sometimes quoted by lobbyists is the alcoholic who fails to buy milk for his children because of the tax he pays on liquor.) Responses to higher taxes increase as producers and consumers have time to adjust, however. Second, the absolute burden of these taxes may be particularly heavy on low-income families and may result in higher effective tax rates on lower-income families. The tax is applied, after all, on the basis of personal preferences, so the teetotaling millionaire pays less liquor tax than the whiskey-drinking laborer. Third, a problem results from the specific (not ad valorem) nature of these excises. Even though that basis is logical because any social cost involved would be related to the amount of consumption, not its value, it does discriminate against lower-priced brands and those who purchase them. If the tax is $10 per gallon on distilled spirits, the effective rate is much higher on liquor sold for $6 per fifth than on liquor sold for $10 per fifth. This is a special problem if users of the lower-priced brands come from low-income groups. Furthermore, the specific nature of the tax obscures the actual ratio of the tax to the net price, which frequently turns out to be high. It also turns out that how the tax is quoted, specific or ad valorem, has an impact on price competition. Sidebar 10–1 provides an example of that.

Benefit-Base Excises

Benefit-base excises, primarily transportation-related taxes, operate as a quasi-price for a public good.[23] Highway use traditionally involves consumption of motor fuel, so a tax on fuel purchase approximates a charge for the use of the highway. These taxes allocate cost to road users without the cost of administering direct user charges (tolls) for streets, roads, and highways. The motor-fuel tax thus operates as a surrogate for price. It does have difficulties for the truck-to-car relationship because differences in incremental costs of providing highways and of keeping up with

---

[23]The federal logic of certain excises as user charges is discussed in Chapter 12. In terms of incidence, one study finds that the burden of the federal gasoline tax is evenly split between consumers and gasoline wholesalers and the burden of the state gasoline taxes is on consumers. Hayley Chouinard and Jeffrey M. Perloff, "Incidence of Federal and State Gasoline Taxes," *Economic Letters* 83 (2005): 55–60.

Sidebar 10–1
Taxes as Competitive Weapons: Smokeless Tobacco

Moist smokeless tobacco is subject to excise taxation in all states. As of January 2006, 43 states levied a tax based on the wholesale or manufacturer price of the product (ad valorem basis). The others tax according to weight.

One company, UST, has historically had almost the entire market for the product and charged a premium price for it. More recently, competitors have developed lower-priced products, and UST has been losing market share to those products. With this development, the ad valorem tax presents a problem for UST. The company describes the difficulty in its annual report:

> [T]he *ad valorem* method of taxation has the effect of increasing the taxes payable on premium brands to a greater degree than the taxes payable on price-value brands, which further exacerbates the price gap between premium and price-value brands.[1]

As a result, UST initiated efforts in state legislatures to switch taxation from ad valorem to a weight (unit) basis. That would eliminate the tax situation that otherwise put the UST product at an extra price disadvantage. Of course, the low-priced brands lobbied the legislators just as vigorously to retain the ad valorem basis.

The struggle continues.

[1]UST Inc. Annual Form 10-K Report for 2005, p. 9.

SOURCE: Based on Stanley R. Arnold, "Tax Law as a Competitive Weapon," *State Tax Notes* 42 (October 16, 2006): 189–91.

---

highway wear and tear are difficult to calibrate and relate to motor-fuel use, but the system functions to generally distribute the cost of operating the highways to those more heavily using the highways.

There are additional questions: whether motor-fuel tax revenues should be segregated for highway construction and maintenance only, whether these funds should be spent for all transportation (mass as well as highway), and whether motor-fuel tax revenue should receive the same budget treatment as other revenue, with no earmarking for transportation.[24] These questions are not yet answered, but if revenues from the gasoline tax do not go to transportation projects, then they are probably subject to the complaints made against luxury excises. On the other hand, if revenue from the gasoline tax goes exclusively to highways, there is a substantial bias for highways in the total transportation system. In most European countries,

---

[24]Even when strictly earmarked for highways, motor-fuel tax funds normally must pass through the regular appropriation process before they can be spent.

motor-fuel taxes are high, revenues are not dedicated to use for highways, and the taxes are considered part of an environmental strategy to make travel by automobile less attractive relative to mass transportation, not part of a "user pays" strategy for financing highways.[25] Even though the federal government, all states, and some localities in the United States levy motor-fuel taxes, the combined rates are far lower than those imposed in Europe. The high pump prices in Europe that shock Americans are purely the result of those higher taxes because the net-of-tax price of motor fuel is about the same on both sides of the Atlantic.

The benefit-base logic of highway or motor-fuel taxes suggests that the tax should be specific because the number of units of motor fuel used is related to the use of the service. At the same time, however, the specific nature of the tax means that, in times of inflation, there are significant pressures placed on the motor-fuel tax fund because of highway operation and construction cost increases. Some states have attempted to avert the need for legislated rate increases by tying the specific tax rate to the prevailing price of gasoline, so that as the price of gasoline is higher, the specific gasoline tax rate is higher.[26] This strategy has not succeeded over the long run because episodes of declining prices brought significant decreases in revenue and price fluctuations brought major revenue instability. Linking the rate to a general inflation index or to road operation and maintenance costs shows greater permanent promise.

The benefit-base motor-fuel tax has a long-term problem. As motor vehicles become more fuel efficient, the typical gallonage rates will not support highway operation and maintenance, and U.S. lawmakers are wary of increasing fuel tax rates.[27] In addition, as hybrids, all-electric vehicles, and exotic-fuel cars become more prevalent, traditional fuel taxes become ever-more irrelevant for highway finance. Even the vendor-collection method that works well for gasoline and diesel falls apart: how would the tax work when the car owner plugs it into a socket at home to charge up the battery, using the same electricity used for other domestic purposes? Fortunately, technology now permits direct charging for highway use—monitoring of distance traveled, time of travel, and location of travel is feasible—and some version of that charging must replace the fuel tax if highways are to be financed through

---

[25]The difference in approach between the relatively low rate motor-fuel tax earmarked for highways in the United States and the much higher rate tax not so earmarked in other developed countries apparently results from the Great Depression era. Other national treasuries, desperately needing revenue in that period, used motor-fuel tax revenue from high tax rates to help relieve general spending pressures whereas in the United States a coalition of organized motorists and oil, automobile, and road-building industries kept the revenues dedicated for highways and the rates relatively low. Rates had been about the same before that era. Carl-Henry Geschwind, "Gasoline Taxes and the Great Depression: A Comparative History," *Journal of Policy History* 26 (2014).

[26]An extensive review of state gasoline tax problems and of variable-rate structures can be found in John H. Bowman and John L. Mikesell, "Recent Changes in State Gasoline Taxation: An Analysis of Structure and Rates," *National Tax Journal* 36 (June 1983): 163–82.

[27]Increasing the tax rate to accommodate lower quantities of motor fuel being demanded won't automatically fix the problem because the higher rate also affects fuel purchases. A recent study finds that each cent per gallon increase in gasoline price reduces consumption by 0.2 percent. Antonio M. Bento et al., "Distributional and Efficiency Impacts of Increasing U.S. Gasoline Taxes," *American Economic Review* 99 (June 2009): 667–99. As would be expected, the tax base is a function of the tax rate.

payments made by users as opposed to general taxpayers.[28] Fuel taxes won't work anymore. More is discussed about that in Chapter 12 on user charges.[29]

Regulatory and Environmental Excises

Excises may be applied to improve resource use efficiency, much like the sumptuary excises, but without the moral or ethical overtones or explicit revenue objectives. Regulatory excises do such things as tax pollutants (the taxes on ozone-depleting chemicals) and penalize automakers not producing fuel-efficient automobiles (the gas guzzler tax).[30] They reflect the ideas that the polluter must pay and that particular actions should be discouraged or penalized. As described in Chapter 8, they seek to make buyers and sellers cognizant of the full social cost of their actions. The United States is far behind Europe in the use of "green" taxes designed to explicitly make the polluter pay for the cost that pollution imposes on others.[31] The tax may charge for these external diseconomies to compensate society in ways not attainable by the market. Some proponents of environmental excises have argued that there is a "double dividend" from such taxes. First, the imposition of the tax corrects for the external and unpriced damaging impact of the pollutant. Second, the revenue generated by the tax can be used to replace other taxes that distort efficient operations of the economy. Thus, the tax can provide two desirable impacts for the economy, not just one.

The big environmental tax under most serious discussion in the United States today is the carbon tax, a way to induce people and industries to pay attention to carbon emissions that would contribute to global warming. Carbon taxes have been in place in Denmark, Finland, Norway, and Sweden since the 1990s and in British Columbia since 2008, so there is some experience to go on. The carbon excise applies to all fossil fuels in proportion to the carbon dioxide emissions associated with each. The more emissions, the higher the tax rate that applies to that particular fuel. More carbon content per unit of energy means a higher rate: in British Columbia the rate on gasoline is 6.67 cents per liter, and on diesel, 7.67 cents per liter. The idea is to tax according to carbon emission from the fuel, so each fossil fuel would bear a different statutory rate. The intent is to induce users of fuels to respond to the environmental damage that their

---

[28]Oregon has adopted an optional user charge program to replace the motor-fuel tax system of financing highways. The program, OReGO, charges according to miles driven. More about this system is discussed in Chapter 12.

[29]The Congressional Budget Office reviews some options in Alternative Approaches to Funding Highways (Washington, D.C.: Congressional Budget Office, 2011).

[30]The gas guzzler tax applies primarily to very expensive imports. It excludes the major domestic guzzlers—trucks and SUVs—and probably is designed more to give some protection to domestic vehicles than for environmental reasons. The motor-fuel tax probably has more potential for inducing fuel economy than does the guzzler tax.

[31]Recent examples include the plastic bag taxes levied in Ireland (at one-quarter of a euro each, such bags have largely disappeared in the country), South Africa (initially 0.46 rand each, limited success), and in Washington, D.C. (at 5 cents, many fewer bags are used).

consumption entails—at least to pay for the damage and even better to reduce their activities that cause the damage. In British Columbia, carbon tax revenue is used to reduce the provincial income tax, allowing it to levy the lowest income tax of any province.

The big question: how high should the environmental tax rate be? Europeans are more willing to use the market to get corrections made and to collect information from market responses to adjust the tax rates.[32] Americans seem to prefer to use the outmoded command-and-control mechanism of regulations and restraints rather than setting appropriate environmental tax rates and then letting the market function. Of course, we also still have Americans who deny that there might be a climate change problem that merits some attention, so we have two layers of being outmoded that have to be dealt with for progress.

Other Excises

There are some other miscellaneous excises as well. Selective excises on imported items (customs duties) are often levied to raise revenue and to protect local producers.[33] Excises also may be narrowly applied to finance research or trade promotion activities, as with agricultural commodity excises functioning through marketing boards or lodging excises used to promote tourism. Particularly narrow excises are often dedicated to a specific purpose, as with the federal vaccine injury compensation fund financed by an excise on certain childhood disease vaccines or the federal excise on fishing equipment that supports sport fish restoration programs.[34] Across all the selective excises, however, the basic criteria for success include "large sales volume, few producers, inelastic demand, ready definability, and no close substitutes unless these can be included in the base."[35] Few selective excises meet all these criteria.

---

[32]As with other unit selective excises, a carbon tax could be levied at various points in the production-to-consumption chain: upstream on oil and gas wells, coal mines, and importers; midstream on oil refineries, electric utilities, and natural gas pipelines; or downstream on vehicles, households, commercial buildings, and industries. Jonathan L. Ramseur and Larry Parker, Carbon Tax and Greenhouse Gas Control: Options and Considerations for Congress, CRS Report for Congress, Order Code R 40242 (Washington, D.C.: Congressional Research Service, February 23, 2009), 25.

[33]And customs duties create some of the same strange results as with other excises when tax rates vary. Take, for instance, Halloween attire. "Festive articles" such as wigs and beards are imported duty-free, but a bunny costume would face the "garment" duty rate of up to 32 percent. Talk to your member of Congress about that one.

[34]The Affordable Care Act brought the medical device excise, a 2.3 percent tax on the sale price at the manufacturer or importer level of taxable items, as defined by the Food and Drug Administration. Its justification is not clear and its revenue is not consequential. Revenue is not earmarked to particular use. Gravelle and Lowry conclude that it will have only minor impacts on output and employment in the industry, will have a negligible impact on the cost of health care, and will have no impact on the profits of the medical device industry. Jane G. Gravelle and Sean Lowry, "The Medical Device Excise Tax: Economic Analysis," Congressional Research Service Report, January 9, 2015.

[35]Cnossen, *Excise Systems*, 9.

General Taxes on Goods and Services: Retail Sales and Value-Added Taxes

Consumption represents an alternative to income as a general basis for distributing the cost of government among elements of the private economy. Many believe that making a switch from heavy reliance on individual and corporate income taxes would be good public policy. There are two main elements in this argument:

1. **Increase economic growth.** A switch from income to consumption as a tax base "will reduce the difference between the pre- and post-tax return to saving that encourages taxpayers to consume rather than to save, so saving will be encouraged by the change and the growth path of the economy may subsequently move upward."[36] Future consumption (in other words, saving) is not penalized in comparison with current consumption. The higher saving improves rates of capital formation, labor productivity, and standards of living.

2. **Improve fundamental equity.** Consumption represents a fundamentally more equitable way for assigning shares of the cost of government than does annual income: "each individual [measures tax capacity] for himself when, in the light of all his present circumstances and future prospects, he decides on the scale of his personal living expenses. Thus a tax based on actual spending rates each individual's spending capacity according to the yardstick which he applies to himself."[37] Using the amount the individual believes that he or she can afford in purchases of private goods and services as the standard for distributing a major share of the total cost of government would seem to be appropriate for financing government in a market economy. This equity measure is *actual consumption*, compared with the Haig-Simons income concept, which equals maximum *potential consumption* possible without a reduction in wealth.

A general consumption tax may be administered either directly, through administrative systems that follow more or less the same filing and collection structures as the current income tax, or indirectly, through a transaction-based sales tax following either the multistage collection scheme of the value-added tax (VAT) or the single-stage collection scheme of the retail sales tax (RST). The three administrative systems are economically identical ways of taxing consumption.

A direct consumption tax uses the fact that, by definition, individual income less personal saving equals consumption. Therefore, if a household had income of $75,000 and saved $35,000 in the year, then its consumption was $40,000, and that

---

[36]S. Cnossen and C. Sanford, *Taxing Consumption* (Paris: Organization for Economic Cooperation and Development, 1988), 32.
[37]Nicholas Kaldor, *An Expenditure Tax* (London: Allen and Unwin, 1955), 47.

base can be taxed accordingly.[38] No government currently uses such a system, possibly because of some questions about defining and reporting savings. However, because of the several provisions in the federal income tax system that provide preferences for saving (the many retirement savings programs, provision for medical saving accounts, provisions for tax-preferred saving for education expenses, etc.), the current federal tax has been described as a hybrid income-consumption tax rather than a pure income tax. Some proponents of consumption taxation argue that the easiest and least disruptive way to transform the federal system into a pure consumption tax would be to dramatically broaden the preferences for savings already in the system. In other words, a direct tax would build on existing foundations in a manner that would be impossible for an indirect approach. Allow a general deduction for all savings during the year and the income tax is converted to a consumption tax.

There are two alternative systems for collecting an indirect, transaction-based (i.e., on individual purchases or "over the counter" rather than through individual filing), general tax on consumption. The forms are the RST and the VAT. The RST is levied in most states and some Canadian provinces, making it the American format for general sales taxation.[39] The VAT is the format used by virtually all central governments in the industrialized world, including all members of the Organization for Economic Cooperation and Development (OECD) except the United States, all countries of Latin America, all countries of the former Soviet Union, and all countries that are part of or would like to join the European Union (it is a membership requirement). Statutory rates for these taxes may be quoted on either a tax-inclusive or a tax-exclusive basis. Sidebar 10–2 explains the difference and shows how to switch between the two methods of quoting rates.

Both taxes can apply a general, uniform tax on household consumption with minimal distortion of production and consumption choice, but they differ in how each accomplishes that end and, in practice, differ in the extent to which they are general, uniform, and nondistorting. The U.S. RST applies to household consumption by taxing only the last stage of the full production-distribution process. As explained in detail later in this chapter, the system suspends application of tax when a business makes a purchase, thus limiting tax coverage to purchases by households. The VAT applies to each transaction in the full production-distribution process, but, in usual application, every purchaser except the final customer has tax refunded through credits for tax the business has collected on its sales. Thus, when they are functioning properly, both systems relieve tax on all transactions but the last—the one to the final household customer, and are equivalent taxes on household consumption.

---

[38]One careful analysis of such a system: Laurence S. Seidman, *The USA Tax: A Progressive Consumption Tax* (Cambridge, Mass.: MIT Press, 1997). The flat-tax proposals that have emerged periodically over the years often are driven in part by a desire to move toward consumption taxation.

[39]The sales tax is also used in some African countries and local governments in some countries of the former Soviet Union. For a few years, it was an important revenue source for regional governments in the Russian Federation. British Columbia, Saskatchewan, Quebec, and Manitoba levy provincial retail sales taxes. Alberta and the territories levy no sales tax of their own. The remaining provinces levy a sales tax that is harmonized with the national goods and services tax and is administered by the Canada Customs and Revenue Agency.

Sidebar 10–2
Tax-Exclusive and Tax-Inclusive Pricing

Many Americans traveling in Europe are surprised to find that no sales tax is added to their purchases, just as Europeans visiting the United States are surprised when tax is added to their purchases. Sales taxes are levied on both transactions, but the RST tradition is for tax-exclusive pricing ("separate quotation" or adding the tax at the cash register), whereas the VAT tradition is tax-inclusive pricing (including tax in the sticker price). There are exceptions. For instance, some European hotels and car rental agencies quote prices without the VAT and add the tax on final purchase, and American vending machines usually sell at tax-inclusive prices. Nevertheless, it is normal for American RSTs to be added at the cash register and for VATs to be included in prices. Neither treatment is required by the logic of either tax, although tax laws often make the requirement.[1] They are both sales taxes, and they both can switch between the two approaches. The Canadian VAT—the goods and services tax—is added at purchase, so prices there are quoted without including the VAT, just like with an American RST.

Tax laws may quote rates on either a tax-exclusive or a tax-inclusive basis, but conversion between the two styles is simple. If *TE* is the tax-exclusive rate in percent and *TI* is the tax-inclusive rate in percent, then the relationship is as follows:

$$TI = TE/(100 + TE)$$

and

$$TE = TI/(100 - TI)$$

Therefore, a tax-exclusive VAT rate of 20 percent is equivalent to a tax-inclusive rate of 16.7 percent. A tax-inclusive VAT rate of 15 percent is equivalent to a tax-exclusive rate of 17.6 percent.

Which tax is less transparent? Neither the VAT nor the RST paid on a purchase need be hidden. Cash register receipts in many European stores include a statement of how much VAT was paid on the total purchase, breaking out the tax that was included in the posted price of the items being purchased, just as cash register receipts in the United States include a statement of sales tax paid at the bottom of the receipt. The only difference: the U.S. receipt includes the sales tax as part of the calculation of how much is owed, and the VAT receipt includes VAT paid as a separate display after the total payment. And that VAT total is likely more accurate than the RST total on the receipt: RSTs exclude business inputs less completely from the tax than do VATs, so there undoubtedly is RST paid by those businesses that is embedded in the price and that doesn't show up at all in the statement of RST. That makes the VAT more transparent than the RST.

U.S. politicians and commentators who charge that the VAT is a hidden tax haven't traveled much outside the United States, haven't bothered to look at receipts they have been given for European or Canadian purchases, or are fibbing. Or maybe someone else is paying their way, so receipts do not matter to them. It is far easier to know how much personal income tax you have paid throughout the year than to know your total payments of either RST or VAT, because you do have to file an income tax return at the end of the year and you can see your total liability quite easily. But, again, to know you have to look.

[1]When the U.S. states were adopting their first RSTs in the depths of the Great Depression, retailer organizations demanded separate quotation laws so that they would not be blamed for the price increase that would come with addition of the sales taxes. On the other hand, when Russia permitted regional sales taxes in the late 1990s, the national enabling law required that the sales tax be included in listed prices, following the tradition of their VAT. When regional sales taxes were abolished a few years later, there was popular concern that the taxes would end, but the merchants would not lower their prices accordingly and would pocket what otherwise would have gone to the government.

The difference between the two taxes lies in the administrative mechanism. Both mechanisms are described in detail later because they are at the essence of each tax and are the distinguishing feature between the two taxes.

In contrast to direct taxes, indirect taxes are difficult to tailor to individual tax-payer circumstances. A direct tax, administered through a periodic filing procedure, can be adjusted for such factors as size of the taxpaying unit and particular events that have befallen the taxpayer during the filing period. An indirect tax collected on a transaction-by-transaction basis is impersonal and cannot easily be adjusted for those sorts of conditions. There may be allowances for the particular transaction (a preferential rate for food, for instance), but that rate will be the same for all purchasers regardless of their circumstances. This inability to target and limit makes preferences provided in an indirect tax less efficient because taxpayers in all sorts of circumstances have access to them.

Retail Sales Taxes

RSTs in the United States share three common features. All are ad valorem taxes "imposed upon the sales, or elements incidental to the sales, such as receipts from them, of all or a wide range of commodities";[40] all have a system for suspending tax on items purchased for resale; and all encourage separate quotation of the tax in each transaction (in other words, the tax is added at purchase rather than being included in the price on

---

[40]John F. Due, *Sales Taxation* (Urbana: University of Illinois Press, 1957), 3.

the shelf, and tax thus collected is excluded from gross receipts upon which the tax is levied). The taxes—levied by all states but Alaska, Delaware, Montana, New Hampshire, and Oregon and by thousands of local governments, including many in Alaska—yield roughly one-third of the total state tax revenue and rank second to the property tax for local governments, providing something more than 10 percent of tax revenue.[41]

In mid-2016, state tax rates ranged from 2.9 percent (Colorado) to 7.5 percent (California). Twenty-five states levied rates of 6 percent or higher. Piggybacked local rates for city, county, and transit or other special districts add to the total rate in many parts of the country. For instance, in New York City, the rate of 8.875 percent applied on retail purchases combines a 4 percent state rate, a 4.5 percent city rate, and a 0.375 percent Metropolitan Commuter Transportation District rate. In Chicago, state plus local rates equal 10.25 percent (6.25 percent state, 2.75 percent Cook County, and 1.25 percent city).[42] Payment to the state is made by the vendor; returns like that shown in Figure 10–2 from Virginia cover all such transactions for a specified period (quarter, month, year). This state return includes local tax as well because Virginia administers the local taxes.[43] The vendor has, through the reporting period, been collecting tax on each of its many sales; this return accumulates all those transactions for transmission to the government. Reporting on the return begins with total sales of the vendor, and sales that are not taxed are subtracted to obtain taxable sales. The amount of sales tax that is owed comes from reported taxable sales.

Two special evaluation standards apply to sales tax structures: uniformity and neutrality.[44] The first standard holds that the tax should produce a uniform tax on consumer expenditures. Thus, the structure should ease shifting to ultimate consumers, it should apply at a uniform rate to all consumption expenditures unless there is a completely necessary reason otherwise, and it should apply to the transaction amount actually paid by the consumer. Second, to avoid loss of economic efficiency, the tax should not create competitive disturbances among types of distribution channels, methods of doing business, or forms of business organization. Choices should not be distorted because of the tax. Figuring out how to get sales taxes to be uniform and neutral—and as fair, revenue-productive, and collectable as possible—is not a simple task. The next sections on the coverage of nonretail transactions, the problem of equity exemptions, the taxability of services, and the treatment of interstate transactions demonstrate that.

---

[41]The standard reference on general sales taxation is John F. Due and John L. Mikesell, *Sales Taxation, State and Local Structure and Administration*, 2nd ed. (Washington, D.C.: Urban Institute, 1994). Not all state sales taxes have that name in their state laws. For instance, the New Mexico tax is called the Gross Receipts Tax. However, it has the basic features of a retail sales tax, not those of a true gross receipts tax, such as the Washington Business and Occupation Tax or the Ohio Commercial Activity Tax. New Mexico suspends business purchases and accommodates adding tax to price; the gross receipts taxes do not.

[42]Alaska levies no state sales tax, but many localities there do. And some of them levy variable tax rates. For example, Seldovia levies a 5 percent rate in October through March and 7.5 percent the rest of the year. Tourists and other nonresidents are making purchases in the high rate months, and locals are the customers the rest of the year. The arrangement would create collection chaos in more populous areas.

[43]A note for those of you interested in doing tax research: one of the best ways of understanding how a particular tax works is to get a tax return and work through the steps in calculating tax liability. This approach helps clarify when the law, regulations, and instructions become insurmountable.

[44]Due, *Sales Taxation*, 351–52.

Figure 10–2
Virginia Retail Sales and Use Tax Return

Form ST-9 Virginia Retail Sales and Use Tax Return
For Periods Beginning On and After July 1, 2013

- All Form ST-9 filers are required to file and pay electronically at **www.tax.virginia.gov.**

- If you are reporting consolidated sales for business locations in more than one locality or you do not have a fixed location for your business, file Form ST-9B with Form ST-9 to allocate local sales to the appropriate Virginia locality. You must also file Form ST-9R if you are required to File Form ST-9B and you are reporting sales in the Northern Virginia or Hampton Roads Regions.

- See ST-9A Worksheet for return completion instructions.

Name	Account Number 10-
Address	Filing Period (Enter month or quarter and year)
City, State, ZIP	Due Date (20th of month following end of period)

Mailing address: **Virginia Department Of Taxation**
P.O. Box 26627
Richmond, VA 23261-6627

RETAIL SALES AND USE TAX		A - SALES		B - AMOUNT DUE
1	Gross Sales and/or Rentals	1		
2	Personal Use	2		
3	Exempt State Sales and Other Deductions	3		
4	Total Taxable State Sales and Use. Line 1 plus Line 2 minus Line 3.	4		
5	State - Qualifying Food Sales and Use. Enter taxable sales in Column A. Multiply Column A by the rate of 1.5% (.015) and enter the result in Column B	5		x .015 =
6	State - General Sales and Use. Enter taxable sales in Column A (Line 4 minus Line 5, Column A). Multiply Column A by the rate of 4.3% (.043) and enter the result in Column B.	6		x .043 =
7	State Tax. Add Line 5, Column B and Line 6, Column B.	7		
8	Dealer Discount. See Form ST-9A Worksheet.	8		
9	Net State Tax. Line 7 minus Line 8.	9		
10	Additional State Sales Tax - Regional Transportation. See ST-9A Worksheet.			
	10a Northern Virginia. Enter total taxable sales for this region in Column A. Multiply Column A by the rate of 0.7% (.007) and enter result in Column B.	10a		x .007 =
	10b Hampton Roads. Enter total taxable sales for this region in Column A. Multiply Column A by the rate of 0.7% (.007) and enter result in Column B.	10b		x .007 =
11	Total State and Regional Tax. Add Lines 9, 10a, Column B and 10b, Column B.	11		
12	Local Tax. Enter local taxable sales in Column A. Multiply Column A by the rate of 1.0% (.01) and enter the result in Column B. See ST-9A Worksheet.	12		x .01 =
13	Total State, Regional and Local Tax. Add Lines 11 and 12, Column B.	13		
14	Prepaid Wireless Fee. Enter number of items sold in Column A and fee due net of Dealer Discount in Column B. See ST-9A Worksheet.	14		14
15	Total Taxes and Fees. Add Lines 13 and 14, Column B.	15		
16	Penalty. See ST-9A Worksheet.	16		
17	Interest. See ST-9A Worksheet.	17		
18	Total Amount Due. Add Lines 15, 16 and 17.	18		

Declaration and Signature. I declare that this return (including accompanying schedules and statements) has been examined by me and to the best of my knowledge and belief is true, correct and complete.

_____   _____   _____
Signature   Date   Phone Number

ST-9 6210051   Rev. 03/13 *

Exclusion of Producers' Goods

Business purchases are a tempting target for taxation. The overall RST base is greater when business purchases are taxed, so a given statutory tax rate raises more revenue and a large piece of the tax burden is hidden to household consumers. These business purchases are not consumption, but the lure of revenue without higher statutory rates is attractive: such purchases constitute an estimated average of around 40 percent of state sales tax bases.[45] If businesses must pay tax on inputs to their business operations (raw materials, supplies, utilities, machinery and equipment, structures, etc.), their costs are higher (input price plus tax paid equals cost). Consequently, prices are higher because of those input taxes, but customers do not see the embedded effect of the producer sales tax on prices, a clear violation of the transparency standard, as well as a source of economic distortion. If producers' goods are not excluded, the tax is not a uniform percentage of consumer expenditures (some consumption items require use of more producers' goods than others), the tax affects choices among methods of production (it makes capital more expensive and may hamper economic development), and it may delay the replacement of old equipment by increasing the after-tax price of new equipment. Furthermore, firms have an incentive to produce goods for their own use rather than purchasing the goods because their internal cost of production is not subject to sales tax. Thus, producers' goods should be excluded from the tax to ensure economic efficiency and equity and to avoid thwarting industrial development.

The U.S. states are stingy in exempting pre-retail purchases. They exempt items purchased for resale (e.g., inventory), component parts of items for resale (e.g., tires purchased by an automobile manufacturer to install on vehicles being sold), and goods used directly in production (e.g., flour purchased by a bakery). Many producer goods (fuel, utilities, fixtures, tools, furniture, machinery, and equipment) remain in the base, despite the clear logic for excluding them. The business purchasing the item is treated as the final consumer, even though its purchase price, tax included, becomes part of the operating cost of the business that the business will include in the price of what it sells. However, legislatures are reluctant to remove the tax from business even though the business is almost certain to transmit the cost to its individual customers. Is the reluctance due to legislatures wanting to hide the tax from the public who will ultimately bear the tax burden, or because they do not want to be appearing to give a tax break to business? Your choice.

What happens when business purchases are not excluded from the sales tax? Figure 10–3 illustrates how pyramiding works and what its impact is. The figure contrasts a typical state sales tax with an ideal sales tax. The difference between the taxes: the ideal sales tax applies only to sales to the household consumer, and the typical sales tax applies to some business input purchases as well as to consumer sales. In the

---

[45]Raymond J. Ring Jr., "Consumers' Share and Producers' Share of the General Sales Tax," *National Tax Journal* 52 (March 1999): 79–90; and Robert Cline, John Mikesell, Tom Neubig, and Andrew Phillips, "Sales Taxation of Business Inputs: Existing Tax Distortions and the Consequences of Extending the Sales Tax to Business Services," *State Tax Notes* 35 (February 14, 2005): 457–70.

Figure 10–3
Retail Sales Tax Pyramiding: Typical versus Ideal

Sales to:	Sales by:			Sales Tax (5% statutory rate)	
	Computer Manufacturer	Appliance Manufacturer	Appliance Retailer	Typical*	Ideal**
Appliance manufacturer					
Computers used in production line	50,000			—	—
Computers used in administration	150,000			7,500	—
Appliance retailer					
Computers used in administration	10,000			500	—
Appliances		800,000		—	—
Household consumers			1,000,000	50,000	50,000
Total sales tax paid				58,000	50,000
Effective tax rate paid				5.80%	5%

*Typical: Exemption of business purchases of inventory and equipment used in direct production process.
**Ideal: Exemption of business purchases of all inputs.

ideal case, all input purchases by businesses are exempt from tax; in the typical case, purchases by businesses of inventory for resale and of goods used in the direct manufacturing process are exempt, but other business purchases are taxed. In this example, there are three businesses: a computer manufacturer, an appliance manufacturer, and an appliance retailer. The computer manufacturer sells computers to the retailer and to the appliance manufacturer. Some of the computers sold to the appliance manufacturer are for administrative work, and some of the computers sold to the appliance manufacturer are used in the production process. The state applies a sales tax rate of 5 percent to taxable sales. In the typical case, the flow of business generates $58,000 in sales tax revenue from $1,000,000 of sales to households—the effective tax rate is 5.8 percent, compared with the statutory rate of 5 percent. The higher effective rate results because $160,000 in computer sales to the manufacturer and to the retailer were taxed; the cost of those computers to the businesses is going to be embedded in the final price of their products, so the value of those computers is being taxed twice— once when the businesses purchase them and again when the products of those businesses get sold to the household consumer. This is sales tax pyramiding.[46]

---

[46]Purchases of inventory for resale are exempt in all state sales taxes. However, the exemption can provide an avenue for tax abuse. An affluent real estate developer and art collector in New York City was found to be purchasing expensive art without paying tax, allegedly because it would be for resale, and displaying it on his own property as if it were his own for extended periods, making it a taxable personal purchase. The settlement for unpaid tax was substantial. (Charles V. Bagli, "Developer Aby Rosen to Pay $7 Million in Suit Over Unpaid Taxes on Art," *New York Times*, May 3, 2016).

Pyramiding causes problems. First, products purchased by households bear differing effective sales tax rates, depending on the way in which products are produced. Those involving more inputs that are subject to tax when businesses purchase them have higher effective rates than those produced without those kinds of purchases. This distorts consumer and business behavior. Second, businesses have an artificial incentive to vertical integration. In the previous example, a firm that made both computers and appliances would have an economic advantage because its appliance branch could obtain administrative computers without facing any sales tax, whereas a firm that was not integrated would need to pay sales tax when it purchased computers on the open market. Third, businesses in states that have limited exemptions for business purchases are at distinct disadvantage in interstate and international competition; they face higher costs of production because of the tax paid on their purchases. Finally, the statutory or advertised sales tax rate understates the true sales tax rate. In the example, the advertised rate is 5 percent, but the true rate on household purchases is 5.8 percent. This violates an important transparency standard: taxpayers need to see what tax they are actually paying. In this example, when lawmakers claim that their state sales tax rate is 5 percent, they are not exactly telling the truth. In spite of the attractiveness of hidden taxes to politicians, it is still difficult to see why lawmakers would want to discourage business investment by taxing business inputs.

RSTs remove transactions from the tax system by suspending collection on those transactions. Figure 10–4 illustrates a suspension certificate prepared by the Multistate Tax Commission for use in its several member states (states also provide their own along the same lines). When a business purchases an item or group of items for an exempt purpose, such as buying inventory for resale or acquiring production equipment, it provides the seller with such a certificate. That turns off the tax on that sale. Sales are assumed to be taxable unless a certificate justifies that the tax should not be collected. The accumulation of such sales during a reporting period is reported on the seller's return (see line 3 in Figure 10–2); deducted sales of otherwise taxable items ultimately need to be documented by certificates provided by the purchaser when tax authorities audit the business. States may have a wide variety of such certificates, depending on the range of exempt purchases in the state law. When states exempt purchases by governments or nonprofit organizations, they provide similar certificates for that purpose.

One enforcement problem in sales taxation is fraudulent use of the exemption certificate: for example, if a business owner presents the certificate to suspend sales tax on the purchase of a computer that will be used at home rather than in an exempt business use. It is the responsibility of the vendor to make a good-faith effort to verify that the certificate is properly used before exempting the purchase. If the vendor erroneously fails to collect, the revenue is probably lost because revenue departments audit only a small percentage of vendors. This is the weakness of RSTs when the statutory tax rate gets particularly high. Purchasers are eager to avoid the tax when buying an expensive item, and vendors are eager not to possibly lose the sale by denying the misused exemption. Cheating might not be worth it when the tax rate is 5 percent, but it might start looking promising when the rate is 10 percent or more.

Figure 10–4
Sales Tax Suspension: Multistate Tax Commission Certificate

UNIFORM SALES & USE TAX CERTIFICATE—MULTIJURISDICTION

The below-listed states have indicated that this form of certificate is acceptable, subject to the notes on pages 2–4. The issuer and the recipient have the responsibility of determining the proper use of this certificate under applicable laws in each state, as these may change from time to time.

Issued to Seller: _____

Address: _____

I certify that: is engaged as a registered
Name of Firm (Buyer): _____   ☐ Wholesaler
Address: _____   ☐ Retailer
_____   ☐ Manufacturer
_____   ☐ Seller (California)
_____   ☐ Lessor (see notes on pages 2–4)
_____   ☐ Other (Specify)_____

and is registered with the below listed states and cities within which your firm would deliver purchases to us and that any such purchases are for wholesale, resale, ingredients or components of a new product or service to be resold, leased, or rented in the normal course of business. We are in the business of wholesaling, retailing, manufacturing, leasing (renting) the following:

Description of Business: _____

General description of tangible property or taxable services to be purchased from the seller: _____
_____

State	State Registration, Seller's Permit, or ID Number of Purchaser	State	State Registration, Seller's Permit, or ID Number of Purchaser
AL	_____	MO	_____
AR	_____	NE	_____
AZ	_____	NV	_____
CA	_____	NJ	_____
CO	_____	NM	_____
CT	_____	NC	_____
DC	_____	ND	_____
FL	_____	OH	_____
GA	_____	OK	_____
HI	_____	PA	_____
ID	_____	RI	_____
IL	_____	SC	_____
IA	_____	SD	_____
KS	_____	TN	_____
KY	_____	TX	_____
ME	_____	UT	_____
MD	_____	VT	_____
MI	_____	WA	_____
MN	_____	WI	_____

Figure 10–4
(Continued)

I further certify that if any property or service so purchased tax free is used or consumed by the firm as to make it subject to a Sales or Use Tax we will pay the tax due directly to the proper taxing authority when state law so provides or inform the seller for added tax billing. This certificate shall be a part of each order which we may hereafter give to you, unless otherwise specified, and shall be valid until canceled by us in writing or revoked by the city or state.

Under penalties of perjury, I swear or affirm that the information on this form is true and correct as to every material matter.

Authorized Signature: _____
(Owner, Partner or Corporate Officer)

Title: _____

Date: _____

Taxation of Services

Most state sales taxes, although applying generally to retail purchases of tangible personal property, apply only selectively to purchases of services. States usually tax the lease or rental of tangible personal property (motor vehicles, videotapes, cement mixers, etc.), the rental of transient accommodations, and some utility services. They may also tax other service purchases; about half the states even tax the repair, installation, or maintenance of the tangible personal property that they tax.[47] However, overall, the omission of services shows a secular vulnerability in the sales tax base. In 1965, 57.4 percent of personal consumption expenditure was of goods; by 2014, that share had fallen to 33.3 percent.[48] Failure to include household purchases of services means that the sales tax base gradually disappears as the economy becomes more service-oriented.

Taxing services on the same basis as goods can close a horizontal equity gap, allow more revenue at any statutory rate, may improve vertical equity, and may improve secular adequacy of the tax. It would even make tax compliance easier, as some businesses would no longer need to segregate sales of goods from sales of service in their billing and bookkeeping processes (auto repair businesses would not need to distinguish between parts and labor, for instance). Why aren't services taxed more widely? The initial objection to taxing services was that the tax on services is a tax on labor income. Of course, labor constitutes much of the production cost of tangible personal property, so the argument lacks merit. And do you think the $75 per hour charge for labor when your car goes in for repair means that the mechanic is being paid $75 per hour? That's a charge by the business for the service, as is

---

[47]John L. Mikesell, "Sales Tax Coverage for Services—Policy for a Changing Economy," *Journal of State Taxation* 9 (Spring 1991): 31–50.
[48]Bureau of Economic Analysis, National Income and Products Accounts. www.bea.gov. Larger changes appear when business purchases of services are included in the analysis.

the charge for the battery you are buying, and it has a lot of cost items (plus profit for the business) rolled into it. A more meaningful reason for exempting services is the frequent absence of a clear line between the worker-client relationship and the worker-employer relationship (e.g., an accountant doing personal tax returns versus an accountant working for a business firm). The latter, a producer-good relationship, should not be taxed. Furthermore, some services, such as medical and possibly legal, for instance, possibly should not be taxed as a matter of social policy. Consumers purchasing these services have enough trouble as it is without adding the sales tax to their bill.

Providing different treatment for purchases of services as opposed to treatment of purchases of goods creates interesting patterns of distortion. Consider the following differences:

(1) if you buy software to prepare your federal income tax, you will almost certainly pay sales tax on the purchase; if you have an accountant or tax preparation firm do it for you, you will almost certainly not pay sales tax on the bill;

(2) if you go to the multiplex to see a movie, you are unlikely to pay sales tax on the ticket; if you rent a video from a vending machine, you are likely to pay sales tax on the rental;

(3) if you arrange for lessons from the tennis pro to improve your game, you will almost certainly not pay sales tax on her charge; if you buy a new racket to improve your game, you will certainly pay sales tax on the purchase;

(4) if you go to a dentist for application of tooth whitener, you almost certainly will pay no sales tax on the bill; if you buy a tooth-whitening product from your local pharmacy, you are quite likely to pay sales tax on the purchase; and

(5) if you pay a lawyer to write your will, you almost certainly will not pay sales tax on the bill; if you buy a book with blank will forms to fill in, you will certainly pay sales tax.

Do these distinctions make any sense at all?

The pragmatic difficulty of taxing services is not surprising, even though the theory is sound and administration generally feasible. Politically, many types of services are sold by businesses with well-developed professional associations (accountants, barbers, lawyers, realtors, etc.), and those associations strive diligently to keep their services outside the sales tax. The problem is not just that these sellers may find adding the sales tax to their bills mathematically challenging (it does require multiplication to compute the 5 percent tax on a $100 purchase, after all). They do understand that adding the tax would have some negative impact on their sales and that dealing with the tax could add to their bookkeeping costs. Only a few states apply broad coverage of consumer services, but the realities of modern society cause extension to many services to be virtually inevitable—and leaving them out of the base of an indirect consumption tax certainly violates the broad-base, low-rate rule for tax policy. The difficult problem is to avoid taxing services sold almost exclusively to businesses; these are politically attractive targets, under the false impression that somehow applying a tax to a business avoids having the cost of government borne by the people.

Commodity Exemptions

RSTs typically exempt some goods that are clearly household consumption expenditures. The most frequently exempted items are food for at-home consumption (more than half the states) and prescription drugs (all but one state). There is a logical reason for these exemptions based on the standard evaluation criteria for taxes. Purchases of these items constitute a higher percentage of the income of low-income families than of high-income families. Excluding them from the tax base gives low-income families greater relief relative to their incomes than it does for high-income families, so the impact is to make the tax less regressive. The reduction of the effective tax rate on income is greater for low- than for high-income families. Hence, excluding the items improves the vertical equity of the tax. However, their exclusion makes the sales tax more difficult to collect (the state must define what items are exempt, stores selling both food and taxed items must maintain segregated accounting records, and audits are more complex), and the tax rate must be higher to yield a given amount of revenue on the smaller base (food constitutes around one-third of a prospective sales tax base).[49] The food exemption poorly targets relief: consumption studies show that households in the highest-income quintile receive double the absolute tax relief from a food exemption than households in the lowest-income quintile receive (because they spend more in total on food than do low-income households). Given that the neediest families automatically receive an exemption when they make purchases using federal SNAP (Supplemental Nutrition Assistance Program) resources because that is a requirement for state participation in the program, adding a general state food exemption almost by definition means that assistance gets misdirected. The net saving beyond SNAP extends exclusively to people other than the neediest families. But it gets worse. Eight states (Connecticut, Massachusetts, Minnesota, New Jersey, New York, Pennsylvania, Rhode Island, and Vermont) have extended commodity exemption to purchases of clothing under the apparent logic of exempting a necessity from the tax base. Unfortunately, clothing expenditures are less concentrated among low-income groups than in the ordinary sales tax base, so the exemption provides about four-and-one-half times more relief to the highest quintile of families, compared to the lowest quintile; does not improve vertical

---

[49]The distinctions for commodity exemptions can be maddening (as well as expensive to operate and downright silly). These examples illustrate the problem. In Illinois, whether a shave cream is considered a medicine (and some are) determines whether its purchase is taxed at a rate of 1 percent or 6.25 percent. The same rate differences apply between types of bottled water and between juices and juice beverages, according to whether they are considered food. In 2009, Illinois experienced a bit of a crisis when it extended its regular sales tax rate to candy (it had previously been considered food and eligible for taxation at a lower rate): was Twix a candy or a food? In Pennsylvania, state and U.S. flags are exempt unless sold with a flagpole. In Texas, plain nuts are exempt, but candy-coated nuts are taxed. A number of states distinguish between a single doughnut and a dozen doughnuts in determining taxability. And Iowa decided, a few years ago, that pumpkins were being sold for decorations and not for food and decided to tax them. People could fill out a form to get an exemption if they swore they were going to eat them. That brought out a firestorm of public complaint, plus the national news media, neither of which made the Iowa tax administrators happy. (Tax people do not, as a rule, ever want to show up on the front page of the newspapers or on CNN.) The administrators changed their decision.

equity of the tax; causes effective rates within income classes to vary according to relative tastes for clothing; complicates compliance and administration; and causes higher rates for given revenues.[50]

Five states (Hawaii, Idaho, Kansas, Oklahoma, and South Dakota) provide an RST credit or rebate as an alternative to commodity exemption for controlling sales tax regressivity. Rather than providing exemption for all purchasers of selected commodities, the credit systems return a fixed sum to taxpayers at year's end, usually equal to estimated payment of sales tax on food purchases by individuals in the lowest-income class. If the prevailing sales tax rate is 4 percent and per capita food purchases by individuals in the under-$15,000-annual-income class are about $10,000, the amount returned would be $400. Return of $400 to all individuals—either by rebate application or as a credit on a state income tax return—would effectively eliminate the sales tax on food purchases by very low-income purchasers. The rebate amount would not increase, however, as food consumption increased through the higher-income classes and, in some states, the rebate is limited only to lower-income families. (High-income people spend more on food than do low-income people; the food exemption works to reduce regressivity because the percentage of income spent on food declines with higher income.) The rebate concentrates assistance where assistance is most needed and eliminates the need for vendors to account for taxed and exempt sales. Overall, the rebate effectively reduces (or even eliminates) regressivity at a lower loss of revenue than commodity exemption. The rebate requires that individuals file returns with the state and that the state make cash payments to individuals, but these would seem small disadvantages relative to the other efficiencies of the device. Canada provides a quarterly payment to low-income individuals and families for the national goods and services tax to accommodate tax that would have been paid on food purchases. There is a similar refund program for provincial sales taxes. The food purchase rebate-credit system allows better targeting of the relief to those in need, thereby getting greater reduction in regressivity per dollar of tax revenue lost and reducing the fiscal impact of the relief provided.

Commodity exemptions (1) narrow the tax base, thereby requiring a higher statutory rate to yield a given amount of revenue, and no good ever comes from high statutory rates applied to anything; (2) increase the probability that family sales tax burdens will differ according to individual tastes and preferences for consumption items; (3) reduce the stability of the revenue base in the face of a business downturn (household consumption of nondurables tends to be less influenced by recessions than is spending on household durables); and (4) complicate administration and compliance by requiring sorting between taxed and exempt. Nevertheless, legislators find exemptions to be popular with the electorate; they create the illusion that responsibility for the cost of government is being avoided rather than being distributed to the public in less transparent ways.[51]

---

[50]John L. Mikesell, "Exempting Clothing from the Sales Tax: The 'Supply Side Message' from the New York Tax Holiday," *State Tax Notes* (March 17, 1997): 835–38.

[51]Over the years, advocates for low income people have worked to switch food credits to food exemptions, thus (apparently) unwittingly improving the tax position of high income households relative to lower income households.

Variation in the State Sales Taxes

The states that levy RSTs do not apply the tax to the same transactions. They vary in the exemptions they provide for household consumption expenditure (food, clothing, nonprescription medicines, motor fuels, magazines, etc.), the extent to which they include service purchases in the tax base, and the degree to which they exclude purchase of business inputs from the tax base. The result of these variations is that the breadth of the tax base differs dramatically across the states. A given statutory sales tax rate yields significantly different revenues from one state to another because of these structural differences. In fiscal 2014, the average ratio of sales tax base to state personal income of the five narrowest states (Massachusetts, Illinois, Virginia, and New Jersey) equaled 0.236, compared with 0.713 for the five broadest (Hawaii, North Dakota, Wyoming, and South Dakota), the result of the differing choices that lawmakers in the two groups of states have made about including transactions in the tax base and some differences in state economies. That means that one percentage point of sales tax rate would yield almost three times as much revenue in the broad-base states as in the narrow-base ones, a considerable fiscal difference.[52] The structure of the base is critical for revenue yield; the broader the base, the more revenue that can be produced from a given rate, and the evidence is that states with broader bases do tend to levy lower statutory sales tax rates.

Although there is a U.S. style for sales taxation that states and localities follow, it is important to remember that there is no single template for these taxes. The structures are established by state lawmakers, and each state is different in how it chooses to structure its own sales tax. The same principle applies in Canada, the only other country making significant use of the RST, where all provinces but one levy either a provincial RST or a general sales tax harmonized with the federal goods and services tax. With the exception of provinces that have chosen to harmonize with the federal tax, the provinces structure their taxes independently and not according to a national standard.

Sales Taxes and Internet Commerce: Remote Vendors and Use Taxes[53]

All sales tax states levy use taxes on the storage, use, or consumption of taxable property on which the sales tax has not been paid (in fact, some state laws call them "*compensating* use taxes" because they compensate for unpaid sales tax) to protect

---

[52]Data from Governments Division of Bureau of Census and Bureau of Economic Analysis and state tax departments.

[53]Although this issue is normally viewed as a retail sales tax problem, it also matters for excise taxes. For example, online merchants physically located on American Indian Reservations and not subject to state excises or in low-tax states also sell cigarettes without remitting tax owed at the destination in Internet sales. By law, the recipient is supposed to pay the excise in his state of residence but very few comply. Evidence indicates that this Internet trade has significantly lessened the yield potential of state cigarette tax rate increases. Austan Goolsbee, Michael F. Lovenheim, and Joel Slemrod, "Playing with Fire: Cigarettes, Taxes, and Competition from the Internet," *American Economic Journal: Economic Policy* 2 (2010): 131–54.

their vendors from untaxed competition and to protect their own sales tax base from sales loss. The tax may not have been paid because the purchase was made in a jurisdiction without a tax on the item (e.g., hunting boots purchased from an outlet store in New Hampshire for use in Chicago) or because the purchase was made in interstate commerce (e.g., purchase of a computer from an Internet vendor located out of state). The rules governing interstate commerce (based on the Commerce Clause of the U.S. Constitution) do not allow either the origination or the destination state to levy a sales tax on such interstate business; however, the destination state may impose the use tax on the purchase after it has come to rest.[54] Protection of vendors and the tax base, not direct collections, really is the primary objective; use tax collections seldom constitute as much as 10 percent of combined sales and use tax collections.

The use tax problem is with enforcement. Transaction taxes can best be collected through vendors—in other words, as indirect taxes rather than as direct taxes collected from purchasers. There are far fewer vendors than purchasers for tax authorities to track, and vendors have far greater record-keeping and accounting capacity than household purchasers. Trying to administer a tax on individual transactions as a direct tax would be virtually impossible.[55] However, that is how most retail activity subject to the use tax, including Internet sales, is expected to be collected—unless the vendor serves as collector. The key to enforcement is getting vendors registered as tax collectors on behalf of the tax administration. The constitutional standard for requiring vendors to register is "physical presence" in the taxing state, as prescribed by the U.S. Supreme Court in *National Bellas Hess v. Department of Revenue,* 386 U.S. 753 (1967), and reaffirmed in *Quill v. North Dakota,* 504 U.S. 298 (1992). The Commerce Clause of the U.S. Constitution prohibits states from placing "undue burden" on interstate commerce, and imposing collection requirements on remote vendors surely could be considered such a burden. The vendor would need to know the base structure and rate wherever sales are made, and that could include taxes for the thousands of taxing local jurisdictions as well as the forty-five sales tax states plus the District of Columbia. A vendor selling nationwide would need to know them all, and vendors selling via the Internet might get an order from anywhere.[56] The Court sought to provide with physical presence a "bright line" standard for firmly establishing when an enterprise would be required to bear the compliance responsibilities of registering to become a sales and use tax collector. If the vendor is physically there, it is not an undue burden for it to learn about the sales and use tax system in place in the jurisdiction.

---

[54]The U.S. Supreme Court, in *Henneford v. Silas Mason Co., Inc.,* 300 U.S. 577 (1937), upheld the Washington State use tax. The tax was on the privilege of use after interstate commerce was complete.

[55]Most states do try to collect use tax directly from individuals, with varying degrees of rigor. For instance, some states provide use tax reporting on their individual income tax return, but revenues are modest. See John L. Mikesell, "Administering Use Tax as Direct Collection through Income Tax Reports," *State Tax Notes* 13 (May 26, 1997): 1603–6.

[56]The court cases establishing the operational principles were based on catalog merchants, not Internet vendors.

The situation can be explained by reference to three classes of purchases and how judicial interpretations of the Commerce Clause of the U.S. Constitution requires that they be handled by state sales and use taxes:

1. **Purchases made from a local storefront.** A local storefront—a store in your local shopping mall—must register with its state as a tax collector and must remit tax from purchases made at that store. Physical presence, registration required. If the purchase is delivered to another state by a common carrier (postal service, package delivery firm, etc.), the sale is in interstate commerce, and the storefront state cannot apply its sales tax. If the storefront uses its own delivery trucks, it has physical presence in the destination state and must collect use tax there. Sidebar 10–3 illustrates one ultimately unsuccessful approach to evading a substantial amount of use tax by fudging place of delivery.

2. **Purchases made from a remote vendor with physical presence in the state.** A remote vendor—Internet seller, mail-order firm, telemarketer, home shopping channel, store in another state, and so on—with any physical presence, not necessarily a retail storefront, in the state must register with that state as a tax collector and must remit tax on purchases made for delivery into that state. The presence might be its delivery trucks, a warehouse, or a repair facility.[57] The tax is a compensating use tax that the vendor is collecting and remitting on behalf of the purchaser. Physical presence, registration required. However, physical presence of a subsidiary does not necessarily constitute physical presence for a parent company; companies have various ways to establish sufficient separation to prevent a registration requirement.

3. **Purchases from a remote vendor without physical presence.** A remote vendor without physical presence may not be required to register as a use tax collector. (Voluntary registration is permitted.) Purchasers owe use tax on their purchases, as in the immediately preceding instance, but they are expected to remit the tax on their purchases directly rather than through the vendor.[58] No physical presence, collection not required for vendors, but purchasers still owe use tax.

How does a state collect its use tax? Some out-of-state vendors collect use tax on sales made in the state, either because they have some physical presence in the state (e.g., some catalog or Internet vendors also have retail or outlet stores) or because they have voluntarily registered as tax collectors. Some use tax is collected when the

---

[57]Or in more interesting fashion. When primary school teachers take orders for Scholastic Books in their classes, a number of states, including California, Ohio, Kansas, Connecticut, and Tennessee, use that to establish physical presence for that publisher for the state. The teacher is regarded as the company's agent.

[58]The problem is primarily one of purchases made through the Internet (or other remote vending format) and delivered through conventional means (postal service, delivery firms, etc.) and not of purchases delivered through the Internet. Only purchases subject to digitization can currently be delivered by electronic means, and that is a small component of the possible tax base. Furthermore, many such purchases are not taxable, even if purchased from a local storefront, because they are not tangible personal property. This is part of the general failure of state sales taxes to keep up with economic change.

Sidebar 10–3
The Not-So-Fine Art of Sales and Use Tax Evasion

Paying the retail sales tax is a normal part of life for most households on most transactions. The vendor adds the tax at purchase and remits the accumulation of those collections on a regular schedule determined by how big the vendor is, with large firms making payments more frequently than do small firms. But that was not a part of the system that Dennis Kozlowski, the former Chief Executive of Tyco International, exploited and attempted to evade when he made over $13 million of taxable purchases of artwork, including paintings by Monet, Renoir, Caillebotte, and others.

Kozlowski evaded the 8.25% New York state and local sales taxes on his purchases with two variants of schemes. In one scheme, he made purchases of artwork in London and had them picked up at the Newark airport for transport to Tyco headquarters in New Hampshire (which levies no general sales tax), from which point they were shipped back to his New York City apartment. State tax departments obtain customs declaration forms when large purchases are brought into the country, and if he had invoiced for delivery to New York City, the tax authorities would have immediately enforced the tax. In another scheme, empty boxes with false invoices showing that they contained paintings were shipped to New Hampshire, but the actual paintings went to New York. In the latter instance, a memo from the art dealer to the shipping company covered it all: "Here is a list of the five paintings that go to NY (wink wink). Please make cardboard boxes or use crates to match the piece count. Cheers & thanks." In these instances, Kozlowski would have owed New York compensating use tax on the artwork purchase because the artwork ended up in New York City shortly after purchase and sales tax to no other state had been paid. It is not entirely clear how the authorities discovered the evasion, but there are suspicions that art dealer might have provided a tip about the scheme.

Kozlowski agreed to payment of $3.2 million in sales tax and interest on unpaid tax on the paintings. The Manhattan district attorney's office was continuing an investigation into transactions involving other art dealers and customers who might have had empty boxes shipped as a device for evading sales tax.

SOURCES: Mark Maremont and Jerry Markon, "Tyco's Kozlowski Is Indicted on Charges of Tax Evasion," *Wall Street Journal* , June 5, 2002; Anemona Hartocollis, "Ex-Tyco Chief to Settle Tax Evasion Charges," *New York Times,* May 13, 2006; and "Kozlowski Sales Tax Deal," The Art Law Blog, May 14, 2006.

---

purchaser registers the item, as with a motor vehicle or a boat. Some use tax is collected when state auditors check a taxpayer's records and discover major purchases made out-of-state without payment of tax (mostly involving audits of businesses). Finally, some use tax is reported by the purchaser, either on a special return or on a "convenience line" added to the state's individual income tax return.

States do not presently have any successful mechanism for enforcing use tax on remote sales, especially through Internet websites, and this is extremely worrisome in terms of fairness of the tax and long-term revenue productivity. States would like to require large firms to register, but Congress has not yet been convinced of the reasonableness of this effort.

Around half the states have voluntarily developed the Streamlined Sales Tax Project (SSTP) to simplify and reduce the compliance burden on remote vendors so Congress would allow required registration. States that participate in the project do not adopt a common sales tax base, but they do agree to certain unified sales tax conditions to make remote vendor compliance easier. In general, the SSTP provisions are these:

1. Any local sales taxes must be state-administered, must apply to the same base as the state tax, and must all use the same tax rate.[59]
2. States must use standard definitions for certain exemptions and exclusions. Important definitions include those for food, drugs, clothing, and tangible personal property. The agreement does not require that the items be exempt, but if they are, the definitions must follow standard lines.
3. States must participate in an online sales and use tax registration system that covers registration in all agreement states. A firm needs to register only once to be registered in all participating states.
4. The agreement provides three sales and use tax remittance options: a certified service provider acts as the firm's agent in all sales and use tax functions; the firm uses a certified automated system to handle tax calculation, remittance, record keeping, and reporting; or the firm does compliance itself according to a performance standard acceptable to each agreement state.
5. States adopt a variety of other changes in how taxes are calculated to make compliance easier. For instance, the state must use brackets consistent with major fraction rounding, the state may not limit the amount of tax due on a particular transaction, and the state must require statewide consolidated returns for multiple-location vendors.

States accept the loss of some fiscal autonomy because they hope to induce Congress to revise the physical presence rule and to use required registration as a means of protecting their local vendors and their sales tax base. That would allow the use tax to be collected as an indirect tax, from the vendors, and not as a direct tax, from the purchasers. Collection from vendors is, in general, the "Holy Grail" in sales tax enforcement.

In addition to the SSTP efforts and absence of congressional action to alter the physical presence standard, some states have sought to get remote vendors into their tax systems through other mechanisms. Some states assert a registration requirement with "click-through" or "affiliate" nexus. This provision in state law establishes a registration requirement when an affiliate with physical presence in a state places a link on its website directing the prospective customer to the online retailer website (e.g., Amazon.com or Overstock.com). If a sale results from that referral, the affiliate entity receives an agreed compensation from the retailer. The law claims that

---

[59]Until recently, tax liability for local taxes had to be based on the destination of the sale (where it was delivered) rather than on the origin (the vendor's shop). This provision is being revised to allow states the choice of the two rules in determining the applicable tax rate and what locality gets the revenue.

this relationship establishes physical presence for the retailer wherever the affiliate is physically present, and the retailer must collect tax on sales to that state. New York passed the first of these laws in 2008, and a couple dozen states now use the approach.[60] The approach has passed initial constitutional challenge.

The second approach is that of required notification by remote vendors. Colorado enacted in 2010 a law assigning three duties to any "retailer that does not collect Colorado sales tax." These retailers must (i) inform Colorado customers that sales or use tax is owed on purchases and that the customer has responsibility to file the appropriate tax return; (ii) send each Colorado customer an end-of-year notice of the date, amount, and category of each purchase made during the year and again remind of the requirement of return filing and tax payment for certain purchases; and (iii) send the Colorado department of revenue an annual statement of purchases made for each in-state customer. Alternatively, the remote vendor may register and collect the tax itself. At present, the law has been held to be constitutional because the *Quill* standard regarding physical presence and undue burden applied to collecting the tax and that the Colorado law deals only with a reporting requirement.[61] That would appear to open the door to getting much broader use tax enforcement and may signal an eventual end to the physical presence standard entirely. States would much prefer a standard based on substantial economic presence in the state to take account of changes in the economy by which remote vendors find it easy to make sales into a jurisdiction with no physical presence in the state. Indeed, Alabama and South Dakota have passed registration requirement laws that totally ignore physical presence in requiring vendor registration. Given likely congressional inaction, the outcome for use tax enforcement will likely be established in the court system.

With regard to the first target of these laws, the actions are gradually becoming moot. Amazon increasingly is establishing distribution centers across the states to provide quicker service and thus is establishing physical presence (sometimes with delayed registration agreements as part of the development effort designed to bring the center to the state). It collects sales tax in at least twenty-six states, including the ten most populous ones. Other online retailers are, of course, another matter.

Collecting the Retail Sales Tax

The RST has a collection advantage: the vendor who remits the tax to the government is something of a third party in the tax transaction between the purchaser, who most likely bears the burden of the tax, and the government receiving the revenue. This indirect tax relationship approximates that of income tax withholding and greatly simplifies administration and compliance. Administration is also simplified by the fact that the sales tax base is concentrated in a relatively small number of

---

[60]Amazon and some other online vendors responded to such laws in some states by canceling affiliate relationships with all entities in the state.
[61]*Direct Marketing Association v. Brohl,* No. 12-175 (10th Cir. Feb. 22, 2016).

firms. Looking across states at vendors in the state with annual retail sales exceeding $10 million gives an idea of this concentration: in Colorado, those vendors constitute 1.8 percent of the total number of vendors and made up 65.4 percent of retail sales volume; in Illinois, 0.5 percent of vendors made up 62.5 percent of sales; in Kansas, 2.1 percent of vendors made up 57.9 percent of sales; in Michigan, 0.9 percent of vendors made up 63.8 percent of sales; in Pennsylvania, 0.4 percent of vendors made up 59.2 percent of sales; in Washington, 0.8 percent of vendors made up 56.5 percent of sales; and so it goes.[62] What this means is that state tax departments can cover an extremely high percentage of the sales tax base with audit and other enforcement work with a relatively small number of firms. That concentration, combined with the third-party nature of the tax, makes for extremely low noncompliance rates for state sales taxes. The Washington State compliance study, done regularly is probably the most comprehensive and careful study of state sales tax noncompliance, estimated sales tax noncompliance at 1.0 percent for 2010.[63] That is in the same range as federal income tax noncompliance for incomes subject to withholding and much lower noncompliance than for the federal tax in total. Noncompliance with the use taxes is much, much greater. Unless the vendor is registered with the state, the state has to hope for direct collection from the purchaser, and payments from purchasers are rare.

Value-Added Taxes

A value-added tax (VAT) provides an alternate mechanism for taxing consumption.[64] Indeed, the VAT may be regarded as how the world (except the United States) levies a general tax on household consumption. This tax applies to the increment in value at each stage of the production and distribution process rather than applying only at the final (retail) stage. In the United States, the VAT over the years has been proposed as a means of financing the social insurance system in place of or in addition to the payroll tax, as a way to stimulate saving and investment through reducing reliance on income taxation, as an avenue to stimulating exports, as a replacement for the property tax as a means for financing primary and secondary education, as a bridge revenue option until sanity is restored to the federal income taxes, and as

---

[62]Small Seller Task Force Committee, "Streamlined Sales Tax Governing Board, September 29, 2008, Report." http://www.streamlinedsalestax.org/Small%20Seller%20Task%20Force%20Committee/Documents/SurveyResults.pdf. In Montgomery, Alabama, the CAFR shows that the ten largest taxpayers remitted 23 percent of all sales tax collections; that's ten taxpayers, not ten percent of the taxpayers.
[63]State of Washington, "Department of Revenue Compliance Study," Research Report No. 2010-4, August 20, 2010. http://dor.wa.gov/Docs/Reports/Compliance_Study/compliance_study_2010.pdf. Use tax noncompliance is much higher, 23 percent.
[64]An excellent reference is Alan A. Tait, *Value-Added Tax: International Practice and Problems* (Washington, D.C.: International Monetary Fund, 1988). The tax may also be designed to approximate an income tax, but the consumption variety predominates.

a revenue source that might unify state fiscal systems. However, none of the arguments has been strong enough for lawmakers to act. Conservative commentators fault the VAT mostly because it is a highly efficient tax, is too effective at raising revenue without doing harm to the economy, and, because of all that, might tempt governments to use it to get bigger. A more disruptive tax might tempt them less. Besides, some argue, the tax is European (German engineered, but first implemented by the French in 1954) and, hence, not to be trusted.[65] Nevertheless, Bruce Bartlett, a former domestic policy advisor in the Reagan and George H. W. Bush administrations, gives the tax high praise: "From the point of view of efficiency, it is generally considered to be the best tax ever invented."[66] Tax analysts swoon; Dutch tax scholar Sijbren Cnossen proclaims: "The nearly universal introduction of the value added tax should be considered the most important event in the evolution of tax structure in the last half of the twentieth century."[67] That might be faint praise.

The value-added tax (or goods and services tax as it is called in, for instance, Canada, New Zealand, and Australia) is collected by businesses on their sales of goods and services to their customers.[68] Each business in the flow of production and distribution from manufacturer to retailer charges VAT on its sales and, in remitting payments to the taxing authority, is permitted to subtract from this amount the VAT that it paid on its purchases.[69] Invoices showing VAT paid must be available to support the VAT credits taken on the return (governments may require electronic invoices to reduce fraudulent invoice claims by facilitating cross-checking and other verification), and credit is provided immediately for tax on all business purchases, including capital goods. Businesses of all types must register as VAT collectors to get the credits, so there will be almost two and one-half times as many firms registered under a VAT than under a RST, in which only retailers need to register.[70] The result of offsetting tax paid on purchases against tax collected on sales is to impose the tax on value added (sales less purchases) at each stage of production-distribution.

---

[65]Denmark introduced the first comprehensive value-added tax in 1967; the French tax did not extend through all stages of production at first. Carl S. Shoup, "Experience with the Value-added Tax in Denmark, and Prospects in Sweden," *Finanz Archiv/Public Finance Analysis New Series,* Bd. 28. H. 2 (1969): 236–52.

[66]Bruce Bartlett, *The Benefit and the Burden, Tax Reform—Why We Need It and What It Will Take* (New York: Simon & Schuster, 2012): 197. Land tax proponents would dispute that.

[67]Sijbren Cnossen, "Global Trends and Issues in Value Added Taxation," *International Tax and Public Finance* 5 (1998): 399.

[68]Although the national value-added taxes follow the same general principles, they do have considerable variation among countries. The taxes in Australia and New Zealand are simpler than those in Europe, with fewer special provisions, exceptions, rate variations, and so on to make compliance complicated. Lawmakers have virtually unlimited capacity to complicate taxes for perceived political advantage.

[69]The tax on the total value of its sales less the tax on the total value of its purchases equals the tax on the value that the business adds. Hence, it is a VAT. A tax on the value of its sales only is a gross receipts or turnover tax. This discussion focuses on the credit-invoice approach to applying the tax, the most frequently used method. Alternatives are examined in Itai Grinberg, "Where Credit Is Due: Advantages of the Credit-Invoice Method for a Partial Replacement VAT," *Tax Law Review* 63 (Winter 2010): 309–58.

[70]John L. Mikesell, "Misconceptions About Value-Added and Retail Sales Taxes: Are They Barriers to Sensible Tax Policy? *Public Budgeting & Finance* 34 (Summer 2014): 15. That trail of invoices that a VAT produces is generally irrelevant to the RST. Only the documentation of inventory sold to the final retailer matters much for enforcement review.

The final consumer, the household, is not a business, has no sales through which VAT paid may be reimbursed, and thus bears the tax. This multistage tax does not pyramid because the tax applies only to the value added at each transaction, not to the total receipts of the transaction, and businesses are reimbursed for the tax that they have paid on their purchases. Why is the VAT equivalent to an RST? The RST applies to the total value of the product (the purchase price at retail) and is levied at the last stage of the production-distribution process; the VAT applies to the value added at each stage of the process, and the accumulation of these increments equals the total value of the product.[71] Sidebar 10-4 outlines the basic math that shows the economic equivalence of the two taxes.

The logic of a VAT can be demonstrated with a simple illustration. Remember in this example that the business is both a taxpayer (on its purchases) and a tax collector (on its sales). The tax that the business pays gets reimbursed (credited or refunded) through the tax that it collects on its sales.

Suppose a 10 percent rate applies in a hypothetical production-distribution process that gets a wool sweater to a customer.[72]

1. A farmer sells wool to a textile company for $20, collects $2 in tax ($20 times 10 percent), and sends the $2 to the government. (The farmer's value added equals sales less purchases; that is, 20 minus 0 equals 20, making the simplifying assumption that the totally self-sufficient farmer buys nothing from any business but grows or makes everything herself.) The textile company receives the wool, for which it has paid $20 plus $2 tax, or $22, and a statement showing that it paid $2 in VAT.

2. The textile company sells the yarn that it spins from the wool to a sweater manufacturer for $50. (Therefore, its value added equals sales minus purchases, or $50 minus $20 equals $30.) The company collects $5 in tax from the manufacturer and sends the government $3 plus the receipt showing $2 already paid when purchasing the wool. The textile company keeps the $2 and is now fully reimbursed for the VAT it paid when it purchased the wool. The sweater manufacturer has the yarn, for which it has paid $50 plus $5 tax, or $55, and a receipt for $5 VAT paid.

3. The sweater manufacturer knits a sweater and sells it to a retailer for $90 (its value added is $90 minus $50, or $40). The manufacturer collects $9 in tax from the retailer and sends the government $4 plus the receipt showing $5 already paid when purchasing the yarn. The retailer has the sweater, for which it has paid $90 plus $9 tax, or $99, and a receipt for $9 VAT paid.

---

[71]Value added by a firm is also equal to the total amount the firm pays to factors of production (rent to land, wages and salaries to employees, interest to capital, and profit to entrepreneurial activity). The VAT base could thus alternatively be calculated by adding these payments—as is done with the New Hampshire tax on business enterprise. At one time the state of Michigan levied a single business tax that was also a value-added tax of this variety.

[72]This illustrates the credit-invoice method of collection, as used in European-style VATs. The subtraction method, an alternate collection approach, would have businesses subtract purchases from sales and pay tax on the difference, without using invoices and credits. Zero rating, removing certain consumption categories from tax by taxing them at a rate of zero, does not work well, however, with the subtraction method.

Sidebar 10–4
The Economic Equivalence of RST and VAT[1]

An ideal RST and an ideal VAT are economically the same; they are just administered in a different fashion. Here is an explanation of the logic behind this equivalence. Assume the following economic chain: an extractor who sells to a manufacturer who sells to a wholesaler who sells to a retailer who sells to a final customer. Notice that one entity's sales are another entity's purchases: for example, the product that represents sales by the wholesaler is the product that represents purchases by the retailer.

Let t equal the VAT or RST rate; S equal sales or purchases; the subscripts e, m, w, and r indicate whether the sale is by extractor, manufacturer, wholesaler, or retailer; and R equal total revenue collected in the production and distribution chain.

RST: The ideal RST applies only to the final retail sales to the household customer. All sales between businesses in the supply chain are not taxed via use of the suspension certificate. Therefore, revenue from the RST equals

$$R = t \times S_r$$

VAT: The ideal VAT applies to value added at each transaction in the production and distribution chain. In other words, it applies to the difference between sales made by the business entity to other entities and purchases made by the business entity from other entities. Therefore, revenue from the VAT equals

$$R = t(S_e - 0) + t(S_m - S_e) + t(S_w - S_m) + t(S_r - S_w)$$

or

$$R = tS_e - tS_e + tS_m - tS_m + tS_w - tS_w + tS_r = tS_r$$

This expression reflects two VAT facts: (1) before the final sale to the household consumer, the purchases of one business are the sales of another business, and (2) VAT paid by a business on its purchases will be refunded from the VAT it collects on its sales.

Conclusion: Although the two taxes are administered in significantly different ways, the two taxes apply to the same final base and will yield equal revenue from a common statutory rate. The VAT accumulates through the stages of production and distribution to be a tax on all household consumption. The RST will tax only household consumption because all tax on all sales or purchases before final have been suspended.

[1]For a more extensive comparison of the retail sales and value-added taxes, see John L. Mikesell, "Is the Retail Sales Tax Really Inferior to the Value-Added Tax?" in *The Sales Tax in the 21st Century,* ed. W. Fox and M. Murray (Westport, Conn.: Greenwood Press, 1997).

4. The retailer sells the sweater to a final customer for $200 plus $20 VAT (the value added by the retailer, $200 minus $90, equals $110). The retailer sends the government $11 plus the receipt showing $9 already paid when purchasing the sweater from the manufacturer. The customer has the sweater and

has paid $200 plus $20 in VAT, or $220. However, in contrast to the businesses in the production-distribution chain, the customer has no avenue to obtain a refund through the next transaction because the customer is the final link in the chain. The customer, not being a business, has no sales upon which the VAT would be applied. The final customer, the household, pays the tax, and the tax paid equals 10 percent of the value of the purchase.

There are, of course, many transactions going on in each of these businesses, but the basic principle of removing the tax from business purchases by refund remains the same. The tax does not pyramid because each business in the chain both pays the tax on its purchases and then receives a refund of that tax when it collects tax on its sales. The tax is not embedded in its operating cost. Notice in the example that the value of the sweater at the end ($200) equals the sum of values added at each stage of production ($20 plus $30 plus $40 plus $110 equals $200), that each cash payment to the government equals the tax rate times value added at that stage ($2, $3, $4, and $11), and that the sum of payments equals the VAT rate times the final value of the sweater. The result is thus equivalent to applying a 10 percent RST to the value purchased by the final customer.

VAT accounting can be simple for a business. Think about the scheme in this fashion. The business has two boxes. One box receives all the invoices for purchases during the month, with each invoice showing the amount of the purchase and the amount of VAT paid on the purchase. The other box receives all the invoices for sales during the month, with each invoice showing the amount of the sale and the amount of VAT collected on the sale. When it is time to do the VAT return at the end of the month, the business owner (1) goes to the purchase record box and tallies all purchases made and the tax paid on those purchases, (2) goes to the sales record box and tallies all sales made and the tax collected on those sales, (3) subtracts total purchases from total sales to get value added during the month, and (4) subtracts total tax paid on purchases from total tax collected on sales to figure the amount of VAT to send to the government. It can get more complicated if the legislature wants to add exemptions or preferential tax rates, but that is how the process works. There are no more records required than for a business income tax, and the calculations from them are less complicated—and the owners of the business are much less likely to bear the burden of the VAT than they are of an income tax.

Figure 10–5 shows a return for the New Zealand goods and service (VAT) tax.[73] Here is the basic structure of the return. The business reports its total sales on line 5, a total that includes VAT that has been collected on these transactions. The business subtracts sales on which it has not collected VAT (in RST terminology, these would be considered exempt sales, but VAT terminology refers to these sales as zero-rated, as in subject to a zero tax rate). The resulting total on line 7 is multiplied by 3 and

---

[73]Why New Zealand? First, the return is in English, so readers of this book will be able to understand it. Second, the return is available. Many countries handle their returns only electronically, with responses individually keyed to each registered business, making the returns generally inaccessible to anyone other than businesses. Third, the New Zealand VAT levies only a single rate, making the process simpler for everyone involved, providing a good model for everyone.

Figure 10–5
New Zealand Value-Added Tax Return

Inland Revenue
Te Tari Taake

Goods and Services Tax Act 1985

Goods and services tax return

You can use the *GST guide (IR 375)* to help you complete this return, which you ll find at
www.ird.govt.nz or call us on 0800 377 776.

GST 101A
July 2007

Registration number **1**

Period covered by the return

from **2** to

This return and any payment are due

If your correct **postal address** for GST is **not** shown above, print it in Box 3. **3**

If your correct daytime phone number is **not** shown here, print it in Box 4 **4**

Area code   Phone number

Goods and services tax on your sales and income

Total sales and income for the period (including GST and any zero-rated supplies) **5** $

Zero-rated supplies included in Box 5 **6** $

Subtract Box 6 from Box 5 and enter the difference here **7** $

Divide the amount in Box 7 by nine (9) **8** $

Adjustments from your calculation sheet **9** $

Add Box 8 and Box 9. This is your **total GST** collected on sales and income **10** $

OFFICE USE ONLY
Operator code   Corresp. indicator
Payment attached   Return cat.

Goods and services tax on your purchases and expenses

Total purchases and expenses (including GST) for which tax invoicing requirements have been met excluding any imported goods **11** $

Divide the amount in Box 11 by nine (9) **12** $

Credit adjustments from your calculation sheet **13** $

Declaration
The information in this return is true and correct and represents my assessment as required under the Tax Administration Act 1994.

Add Box 12 and Box 13. This is your **total GST** credit for purchases and expenses **14** $

Print the difference between Box 10 and Box 14 here **15** $

Signature

Date

If Box 14 is larger than Box 10 the difference is your GST refund
If Box 10 is larger than Box 14 the difference is GST to pay
Has payment been made electronically? Yes No

(Tick one)
Refund
GST to pay

Inland Revenue
Te Tari Taake

Payment slip

GST 700

Registration number

Return for the period ending

This return and any payment are due

Amount of payment $

Use the envelope provided to post your return, payment slip and any cheque payment.

Copy your total from Box 15 and enter it here. Include any late payment penalties for this period only.

then divided by 23 to produce the total VAT collected by the business. How does that make any sense? The statutory VAT rate is 15 percent (tax-exclusive). Its tax-inclusive equivalent, from Sidebar 10–2, would equal TE/(100 + TE) or 15/115 = 0.13. That equals 3 divided by 23, so this calculation yields the amount of VAT collected by the business. The next steps involve total purchases, which include VAT paid on the purchases, and VAT paid equals total purchases multiplied by 3 and divided by 23. Finally, line 15 is the difference between VAT collected and VAT paid—and that difference is paid if collections are higher and is refunded if payments are higher.

The return calculation works exactly like the simple system of a box with receipts showing VAT collections and a box with receipts showing VAT payments, with a netting of the two boxes on a periodic basis.

Value-Added Tax Features

VATs are typically levied by national governments, and those governments rely heavily on revenue from these taxes. As a result, statutory VAT rates are usually much higher than typical RST rates. Table 10–5 displays the standard VAT rate for a number of countries around the world. Rates of 20 percent are common, though there are both higher and lower rates. Countries of the European Union are required to levy a minimum rate of 15 percent. Because the VAT plays such an important role in their revenue systems, most levy rates are higher than that. (Individual income tax reliance is lower as a result.) Many countries also levy special preferential rates on some purchases (food, medicines, etc.) to reduce the regressivity of the tax, and others levy special higher rates on certain luxuries as they attempt to combine excise effects with the general consumption tax. These multirate systems make both compliance and administration more difficult. VAT systems assign a zero rating to goods or services they want to relieve entirely from tax; that relieves the purchaser from tax and allows the seller to have any tax it might have paid to be refunded.

VAT exemptions do not work in the same way that RST exemptions do. An exemption relieves the seller from collecting the VAT on its sales, but it does not relieve the seller from paying the tax on its purchases. There are no purchase suspension certificates in the VAT. For exempt goods and services, the seller of the service is treated like the consumer of its purchases. As a result, with the VAT, businesses usually do not want their product to be exempt even though the tax rates are high; by being registered vendors of taxed goods or services, they have a mechanism for refund of the VAT that they pay on their purchases. Without that registration, they pay the tax without refund. Unless the business purchases very little from other businesses (certain service providers would be an example), so that very little of its operating cost is covered by the VAT, it will much prefer to be selling a taxed rather than an exempt product.

The typical VAT system does not require small businesses to register as VAT collectors. For example, the registration threshold for 2015 in the United Kingdom

Table 10–5
Standard Value-Added Tax Rates in Selected Countries, 2015

Members of the OECD	Rate	Selected Other Countries	Rate
Australia	10	Argentina	21
Austria	20	Brazil	19
Belgium	21	China	17
Canada	5	Columbia	16
Chile	19	Egypt	10
Czech Republic	21	India	12.5
Denmark	25	Indonesia	10
Estonia	20	Kenya	16
Finland	24	Latvia	21
France	20	Lithuania	21
Germany	19	Morocco	20
Greece	23	Nigeria	5
Hungary	27	Peru	18
Iceland	24	Philippines	12
Ireland	23	Russia	18
Israel	18	South Africa	14
Italy	22	Thailand	7
Japan	8	Ukraine	20
Korea	10	Venezuela	12
Luxembourg	17	Vietnam	10
Mexico	16		
Netherlands	21		
New Zealand	15		
Norway	25		
Poland	23		
Portugal	23		
Slovak Republic	20		
Slovenia	22		
Spain	21		
Sweden	25		
Switzerland	8		
Turkey	18		
United Kingdom	20		
United States	none		

SOURCE: EY 2015 Worldwide VAT, GST, and Sales Tax Guide.

was £82,000; any business with annual gross receipts (turnover) below that sum need not register as a VAT collector. That relieves them of VAT compliance responsibilities and reduces administration cost for Her Majesty's Customs and Revenue, the United Kingdom's VAT collectors. Of course, that business would not be able to get VAT it paid on business input purchases refunded. Because this threshold is relatively high, the United Kingdom permits businesses to voluntarily register as

VAT collectors. Many do register because they do not want to become taxpayers. The country loses revenue from the value added by these smaller firms, but reduced compliance and administrative costs are seen as making it a worthwhile loss.[74]

Value-Added Tax versus Retail Sales Tax

The VAT is undoubtedly the global choice for general consumption taxation. Why might a VAT be more desirable than an RST?[75] First, the VAT might help if tax evasion and a lack of vendor cooperation are problems. The VAT induces purchasers to require a documented receipt for vendors for taxes paid because the tax payments shown on those receipts are used to pay part of the taxes the purchasers will owe when they make sales. The VAT does not administer itself, but it certainly encourages a good trail of invoices for audits. (The reports on those invoices tend to be truthful because the buyer has an incentive to overstate the purchase price while the seller has an incentive to understate the purchase price to minimize the value-added in the transaction, and the two incentives cancel out to produce the truth.) The tax authorities have to make sure that VAT collections actually end up in the treasury and that VAT payments claimed as credits are not fraudulent. The RST, on the other hand, puts all its collection eggs in one basket: if the retailer cheats, all revenue is lost.[76] Nevertheless, European experience shows that businesses still cheat—for instance, by claiming credit for VAT not actually paid or for running off with the collections—and that businesses are still delinquent in payment, so the tax authorities continue to have a job to do.[77] However, VATs with high statutory rates have been successfully collected in countries with historically bad compliance environments. Most observers agree that traditional RSTs cannot be successfully administered at statutory rates much higher than 10 percent. If a government intends to levy high statutory rates, for instance, in an effort to replace national income taxes, experience teaches that the VAT is the only feasible choice. However, where compliance analyses have been done, noncompliance is higher for VAT than for RST.

Second, countries are able to remove VAT from international trade and competitiveness considerations. Indeed, this was the primary reason the European Union selected the VAT as the indirect tax of choice for its members. The chain of tax

---

[74]Charities usually must pay VAT when they make purchases, but seldom have a mechanism for having their payments refunded. One of the few exceptions: Canada does provide a rebate of half the goods and services tax that charities pay.

[75]For a more extensive comparison of the RST and VAT, see John L. Mikesell, "Is the Retail Sales Tax Really Inferior to the Value-Added Tax?" in *The Sales Tax in the 21st Century*, ed. W. Fox and M. Murray (Westport, Conn.: Greenwood Press, 1997), 75–87, and John L. Mikesell, "Misconceptions about Value-Added and Retail Sales Taxes: Are They Barriers to Sensible Tax Policy," *Public Budgeting & Finance* 34 (Summer 2014): 1–23.

[76]Furthermore, the RST puts the burden of judging whether the tax should be suspended or collected on the vendor. However, the vendor is almost certainly keenly interested in making a sale and could be willing to sacrifice revenue rightfully owed the state, by failing to deny a doubtful suspension certificate, in order to make the sale. The VAT requires payment of tax, which may be recovered by a business making a successful claim to the revenue department.

[77]Henry J. Aaron, ed., *The Value-Added Tax, Lessons from Europe* (Washington, D.C.: Brookings Institution, 1981).

documentation produced by the VAT makes this extraction simple: the exporter requests a refund of VAT paid at the time inventory is exported, and the importer must pay VAT at the time inventory enters the country. That levels the tax comparison between foreign and domestic products within the country and removes the VAT from prices of goods the country is selling on world markets. This sort of adjustment is not possible with other general taxes.[78] Under the rules of the World Trade Organization, only an indirect tax like the VAT can be adjusted at borders in this fashion. There is no way to remove RST embedded when pre-retail purchases are taxed from export prices, so there is an international competitive problem. A VAT levied at the subnational level would have issues regarding the administration of cross-border credits or rebates, although they could be handled in one way or another (Brazil illustrates how subnational VATs could function, but their operation does involve border checks that somewhat interfere with free trade.) Subnational RSTs are clearly quite feasible; this may be the best level of government to levy such taxes.

Third, the VAT comes closer to being a general consumption tax than does the RST. The VAT provides more complete exclusion of business purchases than does the RST because the credit-refund device politically seems less like a special break for business than does the exemption certificate, and the VAT achieves more general coverage of services purchased by households. The typical RSTs are both too narrow (exempting many household purchases of goods and excluding almost all household purchases of services) and too broad (taxing many business purchases of inputs). Legislatures simply seem unable to accept the idea that exemption of business purchases represents the proper design of the tax base, not an unfair tax advantage to business. Or maybe they just want to delude the public into believing that such a tax paid by businesses will relieve households of tax burden. Legislatures, at least those outside the United States, seem more accepting of the VAT idea of having businesses pay on purchases, but get a refund on their sales, thus permitting the VAT to more closely work as a general consumption tax. Therefore, at higher statutory rates, the VAT is substantially less likely to do damage to economic development prospects and infrastructure investment than is the RST.

Both taxes are typically collected on a transaction basis from businesses and almost certainly the tax is reflected in prices paid by purchasers. The evidence suggests that the compliance gap (the extent to which tax owed is not paid) is somewhat higher for VATs than for RSTs. However, it is not known whether that difference is the result of higher statutory rates typically levied for VATs or the result of something endemic about how VATs are collected.[79]

---

[78]Some suspect that flexible exchange rates may eliminate any impact of the VAT on international trade patterns.
[79]Mikesell, op. cit., 18. Greece has a high VAT rate (23 percent) and high tax evasion (uncollected taxes were estimated to be as much as 15 percent of GDP). Part of the problem is businesses conducting their operations outside their accounting systems through unrecorded cash transactions. In an effort to combat the problem and bring all transactions into the formal structure, a government regulation in 2012 gave customers the right to refuse payment any time they were not given a receipt for their purchase. Indeed, restaurants, widely regarded as major non-VAT collectors, were required to print such a notice on their menu. One guesses that this gave restaurants interested in working off the books an incentive to hire rather large individuals to present bills to customers.

Conclusion

Taxes on goods and services are at the heart of state revenue systems, are an important contributor to local revenue systems, but are relatively unimportant for U.S. federal finance. They are vitally important for finance of other national governments. Though questions of structure persist for each base, there is no doubt concerning the serviceability of these taxes. The case for general sales taxes is much stronger than it is for the selective excises as a general revenue source. Excises are particularly useful when the tax has nonrevenue objectives. The key problem with consumption taxation remains regressivity; no perfect solution exists. VATs and RSTs provide two alternative formats for collecting a tax on general consumption. Although the RST provides an important foundation for state and local revenue systems in the United States, it has significant adverse equity and economic effects. VATs provide an alternative with better economic performance, and these taxes are widely used throughout the world as the mechanism of choice for national general consumption taxation.

QUESTIONS AND EXERCISES

1. Identify the important elements of sales taxation in your state. What governments levy general and selective sales taxes? Identify the following for the RST: What commodity sales are exempt? Are services taxed? What is the nominal rate? Does your state provide sales tax credits/rebates through its income tax? In regard to selective excises: What selective excises are used? Are they ad valorem or specific? What rates apply?

2. It has been proposed that the Foundation for Preservation of the American Badger (*taxidea taxus*) be provided a sales tax exemption for its purchases and for its annual sales of "Badger Booster" cookies. Please analyze according to the general principles of tax policy.

3. The Bureau of Labor Statistics' Consumer Expenditure Survey: 2007 gives the following data:

Income Category of Family	Average Income before Taxes ($)	Alcoholic Beverage Expenditures ($)	Tobacco Products Expenditures ($)
First quintile	10,531	176	259
Second quintile	27,674	272	337
Third quintile	46,213	413	381
Fourth quintile	72,460	506	371
Highest quintile	158,388	917	268

Analyze the likely vertical equity of selective excises on alcoholic beverages and tobacco products.

4. The text worked the logic of a VAT through a production-distribution process from a farmer to the final customer. Work the same process through with a 10 percent turnover or gross receipts tax. Assume that value added at each stage is the same as before, but that no credit for prior tax paid is provided and that each sales price equals tax-inclusive cost of purchases, plus value added at that stage, plus the 10 percent tax. Compute the final price paid by the consumer and the effective tax rate as a percentage of total value added. Make the same computation, assuming the sweater manufacturer and the retailer merge (i.e., there is no taxable sale in this exchange).

5. Vendors at Municipal Stadium sell their wares at prices that include the city, state, and transit district sales taxes; the total of these taxes is 8.25 percent when added to prices that do not include the sales tax.

   a. Convert this 8.25 percent tax-exclusive sales tax rate into its tax-inclusive equivalent rate. (*Hint:* Use the method outlined for VAT calculations.)
   b. A vendor has receipts (including sales tax) at a game of $15,325. What sales tax must the vendor remit to the tax authorities?

6. Several states have declared sales tax holidays, in which the state does not collect sales tax on certain items for a short period of time. In most instances, the holiday has been for clothing, and the period has been a week or ten days in August, the idea being to give a "back-to-school" discount as families get ready for the new school year. However, states have gotten more adventurous with the idea in recent years and have enacted or proposed holidays for hurricane survival supplies, gasoline, Energy Star appliances, and guns and ammunition. Analyze the idea of such holidays according to yield, equity, administration and compliance, and economic impact.

7. When the Russian Federation allowed its regions to levy a retail sales tax, the national value-added tax rate was 20 percent. Many regions levied a 5 percent tax rate, and the rate applied to purchase prices with the national value-added tax included. What is your view about this approach? (This approach has also been used for some Canadian provincial retail sales taxes.)

CASES FOR DISCUSSION

CASE 10–1

Girl Scout Cookies and the Snack Tax

State sales taxes often exempt food purchased for at-home consumption to help relieve regressivity. However, that exemption causes substantial loss of revenue. Furthermore, some people question the nutritional value of certain items exempted under the food label and doubt the wisdom of losing revenue in a tax structure to provide relief to such purchases. In difficult fiscal times in the early 1990s, a few states sought additional revenue by narrowing the food exemption, particularly by removing some of these questionable categories from the exempt list. These new laws and their enforcement have produced policy problems testing the resolve of the legislators and tax administrators.

In the 1991 legislative session, Maine passed a package of tax changes designed to increase revenues by $300 million annually. (Total tax collections in fiscal 1990 were $1,560.9 million.) The changes included higher income taxes, an increase in the state sales and use tax rate from 5 to 6 percent, and a revision to remove snack food from the "sales of grocery staples" category, which was then exempt from the state sales and use tax. The new law was estimated to yield $10 million annually.

The new law taxed snack food, as defined by the legislature:

> 14-C. "Snack food." Snack food means any item that is ordinarily sold for consumption without further preparation or that requires no preparation other than combining the item with a liquid; that may be stored unopened without refrigeration, except that ice cream, ice milk, frozen yogurt and sherbet are snack foods; that is not generally considered a major component of a well-balanced meal; and that is not defined in this section as a grocery staple. "Snack food" includes, but is not limited to, corn chips, potato chips, processed fruit snacks, fruit rolls, fruit bars, popped popcorn, pork rinds, pretzels, cheese sticks and cheese puffs, granola bars, breakfast bars, bread sticks, roasted nuts, doughnuts, cookies, crackers, pastries, toaster pastries, croissants, cakes, pies, ice cream cones, marshmallows, marshmallow creme, artificially flavored powdered or liquid drink mixes or drinks, ice cream sauces including chocolate sauce, ready-to-eat puddings, beef jerky, meat bars and dips. (36 Maine Revised Statutes 1752 [1992].)

The lawmakers soon discovered that the expansion of the sales and use tax base had some unexpected consequences, particularly with regard to the finances of Girl Scouts. Two councils, the Abnaki and Kennebec, served about 19,500 girls in Maine, and 60 to 65 percent of their revenues came from cookie sales. Because neither council was qualified to purchase inventory for resale as a registered retailer, and then charge sales tax on each transaction, the councils now had to pay tax on their cookie purchases. That amounted to around $58,000, or almost 2 percent of cookie revenue (they paid tax on the wholesale price of about 80 cents per box).

The two councils responded differently to the new tax. Abnaki raised its cookie prices from $2.25 to $2.50, but sales fell 7 percent from the prior year. Kennebec lacked sufficient time to react, so it had to absorb about $40,000 in cookie losses. However, neither council thought the new tax was fair. Jo Stevens, executive director of the Abnaki Council, voiced the general view: "We're not selling groceries. We're raising charitable contributions." Of course, the problem for sales tax policy was, indeed, because they weren't selling groceries.

The Joint Taxation Committee was generally sympathetic. Its co-chair, Senator Stephen Bost, said, "We had not intended as a committee to include . . . Girl Scouts in the snack tax." However, proposed legislation to exempt Girl Scouts and related organizations (including the pre-popped popcorn sold by Boy Scouts) would cause a revenue loss of around $175,000 annually, and the state had no clear way to make it up. (Incidentally, candy had been taxed for some time, but candy sales by school groups and parent-teacher organizations are exempt.)

What should Maine do? Here are some options: (1) do nothing—the tax is working as it should; (2) direct the Bureau of Taxation to rewrite the instruction; (3) repeal the snack tax; (4) exempt sales and purchases by the Girl Scouts and similar organizations; (5) require the Girl Scouts to register as retail merchants, buy their cookies using the resale exemption, and collect sales tax on their cookie sales; and (6) exempt sales and/or purchases by all youth or charitable organizations. (You may think of other possibilities.) Use the standards for revenue policy evaluation (yield, fairness, economic effect, and collectability) to test options and provide a recommendation. Explain which approach is most consistent with the logic of sales taxation. Which parties would have an interest in the eventual outcome of the discussion? What is your overall view of the snack tax, without respect to the Girl Scout issue?[80]

CASE 10–2

Pringles and Preferences from the Value-Added Tax Base?

Legislators put many preferences in tax laws with many different objectives in mind: to alter the distribution of tax burden for reasons of equity and to favor certain producers or consumers, to name two. Effects may sometimes be clear-cut, but there may be surprises in their application. There are interesting effects in the conflict between the UK tax authorities and Procter & Gamble UK, the producers of Pringles, as the following describes.

Consider These Questions

1. Explain why Procter & Gamble wanted zero rating and not exemption.

2. Why would the VAT legislation not have explicitly covered Pringles?

3. Tax analysts counsel against tax preferences. How does this case provide support for that position?

4. What are the reasons for the food preference, and what are the reasons for the special treatment of potato crisps? Are there better alternatives for achieving those objectives?

5. Are there lessons for design of a consumption tax in this case?

SOURCE: Data and quotations from "Scouting and Tax Relief," *State Government News* 35 (April 1992): 33.

---

[80]Girl Scout cookies may be a "third rail" for sales tax policy. House Bill 385 in the 2011 Georgia legislature would have, among many other things, applied the state sales tax to Girl Scout cookie sales (along with Boy Scout popcorn sales). The proposal got buried under an avalanche of calls, letters, and lobbying.

The VAT and Pringles

"Are Pringles 'similar to potato crisps and made from the potato'? That is the question."[81] Not as weighty as Hamlet's musing, but that is how Lord Justice Jacob (England and Wales Court of Appeal) began his judgment in a case between the Commissioners for Her Majesty's Revenue and Customs and Procter & Gamble UK, the makers of Regular Pringles. And that is what ultimately determined the decision regarding a tax preference in the United Kingdom value-added tax.

Creating a tax preference is always a tricky business because the tax authorities have to draw a line between what gets preference and what doesn't, and, accordingly, some people end up paying relatively more and others pay relatively less because of where the line is drawn. The principles in the law have to be put into practice in a world of brands, product distinctions, and a consistent desire to reduce tax burdens. The trickiness gets more challenging as activities initially on the wrong side of the preference work to get moved to the other side. That is how, after all, that many tax lawyers and accountants justify their pay. Although the maneuvering occurs with every preference, it gets more frantic when the tax wedge is high, when the tax involves excises (a narrow base), and when substitute alternatives for taxed items are easily available.

The UK value-added tax is levied at a standard rate of 17.5 percent. However, the law makes special provision for sales of food for at-home consumption in an effort to reduce the regressivity. In the UK VAT, "Food of a kind used for human consumption" is zero-rated, meaning it is subject to a tax rate of zero.

However, the tax preference is limited and not applicable to everything that humans might eat. An exception is the following:

> Any of the following when packaged for human consumption without further preparation, namely, potato crisps, potato sticks, potato puffs and similar products from the potato, or from potato flour, or from potato starch, and savoury products obtained by the swelling of cereals or cereal products; and salted or roasted nuts other than nuts in shell.

Those products are subject to the standard tax rate of 17.5 percent. Now the question is: What are Pringles? Many people have pondered this question in the United States as well as in the United Kingdom, although not in court and not with regard to their taxation, since their arrival on the market in 1968. However, such philosophical questions were not what the Procter & Gamble representatives were concerned about here; it was tax rates. Procter & Gamble argued that Pringles should be taxed at zero rate, not the standard rate, because they really are not potato crisps.[82] Their argument primarily hinged on the fact that the Pringle is only around 40 percent potato and the majority was something else, although no other single ingredient made up as much of the total as potato. Therefore, they argued that it wasn't a *potato* crisp and should be zero rated along with other items for human

---

[81]*Revenue & Customs v. Procter & Gamble UK* (2009) EWCA Civ 407 (May 20, 2009). In the UK, a "crisp" is what Americans call a "potato chip." A "chip" in the UK is what we call a "french fry."
[82]It should be noted that another Procter & Gamble product, Pringles Dippers, had been judged to be zero-rated, apparently because they were to be dipped in salsa or whatever, like tortilla chips, and were not fully prepared for immediate human consumption.

consumption. Strictly, Pringles were not "made of" potatoes. That would allow consumers of Pringles to pay less and would also allow Pringles a price advantage in the snack food market (although Procter & Gamble did not point that out in their argument). It should be noted, however, that there are other vegetable crisps available on the UK market (e.g., turnip crisps), and they were not excluded from the preference.

The judge was not impressed: "the VAT legislation uses everyday English words, which ought to be interpreted in a sensible way according to their ordinary and natural meaning. The 'made from' question would probably be answered in a more relevant and sensible way by a child consumer of crisps than by a food scientist or a culinary pedant."[83]

The ruling meant around $155 million in back taxes (which had not been collected from purchasers because of an earlier ruling) and much more to be collected in the future. If it crunches like a potato crisp, looks generally like a potato crisp, and pretty much tastes like a potato crisp, it should be treated like a potato crisp, no matter what the lawyers make their living by arguing. Child consumer trumps food experts.[84]

CASE 10–3

A Simple Tax? Gross Receipts Tax Problems

A gross receipts or turnover tax appears simple. The tax applies to the gross receipts of every market transaction, usually without any deductions or exemptions and without any structural provision to accommodate the seller to add tax to the sales transaction. Along with that apparent simplicity, supporters praise its broad base, ability to generate considerable revenue at a low statutory rate, stability of revenue, and apparent fairness from having one rate apply to all.

The taxes have a long history, dating to the thirteenth century in Europe and the mid-nineteenth century in the United States. They were the tax that the Nazis installed in countries they intended to annex and continued in importance in Europe until they were gradually replaced by value-added taxes. Several states, including West Virginia, Mississippi, Georgia, Indiana, Delaware, and Washington, adopted them as desperation revenue measures in the Great Depression to support collapsed state finances. All but Delaware and Washington replaced the taxes with sources that had more sensible burden distributions and fewer dislocating impacts, and only the latter collects a sizable share of state revenue from the tax. However, in recent years, there has been a resurgence in interest in the tax, with adoptions in Ohio, Nevada, and Texas and proposal for adoption in Oregon. At least in the minds of some lawmakers, the gross receipts tax is the next new thing even though it is, in fact, an old thing with few reasons for it to be brought back.[85]

---

[83]*Revenue & Customs,* op. cit.

[84]An older VAT case involved Jaffa Cakes: if cakes, then food and not taxed; if biscuits (cookies), then subject to the standard rate. The court decided on the basis of what they do when they go stale: cookies go soft and cakes go hard. Jaffa Cakes go hard. (I am not making this up.) And if you are more interested in peanuts than cakes, biscuits, or crisps, how about this: peanuts in the UK are zero-rated if they are in the shell or out of the shell but not roasted or salted. Other nuts are zero-rated unless they are roasted, salted, and deshelled. Surely the United States should adopt a value-added tax if only for the entertaining legal arguments the tax would bring.

The selection that follows gives the viewpoint of the Washington tax from a tax practitioner who deals with the tax on a daily basis.

Consider These Questions

1. Why might a state choose a gross receipts tax as an addition to its revenue system?

2. Explain the political and economic logic behind the tax.

3. The Washington tax starts simple but the rate classification becomes complex. Why?

View from the Other Washington[86]

Washington's business and occupation (B&O) tax system is a lot like Mount Rainier: Both have a dominating size and a pyramidal structure . . . [T]he B&O tax accounts for about 17 percent of Washington's total tax revenue, a greater proportion than most states' corporate net income taxes. Washington also relies heavily on sales and use taxes, which account for nearly half of state tax revenue.

But back to my analogy. Mount Rainier's pyramidal shape is mirrored in the pyramiding structure of gross receipts taxes generally and Washington's B&O tax specifically. Unlike the sales tax, which is imposed only once upon the sale to the final consumer or end-user, the B&O tax is imposed on goods and services at each transaction in the production cycle and supply chain—thus the commonly used description of tax pyramiding.

Using timber products, one of Washington's major natural resources, as an example, B&O tax is imposed on a logger's activity of cutting down marketable timber. B&O tax is also imposed on the person who de-limbs and debarks the felled timber to prepare it for transportation to the lumber mill. The tax is then imposed on the lumber mill that cuts the timber into lumber, and another B&O tax is applied on the person who manufactures plywood from the byproducts of milled lumber. But it doesn't stop there. Additional B&O taxes apply to both the wholesale price of the plywood to a distributer and then to retail sales of the finished product by the retail store. And the more distributors in the supply chain, the more times a B&O tax is imposed.

Consequently, although the nominal tax rates may be relatively low compared with net income tax rates, the repeated imposition of tax at each level makes the effective tax rate much higher than the nominal rate. Moreover, the amount of pyramiding varies widely from industry to industry. A 2002 study of Washington's tax system found that across all industries, the tax on average pyramids about 2.5 times, with service industries experiencing a relatively low level of pyramiding (about 1.5 times), while in some manufacturing industries "the rate of pyramiding is over five or six times."

Economists criticize the pyramiding nature of broad-based gross receipts taxes because it encourages vertical integration. While successive activities in the

---

[85]John L. Mikesell, "Gross Receipts Taxes in State Government Finances: A Review of Their History and Performance," Tax Foundation–Council on State Taxation Background Paper, Number 53, January 2007 presents a review of the taxes in state revenue systems.
[86]The selection is from Scott M. Edwards, "View from the Other Washington," *State Tax Notes*, December 7, 2015. Footnotes in the original are omitted.

production/distribution stream are each taxable when performed by separate entities, each paying B&O tax on its gross income from its particular activity, when a single entity performs all those activities in-house those intermediate transactions disappear and the vertically integrated company only experiences one layer of gross income. It should not be surprising that an old-line Washington company like Weyerhaeuser grew into a vertically integrated business that owned timber, logged it, and manufactured the wood, pulp, and paper products derived from its timber. Consolidating those activities within a single company was a rational approach to reducing the impact of the pyramiding structure of the B&O tax.

The 2002 study identified the pyramidal structure of the B&O tax as a primary driver of nonneutrality in Washington's tax system. A special report from the Tax Foundation on the pyramiding effect of gross receipts taxes noted that over time, legislative efforts to alleviate the pyramiding effect of gross receipts taxes led to more complexity.

Washington's B&O tax is a good case study. When first enacted [1933], Washington's B&O tax had the single uniform rate of 0.25 percent. That single rate was likely adopted to avoid the uniformity clause challenge the graduated state income tax faced at the time. However, when the B&O tax was challenged, the state supreme court held that it was an excise tax, not a property tax, and therefore was not subject to uniformity clause limitations.

Today there are more than 40 B&O tax classifications, with rates ranging from 0.138 percent (applicable to such diverse activities as "processing perishable meat products" and "warehousing and reselling prescription drugs") to 3.3 percent (for disposing of "low level nuclear waste"). The major classifications are retailing, at 0.471 percent; wholesaling and manufacturing, at 0.484 percent; and the catchall "service and other activities," at 1.5 percent. No doubt some of the lower tax rates adopted for some classifications (pejoratively referred to as tax preferences) are an attempt to mitigate the structural pyramiding problem inherent in a general gross receipt tax like the B&O tax.

Another adverse impact of the pyramiding nature of gross receipts taxes identified in the Tax Foundation report is discrimination against domestic production. Goods produced in states without a gross receipts tax enjoy a cost advantage because they are not burdened with the tax, while locally produced goods are subject to tax on their manufacturing activity, putting their products at a cost disadvantage to products produced elsewhere—an increasing disadvantage to Washington manufacturers, as technology and transportation improvements create an increasingly global marketplace.

Not surprisingly, when Boeing considered where to build its next-generation airplanes, the Legislature realized that in order to make Washington a viable option for such desirable business activity, it needed to create a B&O classification applicable to such activity and establish a lower tax rate than the 0.484 percent imposed on general manufacturing. The aerospace industry has long been a source of good jobs and economic vitality for Washington, with the Space Needle a daily visual reminder of the optimism for the future that thriving industry and technology can provide for the state. One hopes the Legislature will continue to recognize the need to monitor and revise the B&O tax system to counter the adverse effects of its pyramidal nature to strong economic performance and good jobs.

CHAPTER 11

Major Tax Structures: Property Taxes

Chapter Contents

Annual taxes on property in the United States yield more than $440 billion each year for state and local governments. That considerable yield is substantially less than the total from either income or consumption bases, and much less than states collect from those bases, but the tax on real property—roughly 90 percent of the property tax total—is the lifeblood for fiscal independence of local governments. As Glenn Fisher points out: "There are no taxes capable of financing our current system of local governments that can be locally levied and administered, except the property tax."[1] Tax experts argue the case for local property taxes because of their efficiency, equity, facilitation of fiscal decentralization, and transparency, but they are unpopular with the electorate and with enlightened and craven politicians alike. They endure because they produce reliable, stable, independent revenue for the governments closest to the people, and there is no better alternative for providing local fiscal autonomy. Property taxes of various designs are levied throughout the world, although governments in the United States and Canada raise relatively more of their tax revenue from them than is the case elsewhere. Because of their utility for providing a source of revenue subject to local control, they are an important element

---

[1]Glenn W. Fisher, *The Worst Tax? A History of the Property Tax in America* (Lawrence, Kans.: University Press of Kansas, 1996), 210. Contrary to the title, Fisher does not believe that the property tax is the worst tax.

in fiscal decentralization programs in many countries of Central and Eastern Europe and in China.[2]

Property taxes were once the primary tax for both state and local government finance. Indeed, in 1932, property taxes produced almost three-quarters of all state and local tax revenue and 92.5 percent of local government tax revenue.[3] But in the depths of the Great Depression, much property tax could not be collected from farmers, businesses, and individuals who had lost their usual sources of income, and states began to develop transaction-based taxes on goods and services, especially retail sales taxes and motor-fuel excises. These new taxes offered high yield and greater reliability in those difficult times, not to mention their less harsh enforcement mechanisms (enforcement of uncollected property tax on a house or farm, for example, meant seizure and sale of that property). State governments, especially, financed their post–World War II responsibilities with more non-property tax revenues. Local governments overall continue a heavy reliance on the property tax, although large cities in some states make significant use of other options. Even during the recent Great Recession, local property tax revenue held up better than did collections from other broad-based local taxes (retail sales and income, in particular). Those local governments that had not diversified away from the property tax suffered a less severe revenue collapse, and property tax reliance preserved local revenues better than did the more diversified state revenue systems.

Table 11–1 offers an overview of property tax reliance in the United States. Although states obtain less than 2 percent of their tax revenue from these levies, local governments collect more than 70 percent of their tax revenue from it. Independent school districts rely more heavily on the property tax than does any other type of government, raising over 95 percent of their tax revenue from that source. Because schools receive substantial intergovernmental aid, mostly from their states, the share of their total revenue from the property tax is much lower (around 35 percent), but they still receive more than 40 percent of all property tax collected. Cities and counties both receive more than 20 percent of property taxes, but cities rely somewhat less heavily on property taxes than do counties. Despite the continuing unpopularity of the property tax, property tax collections have grown at a compound rate of 5 percent annually from 1999-2000 to 2011-2012, a period when the rate of inflation was only around 2 percent.[4]

---

[2]The best source on how property taxes are structured and administered and why they make sense for finance of local government is Joan Youngman, *A Good Tax, Legal and Policy Issues for the Property Tax in the United States* (Cambridge, Massachusetts: Lincoln Institute For Land Policy, 2016).

[3]U.S. Bureau of the Census, *Financial Statistics of State and Local Governments: 1932 (Wealth, Public Debt, and Taxation)* (Washington, D.C.: U.S. Government Printing Office, 1935). The federal government has levied property taxes twice, in 1798 and in 1813. The taxes were apportioned among the states, as required for direct taxes by the U.S. Constitution. See Dall W. Forsythe, *Taxation and Political Change in the Young Nation, 1781–1833* (New York: Columbia University Press, 1977).

[4]Private groups also levy property taxes. Every state but Wyoming has "business improvement districts," areas in which property owners have agreed to levy a tax on themselves to provide certain services (beautification, security, marketing, etc.) within the area. A good source on these BID taxes is Lindsay Kuhn, Sarah Larson, Carolyn Bourdeaux, "Georgia's Community Improvement Districts (CIDs)," Center for State and Local Finance, Andrew Young School, Georgia State University, June 24, 2016. Logically they represent participatory budgeting done right.

Table 11–1

Property Taxes in U.S. Government Finances, 2012

	Total ($ Thousands)	% of General Revenue	% of Tax Revenue	Share of Total Property Tax Revenue
State and Local Governments	446,120,120	17.2%	32.1%	100.0%
State Governments	13,110,672	0.8%	1.6%	2.9%
Local Governments	433,009,448	29.7%	73.5%	97.1%
County Governments	103,839,231	27.9%	71.9%	23.3%
Municipal Governments	102,175,406	23.9%	51.7%	22.9%
Township Governments	28,894,412	60.1%	92.2%	6.5%
Special Districts	18,561,041	11.7%	66.9%	4.2%
School Districts	180,539,358	36.6%	95.6%	40.5%

SOURCE: U.S. Bureau of Census, Governments Division, Annual Survey of Finances of State and Local Governments. www.census.gov

Property taxes are the closest approximation to annual wealth taxes currently levied in the United States.[5] They are not, however, true net-wealth taxes because they typically exclude some types of wealth (e.g., personal property owned by individuals); they apply to gross, not net, wealth (e.g., the debt against a house or car is seldom completely subtracted from taxable value); and they may apply twice to certain wealth (some states tax the value of both corporate stock and properties owned by the corporation). Because they apply to accumulated wealth, not income, they may also have less effect on work and investment incentives than do income taxes. They are not based, however, on current transactions (as is usually the case

---

[5]There are federal, state, and local transfer taxes, however. The federal estate tax is the most widely known, although it produces only modest revenue (1.5 percent of total receipts in 2008). In spite of the fact that it is paid by very few estates (fewer than 1.3 percent of estates are covered by the tax because of large exclusions before the tax begins to apply) and is highly progressive in burden, it is extremely unpopular. Because much of the money taxed by the estate tax represents unrealized capital gains that have not been taxed by the income tax, the tax fills a gap in the fiscal system and does not represent a double tax on income. Nevertheless, a small group of holders of great inherited wealth stand a good chance of getting the tax entirely abolished. See Michael J. Graetz and Ian Shapiro, *Death by a Thousand Cuts: The Fight over Taxing Inherited Wealth* (Princeton, N.J.: Princeton University Press, 2005), for the drama and for how the wealthy few convinced people who have absolutely no chance, barring a huge lottery win, of ever owing any estate tax that the tax would keep them from passing their wealth, bank accounts, farms, businesses, and collections of baseball cards to their children. A number of states and many localities levy real estate transfer taxes, levied when a parcel exchange is recorded and applied against the value of the parcel being transferred. Amounts collected constitute only a modest component of total tax revenue and that revenue is extremely volatile. These taxes are discussed in Patricia Atkins, Catherine Collins, and Lisa Lowry, "Real Estate Transfer Taxes: Widely Used, Little Conformity," *State Tax Notes*, October 19, 2015, 235-45. Of course, things get strange in some places. New York state levies a 1 percent transfer tax on properties exchanging for $1 million or more (formerly a "mansion tax," but not so much anymore at New York prices), not on the amount above $1 million but on the entire amount. That means that an increase in transfer price from $999,999 to $1 million would change the tax paid from zero to $10,000, an increase that surely creates some interesting manipulations.

for income and sales taxes), so the tax requires a value-estimation procedure (assessment). That procedure is the primary weakness of property taxation and is discussed later in this chapter.[6]

Property taxes cannot be simply summarized. As Richard Almy observes,

> In the United States, "the" property tax is composed of fifty-one separate state level property tax systems, each subject to numerous legal and extralegal local variations and each changing in some fashion over time—through constitutional revision, enactment of statutes and ordinances, changes in administrative procedures, court decisions and changes in the capabilities of tax administration.[7]

Property within the scope of taxation may be either real or personal. *Real property* means real estate, realty, or land and improvements on that land.[8] It encompasses soil and things permanently fixed to it by nature (trees, crops, grass, water, minerals, etc.) or by people (buildings, fences, etc.). Real property may also include air rights, the space above that land, but only when that space is actually used. *Personal property* includes everything that can be owned that is not real property. The category includes machinery and equipment, jewelry, automobiles and other rolling stock, inventory, household furnishings, stocks and bonds, and much more. Personal property generally is more easily moved than real property, but there is no general dividing line between the types. Each government develops its own definitions and distinctions, usually resorting to lists of property types to make borderline distinctions.[9] The distinction is crucial because some governments tax personal property more heavily than real property, whereas others exempt certain personal property. The personal property share of the locally taxable property base in national totals is small, only around 10 percent, but it is much higher in a handful of states and in some cities.[10] The biggest share of taxable personal property when it is taxed is business capital equipment and machinery and, in cities in which that property is taxed, this property can be one-third or more of the total tax base. In most states, real property is assessed by local assessors, subject to state rules and regulations and some supervision and evaluation of the work that has been done. Personal property is normally self-reported.

---

[6]The tax may have development and redevelopment disincentives as well, depending on its structure.

[7]Richard Almy, "Rationalizing the Assessment Process," in *Property Tax Reform,* ed. George Peterson (Washington, D.C.: Urban Institute, 1973), 175.

[8]Property taxes have a long history internationally, and trying to get property tax bills to be logically related to property values has always been a challenge. An early tax in England was the window tax (1696–1851), a levy that was based on the number of windows in the residence. It replaced a similar hearth tax, a more difficult to administer tax because it required entry into the building. Windows were important as a source of light (no electricity) and ventilation, but it was expensive to put in a window so properties with more windows certainly were of greater value. Therefore, more windows brought a higher tax bill. Of course, property owners responded by bricking up windows to avoid the tax, and new houses were built to minimize the number of windows. Wallace E. Oates and Robert M. Schwab, "The Window Tax: A Case Study in Excess Burden," *Journal of Economic Perspectives* 29 (Winter 2015): 163–80.

[9] Are mobile homes real or personal property? States use rules including permanency of foundation, presence of wheels or axles, highway licensing, and so forth, but there is no general division.

[10]John L. Mikesell, "Patterns of Exclusion of Personal Property from American Property Tax Systems," *Public Finance Quarterly* 20 (October 1992): 528–42.

Another distinction is between tangible and intangible personal property. *Tangible personal property* is property held for its own sake, including cars, machinery, inventories of raw materials and finished products, and household items. *Intangible personal property* is property valued because it represents an ownership claim on something of value, like stocks, bonds, and other financial assets. Property taxes vary widely in the extent to which they apply to these properties. Many types of tangible personal property are both difficult to locate and, once located, difficult to value (what is the value of a ten-year-old television set or the old sofa where the cat sleeps, after all?); intangible personal property can often be easily valued, but may be difficult to locate. Intangible property is sometimes exempt by law and sometimes exempt by local practice. Seldom is taxation complete.[11]

The conventional real property tax is a levy on the property parcel, including both the land and structures built on that land. An alternative to the conventional property tax is the land or site value tax. It has many advantages over the traditional property tax and has been advocated by many reform advocates over the years, particularly those interested in improved land use and urban development, but it has never gained many adoptions in the United States. Sidebar 11–1 describes the logic and advantages of the tax.

Sidebar 11–1
An Alternate Approach: Land or Site Value Taxes

Even more than they like property taxes as a means of financing local governments, tax analysts, particularly economists, like a particular variant of the property tax—the land tax. Noble laureate economist William Vickery summed it up: "The property tax is, economically speaking, a combination of one of the worst taxes—the part that is assessed on real estate improvement . . . and one of the best taxes—the tax on land or site value. . . . A tax on land, properly assessed . . . is virtually free of distortionary effects . . . while the tax on improvements imposes serious burdens on construction."[1]

Why is that? The answer lies in the power of taxes to discourage and distort. A property tax on improvements adds to the cost of new development, and that discourages the development activity. Additions to the built infrastructure contribute to the standard of living—so why on earth would it be good policy to tax in a way that discourages development and renewal of that infrastructure? If the property owner upgrades or restores a building or builds a new structure on the site, the owner's property tax bill increases, thereby reducing the return on the activity and, at the margin, reducing the likelihood that development will occur. Does discouraging economic development make sense? That is what a conventional property tax does.

---

[11]John H. Bowman, George E. Hoffer, and Michael D. Pratt, "Current Patterns and Trends in State and Local Intangibles Taxation," *National Tax Journal* 43 (December 1990): 439–50.

**Sidebar 11–1
(continued)**

A property tax on land does not have that impact. Land at a particular site is in fixed supply. Applying a tax to the land value does not have an impact on the supply of land, given that it is fixed. Amounts supplied are not increased when return is higher, and amounts supplied are not reduced when return is lower. Indeed, a tax on land value makes sense because the value of that land is determined by the community that surrounds it—the transportation network, the amenities, the utilities, the government services, and so on—and not the efforts of the owner of that land. The tax on land does not influence investment choices in the way that a tax on improvements on that land does and, hence, does not discourage economic development. If the land is taxed according to its market value, its value in the best possible use, then what the landowner does with the land has no impact on the tax bill. Letting the land stand idle and generating no income will not reduce the tax bill, so there is no savings from leaving land fallow. (Conventional property taxes that capitalize income flows to estimate value can support keeping productive land idle.) There is no support for engaging in land speculation or delaying the development of land for strategic gain with a site value tax. The pure land tax is the rarest of revenue sources: one that has no adverse economic impact.

A variant of the land tax is the graded tax or split-rate system, in which improvements are taxed, but at a lower rate than land. Some experience with this approach in around eighteen cities in Pennsylvania, including Pittsburgh from 1913 to 2001, and more than two dozen other nations suggests that the system is feasible, can provide adequate revenues for local finance, and can improve the prospects for economic development relative to the conventional property tax. A number of Pennsylvania cities with split-rate systems managed to have less urban decline, and even growth, when comparable "rust-belt" cities were experiencing considerable decay and blight, and observers believe that the tax system was an important contributing influence to the difference.[2] Critics complain that property assessors would have great difficulty separating the value of the land from the value of any improvement to the land. But even a rough separation would have better development affects than the current system, could produce as much revenue as the current system, and, given the state of many U.S. cities, certainly would seem worth a try.

[1] Quoted in Kenneth Wenzer, *Land Value Taxation* (Armonk, N.Y.: M. E. Sharpe, 1999), 17–18.

[2] An excellent source for more about land taxation, Richard F. Dye and Richard W. England, *Land Value Taxation: Theory, Evidence, and Practice* (Cambridge, Mass.: Lincoln Institute for Land Policy, 2009), includes essays on the logic of land taxation, its administrative practicality, and its impacts on growth and development. Evidence on the development impact of split rates in Pittsburgh appears in Wallace E. Oates and Robert M. Schwab, "The Impact of Urban Land Taxation: The Pittsburgh Experience," *National Tax Journal* 50 (March 1997): 1–21.

Good Tax, Bad Tax?

Academicians and tax analysts like property taxes more than do politicians, the media, and most of the general public. Property tax advocates believe that real property taxation is synonymous with fiscal autonomy for local government. There are no broad-based revenue options that are as well suited for local use as is this tax. If local governments do not have access to a property tax and flexibility to use the tax to cover their service obligations, then they are almost certainly destined to become fiscal wards of their state. There simply is no satisfactory tax option available for local use to replace the lost property tax revenue. Local fiscal autonomy means local property taxation. The specific advantages of the tax for local finance are significant:[12]

1. The base is immobile, so the tax can be administered without fear that it will escape the locality before the tax is collected. Even if the owner of the property skips town or declares bankruptcy, the property itself remains, and the tax authorities can take action against (i.e., sell) the property to collect the taxes. The tax does not create the distortions of economic behavior that other taxes induce, thus making it a rather efficient device for raising revenue.

2. Revenue from the property tax is more stable in the face of recession than is revenue from other broad-base taxes (general sales and income in particular). The Great Recession had less impact on localities that remained dependent on the property tax than it did on those that had diversified to other broad-base local taxes or who relied heavily on state aid (states tend to cut aid to local governments as a way of dealing with their own budget problems). Total local property tax revenue increased by 21.7 percent from fiscal 2007 to fiscal 2010 (start through end of the recession) whereas local general sales tax revenue fell by 1.9 percent and local individual income tax revenue fell by 10.3 percent over those same fiscal years, according to Governments Division, U.S. Bureau of Census data. In fact, property-tax-dependent localities fared better than did most states because states rely heavily on the less stable income and general sales taxes.

3. The tax rate can vary within small geographic areas to support even the smallest local governments. The average effective property tax rate on owner-occupied housing is around 1 percent of market value, although there are considerable variations by region and by jurisdiction (city, suburb, rural).

4. The services typically supported by local property taxes provide direct protection to real property (fire and police protection, for instance) or contribute to making real properties valuable (high-quality local schools, for instance). The property tax is a charge for these services.

5. The property tax base associated with industrial development provides a way of compensating those living around the property for the inconvenience (noise, traffic, pollution, etc.) associated with such activity. Property tax revenue is a way of reducing the "not in my backyard" (NIMBY) opposition to economic development.

---

[12]In China, property taxes have been advocated as a mechanism for controlling the dramatic increase in housing prices, not directly as a means for generating tax revenue. Pilot property tax programs in Shanghai and Chongquing apply only to newly purchased or luxury homes in an effort to constrain price increases. Similar taxes are under discussion for other cities, although the effectiveness of the existing programs is not yet proven.

6. Property taxes are visible, and the decisions made about them are close at hand, thus bringing people directly into the fiscal process, as should be the case in a democracy. That visibility certainly contributes to the popular objections to property taxation.

7. Many decisions made by local government have a direct impact on the value of real property. A property tax gives the government a direct stake in the quality of those decisions, while leaving property ownership, management, and allocation in private hands.

8. The tax applies to extremely valuable properties, including properties owned by people who have managed to avoid being taxed as their income was received, either because of poor administration or because of generous tax preferences. It can lead to large property tax bills for people with extremely expensive property; but if they can afford the huge house, then they surely also can afford the associated bill for providing government services to that household. These people often have considerable political clout, certainly creating a barrier to effective use of the tax because they would prefer not to pay the tax.

Popular opinion does not hold property taxes in such high regard, and politicians regularly build their campaigns on anti–property tax platforms. There are several main complaints.

1. Property taxes are seen as regressive. Some state studies do generally show that the effective property tax rate declines as income is higher. The degree is, however, usually not as great as with sales taxes. Nonetheless, the standard view among economists holds that the basic property tax is progressive because ownership of land and capital is concentrated among high-income households.[13] Abnormally high property taxes in a locality may behave like selective excises, but the normal tax likely is progressively distributed. Furthermore, the tax may be simply a charge for services provided the property, in which case the distributional equity is irrelevant. In spite of the evidence, the belief that shapes the political discussion is the regressivity opinion and, as is often the case in modern American life, evidence to the contrary has made little impact.

2. Property taxes are horizontally inequitable. There is truth to this complaint. The effective property tax rate varies substantially across properties of similar value, and property taxes borne by families of similar affluence also differ significantly. The former is the result of how property taxes are structured and administered; the latter is the result of differing household preferences

---

[13]Wallace E. Oates, "An Overview and Some Reflections," in *Property Taxation and Local Government Finance,* ed. Wallace E. Oates (Cambridge, Mass.: Lincoln Institute for Land Policy, 2001). There are three primary views of property tax incidence: the "traditional view" that the property tax is shifted to consumers in the form of higher housing prices, the "benefit view" that the property tax is simply a charge for services provided by local government, and the "new or capital tax view" that the property tax is a distortionary tax on the use of capital within the local jurisdiction. See George R. Zodrow, "The Property Tax as a Capital Tax: A Room with Three Views," *National Tax Journal* 54 (March 2001): 139–56. Only the traditional view would cause the property tax to be significantly regressive.

for property ownership. There is much evidence of this horizontal disparity problem.[14] Inept assessors working in an inept system are the culprits here. It appears that high-quality assessment is no more expensive than low-quality assessment: factors other than the cost of assessment determine the quality of the assessment, not how much is spent on the work.[15]

3. Local property taxes create a pattern of fiscal affluence and fiscal poverty (fiscal disparity or horizontal fiscal imbalance). Some localities have great endowments of property values (those with manufacturing facilities, for instance), and some have minimal property tax values. That creates great disparity in the type and quality of public services that the localities can provide their citizenry. The problem can be particularly acute when elementary and secondary education is driven by the local property tax endowment.[16] These issues are discussed at greater length in Chapter 14, which focuses on intergovernmental finances.

4. Property tax burdens can become shockingly high for people living in areas with increasing property values and can become difficult for people with low incomes. Long-time residents of an area that has suddenly become trendy can experience sudden increases in their property tax bills because of the unexpected increase in value of their properties, and those bills can confront them with difficult choices. Those owning agricultural land on the fringes of rapidly growing urban areas also can suffer the shock of owning unexpectedly valuable land and the higher property tax bills that can result. And sometimes tax bills change in ways that just don't seem right. If a factory that constitutes a sizable share of the property value in a jurisdiction closes, other property owners in the area will own a higher share of the total property base, their share of the total cost of government increases, and they may receive a higher property tax bill—even though they know that the value of their property hasn't increased. That result stabilizes government finances, but doesn't make the tax popular. The solution—downsizing local government services and expenditures to reflect the reality of a city without the factory—is not politically easy.

5. A property tax can reduce the prospects for economic development by reducing the after-tax rate of return that can be earned from building productive facilities or refurbishing deteriorated properties. With upgrading come higher values, which cause higher tax bills, thus reducing the return from development. (Refer to Sidebar 11–1 for the solution.)

---

[14]There are some systematic problems with the horizontal disparity. For example, Harris finds that majority-minority neighborhoods are assessed at higher effective ratios than are majority-white neighborhoods. Lee Harris, "'Assessing' Discrimination: The Influence of Race in Residential Property Tax Assessments," *Journal of Land Use and Environmental Law* 20 (Fall 2004).

[15]Olha Krupa, "Vertical Consolidation of Indiana's Property Tax System," *State Tax Notes* (October 12, 2015): 165–75. In addition, the study found that moving assessment from township to county level significantly reduced system cost in each county, mostly by reducing the assessor headcount, without harming quality of work done.

[16]Because all major tax bases are distributed unequally across local areas, this disparity complaint is more correctly a complaint against local financing, rather than solely against the property tax.

Arithmetic and Application of Rates, Levies, and Assessed Value

Understanding how property taxes operate requires an understanding of the basic property tax rate equation because property taxes can work differently from other major taxes. Most tax rates change only with special legislative action and are not established as part of the annual legislative process. They are the portion of the fiscal system that is most strictly incremental, in the sense of small changes made to a permanent base. That is the case, for example, with state sales taxes and state and federal income taxes. These taxes are adopted and continue in place year after year without further legislative action. Although the property tax rate may be established in a tax code and thus remains in place from one year to the next in the same way as other taxes, local property tax rates in the United States have traditionally been set as a part of the annual budget process, with rate setting as the climax to the process establishing how much will be spent. The rate in most circumstances will be annually readopted at a level sufficient to yield enough revenue to balance the operating budget and to cover current costs of servicing debt obligations (interest to be paid plus any maturing principal).

Property tax rate setting mechanics are conceptually straightforward. Rates are driven by the budget choices that local governments make within the limits of the tax base and other revenue resources available to them and the controls placed on them by their state governments. The determinations involve both economics and politics and are summarized in the basic statutory property tax rate formula that follows:

$$R_a = (E - T)/[A_a + (W_b \times A_b)]$$

where

R_a = statutory tax rate applied to the class of property intended to face the lowest statutory rate (often single-family, owner-occupied housing),

E = planned local government expenditure for the budget year,

T = expected non-property tax revenue in that year,

A_a = taxable (or net assessed) value of property in the lowest rate class,

A_b = taxable (or net assessed) value of property in a higher rate class, and

W_b = intended multiple of the statutory rate applied to the lowest rate class that rate class b will bear.

There may be several rate classes, each entering into the rate calculation equation as the value in that class multiplied by the multiple of the lowest rate class that that type of property is intended to bear. If all properties are to be taxed at the same statutory rate, then all property weights equal one.

Here is how such a calculation works for a government with three classes of taxable property. Suppose the following information enters the rate calculation process:

planned local government expenditure (E) = \$8,500,000; estimated revenue from sources other than the property tax (T) = \$500,000; taxable value of property in the lowest rate class (A_a) = \$60,000,000; taxable value of property in the next lowest rate class (A_b) = \$100,000,000; multiple of intended rate in class b to intended rate in class a = 2; taxable value of property in the third lowest rate class (A_c) = \$50,000,000; multiple of intended rate in class c to intended rate in class a = 3.

The statutory tax rate for class A_a is calculated as follows:

$$R_a = (8,500,000 - 500,000)/ [60,000,000 + (2 \times 100,000,000) + (3 \times 50,000,000)]$$
$$= 8,000,000/[60,000,000 + 200,000,000 + 150,000,000]$$
$$= 8,000,000/410,000,000 = 0.0195122 \text{ or } \$1.05122 \text{ per } \$100 \text{ of assessed valuation}$$

Rates for the other classes are calculated by use of the multiples:

$$R_b = 2 \times R_a = 2 \times 0.0195122 = 0.0390244 \text{ or } \$3.90244 \text{ per } \$100 \text{ of assessed valuation}$$
$$R_c = 3 \times R_a = 3 \times 0.0195122 = 0.0585366 \text{ or } \$5.85366 \text{ per } \$100 \text{ of assessed valuation}$$

A classified property tax structure means that all property uses are not the same in terms of fiscal yield. Switching land use from a lower rate category to a higher rate category will improve the revenue potential for that land, allowing other properties the benefit of given services while paying lower taxes or of a higher level of services at the same tax rate. The land use categories that typically bear higher multiples (industrial, commercial, and utility) yield more assessed value per acre than do other uses, so classification adds to the existing revenue bias. Higher rate category land use yields fiscal dividends to other properties in the taxing jurisdiction, and assessors do have an incentive to classify properties in higher rate classes for revenue purposes.

This relationship applies for each government unit levying the property tax. Some units may face limits on levies or may need to raise set sums to cover contractual debt service, others have constrained rates, and others have considerable freedom to establish what rate is necessary to balance their budgets. Regardless of the conditions, however, the formula links those terms and applies to each government using the tax.[17]

This rate-setting process goes on independently for each of the several local governments serving an area (the county, cities, school districts, special districts, etc.) as if the other jurisdictions do not exist.[18] One conclusion from the rate equation

---

[17] Joseph K. Eckert, ed., *Property Appraisal and Assessment Administration* (Chicago: International Association of Assessing Officers, 1990), 20.

[18] Some states, including California and Indiana, have established overall rate limits within which totals must fall. That then requires some superior body to divide the overall limit among the jurisdictions having taxing authority, an extra complication to the taxing process. At the other extreme, Massachusetts has only one layer of local government so its overall rate limit—established by Proposition 2 ½—can be applied rather simply. And the Massachusetts system is transparent: property owners know exactly what government is responsible for their tax bill without having to do any research.

is that, if the assessed values of all properties in a jurisdiction increase by around 10 percent, then unless the planned expenditures increase, the property tax rate will decline by around 10 percent, and property tax bills will not change. If assessed values in a jurisdiction fall, as happened in some areas during the Great Recession, and the taxing jurisdiction does not decrease its planned spending, rates will increase to maintain property tax levies needed to finance the spending.

The actual property tax bill received by a property holder is usually like a layer cake of rates imposed by each jurisdiction in which the property is physically located: for instance, $4.58 for the village, $1.22 for the county, and $3.25 for the school district, with a total rate of $9.05 on the net assessed value of the property. Another property located in the same county would face a somewhat different set of rates if it was not in the village (or was in a different village) and in a different school district. The property holder will ordinarily make one payment to cover all the taxes; a single property tax collector (possibly a county treasurer) collects and disburses to each taxing unit. Each of those taxes would have been set in the same way that the village rate was set, but each is done independently.[19]

These legal (or advertised) tax rates cannot be directly compared across governments. For instance, suppose that the combined rate in one city is $10.00 per $100 of net assessed value and the rate in another city is $15.00 per $100 of net assessed value. Would it be reasonable to assume that a property worth $100,000 in the second city would face a tax bill that is 50 percent higher than that for a property of equivalent value in the first city? To make the comparison, we must adjust the legal or statutory tax rate for differences in the assessment ratio, the ratio between the value of the property as established in the assessment process and its market value (the price at which a willing buyer and a willing seller would reach agreement on a sale). As we shall see in the next sections, not all property tax systems define the value for tax purposes to be full market value, and not all property tax assessors are equally adept at hitting the legal assessment target. Therefore, to compare property taxes, it is necessary to adjust legal tax rates for differences in assessment ratios to look at effective property tax rates. The effective tax rate (ETR) on a parcel of property equals the property tax (T) divided by the market value of the property (MV):

$$ETR = T/MV$$

The property tax equals the legal tax rate (r) multiplied by the assessed value of the property (AV):

$$T = r \times AV$$

---

[19]A government may, of course, see the computed rate, worry about the consequences, and revise the amount of levy it chooses to raise.

Therefore, the effective tax rate equals the statutory tax rate multiplied by the assessment ratio (the ratio of assessed value to market value):

$$ETR = (r \times AV)/MV = r\,(AV/MV)$$

In the previous example, if the assessment ratio was 100 percent in the first city and 50 percent in the second, the effective tax rate would be higher in the first ($10.00 per $100) than in the second ($7.50 per $100), the reverse of the legal rates. Comparisons across jurisdictions—and even across properties in a single jurisdiction—absolutely require consideration of assessment ratios!

There is normally a separation of function in property tax administration. The property assessor is responsible for determining the taxable value of parcels in the jurisdictions, the local governing bodies determine the amounts to be raised for their budgets from the property tax, a clerk or auditor calculates the statutory property tax rate for each jurisdiction, and the treasurer collects the tax owed on each parcel and distributes the collections to the proper governments. The separation of functions, whether the officers are elected or appointed, is consistent with the logic of internal control.

Doing Assessments: Standards

The hard part about property taxation is property assessment. Property taxation requires a basis for distributing the tax burden among property holders. Because the tax base includes property holdings (accumulated asset values) rather than current flow of property sales during the year, values must be estimated.[20] This estimation—or assessment—determines what the tax value is for each property parcel and, by aggregation, the total tax value of the government; it is the heart of the property tax system. When a reassessment changes property values for tax purposes, some properties pay a higher share of the tax burden and others a lower share, compared with shares before reassessment. This adjustment of tax payments to more closely match perceived capability to pay the tax—as measured by property value—is the objective of assessment.

What is the standard for property appraisal? The most widely used and accepted standard is market value: "Market value is the cash price a property would bring in a competitive and open market."[21] This hypothetical exchange value—the same concept used by banks, insurance companies, and other institutions to determine a property's value for insurance, mortgage, and related purposes—assumes that (1) markets have adequate time to function, (2) no undue pressure is exerted on either

---

[20]The current value approach ("capital value") to establishing the tax base is used in the United States and Canada, but other approaches are also used. Some countries, particularly former British colonies such as India, Nigeria, and Trinidad, for instance, base tax on the annual rental value of land and buildings ("rates"). Other countries use land or building area as the base. Eckert, *Property Appraisal,* 7.
[21]*Ibid.,* 35.

buyer or seller, (3) both parties are well informed about the parcel at sale, and (4) the transaction is at arm's length.[22] Actual transaction prices—that is, what someone just paid for a property—may provide information about market value, but they are not necessarily that value, both because those conditions may not be met and because the price may include sale of something in addition to the parcel itself.[23] Market value, internationally recognized in both public and private finance, is a standard with the same meaning everywhere, a meaning that is not linked to any particular tax law, legal system, or government structure. Although these value estimates are hypothetical, they can be tested against actual transactions and can be challenged on an objective basis.[24] As is described shortly, a few states in the United States do not use market value as the statutory standard, but it is the assessment basis most widely used.

Within market assessment systems, there frequently are special procedures for certain property groups, often agricultural land. An ordinary appraisal assumes that a prospective buyer may put the newly acquired property to a different use; that is, the farmland close to the growing city might be developed into a shopping center, an apartment complex, or a housing subdivision, or a single-family residence near a university might be converted into apartments or offices. That potential for different use might, indeed, be a principal influence on current market value. *Current-use assessment,* however, assumes that the buyer would continue the same use of the parcel. For most parcels, there would be no difference between the market and current-use assessments because there is but a trivial chance that a market-driven prospective buyer would change how the property is used—a cornfield in central Illinois far from any city or interstate interchange is unlikely to sprout anything but corn, soybeans, or a comparable agricultural crop when the new buyer takes control. However, the difference can be important where markets are changing with urban or other development and expansion. Generally, the idea is to protect existing property holders from the tax implications of the higher values of the properties and

---

[22]House appraisals for mortgage lending are increasingly done through automated systems using computer models provided by Fannie Mae (Federal National Mortgage Association) and Freddie Mac (Federal Home Loan Mortgage Corporation) to quickly estimate values for mortgage loans. These appraisals cost much less than traditional in-house appraisals. They are done by mining databases that list selling prices for homes in the neighborhood and comparing those properties with the one being appraised. Freddie Mac and Fannie Mae operate as financial intermediaries by acquiring, packaging, and then securitizing mortgages originated by various entities. The appraisals are done primarily to test the reasonableness of the proposed transaction price for the appraised property—to verify that the property being purchased has sufficient value to protect the lender if the loan goes bad—and are less concerned with great accuracy. However, the principles are consistent with other appraisals, including for property tax purposes. Patrick Barta, "Lenders Tout Home Appraisals by Computer; Human Appraisers Demur," *Wall Street Journal,* July 20, 2001, B1, B3. Both these entities were badly damaged, both financially and in reputation, during the Great Recession. They helped facilitate the bad mortgage loans that were at the heart of the financial collapse.

[23]Such additions may include, for instance, some personal property or some special financing from the seller.

[24]If a property assessed for $75,000 sells for $300,000, we can be reasonably certain that it was assessed at considerably less than current market value. Therefore, current market value estimates are testable and, hence, refutable.

prevent tax-induced conversion away from agriculture and open-space uses.[25] It can also become a good tax dodge: in Florida, land developers rent cows to put on their land so the property will qualify as farmland and be assessed at a lower rate.

A few states legally require some general assessment standard other than market value.[26] One such alternative standard is the *acquisition value* or assessment-on-sale system required in California by Proposition 13 (1978), required for homestead property in Florida by the 1992 referendum that approved Amendment 10, and introduced in Michigan with the revision of school finances in 1994. In this system, properties are revalued for tax purposes only when they are sold and then at the new transaction price.[27]

This structure of reassessment only on sale disrupts the property market (because prospective buyers would face a different property tax than would the prospective seller), creates a property record substructure of sales without recorded deeds as individuals seek to avoid the property tax adjustments that would accompany a recorded sale, and causes owners of similarly situated properties to pay widely different property taxes. This last problem is especially difficult because it directly conflicts with assessment uniformity, the primary concern of the assessment task. Indeed, in a 1989 case involving the assessment of coal properties in West Virginia, the U.S. Supreme Court unanimously held that valuation of some properties at their recent purchase price when similar parcels are valued on earlier assessments violates the equal-protection clause of the Fourteenth Amendment of the U.S. Constitution. Chief Justice Rehnquist wrote, in a classic statement of the horizontal equity standard, that "the constitutional requirement is the seasonable attainment of a rough equality in tax treatment of similarly situated property owners."[28] In that case, the plaintiff's property, because more recently purchased, was assessed at values eight to thirty-five times the value of comparable neighboring property, and nothing was bringing the assessments closer together. However, the assessor followed this

---

[25]John H. Bowman and John L. Mikesell, in "Assessment of Agricultural Property for Taxation," *Land Economics* 64 (February 1988): 28–36, find use-value assessment to improve the uniformity of property assessment. However, many studies question the effectiveness of such laws in influencing land use, their primary objective. See, for example, David E. Hansen and S. I. Schwartz, "Landowner Behavior at the Rural-Urban Fringe in Response to Preferential Taxation," *Land Economics* 51 (November 1975): 34–54. A good examination of preferential assessment of farmland, its impacts, and some alternatives is provided in Richard W. England, "Reconsidering Preferential Assessment of Rural Land," *Land Lines* (April 2012): 2–7.

[26]Assessment may also be done with uniform application of an administrative formula. It is virtually impossible for a property owner to know whether his or her parcel is over- or underassessed in the system because the owner cannot tell the extent to which the formula has been properly applied to other parcels. If the owner's parcel is properly assessed and other parcels are underassessed, then the owner is overassessed in the system. The only test the owner has is to verify parcel data and application of the formula to his or her parcel.

[27]Both California and Florida apply across-the-board adjustment increases, but realignments between parcels occur only when parcels exchange hands. Allen Manvel noted the precipitous decline in assessment quality produced by that system. See "Assessment Uniformity—and Proposition 13," *Tax Notes* 24 (August 27, 1984): 893–95. Other states with one form of acquisition value assessment or another include Arkansas, Georgia, Illinois, Maryland, Montana, New Mexico, New York, Oklahoma, South Carolina, and Texas. Terri Sexton, "Proposition 13 and Residential Mobility," *State Tax Notes* 50 (October 6, 2008): 29–36.

[28]*Allegheny Pittsburgh Coal Co. v. County Commission of Webster County, West Virginia,* 488 U.S. 336 (1989).

procedure contrary to the state law. It was, as the Court labeled it, an "aberrational enforcement policy."

A test of acquisition value assessment as the legal state standard came from California in *Nordlinger v. Hahn.*[29] Stephanie Nordlinger found that, when she purchased a house in the Baldwin Heights neighborhood of Los Angeles County, the accompanying reassessment on acquisition brought a 36 percent increase in property tax, from $1,247.40 to $1,701 per year. She later discovered she was paying about five times more in taxes than some of her neighbors who owned comparable homes within the same residential development. For example, one block away, a house of identical size on a lot slightly larger than the petitioner's was subject to a general tax levy of only $358.20 (based on an assessed valuation of $35,820, which reflected the home's value in 1975 plus the up-to-2-percent-per-year standard inflation factor). The general tax levied against her modest home was only a few dollars less than that paid by a pre-1976 owner of a $2.1 million Malibu beachfront home.

Nordlinger believed this pattern to be both patently unfair and contrary to constitutional requirements for equal protection. The state, however, disagreed, arguing that the system represented a rational system of classification because there was a legitimate state interest in allowing longer-term owners to pay a lower tax than newer owners of property (1) to avoid taxing property holders on unrealized gains on their properties and possibly taxing people out of their homes, (2) to ensure predictability of tax payments for property owners, and (3) to achieve revenue stability for local governments. The Supreme Court, although showing considerable sympathy for Nordlinger's argument and noting that most of these state objectives could have been better achieved through other means, chose to accept that there was some rational basis for the system—despite the dramatic differences in property tax paid by similarly situated individuals. Furthermore, evidence indicates that Proposition 13 did induce homeowners and renters to stay put and avoid higher tax rates than they would face when buying new properties: from 1970 to 2000, the average tenure for owners and renters in California increased by slightly more than one year and slightly more than three-quarters of a year, respectively, relative to comparison states.[30] Ordinarily, reduced mobility is regarded as an impediment to economic growth and, hence, regarded as undesirable public policy in market-driven economies. The Court found that there was a rational basis for the assessment scheme and, in contrast to the West Virginia situation, the acquisition value system was constitutional. The system, which also rigidly controlled the property tax rate, strangled the revenue capacity of local governments.

Two other valuation standards are worth noting. These are an area-based assessment, in which the tax is driven exclusively by the size of the property, and a formula-based or cadastral assessment, in which the assessment is driven by the

---

[29] *Stephanie Nordlinger, Petitioner v. Kenneth Hahn, in His Capacity as Tax Assessor for Los Angeles County,* 505 U.S. 1 (1992).

[30] Nada Wasi and Michelle J. White, "Property Tax Limitations and Mobility: The Lock-in Effect of California's Proposition 13," National Bureau of Economic Research Working Paper 11108, Cambridge, Mass., February 2005. www.nber.org/papers/w11108.

application of a legal formula that uses physical attributes (size, design, location, soil type, etc.) of each property. The test of a cadastral assessment is not whether it approximates a certain value, but whether the physical attributes have been correctly recorded and whether the formula has been accurately applied to them. These systems are usually applied in situations in which there are few reliable market transactions of the property being taxed, as in developing countries or in countries transitioning from centrally planned to market economies. Sidebar 11–2 illustrates the use of an adjusted area-based system during the recent Greek fiscal crisis.

Local governments in the United Kingdom rely on value-based property taxes to finance their operations. However, they deal with the tricky task of assessment in a fashion that differs from that of the United States and Canada, two other heavy users of property taxes for local finances. The UK system of "banding" is discussed in Sidebar 11–3. This system can be particularly useful when value data are sparse or when values are fluctuating significantly.

Doing Assessments: Cycles

The assessment cycles that governments in the United States use fall into three general categories: *mass cyclical assessment, segmental assessment,* and *annual assessment.* With mass cyclical assessment, all properties in a taxing jurisdiction are valued for tax purposes in a particular year; that value does not change until the next scheduled mass assessment except for new construction, demolition, or change in use of a property. States prescribe mass cyclical assessment at intervals ranging from two to ten years. Examples include Iowa (two years), Maine (four years), Minnesota (four years), Indiana (ten years), and Connecticut (ten years).[31] Some states explicitly indicate that a physical inspection of real property will be made with the reassessment. Many jurisdictions that operate under a mass cyclical assessment system choose to contract the reassessment with a private appraisal firm so that they do not face great changes in staffing between normal and reassessment years. Some states provide for some adjustment ("trending") of property assessments between reassessment years based on property market price changes in local areas to reduce the amount of change in the reassessment year.

Segmental assessment is a procedure by which a specified fraction of real property parcels in a jurisdiction is reassessed each year, moving through the assessing unit in sequence. Thus, if a three-year cycle is used, one-third of the properties in the area are reassessed each year, with all properties reassessed in three years. The last-valued taxpayers can complain about the inflation in their valuations, which is absent from earlier-valued parcels, but administrative convenience and the fact that all parcels take their turn as last valued have preserved the method. Examples include

[31]U.S. Bureau of the Census, *1992 Census of Governments, Vol. 2, Taxable Property Values,* No. 1, Assessed Valuation for Local General Property Taxation (Washington, D.C.: U.S. Government Printing Office, 1994), D-1–D-3.

Sidebar 11–2
A Property Tax Alternative: The 2011 Greek Property Tax

Greece was in fiscal crisis in 2011 (and several years thereafter). Many years of substantial government deficits had accumulated into a level of debt that could not be sustained, around 160 percent of gross domestic product at the time. Private lenders were not willing to lend to the government to refinance the existing debt or to support the continuing deficit because they were skeptical of the ability of the government to pay the promised interest or to repay the principal loaned. The government didn't have the capability of covering its obligations by printing more money because it was part of the euro-zone and didn't control its own currency. To obtain loans from the International Monetary Fund and European institutions, the Greek government had to devise an austerity program to close its deficit, even though a deep recession continued to haunt the nation.

Part of the government strategy to reduce the deficit was additional revenue from a new national property tax. Official rates for the national income and value-added taxes were already high, thus limiting the capacity to raise revenue by increasing them. Furthermore, tax compliance in Greece has been notoriously low, and raising tax rates would promise to worsen what was already a low compliance rate. That created the need for a new tax, one that had features appropriate to the operating environment. The tax would need to yield revenue quickly, and it had to be generally reliable and involve as little scope for private noncompliance as possible. The current revenue system would not work.

The new Greek property tax has been designed to perform in this difficult environment. The emergency tax applies to all commercial and residential properties in the country. The tax is determined according to the size of the property in square meters. Properties between 0 and 25 years of age are assessed a surcharge of 5 to 25 percent, inversely proportional to age; that is, the surcharge is higher for newer properties. Properties are taxed at a zone rate determined by the physical location of the property, with rates ranging from 0.50 to 16 euros per square meter.

The tax calculation is the number of square meters times the surcharge determined by the age of the property times the zone tax rate. Some parts of the country do not have zones, and properties located there are subject to a rate of 3 euros per square meter. The taxes are calculated with data already available to the tax officials (and with data not subject to manipulation or to reporting errors by taxpayers, including information from Google Earth).

The government needed the tax revenue quickly, and there was reluctance to use the existing tax collection structures. Therefore, property owners received billing through their bills from the government-owned electric company, two installments for the first year of the tax and five installments for the second year of the tax. Initially, payments were made with payment of the electric bill, and those not paying the tax were subject to having their electricity cut off.

Power cuts were instituted in January 2012 for nonpayers, but were halted when harsh winter weather hit. Also, nonpayment of electric bills increased so much that the electric utility faced a cash crunch. The electricity cutoffs for nonpayment of the property tax portion of the bills were eventually found to be unconstitutional, eliminating the government's primary collection tool. Enforcement was changed to garnishment of wages or pensions or seizure of properties.

(continues)

Sidebar 11–2
(continued)

The tax avoided the creation of more disincentives from adding to the income or value-added taxes, eliminated the possibility that taxpayers might cheat on tax returns, could be put into place quickly, and used a collection system that could yield revenues quickly. It was not based on current market values of properties.

SOURCES: Charles Forelle, "At Core of Greek Chaos, a Reviled Tax," *Wall Street Journal,* May 31, 2010, A9; "Greece's New Property Tax," *Living in Greece,* September 19, 2011. http://livingingreece.gr/2011/09/19/new-property-tax-greece/.

Sidebar 11–3
An Alternative Scheme for Taxing Property to Finance Local Services: Banding

The United Kingdom introduced property value banding when a short-lived poll tax experiment for financing local government services came crashing down.[1] The population rebelled against the poll tax system under which all residents of a jurisdiction paid exactly the same tax amount regardless of income or affluence—a nice idea for inducing everyone to push for efficient delivery of services in the jurisdiction but pretty terrible for vertical equity. Although the system—a replacement for a property tax based on property rents—was simple and transparent, it also seemed patently unfair.

The replacement, since 1993, has been the banding system for residential properties (combined with a rental value property tax for nonresidential parcels). With this system, tax payment is determined according to (1) the number of bands into which properties are to be divided, (2) the width of the bands in terms of estimated property value, and (3) the tax rate structure. The system is, in essence, a poll or head tax, but with some adjustments for differences in property values. In the UK, eight tax bands were established, with one scheme each for England, Scotland, and Wales. The system in England is described here:

Band in England	Property Value Range (£)	Ratio to Base Band
A	Under 40,000	6/9
B	40,001–52,000	7/9
C	52,001–68,000	8/9
D (Base Band)	68,001–88,000	9/9
E	88,001–120,000	11/9
F	120,001–160,000	13/9
G	160,001–320,000	15/9
H	320,001 and above	18/9

Sidebar 11–3
(continued)

A tax ratio is established for each band in terms of the identified base band; in other words, each tax band has a set ratio relative to the base. In England, band H tax will be double the base band (and triple that of band A).

Suppose a local jurisdiction has 7,750 dwellings and seeks to raise £1,000,000. The following table presents the distribution of dwellings by band and calculates the base band equivalence in each band.

Band	Dwellings in Band	Ratio to Base	Base Band Equivalent Properties
A	500	6/9	333
B	1,200	7/9	933
C	1,500	8/9	1,333
D	1,000	9/9	1,000
E	2,000	11/9	2,444
F	900	13/9	1,300
G	500	15/9	833
H	150	18/9	300
Totals	7,750		8,476

Therefore, base tax equals 1,000,000 ÷ 8,476 = 118. Band D property pays £118, and other bands pay the appropriate ratio times 118.

Band	Number of Properties	Ratio	Band D Equivalent	Tax Bill per Property (£)	Total Tax (£)
A	500	6/9	333	79	39,500
B	1,200	7/9	933	92	110,400
C	1,500	8/9	1,333	105	157,500
D	1,000	1	1,000	118	118,000
E	2,000	11/9	2,444	144	288,000
F	900	13/9	1,300	170	153,000
G	500	15/9	833	197	98,500
H	150	18/9	300	236	35,400
					1,000,300

Property tax bills increase as properties are in higher-value bands. However, the effective rate (tax bill divided by average property value in the band) does fall as the band value is higher—the pattern is regressive.

(continues)

Sidebar 11–3
(continued)

The advantages of the system are these:

1. Simplicity: The system does not require detailed estimates of the value of properties. There are no complex valuation models required and no detailed data requirements.
2. Stability: The system does not require a short revaluation cycle to keep values up to date. So long as properties do not move from one band to another, there is no reason for a new rebanding exercise.
3. Acceptance: The system is generally accepted and understood by the taxpaying public.
4. Administrative cost: The system is not expensive to implement, the process is quick, and the number of appeals is low.
5. Fiscal transparency: Decisions made about government spending drive the tax bills, and that is completely apparent in the process. Changes in property values do not change the tax bills.

The disadvantages of the system are these:

1. Regressivity: Effective rates fall as property values are higher, and it is not easy to remove that pattern.
2. Applicability: The system is applicable only to residential properties.
3. Complexity: Establishing the number and range of bands and the ratios is a policy challenge.

[1]Peter Smith, "Lessons from the British Poll Tax Disaster," *National Tax Journal* 44 (December 1991): 421–36.

SOURCE: Based on Frances Plimmer, William McCluskey, and Owen Connellan, "Property Tax Banding: A Solution for Developing Countries," *Assessment Journal* 9 (2002): 37–47.

a three-year cycle in both Maryland and Cook County, Illinois.[32] Idaho requires that 20 percent of property in each assessment class be appraised each year.

The final system is annual assessment, a process that assumes updated values for all real property parcels each year. Computers and modern information technology make frequent reappraisals possible, but a physical inspection and inventory of all parcels, the traditional mark of reassessment, is unlikely at that pace. More often than not, annual valuation employs the physical characteristics of properties as identified in earlier parcel inventories with new value weights applied to those characteristics and a realignment of the significance of neighborhood location to keep up with changing markets. For instance, in earlier years, a fireplace might have added $1,000

---

[32]In Cook County, the cycle through reassessment works like this: 2009, reassess City of Chicago; 2010, reassess north suburbs; 2011, reassess south suburbs; 2012, reassess City of Chicago; and so on. See John E. Petersen and Kimberly K. Edwards, "The Impact of Declining Property Values on Local Government Finances," Urban Land Institute Research Working Paper 626, Washington, D.C., March 1993, 49.

to the value of a house; this year it is estimated to add $1,800. Or, after adjusting for other charges, certain types of properties in one area may have values altered by 1 percent, whereas in other areas the change may be 2 percent. In that fashion, new value estimates emerge from old physical feature data. Much of the revaluation may be done according to analysis of zones within the jurisdiction, identifying zones in which values seem to be increasing at a particular rate, compared to a different rate in another zone. Of course, annual reassessment can become no reassessment if last year's forms are simply recopied or if all parcels have values increased or decreased by a flat factor of, for example, 3 percent.[33] That process destroys the equity of the property tax because no adjustments are made for properties whose value has either fallen or increased.

Modern information technology, often involving geographical information systems, makes good-quality annual updates feasible and equitable so long as there is process transparency, careful monitoring of changes in real estate markets, and an appeal process that property owners can navigate without great difficulty. These are conditions infrequently found in local assessing systems in the United States.[34]

Doing Assessments: Approaches

Assessment is a technical process, and each system has distinct peculiarities. There are, however, three general approaches to estimating real property values employed in state and local systems; all are offshoots of private property appraisal techniques used by realtors, banks, and others needing estimates of value. The approaches are (1) the market data or comparable sales, (2) the income, and (3) the cost or summation.[35]

1. **The market data or comparable sales approach** estimates value of a parcel by comparing it with similar properties that have recently been sold. The approach uses information directly produced by the market about how property owners and prospective owners value properties that are generally like that being assessed. Of course, the approach requires a number of actual transactions for meaningful comparisons. It does not work for unique

---

[33]As recent experience certainly demonstrates, up is not the direction that housing values go every year, and, when property values are changing, not all values in a locality move together. In the Boston area, "sales of single-family homes in the upscale town of Wellesley fell 2.2 percent in 1992, with an increase in the median sales price of 8.6 percent. In nearby Malden, a lower-middle-class town, single-family home sales grew 8.3 percent, but median prices fell 2 percent." Christopher J. Mayer, "Taxes, Income Distribution, and the Real Estate Cycle: Why All Houses Do Not Appreciate at the Same Rate," *New England Economic Review* (May/June 1993): 40. Uniform adjustments in assessments cannot substitute for reassessment in improving fairness. The larger the area included, the greater the disparity in changes in value, so standard value adjustments may be feasible in small, but not large, areas.

[34]At least U.S. governments try to keep assessments fresh. Austria applies 1973 values, and the United Kingdom uses 1991 values for residential properties. Germany works with 1964 values, and Belgium uses 1975 values, although both index the values for inflation. Enid Slack and Richard Bird, "The Political Economy of Property Tax Reform," OECD Working Papers on Fiscal Federalism, No. 18 (2014). http://dx.doi.org/10.1787/5jz5pzvzv6r7-en.

[35]Eckert, *Property Appraisal,* chaps. 6–13.

properties because it requires property transactions involving properties similar in economically relevant details.[36] A reasonably good comparison is usually possible for residential property (there are many three-bedroom, split-level houses with about 2,500 square feet of living space in most cities, after all, and some have probably sold recently), but uniqueness can create a virtually impossible problem for most commercial or industrial parcels and some residential parcels.

2. **The income approach** converts the future returns from ownership of a parcel into their present-value equivalent to estimate how much a willing and knowledgeable investor would pay for the future income flow. The approach requires an estimate of the gross return from holding the parcel, the expenses associated with holding the parcel, and a rate at which the resulting net annual return would be capitalized into a current-value equivalent. The approach applies the concept of discounting to convert the flow of future income into its net present value, exactly as discussed in Chapter 7. The approach is most attractive for estimating the value of income-producing properties (apartments, stores and offices, agricultural land, parking lots, etc.). On the market, how many multiples of net annual return are being paid for such properties? That comparison provides the value estimate.

3. **The cost or summation approach** estimates value by adding the depreciated cost of improvements on a parcel to the estimated land value of the parcel. In contrast to the other two approaches, rather than valuing the parcel as a whole (land plus improvements), this approach values each component of the parcel separately. The land value is normally estimated from either sales comparison or income capitalization, the previously noted approaches for general valuation. Often the land valuation uses value zone maps that identify the value per acre (or square foot) from transactions occurring within the zone, with the idea that this information will be used to estimate the value of all land in the zone. In estimating the value of the improvement, the approach typically determines the cost of constructing a standard (average) grade structure such as the one being assessed at a particular date (with the labor and materials prices of that time, using the prevailing technology, and in the size and type as the subject property). That cost is adjusted to account for nonstandard construction materials and workmanship of the property being assessed, either higher or lower than standard. To that cost are added extra features not found in the standard unit, such as extra bathroom fixtures, fireplaces, central air conditioning, and so on for residential units; escalators, sprinkler systems, vaults, and so on for commercial units; and cranes, elevators, air handling systems, and so on for industrial units. The "new cost" improvement value is calculated by either of two conceptual methods:

   a. *Reproduction cost,* the cost of constructing an exact replica of the building at current prices.

---

[36]Estimates using forms of regression analysis implicitly use sales comparisons, but the approach is also used without regression equations.

   b. *Replacement cost,* the cost of constructing a building having equivalent utility to the subject building at current prices: the building would be built
   with modern materials and using current standards and design, but would
   have the same utility as the existing building and ignoring the cost of
   structural elements in the building that provide no utility; for example,
   the unused second story of a warehouse could be ignored.

Both the reproduction and the replacement methods should reasonably lead to the
same value estimate through logically different adjustments for *accumulated depreciation.* In general, that accumulated depreciation can be from physical wear and
tear from elements, and may be curable (primarily from deferred maintenance) or
incurable (correction expenses would be enormous and impractical); from functional
obsolescence due to lack of utility or desirability in property design (inadequacy or
absence of features and superadequacy or presence of nonuseful features); or from
economic obsolescence due to changes external to the property (changes in the
neighborhood). The depreciation estimate would vary depending on whether "new
cost" was estimated using reproduction or replacement concepts.

   The three approaches are alternatives, but each has special strengths in the
assessment process. The income approach is best used for properties bought and
sold largely on the basis of income production: office buildings, apartments, motels
and hotels, and some types of land. The cost approach, although applicable to most
improvements, is especially suitable for special or unique properties that are seldom
exchanged on the market (e.g., a purpose-built manufacturing facility) and properties that generate no income (e.g., a public museum). It also, along with the income
approach, is vital for use-value assessment. The market data approach applies in any
circumstance for which a sufficient number of reliable transactions occur, particularly single-family, owner-occupied housing. The market data and cost approaches
are particularly amenable to the requirements of mass reassessment. Each would
be tested by the extent to which the value estimate it generated matches the price
received in a voluntary, arm's length, knowledgeable exchange of a parcel.[37] When
a property owner is appealing an assessment, it is normal for all three approaches
to valuation to be applied, even though the assessor likely relied on only one in the
initial assessment.

Fractional Assessment and Assessment Disparity

The heart of the property tax is assessment, the determination of property value for
distributing total tax burden. Tax law may or may not value property at current market value (what most people understand to be the meaning of "What is it worth?").

---

[37]Another special case for assessment involves public utility and transportation properties. These properties are usually assessed by the state government rather than by local assessors, and the value of each such
property is calculated as an operating unit and divided among local jurisdictions by formula rather than
having the value calculated on a property-in-place basis.

Even where assessment ties to current market value, prevailing assessment practices may cause substantial difference between market and assessed values. For example, according to the *1982 Census of Governments,* the national median-area assessment rate (assessed value to market value) for single-family, nonfarm houses in 1981 was 36.9 percent (an assessment ratio of 0.369).[38] State median-area rates ranged from a high of 86.8 percent in Idaho to a low of 0.6 percent in Vermont.[39] Much to the chagrin of tax analysts, the *Census of Governments* no longer reports any data having to do with market value, so we cannot tell whether national performance has improved or deteriorated since then. Many states do collect the data as part of their performance evaluation programs, but the information is not comparable across states.[40]

Under normal circumstances, the overall assessment rate has little impact on absolute property tax burdens because assessment levels can be counteracted by differences in the statutory tax rate. For instance, suppose a municipality seeks $5 million from its property tax and the market value of taxable property is $80 million. If the assessment rate is 100 percent, a property tax rate of $6.25 per $100 of assessed value will yield the desired revenue. If the assessment rate is 50 percent, a property tax rate of $12.50 per $100 of assessed value will produce the desired levy total. Low assessment rates produce compensating statutory rate adjustments.

Fractional assessment, meaning assessment at less than full market value, creates inequities and other complications.[41] First, low assessment rates increase the likelihood of unfair individual assessments because an individual parcel holder will probably be unaware of any overassessment. Suppose the legal assessment standard is one-third of market value, but the prevailing practice is 20 percent. If a parcel worth about $40,000 is assessed at $10,000, an unwary owner will believe that he or she has a favorable assessment. The tax assessor has valued the property far below the market value and, should the parcel owner know about legal standards, even below the one-third value standard. In fact, the parcel is overassessed—a 25 percent assessment, compared with the prevailing 20 percent—so the parcel bears an artificially high effective tax rate. Unless the parcel owner understands the ways of property taxation, he or she will never realize the inequity.[42] As John Shannon observed,

---

[38]The single-family, nonfarm home is a benchmark for assessment evaluation because almost every assessing district contains several parcels of that class and that grouping tends to be more homogeneous than other property types. Furthermore, markets for such properties usually have many transactions in comparison periods.

[39]U.S. Bureau of the Census, *1982 Census of Governments, Vol. 2, Taxable Property Values and Assessment—Sales Price Ratios* (Washington, D.C.: U.S. Government Printing Office, 1984), 50.

[40]There have been studies of individual states, however. For instance, evidence shows that efforts to reform the Indiana property tax assessment system—current market value assessment standard, trend adjustments between reassessments, consolidation of assessment—initially appeared to improve assessment quality, but more recently quality has declined substantially. Olha Krupa, "An Analysis of Indiana Property Tax Reform: Equity and Cost Considerations," *State Tax Notes* 65 (September 3, 2012).

[41]Rigid statutory rate ceilings, however, may combine with fractional assessment to create revenue constraints more severe than intended by the law.

[42]There is an extra pitfall in the process. The legal standard is 33 percent; the parcel is valued at 25 percent. Some appeal mechanisms suggest that the appropriate action is an increase in assessed value to the legal standard. That is not, however, the view of the U.S. Supreme Court: see *Sioux City Bridge Co. v. Dakota County,* 260 U.S. 441 (1923).

"The lower the assessment level, the larger becomes the administrative graveyard in which the assessor can bury his mistakes."[43]

Second, fractional assessment can make state-imposed property tax rate ceilings and debt limits linked to assessed value more restrictive than intended. Many states permit local government debt levels to be no higher than, say, 2 percent of total local assessed value. If assessment rates are low (for instance, assessment at 20 percent of value rather than at 50 percent), that limit becomes artificially restrictive and creates extra incentive to avoid those debt limits. Furthermore, the practice can cause uneven distributions of any state property tax rate across local areas with differing assessment rates. The effective state property tax rate is higher in areas with high assessment rates than in other areas. Finally, state grant assistance, especially aid to local school districts, is frequently distributed in formulas keyed to local assessed value: the lower the assessed value in an area, the greater the amount of state aid. Fractional assessment obviously can distort that distribution, so states typically develop equalization multipliers to get assessed values to a common assessment level for aid purposes. If an area has an assessment rate of 25 percent and the state-wide standard is 50 percent, its assessed value would be doubled for aid formula calculations. These equalization multipliers may or may not be applied to individual parcel values for computing tax bills. If rates are flexible and all parcels in a taxing area receive the same multiplier, the process makes no difference.

The major difficulty with fractional assessment occurs, however, when assessment rates of parcels within a taxing area differ. When this occurs, as it does to some extent in all systems, the effective tax rate is no longer uniform, and similarly situated properties bear different property tax burdens because of the assessment system. Thus, if property A is assessed at 30 percent of value and property B is assessed at 20 percent, a property tax of $10 per $100 of assessed value translates into an effective rate of $3 per $100 on property A and $2 per $100 on property B. No tax should be so capricious. Unfortunately, property taxes do show such dispersion in operation. The coefficient of dispersion (*CD*) measures the extent of dispersion (or the absence of uniformity) in assessment ratios and, hence, the extent to which effective property tax rates vary within a taxing unit. The CD—the average absolute deviation of parcel assessment ratios from the median divided by the median multiplied by 100—equals

$$CD = \left[\frac{\sum_{i=1}^{n} |A_i - M|}{n} \right] \left[\frac{1}{M} \right] \times 100$$

where

A_i = assessment ratio for an individual property parcel,

M = median assessment ratio for all parcels sampled, and

n = number of parcels in the sample.

[43]John Shannon, "Conflict between State Assessment Law and Local Assessment Practice," in *Property Taxation—USA,* ed. Richard W. Lindholm (Madison: University of Wisconsin Press, 1969), 45.

Table 11–2
Statistics of Assessment Quality: Assessment Ratio, Coefficient of Dispersion, and Price-Related Differential

Parcel	Assessed Value ($)	Market Value ($)	Assessment Ratio	Absolute Dispersion
A	45,000	75,000	0.60	0.00
B	60,000	105,000	0.57	0.03
C	80,000	175,000	0.46	0.14
D	90,000	140,000	0.65	0.05
E	155,000	250,000	0.62	0.02
TOTAL	430,000	745,000		0.24

Median Assessment Ratio = 0.60
Mean Assessment Ratio = 0.58
Average Absolute Dispersion = 0.24/5 = 0.048
Coefficient of Dispersion = [0.048/0.60] × 100 = 8.0
Price-Related Differential = 0.58/[430,000/745,000] = 0.58/0.577 = 1.005

If assessment ratios of individual properties are clustered closely around the median ratio, the CD is low, and assessments are relatively uniform. If individual ratios vary widely from the median, the CD is high; properties are not uniformly assessed, and the property tax burden is not fairly distributed among taxpayers. Table 11–2 illustrates CD computation. The CD of 8.0 means that the average parcel is assessed 8.0 percent above or below the median assessment ratio. In practical terms, it means that equally situated properties pay different effective tax rates. Referring to the table, the owner of property D pays an effective tax rate 41.3 percent higher than the rate paid by the owner of property C simply because of lack of uniformity in the assessment process. The higher the CD, the greater the difference of effective rates in the jurisdiction.

Property market fluctuations make it impossible to maintain completely uniform assessment ratios. However, the International Association of Assessing Officers does prescribe standards for uniformity as measured by the coefficient of dispersion. For single-family residential properties, "The [CD] for single-family homes and condominiums should be 15.0 or less. In areas of newer or fairly similar residences, it should be 10.0 or less."[44] The uniformity reflected in Table 11–2 is, thus, pretty good.

Another measure of assessment quality is called the price-related differential (PRD), a measure of assessment regressivity or progressivity. That is, it measures whether higher-valued properties tend to be assessed lower (have lower assessment ratios) or higher (have higher assessment ratios) than lower-valued properties. The PRD is calculated as the mean assessment ratio of all parcels divided by the sum of all assessed values in the sample divided by the sum of all market values in the sample.

PRD = Mean Assessment Ratio/(Sum of Assessed Values/Sum of Market Values)

---

[44]"IAAO Standard on Ratio Studies," *Assessment Journal* 6 (September/October 1999): 60.

A PRD of 1.0 indicates no assessment bias according to value; a PRD greater than 1.0 suggests that higher-value properties are underassessed relative to lower-value parcels (a sort of regressivity); a PRD less than 1.0 suggests that higher-value properties are overassessed relative to lower-value parcels (a sort of progressivity). In other words, if there are differences in assessment ratios, who is getting the better deal: high-value parcels or low-value parcels? Table 11–2 shows the calculation of the PRD.

Many states conduct annual assessment/sales ratio studies that calculate average assessment ratios, coefficients of dispersion, and price-related differentials for each local assessment district. These studies perform three important functions. First, the state uses these results to equalize assessed values (i.e., to ensure that properties are valued according to the same standard) for use in aid distribution to local governments, for application of a state property tax rate, for equity when local tax rates extend beyond one assessing jurisdiction, and for calculation of local government debt limits. Without such equalization, there is an incentive for competitive underassessment to shift costs to other areas. Second, the studies give property owners a better idea of whether their property assessment is generally consistent with that of other taxpayers. The property holder knows that an assessment of $36,000 on a house worth about $120,000 is no bargain if the assessment study shows the mean ratio in the community to be 20 percent; without the ratio study, the holder might celebrate good fortune rather than appeal. Finally, the ratio studies are necessary for evaluation of the work done by property tax assessors. A high CD, in particular, means considerable horizontal inequity in the distribution of the tax burden. A coefficient of 25 means that the average property holder pays property tax that is 25 percent lower or higher than it would be if all properties were assessed at the same ratio. Sidebar 11–4 illustrates the meaning of the CD with a practical application. Although many states now prepare assessment quality studies for all assessing jurisdictions, Illinois takes assessment quality particularly seriously. Assessment/sales ratio studies are prepared annually, and assessors qualify for a pay bonus if they meet a standard defined in terms of median assessment ratio and CD.[45]

The property tax rate, defined statutorily as the same for all property overall or within a class, differs substantially as it applies to particular parcels when assessments are not uniform. A high CD means big differences in assessment ratios and big differences in effective rates paid by comparable properties. A number of studies have tried to identify what might improve the uniformity of property tax assessment. Evidence shows higher uniformity results where assessment ratios are high, reassessments are frequent, assessment personnel are full-time and specifically trained, assessment technology is available (tax maps are current, computer-assisted mass appraisal is used, building permit and deed transfer data are available, etc.), and formal relief mechanisms are available for dealing with perceived inequities (circuit breakers for elderly homeowners facing a high ratio of property tax to current income, use-value assessment, etc.). Size of assessing district, use of contract

---

[45]See Illinois Department of Revenue, *Property Tax Statistics: Assessment Ratios 2013.* http://www.revenue. state.il.us/AboutIdor/TaxStats/PropertyTaxStats/Table-1/2013-AssessmentRatios.pdf

---

Sidebar 11–4
What the Coefficient of Dispersion Means for Property Tax Bills

The CD measures the extent to which assessment ratios (assessed value divided by selling price) of property parcels recently sold differ from uniformity. If all parcels were assessed at the same ratio, then the effective property tax rate—the property tax owed divided by the value of the property—would all be the same (the rate would be uniform) and the CD would be zero. As there are differences in assessment ratios, the CD rises. The implications of this disparity, or lack of uniformity, can be demonstrated in a simple illustration.

During 2007, sales disclosure records provided 502 sales of single-family residential properties in Montgomery County, Indiana, that were valid transactions for analysis (i.e., not foreclosures, not between family members, not including substantial personal property in the transaction, etc.). Analysis of the data showed the median assessment ratio to be 89.3 percent (the state law prescribed 100 percent) and that the coefficient of dispersion was 15.7. That means that the average house was assessed at 15.7 percent above or below 89.3 percent of its market value as measured by comparable transaction prices. In these sales data from disclosures to the Indiana Department of Local Government Finance, the median selling price was $105,000.

What do these data tell us about the property tax bill and the effective property tax rate paid by the typical property?[1] In Montgomery County, thirteen properties sold at a price of around $105,000—in other words, from $103,000 to $107,000. Assessment ratios for these parcels ranged from 0.3933 to 1.3495. The statutory property tax rate in Montgomery County varies according to the particular overlaying governments serving a particular location, but in one part of the county seat (Crawfordsville) the rate is around $4.30 per $100 of assessed value. Therefore, for the property with the highest assessment ratio, the annual property tax bill would have been $6,209; for the property with the lowest, the annual bill would have been $1,759. The properties are of essentially the same market value, but there is a huge difference in property tax bills simply because the assessor estimated a different taxable value for the properties—and the CD here is not even in the horrible class. The CD gives a measure of how large, in general, this degree of assessment disparity is, and how large the disparity of tax bills will be. The higher the CD, the greater the variation in effective property tax rates and the greater the horizontal inequity of the tax.

[1]Effective property tax rates are normally calculated relative to the market value of the property rather than relative to income of the property holder because the tax applies to the property (*in rem*) and not who owns it. Distributional analysis may link owners and their income to properties, but that involves a set of questions different from the success of achieving uniform and unbiased assessment of property parcels.

---

appraisal firms, and whether assessors are elected or appointed seem not to matter much. Uniformity is greater when property tax rates are higher, presumably because more is at stake. However, much of actual performance depends on local property market and economic conditions.[46]

---

[46]John H. Bowman and John L. Mikesell, "Improving Administration of the Property Tax: A Review of Prescriptions and Their Impact," *Public Budgeting and Financial Management* 2 (November 1990): 151–76.

Collecting the Tax

Real property tax collection and enforcement process differs from that employed for other major taxes. Administration is taxpayer passive. Government officials maintain property records, determine the value of the parcel upon which the tax is applied, compute the tax bill from all entities applying a rate to the parcel, and transmit the resulting bill to the parcel owner. A government treasurer receives resulting payments and can calculate the amount of unpaid tax by subtracting tax paid from tax billed. They know who has not paid, they know how much has not been paid, and they report the amount of tax levied but not collected in their comprehensive annual financial reports, data not possible for income and sales taxes.

Collection action is normally against the property and not the owner, and that action involves an auction for collection of the taxes owed. In somewhat more than half the states, liens against parcels with delinquent tax are auctioned each year, with bids being required to cover at least delinquent tax, fees, and penalties. The highest bidder then has a lien against the property, and the property owner can redeem that property by paying the lienholder everything owed plus substantial interest defined in the delinquent tax law. If the property owner does not discharge the lien within a specified period, the lien purchaser may start proceedings to own the property. Another group of states manage delinquent tax collection by auctioning tax certificates with bids of interest rates that will be accepted by the certificate investor. The investor with the lowest rate bid pays the tax and receives the certificate. The property owner has a limited period of time in which to pay the tax owed plus the interest to the certificate holder. If the payment is not made, the certificate holder can start the process toward property ownership. In both tax sale arrangements, the interest rates are usually attractive and bidders are seeking to earn the interest, not to end up owning the property. The taxing jurisdictions receive delinquent tax immediately and the property owner can clear up the problem to restore clear ownership later by dealing with the winning bidder. In normal times, what could be called the property tax compliance gap is tiny.[47]

Property Tax Relief Mechanisms

Governments provide a number of different systems of property tax relief. They may involve reductions in the tax base (exemptions or reduced assessment ratios), preferential tax rates, or direct credit against tax owed. The relief may be provided because of (1) the character of the owner (e.g., exemptions for the elderly), (2) the

---

[47]Recent years have not been normal for cities like Detroit, Milwaukee, and Cleveland, where property tax delinquencies have been considerably above the 1 to 3 percent normally encountered. John L. Mikesell and Cheol Liu, "Property Tax Stability: A Tax System Model of Base and Revenue Dynamics Through the Great Recession and Beyond," *Public Finance and Management* XIII (Number 4, 2013). Delinquencies were a much greater problem in the Great Depression of the 1930s and many people lost their farms, homes, and businesses in that era.

type of property (e.g., owner-occupied residential property), or (3) how the property is (or is going to be) used (e.g., facilities for pollution abatement).[48] Most programs are established by state legislation for all localities in the state, even though most property tax revenue goes to local government. Some state programs do allow some local choice about granting the relief. Figure 11–1 diagrams the alternative approaches to providing residential property tax relief, all working through the rate calculation equation previously described. Those on the left branch work on the general rate and have an impact on all properties; those on the right branch are focused on particular property groupings, usually residential, although sometimes agricultural. The right-branch reliefs can be more targeted than those on the left, although some can be extremely broad in practice.

Exemptions, Credits, and Abatements

Property tax systems almost always include provisions that subtract a portion of assessed value from the taxable holdings of certain individuals or institutions. Thus, if an individual holding property with assessed value of $8,500 qualifies for a veterans' exemption of $1,500, that person's tax bill would be computed on a net assessed value of $7,000. The exemption reduces the tax base. In most instances, the exemptions are additive, so if a parcel holder qualifies for exemption because of age and veteran status, for example, the property tax base would be reduced by the sum of both exemptions. If the relief is granted as a credit, the reduction from the relief is on the tax bill and not on the tax base.

Exemptions may be granted to certain individuals or institutions, or they may be granted to certain types of property. In the first group are exemptions granted conditional on ownership: (1) government property (federal, state, or local, as well as foreign government property not used for commercial purposes); (2) property held by religious, educational, charitable, or nonprofit organizations; and (3) residential property (through homestead, veterans', mortgage, or old-age exemptions). The second group includes preferential incentives intended to induce favored activities without regard for the otherwise taxable nature of the property holder. These include exemptions for economic development (new plants or equipment), pollution control facilities, and land maintained in an undeveloped, natural state. Closely related are abatements, negotiated contracts between a locality and a parcel holder under which some share of assessed value is not taxed for an agreed-upon period of time. The negotiations are normally arranged to induce developers to undertake projects they would not otherwise have done. Whether abatements actually have that effect is not entirely clear. In most environments, to abate the tax on certain properties means that properties without abatement in the taxing unit pay higher

---

[48]Property tax incentives, i.e., relief mechanisms in the form of exemptions, abatements, credits, etc., for business are examined in detail in Daphne A. Kenyon, Adam H. Langley, and Bethany P. Paquin, *Rethinking Property Tax Incentives for Business* (Cambridge, Mass.: Lincoln Institute of Land Policy, 2012).

Figure 11–1
Forms of Property Tax Relief

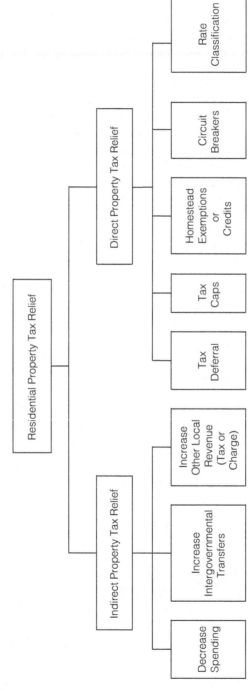

SOURCE: Based on John H. Bowman, Daphne A. Kenyon, Adam Langley, and Bethany P. Paquin, Property Tax Circuit Breakers: Fair and Cost-Effective Relief for Taxpayers. Cambridge, Massachusetts: Lincoln Institute of Land Policy, 2009, p. 5. Reprinted with permission.

tax to support government services; other taxpayers, not the government offering the abatement, bear its cost.[49]

Individuals qualify for many different classes of exemptions. Some of the more important classes used by states (in terms of size of value) are homestead, veterans', and old-age exemptions. Homestead exemptions allow homeowners a given assessed value base before any property tax bill is levied against property. Veterans' and old-age exemptions provide similar partial exemption from the tax. These exemptions can dramatically reduce the base on which the tax can be applied. Nationwide, the partial exemptions reduced gross locally assessed property values by 3.6 percent in 1991. However, the loss of value exceeded 10 percent in several states: Alabama (12.3), Florida (14.1), Hawaii (13.4), Idaho (15.0), Indiana (10.6), and Louisiana (27.5).[50] The redistributions of the cost of government are not trivial.

Such exemption programs are politically popular because of their apparent tax savings, but they have a number of important problems. First, the programs usually have a statewide purpose, but because property taxes primarily support local government, the revenue consequences are local. They may become a way for state legislatures to win votes without losing state revenue. Abatements are locally arranged, but one government (e.g., a city) may contract away a property tax base important to another entity (e.g., a school district). Second, the programs do not focus tax relief on the needy. All people falling into the specific demographic categories (e.g., homeowners or veterans) receive aid, regardless of their specific needs because there is no income or means test for receipt of the exemption.[51] Despite trials and tribulations, homeowners probably are better off than renters, and not all homeowners are equally well (or poorly) situated. Third, if the exemption program is sufficiently widespread, as in the case of general homestead exemption programs, the effect may be substantially higher property tax rates to recover lost revenue. For properties not completely exempted from the base, actual relief may be more psychological than real because the owner pays a higher rate on a smaller base, with about the same total tax bill. Fourth, individual exemption programs ordinarily do not apply to rental properties, and renters tend to be considerably less affluent than are property owners.

Exemptions also apply to some commercial and industrial property.[52] Cities and counties often seek to encourage economic development within their boundaries through exemptions. Property tax payments made by the benefited facility are reduced; local governments serving that facility either receive less property tax revenue or replace the lost proceeds by increasing their statutory rates on the other

---

[49]Abatements are discussed in greater detail in Esteban Dalehite, John L. Mikesell, and C. Kurt Zorn, "Variation in Property Tax Abatement Programs among States," *Economic Development Quarterly* 19 (May 2005): 157–73. Abatements can be thought of as a partial and short-term version of a split-rate property tax: a tax reduction for the improvement but not for land.

[50]U.S. Bureau of the Census, *1992 Census of Governments, Vol. 2, Taxable Property Values, No. 1, Assessed Valuation for Local General Property Taxation,* XI. More recent national data are, unfortunately, not available.

[51]Sometimes a state will do some targeting of exemptions. For instance, Indiana provides an old-age exemption in its property tax but conditions receipt of the exemption on the adjusted gross income of the property owner.

[52]The best general source of information on these programs is Steven Gold, *Property Tax Relief* (Lexington, Mass.: Heath, 1979). Unfortunately, it is severely out of date.

taxable properties in their jurisdictions. If all works well, the fiscal impacts of the relief will be bearable because the fruits of economic development, by reducing social expenditure demands and increasing taxable base, will restore the finances of the localities. The exemption may be complete and permanent, or it may abate all or a portion of property tax for a specific period of time. It may also exempt portions of an otherwise taxable parcel, such as pollution-control equipment or solar energy equipment. Some areas also provide special exemptions for rehabilitated property. The idea is to stimulate economic activity of particular types at defined locations. Evidence suggests things other than property taxes—particularly accessibility to markets, resource availability, transportation networks, and environmental amenities—are much more significant in determining the location of commercial and industrial facilities. Thus, the expected return from such exemptions is low. An even greater problem than low return from the exemption, however, may be the effect on existing property in the area if the incentive works. New industries create a demand for public services (police protection, fire protection, planning, etc.), and new people in the area will likely demand more services than can be covered by the residential tax base they bring. With the new industrial property exempt, those costs must be borne by the existing tax base. This system, at best, is discriminatory and, at worst, may eliminate some marginal businesses. Those properties not qualifying for the exemption face artificially high property tax rates because of the assistance provided the new arrivals.

A final exemption group includes properties that are fully exempt because of the religious, governmental, educational, or charitable nature of the owner. An accurate estimate of the total amount of the potential tax base removed by these exemptions is not available because where the law requires assessment of these properties, officials do not devote much effort on properties that yield no tax revenue. The revenue loss is a particular problem because such properties are unequally distributed among localities. Cities, counties, or school districts with major state installations (e.g., universities and state parks) can be particularly affected. They must provide for the peak and special service demands created by users of that facility without the power to include that facility in the tax base. Thus, taxpayers of that locality must subsidize the citizenry of the state. The problem is reduced somewhat when exemptions are conditioned on both ownership and use of the facility (a university classroom building may be exempt, but not a university-owned hotel), but the dual requirement is neither universal nor applied without interpretation problems. The federal government does make in-lieu-of-property-tax payments to state and local units hosting certain federal installations, but states seldom provide similar relief to their local governments. As discussed in Chapter 12, local user charges may well be an attractive option in such instances. In other words, the university may be exempt from the local property tax, but if it wants to have the city pick up its trash, it will have to pay for the service.

Abatements have historically been a tool used to benefit commercial activities with little formal attention to the amounts of revenue being sacrificed. That changes with Government Accounting Standards Board Statement No. 77, effective for financial statements for periods beginning after December 15, 2015. The statement requires governments to disclose certain essential information about abatement agreements they have arranged. The disclosure includes the purpose of the tax abatement program, the tax being abated, the dollar amount of tax abated, the provisions regarding recapture of abated taxes if promised actions do not materialize, the type of commitments made by abatement recipients, and other commitments made by the government in the abatement agreement, such as promises to build infrastructure. This disclosure is intended to improve transparency of fiscal process; it is not entirely clear how the disclosures will actually be applied and the extent to which they will apply across the entire state-local tax portfolio. But the requirement certainly will include property tax deals given to particular firms.

Circuit Breakers

Property tax exemptions to individuals fail to target property tax relief to those individuals most in need. That problem can be reduced by conditioning property tax assistance on individual income levels, as is done by property tax circuit breakers. Residential-property circuit breakers, used by thirty-three states and the District of Columbia, pinpoint relief of property tax overload (defined in terms of the ratio of property tax payment to current family income) through integration of the local property tax and the state individual income tax structure.[53] The taxpayer reports, on his or her income tax return, the amount of property tax paid for the year. The property tax paid is compared with the taxpayer's income. If the ratio of property tax to income is excessive as defined in the circuit breaker law (an "overload"), the state returns some portion of overload to the individual as an addition to his or her income tax refund, a reduction in income tax owed, or a direct cash payment. Thus, the circuit breaker reduces the property tax overload at state expense. In addition, the circuit breaker relief is targeted to those identified as being in need of relief— simply paying high property taxes alone would not be grounds for giving relief.

Critical structural elements for circuit breakers include age restrictions, income definition and limits, renter status, and benefit formulas. Many programs limit overload relief to the elderly, at least partly to reduce program cost. Elderly individuals, however, may be especially susceptible to overload because the property tax bill on property they accumulate during their work careers does not fall as their income falls with retirement. The property tax bill that was reasonable in relation to salary may consume an excessive chunk of the pension. The circuit breaker can reduce the need for forced sale and can ease retirement. Nonelderly low-income homeowners, however, may face similar overloads, particularly in the early years of home ownership or when a family income earner becomes unemployed.

Income limitations for the circuit breaker program are another design question. States do not provide circuit breaker formula relief to all, but rather impose income ceilings beyond which the system does not apply. The ceilings reduce program cost and concentrate assistance on lower-income people. For these purposes, however,

---

[53]John H. Bowman, Daphne A. Kenyon, Adam Langley, and Bethany P. Paquin, *Property Tax Circuit Breakers: Fair and Cost-Effective Relief for Taxpayers* (Cambridge, Mass.: Lincoln Institute for Land Policy, 2009).

income must be defined more broadly than federal or state taxable income to include nontaxed retirement income sources. If it is not, individuals who are reasonably well off because of pension, Social Security, and other nontaxed incomes would qualify, reducing aid available for the truly unfortunate.

Renters pose a third design issue, under the assumption that they bear a portion of the property tax burden on units they occupy, that is, if the property tax is partially shifted forward. A circuit breaker limited to homeowners would provide renters no assistance, even though many renters are much less affluent than the poorest homeowners. Renter relief, where given, presumes a property tax equivalent as a specified percentage of rent paid. The share is not scientifically determined because analysts have been unable to estimate the extent (if any) to which property tax is shifted to renters. With reasonable income limits, however, the program can be seen as a part of general assistance regardless of property tax conditions.

The final design element is the choice between threshold and sliding-scale relief formulas. The former approach defines a threshold percentage of income as the overload level (somewhat more than half the circuit breaker states use this approach). Property tax payments above that overload level are subject to partial relief. Relief computation follows the formula

$$R = t(PT - kI)$$

where

R = relief to be provided (subject to a lower limit of zero),

t = percentage of the overload that is relieved,

PT = property tax payment,

k = overload threshold percentage, and

I = family income.

Suppose a family has an income of \$12,000 and pays property tax of \$900. If it lives in a state that defines the overload threshold as 5 percent and grants 60 percent overload relief, the family would receive circuit breaker relief of \$180. Some states further reduce their cost by increasing the threshold percentage as income increases (in other words, they have multiple thresholds)—a further effort to economize and focus aid.

The second formula is the sliding-scale approach. In this formula, relief is computed as a percentage of the property tax payment, with the percentage falling as family income increases:

$$R = z \times PT$$

where z is the percentage of property tax relieved for the income class and R and PT are as previously defined. Unless the relief percentage falls to zero at high incomes, all taxpayers receive assistance under this approach, so it is more like general property tax relief than the specific relief of the property tax overload. It does differ, however, from general property tax relief in that (1) there is usually an upper limit to circuit breaker relief available to a parcel holder, (2) taxpayers must file to obtain this relief, (3) only homes occupied by the owner receive the circuit breaker relief (although some states extend the assistance to farm property), and (4) relief is conditioned on income of the property owner.

Circuit breakers are flexible and easily administered in conjunction with the state income tax. Circuit breakers improve property tax equity by targeting relief to those in greatest need and, furthermore, are financed from state, not local, revenue. They provide no incentive, however, for improved property tax administration and may encourage greater use of local property taxes, as some property tax costs are shifted to the state.

Deferrals

Property tax deferrals provide relief for the special property tax problems of the elderly, people with disabilities, those with limited income, and farm owners on the fringe of developing areas. With this mechanism, individuals whose property values have risen dramatically through no fault of their own are permitted to pay tax on the basis of old values, with records kept on the difference between that payment and what it would have been at full property value. That difference is deferred to a later time, but not forgiven. In the case of the agricultural property, it is collected when the farmland converts to a different (higher-value) use. In the case of the elderly individual, the deferred tax becomes a claim against that individual's estate.

These recaptures can be complete or partial, and interest may or may not be charged; state approaches vary. The tax deferral relieves special property tax burdens without creating the problems that circuit breakers and special exemptions often create. Deferrals can relieve without special subsidization—a rare combination in tax policy.

Classification

Some states intend that all properties bear the same statutory tax rate, but others provide classified rates that apply higher rates to certain types of property. Table 11–3 divides the states between those who provide a classified structure and those who intend a uniform rate for all properties. The classification is provided either by prescribing different assessment ratios for type of property or by providing for statutory tax rates that differ by class of property. Classification assumes that certain property classes have superior taxpaying capability over other classes and should pay higher effective property tax rates. Tax-bearing capability, however, varies dramatically within classes, often to a greater extent than variation between classes. In other words, there are affluent and not-so-affluent homeowners, prosperous and poor farmers, and profitable and bankrupt businesses. The classification systems, however, treat each ownership class or property type as if all units in that class were alike. Furthermore, classification is more likely to be based on political clout or the expected ease of shifting the tax to someone else than on any reasonable justification for allocating appropriate tax burdens.

Table 11–3
Property Tax Classification across the States

State	Classification Method
Alabama	Assessment Ratios
Alaska	None
Arizona	Assessment Ratios
Arkansas	None
California	None
Colorado	Assessment Ratios
Connecticut	None
Delaware	None
District of Columbia	Rates
Florida	None
Georgia	Assessment Ratios
Hawaii	Rates
Idaho	None
Illinois	None
Indiana	None, but there are all-taxing-jurisdiction combined rate ceilings that differ by class of property
Iowa	Assessment Ratios
Kansas	Assessment Ratios
Kentucky	Rates
Louisiana	Assessment Ratios
Maine	None
Maryland	Rates
Massachusetts	Rates
Michigan	Rates (school district only)
Minnesota	Assessment Ratios
Mississippi	Assessment Ratios
Missouri	Assessment Ratios
Montana	Assessment Ratios
Nebraska	Assessment Ratios
Nevada	None
New Hampshire	None
New Jersey	None
New Mexico	Rates
New York	None / New York City: Rates and Assessment Ratios
North Carolina	Assessment Ratios
North Dakota	Assessment Ratios
Ohio	None
Oklahoma	Assessment Ratios
Oregon	None
Pennsylvania	None
Rhode Island	Rates
South Carolina	Assessment Ratios
South Dakota	Rates (school district)
Tennessee	Assessment Ratios

(continues)

Table 11–3
(continued)

State	Classification Method
Texas	None
Utah	Assessment Ratios
Vermont	Rates
Virginia	Rates
Washington	None
West Virginia	Rates
Wisconsin	Assessment Ratios
Wyoming	Assessment Ratios

SOURCE: Lincoln Institute of Land Policy and George Washington Institute of Public Policy, *Significant Features of the Property Tax* www.lincolninst.edu/subcenters/significant-features-property-tax/Report_State_Summaries.aspx

Classification can be accomplished by either variation in assessment ratios or variation in statutory rates. New York City applies rates that differ by type of property, as shown in these rates for 2011-2012: Class 1: includes most residential property of up to three units (family homes and small stores or offices with one or two apartments attached) and most condominiums that are not more than three stories, 18.025%; Class 2: includes all other property that is primarily residential, such as cooperatives and condominiums, 13.433%; Class 3: includes utility property, 12.473%; and Class 4: includes all commercial and industrial property, such as office and factory buildings, 10.152%. Most states employ different assessment ratios. For instance, the Alabama classification by assessment ratios works like this: Class I property (public utility property) is assessed at 30 percent of appraised value; Class II property (real and personal property not falling into any of the other classes) is assessed at 20 percent of appraised value; Class III property (agricultural and forest, historic buildings and sites, and residential property) is assessed at 10 percent of appraised value; and Class IV (private automobiles and trucks) is assessed at 15 percent of appraised value. Both systems result in an effective property tax rate—the rate on market value of the property—that differs according to classification of the property.

Each method can produce the same effective-rate pattern, as Table 11–4 demonstrates. Classification by statutory rate variation is more straightforward and transparent and interferes less with the assessment process. If classification is to be adopted, that approach is preferable, although Table 11–3 showed it to be less frequently used than classification by ratios.

Limits and Controls

Extraordinary tax rate limits and controls—beyond the normal process of rate setting—establish a special structure for property tax operation. A categorization of controls appears in Table 11–5. A number of the special controls date from the 1970s, although several have more lengthy heritages. The "tax revolt," especially

Table 11–4
Property Classifications by Statutory Rates and Assessment Ratios: An Illustration

Classes of Property	Rate Classification			Ratio Classification		
	Statutory Rate ($)	Assessment Ratio (%)	Effective Rate ($)	Statutory Rate($)	Assessment Ratio (%)	Effective Rate ($)
Owner-Occupied Housing	2.00	50	1.00	4.00	25	1.00
Farms	1.00	50	0.50	4.00	12.5	0.50
Commercial and Industrial	4.00	50	2.00	4.00	50	2.00
Public Utilities	8.00	50	4.00	4.00	100	4.00

Proposition 13 in California and related referenda in other states from 1978 through 1980, was partly the product of high and rising effective property tax rates on owner-occupied housing. The rising taxes were created by, among several forces, demands for local public service, limited access to non-property tax revenue, waste in local government, and special exemptions provided to some property types. A large part of that rebellion, however, surely reflected irritation with government in general and the feeling of powerlessness to do anything about federal or state taxes—those taxes rose without any statutory rate increase for which elected representatives were clearly responsible. The property tax was another matter. The rate would normally vary each year, so it presented an ideal focal point for those concerns. It became the lightning rod for government finance nationwide during the periods of taxpayer discontent.

Property taxes have been subject to extraordinary limitations at least since the Great Depression of the 1930s. Those limits, however, traditionally controlled local statutory tax rates, either in state statute or in the constitution. These controls on the tax rate appeared ineffective as assessed values increased dramatically, both in total and for individual property parcels, during the high-inflation 1970s. Governments could adopt statutory property tax rates no higher than those of the prior year and within the statutory limit and still obtain dramatically increased revenue because of the higher assessed values. Property owners whose parcels had been reassessed would face increased property tax bills at the controlled property tax rate. Thus, controls on statutory rates, whether through a statutory rate limit or a rate freeze, seemed powerless as constraints on either local governments or property tax bills.

The approach taken in the 1970s was the levy or expenditure limit, which capped total dollars, not the rate applied to the tax base. That approach does constrain the growth of government activity and prevents assessed value increases from being

Table 11–5
Property Tax Control Structures and Their Impacts

Type of Limit	Example	Impact on Property Tax Rate	Impact on Property Tax Levies	Impact on Expenditures
Legal limit on statutory property tax rate	Cities limited to rate of $5.00/$100 assessed value.	Same ceiling rate statewide.	Levy can increase as assessed value increases or with rate increase for jurisdictions not at legal limit.	Same as levies, plus possible increases from other revenue sources.
Property tax rate freeze	Cities limited to statutory rate applied in 2010.	Ceiling rate varies across state.	Levy can increase only as assessed value increases.	Same as above.
Property levy limit	Cities' 2010 levy cannot exceed 105% of 2009 levy.	Depends on change in assessed value.	Constrained to limit	Depends on access to nonproperty tax revenues.
Expenditure limit	Cities' 2010 appropriations cannot exceed 108% of 2009 appropriations.	Depends on change in assessed value and on change in other revenues.	Depends on access to nonproperty tax revenues.	Constrained to limit.
Assessed value increase limit	Assessed value of any property (or properties) in city may not increase by more than 5% in 2009 regardless of reassessment result.	Depends on regular rate calculation.	Depends on local budget process/race calculation.	Depends on local budget process.
"Truth in taxation"/full disclosure	Cities announce impact of new assessed values on tax levy if rates maintained, what rate reduction would maintain old tax levy and, proposed new tax rate, and call for public input on their decisions.	Depends on regular rate calculation.	Depends on local budget process/ rate calculation.	Depends on local budget process.

SOURCE: Daniel Mullins and Bruce Wallin, "Tax and Expenditure Limitations: Introduction and Overview," *Public Budgeting & Finance* 24 (Winter 2004): 2–15.

Table 11–6
Rate Computations for a Levy Control: Levy Increase Limited to 5 Percent, Assessed Value Grows by 8 Percent

Budget Year	Assessed Value ($)	Levy ($)	Property Tax Rate ($)
1	5,000,000	250,000	5.00 per 100
2	5,400,000	262,500	4.86 per 100

automatically translated into higher tax collections and higher tax bills for parcels. With a levy freeze, a general assessed-value increase will require a reduction in tax rates. For example, suppose that a control law permits 5 percent levy growth from one year to the next and that assessed value increases by 8 percent. Rate computations might look like those in Table 11–6. With this control structure, property tax levy ceilings dominate the budget process. Maximum growth in the levy establishes the budget size, and total budget requests must keep within the limit. As soon as assessed value figures are known, property tax rates can be computed because law establishes the total levy. The only unknown is the manner in which the total is appropriated among operating units. In this case, the budget total is not made up of its operating components; rather, the budget total is divided among the operating components, and one extra dollar provided to one agency is truly a dollar not available to any other agency. The total budget cannot expand to accommodate any additions.

Limits of the 1970s were obviously more stringent than the earlier rate controls.[54] They led local governments to adopt a consistent set of responses. First, governments have sought to get other governments or nonprofit organizations to take over services the controlled government has been providing. If the approach succeeds, the services in question are provided, but the controlled government retains the previously committed resources for other activities. Second, governments have sought increased intergovernmental aid (grants, shared taxes, etc.) to continue services without the use of local resources. This search is particularly intense to finance mandated services, that is, services the government provides largely because it has been required to do so by another government. If that government both restricts taxing powers and mandates new expenditure, the intergovernmental strain is especially intense. Finally, governments have levied charges and non-property taxes not covered by the limits. The charges are sometimes merely disguised property taxes (e.g., fire or police protection fees based on property characteristics), but they can be welcome additions that improve both the efficiency and the equity of service finance. Expanded use of legitimate charges is in fact the most attractive side effect of the new limitation movement. Sometimes limits get circumvented by creation of new special districts to take over provision of certain governmental services, with new taxing authority being provided outside the previous limits.

---

[54]The exception is for governments experiencing assessed value decline. A levy control for these units permits the accommodating rate increases that rate control does not.

Another approach limits the growth in assessed value. In this case, when properties are reassessed, the increase in value cannot exceed a particular percentage. Over time, the full increase in valuation is permitted, but it is gradual. It is primarily a control over reassessment shock and the danger that local governments will not adjust their statutory rates when the increase in assessed value hits their budget system. The control can have discriminatory effects. For instance, in New York City, tax increases for some buildings may not increase by more than 6 to 8 percent per year or 20 to 30 percent over five years. That shifts city tax burdens from areas in which property values are increasing dramatically (making their owners even more wealthy than they were before) to blighted areas where prices are not rising. Inexpensive properties tend to bear higher effective tax rates.

A final approach to controlling property tax increases, but without the direct constraints previously noted, is the "truth in taxation" or full disclosure requirement, a system in place in several states, including Arizona, Texas, and Michigan. This system requires local governments to call attention to the fact that assessed values have increased and that their property tax levies will increase unless they reduce their statutory property tax rates to allow for the higher assessed values. An illustration of a "truth in taxation" notification appears in Figure 11–2. This notification from the Pima County (Arizona) Community College District warns its citizens that the District intends to increase its property tax levy and that the increase is in addition to any increase that would result from a higher property tax base (the increase from new construction). The district is thus both taking the proceeds of the higher property tax base and adding an increase in the property tax rate to all parcels. The notice announces a public hearing at which the public can express its views about the tax proposal. The idea is to bring more transparency into the rate-setting process and to allow for public response in fiscal decisions. Similar increases in the tax base, of course, occur with taxes on income and consumption, but there are no laws requiring such "truth in taxation" notifications for them.

Tax Increment Financing

Tax increment financing (TIF) offers support for economic development in targeted, usually blighted, areas. A TIF program "largely freezes the assessed valuation of all property parcels in a designated area (the TIF district) for a specific period of years. Property taxes levied in this frozen tax base continue to accrue to local taxing bodies, but taxes derived from the increases in assessed values (the tax increment) resulting from new development are used to pay for infrastructure needs and development expenditures in the TIF district. Thus, TIF serves as a geographically targeted tax, expenditure, and regulatory inducement to a specific location."[55] In logic, the

---

[55]Joyce Y. Man, "Introduction," in *Tax Increment Financing and Economic Development: Uses, Structures, and Impact,* ed. Craig L. Johnson and Joyce Y. Man (Albany, N.Y.: State University of New York Press, 2001): 1. Some states have included non-property taxes in the TIF as well, although this is not common.

Figure 11–2
Truth in Taxation Notification: Pima County (Arizona) Community College District for 2016

TRUTH IN TAXATION HEARING

NOTICE OF TAX INCREASE

In compliance with section 15-1461.01, Arizona Revised Statutes, Pima County Community College District is notifying its property taxpayers of Pima County Community College District's intention to raise its primary property taxes over last year's level. The Pima County Community College District is proposing an increase in primary property taxes of $1,814,406 or 2.0%.

For example, the proposed tax increase will cause Pima County Community College District's primary property taxes on a $100,000 home to increase from $112.59 (total taxes that would be owed without the proposed tax increase) to $114.84 (total proposed taxes including the tax increase).

This proposed increase is exclusive of increased primary property taxes received from new construction. The increase is also exclusive of any changes that may occur from property tax levies for voter approved bonded indebtedness or budget and tax overrides.

All interested citizens are invited to attend the public hearing on the tax increase that is scheduled to be held Wednesday, June 20, 2012 at 6:30 p.m. in the Community/Board Room at the District Office of Pima Community College, 4905 E. Broadway, Tucson, Arizona 85709-1005.

PimaCommunityCollege

Pima County Community College District
Board of Governors
District 1 Dr. Brenda B. Even, Secretary
District 2 David Longoria
District 3 Sherryn S. Marshall
District 4 Scott A. Stewart, Chair
District 5 Marty Cortez
Dr. Suzanne L. Miles, Interim Chancellor

(520) 206-4500
www.pima.edu

Pima Community College is an equal opportunity, affirmative action employer and educational institution committed to excellence through diversity. Reasonable accommodations, including materials in an alternative format, will be provided for individuals with disabilities when a minimum of five working days' advance notice is given. For the general public, please contact the PCC information line at (520) 206-4500 (TTY 206-4530); for PCC students, contact the appropriate campus Disabled Student Resources office.

Table 11–7
Tax Increment Financing

	Assessed Value ($)	Tax Rate ($/$100)	Yield to Overlapping Governments ($)	Yield to TIF District ($)
Base (predevelopment)	5,000,000	8.00	400,000	0
Year 1	6,000,000	8.10	405,000	81,000
Year 2	7,000,000	8.15	407,500	163,000
Year 3	8,000,000	8.15	407,500	244,500
Year 4	8,000,000	8.20	410,000	246,000

public capital infrastructure needed for a private development project would be self-financed from property taxes from the project. Here is how the scheme could work. Suppose a large manufacturing plant wants to build on a site that lacks certain critical infrastructure normally provided by local government (roads, storm and sanitary sewers, water, etc.). A sponsoring local government could borrow to finance the improvements with payment of debt service (principal and interest) coming from the property tax proceeds from the increased property tax base. Table 11–7 illustrates the general idea of a TIF. If property assessments before development totaled $5 million, taxing units would receive tax proceeds on that base as usual. As assessments rise with development, say, to $8 million, property tax collections on that higher base, regardless of the government levying the tax rate, will be diverted to service the infrastructure debt: property tax on $5 million goes to the overlapping local governments, and property tax on $3 million (the increment) goes to service the debt that allowed the infrastructure making the development feasible.

TIFs have proven popular with industry and development officials, but they often irritate other local officials, especially those operating schools, because the transfer of revenue can seriously strain the finances of general government. Also, use of TIF revenues is so uncontrolled in some jurisdictions that they can be returned to developers to recoup costs not related to improving the public infrastructure around the project—something like a tax "kickback."

Conclusion

The property tax is the predominant tax source for local government, the state and federal governments having taken the other major bases. That may be a good thing, because many elements of a market-value-based property tax make it particularly suited for local use. Though property taxes represent an opportunity to tax accumulated wealth not offered by levies on other bases, that advantage is overshadowed by haphazard and capricious assessment of the tax base. Because the tax applies to values defined by applying regulations, not values from market transactions, assessment is troublesome and requires special attention. Most problems with the property tax, outside of valuation, can be largely resolved by circuit breakers, deferrals, and the like.

It would be unfortunate if the advantages of the tax were sacrificed solely because of unwillingness to improve administration. The advantages of the property tax for local government finance are several. The base is visible, easily attached in an enforcement action, and physically immobile. The tax can be administered at a leisurely pace, and the rate can be adjusted to a fine degree. Those supporting a considerable degree of fiscal independence for the government closest to the people should consider how important the real property tax is to this independence.

QUESTIONS AND EXERCISES

1. Identify these elements of the property tax in your state: Who assesses property? Are some types assessed locally and some types by the state? What valuation standard is used? When was the latest reassessment of real property? Is personal property taxed? What classification system (if any) is used? What circuit breaker type (if any) is used? Does the circuit breaker extend beyond residential property owned by the elderly?

2. Why is the acquisition value or assessment-on-sale assessment system sometimes called the "Welcome Stranger" assessment system?

3. Central County includes five townships (Nixon, Reagan, Davis, Greasy Creek, and Navaho) and one city (Booneville). It is served by two independent school districts: Seagram United Schools (Davis and Greasy Creek Townships) and Clinton Consolidated Schools (Nixon, Reagan, and Navaho Townships). Each government in the county levies a property tax to finance its activities, although Booneville has also enacted a local earned income tax (it is expected to yield $750,000 in the next year). Property tax rates are applied to assessed value, defined to equal 50 percent of fair cash value. Local unit tax rates fully overlap. The county assessor reports the following fair cash values for units within the county:

Nixon Township	$69,535,000
Reagan Township	$35,000,000
Davis Township	$23,720,000
Greasy Creek Township	$15,922,000
Navaho Township	$27,291,000
Booneville (Davis Township)	$88,450,000
Booneville (Greasy Creek Township)	$75,392,000

The township value data are for the area outside of any city or town that resides in the township. Values within a city must be added to obtain the township total.

The following presents the amounts that each taxing unit has budgeted to spend in the next year:

Central County	$3,428,000
Booneville City	$4,539,000
Nixon Township	$ 99,000
Reagan Township	$ 150,000
Davis Township	$ 250,000
Greasy Creek Township	$ 175,000
Navaho Township	$ 83,000
Seagram United Schools	$6,350,000
Clinton Consolidated Schools	$3,800,000

a. Set the property tax rate for each taxing unit. Report each rate in dollars per $100 of assessed value.
b. The Knight family owns property with a fair cash value of $100,000 in the Davis portion of Booneville. Prepare an itemized tax bill for the Knights.
c. Suppose the current market value of the Knights' property is actually $225,000. What is their assessment ratio? What effective total property tax rate do they pay?
d. There are 1,800 students in Seagram United Schools and 600 students in Clinton Consolidated Schools. How many dollars per pupil would a tax rate of $1 per $100 of assessed value yield in each district? Explain the significance of this comparison.
e. A factory with an estimated fair cash value of $15 million may be built in Navaho Township. If the factory has no impact on spending by any local government (i.e., levies do not change) and there are no other changes in the county assessed values, what total property tax bill would the factory face?
f. Suppose that the county undergoes a general reassessment that doubles the assessed values of every taxing unit and that state law forbids any taxing unit from increasing its property tax levy by more than 3 percent. (The factory from part e, sadly enough, ends up in Mexico, so there is no impact from its value.) Assume that the property owned by the Knights (as above) doubles in assessed value and that the city, county, and school districts increase their levies by the maximum allowed, but that there is no increase in levies by any township. What is the Knights' new property tax?

4. The state owns 16,500 acres of state forest land in a county. Forest and untilled open areas (the kind of land largely within the boundaries of the state forest) are valued at $180 per acre on average when in private ownership. Assessed value is one-third of that value. The forest area is in two townships of the county. Sixty percent is in a township with a tax rate of $1.80 per $100, and the remainder is in a township with a rate of $1.64 per $100. According to the aid formula for compensating local governments containing substantial amounts of untaxed state property, the county receives in-lieu-of-property-tax payments of $18,000 per

year for division among the affected taxing units of the county. Is the state payment about right in comparison to the equivalent property tax the land would bear? Explain.

5. Mr. and Mrs. Woodward, an elderly couple with no dependents, have taxable source income of $8,000 and Social Security income of $26,000. They own property assessed at $80,000 (current market value of $190,000) and are subject to a property tax rate of $5/$100 of assessed value. They each receive an old-age property tax exemption of $500. They are eligible for the state property tax circuit breaker. The relief threshold is 6 percent of total money income; 25 percent of any overload is returned by the state in an income tax credit. Maximum relief paid is $600 per couple.

   a. What property tax would they pay without circuit breaker relief?
   b. For how much circuit breaker relief are they eligible?

6. The following data are for the town of Paragon in the fiscal year starting January 1, 2016.

Budgeted town expenditures	$20,000,000
Estimated revenue from grants, fees, and licenses	$6,000,000
Assessed value of property	$142,000,000

   a. What is the town property tax rate in dollars per $100 of assessed value?
   b. The Wooden family has property with a fair cash value of $90,000. The assessment ratio is one-third. The family is entitled to a mortgage exemption of $5,000. That is taken against assessed value. What is their property tax bill from Paragon?
   c. Suppose that, for 2017, properties in Paragon are not reassessed, but that new construction increases total assessed values by 5 percent. The state institutes a levy control, allowing 2017 levies to increase by 6 percent over their 2016 level. Non-property tax revenue is estimated to be $6.5 million. What is the maximum 2017 property tax rate permitted, what is the maximum town expenditure, and what property tax bill would the Wooden family face?
   d. Suppose that, for 2018, properties in Paragon are not reassessed, but that new construction increases total assessed value by 9 percent. The state enacts a new property tax control that allows the 2018 levies to increase only by $1.80 over the 2017 levies. Non-property tax revenue is estimated to be $6.75 million. What is the maximum 2018 property tax rate permitted, what is the maximum town expenditure, and what property tax bill would the Wooden family face?

7. The town of Stratford is setting its property tax rate for the upcoming year. Its budget calls for spending of $220,000,000, and it anticipates receiving $700,000 in non-property tax revenue. It levies a classified rate structure: nonresidential properties pay a rate that is double that applied to residential property. Its residential assessed value equals $4,000,000,000, and its nonresidential assessed value equals $2,800,000,000. What property tax rates will the town set for residential and nonresidential property?

CASES FOR DISCUSSION

CASE 11–1

Property Taxes and a World-Class House

Consider These Questions

1. What approaches may apply in this assessment question, and what problems do they have?

2. What is your view of the assessment system briefly outlined here?

3. What help does the asking price for the rental property give the assessor?

Ross Perot, Texas billionaire and candidate for president in 1992, owns an 8,264-square-foot house with four fireplaces and five baths on more than twenty-five acres of land in North Dallas. His estate also has a 5,327-square-foot rental house with 2.2 acres he purchased around 1988. This parcel has been for sale for about a year, with an asking price of $1.2 million. In 1992, the Dallas Central Appraisal District assessed the main house and land at $12,279,600 and the rental property at $1,220,340. (Those had been the assessment levels for three years.) For 1993, the values were $11,870,550 and $1,200,000 in recognition of declining residential property values in Texas. The district uses full-market-value assessment in its appraisals, but often estimates values by area rather than conducting detailed assessments of each parcel.

The district received 65,000 assessment protests in 1993, one of them being from Mr. Perot. He had not protested in earlier years, but comparable sales in the neighborhood led him to conclude that his properties were overassessed. After the initial hearing, his assessment was reduced by $96,100; he filed suit for further reduction in state district court, the normal avenue to continue the appeal. Following routine procedure, assessing officials will inspect and appraise the property; that is the normal approach to beginning negotiations.

SOURCE: This case was assembled from Scott McCartner, "There Is One Thing We Can Be Sure Of: It's a World-Class House," *Wall Street Journal,* September 2, 1993, B-1; Anne Beilli Gesalman, "Perot Sues over Home Appraisal," *Dallas Morning News,* September 1, 1993, 25-A; and Steven R. Reed, "Perot Files Suit to Lower Taxes on His Estate," *Houston Chronicle,* September 2, 1993, 29.

CASE 11–2

Local Finances and Property-Tax-Exempt Organizations

Nonprofit organizations and governments are often exempt from payment of property taxes. The conditions and standards are not the same for all states or even necessarily for all localities within a state, although state law defines the terms for exemption. Furthermore, not all types of nonprofit organizations receive the same exempt treatment. For instance, property owned by governments, churches, educational institutions, and hospitals may be exempt from property taxation, but property owned by other nonprofit organizations may be taxable. The state standards for qualifying as an exempt nonprofit organization are not always the same as those used by the federal government. Local governments that host major exempt organizations (for instance, large private universities or federal or state government facilities) are in a complex situation. On one hand, there can be considerable benefits in terms of economic impact and prestige associated with hosting the entity (Cambridge, Massachusetts, is proud of being the home of both Harvard University and the Massachusetts Institute of Technology, for instance). On the other hand, the exempt property owned by the institutions provides no tax base for use in providing police and fire protection, primary and secondary education, and other services to the community.

When local governments that rely on their property taxes for the finance of government services face fiscal difficulty, their leaders look toward broadening the tax base as a source of revenue. Getting payments from financially large nonprofit organizations and entities of other governments looks attractive to many. It has been estimated that, nationwide, nonprofit organization exemptions reduced property tax collections by 10 percent, with higher shares in areas with particularly large nonprofit sectors. The discussions become particularly focused when the local government is financially stressed while large tax-exempt organizations it hosts appear prosperous.

The case that follows deals with a dispute between Providence, Rhode Island, and Brown University over the amount that tax-exempt Brown would contribute to the city.

Consider These Questions

1. Why should nonprofit organizations be exempt from payment of local property taxes? Don't they benefit from local services just as much as proprietary businesses? For instance, why should a nonprofit hospital be exempt from the local property tax, while a similar proprietary hospital is taxed? Is the argument for exemption different for a state university compared with a similar private university?

2. If they are to be exempt, what standards would you establish for giving the exemption? Should all nonprofit organizations and government entities be in the same boat? What about state universities, state parks, and the state capitol building?

3. What would be the effect of having a large share of the total potential property tax base in a city owned by tax-exempt organizations? Would it mean lost property tax revenue or higher property taxes paid by taxable entities? Any idea how it might be possible to see whether the impact is higher tax paid by others or lower property tax revenue?

4. In some jurisdictions, there are provisions for exempt entities to make payments in lieu of taxes (PILOTs). Should the PILOT amount be voluntary, or should it

be calculated according to a legislated formula? How should the PILOT be calculated? Should the PILOT approximate the amount of property tax payment on the property? If so, why bother exempting the property?[56] Massachusetts legislators have been considering a proposal to levy a 2.5 percent annual assessment on assets of universities with endowments above $1 billion (the Harvard endowment is $35 billion) and Connecticut has been considering a tax on property owned by Yale University (both universities already make voluntary payments to host local governments). Would that be a sensible approach? Does your university make a PILOT to its host local governments? Do other nonprofits in your state make a PILOT payment?

5. State law typically establishes what entities qualify for local property tax exemption. That being the case, should the state government provide payments to local governments to compensate them for any lost revenue?

6. Would you judge the amount ultimately paid by Brown to be about right? What standard would you apply to decide?

Providence and Brown: Bearing the Cost of Government Services

Providence, Rhode Island, in common with many city governments across the United States, has suffered considerable fiscal stress in the years during and after the Great Recession. Indeed, the Providence mayor, Angel Taveras, warned that the city would run out of money in June 2012 and might need to file for federal bankruptcy protection. Its deficit was around $22.5 million, and that amount could not be managed by the city without devastating cuts in services or huge increases in taxes. Many taxpayers had already seen their taxes increased by 13 percent to get even to that deficit level. The deficit in the previous year was $110 million, so the mayor had made considerable progress. To prevent further service cuts or tax increases, the mayor argued that tax-exempt Brown University should make a greater contribution to the support of city services. Indeed, he thought that an extra $5 million per year would be about right.

Rhode Island law exempts private universities, along with many other types of nonprofit organizations, from payment of property taxes. However, Brown—along with many other exempt entities in Providence—had been making voluntary payments to the city, an amount that recently had been around $4 million per year ($1.2 million under a memorandum of understanding between city and university signed in 2003 plus taxes on buildings not used for educational purposes, such as the for-profit bookstore; in contrast with many other states, tax does not apply to these noneducational facilities, so that payment was voluntary as well). The mayor

---

[56]Boston and its nonprofit universities have a program under which the universities pay the city to help cover the costs of police and fire protection, snow removal, and other services. In fiscal 2015, thirteen of the nineteen colleges in the city paid less than the amount the city had requested. For instance, Harvard paid 44 percent, Suffolk University paid just over 50 percent, Northeastern University paid 13 percent, and Boston College paid 2.3 percent. Matt Rocheleau, "Many Colleges Missing Mark on Voluntary Payments to City," *Boston Globe*, July 21, 2015.

believed that the current amount was not enough. City data show that tax-exempt organizations like Brown hold more than half the land in Providence, amounting to 41 percent of assessed value (if those figures can be trusted; assessors throughout the nation do not devote their greatest care to assessing parcels that generate no revenue). Only a significant minority of colleges and universities across the United States make any such voluntary payment, so Brown is already ahead of the norm.

It would be difficult to argue that Brown suffers from grinding fiscal distress. Its endowment had reached $2.5 billion, having grown by 18.5 percent in the previous year. Its budget was $865.2 million (compared to $614 million for the city). Its campus included more than 200 buildings, with a value of more than $1 billion. That property, if taxed at the commercial rate levied by the city, would face a tax bill of roughly $38 million. However, the Brown administration believed that an additional $5 million would be fiscally crippling to the university. Undergraduate tuition for 2011-2012 was $41,328; room, board, and required fees made the total cost $53,136. The university has 8,000 students, employs around 4,500 people (the sixth largest employer in Rhode Island), and spends around $65 million annually with local vendors. It is an economic force in both the city and the state, in addition to being an important educational institution.

After considerable negotiation, Brown finally agreed to pay Providence $31 million more over the next eleven years. At last report, Providence had not filed for federal bankruptcy protection.

SOURCES: Daphne A. Kenyon and Adam H. Langley, *Payments in Lieu of Taxes, Balancing Municipal and Nonprofit Interests* (Cambridge, Mass.: Lincoln Institute of Land Policy, 2010); Michael McDonald, "Harvard's Voluntary Tax Spurs Providence to Press Brown," *Bloomberg,* February 8, 2012. http://www.bloomberg.com/news/2012-02-08/harvard-s-voluntary-tax-spurs-ailing-providence-to-press-brown.html; Erika Niedowski, "Brown University Taxes; Providence Takes on School in Town-Gown Money Clash," *Huffington Post,* February 12, 2012. http://www.huffingtonpost.com/2012/02/13/brown-university-taxes-pr_n_1272785.html; Stephanie Strom, "Tax Exemptions of Charities Face New Challenges," *New York Times,* May 26, 2008.

CHAPTER 12

Revenue from User Fees, User Charges, and Sales by Public Monopolies

Chapter Contents

User Fees and Licenses

User Charges
  Advantages of User Charges
  Limitations of User Charges
  Charge Guidelines

Public Monopoly Revenue: Utilities, Liquor Stores, and Gambling Enterprises

Government Utilities
Liquor Stores
Government Gambling Enterprises: Lotteries and Offtrack Betting

Conclusion

Governments normally collect revenue through their sovereign taxing power. That establishes the payment owed without any connection to the value of any public product or service received by the taxpayer.[1] When public goods are involved, these market processes will fail. However, governments do sell some goods and services and people can buy them or not, according to tastes, preferences, and affluence. Impacts on others from those purchases are so small that provision is not a public problem. In these instances, revenue to finance these services can be raised without the compulsion of taxation, but rather through voluntary exchange.

There is almost certainly a wide, but not wide-open, territory that governments should explore for such financing, which relieves the general revenue system by requiring specific "customers" to pay for the services they receive. It is good to remember that when government services (parks, cultural events, garbage collection,

---

[1]Civil forfeiture, a controversial tool now widely used by law enforcement officials, operates as a tax in that revenue arises from application of the system of laws. Police agencies have no more special right to these proceeds than the Internal Revenue Service (IRS) has a special claim to revenues from the individual income (or other) taxes that it collects. Because assets are seized without any judicial review to ascertain whether any crime has been involved and because it is difficult for owners to get property returned in full, even if no crime ever is proven, many seek substantially greater control over the technique and the use of any funds obtained by it.

etc.) are provided without direct charge for their use, those services are not, as they are frequently advertised, "free." Instead, they are "taxpayer paid for," or, more precisely, paid according to the tax system rather than according to use of the service. The choice is not between free services and services available through user charge. The choice is between whether the people who use the services pay for them or whether the tax system places the cost on somebody who may or may not use the service and whose payment bears no necessary relationship to the extent of use. Which alternative distribution of cost seems generally more reasonable to you?

Sales revenue can be tantalizing for governments. By appearing to behave like a private business, government leaders can blunt some critics of tax-and-spend politics. Although the sums involved may be relatively small in the full scheme of public finance, the revenues do make a contribution, possibly without the complication of public revulsion to paying taxes. Most important, however, public prices may improve both the efficiency of resource allocation and the equity in distributing the cost of public services. They make the government behave more like a private business and less like an intractable bureaucracy.

This chapter discusses three different sorts of "private" government revenue:

1. **User fees** derived from government sale of licenses to engage in otherwise restricted or forbidden activities;
2. **User charges,** or prices charged for voluntarily purchased, publicly provided services that, although benefiting specific individuals or businesses, are closely associated with basic government responsibilities; and
3. **Fiscal monopoly** revenues that the government receives from exclusive sale of a private or toll good or service, including revenue from government-operated utilities, state liquor stores, and state lotteries.[2]

Table 12–1 and Table 12–2 present recent sales data for U.S. governments. These receipts are modest in comparison with those from taxation, and that is not surprising. The principal economic reason for governments is, after all, market failure, and that implies that prices will not function properly. Pricing often simply is not feasible and not desirable, and that is what the revenue patterns reflect. If pricing is entirely feasible, then why is a government doing it? Nevertheless, collections from market transactions play an important role in government finance at the margin, and their role is likely to continue to increase for reasons related to both political pragmatism and the quest for improved government—efficiency.

Charges amount to 15.6 percent of own-source state revenue, including as own-source the regular own-source revenue, utility revenue, and liquor store revenue.[3]

---

[2]Some countries have operated fiscal monopolies on tobacco products, matches, salt, sugar, caviar, and playing cards. See Sijbren Cnossen, *Excise Systems, A Global Study of the Selective Taxation of Goods and Services* (Baltimore, Md.: Johns Hopkins University Press, 1977), 84–98. They offer an alternative to excise taxation. Some governments operate a fiscal monopoly to sell the product, but also add an excise to it, doing a fiscal double-dip.

[3]Government sales revenues are not all reported on a consistent basis. For instance, the Governments Division of the Census Bureau reports user charge and utility revenue on a gross basis, without offset for production or acquisition cost. Lottery revenue reported as part of the miscellaneous revenue category is included on a net basis.

Table 12–1

State and Local Government Sales Revenue: User Charges and Miscellaneous Revenues, Fiscal 2012

	State & Local Government. Total ($K)	% Total	State Government Total ($K)	% Total	Local Government ($K)	% Total
Own-Source General Revenue Plus Utility and Liquor Store Revenue	2,174,084,384	100.0%	1,115,719,689	100.0%	1,058,364,695	100.0%
Taxes	1,387,916,303	63.8%	797,953,030	71.5%	589,963,273	55.7%
Charges and Miscellaneous	625,861,023	28.8%	297,025,966	26.6%	328,835,057	31.1%
Current Charges	426,419,887	19.6%	174,233,882	15.6%	252,186,005	23.8%
Education	114,579,373	5.3%	90,352,156	8.1%	24,227,217	2.3%
Higher Education	98,825,472	4.5%	89,227,546	8.0%	9,597,926	0.9%
Hospitals	122,969,125	5.7%	49,790,723	4.5%	73,178,402	6.9%
Highways	13,412,958	0.6%	7,321,828	0.7%	6,091,130	0.6%
Air Transportation	19,783,565	0.9%	1,449,276	0.1%	18,334,289	1.7%
Parking Facilities	2,573,108	0.1%	20,474	0.0%	2,552,634	0.2%
Sea and Inland Ports	4,407,269	0.2%	1,265,089	0.1%	3,142,180	0.3%
Natural Resources	4,530,218	0.2%	2,625,753	0.2%	1,904,465	0.2%
Parks and Recreation	9,720,558	0.4%	1,508,961	0.1%	8,211,597	0.8%
Housing and Community	6,354,884	0.3%	626,449	0.1%	5,728,435	0.5%
Sewerage	47,369,106	2.2%	625,464	0.1%	46,743,642	4.4%
Solid Waste Management	16,751,969	0.8%	425,627	0.0%	16,326,342	1.5%
Other Charges	63,967,754	2.9%	18,222,082	1.6%	45,745,672	4.3%
Utility Revenue	151,957,456	7.0%	13,626,445	1.2%	138,331,011	13.1%
Liquor Store Revenue	8,349,602	0.4%	7,114,248	0.6%	1,235,354	0.1%

SOURCE: U.S. Census Bureau, Governments Division, State and Local Government Finances.

Charges by state institutions of higher education are the single largest source of such revenue. However, localities have more opportunity for charge revenue because they provide more individual beneficiary services than do other governments; these services produced 23.8 percent of revenue raised by local governments in 2012. Adding utility revenue increases the percentage to 35.9 percent. Charges for hospitals, sewerage, and utilities are particularly important to localities. Because tax alternatives available to local governments are often tightly controlled by their states, these governments have special incentive for seeking out charge revenues. However, even these governments seldom exhaust possibilities for charging. Among the types of local governments, charges are most important for counties (hospitals) and special districts (hospitals and utilities). For municipalities, utility and sewerage charges are the most important, although overall charge reliance is less than it is for counties and special districts. Special districts—entities providing services such as water, solid waste management, airport operations, or mass transit—survive on charges for services provided: regular charges and utility revenue combine to create more than 70 percent of their own-source revenue. That is reasonable, in that special districts often exist to provide a particular service to particular customers, the ideal environment for self-financing through charges.

Table 12-1
(Continued)

County Government ($K)	% Total	Municipal Government ($K)	% Total	Township Government ($K)	% Total	Special Districts ($K)	% Total	School Districts ($K)	% Total
243,865,414	100.0%	399,643,166	100.0%	40,298,490	100.0%	153,268,813	100.0%	221,288,812	100.0%
144,512,840	59.3%	197,542,590	49.4%	31,334,628	77.8%	27,741,668	18.1%	188,831,547	85.3%
93,028,343	38.1%	117,765,222	29.5%	6,722,667	16.7%	78,861,560	51.5%	32,457,265	14.7%
73,360,358	30.1%	86,899,255	21.7%	4,767,886	11.8%	67,290,678	43.9%	19,867,828	9.0%
3,397,899	1.4%	691,539	0.2%	269,990	0.7%	-	0.0%	19,867,789	9.0%
1,987,442	0.8%	274,325	0.1%	-	0.0%	-	0.0%	7,336,159	3.3%
30,684,977	12.6%	10,147,662	2.5%	74,762	0.2%	32,271,001	21.1%	-	0.0%
1,264,097	0.5%	2,340,012	0.6%	33,635	0.1%	2,453,386	1.6%	-	0.0%
2,654,224	1.1%	8,944,625	2.2%	33,761	0.1%	6,701,679	4.4%	-	0.0%
102,285	0.0%	2,085,108	0.5%	43,963	0.1%	321,278	0.2%	-	0.0%
265,098	0.1%	1,339,828	0.3%	8,872	0.0%	1,528,382	1.0%	-	0.0%
195,240	0.1%	352,934	0.1%	4,508	0.0%	1,351,744	0.9%	39	0.0%
1,428,532	0.6%	4,667,259	1.2%	443,067	1.1%	1,672,739	1.1%	-	0.0%
367,646	0.2%	2,263,343	0.6%	27,758	0.1%	3,069,688	2.0%	-	0.0%
5,794,977	2.4%	30,800,602	7.7%	2,200,802	5.5%	7,947,261	5.2%	-	0.0%
5,094,849	2.1%	9,331,174	2.3%	628,250	1.6%	1,272,069	0.8%	-	0.0%
22,110,534	9.1%	13,935,169	3.5%	998,518	2.5%	8,701,451	5.7%	-	0.0%
5,667,902	2.3%	83,756,329	21.0%	2,241,195	5.6%	46,665,585	30.4%	-	0.0%
656,329	0.3%	579,025	0.1%	-	0.0%	-	0.0%	-	0.0%

The federal scheme for reporting charge revenue is somewhat convoluted. In federal budgetary accounts, most charge revenues are called *offsetting collections* or *offsetting receipts,* and they do not appear directly in tallies of federal revenue. These are payments for goods and services sold to the public and include such charges as those for postal services, for insurance coverage, for admissions to national parks, for sale of public lands, and for sale of commemorative coins, as well as oil extraction royalties from the Outer Continental Shelf. Table 12–2 identifies some of the more significant revenue producers. The largest sums came from postal services and insurance premiums for certain Medicare coverage. Total collections of $238 billion represent a modest sum in comparison with the total federal receipts of over $2.5 trillion.[4]

These federal charge revenues are not reported in the way that tax revenues are because they are deducted from gross outlays of agencies in the budget

---

[4]The federal government also receives profits earned by the Federal Reserve System, largely interest earned from assets the system owns less its operating costs. That amounted to $98.7 billion in 2014, a record amount driven by the large volume of securities it had purchased in its effort to stimulate the economy during the Great Recession.

Table 12–2
Federal User Charge Receipts, Fiscal 2008 ($ Millions)

Corps of Engineers: Harbor maintenance fees	1,467
Department of Commerce: Patent and trademark, fees for weather services, and other fees	1,998
Department of Defense: Commissary and other fees	10,797
Department of Health and Human Services: Food and Drug Administration, Centers for Medicare and Medicaid Services, and other charges	1,743
Department of Homeland Security: Border and Transportation Security and other charges	2,202
Department of State: Passport and other charges	1,807
Department of Treasury: Sale of commemorative coins and other charges	2,588
Department of Veterans Affairs: Medical care and other charges	2,598
Department of Agriculture: Crop insurance and other charges	2,869
Department of Defense: Commissary surcharge and other charges	2,327
Department of Energy: Proceeds from sale of energy, nuclear waste disposal, and other charges	4,303
Department of Health and Human Services: Medicare Part B and Part D insurance premiums	59,435
Department of Homeland Security: Customs, immigration, and other charges	8,609
Department of Interior: Recreation and other charges	6,187
Department of Labor: Insurance premiums to guaranty private pensions and other charges	3,753
Department of Veterans Affairs: Veterans life insurance and other charges	2,358
Office of Personnel Management: Federal employee health and life insurance fees	12,110
Postal Service: Fees for postal services	75,129
Tennessee Valley Authority: Proceeds from sale of energy	10,307
Outer Continental Shelf receipts and other collections	18,285
Department of Energy: Federal Energy Regulation Commission, power marketing and other charges	1,223
Department of Treasury: Bank regulation and other charges	1,170
Federal Deposit Insurance Corporation: Deposit insurance fees and recoveries	2,922
Department of Commerce: Digital Television Transition and Public Safety Fund	1,779
Total User Charges	237,966

SOURCE: Office of Management and Budget, *Budget of the Government of the United States, Fiscal Year 2010, Analytical Perspectives* (Washington, D.C.: U.S. Government Printing Office, 2009).
Note: Only categories exceeding $1,000 million are separately identified.

process. For offsetting collections, the charges are credited directly to the account from which they will be spent and, usually, may be spent without further legislation. As an example, the postal service may use its charge revenue to finance its operations without annual appropriation. For offsetting receipts, the charges are offset against gross outlays but are not credited directly to expenditure accounts.[5] Because of this offsetting process, the regular budget displays understate both total government spending and collections from the public, and the procedures do violate transparency standards. However, the amounts are small in the overall

---

[5]Office of Management and Budget, *Budget of the Government of the United States, Fiscal Year 2010, Analytical Perspectives* (Washington, D.C.: U.S. Government Printing Office, 2009), 282–95. This offsetting provided a way around the outlay controls of the Budget Enforcement Act of 1990.

tally of government operations, as is apparent from the data reported in the prior paragraph.

User Fees and Licenses

Governments levy a number of user fees that have some features of public prices but that reflect the revenue-raising potential of the rule of law rather than voluntary exchange in the private market. (As described in Sidebar 12–1, terminology in the federal budget, rather unhelpfully, broadens the user-charge concept to include narrow-base taxes.) They are not user charges or public prices, even though these fees may share some equity and fiscal advantages of prices.

A license tax is a fee—established as a flat amount, an amount graduated by type of activity, an amount related to business receipts, or whatever—levied as a condition for exercise of a business or nonbusiness privilege. License taxes imposed to regulate specific activities for the benefit of the general public (e.g., massage parlor licenses, hunting licenses, and licenses associated with the ownership or operation of motor vehicles) offer one example. Without the license, one or more governments forbid the activity. The license is a necessary condition for operation, but it does not "purchase" any specific government service. It may thus be distinguished from a user charge, which may be avoided if any individual or firm chooses not to purchase the supplied item or service and the payment of which entitles the individual or firm to a commodity or service, and from fees that are indirectly related to particular privileges. In 2014, licenses yielded more than $51.1 billion to state governments. The largest category was motor vehicle licenses, 46.6 percent of the total license revenue. Over $6 billion came from state corporate licenses.[6]

The license tax must also be distinguished from the franchise fee. The latter (1) involves contracts detailing rights and responsibilities of both the franchisee and the issuing municipality, (2) entails a requirement to service the entire population in the servicing area, and (3) brings a presumption of rate and quality of service regulation. A license simply permits a holder to undertake an activity otherwise forbidden and involves no contractual or property rights.[7] In general, franchises are provided in very limited numbers, whereas licenses are sold to virtually all applicants.

The definitions usually do not differentiate between licenses for revenue and those for regulation. Both varieties are based on the inherent police power of a state. States delegate this power to municipalities by constitution, statute, or city charter grant. Revenue and regulation motives may be hopelessly entangled. Nevertheless, a tentative separation can be suggested. A license ordinance that does not require inspection of the business or articles sold or that fails to regulate the conduct of the business in any manner is a pure revenue license, particularly

---

[6]U.S. Census Bureau, Governments Division, 2014 State Government Tax Collections. www.census.gov.
[7]Charles S. Rhyne develops this logic further in *Municipal Law* (Washington, D.C.: National Institute of Municipal Law Officers, 1957), 655.

Sidebar 12–1
Charging Fees: The Federal System

Most federal revenue comes from taxes that have no relation to any benefits received by the person paying the tax and that are not related to any particular service provided by the government. That is the case with the broad-base taxes on income and payrolls that constitute the great majority of federal revenue. User fees, however, can be appropriate and are feasible when the government can deny use of service to nonpayers or when the government can prohibit activities by nonpayers. Also, as described in Chapter 10, some narrow-base excises can serve to allocate costs to those using certain government services or can cause private entities to recognize the social implications of their actions.

The Congressional Budget Office calls both these fees and narrow taxes user charges and divides them into four classes:

1. User fees are payments for goods or services sold or rented by the government, voluntarily purchased, and not generally shared. They include natural-resource royalties, tolls, insurance premiums, leases and rentals, revenue from sales of resources, fees from use of federal land, admission to federal parks, charges for postal service, and permits or licenses not associated with regulation.
2. Regulatory fees are payments based on government authority to regulate particular businesses or activities that stem from the sovereign powers of the government. They include regulatory and judicial fees; fees from immigration, passport, and consulate services; customs fees; fees for testing, inspecting, and grading; fees for patent, trademark, and copyright services; and licenses through regulatory programs.
3. Beneficiary-based taxes are levied on bases correlated with the use of particular government services (the good or service taxed and the public service are close complements). They include the transportation-related excises (highway, airway, inland waterway, and harbor) and the excises on fuel and equipment associated with boating safety programs.
4. Liability-based taxes are levied for the purpose of abating hazards, discouraging damaging activities, or compensating injuries. They include excises on certain chemicals that are dedicated to the Hazardous Substance Trust Fund, taxes on certain fuels dedicated to the Leaking Underground Storage Tank Trust Fund, taxes on crude oil dedicated to the Oil Spill Liability Trust Fund, taxes on domestically mined coal dedicated to the Black Lung Disability Trust Fund, and taxes on childhood-disease vaccines dedicated to the Vaccine Injury Compensation Trust Fund.

Revenues in the first two groups can be particularly attractive under the Budget Enforcement Act of 1990 control structures because they may be offsetting collections—that is, they are netted against a particular budget outlay. Congressional committees can thus meet outlay ceilings by adding fees rather than cutting programs.

The Government Accountability Office outlines three important questions to consider when developing fees:

1. Who benefits from the program? If a program benefits the general public, then it should be financed by general revenue, not program fees. If the program benefits identifiable users, then it should be financed from fees.

2. Are there mechanisms for ensuring that fees will cover the intended share of total program costs over time? Costs and other revenues will change as years go by, so a regular approach is needed to make sure that shares continue as intended. Stable fees are not likely a virtue if there is an intended share of cost to be paid by users.

3. Are there mechanisms for determining how much the program costs and for establishing how that cost will be distributed among users? There need to be clear standards for identifying program costs (what activities will be included) and for distributing that cost. There may be different incentives intended for the cost distribution, and these need to be clear.

SOURCES: Congressional Budget Office, *The Growth of Federal User Charges* (Washington, D.C.: U.S. Government Printing Office, 1993); and Government Accountability Office, *Federal User Fees: A Design Guide,* GAO-08-386SP (Washington, D.C.: Government Accountability Office, 2008).

if license applications are never denied. If controls apply or if licenses are difficult to obtain (not just expensive), the license is regulatory. The distinction may not always be clear. Some states require that license charges be reasonably related to the cost of issuing, policing, or controlling the thing or activity being licensed. When that stipulation applies, it is especially important to review cost and adjust charges frequently.

Both user charges and fees attempt to relieve burdens on the general revenue system by extracting greater contribution from service beneficiaries, but the former more closely resembles private enterprise pricing.[8] Fees can compensate government for extra costs incurred in providing special services to identifiable entities or completing administrative paperwork for individuals. Thus, governments often charge fees for traffic direction or crowd control and for many legal filings. Fees, however, seldom involve the direct sale of a good or service, but rather involve payment for some privilege granted by government. The exercise of that privilege may cause government to incur a cost that the fee seeks to recoup in part or in total.[9]

---

[8]In recent years, many communities have adopted exactions, in-kind or financial payments, on real estate developers as a condition for permits, access to public facilities, and so on. Development for impact fees are one type of exaction. See Alan A. Altshuler and Jose A. Gomez-Ibanez with Arnold M. Howitt, *Regulation for Revenue* (Washington, D.C./Cambridge, Mass.: Brookings Institution/Lincoln Institute for Land Policy, 1993). Such fees have assumed a position of some fiscal significance in developing areas of the western United States.

[9]If the licensing system is being operated to generate revenue, it is important to consider whether the charge is an effective revenue producer. If demand for the licenses is elastic, then increasing the charge will have enough impact on licenses being purchased to cause total revenues to decline. If demand is inelastic, then increasing the charge will increase total revenues. However, charges for most licenses (hunting, fishing, etc.) are relatively low, and demand is relatively inelastic. In that case, increasing the charge would produce additional revenues that could be used to improve the services provided by agencies.

User Charges

User charges can induce production and consumption efficiency while gauging citizen preferences and demand for government services. User charges can function only when activities financed have two necessary conditions: benefits separability and chargeability. These are the features absent from pure public goods (see Chapter 1). The further a good or service departs from publicness and the closer it approximates a private good, the more feasible are user charges—and the more one wonders why it isn't being handled by a private firm.[10]

First, user charges are feasible when identifiable individuals or firms, not the community as a whole, benefit from the service. Services to a narrow segment of the community financed by general revenues provide an opportunity for that segment to profit at the expense of others. Those using the service benefit, but pay no more than similarly situated citizens who do not benefit. A user charge prevents that systematic subsidization. If recipients of benefits cannot be identified or if the community in general benefits, a user charge is neither feasible nor desirable. Thus, charges for elementary education would be inappropriate, but charges would be desirable for an adult auto mechanics course. Relying on voluntary provision in the first instance would be foolish. Milton benefits if his neighbor's children receive an elementary education because they help choose his government, they read traffic signs, they go on welfare less often, and so on. In the latter instance, the mechanic does help the community, but that help is for a fee. If Milton's car is repaired, he pays the bill—there are no uncompensated community benefits. However, governments too often lose their resolve to be entrepreneurial adherents to the "user pays" principle when they give away costly services to businesses in the name of economic development.

Second, user charges require an economical method for excluding from service benefits those who do not pay for the service. If exclusion cannot be efficiently accomplished, the charge cannot be collected. Furthermore, resource allocation gains are greatest if service use can be metered, as with water meters, toll booths, and the like, so that heavy users pay more than light users and any user pays more than nonusers. Some discretion is needed here, however, because everything that can be gauged may not be worth gauging. Use of city streets could be metered using the tollgate technology of turnpikes and toll bridges; however, the costs involved, including the time waiting in lines, make that option challenging. Administrative cost—measuring customer service use (metering), calculating charges according to service cost, and billing and collecting computed charges—and compliance cost must not be excessive. Many services can, however, be gauged and controlled by meters, fences, turnstiles, decals, and the like. Sidebar 12–2 discusses two alternative charge systems used for direct charge financing of highway facilities. Others may be indirectly measured: many cities gauge residential sanitary-sewer use by water use, a reasonable proxy for volume down the drain and into the sewerage system. (Industrial use is more difficult

---

[10]Federal policy on and administration of user charges for purchase or use of government resources is described in OMB Circular No. 25 (July 8, 1993).

Sidebar 12–2
Charging for Highway Usage

States have historically relied on revenues from motor-fuel excise taxes to finance the construction, operation, and maintenance of their highway networks. Unfortunately, this approach has become unsustainable with greatly improved gasoline mileage of vehicles, the unwillingness of lawmakers to increase the per gallon taxes to keep up with increasing highway cost and improved fuel efficiency, and the development of vehicles that do not run on motor fuel. These forces have driven some governments to work on alternative methods for obtaining financial support from users of highways even as the linkage between highway use and motor-fuel purchase has broken. Two particularly notable approaches have been deployed: the tag system and the direct road usage charge.

Tag or plate reading systems have been developed for users of particular highway facilities. Electronic tags on automobiles using a toll facility reduces collection costs for frequent users (like the E-ZPass program that is used in fourteen northeastern and midwestern states in the United States or the tag program used by the Golden Gate Bridge in California). Sensors read the tags as the vehicle passes through and either a deduction is made from the account of the vehicle owner or a bill is sent to the owner of the vehicle. Technology can read the license plate of the vehicle as it passes through, and the bill is sent to the vehicle owner if it is not in the pass program. No vehicles need to even slow down as they pass through the tolled facility. Germany uses a global positioning satellite system for charging truck tolls (16 cents per kilometer for trucks weighing over 12 tons) on its autobahns. Billing goes to a data center, or drivers may pay manually at roadside terminals. Charges are based on distance traveled, number of axles, and the vehicle's emission class. A private company (Toll Collect GmbH) operates the collection system for the German government. Microwave sensors are used for collecting tolls in Austria and some other European countries.[1] Switzerland and Austria use a "vignette" system, in which motorists must purchase a sticker to place on their windshields to permit usage of autobahns in their countries. Those entering from another country purchase the sticker on entry, or shortly thereafter, or face a considerable fine.

The direct road usage charge system is in operation in Oregon. OReGO provides residents the option of either paying a road usage charge of $0.015 per mile or continuing to pay Oregon fuels tax. The program is initially available to 5,000 light vehicles registered in the state, with no more than 1,500 vehicles with fuel efficiency rating of less than 17 mpg and no more than 1,500 vehicles with rating of at least 17 mpg and less than 22 mpg. After entering the program, the volunteer receives a mileage reporting device that reports miles driven directly to an account manager. Volunteers may choose between a private contractor manager or the Oregon Department of Transportation, depending on what entity the volunteer feels more comfortable about having their vehicle usage data. The account manager computes the fuels tax that the volunteer would have paid based on the vehicle's mpg and reconciles the charge owed against the tax paid for rebate to the volunteer of any excess. The intent is that those driving more will pay more and the payment will be based on actual utilization of the roads. For those in the OReGO program, payment of the fuels tax represents an advance payment of the direct usage charge, much as

(continues)

Sidebar 12–2
(continued)

---

withholding is an advance payment of individual income tax ultimately owed. Because vehicles not in the direct road usage charge system are also traveling state highways, the motor-fuel tax has to remain in place to obtain payment from that travel. Oregon was the first state with a motor-fuels tax (1919) and is the first state to aggressively experiment with a replacement for the tax.[2]

[1]Congressional Budget Office, *Using Pricing to Reduce Traffic Congestion* (Washington, D.C.: Congressional Budget Office, 2009).

[2]Oregon Department of Transportation, "Oregon Road Usage Charge, Category: Emerging and Innovative Technologies." http://www.nascio.org/portals/0/awards/nominations2015/2015/2015OR5-Oregon-ODOT-2015%20-%20Road%20 Usage%20Charge%20Program.pdf.

---

to gauge because there is a problem with quality of the discharge in addition to quantity.) Without enforceable charge barriers, user charges are inappropriate.

Charges are particularly appropriate when substantial waste would occur if the individually identifiable service was unpriced. Resources are not unlimited and a charge can service to discipline demand and ration those scarce resources. Waste would undoubtedly result if, for instance, water was provided through property tax financing. Under that system, efforts to economize on water use would yield the individual consumer no direct return. Payments for water would be determined by property holdings, not the amount of water used. Usage would be much inflated. Investment in supply facilities would have to be abnormally great, and artificially expanded amounts of water would have to be treated. Appropriate user charges could substantially reduce water waste and total water supply cost. By charging higher prices during periods when capital facilities, such as highways or airports, are heavily congested, usage may be redistributed, and the need for new construction may be reduced.[11]

Advantages of User Charges

User charges have four advantages beyond the naked pragmatism of additional revenue for government functions.[12] These advantages include both the important

---

[11]It was common in countries of the former Soviet Union for heating, gas, electricity, water, hot water, and other services to be paid for by residents through a flat "communal charge." Nothing was metered, so there were no incentives to economize on resource use. For instance, if the apartment got too hot in the winter, the temperature was regulated by opening windows–no meters, no thermostats, wasted resources.

[12]When services can be financed by tolls, public facilities can be built and operated without facing the public resistance to use of tax revenue. For instance, private toll road companies operate in public-private-partnerships in Texas, and the use of toll roads has rapidly expanded in Florida. The public is often not amused by the tolls that must be paid because free always seems to be nicer. According to Federal Highway Administration data, there were over 5,400 miles of toll roads in the United States in 2013, 15 percent more than a decade earlier.

efficiency effects of appropriately designed charge structures and the improved equity from direct pricing. First, user charges can register and record public demand for a service. Suppose a city is considering supporting extensive summer softball leagues for adults. If these leagues are financed by user charges (to either team sponsors or individual participants), the city receives important information on choices about service type, quality, and quantity. Without a user charge, there would be continual—and inconclusive—debate about program advisability and structure. However, as rural philosopher Kin Hubbard observed: "Nothing will dispel enthusiasm like a small admission charge."[13] The charge offers a conclusive test of demand for the service. Furthermore, a program that, through user charges, covers its provision cost is not likely to be eliminated and will not burden other government activities. Not incidentally, citizens who do not want the service do not have to receive it and do not have to pay for it. A user charge system not only provides a tangible way for citizens to register their preference for particular services, but also provides some funds for providing those services. That's pretty much the same way the private sector works, so user charge financing represents the ultimate in service privatization, only one step before leaving provision to the private sector.

Those extra funds can be a problem, however, when the charge does not cover all incremental costs of the service. During periods of tight finances, decision makers are tempted to expand revenue-generating activities, often reasoning that any revenue will help with the fiscal problem. Unfortunately, such expansion can worsen the overall budget condition. For example, a city may expand its summer tennis instruction program because it generates $25 per person in revenue. If recreation department costs increase by $30 per person enrolled in the program, the expanded revenue produced actually increases any city deficit.[14]

Second, the user charge can dramatically improve financing equity for selected services. If the service is of a chargeable nature, its provision by general tax revenues undoubtedly subsidizes service recipients at the expense of the general taxpaying public. User charges can obviously prevent that problem. Less obvious, but equally significant are two related equity problems that user charges can reduce: the problems created by nonresident service recipients and by tax-exempt entities. Many urban services, particularly cultural and recreational, can easily be used by anyone in the region. General revenue financing subsidizes nonresident consumers; a user charge prevents that subsidy. It is a simple and direct way to reduce burdens placed on one government by citizens of neighboring governments. A user charge also provides a mechanism for obtaining financial support from tax-exempt institutions. Many cities, for example, use property tax revenue to subsidize refuse collection. Charitable, religious, or educational institutions exempt from property tax would contribute nothing to finance refuse collection, even though they receive the service, whose cost must be borne by general taxpayers. If, however, refuse collection was fully financed by user charges, that cost shifting would not occur. Just as

---

[13]Quoted in *Forbes*, October 21, 1985, 216.
[14]The program may still be worth expanding, even if the charge does not cover the cost of providing the service. That would depend on the social benefits, if any, that extend beyond the participants paying the direct charge. The point here is that such a program should not be expanded because of *revenue* considerations.

these entities must pay for gasoline purchased from a private firm, they would pay the refuse collection charge. Tax exemption does not ordinarily exempt institutions from paying for goods or services bought on the open market. For both nonresidents and exempt institutions, the user charge allows governments to extract revenue from entities outside their tax network; if they use, they must pay.

Third, a user charge program may improve operating efficiency because agency staff must respond to client demand. Agencies usually operate with funds obtained from and justified to a legislative body. That justification elaborates needs as estimated by the agency staff and is defended according to performance criteria established by the agency staff. Those agencies with the best bureaucratic expertise—the ones best able to prepare convincing budget justifications and apply the strategies of the budget process described in previous chapters—are the ones most likely to receive appropriations. User charge finance that allows facilities to retain a considerable share of charge revenue, however, requires a shift to preferences articulated directly by customers. The agency must provide services that are desired by consumers, or it will fail the financial test for survival. It cannot define what clients should want in its budget defense; it must provide the services clients actually will purchase.

Finally, a user charge may correct cost-and-price signals in the private market. Suppose a manufacturing plant places extraordinary demand on traffic control in a neighborhood. That special demand requires additional police officers at a handful of intersections in that area during factory shift changes. The way the plant operates thus produces extra costs for the community. If the plant must pay the extra traffic-control costs its operations require, its management has a direct financial incentive to consider whether its current operating pattern (with attendant traffic-control charges) is cost effective. The plant's management may decide that lower peak-flow traffic produced by staggered shifts, van pooling, subsidies for mass-transit use, and so on is less expensive than paying for traffic control. The user charge makes the decision-making unit recognize and respond to the true social cost of its action.

In summary, user charges make the public recognize that the services provided are not costless. The public can choose whether it wants the service and, if so, how much to purchase. People may save money by economizing on the service, and receiving the service does not place costs on others. In charge-financed areas, the government has an excellent gauge of what services the public wants and is willing to pay for, and that willingness may change over time, making for greater instability than appropriations from the general fund might bring.

Limitations of User Charges

User charges cannot generally substitute for taxes to finance government services because many public services—in fact, most services provided by most governments—simply do not fit the requirements for user charge financing. First, activities that have substantial benefits extending beyond the principal recipient are not candidates for user charge financing. Basic fire protection in an urban area could not, for example, be considered for user charge financing because fire tends to spread;

extinguishing a fire in one building protects surrounding units. Thus, protection financed by one individual automatically protects others; nonpayers are not excludable, so the service cannot be financed by charges. There is a corollary to the external-benefit issue when there are some services for which charges can be collected. The ability to charge for particular services can distort agency decision making. For example, a high school football team may receive magnanimous resources because gate receipts are sizable (even though unlikely to cover even a decent percentage of the program's cost), whereas the girls' volleyball team gets hand-me-downs. The question for resource allocation is contribution to the purposes of the community (or social benefits). The flow of cash is not an unambiguous indicator of what program has the greatest community benefit.

Second, services may intentionally subsidize low-income or otherwise disadvantaged recipients. Charges for these services could be counterproductive.[15] Beneficiaries should not pay if the service has welfare elements. In a related fashion, some have argued that user charges in general are unfair because they often produce a regressive-burden pattern, taking a larger percentage of a low-income consumer's income than of a higher-income consumer's income.[16] That argument is not a convincing attack on user charges for several reasons. For one thing, low-income families not using the service clearly are better off with the user charge system—no charge to be paid and no tax to be paid to subsidize the service used by others. Furthermore, tax-financing devices may have a more regressive burden than user charges, even if the service is widely used by disadvantaged citizens. Finally, it may be possible to design "payability" tests for the charges because the services are received by identifiable individuals.[17] Suppose a city charges an admission fee to swimming pools. This is a good candidate for financing with charges because benefits are primarily individual (to the swimmer and family), prices can be enforced using fences and turnstiles (public health and safety requires access control regardless of financing technique), and overcrowding may otherwise result when children are dumped at the facility for "free" (or taxpayer-provided) babysitting. Charge opponents argue that free pools are a significant recreation option for low-income families; a charge would harm that redistributive function. Charges, however, can function equitably and efficiently if disadvantaged families receive season passes at no cost or if pools located in low-income areas are free, and charges apply at other pools. In general, protection of the disadvantaged should not be an excuse for subsidizing the well-to-do.

Third, some charges, though technically feasible, may be expensive to collect. Spending a considerable share of the revenue raised in collecting that revenue is not likely to be a wise use of agency resources. The high cost suggests a degree of publicness that makes the appropriateness of the charge itself questionable. Technology

---

[15]There are, of course, more efficient ways of redistributing income in society than providing government services. However, once that method is selected, it should not be thwarted by charges.

[16]Willard Price, "The Case against the Imposition of a Sewer Use Tax," *Governmental Finance* 4 (May 1975): 38–44.

[17]Selma J. Mushkin and Charles L. Vehorn coined the "payability" phrase in "User Fees and Charges," *Governmental Finance* 6 (November 1977): 46.

can, however, provide new, less expensive options for charge revenue, as with GPS-type technology that makes tolling even for city streets potentially feasible.

Fourth, there are important political issues when proposing that a tax-supported service shift to charge financing. The charge may face considerable public resentment based on the view that, having paid taxes, the person is entitled to the public service without any additional payment.[18] Although this argument is roughly the same as arguing that, because you purchased bread, the store should provide meat for the sandwich at no charge, it does often accompany shifts toward charge finance. However, in addition to public opposition, there is frequently bureaucratic resistance. Service providers understand that moving from tax finance to a user charge means that, for the client, the service price is increased from zero (though there are costs of providing the service, those costs are borne by other parts of the fiscal system, with no difference in payment according to use) to some positive amount (the price). This change will ration out some use of the service, a change that goes against the attitudes of public officials. Both service providers and clients tend to offer a unified opposition to user charges in all but fiscally distressed environments. However, the fact that service use may decline when a charge is imposed or raised is not a flaw of the charge, but simply what one expects from downward-sloping demand curves.

Finally, there is the ultimate reality in user charge finance that those who do not pay need to be denied service, and this is often unpopular. If the water bill is not paid, service needs to be shut off for the charge system to be effective, even though the service is necessary. The charge is intended to raise money and to regulate use of the service and, for it to have the intended effects, delinquent accounts cannot be tolerated. If government officials do not have the stomach to pull service from those who are not paying, they should forget about user charge finance. Unfortunately, enforcement can be painful and inevitably generates stories in the media and from some politicians of the crisis that enforcement causes for some low-income and elderly people. When Detroit Water and Sewage Department began disconnecting water service from customers who had not paid their bills, the city got a visit from United Nations representatives who declared that the city was violating the Universal Declaration of Human Rights.[19] That isn't very helpful for a city struggling with bankruptcy.

The government needs some sort of safety net or lifeline program to deal with the toughest cases before nonpayment occurs, done in an open and transparent fashion. However, if the delinquents are not successfully pursued, then the cost of

---

[18]Private toll road operators in Texas get around public grumpiness about paying for highways by having a speed limit on the toll roads that is higher than the normal limit (the road operators paid the state for this dispensation). The desirability of going faster overwhelms the unhappiness about paying for the service. Nathan Koppel, "Toll Road Offers Fast Cash to Texas," *Wall Street Journal*, September 8–9, 2012: A3. Long-distance truckers in Russia were not pleased with a new road usage charge applied in 2015 to help with the country's budget problems: they converged on Moscow and blocked traffic on the ring road for some time to show their unhappiness with the charges—and possibly that the system was contracted out for the benefit of a political ally of the president. ("Angry Truck Drivers Converge on Moscow," *Wall Street Journal,* December 5, 2015).

[19]"In Detroit, city-backed water shut-offs 'contrary to human rights,' says UN experts," United Nations News Center, October 20, 2014. http://www.un.org/apps/news/story.asp?NewsID=49127#.VkY9UnarSUk

providing them service is borne by others—including low-income and elderly customers who do not cheat on their bills. That isn't fair at all.[20]

Charge Guidelines

Governments differ in the extent to which they charge for services, partly because of the different services they provide (e.g., national defense, welfare, and highway patrol are hardly priceable) and partly because of political attitudes toward pricing public goods. Outside those constraints, there are some guides for user charge preparation and manipulation. Any service showing the aforementioned features (individual benefit, susceptibility to excluding nonpayers, and an absence of redistributive elements) is a reasonable candidate for user charge financing. The short list in Table 12–3 provides some options. Selma Mushkin and Richard Bird nominate for charge (1) household support functions (water, refuse collection, sewerage), (2) industrial development support (airports, parking, special police or fire services, etc.), (3) "amenities" (specialized recreation facilities, cultural facilities, etc.), and (4) services provided to tax-exempt entities.[21] The list and its classifications should give ample direction. Anytime the service is to an identifiable household or business and there are no discernible external impacts of the service, the service belongs on the candidate list.

When a government decides that a particular service can be financed by a user charge, the appropriate level of that charge must be determined. That determination is not simple. Frederick Stocker reports: "Evidence suggests that pricing policies used by municipal governments are often fairly unsophisticated, perhaps understandably so in light of the difficulty of determining price elasticities, marginal costs, distribution of benefits and other things that enter into economic models of optimal pricing."[22] The municipality, however, may get some guidance from fairly simple concepts about service costs.[23] In particular, the government should separate its service costs into

---

[20]In 2009–2010, Washington state began moving its state park system away from reliance on general tax support to revenues from fees for service (mostly camping and overnight lodging charges) and donations. The result was significant downsizing of the agency and more uncertainty about revenues and service levels. But the state intends no return to the primarily tax supported system. Because it is believed that the park system benefits all, some general funding is appropriate, even with greatest reliance on revenues earned by the parks. Washington State Parks and Recreation Commission, "Efforts to Increase Revenue, Status Update on the Fiscal Health of the State Park System," Report to the Office of Financial Management and Legislature as Required by ESSB5034 (2013 2nd Special Legislative Session), October 28, 2013.

[21]Selma J. Mushkin and Richard M. Bird, "Public Prices: An Overview," in *Public Prices for Public Products*, ed. S. J. Mushkin (Washington, D.C.: Urban Institute, 1972), 8–9.

[22]Frederick D. Stocker, "Diversification of the Local Revenue System: Income and Sales Taxes, User Charges, Federal Grants," *National Tax Journal* 29 (September 1976): 320.

[23]Paul Downing maintains that an appropriately designed user charge would have three components: a portion that reflects short-run production costs and varies with output consumed, a portion that reflects plant and equipment costs (possibly allocated as an individual's share of its designed capacity), and a portion based on the cost of delivering the service to a specific customer location. The first portion may vary by the time of day, depending on whether the system is at peak utilization. If so, the charge would be increased. See Downing's "User Charges and Special Districts," in *Management Policies in Local Government Finance*, ed. J. Richard Aronson and Eli Schwartz (Washington, D.C.: International City Management Association, 1981), 191–92.

Table 12–3
Selected Government Services Amenable to Public Pricing

Special police work	Service for stadium events, alarm servicing
Parking	Garage, meters
Solid-waste management	Collection, disposal (pay-as-you-throw)
Recreation	Golf courses, tennis courts, swimming pools, park admissions, concessions, rescue insurance, instruction, team registration
Health and hospitals	Ambulance charges, inoculations, hospital rates, health insurance premiums
Transportation	Transit fares, bridge and highway tolls (many public-private-partnership arrangements), limited-access toll lanes, airport landing (departure fees, hangar rentals), lock tolls, congestion charges
Education	Rentals of special books, equipment, or uniforms; college or technical school tuition; facility rentals; special training programs for individual businesses
Resource management	Surveys, extension service inquiries, tree nursery and development stock, livestock-grazing fees, mineral royalties
Sewerage	Treatment, disposal
Utilities	Water, electric, gas, transit
Other	Licensing for use of institution, name, miscellaneous special services provided an individual household or business

SOURCE: Based on Selma J. Mushkin and Richard M. Bird, "Public Prices: An Overview," in *Public Prices for Public Products,* ed. S. J. Mushkin (Washington, D.C.: Urban Institute, 1972): 8–9.

two categories: (1) costs that change as a result of the service being provided (incremental cost) and (2) costs that do not change with service provision (fixed costs). The latter includes any cost that would continue, regardless of decisions concerning that service, and thus can be disregarded in the charge analysis. Prices need to be based on market conditions—that is, on demand for the service being sold—and on the offerings of competitive providers of that service. The prospective purchaser is not driven by what it costs the municipality to produce the service, so the municipality is not able to determine what price it should charge from its costs.[24] A knowledge of cost, however, lets the municipality understand to what extent the particular service, after allowance for revenue from the price charged for the service, contributes to or must be subsidized by the remainder of government finances. And some services are likely to be seen as worth subsidizing, sometimes for certain members of the

---

[24]A good analysis of government price setting appears in Chapter 8 of David L. Rados, *Marketing for Non-Profit Organizations* (Boston: Auburn House, 1981). Peter F. Drucker calls *cost-driven* pricing one of "The Five Deadly Business Sins," in *Wall Street Journal*, October 21, 1993, A-22. Cost tells the business whether it is making or losing money, but customers will tell the business what they believe the product is worth and the price they are willing to pay.

population, such as the elderly or low-income households, and sometimes for everyone, if general consumption of the service is worth encouraging. A price that recovers the incremental cost of providing a particular service means that the provision of that user-charge-financed service does not burden other functions of government.[25] Prices above that level are possible, subject to the demand for the service and the government's desire to use surplus to support other government activities.

How can the government arrive at a reasonable price for the services it has chosen to sell? Sometimes the government may find similar services being sold by private firms and can use this market information as a guide for setting its own prices. Sometimes there may be no similar service being sold, and the government may decide to set its price at some markup of its incremental cost. In either case, the initial price will probably need to be adjusted up or down as customers' responses provide the government with more information about what their preferences really are and as government agencies get better insights into how their operating costs change as the amount of service provided varies. The government must also be aware of undesirable side effects. For instance, if imposing a landfill usage fee results in lots of additional dumping on vacant lots and along highways, then the government needs to consider a considerable reduction of the fee, even possibly eliminating the fee for households and charging only large commercial haulers who are less likely to do small-scale, illegal, and hard-to-trace illegal dumping.

The government may use pricing as a dynamic resource allocation tool. For instance, San Francisco adopted a system of charging for on-street parking that varies by location and by time of day, breaking the standard approach of same price all day. The price of curb parking in selected zones of the city varies according to occupancy rates in the zone (occupancy is determined by sensors installed in spaces), making adjustments in prices around every two months. Adjusting prices according to observed customer demand does a better job of allocating the scarce resources among the interested customers and, by doing that allocation, improves the overall occupancy rate of the parking stock. As the city gathered more data about parking demand patterns, it was able to stabilize the parking rates and obtain much higher overall parking occupancy rates (very desirable for merchants), thus reducing waste of unused parking spaces.[26] In addition, the government almost certainly will learn from the political response when it moves certain services from tax finance to charge finance. However, decisions are not permanent, and there is no reason the government cannot experiment with various prices for its services to determine their effect on the amount of service purchased and on net revenue to the government. There

---

[25]James Johnson has identified six elements in existing municipal sewerage service charges: water use (a volume proxy), flat charges, number of plumbing fixtures used by the customer, size of water meter or sewer connection, property characteristics (assessed value, square footage, front footage), and sewage strength. Water use is the most frequently encountered user charge element. See James A. Johnson, "The Distribution of the Burden of Sewer User Charges under Various Charge Formulas," *National Tax Journal* 22 (December 1969): 472–85.

[26]Gregory Pierce and Donald Shoup, "SFpark: Pricing Parking by Demand," *Access* 43 (Fall 2013). The program was aimed at better utilization of curb parking and not so much at maximizing revenue from the parking program.

is no special economic virtue in maintaining stable prices, although it may be politically convenient.

A final consideration about user charges concerns their method of application. Alfred Kahn writes, in an analysis of public utility pricing, "The only economic function of price is to influence behavior. . . . But of course price can have this effect on the buyer's side only if bills do indeed depend on the volume of purchases. For this reason, economists . . . are avid meterers."[27] A similar principle applies to user charges. Buyer behavior will not change unless changes in behavior will influence payments owed. If a refuse-collection customer pays $25 per year for that service, regardless of whether two or fifteen trash cans are collected per week, the customer cannot be expected to change the number of trash cans set out for collection. A charge sensitive to usage, however, does induce behavioral changes by some customers; payment per bag—"pay as you throw"—is more effective than payment per month. To obtain the full benefits of user charge financing, then, the service must be metered and made usage sensitive. Dividing estimated total costs by the number of entities served and presenting a bill to each entity does not produce the desired effects of public prices.

Public Monopoly Revenue: Utilities, Liquor Stores, and Gambling Enterprises

Government power to own and operate business enterprises, to sell private goods, is extensive, although contrary to the global wave of privatization. Government ownership is the exception, not the rule, in the United States. Whenever a public interest is identified that competitive pressures cannot handle, the normal approach in the United States is for the government to regulate the private firm, not for the government to own and operate the enterprise. A government official seeking long-term public ownership of a private business has not paid sufficient attention to the lessons from the collapse of the Soviet Union or from the struggles of Venezuela in 2015–2016.

Government Utilities

Some services are widely provided by municipal utilities, especially in water supply, electric power, intracity transit, and gas supply.[28] The great majority of cities with a

---

[27]Alfred E. Kahn, "Can an Economist Find Happiness Setting Public Utility Rates?" *Public Utilities Fortnightly* (January 5, 1978): 15. One of the problems that countries of the former Soviet Union faced as they transitioned to a market economy in the 1990s was the absence of electric, gas, and water meters on the premises of users. "Communal charges" under the old system were flat payments without any metering. To get a sensible system going required the purchase and installation of lots of meters.
[28]Solid-waste management, a candidate for utility finance, is typically managed within general government or by a special district if not provided by a private firm.

population over 5,000 are serviced by municipal water utilities. However, municipal electric-power systems, usually distributors of power produced by others, operate mostly in small communities. Gas supply is predominantly through private owner-ship. Intracity transit has made something of a resurgence with the failure of private transit systems, but the public systems have been as unprofitable as their private predecessors. Table 12–1 reported the extent to which state and local governments generated utility revenue in fiscal 2012.

Why should a municipality choose to operate a utility rather than allowing a private firm to do it? Surely government can better allocate its time to more press-ing public concerns than to focus on the mundane questions of utility management. Motivation is, not surprisingly, usually mixed. In some instances, the governing body believes that it can use utility-operation profits to subsidize the operations of the general government. In fact, some decades ago, some cities could boast of being tax-free towns because of profits from electric utility systems. That era has passed, however, and the best that one could hope for is some assistance from the utility to the city, not a fiscal bonanza.[29]

In other instances, the government owner may be more interested in keeping the price of the service as low as possible, perhaps even providing the service at less than cost. That policy requires some subsidization of the utility by the sponsoring government. This practice can be politically appealing—the low-cost service can be an important element in reelection strategy and may be supported by a desire to encourage economic development—but the government decision makers must be certain that other important city services are not shortchanged by subsidizing the utility. Otherwise, the practice can contribute to the city's fiscal decay. However, experience suggests that, compared to private owners, government operation may be less greedy in pricing, but probably not more efficient in producing the service.

Liquor Stores

Seventeen states report revenue from a radically different sort of monopoly: the sale of alcoholic beverages, either through wholesale distributorships or through operation of retail establishments. In monopoly states, some, if not all, alcoholic beverage sales are made in the state-owned stores.[30] The state establishes a markup over inventory cost sufficient to cover its operating cost, as well as to return a profit for other state operations. In some instances, the state will also add an excise to the price. Table 12–1 reports liquor store revenues, again following the census prac-tice of not netting out cost. In contrast to the utility case, however, liquor stores return a profit to their parent governments. Only in New Hampshire, a state with

---

[29]Cities can move costs to the utility operation by charging the utility for services rendered it by city gov-ernment (charges for the mayor, the city council, use of space in the municipal building, etc.) or by getting free utilities for city operations if direct payments are difficult or legally restrained.

[30]In Canada, all provinces but Alberta run retail liquor monopolies. Such monopolies are also prevalent in the Nordic countries.

neither general sales nor individual income taxes, do these profits make more than a negligible contribution to state finances (in 2013, liquor store sales exceeded liquor store expenditures by $96.2 million, compared with total state general revenue of $6,132.4 million).[31]

Government Gambling Enterprises: Lotteries and Offtrack Betting

In 2009, the total gross gambling revenue in the United States exceeded $89 billion.[32] Even though that is a small piece of the over $14 trillion U.S. economy, it does offer an attractive revenue opportunity for governments because it is a sector that is politically vulnerable because of the social and moral concerns about evils that gambling might bring. Indeed, that ambivalence can be seen in how governments respond to gambling: as *The Economist* keenly headlined, "That's So Wicked We'll Do It Ourselves." States restrict its availability, they subject it to high taxes, and they keep the promotion of some forms of it to themselves. Their defense is the same nearly everywhere: gambling is a bad thing, so you should have tight rules to ban or restrict it; where it is permitted, it should be discouraged by high taxes; even so, the profits may be substantial, so the state should run some gambling itself.[33]

States selectively allow pari-mutuel gambling on certain events (horse racing, greyhound racing, jai alai, and, in Nevada, other sporting events),[34] casinos (either land-based or on riverboats), racinos (casinos at race tracks), bingo, card rooms, and lotteries. In addition, Native American reservations may operate gaming operations on tribal lands under regulation of federal laws. All states but Hawaii and Utah collect revenue from at least one type of commercial gaming.

State revenue normally flows from taxes on gambling activities—through the regular income, property, and sales tax structures and, as noted in an earlier chapter, through selective excises or licenses directly on operators or applicants for licenses to operate. The gambling excises may be on the number of admissions (a tax on each person going on a riverboat, for instance), on the total amount wagered in the establishment, or on the number of tables or other gaming devices in the establishment. Casinos offer strong competition for other gambling formats, being identified as an important factor in the demise of some horse and greyhound racetracks and in slower lottery revenue growth—even some decreases—in several states. State revenues from casinos are unstable, driven as they are by private management decisions and competitive forces in the gaming market; are cyclically sensitive to national and

---

[31]U.S. Census Bureau, Governments Division, State Government Finances: 2013. www.census.gov.

[32]U.S. Census Bureau, *Statistical Abstract of the United States*, 2012 (Washington, D.C.: U.S. Government Printing Office, 2011), 774.

[33]"That's So Wicked We'll Do It Ourselves," *Economist* (April 11, 1992): 24.

[34]The pari-mutuel system is one in which those backing the winner divide, in proportion to their wagers, the total pool bet, after a percentage has been removed by those conducting the event. Some lottery games are pari-mutuel as well.

regional economies; and are expensive to collect. Because the market for gaming is finite, revenues from a casino in one state are affected by casino operations in adjacent states. Furthermore, except possibly for play at destination resorts, casino gambling appears to be distributed regressively.[35]

Seldom do U.S. governments actually operate the gaming facilities, however, preferring to leave the business to private operators who specialize in those activities and limiting the government's role to regulating and to collecting taxes.[36] There are two exceptions. Offtrack betting may have state (or local, in New York City) government proprietors, and state-operated lotteries have become a standard component of state fiscal systems. Government-operated offtrack betting has seldom been particularly profitable and has not spread beyond the northeast quadrant of the nation, although private operations are common at casinos and race tracks and are permitted as free-standing businesses in some states. Lotteries merit some additional attention because they are state-owned (although sometimes operated under contract with private management firms), have spread throughout the nation, and produce more net revenue for states in aggregate than other gambling activities, although casino excise collections are larger in some individual states.[37] The spread of state lotteries in the 1980s—when they became a standard element in state government fiscal operations—probably paved the way for public acceptance of casinos and pari-mutuel gaming in the 1990s. Indeed, in some states, constitutional amendments in that era to permit lotteries also opened the door to casinos.

In 1964, New Hampshire initiated the first state lottery since the demise of the corrupt Louisiana lottery in 1894. New York followed in 1967, but proceeds in both were disappointing. Greater success came with better merchandising and attention to customer tastes, the approach pioneered by New Jersey in 1970 to generate remarkable revenue totals and substantial public excitement. That approach

---

[35]Ranjana G. Madhusudhan, "Betting on Casino Revenues: Lessons from State Experiences," *National Tax Journal* 49 (September 1996): 401–12. Casinos may also reduce state sales tax revenue. See Jim Landers, "The Effect of Casino Gambling on Sales Tax Revenues in States Legalizing Casinos in the 1990s," *State Tax Notes* 38 (December 26, 2005): 1073–83.

[36]Casinos operated by Native American tribes, a special type of government, are obviously an exception, although, even here, outside management has been the rule. Tribe members are, however, developing expertise for a more active role. The U.S. Supreme Court, in *California v. Cabazon Band of Mission Indians*, 480 U.S. 202 (1987), effectively removed all existing restrictions on gambling on Native American reservations, thereby transforming a small and isolated activity often limited to bingo halls into a growth industry. The congressional response, the Indian Gaming Regulatory Act of 1988, specifically authorized casino gambling on Indian reservations, established a regulatory framework for this gambling, and created the National Indian Gaming Commission to oversee the industry. Native American casino gaming greatly expanded under this system; the largest casino in the world is a Native American casino. More than half the states host at least one Native American casino.

[37]During the Great Recession era, a number of states considered selling their lotteries to private businesses to receive a large lump-sum payment to help with state finances, much as some governments sold public facilities to private operators. However, the Department of Justice issued a memorandum opinion that federal exemptions provided state lotteries would not apply to private operations, thereby killing the possibility of fast cash from a sale. http://www.justice.gov/olc/2008/state-conducted-lotteries101608.pdf. States may contract with private businesses to operate their lotteries so long as ultimate authority rests with the state. That is the recent format that lottery privatization has taken. A private operator runs the lottery, often with a guaranteed revenue payment for the state, regardless of how profitable the operation turns out to be.

Table 12–4
State Lottery Performance, Fiscal Year 2013 ($ in Thousands)

	Year of First Play	Ticket Sales ($)	Net to State ($)	Net as % Own-Source General Revenue	Net as % Ticket Sales	Administrative Cost as % Ticket Sales	Administrative Cost as % Net Proceeds
Arizona	1981	645,853	176,703	0.95	27.36	6.66	24.34
Arkansas	2009	414,561	87,666	0.76	21.15	8.39	39.66
California	1985	4,445,874	1,569,716	0.97	35.31	5.04	14.27
Colorado	1983	524,074	138,813	0.84	26.49	7.56	28.54
Connecticut	1972	1,059,930	317,575	1.63	29.96	4.08	13.63
Delaware	1975	452,962	309,189	5.33	68.26	9.83	14.40
Florida	1988	4,741,570	1,431,093	2.81	30.18	3.11	10.31
Georgia	1993	3,407,047	928,988	3.91	27.27	4.27	15.67
Idaho	1989	182,232	48,177	1.00	26.44	6.13	23.18
Illinois	1974	2,832,575	771,193	1.60	27.23	11.22	41.20
Indiana	1989	870,510	225,502	1.01	25.90	7.31	28.23
Iowa	1985	339,252	85,886	0.68	25.32	15.49	61.20
Kansas	1987	230,469	72,174	0.63	31.32	8.57	27.35
Kentucky	1989	758,665	225,989	1.52	29.79	4.98	16.71
Louisiana	1991	422,633	160,521	1.10	37.98	6.14	16.17
Maine	1974	212,886	54,068	1.05	25.40	6.99	27.52
Maryland	1973	2,021,118	641,651	2.62	31.75	16.87	53.14
Massachusetts	1972	4,565,196	947,010	2.92	20.74	2.07	9.96
Michigan	1972	2,260,945	696,672	1.92	30.81	3.13	10.17
Minnesota	1990	527,007	135,784	0.54	25.77	4.82	18.70
Missouri	1986	1,116,996	314,029	1.94	28.11	4.48	15.92
Montana	1978	60,188	20,021	0.56	33.26	13.28	39.91
Nebraska	1993	170,807	60,681	0.92	35.53	9.97	28.07
New Hampshire	1964	263,794	74,476	1.75	28.23	6.05	21.43
New Jersey	1970	2,663,519	883,588	2.24	33.17	2.66	8.02
New Mexico	1996	139,267	41,390	0.47	29.72	13.16	44.28
New York	1967	7,697,675	3,090,107	3.30	40.14	5.05	12.57
North Carolina	2006	1,570,874	474,307	1.49	30.19	4.60	15.23
North Dakota	2004	26,603	8,285	0.13	31.14	15.42	49.50
Ohio	1974	2,531,002	763,092	1.92	30.15	3.95	13.09
Oklahoma	2005	200,209	72,105	0.53	36.01	11.81	32.79
Oregon	1985	864,231	587,196	3.96	67.94	8.12	11.95
Pennsylvania	1972	3,441,263	1,069,964	2.21	31.09	2.10	6.76
Rhode Island	1974	539,026	379,616	8.32	70.43	1.15	1.63
South Carolina	2002	1,114,410	301,857	2.02	27.09	3.33	12.29
South Dakota	1987	146,536	106,351	4.38	72.58	5.30	7.30
Tennessee	2004	1,278,328	501,029	3.04	39.19	4.46	11.39
Texas	1992	4,139,450	1,190,125	1.58	28.75	4.40	15.29
Vermont	1978	96,067	22,892	0.61	23.83	8.97	37.65
Virginia	1988	1,594,265	488,363	1.57	30.63	5.06	16.53
Washington	1982	534,041	144,721	0.56	27.10	9.35	34.52
West Virginia	1986	713,850	564,723	7.00	79.11	4.61	5.83
Wisconsin	1988	566,103	198,746	0.86	35.11	6.74	19.20
U.S. Totals		62,383,863	20,382,034				
U.S. Mean				1.98	34.72	6.90	22.22

featured "(a) lower priced tickets; (b) more frequent drawings; (c) more numerous outlets; (d) numbered tickets in lieu of recording purchasers' names and addresses; (e) somewhat better odds; and (f) energetic promotion."[38] By 2015, all states but Alabama, Alaska, Hawaii, Mississippi, Nevada, and Utah plus the District of Columbia operated lotteries.[39] Table 12–4 indicates the lottery revenue generated in 2013, a tiny amount in comparison with taxes, but larger than some user charge categories.

The major lottery formats are these:

1. **Passive.** The customer receives a prenumbered ticket with a winner selected at a periodic drawing. States used this format in early days, but it has been superseded by other games.
2. **Instant or Scratch Off.** The player buys a ticket and rubs off a substance to reveal whether the ticket is a winner. Some state lotteries offer a video-terminal version of the game, creating a product much like casino slot machines.
3. **Numbers.** The player selects a three- or four-digit daily number and places a bet on an online computer terminal.
4. **Lotto.** This is a pari-mutuel game in which the player selects a group of numbers out of a larger field of possible selections (e.g., six of a possible forty-four). If no ticket has been sold for the particular group of numbers picked in the weekly drawing, the amount not won rolls over to the next week. Top prize money can grow rapidly, producing multimillion-dollar prizes that are divided among all players who have picked the selected numbers for that week. Even if a couple of people pick all numbers and share the prize, the payoff can be huge, much larger than produced in other formats.[40] Such huge prizes are not produced in the other formats. The lotto games may be offered by a single state or by multistate groups (such as those operating the Powerball and MegaMillions games in the United States). Lotto produces more revenue than the other products currently offered. The multistate lotteries are the ones that periodically produce the jackpots that are advertised as being about as much as a small college endowment.
5. **Keno.** This is a casino-type game in which a player can make a variety of bets, involving long or short odds and large or small prizes, on the selection of numbers from a large field. Play is virtually continuous, with many draws during the day. Play is in sites, often bars, connected to a statewide system.

---

[38]Frederick D. Stocker, "State Sponsored Gambling as a Source of Public Revenue," *National Tax Journal* 25 (September 1972): 437.

[39]Not included is the special state-sanctioned, privately operated statewide lottery for charities in Alaska.

[40]Any combination of numbers is as likely to be a winner as is any other (selection is random), so your shot at getting a big jackpot that need not be shared is less if you include popular numbers in your selection. For example, evidence shows that many people include 11 or 7 in their picks, and few people include. 37. Let the computer pick your numbers randomly to get a meaningless combination not likely to be duplicated by any other player. It's as likely to get selected as any numbers you pick yourself. Jo Craven McGinty, "Lucky Lotto Numbers Will Only Win You Less," *Wall Street Journal,* October 10–11, 2015, A2.

Lotteries appear to be a painless, voluntary, and enjoyable approach to government finance. What are their limitations? Some answers may be deduced from Table 12–4. First, lottery proceeds, although large in several states, contribute but a small amount to overall state finances. In a few states, the lottery contributes more than 5 percent of state own-source general revenue, but the national share across all lottery states is only 1.98 percent. These amounts are not sufficient to provide either significant tax relief or support for crucial state functions, no matter how politically easy the revenue might be to generate. If a state has a serious fiscal imbalance, a lottery is unlikely to correct it. Second, lottery revenue is expensive to produce. Both security and advertising are crucial for lottery success; neither is cheap, and the advertising seldom reveals the real chances of winning. If evaluated on roughly the same basis that a tax would be, the ratio of administrative cost to net proceeds to the state, not including commissions of 5 or 6 percent of sales paid directly to lottery vendors, was 22.22 percent. Even though there is no compliance cost to add in for the lottery, advertising, security, and commission costs are much greater than collection cost for taxes. Third, lottery proceeds are subject to considerable change from year to year, making them an unstable base for financing. Lottery sales have an extremely high elasticity to state income. One estimate indicates a 3.9 percent increase in sales for each 1 percent increase in state personal income. That response is tempered by response to the state unemployment rate. Apparently, lower prospects of employment in the economy make the small, but real chance of the lottery jackpot more attractive for households.[41] Fourth, evidence suggests that low-income families spend a higher percentage of their income on lottery tickets than do high-income families, thus producing a regressive burden distribution. Although it is a voluntary burden, it does remain a burden that makes distributive correction by other parts of the tax or expenditure system more difficult.[42]

Finally, Charles Clotfelter and Philip Cook raise a fundamental question about state lotteries that is even more important than their fiscal implications: "The lottery business places the state in the position of using advertising that endorses suspect values and offers deceptive impressions instead of information."[43] Should this line of business be something that states operate regardless of the money it might be able to raise from such an operation?

Lottery proponents note that profits are often dedicated to the support of important and valuable state programs, especially education. The revenue, however, is fungible, leading to the possibility that the lottery profits going to the dedicated program will simply substitute for other budget resources that would have gone to the program anyway. One analysis done of the Illinois lottery's support for education speaks directly to the point: "lotteries which are designated to support education, in

---

[41]John L. Mikesell, "State Lottery Sales and Economic Activity," *National Tax Journal* 47 (March 1994): 170.
[42]Some have suggested that lotteries can cut into the profits of gambling operated illegally. Unfortunately, lotteries typically offer worse odds than do illegal operations, do not offer regular gambling on credit, and report large winnings to tax authorities, so the competition presented by state systems is not likely to be effective.
[43]Charles T. Clotfelter and Philip J. Cook, *Selling Hope* (Cambridge, Mass.: Harvard University Press, 1989), 249.

all likelihood, do not. Further, there is no reason to believe that other specific programs designated as lottery fund recipients are any more likely to be truly supported by the lottery funds."[44] Money mixes in government operations, and dedication to useful purposes does not ordinarily change the basic points in the case for or against lotteries as an element in government finances.

Conclusion

Public prices can be an attractive alternative to tax financing. Public prices avoid citizen resistance to taxes and can improve both equity in finance and efficiency in service provision. Of the various government levels, cities currently make greatest use of user charges in the United States. User charges have the advantage of voluntarism not found with taxes, but only services with some considerable degree of benefit separability and chargeability are reasonable candidates for user charge financing. Basic services provided by government usually lack those features. Most governments could increase their user charge revenues, but seldom can true user charges (not disguised taxes) constitute a major portion of financial support. A similar conclusion is warranted for municipal utilities and state liquor monopolies; it is not clear why, if a government operates such facilities, it would not seek roughly the same objectives as a private owner. Lotteries in recent years have produced, relatively speaking, more public attention and acclaim than revenue.

QUESTIONS AND EXERCISES

1. The Fernwood Wastewater District—at the gentle insistence of both state and federal agencies—is changing methods of financing the operating and maintenance costs of its system. Presently, all users of the system (residential, commercial, agricultural, industrial, etc.) pay for the system by a property tax; payments to the district are assigned according to individual holdings of property value. If a car wash constitutes 0.0001 of total property in the district, the car wash pays 0.0001 of the operating and maintenance costs of the system. The proposed effluent-charge system would assign cost on the basis of estimated toxic-waste quality and quantity introduced into the system. The structure could easily be applied because a federal agency has data on the amount and type of waste that production and consumption processes generate annually, based on national data. These data would then be used to assign

[44]Mary O. Borg and Paul M. Mason, "The Budgetary Incidence of a Lottery to Support Education," *National Tax Journal* 41 (March 1988): 83.

an annual effluent charge to each user, based on the total costs of the district. How do the two systems differ in terms of incentive to reduce wastewater quantity and toxicity?

2. In mid-1985, the U.S. Customs Service proposed a user charge system for partial support of its services. The system would charge $2 for every passenger arriving on an international flight, $0.25 for every passenger arriving by train from a foreign destination, and $2.50 for every passenger arriving by boat. Fees to inspect airplanes would be $32 and to check passenger and freight carriers, up to $397. The customs system currently was financed by general revenue. Does the proposal seem reasonable? Discuss its logic, advantages, and disadvantages.

3. Here is a list of miscellaneous revenue sources received by governments. Categorize them as best you can as (1) user charge, (2) license tax, (3) franchise fee, or (4) fiscal monopoly, using the standards established in the chapter.[45] Explain your logic. What are the incentive impacts of each one of the revenue sources?

   a. A fee for disposal of used tires
   b. A fee to reserve books at the library
   c. A charge for processing the arrest of a convicted drunk driver
   d. A charge for emergency services required when a driver causes an accident through negligence
   e. A charge by the fire department to pump water from basements flooded by a downpour
   f. A fee for the services of a probation officer
   g. A fee for reviewing a developer's plans
   h. A fee for police response to a malfunctioning alarm system
   i. A charge for ball field use by the youth athletic league
   j. Admission to the city zoo
   k. A mandatory fee for municipal garbage collection
   l. A charge for use of the city municipal garbage collection
   m. A charge for yacht owners who dock at the city marina
   n. Fees for a summer day camp run by the city parks department

4. Due City has decided to shift municipal garbage-collection financing from the property tax to user charges. Describe some ways in which such a system could be implemented. Make certain that your system is primarily one of user charge, not a disguised tax.

5. A city council member of a midwestern university town proclaims that all parking meter revenue generated within his district should be spent to provide services to the population of that district. He argues that to use the money for services anywhere else in the city would represent an unfair transfer away from those who are paying those meter fees. What do you think about this proposal?

---

[45]Most of these examples have been taken from Penelope Lemov, "User Fees, Once the Answer to City Budget Prayers, May Have Reached Their Peak," *Governing* (March 1989): 24–30.

CASES FOR DISCUSSION

CASE 12–1

User Charges for Correcting Externalities: London Congestion Charge

Consider These Questions

1. How is this charge system different from simply adding a new annual license charge to all motor vehicles in the London area? Why might this approach be more effective at getting at congestion?

2. Does the logic of the charge depend on how the revenue from the charge is used? Explain.

3. Pick a large city with which you are familiar: Los Angeles, Boston, New York, Beijing, Moscow, or any other. Would a congestion charge system be sensible and feasible there? What are the political, geographic, or economic barriers (or advantages) to applying a congestion charge in the selected city? New York City has sought authority for such charges, but the state legislature has denied that authorization.

4. It has been suggested that congestion charges could be a solution to airport flight delays—in other words, flights would be charged higher takeoff and landing fees at times when the airport was congested and lower fees at off-peak periods—a cheaper response than building more airports or runways. What do you think about this approach?

The London Example

At the beginning of the twenty-first century, traffic in the center of London moved about as quickly as it did in the horse-and-buggy era. The 200,000 or so cars and trucks that entered the city center made their way down narrow and winding streets that were laid out in the Middle Ages. Congestion was so bad that any small mishap brought traffic from its normal slow crawl to a complete stop. Total gridlock hung as an impending threat over the city every day.

The traditional engineering approach—providing more lanes for traffic—was not possible. All the properties in the congested space were occupied by buildings, including many of historic importance. Even if solving the problem with wrecking crews and bulldozers was technically feasible, voters were unlikely to accept the considerable tax burden this approach would involve. Furthermore, the city was reluctant to use a regulation approach—such as permitting cars access only on alternate days, based on license plate numbers. The mayor of London, Ken Livingstone, developed a radical approach built on the principles of basic microeconomics: a daily congestion charge for driving in the eight square miles of London. As with many other excellent policy applications of microeconomics, the idea of congestion pricing initially was proposed by Nobel laureate in economics William Vickery—in the 1950s—so the implementation was the new part of the proposal.

A Congressional Budget Office study explains the program.

The Central London congestion charging zone applies cordon pricing to an approximately 15-square-mile section of the city. The zone first covered an 8-square-mile area in February 2003 and was approximately doubled to its current size in February 2007 by including an area west of the original zone. That western extension is now intended to be removed from operation, but no earlier than 2010. . . .

Drivers pay a daily charge of £8 (about $11 at current exchange rates) to drive or park on a street within the zone; the charge was £5 when first implemented in 2005. The congestion charge applies on Monday through Friday, from 7:00 a.m. to 6:00 p.m. Motorbikes, mopeds, taxis, buses, emergency vehicles, and vehicles using alternative fuels are exempt, as are vehicles whose drivers are disabled, and residents of the zone receive a 90 percent discount. The congestion fee may be paid in advance on a daily, weekly, monthly, or annual basis by phone, mail, or Internet or at retail outlets. If paid on the following day, the charge is £10 (about $14 at current exchange rates).

Entry into the congestion zone is indicated by street signs or pavement markings. The license plates of vehicles moving into or within the zone are recorded by a network of fixed and mobile cameras. Drivers encounter no toll booths, gantries, or barriers on entering the zone, and traffic does not have to stop. License plate numbers are compared with those in a database of vehicles for which the fee has been paid, and a £120 fine (about $166 at current exchange rates) is assessed to the vehicle owner if the fee has not been paid. The fine is reduced to £60 (about $83) if paid within 14 days. Authorities may apply a "boot" to immobilize vehicles with multiple outstanding fines.

Implementation costs for the first two years of the project were £190 million ($348 million at then-current exchange rates), more than twice the amount expected. Approximately £140 million in costs ($258 million at then-current exchange rates) were incurred in extending the zone to the west. Annual operating expenses for the entire tolling system are approximately £130 million ($246 million). [An aside: The U.S. Embassy claims exemption from the charge for its 200 London employees, arguing for diplomatic immunity and citing the 1960 Vienna Convention on Diplomatic Relations. That included a charge for President Obama's armored Cadillac limousine and the accompanying motorcade when he visited in 2011. London was not impressed, pointing out that a user charge is not a tax. The unpaid Embassy bill at that time was around $8.7 million. The United States was not alone: diplomatic missions owed a total of $83 million in congestion charges.] The system has covered its capital and operating expenses every year since its inception. In a typical day, the system handles 78,000 payments from nonresidents, 60,000 from residents, and 20,000 from operators of fleets. All together, in the fiscal year ending in June 2008, the congestion fees totaled £268 million ($507 million). All proceeds from the program must be spent on improving transport within Greater London.[46]

Drivers entering the congested area would normally take no account of the fact that their presence had the effect of slowing the progress of other travelers. The congestion charge was intended to make drivers pay attention to the cost they imposed on others—slowed traffic—when they added their vehicles to the mass of metal choking London streets. When drivers must bear this cost, many decide that the trip can be postponed to a less congested time, can be canceled, or can be undertaken on public mass transport (bus or train) rather than by private vehicle because the full cost of the trip is greater than the value of the journey. The hope was that the number of vehicles entering the center would fall by 15 to 20 percent, thus allowing travel at speeds faster than horse and buggy. After paying for the cost of the control equipment, all profit was earmarked for transportation system improvements.

Critics had several complaints in addition to the skeptical view that the system was technologically untested and certain to fail. The criticisms included:

1. The concern that the fee put greater burden on low-income than high-income vehicle owners and was thus inherently unfair;
2. The fear that people would be forced off the roads and onto the bus and train system, creating a crisis there;
3. The complaint that the scheme amounted to charging the public to use public property; and
4. The argument that so many people would be discouraged from entering the charge area that there would be a devastating collapse of economic activity there.

What has been the result of the charges? It is too early to know the long-term effects, but comparisons of traffic measurements in the congestion zone show that traffic congestion in the charge area has fallen by 30 percent (as measured by delay per kilometer traveled), traffic entering the charge zone is down by 18 percent, average driving speed in the zone has increased by 20 percent, and 90 million pounds are being generated yearly from the charges, with the bulk of the revenue going to improve London bus services. There have also been reductions in personal injury accidents and in emissions (carbon dioxide, nitrous oxide, and particulate matter) with the changed traffic. The economic impacts on businesses in the zone are in dispute.

There have been erroneous billings, and a new scam has developed: people locate cars of the same make, model, and color of their own and produce a phony license plate with that car's number so that the owner of the other car receives the bills and fines, based on photographic evidence of that car violating the charge controls. In addition, there have been considerable impacts outside the charge zone as drivers divert around the charge zone, creating congestion

---

[46]Congressional Budget Office, Using Pricing to Reduce Traffic Congestion (Washington, D.C.: Congressional Budget Office, 2009), 23–24. Footnotes in source are eliminated.

where there was none before, and as drivers park at the charge zone border to take public transportation for the rest of their travel. However, the experiment is seen as an overall success: national politicians who opposed the idea before it was implemented have now started to refer to the congestion charges as a transportation success worth replicating elsewhere, and the person who devised the specifics of the system in London resigned to undertake a new career designing similar systems for other cities.

The system has survived a change in mayors, and similar systems have been adopted in Stockholm (voters chose to continue the system after an initial trial there) and Singapore (Singapore started its program in 1975). The state legislature in New York, however, blocked implementation of such a system in New York City.

SOURCES: "Congestion Charging: Ken Livingstone's Gamble," *Economist* (February 15, 2003): 51–53; Glenn Frankel, "Toll Zone Put to Test in Divided London," *Washington Post,* February 17, 2003, A2; and Transport for London, *Central London Congestion Charging, Impacts Monitoring, Fourth Annual Report* (June 2006). http://www.tfl.gov.uk/assets/downloads/ FourthAnnualReportFinal.pdf. For an excellent overview of congestion pricing, see Kiram Bhatt, "Congestion Pricing: An Overview of Experience and Impacts," in *Climate Change and Land Policies, Proceedings of the 2010 Land Policy Conference,* ed. Gregory K. Ingram and Yu-Hung Hong (Cambridge, Mass.: Lincoln Institute of Land Policy, 2011): 247–71. The Federal Highway Administration also offers its ideas: *Congestion Pricing, A Primer,* FHWA-HOP-07-074, December 2006.

CASE 12–2

Charging for Firefighting: A Reasonable Financing Option?

Fighting wildfires is expensive. Who should bear that cost? The general taxpayers or the people whose properties the firefighters are working to protect? Global climate change seems to have worsened the conditions for wildfires in the American west, and huge fires in California, Arizona, Colorado, and New Mexico have made national headlines in the past several years. The problem seems to worsen with each year because the fire season starts earlier and ends later than it did in the past. The problem promises not to go away and California, along with the other western states, has not developed a good solution to financing the cost of fighting these fires.

Consider These Questions

1. What are the general alternatives that a state would have for financing state services?

2. Would financing this wildfire fighting through some sort of charge make sense? Discuss this alternative as opposed to using general funds. What would be the advantages and disadvantages?

3. If you were to finance by a charge, how would you design the charge, and how would you enforce it? Would your charge include incentives that could lead to reduced fire damages?

4. Is the case for financing CalFire through direct charges different from the case for financing the fire department of, say, San Francisco by charges?

U.S. News: California Ponders Who Should Pay Firefighting Bill; Some Want Owners of Wooded Property to Bear More of Cost, by Peter Sanders

California's fire season has barely begun, but in the past three weeks alone, blazes have burned through 631,000 acres—and at least $112 million in state money. That is stoking a statewide debate: Who should pick up the bill? The state's costs for fighting wildfires over the past 12 months have soared to an estimated $950 million, a 41 percent increase over the same period a year ago. This doesn't include the cost to various local and federal firefighting agencies. The most intense months for wildfires, typically August through October when local vegetation is driest, are still to come, and some officials worry the hefty price tag could further strain an already overstretched state budget. That has prompted several new fund-raising proposals, including one advanced by Gov. Arnold Schwarzenegger.

But some officials are raising the question of whether Californians are paying firefighting costs to protect forests or to protect homeowners who willingly built property in woodlands, which go up in smoke with increasing frequency.

"The fact is the residents of California are simply not paying enough for fire protection," says Christine Kehoe, a Democratic state senator from San Diego. She argues that frenzied building in rural areas increases the burden on state firefighters to defend homes and property and that people who choose to live in those areas should shoulder more of the firefighting costs. "It's a very tough discussion for citizens and politicians to have."

Covering rising firefighting costs is an urgent issue as California battles a budget deficit currently estimated at $17.2 billion. In his proposed 2008–2009 budget, Mr. Schwarzenegger has tried to find new firefighting funds with an insurance surcharge on all home and business owners that would raise an estimated $130 million extra annually. Some of that money would help cover the costs of the state's fire department, known as CalFire.

But the state's nonpartisan Legislative Analyst's Office [LAO] doesn't recommend the governor's proposed insurance fee because, it argues, it would unfairly burden taxpayers who aren't threatened by the wildfires. "Because the state provides a service—fire protection—that directly benefits a particular group. it is appropriate that those beneficiaries pay for a portion of the state's cost for fire protection," the LAO wrote in a recent report. It is in favor of a property-tax surcharge on residents who live in areas protected by CalFire.

Ms. Kehoe has introduced a bill in the state legislature similar to what the LAO is proposing, an annual fee paid by residents who live in more rural areas to help offset the costs of firefighting.

Since June 20, more than 20,000 local, state and federal firefighters have fought nearly 1,800 fires. The two biggest—one near the coastal tourist hamlet of Big Sur and another north of Santa Barbara—continue to burn as more hot, dry weather rolled into the state Tuesday.

CalFire has taken the lead in combating more than 1,000 of the fires and as of Tuesday was still fighting nearly 60. The department has 4,700 full-time and 2,200 seasonal firefighters, in addition to thousands of local volunteers and prison inmates it uses to fight wildfires.

CalFire's budget, which last year was about $870 million, comes largely from the state's general fund footed by all California taxpayers. The budget covers such costs as those of buildings and fire trucks as well as of firefighting itself.

When the department needs extra money to fight a big fire, it makes a request for emergency funding to the legislature. For the fiscal year ended June 30, state budget officials had anticipated CalFire would make $82 million in emergency fund requests to fight the year's big fires. The officials are now saying those emergency requests will likely reach about $400 million.

Rampant development in places like San Diego County and Riverside County, which abut wilderness, have brought more fires. But because of the proximity of those fires to populated areas, firefighting costs have grown at an even faster clip.

Typically, the costs are highest when firefighters are trying to protect homes in wooded areas. Using fire engines, helicopters, and airplanes to make a stand is vastly more expensive than using smaller crews to monitor and contain a remote wilderness fire.

"When you are forced to move resources in defense of structures, it means you're often taking resources away from other areas of the fire, or entirely separate fires, which means those fires are harder to contain with less resources," says Timothy Duane, professor of environmental planning and policy at the University of California, Berkeley. "You have to deal with life and property and natural resources, in that order, and when you're dealing with the first two, it increases the extent of the fire and the time period before you can put the fire out."

In 1999, Mr. Duane published a study that noted that between 1970 and 1985 the state's population rose 97 percent, while fires rose 90 percent and acreage burned rose 95 percent. But the cost of fire damage in the same period rose 5,000 percent. CalFire's mission has changed as well. The service is charged with protecting 31 million acres of wildland, including the state's timber stands, watershed and vast agriculture lands. Increasingly, however, the service has to divert resources to protecting the growing number of homes sprinkled throughout the forests.

"CalFire protects land that benefits the public at large," says Brendan McCarthy of the state's LAO. "But there is now an increased burden on the department to do whatever they can to protect neighborhoods. . . . It's more expensive . . . because it's harder to defend a neighborhood."

Development is approved at the local level, and the local governments then bear little fiscal consequence if the state is responsible for firefighting in the jurisdiction.

Says Ms. Kehoe: "Local land-use approvals for residential development in the backcountry should be tied to the future cost of firefighting. If they want to approve a new development, they should be required to plan for ongoing fire prevention; otherwise, this problem will continue without interruption."

CHAPTER 13

Revenue Forecasts, Revenue Estimates, and Tax Expenditure Budgets

Chapter Contents

Revenue Forecast (or Baseline)
General Guides for Revenue Forecasts

Monitoring and Evaluating
Alternative Methods for Forecasting
Choosing the Method for the Budget Forecast
Forecasts for the Long Term
Wrong Forecasts

Revenue Estimating (or Scoring)
The Macro-Dynamic Argument
Accuracy in Scoring/Estimating

Tax Expenditure Budgets

Conclusion

Reliable and trusted revenue predictions provide the foundation for fiscal discipline and for the adoption of an executable public budget. Participants in the budget process need to know how much money the revenue system will yield in the budget period—first as it exists and then with proposed changes. Budget participants and the public also need to know the cost of carrying out subsidy programs through tax system preferences rather than through direct expenditures. The predictions are never certain because private economic behavior is not certain, and if the private economy—the source of government revenue in a market economy—is uncertain, so, too, will be revenue yield. Nonetheless, best available predictions are necessary for developing and executing the budget, for preparing long-term fiscal profiles, for understanding the implications of fiscal decisions, and for forecasting short-term cash flow. Financial management without trustworthy revenue predictions is impossible.

Three distinct revenue prediction tasks play a prominent role in public financial management: the revenue *forecast* (or baseline), revenue *estimates* (or fiscal notes or scores), and *tax expenditures*. Approaches, methods, and skills required as well as organizational responsibility for their preparation typically differ, although the tax-collecting agency—the tax service, treasury, or revenue department—is the repository of basic data used in each. The tax collection agency (mostly accountants and lawyers) likely does not have the appropriate technical staff (mostly economists and statisticians) to develop the models and procedures necessary for the predictions, but the collectors serve as a conduit of data to those preparing the predictions. Official forecasts and estimates may come from budget agencies, legislative fiscal staff, or consensus groups representing both the legislature and the executive. Of course, there are many interest groups, lobbyists, consultants, and so on who devise their own forecasts and estimates of varying trustworthiness for their clients and distribute them to whomever will pay attention.[1]

Revenue Forecast (or Baseline)[2]

As the wise philosopher Yogi Berra pointed out, "It's hard to make predictions, especially about the future." The revenue forecast predicts the revenue baseline, meaning the forecast of what revenue will be collected in the budget period under current law. It is driven by forecasts of economic, demographic, administrative, and other structural conditions in the tax-collecting environment, but it assumes no change in tax policy or administration as represented in the current tax structure. If current law has in place a tax change that will take place during the forecast period, then that change would be part of the revenue baseline.

At the federal level, the Office of Tax Analysis in the Department of Treasury prepares revenue forecasts that the Office of Management and Budget (OMB) uses in development of the president's budget, whereas the Congressional Budget Office (CBO) prepares baseline forecasts for the congressional Budget Committees, as well as other fiscal committees.[3] These forecasts drive executive budget development, advise the congressional Budget Committees as they develop the budget resolution, and form the basis for the midsession reviews by the OMB and CBO.

States organize their revenue forecasting in one of three general patterns.[4]

(a) In a few states, legislative and executive branch entities prepare independent forecasts. The entities sometimes cooperate, producing forecasts that usually do not differ substantially. That is the case in Wisconsin, for instance, where the Department of Revenue and the Legislative Fiscal Bureau both do forecasts, but usually cooperate. However, that is

---

[1] Many of these consultants started out as government fiscal staff, so their predictions can be of excellent quality. However, many interest group forecasts are so tinged with self-interest as to be worthless.
[2] An excellent basic source on general techniques of forecasting is "Chapter 5: Forecasting Techniques," in *The Economist Numbers Guide: The Essentials of Business Numeracy* (London: Profile Books, 1997), 92–119.
[3] Congressional Budget Office, *The 2015 Long-Term Economic Outlook* (Washington, D.C.: U.S. Government Printing Office, 2015); and Office of Management and Budget, *The Fiscal 2016 Mid-Session Review, Budget of the U.S. Government* (Washington, D.C.: U.S. Government Printing Office, 2015), for example.
[4] For an excellent overview of how governments in the United States forecast and estimate, see Marilyn Marks Rubin, J. L. Peters, and Nancy Mantell, "Revenue Forecasting and Estimation," in *Handbook on Taxation*, ed. W. Bartley Hildreth and James A. Richardson (New York: Marcel Dekker, 1999), 769–99.

not always the case and that creates considerable tension in the process of developing and adopting a state budget, as with recent disputes between the New Jersey Department of Treasury and Office of Legislative Services.

(b) Several states work with a revenue forecast prepared by a state executive agency, the state budget agency, the department of revenue, the comptroller's office, and so on. That is the case in slightly less than half the states.

(c) Slightly more than half the states use a consensus forecasting process that explicitly involves both legislative and executive representation in the group that develops the forecast, with the understanding that a single revenue baseline will be used by all budget participants in development and enactment of the budget. That approach, when it produces a generally accepted baseline, helps focus attention on fundamental resource allocation issues without diluting attention to arguments about how much revenue might be available. It is believed that this approach, particularly one that insures representation from both political parties, helps maintain attention to the goal of adopting a fiscally sustainable expenditure program.[5]

Because revenue forecasts can become political tools to either boost or constrain expenditure, there can be considerable advantage to an open, consensus forecast process so that neither executive nor legislative branch can manipulate the baseline. Local revenue forecasts for all but the largest governments tend to be informal, simply done in the budget or finance office.[6] Revenue forecasts are often a controversial part of the state and local budget process. However, they seldom are subject to much dispute at the federal level.

Revenue forecasts are made using several different approaches, and seldom will all revenues collected by a government be forecast by exactly the same approach. The more important formal approaches in current use include (a) extrapolation or projection, (b) deterministic models, (c) multiple regression equations, (d) econometric equation systems, and (e) microsimulation from taxpayer data files. All but the first are "cause-and-effect" approaches that try to link economic, demographic, or other influences to revenue sources and then exploit that linkage to forecast revenue.[7] Some forecasts are heavily judgmental or nearly subjective, based on the personal experience, intuition, and guesswork of public finance staff from the revenue department, budget or finance agency, or legislative fiscal committees. Each method has its appropriate uses in the revenue forecast environment, and all are ultimately time-series estimates because they consider revenue flows across years, quarters, months, or weeks into the future.

---

[5]John L. Mikesell and Justin Ross, "State Revenue Forecasts and Political Acceptance: The Value of Consensus Forecasting in the Budget Process," *Public Administration Review* 74 (March/April 2014): 188–203.

[6]The revenue forecasting approach used by New York City, for instance, is not unlike that used by most states. Tax Policy, Revenue Forecasting and Economic Analysis Task Force, *Tax Revenue Forecasting Documentation, Financial Plan Fiscal Years 2014–2018.* New York City Office of Management and Budget.

[7]Localities are hampered in the use of causal modeling by the lack of usable forecasts of economic and demographic variables (personal income, personal consumption, housing prices, population, etc.) at the local level that would be used to drive such a forecasting approach.

General Guides for Revenue Forecasts[8]

Before discussing each method, several general points about revenue forecasting need to be highlighted. The first and most fundamental principle is that the forecaster must understand the tax being forecast, how it is administered, and the procedures that generate collection data. That is the reason this chapter about forecasting comes after the chapters dealing with each of the major taxes: the forecaster needs to understand the structure and administration of the tax before even attempting to do the forecast. It is folly to try to forecast the state insurance tax, for instance, if you do not fully understand the nature (structure and administration) of that tax; having what you believe to be a consistent series of collections data for the tax is not enough. Novice revenue forecasters usually underestimate the problems involved in developing a consistent data series for each tax to be forecast. Messy little transactions (changes in rates or exemptions, failure to properly record receipts for an unspecified period, changes in filing or revenue-processing schedules, loss of revenue reports, a court case lost in a dispute with a major taxpayer, inconsistent or improper revenue accounting, etc.) confuse almost every revenue series, causing the revenue estimator to spend many hours to obtain a clean and consistent data series. Sometimes the forecaster may discover that some historical revenue data have been lost forever. Many possible adjustments can remedy problems with independent variables, including the decision to substitute some other variable to drive the forecast, but estimation based on incorrect, misunderstood, or inconsistent revenue data is nearly hopeless. Furthermore, the forecast is always subject to sabotage, usually accidental, through a repeat of the episodes that messed up the initial data.[9] These problems haunt every revenue forecaster.

Second, the cleaned revenue series to be forecast should be plotted in a simple graph against time. An examination of the graph offers insights into the forecasting task (expansion or decline? large change or small? smooth changes or major fluctuations?) and identifies important questions: When were there large increases or decreases in revenue, and what caused the changes? Are the overall patterns consistent with general forces in the regional or national economy? Sometimes the plots will alert the forecaster to the fact that her revenue data have some errors that need to be straightened out before further work is done. Additional plots, sometimes against time and sometimes against independent variables ("causes") thought to influence revenue, can be helpful throughout the forecasting process as tests of logic and of strength of relationship.

---

[8]A number of forecasting issues, as well as practical illustrations of forecasting applications, are provided in Jinping Sun and Thomas D. Lynch, eds., *Government Budget Forecasting, Theory and Practice* (Boca Raton, Fla.: CRC Press, 2008).

[9]Some revenues are subject to some control by program administrators. For instance, state lotteries can manipulate the introduction of new games, payout rates, or advertising programs and so influence at least the timing of net proceeds to government. Therefore, revenue forecasters must give great deference to what their administrators forecast for their operations; an irritated lottery director can make external forecasters look inept.

Third, openness in forecasting is a virtue. As noted earlier, both legislative and executive branches occasionally seek artificially high or low revenue forecasts as a part of a political budget strategy to increase or reduce expenditure. An open and transparent process reduces the opportunity for such manipulation and keeps the forecaster from being blamed for a revenue forecast error that was actually the work of politicians rigging the numbers. The general public seldom wins when several different revenue estimates are strategically unveiled during budget sessions. A wrong forecast used by all in crafting a budget leads to more responsible budget development and adoption than does a process with many competing forecasts from executive and legislative branches, from each political party, or from factions within parties—even if one of the competitors happens to be absolutely correct. What is really critical is that those preparing and adopting the budget agree to accept the same revenue forecast so that work will be done within a single, hard budget constraint. That is the logic behind the consensus forecasting discussed earlier.[10] Huge forecast errors are most frequent when the business cycle turns (and downturns are difficult to predict accurately) or when politicians intervene to create phantom revenue needed to close a budget gap. An open, consensus forecast prevents the latter problem. State and local government forecasts (and estimates) tend to be more openly prepared than those in the federal government.[11] Historically, political manipulation of revenue forecasts has been more common at the state and local levels than at the federal level, possibly because the federal government has not been as concerned about keeping spending within the revenue baseline as have states and localities.

Fourth, the approach selected often depends on the tasks to be served by the model. If one seeks revenue forecasts for the annual budget process, the multiple regression approach ordinarily yields good results. If one needs to divide annual revenues into amounts expected within the year (quarterly or monthly), univariate analysis may be appropriate. If one seeks the impact of a structural change, in the economy or in the demographic character of the population, microsimulation may be more appropriate. If estimates are needed for long-range plans, trend extrapolations—sometimes adjusted for guesses about structural changes—are as good as anything. In summary, no single approach is ideally suited for all revenue forecasting tasks.

Fifth, individual revenue sources normally are forecast separately. It would be extremely unusual, for instance, to forecast general fund revenue for a state as a single aggregate instead of adding forecasts of each individual revenue source to obtain the total. Different revenue sources respond to different factors, and they should be separately examined. Furthermore, compensating errors in the separate source forecasts can cause the total forecast—the one upon which the budget is based—to be closer to the actual revenue than any of the individual forecasts.

---

[10]Pew Center on the States—Rockefeller Institute, *States' Revenue Estimating, Cracks in the Crystal Ball* (Washington, D.C. and Philadelphia, Penn.: Pew Trust, 2011), 32
[11]Thomas F. Field, "Transparency in Revenue Estimating," *Tax Notes* (January 17, 2005): 329–61.

Alternative Methods for Forecasting

The problem in revenue forecasting is not in finding a method for doing the forecast, because there are many options from which to choose. It is selecting from among the many methods to produce a satisfactory forecast. Which ones will work best for the current forecast? Unfortunately, you won't know for sure until after the year is over, and that is definitely too late to help with adopting a budget.

UNIVARIATE PROJECTIONS, TRENDS, AUTOCORRELATIONS, AND EXTRAPOLATIONS

Forecasters do projections and extrapolations because they can be quick, inexpensive, done without much data, and are sometimes accurate enough. These forecasts, through complex or simple means, extend past revenue patterns into the future. They offer no cause-effect relationship between some economic or other force and the revenue being forecast. This presents a problem for most tax forecasters: they want to understand causal influences in the revenue system, and so do their legislative and executive agency bosses. The need to understand causes is particularly great when the forecaster must explain a revenue shortfall. Nevertheless, these projections can sometimes be the best choice for the forecaster.[12]

Simple and complex univariate methods share a common feature. Only past revenue data are used to forecast future revenue data (e.g., sales tax collection data for the last fifteen years are used to forecast sales tax collections for the budget year and the out-years). No other economic, demographic, social, or cultural variables are involved.

One method is a simple time-series extrapolation or regression against time. These extrapolations may be by (1) constant increments (collections increased by $5,000 in each of the last five years, so they are estimated to increase by $5,000 this year); (2) constant percentage changes (collections increased by 5 percent in each of the last five years, so they are estimated to increase by 5 percent this year); (3) simple growth models using the average annual compounding formula developed in Chapter 3; or (4) linear or nonlinear time trends in which revenue for the budget year is estimated as an arithmetic function of time ($R = a + bt$) or as a logarithmic function of time ($\ln R = a + bt$), where R equals collections from the revenue source and t equals a time index, choosing between the trends according to which is judged most likely to produce a reasonable estimate. Many local governments use these approaches because they lack the data on the local economy—both historical for identifying the relationships and forecasted for creating the revenue baseline from the relationships—requisite for developing cause-and-effect models. States often use the approach for minor revenue sources when improved estimates have no consequential impact on the overall fiscal pattern. Everybody uses them when there is insufficient data or insufficient time for other methods or when the revenue item is too small to merit much attention.

---

[12]You will recall from an earlier chapter that lots of expenditure proposals in the budget request will be constructed with simple projections of workloads, prices, and so on.

Another simple univariate short-term forecasting approach that can be usable in periods of general stability is the moving average technique. A moving average forecast operates with the following procedure:

$$R_t = (R_{t-2} + R_{t-3} + \ldots + R_{t-N})/N$$

where

R_t = revenue for the forecast period,

R_{t-2} to R_{t-N} = actual revenue for previous periods included in the average (data for year $t - 1$ seldom is complete when the forecast is prepared, so data from $t - 2$ will be the most recent year included in the forecast), and

N = the number to periods use in calculating the average.

For instance, a forecast of motor vehicle license revenues in 2017 might be prepared during 2016 as the average of actual revenues in 2015 (the most recent year for which actual data are available), 2014, and 2013. The forecaster selects the number of periods according to an expectation about how many will keep the forecast error to a minimum—in general, fewer periods when there have been recent significant fluctuations and more periods when there has been general stability.

Other univariate approaches work with autoregression techniques, more complex moving average approaches (the Box-Jenkins autoregressive integrated moving average model being one example), and various smoothing techniques (spreadsheet programs usually offer several alternatives). The applicability of the more sophisticated techniques is limited by the need for lengthy data series; revenue forecasting seldom has data series that extend for long periods without considerable shocks from change in the fundamental structure of the tax. Again, revenue forecasters do use these techniques for causal variables (such as personal income, population, inflation rates, etc.) entering their models.[13]

DETERMINISTIC MODELING

Deterministic models use a pre-established formula (or "rule of thumb") that "ought" to forecast revenue. In other words, there should be a link between gross domestic product (GDP), personal income, or some other broad economic aggregate and tax revenue; the forecast results from multiplying that aggregate by the formula coefficient for that particular source. For instance, data from several countries show the value-added tax (VAT) to yield, on average, 0.37 percent of

---

[13]It is wrong to reject these simple models out of hand because they can be remarkably successful in forecasting. For instance, Faust and Wright find that a simple univariate autoregressive forecast of GDP growth is as accurate as substantially more complicated models. Jon Faust and Jonathan Wright, "Comparing Greenbook and Reduced Form Forecasts Using a Large Realtime Dataset," National Bureau of Economic Research Working Paper 13397, Cambridge, Mass., September 2007. In other words, an accurate forecast of GDP growth would result by regressing GDP growth rates against four lagged periods of past GDP growth rates.

GDP for each percentage point of tax rate.[14] The forecaster could use that ratio to develop a rough forecast of VAT yield from a forecast of GDP—possibly developed itself by application of a simple guess about annual growth rates. Or there might be an expected elasticity relationship between growth in revenue from a tax and growth in some aggregate measure of economic activity. The forecaster might believe that every 1 percentage point increase in personal income will generate a 1.2 percentage point increase in the income tax, and from that the revenue forecast emerges. Forecasters working in data-scarce environments regularly use such approaches in developing budget numbers. Such conditions may occur, for example, when the revenue source is relatively new and there are insufficient data for meaningful statistical modeling (fitting equations makes little sense when there are only two or three data points), when the national economic environment is too unstable for the results of statistical modeling to be usable with confidence, or when data are of insufficient reliability to make statistical modeling meaningful. For instance, in countries undergoing transition from components of the Soviet Union to independent nations in the early 1990s, there was great economic instability, there were few data points (the nations were formed in 1991), and all the tax sources were new. There was little reason to use sophisticated causal models in that environment.

Another application of such rule-of-thumb forecasting is when one is attempting to provide a perspective on fiscal conditions. For instance, here is a statement by some macroeconomists about state and local fiscal frameworks:

The "Golden Rule of Thumb" for short-run forecasting:

- Expect each 1 percent rise in the state unemployment rate to cut over 5 percent from trend state revenue growth.
- This 5:1 multiplier is the average impact. Governments with a greater reliance on sales and excise taxes or business profits taxes are more vulnerable, and their golden rules would have notably higher multipliers. California, for example, has a multiplier of eight.[15]

A government budget would not ordinarily be built around such a rule-of-thumb forecast, but it could be important in constructing a longer-term fiscal framework for a government. Many longer-term forecasts use such approaches, not because of a shortage of historical data, but because secular change is likely to alter any relationship that formed a model based on those data. It is fantasy to use complex methods for long-term projections and expect to have anything other than an early-warning device about conditions that should be prevented.

---

[14]Vito Tanzi and Parthasarathi Shome, "A Primer on Tax Evasion," *IMF Staff Papers* 40 (December 1993): 823. This is sometimes called "Cnossen's Rule." Some people thinking about a U.S. federal value-added tax use a more optimistic standard: each 1 percent of rate would yield half a percentage point of GDP in revenue. It is not clear why they do not use the internationally accepted Cnossen standard.

[15]Roger E. Brinner, Joyce Brinner, Matt Eckhouse, and Megan Leahey, "Fiscal Realities for State and Local Governments," *Business Economics* 43 (April 2008): 62. The authors are not actual revenue forecasters.

MULTIPLE REGRESSION

The multiple regression model, the most widely encountered forecasting device, forecasts revenue as a function of one or more independent variables determined outside the revenue model. Each equation used to estimate a revenue source is independent of the others. For instance, a state might forecast quarterly retail sales tax collections with an equation like the following one, which was estimated from an ordinary least squares regression program:

$$ST = 5.523 + 0.926PI + 0.034P - 0.773R + 0.022Q_1 + 0.011Q_2 + 0.032Q_3$$

where

$$ST = \text{retail sales tax collections for the quarter in logarithmic form,}$$
$$PI = \text{state personal income in logarithmic form, lagged one quarter,}$$
$$P = \text{the inflation rate measured as a percentage change in the}$$
$$\text{GDP deflator in logarithmic form, lagged one quarter,}$$
$$R = \text{the statutory sales tax rate applicable in the state, and}$$
$$Q_1, Q_2, \text{ and } Q_3 = \text{categorical dummies to indicate the quarter of the year (sales tax}$$
$$\text{revenues being subject to seasonal variation through the year).}[16]$$

The economic data are lagged because allocation processes are such that economic activity in one period generates tax revenue that is received by the government in the next period. In other words, there is a mismatch between when the taxable activity occurs and when the collections from that activity show up in the state treasury. The lagged economic data in the forecasting equation account for that mismatch. Of course, there are several different ways to measure the economic activity that is producing the sales tax revenue, including state or national GDP or state or national personal income. Each of these measures has some logical attractiveness as a drive force for forecasting state sales tax revenue. The forecaster will almost certainly experiment with each of these possible measures until he settles on the one that seems most likely to reliably track the actual path of tax revenue. The forecaster also will experiment with lags of different lengths and with other formats for the relationship.

Forecasts for the independent or causal variables (personal income and the inflation rate in this example) come from analytic and forecasting work outside the tax equations. To use this approach, estimates of the independent variable must be available for the forecast period: an estimating equation for sales tax collections that uses a stock market index, for instance, will not be usable if the necessary index is not available until three-quarters of the way through the budget year because, for

---

[16]Because tax collections, personal income, and tax rate are in logarithmic transformation, the coefficients in the equation are interpreted as elasticities. That is, the estimating equation shows that a 10 percent increase in personal income produces a 9.3 percent increase in tax collections and that a 10 percent increase in the statutory tax rate produces only a 7.7 percent increase in tax collections. This evidence is consistent with the idea that the retail sales tax grows more slowly than the economy and that rate increases do have a negative impact on the tax base—but that this tax is not on the downward sloping side of the rate–revenue curve. The forecasting equation is for Indiana with data from third quarter 1977 through first quarter 2005. It is for illustration only and is not the model actually used by the state.

budget preparation, the revenue forecast has to be presented well before the start of the budget year. Dummy variables offer an approach to allowing for the influence of unusual qualitative experiences in the past. For instance, a dummy may identify two years in which budget constraints prohibited any out-of-state audits, a tax amnesty, or a period in which the regulations for certain sales tax exemptions differed from those currently in effect.

The equation estimated by multiple regression ordinarily is selected based on the extent to which estimates from the equation coincide with actual revenue collections in prior years. Because many alternative specifications yield similar fit to historical data (several specifications will be almost indistinguishable in terms of normal tests of goodness of fit and forecast error), trial predictions (simulations or "out of sample forecasts") for earlier years are also prepared: Suppose data are available for 1960–2017 and a forecast is being prepared for the 2019 budget year (the estimate is being prepared during 2018). Possible equations can be developed from 1960 to 2016 and test "predictions" made for 2017. The equation coming closest to the known 2017 result is selected.

Ordinarily, separate equations are prepared for each major revenue category to allow for different responses to changes in independent variables. That is, equations are developed for individual income tax, corporate income tax, retail sales tax, and so on rather than simply for all tax revenue. Careful application of multiple regression models should produce overall predictions within 1 to 3 percent of actual collections, although forecasting success falls off dramatically when the economy turns from expansion to recession or when the economy is in severe recession.[17] During the Great Recession, state revenue forecasters struggled to adjust their forecasts downward to keep up with disappointing revenue results each month.

ECONOMETRIC MODELS

Econometric models estimate revenue within a simultaneous system of interdependent equations that express theoretical and empirical relationships between economic and fiscal variables.[18] These models are particularly important when revenue sources are not truly independent (as when the state personal income tax allows a deduction for the state sales tax) and may provide useful insights into the way state economies operate and the way in which they respond to external shocks. Economists generate forecasts from the system of equations by putting current values of

---

[17]Accuracy matters much more for governments facing a severe need for low deficits in the executed budget, such as states and localities. The federal government, with its deficit-running capacity, is less constrained. The CBO reports that its mean absolute error (the average of errors without regard to whether they are positive or negative) for the year after it is published was 5.2 percent over the 1982–2014 period (Congressional Budget Office, *CBO's Revenue Forecasting Record*, November 2015). Errors are greater for forecasts further into the future.

[18]The independent variables used in the multiple regression approach (possibly state personal income or U.S. GDP) often are the product of larger econometric models of the region of the nation. State and local governments obtain these estimates from numerous sources, including proprietary economic forecasting companies, universities, committees of technical advisors, and government economists.

key variables into the models and working them through the estimating equations. As a practical matter, however, states have generally found that the revenue predictions from econometric models are seldom more accurate than the forecasts that multiple regression models produce, and the regression models are less expensive and have smaller data requirements.[19] The interrelationships that are inherent in these systems also have the impact of causing escalating errors, in that an error in one variable creates errors in others.

MICRODATA MODELS

The Office of Tax Analysis of the U.S. Treasury, the CBO, and some states use microsimulation from sample data files for tax forecasting (and for estimating the effect of tax changes as well).[20] Sidebar 13–1 describes the steps in the CBO's forecasting method for its ten-year baseline projection of the federal individual income tax. In general, microdata approaches start with a computer file of tax-return data from a sample of taxpayers (information technology now allows use of extremely large samples). Tax calculator models use this file to forecast how economic activity expected in the budget year tracks into its impact on the taxpayers in the sample. A program figures the tax liability for each taxpayer in the sample, the effect within the sample is expanded to the entire population it represents, and the result is the forecast of tax revenue for the new budget year. Full microsimulation models use the same files as the simpler tax calculator models, but they allow the underlying tax return to vary as taxpayers react to changes in tax policy.[21] Much effort is involved in selecting and preparing the microfile, so uses beyond the forecast improve the economic viability of such an effort. As is discussed later, the microfile is extremely helpful in fiscal note preparation, that is, in estimating the revenue consequences of legal changes in the tax structure. However, data in the microfile need to be refreshed as return years go by and modified when new tax provisions are enacted; the sampling must be a continuing process.

---

[19]C. Kurt Zorn, "Issues and Problems in Econometric Forecasting: Guidance for Local Revenue Forecasters," *Public Budgeting & Finance* 2 (Autumn 1982): 100–10.

[20]The approach employed by the U.S. Treasury is described in Howard Nester, "The Corporate Microdata File Employed by the Office of Tax Analysis," *Proceedings of the National Tax Association–Tax Institute of America* 70 (1977): 293–306; and James M. Cilke and Roy A. Wyscarver, "The Individual Income Tax Simulation Model," in U.S. Department of Treasury, Office of Tax Analysis, *Compendium of Tax Research 1987* (Washington, D.C.: U.S. Government Printing Office, 1987). Forecasting by the Congressional Budget Office is described in CBO, Description of CBO's Models and Methods for Projecting Federal Revenues (Washington, D.C.: CBO, 2001) and Congressional Budget Office, *Improving CBO's Methodology for Projecting Individual Income Tax Revenues, Background Paper* (Washington, D.C.: CBO, 2011). The microsimulation model developed for New York State is described in T. N. McCarty and T. H. Marks, "The Use of Microsimulation Models for Policy Analysis: The New York State Personal Income Tax," *Proceedings of the Eighty-Sixth Annual Conference on Taxation of the National Tax Association* (1994): 179–85. The Oregon Legislative Revenue Office uses a microsimulation model called the Oregon Tax Incidence Model (OTIM) for much of its analysis.

[21]For revenue forecasting, tax calculator and full microsimulation models are not distinguishable in operation because there are no policy changes in the baseline revenue forecast. The approach is particularly valuable in the analysis of policy changes, but it can also be employed in regular forecasting.

Sidebar 13–1
The Congressional Budget Office Approach to Individual Income Tax Forecasting, Fiscal 2001–2011

Note: The CBO prepares forecasts for the fiscal year under way when the forecast is prepared, the budget year, and nine out-years.

Step 1. Begin with a sample of 1998 tax returns. "Age" the sample to match

- Projected demographic changes (such as in population and employment).
- Projected incomes based on the CBO's macroeconomic projections (such as for wages, interest, and dividends), outlay projections (for program benefits), and other projections (such as for capital gains and retirement income).

Result: the projected tax base for 1999 through 2011.

Step 2. Apply the tax calculator (a mathematical formula that represents the calculations required by the tax structure), incorporating

- Tax law parameters.
- CBO's macroeconomic projection of the consumer price index.

Result: projected tax liabilities on individual income tax returns for 1999 through 2011.

Step 3. Adjust projected tax liabilities for consistency with actual collections of owed taxes in 1998 through 2000.

Result: projected collections liabilities for 2001 through 2011.

Step 4. Convert projected liabilities into fiscal year payments by

- Breaking down liabilities by type of payment.
- Applying recent experience in the timing of payments.
- Adjusting for recent legislation not incorporated in step 2.
- Adding fiduciary taxes and back taxes.

Result: projected tax payments for fiscal years 2001 through 2011.

SOURCE: Congressional Budget Office, *Description of CEO's Models and Methods for Projecting Federal Revenues* (Washington, D.C.: Congressional Budget Office, 2001), 8.

Choosing the Method for the Budget Forecast

Revenue forecasts need methods that predict well enough to satisfy the requirements of those developing, adopting, and executing budgets and that can be explained to the satisfaction of executive and legislative tax and budget policymakers. They almost always use a combination of the several forecast approaches to predict the revenue baseline for the executive or legislative budget. In revenue forecasting, the ultimate choice would be whichever produces estimates closest to final yield, but that is something the forecaster finds out after the year is over, too late to be a guide. Among the factors that may enter into the choice of method are the following:

1. **The resources that are available.** The tools of cause-and-effect estimation—computers, software, and data analysts—have come within easy reach of every government with a reliable electricity supply. The resources that may not be available are sufficient time to perform the tasks necessary to prepare and test more complex estimating formats and the data necessary to employ some approaches. For example, microsimulation approaches require complex data files on a sample of taxpaying entities; the approach cannot be contemplated unless the government has devoted the time and money to develop the files. Some governments simply choose to do forecasting on the cheap and do pretty well most of the time. No matter how much money is spent, nobody forecasts downturns very well, and the Great Recession humbled even the best state revenue forecasters.

2. **The materiality of the forecast.** How critical is an error in the forecast being made? If the revenue source constitutes but a small amount of the total, it is a poor use of analytic resources to devote much effort to forecasting it. Forecasting retail sales tax revenue is more important than forecasting the dog tax, so much more attention will be given to forecasting the former than the latter.

3. **The availability of historical revenue data.** Unless a long data series is available to test relationships under a considerable variety of economic and other environments, trying to create a reliable causal model is not likely to be productive. Indeed, an inadequately clean historical series can be a problem for more complex projection models themselves.

4. **The availability and quality of causal data.** A forecasting model with excellent statistical properties does not provide usable forecasts if causal data (the "drivers") needed for the forecast period are not available or if the available forecasts of them are unreliable. For instance, a regression equation may show a strong and reliable relationship between corporate profits and state corporate profits tax collections. Unless there is a good forecast of corporate profits, this equation is useless for the revenue forecast.

5. **The time period of the forecast.** Long-term forecasts—the years beyond the out-years—will be done with cruder approaches than will budget-year forecasts. Technological, political, and economic forecasts are not terribly reliable in the longer term, and a revenue forecast based on "cause-and-effect" models cannot rise above problems in forecasts of the causes.

6. **The "explainability" of the forecast.** A forecast number is not enough. There must be a story that goes with it for the budget director, the legislative fiscal committees, and the media. "Black boxes" have difficulty surviving the first shaky episode.

These forecasts establish the amount of current revenue that will be available to budget for spending during the fiscal year. For many governments, their presentation is an event of considerable importance because it sets the tone for the deliberations—executive and legislative—that produce appropriations to operating agencies. It does not, however, matter much for the federal government; the forecast is in the budgets but the attention is primarily directed to expenditures. Although there is no standard template for such presentations, they frequently are organized according to the following format:

1. **A Look Back:** a review of the forecast for the last budget year and why it was wrong;
2. **The Future Environment:** a prognosis of economic conditions for the next year for the nation and, for subnational government forecasts, for the state or local economy that will drive the revenue being forecast;
3. **The Approach:** an explanation of the general approach being used for the forecast; and
4. **The Forecast:** the forecast itself, divided among the major revenue sources.

You should not discuss all the approaches you tested before you picked the technique you ultimately used or why you picked the one that you did. It goes without saying that you used every approach available to you and you picked the one that you thought would yield the forecast closest to the actual. Your boss automatically assumes all that, and, if those assumptions aren't accurate, then you aren't long for the job. The presentation normally has charts and tables as appendixes accompanying the actual forecast document.

Forecasts for the Long Term

Governments develop longer-term, multiyear revenue (and expenditure) outlooks that extend beyond the annual budget horizon. These prediction tasks vary widely in their sophistication, depending on the term for which they are prepared and on their intended use. They may be prepared, for instance, (a) to guide a city as it prepares an infrastructure development program that fits within likely revenue resources, (b) to show a credit-rating agency what revenue flows might be during the term of a loan to a state or local government, (c) to let planners know the probable financial implications from some major development (a theme park or a truck assembly plant, for instance) in the community, (d) to inform the public or oversight boards what the prospects are when a local government is on the brink of a severe financial emergency, (e) to inform the legislature and the executive what the longer-term implications are of the financial program that the government has in place or might be considering, or (f) as an element in a medium-term economic framework for the development of government policies within available revenues. Indeed, the Governmental Accounting Standards Board has considered requiring that state and local governments report five-year projections of cash inflows, outflows, and financial obligations as supplemental information in their financial statements. (The proposal is called "Economic Condition Reporting: Financial Projections.")

Revenue predictions for the out-years—the ten-year budget horizon for federal budget controls—have been particularly important for federal budget resolutions, especially when deficits turned to surpluses and lawmakers began discussion about new spending and tax reduction programs to get rid of the projected surpluses at the end of the twentieth century (which they decisively did). Longer-term outlooks also can be used to trace the likely impacts of demographic developments on finances.[22] These outlooks are vital for the development of Social Security and Medicare programs, in which present revenues are expected to finance benefits paid many years in the future.

The longer the outlook is, the less sophisticated the method should be because of the great imprecision associated with economic, political, demographic, and technological factors that shape underlying forecasts. Available methods are generally the same as those used for budget-year revenue forecasts, although more attention has to be given to estimating the longer-term economic, demographic, and structural trends that themselves will drive the revenue flows, and huge uncertainties cloud the process. Medium-term forecasts—three, five, or even ten budget out-years—done by the CBO and similar bodies to identify the impact of policy changes, demographic drift, macroeconomic conditions, and so on are done with considerable care to understand links and to identify policy options and are of considerable quality and value. The distant out-year forecasts are important primarily as political drama and advance warning to inform about actions that need to be taken to avoid the forecasted consequences.

Longer forecasts are usually not tested against actuals in the way that budget-year estimates are, and they are replaced by shorter-term forecasts when budget-year choices are being deliberated. Indeed, they often cannot be so tested because they have served their purpose as warning devices and the dangerous practices have been corrected. It must be emphasized that, by their nature, such reports should not be viewed as budget forecasts. The five-year forecast for 2011 for Clearwater, Florida, identifies the role of such analysis: "A financial plan is not a forecast of what is certain to happen, but rather a device to highlight significant issues or problems that must be addressed if goals are to be achieved."[23] Seldom should the predictions be expected to provide great precision; they can, however, assemble information to help with difficult choices and to cause policy changes that keep the projected result from occurring.

The multiyear forecast ordinarily will be prepared with fairly simple, univariate extrapolation methods because forecasts of underlying economic forces in that more distant time horizon are particularly unreliable, because structural relationships between economic factors and the revenue system are not stable for long periods, and because it is quite likely that there will be substantial changes in revenue or expenditure programs over the longer horizon that make forecasts using the baseline conditions wrong. The extrapolations may be adjusted for "known" future events—if the city is going to host a world's fair in the forecast horizon, for instance—but

---

[22]An excellent example of such an outlook study: Congressional Budget Office, *The 2015 Long-Term Budget Outlook* (Washington, D.C.: U.S. Government Printing Office, 2015). Pages 18 to 21 outline the CBO approach to making the long-term projections.
[23]City of Clearwater General Fund Five-Year Forecast, October 2011. [http://ebookbrowse.com/a-five-year-financial-forecast-pdf-d295192606

usually future uncertainty is sufficient that adjustments to the simple projection are not supportable.[24] Multiyear forecasts are not tested according to how close they come to actual outcomes because their purpose is often to warn against outcomes and elicit policy changes that will cause the forecast not to materialize. They are projections of a possible fiscal state based on certain specified assumptions. They cannot have the accuracy expected of financial statements, and accuracy isn't even an appropriate test for them. Longer-term predictions may provide a range of forecast values because of the considerable uncertainty involved; however, forecasts for preparation of the annual budget need to be single numbers.

Monitoring and Evaluating

Revenues need to be monitored carefully and on a regular schedule against the forecast. A single month's variation, although potentially troublesome, can disappear later in the fiscal year, and comparisons between year-to-date actual cumulative and estimated cumulative revenues are more helpful than the comparison for a single month.[25] However, the record needs to be continuously evaluated to maintain control of overall government finances. That performance becomes important information for the development of future revenue forecasts.[26]

If you plot the revenue series on a monthly or quarterly basis for the past several years, the seasonal pattern will almost certainly become apparent. You can use that pattern as your guide to how your forecast is doing against actual collections throughout the year, and you can use that pattern to help develop a cash budget for the year (i.e., to see if there are likely to be points during the year when the government may not have enough cash on hand to cover its payments). Monitoring throughout the year usually involves comparisons of revenue collected in months or quarters against shares of annual totals collected in comparable periods in previous years. If the recent historical record shows that 45 percent of total annual retail sales tax revenue has typically been collected by the end of June and this year only 41 percent of the forecasted total has been collected, then the budget agency might want to constrain the pace of spending because the adopted budget may not be able to be executed without unplanned borrowing or reduction of government reserves.

Figure 13–1 presents a monitoring report from Indiana. The report gives performance information for each major tax for the first five months of the fiscal year.

---

[24]Beware that boosters of big events (expos, big-time sporting events, etc.) notoriously inflate the economic impact that their event will have on the local event.

[25]In other words, rather than comparing April actual with April forecast, a better comparison would be the actual for all the fiscal year through April against the forecast for all the fiscal year through April. That gives a better understanding of whether the fiscal year forecast is likely to be on target than looking at a single month.

[26]Useful standards for revenue estimation are presented in National Association of State Budget Officers/ Federation of Tax Administrators, *Good Practices in Revenue Estimating* (Washington, D.C.: National Association of State Budget Officers, 1989).

Figure 13–1
Monthly Revenue Forecast Status Report

Indiana State Budget Agency
FY 2016 Report of Monthly General Fund Revenue Collections
For the month ending
November 30, 2015

All amounts in millions of dollars
Estimates per April 16, 2015 State Revenue Forecast*

	General Fund Actual Revenue Y-T-D	Comparison to Monthly Estimates			Comparison to Prior Year-to-Date		
		Estimated Revenue Y-T-D	Difference Amount	Difference Percent	Actual Revenue Prior Y-T-D	Change Amount	Change Percent
Major Taxes							
Sales & Use	$3,017.6	$3,120.0	-$102.5	-3.3%	$3,031.1	-$13.5	-0.4%
Individual AGI	$2,038.7	$1,935.5	$103.2	5.3%	$1,973.7	$65.1	3.3%
Corporate—AGI, URT, USUT, FIT	$213.9	$263.4	-$49.5	-18.8%	$261.9	-$48.0	-18.3%
Riverboat Wagering	$75.3	$74.6	$0.7	1.0%	$76.4	-$1.1	-1.4%
Racino Wagering	$40.5	$39.3	$1.2	3.0%	$38.4	$2.1	5.4%
Subtotal Major Taxes	**$5,386.0**	**$5,432.9**	**-$46.9**	**-0.9%**	**$5,381.4**	**$4.5**	**0.1%**
Other Revenue							
Cigarette	$110.1	$107.8	$2.3	2.1%	$106.9	$3.2	3.0%
Insurance	$58.2	$60.9	-$2.7	-4.4%	$58.0	$0.2	0.3%
Inheritance	$0.3	$0.0	$0.3	N/A	$3.1	-$2.7	-89.3%
Alcoholic Beverages	$7.7	$7.8	-$0.1	-1.4%	$7.5	$0.3	3.6%
Riverboat Admissions	$5.7	$5.8	-$0.1	-2.3%	$5.9	-$0.2	-4.2%
Interest	$9.1	$7.8	$1.2	15.7%	$7.9	$1.2	15.2%
Motor Vehicle and Commercial Vehicle Excise	$0.0	$0.0	$0.0	N/A	$0.0	$0.0	N/A
Miscellaneous Revenue	$47.9	$42.0	$5.9	14.1%	$36.5	$11.4	31.2%
Subtotal Other Revenue	**$239.1**	**$232.2**	**$6.9**	**3.0%**	**$225.7**	**$13.3**	**5.9%**
Total General Fund	**$5,625.0**	**$5,665.1**	**-$40.1**	**-0.7%**	**$5,607.2**	**$17.9**	**0.3%**

*The totals, changes, and percent changes in this report are based on unrounded amounts.

It shows how much was collected to date (actual), how much revenue would have been expected to be collected in that period according to the annual forecast (estimated), provides the difference between actual collections and expected collections, and provides a comparison against the five month collections from the prior fiscal year. For example, examination of several prior years showed that 41.58 percent of total sales and use tax revenue for the year would have been collected in those first five months. Multiplying that percentage by the total forecast for the year gave the estimated total for the period ($3,120.0 million). That total compares with actual collections of $3,017.6 million, meaning that sales and use tax collections fall 3.3 percent behind the forecast. If that shortfall carried throughout the forecast, then the governor would likely need to consider restraining previously approved state spending. However, some other taxes are above forecast, leaving the total forecast for the period off by only 0.7 percent, not enough of an error to require immediate action.

At the close of the fiscal year, the success of the forecast needs to be evaluated to permit improvements in future outcomes. This is the forecaster equivalent of an autopsy, trying to figure out what went wrong and to use that information to make improvements for the future. Where "cause-and-effect" models are used, variances from the actual need to be divided into (a) the part caused by errors in forecasting the cause(s), (b) the part due to errors in the model, and (c) the part attributed to legislative changes that make the tax for which the forecast was prepared different from the one that produced the revenue.[27]

Wrong Forecasts

There is one sad fact about your baseline forecast: you will be wrong. Expect it and get used to it. You will be wrong when you do your first, and you will be wrong when you have years of experience. The result is that you will seek to constrain your error so that you produce a trusted and reliable baseline. Billy Hamilton, a long-time revenue forecaster for the state of Texas, sums up the situation:

> After you have prepared your forecast, you report the results, and then put the results into some sort of tracking system and wait for collections to prove you wrong—because inevitably you will be. The only thing in question is how far off you are, and that makes a great deal of difference. It's like hitting in baseball. One-in-three hits over a career is a ticket to the Hall of Fame. One-in-five equals a short career and a somewhat less iconic future as an insurance salesperson. My boss demanded accuracy within 2 percent—and 2 percent lower than actual, not higher. Higher is a problem.[28]

---

[27]In other words, suppose the retail sales tax (S) was forecast as a function of personal income (I):

$$S = 389.7 + 0.782I$$

Actual collections could differ from forecast collections because (1) an error was made in the personal income forecast (I) or (2) the forecast relationship between personal income and retail sales did not hold. Legislative changes are a shock from outside the model.

[28]Billy Hamilton, "Sympathy for the Bedeviled Revenue Estimators," *State Tax Notes* 51 (February 2, 2009): 350.

In case you haven't gotten the message already: your forecast will be wrong. To test how bad your error is for a state revenue forecast, check the leading newspaper in the capital city when the revenue results for a period (month, quarter, or year) are in. If the forecast results appear on the front page, your error is too big.[29]

Economic forecasts tend to be less accurate when the economy is in recession (the errors during the recession that began in December 2007 were huge in most states), but errors occur in happier times as well.[30] Perfection is not the standard against which any revenue forecasting method should be tested. The appropriate test is the accuracy of other feasible forecasting approaches, and there is evidence that formal forecasting methods are better than simple rules of thumb or pronouncements of politicians.[31] If another forecasting method that can be adopted within available resources can produce more accurate results for the budget, then it should be used. However, it, too, will be wrong eventually. The test can never be perfection, just better than feasible alternatives, not subject to political bias, and accepted as binding by lawmakers when the budget is being adopted. When revenue forecasters look at their performance over time, they do not check the simple average percentage error because that would cause large over-forecasts to be canceled out by large under-forecasts and that would defeat the examination of accuracy. (Errors of −10 percent and +10 percent would cancel out, giving an average of 0 percent, which doesn't tell the true story.) They look at average *absolute* errors, so that positive and negative errors will not cancel. (An average of absolute errors of −10 percent and +10 percent would equal 10 percent, a better gauge of typical error.)

Should the forecast be deliberately pessimistic? That is an open question even among government revenue forecasters.[32] However, deliberately optimistic forecasts can be rejected as a violation of the fiscal sustainability principle because they do not provide a reasonable baseline for spending that can occur without producing a deficit.

---

[29]It could be worse. Shortly after levying a tax on witches and fortune-tellers, the Romanian parliament began consideration of a law that would fine or imprison them if their predictions did not come true. One witch complained that the action should be taken against the cards they use in their procedures, not against the witches themselves. So maybe revenue forecasters could blame their evil computers? "Romania: False-Prophecy Penalty," *New York Times*, February 8, 2011.

[30]Michael W. McCracken, "How Accurate Are Forecasts in a Recession?" *National Economic Trends* (Federal Reserve Bank of St. Louis, February 2009): Inability to detect turning points and a bias toward optimism are the major problems. Did you realize that economists, practitioners of the "dismal science," are actually optimists?

[31]Stephen K. McNees, "An Assessment of 'Official' Economic Forecasts," *New England Economic Review* (July/August 1995): 13–23.

[32]It is an open question in international discussions as well. See Ian Lienert, "Should Budgetary Revenue Projections Be Deliberately Pessimistic?" Public Financial Management Blog (International Monetary Fund), January 14, 2009, http://blog-pfm.imf.org/pfmblog/2009/01/should-budgetary-revenue-projections-bedeliberately-pessimistic-.html. One study of thirty-three countries found that forecasts had an overall positive bias (too much money), greater bias in booms, and more bias in the three-year horizon than in shorter horizons. Jeffrey A. Frankel, "Over-Optimism in Forecasts by Official Budget Agencies and Its Implications," National Bureau of Economic Research Working Paper 17239, Cambridge, Mass., July 2011. Both the CBO and the administration tend to over-forecast federal revenue.

Revenue Estimating (or Scoring)

Revenue estimating (called scoring in the federal system, tax costing in the United Kingdom, and preparation of fiscal notes in many states) gives the government a prediction of how revenue will change from the baseline if a new law is passed or administrative processes change. The revenue estimate is the difference between receipts under the current law and receipts under the proposed new law.[33] To keep operations on a fiscally sustainable basis, governments need to know what the fiscal impact will be of legislation that is being deliberated. The question for scoring is of this variety: by how much would revenue increase if the personal exemption in the income tax were reduced by $500, or by how much would revenue fall if the capital gains tax rate were reduced by another 10 percentage points?

The pay-as-you-go (PAYGO) requirement in the federal budget system demands these scores or estimates, most states have prepared such fiscal impact notes for many years, and reports from the Senate Finance and House Ways and Means Committees have carried these estimates since the 1974 Congressional Budget and Impoundment Control Act.[34] The Office of Tax Analysis of the Department of Treasury prepares the executive branch revenue estimates.[35] From the legislative side, the Joint Committee on Taxation scores all tax legislation, and the CBO scores tariffs and user charges (along with spending proposals). The CBO incorporates these estimates from any legislation that passes into its ten-year baseline forecast. For states, fiscal notes attached to revenue proposals often come from the legislative fiscal office, although they may also come from a legislative tax committee, the state budget agency, or the state tax department.[36] Because legislative fiscal offices are usually nonpartisan, estimates produced there are likely unbiased by political agendas.

Revenue estimates often must be rough because existing data sets do not categorize information in the same way that the proposed legislation does. For instance, the revenue loss from a sales tax exemption for grass seed purchases by homeowners in blighted urban areas would be a difficult estimate because neither sales tax collection nor household spending data are tracked to that detail in total, let alone by geographic

---

[33]It should be clear that nothing is simple in federal government, including determining what is the baseline. The baseline could be current law, including the impact of provisions that will be expiring within the forecast/estimate horizon as part of the baseline, or current policy, excluding the impact of those legal provisions because it is expected that the law will be changed to continue those provisions expiring within the forecast/estimate horizon as part of the baseline. The Office of Tax Analysis uses current policy, and the Joint Committee on Taxation uses current law. Thus, tax cuts that are within the horizon will affect the baseline, causing some proposed laws to have scores with different impact signs coming from the two estimating groups.

[34]The revenue-impact estimating method used by Congress is described in Joint Committee on Taxation, "Overview of Revenue Estimating Procedures and Methodologies Used by the Staff of the Joint Committee on Taxation," JCX-1-05, Washington, D.C., February 2, 2005.

[35]Emil M. Sunley and Randall D. Weiss, "The Revenue Estimating Process," *Tax Notes* 51 (June 10, 1991): 1299–1314.

[36]State scoring practices are described and analyzed in John L. Mikesell, "Revenue Estimation/Scoring by States: An Overview of Experience and Current Practices with Particular Attention to the Role of Dynamic Methods," *Public Budgeting & Finance* 32 (Summer 2012): 1–24.

areas. However, even when developed only as rough approximations, the estimates provide an important discipline for the budget process. They estimate the change in the baseline. Federal estimates normally are for the ten-year budget horizon; state estimates may be much shorter. Lawmakers, the media, and the public tend to regard these estimates as far more accurate than do those who actually have prepared them.

These estimates usually are prepared from a sample of existing returns, supplemented with additional data sources because categories of information on those returns seldom match what the new law has in mind. In effect, they represent microsimulations, although at widely varying degrees of sophistication. The Office of Tax Analysis uses an extremely complex model created from a large sample of individual tax returns, whereas a state legislative fiscal office may use an extremely informal estimating process. The tax returns give information about transactions currently reported in the tax system and, to the extent the new provision changes those reported lines, can provide a basis for the estimate. However, not all proposed changes will be to transactions reported on those returns. Therefore, information usually needs to be taken from outside the tax system.

Three distinct protocols may be used in preparation of revenue estimates.

1. **Completely static estimation/scoring.** This approach assumes that the change in the tax law will have no impact on taxpayer behavior or on the level of economic activity. The estimate is based on tax return data, plus supplemental data about taxpayers that may be necessary to estimate the new tax base for each return, and a tax calculator that computes the tax paid on each return under both the baseline law and the proposed changed law. For example, a static estimate of changing the capital gains tax rate would use capital gains reported on each tax return and recalculate the tax at the new rate instead of at the rate under existing law. Adding all returns gives the impact estimate. Revenue estimators usually use this approach only when they have no basis at all for estimating the degree of taxpayer response to a change in the tax law. In the absence of trustworthy data, tax professionals prefer the fiscally conservative approach to their estimates. Neither the Joint Committee on Taxation, the Congressional Budget Office, nor the Office of Tax Analysis regularly uses a static approach, and neither do most state entities charged with preparing estimates.

2. **Microdynamic estimation/scoring.** The approach recognizes that taxpayer behavior will shift in response to the incentives added or subtracted by the tax law and, as a result, the tax base with the new law will differ from what it would have been under the old law. The microeconomic behavioral effects may include shifts in the timing of transactions, changes in portfolio holdings, shifts in consumption, use of tax planning and avoidance strategies to reduce liability, changes in work effort, and so on—all impacts that would involve microeconomic behavior. For instance, (a) a higher tax on cigarettes will cause fewer cigarettes to be sold, (b) a lower capital gains tax rate will induce businesses and individuals to realize capital gains that would otherwise have been deferred and to convert ordinary income to formats judged to be capital gains, and (c) a new tax credit for college tuition will induce more students to attend college. Static estimates of revenue from these tax

proposals would need to be adjusted for these effects.[37] In these instances, simple use of historical data on cigarette consumption, capital gains, and college tuition would not be sufficient to produce the estimate and would need to be adjusted for behavioral responses. The problem is that the effects are difficult to gauge because the data required may be unavailable and the size of taxpayers' response (the demand and supply elasticities) is unknown. Revenue estimates at the federal level and in most states do include these microeconomic impacts when estimating or scoring tax law changes when there is a basis for estimating them, and estimators do make "seat-of-the-pants" guesses if all else fails. There is no debate among professionals that such adjustments are appropriate. The greatest barrier is always the extent to which there is a firm basis for making the behavioral adjustments.

3. **Macrodynamic estimation/scoring.** Macroeconomic dynamic scoring adds the impact on revenue from changes in outputs, interest rates, or other macroeconomic elements to the impact from microdynamic scoring (the microdynamic score is the starting point for the analysis). The microeconomic dynamic estimates work under an assumption of fixed total economic activity (GDP or gross state product). Macroeconomic dynamic scoring seeks to add to the estimate the effect of any change in total economic activity on tax collections. In other words, a tax reduction may have an impact on aggregate economic activity, inflation, interest rates, and so on, and these effects will cause the tax bases to be somewhat greater than they were before the tax reduction (recall from an earlier chapter that the tax base itself is likely a function of the tax rate). Any resulting change in tax revenue should be included in the estimate. The static estimate and even the microdynamic estimate thus overstate the amount of the revenue cost from the tax reduction. For instance, the reduced capital gains tax rate may increase aggregate economic activity, and that will cause more tax to be collected from several federal taxes, all of which would be included as part of the estimated impact of the tax reduction. Federal estimates traditionally have not included a macroeconomic component, largely because of considerable uncertainty about size of effects and the great cost of systematically trying to find out what the effects are. Both the CBO and the Joint Committee on Taxation have developed some macrodynamic estimates in the past (they do not change the traditional microdynamic estimates by very much).[38] Starting in 2015 (through the 2016 Budget

---

[37]A CBO analysis of the impact of increasing the cigarette excise tax clearly shows the way in which microeconomic and behavioral responses are integrated into the CBO's work. Congressional Budget Office, *Raising the Excise Tax on Cigarettes: Effects on Health and the Federal Budget* (Washington, D.C.: Congressional Budget Office, 2102).
[38]Congressional Budget Office, *Analyzing the Economic and Budgetary Effects of a 10 Percent Cut in Income Tax Rates* (Washington, D.C.: Congressional Budget Office, 2005). Depending on assumptions, as much as one-third of the revenue lost from the reduction might be made up in a decade. The cut would not pay for itself. The Joint Committee on Taxation's experiments are described in "Testimony of the Staff of the Joint Committee on Taxation before the House Committee on Ways and Means Regarding Economic Modeling," JCX-48-11, Washington, D.C., September 21, 2011.

Resolution), both bodies are required to use dynamic scoring in preparing their impact estimates of any legislative changes that would have a gross budgetary effect of 0.25 percent of gross domestic product in any of the ten years after enactment (or when requested by a Budget Committee chair). Thus, they must estimate with all macroeconomic effects that would affect total output of the economy through capital and labor markets. The legislatures in a few states have required that estimates include macroeconomic effects in some instances as well.[39]

The Macrodynamic Argument

A revenue estimate should give lawmakers a reliable understanding of the fiscal cost of whatever statutory provision they are considering. With that in mind, why should there be any fuss about introduction of macrodynamic scoring? Including the full behavioral response to a change in tax law should be a reasonable change for anyone interested in government transparency and fiscal sustainability. More complete information should be all to the good.

The fact is that macrodynamic scoring has been a contentious issue at the federal level since the mid-1990s, particularly since lawmakers have become particularly fervent about cutting taxes while facing a variety of PAYGO requirements forcing tax reductions to be deficit neutral (part of the façade of concern about the budget deficit). As a practical matter, making the estimate dynamic reduces the amount of revenue lost from a tax decrease or added from a tax increase. Arguments about the scoring protocol may be briefly summarized. Policymakers favoring macrodynamic scoring argue that the approach provides additional information about likely impacts and that it may reduce some bias against tax changes that encourage economic growth by ignoring the stimulating impacts of tax reductions. Policymakers opposing macrodynamic scoring argue that models used for doing such estimates are extremely speculative and untested and, thus, the scores that emerge are extremely sensitive to underlying assumptions, not empirical evidence (there are competing macrodynamic models around, and each gives different scores for tax proposals with no way of telling what one is most accurate), that requiring such scoring would impose an impractical workload on estimators without much impact on final estimates, and that assumption-sensitivity could erode confidence in the impartiality and nonpartisanship of the revenue estimators.[40] As a practical matter, the argument among lawmakers is not particularly about getting the revenue estimate

---

[39]State use of macrodynamic scoring is discussed in Mikesell, *Ibid*. Some states have required that protocol but then lost enthusiasm when it was discovered that it did not make much difference in estimated impacts of tax changes being proposed and was not seen as worth the cost of operating the estimation system.

[40]A big issue is that the equations in models used for macrodynamic scoring mostly have to be created by assumptions, not empirical evidence, and the final revenue impact can be manipulated with these assumptions. It is not a comfortable situation for preparation of unbiased estimates. Two models, each created by competent analysts, can and do yield dramatically different scores, and it is impossible to know which is closer to accurate. Results are also sensitive to assumptions about what other things lawmakers might do in later years of the forecasting horizon.

to be as accurate as possible. If that were the case, JCT and CBO would be given simple marching orders: use the best fiscal economists money can buy to provide the most accurate estimate, using the most appropriate tools available to them, of what the revenue impact would be from the proposed tax change and, if the proposal is adopted, compare the estimate with the actual, report on any difference, and use that information to do better next time. Instead, the argument centers around political efforts to make the official revenue loss estimate of reduced tax rates or enhanced tax preferences lower than it would be with only static and microeconomic components included. Evidence does indicate that use of macrodynamic scoring makes only a small difference in the estimates and that much of the revenue recovery occurs in later years of the forecasting horizon, with a resulting increase in the annual deficit in the earlier years. The dream of self-financed tax reductions—that is, tax cuts that pay for themselves with increased tax revenue—is just not supported by the evidence.[41] The revenue does not recover fully in the budget year, in five years, or in ten years; all evidence indicates, even with scoring as dynamic as possible, that tax reductions add to the budget deficit.

Accuracy in Scoring/Estimating

Although revenue forecasts are keenly watched and tested against actual revenue collections, revenue estimates are seldom judged for accuracy.[42] Even the federal government, with its great concern and staffing for measuring and evaluating performance, seldom evaluates scoring. A CBO report states: "[I]t is generally not possible to assess the accuracy of past revenue estimates of enacted legislation. Most legislative provisions are part of a large mix of changes, and identifying the revenues associated with a particular provision is impossible. Often, subsequent legislation obscures the effect of previous actions."[43] The estimate matters when the legislation is being considered—particularly when PAYGO requirements are in place or when balanced budget requirements constrain fiscal actions—and then it is typically forgotten and not tested against actual data, particularly when the legislation involves a change in an existing tax rather than the adoption of a new tax. States have fewer resources and almost never is there any attempt to discover whether the estimate for a change in a state tax is accurate. Usually the estimate is folded into the baseline forecast in later years and that is it.

---

[41]Expenditure proposals have macroeconomic effects that can be at least as large as tax reductions, causing the net deficit impact of increasing expenditure to be less than the amount of the initial increase (increased spending stimulates the economy and that both increases revenue yield and reduces the need for some safety net expenditures). The CBO will use macrodynamic scoring for mandatory spending changes but not for regular appropriations.

[42]Edward D. Kleinbard and Patrick Driessen, "A Revenue Estimate Case Study: The Repatriation Holiday Revisited," *Tax Notes* (September 22, 2008): 1191–202, is an exception. They both review the Joint Committee on Taxation's estimate of the foreign dividend repatriation holiday and explain its estimation process.

[43]Congressional Budget Office, *Projecting Federal Tax Revenues and the Effect of Changes in Tax Law* (Washington, D.C.: Congressional Budget Office, 1998), i.

When the change being scored is adoption of a new tax, it is possible to compare the estimates with the actual. For instance, part of the federal health-care program adopted in 2010 was a new 10 percent excise tax on indoor tanning services (the tanning tax), applicable from July 1, 2010. The Joint Committee on Taxation estimated that tax would yield $200 million per year, but through the first nine months of collection, the tax had produced $54.4 million, far less than the expected yield. The estimate anticipated 25,000 businesses would be affected by the tax, but only 10,300 had registered.[44] This illustrates the difficulty with scoring a new tax: was the analysis wrong, was administration of the tax ineffective, or was it a combination of those factors? No one knows, but estimating is tough work when it involves analysis with minimal reliable data to use as the basis. Usually, nobody knows whether the estimates turned out to be right or wrong.[45] Federal battles have usually been about tax estimates, not forecasts, and state battles have usually been about forecasts, not estimates.

Tax Expenditure Budgets

The Congressional Budget and Impoundment Act of 1974 defines tax expenditures to be "revenue losses attributable to provisions of the federal tax laws which allow a special exclusion, exemption, or deduction from gross income or which provide a special credit, a preferential rate of tax, or a deferral of tax liability." The tax expenditure budget, an accumulation of the estimates of revenue lost through these preferences (some dare call them "tax loopholes") thus reflects the dual nature of every tax system—part to generate revenue and part to distribute subsidies—and the conflicting nature of provisions in the system. Some provisions are in the tax system to implement traditional tax policy and should be judged according to the criteria of taxation (they raise revenue), whereas others intend to favor certain economic activities or to relieve personal hardships and should be judged according to budget policy criteria.[46] Table 13-1 identifies the types of tax expenditures in the federal

---

[44]Treasury Inspector General for Tax Administration, "Affordable Care Act: The Number of Taxpayers Filing Tanning Excise Tax Returns Is Lower than Expected," Reference Number 2011-40-115, Washington, D.C., September 22, 2011.

[45]But sometimes wrong estimates can be exciting. For instance, in 2000, Arizona offered a large tax advantage for propane-burning motor vehicles. The estimate was for lost revenue of $3–$10 million. Part of the way through the first year, lost revenue appeared to be around $420 million: the person doing the estimate did not see an error in writing the legislation that effectively made the program open-ended and miscalculated exactly how attractive the program would be. Jim Carlton, "If You Paid Half Price for That New SUV, You Must Be in Arizona—With Big Rebates to Car Buyers, Clean-Air Law Cleaned Out the State's Coffers Instead," *Wall Street Journal*, October 26, 2000, A-1.

[46]In the federal system, both the administration (in the annual budget presentation) and Congress (through the Joint Committee on Taxation) prepare tax expenditure budgets. The latter presents both tax expenditure amounts for each provision and the distribution of benefits from major provisions across household income groups: Joint Committee on Taxation, *Estimates of Federal Tax Expenditures for Fiscal Years 2015–2019*, JCX-141-15, December 7, 2015.

Table 13–1
Individual Income Tax Provisions Creating Tax Expenditures

Tax Expenditure	Description	Example
Exclusion	Excludes income that otherwise would constitute part of the taxpayer's gross income	Contribution employer makes for employee health insurance
Exemption	Reduces gross income for taxpayer because of status or circumstances	Exemption for dependent child
Deduction	Reduce gross income due to expense taxpayer has incurred	Deduction for state and local income tax paid
Credit	Reduces tax liability dollar for dollar, may be fully refundable	Credit for certain dependent children
Preferential tax rate	Reduced tax rate for certain income	Lower rate for capital gains
Deferral	Delay of recognition of income	Delay tax on interest on certain U.S. savings bonds until redeemed

SOURCE: United States Government Accountability Office, *Tax Expenditures: Background and Evaluation Criteria and Questions, GAO-13-167SP*

individual income tax and gives examples of each type. Discussions about broadening the tax base (either to raise additional revenue or to permit lower statutory rates) focus on the tax expenditures. If the base is to be broadened, it will be by elimination of some of these tax preferences.

A tax expenditure is equivalent to having the taxpayer pay the tax that would be owed without the special provision and simultaneously receive a government grant equal to the amount of tax in that provision. A direct expenditure and a tax expenditure are comparable because both provide a benefit to a recipient and reduce public resources available for other uses. However, they look different politically. As Eugene Steuerle points out, tax expenditures "allow politicians to appear to be reducing the size of government (reducing taxes) while actually increasing it (increasing spending)."[47] This represents gross hypocrisy and a clear violation of fiscal transparency. The tax expenditure intervenes in the private choice process while being sold as down-sizing government.[48] The tax expenditure concept and the tax expenditure budget are both tools for adding transparency because they identify who is receiving these otherwise hidden government subsidies.

---

[47]Eugene Steuerle, "Summers on Social Tax Expenditures: Where He's Wrong . . . or at Least Incomplete," *Tax Notes* 89 (December 18, 2000): 1639.

[48]In possibly the greatest hypocrisy of all, social insurance spending by the U.S. government as a share of GDP when tax expenditures are taken into account are only slightly below that of Denmark, a country many Americans view as being overly generous in coddling its citizens.

The development of a tax expenditure budget is "a classification exercise: dividing the provisions of the tax system into a benchmark or norm and a series of deviations from that norm."[49] But what is normal? The practical problem is deciding what components are part of the *baseline* and what components represent the *deviations* from the norm that constitute a tax preference to be measured by the tax expenditure budget. By classifying most of the tax system as part of the norm, the size of the tax expenditure is reduced. Conversely, by defining the norm narrowly, more provisions in the law become suspect, and the tax expenditure budget is large.

Because there are so many specific translations of tax concepts into tax structures, any tax expenditure budget demands a careful explanation of what the baseline means. The federal budget for 2010 describes two alternative specifications for baseline:

> The normal tax baseline is patterned on a practical variant of a comprehensive income tax, which defines income as the sum of consumption and the change in net wealth in a given period of time. The normal tax baseline allows personal exemptions, a standard deduction, and deduction of expenses incurred in earning income. It is not limited to a particular structure of tax rates, or by a specific definition of the taxpaying unit.
>
> The reference tax law baseline is also patterned on a comprehensive income tax, but it is closer to existing law. Reference law tax expenditures are limited to special exceptions from a generally provided tax rule that serve programmatic functions in a way that is analogous to spending programs. Provisions under the reference law baseline are generally tax expenditures under the normal tax baseline, but the reverse is not always true.[50]

The normal tax defines the ideal or standard tax, the tax that follows the textbook concept of what structure would assign shares of the cost of government in a way consistent with the logic of the tax. It starts with a fundamental principle (notice the track from the Haig-Simons comprehensive definition of *income* here; both Treasury and JCT agree on that) and allows some appropriate adjustments to define *normal* or *reference*.[51] Differences from that definition constitute tax expenditures. The reference law approach works from a benchmark law, and deviations from that benchmark represent tax expenditures.

Existing federal tax expenditures encourage selected economic activities (investment, housing, municipal borrowing, support of charities, etc.) or reduce taxpayers' liability in special circumstances (deduction of medical expenses, casualty loss deduction, etc.). Estimates by both Congress (the Joint Committee on Taxation)

---

[49]Organization for Economic Cooperation and Development, *Tax Expenditures: Recent Experiences* (Paris: Organization for Economic Cooperation and Development, 1996), 9.

[50]Office of Management and Budget, *Budget of the Government of the United States, Fiscal Year 2013, Analytical Perspectives* (Washington, D.C.: U.S. Government Printing Office, 2012), 248.

[51]States follow a similar approach with defining normal for their income taxes. They do, however, struggle somewhat with defining normal for their retail sales taxes. Many do get around to accepting the idea that all household expenditures should be taxed and all business purchases should be exempt but some simply and incorrectly list every provision that reduces revenue as a tax expenditure. (John L. Mikesell, "State Tax Policy and State Sales Taxes: What Tax Expenditure Budgets Tell Us about Sales Taxes," *American Review of Public Administration* 42 (March 2012): 131–51.)

Table 13–2
Federal Income Tax Expenditures with Revenue Loss above $20 Billion, Fiscal 2015 (exclusions, deductions, credits, reduced rates)

Provision	Impact ($million)
Exclusion of employer contribution to medical insurance premiums and medical care	206,430
Capital gains (except agriculture, timber, iron ore, and coal)	85,360
Exclusion of net imputed rental income	78,810
Mortgage interest on owner-occupied residences	69,480
Defined contribution employer pension plans	68,040
Deferral of income from controlled foreign corporations (overseas profits not taxed until repatriated)	64,560
Step-up basis of capital gains at death (capital gains tax does not apply to inherited wealth)	63,440
Deductability of nonbusiness state and local taxes other than on owner-occupied homes	47,490
Defined benefit employer pension plans	44,640
Deductability of charitable contributions, other than education and health	44,280
Capital gains exclusion on home sales	36,930
Exclusion of interest on public purpose state and local bonds	31,070
Deduction of property taxes on real property	33,120
Self-employment pension plans	25,480
Social Security benefits for retired workers	27,080
Treatment of qualified dividends (lower tax rate)	26,320
Child credit	23,900

SOURCE: Office of Management and Budget, Executive Office of the President, *Budget of the United States Government, Fiscal Year 2016: Analytic Perspectives* (Washington, D.C.: OMB, 2015).

and the president (Department of Treasury) are a regular part of the executive budget and other presentations.[52] Table 13-2 presents estimates of the income tax expenditures with a revenue impact of $20 billion or more, according to the Treasury. Notice that many of these larger tax expenditures are quite popular with the American public and often have organized interest groups that support the preference. That is why serious action on federal income tax broadening is so difficult. Estimates also are prepared on a regular, although not always annual, basis in about

---

[52]They may be in revenue or outlay-equivalent terms. The latter estimates the dollar amount of direct spending that would provide taxpayers the net benefits equaling what they receive from the tax expenditure.

forty of the states.[53] Appendix 13–1 describes the criteria and measurement principles that Minnesota uses.

Tax policy is generally predisposed against tax expenditures—assuming the normal structure is rationally designed—because the differential provisions distort business and household decisions, because their implementation complicates the tax system, because they continue without regular evaluation and legislative approval (they lack the separate authorization/appropriation steps that characterize direct spending in the federal system), because they are open-ended in amount, and because they are not transparent in enactment, in delivery of benefits, or in overall magnitude. It is hard to associate an approach to subsidization that is hidden, permanent, and open-ended with good governance. These same features of tax expenditures make them a great way for special interests to receive subsidies. However, not all tax expenditures are necessarily bad because conducting some budget policy through the tax system may be a sensible, quick, inexpensive, and feasible approach in comparison with alternative approaches (e.g., direct expenditure or regulation) to achieving a particular objective. There is no need to establish an administrative structure to operate tax expenditure assistance, and the tax expenditure may reach a wider population of beneficiaries than would a freestanding program that requires special application. And, of course, there is the lure of political popularity: nothing enthralls the American public more than the prospect of tax reduction, even when it increases government invasion into private choices.

The critical stage in development of a useful tax expenditure budget is that of defining the normal tax, that is, deciding what basic tax policy is—and that is a question that continues to be debated. Federal budgets presented in the later years of the administration of President George W. Bush, to stress that the current federal income tax is actually a sort of hybrid income-consumption tax, added tax expenditure estimates under a consumption tax base norm. Of course, that causes a different pattern of tax expenditures than under the traditional income tax base norm. In particular, the several tax provisions providing preferences for saving are no longer tax expenditures. The most obvious of these are the several exclusions for contributions for retirement plans shown in Table 13-2. These represent exclusions of savings, so if the normal tax base was consumption, they would become elements that would need to be deducted to produce the normal base (income minus saving equals consumption). This illustrates why a clear consensus on normal tax policy must be reached before the tax expenditure budget can have any practical meaning or utility for policy discussions. If you cannot agree on the basic tax policy, doing a tax expenditure budget is hardly worth the effort.

A properly drawn definition of a benchmark or normal structure provides a defense *against* arbitrary and capricious tax policy. Most fiscal experts would agree

---

[53]An analysis and evaluation of state tax expenditure budgets appears in John L. Mikesell, "Tax Expenditure Budgets, Budget Policy, and Tax Policy: Confusion in the States," *Public Budgeting & Finance* 22 (Winter 2002): 34–51; and John L. Mikesell, "The Tax Expenditure Concept at the State Level: Conflict between Fiscal Control and Sound Tax Policy," *Proceedings of the Ninety-fourth Annual Conference on Taxation of the National Tax Association* (Washington, D.C.: National Tax Association, 2001). The states in general fail to clearly identify the normal structures upon which their tax expenditure estimates are based.

Figure 13–2
Federal Tax Expenditures Reported by Joint Committee on Taxation, 1974–2014 (Real 2009)

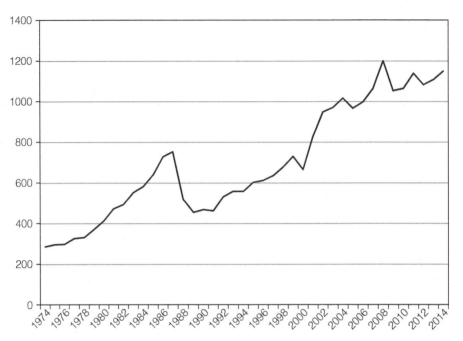

with the Surrey and McDaniel conclusion: "[U]nless attention is paid to tax expenditures, a country does not have its tax policy or its budget policy under full control."[54] The same message applies for U.S. state governments. Without a proper tax expenditure budget, a government has no gauge of the extent to which its revenue system is being used for nonrevenue purposes.[55] According to the Joint Committee on Taxation, tax expenditures now exceed 140 percent of federal nondefense discretionary spending.[56] The record of restraining tax expenditures is not good. Figure 13–2 traces total federal tax expenditures in real terms from 1974 through 2014. The almost permanent upward drift is apparent. Excluding the dramatic reduction around the Tax Reform Act of 1986, the inclination of lawmakers to add more special provisions to the income tax system dominates the data. They like to dole out special deals to favored taxpayers (or nonpayers, as the case may be), seeing the system as a device for generating preferences rather than a structure for raising revenue. No wonder

---

[54]Stanley S. Surrey and Paul R. McDaniel, "The Tax Expenditure Concept and the Legislative Process," in *The Economics of Taxation*, ed. Henry J. Aaron and Michael J. Boskin (Washington, D.C.: Brookings Institution, 1980), 124.

[55]Tax expenditure budgets are common in other national fiscal systems as well: Hana Polackova Brixi, Christian Valenduc, and Zhicheng Li Swift, *Tax Expenditures—Shedding Light on Government Spending through the Tax System, Lessons from Developed and Transition Economies* (Washington, D.C.: World Bank, 2004).

[56]Daniel R. Mullins and John L. Mikesell, "Innovations in Budgeting and Financial Management," in *The Oxford Handbook of American Bureaucracy*, ed. Robert F. Durant (New York: Oxford University Press, 2010), 754–55.

people see the tax code to be overly complicated. Unfortunately, the tax expenditure budget seems not to have dramatically controlled the expansion of tax expenditures; although without these data being presented by JCT and OMB, it is possible that it could have been even worse.

State and local governments have also become interested in an examination of the revenue cost of incentives for economic development inserted into their tax systems, a special sort of tax expenditure. The Governmental Accounting Standards Board now requires that state and local government financial statements include information about tax abatement program current and future obligations, defining a tax abatement to be:

> A reduction in tax revenues that results from an agreement between one or more governments and an individual or entity in which (a) one or more governments promise to forgo tax revenues to which they are otherwise entitled and (b) the individual or entity promises to take a specific action after the agreement has been entered into that contributes to economic development or otherwise benefits the governments or the citizens of those governments.[57]

In a similar vein, a number of states are now preparing tax incentive reports on a regular cycle that, for each development incentive inserted into their tax structure, identify the amount of revenue lost, the number of entities receiving the incentive, and some assessment of the effectiveness and economic impact resulting from that incentive.[58] These reports are the result of a growing suspicion that many incentives may not be worth the revenue loss that they entail because they do not have a significant impact on economic growth and may serve primarily to line the pockets of wealthy owners of businesses.[59] They have not successfully quenched the desire of lawmakers for constituent tax preferences, but they do add transparency to the give-aways that the laws are delivering.

Conclusion

Revenue prediction, a portion of administration particularly vital for budget preparation, has three significant divisions: forecasting collections in future fiscal years, estimating the impact of proposed changes in tax law, and calculating revenues currently sacrificed by existing elements of the tax law. The first activity normally produces excellent accuracy (1 to 3 percent error) when it is professionally done and when the forecasts are not politically driven. Errors are usually greater when the country enters a recession. Revenue estimates are important to let policymakers

---

[57]Statement No. 77 of the Governmental Accounting Standards Board, Tax Abatement Disclosures, No. 353, August 2015.

[58]One example: Office of Fiscal and Management Analysis, Indiana Legislative Services Agency, *2015 Indiana Tax Incentive Evaluation* (Indianapolis, In.: LSA, 2015).

[59]Governments and businesses have little shame with regard to delivery of tax breaks. For instance, Memphis and the state of Tennessee recently gave the company that operates Elvis Presley's Graceland estate $79 million in tax incentives for improvements at the facility. Possibly they were concerned that the attraction would move to West Virginia. (Michael Rapoport and Theo Francis, "Elvis and a Big Hunk o' Tax Breaks," *Wall Street Journal*, October 6, 2015.) Such abatements are the sort that would be covered by the provisions of GASB Statement No. 77.

know what the fiscal cost of their policies is likely to be. Tax expenditure budgets tally the revenue effects of provisions in existing tax laws. The practice of revenue prediction, especially forecasting and estimating, has a high degree of art mixed with the quantitative science in its real-world application.

QUESTIONS AND EXERCISES

1. A state intangibles tax is levied on the holders of intangible personal property in the state. The tax base is market value of the item of property on the last day of December; for most taxpayers, intangible holdings in December establish tax due by April 15 of the next year (paid with the annual income tax return). Tax rates have been 0.0025 percent, but a phase-out of the tax begins in calendar year 2017. In that year, the rate will be 0.00233 and in the following year, 0.00217.

   Fiscal year (July 1–June 30) collections for the tax from 2009 through 2015 follow, along with estimates previously prepared for fiscal 2016 and 2017 and calendar-year data on state personal income.

	Collections (millions $)	Personal Income (millions $)
2009	15.6	26,158
2010	17.8	27,776
2011	14.7	26,816
2012	14.1	26,206
2013	16.6	34,132
2014	17.4	36,487
2015	19.2	40,279
2016 (forecast)	19.4	Not available
2017 (forecast)	19.6	Not available

   Forecast revenue from the tax for fiscal years 2017, 2018, and 2019 using any method that is appropriate. (An independent commission has estimated state personal income for the three years to equal $48,660 million in 2017, $52,800 million in 2018, and $57,500 million in 2019.) Describe the method you used and indicate why it is better than other alternatives available.

2. States differ with respect to how they handle the revenue portion of their budgets.

   a. Who does revenue forecasts for your state budget? Is it an executive branch or a legislative branch agency or a consensus process?

   b. What entity in your state government prepares revenue estimates for tax legislation? Are the estimates easily available on a state website?

   c. Does your state develop a tax expenditure budget? If so, what are the largest tax expenditure categories for the two taxes that generate the most revenue for the state? Does the tax expenditure budget identify the normal structure for each of those taxes?

3. A state in the southeastern region of the United States operates state liquor stores. Prices at the stores are set in the following fashion: add 41 percent to the wholesale price at which the system acquires the product. To that is added an excise of $8.10 per case. The state sold roughly 36 million cases. The state, however, increases the excise rate to $9.10 per case, and a tentative revenue estimate shows that excise revenue will increase by $36 million. The state economist objects: "The demand for liquor is inelastic, so sales will be relatively insensitive to a tax increase. Therefore, revenue will increase by more than $36 million." What is your reaction to this objection?

4. Your state plans to adopt a tuition tax credit for college students. How would you estimate the revenue impact of this provision? How would the decision to use static, microdynamic, or macrodynamic approaches influence your estimate?

5. When the Soviet bloc broke up in the early 1990s, the Republic of Vardar declared its independence. As the country established a monetary system, democratic processes, and a controlled fiscal system, the early problems of hyperinflation, unemployment, and declining standards of living slowly subsided. In late 1997, the country initiated a personal income tax, heavily dependent on taxes withheld by large employers on wages and salaries, but still broad in coverage. The country has been collecting about 30 percent of its tax revenue from that tax, although a law passed in 2000 is expected to reduce personal income tax collections by 25 percent in the short term. The lower tax rates are expected to stimulate economic activity and to encourage business to move from the shadow to the official (tax-paying) economy, so some of the revenue loss will ultimately be recovered. The Ministry of Finance forecasts collections of 7,789,000.0 thousand markka (MK) for 2001. Data on tax collections are reported below.

   a. From this information, would you advise the ministry to revise its 2001 forecast? Explain.

   b. What factors may influence the patterns you see in the data?

   c. What other issues would you pursue in addition to the data presented here? Collections are in MK thousand.

	1998	1999	2000	2001
January	668,534.0	625,149.1	559,070.9	714,981.0
February	782,026.6	754,396.9	874,000.0	575,115.0
March	738,856.7	811,506.7	988,047.2	583,592.0
April	826,622.9	880,075.8	916,030.7	586,743.0
May	678,031.1	756,507.9	800,876.8	
June	736,974.5	831,054.5	940,975.1	
July	824,343.7	978,485.6	967,098.4	
August	668,708.8	743,718.4	841,267.5	
September	766,271.3	898,210.0	874,308.1	
October	759,679.8	846,494.2	887,091.4	
November	742,371.5	847,950.2	936,090.7	
December	984,911.2	1,259,467.1	1,204,961.7	

6. These are the collections from a state liquor excise tax for a number of years. There have been no changes in the structure or administration of the tax in that period of time. Collections are in thousands of dollars, and fiscal years end on June 30. Your job is to forecast collections for fiscal years 2017 and 2018. It is a minor source of revenue to the state, so use of causal economic modeling is not likely to be seen as worthwhile.

2006: 144,990

2007: 153,831

2008: 162,083

2009: 170,469

2010: 193,181

2011: 195,179

2012: 212,501

2013: 223,036

2014: 239,494

2015: 245,693

CASE FOR DISCUSSION

CASE 13–1

Estimating Revenue from a New Tax

The preparation of revenue estimates is particularly challenging when the tax change being proposed is for a new tax. In that instance, the tax system typically provides no relevant information for preparing the estimate, meaning that the estimate will be prepared from a grab bag of data pulled from many sources, none of which exactly match the terms of the new tax law.

Consider These Questions

1. What estimating protocol is used for the tax? Do you think this is the appropriate approach in this instance?

2. What are the special problems that the revenue estimators had to confront in the case?

3. What changes would you make to their estimating approach? What difference would your changes make to the final estimate?

In November 2014, the voters of Alaska approved a citizen-initiated proposal to legalize the sale of marijuana and to tax it at $50 per ounce. Although revenue production may not have been the most important thing on the minds of voters of the state, the revenue does go to the state budget and, hence, it has to be estimated in the budget-making process. It is a new tax, applied in a market that does not yet exist, so preparing the estimate will be a challenge.

What might the revenue estimators do? First, look for any usable data. It turns out that there is a 2009-2010 National Survey of Drug Use and Health. That survey estimated that 37 percent of people from 21 to 25 years old had used marijuana in the past year and that 14 percent of people 26 and older had used marijuana. Working from state population data, that meant that 19,258 people from 21 to 25 years old and 65,445 people over 26 would be estimated as marijuana users. However, the survey was picking up responses about use of an illegal product, and people might well be likely to underreport their illegal activity. Thus, we will add 20 percent to the number of people using the product and to allow for some possible growth in usage rates. That means 23,110 users in the younger age group and 78,534 users in the older group.

Now for some more guessing, or estimating. The state thinks the younger group would average a usage rate of 3.4 ounces per year, and the older group would average 3.7 ounces per year. Multiply usage rate by number of users to get 369,148 ounces per year.

The state has an existing medical marijuana law, and some people are likely to move from that market to the now-legal market because it is likely to be more convenient and possibly less expensive. That movement might total 1,240 users, estimated to be purchasing 4,588 ounces. Add this consumption to that previously estimated to obtain 373,736.

A tax of $50 per ounce is pretty steep. There will be a response in quantity demanded from this shock, suppose possibly a 5 percent reduction, leaving consumption of 355,049 ounces. Finally, the consumption data from the survey dealt with illegal consumption entirely. With marijuana now being a legal product, there probably will be an increase in consumption (somewhat dampened by leakage back to illegal suppliers because of the high tax rate). Let's suppose the increase is 25 percent. That means that consumption of 443,811 ounces. Taxed at $50 per ounce, that would yield $22,190,550.

Is that how much money the state will collect in the 2016 fiscal year? We do not know, and we can find lots of problem areas in the estimate. Fortunately, the amount of revenue from this tax is not likely to make or break the Alaska state budget. The revenue estimated here is lots of money for almost any household budget, but it is only around one-half of one percent of total tax revenue collected by the state.

SOURCES: Laurel Andrews, "The State Weighs In: How Much Will Marijuana Bring to Alaska?" *Alaska Dispatch News*, July 7, 2015; U.S. Bureau of Census, Governments Division, *State Tax Collections in 2014.* www.census.gov

APPENDIX 13–1

The State of Minnesota Tax Expenditure Budget: Criteria and Measurement

The state of Minnesota prepares a tax expenditure budget on a two-year cycle, delivered on the off-year from the governor's biennial budget. It is notable for the care taken to make it a meaningful document by setting clear standards for identifying the tax expenditures and can serve as a useful model for any jurisdiction considering the development of such a budget. The selection that follows is taken from the 2012–2015 document.[60] Notice the section at the end that discusses the difference between the tax expenditure budget estimates and the numbers that would appear in a revenue estimate for a proposed change in tax law.

The Tax Expenditure Concept

"State governmental policy objectives are sought to be achieved both by direct expenditure of governmental funds and by the granting of special and selective tax relief or tax expenditures." (Minnesota Statutes, Section 270C.11, Subd. 1, in part, reprinted in Appendix A.)

Tax expenditures are statutory provisions which reduce the amount of revenue that would otherwise be generated, including exemptions, deductions, credits, and lower tax rates. These provisions are called "expenditures" because they are similar to direct spending programs. Both tax expenditures and direct expenditures are used for public policy goals, such as funding or encouraging specified activities or providing financial assistance to persons, businesses, or groups in particular situations.

A tax expenditure is different from a direct spending program in two major respects:

- A direct spending program continues only if funds are appropriated for each budget period, but the continuation of a tax expenditure does not require legislative action. Unless a tax expenditure provision has an expiration date, it continues indefinitely.
- Direct spending programs are itemized on the expenditure side of the budget. Tax expenditures are reflected on the revenue side of the budget and are not itemized. Revenues shown in the state budget are net of tax expenditures.

The Purpose of the Tax Expenditure Budget

The purpose of the tax expenditure budget is to provide information to facilitate a regular, comprehensive legislative review of tax expenditure provisions. Tax expenditure provisions are identified and listed in the report, along with the legal citation, explanation, history, and fiscal impact for each provision.

---

[60]Tax Research Division, Minnesota Department of Revenue, *State of Minnesota Tax Expenditure Budget, Fiscal Year 2012–2015* (St. Paul: Minnesota Department of Revenue, 2012).

Minnesota Statutes, Section 270.067, enacted in 1983, required a tax expenditure budget to be submitted as a supplement to the governor's biennial budget. In 1996 the law was changed so that the report is due in each even-numbered year, rather than at the same time as the governor's biennial budget in the odd-numbered years. In 2005 the statute was recodified as Section 270C.11 (reprinted in Appendix A).

Tax Expenditure Criteria

Not every exemption, deduction, credit, or lower tax rate is a tax expenditure. A conceptual framework governs the identification of tax expenditure provisions. Each tax provision is evaluated against a list of criteria. Seven criteria are used to determine if a provision is a tax expenditure. Some of the criteria are taken directly from the authorizing statute; some are based on concepts used in the preparation of federal tax expenditure reports; and others are based on what is believed to be a logical application of the tax expenditure concept. A provision must meet all the criteria in order to be a tax expenditure. A provision is a tax expenditure if it:

- has an impact on a tax that is applied statewide;
- confers preferential treatment;
- results in reduced tax revenue in the applicable fiscal years;
- is not included as an expenditure item in the state budget;
- is included in the defined tax base for that tax;
- is not subject to an alternative tax; and
- can be amended or repealed by a change in state law.

The first four criteria are based on the statute requiring the tax expenditure budget.

Statewide Tax: The tax expenditure budget is required by statute to include every state tax and any local tax that is applied statewide. A local tax imposed pursuant to a special law is not included in the report. Only taxes that contain tax expenditure provisions are included in the report.

Preferential Treatment: Preferential treatment is a key concept in determining tax expenditures. The first sentence of the authorizing statute, quoted at the beginning of this introduction, uses the words "special and selective." Also, the statutory definition of a tax expenditure uses the word "certain." Minnesota Statutes, Section 270C.11, Subd. 6(1)(emphasis added):

> "Tax expenditure" means a tax provision which provides a gross income definition, deduction, exemption, credit, or rate for *certain* persons, types of income, transactions, or property that results in reduced tax revenue.

If a provision is not preferential, it is not a tax expenditure. The personal exemption for the individual income tax is not preferential because the amount of the exemption is the same for each taxpayer, spouse, and dependent. Likewise, the graduated rate structure of the individual income tax is not considered a tax expenditure because each taxpayer with the same amount of tax base pays at the same rate.

Reduction in Revenue: In the statute quoted above, a requirement is that the provision "results in reduced tax revenue." A provision that would otherwise qualify is not considered a tax expenditure if it is not being used or is not likely to be used during fiscal years 2012 through 2015.

The federal law (Congressional Budget Act of 1974, Public Law 93–344) that requires a list of tax expenditures to be included with the federal budget includes in its definition of tax expenditures "provisions of the Federal tax laws which allow . . . a deferral of liability." The Minnesota law does not specifically mention deferral of liability. However, this concept has been adopted in the preparation of the report because a deferral of liability results in reduced tax revenue for a given year.

A deferral of liability involves the time value of money and affects primarily the individual income and corporate franchise taxes. A deferral can result either from postponing the time when income is recognized or from accelerating the deduction of expenses. Taxable income is lower in that year than it would be otherwise, and an adjustment is made in a future year. The deferral of liability is similar to an interest-free loan for the taxpayer.

Not an Expenditure in the State Budget: The tax expenditure budget is intended to supplement the regular state budget and therefore does not include provisions that are itemized as expenditures in the state budget. The state-funded property tax relief provisions are similar to tax expenditures, but they are not included in this report because they are itemized in the state budget as expenditures.

Included in Defined Tax Base: The tax base for each tax must be clearly defined so that exceptions to that base can be identified. Some tax provisions help to define the base; others are exceptions to the base. The tax base for a tax is the working definition used for this report and is not intended to define the ideal tax base. The defined tax base for each tax is explained in the chapter introduction for the tax. Knowing the tax base is important to understanding how tax expenditures are determined for that tax.

Not Subject to an Alternative Tax: In some instances, one tax may be in imposed in place of another tax, and it would not be reasonable for a taxpayer or activity to be subject to both taxes. Therefore, the exemption from one tax is not considered a tax expenditure if the alternative tax is imposed.

The application of the alternative tax concept for this report was limited to these situations:

- The income from taconite and iron mining is subject to the occupation tax in lieu of the corporate franchise tax.
- The purchase of a motor vehicle is subject to the motor vehicle sales tax (Chapter 5) in lieu of the general sales and use tax (Chapter 4).
- Cigarettes are exempt from the general sales and use tax but are subject to a tax in lieu of the sales tax at the wholesale level.
- The solid waste management taxes are imposed in lieu of the general sales tax.

- A number of taxes are imposed in lieu of the general property tax, including the motor vehicle registration tax and the taconite production tax.
- Noncommercial aircraft are taxed under the aircraft registration tax, and commercial airflight property is taxed under the airflight property tax.

Subject to Legislative Authority: The statute requiring the tax expenditure budget specifies that it is to be submitted to the legislature. Therefore, the report contains only state law provisions that the legislature can propose to repeal or amend. Tax provisions that are contained in the Minnesota Constitution, federal law, or the United States Constitution are not included in the tax expenditure budget.

How Tax Expenditures Are Measured

The fiscal impact of a tax expenditure measures the revenue loss from that one provision under current law. Each provision is estimated in isolation, and other provisions in that tax and in other taxes are held constant. The impact of that provision on other tax provisions is not taken into account. Because the estimates measure the impact of the provision as it exists, no change in taxpayer behavior is assumed.

The estimates for provisions that result in the deferral of tax are the net impact for that year. For example, contributions to a traditional individual retirement account (IRA) are deducted in the year that the contribution is made, earnings are not taxed in the year they are earned, and distributions are included in taxable income in the year received. The tax expenditure impact for a given year measures for all traditional IRAs the deduction for contributions made that year plus the exclusion of earnings accrued that year less distributions included in taxable income in that year.

The precision of the estimates varies with the source of the data and with the applicability of the data to the tax expenditure provision. Data from Minnesota tax returns were used whenever possible. Other sources included federal tax expenditure estimates, data from federal tax returns, census data, and numerous other economic and industry sources of data for Minnesota and the nation.

The methodology used to estimate tax expenditures can produce misleading results if the estimates for two or more provisions are totaled. Depending upon the situation, the combined impact of two or more provisions could be more or less than the total of the provisions estimated separately.

When two tax expenditures overlap, generally the overlap is not included in either estimate. For example, the sales tax exemption for Job Opportunity Building Zone (JOBZ) businesses includes purchases that would also qualify under the capital equipment exemption. Neither the JOBZ sales tax exemption nor the capital equipment exemption includes capital equipment purchases by JOBZ businesses. Adding together the two estimates done separately would understate their combined impact.

The graduated rate structure of the individual income tax is another reason that adding together tax expenditure estimates results in misleading information.

As income increases, the marginal tax rate increases. The estimate for each exclusion and deduction uses a marginal tax rate appropriate for that provision. If two or more exclusions or deductions were repealed together, the marginal tax rate for the combined impact would be higher than the rate used for each provision. In that case, adding together the estimates done separately would understate their combined impact.

The itemized deductions for the individual income tax illustrate the distortion that can result from adding together tax expenditure estimates. Because other provisions are held constant, the estimate for each itemized deduction compares the total of the remaining itemized deductions to the standard deduction. For taxpayers who would lose the benefit of itemizing by the loss of that one deduction, the tax expenditure estimate measures the incremental benefit over the standard deduction. Adding together the tax expenditure estimates for two or more itemized deductions ignores the fact that the incremental benefit over the standard deduction may be different when estimating them together compared to estimating each one separately.

The report contains six itemized deductions (Items 1.66 through 1.71). If the FY 2013 estimates for the six separate provisions were added together, the total is $766.2 million. However, when the six provisions are estimated together, the combined estimate is $521.1 million. Adding together the six estimates done separately would overstate the combined impact by $245.1 million, or about 47%.

How the Measurement of Tax Expenditures Differs from Revenue Estimates for Proposed Law Changes

The fiscal impact of a tax expenditure provision is not necessarily the same as the revenue that would be gained by repeal of the provision. This distinction is important.

Estimating the repeal of a provision would take into account interactions within a tax or between taxes and may include changes in taxpayer behavior. As explained in the previous section, if two or more provisions were repealed at the same time, the combined impact would be estimated and could be larger or smaller than the sum of the provisions estimated separately.

The chart below summarizes in general how various factors are different for tax expenditures estimates compared to estimates of proposed law changes.

	Tax Expenditures	Proposed
Estimates take into account:		
Changes in taxpayer behavior	No	Yes[1]
Impact on other tax provisions	No	Yes[1]
Combined impact of two or more provisions	No	Yes[1]
Effective date	No[2]	Yes
Other factors, including collectability	No	Yes[1]

[1]As appropriate
[2]Only effective date of changes under current law

CHAPTER 14

Intergovernmental Fiscal Relations: Diversity and Coordination

Chapter Contents

Correspondence and Subsidiarity
Is Bigger Better?
Fiscal Disparity
Coordination and Assistance: Tax Systems
Coordination and Assistance: Grants
  Categorical Grants

  Block Grants
  Revenue Sharing (General-Purpose Fiscal Assistance)

States and School Aid
Coordination and Assistance: Mandates
Conclusion

Federal, state, and local governments provide and finance public services in the United States, sometimes independently, sometimes cooperatively. Governments of each level are selected by their own electorates, and no government level functions as a regional department of another. Even though the localities add up to the state and the states add up to the nation, the balance of choices differs among localities in a state and among states in the nation. Because of that diversity of choice, state and local governments have an important and independent role in providing and financing government services. That includes the power to spend, as well as the responsibility to raise revenue adequate to support that spending.[1] In contrast to the case with subnational governments in many countries, U.S. state and local governments have considerable responsibility for raising the revenue that they spend. In some countries, these subnational units operate mostly as departments of the national government and have only limited independent authority for either service or revenue decisions.

Completely independent and uncoordinated operation of these levels would, most argue, produce unacceptable results. Such a posture would undoubtedly leave the public without desired and affordable services, inflict severe burdens on some unluckily placed individuals and businesses, and leave some lower-level governments

---

[1]The analysis of the vertical structure of public finance and the practice of government finance across tiers of governmental entities in a nation is called "fiscal federalism."

in chronic fiscal crisis. Those problems highlight the importance for regularized fiscal interrelationships among governments.[2]

Subnational governments allow fiscal diversity and choices about which government should provide which services. Although the federal government continues as sole government provider of national defense and postal services, other significant government functions are divided among federal, state, and local governments. As discussed in previous chapters, state and local governments are dominant for the services of public safety (police, fire, and protective regulation), education (primary, secondary, and higher), recreation and culture, and transportation (highways, air, water, and urban mass transit). They also run elections that select officials for all governments.

States and localities can adjust both levels and types of government services they provide as they respond to the preferences of a heterogeneous population. Maintaining service responsibility at state and local levels almost certainly means great diversity in what services are provided and how they are financed. It may also bring efficiencies in service provision as jurisdictions compete to keep the cost of government service affordable. Centralization would mean greater uniformity and possibly more secure financing. In addition, centralization makes for clear governmental responsibility: with only a single government, there would not have been the competitive finger pointing to identify which government was responsible for mishandling the response to Hurricane Katrina, for instance. What establishes the level of government that should have primary responsibility for providing particular services, and how should intergovernmental financing be arranged? To what extent should diverse provision be constrained or coordinated? And to what extent should subnational governments expect to receive revenue from the central government, as opposed to being required to raise the revenue they spend from their own taxing powers?[3]

Correspondence and Subsidiarity

The critical factor in identifying the level of government that should provide (but not necessarily produce) a public service is the range of benefit spillover. A structure of governments "in which the jurisdiction that determines the level of provision of each public good includes precisely the set of individuals who consume the good" satisfies the *correspondence principle* in defining geographic boundaries and

---

[2]Not all federations are characterized by the degree of political independence between federal and regional governments that characterizes the United States, Australia, and Canada. For instance, Russia and India have systems in which regional chief executives are selected in a process that gives considerable control and influence to the national chief executive rather than the free election of state officials that is the practice in the United States and Canada. Also, recall from Chapter 1 that many nations are unitary, not federal. In these countries, the lower tiers of "government" function as subordinates to the central government.

[3]Among countries of the Organization for Economic Cooperation and Development, Canada and the United States are the leaders in terms of expecting regional and local governments to raise their own revenues. Julia Darby, V. Anton Muscatelli, and Graeme Roy, "Fiscal Consolidation and Decentralization: A Tale of Two Tiers," *Fiscal Studies* 26 (2005): 173.

government size.[4] Making the spillover area and the decision unit coincide concentrates government attention on the important matters and prevents the problems that occur when beneficiaries do not pay for a service.

The correspondence principle, using the geographic extent of primary spillovers, defines a hierarchy of public services. A completely private good would have no spillovers. In that case, no distortions result from permitting private individuals to decide on the provision of purely private goods. Public goods and services, however, yield external benefits over areas of widely different geographic range. For instance, a neighborhood park benefits a small community of households around it, benefits from basic police and fire protection spill beyond the neighborhood to a broader local community, and interregional mobility causes benefits from elementary and secondary education to extend to whole regions, whereas the benefits of national defense and international relations extend to the entire nation (and beyond). The correspondence rule for assigning responsibilities to governments is that expenditure and service responsibilities (in other words, the size of the government) should align with the benefit areas for each government service. Therefore, services whose benefits do not spill beyond the local community should be locally provided, services that benefit a number of communities should be state (or regionally) provided, and services that benefit the entire country should be nationally provided. Failure to match spillover range and provision range, at least in general terms, can produce substantial misallocations in resources, overspending for some services, underspending for other services, poorly served citizens, badly managed service delivery, and poorly structured revenue systems.

There is a second general principle in assigning responsibility for government services, the principle of *subsidiarity*. The principle is that government responsibility for a function should be at the lowest level of government that can deliver the function efficiently. Jorge Martinez-Vazquez explains why:

> Because subnational governments are closer to the preferences and needs of taxpayers, they are more likely than the central government to deliver services that local residents want. And, to the extent that preferences for public services differ, efficiency will lead to (indeed, will require) diversity among subnational jurisdictions. Reliance (to the extent possible) on locally imposed taxes to finance subnational expenditures internalizes the costs of providing these services and leads residents in turn to demand more accountability from public officials. When the beneficiary pays, there is greater efficiency and responsibility in government decision-making.[5]

Subsidiarity brings devolution, moving government responsibility to lower levels of government. The devolution trend "is largely a reflection of the political evolution toward more democratic and participatory forms of government that seeks to improve the responsiveness and accountability of political leaders to their electorates, and to ensure a closer correspondence between the quantity, composition, and quality of publicly provided goods and services and the preferences of recipients."[6]

---

[4]Wallace E. Oates, *Fiscal Federalism* (New York: Harcourt Brace Jovanovich, 1972), 34.
[5]Jorge Martinez-Vasquez, "Expenditures and Expenditure Assignment," in *Russia and the Challenge of Fiscal Federalism,* ed. Christine I. Wallich (Washington, D.C.: World Bank, 1994), 99.
[6]Teresa Ter-Minassian, "Decentralizing Government," *Finance and Development* 34 (September 1997): 36.

Efforts of the U.S. Congress to shed responsibility to the states, of the United Kingdom to give more power to Scotland and Wales, for division of responsibilities between the European Union and its component nations, for making subnational entities more robust in China, for responding to minority populations in Canada and Belgium, and for efficiently rebuilding governments in countries formed from the former Soviet Union have all been driven by the dual principles of subsidiarity and correspondence in deciding which government will do what so that governments serve the people most effectively and efficiently. Surely the desire to have decisions made close to the population was part of the 2016 vote for the United Kingdom to leave the European Union.

A mismatch between spillover range and government jurisdiction can distort the use of public resources. Suppose a city can construct a local sports complex that would cost $1 million with only $50,000 of its own resources, the difference being financed by the federal government. The city would reasonably behave as if the full capital cost of the project is $50,000, even though the project uses $1 million of resources. If the project has minimal beneficial impact beyond the city, there is no significant spillover that federal financing corrects. Thus, the lack of correspondence causes the city to behave as if $1 million of resources have a value of only $50,000. Had the city been required to finance the project itself, it would have been unwilling to pay the $1 million if the project did not return at least $1 million in benefits to the community. When the correspondence principle is not followed, wasted resources are likely.

However, a broader geography for financing can also correct misallocations from spillovers. Consider a situation in which city A's sewage treatment plant dumps partially treated waste into a river. That river flows past city B, which draws river water for the municipal water utility. City A also draws water from the river, but it gets water from a point upstream of the sewage treatment discharge point. The more complete the sewage treatment is by city A, the lower the water-treatment costs are for city B, and the more attractive the river is to the residents of city B. The primary beneficiaries of city A's sewage treatment are residents of city B. Without some intervention by a geographically larger government—assistance designed to relieve city A of treatment plant expense incurred primarily for the benefit of those downstream—socially desirable actions probably would not be undertaken. City A's decision would be made by comparing returns to its residents (only a small portion of total returns) against the full cost of the complex. In this case, federal (or state) financing of a large share of project cost is justified (absent a politically difficult payment from city B to city A to pay for the treatment plant). That financing would allow city A to pay only to the extent its residents receive benefits, whereas federal (or state) taxpayers pay for returns received by outsiders.

Is Bigger Better?

Correspondence and subsidiarity imply relatively small size for providing many government services, subject only to the problems of externalities for some services. However, that ignores the possible unit-cost advantage of larger governments. Economies of scale, in the sense used in government finance, exist if the cost per person served decreases as the size of the service entity increases.[7] In other words, the cost per person of delivering a given level of fire protection would be smaller for a 100,000-person service district than for a 10,000-person service district. The scale advantage may also reflect the nonexhaustion property of public goods. In other words, up to a congestion point, the total cost of providing additional service does not rise as more people are served, so the cost per unit declines with size. If it costs $1,000,000 to provide a given level of public service, expanding the population served from 50,000 to 60,000 reduces unit cost from $20 per person to $16.67 per person. If such scale economies exist, then governments can economize by growing and consolidating regardless of the advantages the correspondence principle tells us are available in getting small units to better capture citizen preferences.

There are two problems with the general idea that larger governments operate more economically. First, empirical evidence shows there to be few traditional state and local government services that show substantial economies of scale except at small population sizes. Economies of scale do exist for capital-intensive services such as water supply, wastewater treatment, electricity, and gas distribution; however, for services such as police and fire protection and elementary and secondary education, unit cost seems not to vary much over a wide range of operating scales. That would be expected for most labor-intensive services.[8] In other words, the cost per person of delivering the service is pretty much the same for a small government provider as it is for a large government delivering the same service. Cost economies from bigness do not stand in the way of achieving the advantages of correspondence and subsidiarity from relative smallness.

Second, economies of scale refer to the conditions of production only. Size of government matters only if production and provision of the service are necessarily joined. If production by an external contractor is feasible, then scale economies are of no particular importance for determining size for provision decisions. Just as households need not be large enough to actually build an automobile at low cost in order to buy an inexpensive car, neither do governments need great size to provide service at an attractive price.[9] They may deal with larger governments, form cooperative supply arrangements with other small governments, or contract with

---

[7]From microeconomic theory, economies of scale occur in production when doubling all inputs—a double plant size, in other words—more than doubles output: "Because larger scale permits the introduction of different kinds of techniques, because larger productive units are more efficient, and because larger plants permit greater specialization and division of labor, the long-run average cost function declines, up to some point, with increases in output." Edwin Mansfield, *Microeconomics*, 7th ed. (New York: Norton, 1991), 199. In analysis of government services, the focus is commonly on population served and per capita cost rather than on cost per unit of product.

[8]Roy W. Bahl and Walter Vogt, *Fiscal Centralization and Tax Burden: State and Regional Financing of City Services* (Cambridge, Mass.: Ballinger, 1975), 13–14.

[9]There may be economies of scope. If that is the case, then a single firm may produce more than one product more cheaply than if each product was produced by a separate firm. For government operations, this would mean that there would be savings to be had from having one government provide a number of government services rather than having a separate government responsible for each distinct service. A merged public safety district would be less expensive than having a fire protection district and a police protection district.

private businesses for service provision depending on the circumstances. Therefore, even where there are cost advantages from large size, those advantages are from *producing* the service. Smaller units, designed under the principles of correspondence and subsidiarity, can make the provision decisions and contract with larger units for production, thereby gaining the best of large size for production and small size for purchase. Small local governments can provide a full range of local services without owning any resources for production or having any employees by contracting for service provisions with other governments or private firms. There are around forty contract cities in California that provide a complete array of municipal services for their population but have virtually no employees: the services are produced by other cities, by overlapping county governments, or by private firms according to city contract.[10] If the city is dissatisfied with either the cost or quality of the work being done, it can move on to another contractor or even start producing the service itself. That competition among competing providers can also help to reduce service cost and improve service quality.

The bottom line is that bigger might be better, but don't conclude that it is until after you have run the numbers and don't conclude that this would require a big government. Smaller is almost always going to be more responsive to local preferences.[11]

Fiscal Disparity

Another complication in intergovernmental service-delivery questions is disparity between regions. Some parts of a country or state are likely to be more affluent than others. Within the United States, per capita income of states ranges significantly—from an average of $34,431 in Mississippi and $36,132 in West Virginia to an average of $64,864 in Connecticut and $58,737 in Massachusetts in 2014.[12] Within each state, some localities have residents with considerably greater affluence than do others. Although resident incomes and affluence do not directly translate

---

[10]There is even an association of these cities (the California Contract Cities Association) that keeps track of common interests of localities choosing this form of government operation.

[11]One thorough analysis of the possibility of cost saving from consolidation in production of local government services characterized by heavy reliance on capital equipment, technology, or specialized skills—particularly 9-1-1 call handling and dispatch, public health, and high-level administrative and financial functions—in New England found considerable potential savings. Yolanda Kodrzycki, "The Quest for Cost-Efficient Local Government in New England: What Role for Regional Consolidation?," New England Public Policy Center Research Report 13-1 (February 2013).

[12]U.S. Department of Commerce, Bureau of Economic Analysis. An alternate measure, total taxable resources, prepared by the Office of Economic Policy of the Department of Treasury, more specifically gauges base available for states to tax. Per capita total taxable resources in 2009 ranged from $35,988 in Mississippi and $38,015 in West Virginia to $74,699 in Delaware and $74,021 in Connecticut, again a wide disparity in fiscal capacity. Disparity measured by total taxable resources is discussed in detail in John L. Mikesell, "Changing State Fiscal Capacity and Tax Effort in an Era of Devolving Government, 1981–2003," *Publius: The Journal of Federalism* 37 (2007): 532–50.

into an available tax base, similar differences occur in the tax base available to governments.[13] If fiscal resources differ among governments, otherwise equally situated individuals will have considerably different access to public services because of the relative affluence of their government.

The property tax provides a simple demonstration. Suppose Smith and Jones each own houses assessed at $10,000 for the property tax. Smith lives in a community with a property tax base of $40,000 per pupil in its public schools; Jones lives in a community with a property tax base of $20,000 per pupil. If a quality education uses resources costing $1,500 per pupil, Smith's community need levy only a property tax of $3.75 per $100 of assessed value to meet that cost. Jones's community would require a tax of $7.50 per $100. When both communities spend the same amount per pupil, the Jones's property must pay twice as much as the Smith's property for the same quality education ($750 versus $375). Thus, services rendered from a given tax rate—or level of *tax effort*—are greater where the capacity endowment is greater. Because there often is a mismatch between need for government services and capacity to finance those services, higher governments intervene by providing various fiscal assistance. Higher-level governments can use their tax systems to raise revenue and then distribute that revenue to lower-level governments, using that distribution to even out the disparities in fiscal capacity among those lower-level governments. As is discussed later in this chapter, state governments are particularly concerned with disparity problems as they affect local school finances.[14]

Fiscal disparity can be particularly acute between cities and their suburbs. In any metropolitan area, some parts are considerably more prosperous than others, and the distribution of the local government tax base may not be related well to where the needs for local government services are greatest. Localities with a revenue-rich economic base—for instance, a regional shopping center or an auto-sales mall for local sales tax communities or an electricity generating plant or a major industrial plant for real-property tax communities—can have huge fiscal affluence without much population at all; workers and shoppers generating that revenue base live in many other locations in the metropolitan area, and where they live is where the need for schools, police and fire protection, parks and recreation, and other local services is. A small number of metropolitan areas use *regional tax-base sharing* of the property tax to assist with the disparity problem (as well as to reduce competition

---

[13]An effort to calibrate total fiscal capacity and compare it with actual effort is the Advisory Commission on Intergovernmental Relations' representative tax system: Advisory Commission on Intergovernmental Relations, *1988 Fiscal Capacity and Effort*, M-170 (Washington, D.C.: Advisory Commission on Intergovernmental Relations, 1990). The representative tax system estimates how much revenue a jurisdiction would raise if it applied typical (national average) tax rates to the major tax bases; an index of that representative yield is the capacity estimate. Tracy Gordon, Richard Auzier, and John Iselin, "Assessing Fiscal Capacities of States, A Representative Revenue System—Representative Expenditure System Approach, Fiscal Year 2012," Urban Institute Research Report (March 2016) estimates per capita revenue capacity in North Dakota to be 2.125 times as great as that in Mississippi, clearly demonstrating the disparity issue. Canada uses a representative tax system measure of fiscal capacity in its primary financial aid program across provinces and territories.

[14]The disparity issue also applies to other local governments: Katharine Bradbury and Bo Zhao, "Measuring Non-school Fiscal Disparities among Municipalities," *National Tax Journal* 67 (March 2009): 25–56.

among local governments for new base-rich development). In these plans, a portion of commercial and industrial property assessment growth is pooled—the Minnesota Twin Cities program for seven counties captures 40 percent for the pool—to provide revenue for all the localities. A portion of local fiscal independence is surrendered for the common good of the metropolis and to smooth the tax spikes between localities that certain economic activities can produce. However, the sharing concept has critics as well: economic developments that are particularly rich in tax base are often not desirable neighbors, bringing noise, smells, traffic, and so on. That extra tax base—which can be used to enrich local services or to reduce local tax rates—may be a way of compensating the host community for those factors. Fiscal disparity can also be great between urban and rural areas within a state.

The United States differs from many other federations in that the federal government provides no general transfer programs to reduce differences in fiscal capacity among its subnational governments. Equalization grants are important programs in Australia, Canada, Germany, and elsewhere, all designed to reduce significant variation in fiscal resources among the component jurisdictions—regions, states, provinces, and so on. For instance, Section 36 of the Canadian Constitution states that equalization policies will "ensure that provincial governments have sufficient revenues to provide reasonably comparable levels of public service at reasonably comparable levels of taxation."[15] There are equalizing elements in some federal grant formulas, but no general program of fiscal equalization among states. Disparity equalization, to the extent it exists, is something that states do among their localities.

Coordination and Assistance: Tax Systems

Governments can tailor their revenue structures to provide mutually beneficial financial and administrative assistance. Such assistance, although not bringing new resources into a government, may improve access to the existing revenue base and may be arranged with minimal interference to local autonomy. The two general classes of revenue assistance are (1) relief in tax-base use and (2) assistance with revenue administration and compliance.

Revenue relief includes deductions and credits granted to the taxes of one unit in tax computations made for another unit. Both are important, but they work differently and have different clout. Deductibility causes the federal government to, in effect, pick up part of the burden of selected taxes paid to state or local government. For example, the federal individual income tax permits deduction of certain state and local taxes from the federal income tax base. The power of deduction can be demonstrated with a simple example. Suppose a taxpayer is in the 35 percent

---

[15]Part III, Equalization and Regional Disparities, Section 36, Constitution Act, 1982. Equalization Transfers go to all Territories and Provinces except Ontario and Alberta. All Provinces Receive Transfers For Support of the Health and Social Systems.

federal tax bracket. If his or her state income tax increases by $100, the taxpayer's net tax burden increases by only $65 because deducting that state tax reduces his or her federal liability by $35. The deduction rewards state and local governments that use deductible taxes by making their net cost to taxpayers less.[16] Increasing a deductible tax (like an individual income tax) is cheaper for residents of a state than is increasing a nondeductible excise tax or applying a user charge. Of course, the coordination effects are not extraordinarily strong (states continue to use nondeductible taxes), deductibility does not equalize wealth among lower units, and only taxpayers who itemize get the advantage of the deduction. Furthermore, taxpayers in high-tax states are likely to lose the deduction through the operation of the alternative minimum tax.[17]

A stronger device is the tax credit, an arrangement in which the tax levied by one government unit acts as full or partial payment of the liability owed to another government. That was the case for the federal tax on transfer of assets on death. A qualifying state tax would, up to a limit, be a credit against liability for the federal tax, meaning that the state tax would mean no net liability for the estate. That gave an almost overwhelming incentive for states to levy the tax—essentially free money to the state. But a credit does not alter the basic distribution of resources among states or localities. Affluent units remain affluent, and poor units remain poor, leaving one intergovernmental issue untouched. In general, the credit involves substantial implicit control of the lower government unit by the higher government unit.

Deductions and credits create a curious effect for state (or local) tax reductions—the loss of state tax revenue when such a tax cut is greater than the increase in disposable income available to its taxpayers. The other beneficiary of such a state or local tax cut is the federal government. Estimates suggest, for instance, that federal income tax revenue increased by between $1 billion and $1.7 billion in 1979 as a result of California's Proposition 13 property tax reduction.[18] Every state or local property or income tax reduction program brings more federal tax revenue because of the smaller federal deductions received by taxpayers in the jurisdiction—the state or locality loses revenue, taxpayers in the jurisdiction have increased disposable income, and federal tax collections from taxpayers in the jurisdiction increase. In other words, when your governor cuts taxes in your state, the U.S. Congress should send a note of thanks for the extra federal revenue.

Another set of revenue tools can assist with that part of the intergovernmental fiscal problem. These devices include source separation, cooperative administration, coordinated tax bases, tax supplements, and centralized administration, arrayed in order of high to low amounts of lower-level government involvement in operations.

---

[16]In the pre-1964 tax-reduction period—when marginal rates were as high as 91 percent—deductibility prevented taxpayers from encountering marginal rates above 100 percent.

[17]The tax deductibility issue is discussed in detail in Congressional Budget Office, *The Deductibility of State and Local Taxes* (Washington, D.C.: Congressional Budget Office, 2008).

[18]Report to the Comptroller General of the United States, *Will Federal Assistance Be Affected by Proposition 13?* GGD-78-101 (Washington, D.C.: General Accounting Office, 1978). Some state income taxes provide a tax deduction for federal income tax paid. Taxpayers in those states found that the federal income tax rebates of 2001 were taxable under the state income tax because their deduction for federal income tax paid was lower.

Table 14–1

Tax Source Separation, 1970 and 2013: Percentage of Revenue Collected by Level of Government

	Federal		State		Local	
	1970	2013	1970	2013	1970	2013
Reliance of Levels of Government on Tax Sources						
Taxes on Property	0	0	2.3	1.5	84.9	76.5
Taxes on Individual and Corporate Income	84.4	95	26.9	41.8	4.2	6.4
Taxes on Sales or Gross Receipts	12.5	3.1	56.8	46.5	7.9	12.6
Other Taxes	3.1	1.9	14	10.1	3	4.6
Distribution of Tax Sources by Level of Government						
Taxes on Property	0	0	3.5	2.9	96.8	97.1
Taxes on Individual and Corporate Income	89.4	86.6	9.4	12.1	1.2	1.3
Taxes on Sales or Gross Receipts	37.6	15.2	56.1	71.5	6.3	13.2
Other Taxes	36.6	31.2	53.9	52.7	9.4	16.2

SOURCES: Bureau of Census, Governments Division, Annual Survey of State and Local Government Finances and Executive Office of the President, Budget of the United States Government.

Separation of tax sources prevents tax overlapping. Vertical overlapping occurs when governments at different levels (say, federal and state) apply a tax to exactly the same base; horizontal overlapping occurs when more than one government at the same level (say, two different states) applies a tax to the same base. Overlapping not only may produce the nuisance of multiple taxpayer filings, but also may distort economic activity. If each level of government were guaranteed an exclusive use of particular tax bases, the vertical-overlap problem would be effectively eliminated. Table 14–1 presents the record on source separation in 1970 and 2013. Local governments dominated use of the property tax base in both years: more than 95 percent of all property tax collected in 1970 and 2013 went to local governments. Local governments did somewhat reduce their reliance on that tax over the years, from 84.9 percent of total tax revenue to 76.5 percent, but it remains the dominant local tax. States were the heaviest user of taxes on sales and gross receipts, 56.1 percent of total collections in 1970, increasing to 71.5 percent in 2013. That base plays a critical role in state tax structures, constituting 56.8 percent of their tax revenue in 1970 and 46.5 percent in 2013. The federal government collects just less than 90 percent of total taxes on individual and corporate income and that base is dominant in the federal tax structure, yielding 95 percent of the total in 2013. However, the importance of that base in state tax structures has increased substantially, from 26.9 percent in 1970 to 41.8 percent in 2013. In sum, there is some separation of use of the taxes, with federal domination of the income base, state domination of the sales and gross receipts base, and local domination of the property base, but the separation is distinct only with the latter. That may be because state and federal governments do not want the property base and local governments are stuck with it.

Governments show little taste for source separation as a response to vertical-coordination problems because all want access to the "better" sources regardless of how that may confuse tax administration, compliance, and transparency of the levy. Only sources viewed rightly or wrongly as inferior (such as the property tax) are likely to be happily shed by any level of government. Although source separation would be orderly, most governments would prefer expanded revenue options. The exception is, of course, the federal government, which steadfastly sticks with the income base.

Fortunately, there are coordination mechanisms that accommodate more than one level of government using a single tax base. These include (1) cooperative administration, (2) coordinated tax bases, (3) tax supplements, and (4) centralized administration.[19] *Cooperative administration* involves continuous contact and information exchange among taxing units. Sales tax administrators may inform their peers when a firm is found to be violating tax laws in a manner that would generate liability in other states. Income tax administrators may exchange information about audits. The Internal Revenue Service (IRS) may inform a state about audit findings for an individual living in that state. State business tax administrators may exchange information about contractors who should be registered to pay taxes in other states. Coordination is weak, but profitable for the parties because work done by one administration can generate revenue for another with little or no additional work. Bases, rates, and rate structures need not coincide among governments for this cooperation, but all governments can gain from the exchange. Indeed, every state in the United States links its income tax administration closely to the work of the IRS, has information exchange agreements with the IRS, and relies heavily on IRS enforcement for collection of income taxes.[20]

With *coordinated tax bases,* one government links its tax to some point in the tax structure of another government. For example, several states key their individual income tax to federal adjusted gross income, and a number of localities begin their local sales tax ordinances with definitions taken from their state sales tax. Other elements of the tax may differ from that point—different exemptions, rate patterns, rate levels, and so on—but the higher- and lower-level taxes have important common elements. The links reduce taxpayer compliance problems (one set of records can be used for both taxes, and some of the computations need not be replicated) and simplify administration across governments. However, substantial differences between the taxes reduce the gains in both compliance and administration.

Tax supplements provide more coordination, either through applying a lower-level rate on the base used by the higher level (many state sales taxes have supplements

---

[19]George Break, *Financing Government in a Federal System* (Washington, D.C.: Brookings Institution, 1980), 34.
[20]Evidence shows that the federal income tax audit rate does have an impact on state income tax compliance, generally allowing states to do almost no individual income tax audits on their own. Liucija Birskyte, *The Effects of IRS Audit Rates on State Individual Income Tax Compliance*, PhD dissertation, Indiana University (2008).

added by localities) or through applying a lower-level rate that is a percentage of tax paid to the higher level. This method dramatically reduces compliance requirements for taxpayers and cuts administration expenses when the supplementing unit refrains from adding extra features. Few government units can refrain from at least a few changes, and each change cuts the savings to taxpayers.

The final coordination system is *central administration* of a "piggyback" tax, a system in which a lower government unit applies its own rate to the tax base used by higher government. Full piggybacking would have the higher unit doing all administrative and enforcement work: the taxpayer reports on a single form to the higher unit, which records for and remits collections to the lower unit. Lower units must adopt the tax to receive revenue (it is not simply a system of tax sharing), but they cannot select a base structured differently from that used by the higher unit. Administrative economies are possible with single-unit administration, and the taxpayer can comply with multiple obligations at one time. Supplemental tax rates, however, do not permit a redistribution of resources among lower units. Most local sales taxes piggyback on their state sales tax—often, the local tax return consists only of some extra lines on the state sales tax return (that is the intent of the Sales Tax Streamline Program discussed in Chapter 10)—and local income taxes in Maryland, Indiana, and Iowa are similarly supplements to the state return. Most localities levy income taxes, however, that are not related to either federal or state taxes, often limiting the tax to wages and salaries ("earned" income). States that continue a state property tax apply them to the locally administered base, a rare example of piggybacking from state to local.[21] Piggybacking obviously provides considerable economy in collection, but at the cost of transparency in taxation. Taxpayers seldom know, without considerable checking, which government is levying what portion of the tax that they pay.

Coordination and Assistance: Grants

Grants transfer spending power from one government to another. In a multilevel governmental relationship, such as that between the federal government and the states or between a state and its localities, grants can compensate governments for benefit spillovers to nonresidents, reduce the problems created by fiscal disparity, encourage programs of special national merit, reduce special problems associated with regional economic decline, and encourage governments to implement management reform by making it a condition for receiving aid.[22] In other words, they can have a purpose in a federal system beyond simply using the supposedly

---

[21]In Canada, the federal government administers provincial individual and corporate income taxes, and most provincial sales taxes are harmonized with the national goods and services (value-added) tax for federal collection. In Quebec, provincial authorities administer the national goods and service tax along with the provincial retail sales tax.

[22]General Accounting Office, *Federal Grants: Design Improvements Could Help Federal Resources Go Further*, GAO/AIMD-97-7 (Washington, D.C.: U.S. Government Printing Office, 1996). A number of local governments instituted external financial audits for the first time because that was a condition to receive federal revenue-sharing funds.

stronger revenue administration capacity of the higher level to raise money for the lower level.

There is a classic conflict between the donor and the recipient in transfer systems, a conflict that can never be entirely resolved. The donor government raises the revenue, bearing whatever political burdens may be associated with the revenue function. The recipient government gets any political benefits associated with service delivery. Because the recipient did not have to raise the money, might it be likely that the funds will be mismanaged or misallocated? To prevent such carelessness (or worse), the donor seeks controls, or "strings," on the use of the funds. The recipient government, of course, views the situation differently. The granting government is less familiar with local conditions, needs, and priorities. Any controls make service delivery more difficult and reduce the ability to provide needed services. The controls that the donor seeks to ensure accountability are viewed by the recipient as barriers to effective response.

A significant amount of the money spent by state and local governments comes from assistance provided by other levels of government. The general pattern of intergovernmental aid between 1971-1972 and 2011-2012 appears in Table 14–2. In 2011-2012, 32.74 percent of state revenue and 37.04 percent of local revenue consisted of assistance in the form of grants from other levels of government, transfers to states being a somewhat higher share than forty years earlier but transfers to localities about the same. Aid to states was mostly from the federal government, and aid to localities was mostly from their states; that continues today. Among local governments, aid is particularly vital to school districts; they received 59.55 percent of their general revenue from aid in 2011-2012, with 88.49 percent of that coming from states. In spite of all the talk from federal politicians about American elementary and secondary education, the finances are mostly state and local, although the federal share has increased from 4.24 percent in 1971-1972 to 9.07 percent in 2011-2012. States received a somewhat increased share of revenue from aid in 2011-2012 compared with 1971-1972 (from 28.37 percent to 32.74 percent), and the share to localities has remained about the same (from 37.72 to 37.04 percent). Aid to school districts has increased significantly for reasons that are discussed later in this chapter.

The flows of federal aid to state and local governments have recently increased. As Table 14–3 shows, aid rose through the late 1970s to the mid-1980s to more than 20 percent of total state-local general revenue, but then fell as the environment became what John Shannon called "fend-for-yourself federalism," one in which governments spending money were expected to raise that money.[23] Recently, the share has risen again, driven by what the federal budget classifies as outlays for state and local government aid for payments to individuals, including Medicaid and certain welfare programs, through which state administrative agencies distribute this federal assistance. (It has also increased somewhat with assistance to help states and

---

[23]John Shannon, "The Return to Fend-for-Yourself Federalism: The Reagan Mark," *Intergovernmental Perspective* 13 (Summer–Fall 1987): 34–37. The United States expects subnational governments to raise a considerably greater share of the money spent than do most other nations, including the major federal states (Australia, Canada, and Germany)—it always has, and probably always will.

Table 14–2
Source of Intergovernmental Revenue ($ Millions)

	Total General Revenue ($M)	Total Transfers ($M)	Transfers from Federal ($M)	Transfers from State ($M)	Transfers from Local ($M)	Total as % General Revenue	Transfers from Federal (% Total Transfers)	Transfers from State (% Total Transfers)	Transfers from Local (% Total Transfers)
1971–1972									
State	98,632	27,981	26,791	–	1,191	28.37%	95.75%	0.00%	4.26%
Local	105,243	39,694	4,551	35,143	–	37.72%	11.47%	88.53%	0.00%
Cities	34,998	11,528	2,538	8,434	556	32.94%	22.02%	73.16%	4.82%
Counties	23,652	9,956	405	9,252	299	42.09%	4.07%	92.93%	3.00%
School districts	39,256	17,653	749	16,471	433	44.97%	4.24%	93.30%	2.45%
1991–1992									
State	608,804	169,928	159,068	–	10,861	27.91%	93.61%	0.00%	6.39%
Local	579,083	217,996	20,107	197,890	–	37.65%	9.22%	90.78%	0.00%
Cities	175,116	49,474	8,103	37,380	3,992	28.25%	16.38%	75.55%	8.07%
Counties	148,367	55,292	3,243	49,663	2,386	37.27%	5.87%	89.82%	4.32%
School districts	198,320	107,160	1,354	103,084	27,222	54.03%	1.26%	96.20%	25.40%
2001–2002									
State	1,062,628	33,543	317,583	0	17,851	3.16%	946.79%	0.00%	53.22%
Local	995,779	398,641	42,964	355,677	0	40.03%	10.78%	89.22%	0.00%
Cities	286,036	85,290	15,212	62,538	7,539	29.82%	17.84%	73.32%	8.84%
Counties	257,167	99,122	7,539	86,759	4,823	38.54%	7.61%	87.53%	4.87%
School districts	350,793	199,544	3,632	191,145	4,767	56.88%	1.82%	95.79%	2.39%
2011–2012									
State	1,630,035	533,658	514,139	0	19,519	32.74%	96.34%	0.00%	3.66%
Local	1,456,674	539,507	70,360	469,147	0	37.04%	13.04%	86.96%	0.00%
Cities	425,930	110,748	23,642	77,426	9,680	26.00%	21.35%	69.91%	8.74%
Counties	368,757	132,110	14,012	110,698	7,400	35.83%	10.61%	83.79%	5.60%
School Districts	493,487	293,857	26,643	260,042	7,172	59.55%	9.07%	88.49%	2.44%

SOURCE: U.S. Bureau of Census, Governments Division, State and Local Government Finances. www.census.gov

Table 14-3
Federal Aid to State and Local Governments

Fiscal Year	Federal Outlays for Grants to State-Local Governments ($ billions of constant 2009)	Grants for Individuals	Grants for Capital Investment	Grants for Other	Percent of Grants by Function — Transportation General	Education	Health	Income	Federal Aid as % State-Local Revenue
1960	52.4	13.3	19.6	12.3	42.7	7.5	3.0	37.5	13.7
1965	76.4	18.8	27.9	19.2	37.6	9.6	5.7	32.2	14.9
1970	142.7	37.3	31.4	55.0	19.1	26.7	16.0	24.1	16.7
1975	215.3	53.5	30.0	103.4	11.8	24.4	17.7	18.8	20.6
1980	264.7	71.1	44.9	111.1	14.2	23.9	17.2	20.2	21.7
1985	217.6	83.5	39.5	66.6	16.1	16.1	23.1	26.3	17.8
1990	224.3	107.6	37.6	53.0	14.2	16.1	32.4	27.2	16.1
1995	318.7	175.7	50.0	57.9	11.5	13.7	41.6	25.9	19.2
2000	366.9	203.2	56.5	67.0	11.3	12.8	43.7	24.0	18.5
2005	480.4	273.9	60.8	93.3	10.1	13.4	46.2	21.2	21.1
2010	603.0	342.1	74.4	110.5	10.0	16.0	47.7	18.9	n.a.
2013	509.7	349.3	74.0	86.3	11.0	11.5	51.8	18.7	n.a.

SOURCE: Bureau of Census, Government Division and Executive Office of the President, Office of Management and Budget, *Historical Tables: Budget of the United States Government, Fiscal Year 2014.* (Washington, D.C.: USGOR, 2013).
n.a., Data not available.

localities during the Great Recession, although the increase has not been as significant as in other recent recessions.) That category now constitutes almost two-thirds of the total.[24] A considerable amount of the capital-investment aid comes through trust funds supporting highways and airports. That share is far less now than it once was, which is an important contributor to our crumbling public transportation infrastructure. In terms of government function, virtually all federal aid comes through four categories: health, income security, education, and transportation, as Table 14–3 shows. Growth in Medicaid spending is particularly important for the increase, and it is the largest single federal grant program to state and local governments.

Both federal and state governments operate intergovernmental assistance programs. Many problems and structural features are common to both. The federal grant system has included three types of assistance: (1) categorical grants, (2) block grants, and (3) from 1972 through 1986, general revenue sharing.[25] The last is a type of general fiscal assistance, a more common element of state-to-local grant programs. There is much hybridization of grant styles, making clear classification difficult. However, the great preponderance of federal grant programs—measured in both numbers and outlay totals—are categorical grant programs.[26] A federal website provides the *Catalog of Domestic Federal Assistance* (http://www.cdfa.gov) to guide anyone through the 2,312 federal assistance programs (the count as of 2015).

State aid systems have some elements similar to the federal system, although each state has its own peculiar mix. State grants to general-purpose local governments (mostly cities and counties) have always been for relatively broad purposes. The grants sometimes distribute earmarked percentages of certain state taxes. In a later section, we examine state aid to schools, a major component of total state aid.

Categorical Grants

Categorical grants finance specific and narrowly defined programs, usually limited to spending for certain activities, such as constructing a wastewater-treatment plant or paying salaries of special education teachers. Such aid seeks to induce the recipient government to behave in a fashion other than the way it would behave without the aid. The grants encourage recipient governments to shift expenditures to particular functions or to guarantee provision of certain recipient government services in a

---

[24]Medicaid provides medical assistance for low-income people who are aged, blind, disabled, members of families with dependent children, and certain other pregnant women and children. States establish their own coverage rules, scope of benefits offered, and amounts paid for services, all within guidelines established by the federal government. The federal government then pays a portion of the total spent by the state, according to an annually adjusted rate that ranges between 50 and 83 percent; the rate is inversely related to state per capita income. This is a categorical formula grant program.

[25]The federal government also assists state and local governments through credit, either directly via loans and advances or indirectly through loan guarantees.

[26]Advisory Commission on Intergovernmental Relations, *Characteristics of Federal Grant-in-Aid Programs to State and Local Governments: Grants Funded FY 1995,* M-195 (Washington, D.C.: Advisory Commission on Intergovernmental Relations, 1995), 3.

manner consistent with national interest. In these areas, narrow local interest and national interest presumably do not coincide. The grant changes the returns as seen by the recipient to make certain activities more attractive—the federal share makes the aided activity cheaper for the lower-level government—so that recipient actions coincide with national interest.

Categorical grants may be:

1. **Formula,** in which aid is distributed among eligible governments according to a legislatively or administratively determined formula. Formula elements may include population, population in certain demographic categories, per capita income, unemployment, energy use, housing categories, fiscal capacity, program performance, highway lane miles, or other measures. For example, the Dingell-Johnson Sport Fish Restoration Program (Federal Aid in Sport Fish Restoration Act of 1950) distributes funds to state fish and wildlife agencies according to a formula that includes the state share of land and water area, miles of coastline, and paid fishing license holders.[27]

2. **Project,** in which aid is distributed at the discretion of the administrator for particular projects. These grants are usually awarded on a competitive basis from applications made to support a particular proposal from a state or local government (or other entity).

3. **Project/formula,** in which aid is distributed at the discretion of the administrator within constraints set by a formula that limits amounts awarded in a state. For instance, the Recreational Trails program in the Department of Transportation provides formula assistance for development of trails for nonmotorized and motorized use with an 80 percent matching requirement.[28]

These grants may have *matching* provisions that require the recipient to spend a specified sum for each dollar spent by the federal government in the grant (the match can often be in-kind contributions to a program, such as office space, rather than cash) or *maintenance of effort* provisions that require the recipient to continue a specified level of spending in a specific area to receive the federal funds and to use the funds to supplement, not supplant, spending.[29]

Project grants—about 70 percent of all categorical grant programs, but considerably less than half of total categorical aid outlay—are the realm of the grants person, the individual assigned by many state and local governments and nonprofit agencies to manage the quest for external assistance. (Formula and reimbursement categories, plus the block and revenue-sharing assistance examined later, do not require competitive application to receive the funds but do require competent reporting of use of the funds.) This person becomes familiar with the activities of federal agencies and

---

[27]Find it in the *Catalog of Federal Domestic Assistance.* https://www.cfda.gov/index?s5program&mode5for m&tab5step1&id529bb1c73e764c9635937ebbdd1140393

[28]Ibid. https://www.cfda.gov/index?s5program&mode5form&tab5step1&id597e2194928c0e1bde5aaf7-b62023b196

[29]Evidence indicates that about 60 cents of each federal grant dollar substitutes for state funds that would have been spent anyway. General Accounting Office, *Federal Grants*, GAO/AIMD-97-7 (Washington, D.C.: General Accounting Office), 2.

private foundations (state governments tend not to use project grants) and watches available funding announcements published in sources such as the *Federal Register* and the *Catalog of Federal Domestic Assistance*. When project requirements and the activities of the government coincide, the manager prepares a project proposal. The funding agency awards go to proposals evaluated as best according to legislative and regulatory constraints. Decisions are based on the extent to which the proposal responds to the requirements presented in the funding advertisement, the extent to which the proposer demonstrates ability to carry out the project, and other factors such as the creativity or novelty of the project approach or the possibility that results may be used elsewhere. Selection criteria and weighting among factors are usually published with program announcements. Skeptics stress the significance of noncompetitive, political factors in some assistance programs, however. These are the earmarked or pork-barrel projects described in an earlier chapter. Sidebar 14–1 outlines basic rules for writing a grant proposal to a government or nongovernment donor.

Sidebar 14–1
Some Basic Guides for Writing Grant Proposals

Most federal assistance to state and local governments is provided on a noncompetitive basis for particular programs, as is virtually all state aid to their local governments. However, some assistance is awarded competitively to particular projects on the basis of grant proposals, as are awards from foundations and other nongovernmental organizations. Although grant writing is more art than science, a few simple steps can assist in grant proposal preparation.

1. Read the materials provided by the granting entity with great care. Often the information comes in the form of a "request for proposals" (RFP), and the instructions included there are to be followed scrupulously. The RFP indicates deadlines for submission (which, for federal agencies and most other donors, are rigidly enforced), instructions for submission, format and style for the submission, and a description of the kinds of projects that can be proposed. The proposed project must fit the intent and guidelines of the competition. If it doesn't, then writing the proposal is just a waste of time. If you are not sure whether what you have in mind is the sort of thing that might be competitive, then check with the program officer before devoting much time to the proposal.
2. Write the proposal in the language of the RFP. The proposal should use exactly the same terminology, key phrases, concepts, and so on that the RFP uses. One grantsperson has described this as "writing the RFP back to the agency." This approach is effective in part because the people who wrote the RFP are likely to be evaluating the proposals and seeing their own words coming back is a nice form of flattery. Besides, they are experts in the area being supported, and this degree of consistency is only logical. If you can't use the terminology of the RFP in what you are proposing, then probably this isn't the right grant competition for the project you have in mind.
3. Keep in contact with the granting entity. Unless there are rules that forbid advance contact, you should let the agency know that your proposal will be coming, and you should find out as much

about the agency's interests as you can. Part of this work involves studying proposals that have been funded by the agency in the past, if they are available for public inspection, so that you can get hints about what might be sensible in your project and how successful projects have been structured. Even if full proposals are not available, you should be able to obtain brief abstracts, and these can be helpful as you develop your proposal. Many grant competitions have "no contact" periods after the submission deadline. You may not contact the agency about your proposal after that date, and you must take care not to cross the line and have your proposal ruled ineligible by accident.

4. Follow the traditional guidelines for preparing budget requests (review the relevant sections of Chapter 3) in your proposal because, after all, a budget request and a grant proposal are logically the same. The proposal must describe what is intended in the project, what resources will be necessary, what funds are requested, and what results of the project are expected—just as with a fully developed agency budget request. The RFP frequently specifies a format for the submission, and it usually specifies a particular budget classification structure and certain standards for the budget. These requirements need to be followed to make the proposal eligible for consideration. If the instructions say "double-space," then the proposal absolutely must be double-spaced. No exceptions.

5. Agencies frequently enter into negotiations about the proposal after the first review of competitors. To receive a call for further information or for revisions of your proposal is usually a good sign because it means that your proposal has passed the first set of tests and the chances that your proposal will be funded are very good.

Grant proposals, even for good projects, are not always successful. Following these simple steps can improve the likelihood that a strong project—and some not-so-strong ones—will receive support.

One peculiarity of the categorical grant must be recognized. For the recipient, the grant is most valuable if it supports an activity the recipient was going to undertake even without the assistance. In that case, there is minimal disruption of local interest, and resources are released for use in accord with local priorities. For the donor, the grant is most powerful when it supports activities not ordinarily undertaken at levels consistent with the donor's interest. Thus, there is some divergence of interest between recipient and donor in a well-designed categorical grant.

Critics of the categorical grant system emphasize three particular difficulties. First is the administrative complexity of the categorical grant system. In an effort to ensure that federal policy objectives are met as nearly as possible by the recipients, federal programs establish elaborate control mechanisms to monitor and shape actions taken by the recipient. These mechanisms usually have different planning, application, reporting, and accounting requirements—none of which coincide with those ordinarily used by the recipient government. Not only are these controls an irritation, but also they divert state and local resources to the administrative process. Some programs may be deemed to have so many controls and required expenditures that they are not worth applying for.

A second criticism is the program overlap and duplication that has emerged in the federal grant system. Complexity means that some communities do not participate, leaving their residents less well served than would be desirable. Other local governments aggressively seek funds, producing extraordinary assistance for their residents. Governments may even use funds from one program to meet another program's matching requirements, thus thwarting the intention of matching to stimulate local expenditure.

Third, critics complain that categorical grants distort local priorities. Although grant requirements try to reflect national interests, the distortion may exceed the level justified by the traditional spillover-of-local-action argument. Furthermore, the aid may not be reliable. Aid may be eliminated after a few years, leaving state and local governments with program responsibility, but no resources. The combination of these criticisms has been instrumental in movement toward block assistance and calls for a return to general-purpose assistance.

Block Grants

Block grants are usually distributed to general-purpose governments (categorical grants often go to special-purpose governments or non-governments) according to a statutory formula to finance activities in a broad functional area. Recipients have considerable discretion in how to spend the money. Among the features of federal block grants are these: "[A]id is authorized for a wide range of activities within a broadly defined functional area; recipients have substantial discretion to identify problems, design programs, and allocate resources; administrative, fiscal reporting, planning, and other federally imposed requirements are limited to those necessary to ensure that national goals are being accomplished; and federal aid is distributed on the basis of statutory formula with few, if any, matching requirements and, historically, spending has been capped."[30] Federal block grants support programs that include health (Community Mental Health Services, Prevention and Treatment of Substance Abuse, Maternal and Child Health Services, Preventive Health and Health Services), crime control (Local Law Enforcement, Juvenile Accountability Incentive), community development (Community Development), social services (Social Services, Child Care and Development, Low-Income Home Energy Assistance, Community Services), aid for the needy (Temporary Assistance for Needy Families), and emergency management (Emergency Management Performance).[31] Some federal lawmakers prefer block grants because they do cap federal spending and may encourage recipient agencies to be more efficient in use of grant resources.

---

[30]General Accounting Office, *Block Grants: Issues in Designing Accountability Provisions,* GAO/AIMD-95-226 (Washington, D.C.: General Accounting Office, 1995), 4.
[31]Plus special block grants for Native Americans.

The largest single surge of conversion from categorical to block grants in terms of programs involved was in the Omnibus Reconciliation Act of 1981 (P.L. 97–35), when fifty-seven categoricals were consolidated into nine block grants (social services; home-energy assistance; community development; elementary and secondary education; alcohol, drug abuse, and mental health; maternal and child care; community services; primary health care; and preventative health and health services). Federal welfare reform, through the Personal Responsibility and Work Opportunity Reconciliation Act of 1996 (P.L. 104–193), added welfare to the list of block grants to states by replacing Aid to Families with Dependent Children (AFDC), a formula entitlement paid to states for distribution to needy mothers and children, with a multiyear, fixed-appropriation block grant to states for support of the welfare programs. The new program is Temporary Assistance to Needy Families or TANF. The appropriated amount is distributed among states by a formula based on money each state received for programs it replaced—either the higher of fiscal 1994 or fiscal 1995 or the average of fiscal 1992–1994. State programs must be within certain federal standards, and states must achieve certain performance goals to continue to receive the funds.

The Advisory Commission on Intergovernmental Relations maintained that block grants with "well-designed allocation formulas and eligibility provisions" could:

1. Provide aid to those jurisdictions having the greatest programmatic needs and give them a reasonable degree of fiscal certainty.
2. Accord recipients substantial discretion in defining problems, setting priorities, and allocating resources.
3. Simplify program administration and reduce paperwork and overhead.
4. Facilitate interfunctional and intergovernmental coordination and planning.
5. Encourage greater participation on the part of elected and appointed generalist officials in decision making.[32]

Block grants should not be expected to stimulate new recipient-government initiatives and should be confined to activities for which a broad consensus already exists. Block grants are not designed to bend local choices in a direction more consistent with national interest or to cause local government units to change their operating methods. They may replace groups of similar categoricals that have already established strong local clienteles. However, critics complain that block grants, especially community development block grants, usually aid affluent as well as poor communities and that some funds get used in ways that would stretch congressional intentions. Donors worry about how the programs can ensure accountability for spending and for outcomes. Federal block grant funding has recently been restrained as one casualty on the path toward expenditure constraint.

---

[32]Advisory Commission on Intergovernmental Relations, *Characteristics,* 24.

Revenue Sharing (General-Purpose Fiscal Assistance)

The third variety of federal grants is revenue sharing, a formula distribution with few or no restrictions on the use of funds provided.[33] The federal revenue-sharing program, started in 1972, used a formula to distribute multiyear appropriations to states and general-purpose local governments. The funding approach—appropriation rather than a share of certain taxes—provided some greater certainty of aid during the appropriation's life (unforeseen changes in federal revenue did not influence distributed shares), but the funds had to be appropriated again when the appropriation period expired. The program was the primary source of the increase in the federal share of state and local general revenue in 1975 and 1980 that was shown in Table 14–3. Each renewal raised questions about the program's continuation; the entire program was excluded from the 1986 budget. Similar (and older) state tax-sharing programs typically dedicate a given share of selected taxes (e.g., 1 percentage point of the state sales tax rate) to a local-aid formula. Such programs are used in a large number of states for support of a wide array of local services, and the service to be supported is often targeted in the program (e.g., a portion of the state motor-fuel tax for support of local streets and roads).

Federal revenue sharing distributed funds according to a formula that combined population, percentage of urban population, tax effort, income tax effort, and per capita income to define the appropriate shares. State governments initially received one-third of revenue-sharing funds, but were gradually removed. Checks were sent to each eligible government without application and with only minimal restrictions concerning use (there had to be a publicized appropriation process, there could be no discrimination in hiring or compensation, funds could not be used for grant matching, use had to be subject to external financial audit, etc.).[34]

Although federal revenue sharing ended at the national level in 1986, such programs continue as an important feature of several state fiscal systems, including those of Michigan, Alaska, Louisiana, Florida, Maine, and Wisconsin. The distributions are sometimes of dedicated shares of particular taxes and sometimes of specific appropriations. The distributions are by formula, and the funds are for general use by the recipient government with few, if any, controls. When these distributions are on a per capita basis, they reduce fiscal disparity to an extent because the per capita amount provides greater relative assistance to lower-capacity areas than to higher-capacity ones. High-capacity areas pay more into the state aid pool than they receive in return.

Programs of revenue or tax sharing can strengthen local spending power and reduce differences in fiscal capacity across governments. Such programs would not shape local priorities to make them more consistent with national interest because

---

[33]Although they are not general, the federal government does have a few shared taxes, levied at the federal level for formula distribution to state government for specific use. The most significant of these support the highway and airport and airway trust funds. These funds do have to be appropriated, however; they are not automatically distributed to states.

[34]Some large American cities had never had an external financial audit before the general revenue sharing era. Inducing them to be audited can be counted as a benefit of the program, over and above any services ultimately delivered by the grant revenue.

of the lack of controls placed on the assistance. They would not be particularly effective as a way to aid disadvantaged groups because advantaged and disadvantaged tend, with few exceptions, to live in the same political jurisdictions. General aid to the jurisdiction can improve capacity to provide services (or reduce taxes with no change in services) for anyone, and probably the advantaged will do better because they usually have greater political clout. Revenue sharing should not be expected to achieve the targeting and revision of public action that categorical programs can produce. Revenue sharing can reduce fiscal disparity among governments and strengthen the expenditure capability of government units with constrained taxing powers.

Tax-sharing programs from central to subnational governments are a common feature of the finances of many countries, including both unitary and federal systems and many countries of the former Soviet Union, but not the United States. In these programs, the central government adopts a tax (for instance, an individual income tax) and establishes what share of collections will be assigned to regional or local governments (for instance, 25 percent). In this example, 25 percent of individual income tax collected in each region or locality is distributed to that government. Fiscal choices are made centrally, but a share of the tax accrues to the lower-tier government. Shared revenue may be returned to the region from which it was collected or it may be distributed by formula (for instance, equal per capita shares).

States and School Aid

Elementary and secondary education in the United States has traditionally been a local activity, either of independent school districts or, in some larger cities, of city governments. That arrangement allows local decision making and control so that choices can be made by governments close to the families affected most by the schools. However, state governments have ultimate responsibility for the provision of education; state constitutions contain education clauses that require the state to provide statewide systems of education that are "equitable," "thorough and efficient," "adequate," "general and uniform," and so forth.[35] Local finance seems likely to violate the idea of a "statewide" system because local fiscal capacity (the local tax base) per pupil—and thus access to educational resources—varies widely among

---

[35]Earlier concerns with equal-protection violations of the U.S. Constitution were resolved in favor of the states in 1973. See *Rodriguez v. San Antonio Independent School District,* 411 U.S. 1 (1973). Recent challenges have involved state constitutional requirements. Some of the challenges have brought increased school spending, but some appear to have caused spending to be less than would otherwise have been expected. See Robert L. Manwaring and Steven M. Sheffrin, "Litigation, School Finance Reform, and Aggregate Education Spending," *International Tax and Public Finance* 4 (May 1997): 107–27. Only Delaware, Hawaii, Mississippi, Nevada, and Utah have not had a lawsuit over such school finance issues. Jennifer Carr and Cara Griffith, "School Finance Litigation and Property Tax Reform: Part I, Litigation," *State Tax Notes* (June 27, 2005): 1015.

Table 14–4
Public School District Revenues by Source of Funds, Percentage of Total

School Year	Federal (%)	State (%)	Local (%)
1939-1940	1.8	30.3	68.0
1949-1950	2.9	39.8	57.3
1959-1960	4.4	39.1	56.5
1969-1970	8.0	39.9	52.1
1979-1980	9.8	46.8	43.4
1989-1990	6.1	47.1	46.8
1999-2000	7.3	49.5	43.2
2009-2010	12.7	43.4	43.9
2012-2013	9.3	45.2	45.5

SOURCE: U.S. Department of Education Sciences, National Center for Education Statistics, *Digest of Education Statistics* [online].

districts. Not all local school districts are created equal, so how can the education that they provide be considered equitable across the state? How can this state-provided system of education be accommodated with local control when localities have significant differences in preferences for schooling and in fiscal resources to fund those schools?

There are no simple answers to the dilemma, but one response has been an increased state role in public school finance (Table 14–4). The trend shows an expanding state role in finance, from 30.3 percent of total revenues in 1939-1940 to 45.2 percent in 2012-2013, and a falling local role, 68.0 percent to 45.5 percent in the same period. (The federal role is greater as well, having increased from 1.8 percent to 9.3 percent, but is still small.) However, 2012-2013 state shares do vary widely, from 26.1 percent in Illinois to 88.9 percent in Vermont.[36] Local school revenue remains almost exclusively a matter of the property tax (90.7 percent of school revenue from local sources), whereas state finances are usually balanced between sales and income taxes and provide an opportunity for state-aid systems to offset disparities in resources among local districts. In some states, property tax relief has been provided by having the state government assume a greater share of the cost of local schools.

There are two big catches with the increased state role in public school finance. First, when the state pays the bills, the state will almost certainly want increased control over what goes on in the local schools. The greater the extent of state financing, the less local officials will have to say about local programs and policies. Second, local school finances become vulnerable to the fiscal condition of state government.

---

[36]U.S. Census Bureau, Governments Division, *Public Education Finances Report: 2012-2013*. http://www.census.gov

A frequent state response to the difficult finances of the recession that started in 2007 was to reduce the amount of money provided to school districts in the state, a common response whenever states experience some fiscal difficulty. The state problem gets punted away to the localities. The local districts then get to decide what to do: cut programs, find more revenue, or implement some combination. The choices get even more difficult if the state has placed strict limits on use of the property tax. A local property tax has considerably greater stability than aid from state government.

School-aid systems that states use are remarkable for their complexity as legislators seek to balance local control, state responsibility, and protection for their home districts. It should be no surprise that distribution formulas combine various philosophies. Three general systems have been devised to distribute basic state aid:[37]

1. **Flat grants, general and categorical.** In a few states, every school district receives the same dollar amount per pupil from the state. There is no distinction between high-affluence and low-affluence districts. Some aid may be distributed according to types of students or to finance certain categories of expenditure (such as student transportation on a bus-mile basis).

2. **Foundation grants.** The foundation programs, used in about three-fourths of the states, aid in direct proportion to the number of students and inversely with the local property tax base per pupil. Aid per pupil to a district equals the difference between the per-pupil foundation spending level (the amount of expenditure the state determines to be the minimum acceptable) and the per-pupil revenue the district would collect by applying the statewide target tax rate to the district tax base. States usually require the district to spend at least the foundation amount to receive aid. The aid is designed to fill the gap between the expected foundation spending per pupil and the capacity of the district to finance the spending itself.[38]

3. **Guaranteed tax base (or percentage equalizing).** These formulas provide aid to districts to make up the difference between what the district tax rate raises on the district tax base and what the district tax rate would raise if applied to a guaranteed tax base. Therefore, without regard to actual district affluence per pupil, all districts will raise the same tax per pupil from a given tax rate. Aid systems may add other factors, such as adjustments for differences in operating costs among districts, for service to special client populations, or to prevent substantial aid loss from year to year. The elements in a state formula may change often, as may the money the state puts into state aid. Many states create hybrids that distribute total aid according to more than one logical system.

States generally are uncomfortable with state school-aid systems. A considerable amount of state revenue has to be raised for school support, and many critics

---

[37]Katherine L. Bradbury, "Equity in School Finance: State Aid to Local Schools in New England," *New England Economic Review* (March/April 1993): 25–46.
[38]It is the estimated capacity for self-finance, not actual revenues, to prevent the district from reducing its own taxes to allow more of the cost to be borne by the state.

question whether its distribution satisfies the responsibility that states have for seeing to the provision of this service. Local control and state responsibility are real concerns that no system has fully resolved. Almost every state legislative session will produce new struggles about state assistance to local schools.

Coordination and Assistance: Mandates

A mandate is a constitutional provision, a statute, an administrative regulation, or a judicial ruling that places an expenditure requirement on a government. That requirement comes from outside the government forced to take the action.[39] A state government can mandate local spending, the federal government can mandate either state or local spending, and the judiciary—the branch of government outside the normal budgeting and appropriation flow—can mandate spending at any level. Mandates are like the operating restrictions that governments place on private industry to regulate workplace safety, environmental quality, and so on—or on individuals to purchase health insurance. Indeed, some costly mandates are simply extensions to government of these regulations of the private sector.[40] Much concern about mandates emerges at the local level because these government units typically lack the size needed to respond flexibly to external expenditure shocks (few individual mandates would be sufficiently large, relative to overall expenditure, to significantly disrupt the federal government) and lack the revenue options available to other levels. States also express considerable concern for mandated cost, even as they place such cost on their localities.[41]

Mandates seek to cause governments to behave in some manner other than the way they would ordinarily behave. This changed behavior can be directed toward either (1) services and programs or (2) inputs used (normally, personnel). Examples of the former include such things as hours libraries will be open, provision of special education by local schools, jail-condition standards, water temperature in hospitals, provision of legal defense for indigents, and accessibility of facilities to all. Input use mandates encompass required compensation levels, resources acquired, input

---

[39]Advisory Commission on Intergovernmental Relations, *State Mandating of Local Expenditures* (Washington, D.C.: Advisory Commission on Intergovernmental Relations, July 1978). *Gideon v. Wainwright*, 372 U.S. 335 (1963) and *Argersinger v. Hamlin*, 407 U.S. 25 (1972) illustrate two court mandates (defense attorneys must be provided if the defendant cannot afford to pay).

[40]In *Garcia v. San Antonio Metropolitan Transit Authority*, 469 U.S. 70 (1985), the Supreme Court held that the federal Fair Labor Standards Act of 1938, mandating standards for overtime pay and minimum wages, applied to state and local government. The cost implications are substantial. In *Monell v. Department of Social Services of the City of New York*, 436 U.S. 658 (1978), the Court eroded the idea of sovereign immunity by extending the right of citizens to sue a government for negligent acts of its employees.

[41]Governments also pick up restrictions as a result of accepting grants from federal or state governments. Grant controls create fewer logistical problems than ordinary mandates because the recipient government accepts obligations as a condition of accepting the funds. There is no compulsion to enter the system. The Advisory Commission on Intergovernmental Relations describes the major federal mandates in *Federal Regulation of State and Local Governments: The Mixed Records of the 1980s* (Washington, D.C.: Advisory Commission on Intergovernmental Relations, 1993).

quality and quantity, and the conditions under which the input will be employed. All potentially change the cost of providing any given level of service. Examples include state determination of local welfare department salaries; required employee training; required funding for pension systems; required participation in unemployment insurance or workers' compensation systems; and regulation of wages, hours, and working conditions. Several of this latter group are simply extensions of requirements applied to private employers.

Beyond the mandates, there are many other state controls on local government action because states establish the "rules of the game" for localities: election frequency, budget and finance structures, permissible forms of government, due process definitions, and so on. Many of these standards cause extra expenditure, but we accept them as reasonable costs of an informed democracy. Rules of the game, however, are often designed to reduce local government costs by limiting competition among local units, restricting direct democracy initiatives and official elections, constraining elected officials' salaries, or defining tax processes on a statewide basis. They are clearly of a different nature than the earlier group of mandates. Other interventions determine tax-burden distribution as the scope of local taxation is defined (e.g., residential electricity may be removed from the local sales tax base). Furthermore, these controls, along with controlling the rules of the game, are best considered with the home-rule issue and the balance between local power and state sovereignty. One of the biggest state mandates on local governments in 2009 was the effort by the state of California to force municipalities to "loan" the state $2 billion in property tax revenue to help the state with its huge fiscal problem. States frequently reduce transfers to their localities when state finances are difficult, but this proposal sets new standards for forceful application of Dillon's Rule.[42]

The case for mandates has two logical elements. First, the benefit of a lower unit's action (or the cost of its inaction) may spill beyond the lower unit's boundaries. For example, an irresponsible action by one government can reduce that unit's expenditures (and the taxes paid by those in that unit), while harming residents of adjacent governments; the state government may mandate service levels to prevent damaging innocent bystanders. Second, the legislature or the judiciary may view statewide uniformity as essential. The state may require equal expenditure per unit for schools, sanitation, and so on to prevent individuals from having low service levels solely because of their residence. Expenditure correction thus is mandated.

Against these arguments for mandates are strong counter-cases. First, many argue that the mandating government unit should be responsible for financing the mandate. The mandate can become a political tool for the higher government unit, while the lower government unit bears the burden of finance—a condition not conducive to careful decision making. Second, mandates can threaten other government programs. If limits constrain a government's ability to raise revenue, mandates for certain expenditures can endanger the provision of other desirable services. Third, mandates are characteristically enacted without cost awareness. Although the mandate's result may

---

[42]In another intergovernmental approach to dealing with the state fiscal crisis in 2009, the state proposed to change sentencing guidelines so that inmates sentenced to state prisons could be shifted to local jails. Bobby White, "California Looks to Cut State Prison Population," *Wall Street Journal,* June 13–14, 2009, A3.

be desirable, the cost of its achievement may be excessive, particularly when compared with the return from other uses of government resources. Mandates seldom are imposed in an environment favorable to cost-benefit comparisons. This is particularly true when mandates emerge from the judiciary. More than half the states estimate the cost of state mandates to localities, but there is seldom any effort to identify the cost to the government units that must finance the expenditures. Finally, mandates restrict fiscal autonomy. Mandates are clearly an uneasy companion to home rule.

For decisions about mandates, the appropriate comparison would appear to be whether the resource cost created by the mandate is worth the return generated by the mandate. Inflicting costs on other units may not be a likely way to generate that comparison. Some suggest that mandates without financial assistance sufficient to cover their costs are a violation of intergovernmental fair play. Others point out that governments do not finance mandated activities for private firms or individuals (minimum-wage requirements, safety regulations, etc.); therefore, although mandates may raise questions of appropriate government roles, they do not necessarily require accommodating fiscal transfers.

Concerns about cost imposed on state and local governments induced Congress to pass the Unfunded Mandates Reform Act of 1995 (UMRA; P.L. 104–4) "to end the imposition, in the absence of full consideration by Congress, of federal mandates on state, local, and tribal governments without adequate federal funding." Rather than prohibiting mandates or requiring that mandates be financed, the act requires that the cost of mandates to subnational governments be explicitly identified by Congress before it approves a mandate. The idea is that transparency and accompanying shame might keep Congress from imposing cost on other governments. The act has three critical elements:[43]

1. **The act defines** mandates to be "any provision in legislation, statute, or regulation that would impose an *enforceable duty* on state, local, or tribal governments or the private sector, or that would reduce or eliminate the amount of funding authorized to cover the costs of existing mandates." The definition includes direct requirements for state and local spending, provisions that preempt use of certain revenue sources by subnational governments, and reductions in federal aid that defrays subnational government costs of complying with existing federal mandates.

2. **The act assigns** the Congressional Budget Office the task of informing congressional committees when their bills contain federal mandates. When the total direct costs of government mandates in a bill exceed an inflation-adjusted threshold ($71 million now, initially $50 million) in any of the first five fiscal years in which the mandates are effective, the CBO must estimate those costs (if feasible), and the committees must publish these mandate statements. The CBO statements also assess whether the bill provides funds to cover the costs of any new mandate.

---

[43]Congressional Budget Office, *An Assessment of the Unfunded Mandates Reform Act in 1997* (Washington, D.C.: U.S. Government Printing Office, 1998).

3. **The act provides** an enforcement mechanism. Neither house of Congress may consider legislation that contains mandates unless the bill has a CBO statement about costs of mandates and provides direct spending authority or authorization for appropriations sufficient to cover the costs. However, the provision is not self-enforcing—a member of Congress must raise a formal objection for the requirements to be applied. A majority of the body can pass the mandate anyway, but the provision guarantees debate on the mandate, should any member so wish.

The UMRA controls exclude certain types of mandates, including those preventing discrimination, establishing conditions of grants, and preempting state and local authority to regulate or provide services that do not carry state or local fiscal implications. The exclusion of grant conditions allows the federal government to continue its influence within the realm of state and local affairs. However, new grant conditions or funding caps for eleven entitlement grant programs, such as Medicaid, are defined as mandates under the act if state and local governments lack authority to adjust these changes.

From the effective date of the act in January 1996 through 2014, the CBO reported that only thirteen bills had been enacted that exceeded the mandate threshold established in the act.[44] Whether this congressional restraint has been a result of the act is unknown. However, laws with smaller mandates have been passed, and state and local governments note that nothing has been done about the existing mandates.

Conclusion

Multiple levels of government provide public services in the United States and other federal nations. That diversity allows greater individual choice, but service delivery cannot be entirely uncoordinated because of two factors: intergovernmental spillovers and fiscal imbalance. Spillovers occur when an action by one government has an impact (good or bad) on its neighbors. Intergovernmental intervention can induce governments to allow for those external effects. Imbalance emerges because fiscal capacity is unevenly distributed across the nation and within states. Without an intergovernmental response, some individuals will be unduly penalized by the public sector simply because of where they live.

Those intergovernmental problems can be reduced by three varieties of coordination: revenue adjustments (relief, administrative assistance, source separation, or coordinated use of a single base), grants (categorical, block, or revenue sharing), or mandates. The devices together help retain the advantages of multilevel government without some associated problems.

---

[44]Congressional Budget Office, *A Review of CBO's Activities in 2014 under the Unfunded Mandates Reform Act* (Washington, D.C.: U.S. Government Printing Office, 2015). Theresa Gullo, "History and Evaluation of the Unfunded Mandates Reform Act," *National Tax Journal* 57 (September 2004): 559–70, provides a review and evaluation of the operation of the act.

QUESTIONS AND EXERCISES

1. Your state constitution almost certainly contains an education clause. What does the clause say? How might it be used (or how has it already been used) to challenge the system of financing local schools? On what basis does your state distribute assistance to local schools?

2. Horizontal fiscal balance (or fiscal disparity) is a persistent concern in fiscal federalism. Go to the U.S. Treasury website, which provides data on total taxable resources for each state. Using state population data provided by the U.S. Bureau of Census, compute total taxable resources per capita for the states and analyze the extent to which there is fiscal disparity across the states. What is its implication for American fiscal federalism?

3. Mundane County wants to develop an old railroad right-of-way into a hiking and bicycling trail. Information about available federal grant programs appears at the website http://www.cgfa.gov. Explore that website to determine whether a federal aid program might be available to assist with the program. (This website also is the medium through which federal grant proposals must be submitted, so understanding its features could be useful for your career.) If you do locate an appropriate program, what critical points would need to be in the proposal to improve its chances for success?

4. Which of the government functions listed in the United Nations Classification of Functions of Government (Appendix 6–1) would normally be work for the central government, and which would normally be assigned to subnational governments?

CASE FOR DISCUSSION

CASE14–1

Correspondence, Subsidiarity, and the Tenn-Tom Waterway

You read about the development of the Tenn-Tom Waterway in Case 2–1. Along with political lessons, that case involves dimensions of intergovernmental fiscal relations. In that regard, read the case again.

Consider These Questions

1. According to the principle of subsidiarity, should the Tenn-Tom have been a federal, state, or local project?

2. If principles of subsidiarity and correspondence had been followed, is it likely that the waterway would have been built?

CHAPTER 15

Debt Administration

Chapter Contents

Federal, state, or local government debt results when that government borrows from an individual or institution. Borrowing changes the pattern of purchasing power between the lender and the borrower. The lender forgoes purchasing power now for the promise of repayment later, and the borrower receives purchasing power now with an obligation for repayment later. The bond representing that debt is a long-term promise by the borrower (bond issuer) to the lender (bondholder) to pay the bond's face amount (or par value or the principal of the loan) at a defined maturity date and to make contractual interest payments until the loan is retired.[1] It is a

---

[1]Some governments, notably the British, have sold obligations with no maturity, but paying interest in perpetuity. Holders of these securities, called consols or perpetual notes, may retrieve principal by sale to another investor. Recent interest rates have been so low that the United Kingdom has decided to redeem some of this debt, some dating to the South Sea Bubble, the Crimean War, and World War I. Of course, it is being refinanced, not being paid from a budget surplus. (Tommy Stubbington and Ben Edwards, "U.K. Will Repay Some War Debt," *Wall Street Journal*, November 1-2, 2014). Some debt is sold on a discount basis. The difference between what is paid for the debt instrument by the lender and the amount repaid by the borrower constitutes the interest. Short-term obligations—typically sold on a discount basis by the federal government—are called bills and notes. Massachusetts Institute of Technology,

contract between the borrower and the lender. The borrower is committed to debt service—interest payments as required plus periodic repayment of the principal—through the life of the loan.

Government debt results from (1) covering deficits (annual expenditures greater than annual revenues), (2) financing capital-project construction, and (3) covering short periods within a fiscal year in which bills exceed cash on hand. Not all governments borrow for the same set of reasons. In particular, the causes of the debt of the federal government are not the same as those behind the debt of state and local governments.

Federal Debt[2]

The federal government's debt is the product of war finance, attempts to stabilize the nation's macroeconomy (i.e., to deal with problems of unemployment and slow growth),[3] and miscellaneous political situations that have caused lawmakers to disregard the relationship between federal revenues and federal expenditures. Recall that politicians find it far easier to object to the federal deficit than to take the actions necessary to actually reduce the deficit (i.e., to reduce spending or to increase taxes). The amount of debt is the result of federal choices about spending and raising revenue, not a debt objective itself. The level of debt equals the accumulation of all annual deficits since the start of the federal government less all annual surpluses. It is far easier to run a deficit than a surplus, and, when there is a deficit, there will be an addition to total debt. As the General Accounting Office (GAO) explains:

> The federal deficit . . . is the difference between total federal spending and revenue in a given year. To cover this gap, the government borrows from the public. Each yearly deficit adds to the amount of debt held by the public. In other words, the deficit is the annual amount of government borrowing, while the debt represents the cumulative amount of outstanding borrowing from the public over the nation's history. . . . [Each year] the federal

---

a nonprofit organization, borrowed $750 million with 100-year bonds in 2011, not exactly a consol, but a close approximation. It locked in an interest rate of 5.62 percent, which it regarded as very attractive. Goldie Blumenstyk, "MIT Borrows for the Long Run with a $750 Million 'Century Bond,'" *Chronicle of Higher Education*, May 12, 2011. Not all government debt pays a fixed rate. The U.S. Treasury sold its first floating-rate notes in 2014. On these notes, the rate of interest would be periodically reset to the thirteen-week Treasury bill rate, rather than bearing a fixed interest rate through the life of the obligation, as is the case with other federal debt.

[2]Other national governments, of course, also borrow. All such national government debt is called "sovereign debt" by participants in such markets.

[3]Management of the federal debt, including the mechanics of issuing new debt, is intimately connected to decisions about and implementation of national monetary and fiscal policy. A good history of the federal debt and how it has been managed is Donald R. Stabile and Jeffrey A. Cantor, *The Public Debt of the United States: Historical Perspective, 1775–1990* (Westport, Conn.: Praeger, 1991). Most of the federal debt has been issued by the Treasury, but a small amount, less than 1 percent of total federal debt held by the public, has been issued by agencies directly (Tennessee Valley Authority Corporation, Architect of the Capitol, National Archives, Federal Housing Administration, etc.). This agency debt has little practical difference from the rest and is included with federal totals. Office of Management and Budget, *Budget of the Government of the United States, Fiscal Year 2010, Analytical Perspectives* (Washington, D.C.: U.S. Government Printing Office, 2009), 229–32.

government pays only the interest costs of its debt. The principal is paid off when bonds come due. The cash to pay the principal comes from additional borrowing; hence the debt is "rolled over" or refinanced. To reduce its debt, the government would need to run a budget surplus and use the surplus funds to pay off the principal of maturing debt securities.[4]

There are two important overall measures of federal debt: *gross debt,* which equals all federal debt outstanding, and *debt held by private investors* (or net debt), which equals all federal debt except that held by federal accounts and the Federal Reserve System. Figure 15–1 traces both measures of the federal debt since 1940, each as a percentage of gross domestic product (GDP) to accommodate the considerable difference in the size of the economy over those years.[5] Debt rose dramatically—equaling 122 percent of GDP in 1946—as a consequence of financing World War II. (In absolute terms, the federal government has never eliminated the debt issued to finance World War II. The economy grew, and, over time, that debt lost its economic significance. This is an important point: the United States really does not need to eliminate its debt. It does, however, need to keep it under control relative to the size of the economy, and our elected officials have not done an outstanding job of this in recent years. It hasn't eliminated the debt created from the Civil War or World War I either, but that seems not to have harmed economic progress very much.[6] Refinancing debt as it matured seems to have worked rather well.) From that 1946 peak, the percentage fell almost continuously until the mid-1970s—reaching a low of 33 percent in 1981—as economic growth was greater than the rate of increase of the debt; debt in public hands reached a low of 18 percent in 1974. Occasional surpluses sometimes even allowed debt to be retired. Except for a drop in the 1990s, the record has been one of increases in this ratio. It is likely to continue to rise in the foreseeable future. (Recall the rather alarming CBO estimates presented in Chapter 4 .)[7]

Details on the federal debt appear in Table 15–1. Debt held by private investors is an impressive number—more than $10.6 trillion in 2015—but not as large as the gross federal debt—more than $18.1 trillion. Both have increased dramatically in total and in relation to GDP since the turn of the century. That's what happens when the federal government spends way more than its revenue, and the gap is increasing more rapidly than the economy. The amount of debt in private investor hands depends on accumulated federal deficits (gross public debt), monetary policy actions by the Federal Reserve that involve purchase and sale of federal debt, and

---

[4]General Accounting Office, Federal Debt: Answers to Frequently Asked Questions, GAO/AIMD-97-12 (Washington, D.C.: U.S. Government Printing Office, 1996), 13–16. The exception is the rare years in which there is a federal surplus rather than the persistent deficit.

[5]The federal government started its debt history by assuming the states' Revolutionary War debts in 1789 as part of a deal to get the nation started, so it started life in debt. Secretary of Treasury Alexander Hamilton initiated federal debt by borrowing $19,608.81 in February 1790. The War of Independence was fought with loans from foreign banks—and, with the exception of a brief period in the mid-1830s, the federal government has been in debt ever since. We are the best borrowers in the world.

[6]As noted in an earlier chapter, wars and preparation for them are horribly expensive. Much of our existing debt is a direct consequence of that spending and our unwillingness to pay for it on a current basis.

[7]See Kenneth D. Garbade, "Why the U.S. Treasury Began Auctioning Treasury Bills in 1929," *Federal Reserve Bank of New York Economic Policy Review* 14 (July 2008): 31–47, for a description of Treasury bill auctions, the most common way the federal government borrows, and the reasons behind creation of the auctions.

Figure 15–1
Gross and Net Federal Debt as % of GDP, 1940–2015

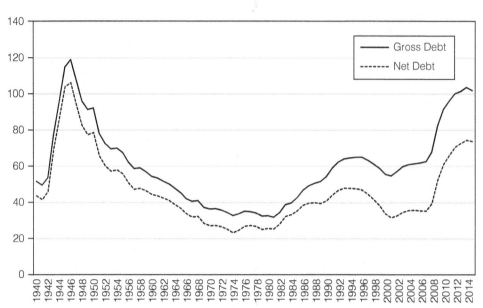

SOURCE: Office of Management and Budget, *Budget of the Government of the United States, Fiscal Year 2017, Historical Tables* (Washington, D.C. U.S. Government Printing Office, 2016).

federal trust funds' investable cash balances. Privately held debt excludes federal debt owned by elements of the federal government; privately held debt represents a net requirement for resource transfer to private holders as the debt is serviced.

Federal agency or trust fund accounts held roughly 28 percent of federal securities in 2015.[8] The Social Security Trust Fund is the largest single holder of federal securities (and, remember from Chapter 4, the value should be even more if the future obligations of the fund are to be met). These agencies and accounts acquire the debt in their cash-management programs because such debt is safe and politically neutral—certainly less hazardous in most respects than, say, holding stock in J. P. Morgan Chase or Exxon Mobil or bonds issued by the German government.[9] This debt is not a *net* claim on federal government resources. The Federal Reserve System conducts monetary policy by sale and purchase of federal debt, so these transactions to change the supply of money in the economy also influence the amount of debt in private hands. Because the Federal Reserve Banks legally must return to the U.S.

---

[8]Details on federal debt holdings throughout this chapter come from the quarterly publication of the U.S. Treasury, the *Treasury Bulletin*.

[9]There's even a section of an amendment to the U.S. Constitution giving assurance: Article XIV, section 4 states: "The validity of the public debt of the United States, authorized by law, including debts incurred for payment of pensions and bounties for services in suppressing insurrection or rebellion, shall not be questioned." So when members of Congress or candidates for president question the value of the assets supporting the Social Security system—those Social Security bonds that sit in a vault in West Virginia— have they committed a treasonable offense? They have questioned the validity of the public debt, which is a constitutional "no-no."

Table 15–1
Federal Debt from 1940 to 2015

End of Fiscal Year	Gross Debt ($ Millions)	Gross Debt as % of GDP	Debt Held by Private Investors ($ Millions)	Debt Held by Private Investors as % of GDP
1940	50,696	51.6	40,314	41.1
1945	260,123	114.9	213,390	94.3
1950	256,853	92.1	200,692	71.9
1955	274,366	67.4	203,009	49.9
1960	290,525	54.3	210,317	39.3
1965	322,318	45.4	221,678	31.2
1970	380,921	36.3	225,484	21.5
1975	541,925	33.6	309,707	19.2
1980	909,041	32.5	591,077	21.1
1985	1,817,423	42.6	1,337,454	31.3
1990	3,206,290	54.2	2,177,147	36.8
1995	4,920,586	64.9	3,230,264	42.6
2000	5,628,700	55.4	2,898,391	28.5
2005	7,905,300	61.3	3,855,852	29.9
2010	13,528,807	91.4	8,207,213	55.5
2015	18,120,106	101.8	10,654,745	59.8

SOURCE: Office of Management and Budget, Budget of the Government of the United States, Fiscal Year 2017, Historical Tables (Washington, D. C.: U.S. G. P. O., 2016)

Treasury sizable portions of interest received and because they are, at least loosely, government agencies, their holdings also—just above 15 percent of the total federal debt in 2015—do not represent an outside claim on the government. For most analytical purposes, it is the debt held by private investors—that debt outside federal agencies, federal trust funds, and Federal Reserve Banks—that is the major concern for federal debt policy. The share of the debt that is privately held—the share that represents a net requirement for resource transfer outside government—declined throughout the 1990s and the first decades of the 2000s, to 57 percent in 2015 from around 68 percent in 1990. The more significant private domestic holders of the debt include private pension funds, state-local government pension funds, insurance companies, depository institutions, and state-local governments.

How does the United States stand in comparison with other countries? The net debt ratio to GDP was 56.6 percent in 2011. That puts the United States somewhat above the median of 42.9 percent for countries of the Organization for Economic Cooperation and Development. Greece (147.8 percent), Italy (109.0 percent), Belgium (96.8 percent), Portugal (88.0 percent), the United Kingdom (85.5 percent), and Iceland (81.3 percent) were at the top in 2010, and Estonia (3.2 percent), Chile (9.2 percent), Australia (11.0 percent), Luxembourg (12.6 percent), Switzerland (20.2 percent), Norway (26.1 percent), and Mexico (27.5 percent) were at the low end.[10]

---

[10]Organization for Economic Cooperation and Development, *Central Government Debt.* http://stats.oecd.org/Index.aspx?DatasetCode=GOV_DEBT

One notable change in historical pattern is the new importance of foreign and international ownership of the federal debt. Until the mid-1970s, foreign ownership of the federal debt was small, considerably less than 10 percent of the total privately held debt. However, those holdings quickly jumped to around 20 percent in the mid-1970s and have expanded since then. At the end of September 2015, 58.2 percent of privately held federal debt was in foreign and international investor ownership. Repayment of that portion of federal debt cannot be casually dismissed with "we owe it to ourselves." Servicing that debt transfers resources from U.S. taxpayers to foreign bondholders, a condition with substantially different standard-of-living implications for the United States than if the payment of debt service was going mostly to other Americans. As long as foreign entities build up dollar reserves in international trade and world investors regard U.S. government debt as yielding a high return without significant risk of political upheaval, such investment will continue. Bond purchases are made by our major trading partners; those countries are the ones with individuals and institutions having dollars to invest. In April 2016, the top ten foreign holders of federal debt were the following: Mainland China (19.9 percent of foreign holdings), Japan (18.3 percent), Cayman Islands (4.1 percent), Ireland (4.1 percent), Brazil (4.0 percent), Switzerland (3.7 percent), Luxembourg (3.5 percent), United Kingdom (3.5 percent), Hong Kong (3.1 percent), and Taiwan (3.0 percent).[11] Compared to other governments in the world, the U.S. federal government is seen as a safe haven for international funds, and that helps keep the interest rate that the federal government pays on its debt low, even with rising debt levels.

The federal debt tends to have a short term to maturity, averaging sixty-one months at the end of fiscal 2015. That is a reflection of the fact that the federal government has historically borrowed to finance its continuing deficits, not to finance long-life capital projects. The maturity has lengthened in recent years, from its low point of two years and eight months at the end of 1975, but it is much shorter than the post-World War II maximum of ten years and five months at the start of 1947.[12] In late 2001, the Treasury stopped selling thirty-year bonds, historically the benchmark bond in many financial markets, with the intention that the longest Treasury bond would have a ten-year maturity. That was in the era in which it was feared that the federal surpluses would wipe out federal debt entirely. However, the return to deficit conditions brought the thirty-year bond back in 2005.[13]

The relatively short maturity combines with the substantial federal debt to create a continued federal presence in debt markets, either refinancing maturing debt or financing new cash needs (i.e., covering the deficit). However, interest rates tend to

---

[11]"Major Foreign Holders of Treasury Securities," June 15, 2016 [http://ticdata.treasury.gov/Publish/mfh.txt].

[12]*Treasury Bulletin* (March 1989), 32.

[13]Most federal debt is in the form of notes or bonds that pay a fixed interest rate through their term to maturity. Another form is the Treasury bill, a short-term maturity instrument with a broad and lively secondary market that allows them to be converted to cash easily. T-bills are sold weekly on an auction basis in which bidders offer less than the face value of the instrument (a discount), with the difference between face value on maturity and the amount paid equaling the return on the investment. The annualized rate of return or yield rate on a discounted bill equals $Y = [(FV - P)/FV] * [360/M]$ where P = the purchase price paid for the bill, FV = the face value of the bill, M = the maturity of the bill, and 360 = the number of days used by banks to determine short-term interest rates. The discount yield for a 182-day T-bill at a price of $9,659.30 for a $10,000 bill would be $Y = [(10,000 - 9,659.30)/10,000] *[360/182] = 0.06739$.

Sidebar 15–1
Inflation-Indexed Bonds

Conventional bonds repay the bondholder the principal of the loan plus a contracted interest rate; an inflation-indexed bond repays the principal adjusted for inflation plus the contracted interest rate applied to that adjusted principal. That prevents the purchasing power of the investment from being eaten away by unexpected price increases. Price increases in the economy will be matched by higher payments from the indexed bond—so holders of indexed bonds are not hurt by inflation. Their real rate of return is protected. The indexed bond should be particularly attractive when expectations of future inflation are high.

A number of governments, including those of Israel, the United Kingdom, Australia, Canada, Sweden, Mexico, Argentina, and New Zealand, have sold such bonds. The U.S. Treasury offered its first index bonds in January 1997—$7 billion worth of ten-year bonds with a 3.45 percent coupon rate—with the intent for quarterly auctions of more such bonds. In contrast with conventional bonds, the principal is adjusted before each semiannual payment to reflect any change in the Consumer Price Index since the issue of the bond. By that adjustment, the real return from the bond remains the same for the bondholder—and the U.S. Treasury knows the real, but not the nominal, cost of this debt. These are now referred to by the Treasury as Treasury inflation-protected securities (TIPS).

Jeffrey Wrase of the Federal Reserve Bank of Philadelphia provides a comparison of payments for conventional and indexed bonds:[1]

> Consider a 10-year conventional nominal bond and a 10-year inflation-indexed bond. Each bond is purchased at its face, or principal, value of $1,000. Although Treasury notes and bonds provide semiannual payments, the bonds in this example are assumed to provide annual coupon payments. Each coupon payment on a conventional bond is the coupon rate stated on the bond times the principal. Each coupon payment on an indexed bond is the coupon rate times the indexed principal. The indexed principal is simply the beginning principal of $1,000 scaled up through time at the rate of inflation. We'll assume that the coupon rate on the indexed bond is 3 percent, and that actual inflation over the 10-year horizon turns out to be a steady 2 percent, equal to expected inflation, and that the coupon rate on the conventional bond is 5.06 percent so that its expected real rate of return equals the coupon rate on the indexed bond.

> A schedule of nominal and real values of payments on the bonds is given below. The real values give the purchasing power of the nominal payments. For example, suppose a given item today costs $1. With 2 percent inflation, at the end of the year the same item will cost $1.02, and $1 will purchase 0.98 (1/1.02) units of the item. So, $50.60 received at the end of year 1 from the nominal bond will purchase 49.61 units.

> As the schedule of payments shows, the nominal value of the conventional bond's principal stays fixed. The real value is eroding through time because of inflation. When received at maturity, the $1,000 principal can purchase 820.35 units of the good. In contrast, when the bond was first purchased, that $1,000 could buy 1,000 units. The payment schedule also shows how the fixed nominal payment of $50.60 per year on the nominal bond has a smaller real value over time because of inflation. Note that for the indexed bond, the real values of the principal and interest payments are preserved for the life of the bond. As the principal gets scaled up, so, too, does the nominal coupon payment to preserve the real return of 3 percent. The indexed bond pays less interest than the nominal bond each year, but that is offset by its larger payment of principal at maturity.

(continues)

Sidebar 15–1
(continued)

Schedule of Payments

	Conventional Bond				Indexed Bond			
Year	Nominal Value of Principal	Real Value of Principal	Nominal Interest Payment	Real Value of Interest Payment	Nominal Value of Principal	Real Value of Principal	Nominal Interest Payment	Real Value of Interest Payment
1	$1,000	980.39	$50.60	49.61	$1,200.00	1000	$30.60	30
2	$1,000	961.17	$50.60	48.64	$1,040.40	1000	$31.21	30
3	$1,000	942.32	$50.60	47.68	$1,061.21	1000	$31.84	30
4	$1,000	923.85	$50.60	46.75	$1,082.43	1000	$32.47	30
5	$1,000	905.73	$50.60	45.83	$1,104.08	1000	$33.12	30
6	$1,000	887.97	$50.60	44.93	$1,126.16	1000	$33.78	30
7	$1,000	870.56	$50.60	44.05	$1,148.69	1000	$34.46	30
8	$1,000	853.49	$50.60	43.19	$1,171.66	1000	$35.15	30
9	$1,000	836.75	$50.60	42.34	$1,195.09	1000	$35.85	30
10	$1,000	820.35	$50.60	41.51	$1,218.99	1000	$36.60	30

Total Nominal Receipts:	$1,506
Real Value of Principal at Maturity:	$820.35
Total Nominal Receipts:	$1,554.07
Real Value of Indexed Principal at Maturity:	$1,000

[1]Jeffrey M. Wrase, "Inflation-Indexed Bonds: How Do They Work?" *Federal Reserve Bank of Philadelphia Business Review* (July/August 1997): 5.

be lower for short-term than for long-term loans, so maturity shortening can reduce the interest cost of serving the debt.

Although some federal debt is sold directly to the public, most is sold through a small group of primary security dealers who acquire the debt at auction for resale to investors.[14] Yields are normally established at those auctions at fixed nominal levels. Most securities sold by the U.S. Treasury pay a set return, but, as Sidebar 15–1 describes, it also sells some securities that pay inflation-indexed returns to investors.[15]

A reasonable question is why worry about the debt of the central government? The federal government is an experienced debtor, having been in debt from the

---

[14]The process through which the Treasury borrows is described in Kenneth D. Garbade and Jeffrey F. Ingber, "The Treasury Auction Process: Objectives, Structure, and Recent Adaptations," *Current Issues in Economics and Finance* (Federal Reserve Bank of New York) 11 (February 2005): 1–11.

[15]A good discussion of the U.S. experience with inflation-indexed borrowing is B. Sack and R. Elasser, "Treasury Inflation-Indexed Debt: A Review of the U.S. Experience," *Federal Reserve Bank of New York Economic Policy Review* 10 (May 2004): 47–63.

instant of its founding to now, except for a brief time in 1835, and has been devoid of crises along the way. The deficit is a concern as a violation of fiscal sustainability, but not if the reason for the deficit is the acquisition of productive capital assets (infrastructure) that will yield a return to the future generations that will face the requirement of paying the service on the debt issued to support the deficit.[16] Federal spending on infrastructure is, however, much smaller than the amount of the deficit. But the debt level relative to the size of the economy can be an economic and financial concern beyond the worries about the accumulated deficits.

First, there is the worry that the debt level will be so large relative to the economy that potential lenders will refuse to lend at all or, if they lend, they will do so only at disastrously high interest rates. Being shut out of the capital market is a major worry because governments need to borrow for capital projects, for bridge financing during the year, and for rollover of maturing debt. In mid-2012, this was the problem that the Greek government faced. Its debt level, around 160 percent of GDP, was so large that lenders were not willing to make loans and international bodies were unwilling to assist without substantial fiscal reforms by the government. The U.S. federal government is not close to this sort of limit and its debt is in U.S. dollars, not a currency controlled by an entity other than the U.S. government, but many believe that some precaution is necessary to prevent that eventuality of being shut out of markets.

The second concern is important, but possibly without all the draconian implications of the first. As debt levels increase, so must the need for debt service, predominantly interest payments if maturing debt is mostly rolled over into new debt. When interest obligations become large, they crowd out other spending programs from available tax revenue. Legislators face the difficult choice between raising taxes to allow both debt service and public programs and reducing public programs to meet debt service without increasing taxes. Both options create difficult political problems. Those problems can be mitigated by controlling the increase in the debt level, which is easier to do gradually than by waiting until the interest crunch truly hits. The federal government has been insulated from this problem in recent years by the extremely low interest rates during the Great Recession and its aftermath. The concern promises to build, however, as the economy improves and interest rates increase and as debt continues to increase. Of course, the way to deal with the debt is to deal with the deficit— and that has to do with taxation and expenditure policy, not directly with debt.

The federal government operates under a statutory debt ceiling. The ceiling was first enacted during World War I when Congress got concerned about the amount of money it was approving for the support of the war and other programs.[17] The ceiling was intended to provide a degree of control over federal spending. This

---

[16]It can also be argued that the costs of fighting the Civil War and World War II (and probably World War I) fall into the category of long-life capital expenditures. The consequences of losing those wars would have been extraordinarily bad for the American public, so the return from the huge, one-time expenditure of fighting the war stretched far into the future. That sounds like a classic justification for debt finance within the context of fiscal sustainability.

[17]Prior to the ceiling, Congress had to approve each individual debt issue. Moving toward an overall ceiling was a change intended to provide simplification and greater flexibility for Treasury borrowing: it didn't have to get approval for each debt issue, and the ceiling provided aggregate control of debt-financed spending.

approach to control was superseded by the enactment of the federal budget process in the Budget and Accounting Act of 1921—it is far better to control spending before it occurs than to prevent payment for services that have already been provided.[18] Although the original purpose of the debt ceiling had been taken care of by an improved mechanism, no Congress got around to eliminating the ceiling, thus continuing control of paying for bills that had already been incurred rather than controlling the spending itself, a remarkably inefficient constraint concept. The absolute amount of the ceiling was increased by congressional action each time before the actual debt reached the limit. However, in the summer of 2011, Congress balked at enacting the necessary increase (as was discussed in Chapter 4), preferring to return to the antiquated World War I control logic and threatening default on federal debt service. The nation's creditworthiness was appropriately adjusted downward—the threat of missing a scheduled payment is sufficient to make lenders nervous.[19] A Government Accountability Office study of the episode found that the delay in increasing the ceiling increased Treasury borrowing cost by $1.3 billion and that there will be additional costs in future years.[20] Of course, those extra costs add to the federal debt. Failing to increase the ceiling after having taken the fiscal actions that created its violation represents the greatest unforced error in American, if not world, history. The country faced a similar crisis in fall 2015 as the ceiling again was breached. Congress ultimately suspended the ceiling until 2017 as part of a deal to increase the defense and domestic discretionary spending ceiling that had been imposed in the 2011 law.

State and Local Government (Municipal) Debt[21]

State and local government debt has similarly grown rapidly since the early 1970s, from $175.2 billion in 1972 to $2,942.3 billion in 2012. This debt—the product of borrowing by states, counties, municipalities, townships, school districts, and special districts (Table 15–2)—is all called municipal debt, distinguishing it from corporate or federal issues. Total local government debts are larger than are total state government debts, and cities have more debt than any other form of local

---

[18]As of January 2016, the ceiling was $18.1 trillion, but it is suspended until March 2017.

[19]Historically, federal government debt has been regarded as the safest, most risk-free debt on the planet and was the standard against which the risk of nonpayment of interest and principle when due was evaluated. The debt was the gold standard of financial certainty. The debt ceiling crisis of 2011 shattered that evaluation; hitting the ceiling would create some uncertainty about whether payment obligations would be honored. Accordingly, U.S. government debt is no longer regarded as risk-free (as explained later in this chapter, the debt is no longer given the highest rating by all rating firms), with some slightly higher interest cost resulting.

[20]U.S. Government Accountability Office, "Debt Limit: Analysis of 2011–2012 Actions Taken and Effect of Delayed Increase on Borrowing Costs," GAO-12-701, July 2012.

[21]The best advanced source on municipal debt is Craig L. Johnson, Martin J. Luby, and Tima T. Moldogaziev, *State and Local Financial Instruments, Policy Changes and Management* (Cheltenham, U.K.: Edward Elgar, 2014).

Table 15–2
Summary of State and Local Indebtedness, 2011–2012 ($ Thousands)

Description	State and Local Government Amount	State Government Amount	Local Government Amount	County Government Amount	Municipal Government Amount	Township Government Amount	Special District Government Amount	School District Government Amount
Debt								
Outstanding	2,942,295,481.00	1,145,576,715.00	1,796,718,766.00	314,411,896.00	694,346,656.00	33,736,333.00	369,816,391.00	384,407,490.00
Short-Term	43,924,608.00	15,463,663.00	28,460,945.00	5,261,896.00	6,865,652.00	3,872,716.00	4,262,061.00	8,198,620.00
Long-Term	2,898,370,873.00	1,130,113,052.00	1,768,257,821.00	309,150,000.00	687,481,004.00	29,863,617.00	365,554,330.00	376,208,870.00

SOURCE: U.S. Census Bureau, State and Local Government Finances. [http://factfinder2.census.gov/faces/tableservices/jsf/pages/productview.xhtml?src=bkmk]

government. The preponderance of this debt is long-term. That differs radically from the federal debt. Furthermore, municipal debt is typically issued for construction of identifiable long-life assets. Much of the debt is for education, transportation, and public-utility infrastructure. The borrowing occurs to finance an identifiable, specific structure. Such an identification of purposes, of course, would not be possible for federal debt.

State-local debt can be either full-faith-and-credit debt or nonguaranteed (limited-liability) debt. Full-faith-and-credit obligations "have an unlimited claim"[22] on the taxes (and other revenues) of the issuing unit; nonguaranteed debt issues lack that assurance and are sold on the basis of repayment from specified revenue sources only. Because public-debt purchasers (the individuals and institutions lending the money to state-local governments) regard the claim on all tax resources as offering greater likelihood that bond principal and interest payments will be made on time, full-faith-and-credit debt bears a lower interest rate than does equivalent nonguaranteed debt. (Later sections suggest why many governments use nonguaranteed debt, despite its higher cost.)[23]

Most municipal debt is long-term. Long-term state government debt is almost three-quarters nonguaranteed; long-term local government debt is about 45 percent full-faith-and-credit. School districts are major users of full-faith-and-credit: more than 95 percent of their debt is of that variety. School districts traditionally have not been operated from user charges (there are strong public policy reasons for providing elementary and secondary education at no direct charge to patrons), so they lack project revenue to support borrowing and must repay from tax and intergovernmental aid revenue. They are the sole sources for repayment, so full-faith-and-credit issues must be the primary mechanism for debt finance for schools. They do establish, however, separate building corporations that issue debt to finance construction with repayment guaranteed by leases charged to a school district, as is discussed later.[24] Other special districts are major users of limited-liability debt—almost 85 percent. Many special districts (waste management, transit, water, etc.) are established on a semi-commercial basis in that they collect charges from their customers and lack a tax base for guaranteeing their debt. Around two-thirds of city debt is limited-liability. Short-term debt at both levels is almost completely full-faith-and-credit.

---

[22]Roland I. Robinson, "Debt Administration," in *Management Policies in Local Government Finance,* ed. J. Richard Aronson and Eli Schwartz (Washington, D.C.: International City Management Association, 1975), 23. How "unlimited" that claim actually is has been tested in some municipal bankruptcy cases since 2012.

[23]U.S. state and local government debt is issued with no explicit or implicit guarantee from the national government. If the debt cannot be repaid, the federal government is not expected to come to the aid of the issuer, no matter how prominent the issuer, as was made clear in the 1970s when bonds associated with New York City went into default—a famous *New York Daily News* headline (October 30, 1975): "[President] Ford to City: Drop Dead." States, as their legal creator, are more likely to provide guarantees to their localities. Some other federal governments, notably those of Canada and Germany, are more likely to be expected to provide assistance to troubled localities, but they are also more likely to be exercising greater control over their normal operations as well.

[24]These building corporations are outside normal fiscal limitations—"off the books" in a manner similar to entities associated with Enron and other private businesses.

Nonguaranteed debt is outside the limits frequently placed on municipal government debt by state statute or constitution. Interest on such debt is, however, eligible for the same exclusion from federal taxation received by municipal debt. That creates a logical inconsistency. To invoke tax immunity, the agency that issues those bonds must show that they are the obligations of a state or subdivision. However, to provide that they are revenue bonds and not subject to the usual debt limitations, the agency must show that they are not the obligations of any such unit.[25] Municipalities thus seek to have it both ways, treating the debt as theirs for federal tax purposes and treating the debt as somebody else's for purposes of state law.

Much revenue bond debt is issued by public authorities, entities with public powers that operate outside the normal constraints placed on government. Governments form authorities to build public projects (bridges, power projects, highways, etc.) and pay off bonds used to finance the construction with charges from users; the authorities seldom have taxing authority. An authority may or may not go out of existence when the bonds are retired.[26] (Special entities created for lease-purchase finance are discussed later.)

The municipal bond market is dominated by revenue bond debt, meaning that revenue from a project (e.g., a parking garage, a sewage treatment plant, or a university dormitory) is pledged for debt service rather than the general revenues (or full-faith-and-credit) of the jurisdiction.[27] This nonguaranteed debt was only 38 percent of all state and local long-term debt outstanding in 1960. It now is around 80 percent of the total. The market has continuously shifted toward nonguaranteed debt to allow governments to avoid legal restrictions placed on general obligation debt and to allow revenue-producing projects to float on their own debt. However, the trend is somewhat troubling for older, large cities: "The economic advantage of cities lies in making the marginal maintenance and repair expenditures that can keep the basic elements of their present infrastructure in adequate working order."[28] Nonguaranteed bonds are not easily adapted to generate financing for reconstruction or maintenance, so the shift indicates special problems for those cities. If the infrastructure (streets, water and sewage systems, etc.) is not maintained, the economic advantage of new cities becomes overwhelming. Debt is not, however, the complete answer to public infrastructure deterioration; much work on maintenance is recurring and should be part of operating financing.

---

[25]B. U. Ratchford, "Revenue Bonds and Tax Immunity," *National Tax Journal* 7 (March 1954): 42.

[26]For a fascinating view of public authority operation, see Robert Caro, *The Power Broker: Robert Moses and the Fall of New York* (New York: Vintage Books, 1975), chap. 28.

[27]Some local governments have added statements about the prospect of using tax revenue if project revenues are not sufficient, in an effort to obtain a lower interest rate. The meaning of such a fuzzy pledge has recently been tested with cities that opted not to come up with the money when project revenues were inadequate and scheduled debt service was not paid (a default). As with most conflicts, the question will be settled in court. Michael Corkery, "The Next Credit Crisis? Munis," *Wall Street Journal*, November 20, 2010, C1. In a Menasha, Wisconsin, case, a settlement was eventually negotiated, with the city using its municipal electric utility in a lease-purchase agreement with a private utility to come up with funds for the settlement, suggesting that the pledge does have some meaning.

[28]George E. Peterson, "Capital Spending and Capital Obsolescence—The Outlook for Cities," in *The Fiscal Outlook for Cities*, ed. Roy Bahl (Syracuse, N.Y.: Syracuse University Press, 1978), 49.

Municipal Bonds, Tax-Exempt Interest, and the Tax Reform Act of 1986

The federal income tax adopted in 1913 specified that interest on state and local government bonds would be exempt. The reasoning apparently reflected the doctrine of intergovernmental tax immunity reflected in the 1819 decision in *McCulloch v. Maryland* (17 U.S. 316), in which the Supreme Court stated that "the power to tax is the power to destroy," and furthered in the 1871 decision in *Collector v. Day* (78 U.S. 113), in which the Court found that the federal government could not tax state judicial officers' salaries. Indeed, the Court's 1895 decision in *Pollock v. Farmers Loan & Trust Company* (157 U.S. 492) that the income tax would require apportionment as a direct tax also ruled on a provision that would have included state and local debt interest in the base: "The tax in question is a tax on the power of the states and their instrumentalities to borrow money, and consequently repugnant to the Constitution." Therefore, the constitutional principle appeared clear.

Economic impacts and equity effects, however, soon muddied the issue.[29] Because interest payments on municipal bonds were not subject to tax, municipalities could borrow at artificially low interest rates. That created the possibility of capital-market distortions between taxed and tax-exempt activities and certainly caused lost federal revenue. Furthermore, as marginal tax brackets rose over the years, interest payments that were not subject to federal tax became more attractive to high-income taxpayers as a safe avenue for tax avoidance. That avoidance reduced the progressivity of the federal system, along with reducing federal revenue. After Mississippi (in 1936) introduced industrial development bonds (IDBs), a mechanism whereby a tax-exempt borrower constructed a plant for a private firm and serviced the debt with lease payments from the firm, the distortion problems became especially troubling. Some controls on exempt bonds were inevitable.

Although controls on the bonds started with limits on IDBs in 1968, the most dramatic changes came in the 1986 Tax Reform Act.[30] The law distinguishes between two municipal debt categories: private activity (taxable) and public purpose (tax-exempt). The law and regulations putting the categories into effect are complex; here is a simplified version: (1) Private-activity and taxable bonds pass the private-business-use and private-loan tests.[31] The bond issue is in this category if (a) more than the greater of 5 percent or $5 million of bond proceeds are used for loans to nongovernment entities (the private-loan test) or (b) more than 10 percent of the bond proceeds are used by a nongovernment entity in a trade or business and more

---

[29]For an excellent analysis of the equity and efficiency problems of the municipal bond market, see two articles by Peter Fortune: "The Municipal Bond Market, Part I: Politics, Taxes, and Yields," *New England Economic Review* (September/October 1991): 13–36; and "The Municipal Bond Market, Part II: Problems and Policies," *New England Economic Review* (May/June 1992): 47–64.

[30]The control legislation is chronicled in Robert L. Bland and Li-Khan Chen, "Taxable Municipal Bonds: State and Local Governments Confront the Tax-Exempt Limitation Movement," *Public Administration Review* 50 (January/February 1989): 42–48.

[31]*Bond Buyer 1997 Yearbook* (New York: American Banker, 1997). Such bonds can tap foreign capital markets because of the higher yield that the absence of federal tax advantage requires.

than 10 percent of the debt service is secured by or derived from payments from property used in a trade or business (private-business-use test).[32] (2) Public-purpose and tax-exempt bonds are issued by a state or its political subdivision in registered form and do not pass these tests. Passing these tests would ordinarily not be a good thing for the borrower, in terms of likely interest costs.[33]

Certain private-activity bonds, however, can be tax exempt. Allowable uses include multifamily rental housing; publicly owned airports; publicly owned docks and wharves; publicly owned non-vehicular mass-commuting facilities; hazardous waste disposal facilities; sewage and solid-waste disposal facilities; some student loans; some water, electric, and gas utilities; and some other categories.[34] The annual volume of such bond issues, however, is subject to a state cap of the greater of $50 per capita or $150 million.[35] How states allocate the amounts is their choice. Furthermore, state and local governments may choose to sell their debt in taxable markets; indeed, this accounted for 18.5 percent of outstanding municipal debt at the end of 2011.[36]

The 1986 act clearly reduced the scope of future tax-exempt borrowing. Furthermore, a 1988 Supreme Court ruling in *South Carolina v. Baker* (485 U.S. 505), a case testing whether state and local governments could be required to issue bonds only in registered form, held that the Constitution does not prevent applying the federal income tax to state and local debt interest.[37] As the federal government seeks

---

[32]Some state and local governments do regularly use these hybrids (taxable municipal securities). Such issues can be attractive to foreign investors.

[33]The new Yankee Stadium, approximately $1.3 billion total cost with $942 million worth of tax-exempt bonds, is owned by New York City. To keep the project from being classed as "private activity," the deal was structured with the city as owner. The Yankees pay no rent and pay no property tax because the city is the owner, keeping away from the private-activity categorization. However, the Yankees make payments in lieu of taxes (PILOTs) that are theoretically equal to the property tax that would have been owed—except the stadium value is inflated for tax purposes to make the payments look like tax and not like rent, allowing the city to say that the city is paying for most of the stadium cost from tax revenue. That all keeps things away from private activity, the bonds are tax exempt and at a lower rate, and U.S. taxpayers are implicitly subsidizing the Yankees. Joseph Henchman and Travis Greaves, "From the House that Ruth Built to the House the IRS Built," Tax Foundation Fiscal Fact No. 167 (Washington, D.C.: Tax Foundation, April 6, 2009). In many instances, cities have built stadiums with long-term debt and must continue servicing that debt even though the city has built a new stadium to meet the demands of the same team. Amazingly enough, cities contribute substantial resources to professional, for-profit teams, almost certainly contributing much to the value of the professional franchise, without receiving any ownership rights in return. This is not something that a prudent private business would ever do, and city leaders certainly do it only because they are playing with public money and not their own.

[34]The development impact of small-issue IDBs appears doubtful. See General Accounting Office, Industrial Development Bonds: Achievement of Public Benefits Is Unclear, GAO/RCED-93-106 (Washington, D.C.: General Accounting Office, 1993).

[35]Private-activity bonds for airports, docks, wharves, and solid-waste facilities are outside the cap; certain public-purpose bonds (parts earmarked for private activities costing more than $15 million and private portions of advance refunds) are included in the cap.

[36]This includes Build America Bonds, discussed in a later section, as well as other types of taxable issues.

[37]Bonds had been issued as bearer bonds (whoever presents the bonds receives interest and principal owed, no questions asked) or as registered bonds (the owner is explicitly named). There was concern that bearer bonds were being used to launder illicit incomes and to evade gift and estate taxes. The Tax Equity and Fiscal Responsibility Act of 1982 limited tax-exempt status to registered issues alone. The case challenged that provision; the state did not expect the extra comment on tax-exempt status in general. See Bruce F. Davie and Dennis Zimmerman, "Tax-Exempt Bonds after the South Carolina Decision," *Tax Notes* (June 27, 1988): 1573–80.

revenue and reform of its revenue system, municipal bond interest, even for clear public-purpose debt issues, will continue to be one option for base broadening. The preference provided municipal borrowing is a policy choice, not a necessary constitutional requirement.

A New Taxable Municipal Bond Option (Short-Lived)

The American Recovery and Reinvestment Act of 2009 added another layer of complexity to municipal bond markets by creating a new borrowing alternative, the Build America Bonds (BABs) program, an option available for bonds issued in 2009 and 2010 and periodically discussed for revival. This program allowed state and local governments to issue taxable bonds for capital projects, but with a direct federal subsidy (a direct expenditure and not a tax expenditure) equal to 35 percent of the total coupon payments made to investors. That reduced the total interest cost to the bond issuer and made capital projects less expensive.

The program worked like this. Suppose a state or local government issues a BAB and pays the bondholder $100 interest on the bond. With an "Issuer BAB" or "Direct Payment BAB," the U.S. Treasury then pays the issuing government $35, making the net cost $65 on the bond paying $100 to the bondholder. An alternative format, the "Tax Credit BAB," gives the bondholder a nonrefundable tax credit of 35 percent of interest paid each year. The debt might be structured in either format. The program had no volume limitation, so the total amount of subsidy depended on choices made by the states and localities. This program gave financial support for state and local infrastructure programs in amounts controlled by the issuing governments, not by federal granting authorities, just as the traditional tax-exempt bond does, but, in contrast to the traditional format, the tax savings did not vary with the marginal rate of the borrower. The investment could be attractive even for those in low marginal rate brackets. The program converted a tax expenditure to a direct expenditure, thus providing greater transparency, and made municipal bond purchases more attractive to lower-income taxpayers. Congress did not renew it and has continued to resist efforts to create a successor program.

Appropriate Debt Policy

Borrowing provides funds to acquire resources for current public use. The debt from that borrowing must be repaid, with interest, in the future. Therefore, borrowing commits future budgets. Because of the contractual rigidity, debt must be issued with care; unwise use of debt can disrupt the lives of those paying taxes and expecting services in the future (i.e., it may violate the fiscal sustainability standard). The fundamental rule of debt policy is this: do not issue debt for a maturity longer than the financed project's useful life. If the debt life exceeds the useful life, the project's true annual cost has been understated, and people will continue to pay for the project after the project is gone. If the useful life exceeds the debt period, the annual cost has been overstated, and people will receive benefits without payment. The timing-of-payment question is particularly significant across generations and, at the local level, across a citizenry that is frequently changing as people move in and out of the locality.[38]

Long-term borrowing can be appropriate for long-life capital facilities. Economic growth requires expanded public-capital infrastructure, often before any associated expansion of public revenue. A strong case can be made for using debt for these projects when the future revenue stream will be adequate to service that debt. Some governments, however, have elected to employ pay-as-you-go financing, paying for capital facilities only from current-year operating surpluses. Such a policy can produce both inefficiency and inequity. First, with population mobility, users would not pay an appropriate charge for those facilities. Those in taxing range would pay when the facility is built; they may not be there when the facility for which they have paid is actually providing services. Second, the high single-year ticket price of a major project may discourage construction, even when the project is sound and feasible. Third, pay-as-you-go financing can produce substantial tax-rate instability, with artificially high rates during the construction phase and artificially low rates during operation. Such instability is unlikely to help development of the local economy. Furthermore, debt financing produces annual debt-service charges that are fixed by contract. Therefore, when the area tax base grows, the tax rate required for debt service for a project will decline over time. For large, long-life infrastructure, debt finance can be more sensible and fiscally prudent than pay-as-you-go finance. All this suggests the importance of integrating the capital budgeting principles discussed in Chapter 7 with the principles of debt management discussed here.

Debt commits resources for extended periods and can be misused by public officials who seek to postpone the cost of public actions. Potential for misuse does not preclude debt financing, but it does mean that debt needs to be issued with caution. When properly handled, debt is an appropriate financing medium. In fact, strict pay-as-you-go can be as unsound as careless use of debt. Both financing methods can be appropriate tools in the fiscal arsenal. Appendix 15–1 illustrates a debt policy with the principles of debt management endorsed by the New York state comptroller.[39]

---

[38]Temporary cash needs should be covered by short-term borrowing liquidated within the fiscal year. Carrying short-term cash borrowing across a fiscal year (rolling over) would violate the fundamental principle.

[39]Some municipalities now issue bonds with variable interest rates (variable-rate demand obligations or VRDOs) in an effort to take advantage of the tendency of short-term interest rates to be lower than long-term interest rates. These securities require the borrower to continually reenter the bond market (the floating interest rate resets periodically) and have caused a number of jurisdictions considerable financial difficulty (school districts in Pennsylvania and Jefferson County, Alabama, for instance), but others have successfully escaped the problem. In the early days of the bonds, financial advisors did not adequately explain the risks associated with the issues to borrowers, much to the detriment of the citizenry. Risk to the municipal issuer can be higher than with the traditional bond, which locks in a coupon rate for the life of the issue, but these bonds can tap an additional segment of the credit market.

The Mechanics of Bond Values

Bond sales represent transactions in which a lender exchanges payment to a borrower now for the contractual promise of repayment plus interest at a later date. The bond contract specifies the interest the borrower will pay the lender for using the money, typically with a semiannual interest payment. This stated or nominal return on a bond is its coupon rate, the percentage of par value that will be paid in interest on a regular basis. Thus, a 5 percent coupon rate means that the bond pays $50 interest per $1,000 of face value.[40] The yield on a bond may differ substantially from the coupon rate because the current value of the bond itself may differ from the face value. The bond contract, however, states a coupon rate and face value to be redeemed at maturity.[41] Bond calculations thus employ the time value of money, compounding, and discounting techniques discussed in Chapter 7. Recall that

$$FV_n = PV (1 + r)^n$$

and

$$PV = FV_n / (1 + r)^n$$

where

FV_n = a value received in the future,

PV = a value received now,

r = the market rate of interest, and

n = the number of years.

The current bond price equals the present value of cash flow to which the bond-holder is entitled (return of principal plus interest). Therefore,

$$P = \sum_{i=1}^{m} \frac{F \times c}{(1+r)^i} + \frac{F}{(1+r)^m}$$

---

[40]Municipal bonds are normally issued in denominations of $5,000 face value, even though coupon discussions use the smaller face value. Small denomination bonds ("minibonds") are sometimes sold. Lawrence Pierce describes an issue from Virginia Beach, Virginia, in "Hitting the Beach and Running: Minibonds," *Government Finance Review* 4 (August 1988): 29. Minibonds are not a significant component of the bond market. Some issuers are experimenting with sales through the Internet. Most borrowers need money for large capital projects and cannot work with revenue from bond sales that trickles in via sales to individual investors.

[41]For a bond purchaser, the yield-to-maturity is the total annualized return earned on a bond if it is held to maturity. It includes both the coupon and any difference between the amount paid for the bond and its face received on redemption by the borrower. A bond may be zero coupon, in which case the yield is the difference between the amount paid initially and the amount ultimately received back.

where

P = the market value or current price of the bond,

m = the number of years in the future until maturity of the bond,

F = the face value of the bond,

c = the coupon rate of the bond, and

r = the market interest rate available on bonds of similar risk and maturity.

The first term of the formula requires computing the present value of a constant stream of returns in the future, so the annuity-value formula (Chapter 7) provides a quick valuation method. For a bond with semiannual interest payments, the first term—the value of the coupon flow—would be computed using $(2m)$ instead of m and $(r/2)$ and $(c/2)$ instead of r and c.

To illustrate, suppose a Stinesville Water Utility bond matures in fifteen years, pays an 8 percent coupon semiannually, and has a face value of $5,000. The market rate currently available on comparable bonds is 6 percent. The holder receives an interest payment of $(F \times c)/2$, or $200, each six months for thirty periods $(2m)$. At the end of those thirty periods, the holder will receive back the $5,000. The bond price emerges from the formula

$$P = \sum_{i=1}^{30} \frac{(5,000 \times 0.08)/2}{\left(1 + \dfrac{0.06}{2}\right)} + \frac{5,000}{(1+0.06)^{15}}$$

$$= 3,920 + 2,086 = 6,006$$

It is obvious that the value of a bond can change, causing capital gain or loss for its holder, as market interest rates vary. The value of the Stinesville bond will be higher than computed here if the market rate is less than 6 percent and lower if the market rate is above 6 percent. The change would not cause a cash loss or gain for an individual holding the bond to maturity, but would change the return for anyone selling it early. When market interest rates fall, the value of bonds goes up, and when market interest rates increase, the value of bonds goes down.

Debt Structure and Design

After the decision to borrow has been made, a number of debt-structure decisions remain. They are considered here, along with some institutional detail about municipal bond markets.[42] Characteristics should ideally be designed to ensure least-cost

---

[42]The federal government constantly borrows to accommodate the continuing deficit and refinancing of maturing debt. Decisions about debt maturity are driven not by the life of particular capital projects, but by concerns of economic management. A longer term (Treasury bonds, notes) relieves financial markets of the regular disruptions that occur when maturing debt is refinanced, but may interfere with private long-term capital investment. A shorter term (Treasury bills) usually reduces the average initial interest rate on the debt, but requires more frequent financing, probably will cause higher ultimate interest cost, and may make inflation more difficult to control. These are radically different concerns from those in the municipal market.

marketability of the issue, simplify debt management, and provide appropriate cost signals to fiscal decision makers.

One initial decision involves the type of security and its term to maturity (i.e., the period for which the money will be borrowed). Markets respond differently to full-faith-and-credit bonds than to revenue bonds. The greater security behind full-faith-and-credit debt typically causes a lower interest rate to be paid on that offering. Revenue bonds may be desired, however, because of legal restrictions placed on the full-faith-and-credit debt[43] or because revenue debt provides a good way to allocate costs to the project's users. For instance, a city may enter capital markets to obtain funds for pollution-control equipment for a private electric utility. There is no logic to full-faith-and-credit finance here because charges paid by utility customers should be the sole source of debt service. This isn't the sort of project that the general taxpayers (the basis for full-faith-and-credit finance) ought to be paying for.

Debt maturity should roughly coincide with project life to ensure that the project will be paid for and the debt liquidated before replacement or major repair is required. This maturity-matching principle prevents debt financing for operating expenditures and permits those financing an improvement to receive its benefits. Debt-service costs along the project's life roughly represent a rental (or depreciation) charge. The facility users pay charges or taxes to cover those annual costs. The total charge can thus more accurately reflect the service's annual cost, including both capital and operating costs.

A bond issue—for example, an issue with thirty years' overall maturity—can be either term or serial. A term issue would have all bonds in the issue timed to mature at the end of thirty years. Funds to repay principal would be obtained through the bond issue's life (along with interest charges along the way) and placed into a sinking fund maintained by the bond issuer. At maturity, sinking-fund accumulations would be sufficient to repay the principal. A serial issue contains multiple maturities in a single issue. Thus, some bonds would be for a thirty-year term, some for a twenty-year term, and so on. (Issuers often seek to maintain constant total annual debt service—interest plus retirement of maturing bonds—through the length of an issue by gradually increasing the volume of bonds maturing through the life of the issue.) Portions of the project cost would be paid through the overall term of the issue. The serial issue may improve marketability of many municipal issues. Thin secondary markets (meaning there are not many prospective buyers in the market) for municipal debt cause most purchasers of that debt to hold the bond to maturity.[44] With serial issues, the issuing government can sell its debt to purchasers with funds

---

[43]Full-faith-and-credit debt may be limited to a maximum total amount for the jurisdiction, to a maximum percentage of the jurisdiction's tax base (usually assessed value), or by a requirement that voters approve the debt at a referendum. Revenue bond debt generally escapes all these limits. Limits are reported by state in tables 61–63 of Advisory Commission on Intergovernmental Relations, *Significant Features of Fiscal Federalism, 1976–77, Vol. 2, Revenue and Debt* (Washington, D.C.: Advisory Commission on Intergovernmental Relations, 1977).

[44]Purchasers of corporate bonds are reasonably confident that these bonds can be sold to another person if funds are needed prior to maturity. In other words, a strong secondary market exists. Thus, these bonds are ordinarily not serial.

available for several different periods of time. Either term bonds with sinking funds or serial bonds spread a project's financing over the life of the project and provide financing on a pay-as-you-use basis.

Debt maturity plays an important role in determining what the issue's ultimate interest cost will be because there is a relationship between the debt's term of maturity and the interest rate required. This relationship, the term structure of interest rates, is influenced by economic conditions at the time of borrowing and is often, but not always, upward sloping (the longer the term to maturity, the higher the interest rate required to borrow for that period of time) because borrowers must compensate investors for locking up their resources for a longer period. (The yield curve is called *inverted* when long-term rates are lower than short-term rates.) Expectations about the future of interest rate conditions and the economy, especially expectations about inflation, determine the curve's shape at any time.[45] Figure 15–2 illustrates the term structure of the yield curve for U.S. Treasury securities in the middle of January 2016 (the yield curve here is upward sloping, or ascending). Rates at the short end are extremely low, and longer maturities bear significantly higher rates. The continuing issues from the Great Recession complicate financial markets and contribute to the low rates shown here. A similar yield curve can be constructed for any security,

Figure 15–2
U.S. Treasury Yield Curve, January 15, 2016 (x-axis not to scale) (yield in %)

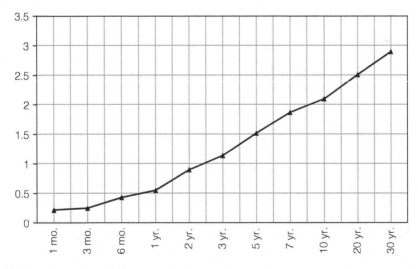

SOURCE: Derived from U.S. Department of Treasury data.

---

[45]When inflation is expected to be mild, the purchasing power of debt repayments in the distant future will be closer to the same as purchasing power given in the initial loan. Interest rates do not need to compensate for purchasing power loss and hence are lower in money terms. See Peter A. Abken, "Inflation and the Yield Curve," *Economic Review* 78 (May/June 1993): 13–30.

Figure 15–3
Bond Buyer 20 GO Municipal and Moody's AAA Corporate Debt Bond Yields,
Monthly 1953–2015

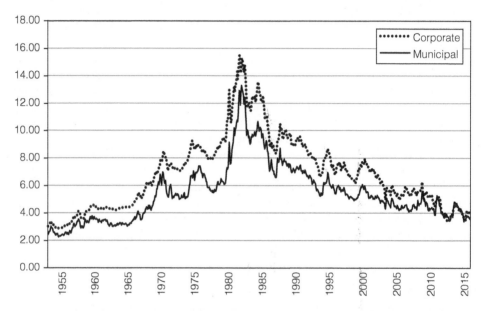

SOURCE: Compiled from FRED, Federal Reserve Bank of St. Louis

such as municipal bonds of a standard quality. Yields for high-quality municipal and corporate securities tend to move together with market conditions, as shown in Figure 15–3. Municipal debt generally bears lower yields than corporate securities as a result of the lower risk that debt service will not be paid and the exempt nature of interest paid by most municipal bonds, although the difference between the yields varies substantially over the years.

Municipalities can protect themselves from being locked into high interest rates on long maturity bonds. A *call provision* in a debt issue allows the borrower to repay debt before the normal maturity. The borrower usually refunds the debt, or borrows to cover the repayment, at the lower interest rates prevalent at the time of the refunding. If interest rates fall sufficiently before the first call date, the municipality may use advance refunding—borrowing at the lower interest rate and using the proceeds to cover debt service until the call date allows the initial issue to be entirely replaced.[46] Of course, the possibility of a call reduces an issue's attractiveness to lenders, so issues with such a provision must compensate the investor (with a call premium above face value) to permit marketability of the original issue.

---

[46]Proceeds of advanced refunding will be invested. The U.S. Treasury provides special securities for this purpose (since 1972) to prevent violation of arbitrage restrictions (municipalities cannot borrow tax exempt while lending on ordinary markets).

Ratings

When risk (the chance that principal and interest payments will not be made on schedule) is greater, lenders demand a higher return for their loans. Therefore, risk is important to both borrowers and lenders, and, in bond markets, commercial rating firms assess the risk of particular bond issues, thus screening and sorting issues for prospective investors. Because the assumption of risk must be compensated by higher returns to lenders, this assessment of risk will be critical in determining the interest rate paid by the borrowing government. Ratings also allow governments to sell on larger capital markets because they convert bonds issued by a locality into a commodity; all bonds with the same rating carry the same estimated risk. Credit risk is low because defaults in the United States are rare, rarer for municipal bonds than for corporate bonds, although less rare for revenue bonds issued by public authorities than for full-faith-and-credit bonds issued by general-purpose governments.[47] The rare defaults by the latter are usually linked to major economic recession, flagrant fiscal mismanagement, or unresolved political disputes. Because capital markets have long memories, governments want to avoid "a reputation-based loss of access to future loans."[48] That makes general-purpose governments especially reluctant to miss scheduled debt service. (As described later in this chapter, default is only one way in which government finances can go wrong.)

Three firms—Moody's Investors Services, Standard & Poor's (a subsidiary of McGraw-Hill, Inc.), and Fitch Investors Service/ICBA—prepare most creditworthiness opinions in the municipal market.[49] These three are the nationally recognized statistical rating organizations. Moody's has been doing municipal ratings since 1919 and Standard & Poor's since 1940; Fitch has only recently undertaken municipal rating, but has been in the market since 1913. A fourth firm, Kroll Bond Rating Agency, was established in 2010, and its share of the market is small. These agencies, for a fee paid by the bond issuer, prepare an opinion of the borrower's credit quality (for full-faith-and-credit issues) or of the particular bond issue (for revenue-bond issues). These rating opinions are widely distributed to the investment community and are used nationally to form portfolio strategies.[50] The agencies also prepare sovereign credit ratings, the ratings for central government debt, as international debt markets

---

[47]The cumulative record shows that for Moody's rated bonds, the default rate for corporate bonds is 97 times that for municipal bonds and for Standard & Poor rated bonds, the corporate rate is 45 times that of municipalities. (House Report 110-835—Municipal Bond Fairness Act.)

[48]William B. English, "Understanding the Costs of Sovereign Default: American State Debts in the 1840's," *American Economic Review* 86 (March 1996): 272.

[49]The Securities and Exchange Commission (SEC) identifies these firms as those whose ratings will be used in valuing bond assets of SEC-registered brokers and dealers. A fourth firm, Duff and Phelps Credit Rating Company, specializes in rating financing for water and public power systems, commercial development, toll roads, airports, and education facilities and does sovereign credit ratings, especially in emerging markets. It has a narrower focus than the other three.

[50]The rating agencies do not always agree on the risk associated with a particular municipality. For instance, in 2015, Moody's gave the city of Chicago a junk bond (non-investment-grade) rating, whereas Standard & Poor gave it an A-minus (investment grade) rating. (Timothy W. Martin and Aaron Kuriloff, "Ratings Rift Rattles Chicago," *Wall Street Journal*, May 21, 2015.) The raters had different views about the significance of unfunded city pension obligations.

have grown; U.S. federal government debt has been generally regarded as fully secure and, historically, was the standard against which risk has been calibrated. However, Standard & Poor's downgraded federal debt in the summer of 2011 when Congress threatened the timely payment of debt service in its debates regarding the statutory debt ceiling. There had been debt ceiling incidents in the past, but the position taken by some members of Congress regarding the ceiling and their statements that a default might not be particularly terrible caused the rating agency to warn its clients that federal debt did have some default risk.[51] The United Kingdom suffered a similar fall from the highest rating category when it voted in 2016 to leave the European Union.

An issue without a rating seldom sells on national markets, but issues can be unrated if local markets will buy them. Notice in Table 15–3 that a full percentage point or more often separates the highest-grade (Aaa) and lower-grade (Baa)

Table 15–3
Yield by Moody's Municipal Rating Group, 1940–2012 (End of Year)

	Aaa	Aa	A	Baa	Composite
1940	1.56	1.78	2.11	2.60	2.01
1945	1.11	1.27	1.62	1.91	1.48
1950	1.42	1.60	1.92	2.17	1.78
1955	2.29	2.46	2.81	3.25	2.70
1960	3.12	3.35	3.60	4.03	3.53
1965	3.39	3.47	3.60	3.78	3.56
1970	5.21	5.33	5.60	5.80	5.49
1975	6.50	6.94	7.78	7.96	7.30
1980	9.44	9.64	9.80	10.64	9.88
1985	7.98	8.31	8.64	9.05	8.50
1990	6.63	6.82	6.96	7.10	6.88
1995	5.40	5.43	5.53	5.66	5.51
2000	5.11	5.18	5.27	5.85	5.35
2005	4.46	4.58	4.68	4.92	4.66
2006	3.76	3.99	4.14	4.26	4.04
2007	4.23	4.35	4.58	4.91	4.52
2008	5.17	5.36	6.15	7.06	5.93
2009	3.89	4.10	4.72	5.86	4.64
2010	4.67	4.92	5.57	6.25	5.35
2011	3.72	3.98	4.71	5.49	4.47
2012*	3.43	3.70	4.23	5.12	4.12

*Based on April.
SOURCE: Mergent Moody's Municipal and Governmental Manual (New York: Mergent, 2012).

[51]Richard Cantor and Frank Packer, "Sovereign Credit Ratings," *Current Issues in Economics and Finance* 1 (June 1995): 1–6. There were similar debt ceiling issues in 1995-1996 and 2002, but they were seen as less serious than the 2011 standoff. Should there actually be a delayed debt-service payment, there would be a ratings impact from all agencies and higher interest payments that would entail considerable extra cost to U.S. taxpayers for many years. Although debt-to-GDP ratios are increasing, they do not constitute a threat to ability to service the debt in the near future. Politics does.

investments. That difference means a lot of money for large debt issues that will mature many years into the future, so municipalities have a considerable financial incentive to preserve a good rating. Grades lower than investment grade (below Baa in the Moody's system) fare less well because many financial institutions are forbidden to hold speculative, lower-rated securities. Table 15–4 relates the ratings definitions of the three major services and suggests the general risk factors associated with each rating.[52]

The rating firms use proprietary schemes for establishing the rating for an issue or a borrower, so we do not know exactly what goes into producing a particular rating. Statements by the rating firms identify four sorts of factors that are important in their reviews and evaluations of creditworthiness:[53]

1. **The economy.** The economy in which the issuing unit operates is important. A strong and growing economy brings a strong revenue base for servicing the debt. That reduces the credit risk of the issue.
2. **Debt.** The debt history and debt position of the issuing unit are important. A high debt burden and high debt-service requirements in relation to government resources raise questions about the credit risk of the issue. Plans for retiring the debt, the maturity structure in relationship to the project being financed, and any prior defaults are also reviewed. Some ratings agencies now explicitly state that they will also consider the level of unfunded pension obligations, the liability for promised future retirement benefits that is not covered by pension fund accumulations, when they do state government ratings. The view is that these are debt burdens, no different from the formal debt obligations.
3. **The government.** The investigation considers the degree of professionalism shown by the issuing government, the capacity of administrators, the quality of the full budget process (audits, documents, appropriations, controls, etc.), and the quality of government financial reports. Delays in approving budgets are not regarded as a favorable factor.[54]

---

[52]The rating agencies also rate corporate debt issues. It has been argued that municipal debt has been given lower ratings than comparable corporate issues, thus causing municipalities to pay higher-than-necessary interest rates—municipal defaults are much less frequent than are corporate defaults, and it is argued that the ratings should reflect that difference. Over the 1970–2008 period, the default rate on double-B municipal bonds was 1.74%, compared to a 2.93% rate for comparably rated corporate bonds, so maybe the critics have a point. Liz Rappaport and Karen Richardson, "What If Muni Insurance Disappeared?" *Wall Street Journal*, February 8, 2008.

[53]In recent years, the rating agencies have become more transparent with regard to the methods they use in producing their municipal bond ratings. They explain their logic: Moody's Investors Service, U.S. States Rating Methodology, Report Number 129816, April 17, 2013; Standard & Poor's Ratings Service, U.S. Local Governments General Obligation Ratings: Methodology and Assumptions, September 12, 2013; and Standard & Poor's, U.S. State Ratings Methodology, January 3, 2011. But do not expect to find the formulae that would allow you to replicate their ratings; that part of the structure remains proprietary.

[54]The congressional indecision about raising the federal debt ceiling certainly contributed to Standard & Poor's downgrade of the U.S. government. The report on the downgrade from AAA to AA+ stated: "The political brinksmanship of recent months highlights what we see as America's governance and policy-making becoming less stable, less effective, and less predictable than what we previously believed. The statutory debt ceiling and the threat of default have become political bargaining chips in the debate over fiscal policy." Standard & Poor's, "United States of America Long-Term Rating Lowered To 'AA+' on Political Risks and Rising Debt Burden; Outlook Negative," August 2, 2011. Debt burden mattered, but playing games with default mattered as well.

Table 15–4
Credit Ratings by Moody's, Standard & Poor's, and Fitch

Moody's	Symbol
Highest quality; minimal credit risk	Aaa
High quality; subject to very low credit risk	Aa
Upper-medium grade; subject to low credit risk	A
Moderate credit risk; medium grade; possess certain speculative characteristics	Baa
Have speculative elements; subject to substantial credit risk	Ba
Considered speculative; subject to high credit risk	B
Judged to be of poor standing; subject to very high credit risk	Caa
Highly speculative; are likely in, or very near, default; some prospect of recovery of principal and interest	Ca
Lowest rated class and are typically in default, with little prospect for recovery of principal or interest	C

Standard & Poor's	Symbol
Extremely strong capacity to meet financial commitments; highest rating	AAA
Very strong capacity to meet financial commitments	AA
Strong capacity to meet financial commitments; somewhat susceptible to adverse economic conditions and changes in circumstances	A
Adequate capacity to meet financial commitments; more subject to adverse economic conditions; lowest investment security rating	BBB
Less vulnerable in the near term; faces major ongoing uncertainties to adverse business, financial, and economic conditions; highest speculative grade	BB
More vulnerable to adverse business, financial, and economic conditions; currently has the capacity to meet financial commitments	B
Currently vulnerable; dependent on favorable business, financial, and economic conditions to meet financial commitments	CCC
Currently highly vulnerable	CC
Bankruptcy petition has been filed or similar action taken; payments of financial commitments are continued	C
Payments default on financial commitments	D

Fitch	Symbol
Highest credit quality: exceptional strong capacity to pay: unlikely to be affected by foreseeable events	AAA
Very high credit quality: very low default risk, strong capacity for payment	AA
High credit quality: low default risk, strong ability but more vulnerable to adverse changes in economic conditions and circumstances	A
Good credit quality: low default risk, adequate capacity for payment	BBB
Speculative: elevated vulnerability to default risk, particularly in the event of adverse changes in business or economic conditions over time	BB
Highly speculative: default risk is present; limited margin of safety remains	B
Substantial credit risk: default is a real possibility	CCC
Very high levels of credit risk: default of some kind appears probable	CC
Exceptionally high levels of credit risk: default is imminent or inevitable	C
Restricted default: experienced an uncured payment default; has not entered into bankruptcy filings, receivership, liquidation, etc.	RD
Default: entered into bankruptcy filings, receivership, liquidation, etc.	D

NOTE: Moody's designates with 1 those bonds with the strongest investment attributes (i.e., Aa1). A plus or a minus attached to an S&P or Fitch rating indicates upper or lower segment of the rating category.

4. **Financial analysis.** The investigation covers fund balances, trends in revenues and expenditures, adequacy of the revenue base, vulnerability to new liabilities (pension requirements, etc.), adequacy of financial planning, and so on.

Revenue bond analysis is primarily concerned with the enterprise's revenue potential and the legal protection of bondholders in the bond resolution's covenants. There is little concern with the associated government because there is no precedent requiring bailout of revenue bonds. For instance, in two well-publicized incidents, neither the city of Chicago nor the state of West Virginia prevented default of associated revenue bond issues (the Chicago Skyway and West Virginia Turnpike, respectively).[55] No government intervened to assist the Washington Public Power Supply System in its $2.25 billion default in 1983. Thus, revenue bond analysis presumes the project must stand on its financial merits.

The current problem with the traditional ratings agencies is that they made massive misjudgments in the financial collapse of 2007–2008.[56] Indeed, some claim they were instrumental in both creating and deepening that collapse. The rating agencies dramatically understated the risks associated with mortgage-backed securities (moving far away from their traditional work in the municipal bond market), giving stellar ratings to many securities that turned out to be nearly worthless. Some of these issues were novel with no track record regarding performance and so complex that risks were almost impossible to quantify, but the rating agencies swallowed the risk claims of the issuers. This record of failed bonds with high ratings created grave doubts about the credibility of all work done by the agencies, even though the problems were with a relatively modest amount of total rated issues, and not at all with traditional municipal bonds. In addition, conflict of interest issues emerged: the rating agencies are paid by the issuer, and, if a rating is low, that issuer may not continue to be a client of that agency. Skeptics saw in this the possibility that ratings would get skewed from that desire to do business in the future. The problems cast a shadow over all work by the ratings agencies, a cloud from which they only now are beginning to emerge.

What to do is an unresolved question. The work of the rating agencies provides an important link in financial intermediation, but it needs to be seen as credible. One approach could be a public rating agency financed in a way that eliminates the conflict apparent in the issuer-pays system.[57] Other approaches would involve greater regulation of private rating firms and finance of ratings from the users of

---

[55]The finances of the Chicago Skyway have been straightened out, and the city was able to lease the Skyway for 99 years to a private Spanish-Australian consortium for $1.82 billion in 2004.

[56]The Securities and Exchange Commission examined the problems in *Summary Report of Issues Identified in the Commission Staff's Examinations of Select Credit Rating Agencies* (Washington, D.C.: Securities and Exchange Commission, 2008). In general, it found that the agencies were swamped by the number and complexity of issues being rated—and also may have been influenced by conflicts of interest in relationships with the issuers. The movie *The Big Short* provides a good portrayal of the many things that went wrong in the mortgage crisis, the ratings errors, and associated recession of 2007–2009. Watch it the next time you feel like goofing off in a productive way.

[57]M. Ahmed Diomande, James Heintz, and Robert Pollin, "Why U.S. Financial Markets Need a Public Credit Rating Agency," *The Economists' Voice* 6 (June 2009): 1–4.

ratings rather than from the rated entities. No clear solution has yet emerged, and, in the tradition of the U.S. Congress, nothing substantial has happened.[58] It is difficult to empirically test the work of the agencies rating state or local general obligation debt because default on this sort of debt is so rare—testing the accuracy of the ratings would involve checking ratings variations of predicted probability of an event happening, even though the event hasn't happened. Good tests of ratings quality are not simple.

Credit Enhancements

Some municipal bonds have been supported by credit enhancements that may reduce the interest rate that the bond bears by adding a third-party guarantee that service will be paid when due.[59] Such a guarantee would reduce the risk associated with the bond. There have been three sorts of guarantees provided in the bond market: (1) state credit guarantees, (2) bank letters of credit, and (3) municipal bond insurance. Their relevance has changed in recent years.

The state credit guarantees are an "explicit promise by the state to a local unit bondholder that any shortfall in local resources will automatically be assumed by the state. In its strongest form, a state guarantee places the full-faith-and-credit of the state behind the contingent call on state funds."[60] The guarantee may take the form of a state insurance fund into which local issuers make premium payments, the program may guarantee only portions of debt service, the guarantee may not automatically pledge the full-faith-and-credit of the state, or there may be other conditions placed on the backing. About twenty-four states have credit enhancement programs, many for school districts (seldom are they available for all types of local government in the state). These often enhance the credit by having a system in place to intercept state aid to the district for debt service, thus dramatically improving the chances that debt service will be paid before any other obligations the district might have. In the final analysis, the guarantee can hardly be stronger than the state's finances and even that strength is always at jeopardy from the whims of state politicians. Those complications, plus the many different shades of the guarantee, makes generalizations about this form of third-party credit strengthening particularly hazardous.[61]

---

[58]The Dodd-Frank Act requires the Securities and Exchange Commission to adopt additional rules regarding the nationally recognized rating agencies and the commission has required some additional disclosures. In characteristic American political fashion, opinions range from the view that this is too aggressive to not nearly aggressive enough.

[59]Rating agencies may give municipal issues two ratings, a credit-enhanced rating and an unenhanced rating.

[60]Ronald W. Forbes and John E. Petersen, "State Credit Assistance to Local Governments," in *Creative Capital Financing for State and Local Governments,* ed. John E. Petersen and Wesley C. Hough (Chicago: Municipal Finance Officers Association, 1983), 226.

[61]There is considerable doubt about the wisdom of such guarantees because they reduce the incentive for fiscal responsibility by the borrower. In no case should the guarantees be open-ended.

A second form of guarantee is the bank letter of credit (LOC). The LOC is a commercial bank guarantee of payment of principal and interest on a bond if the issuer cannot do so. The bank LOC, always a relatively small element of the municipal market, has fallen in significance because major money-center banks—the ones most likely to be able to offer LOC enhancement—have lost their high credit ratings. There aren't any triple-A rated U.S. banks; they are safe, but do not have the high credit rating. Without the high credit rating, the LOC isn't worth the annual fee charged for the coverage. They were used mostly for short-term obligations.[62]

The third bond guarantee, municipal bond insurance, has historically been the most widely used since its inception in 1971. This insurance, purchased by the bond issuer, guarantees timely payment of principal and interest on that issue and thus allows a low-rated issue with insurance to sell at roughly the same interest rate as a higher-quality issue. The insurance premium is paid when the bond is initially issued. The recent problem is that insurance is only as good as the insurance company that sells it, and insurance company quality has plummeted.

The first insurance was sold in the early 1970s, and 3 percent of issues were insured in 1980. Insurance coverage became common, and in 2007, approximately 60 percent of issues were insured. In 2007, these bond insurers enjoyed triple-A ratings from the ratings agencies: Ambac, Assured Guaranty Corporation (AGC), CIFG Assurance North America, Financial Guaranty Insurance Company (FGIC), Financial Security Assurance, MBIA, and Syncora Guarantee (XLCA).[63] Two other firms—ACA and Radian—lacked the highest ratings but specialized in small sectors of the market. Purchasing insurance meant that security from the finances of the highly ranked insurance company was added to the finances of the bond issuer. However, the insurance companies expanded their markets from the sure profits of insuring municipal bonds, which were extremely unlikely to default, to insuring complex debt obligations tied to the subprime mortgage market. Part of the problem was associated with the fact that the ratings agencies had the ratings wrong for these obligations and, accordingly, the insurance companies had bad data for setting their premiums for covering this debt because they misjudged the default risk of the securities. But it is also true that the insurance companies did not fully understand the instruments that they were insuring and, when the claims on defaulted obligations came in, the insurers were not prepared. The claims and the exposure to more claims in the future threatened the capacity of the insurance companies to meet their obligations, and, by late 2008, none of the bond insurers enjoyed triple-A ratings from all ratings agencies. By 2014, ACA, Ambac, CIFG, FGIC, MBIA, Radian, and XLCA had discontinued writing bond insurance and were facing bankruptcy. Most issuers find no added value from insurance and prefer to sell based on their own financial prospects (recall that municipal defaults are extremely rare). While there is

---

[62]Banks are likely less interested in providing the LOCs because the SEC now requires full liquidity coverage on LOC lines and, accordingly, banks may find other uses of their resources more lucrative.

[63]Congress established the for-profit firm, the College Construction Loan Insurance Association, with federal seed money in 1986 to insure low-rated issues (S&P's BBB or lower) from higher education institutions. "Connie Lee" covered less than 1 percent of all insured issues in 1996—a poor fifth place among insurers. Some have argued for an extension of its role. Private insurers are not amused.

likely a market for the insurance and it is likely to return, finances of the insurance companies must be significantly better if they are to provide value to borrowers. [64] In the meantime, default rates on municipal bonds remain low, and the market has adjusted to bonds without insurance.

The market has changed. In 2005, the peak year, 63 percent of municipal issues by principal issued were sold with credit enhancement of one type or another. By 2009, only 17 percent had credit enhancement, a percentage that continued for 2010 and 2011.[65]

Underwriting, Interest Rates, and Ownership

Bond issues are usually too large to be bought by a single investor, and the issuer cannot effectively market the issue to large numbers of individual investors. Thus, bonds are typically sold to an underwriter, a firm that purchases the entire issue. The borrower receives the entire issue's proceeds quickly, without worrying about marketing. The underwriter hopes to resell the issue at a profit to investors. The gross profit (or underwriting spread) equals the difference between the price the firm pays for the bonds and the price the firm receives from their sale to investors. From that spread, the firm will pay all costs of distribution involved in the transaction. An increase in market interest rates can cause bond values to fall, so underwriters typically want to sell the bonds quickly.

Underwriting firms are selected either by negotiation or by competitive bid. In the former case, the underwriter is selected as the bond issue is being designed. An interest rate is negotiated between the borrowing unit and the underwriting firm. The underwriter engages in presale marketing and assists the borrower with such organizational services as preparing official statements, structuring the bond issue, and securing credit ratings. Negotiated bond sales dominate the revenue bond market (three-quarters of the issues by dollar volume), and competitive sales dominate the general obligation market (three-quarters of the issues by dollar volume). Unfortunately, noncompetitive selection opens the door for possible favoritism and bribes and eliminates market forces that reduce the spread.[66] Fifteen states have

---

[64] An additional company, Berkshire Hathaway Assurance, was briefly in the market in 2008. It withdrew quickly as Warren Buffett, its founder, found the risks to be excessive relative to the premiums that could be charged. Assured Guaranty remains in the market. A new firm, Build America Mutual Assurance, entered the market in 2012. It is a mutual company, thus owned by the entities it insures, and has a Standard & Poor AA rating. It wisely intends to limits its insurance to municipal issues.

[65] U.S. Securities and Exchange Commission, *Report on the Municipal Securities Market* (July 31, 2012), p. 50.

[66] The Public Securities Association recommended in 1993 a moratorium on political campaign contributions to candidates in states where public finance firms do bond business. This represents a major change in prior practice. Some scandals involving the selection of underwriters in that year produced that recommendation, but similarly piqued the interest of the federal SEC. The SEC has historically provided little supervision of municipal securities, but, to prevent market abuses, it proposed in 1994 to pursue securities-fraud charges against state and local government officials if they (1) fail to disclose conflicts of interest, including the acceptance of political contributions from underwriters or financial advisors; (2) fail to issue annual financial statements and inform investors of significant financial developments; (3) fail to disclose terms and risks of bonds; or (4) make inaccurate statements of the finances of the jurisdiction. The idea, if fully implemented, would make municipal-security information requirements more consistent with those placed on private issuers.

bond banks that underwrite and provide other services for municipal offerings; these sales are also negotiated.[67]

Two important documents must be prepared during the sale of bonds: the official statement and the legal opinion. The *official statement,* a requirement when the underwriter will be selected by competitive bid, contains two sections providing information prospective underwriters and investors need before committing funds to the borrower. One section provides information about the borrower's ability to repay its debt: a description of the community and its industries, its major taxpayers, debt currently outstanding, a record of tax collections and bond repayments in the past five years, and future borrowing plans. The other section describes the proposed bond issue: purpose, amount, and type of issue: its maturity structure and interest payment schedule: all provisions: date and place of bidding: whether a bond rating has been applied for: the name of the counsel preparing the legal opinion (described later): and where bonds will be delivered. The official statement also indicates any maximum interest rate and discount. Most official statements include a disclaimer indicating a right to refuse any and all bids, even though that right will seldom be used by units intending to maintain good relations with underwriters.[68]

The second document is the *legal opinion* prepared by a bond counsel, a certification that the bond issuer has complied with all federal, state, and local legal requirements governing municipal debt. Seldom will local law firms do this work; underwriters and large private investors require opinions from specialist law firms. The bond counsel ensures that the issuer has legal authority to borrow, that the revenue source for repayment is legal and irrevocable, and that the community is legally bound by provisions of the bond. The bond counsel also indicates whether interest paid on the debt will, in its opinion, be exempt from federal and state income tax. The bond counsel offers no judgment about the borrower's capacity to repay the debt; the bond counsel's concern is with how tightly the contract to repay binds the borrower. Without a satisfactory opinion, the bond issue is virtually worthless on the tax-exempt market.

A competitive bid is the typical method of selecting underwriters for full-faith-and-credit bonds and for many revenue issues. In this method, the issuer selects the amount of principal to mature at various years through the issue's life, and underwriters bid on the interest rate the issuer would have to pay. The rates, of course, need not be the same for different maturities, but would be the same for all bonds in a single maturity. The issuer chooses the underwriter bidding the lowest interest rate for the total issue. The winning underwriter bid determines what the interest cost will be to the issuer.

---

[67]Bond banks reduce interest costs to local borrowers. See Martin T. Katzman, "Municipal Bond Banking: The Diffusion of a Public-Finance Innovation," *National Tax Journal* 33 (June 1980): 149–60; and David S. Kidwell and Robert J. Rogowski, "Bond Banks: A State Assistance Program That Helps Reduce New Issue Borrowing Costs," *Public Administration Review* 42 (March/April 1983): 108–12.

[68]SEC rules effective in 1990 have placed extra controls on municipal disclosure in the official statement. Although the rules are directed at underwriters, the statements to which they apply are those produced by municipal borrowers. See John E. Petersen, "The New SEC Rule on Municipal Disclosure: Implications for Issuers of Municipal Securities," *Government Finance Review* 4 (October 1988): 17–20.

Two methods are used to compute interest cost when determining the lowest underwriter bid: net interest cost (*NIC*) and true interest cost (*TIC*). Both represent *weighted averages* of the several coupon rates in the serial issue. The *NIC* method computes cost according to the formula

NIC = Total Interest less Premium or plus Discount/Bond Dollar Years

It produces an average annual debt cost as a percentage of the outstanding principal of the debt. First, compute *N*, the total dollar cost of coupon payments over the life of the bond:

$$N = \sum_{i=1}^{n} (C_i \times A_i \times Y_i) + D$$

where

N = net dollar interest costs;

n = number of different maturities in issue;

C = coupon rate on each maturity;

A = par amount, or face value, in each maturity;

Y = number of years to maturity; and

D = bid discount (bid premium is a negative discount).

N equals the total interest paid through the life of the bond issue. The bond dollar years (*BDY*) formula is

$$BDY = \sum_{i=1}^{n} (A_i \times Y_i)$$

BDY represents the amount borrowed and the time for which it is borrowed: $1 borrowed for two years equals two bond dollar years, $2 borrowed for five years equals ten bond dollar years, and so on.
Thus,

$$NIC = \frac{N}{BDY}$$

The *TIC*, or the Canadian interest cost, method is more complicated because it takes into account the time profile of interest-payment flows, that is, a dollar paid in twenty years is not exactly the same as a dollar paid next year, and it is the norm in competitive bidding. If two bids have the same net interest cost, but one bid involves higher interest payments in the early maturities of the issue and lower interest payments in the later maturities (frontloading), then that bid would be less attractive because it requires the issuer to surrender resources earlier and thus to lose the return that could have been received from use of those resources. The second bid is, in present value terms, lower than the first. True interest cost is the interest rate that equates the amount of dollars received by the bond issuer with the present value of the flow of principal and interest payments over the issue's life.

The *TIC* formula is

$$B = \sum_{i=1}^{m} \frac{A_i}{(1+TIC)^i} + \sum_{i=1}^{m} \frac{I_i}{(1+TIC)^i}$$

where

B = aggregate dollar amount received by the issuer (the amount borrowed less discount or plus premium),

i = number of years until a cash payment occurs,

m = number of years to final maturity,

A_i = annual principal in dollars repaid in period i,

TIC = true interest cost, and

I_i = aggregate interest payment in period i (assuming one interest payment per year).

In a *TIC* computation for a municipal bond sale, the bid price or amount to be paid by the underwriter to the issuer (B) and the stream of debt-service payments (I_i) are specified by the bidder. The issuer defines the number of years to future payments (the maturities). The implied interest rate (*TIC*) is solved by iteration for successive approximations until the left and right sides of the equation balance.[69] Larger offerings require computer assistance for *TIC* calculation, but smaller issues can be handled using standard methods for approximating the internal rate of return. Table 15–5 illustrates *TIC* and *NIC* computation.[70]

The successful underwriting firm or syndicate (a group of firms) then sells the bonds to investors. Underwriters cover their costs and make any profit from the difference between the price the underwriters pay the issuer and the price the underwriters receive from purchasers (the spread).[71]

Table 15–6 reports the types of entities holding municipal bonds. Ownership in any class is concentrated among units in higher tax brackets—those are the purchasers to whom the tax-exempt status of municipal bond interest is especially

---

[69]The internal-rate-of-return function on spreadsheet programs quickly performs the calculations. This is one calculation you will not want to try with pencil and paper, although it is theoretically possible.
[70]In this illustration, *NIC* and *TIC* are about the same. Bids may manipulate *NIC* by use of high coupons on debt with shorter maturity and low coupons on long maturity (frontloading), keeping *NIC* low while *TIC* is increased. The illustration in the table does not involve frontloading.
[71]In 2007, the average gross spread was $5.27 per $1,000 face value of bonds, averaging $5.40 for negotiated issues and $4.09 for competitive issues. The competitive spread typically is less than the negotiated spread, however. For comparison, the average spread was $8.10 in 1995. *The Bond Buyer/Thomson Financial 2008 Yearbook* (New York: Source Media, 2008), 61.

Table 15–5
A *TIC* and *NIC* Computation Worksheet

Bonds Sold July 1, 2017, and Interest Payable on July 1 Thereafter. Bid Amount = $128,000

Maturity Date	Amount ($)	Bid Interest Rate (coupon) (%)	Annual Paid ($)	Bond Years	Bond Dollar Years
July 1, 2022	30,000	1.25	375	5	150,000
July 1, 2027	50,000	2.00	1,000	10	500,000
July 1, 2032	50,000	3.50	1,750	15	750,000
TOTAL	130,000				1,400,000

Schedule of Payments by Dates Paid

Payment Date	Interest ($)	Principal ($)	Total ($)
July 1, 2018	3,125	–	3,125
July 1, 2019	3,125	–	3,125
July 1, 2020	3,125	–	3,125
July 1, 2021	3,125	–	3,125
July 1, 2022	3,125	30,000	33,125
July 1, 2023	2,750	–	2,750
July 1, 2024	2,750	–	2,750
July 1, 2025	2,750	–	2,750
July 1, 2026	2,750	–	2,750
July 1, 2027	2,750	50,000	52,750
July 1, 2028	1,750	–	1,750
July 1, 2029	1,750	–	1,750
July 1, 2030	1,750	–	1,750
July 1, 2031	1,750	–	1,750
July 1, 2032	1,750	50,000	51,750
TOTAL	38,125	130,000	168,125

Solving for *NIC*:

$$NIC = [23,925 + 2,000] / 1,400,000 = 2.866 \%$$

Solving for *TIC*:

$$128,000 = [3,125 / (1 + TIC)] + [3,125 / (1 + TIC)^2] + [3,125 / (1 + TIC)^3]$$
$$+ [3,125 / (1 + TIC)^4] + [33,125 / (1 + TIC)^5] + [2,750 / (1 + TIC)^6]$$
$$+ [2,750 / (1 + TIC)^7] + [2,750 / (1 + TIC)^8] + [2,750 / (1 + TIC)^9]$$
$$+ [52,750 / (1 + TIC)^{10}] + [1,750 / (1 + TIC)^{11}] + [1,750 / (1 + TIC)^{12}]$$
$$+ [1,750 / (1 + TIC)^{13}] + [1,750 / (1 + TIC)^{14}] + [51,750 / (1 + TIC)^{15}]$$
$$= 2.8552\%$$

Table 15–6
Distribution of Municipal Debt by Major Holding Entity (End of Year)

	1985	1990	1995	2000	2005	2010	2015
Total outstanding	100%	100%	100%	100%	100%	100%	100%
Households	46	55	42.1	35.9	36.9	33.7	41.7
Money market funds	4.2	7.1	10.1	16.4	15.1	18.5	6.9
Mutual funds	4.1	9.6	16.6	15.6	14	14.5	18.5
Non–life insurance companies	10.3	11.6	12.7	12.4	14.1	14.2	8.7
Commerical banks	27	10	7.4	7.7	7.1	8	13.2
Closed-end funds	0.1	1.2	4.6	4.6	4	2.9	2.3
Government-sponsored enterprises	0.2	0.3	0.6	2	1.8	1.2	0.2
Nonfinancial corporate business	3	2.1	2.9	2.2	1.4	1	0.4
Brokers and dealers	2.3	0.7	1	0.8	1.9	1.4	0.4
Life insurance companies	1.1	1	0.9	1.3	1.5	1.8	4.1
State and local governments	1.1	1	0.4	0.2	0.2	0.2	0.4
State and local retirement funds	0.1	0	0.1	0.1	0.1	0.1	0.1
Other	0.5	0.4	0.6	0.8	1.9	2.5	3.1

SOURCE: Board of Governors of Federal Reserve System, *Flow of Funds Accounts of the United States* (Z1 Release).

attractive. Household holdings are a smaller share than twenty years ago, although they still account for roughly one-third of the total. They would own more indirectly through money market and mutual funds. The role of commercial bank purchases has declined. Banks lost the ability to deduct from income for federal tax purposes the interest they paid on deposits used to purchase tax-exempt bonds in tax reforms in the 1980s, which substantially reduced the attractiveness of these bonds to banks. Commercial banks have recently started direct loan programs to municipalities, avoiding the traditional bond market, as a generally safe use of their funds. The loans generate tax-exempt interest (within limits), and most lending expenses are deductible. They replace in part the letter-of-credit line of business the banks once had. The loans, however, have some extra risk for the borrowers because there could be a call for early repayment that would not be part of a regular bond issue.[72] Other bondholding entities' shares have been rather stable and rather small except for the development of mutual and money market funds as an important financial intermediary.

---

[72]Michael Corkery, "In Shift, Municipalities Turn to Banks for Loans," *Wall Street Journal*, July 14, 2011.

Lease-Purchase Finance and Certificates of Participation

Leases and certificates of participation provide governments with a backdoor method for purchasing capital assets (structures and equipment). Governments utilize two types of leases: operating leases and capital leases. Although there may be other reasons driving some of these transactions, capital leases are often used to avoid legal and procedural constraints on issuing debt to construct capital projects. From an accounting perspective, operating leases are treated like rentals. At the end of an operating lease, the leased equipment is returned to the lessor. If any one of the following conditions is met, then the lease is not an operating lease but instead is considered a financing arrangement or capital lease:

- There is a bargain purchase option.
- The lease transfers the title of the property to the lessee.
- The term of the lease equals or exceeds the full life of the property.
- The lease payments plus interest exceed the fair value of the property.

Capital leases, or lease-purchase financing, resemble an installment purchase. A lessee—in this case, a government—buys a property from the lessor through installment payments made over a given period of time. The capital lease is treated as debt instead of an expense in the government's accounts. Unlike an operating lease, the government carries the equipment on its books as the owner.[73] From an accounting perspective, interest paid on a capital lease may be treated as debt; from a legal perspective, it can be exempt from debt ceilings through the use of a nonappropriation clause, which means that lease payments have to be appropriated annually. Often nonappropriation clauses contain restrictions to protect the lessor from the replacement of equipment should the lease not be appropriated. For instance, a leased telecommunications system might have a covenant restricting the purchase or lease of a new system should the lease be terminated.[74]

On larger transactions, investors buy certificates of participation (COPs), which give them a share of lease payments made on that property; for smaller purchases, a bank or other financial intermediary may handle the entire transaction. The interest portion of these lease payments also can be exempt from federal taxation if the standards for issuer and purpose are met: if certain state-specific conditions are met, the financial obligation is not subject to constitutional or other limits with regard to voter approval, capacity ceilings, and so on because they are not strictly debt obligations. More issues have been raised in California than in any other state because of high infrastructure demand and strict controls on traditional finance there, but Arizona, Colorado, Florida, Georgia, Illinois, New Jersey, New York, North Carolina, South Carolina, and Washington each issue high volumes.[75]

---

[73]Federal lease-purchases generally are recognized as borrowing from the public in the budget. See Office of Management and Budget, *Budget of the Government of the United States, Fiscal Year 2006, Analytical Perspectives* (Washington, D.C.: U.S. Government Printing Office, 2005), 251.

[74]Richard Baker, "Public Policy Implications of Tax Exempt Leasing in the United States," *International Journal of Public Policy* 1(2005): 148.

[75]Craig Johnson and John L. Mikesell, "Certificates of Participation and Capital Markets: Lessons from Brevard County and Richmond Unified School District," *Public Budgeting & Finance* 14 (Fall 1994): 42.

Figure 15–4
A Certificate-of-Participation Arrangement

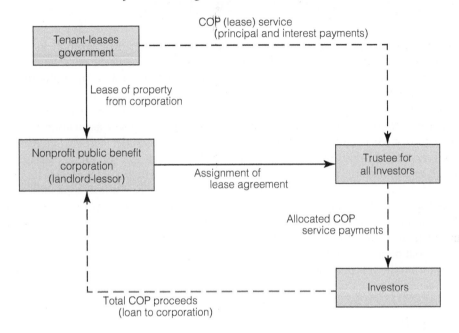

Figure 15–4 illustrates the flow of transactions in a COP arrangement. Suppose a government wants to acquire a new jail. It would arrange for the establishment of a nonprofit building corporation from which it would lease the new jail. The building corporation would borrow from private investors enough to build the jail, using the promised lease payments as the basis for prepayment of the loan.[76] A trustee, usually a bank, handles the distribution of lease payments, as they come from the government, to individual COP holders and manages any legal proceedings if lease payments do not arrive. The COP provides lenders less security than bonds because funds normally must be appropriated on a year-to-year basis and politics may intervene. This flow has been a problem in the Great Recession era, as revenues supporting the leases have faltered and leaseholders have limited capacity, at best, to sue localities associated with the leased facility.[77] However, the requirement for annual appropriations, a nonappropriation clause, is legally critical to distinguish these transactions from debt subject to referenda, ceilings, and the like.

---

[76]There is another variety used to patch deficits. In this approach, a government sells an existing facility to a holding corporation, uses the cash for government operations, and then leases the facility back from the corporation. For a particularly unfortunate example, see Craig Johnson and John L. Mikesell, "The Richmond School District Default: COPs, Bankruptcy, Default, and State Intervention," in *Case Studies in Public Budgeting and Financial Management*, ed. A. Khan and B. Hildreth (Dubuque, Iowa: Kendall/Hunt, 1994).
[77]Mike Cherney, "Cities' Rentals Hurt Bonds," *Wall Street Journal*, May 11, 2012, C1.

When Government Finances Go Horribly Wrong: Debt and Other Claims

The process of fiscal choice can go badly wrong, sometimes through economic or social misfortune, sometimes through incompetence or fiscal mismanagement, sometimes from corrupt practices, sometimes through a stubborn unwillingness to make tough choices, sometimes through political deals, and often through a combination of causes. When spending requirements exceed the productive capacity of the revenue system, the consequences are unpleasant for everyone associated with the government. At the worst, governments may face or consider default, repudiation, receivership, or bankruptcy as an outcome of fiscal crises that cannot be managed by tough manipulation of finances to reduce spending or to increase revenue. The terms are often carelessly used in public discussion; they do have different meanings and different consequences. All are, for U.S. general-purpose governments, extremely rare–but all can be found in a global review of government finances. Although the problems are not always the product of excessive borrowing or mismanagement of municipal debt, their ramifications frequently spill into the municipal bond market either directly or indirectly.

Default

A government defaults when it does not meet a scheduled payment of principal or interest on a debt issue. It is believed that the first municipal bond default was by Mobile, Alabama, in 1839. Defaults are notorious because they represent a clear violation of the public trust and, probably more important, because they are extremely rare in normal economic environments. There were many defaults during the Great Depression of the 1930s, but there have been few during the recent Great Recession. Widely publicized defaults in the municipal securities market over the past few decades include New York City and Cleveland in the 1970s and the Washington Public Power Supply System in the 1980s. In the New York case, the issuer defined the episode to be a "technical default" because it unilaterally announced a slower-than-contracted payment schedule. Bondholders may not have appreciated the distinction. Most defaults are of small issues by special-purpose districts, often involving industrial development projects. The 1978 Cleveland default was the first general obligation bond default since the Great Depression (Arkansas and Louisiana). Some defaults are permanent, as with that of the Washington Public Power Supply System bonds; some defaults are only temporary, as with those of the New York City and Cleveland bonds. Bondholders may be protected from the economic consequences of default by bond insurance purchased by the issuer.

Municipal bond defaults are exceedingly rare, rarer than are corporate bond defaults. Over the 1970 to 2011 period, there were seventy-one municipal bond defaults in total among bonds rated by Moody's, only five of them being general obligation bonds. Most defaults were for housing and hospital and health service provider bonds. Between 2009 and 2011, a period tainted by the problems of the Great Recession, there was only one general obligation bond default—that of Harrisburg, Pennsylvania in 2010. That is a very low rate: Moody's had ratings established for roughly 9,700 issues at the end of 2011. The ultimate recovery rate on municipal defaults, in other words, the amount of debt service that gets paid, was 65 percent over the 1970–2011 period, considerably higher than the 49 percent rate for corporate issues.[78]

The default may occur without any discernible impact, at least in the short term, for those receiving services from the defaulting government, but the impact is felt when the government proposes to borrow again and faces higher interest rates because of the market reaction to the earlier default. A number of states defaulted in the 1840s (Arkansas, Florida, Illinois, Indiana, Louisiana, Maryland, Michigan, Mississippi, and Pennsylvania) and a few more in the 1870s (Alabama, Florida, Georgia, Missouri, North Carolina, South Carolina, Tennessee, Virginia, and West Virginia). Mississippi still has not made good on its obligations. There have been no state general obligation defaults since then.[79] National governments also default on their debt issues. Hatchondo and colleagues tally fifty-six separate sovereign defaults in the period from 1976 to 2003, for instance.[80]

---

[78]Moody's Investment Service, Special Comment: U.S. Municipal Bond Defaults and Recoveries, 1970–2011 (New York: Moody's Investment Service, 2012).

[79]The Commonwealth of Puerto Rico, a U.S. territory, is neither state nor local government. It has experienced great economic problems and bears a substantial public debt burden—roughly $73 billion in debt, compared with a territory gross domestic product of $103.1 billion and a population of 3.6 million—because of many years of poor fiscal choices. Obligations to pay for current services, pension payments for work in the past, and debt service exceeded its revenue yield, so something had to give beyond the tax increases, service reductions, and pension reductions that had already been implanted. Its first default was in August 2015 when it did not pay $58 million to its Public Finance Corporation. It would likely have filed for bankruptcy, claiming inability to deal with its obligations, except it lacks authority from the U.S. government to do so, and Congress was not receptive to extending that process to that government, possibly because it feared that states would then seek similar authority. With no established process for dealing with the obligations, the government defaulted without any scheme for negotiating with lenders. By early 2016, problems had not been resolved and the Commonwealth defaulted again in 2016, first on debt issued by its development bank and then on debt with full constitutional guarantee of repayment (roughly, full-faith-and-credit debt). Things were complicated by a clause in the territory constitution that made repayment of general obligation debt a first claim on revenues, to be paid before anything else. The territory had no orderly process for parsing claims, that is, systematically arranging who wouldn't get paid, so it put all finances of the government in great jeopardy. Shortly after the default on the guaranteed debt, Congress passed the Puerto Rico Oversight, Management, and Economic Stability Act that created an oversight board with extraordinary powers to revise territory finances, adjust agreements entered into by the territory (including debt, pensions, and other payments), and audit finances. It did not guarantee that bondholders would be paid.

[80]Juan Carlos Hatchondo, Leonardo Martinez, and Horacio Sapriza, "The Economics of Sovereign Defaults," *Economics Quarterly* 93 (Spring 2007): 163–87. Recently there have been concerns about sovereign default by Greece, a country facing high amounts of debt relative to the size of the economy and the tax-collecting capacity of the government. The country has a special problem because the debt is in euros, not an independent national currency, so the government cannot service its debt by having its treasury and central bank produce more of its own currency. Whether that approach might make economic sense or not is beside the point. It simply is not an option open to the country. That is not the case, however, for the U.S. federal debt; it is dollar denominated and the government has the power to create more dollars for itself in a possibly worst case scenario. Other recent defaults have involved transition or developing countries only.

Receivership/Emergency Managers

About twenty states have provisions for state assistance and control for local governments in fiscal distress. In many respects, the receivership is a state-controlled approach that avoids the federal bankruptcy program (or may be a required step before a bankruptcy filing is permitted, as is the case in Michigan). A government enters receivership when an appointed third-party manager takes control of operations of the government. The receiver, appointed by a superior government (the state) or by a court, has the responsibility to protect the assets of the unit and to meet legitimate demands made by those owed money by the government. The receiver usually has authority to change employment contracts and benefit programs for retirees, as well as to fire employees without the normal termination procedures. In many cases, the receiver completely replaces all elected officials of the jurisdiction. States often appoint receivers or trustees to manage the finances of local governments in great jeopardy; for instance, Massachusetts appointed a receiver to take over the management of the city of Chelsea in the face of major financial irregularities, including alleged theft of city funds and properties, discovered there. School districts in California have also been placed in receiverships by the state. State control boards—in which states take over financial operations of particular localities (usually cities)—behave something like receiverships. Examples include the Pennsylvania Intergovernmental Cooperation Authority (for Philadelphia in 1991, Pittsburgh in 2004, and several smaller jurisdictions since the state created the oversight law called Act 47 in 1987), the Miami Financial Emergency Oversight Board (1996), the Buffalo Fiscal Stability Authority (2003), and the New York State Financial Control Board (for New York City in 1975). There are also emergency procedures for municipalities in Ohio. The Michigan Local Government and School District Fiscal Accountability Act (Public Act 4, 2011) gives emergency managers installed by the state powers to void collective bargaining agreements, fire elected officials, and privatize or sell government assets. Emergency managers have been in place for various periods in the past in Allen Park, Benton Harbor, Detroit, Ecorse, Flint, Hamtramck, Highland Park, Inkster, Lincoln Park, Pontiac, River Rouge, Royal Oak Township, Wayne County, Benton Harbor Area Schools, Detroit Public Schools, Highland Park School District, Muskegon Heights School District, and Pontiac Public Schools.[81] Atlantic City entered a program of strong state fiscal control in 2016, an intervention reportedly to prevent the need for full state takeover of city finances or a bankruptcy filing. Washington, D.C., lost most of its fiscal independence to a congressionally appointed board in 1997, for similar reasons.

---

[81]The Flint emergency manager, using his broad powers to act without approval from local elected officials, decided to save money by switching the city water source from the City of Detroit to the Flint River. Unfortunately, the treatment process for the river water resulted in high levels of lead in the water supplied to the public and some evidence that the water was causing lead poisoning in local children (not to mention many public complaints about general water quality). The city switched back to Detroit water in 2015, although the health and financial consequences from the river water have not been resolved. There is some thought that, had local officials been in charge, there would have been greater sensitivity to water quality, less pure focus on cost reduction, and the health crisis would have been avoided.

Courts may also appoint receivers for public entities, although less frequently than for private firms or nonprofit organizations. In 1986, the Wayne County Circuit Court appointed a receiver to operate the city of Ecorse, Michigan, after suits by Detroit Edison, the Detroit Water and Sewerage Department, and others for nonpayment of bills. The city emerged from this receivership, but later fell into the emergency manager system. Receivers may well dramatically change the services supplied by the government and possibly the taxes it levies, so the population almost certainly will see a difference from the experience.

Bankruptcy

Governments enter bankruptcy by a formal filing with a federal court under Chapter 9 of the federal bankruptcy code (a chapter created during the Great Depression of the 1930s).[82] After the filing has been accepted, the court protects the government from financial claims while the government develops a plan under which it can pay a large share, but usually not all, of its financial obligations. Only municipalities fall under the bankruptcy process because the Tenth Amendment to the United States Constitution provides for the sovereignty of states, thus apparently forbidding Congress from imposing an involuntary debt restructuring plan on the states, although some have suggested that something approximating bankruptcy may be appropriate for states like Illinois which face nearly overwhelming debt and pension obligations and little demonstrated ability to deal with the problems. Seldom does the bankruptcy result from an excessive amount of bonded indebtedness because debt service normally is only a small portion of total spending. The bankruptcy may or may not involve default on debt service. It does often result from poor decisions made by public managers and elected officials about investments, public projects, and compensation to employees.[83] It results when the government lacks the resources to pay its bills when they are due; it does not involve a bad looking balance sheet or prospective future liabilities.

The precise rules for municipal bankruptcy are less well defined than the rules for corporate bankruptcy because municipal bankruptcies are so rare (fewer than 600 since the 1930s, mostly involving special districts, out of a current count of over 80,000 jurisdictions). However, it is clear that in order to receive bankruptcy

---

[82]The complex law of municipal bankruptcy and a review of notable cases is discussed in Kenneth E. Noble and Kevin M. Baum, "Municipal Bankruptcies: An Overview and Recent History of Chapter 9 of the Bankruptcy Code," *Pratt's Journal of Bankruptcy Law* (July/August 2013): 458–483. It includes a helpful chart that compares municipal bankruptcy features with those of commercial bankruptcy.

[83]Why municipalities file for bankruptcy is not entirely clear, partly because general purpose government bankruptcy is so rare that there is insufficient data for analysis. One investigation of the fiscal health of three larger cities that filed for bankruptcy in California (San Bernardino, Stockton, and Vallejo) finds evidence suggesting that the filing is a political or managerial mechanism, as much as a decision driven by acute fiscal stress. Akheil Singla, James Comeaux, and Charlotte L. Kirschner, "Bling, Broke, and Bedlam: Differentiating Fiscal Stress from Bankruptcy in California," *Public Finance and Management*, 14 (Number 3, 2014): 306–28. They suggest that other cities do not file for bankruptcy because of political and legal costs and the potential stigma associated with filing.

protection, the municipality must be insolvent, meaning that the municipality is not able to pay its bills when they come due. The strong prospect that the municipality will not be able to pay its bills at some point in the near future is not enough (to emphasize again: a suspicious balance sheet is not a reason for bankruptcy).

The bankruptcy aims to ensure that the government can continue to provide services to its citizenry and retain its assets. The bankruptcy court cannot in practice force the jurisdiction to either raise taxes or reduce spending. In contrast to corporate bankruptcies, liquidation of the bankrupt municipality is not permitted. It is, in fact, not clear what liquidation of a city would mean. Also in contrast to individual or corporate bankruptcies, governmental bankruptcies can only be voluntary. That is, they cannot be forced into bankruptcy by creditors. In many respects, bankruptcy is more lenient than state receivership programs. After the 1991 effort by Bridgeport, Connecticut, to declare bankruptcy, Congress changed the bankruptcy code to require specific state authorization before a municipality may file for bankruptcy. Historically, bondholders have been superior creditors, so debt service ordinarily flows on schedule (besides, the government wants continued access to municipal capital markets), but other contractual obligations may not be met.[84] For instance, wages and salaries may be reduced from the previously agreed-to levels, and pensions for retirees are a frequent target for reduction. In some recent bankruptcies, the jurisdiction has defaulted on debt service to reduce the need for other cutbacks.[85] In order for the municipality to enter into bankruptcy, it must be insolvent—in other words, unable to pay its obligations when they come due—a stronger requirement than for corporate bankruptcy filing. The municipality may or may not have bonded debt outstanding when filing for bankruptcy protection. Only slightly more than half the states permit their local governments to declare bankruptcy. Recent bankruptcy filings of city, town, or county governments include Detroit, Michigan (population 688,701) in 2013; Vallejo, California (population 117,000) in 2008; Stockton, California (population 291,000) in 2012; Jefferson County, Alabama (population 659,000) in 2011; Harrisburg, Pennsylvania (population 49,188; the city was under state receivership) in 2011; Pritchard, Alabama (population 22,000) in 1999 and 2009; Orange County, California (population 3 million) in 1994; Boise County, Idaho (population 7,500) in 2011; San Bernardino, California (population, 213,000) in 2012; Westfall Township, Pennsylvania (population 2,300) in 2009; Moffett, Oklahoma (population 127) in 2007; Hillview Kentucky (population 7,905) in 2015; Mammoth Lakes, California (population 8,073) in 2012; and Central Falls, Rhode Island (population 9,000;

---

[84]The private sector bankruptcies of Chrysler and GM in 2009 did not follow the principle of bondholders as superior creditors. It is not clear whether this would be generalizable to municipal bankruptcies in the future. The 2012 Stockton bankruptcy filing identified bondholders and city employees as the groups most likely to be affected by the bankruptcy.

[85]Moody's reports that median debt service as a percentage of expenditures for state and local governments is in the 5 to 8 percent range. Moody's Investors Service, "Municipal Market Investor Confidence: Linkages to Credit Quality," January 6, 2011. Unless the government has debt service considerably above the typical level, trimming debt service is not going to be as important as reducing a cost category that is more significant in the total budget—hence, the particular attention to labor costs, current and past, in bankruptcy discussions. Debt service was not met in bankruptcies or receiverships in Vallejo, Jefferson County, Harrisburg, Stockton, Detroit, and San Bernardino, for instance.

there had been a state receivership before the bankruptcy filing) in 2011.[86] The bankruptcy court rejected the Boise County, Harrisburg, and Mammoth Lakes filings. There are roughly 39,000 general purpose local governments in the United States at the most recent Census of Governments count, so the number of bankruptcies is a tiny percentage of that total.[87] Although the Great Recession created substantial fiscal problems for localities, the Recession produced no run to bankruptcy protection for local governments.

The big question in bankruptcy is whether bondholders, current employees, or retirees are going to get stiffed because that is what the bankruptcy involves. In contrast to private businesses, governments seem to regard breaking contracts freely arrived at as something more weighty than just getting a fresh start. One problem with a bankruptcy is the reputational impact on neighboring jurisdictions. For example, as Birmingham, Alabama, was preparing for a bond issue in 2012, the city took great pains to distinguish itself from the bankrupt county (Jefferson) in which it is located. Although it had substantial cash reserves and a AA rating on its general obligation debt, it seemed likely that a bond issue for capital projects would have to pay a slight premium because of the negative bankruptcy halo.[88]

Although there has been no avalanche of municipal bankruptcies in the aftermath of the Great Recession, there is some concern that municipalities may start viewing them as a viable strategy. That has not historically been the case: "Municipalities traditionally have believed that using bankruptcy as a tool to put their finances in order wasn't worth the risk of alienating creditors and being closed out of the $3.7 billion municipal bond market."[89] Because of their rarity, it is not clear what the ramifications would be when a general purpose government—a city or a county—emerges from bankruptcy. The government is likely to be smaller, providing fewer services, and taxes may be higher. For example, Vallejo, California,

---

[86]The several mistaken choices that led to the Jefferson County bankruptcy are analyzed in Michael E. Howell-Moroney and Jeremy L. Hall, "Waste in the Sewer: The Collapse of Accountability and Transparency in Public Finance in Jefferson County, Alabama," *Public Administration Review* 71 (March/April 2011): 232–42. The county had suffered through many years of fiscal mismanagement leading up to the bankruptcy filing. It has been presumed that revenue bond service would be immune from bankruptcy filings of a government. These bonds do not pledge the resources of the government, but only project revenues. In the Jefferson County, Alabama, filing, the county sought to reduce payments to holders of sewer project revenue bonds to protect other operations of the county from cuts and even to repair the sewer system itself. Municipal bankruptcy filings are so infrequent that the law is not clear on how bondholders, either general obligation or revenue, are to be treated, although it was presumed that they were superior claimants. It is no longer clear. Presumably, Jefferson County plans never again to try to borrow at normal rates. Kelly Nolan, "Muni Market Sounds Alert," *Wall Street Journal*, November 29, 2011, C4; and Michael Corkery and Katy Stech, "County Bond Fight Begins New Round," *Wall Street Journal*, April 17, 2012, C1. Rhode Island passed a law in 2011 that places bondholders ahead of all other creditors in a municipal bankruptcy in an effort to make sure that Rhode Island jurisdictions would not face an interest rate penalty because of the Central Falls problem. The Moffett, Oklahoma, bankruptcy is curious. The tiny town was an infamous speed trap, and when state action ended its ability to get traffic ticket revenue, its finances collapsed.

[87]Bankruptcy court records show that in federal fiscal 2012, there were 1,261,140 bankruptcy filings, of which twenty-three were under Chapter 9. In the prior year, there were eight Chapter 9 filings out of 1,467,221 total.

[88]Michael Corkery, "Birmingham Angles for Extra Credit," *Wall Street Journal*, June 26, 2012, C1.

[89]Michael Corkery, "Muni Blues Worry Investors," *Wall Street Journal*, July 26, 2012, C1.

emerged from three years under bankruptcy protection in 2011 with a much smaller government, many facilities that formerly provided government services closed forever, renegotiated employee contracts and fewer municipal employees, a continuing obligation to repay a large amount of the debt that had been incurred before the bankruptcy, reduced retiree benefits, a participatory budget system in place, a higher city sales tax rate, and substantial legal bills (bankruptcy lawyers are probably the greatest beneficiaries of a municipal bankruptcy)—plus, almost certainly a renewed appreciation for the importance of the rules for fiscal sustainability.[90]

Repudiation

Repudiation occurs when the borrower announces that it will make no more principal or interest payments on debt, that it will no longer recognize that debt as a liability. This action is rare because bond markets have long memories and a government that has repudiated debt will have difficulty borrowing again. As Spiotto observes, "Repudiation of validly issued public debt destroys the credit rating for the issuer and makes any subsequent return to the public-debt markets problematic at best."[91] Some U.S. states repudiated debt issued in the first half of the nineteenth century to finance canals, roads, railroads, and other internal improvements, and some others in the South did so after the Civil War. Some of the projects were absolutely scandalous, and money almost certainly was stolen by both government and private thieves. However, these repudiating governments faced premium interest rates on their borrowing well into the twentieth century because the capital markets remembered that experience. The bond market affects even radical changes in government. For instance, questions about payments on Russian tsarist debt issued in France from 1822 to 1914 complicated Russia's entry into international bond markets in 1996. A French bondholders' association (Association Francaise des Porteurs d'Emprunts Russes) kept rating agencies informed and warned prospective investors. Eventually, the governments of Russia and France reached an agreement for at least partial payment of that old debt, and the new Russian government was able to enter the market. Bond markets collectively have long memories, and repudiation is a distinctly poor option for dealing with difficult debt obligations.

---

[90]There have been a few detailed studies on the actions and economic forces that cause localities to end up in bankruptcy. A couple of these are Craig Johnson and John L. Mikesell, "The Orange County Debacle: Where Irresponsible Cash and Debt Management Practices Collide," *Municipal Finance Journal* 17 (Summer 1996); and Douglas J. Watson, Donna Milam Handley, and Wendy L. Hassett, "Financial Distress and Municipal Bankruptcy: The Case of Pritchard, Alabama," *Journal of Public Budgeting, Accounting, and Financial Management* 17(Summer 2005).

[91]James E. Spiotto, "Financial Emergencies: Default and Bankruptcy," in Robert D. Ebel and John E. Petersen, eds., *The Oxford Handbook of State and Local Government Finance* (New York: Oxford University Press, 2012): 759.

Sidebar 15–2
Capital Appreciation Bonds

Municipal bonds typically deliver coupon payments (payment of interest) on regular dates through the maturity of the bond. When the bond matures, that last debt service payment will be of interest earned since the last coupon payment plus the face value of the bond. Hence there is a stream of interest payments through the life of the bond. These bonds are sometimes called current interest bonds.

The capital appreciation bond is different. No payment to investors is made until the bond matures. At that date, the face value of the bond plus all the accumulated interest through the life of the bond is paid, sort of a balloon payment at the end of the issue. If the bond has a maturity of ten, fifteen, or more years, that payment will be several times the amount borrowed at the time of the bond issue, an order of magnitude larger if the term is long enough and the interest rate is high enough. That isn't surprising because that is the way interest accumulates. The difference between current interest and capital appreciation (or zero coupon) bonds is most significant when the term to maturity is long and issues raised by capital appreciation bonds are least when maturity is short.

The idea behind capital appreciation bonds is that the borrower receives funds to develop infrastructure for the jurisdiction without having the population pay for the infrastructure at the time is developed or even for some years into the future. The economy will grow, the tax base will grow, and the bond issue repayment at a date in the future will be a more manageable burden on that larger economy. At least that is the cover story. In pragmatic terms, the population will have had services of that infrastructure for a number of years without having to pay for it, the people who ultimately have to pay for the infrastructure will have had no say in the decisions involving that infrastructure and may have other things that they would prefer their tax dollars pay for than infrastructure of the past, and the politicians involved will have enjoyed the credit for the infrastructure spending and will undoubtedly have moved on to other things when the bills ultimately come due. Because the bond proceeds appear to be free money at the time of issue, their political attraction is obvious. Of course, the municipality could mitigate these incentive and intergenerational equity problems by accumulating a fund through the life of the infrastructure, making payments each yea that will be adequate to cover the bond when it comes due. That would work something like the process for funding a defined benefit pension program. That has been a big success in terms of fiscal sustainability and good government, hasn't it?

Among the jurisdictions that have used these bonds are California school districts (recent laws there have considerably constrained the conditions of their use) and Chicago.

Conclusion

Government debt exists because expenditure has exceeded revenue. Federal debt represents the accumulated effects of annual deficits, whereas state and local government debt largely represents the outcome of capital-project financing. State and local government debt costs can be managed through care to maintain good creditworthiness (ratings), careful tailoring of maturities and timing of debt issues, use of the recently narrowed ability to issue federal tax-exempt debt, and use of available debt guarantees. Debt itself is not necessarily evidence of poor fiscal management.

QUESTIONS AND EXERCISES

1. What restrictions are placed on state and local government debt in your state? What methods are used to avoid those limits? Is there a state bond bank? Does your state have any program for credit enhancement for local debt?

2. Investigate the debt and debt-rating history for a large city of your selection. Have debt issues been full-faith-and-credit or limited-liability? Have issues been insured?

3. A city advertised for bids for the purchase of $2 million principal amount of Sewage Works Revenue Bonds. Bonds will be delivered on April 1, 2017, and interest will be paid on April 1 of the following years. The bonds mature as follows:

Maturity Date	Amount ($)
April 1, 2022	50,000
April 1, 2023	50,000
April 1, 2024	50,000
April 1, 2025	100,000
April 1, 2026	100,000
April 1, 2027	100,000
April 1, 2028	150,000
April 1, 2029	150,000
April 1, 2030	150,000
April 1, 2031	550,000
April 1, 2032	550,000

Two bids were received:

From Five Points Securities:

Pay $2 million
The interest rates for each maturity:
2012 through 2020, 5.50 percent
2021 through 2022, 6.25 percent

From Wellington-Nelson:

Pay $2 million
The interest rates for each maturity:
2022 through 2024, 4.19 percent
2025 through 2030, 5.75 percent
2031 through 2032, 6.50 percent

For each bid, compute the net interest cost (NIC) and the true interest cost (TIC). Which bid is more advantageous to the city?

4. An Eminence Water Utility Revenue Bond matures in fifteen years, pays a 5.5 percent coupon rate semiannually, and has a face value of $5,000. The market interest rate for similar risk and maturity municipal bonds is 4 percent. What is the current price of the bond? What would be its price if the market rate was 6 percent?

5. Solomon Keith, a bank janitor, won a large prize in the New York lottery in 1987. Unfortunately, Mr. Keith died before he could collect all of the twenty annual payments of $240,245 each to which he was entitled. To pay taxes and legal fees (as well as to distribute some of this estate to heirs), an auction was held in early July 1992 for rights to the sixteen annual payments remaining in the prize (the first to be paid on July 15, 1992). Presidential Life Insurance Company was the winning bidder, paying $2.1 million for the prize. Suppose other comparable investments of Presidential's funds could have earned about 5 percent annual interest. What do you think of the wisdom of its investment?

6. Does your state permit its localities to file for bankruptcy protection? Is there some sort of state receivership or similar program for fiscally distressed localities? Are there any localities in your state in such a program? Are there municipal bond issues in your state that are in default?

APPENDIX 15–1

General Principles of State Debt Management

The following principles outline the debt management policies endorsed by the comptroller of the State of New York. They are consistent with the concept of fiscal sustainability and could serve as a reasonable model for any state or local government for guiding its use of debt.

1. Do not use refinancing to extend debt maturity.
2. Ensure present value and cash flow savings in every year.
3. Maximize the economic benefits of debt refunding.
4. Integrate the capital and financial planning process.
5. Update both plans quarterly and provide realistic four-year projections.
6. Maximize the use of PAYGO financing.
7. Target projects with low periods of probable usefulness.
8. Maximize the use of surplus revenues to retire older and expensive debt.
9. Use nonrecurring revenues for capital spending/debt reduction.
10. Issue long-term debt for capital purposes only.
11. Issue no debt for operating expenses.
12. Issue debt for capitalized interest only in extraordinary circumstances, such as a pending construction of a revenue-producing facility.
13. Keep debt to an affordable level.
14. Limit outstanding debt and debt issuance.
15. Minimize the costs of debt issuance.
16. Limit the term of debt to maximize intergenerational equity.

17. Issue no debt beyond the period of probable usefulness.
18. Provide comprehensive and clear debt reporting.
19. Continually strive toward superior disclosure practices.
20. Use competitive sales rather than negotiated sales.

SOURCE: *New York State's Debt Policy, A Need for Reform* (Albany, N.Y.: Office of New York State Comptroller Alan G. Hevesi, February 2005), 101.

Index

Note: Page numbers followed by letters indicate the following: f indicates figures, n indicates notes, s indicates sidebars, and t indicates tables.